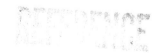

Contemporary
Literary Criticism

Guide to Gale Literary Criticism Series

For criticism on	Consult these Gale series
Authors now living or who died after December 31, 1999	*CONTEMPORARY LITERARY CRITICISM (CLC)*
Authors who died between 1900 and 1999	*TWENTIETH-CENTURY LITERARY CRITICISM (TCLC)*
Authors who died between 1800 and 1899	*NINETEENTH-CENTURY LITERATURE CRITICISM (NCLC)*
Authors who died between 1400 and 1799	*LITERATURE CRITICISM FROM 1400 TO 1800 (LC)* *SHAKESPEAREAN CRITICISM (SC)*
Authors who died before 1400	*CLASSICAL AND MEDIEVAL LITERATURE CRITICISM (CMLC)*
Authors of books for children and young adults	*CHILDREN'S LITERATURE REVIEW (CLR)*
Dramatists	*DRAMA CRITICISM (DC)*
Poets	*POETRY CRITICISM (PC)*
Short story writers	*SHORT STORY CRITICISM (SSC)*
Literary topics and movements	*HARLEM RENAISSANCE: A GALE CRITICAL COMPANION (HR)* *THE BEAT GENERATION: A GALE CRITICAL COMPANION (BG)* *FEMINISM IN LITERATURE: A GALE CRITICAL COMPANION (FL)* *GOTHIC LITERATURE: A GALE CRITICAL COMPANION (GL)*
Asian American writers of the last two hundred years	*ASIAN AMERICAN LITERATURE (AAL)*
Black writers of the past two hundred years	*BLACK LITERATURE CRITICISM (BLC-1)* *BLACK LITERATURE CRITICISM SUPPLEMENT (BLCS)* *BLACK LITERATURE CRITICISM: CLASSIC AND EMERGING AUTHORS SINCE 1950 (BLC-2)*
Hispanic writers of the late nineteenth and twentieth centuries	*HISPANIC LITERATURE CRITICISM (HLC)* *HISPANIC LITERATURE CRITICISM SUPPLEMENT (HLCS)*
Native North American writers and orators of the eighteenth, nineteenth, and twentieth centuries	*NATIVE NORTH AMERICAN LITERATURE (NNAL)*
Major authors from the Renaissance to the present	*WORLD LITERATURE CRITICISM, 1500 TO THE PRESENT (WLC)* *WORLD LITERATURE CRITICISM SUPPLEMENT (WLCS)*

b10277390

ISSN 0091-3421

Volume 274

Contemporary Literary Criticism

Criticism of the Works
of Today's Novelists, Poets, Playwrights,
Short Story Writers, Scriptwriters, and
Other Creative Writers

Jeffrey W. Hunter
PROJECT EDITOR

 GALE
CENGAGE Learning

Detroit • New York • San Francisco • New Haven, Conn • Waterville, Maine • London

Contemporary Literary Criticism, Vol. 274

Project Editor: Jeffrey W. Hunter

Editorial: Dana Ramel Barnes, Lindsey J. Bryant, Kathy D. Darrow, Kristen Dorsch, Jelena O. Krstović, Michelle Lee, Thomas J. Schoenberg, Lawrence J. Trudeau

Content Conversion: Katrina Coach, Gwen Tucker

Indexing Services: Laurie Andriot

Rights and Acquisitions: Margaret Abendroth, Sari Gordon, Tracie Richardson

Composition and Electronic Capture: Gary Oudersluys

Manufacturing: Cynde Bishop

Associate Product Manager: Marc Cormier

For product information and technology assistance, contact us at
Gale Customer Support, 1-800-877-4253.
For permission to use material from this text or product,
submit all requests online at **www.cengage.com/permissions.**
Further permissions questions can be emailed to
permissionrequest@cengage.com

While every effort has been made to ensure the reliability of the information presented in this publication, Gale, a part of Cengage Learning, does not guarantee the accuracy of the data contained herein. Gale accepts no payment for listing; and inclusion in the publication of any organization, agency, institution, publication, service, or individual does not imply endorsement of the editors or publisher. Errors brought to the attention of the publisher and verified to the satisfaction of the publisher will be corrected in future editions.

Gale
27500 Drake Rd.
Farmington Hills, MI, 48331-3535

LIBRARY OF CONGRESS CATALOG CARD NUMBER 76-46132

ISBN-13: 978-1-4144-3447-6
ISBN-10: 1-4144-3447-2

ISSN 0091-3421

Printed in the United States of America
1 2 3 4 5 6 7 13 12 11 10 09

Contents

Preface vii

Acknowledgments xi

Literary Criticism Series Advisory Board xiii

Preface

Named "one of the twenty-five most distinguished reference titles published during the past twenty-five years" by *Reference Quarterly,* the *Contemporary Literary Criticism* (*CLC*) series provides readers with critical commentary and general information on more than 2,000 authors now living or who died after December 31, 1999. Volumes published from 1973 through 1999 include authors who died after December 31, 1959. Previous to the publication of the first volume of *CLC* in 1973, there was no ongoing digest monitoring scholarly and popular sources of critical opinion and explication of modern literature. *CLC,* therefore, has fulfilled an essential need, particularly since the complexity and variety of contemporary literature makes the function of criticism especially important to today's reader.

Scope of the Series

CLC provides significant passages from published criticism of works by creative writers. Since many of the authors covered in *CLC* inspire continual critical commentary, writers are often represented in more than one volume. There is, of course, no duplication of reprinted criticism.

Authors are selected for inclusion for a variety of reasons, among them the publication or dramatic production of a critically acclaimed new work, the reception of a major literary award, revival of interest in past writings, or the adaptation of a literary work to film or television.

Attention is also given to several other groups of writers—authors of considerable public interest—about whose work criticism is often difficult to locate. These include mystery and science fiction writers, literary and social critics, foreign authors, and authors who represent particular ethnic groups.

Each *CLC* volume contains individual essays and reviews taken from hundreds of book review periodicals, general magazines, scholarly journals, monographs, and books. Entries include critical evaluations spanning from the beginning of an author's career to the most current commentary. Interviews, feature articles, and other published writings that offer insight into the author's works are also presented. Students, teachers, librarians, and researchers will find that the general critical and biographical material in *CLC* provides them with vital information required to write a term paper, analyze a poem, or lead a book discussion group. In addition, complete bibliographical citations note the original source and all of the information necessary for a term paper footnote or bibliography.

Organization of the Book

A *CLC* entry consists of the following elements:

- The **Author Heading** cites the name under which the author most commonly wrote, followed by birth and death dates. Also located here are any name variations under which an author wrote, including transliterated forms for authors whose native languages use nonroman alphabets. If the author wrote consistently under a pseudonym, the pseudonym will be listed in the author heading and the author's actual name given in parenthesis on the first line of the biographical and critical information. Uncertain birth or death dates are indicated by question marks. Single-work entries are preceded by a heading that consists of the most common form of the title in English translation (if applicable) and the original date of composition.

- The **Introduction** contains background information that introduces the reader to the author, work, or topic that is the subject of the entry.

- The list of **Principal Works** is ordered chronologically by date of first publication and lists the most important works by the author. The genre and publication date of each work is given. In the case of foreign authors whose works have been translated into English, the English-language version of the title follows in brackets. Unless otherwise indicated, dramas are dated by first performance, not first publication.

- Reprinted **Criticism** is arranged chronologically in each entry to provide a useful perspective on changes in critical evaluation over time. The critic's name and the date of composition or publication of the critical work are given at the beginning of each piece of criticism. Unsigned criticism is preceded by the title of the source in which it appeared. All titles by the author featured in the text are printed in boldface type. Footnotes are reprinted at the end of each essay or excerpt. In the case of excerpted criticism, only those footnotes that pertain to the excerpted texts are included.

- A complete **Bibliographical Citation** of the original essay or book precedes each piece of criticism. Source citations in the Literary Criticism Series follow University of Chicago Press style, as outlined in *The Chicago Manual of Style,* 15th ed. (Chicago: The University of Chicago Press, 2003).

- Critical essays are prefaced by brief **Annotations** explicating each piece.

- Whenever possible, a recent **Author Interview** accompanies each entry.

- An annotated bibliography of **Further Reading** appears at the end of each entry and suggests resources for additional study. In some cases, significant essays for which the editors could not obtain reprint rights are included here. Boxed material following the further reading list provides references to other biographical and critical sources on the author in series published by Gale.

Indexes

A **Cumulative Author Index** lists all of the authors that appear in a wide variety of reference sources published by Gale, including *CLC*. A complete list of these sources is found facing the first page of the Author Index. The index also includes birth and death dates and cross references between pseudonyms and actual names.

A **Cumulative Nationality Index** lists all authors featured in *CLC* by nationality, followed by the number of the *CLC* volume in which their entry appears.

A **Cumulative Topic Index** lists the literary themes and topics treated in the series as well as in other Literature Criticism series.

An alphabetical **Title Index** accompanies each volume of *CLC*. Listings of titles by authors covered in the given volume are followed by the author's name and the corresponding page numbers where the titles are discussed. English translations of foreign titles and variations of titles are cross-referenced to the title under which a work was originally published. Titles of novels, dramas, films, nonfiction books, and poetry, short story, or essay collections are printed in italics, while individual poems, short stories, and essays are printed in roman type within quotation marks.

In response to numerous suggestions from librarians, Gale also produces an annual cumulative title index that alphabetically lists all titles reviewed in *CLC* and is available to all customers. Additional copies of this index are available upon request. Librarians and patrons will welcome this separate index; it saves shelf space, is easy to use, and is recyclable upon receipt of the next edition.

Citing *Contemporary Literary Criticism*

When citing criticism reprinted in the Literary Criticism Series, students should provide complete bibliographic information so that the cited essay can be located in the original print or electronic source. Students who quote directly from reprinted criticism may use any accepted bibliographic format, such as University of Chicago Press style or Modern Language Association (MLA) style. Both the MLA and the University of Chicago formats are acceptable and recognized as being the current standards for citations. It is important, however, to choose one format for all citations; do not mix the two formats within a list of citations.

The examples below follow recommendations for preparing a bibliography set forth in *The Chicago Manual of Style,* 15th ed. (Chicago: The University of Chicago Press, 2003); the first example pertains to material drawn from periodicals, the second to material reprinted from books:

James, Harold. "Narrative Engagement with *Atonement* and *The Blind Assassin.*" *Philosophy and Literature* 29, no. 1 (April 2005): 130-45. Reprinted in *Contemporary Literary Criticism.* Vol. 246, edited by Jeffrey W. Hunter, 188-95. Detroit: Gale, 2008.

Wesley, Marilyn C. "Anne Hèbert: The Tragic Melodramas." In *Canadian Women Writing Fiction,* edited by Mickey Pearlman, 41-52. Jackson: University Press of Mississippi, 1993. Reprinted in *Contemporary Literary Criticism.* Vol. 246, edited by Jeffrey W. Hunter, 276-82. Detroit: Gale, 2008.

The examples below follow recommendations for preparing a works cited list set forth in the *MLA Handbook for Writers of Research Papers,* 5th ed. (New York: The Modern Language Association of America, 1999); the first example pertains to material drawn from periodicals, the second to material reprinted from books:

James, Harold. "Narrative Engagement with *Atonement* and *The Blind Assassin.*" *Philosophy and Literature* 29.1 (April 2005): 130-45. Reprinted in *Contemporary Literary Criticism.* Ed. Jeffrey W. Hunter. Vol. 246. Detroit: Gale, 2008. 188-95.

Wesley, Marilyn C. "Anne Hèbert: The Tragic Melodramas." *Canadian Women Writing Fiction,* edited by Mickey Pearlman. Jackson: University Press of Mississippi, 1993. 41-52. Reprinted in *Contemporary Literary Criticism.* Ed. Jeffrey W. Hunter. Vol. 246. Detroit: Gale, 2008. 276-82.

Suggestions are Welcome

Readers who wish to suggest new features, topics, or authors to appear in future volumes, or who have other suggestions or comments are cordially invited to call, write, or fax the Associate Product Manager:

Associate Product Manager, Literary Criticism Series
Gale
27500 Drake Road
Farmington Hills, MI 48331-3535
1-800-347-4253 (GALE)
Fax: 248-699-8983

Acknowledgments

The editors wish to thank the copyright holders of the criticism included in this volume and the permissions managers of many book and magazine publishing companies for assisting us in securing reproduction rights. Following is a list of the copyright holders who have granted us permission to reproduce material in this volume of *CLC*. Every effort has been made to trace copyright, but if omissions have been made, please let us know.

COPYRIGHTED MATERIAL IN *CLC*, VOLUME 274, WAS REPRODUCED FROM THE FOLLOWING PERIODICALS:

American Book Review, v. 29, May-June, 2008. Copyright © 2008 Writer's Review, Inc. Reproduced by permission.—*American Quarterly,* v. 60, September, 2008. Copyright © 2008 The American Studies Association. Reproduced by permission.—*Asian American Policy Review,* v. 14, 2005. Copyright © 2005 President and Fellows of Harvard College. Reproduced by permission.—*Asian Studies Review,* v. 31, June, 2007 for "Narratives, the Body and the 1964 Tokyo Olympics" by Rio Otomo. Copyright © 2007 Asian Studies Association of Australia. Reproduced by permission of Taylor & Francis, Ltd., http//:www.tandf.co.uk/journals and the author.—*Atlantic Monthly,* v. 280, November, 1997 for review of *The Wind-Up Bird Chronicle,* by Haruki Murakami, by Phoebe-Lou Adams. Copyright © 1997 Phoebe-lou Adams. Reproduced by permission of the author.—*Boundary 2,* v. 28, summer, 2001. Copyright © 2001 Duke University Press. All rights reserved. Used by permission of the publisher.—*Comparative Literature Studies,* v. 37, 2000; v. 45, 2008. Copyright © 2000, 2008 by The Pennsylvania State University. Both reproduced by permission of The Pennsylvania State University Press.—*Confluencia: Revista Hispanica de Cultura Y literatura,* v. 19, spring, 2004. Reproduced by permission.—*Contemporary Literature,* v. 43, summer, 2002. Copyright © 2002 by the Board of Regents of the University of Wisconsin System. Reproduced by permission.—*Critique: Studies in Contemporary Fiction,* v. 49, fall, 2007. Copyright © 2007 by Helen Dwight Reid Educational Foundation. Reproduced with permission of the Helen Dwight Reid Educational Foundation, published by Heldref Publications, 1319 18th Street, NW, Washington, DC 20036-1802.—*Irish Marketing Review,* v. 19, 2007. Copyright © 2007 Mercury Publications Ltd. Reproduced by permission.—*Irish Studies Review,* v. 16, August, 2008 for "'Let the Fall Begin': Thomas Kinsella's European Dimension" by Andrew Fitzsimons. Copyright © 2008 Taylor & Francis Group, LLC. Reproduced by permission of Taylor & Francis, Ltd., http//:www.tandf.co.uk/journals and the author.—*Irish University Review: A Journal of Irish Studies,* v. 36, winter, 2006. Copyright © 2006 *Irish University Review.* Reproduced by permission.—*Japan Forum,* v. 16, 2004 for "In Search of the Real: Technology, Shock and Language in Murakami Haruki's 'Sputnik Sweetheart'" by Michael Fisch. Copyright © 2004 BAJS. Reproduced by permission of Taylor & Francis, Ltd., http//:www.tandf.co.uk/journals and the author.—*Journal of Asian American Studies,* v. 9, October, 2006. Copyright © 2006 by The Johns Hopkins University Press. Reproduced by permission.—*Mosaic,* v. 36, June, 2003; v. 40, March, 2007. Copyright © 2003, 2007 *Mosaic.* Acknowledgment of previous publications are herewith made.—*New Republic,* v. 235, October 23, 2006. Copyright © 2006 by The New Republic, Inc. Reproduced by permission of *The New Republic.*—*New Statesman,* v. 134, January 24, 2005; v. 136, June 4, 2007. Copyright © 2005 New Statesman, Ltd. Both reproduced by permission.—*PMLA: Publications of the Modern Language Association of America,* v. 121, October, 2006. Copyright © 2006 by the Modern Language Association of America. Reproduced by permission of the Modern Language Association of America.—*Publishers Weekly,* v. 248, June 18, 2001. Copyright © 2001 by Reed Publishing USA. Reproduced from *Publishers Weekly,* published by the Bowker Magazine Group of Cahners Publishing Co., a division of Reed Publishing USA, by permission.—*Studies in the Literary Imagination,* v. 37, spring, 2004. Copyright © 2004 Department of English, Georgia State University. Reproduced by permission.—*Virginia Quarterly Review,* v. 83, winter, 2007. Copyright © 2007 by *The Virginia Quarterly Review,* The University of Virginia. Reproduced by permission of the publisher.—*Women's Review of Books,* v. 25, May-June, 2008. Copyright © 2008 Old City Publishing, Inc. Reproduced by permission.—*World Literature Today,* v. 77, April-June, 2003. Copyright © 2003 by *World Literature Today.* Reproduced by permission of the publisher.—*Yearbook of English Studies,* 2005. Copyright © 2005 Modern Humanities Research Association. Reproduced by permission of the publisher.

COPYRIGHTED MATERIAL IN *CLC,* VOLUME 274, WAS REPRODUCED FROM THE FOLLOWING BOOKS:

Alonso Gallo, Laura P. From "'The Good, the Brave, the Beautiful': Julia Alvarez's Homage to Female History," in *Evolving Origins, Transplanting Cultures: Literary Legacies of the New Americans.* Edited by Laura P. Alonso Gallo and An-

Gale Literature Product Advisory Board

The members of the Gale Literature Product Advisory Board—reference librarians from public and academic library systems—represent a cross-section of our customer base and offer a variety of informed perspectives on both the presentation and content of our literature products. Advisory board members assess and define such quality issues as the relevance, currency, and usefulness of the author coverage, critical content, and literary topics included in our series; evaluate the layout, presentation, and general quality of our printed volumes; provide feedback on the criteria used for selecting authors and topics covered in our series; provide suggestions for potential enhancements to our series; identify any gaps in our coverage of authors or literary topics, recommending authors or topics for inclusion; analyze the appropriateness of our content and presentation for various user audiences, such as high school students, undergraduates, graduate students, librarians, and educators; and offer feedback on any proposed changes/enhancements to our series. We wish to thank the following advisors for their advice throughout the year.

Barbara M. Bibel
Librarian
Oakland Public Library
Oakland, California

Dr. Toby Burrows
Principal Librarian
The Scholars' Centre
University of Western Australia Library
Nedlands, Western Australia

Celia C. Daniel
Associate Reference Librarian
Howard University Libraries
Washington, D.C.

David M. Durant
Reference Librarian
Joyner Library
East Carolina University
Greenville, North Carolina

Nancy T. Guidry
Librarian
Bakersfield Community College
Bakersfield, California

Heather Martin
Arts & Humanities Librarian
University of Alabama at Birmingham, Sterne Library
Birmingham, Alabama

Susan Mikula
Librarian
Indiana Free Library
Indiana, Pennsylvania

Thomas Nixon
Humanities Reference Librarian
University of North Carolina at Chapel Hill, Davis
  Library
Chapel Hill, North Carolina

Mark Schumacher
Jackson Library
University of North Carolina at Greensboro
Greensboro, North Carolina

Gwen Scott-Miller
Assistant Director
Sno-Isle Regional Library System
Marysville, Washington

Julia Alvarez
1950-

American novelist, poet, essayist, and writer of children's books.

The following entry provides an overview of Alvarez's career through 2008. For further discussion of her life and works, see *CLC,* Volume 93.

INTRODUCTION

A political exile from the Dominican Republic, Alvarez documents the Hispanic American experience in novels, poetry, and essays that address issues of acculturation, alienation, prejudice, and power. She is best known for her novels, which redefine the U.S. Latino identity with a mix of fact, fiction, and autobiography related through the perspectives of multiple narrators. Citing Maxine Hong Kingston's *Woman Warrior* as one of her greatest influences, Alvarez has frequently chosen as subjects women of historical importance to the Dominican Republic, women who, as she wrote in the postscript to her novel *In the Time of the Butterflies* (1994), "can only be understood by fiction, only finally redeemed by the imagination." Alvarez's novels, especially the semi-autobiographical *How the García Girls Lost Their Accents* (1991) and its sequel, *¡Yo!* (1997), are considered important additions to postcolonial literature because of their exploration of the Caribbean diaspora in terms of the U.S. presence in the Dominican Republic.

BIOGRAPHICAL INFORMATION

Alvarez was born in New York City in 1950. When she was just three months old, her parents, both native Dominicans, decided to return to their homeland. Alvarez's father, a medical doctor, actively participated in the underground movement to overthrow U.S.-backed dictator Rafael Trujillo. However, her father was continually spared in the government's regular purges of dissidents because of his wife's wealthy and powerful family, which had strong ties to the United States. According to Alvarez, her parents feigned an obsession with all things American as a strategy for survival, seeking to conceal their opposition to Trujillo's regime. Following an aborted assassination attempt on Trujillo in 1960, the Alvarez family moved

back to the United States. Four months after their escape, the founders of the underground movement, the Mirabal sisters, were murdered. The Mirabal sisters are the subject of Alvarez's *In the Time of the Butterflies,* which was adapted into a popular film starring Salma Hayek in 2001. Trujillo was ultimately assassinated in 1961, ending his thirty-year reign. Growing up in the Bronx, Alvarez and her sisters experienced American culture firsthand. In her first novel, *How the García Girls Lost Their Accents,* Alvarez documents the ambivalence she and her siblings felt toward their adopted country as a result of their prior experience with American government and business infiltration in the Dominican Republic. Alvarez's adolescence is also recollected in the essay collections *Something to Declare* (1998), which includes pieces on her influences as a writer, and *Once upon a Quinceañera* (2007), which describes the long tradition of elaborate celebration surrounding a Latina's fifteenth birthday. Alvarez completed her undergraduate studies at Middlebury College in Vermont in 1971. In 1975 she obtained a master's degree in creative writing from Syracuse University. Since 1988, she has taught at Middlebury College, where she is currently writer-in-residence. In addition to her five novels and two works of nonfiction, Alvarez has published four collections of poetry and several books for children. She frequently travels to the Dominican Republic, where she and her husband, Bill Eichner, have established an organic coffee farm that doubles as a literacy center. Their experience in progressive agriculture is documented in Alvarez's fable for children, *A Cafecito Story* (2001). Alvarez's most recent project is the children's novel *Return to Sender,* (2009) about Mexican migrant workers in Vermont. The title refers to a 2006 dragnet operation in which undocumented workers were seized and separated from their children.

MAJOR WORKS

Alvarez manipulates literary genres in all of her novels, which present both history and autobiography in the form of fictionalized memoirs, the validity of which are further called into question through the device of competing narratives. In this way, Alvarez seeks not authentic documentation, but rather an imaginative view of the past that incorporates the perspectives of its many participants, according none superiority. Alvarez's most personal collective histories are *How the García Girls Lost Their Accents*, a PEN/Faulkner award winner, and *¡Yo!*, both of which are based on her family's immigration experience. *How the García Girls Lost Their Accents* is actually a series of fifteen short stories, told in reverse chronological order and spanning the years from 1956 to 1989. Through the alternating perspectives of the four García sisters—Carla, Sandra, Yolanda, and Sofía—the reader is introduced to the large family compound inhabited by the García clan in the Dominican Republic, where a life of privilege comes at the price of constant fear of government reprisal. Speaking through her double, the poet Yolanda García, Alvarez recalls being punished for inventing stories in an atmosphere where silence was prized. Coming of age in the liberated culture of the 1960s United States, the girls confront ethnic discrimination as well as an onslaught of popular culture urging behaviors that defied their strict Catholic upbringing. The girls' accounts of their resistance to parental authority as they seek to assimilate are mirrored by the Dominicans' rebellion against Trujillo. Alvarez the author emerges as the central character of *¡Yo!* Each chapter of this novel narrates an episode in the life of Yolanda García from the perspective of another person involved in the event, many of whom are friends or family members who appeared in *How the García Girls Lost Their Accents*.

In the Time of the Butterflies is also narrated by four sisters—the Mirabals—Patria, Minerva, Maria Theresa, and Dedé. Set entirely in the Dominican Republic, the sisters' stories document how they came to be leaders of the anti-Trujillo political movement, code-named Las Mariposas (The Butterflies). Three of the sisters were killed in the violence that ensued between the insurgents and the military police. Although Alvarez has been criticized by some scholars for portraying the Mirabals as martyrs, Alvarez claims in her postscript to the novel to have resisted this approach: "As for the sisters of legend, wrapped in superlatives and ascended into myth, they were totally inaccessible to me. I realized, too, that such deification was dangerous, the same godmaking impulse that had created our tyrant [Trujillo]." The novels *In the Name of Salomé* (2000) and *Saving the World* (2006) both juxtapose the life of a nineteenth-century Dominican heroine with that of a more contemporary woman. In the first, Salomé, the poet of the Dominican Republic's struggle for independence from Spain, is viewed in relation to her only daughter, Camila, a professor at Vassar college who in 1960—at the age of sixty-three—joined a literacy brigade in Cuba. The parallel stories in *Saving the World* are those of the real-life Dona Isabel, who embarked on a crusade against smallpox in 1803, and the fictional Latina author Anna Heubling, whose

discovery of Isabel's story makes her regret not being more involved in her husband's work with deforestation and AIDS in the Dominican Republic.

CRITICAL RECEPTION

Alvarez's novels have contributed greatly to critical theories about multiculturalism. She is generally considered one of the earliest writers to move away from the static binaries of home/exile and patriot/expatriate, instead revealing the fluidity of the immigrant experience through shifting narrative perspectives, nonlinear chronology, and geographic flux. For the most part, critics consider Alvarez's novels to embody the author's theory about hybrid identities: "We travel on that border between two worlds and we see both points of view." Critic Karen Castellucci Cox writes, "The mental affliction that signals . . . a split identity, where one experiences authentic citizenship only in the shadowy borderlands between juxtaposed worlds, haunts much of Alvarez's written work."

In a review of *¡Yo!* Ellen McCracken concurs: "Alvarez exemplifies the hyphenated Americans whose formation links them crucially to both the North and the South, and whose writing glides perpetually between these distinct geographic, cultural, and political spaces." This state of spatial transition has been seen to further disrupt the classic dualisms of postcolonial theory. David T. Mitchell writes, "Parallel to other postcolonial writers, such as Salman Rushdie, Michelle Cliff, and Bharati Mukherjee, Alvarez attempts to destabilize the binary of the postcolonial writer's 'absence' or 'presence' in a geographical homeland." Critic Katarzyana Marciniak also addresses the issue of objectivity as related to the displaced writer. She praises Alvarez's approach, claiming that the self-reflexive nature of Alvarez's writing, which calls into question the authority of the author through the use of multiple narrators, serves to "debunk the idea that a transnational position implies a new, liberatory identity that allows an exile-immigrant a special epistemological insight and overall empowerment."

Still, a few critics argue that Alvarez has been too long away from the Dominican Republic to sympathize with its concerns. For example, Trenton Hickman, in a review of *A Cafecito Story*, charges Alvarez with perpetuating colonialism: "Even as [the book] envisions a new future for Dominican coffee growers, it reinscribes the U.S. expansionist policy of Manifest Destiny as a white Nebraska farmer, Joe, seizes control of land as part of a new paternalism." The multiple narrative voices in Alvarez's fiction have also been viewed as a paradigm for the power dynamics of race, class and gender, especially as they relate to the Dominican experience of American capitalism and the authority of history as written from the standpoint of the dominant power. In addition, Alvarez has received much attention from feminist critics, who have adopted her as an important revisionist historian for her portrayal of women in the service of revolution.

PRINCIPAL WORKS

Homecoming (poetry) 1984
How the García Girls Lost Their Accents (novel) 1991
In the Time of the Butterflies (novel) 1994
The Other Side/El Otro Lado (poetry) 1995
Homecoming: New and Collected Poems (poetry) 1996
¡Yo! (novel) 1997
Something to Declare (essays) 1998
In the Name of Salomé (novel) 2000
A Cafecito Story (fable) 2001
How Tía Lola Came to Stay (juvenilia) 2001
Before We Were Free (juvenilia) 2002
Finding Miracles (juvenilia) 2004
The Woman I Kept to Myself (poetry) 2004
Saving the World (novel) 2006
Once upon a Quinceañera: Coming of Age in the USA (nonfiction) 2007
Return to Sender (juvenilia) 2009

CRITICISM

David T. Mitchell (essay date 1999)

SOURCE: Mitchell, David T. "The Accent of 'Loss': Cultural Crossings as Context in Julia Alvarez's *How the García Girls Lost Their Accents*." In *Beyond the Binary: Reconstructing Cultural Identity in a Multicultural Context,* edited by Timothy B. Powell, pp. 165-84. New Brunswick, N.J.: Rutgers University Press, 1999.

[*In the following essay, Mitchell explores Alvarez's use of multiple perspectives in* How the García Girls Lost Their Accents, *arguing that this technique emphasizes the various facets of her characters' identities.*]

> *It would be years before I took the courses that would change my mind in schools paid for by sugar from fields around us, years before I could begin to comprehend how one does not see the maids when they pass by.*
>
> Julia Alvarez, **Homecoming**

For postcolonial novelists, the enunciative position of the exile, émigré, or expatriate serves as an apt metaphor for the paradoxical desire of their fictions to capture the ambivalence of immigrant lives. The "loss" of an ability to depict an absent homeland empirically becomes a key characteristic of postcolonial writing; the central tension is informed by a desire to look back on what has been "lost" in order to restore or regain one's place of origin. The impossibility of such a repossession, imaginative or otherwise, produces profound uncertainties about cultural belongingness and the artistic pursuit of "authentic expression."

This defining ambivalence characteristic of postcolonial writing inscribes the idea of "loss" in terms of a negativity that forever places the postcolonial writer in a subordinate position to those who retain "unhindered" access to the desired artistic object of the homeland. The critique of culturally produced binaries that separate enunciative positions such as home/exile, patriot/expatriate, and citizen/alien serves as the guiding impetus of the postcolonial writer's narrative explorations and calls into question those divisions as flawed and unnatural categories of contemporary cultures and identities that are always already hybrid cultural products.

Crucial to understanding the contemporary postcolonial writer's definitive sense of "homelessness" is the analysis of the ways in which he or she seeks to go beyond the stale binaries of state-imposed identities in narrative. Often this objective is accomplished by demonstrating that each character possesses only some of the pieces that make up an absent or inaccessible whole. Postcolonial writers privilege the culturally mixed heritages and influences of their protagonists in order to de-essentialize nationalist polemics that seek to define the characteristics of the true geographical native. By challenging authorial and authoritative claims to geographic and cultural binaries that falsely legislate what counts as the official experience of a community or place, postcolonial writers strategically foreground and celebrate either the limitations of the first-person perspective or proffer multiple narrators who decenter readerly identifications with a singular or omnisciently controlling narrative perspective.

Such a project informs **How the García Girls Lost Their Accents,** the first novel by postcolonial writer Julia Alvarez. The careful positioning of the verb "lost" at the heart of the novel's title promises a document that will ferret out the moment or moments of cultural extinction/assimilation for the title characters—four sisters who grow up in an upper-class family in the Dominican Republic and are later forced into exile in the United States. Parallel to other postcolonial writers, such as Salman Rushdie, Michelle

Cliff, and Bharati Mukherjee, Alvarez attempts to destabilize the binary of the postcolonial writer's "absence" from, or "presence" in, a geographical homeland. Alvarez's first novel seeks to delineate the complex interplay of colliding ideological and political systems that inform the experiences of her culturally hybrid subjects of the Dominican Republic and the United States. By pluralizing the lost accents of the title, Alvarez presents a novelistic strategy that fragments and multiplies the story of immigrant experience into competing accounts and thus rejects the impulse to reduce the interplay of individual and cultural influences to a static binary of dominated and dominant.

How the García Girls Lost Their Accents, which won the Pen/Faulkner award in the ethnic fiction category, marks Alvarez's debut as a novelist who contemplates the complex intersections of class, nationality and race for her Dominican American characters.[1] Since Alvarez's family was part of a wave of middle-class immigrants who came to settle in New York City during the second half of the twentieth century, her work privileges the cultural limbo of migratory groups as an important site of fictional investigation.[2] The geographical and imaginative terrain of *How the García Girls Lost Their Accents* is consistently saturated with the economic and political influence of an exported U.S. capitalism that has resulted from years of military and market control. As Alvarez explains in an autobiographical essay, **"An American Childhood in the Dominican Republic,"** the two cultures are inextricably bound together:

> [My mother] enrolled her daughters in Carol Morgan's school where we began each day by pledging allegiance to the flag of the United States, which I much preferred to the Dominican one, for it had the lovely red-and-white stripes of the awning at the ice-cream parlor. . . .
>
> We also sang the marine song, "From the halls of Montezuma to the shores of Tripoli," marching in place to the rallying beat. The marines had occupied the country often, most recently when they had installed Trujillo as head of state two and a half decades before, and their song as well as the light-skinned, light-eyed children with American names in the barrios were some of the traces that they had been there.[3]

Such entwined racial and national histories openly inform the narrative trajectory of *García Girls* [*How the García Girls Lost Their Accents*] as well as the novel's oscillation between assimilating into the lifestyles promulgated by middle-class consumer culture in the United States and longing for a lost Dominican origin. The oscillation of her characters between the "promise" and "tragedy" that each cultural experience affords establishes the binary nationalist affinities that compete for authority in the midst of her characters' migratory movements between two countries.

The argument that this essay pursues is located in an analysis of the significance of this nationalist ambivalence in postcolonial narratives. For Alvarez, the infiltration of U.S. culture, military, and governments into the Dominican Republic has produced neither a sense of colonial resentment nor an open ideological embrace of capitalist infiltration. Instead, the writer explores the class and racial dimensions of such a relationship in ways that complicate an understanding of cultural privilege in the colonial commerce of nations:

> What kept my father from being rounded up with the others [political dissidents of the Trujillo Regime] each time there was a purge . . . was his connection with my mother's powerful family. It was not just their money that gave them power, for wealth was sometimes an incentive to persecute a family and appropriate its fortune. It was their strong ties with Americans and the United States. As I mentioned, most of my aunts and uncles had graduated from American schools and colleges, and they corresponded regularly with their classmates and alumni associations. . . . The family subscribed to American magazines, received mail-order catalogues, and joined American clubs and honorary societies. This obsession with American things was no longer merely enchantment with the States, but a strategy for survival.[4]

It is this particular history of cultural appropriations and incestuous political crossings that structures the postcolonial backdrop of Alvarez's novel. As members of a privileged class in the Dominican Republic, the Garcia family has the capacity to negotiate the fraught binaries that exist between nationalist loyalties and political tyranny. Rather than cast the colonialist heritage of the Dominican Republic as a choice between colonial servitude and naive ideological indoctrination, Alvarez's family consciously embraces their Dominicanized version of an exported American culture in order to maintain and bolster their economic and social advantage. By surrounding the family with the accoutrements of a U.S. export economy, they temporarily secure their safety despite their opposition to the United States-backed Trujillo regime. In attending to this aspect of Alvarez's interests, this essay goes on to explicate the ways in which class privilege interrupts and complicates strict nationalist binaries by promoting the alternative values of postcolonial multiplicity.

How the García Girls Lost Their Accents charts the reactions and responses of familial and cultural relations among four sisters: Carla, Sandra, Yolanda, and Sofia. Sociological studies have often endeavored to use sibling groups as a means of charting the ways in which environment and/or genetic inheritance affect the development of children who are brought up in the same environment. Alvarez employs a similar strategy by maintaining a simultaneous focus upon a cast of characters who develop within a shared social and familial milieu. In situating her characters together as a discursive "family," Alvarez seeks to explore the means by which her characters appropriate and recognize their narrative stories as shared and/or separate from a unitary body of gendered familial identities. Throughout the novel, numerous commentators remark on the poor fortune of a family that consists entirely of girls—"what, four girls and no boys?"—while each daughter struggles to free herself from the limitations of a communal designation that strips them of their uniqueness and individuality. Because the label "García Girls" stands in for the plural identities submerged beneath the faceless anonymity of daughters (who, unlike their male counterparts, do not need to be individuated as distinct human beings), Alvarez remains ambiguous about the prospects for her four narrators throughout the novel.

Since multiple narrators (or what I will term multiperspectivity from this point on) afford novelists the opportunity to simulate access to a variety of first- and third-person narrators within the same text, *How the García Girls Lost Their Accents* exploits such a tactic by oscillating between diverging narrative lines that upend and dynamically revise each other. Multiperspectivity succeeds in breaking the binary between narrator and narrated and paves the way for the interruptive force of hybrid postcolonial forms. Rather than explicating one specific response to the dislocating sensations of cultural transition, the novel situates the notion of "loss" in terms of each characters' responses to the intersection and clash of U.S. and Dominican cultures. Alvarez's use of multiple first-person narratives formally mirrors her understanding of the shifting and multiple nature of postcolonial identity itself.

The poster image of the Palmolive woman near the Garcia daughters' home in the Dominican Republic establishes the influence of American postcapitalist forms long before any member of the family ever sets foot in the land of "concrete cities and snow." Because the novel moves backward in time from 1989 to 1956, rather than forward to chart the movement (in some progressive chronological sense) of the Dominican family's transition from the island to the States, readers are set up to anticipate that the novel will present a vision of the Dominican homeland prior to U.S. cultural infiltration and military intervention. Yet the reader's arrival at the multiple first-person narratives of the title characters does not coincide with this notion of a "pure" cultural setting. Despite the narrative's interest in explicating the alienating cultural terrain to which the daughters are exposed in the United States, Alvarez's analysis becomes increasingly geared toward plotting the ways in which such a sense of estrange-

ment seems present from the outset. In doing so, Alvarez attempts to imagine the contradictions inherent in any return to a geographic space once occupied and then relinquished.

Although [. . .] *García Girls* charts numerous reactions on the part of its characters to the move from the Dominican Republic to the United States, the most significant aspect of negotiating such "returns" entails the ability or inability of each daughter to understand her specific relation to the family servants. Unlike the more prototypical plot lines of the immigration novel, *García Girls* details the experiences of characters who operate within the upper echelons of economic status and political power in their homeland. Their cultural positioning is interesting because they literally move from a position of dominance to a racially marginal position in the United States. Alvarez's story contemplates the exploitive social conditions of each culture and refuses to privilege the country of origins over the newly adopted nation—each exists in a dialectical tension within the minds of her narrators in such a way that the binary of national identity gradually falls away to be replaced by the more indeterminate identity of a multinationed clan.

Thus, the move from the Dominican Republic to the United States involves a "fall" from influence for the family. After discovering that they will be forced to leave the family compound because of a failed CIA-backed governmental coup, the family's visionary mother, Mami, explains that the relocation means an abdication of material wealth and relative security:

> So, Laura thinks. So the papers have cleared and we are leaving. Now everything she sees sharpens as if through the lens of loss—the orchids in their hanging straw baskets, the row of apothecary jars Carlos has found for her in old druggists' throughout the countryside, the rich light shafts swarming with a golden pollen. She will miss this glorious light warming the inside of her skin and jeweling the trees, the grass, the lily pond beyond the hedge.[5]

The "lens of loss" that Alvarez uses to underscore Mami's instantaneous sense of desire for the home and countryside she has come to cherish epitomizes the way the novel situates nostalgia for the homeland. In the wake of the class privileges that have been stripped from the island family once they are forced to seek exile to escape Papi's impending imprisonment and the random searches of the government *guardias,* each family members' narrative investigates how their experiences on the island of the Dominican Republic condition their responses throughout their lives. The household accoutrements that Mami longs to retain even before she has stepped outside the compound for the last time indicate the history of acquisitions and purchases that represent the multinational life of consumption she has created for herself and her family.

Such longing for the life that has been lost reverberates throughout the novel, and like Yolanda's craving for guavas, the native fruit she ate as a young girl, all the characters in this fiction attempt to reclaim the present in terms of the past—their experiences in the United States compared and contrasted to their lives before the family's exile. The imaged or imagined homeland that haunts each narrator serves as a barometer to gauge the "success" or "trauma" of the years that follow. The "lens of loss" inevitably alters, however, and as each child relates her story to the reader, individual notions of "loss" shift and a collide. When Yolanda, for instance, arrives on the island after a five-year hiatus in the United States, her memory of the land she left is rekindled and reinvested with the startling beauty of the country and the warmth her relatives provide:

> All around her are the foothills, a dark enormous green, the sky more a brightness than a color. A breeze blows through the palms below, rustling their branches, so they whisper like voices. Here and there a braid of smoke rises up from a hillside—a campesino and his family living out their solitary life. This is what she has been missing all these years without really knowing that she has been missing it. Standing here in the quiet, she believes she has never felt at home in the States, never.
>
> (12)

Yet, despite the apparent parallels between Mami's earlier sense of loss for the island atmosphere and her third daughter's nostalgia for "palms . . . [that] whisper like voices [, . . . and the] solitary life" of the hillside *campesinos,* Yolanda's return is tempered by her growing awareness of the servant classes who make the family's life of relative luxury possible. Rather than smoothly assimilate back into her prior existence as the pampered daughter of a wealthy political official, Yolanda's experiences in the United States provide her with a politicized context of class consciousness that troubles the family's once naturalized Dominican lifestyle. Rather than circulate on the periphery of the family, the maids immediately erupt into Yolanda's description of the scene. The "invisible" labor force that populates and "invisibly" maintains the family estate forms a separate enclave that is openly excluded from the closeness the rest of the family enjoys: "She [Yolanda] pictures the maids in their mysterious cluster at the end of the patio" (11).

Because "home" has taken on differing significances for Yolanda now that she has, like the narrator of the epigraph with which I began, taken "the [college]

courses which would change [her] mind," the homecoming that establishes the narrative tone and mood of *García Girls* is one of tension and profound ambivalence. The mature narrative perspective that begins this novel cannot simply recapture the girlhood geography of her previous recollections. Alvarez invests her imaginative reunion with images that disrupt and revise her protagonist's relationship to the familial and cultural beliefs that she fails to recognize at an earlier age. The benefits she and her immediate family have reaped at the expense of the servant classes they employ and exploit lose their luxurious gloss. Armed with a repertoire of political theories from her college classes and her own racial experiences in the United States, which irreparably change her vision of home, Alvarez points to the ways in which her characters respond to the context of upperclass privilege in the Dominican Republic that once went unarticulated in their day-to-day lives. The racial binary of U.S. culture (dark/light) provides a new context from which to collapse a previously unchallenged binary of self/darker-skinned other that the class system of the Dominican Republic perpetuates.

This exposed "absence" of the novel's working classes does not, nonetheless, allow Alvarez's fictional servants a space from which they may speak their own lives. Although the eldest maid, Chucha, briefly narrates her own response to the family's departure later in the novel, *García Girls* attempts to theorize the significance of the racialized dimensions of class overtly. While the novel engages in the significant political act of articulating the experiences of Dominican Americans who have remained largely invisible in U.S. discourses, her own concerns also focus upon the "others" she cannot quite reach in the Dominican Republic. While the novel offers developed subject positions to its upper-class Dominican characters, it simultaneously acknowledges that granting "voices" to some falls short of "speaking" for other marginalized perspectives.

In fact, the lost accents of the title alludes to the difficulties inherent in the Garcia family's ability to "read" or "represent" the experiences of servants who prove absolutely essential to maintaining the familial fabric. In the wake of becoming political exiles living in the United States, they struggle to understand the changes that assault them once they land on foreign soil—"There have been so many stops on the road of the last twenty-nine years since her family left this island behind. She and her sisters have led such turbulent lives—so many husbands, homes, jobs, wrong turns among them" (11)—but such a volatile transition has not necessarily enabled them to make anything more than a nod in the direction of the "inscrutable" nature that the maids seem to harbor: "In the fading light of the patio, Yolanda cannot make out the expression on the dark face [of the maid, ironically named Illuminada]" (10). For Alvarez and Third World theorists such as Trinh and Spivak, the subject speaking position of these subaltern characters already presupposes the impossibility of capturing the "lost accents" of difference that the title contemplates.[6]

Despite Yolanda's attempts to analyze the meaning of the family's willingness to use its class position at the expense of other island denizens, the sisters' narratives, which conclude Alvarez's novel, completely overlook the hierarchical class system from which their family has benefited. This fact is perhaps most evident in the oldest sister, Carla's, chapter, "An American Surprise." While the adult Yolanda's chapter moves back and forth between her sense of security in the island homestead and her growing dis-ease with the now ever present servant class who fulfill the needs of the Garcia clan, Carla's narrative demonstrates that even her own experience of racial denigration in the United States cannot bring her to an awareness of the Dominican situation.

Because Carla is the oldest of the four sisters, her relationship to the family's live-in maids is the most established of the four sisters. As in Mami's "lens of loss," Carla's chapter begins most forthrightly with a contemplation of her own private sense of loss in the wake of the family's relocation. Unlike the "welcome back" cake that Yolanda is offered as a sign of appreciation from her island relatives, the celebration dinner in "An American Surprise" marks the day the Garcias turn "one American year old." After Carla listens to her father make a speech that misquotes the poem on the Statue of Liberty, she wonders exactly what such a celebration means to her own experience in her newly adopted country: "What do you wish for on the first celebration of the day you lost everything?" (150). The homesickness she feels manifests itself most specifically in terms of her unfamiliarity with English slang and colloquialisms that elude her comprehension. As soon as she asks God to let the family return home and helps blow out the celebration candles that line the cake, she recalls a scene that vividly reminds her of her exclusion from the culture she now circulates within:

> Down the block the neighborhood dead-ended in abandoned farmland that Mami read in the local paper the developers were negotiating to buy. Grasses and real trees and real bushes still grew beyond the barbed-wire fence posted with a big sign: PRIVATE, NO TRESPASSING. The sign had surprised Carla since "forgive us our trespasses" was the only other context in which she had heard the word. She pointed the sign out to Mami on one of their first walks to the bus stop. "Isn't it funny, Mami? A sign that you have to be

good." Her mother did not understand at first until Carla explained about the Lord's Prayer. Mami laughed. Words sometimes meant two things in English too. This trespass meant that no one must go inside the property because it was not public like a park, but private. Carla nodded, disappointed. She would never get the hang of this new country.

(151)

Because language represents one of the most significant barriers to the characters' ability to discover a space from which to speak and be understood, Carla's frustration serves to highlight the fact that accents are not just lost but also get in the way. Her inability to comprehend the alternative context for the trespassing sign (that is, her lack of knowledge about the rules of private property) is highlighted by her "only other context," the Lord's Prayer, which she has memorized as a young girl and carried with her from the Dominican Republic. To the oldest daughter the alien notion of "no trespassing" serves a dual function: to highlight the narrator's inability to contemplate the "meanings" of an Other culture that deviates from the linguistic rules to which she has grown accustomed, and to signal a metaphorical exclusion as well. Not only does Carla sense her loss of cultural privilege in the transition from a social context she understands to one she does not, but Alvarez also wants to foreshadow the impending hostility that will greet the transplanted family in the "new world." The Garcias' relocation to a different culture upends their sense of class privilege and simultaneously challenges the American myth of a classless society. This cultural transition not only thrusts the family into a new national context but also revises the daughter's previously uninterrogated class identity in the Dominican Republic. "No trespassing" represents the loss of access to the institutions of authority and meaning making that matter in an American context.

Parallel to the immigrant-novel tradition from which it hails, ***How the García Girls Lost Their Accents*** explicitly engages in a critique of the inhospitable promised land that remains indifferent and even violent toward its newly arrived inhabitants. Unlike other versions of the genre, such as *The Rise and Fall of David Levinsky, The Breadgivers, China Men, The Borderlands,* and *Jasmine,* Alvarez's novel emphasizes the time before the relocation of her characters.[7] Instead of positing a moment when her characters were fully "at home" on their native soil (that is, a time when the characters believed in their thorough comprehension of cultural codes, customs, and social contracts), Alvarez's attention to the daughters' experiences in their childhood prior to expatriation demonstrates that their collective sense of security is founded upon their familial myths of class and social privilege. The cultural codes that Carla finds obscure and difficult to interpret in the United States may just as easily be located on the island. While Carla moves in and out of the servant circles at her parents' house, the naturalized social hierarchy cannot be unmoored or questioned. The children's acculturation in the naturalized Dominican binaries of racial and class differences proves a necessary ideological component to their participation in their family's privileged status.

Carla's lack of access to Mami's point of view underscores the novel's recurrent theme of impassable cultural boundaries. As Gladys, one of the household's recent arrivals to the servant's quarters, prepares the table for dinner, she sings a popular ditty that Carla listens to from the corridor:

> *Yo tiro la cuchara,*
>
> *Yo tiro el tenedor*
>
> *Yo tiro to' lo' plato'*
>
> *Y me voy pa' Nueva Yor'.*
>
> I loved to hear Gladys' high, sweet voice imitating her favorite singers on the radio. Someday she was going to be a famous actress, Gladys said. But my mother said Gladys was only a country girl who didn't know any better than to sing popular tunes in the house and wear her kinky hair in rollers all week long, then comb it out for Sunday mass in hairdos copied from American magazines my mother had thrown out.
>
> (258)

The young narrator can report but not comment upon the divergent interpretations of Gladys's behavior. Despite Mami's diminutive tone toward Gladys's desire to westernize her appearance, the lines of cultural influence and each character's relationship to them remain tangled. Since the American magazines belong to Mami to begin with, Gladys's appropriation of them seems to be more than a case of her uncomprehending capitulation to American standards of beauty. In fact, the song Carla listens to but fails to analyze would suggest that Gladys thinks of the United States as a place away from the exploitive world of the Dominican caste system. Her desire to free herself from the utensils that signify the tools of her class oppression, implies a refusal to surrender to the order of maids and masters to which the Garcias subscribe.

Despite moments when the household servants communicate their concern and attachment to various family members, the cultural constraints of racial and class identifications prevent empathy or understanding from taking place:

> Chucha held each of our heads in her hands and wailed a prayer over us. We were used to some of this strange stuff from daily contact with her, but maybe it was

because today we could feel an ending in the air, anyhow, we all started to cry as if Chucha had finally released her own tears in each of us.

(221)

In this instance, the unitary "we" pronoun that the second-oldest sister, Sandra, uses to represent her own as well as her sisters' shared perspectives about Chucha's "strange stuff" indicates their inability as a group to accept the maid's sorrow and forge a connection to her. The narrator's own sense of sadness evolves not out of a shared understanding with the "tears" the maid releases "in each of us" but as a result of the "feel [of] an ending in the air." Not only will they leave behind the familiar Dominican world, they also will surrender their lives as social insiders who benefit from sedimented economic stratifications deeply embedded in Dominican society.

Yet, to begin to counter the mystique that surrounds the lower classes of *García Girls,* Alvarez interrupts the textual space separating the first three "I" narratives and the final "I" of the artist figure Yolanda with Chucha's own account of the day her employers vacate the family compound. With her proliferation of multiple first-person accounts, Alvarez seeks to transcend the limitations of the class binaries that separate the Garcias from the servants. The narrative device of multiperspectivity enables the novel to resist closure and more singular readerly identifications by moving from one story to the next, in effect denying the reader's desire to follow through more thoroughly on any single story. Left behind in the wake of the family's sudden exit, Chucha wanders through the empty house imagining what life will hold for the Garcias as they head off to encounter the "pale Americans" who make up "a nation of zombies" (221):

> They have left—and only silence remains, the deep and empty silence in which I can hear the voices of my *santos* settling into the rooms, of my *loa* telling me stories of what is to come . . . I am to close up the house, and help over at Dona Carmen's until they go too, and then at Don Arturo's, who also is to go. Mostly, I am to tend to this house. Dust, give the rooms an airing. The others except for Chino have been dismissed, and I have been entrusted with the keys.
>
> (222)

The "voices" and "stories" that Chucha anticipates hearing positions her as the future curator of the family's multiple histories and identifies her role with that of the novel, which can house so many differentiated stories and accounts. Chucha's social and metaphorical charge to "tend to this house" becomes indicative of Alvarez's own reclamation project where she preserves the neglected stories of the "Dominican" life of the family before exile, which is rapidly fading from view. The deployment of multiperspectivity as an artistic form is an attempt to simulate a reader's access to the personal and personalized narrative lines of individual perceptions, which are in danger of being "lost" forever if they are not reconstituted in writing or some other analogous activity.[8]

Perhaps Chucha describes the dangers and potentialities of such a process most accurately as she imagines the difficulties the daughters will face once they arrive in New York:

> In the girls' room I remember each one as a certain heaviness, now in my heart, now in my shoulders, now in my head or feet; I feel their *losses* pile up like dirt thrown on a box after it has been lowered into the earth. I see their future, the troublesome life ahead. They will be haunted by what they do and don't remember. But they have spirit in them. They will invent what they need to survive.
>
> (223)

The prophetic voice that resonates in Chucha's claim that the girls will "invent what they need to survive" suggests the novelistic weight that Alvarez wants to give to the interruption of the maid's narrative. The prediction she makes serves to underscore that the Garcias transport from one geographic locale to another will not mean the catastrophic "loss" of cultural upbringing, but rather an altered constellation of experiences. Instead of surrendering access to a life that can never be reclaimed, the Dominican past will continue to reverberate in the United States for each family member. For Alvarez, identity is understood not in terms of the binary of being Dominican or American, but as a hybrid invention that mirrors the multiple perspectives that make up her postcolonial narrative. The cultural bricolage that such an adjustment inevitably entails will prove difficult—"They will be haunted by what they do and don't remember"—but the "spirit" that Chucha bequeaths to all of them will allow each Garcia to "invent" what is necessary to her survival. The "losses" that "pile up like dirt thrown on a box after it has been lowered into the earth" metamorphose into the stories that populate Alvarez's fiction, for what is not remembered (or what is too painful to remember) moves underground while continuing to wield influence.

The core of familial identity in this novel ultimately proves difficult to specify for Alvarez and her characters, because unlike Chucha, they all fail to develop a successful critical framework within which to understand their lives. Unlike the narrative voice of the opening epigraph, the "homecoming" in *García Girls* does not prove to hold any particular resonance for any of the daughters. Although each narrator's version of events collides with and contradicts those that

precede and follow, Alvarez remains skeptical about the ability of her characters to assess their present in terms of the past. Ultimately, the novel seeks to fill in the absence of such a process by committing to textual "memory" the child and adult experiences she believes had a significant impact upon her fictional family (the past they do and don't remember). The utilization of multiperspectivity provides an example of what Homi Bhabha terms "living perplexity," the evolution of a minoritized narrative form that is neither "the transcendental . . . idea of History nor the institution of the State, but a strange temporality" where the story oscillates between past and present in a contest to a controlling master narrative.[9]

This reverberation of the past in the narrative present becomes most overtly foregrounded in the final chapter, "The Drum." Since Yolanda's narrative "I" begins and ends the novel, Alvarez's artistic stand-in can be read in terms of the tensions and gulfs that exist for her own immigrant status as an artist in the United States. The story uses the gift of a drum from Yolanda's grandmother as the narrative vehicle for exploring questions of voice. Because we receive more information about Yolanda's experiences in the United States than any other character (the novel devotes six chapters out of fifteen solely to her impressions), the difficulties of negotiating the relocation are largely documented through her particular observations and concerns. Because Yolanda's character evolves into the figure of the writer, the narrative privileging of her memories situates the issue of locating a "voice" or reclaiming "lost accents" as a central preoccupation. How can the experiences of an upper-class Dominican family who move to the United States be recounted and represented effectively? How does the surrender of class privileges figure as a legitimate and understandable narrative concern without embracing a model that justifies exploitation and inequality? Can the Garcias come to comprehend the exploitation of their pasts while simultaneously coping with their marginalized condition in the United States?

Because Yolanda's story line most overtly addresses such concerns, I want to begin by charting the ways in which her perspective acts as a frame for the novel's focus. When we meet Yolanda for first time in the opening chapter she approaches her childhood home with anxiety and a tinge of guilt about the responses her appearance will produce in her island relatives. She immediately anticipates that her experience in the United States will result in disapproval, that her aunts will see her "shabby in a black cotton skirt, . . . her wild black hair held back with a hairband" (3). The internalized gaze that she will turn upon herself in a self-conscious critique of her status as a cultural emissary of a world she "never felt comfortable in" results in a moment of cultural tension that will be maintained throughout the novel. Her ability to create the stories that her relatives will tell themselves about her "fall" in the States—despite their apparent embrace of her return—sets up Yolanda as a product of her childhood environment that comes replete with myths of the fallen western woman who lets herself "go so as to do dubious good in the world" (4). These competing nationalist versions of the cultural other—represented sometimes as the Dominican Republic and sometimes as the United States—are negotiated both at the level of plot and within Yolanda's psyche as the evidence of a subjectivity in transition.

This negotiation of internal conflicts becomes most poignant near the end of the opening chapter when the young writer finds herself alone on a deserted back road with a flat tire. Like her sisters, who are incapable of imagining the perspectives of the family servants who populate their island homestead, Yolanda's concern about the "dark men" who approach her while she waits for help to arrive from nearby results in her own inability to construct counternarratives of Dominican masculinity. Her first impulse is to run as they suddenly appear out of the woods, and once she rejects the idea because she sees that they are "strong and quite capable of catching her" her legs freeze and feel as if they are "hammered into the ground beneath her" (19). Once the men kindly agree to change the flat for her so she can get on her way before she is trapped out in the country on dark back roads, Alvarez leaves the reader to mull over the reasons behind her protagonist's response. Because Yolanda has been subjected to the terror and threat of violation in the patriarchal cultures of the United States and the Dominican Republic, her initial suspicion of the approaching men leaves the racial implications of her response ambiguous.

The complexity of negotiating the dual structure of racism and gendered violence resonates throughout the remainder of the novel. Yolanda's immediate response of fear and flight is highlighted as an understandable reaction; not only has she recently been warned about the unfeasibility of taking a "*camioeta* full of *campesinos*" by her island aunts, she has also been exposed to her older sister's near abduction and traumatic encounter with male sexuality in the United States. In addition, the Dominican daughters struggle throughout the novel for a sense of self-worth in spite of the limited options available to women in both cultures. By placing readers in present time, we are drawn into the confusing interplay of gendered fears and racial assumptions in Yolanda's mind while also being asked to assess the competing cultural origins of such expectations.

Yolanda goes on to encounter discriminatory attitudes about her Dominican background in the United States, demonstrating that racial and gendered attitudes are equally conflictual in both contexts. In one scene Yolanda's boyfriend's parents comment on the pride her parents must feel about the achievement of "her 'accentless' English." This particular inflection upon the loss or repression of an accent as evidence of the nearly seamless "achievement" of acculturated speech further multiplies the valences of "loss" in the title. The parent's centrist statement explains the cultural mire of the immigrant experience, in which one is congratulated for assimilating at the expense and devaluation of the culture one has left behind. Conversely, Yolanda also finds herself retreating into her "native tongue" in order to avoid answering difficult questions about her personal desires put to her by her later lover, John. In this scenario the narrator is able to use her mixed cultural heritage as an escape hatch into a self-willed loss of comprehension. Such a textual conflation of cultural obstacles situates a matrix of meanings behind Alvarez's pivotal notion of "loss" for her characters.

The "American Drum" that Yolanda proudly beats in her yard after being reprimanded for beating it too loudly in the house provides her with the impetus for making herself heard around the family compound. As she struts up and down "saluting the bougainvillea and drumm[ing] until the humming-birds were ready to fly off to the United States of America in the middle of December," she contemplates the unfortunate condition of her banishment to the "outside" at the behest of her mother:

> That was just like my mother to let me have a drum and then forbid me to drum it, ba-bam, ba-bam, in any significantly inspired way. And how could I judge the significance in a drum unless at least one grownup clapped her hands over her ears? And how could I judge inspiration unless there was noise in it, drumming from my ten flexed toes, from my skinny legs that would someday improve themselves, drumming from the hips I swayed when I was womanish, and up, up the rib cage, where the heart sat like a crimson drum itself among ivory drumsticks.
>
> (277)

The narrator's despondency over her ability to provoke a discernible response from her audience—"how could I judge the significance in a drum unless at least one grownup clapped her hands over her ears?"—functions as an artistic question of voice that Alvarez herself desires to allegorize in nearly all of the personal anecdotes that constitute her novel. Since Yolanda represents the artistic conscience of the family, the one whose impulse it is to organize this family tree of stories, the question of a drum's ability to elicit some sign of artistic impact foregrounds the novel's concern with the feasibility of attaining a "voice," or many voices, that can create a stir in her readership. If writing is equated with the desire to drum with authority, then Yolanda's chapter, which ends the collection, sits strategically poised as the novel's central preoccupation with a minority woman's ability to evolve a viable artistic voice.

The close parallels that Yolanda draws between her drumming and her physical development into a "womanish" adult make this goal of attaining a mature artistic "voice" explicit. Because the drum comes from, in her grandmother's words, the "magic store" back in the United States (F. A. O. Schwartz), pure lines of artistic and cultural lineage are blurred even at the furthest chronological narrative moment recorded in the novel. While Yolanda locates her own maturity as a function of growing into a "responsible drumm[er]," the novel posits the nature of such "maturity" as ambiguous and conflicted (277). The imported drum comes to symbolize the business of cultural imports and exports in a novel that refuses to reduce the complexities of individual or social heredity to a matter of one "pure" lineage versus another. Alvarez adopts the imported drum as a crucial piece in the puzzle of familial and cultural identity and influence. The impossibility of locating a truly original version of a homeland culture prior to its infiltration by the United States underscores the novel's interest in exploring the ramifications of accents that are altered but never entirely lost.

Such an ambiguity is further emblematized when Yolanda confesses that she quickly misplaces the original drumsticks (one is mysteriously lost and the other is irreparably broken when her "crazy aunt, Tia Isa," accidentally sits on it) that accompany her grandmother's gift. Despite some valiant attempts on the part of her mother and grandmother to substitute "pencils or the handles of wooden spoons used for making cake batter," Yolanda sadly explains that "the sound was not the same, and the joy went out of drumming" (278). Yolanda's loss of interest in drumming suggests that there is no substitute for the original instruments of a once authentic "voice." Yet this longing for a nonartificial mode of expression proves inevitably flawed. The narratives in *García Girls* can only take shape as a product of the "artificial" and mediating forces of memory, time, and narrative retrospection. The drumsticks are not valuable because they make the drum sound authoritative and drumlike; rather, Yolanda associates the original drumming sound with authenticity and therefore cannot revise her ideas about what a drum should sound like. Thus, Yolanda's story of the drum acts as an allegory for the situation of the hybrid cultural subject who would privilege her

"Dominican" experience only at the expense of sacrificing her Dominican American identity.

Of course, this question of returning to a homeland that represents a life uncomplicated or complicitous in impure discourses of cultural influence is possible for Alvarez in part because she moves her characters from a position of power and authority in the Dominican Republic to one of marginality and relative invisibility in the United States. Unlike, for instance, Toni Morrison's *Beloved,* which posits the possibility of an "other (liveable) place"—that is, Africa prior to the western military invasions and cultural appropriations—Alvarez's task is to unveil the illusion of a romanticized homeland unfettered by the bonds of caste, gender, and racial violence.[10] For Yolanda, the "wailing" that signals "some violation that lies at the center of my art" implies a connection between the "lost accents" of the title and the "void" that sits at the heart of artistic representation. While the impossibility of contemplating the "dark other" seems to place Alvarez as a firm believer in, and documentor of, the logistics of cultural "loss," I want to argue in the remainder of this essay that the text transforms the discursive category of "loss" into a metaphor for the multiple combinations that occur in cross-cultural appropriations and exchanges.

When Yolanda accidentally stumbles upon a kitten in the tool shed that sits tucked away on the back lawn of the family compound, she decides, despite her mother's explicit orders to the contrary, to enter and remove the kitten from the new litter. As she moves away from the scene of the theft she quickly tucks her new pet into the hollow of the drum that she no longer plays but rather wears "riding [her] hips like a desperado's revolver" (278). After dodging the kitten's mother and sneaking through the house to her bedroom, the narrator spends her time trying to quiet the kitten's meowing from the inside of the drum. Her efforts prove futile, and instead of returning her hostage, she lifts the screen and throws "the meowing ball out the window" (288). In the process the small kitten is injured and the narrator returns periodically to the window in order to watch the wounded kitten make "its broken progress across the lawn" toward the shed. The period of time that follows places the howling mother cat at her bedside "wailing until dawn," and the narrator continues to be haunted by her apparition until the family finally vacates the island to the United States. As the novel winds down and the final narrative voice moves toward its conclusion, Alvarez explains the impulse that resides behind her storytelling desires:

> Then we moved away to the United States. The cat disappeared altogether. I saw snow. I solved the riddle of an outdoors made mostly of concrete in New York.

My grandmother grew so old she could not remember who she was. I went away to school. I read books. You understand I am collapsing all time now so that it fits in what's left in the hollow of my story? I began to write, the story of Pila, the story of my grandmother. I never saw Schwarz [the kitten] again . . . I grew up, a curious woman, a woman of story ghosts and story devils, a woman prone to bad dreams and bad insomnia.

(289-290)

For "a woman of story ghosts and story devils," such a denouement seems glaringly inadequate. The haunting nature of the "loss" that she cannot fill—the narrative "hollow of my story"—solidifies around her sense of guilt about the theft and injury of the kitten she "illegally" abducts from its family. Her attempt to "collaps[e] all time" so that its fills in the emptiness she feels now that she has left her island homeland and taken up residence in the United States becomes the impetus for writing. In the hope of recapturing what's been lost or left behind, she begins the process of recording the "story of Pila, the story of my grandmother": all of the stories that have come to make up the very novel we have before us. In leaving the homeland she also leaves behind the fears and anxieties that haunted her as a child, but the adult narrator must reconstruct those repressed sentiments in order to produce a narrative that revives the experience of the lost homeland.

Such a process—the inevitable sense of inadequacy that accompanies any attempt to reinvent a past in the hopes of regaining a whole self, culture, experience, and so on—is the core component of Alvarez's novel. "Lost Accents" become the discursive site of what's found; a narrative production that exploits a sense of loss in order to locate a family/community of voices once invisible (or unvocalized), and now found (or reconstructed). The competing cultural influences in the Dominican Republic and the United States that would propose to usurp or cancel each other out must be seen not as a "loss" but as a productive tension that allows a myriad of influences to coexist. Alvarez seeks to go beyond the binary of a cultural either/or by creating a novel that defines the immigrant subject as an uneasy hybrid product of conflicting social positions such as class, gender, race, and nation.

While Yolanda mourns her inability to capture her artistic object adequately on canvas, Alvarez's novel self-consciously exposes the absence of perspectives that it cannot adequately represent. The stories that each of the García Girls relate in the finale of "I" narratives that bring this novel to a close all situate their inability to imagine various racialized and class perspectives; consequently, the text foregrounds the myriad ways in which all their stories are bound together in a shared project rather than distinctly separate and "lost." The lack of overt narrative commentary on the part of the narrators gestures toward a hybrid narrative space that reflects the multiplicities of Dominican American identity.

For Alvarez, the notion of multiple versions of "loss" situates her attempt to use the very concept of loss as the terrain upon which she can locate the uniqueness of her narrative vision. In a parallel to Gloria Anzaldúa's arguments, finding oneself living between the illusion of monolithic cultural identities must be articulated in and of itself as a speaking position that undermines the very idea of cultural purity. As a Mestiza American woman, she attempts to specify the numerous colliding and contradictory influences she must negotiate each day. Her valorization of the notion of "borderlands" takes shape as the need and desire to vocalize the myriad ways in which cultural subjects find themselves on the cusps of numerous discursive communities:

> I am a border woman. I grew up between two cultures, the Mexican (with a heavy Indian influence) and the Anglo (as a member of a colonized people in our own territory). I have been straddling the *tejas*-Mexican border, and others, all my life. It's not a comfortable territory to live in, this place of contradictions . . . Living on borders and in margins, keeping intact one's shifting and multiple identity and integrity, is like trying to swim in a new element, an "alien" element. . . . Strange, huh? . . . No, not comfortable, but home.[11]

In order to maintain and participate in such a community of "border residents," Alvarez utilizes the narrative strategy of multiperspectivity to suspend and illustrate this notion of "shifting and multiple identity" both thematically and formally. Such a suspension allows Alvarez to write across the boundaries of dueling nationalities in order to present immigrant or border subjectivities as a dynamic hybrid prototype of the postcolonial novel. The narrative tool of multiperspectivity allows Alvarez's text to straddle the divide(s) of personal, political, and cultural interpretive systems, in order to capture the kaleidoscopic arrangements of individual and communal perception.

Notes

1. The Pen/Faulkner award had never been awarded to a first novel before *How the García Girls Lost Their Accents* won in 1991.

2. Immigration data and trends for the Dominican Republic have been compiled by several different studies, but this figure was taken from Peter Winn, *Americas: The Changing Faces of Latin America and the Caribbean* (New York: Pantheon Books, 1992). Winn's portrait of Dominican immigration parallels the trajectory of Alvarez's novel closely:

"Unlike the Puerto Rican migrants, the new Dominican community in New York is largely composed of middle-class people whose educational and financial resources are greater than those of most of their compatriots. Many are children of small landowners from the countryside who were seeking ways to supplement their family incomes or to save money with which to expand or modernize their family farm. Others had owned businesses in Santo Domingo and looked to set up their own enterprises in New York, or else to accumulate the capital to establish a business back home. Most were forced to accept work that was beneath their occupational status in the Dominican Republic, jobs they left as soon as they had accumulated the capital to open their own businesses" (586-87).

3. Julia Alvarez, "An American Childhood in the Dominican Republic," *The American Scholar* 1 (winter 1988): 77-78.

4. Ibid., 80.

5. Alvarez. *How the García Girls Lost Their Accents* (Chapel Hill, N.C.: Algonquin Books of Chapel Hill, 1991), 212. All future references to the novel are made parenthetically in the text.

6. Trinh T. Minh-ha, *Woman, Native, Other: Writing Postcoloniality and Feminism* (Bloomington: Indiana University Press, 1989); Gayatri Spivak, "Can the Subaltern Speak?", in *Marxism and the Interpretation of Culture,* ed. Cary Nelson and Larry Grossberg (Urbana: University of Illinois Press, 1988).

7. Traditionally, the key common denominator of immigrant novels has been the conflict of the underclasses coming to the United States in pursuit of a more economically viable lifestyle. In each of the examples listed here, the United States exists as a prosperous Mecca that lures the immigrant toward its mythic promise of class mobility. The saturation of the Third World with U.S. exports (for example, product lines, films, and corporations) ensnares those cultures that have been subject to U.S. military and cultural occupation while simultaneously obliterating the historical lines of this intervention. Alvarez's novel revises this plot line by demonstrating her characters' manipulation of U.S. dependency rather than making them simply consumers of the mythic vision itself.

8. Part of the failure of Alvarez's novel to imagine the perspectives of her lower-class figures is that Chucha's chapter, which is the only one allotted to any of the servants in the novel, articulates the now largely clichéd role of the loyal domestic slave. Although a great deal of the novelistic weight is offered to Chucha's charge as household retainer, she nonetheless is left to mourn her kind keepers and worry over their turbulent departure from home. Such an impulse has been espoused fairly often in American letters (Faulkner's Dilsey most immediately comes to mind); thus, this mode of characterization seems to mar Alvarez's project despite her apparent cognizance of the "gaps" in her own narrative path.

9. Homi K. Bhabha, *The Location of Culture* (New York: Routledge, 1994), 157.

10. Toni Morrison, *Beloved* (New York: Alfred A. Knopf, 1997), 198.

11. Gloria Anzaldúa, *Borderlands/La Frontera: The New Mestiza* (San Francisco: Spinsters/Aunt Lute Book Company, 1987), i.

Julia Alvarez and Juanita Heredia (interview date 2000)

SOURCE: Alvarez, Julia, and Juanita Heredia. "Citizen of the World: An Interview with Julia Alvarez." In *Latina Self-Portraits: Interviews with Contemporary Women Writers,* edited by Bridget Kevane and Juanita Heredia, pp. 19-32. Albuquerque, N.M.: University of New Mexico Press, 2000.

[*In the following interview, Heredia and Alvarez discuss personal issues, such as the author's childhood, her connection to the Dominican Republic, and her relationship with her family, as well as professional topics, including her literary influences and the themes in her work.*]

Julia Alvarez was born in New York in 1950. She received a B. A. in English at Middlebury College, where she graduated summa cum laude, and earned her M. A. in creative writing at Syracuse University. She spent the first ten years of her life in the Dominican Republic, until her family was forced to move to the United States as political exiles. She now returns often to her homeland. She is currently professor of creative writing and English literature at Middlebury College.

When I met Alvarez at Middlebury College in February 1998, she greeted me with a warm smile and took me to her home. As we drove to her house, we discussed her recent projects, the state of Latino literature, American and Latin American literature, traveling, and a love of good coffee. Sitting in a study room, I noticed bookshelves, plants on her desk, and a window that overlooked the scenic snowcapped mountains of Vermont. As we spoke Alvarez showed me the embroidery and calligraphy of her first collection of poems, *The Housekeeping Book.* Her fellow artist friends, members of the Vermont Women's Art Collaborative, had handmade this piece. Alvarez talked about how, as a young writer, she traveled throughout the United States to teach as a poet in the schools and as a visiting professor, often learning from her students' stories.

After Alvarez published *How the García Girls Lost Their Accents* (1991) she came into prominence as a fiction writer. This novel portrays the coming of age of four sisters who leave their home with their family in the Dominican Republic to seek political asylum in the United States. In 1994 Alvarez received a National Book Critic's Award nomination for her novel *In the Time of the Butterflies*. This work captures the heroic struggle of the Mirabal sisters who founded the underground movement against Trujillo's dictatorship. By combining history and fiction, Alvarez demonstrates that some stories are better told through a poetic sensibility than factual documentation. In the novel *¡Yo!* (1997) Alvarez returns to the characters of her first novel, all of whom respond to the protagonist, Yolanda, who is also considered Alvarez's alter ego. With irony and poignancy she chronicles the life of a writer who has achieved success at the expense of criticism from her circle of family and friends.

All that said, Alvarez is a poet at heart. She has not only written two collections of poems *Homecoming* (1985) and *The Other Side/El Otro Lado* (1995), but she also admires poets of all periods and places. In fact, she pays homage in great depth to Walt Whitman in this interview. In *Something to Declare* (1998), Alvarez gathers a collection of essays on personal experiences and the craft of writing. Before she began to write essays, fiction, or poetry, though, stories occupied an important place in her life as a writer.

[Heredia]: What motivated you to become a writer? Is there any connection to your childhood in the Dominican Republican?

[Alvarez]: I don't think I would have become a writer if I had not come to the United States at the age of ten. I did not have a literary childhood. Seeing people read was a rare thing. I only saw it in school, and I hated books because I did not find much in them that was of interest to me. I was being sent to an American school where we had the Dick and Jane readers in English. This was not my language, and these were not my people. So I was not that interested in those readers. At the same time, though, I think I was in a very storytelling culture. Dominicans are great storytellers! My mother and all the women in my family were great storytellers, so I grew up in a folk culture where stories were very important. But in terms of writing or being one of these bookish people or always having to keep a journal, forget it! When I came into the English language, I discovered books.

Your departure from the Dominican Republic was rather abrupt. How did you feel leaving the homeland?

When my family and I came to the United States, we were really political exiles, as opposed to a large Dominican immigrant population who came around the seventies more for economic reasons. My parents were planning our departure, but it was abrupt and we were not prepared as children. I think it was one of the most traumatic experiences of my life. Suddenly everything changed overnight—the way the air smelled, the way the light felt, the way the people responded, the language in which people responded, the food that was given to us in school, the structure of the family, which was no longer extended and varied but suddenly a nuclear family, which put a lot of pressure on all of us. Before, in the Dominican Republic, among a dozen tías, we had many mothers. Suddenly there was such pressure on Mamí and on each other. That was really hard.

Was the transition to school easier considering the fact that you did attend an American school in the Dominican Republic?

Perhaps . . . But don't forget that U.S.A. street English did not sound the same as classroom, blackboard, verb drill English! When we arrived in New York, I remember having to concentrate to hear the words and not lose the sense at the same time. So I had this sense of anxiety all the time that I would not understand what was being said. I spoke with an accent, which made it hard for people to understand me. I learned to pay attention. So I became very interested in words, the little weights and measures of each word. Why does one say "kind" instead of "generous"? These are the subtleties that you learn as a child when you are learning your mother tongue, almost intuitively, but I was learning a second language as a young girl intentionally. I think this experience was a great influence in my becoming a writer, because I think you have to do that with your own language when you become a writer. That's part of the training and the craft, but I was doing it as a ten-year-old in order to survive in this new country.

I know that you have many sisters. Did you find comfort in their company?

We did not move into a Latino community where there were other people like us, so I really depended on my nuclear family, especially my sisters. Our surroundings were in English, alien to us. All we had was each other. Once Trujillo was killed, we found we had become hybrids, Dominican-Americans! We were no longer "real" Dominicans because we had changed. But we were not mainstream Americans either. We were ni pez, ni carne, neither fish nor fowl. We had experienced situations that our Dominican cousins back on the island had not. Our eyes had seen new things that they had not seen and the same occurred with our U.S.A. friends. We were between worlds. We belonged nowhere. So I sought out books, the homeland of the imagination.

Who were some of your role models in literature? Who were you drawn to?

Well, in high school we were taught the canon that I admired, but I did not connect with these authors. My first chosen mentor was Walt Whitman. He was so, well, so "Latino." In fact, a few years back, I read Borges's Spanish translation of Whitman's *Leaves of Grass.* I thought, my God! I think Whitman wrote *Leaves of Grass* originally in Spanish! The style, the expansiveness, the gestures, the rhetorical way of using this Anglo-Sajón language so that it just rolls off the tongue, the long lines, lush and tropical. No wonder Whitman translates so well into Spanish. Borges does such a wonderful job that I thought, gosh, Whitman is a Latino-American writer. His attitude was also so inclusive. That might have been some of the attraction—a sense of an expansive America that includes so many different kinds of people. If I contradict myself, very well, I contradict myself. I am large. I contain multitudes. That sense of being American, as being diverse: I don't belong in the parlor speaking pretty English. I belong listening to the organ player in the Southern church. I belong wandering the prairies. I belong with the longshoremen in New England. I belong among the Indian princes, traveling. It's this sense of inclusiveness that appealed to me because I was part of that America too. I liked his defiance of being trapped within a limited definition of what it was to be American. I think all of that—his gutsiness, his being marginal, his not wanting to be trapped in a limited self-definition, his wanting to take it all—drew me to him as a writer.

It sounds like a very transient identity, mobile and fluid, moving through landscapes.

Exactly. His rootlessness was part of his being rooted in this country. That kind of mobility appealed to me a great deal. I was also very taken with Emily Dickinson: her intensity, her refusal to be trapped in the typical paradigm of a young woman of her class. Her exact focus on any little thing. She would take a feeling of solitude and mourning and zoom in on exactly how that feels in language. Whitman, Dickinson: I loved both of their intensities in different ways!

How do you recall this period of the 1960s?

The civil rights movement was just getting started. All those movements—women's, multicultural—were in the future. That cracking open of American culture, with people who had long been left out saying, "I, too, sing America," it had not yet happened. Not until college and graduate school did I feel the social world around me include people like me.

Why did you begin to write poetry before prose fiction?

I think the love of the language, the love of each word. Also, I think the brevity of form. There are so many words in a novel. I felt that the wild horses of English would run away with me. I could manage them only in a small arena. In a poem the heart of the language was there that I had not gotten as a child in English.

You have to be very precise with language to write poetry, which I think is more difficult than writing fiction.

A poem is very intimate, heart-to-heart, whereas I think a story weaves a world that you enter. You can feel close to a character or a situation, but it's not that intense one-to-one of a lyric poem in which every word counts. There is nothing else, no narrative world, just the language in a poem, a voice speaking to you.

You have stated in one of your essays that Maxine Hong Kingston was very important in your formation as a novelist and consciousness as a woman writer.

Reading Maxine Hong Kingston's *Woman Warrior,* I realized that here was a Chinese-American woman with a different background but engaged in the same struggle of trying to put together two different worlds, two different languages, two different ways of seeing things. As I read her memoir, I kept saying, "Yes, yes!" It is beautifully written, a real classic. The book also confronted the demon that I had to confront as well. Maxine's first sentence is "'You must not tell anyone, my mother said,' what I am about to tell you.'" Hey, I thought, my Mamí told me that too! Not just my Mamí, but the whole culture she represented— Catholic, female, Old World, being told to keep my mouth shut, being told to keep things entre familia, never to betray ourselves, and all of those things. Maxine showed me the way out of the tight circle of taboos that I had been raised to observe as a Latina woman.

What did you read later on?

I began to read African-American literature—Toni Morrison, Alice Walker, Zora Neale Hurston. Native American writers, Latino writers. I began to search for the literature I had not been taught in school. I found Rudy Anaya's *Bless Me, Ultima,* Ernesto Galarza's *Barrio Boy,* Eduardo Rivera's *Family Installments.* When I began teaching survey courses, I introduced my students to these books, Latino books. At first I did not find many Latina writers except for Nicholasa Mohr's work, *Nilda,* and Lorna Dee Cervantes's *Emplumada.* Then I found Cherríe Moraga and the Kitchen Table group that came out with *Cuentos: Stories by Latinas.* With that collection I discovered that there were other women, like me, writing from a tradition that incorporated our Latina selves as well as our U.S.A. American selves. At Syracuse University, where I went to graduate school, the women in the program started an alternative workshop and we would meet once a week. All the women discussed the literature that we were writing from a different point of view. That gave me experience outside the academic structure in addressing alternative ways of thinking, writing, and reading. Many of these women gave me recommendations to read this or that. So I became acquainted with a different kind of literature than the traditional canon I had known before. I'm glad I had both of these educations.

Could you elaborate on both of those kinds of education, formal and personal?

Both kinds of knowledge are significant. It's important to understand formal verse, for instance, if you want to write free verse. You have to understand a metrical line when you write free verse. But if you don't know what a metrical line is, how can you "explode" it? What is free verse? What is the sonnet structure, and how do you work inside that structure to claim it for yourself? How do you move within? What kind of new structure do you create? I'm glad I had formal training. I read "the canon" because these paradigms formed the culture that I'm working to reform and expand. For example, I have to know *The Tempest* to fully understand *Caliban*. Before dying in a concentration camp, Robert Desnos, the French poet, said that the task was not only to be oneself but to become each one. I love it!

How did you begin to develop your poetic voice?

I first heard my voice with the **Housekeeping** poems. The stuff I was writing before that sounded stilted, and I had not learned to trust my voice. In that alternative workshop people would tell me to close my eyes and listen to the voice inside me, what does it sound like? I was expecting to hear, "Sing in me, muse, and through me tell the story." But when I closed my eyes what I heard were things like, Don't put so much vinegar in the lettuce, you are going to ruin the salad. You call that a blind stitch? I can't see it. This is the way you make a cake. I heard women talking to me about taking care of a house. That was what I heard growing up, voices of women doing things together in a household.

Well, family is certainly important in your fiction, especially your first novel, **How the García Girls Lost Their Accents.** *Do you consider it semiautobiographical?*

[Laughs] Oh, don't call it semiautobiographical! You'll get me in trouble with my family. I think first novels are often a kind of bildungsroman. Young writers are

often trying to work out their stories, the world according to how they were raised, the journey that they underwent, almost as if to clear the slate for other things that are coming. So I think definitely my story is part of that first novel. But not only my story, the stories of my people, Latinos who were also Americans, a hybrid. I was especially interested in Latinas who were also dealing with gender issues, issues about being "nice girls" from Latino families who had to deal with the rough and tough new world to which they had come. This story, the story of women like us, was one I had never read before. That's why I felt it was necessary for me to put it down on paper.

And you continue this story with some of the same characters in ¡**Yo!** *creating a dialogue between your works. How did* ¡**Yo!** *evolve?*

¡*Yo!* is very much a "portrait of the artist." Again, this type of novel follows a very canonical structure: the artist as the aristocrat of spirit is always awarded the point of view. Western literature gives the top position to the artist, especially with romanticism, Wordsworth, and later Joyce and Proust. Well, I've never been interested in hierarchies. That's the reason that I can't stand the placing of "the top Latina writers." I don't like that. It makes me uncomfortable.

In ¡*Yo!* I took the point of view away from the traditional aristocrat, the artist. I gave it to the "little people" who surround the artist, who tell you they are not creative, not storytellers. But these people, who do not consider themselves artistic, tell stories. Even the people I grew up with in the Dominican Republic, whom I told you were nonliterary, those people told wonderful stories, because all of us need stories to survive. This is how we make our lives meaningful, trying to tell ourselves in our heads the story of who we are.

In the workshops, how do you teach writing? What advice do you give students?

Writing is a craft. All I can do is expose students to good writers and texts and follow their own process and progress as they find their voices. I give them a variety of those texts to read, hoping they'll find what they need to put the world together with language. Look at a de Maupassant story or a Sandra Cisneros story. Look at the different tools the authors use, like point of view. Then you have options. When you write your story, you will have choices and models. But being a writer also involves revision: you have to shape what is meaningful to you into something that is meaningful to the reader too. You have to have models. Many times, young writers just want to write. When I ask them about point of view or character or what they are trying to do with dialogue, they can't really say. They are unaware of the options available to them. They have not read enough. If I want to throw a dinner party in a novel, I might read a scene from Tolstoy's *War and Peace*. But I also try to encourage young writers to find out what they need to write about. What are the stories that they have to tell?

Can you tell which students will be prose writers or poets?

I can tell you if a student has promise because he or she is interested in language. I can't say that this person will be a great novelist, or poet, or journalist, but I can say that there is something there. I can't predict. Look at all of us. Sandra [Cisneros] began as a poet. I began as a poet. So many of us. Judith Ortiz Cofer. Learning and controlling the language is going to work no matter what you do with it. I tell them that good writing is good writing. If you write a good memo, that is good writing too. But it is not art. Art begins with that, but it goes further. I can't tell which ones will go further.

Your novel **In the Time of the Butterflies** *pays homage to heroic people, like an ode that reminds me of Keats and Neruda. What made you write this story as a novel instead of poems?*

Since writing a novel is a messy job, you don't get a clean notebook and start off. That's what used to scare me about writing novels. I thought that's how "real" writers wrote novels. Well, that's not how I write them. I discard chapters out the window; a framework I thought was going to be the structure of the novel goes out too. But you remind me that I did begin that novel by writing poems in the voices of each of the characters. Each sister had a poem before each chapter. I envisioned that those poems would form part of the novel, and then the poems fell away. I still have them in folders. I guess I needed them in order to hear essentially, rhythmically, each voice. The sound of each voice came to me via poetry.

What motivated you to write this novel about a specific event in Dominican history?

When I met the surviving Mirabal sister, Dedé, in the Dominican Republic, I realized that I was actually going to write a novel. Before that the Mirabal sisters were legends. But when I met Dedé, I saw the clothes that her sisters were wearing the day they were killed. I held María Teresa's braid that Dedé had cut off before the burial; I saw their bedrooms, sat on their beds. I felt the sisters come to life in all those details that Dedé shared with me. They became real to me because she was real. She was really my entry into the

story. Then I also heard stories from other members of their family, from people who had been in the underground with them. I gathered all these pieces together. Their voices became real to me in an intuitive way. Each one would require something different of me. Patria liked me to read her the Bible. María Teresa liked girls' diaries. Anne Frank, of course. The novel had to end with the sisters still being alive. The murder scene would have taken over the whole novel and would have been what my readers remembered. I wanted the readers to remember their lives, not their deaths. Also, I wanted the readers, like Dedé, the survivor, to have to make sense of their stories.

I can see resemblances to novels about resistance to dictatorships in Latin America or literature of the Holocaust. Which books influenced you in this process?

Certainly I was influenced by literature of the Holocaust and the testimonial literature that comes out of Latin America—that whole tradition, the Mothers of the Plaza in Argentina. I did a lot of reading of women in the Resistance in France during World War II. A lot of the reading I did is not a part of North American literature, except for the narratives of slavery. Political testimonial literature does not come from the U.S.A. tradition. It just goes to show that as a writer I am a mixture of traditions.

How did you feel when you received the National Book Critics' Award nomination for **Butterflies** *[***In the Time of the Butterflies***]? Do you sense an impact in the direction of American literature?*

When I saw the nomination for the National Book Critics' Award, I was shocked, but I tried to put it out of my mind to stay focused on my work. Book biz can be distracting. A writer runs the danger of becoming a creature of publicity. You asked me if I like to go on book tours. It's so easy to get sucked into that star world instead of paying attention to your work. And your work is really bigger than you. The canon is widening to include Julia Alvarez, Sandra Cisneros, Rudolfo Anaya, essentially books that can help because they are deeply meaningful, not just to Latinos, but to all of us as a culture. For me to have read *The Invisible Man* is to have become an African-American. It makes me more of a human being. I enter another reality. That's why the canon should include all of us. It is also important for people to enter the reality of a little Mexican-American girl in *The House on Mango Street* or to enter the reality of Native Americans in *Love Medicine,* just as it's important for them to understand a crazed sea captain on a whaling ship or an indecisive Danish prince. You don't exclude those points of views or those realities. You also don't include books because they present "other" realities but because they are fine books, and they belong there along with the canonical "classics."

What is your present relationship with the Dominican Republic?

Well, Bill [Alvarez's husband] and I have started a project. Coming from there, being one of the lucky ones, having had a good education and having achieved all these things that I had as dreams, that I never thought I could achieve, all of this means that I have a responsibility to give something back. How do I serve now in this part of my life? What Bill and I are starting there is a model farm that will have an artist center for Dominicans. These artist "colonies" exist in this country—a place where a Dominican painter can come and paint for a couple of months. What will be required of the residents is that they do something for the community. They could give a workshop or donate a piece of work that would be part of the foundation so that it can make money to support itself. They could work on the farm, using organic methods that take care of the land. So that's my goal, trying to be a part of both worlds but also trying to do the cross-semination that is already in my work now in terms of the places that I move in.

*In your groundbreaking essay, **"On Finding a Latino Voice,"** you discuss the need to form a literary tradition. You pose the question, "Why couldn't we have a made-in-the-U.S.A. Latino and Latina literary boom"? What do you think happened in the 1990s, and where do you see it going?*

Well, I think what happened is the same thing that happened with African-American literature. Suddenly there was a "discovery" of Richard Wright, Maya Angelou. Suddenly Alice Walker, Toni Morrison, Gloria Naylor, and Ntzoke Shange. The voices were there, but "suddenly" the publishing establishment noticed. And one by one, each voice adds to the critical mass and there is a "boom." You put certain numbers together, and an energy is born that is bigger than the individual parts. Sandra Cisneros, Ana Castillo, Cherríe Moraga, Lorna Dee Cervantes, and Judith Ortiz Cofer, some of us were in touch here and there with one another. But suddenly there was this sense of energy from conversation and dialogue, a chorus that started building, all of these voices in all their diversity, how much we share and how different we all are. On the market level what happened was that publishers realized that these writers really sell and some of them are terrific writers. In this boom there are definitely books and writers whose works are not as strong. Some books will stay, and the others will sink to the bottom. But, as I often tell my students, maybe some of these stories are not so good, but they

have to write those stories to get to their best stories. Over time a culture uses what it can use and the rest falls away and creates literary fertilizer for the next crop coming up.

Do you see a younger generation coming up?

Oh, yeah! Junot Díaz! A Dominican. He is a very talented, wonderful writer. Edwidge Danticat. She is Haitian-American, young, twenty-eight years old. A second wave is now coming up. I think their talent would have thrust them forward, but I think that the market is also ready to receive them because some groundbreaking happened with my generation. Nicholasa Mohr and Lorna Dee Cervantes were the first ones out there, clearing ground. Then Sandra Cisneros, Ana Castillo, Denise Chávez, Cherríe Moraga, Helena María Viramontes, and the rest of us came. Now, new blood! We are taken seriously now as American writers, not as writers of sociological interest only.

*In another essay, **"Imagining Motherhood,"** I thought of the pressures involved in being a writer and a mother. How do you feel about these issues?*

In my book of essays, **Something to Declare,** I was writing both personal essays and essays about craft. **"Imagining Motherhood"** was one of the first essays in which I was trying to come to terms with being childless, especially as a Latina. As you know, this is an important "credential" as a Latina. You have to have your children. I had to come to terms with that, not just as a Latina, but as a woman of an earlier generation in which I was told that was something I was supposed to do. What does it mean to be a "childless woman"? Even the role of stepmother, my present role, has such a bad legacy. What does it mean to make a choice not to have a child and still be a whole woman? All the feelings that come to mind and all the pressures and opinions because I made that choice haunt me! I wrote the essay to address those demons that haunt me, to exorcise them. Where does that hunger to be a mother come from? Part of it as a writer is that you want to know everything. You hunger for experience. That desire was driving me too. There are also other ways to mother and to nurture that do not necessarily have to do with having a child biologically.

Do you feel close to your family now?

Oh, yes, both with my sisters here and with my family in the Dominican Republic. Some of my Dominican family have made very different choices about their lifestyles, their values, how they decide to spend their time. I am sure they find it absolutely crazy for my husband and me to buy land up in the mountains, where there is no electricity, no good roads, no phones, no running water. And here we are, trying to grow organic coffee and be part of a comunidad. But family is always family. I think it's a gene that I got as being part of that culture, that familia is important even if people are different from me. We all belong. Everybody is part of la familia—el loco, la jamona. [Laughs] I do keep up when we go down there, always staying at my favorite tía's house in the capital, visiting the cousins that drop in. Now that we have our own place up in the mountains, we have our own base and connections with people there who are not necessarily family. We already feel a part of this other community, very much so.

What feels like home for you?

As Czeslaw Milosz said in a quote I used as the epigraph to **Homecoming,** my book of poems, "Language is the only homeland." The page is where I've learned to put together my different worlds, where I've put down the deepest roots. Maybe because I am an immigrant, I don't feel those deep loyalties to a piece of land or a landscape. But the world of the imagination is the one I feel most at home in. I am a traveler with this portable homeland of the imagination.

Is that how you would like to be remembered, a traveler?

Yes, a traveler. The writer Terence, born a slave, once said, "I am a human being. Nothing human is alien to me." Not only to be oneself, but to be each one. These phrases mean a great deal to me. What I try to do with my writing is to move out into those other selves, other worlds. To become more and more of us. Here, I am writing in English often about Dominican situations and characters, using Spanish as part of my English—those combinations are happening all over the planet, as populations are on the move. I find this empowering: that we are becoming these mixtures, we are becoming each other. By allowing myself to be those mixtures and not having to choose or repress myself or cut myself off from the other, I have become a citizen of the world.

Karen Castellucci Cox (essay date 2001)

SOURCE: Cox, Karen Castellucci. "A Particular Blessing: Storytelling as Healing in the Novels of Julia Alvarez." In *Healing Culture: Art and Religion as Curative Practices in the Caribbean and Its Diaspora,* edited by Margarite Fernández Olmos and Lizabeth Paravisini-Gebert, pp. 133-48. New York: Palgrave, 2001.

[*In the following essay, Cox draws a connection between the bicultural backgrounds of Alvarez's*

characters and the presence of healing practices in Alvarez's fiction.]

> A borderland is a vague and undetermined place created by the emotional residue of an unnatural boundary. It is in a constant state of transition. The prohibited and forbidden are its inhabitants.
>
> —Gloria Anzaldúa, *Borderlands/La Frontera*

> Illness is the night-side of life, a more onerous citizenship. Everyone who is born holds dual citizenship, in the kingdom of the well and in the kingdom of the sick. Although we all prefer to use only the good passport, sooner or later each of us is obliged, at least for a spell, to identify ourselves as citizens of that other place.
>
> —Susan Sontag, *Illness as Metaphor*

I

While Susan Sontag refers in her classic essay, of course, to the experience of pathologically fatal disease,[1] her reflection could as easily hold for the experience of mental illness or breakdown, that more inscrutable world of psychological dysfunction that resides as much in the human spirit as it does in the physical body. As Western science reaches for new palliatives for the troubled mind, applying medications, therapies, and analytic treatments to the myriad forms of mental affliction, socioreligious communities in Western and non-Western cultures have looked historically to the spirit world for healing. The Caribbean, with its multicultural matrix of blended religions and beliefs, is a unique site of such mystical curatives. While a thorough description of the richly varied tradition of Caribbean religious rites and healing cures is beyond this essay's scope,[2] tracing the influence of Haitian vodou and its healing practices in the fiction of Dominican American writer Julia Alvarez is useful in elucidating the episodes of mental breakdown and recovery in her novels. Though occasional vodou elements appear without elaboration in the novels, as in the "magic waters" that grace her fictional alter ego's desk and windowsills, Alvarez makes neither the sacred practices of Afro-Caribbean spirituality, learned from Haitians in her household, nor the symbolic world of her family's Dominican Catholicism central to her fiction. Rather than treating these competing (and, in the Dominican Republic, often syncretic) traditions overtly, Alvarez addresses the absence of a spiritual realm in the lives of her characters, women who suffer from various maladies for which Western medicine has no adequate cure. It is finally only the memory of a single episode of mystical healing that offers psychological wholeness to these Dominican American women characters living between two cultures in the mental borderland of the exiled.

A writer of novels and poetry, Alvarez spent her early girlhood in the Dominican Republic, living a comfortable, upper-class life within the superficially safe confines of her mother's extended family. Alvarez's father, a medical doctor, was politically active and participated in the underground movement to overthrow dictator Rafael Trujillo. Fearing discovery and serious reprisal after an aborted assassination attempt by his organization, in 1960 Alvarez's father secured passage for his wife and four daughters to move to New York City on a "temporary basis." Four months after the family's escape, the famous Mirabal sisters were killed for their political activities.[3] Shortly thereafter, on May 30, 1961, the same underground group to which Alvarez's father belonged succeeded in assassinating "El Jefe," unwittingly setting in motion a series of unstable governments in the country. The political turmoil of these years encouraged Alvarez's parents to put down roots in the United States and enroll their children in reputable boarding schools to accelerate the transition to American life. Though Alvarez and her sisters would return to "the Island" many times as visiting relations, this original migration to the United States would mark the end of their citizenship in the Dominican Republic.

In much of her work, Alvarez interrogates this tenuous category of belonging fully to neither the homeland nor the adopted country. For participants in the Caribbean diaspora in the United States, whose migrations were precipitated in so many cases by dictatorial persecution or menacing poverty brought on by a (post)colonial culture, the break with the past results in an alienation common to both immigrants and political refugees, who find themselves immersed in a new society that does not recognize the values these newcomers wish to retain. Thus, living between two cultures creates its own kind of "dis-ease"—a discomforting consciousness of things missing, neither a language, nor a culture, nor an extended family within which to position oneself. For people like Alvarez's parents, whose hearts remained with the homeland but whose future dreams were firmly planted in the new country, such a position necessitates an ambiguous melding of divided loyalties and conflicting customs. Julia Alvarez, who characterizes herself as a "U.S.A. Latina"[4] writer, suggests that her identity and many themes in her fiction grow out of this hybridity of two languages and cultures, a potentially positive amalgamation. Yet, the mental affliction that often signals such a split identity, where one experiences authentic citizenship only in the shadowy borderland between juxtaposed worlds, haunts much of Alvarez's written work.

In her first and third novels, Alvarez leans heavily on personal experience to create a fictional Dominican family, the Garcías, whose lives are thrown into turmoil when they must leave all they know to learn to negotiate the 1960s world of New York City. Alvarez's first novel, *How the García Girls Lost Their Accents*,[5] and its sequel, *¡Yo!*,[6] follow the four sisters—Carla, Sandi, Yolanda, and Sofía—as they straddle the borderland between two cultures. Despite the abrupt removal to a foreign country in preadolescence, there are ways in which these young women's initiations into adulthood seem very "American." They sneak away to meet boys, experiment with drugs, elope, marry, divorce, struggle with anorexia, depression, anxiety, and mental breakdown; in short, their lives can be read as not atypical outgrowths of the sixties culture in the United States. Yet, behind these apparently conventional narratives lurks the specter of difference. With every act of American conformity, these Dominican daughters act against a cultural code of behavior that values feminine deference, sexual purity, and familial devotion. The García girls are reminded incessantly that their allegiance lies in another place, their conduct measured by another standard. Even their subtle accents mark them, as they are encouraged as children in the Dominican Republic to "use your English" and then reprimanded as adults visiting the island to "say it in Spanish," as if language were a bulwark against the dangerous influences of the opposing culture, a country all its own, claiming its denizens by voice. Perhaps due to this attention to language, the central character Yolanda experiences her dual (or internally dueling) citizenship as a linguistic balancing act, one in which the requisite split between two languages represents the break between cultures and even the split self that initiates Yolanda's mental breakdown. The pressure of growing up walking a tightrope of conflicting identities is even more apparent in Alvarez's latest book, the collection of essays *Something to Declare*.[7] Episodes recalled here provide important background material and additional evidence for the cycle of hurt and healing present in the novels.

How the García Girls Lost Their Accents is a novel made up of interconnected stories grouped into three segments that move backward through time. Part 1 comprises the years 1989-72, when the girls are teenagers and adults; Part 2 recounts the decade of 1970-60, the first ten years in New York; and Part 3 returns to the years 1960-56, when the family is still in the Dominican Republic. Because the narrative recedes rather than proceeds, the reading experience becomes one of simultaneous loss and recovery. Even as the narrative unfolds in reverse to reveal what feels like the recouping of a relinquished culture, the stories record a past that is not actually recoverable but irretrievably abandoned. Julie Barak has compared this narrative structure usefully to a "widening gyre," which highlights in its "spiral movement the centripetal and centrifugal forces that pull [the García girls] toward and away from their island home, toward and away from the United States, toward and away from an integrated adulthood."[8] The recurring sense of an island community, to which one's belonging is forever altered, is magnified by its disparity to New York City, which offers freedom within anonymity but at the cost of familial identity. The narrative pattern balances this perception of loss with an equal feeling of extrication and salvation, however, in that forays into the past are not simply nostalgic remembrances but critical turning points juxtaposed with increasing frequency against the harsh realities of life under Trujillo's dictatorship. Given the recurrence of anxiety and mental breakdown in the book, the incremental revelation of the narrative, told from the perspective—and occasionally the first-person voice—of different sisters in turn, could be compared superficially to the recursive process of psychoanalysis, during which the patient is directed to peel back the layers of adult protection to discover the repressed childhood nightmares that have given rise to the illness. The crucial difference, however, is that in the case of these characters the methods of Western science fail to alleviate a mental anguish whose original injury and restorative antidote both emanate from a complex Dominican past. The first episode, an experience of violence and violation for the future writer, documents the injunction of silence that plagues her art.

The key scene to which I allude is an episode in the life of the third daughter, Yolanda. Like the author who created her, Yo (her nickname and the Spanish word for "I") is a writer, a teller of stories from childhood who "always lied like the truth is just something you make up."[9] Alvarez identifies both Yo's first muse and her own as a picture-book version of the heroic Scheherazade, whose life is preserved rather than plagued by an inclination toward tall tales.[10] As Yo grows up, her mother seems especially concerned that the child learn the difference between fact and fiction, inflicting punishment on her child whenever Yo tells stories: "Often, I put Tabasco in that mouth hoping to burn away the lies that seemed to spring from her lips. For Yo, talking was like an exercise in what you could make up."[11] In *¡Yo!,* Alvarez interrogates the full measure of what her fictional family's escape and survival has cost each of them, but especially the writer, whose inheritance from growing up in a police state has been a command to silence herself. Like the first novel, its sequel is a collection of stories, each narrated by a different character whose life has been altered by Yolanda's fictionalizing. Alvarez paints a picture of a family frustrated by the writing daughter who insists on turning all their lives into, as one sister puts it, "fictional fodder."[12] And yet, despite a child-

hood of punishments and a family infuriated by her revelatory fiction, Yo's adult struggles with mental breakdown and identity crisis are rooted more deeply in the political turmoil of her homeland, the fallout of that persecution in the private home, and the scars it inflicts on Yo's authorial voice.

The dark episode at the core of Yo's artistic troubles takes place prior to the family's exile. As a member of the underground resistance, Papi knows he is being watched at all times. In addition to having a secret closet where he can hide in times of extreme danger, he has also concealed an illegal gun in the floorboards of his study. Though no one in the household may enter the father's study, Yo has been allowed to play there unsupervised because she has shown such an interest in his medical books. When her father asks what she whispers to the photographs of diseased and misshapen people in the books, she tells him, "I am telling the sick people stories to make them feel better."[13] Despite the girl's childish admiration of her father's medical skill, telling her friends, "My papi can do anything!," the future writer already seeks an alternative healing in words.[14] Through this innocent urge to tell stories, Yo lets slip the inadvertent betrayal that is rehearsed multiple times in the cyclic narrative, as if to repeat this singular event is to unlock the mystery of the writer's artistic urge and anxiety at once.

Each time the third-person narrator or a García speaks the story of Yo's betrayal, its details change and its significance grows. In the first brief telling, Yo remembers that she "told their neighbor, the old general, a made-up story about Papi having a gun, a story which turned out to be true because Papi did really have a hidden gun for some reason . . . and her parents hit her very hard with a belt in the bathroom, with the shower on so no one could hear her screams."[15] Later in this version, the mother silently admits that the parents' reaction was inappropriately harsh but excuses it with the comment, "[Y]ou lose your head in this crazy hellhole, you do, and different rules apply."[16] Interestingly, in a return to the episode early on in the second book, the mother's version of the story has been purged of its unsavory center, and Yo is questioned but not punished. The scene ends with the weeping Mami explaining how she "hated being at the mercy of my own child, but in that house we were all at the mercy of her silence from that day on."[17] From this cleaned-up version in which both the betrayal and the violation have been erased, the narrative gradually moves to the close of the novel *¡Yo!,* where Carlos García, "el Doctor" and patriarch of his family, finally tells what he promises is the "undoctored truth"[18] of that terrible day:

We took her into the bathroom and turned on the shower to drown out her cries. "Ay, Papi, Mami, no, por favor," she wailed. As my wife held her, I brought down that belt over and over, not with all my strength or I could have killed her, but with enough force to leave marks on her backside and legs. It was as if I had forgotten that she was a child, my child, and all I could think was that I had to silence our betrayer. "This should teach you a lesson," I kept saying. "You must never ever tell stories!"[19]

Through the words and the beating, the child learns that her destiny to become a writer is forbidden; the "lesson" burned into her conscious is one of the danger lurking in words. Moments before the punishment, the father describes her shocked face as the lie gradually comes to light: "It was as if she were finally realizing that a story could kill as well as cure someone."[20]

The violent conclusion to Yo's childish storytelling sheds light on the close of *How the García Girls Lost Their Accents,* in which the adult artist laments the "violation that lies at the center of [her] art."[21] As a girl, she had violated the code of silence, and in turn her artistic nature has been permanently marred. The injury done to the artist's sensibility is not simply one of a father's beating, however. That private act of abuse is the outgrowth of a public political climate in which silence is the mandate. Mami notices that her other small girls seem already to have internalized the lesson beaten into Yo: "[S]he sees with a twinge of pain that they are quickly picking up the national language of a police state: every word, every gesture, a possible mine field, watch what you say, look where you go."[22] Alvarez explains that in her actual family, even removal to the United States did little to calm her parents' fears. If the children asked any questions about the state of the Dominican Republic, her mother answered, "'En boca cerrada no entran moscas.' No flies fly into a closed mouth." Alvarez discovered only later that "this very saying had been scratched on the lintel of the entrance of the SIM's torture center at La Cuarenta."[23] For Alvarez's characters, then, silence becomes the partner of dictatorship and death. The trauma of living in an environment of unquestioned obedience, suppression of personal desire, and absolute secrecy, coupled with the father's mandate that the artist must tell no stories[24] together make up Yolanda's violation—and the specter of mental illness that figures in the first novel.

II

Hysterics suffer mainly from reminiscences.
　　　　　　　　—Breuer and Freud, *Studies on Hysteria*

How the García Girls Lost Their Accents documents two episodes of mental breakdown and hospitalization, the first in the older sister Sandi and the second in the

artist, Yolanda.[25] The narratives share important characteristics in their emphasis on speech and silence and on the dangers of the written word. Thus, the fragility of these women in adulthood seems easily attributable to the traumatizing vigilance with which their words and intellects were monitored as children, and to the emotional strain inherent in learning to adapt to a foreign culture and language. At the same time, the sense of a misplaced self that plagues each sister's breakdown could be traced as readily to the types of identity crises characterizing many women's awakenings as the feminist movement gained momentum in the American 1970s. Allowing the complex factors that coalesce in the periods of illness in the novel, I wish to focus principally on the role of the "doctor" in these episodes, both the psychiatrists who treat the women and the father who stands idly by throughout. Though as a child Yo believed her Papi could "cure anything," what comes through in these narratives of mental illness is the ineffectuality of Western medicine to make whole the brokenness of the García sisters. While their cases may in many ways bear the marks of classic depression, anxiety, and psychoneurosis, the real "illness" from which these sisters suffer resists clinical diagnosis and scientific treatment.

It is nearly impossible to read the narrative of Sandi's mental breakdown and not think of the case history of "Fräulein Anna O.," Josef Breuer's famous account of his therapy sessions with Bertha Pappenheim that mark the beginnings of the psychoanalytic movement.[26] Like Anna O., Sandi refuses to eat anything prepared for her, literally starving herself. In this, she displays classic symptoms of anorexia nervosa, a contemporary diagnosis for a historically female illness. Also markedly similar to the first case, Sandi has begun to read obsessively, as if words have replaced physical nourishment. She tells her mother that "[s]he had to read all the great works of man because soon . . . she wouldn't be human."[27] Trapped in a patriarchal canon, Sandi heads her compulsory reading list not surprisingly with the father of psychoanalysis, Freud. Nietzsche and Erikson also figure in the string of great male authors whose books her mother claims are "driving her crazy."[28] Alvarez recalls as a child hearing the same words from an aunt about a poetry-writing cousin and feeling unsettled: "I had never in the world considered that books had that kind of power. They could make a person sick."[29] It is not the books alone that afflict Sandi, however. She is also haunted by a sense that her intellect is deteriorating. Asserting that "[e]volution had reached its peak and was going backward," Sandi worries that she is "becoming a monkey," and eventually loses her ability to speak.[30]

Her clinical aphasia mimics that of Anna O., whose devolving communication skills Breuer documents:

> It first became noticeable that she was at a loss to find words, and this difficulty gradually increased. . . . In the process of time she became almost completely deprived of words. She put them together laboriously out of four or five languages and became almost unintelligible.[31]

Sandi's parents choose hospitalization only when she too reaches a state of complete incoherence, "making these awful sounds like she's a zoo."[32]

In the episode of Sandi's hospital admission, her role is subordinated to the presence of the two doctors, her treating psychiatrist Dr. Tandlemann and her father, "el Doctor" García. The effect of the scene is one of miscommunications, evasions, and half-truths. While Dr. Tandlemann asks mundane, stock questions (How many siblings? Did they get along?, etc.) and even has to glance at the folder to remember the patient's name, the mother offers a subjective case history while anxiously folding and refolding a Kleenex tissue until it disintegrates into bits. The father stands passively to the side, pressing his face tighter against the window, at one point "timing the gardener's treks across the rolling lawns" as if to fix himself in the everyday.[33] Reduced from medical colleague to detached listener, Dr. García makes no effort to help with the case history or diagnosis, breaking in only twice to categorize the breakdown as "small." At the close of this scene, Sandi, outside walking the grounds with a nurse, encounters the gardener's lawn mower, experiencing it as a ferocious animal. Watched by her father, Sandi capitulates to a horror he is powerless to assuage: "The girl screamed and broke into a panicked run towards the building where her father, whom she could not see, stood at the window, waving."[34] A relentless silence closes this section, as the incoherent daughter's screams are muffled behind glass and the father's efforts at contact are equally muted. The failure of these two to speak their terrors only magnifies the disastrous effect of the childhood mandate of silence, distorting words and books—any unchecked speech at all—into a dangerous illness that isolates and dehumanizes.

What is most painfully evident in Sandi's narrative of breakdown is the ineffectual presence of the doctors, whose mundane exchange going on literally above and beyond her cannot begin to offer authentic healing. When the reader encounters Sandi in the text postdischarge, it seems that the only objects shoring up her sanity are the Kleenex tissues and antidepressants she carries in her purse, the first reminiscent of the mother's obsessive attentions, the second of the father's medical correctives. No account is given of her treatment, and she seems to have been left, much

like Breuer's abruptly dismissed Anna O., to fend for herself. She reveals sadly to her sisters, "I just want to forget the past, you know?"[35] But in this statement, relinquishing not just her immediate past but the whole bittersweet past to which she might lay claim, Sandi misses the one possibility for healing that could free her from the sickness of words and make her shattered identity whole.

Like Sandi's breakdown, which begins with her "crazy diet," Yo's depression and mental instability are precipitated by a concrete event, the dissolution of her marriage. The episode is less about relationships, however, than it is about Yo's attempts to reconcile the dual languages that threaten her identity. She complains of the permutations of her very name since she has moved to the United States: "Yolanda, nicknamed *Yo* in Spanish, misunderstood *Joe* in English, doubled and pronounced like the toy, *Yoyo*—or when forced to select from a rack of personalized key chains, *Joey*."[36] Her sense of self is likewise divided into *"head-slash-heart-slash-soul,"* as if to match the multiplying names. When Yo fights with her husband, he pries open her mouth with a kiss, "pushing her words back in her throat" and overpowering her with the old injunction of silence.[37] As if in response, Yo discovers that the English language of her husband has become indecipherable: "[S]he could not make out his words. They were clean, bright sounds, but they meant nothing to her."[38] Contrary to Sandi, who devolves into wordlessness, Yo develops a condition of perseveration, in which she cannot stop talking for months and months, but during which time she invents no ideas of her own. Instead, her voice becomes a stream of others' words, as she quotes and misquotes all the great writers, "drowning in the flooded streams of her consciousness."[39]

Admitted to a private facility, where her doctor can "keep an eye on her," Yo briefly places her faith in the claims of the medical world, though a visit from her parents suggests such reliance will prove futile. In a repetition of the earlier scene with Sandi, the mother talks anxiously and the father averts his eyes out a window—both powerless to restore their daughter's health. When Mami tells Yo that they love her, Papi cannot even say the words, simply adding, "There's no question at all."[40] Recalling life with her medical father, Alvarez describes a similar detachment:

> To take hold of a hand, to graze a cheek and whisper an endearment were beyond him. Tenderness had to be mothered by necessity: he was a good doctor. Under the cover of Hippocrates' oath, with the stethoscope around his neck and the bright examination light flushing out the personal and making any interchange completely professional, he was amazingly delicate: tapping a bone as if it were the fontanelle of a baby,

easing a patient back on a pillow like a lover, his sleeping beloved, stroking hair away from a feverish forehead.[41]

Despite the signs her father has given her that medicine offers only impersonal intimacy and no magical cures, Yo continues to trust in Western science. Calling her psychiatrist "Doc" "secretly for luck," Yo believes he will "save her body-slash-mind-slash-soul by taking all the slashes out, making her one whole Yolanda."[42] Like Anna O., Yo engages in a modern-day "talking cure," daily sharing all manner of personal thoughts with her doctor and even effecting a classic act of transference by falling in love with him.[43] Nevertheless, psychotherapy fails Yo. While the definitive goal in the process of psychoanalysis is to achieve a picture of "the Truth," to uncover the past exactly as it happened and transform those memories into language,[44] this is not the path to healing for the storytelling Yo, who seeks freedom to stray from truth into art.

When Yo loses faith in the power of psychotherapy to repair her "slashed" self, events in the narrative shift toward an alternative to Western medicine, a dependence on the mystical rather than medical to heal the soul. In a small step back toward her roots in a Dominican culture that embraces the corporeal/spiritual duality of life, the writer recognizes the power of words, the spells they cast, and the authority they wield over the artist. At this point, psychotherapy fails to meet Yo's quest for meaning, even as she develops a symbolic allergy to the most important words in both her tongues. Speaking "love" and "amor" aloud, Yo discovers that "[e]ven in Spanish, the word makes a rash erupt on the backs of her hands."[45] Yet she determines to build up an "immunity" to the threatening words and learn how to speak the stories that have been silenced in her.

In his essay "The Healing Word: Its Past, Present, and Future," Thomas Szasz criticizes the usefulness of any "talking cure" that dispels the mystery of words in and of themselves to hurt or heal:

> Since ancient times, people have recognized that words powerfully affect the listener and that, like double-edged swords, they cut both ways. Indeed, our vocabulary possesses numerous adjectives for characterizing both types of speech acts, such as blasphemous, impious, obscene, perjurious, pornographic, profane, and sacrilegious for words deemed to be harmful; and calming, cheering, comforting, consoling, encouraging, heartening, inspiring, motivating, and reassuring for words deemed to be helpful.[46]

In her empowering "speech act," Yo conjures up a hallucinatory vision that enacts a spiritual return to wholeness as an artist, "the real Yolanda resurrecting" in the figure of a "huge, black bird" who emerges from her mouth.[47] Like Poe's black raven perched on Pallas' bust, Yo's personal muse and secret phoenix rises up, seeking out a representative of the force that has silenced its fancy. Finding the doctor sunning outside on the lawn, the bird plummets: "Beak first, a dark and secret complex, a personality disorder let loose on the world, it plunges!"[48] After the murder of Western science, Yo is set free to begin her mental healing. The episode ends far more triumphantly than Sandi's narrative, with the poet mouthing "offending" words, exulting that "[t]here is no end to what can be said about the world."[49]

III

El papel lo aguanta todo.

(Paper holds everything.)

Mami

—Alvarez, **"Ten of My Writing Commandments"**[50]

When Yo unleashes her dark, flying muse and embraces both her languages—Spanish and English—she repudiates the law of the father and frees herself to take up the writing profession. That she achieves such a goal is evidenced by the legions of angry friends and relatives in *¡Yo!,* who complain that the first book exposed their lives. Echoing the father's injunction to "never tell stories," they condemn Yo's lifework and her *destino.* Alvarez describes the actual difficulty she encountered in lifting the silence:

> "My mother told me never ever to repeat this story," Maxine Hong Kingston begins her memoir, *The Woman Warrior.* And those same words could have been spoken to me by any number of women and men in my family. I had transgressed an unspoken rule of la familia. By opening my mouth, I had disobeyed. By opening my mouth on paper, I had done even worse. I had broadcast my disobedience."[51]

For Alvarez's fictional manifestation Yo, personal doubts about her indecorous profession haunt her into middle age, the "violation" at the core of her artistic self. In the final section of *¡Yo!,* the daughter, again anxious and depressed about her life immersed in words, worries that she should have become a mother, followed another path. When her father suggests that it is a blessing to get to fulfill one's destiny, she asks him, "But how can I be sure this is my destino?"[52] Splitting again into halves or "should haves," the artist—Yo or Alvarez in her place—must enact a final ritual of healing that returns to the scene of injury and invents a new story.

While the painful genesis of the artist's anxiety can be traced back to the silence demanded in a police state, the curative for what ails her is likewise located outside Yo's adopted *norteamericana* culture, in the hands of a Haitian maid back in the Dominican Republic. A deceptively minor character in *How the García Girls Lost Their Accents,* Chucha has lived with the de la Torre family for over fifty years, having sought asylum at their compound on the terrible night in 1937 when Trujillo authorized the slaughter of thousands of Haitian canecutters in the Dominican Republic. Chucha's unique religious fervor replicates that of much Haitian spiritual belief in that it is a syncretism of African vodou and the conquistador Catholicism of the family she serves.[53] Unmarried and forever grateful to her guardians, she spends her free days praying in her room for "any de la Torre souls stuck up in purgatory" and insists on sleeping in a coffin to "prepare herself for dying," as in certain monastic orders.[54] Side by side with this eccentric Catholicism. Chucha "always had a voodoo job going, some spell she was casting or spirit she was courting or enemy she was punishing."[55] The other Dominican maids fear and shun the Haitian, gossiping that she "got mounted by spirits" and that "she cast spells on them." Such rumors attest to Chucha's direct connection to her gods, her role as a *hounsi,* a spirit-wife or "horse," as described by Joan Dayan:

> The language of possession, or the *crise de loa*—that moment when the god inhabits the head of his or her servitor—articulates the reciprocal abiding of human and god. The "horse" is said to be mounted and ridden by the god. The event is not a matter of domination, but a kind of double movement of attenuation and expansion. For make no mistake about it, the loa cannot appear in epiphany, cannot be made manifest on earth without the person who becomes the temporary receptacle or mount. And the possessed gives herself up to become an instrument in a social and collective drama.[56]

Despite the García family's skepticism of their maid's strange practices Chucha's connection to the gods is directly instrumental in their protection and safe escape. When a menacing pair of *guardias* visit the house, only little Yo exhibits confidence in the maid's vodou. Dropping a fine powder as she leaves the room, Chucha mumbles under her breath, and "Yoyo knows she is casting a spell that will leave the men powerless, becalmed."[57] Not only is the Haitian spell effective in delivering the family from these thugs, it is finally Chucha's "farewell voodoo," performed hours before the García family flees the Dominican Republic, which casts the right spell to release Yo's artistic muse forever.

The youngest sister, Fifi, narrates the episode of vodou, her only memory of her previous life. Chucha speaks:

> "When I was a girl, I left my country too and never went back. Never saw father or mother or sisters or brothers. I brought only this along." She held the bundle up and finished unwrapping it from its white sheet. It was a statue carved out of wood. . . .

Chucha stood this brown figure up on Carla's vanity. He had a grimacing expression on his face, deep grooves by his eyes and his nose and lips, as if he were trying to go but was real constipated. On top of his head was a little platform, and on it, Chucha placed a small cup of water. Soon, on account of the heat, I guess, that water started evaporating and drops ran down the grooves carved in that wooden face so that the statue looked as if it were crying. Chucha held each of our heads in her hands and wailed a prayer over us. We were used to some of this strange stuff from daily contact with her, but maybe it was because today we could feel an ending in the air, anyhow, we all started to cry as if Chucha had finally released her own tears in each of us.[58]

Barak rightly notes that Chucha's "voodoo good-bye" sits at the very center of the gyre that pulls the sisters away from and back to the Island.[59] The protective ritual the old Haitian maid enacts ties the sisters forever to their Dominican roots, and the final spell she casts after them offers the antidote for whatever still haunts their memories.

When the family has gone, Chucha consults the voices of her *santos* and hears her *loa* whispering stories to her of the future. Swinging her can of "cleaning smoke" in the bedroom of the García sisters, Chucha has a vision of their new American life:

> In the girls' room I remember each one as a certain heaviness, now in my heart, now in my shoulders, now in my head or feet; I feel their losses pile up like dirt thrown on a box after it has been lowered into the earth. I see their future, the troublesome life ahead. They will be haunted by what they do and don't remember. But they have spirit in them. *They will invent what they need to survive.*[60]

Like her role as "horse" to her *loa,* Chucha becomes a temporary receptacle of the daughters' pain. She gives a deathlike quality to the García girls' loss, as if the exile from their homeland is a kind of spiritual burial. She prophesies the coming anxieties, breakdowns, and identity crises that will mar their journeys into adulthood. In all this, Chucha does not deny the long-term repercussions of dictatorial oppression, forced migration to a foreign country, and a life spent negotiating between the haunted past and unpredictable future. The spell that Chucha sends after the children is not a promise of protection from the inevitable but an incantation of healing to equal it. Knowing that the family spirits have already gone (she saw Carlos' *loa* leave out the back door), Chucha invokes the García girls' special voodoo god-spirits to travel with them, to give them *invention,* voices to tell stories with which these silenced daughters can re-create a livable past from words.

This mystical call to invention—originating from the same Dominican past as the edict of silence—is finally what frees the third daughter, the artist, from her anguished self-doubts and mental exhaustion. In the final episode of *¡Yo!*, the father admits his wrong and resolves to return one final time to the scene of the violation in order to reinvent the past: "I beat her. I told her that she must never ever tell stories again. And so maybe that is why she has never believed in her destiny, why I have to go back to that past and let go the belt and put my hands on her head instead. I have to tell her I was wrong. I have to lift the old injunction."[61] Calling it a "magical solution," Papi promises, like a Biblical patriarch, to give his "particular" blessing to the writing daughter. In this part, he plays as well the Afro-Caribbean role of Orúmila or the "witness of destiny, he who knows the whole of our lives."[62] In giving his particular blessing, the father, in effect, heals them both:

> I have promised her a blessing to take the doubt away. A story whose true facts cannot be changed. But I can add my own invention—that much I have learned from Yo. A new ending can be made out of what I now know.
>
> So let us go back to that moment. Let us enter that small, green-tiled bathroom. . . . I lift the belt, but then as I said, forty years pass, and my hand comes down gently on my child's graying head.
>
> And I say, "My daughter, the future has come and we were in such a rush to get here! We left everything behind and forgot so much. Ours is now an orphan family. My grandchildren and great grandchildren will not know the way back unless they have a story. Tell them our journey. Tell them the secret heart of your father and undo the old wrong. My Yo, embrace your destino. You have my blessing, pass it on."[63]

This new story of an old horror should not be read as a classic psychoanalytic catharsis.[64] Not should the Judeo-Christian overtones of the patriarchal blessing prompt a misconstrual of the episode as a Catholic confession.[65] In prompting her father's return to the bathroom episode—the revision that ends with a blessing rather than a beating, a call to speak rather than to suppress the family's stories, the artist has summoned Chucha's decades-old invocation to invent the words that can cure the "dis-ease" of the past. The protective spell Chucha casts echoes the healing cures of the Afro-Caribbean Ifá tradition, a religious system that invests the speech act with medicinal properties. In speaking of Ifá's sacred oracles, Eugenio Matibag explains that in the Afro-Caribbean belief system, "'literature' is medicine, therapy, counsel, soothsaying, and value clarification: it gives equipment, strategies, and instructions for living."[66] This notion exactly parallels the purpose of Chucha's call to the spirits to inspire the García daughters with healing fictions rather than self-limiting truths.

The ending of *¡Yo!*, in fact, has curative powers even beyond its reparation of old wounds between the father and daughter characters. Alvarez has written of the

personal value for her in receiving the rare blessing from a relative, at one time her grandfather and at another an aunt.[67] As for the father's blessing that closes her novel, she reveals in an interview:

> The father's blessing at the end is something I could give myself. We all grow beyond it, but there's a way which we all want the blessing of our *antepasados*. Especially from a Latino culture, you are a bead on a string. You don't think of yourself separately, of me and my feelings and who I really am. I'm also Alvarez and my *abuelito* and my *abuelita*. To feel that blessing coming down from the past, even though I broke the rules of what I should have been as a woman in my culture, it made me feel good—at least on paper.[68]

The ending of *¡Yo!*, then, offers a triple healing in that it first resolves the anxiety of the character Yo, naming her destino and saving her from further depression and crisis. In an equally important capacity, however, the episode allows the father, the original perpetrator of the violent silencing, a fictional forum in which to repent and return his daughter's voice to her.[69] Finally, as the revelation above suggests, these fictional blessings result in a very genuine healing for their creator, Alvarez. The daughter who "broke the rules," she literally invents her own medicine by writing down what she needs to survive.[70]

* * *

The epigraph to this essay, a quote by Gloria Anzaldúa, describes the indeterminacy experienced by those who live on the nameless borderland between two cultures. Anzaldúa's words suggest that the inhabitants of that shadowy country never reconcile themselves to its duality. The novels of Julia Alvarez, on the other hand, assert that a life lived between these binary worlds—in spite of the alienation and pain it engenders—can be embraced and celebrated with words. In fact, Alvarez calls books her "portable homeland,"[71] the country to which she claims a most comfortable citizenship. She also suggests in a recent essay that blazing a trail into the borderland can be the writer's finest role:

> Sometimes I hear Spanish in English (and of course, vice versa). That's why I describe myself as a Dominican American writer. That's not just a term. I'm mapping a country that's not on a map, and that's why I'm trying to put it down on paper.
>
> It's a world formed of contradictions, clashes, comminglings—the gringa and the Dominican, and it is precisely that tension and richness that interests me. Being in and out of both worlds, looking at one side from the other side. . . . These unusual perspectives are often what I write about. A duality that I hope in the writing transcends itself and becomes a new consciousness, a new place on the map, a synthesizing way of looking at the world.[72]

Alvarez's fearless melding in her novels of all the dualities of her life experience—of doubled religions, languages, cultures, and consciousness—suggests that such a "new place on the map" can be traced in the world of books. If writing on the borderland creates such narratives, it assures that Alvarez's fictional double, Yo, had it right from the beginning: stories do in fact have the power to heal.

Notes

1. Susan Sontag, *Illness as Metaphor* (New York: Farrar, Straus and Giroux, 1977), 3.

2. For a more complete study of the wide variety of African-based religious customs in the Caribbean, see *Sacred Possessions: Vodou, Santería, Obeah, and the Caribbean,* ed. Margarite Fernández Olmos and Lizabeth Paravisini-Gebert (New Brunswick: Rutgers University Press, 1997).

3. Alvarez's second novel, *In the Time of the Butterflies,* celebrates the bravery of the martyred Mirabal sisters, who lost their lives under Trujillo (Chapel Hill, N.C.: Algonquin, 1994).

4. Julia Alvarez, *Something to Declare* (Chapel Hill, N.C.: Algonquin, 1998), 174.

5. Julia Alvarez, *How the García Girls Lost Their Accents* (New York: Penguin, 1992).

6. Julia Alvarez, *¡Yo!* (Chapel Hill, N.C.: Algonquin, 1997).

7. In this essay, I will periodically supplement examinations of the fictional Yolanda's experience with Alvarez's personal reflections in her collection of essays *Something to Declare.* While the novels cannot be read as purely autobiographical, or as dependably factual renditions of the Alvarez family's expatriation, the character Yolanda is, by Alvarez's own admission, enough of a composite of her creator to warrant such comparisons.

8. Julie Barak, "'Turning and Turning in the Widening Gyre': A Second Coming into Language in Julia Alvarez's *How the García Girls Lost Their Accents,*" *MELUS* 23 (Spring 1998): 160.

9. Alvarez, *¡Yo!,* 12.

10. Alvarez, *How the García Girls Lost Their Accents,* 231-32, and *Something to Declare,* 135-38.

11. Alvarez, *¡Yo!,* 24.

12. Ibid., 7.

13. Ibid., 300.

14. Ibid., 300.

15. Alvarez, *How the García Girls Lost Their Accents,* 198.

16. Ibid., 202.

17. Alvarez, *¡Yo!,* 28.

18. Ibid., 299.

19. Ibid., 307.

20. Ibid., 305.

21. Alvarez, *How the García Girls Lost Their Accents,* 290.

22. Ibid., 211.

23. Alvarez, *Something to Declare,* 109.

24. In a second instance of censorship in the first novel, the father tears up a speech (a loose plagiarism of Whitman's "Song of Myself") that the adolescent Yo has written, forbidding her to speak such self-congratulatory words in public. Though there is not space to examine the scene closely here, it is another instance of violation brought on by the father's haunting fears of political retribution for speaking aloud. Recognizing the root of her parent's oppression, Yo bitterly flings Trujillo's hated nickname "Chapita" at her father, as she weeps over her second unjust silencing (*How the García Girls Lost Their Accents,* 142-47).

25. By "first" and "second," I refer to the appearance of each episode in the book, an important distinction in shaping the reader's experience of mental illness in the novel. Because the novel moves backward through time, however, the chronological position of each breakdown is actually the opposite (historically, Yolanda's hospitalization occurs prior to Sandi's).

26. Joseph Breuer and Sigmund Freud, *Studies on Hysteria (1893-1895),* trans. James Strachey (New York: Basic Books, 1957).

27. Alvarez, *How the García Girls Lost Their Accents,* 54.

28. Ibid., 55.

29. Alvarez, *Something to Declare,* 8.

30. Alvarez, *How the García Girls Lost Their Accents,* 55, 54.

31. Breuer and Freud, *Studies on Hysteria,* 25.

32. Alvarez, *How the García Girls Lost Their Accents,* 55.

33. Ibid., 53.

34. Ibid., 56.

35. Ibid., 60.

36. Ibid., 68.

37. Ibid., 75.

38. Ibid., 77.

39. Ibid., 80.

40. Ibid., 82.

41. Alvarez, *Something to Declare,* 58.

42. Alvarez, *How the García Girls Lost Their Accents*, 74, 80.

43. For a useful discussion of the talking cure as it is enacted in literary texts, including the psychoanalytic phenomena of transference, countertransference, and resistance, see Jeffrey Berman's *The Talking Cure: Literary Representations of Psychoanalysis* (New York: New York University Press, 1985).

44. In speaking of resistance in psychotherapy, Berman argues: "The psychobiographer thus frees the word from any connotations of a conscious, insincere, or fraudulent reluctance to tell the truth. There is resistance, then, in the nature of all inquiry. Viewed in this way, resistance becomes the natural reluctance to reveal or discover troubling human truths." The goal of therapy is, of course, to overcome resistance in order to uncover the real story, whereas the goal of art might be construed as the creative use of facts as raw material for weaving fictions.

45. Alvarez, *How the García Girls Lost Their Accents*, 85.

46. Thomas Szasz, "The Healing Word: Its Past, Present, and Future," *The Journal of Humanistic Psychology* 38, no. 2 (spring 1998): 8-20.

47. Alvarez, *How the García Girls Lost Their Accents*, 83.

48. Ibid., 84.

49. Ibid., 85.

50. List of "Commandments" in Alvarez, *Something to Declare*, 259-60.

51. Ibid., 123.

52. Alvarez, *¡Yo!*, 296.

53. See Joan Dayan, "Vodoun, or the Voice of the Gods," in Fernández Olmos and Paravisini-Gebert, eds., *Sacred Possessions: Vodou, Santería, Obeah, and the Caribbean*, 13-36.

54. Alvarez, *¡Yo!*, 218, 220.

55. Ibid., 219.

56. Dayan, 19.

57. Alvarez, *¡Yo!*, 200.

58. Ibid., 221.

59. Barak, "'Turning and Turning in the Widening Gyre,'" 162.

60. Alvarez, *¡Yo!*, 221. (My italics)

61. Ibid., 296.

62. Eugenio Matibag, "Ifá and Interpretation: An Afro-Caribbean Literary Practice," in Fernández Olmos and Paravisini-Gebert, eds., *Sacred Possessions: Vodou, Santería, Obeah, and the Caribbean*, 153.

63. Alvarez, *¡Yo!*, 308-9.

64. While the obsessive return to this episode in previous narratives could be seen as cathartic, a bringing to consciousness of an old injury to purge its emotional power, this revised episode is fictional. It finally closes the recursive story by rewriting it, thus halting the cycle of repression and recovery.

65. Though, like psychotherapy, the Catholic confessional can offer relief for mental suffering (see Szasz).

66. Matibag, "Ifá and Interpretation," 166.

67. Alvarez, *Something to Declare*, 11, 129.

68. Marny Requa, "Julia Alvarez: The Politics of Fiction," *Frontera* (5) online: www.fronteramag.com/issue5/Alvarez/

69. While it might be tempting to read this as a disturbingly colonial image—the patriarch as the sole controller of language—it must be remembered that it is the writer, Alvarez, who returns to this episode, in which to rewrite it and free her muse. In effect, she puts words in the mouth of her silencer and blesses *herself*.

70. In her daily writing rituals, Alvarez reveals more than a passing commitment to the syncretic spiritualism of her homeland: "I fill my writing bowl and say hello to my two old cemíes [stone and wooden Taino deities from the Dominican Republic] and make sure my Virgencita has fresh flowers, if it is summer, or a lit candle, in the winter" (*Something to Declare*, 285).

71. Requa, "Julia Alvarez: The Politics of Fiction."

72. Alvarez, *Something to Declare*, 173.

Laura P. Alonso Gallo (essay date 2002)

SOURCE: Alonso Gallo, Laura P. "'The Good, the Brave, the Beautiful': Julia Alvarez's Homage to Female History." In *Evolving Origins, Transplanting Cultures: Literary Legacies of the New Americans*, edited by Laura P. Alonso Gallo and Antonia Domínguez Miguela, pp. 89-100. Huelva, Spain: Universidad de Huelva, 2002.

[*In this essay, Gallo examines* In the Name of Salomé *and* In the Time of the Butterflies, *novels that center on women who played significant roles in the recent history of the Dominican Republic.*]

Julia Álvarez revises the history of the Dominican Republic in the novels ***In the Time of the Butterflies*** (1994) and ***In the Name of Salomé*** (2000). Hers is a fictional account of historical episodes in which she reworks the conventions of literary genres. The writer also plays with multiple viewpoints and discursive polyphony, techniques her readers have become familiar with ever since the publication of her two other novels. *How the García Girls Lost Their Accents* (1991) and *¡Yo!* (1997). Her manipulation of literary genres within the ground of the historical novel consists of the combination of an autobiographical discourse which presents the subject to the reader as an individual, and the *testimonio,* which transforms personal stories into a collective historical memoir. With both novels, Álvarez succeeds in exorcizing the evils inherent to myth and legend, presenting Dominican women whose greatness lies in their humanness, the consistency of their principles regarding family and homeland, and their capacity for commitment. The concepts of nationalism, homeland, and American identity are also examined under the light of great Latin American women's lives.

A Revision of Literary Genres and Aesthetics

In the presentation of the autobiographical self— mother and daughter in *Salomé* [*In the Name of Salomé*] and the four sisters in *The Butterflies* [*In the Time of the Butterflies*][1]—Álvarez constructs the female Latin American subject from within her own position as Latina; that is, as a Dominican, female, and bicultural and bilingual exile. Critics of Latina fiction have argued, since as early as 1989, that for a subject who is not part of the dominant ideology, construction of the self is a far more complex negotiation [than that of the white female]. In constructing herself as a subject, a Latina must dismantle the representation of stereotypes of her Self constructed, framed, and projected by the dominant ideology. (Ortega and Saporta Sternbach 14)

Álvarez creates distinct autobiographical female subjects in order to transcribe them culturally for North American readers whose anglocentric ideology may thus be questioned. By presenting six Latin American women inspired in real historical figures, the writer is informing the non-Latino reader of the Dominican people's history and culture. In an interview, Álvarez declares that her "desire to tell the story was there from the beginning," since "[she] was constantly telling North Americans about the Mirabal sisters, surprised that even [her] well-informed friends had never heard about them ("Conversation" 35). As this essay aims to illustrate, Álvarez critiques some of the stereotypes held by the dominant North American ideology and, at the same time, denounces sexist and patriarchal traits of Dominican society.

I consider both novels to be fictional autobiographies, given Álvarez's intention of building fictional characters upon real women. As she explains in the postscript

to *The Butterflies,* "what you will find here are the Mirabals of my creation, made up but, I hope, true to the spirit of the real Mirabal sisters. . . . I sometimes took liberties—by changing dates, by reconstructing events, and by collapsing characters or incidents" (324). Likewise, she justifies the literary representation of the poetess and her daughter in *Salomé*: "The Salomé and Camila you will find in these pages are fictional characters based on historical figures" (357). Álvarez's narrative style evidences what critics have detected in autobiographical works by Latinas:

> They challenge traditional notions about the genre of autobiography through their form and content. They subvert both Anglo and Latino patriarchal definitions of culture. They undermine linguistic norms by using a mixture of English, Spanish, and Spanglish. All address the question of politics of multiple identities from a position which seeks to integrate ethnicity, class, gender, sexuality, and language.
>
> (Torres 272)[2]

The Dominican writer does not follow the structural paradigms of a linear and logocentric discourse proper to the traditional autobiography. Moreover, when presenting women who form part of official history, Álvarez destabilizes concepts of male authority that have characterized that same history, thus condemning both the North American and Latino ideological systems. Through the use of Spanish words (for example *patria, campesino, papá, calmante, revolución, pohrecito, musa*), typical expressions and sayings (*un clavo saca otro clavo y voz del pueblo, voz del cielo*), and even literal translations of Spanish into English (*to hide the sun with one finger*), Alvarez attempts to subvert the authority of the English language and restitute the power of Spanish. By tropicalizing[3] her literary discourse, the writer reclaims Hispanic culture and reaffirms her Latina identity before the Anglo-American reader.

Along with the fictional autobiography, Álvarez makes use of the *testimonio,* a genre proper to the Latin American literary tradition that enhances the credibility of historical facts in narrative works. The *testimonio* imprints a collective trait onto the stories told by Álvarez's female characters so that individual experience becomes inextricably linked to that of broader social groups. The combination of different viewpoints and the polyphony of discourses reinforce the effect of the *testimonio,* allowing readers to grasp from multiple perspectives the historical reality experienced by family and society.[4] A close examination of structure will reveal the particularities of these narrative techniques.

Salomé is divided into two parts, each composed of four sections and framed by a prologue and an epilogue. The stories of Salomé Ureña and her daughter Camila intertwine in a parallel pattern throughout the book. The poetess's life unfolds in a linear progression, while her daughter's account follows a regressive order, starting at the age of sixty-six in the prologue and gradually going back in each chapter to the age of three, when her mother dies. Camila reappears in the epilogue at the age of seventy-nine, upon her return to the Dominican Republic in 1973, and close to death herself. These parallels, divisions into double discourses, and the alterations in narrative progression, confirm once again that the revision carried out by Latina writers on traditional autobiography, as Torres points out, is a political tool for the defense of their identity.

Mother and daughter's viewpoints dovetail in the novel, but only Salomé speaks in the first person. The guidelines of the *testimonio* are thus respected as the national poetess represents the Dominican female community enduring painful experiences in a patriarchal society. Camila's voice, however, in being filtered through a third-person omniscient narrator, produces an effect of estrangement and suggests that the muse's daughter has never had a voice of her own. In point of fact. Camila is characterized as a fragmented Latina who has not been able to integrate the diverse components of her identity: she appears to be lost in the anonymous world of the United States, and overshadowed at all times by the distinguished members of her intellectual family. She is often identified as the *sister* of Pedro and Max Henríquez de Ureña and *daughter* of the national poetess Salomé and Francisco Henríquez, a short-term President of the Dominican Republic. Aware of her vicarious existence. Camila, as if ventriloquized, admits: "She's done it all her life. Long before she stepped into a classroom, she indulged this habit of erasing herself, of turning herself into the third person, a minor character, the best friend (or daughter!) of the dying first-person hero or heroine" (8).

Nevertheless, in the fast pages of the novel, Camila uses her own discourse. It is in the epilogue that Álvarez grants Salomé's daughter a first-person voice, through which she reveals that at the age of seventy-nine she has come to terms with her life and feels ready to die in peace. At this stage, Camila resolves her long-standing internal conflict in which she viewed an unmarried, childless woman as purposeless, inferior, and disgraceful. She understands that womanliness is not exclusively defined by motherhood: that her mulatto blood is cause for pride; and that her modest work as a teacher has contributed to the larger revolution which great Latin American figures such as José Martí, Simón Bolívar, Eugenio María de Hostos, and her own mother spearheaded. But most importantly, Camila has learned that life entails struggle and the acceptance of uncertainty: "Such a mistake to want clarity above all else! . . . A mistake I myself made over and over all my life" (350). The final testimony of this woman, who thinks of herself as insignificant, stands as a manifesto for all Latinas, whose lives are part of a larger project no matter how small their existence appears to be: "The struggle to see and the struggle to love the flawed thing we see—what other struggle is there? Even the struggle to create a country comes out of the same seed. In the name of Hostos, Salomé, José Martí . . ." (339).

The Butterflies is structured in three parts, which contain four narrative pieces corresponding to each of the Mirabal sisters. The discourses of Patria. María Teresa, Dedé and Minerva tell the story of the women's lives from their adolescence in 1938 through the end of their days in 1960, at which time they returned from La Victoria, the prison where their husbands had been under arrest. The flow of the story stops abruptly at that point; Trujillo's men assassinate them and arrange things to look as if a fatal accident had occurred. Only Dedé, the sister who survived, will give voice to the story, oscillating between the present (1994, the date of the novel's publication) and different moments of the past through subtle narrative digressions.

In order to infuse realism into the story, Álvarez provides Dedé's reconstruction of the 1960 homicide in an epilogue, outside of the other sisters' stories. Dedé did not, however, accompany her sisters to La Victoria, but remained at home. She actually reconstitutes the incidents of the homicide by assembling the stories told to her by people (neighbors, strangers, friends, and even the sisters' husbands) who had witnessed different events before or after the "accident." She collects these fragments in order to figure out the terrible episode. Therefore, Dedé gives readers details of the supposed accident in the style of the *testimonio,* which in this case encapsulates multiple perspectives.[5]

According to the author's account, her literary influences are exclusively neither Latin American nor, despite her literary education, Anglo-American. She recognizes a more universal scope in her literary models, defining herself as "a mixture of traditions":

> I was influenced by literature of the Holocaust and the testimonial literature that comes out of Latin America. . . . A lot of the reading I did is not a part of North American literature, except for the narratives of slavery. Political testimonial literature does not come from the U.S.A. tradition. It just goes to show that as a writer I am a mixture of traditions.

> **("Citizen" ["Citizen of the World. An Interview with Julia Álvarez"] 28)**

By using a variety of literary traditions, Álvarez stresses her cultural *mestizaje,* rendering tribute to the syncretism that defines the history of Latin America. The writer's recourse to genres proper to the Latin American literary heritage seems to allow her to imprint *latinidad* onto the hegemonic discourse, since she writes in English and for the U.S. editorial market. Her revision of such genres adheres not merely to aesthetic considerations, but to a conscious political position that encompasses her Latina condition.

HUMANIZING MYTHS

Julia Alvarez had access to the Henríquez Ureñas' correspondence, one of the first editions of Salomé's poems, and the diary of her son Pedro, where he records the family history (***INS*** [***In the Name of Salomé***] 355-56). These materials allowed the writer to retrieve "the history and poetry and presences of the past," although she insists that her novel is a fictional re-creation where "inventions, opinions, portrayals, errors" are deliberate: "This is not biography or historical portraiture or even a record of all I learned, but a work of the imagination" (***INS*** 357). The writer acknowledges the same fictional re-creation in ***The Butterflies,*** disallowing strict biographical or historical rigor to her version of the Mirabal sisters' story. She argues: "And so it is what you find in these pages are not the Mirabal sisters of fact, or even the Mirabal sisters of legend. The actual sisters I never knew, nor did I have access to enough information or the talents and inclinations of a biographer to be able to adequately record them" (***ITB*** [***In the Time of the Butterflies***] 324).[6]

Therefore, the writer's intention has been to create fiction out of reality and real people's experiences—not out of popular or historical myth—in order to confront the bitterness ingrained in Dominican history. She writes: "For I wanted to immerse my readers in an epoch in the life of the Dominican Republic that I believe can only finally be understood by fiction, only finally redeemed by the imagination" (***ITB*** 324). Indeed, Julia Álvarez wrote both novels with the same purpose: to meditate upon the humanness hidden behind legendary women, and to publicize historical episodes and figures of the island. As a matter of fact, she started writing about the Mirabal sisters so that she could understand for herself the courage of these women, as she avows in the postscript to ***The Butterflies*** (323). Furthermore, the novel is aimed at North American readers, generally unacquainted with Dominican history, so that they may get to know the Mirabals and understand the grief of their people during Trujillo's dictatorship (324). Álvarez's intention of educating non-Latino U.S. audiences in Dominican history, politics, and social issues reveals once again

her political position as a minority writer who is reclaiming Latin American cultural wealth within Anglo-American society. To humanize the Butterflies, whom historians had consigned to the role of sacred national martyrs or simply ignored for decades, was Álvarez's desire from the beginning of her project. "The hard part," she acknowledges, "was that they had become legends: they had become such mythical characters that they had been robbed of their humanity, . . . and I was afraid to make them real. . . . They were robbed of the dignity of being real human beings and robbed of the dignity of what that sacrifice meant" (**"Conversation"** [**"Conversation with Julia Álvarez"**] 35).

Álvarez brings about the humanization of the Mirabal sisters by creating four distinctive characters that narrate in the first person their lives as children and young women. Readers become acquainted with the normalcy of their lives as they grow up, which shatters the popular mythic construct of the sisters. They are presented as daughters, girlfriends, wives, and mothers whose fears, dreams, and disappointments are gradually introduced in the story. Many times in the course of their lives, when imprisoned or harassed by the police, the sisters acknowledge with candor and honesty their weakness and fear. Courageous and daring in the defense of justice as they were, the sisters' attitude speaks for itself of their strong moral fiber. Through the personal stories of the Butterflies, Álvarez has answered the question that prompted her to write about them: "What politicized these women?" As the writer has commented, "women were supposed to be *mujeres de su casa.* In such a patriarchal *machista* culture, these women became politicized at a time when even the males in this culture kept their mouths shut" (Morales 13).[7]

The oldest of the four, Patria, is characterized as a profoundly religious person. She suffers a crisis after a miscarriage, which causes her to teeter on the brink of despair despite her strong faith. Her beliefs end up being completely overturned at the sight of national guards killing young farmers. Patria relinquishes her docile attitude, modeled after the biblical Good Shepherd, to blindly defend the revolution: "The time was now, for the Lord had said, I come with the sword as well as the plow to set at liberty them that are bruised. . . . And so we were born in the spirit of the vengeful Lord, no longer His lambs. Our new name was Acción Clero-Cultural. Please note, action as the first word!" (163-64).[8] Without abandoning her Catholic creed, Patria also painfully but resolutely exchanges her formerly passive acceptance for politically committed struggle against social injustice.

Minerva is characterized as rebellious, passionate, and sagacious. Acquainted from an early age with the many injustices suffered by the Dominican people, Minerva becomes the most politically committed of the four sisters as her resentment toward Rafael Trujillo increases over time. Such commitment may have been fueled by the disappointment that she experienced when she found out that her respected father had a secret, illegitimate family of a wife and four other daughters. Her wholehearted effort in supporting the education of these four sisters, who otherwise would be ignored by the patriarchal Dominican society, evidences the boundless social ethics of this woman.[9] Minerva, who would be given the code name *Mariposa*. Butterfly, by the underground comrades, was the first of her sisters to start working against the system. During her long incarceration in La Victoria prison, she would serve as an example of strength, firmness, and leadership for the other women, including her sisters Minerva and Patria.

After organizing a hunger strike in prison and enduring with dignity the humiliations to which she and the other women of La Victoria were subjected, Minerva is put under house arrest. During that short period she realizes that she has become famous among the Dominicans, who often praise her courage in the streets and acknowledge her plea for justice: "My months in prison had elevated me to superhuman status. . . . I hid my anxieties and gave everyone a bright smile. If they had only known how frail was their iron-will heroine" (259). With such modest remarks Álvarez places her heroine on a human level, drawing a credible and realistic portrait of the legendary Minerva.

María Teresa, the youngest, lacks political convictions. Thus, she complains about the hard time in prison and finds no sense in political struggle. She contends with open honesty: "I wanted an excuse to stay home. Like Dedé, I just didn't have the nerves for revolution, but unlike her, I didn't have the excuse of a bossy husband" (240). Although admitting her terror at being incarcerated at La Victoria, she experiences with profound emotion the sisterhood with the other women and rejoices in the idea of a free homeland. It is her loyalty to her older sisters and solidarity with her husband that give her the fortitude to endure the arduous confinement.

Dedé has neither Minerva's nor Patria's tenacity. Her situation appears to be more complicated than her sisters' as her misogynist husband refuses to become involved in the struggle against Trujillo, thus opposing Dedé's collaboration with her sisters in the underground. Even though the cautious and conservative Dedé understands the danger idealism entails, she eventually leaves her husband in order to join her sisters and support their cause. Honesty, now expressed in Dedé's words, humanizes this character as well: "She was hiding herself behind her husband's fears, bringing down scorn on him instead of herself" (179-80). She does not get involved directly with clandestine activities, however, and her role is that of taking care of the household and the children of Minerva and María Teresa while they are in prison. Hers is a quiet and self-sacrificing struggle. After her sisters' death, she becomes "Mamá Dedé," giving herself eagerly to her maternal role. She devotes her life to raising her nieces and nephews, attempting to shield them from the vanity or rancor of being the children of national heroines. As the only survivor of the homicide, Dedé is tormented by feelings of loss and guilt at being alive. In 1994, thirty-four years after the murder, when she is sixty-nine, Dedé still wonders if the sacrifice of her courageous and beautiful sisters served any noble purpose. In the decline of her life, she observes with much regret Dominican youngsters given to materialistic values: "the boy-businessmen with computerized watches and walkie-talkies in their wives' purses to summon the chauffeur from the car; their glamorous young wives with degrees they do not need; the scent of perfume . . . To them we are characters in a sad story about a past that is over" (318). The novel ends with her troubled thoughts; she is convinced that her own martyrdom inheres in having lived many years. Her final resolution, however, shows some hope, since she wants to believe that her mission has consisted of telling the story, *bringing the past into the present* (313). Like Camila in *In the Name of Salomé*, who asserts that it is "her mission in life—after the curtain falls—to tell the story of the great ones who have passed on" (8). Dedé underestimates her personal merit. Nevertheless. Álvarez does not give these two women the mere role of telling the story of the other great women; in giving all of them equal weight in the novels, she is once again stressing the importance of humanness over myth and legend.

Álvarez's effort to dig into the past in order to understand the present of Latin American nations and peoples is also made evident in *In the Name of Salomé*. The writer has rescued two other female figures of American history who had long been buried in oblivion: Salomé Ureña, the national poetess, and her daughter Camila. In Álvarez's words, "Given the continuing struggles in Our America to understand and create ourselves as countries and individuals, this book is an effort to understand the great silence from which these two women emerged and into which they have disappeared, leaving us to dream up their stories and take up the burden of their songs" (357). To Álvarez, Salomé's merit lies not solely in her artistic talent, nor in her role as muse of patriotic ideals in the political scene of the Dominican Republic during the second half of the nineteenth century, nor in her work as a social reformer. The novel highlights that what was also commendable about Salomé is simply her human condition; that is, her position within the family as both a devoted mother and wife of an unfaithful and politically famous husband. It is the complete portrait of Salomé, and not only the public depiction of the encyclopaedias, that Álvarez tries to recover from history.

Salomé stands out at early age because of her poetic work, which was surprising at the time for a young lady from a distinguished family. The novel emphasizes that young Dominican women in the 1850s were educated in sewing, embroidery, crochet, catechism, mores and civility and manners, and reading but not writing. Salomé, who at age seventeen started publishing some of her poems under a pseudonym and without her father's permission, soon becomes the driving force of the patriotic independence movement of the Dominican Republic. Readers follow the private life of this mulatto woman: her parents' separation arising from her father's infidelities, her mother's efforts to give Salomé a good education, and her marriage to Francisco Henríquez, "Pancho" (who, like the Butterflies' father, has a secret family). Álvarez emphasizes Salomé's facets as mother as well as founder of the Higher Education Institute for Women, where she attempted to carry out a positivist reform of the Dominican Republic in the social sphere. Salomé devotes herself to these tasks passionately until she dies, in marital and political exile, of tuberculosis, Readers learn of the loneliness she suffers as a woman who indefatigably fights for the improvement of her country as well as of her grief over her husband's betrayal. In her final days Salomé is struck by an existential crisis over having ranked her priorities in what she believes to have been the wrong order. From first to last: socio-political (as educational reformer and inspiring figure of political ideas), artistic (as poetess), and personal (as woman, mother and wife).

All of Salomé's anguish seems to be passed on to her daughter Camila, a three-year-old child when her mother dies. Camila does not share her mother's gift for poetry, and is characterized as a disoriented, perpetually exiled woman, who lives for and in the glorious shadow of her mother, father, and brothers. She reaches the end of her life single and, what saddens her the most, without children to hand down to the American future. She devotes herself to education, keeping up her mother's enterprise. But Camila works in the most absolute anonymity, in a small U.S. college and, for some time, in the Cuban schools of Castro's regime. Not until her last days will she understand the true meaning and purpose of her life. Salomé, the Dominican Republic's national icon, with her surpris-

ing intimacy, and Camila, the anti-heroine of ordinary life, appear elevated to the same great human height. Álvarez wants her readers to know both women in their complete humanity.

NATIONALISM AND THE AMERICAN IDENTITY

In her two novels, Álvarez poses questions regarding nationalism, nation, homeland and American identity. In *Salomé,* for example, some of those questions are explicitly formulated throughout the book: *"Who are we as a people? What is a patria? How do we serve? Is love stronger than anything in the world?"* (357). Learning from the lives of diverse characters in both novels, readers come to understand that such questions are impossible to answer as absolutes, for America and its nations are founded on their peoples' fluid sense of community and culture. Through the confessions of several women and the stories of two families, unmasking the myth built for those who left their imprint on history as artists, humanists, intellectuals, politicians or committed individuals, and elevating the humanness of anonymous figures who are and have been ignored by that same history, Álvarez deconstructs the absolute quality of nationalism, unveiling its particularities. Moreover, the writer raises the question of American identity—not specifically Dominican, Cuban or U.S. identities—through Salomé's children. Pedro, Maximiliano and Camila Henríquez Ureña, and indirectly through the figures of José Martí, Eugenio de Hostos and Simón Bolívar. We hear Camila mumbling, "What is it that Martí used to say, . . . Or was it Hostos who said that, or was it Mamá, after all? The beautiful, the brave, the good—that are all running together in my head" (*INS* 350). In the generation of the poetess's children, closer to our time, Álvarez updates those same interests, advocating education and the continuous pursuit of freedom for individuals, and prosperity for nations. According to the writer. Latin America must never forget its history, rich in thought and individuals who are carrying on the forging of its identity. With her stories about these good, brave, and beautiful women, Julia Álvarez reveals the most intimate female self as well as women's capacity to fight for a cause, be it as concrete as the family, or as abstract, subjective and problematic as freedom and patriotism.

Notes

1. Hereafter I will refer to the novels in the abbreviated forms *Salomé* and *The Butterflies,* For parenthetical information I will use the forms *INS* and *ITB* when needed.

2. In her enlightening article, Lourdes Torres analyzes the autobiographical works *Loving in the War Years: Lo que nunca pasó por sus labios* (1983) by Cherrie

Moraga. *Borderlands/La frontera* (1987) by Gloria Anzaldúa, and *Getting Home Alive* (1986) by Rosario Morales and Aurora Levins Morales.

3. I am using the term "tropicalization" according to the analysis of Frances R. Aparicio and Susana Chávez-Silverman in their critical edition *Tropicalizations: Transcultural Representations of Latinidad* (Hanover and London: University Press of New England, 1997).

4. In his article about *In the Time of the Butterflies,* Gus Puleo reviews the chronicle in the literary history of the New World (11-12). The critic sustains that the novel employs the genre known as *falsa crónica,* in the fashion of Ana Lydia Vega, "which serve to humanize historical facts and events. . . . By means of the *falsa crónica,* the one-dimensional and univocal record of society, in which society is defined as a mere result of a military or political movement, opens to an array of personalized events and accounts that reflect the experiences of individuals within a larger community." Puleo also quots Vega, who justifies her use of the *falsa crónica* in her version of the history of Puerto Rico: "Me interné entonces en el denso universo de las bibliotecas públicas y los archivos privados para confirmar la proteica multiplicidad de 'los hechos' y la desconcertante ambigüedad de las perspectives. Sobre las siempre cambiantes versiones de sucesos vividos o escuchados, construí estas que ahora someto a la imaginación de ustedes" (11).

5. The novel also draws on another genre typical of the Latin American literary tradition: the literature of resistance. The Mirabal sisters endured times of political repression on the island, and ended up risking their quiet lives by collaborating with the underground. Álvarez fictionalizes the testimonies of their incarceration, creating poignant and realistic examples of political resistance.

6. In several interviews, essays, and the postscript to *In the Time of the Butterflies,* the writer declares that from the age of ten, when already an exile in the U.S., she had a fixation on the supposed accident. Her curiosity would lead Álvarez in 1992 to meet the only surviving sister, Dedé, who gave the writer first-hand testimony, allowed her to visit the Mirabals' house, and provided her with the young María Teresa's diaries. After this moment, Álvarez asserts, "[the sisters] became real to me because [Dedé] was real. She was really my entry to the story. Then I also heard stories from other members of the family, from people who had been in the underground with them. I gathered all these pieces together. Their voices became real to me in an intuitive way" ("Citizen" 28). More information about the author's personal interest in the sisters' story can be found in Álvarez's essay, "Chasing the Butterflies" (*Something to Declare* 197-209).

7. The murder of the Mirabal sisters had a great impact on Dominican society, even on Trujillo's men themselves. According to the journalist Diederich, the fact that the Mirabals were women mortified the men's *machista* nature: "El general Pupo Román había visitado a las hermanas Mirabal cuando estaban en la prisión, siguiendo instrucciones de Trujillo, y se hahía sentido conmovido. . . . 'Éste es el principio del fin. No me gusta que la gente sea tratada así, especialmente las mujeres.' . . . El cobarde asesinato de tres bellas mujeres, cometido de semejante manera, tuvo un efecto mayor en los dominicanos que la mayor parte de los crímenes de Trujillo. Eso le hizo algo a su 'machismo.' Nunca se pudo perdonar a Trujillo ese crimen. Más que el pleito de Trujillo con la iglesia o con los Estados Unidos, o el hecho de que estaba siendo aislado por el mundo como un leproso politico, el asesinato de las Mirabal templó la resolución de los conspiradores que tramaban su fin." (69)

8. In her review of *In the Time of the Butterflies.* Martinez points to Patria as a representative of the action and beliefs proper to Liberation Theology: "Her long journey from traditional Catholicism to revolution—à journey made by many priests also—is a major theme in this book, as in Latin American Liberation Theology" (40).

9. It is interesting to note that Alvarez hardly provides physical descriptions of the Mirabal sisters. Even though the sisters are the protagonists of her novel, the author concentrates on their psychological and emotional traits. On the contrary, the Peruvian writer Mario Vargas Llosa writes a description of Minerva's physical beauty as well as femininity and intelligence in his novel about the Trujillo regime, *La fiesta del chivo* (182-84).

Works Cited

Álvarez, Julia. *In the Time of the Butterflies.* New York: Plume, 1995.

———. "Conversation with Julia Álvarez." Interview with Heather Rosario-Sievert. *Review: Latin American Literature and Arts* 54 (Spring 1997): 31-7.

———. *Something to Declare.* Chapel Hill. N.C.: Algonquin Books, 1998.

———. *In the Name of Salomé.* Chapel Hill, N.C.: Algonquin Books, 2000.

———. "Citizen of the World. An Interview with Julia Álvarez." Interview with J. Heredia. *Latina Self-Portraits: Interviews with Contemporary Women Writers.* Eds. Bridget Kevane and Juanita Heredia. Albuquerque: University of New Mexico Press. 2000. 19-32.

Aparicio, Frances R. and Susana Chávez-Silverman, eds. *Tropicalizations: Transcultural Representations of Latinidad.* Hanover and London: University Press of New England, 1997.

Diederich, Bernard. *Trujillo. La muerte del dictador.* Santo Domingo: Fundación Cultural Dominicana, 2000.

Horno-Delgado, Asunción, Eliana Ortega, Nina M. Scott and Nancy Saporta Sternbach, eds. *Breaking Boundaries: Latina Writing and Critical Readings.* Amherst: The University of Massachusetts Press, 1989.

Martínez, Elizabeth. "Of Passion and Politics." Review of *In the Time of the Butterflies* by Julia Álvarez. *The Progressive* 59.7 (1995): 39-44.

Morales, Ed. "Madam Butterfly: How Julia Álvarez Found Her Accent." Review of *In the Time of the Butterflies* by Julia Álvarez. *Village Voice Literary Supplement* 130 (Nov. 1994): 13.

Ortega, Eliana and Nancy Saporta Sternbach, 1989. "At the Threshold of the Unnamed: Latina Literary Discourse in the Eighties." Horno-Delgado et al. 3-23.

Puleo, Gus. "Remembering and Reconstructing the Mirabal Sisters in Julia Álvarez's *In The Time of the Butteflies.*" *Bilingual Review* 23 (1988): 11-20.

Torres, Lourdes. "The Construction of the Self in U.S. Latina Autobiographies." *Third World Women and the Politics of Feminism.* Eds. C. Talpade Mohanty, Ann Russo and Lourdes Torres. Indiana: Indiana University Press, 1991, 271-87.

Vargas Llosa, Mario. *La fiesta del chivo.* Madrid: Alfaguara, 2000.

Ellen McCracken (essay date 2002)

SOURCE: McCracken, Ellen. "The Postmodern Self of Julia Alvarez's *¡Yo!*: Identity, Memory, and Community." In *Evolving Origins, Transplanting Cultures: Literary Legacies of the New Americans,* edited by Laura P. Alonso Gallo and Antonia Domínguez Miguela, pp. 223-28. Huelva, Spain: Universidad de Huelva, 2002.

[*In the essay below, McCracken demonstrates how Alvarez uses postmodern techniques to explore the identity of the Latino community living in the United States.*]

Concepts of personal and public identity have long been a contested terrain for Latino immigrants to the United States and subsequent generations. For some, the initial sense of displacement has been attenuated and at times gradually eroded through the ideological metaphor of the melting pot whereby generations of immigrants, their children, and those already assimilated to American society were taught to desire the meltdown of distinct ethnic cultures into an amorphous American unity. Nonetheless, existential self-doubt frequently remained in the face of the *de facto* segregation and second-class citizenship that generations of Latinos experienced.

In the 1960s, the economic upturn fueled by the Viet Nam war provided the material conditions for a new generation of the children and grandchildren of immigrants to question and rebel against the weakening of ethnic identity prescribed by the melting pot model of assimilation. Various groups of Latinos in the U.S. asserted their identity in contradistinction to that of their parents and to the predominant Anglo ideals of mainstream Americanism. Chicano. Nuyorican, or Cuban-American identity provided groups with a new sense of community and self that often militantly demanded recognition and the full rights of American citizenship without forfeiting ethnic identity. Key to the strategies of these political movements was a stable concept of identity and a unifying nationalism that excluded the non-Latino in order to consolidate each group and engender political unity.

In the late 1980s and 1990s in what has been termed the Post-Chicano Movement Period, the influence of theories of postmodernity and new understandings of multiculturalism called into question such stable concepts of identity. Having served a useful purpose in the initial period of the consolidation of political movements, singular and uni-dimensional notions of the self began to be eroded. Gender, sexuality, race, and class helped to problematize and refine the notion of identity, as did the subsequent suspicion of essentialist categorization of complex human identities. As the concept of fixed identity eroded under the aegis of postmodern indeterminacy, some members of minority groups complained that now that they had found a new identity of which to be proud, mainstream theorists conveniently declared the death of the subject and stable identities. On the positive side, however, more complex understandings of identity allow for an evolving, dynamic, and nuanced sense of the self. Some saw an exciting challenge in the broadening and fluidity of notions of identity, in moving beyond the unifying categories that both affirmed and delimited people in the earlier period of Movement politics.

The broader and more complex understanding of Latino identity in the 1980s and 1990s helped to redefine multiculturalism to include less represented minorities and less visible identities. Writers such as Cecile Pineda and John Rechy who had published in the mainstream on themes not perceived to be related to the Movement began to receive critical attention. A burgeoning of Latina fiction called into question the predominant preoccupations of the celebrated male writers of the Movement period. New components of Latino ethnicity received recognition including alternative sexualities, political views, and smaller sub-ethnic cultures representing immigration from various countries in Latin America. Both mainstream and popular varieties of multiculturalism broadened their scope to include Latino writers publishing on non-Latino themes; established Latin American writers who immigrated to the U.S. and now write on U.S. Latino themes such as Isabel Allende; Central Americans who sought refuge in the U.S. and began to publish creative writing; and less well-known immigrants such as Dominicans, Colombians, Chileans, Argentineans, and Spaniards.

The Dominican-American Julia Álvarez emerged in the 1980s as one of the principal new writers to broaden and redefine U.S. Latino identity. Shortly after her birth in New York City in 1950, her family returned to the Dominican Republic where she spent her formative years. In 1960 her family emigrated to the U.S. permanently as political refugees because of her father's involvement in unsuccessful attempts to overthrow the dictatorship of Rafael Trujillo. The formative years of her childhood and adolescence took place in two distinct locales of the Americas—the complicated political and social space of the Caribbean island that she narrativizes in essays such as "An American Childhood in the Dominican Republic," and fiction such as *How the García Girls Lost Their Accents* and *In the Time of the Butterflies*—and the privileged but also difficult space in the U.S. as a Dominican physician's immigrant daughter who attended expensive boarding schools and an elite college. But like Puerto Ricans who are U.S. citizens yet culturally immigrants when they move to New York City, Álvarez exemplifies the hyphenated Americans whose formation links them crucially to both the North and the South, and whose writing glides perpetually between these distinct geographic, cultural, and political spaces.

Álvarez is one of the primary articulators of the complexities of U.S. Latino postmodern identity as we enter the new millennium. Her 1997 novel *¡Yo!* celebrates the hybridity of identity and the epistemological uncertainty that refreshingly distinguishes postmodernism from the master narratives and subtle authoritarian gestures of Movement politics. She carries on the tradition of self-narration important in both realist and modernist texts of the Movement: now, however, the focus is an accessible postmodernist experimentation that invites readers to engage with central questions about the coterminous nature of reality and representation, the continuum between the public and the private, and the construction of the self by the community.

The verbal and visual signs on the front cover of *¡Yo!* present an exotic image of the self in keeping with the romantic view of the Latina Other with which mainstream U.S. publishers market writing by Latinas.[1] The bright colors yellow, fuchsia, and blue chromatically signify the third-world Other as a kind of background or setting for the main message of the cover—the apposition between the central, hand-drawn title "*¡Yo!*," the author's printed name above, and the painting of an exotic reclining nude below. The verbal-visual montage between these three signifiers establishes a triple configuration of the self, linking Julia Álvarez the author, with the various significations of "Yo," and with the exotic woman pictured beneath. The exclamation points that precede and follow the title "**Yo**" signal the Spanish-language context of the signifier and its word play: first, the emphatic assertion of the presence of the self—the exclamation "I am here!" or "This is the story of me!", and secondarily the nickname of the fictional protagonist with autobiographical trappings, Yolanda García who becomes known to the reader in the text proper or is remembered from Álvarez's first fictional book. *How the García Girls Lost Their Accents*. Like the false promises of most advertisements, the picture of the exotic reclining nude lies to readers, for there is no correlative image of the self in the novel and no motivation for the exotic pose, headdress, scarves, and pillows in the image.

The text itself transcends the exotic trappings of the front cover. Álvarez draws readers almost effortlessly into delightful postmodern epistemological and ontological questions that engender complex thinking about identity and representation. Reminding readers of the process of its own construction from the very beginning, the book presents itself as a kind of writer's workshop on its table of contents page; each narrative item is classified as a literary genre, narrative technique, or theme to be attempted. Each chapter represents not only a different person's point of view about the protagonist "Yo," but also a particular technique, theme, or genre that will be the focus. "The Stranger," for example, not only narratively recreates one of Yolanda's visits to the Dominican Republic from the point of view those who see her as a stranger, but focuses on the narrative genre of the epistle as she helps a mother on the island to write a letter to her daughter in the U.S. with advice that she leave the man who is abusing her.

The prologue, entitled "Sisters—fiction," establishes the key questions of representation and reality that underlie the book's larger narrative project. Álvarez's sisters, who have been the subject of some of her previous writing, rebel against the ways in which they have been narratively cast. Perceiving themselves to be "fictionally victimized" (6) and "plagiarized" into fictional characters, the sisters fear that life is losing ground to fiction, that Álvarez's stories about them are becoming more real than reality. We experience the family's fear of the eroding border between the public and the private, truth and lies, and the original and the copy when the story itself draws us into the slippery relation between reality and its simulacra. One sister who is pregnant after having been artificially inseminated with sperm from the Dominican Republic asks that Yolanda not be told so that her baby will not become "fictional fodder"(7) in a published book. Yet we encounter the simulacrum of this baby precisely as we read the details of its conception and birth in the book in our hands. Just as one sister tells her about the soon-to-be-born baby and warns her not to write about it, it has already been written about in the paragraph we're reading. Gestation progresses with the progress of reading the story, and the birth itself is so forceful a life event that it requires narration; the new mother calls her difficult-to-reach famous sister and embarks on a long monologue about the birth to Yolanda's answering machine. The chapters that follow this prologue in the book carry on this motif of allowing characters their chance to talk about the author in long monologues. The book we are reading becomes Yolanda's metaphorical child.

If Latino immigrant identity has been centrally connected to the community in both the Movement and Post-Movement periods. Álvarez establishes this link rhetorically and fictionally by what might be termed the revenge of the characters. Each chapter of the book narrates an episode in the life of "Yo," from the perspective of another person involved in the event. The characters thus tell the "secrets" of the author, turning the author herself into a character. On the surface, each appears to offer a counter narrative to the dominant master narrative of Julia Álvarez's *oeuvre,* a kind of *testimonio* in which the interviewer is the subject rather than the interviewee. But the fiction maker is still ultimately in control, portraying herself in the third person the way she wishes to. By giving first-person voice and the role of narrator to her characters, Álvarez rhetorically recuperates and gives centrality to the community in this collective biography of "Yo," the authorial self.

"I was eight years old when my mother left me in the campo with my grandmother to go off to the United States to work as the maid for the Garcia family" (54). "The Maid's Daughter-report" begins as the *testimonio* of Sarita, the daughter of the Garcías' Dominican maid who later immigrates to the U.S., attends school at the Garcías' expense, suffers through a sense of racial and class inferiority by assuming a fictional life story for herself, and ultimately becomes a successful physician. When Sarita is in school, the privileged college student Yolanda completes a course project by

writing an ethnographic narrative about Sarita's acculturation process. Like Yolanda's sisters in the prologue. Sarita feels that something has been stolen from her when she secretly reads the report. She wants to cross out the nickname the Garcia family has given her mother "Primitiva," and she steals back the report in an attempt to regain control over her identity. Like other narratives in the volume, this episode has the overtone of an apology, a new "report" that Yolanda writes to make up for the shortcomings of the earlier ethnography about Sarita written for a course assignment.

Yolanda herself has become successfully acculturated, and many of the narratives in *¡Yo!* reveal her integration into American society. About half of the *testimonio* voices are those of non-immigrants, but several of Álvarez's collage of revisionist narratives re-elaborate the identity of Dominicans or Dominican immigrants to the United States in their own fictional voices. Those of her cousin, mother, and father connect thematically to her own development as a writer, and while telling these people's stories, she reaffirms the powerful role of fiction and narration in her life. Throughout the book we see at work her role as a writer of conscience who recuperates the personal, familial, and community identity of *dominicanos* on the island and in the U.S. In the last story her father offers his *hendición* to her as a writer, absolving her of a youthful narrative transgression that endangered the lives of her family under the Trujillo dictatorship. The childhood whipping she received to punish the dangerous narrative she told is transformed into the laying of her father's hand on her graying adult head to sanctify her *destino* as a writer: "My daughter, the future has come and we were in such a rush to get here! We left everything behind and forgot so much. Ours is now an orphan family. My grandchildren and great grandchildren will not know the way back unless they have a story. Tell them our journey . . ." (309). The father's blessing urges Yolanda to rewrite life and the past with fiction in order to recover the identity of the exiled immigrant. If the sisters and mother feel violated by Yolanda's fictionalization of them in the first story, the father reasserts the crucial role of fiction and narrative in the formation of immigrant identity, memory, and community in the final story. Álvarez's engagement with issues and techniques of postmodernism in this book is not the unmotivated play of rhetorical tropes like the exotic images on the front cover, but rather a crucial means of recuperating and renewing the self-narrative of an exiled Latino community in the United States.

Note

1. See McCracken. *New Latina Narrative.* 11-39.

Works Cited

Álvarez, Julia. "An American Childhood in the Dominican Republic." *The American Scholar* 56 (1987): 71-85.

———. *How the García Girls Lost Their Accents.* Chapel Hill, N.C: Algonquin Books, 1991.

———. *In the Time of the Butterflies.* Chapel Hill, N.C.: Algonquin Books, 1994.

———. *¡Yo!* Chapel Hill, N.C.: Algonquin Books, 1997.

McCracken, Ellen. *New Latina Narrative: The Feminine Space of Postmodern Ethnicity.* Tucson: University of Arizona Press, 1999.

Kelly Oliver (essay date 2002)

SOURCE: Oliver, Kelly. "'One Nail Takes Out Another': Power, Gender, and Revolution in Julia Alvarez's Novels." In *Foucault and Latin America: Appropriations and Deployments of Discursive Analysis,* edited by Benigno Trigo, pp. 235-46. New York: Routledge, 2002.

[*In this essay, Oliver argues that Alvarez's novels reveal how race, gender, and socioeconomic status influence power dynamics, linking Alvarez's views to philosopher Michel Foucault's theories on power and domination.*]

> Between every point of a social body, between a man and a woman, between the members of a family, between a master and a pupil, between everyone who knows and everyone who does not, there exist relations of power . . .
>
> —Michel Foucault[1]

One of the central themes in Julia Alvarez's novels is the way that power dynamics shift according to race, class, and gender positions. Alvarez's reflections on power, resistance, and domination in *How the García Girls Lost Their Accents, In the Time of the Butterflies,* and *¡Yo!,* can be productively used to exemplify both the strengths and limitations of Michel Foucault's analysis of power, resistance, and domination. On the one hand, Alvarez's reflections on power, in her novels bring to life Foucault's notion of local transformation and immanent resistance. On the other hand, her focus on the power dynamics of race, class, and gender in the private domestic sphere unsettles a Foucauldian analysis more concerned with disciplinary techniques in public institutions such as schools, churches, prisons, and hospitals. Alvarez's use of the conventions of domestic femininity, womanhood, and motherhood, to resist patriarchal authority both at the level of private family life and in public institutions, including government, at once demonstrates Foucault's thesis that resistance to domination must take localized forms and at the same time makes all the more striking the Foucauldian blind spot in terms of sexual difference in relation to power.[2]

In addition, Alvarez's attempts to fragment the authority of a unified centered narrative voice through her use of changing perspectives and voices, and the tensions between domination and resistance raised by such an attempt that become explicit in her latest novel *¡Yo!* are symptomatic of the Foucauldian notion of power which is necessarily both the power to dominate and the power to resist *¡Yo!* can be read as a literary exercise in the necessary tension between the attempt to open one's own discourse onto the voice of the others, on the one hand, and the solipsistic world that attempt can engender, on the other—between having a voice and being silenced, between resisting domination and dominating through resistance.

POWER AND RESISTANCE

Foucault suggests that resistance does not have to originate from outside the system of dominance. In fact, it can't. To say, as Foucault does, that one cannot get outside power is not to say that it is necessary to accept an inescapable form of domination (*Power/ Knowledge,* 141). Foucault insists that "resistance to power does not have to come from elsewhere to be real, nor is it inexorably frustrated through being the compatriot of power. It exists all the more by being in the same place as power. . . ." (*Power/Knowledge,* 142). Moreover, "[i]t would not be possible for power relations to exist without points of insubordination" (*Dreyfus,* 225). Power demands resistance and resistance requires power.

To say that everyone is caught in the machine of power is not to say that there aren't those who benefit and those who suffer. For Foucault, "everyone does not occupy the same position; certain positions preponderate and permit an effect of supremacy to be produced" (*Power/Knowledge,* 156; *Dreyfus,* 223) "Every relationship of power puts into operation differentiations which are at the same time its conditions and results" (*Dreyfus,* 223). The oppressive effects of power relations are very real. And although resistance is part of this power relation, it too is very real:

> [T]here is a plurality of resistances, each of them a special case: resistances that are possible, necessary, improbable; others that are spontaneous, savage, solitary, concerted, rampant, or violent; still others that are quick to compromise, interested, or sacrificial; by definition, they can only exist in the strategic field of power relations. But this does not mean that they are only a reaction or rebound, forming with respect to the basic domination an underside that is in the end always passive, doomed to perpetual defeat.
>
> (*The History of Sexuality* (a), 96)

In fact, Foucault's analysis points to the fragility of systems of domination. They do not have one central power and therefore they do not have only one central weak spot. Rather, they have weakness everywhere. There is potential for resistance on every level. Because power is not possessed and because it doesn't just emanate from the top down, even those disenfranchised by the dominant system are empowered. Power is not possessed; it is not something that belongs exclusively to the oppressors (*Discipline and Punish* (a), 26). Foucault says that "power is not a thing, it is a relationship between two individuals, a relationship which is such that one can direct the behavior of another or determine the behavior of another" ("What Our Present Is," 155).

Foucault suggests that "local, specific struggles" against local forms of power and resistance on all levels can affect change (*Power/Knowledge,* 130-131). If the state is the effect of a multiplicity of institutions, it can be changed by changing those institutions. Changes can ripple through the system. Just as disciplinary patterns are repeated on different levels and cascade upward through the system, so too changes and resistance can move from one location to another throughout the system. Foucault's local strategies provide the hope that individuals can make a difference. Because power dynamics are fluid and always shifting, resistance to domination is possible. In *The History of Sexuality* Foucault concludes that: "one is dealing with mobile and transitory points of resistance, producing cleaves in a society that shift about, fracturing unities and affecting regroupings, furrowing across individuals themselves, cutting them up and remolding them, marking off irreducible regions in them, in their bodies and minds" (*The History of Sexuality* (a), 96).

SHIFTING POWER RELATIONS

Julia Alvarez's first novel, **How the García Girls Lost Their Accents,** is in one sense a study in mobile and transitory points of resistance and shifting power dynamics that fracture unity and affect regroupings. Throughout this novel, Alvarez shows shifting power relations between race, class, and gender. The same individual in different contexts occupies positions of power and disempowered positions. For example in the first chapter, "Antojos," Yolanda Garcia returns to the Dominican Republic after five years without a visit and ventures into the countryside to pick fresh guavas. The first chapter opens with the narrator describing the color-coding of class hierarchy: old aunts in greys and blacks of widowhood, cousins in bright colors, nursemaids in white uniforms, and kitchen help in black uniforms (3). This chapter and the book as a whole repeatedly recount the deferential gestures that signal power relations between race,

class, and gender. When scolded for not having matches on hand to light the candles on the cake, one of the maids, Iluminada, makes a pleading gesture with her hands clasped against her breast (4). When another maid, Altagracia, is asked to explain the word "antojo" to Yolanda, she "puts her brown hands away in her uniform pockets" and "says in a small voice. You're the one to know" (8) These deferential gestures signal class hierarchy and the differential power relation in terms of class privilege.

Later in this chapter, when Yolanda is picking guavas and she gets a flat tire, gender hierarchy displaces class hierarchy and the power dynamics shift. Alone with her car, Yolanda is terrified when two men appear out of the grove with machetes hanging from their belts. She considers running, but she is paralyzed with fear and rendered speechless (19). The narrator describes her repeating the same pleading gesture of Illuminada, hands clasped on her chest (20). Yolanda's class privilege in relation to the maid, and in relation to the young boy, José, who has taken her to pick the guavas, shifts in relation to these two men whose gender privilege is threatening to Yolanda. Now she is the one using deferential gestures.

The power dynamics again suddenly shift in this scene when she begins speaking in English and the two men conclude that she is American. At this point, they are "rendered docile by her gibberish" and when she mentions the name of her aunt's rich friends, the Mirandas, "their eyes light up with respect (20-21). In this scene of shifting power relations, class privilege has given way to gender privilege, and then the relation between gender hierarchy and class hierarchy is reversed again. In the end, when Yolanda tries to confirm her class privilege and express her gratitude by paying the men, they refuse and look at the ground, as the narrator tells us, with the same deferential gestures of Illuminada and the little boy José (22). The chapter ends with José returning from the Mirandas' slapped, shamed, and accused of lying when he tells the guard that a woman is out picking guavas alone. Even Yolanda's dollar bills can't cheer him. The collusion of rigid gender and class structures results in José's punishment which is just intensified when Yolanda offers him money. Even in attempts to make José happy, Yolanda reaffirms her class dominance over him.

Although the novel is full of this type of power reversal and shifting power dynamics, I will mention just one more example of shifting power relations between race, class, and gender from the tenth chapter, "Floor Show." As the novel moves back in time, this chapter takes place in New York when the Garcías' girls are young, shortly after their family has fled the

Trujillo dictatorship. Here the Garcías have been invited to join Dr. Fanning and his wife for dinner at a restaurant. Dr. Fanning had arranged the fellowship that allowed "Papi" Garcías to take his family to New York and was trying to help Papi get a job. For days "Mami" gave the girls instructions on how to behave, and on the evening of the dinner she dressed them in binding braids and tights in the hopes of disciplining not only their behavior but also their bodies. The dinner scene is very tense because the Garcías, used to having class privileges in the Dominican Republic, are financially beholden to the Fannings. In their presence both Mami and Papi García display deferential gestures and repeatedly look down at the floor.

This chapter displays several reversals between race, class, and gender hierarchies. First, because Mami García studied in the United States as a girl, her English is better than Papi's and this gives her more power than him in social situations: "Mami was the leader now that they lived in the States. She had gone to school in the States. *She* spoke English without a heavy accent" (176). The power dynamics between mother and father are reversed by the power of linguistic access. Class dynamics shift when the Garcías, struggling to make ends meet in the United States, no longer have class privilege. Papi no longer has the honor of paying for dinner. The Fannings, who appeared in the Dominican Republic as silly-looking tourists speaking bad Spanish, now make the Garcías look small (184). Gender dynamics shift when Mrs. Fanning kisses Papi García on the way to the bathroom. In this context his class and race deference to Mrs. Fanning make him powerless to object to her flirtations. Power dynamics shift again when Sandi, who witnessed the kiss, uses what she saw to blackmail her father into allowing her to get a doll that they cannot afford and for which the Fannings end up paying. In this chapter Sandi recognizes the value of passing as a white American when she studies her fair-skinned and blue eyed beauty in the mirror after she has seen the power Mrs. Fanning exercised over her father with the kiss.

Shifting power dynamics are also central to Alvarez's second novel, *In the Time of the Butterflies*. Here, there is a scene similar to "Floor Show" where a daughter becomes more powerful than her father when he wants her to keep a secret from her mother. When Minerva Mirabal discovers that her father has a secret second family, she gains power over her father; gender and generation power relations shift. In the end, it is this second illegitimate family, much poorer and less powerful than the first, that smuggles letters and care packages back and forth between the girls in prison and their family at home; the power dynamics of class shift when the lower-class family has access to the guards in a way unavailable to the upper-class family.

The narrative structure of Alvarez's third novel, *¡Yo!,* is motivated by shifting power dynamics. Like her earlier two novels, *¡Yo!,* is written from different perspectives and in different voices, but with the third novel, perspective and voice become the focus of the novel itself; even the plot revolves around the question of narrative voice. In the first novel, the story of the Garcia girls is told as the stories of the four daughters and their parents. The chapters are written about each of them and, with the exception of Yolanda's chapters written in the first person and the unidentified "we" of the chapter "A Regular Revolution," the narrator refers to them all in the third person. We still have one omniscient narrator who sees and describes the inner lives of the different protagonists. In the second novel, the chapters are written from different first-person perspectives. Although there is still a thin narrator, each chapter is written from the perspective of one of the four Mirabal sisters. While the first novel gives us different perspectives by telling different stories, it does not give us different voices. The second novel gives us different perspectives by giving us different voices. This shift in perspective as well as voice unsettles the power of the narrator or any one character to direct the point of view of the novel. In the third novel, perspective and voice even become plot themes. Characters in the novel challenge the narrator's authority. In addition, for the first time in Alvarez's novels, chapters are written from the perspectives and in the voices of minor characters, who challenge the point of view of major characters and the narrator.

Alvarez's fictional account of shifting power relations embodies Foucault's theory of mobile and transitory sites of resistance that reconfigure always shifting power relations. These novels exemplify some of the ways in which, as Foucault says, individuals are furrowed by intersecting axes of power, cut up and remolded and marked by their various positions in shifting power relations that constantly regroup them in terms of race, class, and gender, among other alliances. While Foucault's genealogies are peopled with boys and men locked into mental and penal institutions, Alvarez's novels are peopled with girls and women locked into patriarchal conventions. The contrast between the everyday lives of ordinary women incarcerated in their own homes and disciplined through mundane practices and Foucault's descriptions of public disciplinary practices used to crush "insane," "criminal," and "perverted" boys both expand a Foucauldian notion of power to include domestic space and highlights the lack of attention to this feminine space in Foucault's own work. While the logic of power determines that it shifts between resistance and dominance, Alvarez's novels make clear that the differential norms for masculinity and femininity within patriarchal cultures circumscribe power relations differently for men and women.

In her depiction of shifts in power relations, Alvarez is not only sensitive to the ways in which individuals move between positions of relative power but she also shows how individuals are marked and excluded by group identities that divide them against themselves. Alvarez's focus on shifting power relations of race, class, and gender show how these group identities work as what Foucault calls "dividing practices" that split individuals and individuality itself (*Dreyfus,* 208). Foucault describes how the individual needs to be recognized in his individuality but not to the point that his identity or individuality is used to exclude him. Individuality itself is a dividing practice that divides us against ourselves. Foucault says that the power of dividing practices: ". . . applies itself to immediate everyday life which categorizes the individual, marks him by his own individuality, attaches him to his own identity, imposes a law of truth on him which he must recognize and which others have to recognize in him. It is a form of power which makes individuals subjects" (*Dreyfus,* 212). Alvarez's fiction is a study in how individuals become subjected to race, class, and gender in ways that mark them, cut them up, remold them, and reconfigure them relative to their position in relation to the shifting power dynamics of racist, classist, and patriarchal cultures.

REVOLUTION

Revolution is a recurring trope in all of Alvarez's novels. Like Foucault, Alvarez is concerned with local resistance to domination and exclusion. The revolutions of Alvarez's novels, however, are not monumental actions that overthrow governments but the everyday struggles with authority that enable and empower resistance. Alvarez's revolutions are localized sites of resistance that often use the very structure and traditions of domination itself against domination. They are Foucauldian revolutions. As Foucault says: "points of resistance are present everywhere in the power network. Hence there is no single locus of great Refusal; no soul of revolt, source of all rebellions, or pure law of the revolutionary. Instead, there is a plurality of resistances, each of them a special case. . . ." (*The History of Sexuality* (a), 95-96). More specifically, Alvarez is concerned with the ways in which the very trappings of femininity, womanhood, and motherhood can be used against patriarchy in order to open up a space for women's resistance to patriarchal domination.

How the García Girls Lost Their Accents documents various localized struggles of women against patriarchal domination. In a chapter entitled "A Regular Revolution," Alvarez suggests that revolution is a matter of "constant skirmishes" on an everyday mundane level (111). She compares the four daughters' revolt against their parent's authority and against patriarchal authority to their father's participation in the revolt against the Trujillo dictatorship. This comparison itself suggests that revolution happens continually through everyday resistance rather than "global" overthrow. The girls plot their revolution using the accepted patriarchal codes for chaperones and young ladies' proper behavior against those very codes. Alvarez shows how the patriarchal traditions are turned against themselves in order to undermine patriarchal authority. Everyday practices of domination also open up everyday modes of resistance. Alvarez's novels deliver the Foucauldian message that power is not only the power to dominate but also the power to resist.

In "A Regular Revolution" three sisters, Carla, Yolanda, and Sandi, are trying to rescue the fourth, Fifi, from getting pregnant and stuck marrying their very traditional sexist island cousin Mundín. Here, Mundín is called a "tyrant" and the girls are staging a "revolution," "a coup on the same Avenida where a decade ago the dictator was cornered and wounded on his way to a tryst with his mistress" (127). The girls use the traditional restrictions on girls and women to their advantage when they insist that their cousin and chaperone Manuel take them home early without the lovers Mundín and Fifi. They use Manuel's responsibility for them to combat the "male loyalty" that "keeps the macho system going" (127). Manuel is forced to take them home without the lovers, which blows their cover. The "first bomb" explodes on women's side of the patio when the girls answer that Fifi is with Mundín and then "there is an embarrassed silence in which the words *her reputation* are as palpable as if someone had hung a wedding dress in the air" (129). The girls use the patriarchal convention that girls are not to be left alone without their chaperone to expose the breach of another convention that girls are not to be left alone with their *novios*. Their motives, however, are not to protect their sisters' reputation or virginity but to protect her from the oppressive patriarchal culture that would demand and circumscribe marriage, family, and subservience to her husband.

The plot of Alvarez's *In the Time of the Butterflies* revolves around revolution, specifically the Mirabal sisters' involvement in the underground revolution against Trujillo. Again revolution and resistance are not painted in the broad strokes of bloody battles and guerilla uprisings but in the mundane makeup of femininity. Alvarez's story of the Mirabal sister's revolution against Trujillo is as much about their own local revolutions against the restrictions of patriarchy as it is about a rebellion against the restrictions of dictatorship. In fact, the dictator's authority is depicted as founded on the macho image of a patriarch who has his ways with women.

Like *How the García Girls Lost Their Accents, In the Time of the Butterflies* describes how patriarchal conventions are used to undermine patriarchy and how the trappings of femininity are used to fuel revolution, this time political as well as personal revolution. The church, crucifixes, and praying become forms of rebellion (237). The sisters use the script they learned from the nuns for writing out Bible passages to list the ammunition in their hiding places (168). The sisters' mental and physical discipline while in prison is compared to keeping the baby on a feeding schedule (235). Maté uses her long hair and hair ribbons to smuggle news stories to other prisoners and secret notes detailing the human right's abuses of the Trujillo regime to the Organization of American States representatives when they visit the prison (246, 252). A young woman's diary becomes incriminating evidence against the dictatorship's human right's abuses. The election of "Miss University" becomes the promise of democratic elections. Minerva tells Maté that "this country hasn't voted for anything in twenty-six years and it's only these silly little elections that keep the faint memory of democracy going" (136).

For the Mirabal sisters, love, family, and revolution are inseparable. Passion between lovers feeds passion for revolution, and the common struggle against the dictator fuels personal passion. The struggle for freedom keeps Minerva and Manolo together through difficult personal times. Maté falls in love with Leandro when she meets him delivering ammunition for the revolutionaries. She sees the revolution as her chance for personal independence from a family that treats her like the baby. More than that, she realizes that her looks and easy manner with men can serve the revolution. She writes in her diary: "now I can use my talents for the revolution" (143). Patricia becomes involved after her church group witnesses young guerillas attacked by Trujillo's soldiers. She sees the face of her own son Nelson in the face of a dying young guerilla and from that moment on is committed to saving her family by fighting Trujillo. While these women are fighting against the national patriarch, Trujillo, they are also fighting against their own local patriarchs at home. They all have various skirmishes with their father and their husbands in order to assert themselves against patriarchal conventions.

If, as Minerva Mirabal says of the dance that cures her headache, "one nail takes out another," then she is the

hammer (97). She knows how to strike one nail of patriarchy against another in order to get what she wants. When her father won't let her leave the farm to go to law school, and when El Jefe (Trujillo) wants to make her his mistress, she eventually convinces Trujillo to allow her go to law school to be near him in the city (98). She pits the authority of Trujillo against her father's authority. When Trujillo suggests private meetings, she uses the patriarchal conventions of propriety and honor to argue that it would not be honorable of her to meet him alone (111). One nail of patriarchy takes out another.

GENEALOGY AND SUBJUGATED KNOWLEDGE

In his own work, Foucault attempts strategically to recall points of resistance in the form of subjugated knowledges. "Subjugated knowledges," he says, are those "blocs of historical knowledge which were present but disguised within the body of functionalist and systematizing theory." Subjugated knowledge is by definition differential knowledge. It is oppositional knowledge. It is knowledge which is concerned with historical struggles (*Power/Knowledge,* 82-83). Foucault suggests that the genealogist uses subjugated discourses in order to effect a resistance to domination. Genealogy, says Foucault, is the "union of erudite knowledge and local memories which allow us to establish a historical knowledge of struggles and then make use of this knowledge tactically today" (*Power/Knowledge,* 84).

Julia Alvarez's *In the Time of the Butterflies* is a type of Foucauldian genealogy. In her fictional account of the Mirabal sisters' participation in the resistance to the Trujillo dictatorship, Alvarez documents/imagines a resistance not only to the patriarchal power of the dictator but also localized and more mundane patriarchal power that subordinates women in their everyday lives. In her postscript to the novel, Alvarez says that she presents neither the real Mirabal sisters of fact nor the Mirabal sisters of legend, but tries to demythologize their courage by describing ordinary people. Perhaps paradoxically, even as she creates them in her fiction, she wants to avoid making these women into deities under the sway of "the same god-making impulse that had created our tyrant" (324).

Alvarez's novel describes the ways in which femininity and women's restricted and stereotypical roles as guardians of the family and of religion are put into the service of revolution—revolution against the dictatorship and revolution against patriarchy. Confessional diaries become means not only for personal therapy and Foucauldian self-surveillance but also for testimonies of injustice and suffering. The trappings of femininity, for instance, beautiful long hair, become means to deliver secret messages to the outside world. In a Foucauldian vein, Alvarez's *In the Time of the Butterflies* not only documents the subjugated knowledge of women subject to patriarchal oppression, but also shows some of the ways in which the very trappings of domination can be used to resist that domination. Insofar as women's knowledge is subjugated knowledge within patriarchal cultures, all of Alvarez's novels in various ways give voice to the subjugated knowledge of girls and women.

Alvarez's third novel, *¡Yo!,* attempts to give voice to knowledge and perspectives subjugated within her first novel, *How the García Girls Lost Their Accents.* The book begins with one of the Garcia sisters, Fifi, complaining about her sister Yolanda becoming a famous novelist and at once exposing and distorting the family history. Many of the subsequent chapters in the novel are written from the perspectives of both major and minor characters from the first novel—a cousin Lucinda, the maid's daughter Sarita, the mother, the father, the sister Fifi. Often these characters correct and revise the story as told by Yolanda, the famous novelist. Both Alvarez's use of the first person only from Yolanda's perspective in her first novel and the depiction of Yolanda as a famous author who wrote a book about "the hair and nails cousins" and other characters from *How the García Girls Lost Their Accents.* suggest that as readers we are to identify Alvarez with the character Yolanda.

Yet, *¡Yo!* makes us suspicious of Yolanda and of our author. The novel is written not only from different perspectives but also from those perspectives that challenge the perspective of the novelist character, Yolanda. Even when they don't challenge Yolanda's story, Yolanda is the center of attention, so much so that if we are supposed to identify Alvarez with Yolanda, this third book seems self-indulgent. For example, the last chapter begins with the father saying "of all my girls, I always felt the closest to Yo" (292). Characters throughout the novel question the stories told by others. The reader is continually told that an author lies, exaggerates, and manipulates the truth. This move within the novel itself to challenge the authority of the novel puts the reader in the liar's paradox: Do we believe what the characters tell us, that the novel is not telling the truth? Or, do we disbelieve what the characters tell us, and believe that the novel is telling the truth? We are caught within a paradox of saying that the truth is that there is no truth.

The reader is put into an even more problematic position in relation to the alternative perspectives presented by the minor characters insofar as they are also the creations of Julia Alvarez, identified with Yolanda Garcia. If Alvarez (as Yolanda) is trying to give a voice to the silent minor characters of her first novel in her third novel, she does so by co-opting their voices, speaking for them, and thereby manipulating her readers. This tension between opening up space for voices other than the author's unified individual voice and speaking for others is symptomatic of the Foucauldian project of giving voice to subjugated knowledges. How is it possible to write or speak or describe subjugated knowledge without also reinscribing it within another dominant discourse and subjugating it even while attempting to liberate it? In other words, how can Foucault or anyone else write about subjugated knowledge or discourse silenced by other dominant discourses without reinscribing the subjugated discourse within his own discourse, and, more than that, reinscribing it *as subjugated*? So, too, how can the author of *¡Yo!* speak for all of the characters who didn't have a chance to tell their stories in the first novel (*How the García Girls Lost Their Accents*) without, as Fifi accuses Yolanda, putting words in their mouths? This tension is inherent in all attempts to speak for others, even if those attempts are motivated by a concern to give voice to subjugated knowledge.

With *¡Yo!* we have the mind-bending situation of a character telling us that her husband didn't speak the way that he does until he read her sister's novel, which put the words into his mouth. This novel, which begins with one sister making fun of the other for mouthing clichés on the radio about art mirroring life, ends up confusing the relation between life and art. At the end of *How the García Girls Lost Their Accents,* in a chapter entitled "Yoyo" the first-person narration concludes: "I grew up, a curious woman, a woman of story ghosts and story devils, a woman prone to bad dreams and bad insomnia. There are still times I wake up at three o'clock in the morning and peer into the darkness. At that hour and in that loneliness, I hear her, a black furred thing lurking in the corners of my life, her magenta mouth opening, wailing over some violation that lies at the center of my art" (290). Who is the author? Whose words and voices are these? In *¡Yo!* Alvarez ties the text in knots around the question of the author's authority. By so doing, she at once challenges and fragments the authority of the author and at the same time exposes the fiction of speaking for and as others. This double movement again suggests the Foucauldian lesson that the power to resist is also the power to dominate, and visa versa.

At this point, the postscript to *In the Time of the Butterflies* reads as a warning. Alvarez, presumably now in her own voice, tells us that "a novel is not, after all, a historical document, but a way to travel through the human heart" (324), and that an epoch of life, at least that of the Trujillo regime in the Dominican Republic, "can only be understood by fiction, only finally be redeemed by the imagination" (324). Fiction, then, tells us something about life that history can't. It speaks to the heart in a way that "immerses" readers in an epoch and helps them to "understand" it. Like a Foucauldian genealogy, Alvarez's fiction uses and creates local memories "which allow us to establish a historical knowledge of struggles and then make use of this knowledge tactically today" in order to understand the dynamics of patriarchal oppression.[3]

Thanks to Benigno Trigo for helpful suggestions and continuing a dialogue from which this essay is formed.

Notes

1. Foucault *Power/Knowledge,* 187.

2. Although Foucault analyzes the normalization of heterosexuality, he pays little attention to the effects of patriarchal power on women. For feminist criticisms of Foucault on the question of sexual difference see: Alcoff; Butler, *Gender Trouble*; Diamond and Quinby; Fraser; Heckman; Biddy Martin; McNay; McWhorter: Sawicki.

3. Benigno Trigo has suggested that there is a tension between what Alvarez says she does in her novels—provides what is missing in history, the story of the human heart—and what she actually does in her novels. The tension between what Alvarez says she is doing and what she does points to tensions between any author's intentions and her products especially when those intentions are to speak what has not been spoken or heard within dominant culture. Foucault has problematized any straightforward discussion of the transparency of the author's intentions or authority in ways that speak to this tension in Alvarez's writing. While Alvarez describes the feminine domestic space that Foucault ignores, she is not as self-reflective about the ways that her writing is inscribed in process of the production of truth and authority as is Foucault.

Kelli Lyon Johnson (essay date June 2003)

SOURCE: Johnson, Kelli Lyon. "Both Sides of the Massacre: Collective Memory and Narrative on Hispaniola." *Mosaic* 36, no. 2 (June 2003): 75-91.

[*In the following essay, Johnson compares* In the Time of the Butterflies *to Haitian writer Edwidge Danticat's novel* The Farming of Bones, *contending that both Alvarez and Danticat use the form of the novel to explore the collective memory of women in the Dominican Republic and Haiti.*]

Together, Haiti and the Dominican Republic form the island named Hispaniola, and between Haiti and the Dominican Republic runs the Massacre River, named for the slaughter of thirty buccaneers by Spanish colonials in 1728. The river earned its name again in 1937, when Generalisimo Rafael Leonidas Trujillo ordered the massacre of thousands of Haitians living on the border in the Dominican Republic. As Michele Wucker points out in *Why the Cocks Fight: Dominicans, Haitians, and the Struggle for Hispaniola,* the memory of the massacre in 1937 is still so strong that "even now, it is nearly impossible for Dominicans and Haitians to think of each other without some trace of the tragedy of their mutual history" (44). Remembering that mutual history and the regime that initiated it—the *trujillato,* the thirty-year reign of Trujillo in the Dominican Republic (1930-1961) is for both Haitians and Dominicans a painful negotiation of race, nation, and identity. As Neil Larsen asks "Como narrar el trujillato?", we also ask, How do Dominicans and Haitians remember, and commemorate, the *trujillato*? Trujillo commemorated himself frequently and on a grand scale. Monuments, parades, and rituals were devoted entirely to him, earning him, for a time, a place in the *Guinness Book of World Records* as the leader who built the most statues in his own honour (Wucker 69). Those commemorations were the space Trujillo claimed for himself in which to construct the national identity of the Dominican Republic, his own attempt to shape the country's collective memory and identity.

Theorists of collective memory have revealed two opposing constructions of both its function and location. Pierre Nora has argued that memory attaches itself to sites, which he calls *lieux de mémoire,* in contrast to history, which attaches itself to events (22). Because "memory takes root in the concrete, in spaces, gestures, images and objects," *lieux de mémoire* make concrete the abstract. These sites, Nora argues "are *lieux* in three senses of the word—material, symbolic, and functional" (18-19), and these *lieux* are the very monuments that Trujillo constructed, the portraits he commissioned, the ceremonies he commanded. In contrast to such sites, Susan Crane argues that "groups have no single brain in which to locate the memory function, but we persist in talking about memory as 'collective,' as if this remembering activity could he physically located." According to Crane, "collective memory ultimately is located not in sites but in individuals" (1,381).

At issue in these two opposing locations for collective memory is space: the social, political, and personal space necessary for assertions of national and individual identity. Such postcolonial contests for space—geographical, political, linguistic, and cultural—define the recent history of Hispaniola as well. Homi Bhabha suggests in *The Location of Culture* that postcolonial cultures must create and inhabit "in-between spaces" that "provide the terrain for elaborating strategies of selfhood—singular or communal—that initiate new signs of identity, and innovative sites of collaboration, and contestation" (1-2). For Dominican American writer Julia Alvarez and Haitian writer Edwidge Danticat, that in-between space is entextualized in the novel: between history and memory, the vernacular and the official, fiction and fact. The novel thus becomes a new narrative space. These novelists create and claim a new, literary space in which collective memory expresses a national identity that includes members of the memory community previously excluded from historical discourse because of racial, class, sexual, or national identity.

Alvarez and Danticat not only include members of Dominican and Haitian society marginalized by traditional discourses of history, but they also include their reading audiences—the English-speaking audience and those who read the translations in a variety of countries across the world. As a form often called "democratic" because of its accessibility, the novel becomes a literary space in which Alvarez and Danticat remember the *trujillato* by locating collective memory both within individuals and in a specific location—the novel itself. By locating the collective memory of the *trujillato* in the novel, they reconceive collective memory as existing in a shared space (the narrative) and in the individual (the narrator/s).

Maurice Halbwachs first recognized that "every collective memory unfolds within a spatial framework" (140). Members of a memory community share not only a geography, an infrastructure, and natural resources but also other spaces of collective memory beyond the physical: legal, economic, and religious. Similarly, Alvarez and Danticat explore the relationship between narrative space and collective memory, creating a site for memory belonging to the people who suffered under Trujillo's regime. While religious and historical accounts may occur within an elite discourse inaccessible to marginalized communities, the narrative space created by Danticat and Alvarez fills with the voices of women, the poor, and the disenfranchised on both sides of the Massacre River.

The individuals who give voice to the narratives in these novels are women. Collective memory, in general, may be explicitly gendered because, as James Fentress and Chris Wickham suggest, "in most Western societies, women, rather than men, have the responsibility of encapsulating (sanitizing, moralizing) accounts of the experienced past for young children, as part of the process of socialization" (142). Gendered in this way, collective memory reveals national identity and history through women's eyes, in stark contrast to traditional history, which focusses on the lives, ac-

tions, decisions, deaths, and wars of men. When remembering the *trujillato*, Alvarez and Danticat focus on both the perceived dichotomy between memory and history and the reality that women's stories have long been absent from traditional historical discourse. Dominicans and Haitians under the dictatorships that characterized much of their history in the twentieth century have seen history books written that neglect their stories—as the poor, the disenfranchised, the silent, and the "disappeared." Women have been further marginalized by their inability to participate in politics, education, and the economy, all sources of the male narrative of history. The distinction between history and memory thus creates divisions of gender, race, and nationality, ultimately devaluing collective memory as inferior to the "objective" events and materials of history. In *The Farming of Bones* and **In the Time of the Butterflies,** however, Danticat and Alvarez re-value the memory of women's experiences during Trujillo's regime by writing from women's perspectives, largely ignored in other narratives of the *trujillato*.

Neatly framing Trujillo's regime, Danticat's *The Farming of Bones* and Alvarez's **In the Time of the Butterflies** tell the stories of women's lives during the *trujillato*, based on real events in Haitian and Dominican history. Danticat's novel opens in 1937, near the beginning of the *trujillato*, recounting the story of the Haitian massacre and its aftermath. Danticat presents *The Farming of Bones* through the voice of Amabelle Désir, a Haitian *restavèk* 'live-in servant' for a prominent Dominican family, living near the border between the two countries. Hearing rumours of mass Haitian executions, Amabelle flees her post in search of her lover and, when she survives the massacre, returns to Haiti to try to create a life out of the memory of the genocide she has witnessed. In contrast, Alvarez's novel, set on the other side of the Massacre River, focusses on events at the end of the *trujillato*, telling the lives of the real Mirabal sisters—Minerva, Patria, and Maria Teresa—and their assassination in 1960. Alvarez writes their lives through their own voices and through the reconfigured voice of Dedé, the surviving sister. Both of these novels commemorate the women, and not Trujillo himself, creating of the novel a gendered space of the collective memory of these historical events.

The Farming of Bones and **In the Time of the Butterflies** explore the role of commemoration in the *trujillato* and its effect on national identity and collective memory in Haiti and the Dominican Republic. In practice, commemoration is frequently accomplished by designating an object, location, or ritual as meaningful, and those multiple meanings are both constructed and contested, as people assimilate them into the (hi)story they tell themselves about their nation. Traditionally, commemoration is manifest in museums, parades, monuments, and other sites and ceremonies, providing a specific space in which to mark the memory of historical events and people. Danticat and Alvarez come from two very different traditions of commemoration: The official silence of commemoration in Haiti contrasts sharply with the cacophony of the Dominican Republic, in which the truth of the *trujillato* must be distinguished amid too many stories, memories, monuments, markers, and rituals.

The nationalism that has characterized the Dominican and Haitian experience is largely predicated on memory, recollections of occupation, war, and political struggle. John Augelli suggests that such "memories of bitter conflicts reinforce the national contrasts between Haiti and the Dominican Republic" (21-22). Silvio Torres-Saillant similarly points out that the Dominican national identity is dependent upon Haitians, against whom Dominicans define themselves, thus constructing "a nation-building ideology based primarily on self-differentiation from Haiti" (54), in which "anti-Haitianism becomes a form of Dominican patriotism" (55). Trujillo reinforced this anti-African sentiment in his campaign to "whiten" the Dominican Republic. Moreover, during the *trujillato,* "anti-Haitianism served a two-fold purpose: to furnish a nationalistic ambience that would stimulate unquestioning patriotism and to provide an international concern around which the Dominican people could be induced to rally so as to quell the forces of potential domestic dissent" (55).

Danticat addresses Dominican nationalism in *The Farming of Bones,* particularly the anti-Haitianism that characterized the *trujillato.* She puts the patriotic ideology in the mouth of a Haitian priest who is caught and tortured during the massacre, forced to repeat the nationalist and racist anti-Haitianism that shaped Dominican identity: "Our motherland is Spain; theirs is darkest Africa, you understand? They once came here only to cut sugarcane, but now there are more of them than there will be cane to cut, you understand? [. . .] We, as Dominicans, must have our separate traditions and our own way of living. If not, in less than three generations, we will all be Haitians" (260-61). To the Dominicans, writes Danticat, Haitians "were those people, the nearly dead, the ones who escaped from the other side of the river" (220). In constructing their own identity against the Haitians, Dominicans also had to construct Haitian identity, an ideology that depended, in part, on dehumanizing beliefs "about [Haitians] eating babies, cats, and dogs" (190) as well as questions of race and religion. While many scholars have pointed to the productive use of

collective memory in nationalist projects in the nineteenth and twentieth centuries, Danticat and Alvarez reclaim collective memory for their own purpose of instantiating a new collective memory of the *trujillato.* By revealing the lack of commemoration in Haiti and its misuse in the Dominican Republic, these two women writers undermine traditional state uses of collective memory and use the narrative space of their novels to write a new collective memory.

In constructing their own identity, Haitians look to a history of rebellion, revolution, and independence. The first country in Latin America to win and declare its independence—the second independent state, after the United States, in the western hemisphere—Haiti is a country of people who resisted and continue to resist imperial and patrimonialist domination and interference. The slave rebellion that led to Haiti's independence in 1804 left in its wake many years of instability and political isolation. In order to preserve their independence throughout such volatile times, Haitians progressively dismantled or destroyed the social, political, and economic structures established by the colonial invaders, structures that had created and maintained the plantation system. Haiti, suggests Franklin Knight, was confronted with a hard choice: "independence or general well-being. [. . .] The Haitians opted for independence, which meant nothing short of the total physical destruction of every institutional form which made plantation society possible" (63). As a result, there is little evidence that the people of Haiti locate their national identity within physical institutions such as universities, museums, historical markers or monuments in the same way that Trujillo invested these sites with meaning and history. This sense of rebellion continues to inform Haitian life, engendering a marked disrespect for the very monuments and markers that Trujillo used to foster national identity. In 1986, for example, when a military coup overthrew Haitian President Jean-Claude "Baby Doc" Duvalier, jubilant Haitians "marched to downtown Port-au-Prince and mobbed the statue of Christopher Columbus that the Italian government had helped erect years before. Throngs of exuberant protesters tore the bronze Columbus off his base and cast him into the ocean that had brought him to Hispaniola" (Wucker 76).

Not surprisingly, then, the Haitian massacre of 1937 is not commemorated by monuments or ceremonies in Haiti. "There were no graves, no markers," Amabelle says in *The Farming of Bones* (Danticat 270). Absence, however, can also frame the past, according to Iwona Irwin-Zarecka, who sees "the challenge of grieving without graves" and asks, "What becomes of mourning when there is no place?" (24). Without a monument in which to root memory, Danticat turns to the

Massacre River, which she visited before she began writing the novel. She believed, "As soon as I got there, I would sense the history, that I would see it as though unfolding on a screen." What she discovered, however, was "the ordinariness of life" (Wachtel 107). In *The Farming of Bones* Danticat writes, "At first glance, the Massacre appeared like any of the three or four large rivers in the north of Haiti. On a busy market day, it was simply a lively throughway beneath a concrete bridge, where women sat on boulders at the water's edge to pound their clothes clean, and mules and oxen stopped to diminish their thirst" (284). For Danticat, it was not what she found at the Massacre River but, rather, she says, "what I didn't find there that most moved me" (Wachtel 107). Visiting Haiti and the Dominican Republic "to research the massacre, I was really sad because there was nothing that reaffirmed what had happened. No memorial plaques. No apologies. Life was just going on. That's when I realized how fragile memory is. It can just vanish in the air if we let it." Because of the lack of sites or commemoration in Haiti, she says, "we ourselves are the museums" (Shea 21).

Where there are no markers and no physical spaces to commemorate thousands of deaths, Danticat creates a narrative space in her novel, locating Haitian collective memory of the massacre in a space that is truly collective. The massacre, she says in an interview, is "a part of our history, as Haitians, but it's also part of the history of the world. Writing about it is an act of remembrance" (Charters 43). In writing the novel, she had "one of the less solitary writing experience because it felt like [she] was collaborating with those who had existed once" (Anglesey 36-37). Other Haitians were "collectively invested in the story," inviting her to hear their stories, but, she says, "I didn't always think of it as research. I felt like I was reclaiming a lot of my own history, learning about my country, our people, the different lives we've been forced to live, the different types of migration we've experienced" (Shea 15). She heard many different versions, depending "upon where people were along the borders. I traveled along border towns both in the Dominican Republic and in Haiti, and there are a lot of differences in how people remember it" (16). This multiplicity of memory is mitigated through Danticat's use of a single narrator. Because the story is a first-person narrative, Danticat creates "one person telling of the historical events. It's not really objective, but rather the moment as she, the narrator, lives it" (Anglesey 39).

In *The Farming of Bones,* Amabelle herself is haunted by memory: the death of her parents in the Massacre River, the loss of Sebastian in the massacre, and her flight from the Dominican Republic. For Amabelle,

"when you have so few remembrances, you cling to them tightly and repeat them over and over in your mind so that time will not erase them" (45). In the novel, memory plays an important role in the lives of all the Haitians living in the Dominican Republic, where they spend much of their time recounting memories of their homeland, which "was how people left imprints of themselves in each other's memory" (73). These memories also allow for the construction and maintenance of a national identity for those Haitians working in exile, one that challenges the dominant Dominican construction of Haitians in the land where they are working and living. Before the massacre, in Father Romain's sermons "to the Haitian congregants of the valley, he often reminded everyone of common ties: language, foods, history, carnival, songs, tales, and prayers. His creed was one of memory, how remembering—though sometimes painful—can make you strong" (73). In the absence of concrete markers and ceremonies of commemoration, memory creates bonds among Haitians.

Danticat also insists on the fragility of memory revealing how it resists the materiality of a historical record as her own method of research resists the material remains of history in favour of individual memory and story. In preparing to write *The Farming of Bones,* she says, "I mentally collected oral history by talking to people living on both sides of the river to hear their perceptions of the event" (Anglesey 37), but she didn't take notes or tape record stories. If the story is not told, if memory is not iterated, does it cease to exist? Danticat's novel ensures the existence and persistence of Haitian memory and, thereby, the world's memory, of her people's massacre. Because "nature has no memory" (309) and because there are no markers to the massacre, Danticat has written a novel that consecrates a location for the collective memory of Haitian identity and history.

On the other side of the border, in the Dominican Republic, memory plays a significant role in the construction of Dominican history, as reflected in Alvarez's novel. The space consecrated to the *trujillato* in the Dominican Republic, however, has traditionally been a masculine space, leaving little room for the iteration of women's memories. Out of Trujillo's long tradition of commemoration emerge monuments dedicated to the Mirabal sisters and their resistance to Trujillo's dictatorship, monuments that themselves are social constructions of memory. National identity and memory are often located in museums, which are themselves, argues Irit Rogoff, "a twentieth-century critical discourse, a theorization of the cultural practices of collecting, classifying, displaying, entertaining, and legitimating various histories through selected objects within staged environments" (231).

Part of our cultural interest in museums as institutions of memory lies in our feeling of obligation "to collect remains, testimonies, documents, images, speeches, any signs of what has been" (Nora 13). Because visitors to museums may remember their trip to the museum rather than the events themselves, these material artifacts of history can replace memory rather than represent it, rejecting the stories and experiences of those who do not have access to institutions of history. Museums, as locations and inventories of history, may also exclude the histories of the silent and invisible. If museums are to be what Crane calls "memory institutions," sites that create and re-create history for their visitors, their discourses must legitimize testimony and experience—creating "the multiple pasts" (Crane 1,382)—as much as documents and artifacts.

The museum commemorating the Mirabal sisters is located in their house, a domestic space that immediately genders the country's collective memory of their lives. Alvarez writes in **Something to Declare,** "As I entered the Mirabal house, as I was shown the little patio where Trujillo's secret police gathered at night to spy on the girls, as I held the books Minerva treasured (Plutarch, Gandhi, Rousseau), I felt my scalp tingle" (199). Alvarez notes the "little clothes that the girls had made in prison for their children," their jewellery, their dresses, and María Teresa's braid (200). These artifacts of memory—jewellery, clothing, hair—are also gendered markers of the sisters' identity as women rather than national heroines. Because "gender is a covert signifying process," Rogoff argues, the feminization of museums and their contents alters memory and history both by shifting the focus onto feminized elements of a nation's history. Rogoff has remarked that German museum displays of the Nazi era are sometimes feminized, "characterized by a disproportionately high representation of the lives of women, domestic economies, and the culture of survival" (231). This feminization of fascism emphasizes "the realities of women's lives (*civilian* lives), and focus[ses] on the remains as *debris* rather than *ruins* and on the protagonists as victims rather than *vanquished,*" thus rewriting "the entire relation of the nation to its fascist heritage" (242, emph. Rogoff's). Such exhibits devalue the lives of all Germans under the Nazis because they equate women's lives with defeat and victimization. A similar feminization of the space of Dominican collective memory about the *trujillato*—the Mirabal museum and its contents—risks the marginalization of the sisters in Dominican history, a de-centring that Alvarez resists by providing them literary space in the novel that focusses on their whole lives, including in particular their education and political activities outside the domestic space of the home. The museum dedicated to the Mirabal sisters in the

Dominican Republic is not a national museum and is generally absent from guidebooks and tourist literature about the island. That the museum lacks federal funding, a reliable influx of visitors, and trained personal in the creation of historical narratives through exhibition exposes the potential loss of the Mirabal story to both Dominicans and visitors to the country.

Alvarez also relies on documents and sites—Nora's *lieux*—in her reconstruction of the memory of the Mirabal sisters. She reads the letters passed between Minerva and Manolo, documents of their relationship and experiences, and she "combed for information about the Trujillo regime" in the National Archives (**Something** [**Something to Declare**] 204). She and her husband visited the Gonzalez farm, Minerva and Manolo's house in Monte Cristi, the family church, Minerva's friend Sinita's home, and the site of the "accident," which is not marked but is located in the memories of Dominicans. In her research, some local Dominican boys offered to show Alvarez and her husband where the sisters had been killed. "Many of the old people heard the crash," one of the boys tells her. "You want to talk to someone who remembers?" At that time, Alvarez refused the offer, but she left with an understanding that the Dominican people remembered the Mirabal sisters and their murder even without the markers that so characterize the rest of the *trujillato*.

The physical vestiges of history have traditionally granted legitimacy to individual memories of events, which might not otherwise be included as part of history. Alvarez recognizes the relationship between material remains and memory in **In the Time of the Butterflies.** Dedé, as the surviving sister, becomes the guardian of the girls' memory. She sets up a museum, "just five minutes away and everyone shows up there wanting to hear the story firsthand" (311-12). When the "gringa dominicana," a double for Julia Alvarez, arrives at the beginning of the novel, Dedé knows that the material memories—"books and articles, [. . .] the letters and diaries" (7)—represent the expectations of those in search of history and memory; they are the stuff of the *gringa*'s "research." Before Dedé "knows it, she is setting up her life as if it were an exhibit labelled neatly for those who can read: THE SISTER WHO SURVIVED." In the museum, there are also "three pictures of the girls, old favorites that are now emblazoned on the posters every November, making these once intimate snapshots seem too famous to be the sisters she knew" (5). For Dedé, those pictures are now markers of something else, not her sisters but the national heroines, *las martires* of the *trujillato*. As the pictures become part of the collective memory, they cease to be part of Dedé's personal memories.

Other surviving remains of the sisters' lives come from the site of the "accident," the belongings found in the car. Dedé takes an inventory of "the losses. I can count them up like the list the coroner gave us" (314). She can say them like a catechism:

> One pink powder puff.
> One pair of red high-heeled shoes.
> The two-inch heel from a cream-colored shoe.
> [. . .]
> One screwdriver.
> One brown leather purse.
> One patent leather purse with straps missing.
> One pair of yellow nylon underwear.
> One pocket mirror.
> Four lottery tickets.
> [. . .]
> One receipt from El Gallo.
> One missal held together with a rubber band.
> One man's wallet, 56 *centavos* in the pocket.
> Seven rings, three plain gold bands, one gold with a small diamond stone, one gold with an opal and our pearls, one man's ring with garnet and eagle insignia, one silver initial ring.
> One scapular of Our Lady of Sorrows.
> One Saint Christopher's medal.
>
> (314-15)

That Alvarez includes these gendered artifacts in the novel reveals her own consciousness of the domestic reality of these women's lives, in spite of what they could represent to those in search of history. Alvarez is not feminizing their story to portray the Mirabal sisters and all Dominicans as victims. Rather, she emphasizes the everyday nature of their lives as women—the domestic reality of the Mirabal sisters' history—to show that we must not dismiss "the challenge of their courage as impossible for us, ordinary men and women" (324). Moreover, Alvarez genders the narrative space of her novel to reflect a cultural belief that "the most enduring Dominican legends of strength and redemption are female: the Mirabal sisters [. . .] and the Virgin Mary" (Wucker 7).

The most salient aspect of the location of collective memory in the novel is the means of transmission of the memory: language. Language, writes Juan Flores, is "the supreme mnemonic medium, the vehicle for the transmission of memory" (283). Moreover, because it was a key instrument of Trujillo's control of the Dominican Republic, language plays a double role in the novel, both a means of control by the regime and a means of resistance and remembering by the people. Dominicans dreaded "words repeated, distorted, words recreated by those who might bear them a grudge, words stitched to words until they are the winding sheet the family will be buried in when their bodies are found dumped in a ditch, their tongues cut off for speaking too much" (*Time* 10). Under Trujillo, Miner-

va's friend Sinita points out, "people who opened their mouths didn't live very long" (18). In this way, silence becomes as meaningful as language, a mechanism of survival. Even the journal that Maria Teresa keeps while in prison is full of silences, missing pages, and she herself censors a report to the visiting O.A.S. Peace Committee investigators, blotting out the identities of those involved in prison violence.

The Mirabal family thus recognizes the power of language in the *trujillato*. In their efforts to protect Minerva, who interests Trujillo at first personally and later politically, her family repeatedly silences her, providing her with their own words, which they see as less dangerous for her. María Teresa writes a speech for Minerva "praising El Jefe at the Salcedo Hall." Mate (María Teresa) points out that "it worked, too. Suddenly, she got her permission to go to law school" (*Time* 121). When Minerva is called to police headquarters in the capital city, her mother, who generally "doesn't say a word in public" (106), speaks for her, saying, "All my daughter wants is to be a good, loyal citizen of the regime" (114). Later, at a command performance for Trujillo, a lavish party that the Mirabals are "requested" to attend, "Papa says to Minerva, 'you keep quiet'" (93), and Patria begs her, "*Ay, Minerva, por Dios,* keep that tongue in check tonight" (94). In one of the most poignant scenes in the novel, as Minerva and Dedé are travelling together, they are pulled over by five *calíes*. Minerva says, "I will never forget the terror on Dedé's face. How she reached for my hand. How, when we were asked to identify ourselves, what she said was—I will never forget this—She said, 'My name is Minerva Mirabal'" (277). Dedé speaks for Minerva, willing to take her sister's identity and risk the punishment meant for Minerva.

Danticat in *The Farming of Bones* also explores the role that language plays in the *trujillato*, demonstrating in particular how rumours shape Haitian life. In the Dominican Republic, Haitian workers "were always hearing about rifles being purposely or accidentally fired by angry field guards at braceros or about machetes being slung at cane workers' necks in a fight over pesos at the cane presses" (70). Such rumours serve to quell worker rebellion or other unrest resulting from the substandard working and living conditions of Haitian cane workers in the Dominican Republic. Language also serves as a weapon of social control when Trujillo orders the slaughter of all Haitians living on the border. He uses a linguistic test to identify Haitians "of dubious nationality" (Augelli 24). Haitians were "being killed in the night because they could not manage to trill their 'r' and utter a throaty 'j' to ask for parsley, to say perejil" (Danticat 114). Estimates of the number of casualties in the massacre fall between 18,000 and 35,000 (Farmer

103), which Trujillo justified by claiming that "Haitians are foreigners in our land. They are dirty, rustlers of cattle, and practitioners of voodoo. Their presence within the territory of the Dominican Republic cannot but lead to the deterioration of the living conditions of our citizens" (qtd. in Farmer 103). Amabelle voices the question all Haitians must have had: Why "parsley? Was it because it was so used, so commonplace, so abundantly at hand that everyone who desired a sprig could find one? We used parsley for our food, our teas, our baths, to cleanse our insides as well as our outsides. Perhaps the Generalissimo in some larger order was trying to do the same for his country" (203). Parsley becomes a new symbol in the collective memory of Haitians—identity, nationalism, and death.

Language is also the means through which the testimonies of the victims of the massacre are transmitted. A testimony, or *testimonio* in the Latin American tradition, is what René Jara calls a *"narración de urgencia"* 'a story that needs to be told' (Jara and Videl 1). Testimonies themselves are collective, as Latin American *testimonio* "speaks for all those oppressed, disappeared, imprisoned 'without a name'" (Rice-Sayre 68), belonging to the entire people. Testimony "derives from a long oral history of witnessing" (49), a process that, according to Dori Laub, "includes the listener. For the testimonial process to take place, there needs to be a bonding, the intimate presence of an other—in the position of one who hears" (Laub and Felman 70). In this way, "testimonies are not monologues; they cannot take place in solitude" (70-71). In the Latin American tradition, however, *testimonio* is not a novel, as John Beverley points out in his oft-cited article, "The Margin at the Center: On Testimonio." His delineation of the form, which he understands to be "at best provisional, at worst repressive" (13), exceeds the scope of this essay, but it is worth noting that "*testimonio* is a fundamentally democratic and egalitarian form of narrative in the sense that it implies that any life so narrated can have a kind of representational value. Each individual *testimonio* evokes an absent polyphony of other voices, other possible lives and experiences" (16). Danticat, therefore, serves as witness on two levels: she is a witness as she listens to the testimonies of survivors and the families of both victims and survivors of the massacre, but she is also a witness who assumes a voice for those people, telling their story in the novel. Conscious of the role of language in such testimonies, Danticat explains, "I was purposely questioning myself and what I was doing—writing this story in English, stealing it, if you will, from the true survivors who were not able or allowed to tell their stories" (Shea 17-18).

Locating testimonies in the narrative space of the novel mitigates the objectification of the stories of the survivors and draws attention to the role of testimony in the collective memory of the massacre. Immediately after the massacre, on the other side of the Massacre River in Haiti, "people gathered in a group to talk. Taking turns, they exchanged tales quickly, the haste in their voices sometimes blurring their words, for greater than their desire to be heard was the hunger to tell" (209). When Yves and Amabelle have returned to Yves's home in Haiti, Yves hears that "'there are officials of the state, justices of the peace, who listen to those who survived the slaughter and write their stories down. [. . .] The Generalissimo has not said that he caused the killing, but he agreed to give money to affected persons. [. . .] To erase bad feelings'" (231). Haitian survivors gather around a civic building, waiting in line all day, for several days, for the opportunity to testify to their experience. One woman who is finally able to enter the building returns to tell the crowd what had happened. She says, "'He writes your name in the book and he says he will take your story to President Sténio Vincent so you can get you money.' She kept her eyes on the crowd, no longer watching the soldiers for approval. 'Then he lets you talk and lets you cry and he asks you if you have any papers to show that all these people died'" (234).

The insistence on papers and the bureaucratic preoccupation with documentation reiterates Trujillo's policies in the Dominican Republic where documents and papers of identification had become paramount. The book in which the stories are supposedly inscribed represents government, civility, and order, which Haitians long for after the chaos of the massacre. The book, however, contains the civil servants' versions of the testimonies, appropriated and recast to fit the government's purposes, both on the Haitian side and the Dominican side of the border. One woman reports, "You tell the story, and then it's retold as they wish, written in words you do not understand, in a language that is theirs, and not yours" (246), echoing Danticat's own feelings about the writing of the novel. In her collection of testimony, however, Danticat is inscribing not only the individual stories but also the collective memory of the event, what remains in Haitian memory more than sixty years after the massacre.

Continuing their tradition of rebellion, the Haitians who had gathered to tell their stories stage a small revolt when the government stops listening to the testimonies. When a functionary announces "that there would be no more testimonials taken" because "all the money had already been distributed" (Danticat 235), the waiting crowd "charged the station looking for someone to write their names in a book, and take their story to President Vincent. They wanted a civilian face to concede that what they had witnessed and lived through truly did happen" (236). These Haitian survivors understand the traditions of history: if an event is written, documented, contained in a book, it is real. As part of the written record, their testimonies somehow will become truth. These survivors—the poorest of Haitians driven from their own country by economic need—do not distinguish among the history books from which they are excluded, the civil servants' record of the massacre appropriated from them for political reasons, or novels such as Danticat's to which they would have no access as the most illiterate and marginalized of the country. In telling the story of these survivors, Danticat seeks to create a new kind of book that includes their stories not for the political or economic purposes of the government but for the sake of locating the vivid memory of the massacre in the safe space of *The Farming of Bones.*

Alvarez similarly uses *testimonio* as an expression of collective memory in her novel, which Ellen Mc-Cracken notes in her book *New Latina Narrative,* writing that **In the Time of the Butterflies** "might be viewed as a kind of collective autobiography or *testimonio* of the women" (84). It might seem unreasonable to take such a view of a novel that does not, as Danticat's does, take the voice of one narrator to stand for all those oppressed under the *trujillato*; however, in her postscript to the novel, Alvarez exhorts her readers to take on the challenge of the lives of her characters, "ordinary men and women" (324), suggesting that the story of the lives of the Mirabal sisters exemplify the ordinary lives of all Dominicans under the *trujillato.*

Alvarez draws on the tradition, including in the novel the *testimonio* of witnesses to the sisters' assassination. Just after the "accident," Dedé listens to the testimonies of those who had seen the girls on their last day. She says, "They would come with their stories of that afternoon," all wanting "to give me something of the girls' last moments." She creates memory from these witnesses' stories, "composing in my head how that last afternoon went" (301). Testimony becomes her memory. Years later, Dedé is no longer the listener but the teller, testifying and witnessing the girls' lives. She wonders when her life changed "from [her] being the one who listened to the stories people brought to being the one whom people came to for the story of the Mirabal sisters" (312). When Trujillo was assassinated and the country was plagued by a succession of unstable governments, Dedé tells the *gringa dominicana,* "We were a broken people. [. . .] Instead of listening, I started talking. We had lost hope, and we needed a story to understand what had happened to us" (313). In telling her own story and the story of the girls and of the Dominican people, Dedé can pass on the memory to the *gringa dominicana,* who in turn passes it on to the world in the novel. In passing on

the memory, by making it part of the collective memory, Dedé feels that "the future is now beginning. By the time it is over, it will be the past, and she doesn't want to be the only one left to tell their story" (10). In this way, testimony serves as part of the collective memory and as part of the healing process of those who survived Trujillo's regime. Alvarez's novel itself thus serves as *testimonio,* for the Mirabal sisters and for the Dominican people.

In the Time of the Butterflies and *The Farming of Bones* constitute the space in which to iterate the collective memory of the inhabitants of Hispaniola, the children of the survivors of the *trujillato.* Alvarez's novel reflects the tradition of commemoration in the Dominican Republic, now a significant component of Dominican national identity, but she takes it in a new direction by seeking to fill the absences still left from the silences of the *trujillato.* In the national tradition of commemoration, Dominicans even commemorated the end of the *trujillato*: "Years later, at the very spot on the renamed 30th of May Highway where the dictator died, they erected a memorial of concrete and twisted, rusted steel—a tribute to the pain he had inflicted" (Wucker 69). In this memorial Dominicans have created a site consecrated to Trujillo's death, in contrast to the absence of a marker commemorating the deaths of the Mirabal sisters, an assassination in which some Dominicans found themselves complicit— the very high-ranking Dominicans responsible for Trujillo's assassination—because of their own silence. Alvarez's novel becomes that marker for the Mirabal sisters. Another monument to Trujillo, this one constructed during his regime, is *el obelisco macho.* Wucker points out that "this phallic obelisk has been repainted with images of the Mirabal sisters" (231), by which Dominicans seek to inscribe a new history, a new national memory of the *trujillato,* modifying it, obscuring it, erasing it. As with Alvarez's novel, the inscription of the feminine over the phallic obelisk serves to include those excluded by Trujillo's tyranny.

In stark contrast, on the Haitian side of the Massacre River, there are no markers. The official silence about the *trujillato* and its aftermath have created in the Haitian imagination the sense that their history must be made salient and available not only for Haitians but also for the world. Danticat breaks that official silence, creating from her own research and the collective memory of those to whom she spoke a narrative of the history of the victims and the survivors of the Haitian massacre.

Ultimately, despite differences in monuments and commemoration, both Alvarez and Danticat create a space for the collective memory of the *trujillato* within the novel, giving collective memory a face, a voice, and a story. These faces, these voices, and these stories belong to women, who create a history that includes, rather than excludes, the experiences of women and revalues their role in the preservation of collective memory and the construction of national identity. As Michael Bernard-Donals and Richard Glejzer tell us, novels about the Shoah demonstrate the possibility that "the language of fiction" may be "the best means that we have to approximate the heat of the fire itself," the actual event (81). In her postscript to **In the Time of the Butterflies,** Julia Alvarez writes, "I wanted to immerse my readers in an epoch in the life of the Dominican Republic that I believe can only finally be understood by fiction, only finally be redeemed by the imagination. A novel is not, after all, a historical document, but a way to travel through the human heart" (324). In her novel, on the last day of the Mirabal sisters' lives, as they finish their visit to their husbands in prison, they "said [their] hurried goodbyes, [their] whispered prayers and endearments. Remember, . . . don't forget" (295). Such is the spirit of **In the Time of the Butterflies** and *The Farming of Bones,* which transform the silences and din of the *trujillato* into memory.

Works Cited

Alvarez, Julia. *In the Time of the Butterflies,* New York: Plume, 1994.

———. *Something to Declare.* Chapel Hill, NC: Algonquin Books of Chapel Hill, 1998.

Anglesey, Zoe. "The Voice of the Storytellers: An Interview with Edwidge Danticat." *Multicultural Review* 7.3 (September 1998): 36-39.

Augelli, John P. "Nationalization of Dominican Borderlands." *Geographical Review* 70.1 (1980): 19-35.

Bernard-Donals, Michael, and Richard Glejzer. *Between Witness and History: The Holocaust and the Limits of Representation.* Albany: State U of New York P, 2001.

Beverley, John. "The Margin at the Center: On Testimonio." *Modern Fiction Studies* 35.1 (Spring 1989): 11-28.

Bhabha, Homi. *The Location of Culture.* London: Routledge, 1994.

Charters, Mallay "Edwidge Danticat: A Bitter Legacy Revisited." *Publishers Weekly* 245.33 (17 August 1998): 42-43.

Crane, Susan. "Writing the Individual Back into Collective Memory." *American Historical Review* 102.5 (December 1997): 1,372-85.

Danticat, Edwidge. *The Farming of Bones.* New York: Penguin, 1999.

Farmer, Paul. *The Uses of Haiti.* Monroe, ME: Common Courage, 1994.

Fentress, James, and Chris Wickham. *Social Memory.* Cambridge, MA: Blackwell, 1992.

Flores, Juan. "Broken English Memories." *The Places of History: Regionalism Revisited in Latin America.* Ed. Doris Sommer, Durham, NC: Duke UP, 1999. 274-88.

Halbwachs, Maurice *On Collective Memory.* Ed. and Trans. Lewis A Coser. Chicago: U of Chicago P, 1992.

Irwin-Zarecka, Iwona. *Frames of Remembrance: The Dynamics of Collective Memory.* New Brunswick, NJ: Transaction, 1994.

Jara, René, and Herman Vidal. *Testimonio y Literatura,* Minneapolis: Institute for the Study of Ideologies and Literature, 1986.

Knight, Franklin. *Toward a New History of Caribbean Literature: Process of Unity in Caribbean Society.* Ed. Ileana Rodriguez, Mare Zimmerman, and Lisa Davis. Minneapolis: Institute for the Study of Ideologies and Literature, 1983. 132-41.

Larsen, Neil. "Como narrar el trujillato" *Revista Iberoamericana* 54. 1-2 (January—March 1988): 89-98.

Laub, Dori, and Shoshana Felman. *Testimony: Crises of Witnessing in Literature, Psychoanalysis, and History.* New York: Routledge, 1991.

McCracken, Ellen. *New Latina Narrative: The Feminine Space of Postmodern Ethnicity.* Tucson: U of Arizona P. 1999.

Nora, Pierre. "Between Memory and History: *Les Lieux de Memoíre"* *Representations* 26 (Spring 1989): 7-24.

Rice-Sayre, Laura P. "Witnessing History: Diplomacy versus Testimony." *Testimonio y Literature. Ed.* René Jara and Herman Vidal. Minneapolis: Institute for the Study of Ideologies and Literature, 1986. 48-72.

Rogoff, Irit. "From Ruins to Debris: The Feminization of Fascism in German History Museums." *Museum Culture: Histories, Discourses, Spectacles.* Ed. Daniel J. Sherman and Irit Rogoff, Minneapolis: U of Minnesota P. 1994.

Shea, Renee H. "'The Hunger to Tell': Edwidge Danticat and *The Farming of Bones.*" *Macomere* 2 (1999): 12-22.

Torres-Saillant, Silvio. "Dominican Literature and Its Criticism: Anatomy of a Troubled Identity." *A History of Literature in the Caribbean,* Vol. 1, Ed. A. James Arnold, Julio Rodriguez-Luis, and J. Michael Dash. Amsterdam: Benjamins, 1994. 49-64.

Wachtel, Eleanor. "A Conversation with Edwidge Danticat." *Brick* 65-66 (Fall 2000): 106-19.

Wucker, Michele. *Why the Cocks Fight: Dominicans, Haitians, and the Struggle for Hispaniola* New York: Hill and Wang, 2000.

Ibis Gómez Vega (essay date spring 2004)

SOURCE: Gómez Vega, Ibis. "Radicalizing Good Catholic Girls: Shattering the "Old World" Order in Julia Alvarez's *In the Time of the Butterflies*." *Confluencia: Revista Hispanica de Cultura y literatura* 19, no. 2 (spring 2004): 94-108.

[*In the following essay, Vega analyzes the Mirabal sisters as characters in* In the Time of the Butterflies. *She concludes that in fighting oppression, these women challenged and transformed the role of all Dominican women.*]

Julia Álvarez's *In the Time of the Butterflies* is a political novel, a record of the violence which led thousands of people into exile or to death in the hands of the Dominican government's military police. In it, Álvarez documents the lives of four Dominican women caught in the maelstrom of Dominican politics and history, but she insists in her postscript to the women's stories that "a novel is not . . . a historical document, but a way to travel to the human heart." Through her fictional rendition of the Mirabal sisters' stories, Álvarez claims to be presenting not the "real" historical women who sacrificed their lives for a better world but "the Mirabals of my creation." Her purpose, she says, is "to immerse [her] readers in an epoch in the life of the Dominican Republic that . . . can only be understood by fiction, only finally redeemed by the imagination" (*In the Time of the Butterflies* 324).

The imaginary women whom she creates are traditional upper-class Dominicans who are also good Catholics, devout, the kind of women who do not question the status quo and ask their father's permission to attend the university. Throughout the novel, Álvarez documents, methodically, the sisters' dedication to their religion, their families, and the traditional, albeit patriarchal, Dominican way of life. In their world, men rule, both in the private and public spheres, and their rule is seldom questioned or challenged. Through the Mirabal sisters' revolutionary struggle against President Trujillo, however, Álvarez creates a new kind of Dominican woman who dares to challenge the "old world" order of the patriarchy without being too strident about it. The Mirabal sisters join a revolution not because they want to challenge the patriarchy but because it is the right thing to do. Through their involvement in the political movement against Trujillo's tyranny, they redefine what it means to be a good Catholic and a good Dominican woman.

Because the Mirabal sisters are historical characters, much of the criticism written by Dominican critics focuses on the liberties taken by Álvarez in creating the fictional Mirabal sisters. Fernando Valerio Holguin argues in "Una reinterpretación de la historia" that, in writing this novel, Álvarez answers Neil Larsen's call to write the definitive novel about Trujillo's reign in "Cómo narrar el trujillato?" Valerio Holguín claims that Álvarez "propone una alegoría política de la República Dominicana durante la dictadura de Trujillo," an allegory in which "el cuerpo de las Mirabal se convierte en texto político gracias a la inscripción de lo público en lo privada de lo político en el poético" because "la novela de Álvarez inserta la política y la historia en la vida privada de la familia Mirabal" (96). Valerio Holguín's point is that Álvares means to "devolverles el carácter de sujetos históricos" to the Mirabal sisters in order to "restituir el cuerpo político escamoteado por la leyenda y el mito" (95).

Of the three sisters who become revolutionaries, only Minerva dares to stray from the prescribed gender specific role of the Dominican female. She understands even as a girl in high school that something is wrong with the government in her country because people behave in ways that are not consistent with religious teaching or even decent human behavior. At the Mirabal sisters' private Catholic school, for example, the talk is that girls disappear from school because they move on to live in homes provided by Trujillo. When her own father points out "a high iron gate and beyond it a big mansion with lots of flowers and the hedges all cut to look like animals," he tells her, "Look, Minerva, one of Trujillo's girlfriends lives there, your old schoolmate, Lina Lovatón." Minerva's immediate response is to question the president's behavior. "But Trujillo is married," she exclaims. Minerva's father

> Looked at [her] a long time before he said, 'He's got many of them, all over the island, set up in big, fancy houses. Lina Lovatón is just a sad case, because she really does love him, *pobrecita*.' Right there he took the opportunity to lecture [her] about why hens shouldn't wander away from the safety of the barnyard.

> (*Butterflies* [*In the Time of the Butterflies*] 23)

Girls in Dominican society are not expected to "wander from the safety of the barnyard," but when they do wander into the homes of powerful men the rest of the well-bred Dominican society pretends that nothing has happened. Minerva, however, is not capable of pretending.

Although three Mirabal sisters, Minerva, Patria, and María Teresa, join a revolution and are eventually murdered because they dare to challenge the rule of the Dominican patriarchy, they are not radical or subversive in any recognizable sense of the word. As girls, they attend Catholic school; as young adults, they look forward to marrying and having children. Their lives are ordinary by anyone's standards. In fact, Minerva's most radical expectation is that she be allowed to attend the university to study law, something denied to most Dominican women and especially to Dominican women of her class. In the 1950s and 1960s, the time when the events in the book take place, the roles of women as caretakers and housewives were clearly defined. It takes a special kind of emotional and religious awakening for the Mirabal sisters to join the struggle for liberation against Trujillo.

Perhaps because the characters in the novel are drawn as traditional and recognizably Hispanic women, some readers want to place Álvarez's novel within the Latin American literary tradition. Gus Puleo argues in "Remembering and Reconstructing the Mirabal Sisters in Julia Álvarez's *In the Time of the Butterflies*" that in this novel "Álvarez places herself within two of the oldest cultural traditions in Latin America—orality and the written chronicle" (Puleo 11). He explains that the "written chronicle" or *crónica* is "the one-dimensional and univocal record of society, in which society is defined as the mere result of a military or political movement." The *crónica* emphasizes "the role of the witness who saw and now tells what actually happened and the role of the writer or compiler." In Álvarez's novel, Dedé, the one sister who does not become involved in political activities, is the long survivor, the witness who tells her sisters' stories. The compiler or narrator is a *gringa dominicana* (*Butterflies* 3) whom most readers recognize as Julia Álvarez, the writer who returns to Santo Domingo to research and document the story. Gus Puleo recalls attending one of Álvarez's lectures and watching slides of her visit to Santo Domingo during the time when she was researching the book. He alludes to Álvarez's personal interest in the lives of the Mirabal sisters and calls her novel "a novelized autobiographical chronicle in English that deals with recovery, with recapturing a lost past and a lost self" (13). He also reminds his readers that bell hooks "describes this mode of storytelling as "a process of historization that does not remove women from history but enables [them] to see [themselves] as a part of history'" (quoted in Puleo 13).

Like Gus Puleo, Concepción Bados Ciria notes the importance of including the female voice in the Latin American *crónica*. "*In the Time of the Butterflies,* by Julia Álvarez: History, Fiction, *Testimonio* and the Dominican Republic," Bados Ciria argues that the novel "offers an alternative reading to the autobiographical canon" (408) and to the previous tradition of

writing *testimonios,* which "until now [were] only written by men" (409). Elizabeth Coonrod Martínez, likewise, focuses on the inclusion of women's voices in the Dominican Republic's *crónicas*. She points out that the novel "represents Dominican history through women's lives, a feature unavailable in traditional Spanish-language Dominican novels" ("Recovering a Space . . ." 264). She finds the novel to be "a beautiful tribute to intelligent women who struggle alongside their men, against governments that continue the Spanish colonial philosophy of an autocratic, elitist, and racist white power controlling the nation," and she argues that

> The Dominican woman, as well as her counterparts in other countries, needs to be found in the place she disappeared, her own context, her own participation in her struggle. Only in that space—between the West and the Third World, between patriarchy and imperialism—can the sexed subject speak.
>
> ("Recovering a Space . . ." 267)

That Julia Álvarez presents Dominican history through the lives of four women adds another dimension, one in which gender becomes important, to Dominican literature. Through this novel, Julia Álvarez introduces her country's painful history to the world at large and, specifically, the English-reading world. For her, keeping the Mirabal sisters' stories from being forgotten is significant; sin querer, however, she also provides clear evidence of the radicalizing influence of a traditional Catholic upbringing on women who understand what it means to have religion in their lives.

Julia Álvarez's *In the Time of the Butterflies* may not be a novel about religion, but it is a novel about women for whom religion means something. While Álvarez chronicles the radical political choices made by the Mirabal sisters, she also documents the subtle process of radicalization that forces the three sisters to ask themselves, "what is a good Christian to do?" Their answer is simply that, when faced with a tyrannical oppressor, a good Christian must join the struggle for liberation. Their choice to join the revolution places their story within the realm of what Lois Parkinson Zamora defines as literature that carries "the conviction that historical crisis will have the cleansing effect of radical renewal" (*Writing the Apocalypse* 12). According to Parkinson Zamora,

> Apocalypse is *not* merely a synonym for disaster or cataclysm or chaos. It is, in fact, a synonym for 'revelation,' and if the Judeo-Christian revelation of the end of history includes—indeed, catalogues—disasters, it also envisions a millennial order which represents the potential antithesis to the undeniable abuses of human history.
>
> (12)

Parkinson Zamora warns that "while it is true that an acute sense of temporal disruption and disequilibrium is the source of, and is always integral to, apocalyptic thinking and narration, so is the conviction that historical crisis will have the cleansing effect of radical renewal" (12).

An apocalyptist writer, Julia Álvarez means not only to document the chaos of history in Santo Domingo during the reign of General Trujillo, to answer Neil Larsen's call and "write" the "trujillato," but also to herald the advent of the new woman. Although the Mirabal sisters become victims of the chaos rampant in their country, their political involvement in the revolutionary movement against Trujillo's reign allows them to make choices that other Dominican women of their class had never made before. Their awareness of Trujillo's violations and their decision to oppose his tyranny through active participation radicalize them and, thereby, create a new woman capable of defying patriarchy and the status quo.

As a novelist documenting a political event, Julia Álvarez insists on investing the sacrifice of the Mirabals' lives with historical meaning. Apocalyptist writers "use the historical vision and narrative forms of apocalypse to explore the relationship of the individual, the community, and the novel itself to the process of history" (4). They place their characters within the historical reality of their respective countries and move their stories toward an apocalyptic ending, but in order to study the writers whom she defines as apocalyptists, Parkinson Zamora first defines the different ways in which prophets and apocalyptists see history. According to her theory, "the prophet sees the future as arising out of the present and exhorts his listeners on the basis of an ideal to be realized in this world." Parkinson Zamora points to the works of the early Spanish settlers and the Puritan writers who come to the New World to escape the chaos of the Old World and find a Paradise on earth. For these writers, exhortation for "the ideal to be realized in this world" becomes the message, but "the apocalyptist, on the contrary, sees the future breaking into the present, and this world being replaced by a new world under God's aegis" (11).

Replacing the old world order with a better world is precisely what the Mirabal sisters are attempting to do in Julia Álvarez's *In the Time of the Butterflies*; however, Álvarez's characters are not radical. They are ordinary women of a certain class and religion, and they lived before the women's liberation movement could provide them with the language and the method for rebellion. Minerva, Patria, and Maria Teresa (Mate) are Catholic women in a patriarchal world. For them, revolution and liberation must come through the one thing they know best, their Catholic religion,

which explains why Parkinson Zamora's theory of the apocalyptist writer resonates through Álvarez's novel. Álvarez's characters are such good Catholics that their stories become heavily invested in religious imagery and language; as a result, their choices and their fictional lives can only be understood through a clear understanding of what living like a Catholic means to the awakening revolutionary Catholic. Since the language and symbols of religion are all they know, they use it to question the roles prescribed to them by the Church and by their own social class.

A perfect example of how religious imagery and symbols help define the characters' rebellion is the chapter in which Patria joins Minerva and Mate in the revolutionary struggle against Trujillo. Patria's conversion from a traditional Catholic woman into a radical revolutionary takes place in a religious retreat in the mountains. There, she witnesses the slaughter of the innocent. Her revolutionary epiphany "happened on the last day of our retreat." Patria notes that "the shelling happened in a flash, but it seemed the chaos went on for hours. I heard moans, but when I lowered my chair, I could make out nothing in the smoke-filled room." She remembers "an eerie silence, interrupted only by the sound of far-off gunfire and the near by trickle of plaster from the ceiling." Like good Catholics,

> Padre de Jesús gathered us in the most sheltered corner, where we assessed our damages. The injuries turned out to look worse than they were, just minor cuts from flying glass, thank the Lord. We ripped up our slips and bandaged the worst. Then for spiritual comfort, Brother Daniel led us through a rosary. When we heard gunfire coming close again, we kept right on praying.
>
> (161)

Patria's statement reveals the lack of involvement that characterized not only the church but also its members during the thirty-one years of Trujillo's reign of terror. When the gunfire is "far off," Catholics pray. Before too long, however, the gunfire gets too close for comfort.

As the people gathered in the room pray, the revolution rages on outside. The outside world barges in and forces itself on the people who had been gathered by their priest "in the most sheltered corner." That they are gathered "in the most sheltered corner" speaks volumes for the role of the church during Santo Domingo's time of crisis. Good Catholics found shelter away from the dangerous things happening outside the church as priest acted as if nothing was happening. On this day, however, Patria faces her own complicity in the events that take place. She remembers that

> There were shouts, and four, then five, men in camouflage were running across the grounds towards us. Behind them, the same *campesinos* we'd seen on our

walk and a dozen or more *guardias* were advancing. Armed with machetes and machine guns. The hunted crouched and careened this way and that as they headed towards the cover of the motherhouse. They made it to the outdoor deck. I could see them clearly, their faces bloodied and frantic. One of them was badly wounded and hobbling, another had a kerchief around his forehead. A third was shouting to two others to stay down, and one of them obeyed and threw himself on the deck. But the other must not have heard him for he kept on running toward us. I looked in his face. He was a boy no older than Noris. Maybe that's why I cried out, 'Get down, son! Get down!' His eyes found mine just as the shot hit him square in the back. I saw the wonder on his young face as the life drained out of him, and I thought, Oh my God, he's one of mine!

(161-162)

When the country is in chaos, no one is safe. Patria admits that, after the event, she "cried all the way down that mountain" as she "looked out the spider-webbed window of that bullet-riddled car at brothers, sisters, sons, daughters, one and all, my human family." The good Catholic attempts to make sense of what happens, but she finds no answer. She cannot even find a hint from God when she tries to look "up at our Father, but [she] couldn't see His Face for the dark smoke hiding the tops of the mountains."

What Patria learns on the last day of her retreat in the mountains is that there is no place to hide from injustice. The good Catholic must make choices. She admits that on her way down the mountain, she makes herself pray, but her "prayers sounded more like I was trying to pick a fight" with God. For some reason that she cannot yet understand, she is angry with God, but she is beyond asking why bad things happen to good people. On her way down that mountain, Patria tells God, "I'm not going to sit back and watch my babies die, Lord, even if that's what You in Your great wisdom decide" (162). The good Catholic who goes up the mountain to her safe religious retreat comes down as a radical revolutionary steeped in the knowledge that no one is safe. She learns to question not only what she has been taught to identify as God's will but also her own role as an instrument of His will.

Before her moment of epiphany in the mountains, Patria reassesses her life and her sisters' lives through what appears to be a symbol of security. This very revealing chapter opens with an almost religious account of the houses in which the sisters live.

> Build your house upon a rock, He said, do my will. And though the rain fall and the floods come and the winds blow, the good wife's house will stand.
>
> I did as He said. At sixteen I married Pedrito González and we settled down for the rest of our lives.

My boy grew into a man, my girl into her long, slender body like the blossoming mimosa at the end of the drive. Pedrito took on a certain gravity, became an important man around here. And I, Patria Mercedes? Like every woman of her house, I disappeared into what I loved, coming up now and then for air. I mean, an overnight trip by myself to a girlfriend's, a special set to my hair, and maybe a yellow dress.

> I had built a house on solid rock, all right.

(***Butterflies*** 148)

The "good wife," Patria, builds a house on "solid rock" and feels trapped by it because her social class requires that she refuse to see what is happening in her country. If she wants to preserve her house and her family, she must ignore the obvious abuses taking place, but after eighteen years of marriage and security, Patria admits that "all of us were praying for a change this new year. Things had gotten so bad, even people like me who didn't want anything to do with politics were thinking about it all the time" (149).

After many years of marriage, Patria realizes that she has taken her security for granted. Her solid rock home begins to seem less secure when she learns that Nelson, her teenage son, has been talking to his uncles about politics and may, in fact, be involved in the counter-revolutionary movement against Trujillo. The good wife/good mother fears for her son and begins to think about her own sisters' lives through their houses, the only terms that she can understand. She complains that her sisters, Minerva and Mate, "were so different! They build their homes on sand and called the slip and slide adventure." According to her, "Minerva lived in a nothing house . . . in that godforsaken town of Monte Cristi" (148), the distant town where Minerva and Manolo move so that they can better serve the revolution. Like Minerva, "Mate and Leandro had already had two different addresses in a year of marriage. Renters, they called themselves, the city word for the squatters we pity in the country" (149). Minerva's and Mate's homes are built on sand because they are redefining the role of the Dominican woman during the revolutionary period; although they are wives and mothers, they are revolutionaries first and good wives later.

Patria decides to fight Trujillo's tyranny after she witnesses the killing of her country's "babies" (162) during her religious retreat in the mountains. Soon after her conversion experience, she returns to her church to learn that she is not alone in her determination to fight the tyrant. It takes thirty years of tyranny to move the church to action, but little by little, a priest at a time, the church joins the struggle. As Patria attends a cultural gathering sponsored by her church, she finds that "the room was silent with the fury of avenging angels sharpening their radiance before they strike." The priest and several of the people who had also lived through the experience in the mountain retreat "invited only a few of us old members whom—I saw later—they had picked out as ready for the Church Militant, tired of the Mother Church in whose skirts they once hid" (163). The experience in the mountain retreat radicalizes the people involved, and "the priests had decided they could not wait forever for the pope and the archbishop to come around." Patria is surprised. She says that

> I couldn't believe this was the same Padre de Jesús talking who several months back hadn't know (sic) his faith from his fear! But then again, here in that little room was the same Patria Mercedes who wouldn't have hurt a butterfly, shouting, 'Amen to the revolution.'
>
> And so we were born in the spirit of the vengeful Lord, no longer His lambs.
>
> (163-64)

Patria's conversion, her radicalizing experience, comes through her involvement with the church. As a Christian, she cannot stand by and bear witness to the slaughter of the children, the young people who, like her son Nelson, joined the struggle and performed many of the most dangerous acts of defiance. Her religious convictions demand that, pregnant as she is at the time of her conversion, she join the cause; thus, she speaks of her co-conspirators as "avenging angels" who are "born in the spirit of a vengeful Lord," but the real message is that, like her sisters Mate and Minerva, Patria is no longer willing to play her socially prescribed role of the "good wife" at the expense of her conscience. She may not have been born a radical, but she becomes one.

Of the four Mirabal sisters, Minerva is the natural born rebel. She is the one who asks herself "What's more important, romance or revolution?" and hears "a little voice [that] kept saying, *Both, both, I want both*" (86). When the Mirabal family is invited to a state dance in Trujillo's honor, they realize that Trujillo has his eye on Minerva, the eldest of the four sisters. They try to get out of attending the dance, but they know that it is too risky an act to defy Trujillo by ignoring his invitation. Once at the dance, Trujillo asks Minerva to dance, an act that would have impressed most Dominican girls of Minerva's class, but during the dance

> He yanks me by the wrist, thrusting his pelvis at me in a vulgar way, and I can see my hand in an endless slow motion rise—a mind all its own—and come down on the astonished, made-up face.
>
> (100)

The slap on the face resonates through the room and sets in motion the chain of events that will determine the future of the Mirabal family. Shortly after the dance, Minerva's father, Don Enrique Mirabal, is arrested. When he is finally released from jail, he "is such a pitiful sight. His face is gaunt, his voice shaky; his once fancy *guayabera* is soiled and hangs on him, several sizes too large" (112).

Don Enrique, whose only crime is being Minerva's father, emerges from prison a broken man who greets his family speaking nonsense. Although he tells the family that he is "'feeling much better,'" he also adds, "'I just hope the music hasn't spoiled the yuccas while I've been gone.'" His wife reminds him that they have not planted yuccas in years, but the family soon realizes that the old man's mind is gone. When his wife asks him to explain his comment about the yuccas, his reply is, "every time there's a party, half the things in the ground spoil. We've got to stop feeding the hogs. It's all human teeth anyhow" (112). Thus Don Enrique becomes the first casualty in the struggle between Trujillo and Minerva Mirabal, between the tyrannical old order of Dominican men and the new Dominican woman.

Shortly after Don Enrique is released from prison, the Mirabal family must sign a letter of apology in Trujillo's presence. Defeated, Minerva, Don Enrique, and Señora Mirabal are taken to the general's office to sign their names to the dreaded letter. Minerva, however, will not leave well enough alone and manages to manipulate Trujillo into allowing her to attend the university. Having noticed two sets of dice, one loaded and one not loaded, sitting on the scales held by the statue of Justice, Minerva offers to roll the dice for her "dream of going to law school." As it happens, the two sets of dice were a gift given to Trujillo by one of Minerva's relatives, so Trujillo, knowing that one of the sets is loaded, agrees to roll the dice with another gambling Mirabal. "'You win, you get your wish. I win, I get mine'" (115), he tells her. Minerva, of course, picks up the loaded dice and wins the game, a win that guarantees that her parents can no longer object to her going to school. Once Trujillo agrees to grant Minerva's wish, the father must also agree or risk incurring Trujillo's wrath. Nor being a man of integrity, however, Trujillo thwarts Minerva's plan by allowing her to study at the university and receive her diploma but denying her the license to practice law in her country once she finishes her studies.

In spite of the spunk that leads her to defy the system, Minerva can only go as far as the men in her country are willing to let her go. She lives in a world where good Catholic girls are expected to protect their reputations, but slapping the wrong man for abusing that reputation can cost her and her family their freedom. Still, by the time she acquires her law degree, Minerva has become a central figure in the underground movement working against Trujillo's regime, which explains why Trujillo denies her the license. She has also married and given birth to a child, but she does this while becoming more and more involved in dangerous revolutionary activities. Through her involvement with the revolution, Minerva succeeds in redefining the role of the woman as wife and mother in the world that she helps to create.

As a young woman living in her parents' home, Minerva also redefines the role of the daughter when she discovers that her father has another family living near her own family home. Like Celia in *Dreaming in Cuban,* Minerva recognizes her own half sisters. She notices that

> Every time I drove the Ford, these raggedy girls came running after me, holding out their hands, calling for mints.
>
> I studied them. There were three that ran to the road whenever they heard the car, a fourth one sometimes came in the arms of the oldest. Four girls, I checked, three in panties, and the baby naked. One time, I stopped at the side of the road and stared at their Mirabal eyes. Who is your father?' I asked point blank.
>
> (85)

The answer to her question is that her own father is the girls' father, but Minerva reacts to the knowledge of her father's illegitimate children with sympathy rather than anger. She demands to be introduced to them, and she visits them often after their initial meeting. When her father realizes that his life is in danger and that he may die in Trujillo's prison, he asks Minerva to take over the job of providing a monthly check for the girls' support, a job that she performs until she herself becomes a prisoner.

The old-fashioned Dominican woman would never have helped support her father's illegitimate children, but Minerva not only delivers the monthly checks that her father asks her to deliver but she also makes sure that her sister Dedé knows to take money "out of her inheritance for those girls' education." Dedé is so moved by Minerva's act of compassion towards the illegitimate Mirabals that she also decides to "put in half" (211) of her own money, which is not much to begin with. The money provided by Minerva and Dedé allows Margarita, the eldest, to get a pharmacy degree. When she starts work as a pharmacist, she helps the other three sisters with their own education, an education which they owe entirely to Minerva's intervention in their lives. One of Minerva's first acts after her father is released from prison is to deliver the first check to his father's mistress and ask that the girls, who had never attended school, be allowed to attend. The illegitimate girls thus benefit from Minerva's audacity and kindness, from her ability to see not class but people.

Patria, Minerva's sister, admits that she "had always kept [her] distance" from her father's illegitimate daughters because she "did not want to be associated with the issue of a *campesina* who had had no respect for the holy banns of matrimony or for the good name of Mirabal." Associating with a *campesina,* a farm girl beneath Patria's social class, is part of the reason why Patria cannot even consider acknowledging that the illegitimate children exist. Minerva, however, acts with acceptance and compassion towards the ones who would normally have been ostracized by the community, and her behavior reveals the new kind of woman that her revolutionary ideals are shaping. In the post-Trujillo Santo Domingo that Minerva wants to forge, the separation between the social classes will no longer be an issue, and the social stigma of illegitimacy will no longer separate families. In fact, in Minerva's case, it is Santicló, a cousin of her father's mistress, who smuggles the Mirabal family's care packages into prison during the many months of the women's imprisonment. Margarita Mirabal, the illegitimate family's oldest daughter, visits the Mirabal family home and offers her services to Patria. She tells Patria about her mother's cousin who works at La Victoria prison where the sisters are detained; she also tells her to leave the care packages with her at the pharmacy where she works, the pharmacy where Patria has been purchasing her medicine for years. Patria has probably been dealing with Margarita for years, but she has also been denying the family resemblance that Minerva recognizes and acknowledges at once.

That simple act of solidarity between the illegitimate family members and the legitimate family members breaks the code of behavior by which the Dominicans of the old world order lived. Necessity forces even the legitimate daughter, Patria, to accept the assistance provided by her father's illegitimate children, the ones whom she had never before acknowledged, and she tells herself

> I sat down on the bench by the birds of paradise, and I had to laugh. Papá's other family would be the agents of our salvation! It was ingenious and finally, I saw, all wise. He was going to work several revolutions at one time. One of them would have to do with my pride.
>
> (210)

Whether the "He" who will work revolutions is her dead father or God is not very clear. What becomes clear is that Minerva's kindness to her father's illegitimate family brings the two families together and pays off in the way that the girls behave when the legitimate Mirabal sisters are in prison. Margarita Mirabal risks her job and her life to help her half sisters.

Minerva's acceptance of her father's illegitimate children and her new way of living as a fully involved citizen redefine the Dominican woman's role in Dominican society. In many ways, her life represents the new world order that she hopes to create after the tyrant has been defeated. Although she is a daughter, her life is not restricted by her parents' wishes. After she becomes a wife and mother, she still does not relinquish her involvement in the political struggle that she hoped would bring about a new way of life for her compatriots. Minerva's struggle represents the apocalyptist writer's ideal for a new world order, and in the process she also redefines the role of the woman in Santo Domingo. That she pays for her efforts with her life simply reminds the reader of the cost of freedom in countries where political chaos reigns.

Julia Álvarez's *In the Time of the Butterflies* is a novel about revolutionary characters because it documents the revolutionary ways in which people deal with the tyranny of oppression. When Patria's husband, Pedrito, is arrested, he is not only physically tortured but he is psychologically tortured as well. His imprisonment is also used to torture the relatives who are presumably "free," not in prison. When Patria, in her attempt to find out what has happened to her husband, visits the office of Captain Peña, a presumed "friend of the family," and pleads for news about Pedrito, she realizes that the Captain "got some thrill out of having me plead for information." The Captain, however, tells her that

'Your husband was offered his freedom and his farm back—

'My heart leapt!'

—if he proved his loyalty to El Jefe by divorcing his Mirabal wife.'

'Oh?' I could feel my heart like a hand making a fist in my chest. Peña's sharp, piglike eyes were watching me. And then he had his dirty little say. 'You Mirabal women must be something else'—he fondled himself—to keep a man interested when all he can do with his manhood is pass water.

(204)

Captain Peña's remark reminds one of the sadistic nature of tyrants, but it also stresses the fact that the Mirabal women are "something else." They are the new women of Santo Domingo, the ones who will not sacrifice their consciences to the socially prescribed roles of mothers and wives. When confronted with such a woman, a man like Captain Peña would naturally find nothing better to do with his "manhood" than pass water, but Pedro, Manolo, and Leandro know that their wives are equal partners in a revolutionary ideal for a better world.

Although the Mirabal sisters, the butterflies, help bring about an end to oppression, their one surviving sister, Dedé, questions the purpose of their sacrifice. As a character, Dedé also questions the novelist's purpose in writing the novel. Long after her sisters have been murdered, Dedé finds herself one day talking to Lío, an old friend who had also been involved in the revolutionary struggle. Lío, however, was lucky enough to leave Santo Domingo before he was arrested. She says that, through their conversation, they "are working their way towards the treacherous past, the horrible crime, the waste of young lives, the throbbing heart of the wound" (318). Lío had once dated Minerva, so his pain over the loss is as significant as Dedé's pain, but when he tells her to "look at what the girls have done," Dedé thinks,

He means the free elections, bad presidents now put in power properly, not by army tanks. He means our country beginning to prosper, Free Zones going up everywhere, the coast a clutter of clubs and resorts. We are now the playground of the Caribbean, who were once its killing fields. The cemetery is beginning to flower.

(318)

For Dedé, the sacrifice of her sisters' lives means more than whatever it presumably accomplishes because, in Santo Domingo, as in most Latin American and Caribbean countries, one bad government succeeds another one. There is no antidote for what ails politics in these countries, and people like Dedé have resigned themselves to simply surviving as best as they can by leaving the country or staying and waiting it out. Like the angel in Walter Benjamin's "Theses on the Philosophy of History," they are witnesses to the wreckage of their countries and their lives, but they do not become active participants in effecting change.

Dedé's skepticism about the role played by her sisters in Santo Domingo's history becomes more evident when she overhears two apparently wealthy young women, members of the new elite, discussing a revolution in another country. "'Oh yes,' I hear one of the women say, 'we spent a revolution there'" as if spending the revolution in a Latin American or Caribbean country were the same as spending time in a vacation resort. The casual tone and the flippancy of the woman's statement belie the sacrifice of human lives that revolution requires. The young women overheard by Dedé have no clear understanding of the sacrifice made by the Mirabal sisters. They commodify it because they understand only what their sacrifice accomplishes; the country has prospered. For the ones like Dedé who suffered through the sleepless nights of worrying about her sisters and later crying about their deaths as well as raising their orphaned children, the sacrifice is measured in the private grief that cannot be assuaged. Dedé says that she "can see [the young women] glancing at us, the two old ones, how sweet they look under that painting of Bidó. To them we are characters in a sad story about a past that is over" (318). For Dedé, however, the past is not over. She lives with the loss of her sisters every day of her life.

When Dedé wonders, "Was it for this, the sacrifice of the butterflies?" (318), she questions not only the purpose of her sisters' lives and deaths but the way in which Julia Álvarez intends her novel to be read. Álvarez admits in the postscript to her novel that

> When as a young girl I heard about the 'accident,' I could not get the Mirabals out of my mind. On my frequent trips back to the Dominican Republic, I sought out whatever information I could about these brave and beautiful sisters who had done what few men—and only a handful of women—had been willing to do. During that terrifying thirty-one-year regime, any hint of disagreement ultimately resulted in death for the dissenter and often for members of his or her family. Yet the Mirabals had risked their lives. I kept asking myself, what gave them that special courage?
>
> (323)

Clearly, Julia Álvarez intends her novel to be read as a *crónica,* a testimony to the things that were done during the thirty-one years of Trujillo's regime; however, she also creates in Dedé a character who catalogues what is left of her sisters' lives after their ordeal is over and, thereby, questions not only the significance of her sisters' sacrifice but the meaning of Álvarez's *crónica.*

Having been the only one to survive, Dedé is also the only one left to pick up her sisters' remains and their personal belongings. Unlike her sisters, she stands by, like Walter Benjamin's angel, and simply witnesses what is happening in her country. After having to collect what remains of her sisters, however, Dedé begins to count "the losses. I can count them up like the list the coroner gave us, taped to the box of things that had been found on their persons or retrieved from the wreck." She admits that what remains is "the silliest things, but they gave me some comfort," and she calls out the items on the list "like a catechism, like the girls used to tease and recite 'the commandments' of their house arrest" (314). For Dedé, her sisters' lives have become

> One pink powder puff.
> One pair of red high-heeled shoes.
> The two-inch heel from a cream-colored shoe.

After the women are gone, the only tangible things that remain are their personal belongings, but these things are not enough. She can find no meaning in their sacrifice because she never shares their revolutionary zeal. Dedé sees only the waste in the loss of her sisters' lives.

While reading through the list of what remains, Dedé also catalogues a different type of loss. After the sisters are murdered, the Mirabal family dissolves, one person at a time, and Dedé catalogs those losses too, beginning with the collapse of her own marriage. She writes that Jaimito, her husband, who also had had no involvement in the revolution,

> went away for a time to New York. Our harvests had failed again, and it looked as if we were going to lose our lands if we didn't get some cash quick. So he got work in a *factoría,* and every month, he sent home money. I am ashamed after what came to pass to say so. But it was gringo dollars that saved our farm from going under.
>
> (314)

The gringo money that once helped to sustain Trujillo's government becomes Dedé and Jaimito's salvation, but it also helps to bring home the point that their marriage could not survive what had happened. Dedé catalogues the remains as if they were a litany because she must grasp the meaning of what has happened by enumerating what is left. Reality, however, interferes with her list because the fact remains that, for her and all the others who survive, life goes on. The farm must be saved; the children must be fed.

The catalogue of her sisters' private belongings allows Dedé to also catalogue the personal changes through which the surviving members of the family evolve. Clearly, the revolution changes more than the lives of the revolutionaries involved in the struggle. Dedé says that when her husband, Jaimito, returns from New York, "he was a different man. Rather, he was more who he was. I had become more who I was, too . . . we had already started on our separate lives" (314-15). As her own personal life with her husband falls apart, the list continues with

> One screwdriver.
> One brown leather purse.
> One red patent leather purse with straps missing.
> One pair of yellow nylon underwear.
> One pocket mirror.
> Four lottery tickets.
>
> (315)

The end result of the historical sacrifice of the butterflies' lives is a personal tragedy as "we scattered as a family, the men, and later the children, going their separate ways."

After the women are murdered, the men lose their bearings. The first to go is Manolo, Minerva's husband, "dead within three years of Minerva." The revolutionary struggle had been the focus of Minerva's and Manolo's lives; without it and without Minerva, Manolo could not function. He goes "off to the mountains" to continue the fight for the socialist society that he and Minerva once envisioned, but he does not live long. The other two surviving husbands, Leandro, Mate's husband, and Pedrito, Patria's husband, fare differently.

> After Manolo died, Leandro got out of politics. Became a big builder in the capital. Sometimes when we're driving through the capital, Jacqueline points out one impressive building or another and says, 'Papá built that.' She is less ready to talk about the second wife, the new, engrossing family, stepbrothers and sisters the age of her own little one.
>
> (315)

Leandro starts a new life and becomes successful. Pedrito also attempts to do the same, but the memory of his past life haunts him. Dedé claims that Pedrito

> Had gotten his lands back, but prison and his losses had changed him. He was restless, couldn't settle down to the old life. He remarried a young girl, and the new woman turned him around, or so Mamá thought. He came by a lot less and then hardly at all. How all of that, beginning with the young girl, would have hurt poor Patria.
>
> (315)

For the men, life without their revolutionary wives becomes as significant a struggle as it is for Dedé. Although they attempt to carry on by remarrying and starting new families, the ghost of the past stays with them. They sever their ties with their past by visiting as little as possible, but the memory of their experiences never goes away.

For Dedé, the only comfort available is the list of what remains, and she continues the count by acknowledging that her sisters, at the moment of their deaths, had with them,

> One receipt from El Gallo.
> One missal held together with a rubber band.
> One man's wallet, 56 *centavos* in the pocket.
> Seven rings, three plain gold bands, one gold with a
>   small diamond stone, one
> gold with an opal and four pearls, one man's ring
>   with garnet and eagle insignia,
> one silver initial ring.
> One scapular of our Lady of Sorrows.
> One Saint Christopher's medal.
>
> (315)

History having taken its course, the wreckage that remains is made up of things that seem to have no meaning in and of themselves. Only the ones who recognize the items as part of the whole, items belonging to the living women who once wore the shoes and the rings, can actually gauge the meaning of the wreckage.

Through the catalogue of her sisters' belongings, a very personal statement of loss, Dedé questions the purpose of Julia Álvarez's novel. While Álvarez, as a writer, seems to assume the task of interpreting Dominican history for her audience and investing the sacrifice of the Mirabal sisters with historical meaning, Dedé, as the surviving sister, denies that there is any meaning other than the losses suffered by the family. The author and her character disagree on what it means to be an active participant in the historical process. The writer may want to romanticize history to invest it with meaning; she may want to argue that freedom is worth the sacrifice of human life, but the people who survive the wreckage of history know better than to think that there is anything more important than the loss of their loved ones. For Dedé, Santo Domingo's freedom is not worth her sisters' lives. In spite of Dedé's ambivalence about the purpose of her sisters' death, the most important message emerging from Julia Álvarez's *In the Time of the Butterflies* is the significance of the Mirabal sisters' resistance to oppression and the sacrifice of their lives. Through their stories, Álvarez presents a new woman who is willing to defy the old world order to redefine herself and the role of Dominican women in the process. The message clearly is that Santo Domingo is a better place because women like Minerva, Patria, and Maria Teresa are not content to merely witness the wreckage of history but find a way to act and leave their marks on their world.

Works Cited

Álvarez, Julia. *In the Time of the Butterflies*. North Carolina: Algonquin Books of Chapel Hill, 1994.

Bados Ciria, Concepción. "*In the Time of the Butterflies*, by Julia Álvarez: History, Fiction, *Testimonio* and the Dominican Republic." *Monographic Review/Revista Monografica* 8 (2000): 406-416.

Benjamin, Walter. "Theses on the Philosophy of History." *Illuminations*. 1968. Trans. Harry Zohn. New York: Schocken Books, 1985. 253-261.

Coonrod Martinez, Elizabeth. "Recovering a Space for a History between Imperialism and Patriarchy: Julia Álvarez's *In the Time of the Butterflies*." *Thamaris* 5.2 (1998): 263-279.

Larsen, Neil. "¿Cómo narrar el trujillato?" *Revista Iberoamericana* 142 (1988): 89-98.

Parkinson Zamora, Lois. *Writing the Apocalypse: Historical Vision in Contemporary U. S. and Latin American Fiction*. Cambridge: Cambridge University Press, 1989.

Puleo, Gus. "Remembering and Reconstructing the Mirabal Sisters in Julia Álvarez's *In the Time of the Butterflies*." *The Bilingual Review/La Revista Bilingüe* 23.1 (January-April 1998): 11-20.

Valerio Holguin, Fernando. "*En el tiempo de las mariposas* de Julia Álvarez: Una reinterpretación de la historia." *Chasqui* 27.1 (1998): 92-102.

Trenton Hickman (essay date 2005)

SOURCE: Hickman, Trenton. "Coffee and Colonialism in Julia Alvarez's *Cafecito Story*." In *Caribbean Literature and the Environment: Between Nature and Culture,* edited by Elizabeth M. DeLoughrey, Renée K. Gosson, and George B. Handley, pp. 70-82. Charlottesville, Va.: University of Virginia Press, 2005.

[*In the following essay, Hickman praises the environmental message of* A Cafecito Story *but criticizes the book's stereotypical view of the Caribbean.*]

In *A Cafecito Story,* renowned Dominican-American writer Julia Alvarez adventures into the world of progressive coffee cooperatives bent on "environmental, social, economic, and educational sustainability" by telling the story of an American named Joe who successfully aids a Dominican shade-coffee grower named Miguel in his quest to farm coffee in "the old way." The story's afterword, written by Julia Alvarez's husband, Bill Eichner, details the couple's real-life forays into the coffee business and their own dedication to environmentally friendly coffee cooperatives in the Dominican Republic. Certainly, Alvarez's *A Cafecito Story* merits a long list of praise from those concerned about the degradation of the Caribbean landscape by unwise farming practices and the exploitation of its family farmers. The text itself is published by Chelsea Green, an ecologically friendly press that has lavished all the right sort of attention on Alvarez's eco-parable and that makes clear that Alvarez's narrative, though fictional in one regard, is based on Alvarez's real-life coffee cooperative in the Dominican Republic. The book's attractive woodcut illustrations have been commissioned to a Dominican artist, Belkis Ramírez; it includes an appendix, "A Better Coffee: Developing Economic Fairness," which advocates principles of fair trade, environmental sustainability, and the economic independence of less-privileged nations as well as includes a long list of resources and websites committed to such causes; and the final page of the book promote the sale of other Chelsea Green books, recordings and products committed to "sustainable living."

Even as I acknowledge these merits, I contend that although Alvarez's narrative ostensibly clears space for a new future for Dominican coffee growers, it also reinscribes the U.S. expansionist project of Manifest Destiny as a white Nebraskan farmer, filled with a yearning to carve his own homestead out of the "frontier," does so by seizing control of what Alvarez genders as "female" coffee and land as part of a new paternalism. In this manner, the exoticism of coffee grown in forests "filled with songbirds" actually renews age-old market paradigms first deployed in the old imperial centers of Europe and then in the United States. In the end, readers of Alvarez's book must ask themselves to what degree environmentally friendly farming practices in the Dominican Republic can shed their colonialist roots if the tropology to make such practices attractive to U.S. readers merely reiterates stereotypes about the land and resources of the Caribbean. As long as these "new" paradigms merely content themselves with renewing the old colonial relationships of paternalist, Euroamerican whites overseeing subservient filiations of mixed-race people of color, has much changed in the way the Caribbean is perceived? Also, I argue that close study of *A Cafecito Story* foregrounds for its readers the difficulty for writers to "see" the land of the Caribbean on its own merits and not simply as a site to superimpose their own desires onto the landscape through the telling of another unfortunate spatial story.

COFFEE CULTIVATION IN THE DOMINICAN REPUBLIC

Frequently in its narrative, Alvarez's *A Cafecito Story* mentions a return to "the old way" of coffee cultivation, invoking the superiority of shade-coffee cultivation (that is, the cultivation of full-grown coffee trees underneath an "overstory" of other tropical foliage) to the "new" farming of what has been termed "sun-grown coffee" (the growth of coffee "bushes" in full sunlight with heavy doses of artificial fertilizers and pesticides, which generates weak plants but larger, more quickly grown harvests). But when Alvarez's text tells us that Miguel "planted with coffee the old way," or when the narrative's white U.S. protagonist, Joe, passionately argues to the impoverished mestizo farmers that they "need to keep planting coffee your old way," the narrative also invokes a nostalgia for that which is "original," "foundational," or "natural" in the island of Hispaniola, a pseudo-Edenic revisiting of island ways whose historical presence has only recently been displaced by the machinations of corporate greed (15, 22). Hasn't the cultivation of coffee in the Dominican Republic always existed, Alvarez's text seems to ask? Can the cultivation of coffee be separated from the "ways" of the islanders that farm it?

At a fundamental level, Alvarez's nostalgia for the "original" points to an age-old history that never existed, for coffee cultivation in the Caribbean is relatively new, historically speaking, having arrived as part of the European colonial project and finally cultivated as an extension of capitalist development in the region.[1] That the introduction of *coffea arabica* was seen as an unnatural, even violent change for the Caribbean can be seen in the words of none other than Karl Marx, who as part of a critique of free trade noted: "You believe, perhaps, gentlemen, that the production of coffee and sugar is the natural destiny of the West Indies. Two centuries ago, nature, which does not trouble itself about commerce, had planted neither sugar-cane nor coffee trees there. And it may be that in less than half a century you will find there neither coffee nor sugar, for the East Indies, by means of cheaper production, have already successfully broken down this so-called natural destiny of the West Indies" (205).

It is true that Marx's conflation of the cultivation of coffee and sugar betrays his ignorance of the differences between the production and cultivation of the two crops, and his forecast of the disappearance of both cash crops from the Caribbean by the end of the nineteenth century proved dead wrong. Still, his perception that a discourse already existed that would "naturalize" the history of both crops in the Caribbean imbricates coffee cultivation and the presence of European capital in the region, explaining the ideological investment in portraying coffee as an "original" part of the landscape.

While it is true that the French employed slave labor to grow and harvest coffee during their dominance of Saint Domingue in the seventeenth and eighteenth centuries (Randall and Mount 16), the majority of coffee cultivation in the Dominican Republic occurred in *minifundias*—small, peasant-owned parcels of land where coffee was initially grown more for local consumption than for export—rather than on the large *latifundia* plantations (Topik 242). In the last half of the nineteenth century, the cultivation of coffee in the Dominican Republic "expanded enormously," becoming more widespread along with the farming of cotton, cocoa, and tobacco, and in the coffee-growing north a "decentralized peasant society evolved whose products were exported by a class of urban merchants" (Baud 135-36). Randall and Mount point out that until 1912, "the Dominican Republic's exports were overwhelmingly cocoa and sugar, with coffee consistently a very distant third," but when General Rafael Trujillo assumed dictatorial control of the Dominican Republic in 1930, he realized the attractiveness of coffee as one of the premier cash crops of the country (51). By 1955, Trujillo had created the "Café Dominicano" Company, an enterprise controlled by investment from Trujillista cronies that dominated the coffee revenues of the country.[2] Even though the small coffee grower suffered from the unfair competition generated by Trujillo's

consolidation of coffee production and distribution and his preferential taxation of large-scale coffee growers allied to his cause, over half of the coffee production in the Dominican Republic in 1960 came from farms smaller than 100 acres.[3]

The most serious challenge to the small coffee grower in the Dominican Republic came not at the hands of Trujillo, however, but from those who seized control of the coffee industry in the wake of Trujillo's assassination and the abolition of his coffee enterprise. Adriano Sánchez Roa demonstrates that between 1967 and 1988, eight families created a de facto cartel that controlled 66 percent of the coffee production in the Dominican Republic (Sánchez Roa 9). These families, whose power enabled them to broker the price for Dominican coffee on the international market and that dictated the legislation of laws regarding coffee production and sales for all the producers in the Dominican Republic, are most likely the *"compañía"* that Miguel alludes to in *A Cafecito Story.*

The Coffee, The Land, and Alvarez's Songbirds

The development of high-yield varieties of coffee during the so-called "green revolution" of the 1970s increased the number of coffee trees that could be commercially cultivated "from 1,100-1,500 to 4,000-7,000 trees per hectare" (Waridel 34). These new, sun-resistant varieties of coffee encouraged many growers to bulldoze their shade-coffee crops in hopes of increased revenue and at the behest of the large coffee brokers. The resultant monocropping devastated the habitats that had existed in the shade-coffee plantations, which had depended on an overstory canopy of shade trees in order for their crop to grow and which had supported a dramatic biodiversity of insects, animals, and plants (Waridel 34-35). Once the sun-grown coffee filled the fields and this biodiversity largely vanished, other environmental problems occurred, including agrochemical pollution from fertilizers and pesticides and pronounced soil erosion (Waridel 35). In *A Cafecito Story,* Alvarez dramatizes Joe's first exposure to these degraded environmental conditions:

> As the truck heads up the narrow, curving road, Joe notices the brown mountainsides, ravaged and deforested, riddled with gullies. The road is made even more narrow by huge boulders. They must roll down during rainstorms. No trees to hold back the eroding soil. Suddenly, the hillsides turn a crisp, metallic green. A new variety of coffee grown under full sun, the old man beside him explains. A young man with a kerchief over his mouth his spraying the leaves. ¿Qué es? Joe asks the old man. Veneno, he answers, clutching his throat. A word Joe doesn't have to look up in his dictionary. Poison.
>
> (12-13)[4]

In fact, Alvarez echoes the words of earlier scholars about the ecological disaster that these coffee fields represent. Eduardo Galeano refers to "the story of coffee" in *Open Veins of Latin America* as that "which advances, leaving deserts behind it" (73); earlier in the century, Fernando Ortiz had labeled coffee one of the "four devils" of colonialist agriculture in the Caribbean (209).

In producing her account of the environmental impact of the coffee fields, Alvarez employs "songbirds" as special symbols to be metonymous for all that will be lost if the sun-grown coffee producers triumph. But Alvarez's prose, which has elsewhere condensed the data of complex environmentalist critiques into terse, gritty glances at the landscape, suddenly veers toward the romantic and the exotic when speaking of these birds. "In the midst of the green desert," she writes, "Miguel's land is filled with trees. Tall ones tower over a spreading canopy of smaller ones. Everywhere there are bromeliads and birdsong. A soft light falls on the thriving coffee plants. Perched on a branch, a small thrush says its name over and over again, chinchilín-chinchilín. A flock of wild parrots wheel in the sky as if they are flying in formation, greeting him" (13). Not only does Alvarez stage this scene to be lush and comfortable in contrast to the harsh "green deserts"— "bromeliad" flowers are in the trees, the lighting is "soft," the plants "full" and "thriving"—but the birds are made to be exotic and inviting, even "greeting" Joe's foreign gaze. Alvarez makes her thrush sound as if it speaks some tropical variant of Spanish, and her "wild parrots" invoke whole generations of literary texts that mark tropical exoticism with a similar plumage. Alvarez continues this pattern of exoticism as the narrative progresses, as the birds "sing to the cherries" to help ripen them (15). Finally, when Joe succeeds in luring the woman who becomes his wife to join him on the cooperative in the Dominican Republic, Alvarez extends an invitation to readers of *A Cafecito Story* that seems intended to ripen their own favorable reading and interpretation of the text: "Read this book while sipping a cup of coffee grown under birdsong. Then, close your eyes and listen for your own song" (37).

In reality, Alvarez's exoticism of the birds and their song depicts only a portion of the birds actually populating the shade-coffee forests of the Dominican Republic. Joseph Wunderle, the ornithologist who has carried out the most extensive recent research on avian distribution in the shade-coffee plantations of the Dominican Republic, reports that "a variety of resident and migrant bird species occupy these [coffee] plantations" and demonstrates that many of these "songbirds" are "Nearctic migrants" to the area; simply put, many of the birds that inhabit the groves that Alvarez details

in *A Cafecito Story* are actually birds from North America that winter in the warm overstory of the shade-coffee plantations.[5] Nowhere in the ornithology research on the avian inhabitants of Dominican shade-coffee groves do we read of "wild parrots" populating these plantations, though birds that would be unfamiliar to Alvarez's U.S. readers (the lizard cuckoo, the Hispaniolan emerald, and local varieties of woodpecker, tody, tanager, and oriole) are mentioned in the study, and resident varieties of the "thrush" that Alvarez names do appear in the scientific data (Wunderle 64). Interestingly, Wunderle's research as well as the research of other ornithologists also deflates Alvarez's notion that these birds are drawn to the coffee plants themselves.[6]

EXOTICISM, DESIRE, AND NOSTALGIA IN
ALVAREZ'S TEXT

Why would Alvarez stay faithful to many of the small details of environmentalists' critique of sun-grown coffee fields and to their corresponding campaign to energize the shade-coffee industry but not accurately portray the songbirds around which she spins the more romanticized aspects of her narrative? I contend that Alvarez's text wants to reinscribe a very traditional set of historical desires and nostalgias onto the Dominican landscape, using the exotic romance of the songbirds as part of a larger strategy to feminize the coffee production that she chronicles and to accentuate the sexualized desire with which she colors the consumption of the shade coffee in her narrative (and, by extension, the land). By feminizing the coffee, its production, and its consumption, Alvarez's text clears a space for Joe, her nostalgic Nebraskan narrator, to reclaim the family farm he lost to agribusiness in Nebraska by means of a "new" homestead in the Dominican Republic, Joe sees his gesture, itself a smaller version of the same Manifest Destiny of which his ancestors were a part, as a "masculine" means to oppose the forces of globalization.

Unlike many of the writers who have composed narratives in the wake of the colonial encounter in the Caribbean, it is true that Alvarez is at one level sensitive to the colonial discourse about the Dominican Republic that she's inherited. She notes, for instance, how the advertisements that hawk their fun-in-the-sun vacations in the Dominican Republic to Joe speak of "the land Columbus loved the best," and she registers the tendency of these same advertisements to paint their tourism in terms of "barely clad beauties tossing beach balls with waves sounding in the background" (6). When Joe arrives at the beach resort, he is dismayed to see that "no natives are allowed on the grounds except the service people who wear Aunt Jemima kerchiefs and faux-Caribbean costumes and perpetual, desperate smiles of welcome" and that, what's more, "the barely clad beauties come with men already attached to their arms" (9).

Indeed, it is Joe's disenchantment with commerce in these worn-out exoticisms that initially compels him to visit Miguel's *minifundio* in the mountains. But Alvarez's postcolonial critique of the Dominican Republic as a simulacrum of post-Columbian sex-and-sun ends when Joe drinks his mystical first cup of shade coffee. Suddenly, Joe, the white divorcé who came to the Dominican Republic seeking an exotic, dark-skinned woman's love, finds himself seduced not by a half-naked, dark-skinned Dominican "beauty" but by a similarly exoticized cup of coffee. "Coffee comes in one denomination," Alvarez writes, "a dollhouse-sized cup filled with a delicious, dark brew that leaves stains on the cup. Joe closes his eyes and concentrates on the rich taste of the beans. He hears the same faint whistle he heard on the plane, getting closer" (10). This "whistle," which we've been told sounds like "a faint whistling of birdsong" that Joe imagines he can hear on the flight south while dreaming of the "barely clad beauty" he'll surely claim on the island, ties the coffee to the very exoticism that Alvarez seemed to critique earlier in the narrative, and the fact that this coffee comes in a "dollhouse-sized cup" only heightens the uncomfortable connection between the "dolls" of the Dominican Republic that Joe thought he would seek out upon his arrival and the exoticized Dominican coffee. When Joe arrives at Miguel's coffee farm and Miguel instructs him in the nuances of shade-coffee production, Alvarez extends the connection between coffee and the exoticized female even further as Miguel explains "When a bird sings to the cherries as they are ripening, it is like a mother singing to her child in the womb. The baby is born with a happy soul" (15). Miguel goes on to explain: "The wet granos [coffee beans] we take to the river for washing. They must be bathed with running water for eight or so hours—a watchful process, as we have to get the bean to just that moment when the grains are washed but no fermentation has begun." It is not unlike that moment with a woman—Miguel smiles, looking often toward the mountains—when love sets in" (19).

By helping her readers understand that processing coffee beans to have a full-bodied flavor is like coaxing "love" out of "that moment with woman," Alvarez sexualizes the coffee in a way that reinvokes the heterosexual colonial stereotypes about the exotic female nature of the Caribbean that she seemed to have dismissed earlier in the narrative. Alvarez reminds us of this link between coffee and a sort of exotic sensual pleasure once again as Miguel informs Joe that the "coffee tastes better than anything" because Joe, as "a farmer's son," can "taste with [his]

whole body and soul" (20). Only a few pages later, when Joe's sister invites him to a visit in Nebraska and asks if he'll stay, Joe replies, "I have a family," and Alvarez's narration explains, "Although he has never married, he has become a husband to the land," and we also learn that the progeny of Joe's marriage to the Dominican landscape is "his large campesino [peasant] familia, all of whom he has taught to read and write" (26).

Through these associations, Alvarez renews the paternalism that had existed for centuries between plantation owners and their "family" of workers in Caribbean societies and allows a white male to figuratively "inseminate" himself into the "colored," "feminine" land of the Dominican Republic. By tasting the coffee, Joe tastes and ultimately possesses the feminine in the Dominican Republic's exoticized landscape—if he comes to the Dominican Republic looking for a romance, he gets it. Once wedded to the female body of the Dominican coffee plantation, Joe "fathers" the awakening of his Dominican "child" workers into literacy and modernity.[7]

In this way, Joe enables himself to achieve a new sort of masculinity, one rooted in his identification with his Nebraskan farmer father. At the beginning of *A Cafecito Story*, Joe has failed to be a man like his father, who once successfully maintained a large farm in the Nebraskan prairie, where "gulls," "swallows," and "sparrows" enriched the land with their own birdsong before he was forced out by big agribusiness (3-4). This loss of a chance to be a farmer like his father emasculates Joe; Alvarez writes that "something seemed to be missing from [Joe's] life" and credits Joe's divorce to his first wife, a "city girl," in part to the fact that Joe felt "adrift, a little lost" (4-5).

At least part of Joe's characterization as a male-made-man-through-farming likely derives from Julia Alvarez's awareness of her husband Bill Eichner's own attitudes toward the land of the Dominican Republic. Although Eichner makes a specific point of informing his reader that "my wife Julia and I are not the man and the woman of the parable," he concedes that "our story is related to this parable" and goes on to state that he is "from farm stock in Nebraska" and that he had not "realized that the same kind of technification that had eliminated sea gulls and family farms in Nebraska was now doing a job on traditional shade-coffee farms in the tropics" (Eichner 39-40). Eichner concludes, "Julia and I saw first-hand how globalization was changing the *campo,* or countryside, that we had both known as youngsters" (40).

If Alvarez's and Eichner's texts want us to understand Joe's fight against the "globalization" of agribusiness as a worthy cause on the environmental and social levels, the texts' tropes also necessitate that we see their story as the ideologically problematic struggle of a Nebraskan family farmer to carry on a masculine Manifest Destiny on a new female "frontier" found in the Dominican shade-coffee plantation. In this manner, the unfortunately familiar hue of European-American paternalism over the "mismanaged," "exotic" land of the Caribbean emerges anew in Alvarez's narrative.

SPATIAL STORIES AND THE LAND OF THE DOMINICAN REPUBLIC

Michel de Certeau has argued that when an individual or social entity needs to exert its authority over a certain physical space but worries that the legitimacy of the authority over that space will be questioned, a "spatial story" is invented that enables the corresponding appropriation of that space.[8] In Julia Alvarez's *A Cafecito Story,* we encounter a spatial story that seeks to rewrite the economic and social history of Dominican shade-coffee farming by giving us what it calls a "parable" to illustrate the environmental and social woes that are the fruit of a long history of abuse culminating in the latest exploitation of the Caribbean by the multinational capital of agribusiness. The other part of the spatial story that Alvarez tells wants readers to see the coffee and island of the Dominican Republic as one more "colored" female landscape in which a white male presence can figuratively inseminate itself; the "love" of this land is meant to be the love of the supervisory gaze of man for the woman of the landscape. Will this combination of spatial stories enable its readers to escape the abusive paradigms of the past, as Alvarez's text ostensibly aims to facilitate? In raising this question, I do not suggest that Alvarez's text is guilty of a unique or unusual problem; indeed, I argue that because *A Cafecito Story*—a narrative composed by an admirable, engaging writes who has proven herself sensitive to many aspects of the diasporic Caribbean and to its history—perpetuates colonialist views of the Caribbean, its people, and its environment, we should reassess the contributions of all narratives, fictional or otherwise, in their contributions to how one perceives the "nature" and the "natural" history of the Caribbean and its islands.

For if we continue to think of the land, in the Caribbean and its islands as female and of the modification of that land in the name of "progress" a male, then we will not be able to conceive of a progressive economics and environmentalism that doesn't first involve the "seduction" and "impregnation" of the land, first metaphorically and then literally by the violent introduction of alien crops, settlements, and societies. In making this point I would suggest that writers like Alvarez who, like many of us, wish to write about the land in progressive terms don't *intend* to perpetuate

these patterns of thinking. But because these writers perhaps wish to honor and conserve a land's "beauty" and have understood the "beautiful" to be equated with the feminine, pejorative male associations with the handling of the land inevitably insinuate themselves into their texts. It is ironic but true that the act of embracing the best qualities of the land through the use of female-associated language simultaneously enables the language of rape and despoilment that cages our view of the land as a victimized, passive entity in the clutches of a malignant male embrace.

As it tells its spatial story, Alvarez's *A Cafecito Story* also relegates the voice of the Dominican shade-coffee farmer to second-tier status, asking a character like Miguel to function as a mere enabler for Joe's Manifest Destiny in the tropics. Miguel knows much about coffee cultivation but is portrayed as one almost completely disconnected from a knowledge of the flow of multinational capital. This, too, is part of Alvarez's spatial story, one that would validate a Dominican-American writer returning to the island of her childhood as a more benevolent, environmentally progressive colonizer of the land, "civilizing" the undereducated coffee farmers through ambitious literacy projects. But as Édouard Glissant has argued on behalf of the so-called "peasantry" of the Caribbean: "It is certainly true that we . . . are no longer the country people we used to be, with our same old instinctive patience. Too many international parameters come into this relationship. A man involved in agriculture is inevitably a man involved in culture: he can no longer produce innocently" (*Poetics* 149). The "innocence" and naiveté that Alvarez ascribes to Miguel and his compatriots would, against the reality that Glissant presents, credit the Dominicans with little more than a vague awareness of the "international parameters" of their situation, and in doing so would absolve Alvarez's spatial story of its obligation to present or represent the ideological commitments of the community in more than a passing, romanticized manner. For Alvarez's spatial story wants to convert Miguel and his family into something not unlike the exotic songbirds that flutter through *A Cafecito Story*: quaint, simple, and unproblematically beautiful in their ties to the earth and in their eroticizing role in the shade coffee's production and consumption.

There would appear to be much more work to be done before we really hear the "birdsong" and "see" the plantations of the Dominican Republic. Glissant has suggested that embracing "an aesthetics of the earth" rather than thinking of the earth as "territory" would offer the possibility of this peeling away of dated spatial imaginations of the Caribbean. He argues: "Territory is the basis for conquest. Territory requires that filiation be planted and legitimated. Territory is defined by its limits, and they must be expanded. A land henceforth has no limits. That is the reason it is worth defending against every form of alienation" (*Poetics* 151). Glissant understands that abandoning an "aesthetic of the earth" for genealogies of economic, historical, and cultural affiliations only inscribes extra-environmental ideologies on the land. The earth, as Glissant apprehends it, could conceivably be loved on its own merits: not on its ability to produce crops, not on a vision of its personification as a feminized Other, and not as a site to enact policies of hopeful postmodern social programs pre-viewed as counterbalances to the heartlessness of globalization.

If this revisioning of the earth is to be realized, it will require that the dualities inherent in spatial stories like Alvarez's (narratives of self/Other, the banal/the exotic, civilized/uncivilized, male occupier and cultivator of the land/female landscape) be collapsed. As Ben Heller has noted, this rhizomatic and "relational" model that Glissant proposes "is not a rejection or abandonment of the self, but an errancy that finds/founds the self through relation with the Other" (405). The "errancy" to which Heller alludes speaks to Foucault's argument that the "see/being seen dyad" is what must be eliminated in order to frustrate the supervisory gazes that warp fundamental perceptions of power distribution in society[9]; if we want to be able to find an "aesthetic of the earth," perhaps for the first time, we must always understand the "errancies" of our gaze of that earth and how the "errant" gazes of the Other are, in turn, supervising and constructing us in their own errant ontological strategies.[10]

In the case of Alvarez's story, a refusal to make the earth of the Dominican Republic metonymous for desires that at a basic level have nothing to do with the tropical landscape itself would seem to be the first step in being able to see the earth and its "aesthetic" for the first time. This would create a rupture of perception that would direct the reader's gaze not toward territorial definition and inevitable "conquest" of the land but toward the earth as an entity worthy of independent consideration. For Alvarez, a writer who wishes to connect herself to new goals for the land of the Dominican Republic, such a consideration would offer the possibility of entirely new solutions—not ones that seek to "impregnate" the "female coffee plantations of the Dominican Republic with a slightly more benefit cent deployment of U.S. capital, but ones that understand how the future of the shade-coffee groves and its songbirds has more to do with the earth, its flora and fauna, and the fluvial movements of its wildlife from one ecosystem to another outside of the recent advent of colonialism, capitalism, and the United States' infatuation with the elusive cup of perfect flavored coffee.

Notes

1. This is especially true with the "heirloom" coffees cultivated on the real-life cooperative owned by Alvarez and Eichner and detailed in the afterword to *A Cafecito Story,* which descend from *coffea arabica* beans brought from the Middle East in the years following Columbus's "discovery" of Hispaniola and during the epoch in which European states saw in coffee a new mercantilist opportunity. See Topik 229.

2. Of the million pesos invested in the enterprise, around half came from Trujillo's personal coffers, though it was invested by his friends Tirso Rivera, Féderico García Godoy, and Manuel de Moya Alonso. See Sánchez Roa 15.

3. Sánchez Roa 17. It would make sense to see the narrative of *A Cafecito Story* indirectly attack Trujillo's legacy, since two of Alvarez's earlier novels, *How the García Girls Lost Their Accents* and *In The Time of the Butterflies,* critique the abuses of Trujillo's regime. Alvarez's critique of Trujillo, however, seems less a critique of the United States' involvement in the economic practices of the Trujillo regime. In fact, Trujillo's economic commitments consistently played to U.S. desires for regional economic "stability," which meant that *Trujillista* economics were, at an important level, U.S. economic policies for the island.

4. Alvarez's description, which would seem to collapse the entirety of the environmental stress that these new coffee fields place on the Dominican ecosystem into one glance, accords with Eichner's account in the book's afterword, where he notes: "While there [in the mountains of the Dominican Republic where the bulk of the coffee is grown], we were shocked by the "green desert" of the surrounding modern coffee farms. By the uniformity of the monoculture—hillside after hillside without a single fruit or shade tree. No sign of life except coffee plants and a single masked worker walking down the rows in a cloud of chemicals he was spraying on the coffee." See Eichner 39-40.

5. See Wunderle 59; and Wunderle and Latta, "Winter Site" 596-614.

6. See Wunderle 65-68; Wunderle and Latta, "Avian Resource Use" 273-80. Similar findings can also be seen in Perfecto et al. 601. In fact, a study published in the American Ornithologists.' Union's quarterly journal points out that the American redstarts, perhaps one of the best examples of a bird that actively forages in the coffee plants by eating the coffee berry borer (its larva destroys the coffee cherries themselves), aren't exclusive to the shade-coffee plantations that Alvarez would champion but also can be found preying on the insects in sun-grown coffee fields that Alvarez condemns. See Sherry 563-66.

7. That Joe returns to the United States to bring back an actual woman to be his literal wife is but an afterthought in the narrative, a way during the nar-

rative's denouement to have the would-be-writer wife give birth to Joe's narrative of how he has placed seed in the Dominican Republic.

8. See de Certeau 115-30.

9. See Foucault, *Discipline and Punish* 202.

10. In other words, the propensity of individuals to think of the Caribbean in terms of "filiation" instead of "relation" means that the landscapes of the Caribbean don't have an existence outside of the colonial genealogies that have overdetermined our perceptions since Columbus. We can't see the Caribbean as a site where different groups have creolized relationships; we only see the Caribbean as a family tree instigated by the colonial project, peppered with the race-mixing of colonial desire (Glissant, "Creolization" 269-75).

Katarzyana Marciniak (essay date 2006)

SOURCE: Marciniak, Katarzyana. "Accented Bodies and Coercive Assimilation: The Trespasses of the García Girls." In *Alienhood*, pp. 57-75. Minneapolis: University of Minnesota Press, 2006.

[*In the essay below, Marciniak studies* How the García Girls Lost Their Accents *in terms of the novel's focus on American transnational identities.*]

> Thus the act of determining the "character" of a nation involves regulating who may and may not come in, who are "family" and who are strangers.
>
> —David Jacobson, "Introduction: An American Journey"

> A foreigner in principle is already a spy.
>
> —Trinh T. Minh-ha, in *Surname Viet Given Name Nam*

At the turn of the millennium, as a visitor to the American Museum of Natural History in New York City, I received a sleek pass, allowing me to enter the Rose Center for Earth and Space. This pass—an identity card of sorts, titled "Passport to the Universe," and also calling itself "Official Cosmic Passport"—is a fascinating cultural artifact, figured as a dark bluish rectangle to resemble an actual U.S. passport. The front cover features a hologram with an image of the cosmos and bears such words as "Earth," "Solar System," "Milky Way Galaxy," and "Observable Universe." The back of the card contains a blank line for the visitor's signature and, above it, the following text:

> The American Museum of Natural History hereby requests all whom it may concern to permit the citizen of the cosmos named below to pass without delay or hindrance. The bearer is empowered by knowledge and imagination to travel anywhere in the universe.

As someone who has been teaching within the area of transnational cultural studies, I have been captivated by the notions put forth by the "Passport to the Universe" and its celebratory mapping of what might be called a "transnational identity" in relation to the United States, a notion that is intimately connected to the cultural experiences and discourses of immigration. This particular model of an empowered citizenry interestingly speaks to the much-debated clash between current *discursive* liberatory renditions of mobility, travel, and border crossings and painful limitations that immigrants themselves often acutely experience. Undoubtedly, the visual-conceptual landscape of the "Cosmic Passport" offers provocative connotations, especially if we consider recent discussions within transnational studies that ask us to be wary of the favorable renditions of transnational positions.[1]

First, the "passport" plays on the idea that the contemporary era of transnational capitalism alters our national and cultural mobility in affirmative ways. The traditional idea of a U.S. citizen is stretched to include the notion of a citizen of the cosmos, inviting a reflection that such a citizen is free to roam the cosmic space. This freedom, of course, implies the unhindered ability to cross national borders, including venturing into outer space. Moreover, one could argue that this conceptual shift from American citizenry to cosmic citizenry reflects not only an ontological empowerment but an epistemological one as well, because the traveler is promised special access to "knowledge and imagination." Thus, the "Official Cosmic Passport," with its implication of the citizenry of the universe, opens up a space for an understanding of transnational crossings as a formation of a hypercosmopolitan identity ("the bearer is empowered . . . to travel anywhere") and as a presumably carnivalesque possibility for the museum's visitor to indulge in the fantasy of cosmic subjectivity. However, while the "Passport to the Universe" as a transnational text offers a flexible idea of the nation and the national self, it does so only by concealing the imperial desire of "America" to extend itself beyond all imaginable borders via the Eurocentric logic of domination. For a critical reader of such a transnational representation, the important issue is the interrogation of what kinds of national identities would be permitted to occupy the privileged position of a citizen of the cosmos. In other words, metaphorically speaking, who can use the "Official Cosmic Passport"?

To develop this discussion, I want to situate this question in the context of Nina Glick Schiller and Georges Fouron's explication of transnational migrations:

> Little research has been done on transnational relationships and their economic and political implications, because of a flawed historiography and ethnography of

migration that, since the 1950s, has portrayed immigrants in the United States as displaced persons permanently uprooted from home and family. Current transnational research can correct these weaknesses only if we move beyond the stage of celebrating transnational connections and proclaiming the agency of transmigrants.

(Schiller and Fouron 2001, 326)

Schiller and Fouron define "transmigrants" as those who "maintain multiple familial, social, economic, and political ties to both their country of origin and their country of settlement and live their lives across national borders" (322). In doing so, they call for a re-conceptualization of immigrant identities not as permanently uprooted and alienated from their native cultures but in the context of transnational connections, more and more enabled by a global economy. In other words, they propose to revise the traditional meaning of immigration and exile via transnationalism. Linda Basch, Schiller, and Cristina Szanton Blanc define transnationalism as the "processes by which immigrants forge and sustain multi-stranded social relations that link together their societies of origin and settlement" (1994, 7). They caution, however, against a salutary understanding of those connections. These contentions interestingly expand on my previous question about the "Passport to the Universe": How do transnational bonds alter an understanding of immigrants in the United States? By implication, how do they modify the traditional grasp of American immigrant literature?[2] What does it mean to claim transnationality as one's mode of location? Who precisely might have access to a transnational subjecthood? What are the risks involved in theorizing such subjecthood in emancipatory ways?

Although a lot of groundbreaking work in the field of transnationalism has been carried out by anthropologists, sociologists, political scientists, and post-colonial theorists, relatively little attention has been devoted to the literary explorations of transnationalism in the context of current American literature. As Basch, Schiller, and Szanton Blanc observe: "individuals, communities, or states rarely identify themselves as transnationals. It is only in contemporary fiction that this state of 'in-betweenness,' has been fully voiced."[3] Indeed, contemporary American transnational literature, written by "bicultural" authors, many of whom are women of diverse ethnic and racial backgrounds, is an especially fertile ground for an exploration of the polysemous representations of transnationalism and its predicaments.[4] The recent "exilic" narratives I am referring to include the writings of such transcultural authors as Diana Abu-Jaber, Julia Alvarez, Edwidge Danticat, Chitra Banerjee Divakaruni, Ariel Dorfman, Cristina Garcia, Eva Hoffman, Jamaica Kincaid,

Chang-Rae Lee, Bharati Mukherjee, Loida Martiza Pérez, and Esmeralda Santiago.[5] Overwhelmingly, their texts feature binational characters who transgress the boundaries of established nationhood by moving across national borders, languages, cultures, and competing ideologies.[6] In doing so, they explore and question the notion of privileged Americanness: they show how liminal identities, with their shifting subject positions, complicate the dichotomous hierarchy of citizen-legal subject/stranger-illegal other. What is particularly engaging about these narratives is the way they foreground the textual representation of exile as a critique of nationalism and accentuate the way that identities of "trespassing" strangers-foreigners unsettle monocultural narratives of the nation. Most of these texts, while insisting on the historical specificity and heterogeneity of their racial, ethnic, and gender modalities, enact transnationality thematically and stylistically. Emphasizing fragmentation, multiple and often conflicting points of view, and nonchronological narrative movements, the themes that emerge ask readers to think about what it means to be perceived as foreign or alien in the contemporary culture of the United States, or alternately, what it means to occupy the space of sanctioned citizenhood. In a variety of differing geopolitical contexts, these texts center on the experience of alienhood and give space to the often dispersed voices of those who do not quite fit within the validated limits of a nation.

With these concerns in mind, I inspect the voicing of transnational identities in Julia Alvarez's well-recognized, semiautobiographical first novel, *How the García Girls Lost Their Accents*.[7] Although I will approach the text through a textual close reading, my broader goal is to use Alvarez's novel as a starting point for a series of reflections on the need to scrutinize the idea that a transnational position implies a new, liberatory identity that allows an exile-immigrant a special epistemological insight and overall empowerment. The need to recognize the asymmetries of power of privilege that affect immigrants, refugees, and various border crossers in relation to U.S. territory prompts us to dissect the specific dangers in seeing the character of transnational connections as solely affirmative.

I focus on Alvarez's text as a representative example of American transnational literature for a number of interrelated reasons. First, the novel, self-conscious of the public rhetoric of multiculturalism in the United States, which often manifests itself in "happy pluralism" and "management of diversity" (Grewal and Kaplan 1999, 349), shows the dangers of the liberal multicultural model that often eagerly accepts, but also disciplines and consumes, difference through a subtle mixture of xenophobic and xenophilic undertones.[8]

This notion is perhaps best represented through a nuanced textual portrayal of various accented identities that reveal that *accentless bodies* remain the markers of authentic Americanness.

Second, the Garcías' transnational status as political refugees from the Dominican Republic to the United States who maintain familial ties with the island mobilizes an interesting tension: even after the García family members have successfully crossed the border and begun to function as legal subjects in the United States, the stigma attached to them as trespassers haunts their unstable cultural positions. The narrative emphasizes their location as that of dubious strangers and foreign intruders whose national belonging is suspect: "The Garcias were only legal residents, not citizens."[9] As I will suggest, the trope of trespassing is interestingly woven into the text to carry a dual, bidirectional, function: it comments on the Garcías' position in the United States as metaphoric trespassing transnationals, and it also helps us read the cultural dynamics surrounding the transnational returning to her homeland. I will link the moments of trespassing to the underscoring logic of purity that, although manifested differently in the United States and the Dominican Republic, symbolically invests in "clean," that is, monocultural, identities.[10]

Third, keeping in mind Trinh T. Minh-ha's point that "the experience of exile is never simply binary," I will propose that *How the García Girls Lost Their Accents* represents what might be called an "exilic quivering" by foregrounding the experiences of transnational identities that, in a dissonant way, function in a precarious space of liminality as fragile yet threatening, privileged yet dispossessed. Placing Alvarez's novel within a context of other recent bicultural American narratives, I will focus on the portrayal of liminars whose multiple national belongings are frequently figured in various texts through a dialectics of pain *and* pleasure. Such representations of transnational subjectivities that occupy, to use Trinh's words again, "hyphenated reality" (1994, 13, 17) compellingly intervene in the celebratory discussions of transnationalism and in what Ali Behdad and Laura Elisa Pérez, for example, term a "multicultural euphoria" (1995, 70).

Finally, although *How the García Girls Lost Their Accents* has been traditionally read as an example of U.S. Latina literature (Vázquez 2003), I will turn to Alvarez's essay writing to discuss why the category of Latina/o literature, although certainly suitable and historically valid, seems insufficient in addressing the transnational location of the writer who belongs in the interstices of two cultures. As Alvarez remarks: "We travel on that border between two worlds and we can see both points of view."[11]

ACCENTED BODIES AND THE TROPE OF TRESPASSING

André Aciman compellingly describes accented identity: "An accent marks the lag between two cultures, two languages, the space where you let go of one identity, invent another, and end up being more than one person though never quite two" (1999a, 11). This sense of fractured doubleness that Aciman expresses—of cultures, languages, and identities—infiltrates the narrative of *How the García Girls Lost Their Accents,* especially since the text foregrounds the representations of the foreign bodies of exiles—the accented body, as I call it—whose exilic subjectivity comes into being through the process of border crossing. The experience of varied transnational crossings between the Dominican Republic and the United States permeates most of Alvarez's work: the poetry collections, *Homecoming* (1984) and *The Other Side/El Otro Lado* (1995); her novels, *In the Time of the Butterflies* (1994), *¡Yo!* (1997), *In the Name of Salomé* (2000); and her collection of essays, *Something to Declare* (1998). And Alvarez, positioned as a writer in the United States who grew up in the Dominican Republic and still cultivates strong family and activist ties to the island, has frequently commented on her doubleness and the fact that "being in and out of both worlds" allows her to "[map] a country that's not on the map" (1998b, 173). Asked about her national identity in one of the interviews, she stresses her hybrid position: "I am not a *Dominican* writer. I can't pretend to be a *Dominican.* By the same token, when people ask me if I'm an American writer, I have to say I don't think of myself as being in the same tradition as Melville or Hawthorne. I am a hyphenated person interested in the music that comes out of a language that hears both languages. My stories come out of being in worlds that sometimes clash and sometimes combine."[12]

The friction Alvarez speaks about is poignantly reflected in *How the García Girls Lost Their Accents,* whose intricate narrative structure at first glance moves us straightforwardly from the United States to the Dominican Republic, and unfolds from the present to the past, from 1989 to 1959. The novel is divided into three sections, each segment shifting backward in time, with the narrative focus on members of the upper-class García family who are forced into exile by the Dominican regime of Rafael Trujillo in 1960 because of the father's secret involvement in the underground political movement against the dictatorship. But even though it appears that the narrative takes us from the American immigrant present into the Dominican native past, the text clearly refuses any direct trajectory. Instead, while the larger diegetic framework moves us back in time, simultaneously we are asked to read the fragmented exilic textual space of the in-between. The narrative often impedes temporal consistency, moving back and forth between the two cultures, languages, and their ideological and ethical systems, not allowing us to anchor the characters according to the logic of monolithic cultural identity. In explaining her desire to experiment with the consistency of the narrative structure, Alvarez notes: "I wanted the reader to be thinking like an immigrant, forever going back" (1998a, 132). The effect is performative: the fragmented narrative the reader is asked to sieve through in *How the García Girls Lost Their Accents* reflects the sense of painful disorientation and confusion the characters experience as they cope with their exilic in-betweenness.[13]

Additional complexity of the novel is underscored by what David Mitchell calls multiperspectivity, that is, a lack of a singular enunciative position, or a lack of a coherent, narrating point of view (1999, 168). As Alvarez has acknowledged, all her novels give space to multiple points of view that, unlike the single perspective, do not privilege the protagonist and his or her singular story (Alvarez 1998a, 132). For example, her third novel, *¡Yo!*, often thought of as a sequel to *How the García Girls Lost Their Accents*, performs a compelling experiment with the diversity of narrating voices. One could say that *¡Yo!* is about Yolanda, a writer and poet, except that she does not utter a word in the text.[14] She remains the curious absence at the heart of the narrative, displaced as the authorial voice. Instead, the book is a weaving of interrelated stories that come from various characters whose voices speak about their lives being intertwined with Yo's: there is a story from the sisters, from Yo's mother, from her father, from her stepdaughter, her third husband, her best friend, and a Midwestern landlady. All get a space to express their point of view except Yo. Alvarez says that she appreciates "listening and being taken over by other voices": "We get the story of how this woman got to be a writer, but not from the writer's point of view" (1998a, 133). This intentional dispersal of an authorial voice is also movingly played out in Alvarez's most recent novel, *In the Name of Salomé*. A story of a Dominican poet, Salomé Ureña and her daughter, Salomé Camila Henríquez Ureña, the novel has an elaborately structured narrative, allowing the voices of the two women to speak about their struggles with exile, poetry, family, identity—all wrapped up in the larger questions of cultural and national belonging.

In *How the García Girls Lost Their Accents*, too, we are invited to listen to different narrators. The multiperspectivity, or what might be called a dispersed focalization, allows various voices of the García sisters—Carla, Sandra, Yolanda, and Sofía—or "the four girls" as they are called, to speak their own vi-

sion of the exile, switching from a first- to a third-person narrative to a multiple "we." Yolanda, the poet in the family, also known as Yo (meaning "I" in Spanish), Joe, or Yoyo, has the strongest voice in the novel and occupies the space of a textual navigator who records the family's history.[15] The novel opens and closes with sections privileging Yolanda's experiences: the first part, "Antojos," is told in the third person; in the last part, "The Drum," Yolanda's point of view is emphasized by the first-person narration. By the end of "The Drum," in a self-conscious moment, she identifies herself as a diegetic creator and temporal manipulator by directly addressing the readers: "You understand I am collapsing all time now so that it fits in what's left in the hollow of my story?" (289).

The novel's title emphasizes the notion of an accented identity and its perceived loss, an experience that is often coded in the text as desirable because accentless identity, at least in an American popular imaginary, supposedly allows an immigrant to masquerade as a native. For example, "The Rudy Elmenhurst Story," a section that focuses on Yolanda's years in college and her failed romantic relationship with Rudy, explicates how the cultural mechanisms of coercive assimilation project the idea of an accentless speech as desirable. This explication is a result of Yolanda's critical dissection of her involvement with Rudy: "Why I didn't just sleep with someone as persistent as Rudy Elmenhurst is a mystery I'm exploring here by picking it apart the way we learned to do to each other's poems and stories in the English class" (88). This is the way Yo remembers her encounter with Rudy's parents: "His parents did most of the chatting, talking too slowly to me as if I wouldn't understand native speakers; they complimented me on my 'accentless' English and observed that my parents must be very proud of me" (100). The space of enunciation belongs to Rudy's parents who, assuming the authority of language, patronize Yolanda. Their comment plays on a common belief that an alien can pass as one of "us" once she removes foreign marks that code her as a suspicious stranger. Accented speech is obviously one such marking. It is thus the accented body—the body coded semiotically as an alien—that marks the García girls as strangers-hybrids and attracts the often violent force of coercive assimilation that manifests itself in subtle, invisible ways. The comment Yolanda hears invites her to lose her accented speech quickly so that she can begin to function socially at the level of a normative subject—successfully Americanized and gratefully assimilated.

In fact, many of the reviews of Alvarez's text echo these nativist sentiments. Donna Rifkind, for example, opens her review by saying that "to speak without an accent is the ultimate goal of the immigrant," clearly presupposing an immigrant universal desire of complete assimilation manifested by the perceived necessity of losing the accented speech. Similarly, Judith Freeman discusses the notion of a full American identity as one characterized by accentless articulation when she describes the García girls' cultural predicament: "The only choice left to them is to become fully American—lose their accents and plunge in."[16] I refer to these reviews not so much to point out how these critics failed to read the idea of an accent as transgressive, but rather to show how their formulations are indicative of a larger cultural logic that is conventionally applied to the immigrant identity. What motivates such statements is the reliance on the dichotomous thinking that privileges, even glorifies, the notion of speaking like a native over accented speech. Rifkind, indeed, sets up her review by displaying these binarisms up front, addressing the threshold "between accent and native speech, alienation and assimilation." Having an accent is hence equated with the perpetual mode of alienation, suggesting that an accented identity is always branded with strangerhood and doomed to cultural scrutiny and exclusion.

To lose an accent, however, does not necessarily mean to accelerate the desired acculturation. In Alvarez's novel we are confronted with subversive resistance to the metaphoric idea of losing an accent because to lose it means to obliterate the culturally and historically specific position marked by exile and to instantiate the idea of a full American whose uneasy, un-American differences have been successfully appeased or erased. Yolanda initially has no access to a conceptual apparatus that would allow her to dissect Rudy's parents' assumed position of privilege as natural Americans who cast her as a foreign object useful in their son's multicultural experiences:

> They encouraged him, his parents, to have experiences with girls but to be careful. He had told them he was seeing "a Spanish girl," and he reported they said that should be interesting for him to find out about people from other cultures. It bothered me that they should treat me like a geography lesson for their son. But I didn't have the vocabulary back then to explain even to myself what annoyed me about their remark.
>
> (98)

This is the moment that performs what might be called a conservative multiculturalism,[17] that is, the idea that ennobles the nativist vision of an American identity as the imperial center that, in a benevolent gesture, welcomes the encounter with difference, while still holding on to a politics of binary oppositions.[18] What I mean by a conservative multiculturalism is the traditional coercive acceptance of otherness under the slogans of "embracing difference" and "celebrating

diversity."[19] The logic of binary oppositions that we encounter in this passage invests Rudy's parents with ontological superiority that allows them to entertain the idea that their son's education is enriched via multiethnic encounters. Yolanda becomes "a geography lesson" for Rudy, an attractive object of study to spice up his college life. In fact, Rudy loses his interest in Yolanda once he realizes that she does not conform to his vision of the hot-blooded Latina who can be useful as an erotic/exotic Spanish body (99).

The condescending comment about finding out "about people from other cultures" in many ways parallels the prevalent academic notion that students, especially education majors, should take world literature courses to be exposed to multicultural texts, which will help them learn about other cultures. Within this paradigm, the texts to be studied in such world literature courses are often positioned outside the realm of American literature, creating an impression that multiculturalism comes from the outside, or alternately, that it belongs to a subcategory of other cultures situated within the United States.[20] Thus, within this discourse, Rudy is already positioned as the full subject who does not need to question his privileged cultural location and who, certainly, does not need to lose an accent.

While Alvarez posits the idea of an accented subjectivity as the driving force of the narrative and prompts the readers to question the ideology behind the assumed necessity of an exile to lose an accent, *How the García Girls Lost Their Accents* does not necessarily celebrate the accented identity as liberatory. On the contrary, Yolanda and her sisters frequently reflect on the feeling of discomfort of being coded as different by an accent. In the section titled "Trespass," Carla, the oldest sister, a seventh grader in a Catholic school, becomes the object of violence of a gang of schoolboys:

> Out of sight of the nuns, the boys pelted Carla with stones, aiming them at her feet so there would be no bruises. "Go back to where you came from, you dirty spic!" One of them, standing behind her in line, pulled her blouse out of her skirt where it was tucked in and lifted it high. "No titties," he snickered. Another yanked down her socks, displaying her legs, which had begun growing soft, dark hairs. "Monkey legs!" he yelled to his pals.
>
> (153)

First, through the logic of dirt—that is, through the idea that cleanliness has been traditionally associated with whiteness, purity, and the right to racial superiority—Carla is being marked as an unerotic and undesirable dirty body. Her rapidly changing young female body becomes an object of ostracism, showing us how the racist discourse is in this context rooted in patriarchal violence. The epithet "monkey legs" painfully stigmatizes Carla as some savage, unclean creature. Second, the customary comment about going back to where one comes from rests on the unquestioned (and perhaps unconscious) right the boys feel as the legitimate possessors of the national space. It is this right that allows them to cast Carla as a usurper of a place that, as if organically, does not belong to her. And the feeling of not belonging is an emotion that Carla knows quite intimately. She hates, for example, being asked for directions in the street: "'I don't speak very much English,' she would say in a small voice by way of apology. She hated having to admit this since an admission proved, no doubt, the boy gang's point that she didn't belong here" (156). She is haunted by the boys' racist insults, remembering their "high voices squealing with delight when [she] mispronounced some word they coaxed her to repeat." And even after the tauntings stop, their voices and faces persecute Carla:

> But their faces did not fade as fast from Carla's life. They trespassed in her dreams and in her waking moments. Sometimes when she woke in the dark, they were perched at the foot of her bed, a grim chorus of urchin faces, boys without bodies, chanting without words, "Go back! Go back!"
>
> (164)

This oppressive imagery of "boys without bodies," which weighs on Carla's conscious and unconscious visions, reveals the devastating impact of discursive violence that pins her down as an unacceptable intruder who is repeatedly told to "go back."

In her fantasy of constructing possible defenses against this anti-immigrant abuse, she imagines herself being driven to school "in a flashy red car the boys would admire" (155). Although it is evident that Carla's desire is influenced by capitalist consumption (which she learns from the boys whom she observes being in awe over cars), at this point this is the only imaginary weapon she can call forth to counter the violation she feels.[21] But she realizes that even this fantasy cannot work: "Except there was no one to drive her. Her immigrant father with his thick mustache and accent and three-piece suit would only bring her more ridicule" (155). The accent is thus perceived as a burden, an unmistakable label of unwanted otherness that trespasses the protected boundary of privileged citizenhood. The exclusionary logic at work here that Carla senses is that even if she loses *her* accent, her parents' marked articulation will always serve as an unwelcome familial signifier that pins her down as a foreigner. Similarly, when Yolanda compares her parents with Rudy's parents, who "looked so young and casual—like classmates," she feels awkwardly self-conscious,

sensing her parents' difference, not just audible in their accented speech but also written all over their bodies:

> My old world parents were still an embarrassment at parents' weekend, my father with his thick mustache and three-piece suit and fedora hat, my mother in one of her outfits she bought especially to visit us at school, everything overly matched, patent leather purse and pumps that would go back, once she was home, to plastic storage bags in her closet.
>
> (98)

Yolanda intuits that her parents' visible old worldness draws attention to her very self and singles her out as not quite adequate.

The idea of the García family as trespassers is interestingly figured in the opening of the section "Trespass," which underscores Carla's exclusion from the dominant culture:

> Down the block the neighborhood dead-ended in abandoned farmland that Mami read in the local paper the developers were negotiating to buy. Grasses and real trees and real bushes still grew beyond the barbed-wire fence posted with a big sign: PRIVATE, NO TRESPASSING. The sign had surprised Carla since "forgive us our trespasses" was the only other context in which she had heard the word. She pointed the sign out to Mami on one of their first walks to the bus stop. "Isn't that funny, Mami? A sign that you have to be good." Her mother did not understand at first until Carla explained about the Lord's Prayer. Mami laughed. Words sometimes meant two things in English too. This trespass meant that no one must go inside the property because it was not public like a park, but private. Carla nodded, disappointed. She would never get the hang of this new country.
>
> (151)

On a manifest level, Carla simply does not comprehend nuances of signification in English because the only context available to her is that of a Catholic upbringing in the Dominican Republic. Quite simply, she does not know yet that meaning is contextual. We see how at this point she does not have a position to speak from in the new culture, and she certainly has no access to a voice, understood, of course, not just as the ability to speak but also as an enunciative place of agency. The comment about Carla's inability to speak "very much" English, which I quoted earlier, also emphasizes that she expresses herself "in a small voice." This notion of a small voice underlines how Carla does not want to attract attention to herself as an accented identity and instead hopes to appear inaudible. But this passage is not only about how Carla does not know yet that "words sometimes meant two things in English." The no trespassing sign becomes a metaphorical warning that signals the prevailing aura of hostility frequently experienced by foreigners in the United States. This idea is aggressively expressed through the imagery of the barbed-wire fence as a protector of the purity of a nation.

The community that Carla scrutinizes in "Trespass" is characterized by patterns of sameness and cleanliness: "[T]hey had moved out of the city to a neighborhood on Long Island so that the girls could have a yard to play in, so Mami said. The little green squares around each look-alike house seemed more like carpeting that had to be kept clean than yards to play in" (151). The look-alike houses with neat carpetlike lawns embody the homogeneous vision of community that rests on orderly sameness, which Carla finds uninviting as a space of pleasure. She reads it as a place of exclusion—inhospitable and forbidding. She hungers for the greenery in the Dominican Republic: "Carla thought yearningly of the lush grasses and thick-limbed, vine-ladened trees around the compound back home" (151). In her childlike way, Carla romanticizes the vision of "back home" and invites the readers to perceive her world in a dichotomous, uncritical way: the luscious beauty of the island is clearly privileged over the mundane and a sensual landscape of a Long Island neighborhood.

LIMINALITY: DIALECTICS OF PAIN AND
PLEASURE

Although in "Trespass" Carla clings to the sentimentalized vision of home, ***How the García Girls Lost Their Accents,*** as a whole, refuses the predictable pleasant home/painful exile binary. Instead, the text creates a much more complex representation of exilic selfhood, which does not allow us simply to romanticize the Dominican Republic and to remain critical of hostility in the United States. This complexity is poignantly represented already in the first section of the novel, "Antojos," meaning "cravings," in which Yolanda realizes, to use Bharati Mukherjee's words, that she "flutters between worlds" (1988, 189). We begin to see how Yolanda's liminal position unmoors her sense of belonging to one nation and are invited to question the assumed natural connection between a person and her place of birth. Even though Yolanda is "the true geographical native" of the Dominican Republic (Mitchell 1999, 166), in an ironic and painful twist, "Antojos" shows that the space of home can be as unfamiliar and strange as the place of exile. Feelings of ambivalence, discomfort, and uncertainty permeate this section of the novel, as Yolanda tries to perform her homecoming.

Her wish to re-belong to the island is enacted by her desire to eat guavas, which she remembers from her childhood as an experience of pleasure, a desire that is underscored by the title of this section. Ironically, however, Yolanda is unable to figure out the meaning of *antojo*. This inability to capture signification parallels, of course, Carla's inability to understand the multiple meanings of "trespass," except that in Carla's case, we realize that she is still learning English, hence her lack of comprehension appears understandable. For Yolanda, however, her inability to understand *antojo* signals her estrangement from her native language and culture. In an interesting twist, Yolanda learns from her relatives that there is no one way to capture the meaning of *antojo*. Tía Carmen says, "it's not an easy word to explain." She translates it as "a craving for something you have to eat," while Altagracia, one of the family's maids, adds that "a person has an *antojo* when they are taken over by *un santo* who wants something" (8). Thus, the various shades of meaning that arise out of these translations mark *antojo* as an ambivalent desire, and this equivocal tension is associated with Yolanda as a character who has a craving that cannot easily be figured out.

"Antojos" opens with Yolanda's return to the island and it paradoxically establishes her position as a trespasser and foreigner. Instead of performing a pleasant encounter with the native culture, the beginning of the novel defamiliarizes the Dominican Republic for Yolanda. We learn that, after twenty-nine years of exile (and five years after the last visit), Yolanda secretly hopes to recover her old place among her extended family: "This time, however, Yolanda is not so sure she'll be going back. But that is a secret" (7). She is affectionately greeted by her aunts and cousins who prepare a cake to welcome her home. Yolanda is urged to make a wish:

> She leans forward and shuts her eyes. There is so much she wants, it is hard to single out one wish. There have been too many stops on the road of the last twenty-nine years since her family left this island behind. She and her sisters have led such turbulent lives—so many husbands, homes, jobs, wrong turns among them. But look at her cousins, women with households and authority in their voices. Let this turn out to be my home, Yolanda wishes.

(11)

The yearning for home is problematized when Yolanda takes her family's car to search for guavas in the countryside. Even before she leaves, her aunts warn her about potential dangers: "This is not the States. A woman just doesn't travel alone in this country" (9). When her car gets a flat tire on a secluded road and she is met by two native farmers who offer their help, Yolanda is petrified, seeing the men as "strong and quite capable of catching her if she makes a run for it" (19). In her fear, she initially does not speak and is mistaken for an American tourist: "'*Americana,*' he says to the darker man, pointing to the car. *'No comprende.'* The darker man narrows his eyes and studies Yolanda a moment. *'Americana?'* he asks her, as if not quite sure what to make of her" (20).

We immediately understand the irony of Yolanda's position. Not only are the men "not quite sure what to make of her," but she does not know what to make of herself. Her inability to choose whether she is Dominican or American dramatizes her hyphenated, hybridized sense of selfhood and reveals her liminality. This liminality manifests itself bodily. She speaks and understands Spanish, but, being paralyzed by fear, she literally cannot articulate her cultural position: "[H]er tongue feels as if it has been stuffed in her mouth like a rag to keep her quiet" (20). Eventually, she admits to being *Americana* and begins explaining in English what happened to her car. The readers cannot miss the fact that Yolanda "others" the Dominican men (her "own people"), perceiving them as dark and dangerous, as if reenacting the xenophobic racism that her own family has experienced in the United States.[22]

The subsequent irony emanating from Yolanda's "choice" to present herself as *Americana* to the island's *campesinos* is underscored by an earlier moment in this section when, at her cousin's party, she is asked about her identity: "That poet she met at Lucinda's party the night before argued that no matter how much of it one lost, in the midst of some profound emotion, one would revert to one's mother tongue. He put Yolanda through a series of situations. What language, he asked, looking pointedly into her eyes, did she love in?" (13). The point about speaking one's mother tongue in the moment of emotion foreshadows, of course, Yolanda's encounter with the men on a secluded country road and sets up expectations that, in a situation like this one, she would naturally resort to Spanish. Additionally, these expectations are heightened by the fact that Yolanda, as a poet and crafter of words, obsessed with the workings of signification, is marked by the text as a character for whom language is not merely a tool of communication but mostly an aesthetic space of invention, reinvention, and enunciation of the self. Yolanda is not only hyperconscious of the process of meaning making, but she also treats language as a shelter: "In New York, she needed to settle somewhere, and since the natives were unfriendly, and the country inhospitable, she took root in the language" (141). All these expectations are foiled in the incident with the *campesinos,* pointing out that even the supposedly most intimate links like the one between one's native tongue and one's identity are not inherently stable. Thus, this performative moment of confused identity suggests that an exilic ontology is about quivering that is not always liberatory. That is, while Yolanda certainly has (unequal) access to two

cultures, the episode on the country road shows us that her quivering is first and foremost viscerally painful. Later on, in "The Rudy Elmenhurst Story," Yolanda expresses this idea poignantly: "For the hundredth time, I cursed my immigrant origins" (94); "I saw what a cold, lonely life awaited me in this country" (99).

Contrapuntally, I am reminded of an intriguing 1998 *New York Times* article, "The New Immigrant Tide: Shuttle between Worlds." Focusing on binational immigrants who "lead a double life, with gusto," the article is permeated by the tone of cheerful exhilaration describing transnational crossings. The authors explicate the idea of modern immigrants who, supposedly able to straddle two worlds freely, live out "this here-there phenomenon" in ways not experienced by earlier immigrants and migrants: "Still, for the newest immigrants, technological advances and global political and economic changes have revolutionized the relationship with the homeland—just as the American embrace of multiculturalism allows it to flourish as never before." The article opens with the story of Fernando Mateo, a dual citizen of the Dominican Republic and the United States, who "simply commutes" between the two countries, conducting his business. The authors conclude, "There is nothing fractured about his existence." And Mateo himself confirms this point: "I believe people like us have the best of two worlds. We have two countries, two homes. It doesn't make any sense for us to be either this or that. We're both. It's not a conflict."[23]

In applauding the experience of national doubleness and refusing the either/or model of monocultural identity, Mateo speaks about a hybrid selfhood as empowering and unproblematic. In a sense, we could say that this is a transnational person who metaphorically owns the "Cosmic Passport" and uses it with gusto. Although I think that most who live exilic lives understand the notion of multiple belonging, accepting the idea that a transnational existence is "not a conflict" seems prematurely celebratory. The *New York Times* article does not even mention those who, despite their wish to be transnational, often cannot go back home (political refugees, for example). Additionally, it is hard to miss the point that the idea of an "unfractured existence" that the authors foreground in their discussion of transnational identities takes us back to the humanistic notion of the "I" that historically is positioned as a whole, unfractured subject. Hence, even though Mateo's life is located between "yucca and plantains" and "bagels and lox,"[24] his in-betweenness is paradoxically refashioned as a postmodern wholeness. After all, Mateo is a shuttling transnational.

I refer to "The New Immigrant Tide" not because I want to discount the compelling experiences of people like Mateo, but because I am struck by the difference between how this article invites the general public to think about contemporary transnational crossings and the way *How the García Girls Lost Their Accents* and other exilic literature I mentioned earlier represent transcultural identities. Overwhelmingly, the transnational characters we encounter in these texts, through their unstable positioning in relation to the presumed stability of the Western self, exhibit how their identities are created in the dialectical space between pain and pleasure. And they show us how, to use Edward Said's words, "exile is fundamentally a discontinuous state of being," which complicates the logic of national identity (1984, 51). Furthermore, in Yolanda's case, her liminality reveals how she does and simultaneously does not belong to either the Dominican Republic or the United States. That is, in many ways *How the García Girls Lost Their Accents* and other above-mentioned texts are about strangers, about those who—like the Derridean idea of the *pharmakon,* signifying both remedy and poison—remain in the space of undecidability, forever quivering.

Zygmunt Bauman's theorizing of the position of the stranger is helpful to explicate my point further:

> The strangers are not, however, the "as-yet-undecided"; they are, in principle, undecidables. They are that "third element" which should not be. The true hybrids, the monsters: not just unclassified, but unclassifiable. They therefore do not question this one opposition here and now: they question oppositions as such, the very principle of the opposition, the plausibility of dichotomy it suggests. They unmask the brittle artificiality of division—they destroy the world. [The stranger] is a constant threat to the world order.
>
> (1990, 148-49)

His discussion helps us to reflect on Yolanda's complex subject position that, as an unclassifiable third element, occupies the neither/nor exilic territory. However, Bauman does not suggest that strangers are merely occupying some neutral gray area that gives them the power to be perceived as a threat to the established social order. Nor does he suggest, I believe, that the ontological position of such strangers-hybrids as "undecidables" is necessarily a liberatory one. Rather, what underscores Bauman's discussion is what I came to call a quivering subjectivity that is both dangerous and in danger. For an exile's quivering self—neither firmly here nor there, but in the space of unclassifiable categories—constantly threatens to undo the normative idea of the self, one supposedly securely positioned in a given national territory. Simultaneously

then, this exilic identity is in danger because, although it is a challenge to the historically privileged notion of the "I," it does not often count as a valid, sanctioned subject.

Interestingly, "The New Immigrant Tide" privileges the uplifting narrative of Mateo, but it also mentions Mersuda Guichard's family, whose story explores what it means to live the dangerous and in danger multicultural identity I am referring to. Although Guichard was born in Trinidad, her children "are a hybrid: part West Indian, part American—and all New Yorker." Despite the article's overall cheerful tone, the authors allow the strangerhood to speak its troubling modality in a rare moment: "The back and forth can be confusing, and some feel they fit in neither here nor there. 'Here they say, "You're from the islands,"' Starr [Guichard's daughter] said. 'In Trinidad, they call me a Yankee, and that's considered an insult.'"[25]

The sentiments that Guichard's daughter expresses are indicative of the way many American transnational exilic narratives foreground the neither/nor territory I am discussing. For example, the narrator of Hoffman's *Lost in Translation* (1989), Ewa, a Jewish-Polish exile residing in the United States, compellingly speaks of her location as being ridden with continual tension: "Of course, one of the shards sticking in my ribs suggests that maybe I'll never belong comfortably anyplace, that my sensibilities and opinions will always be stuck in some betwixt and between place." As Ewa uses the bodily imagery as a site of knowledge that foregrounds a sense of her hybrid self oscillating in the in-between space between different "I's"—past and present, Polish-Jewish and American—we see that, as she writes, "the gap cannot be fully closed" (216, 274). The "shards sticking in [her] ribs" become a metaphor for a sense of her flesh being torn and fragmented, and the place "betwixt and between" is not some idealized moment of suspension, but rather a lived experience that is both daunting and empowering. This experience of unresolvable doubleness also permeates Divakaruni's stories in *Arranged Marriage* (1995). For instance, in "Doors," Preeti, born in India but living in the United States since she was twelve, is paradoxically marked as "Indian and yet not Indian" by her husband, Deepak, who is "straight out of India" (189, 183). Ironically, Deepak thinks of Preeti's cultural location as exotic and mysterious; a sense of her mystery manifests itself in his inability to understand her desire for closed doors—for intimacy and privacy. Similarly struggling with the experience of bifocality, Jemorah, one of the protagonists of Diana Abu-Jaber's *Arabian Jazz* (1993), born in the United States of a Jordanian father and an American mother, wonders where she and her sister, Melvina, belong. Having experienced xenophobia, she probes the meaning of a legitimate Americanness: "It's not enough to be born here, or to live here, or speak the language. You've got to *seem* right." When for a moment she fantasizes about relocating to Jordan in search of "home," her cousin's words compel Jemorah to acknowledge her in-betweenness: "[T]his 'home' that you seek is not there. . . . People like you and Melvina, you won't have what your grandparents might have had. To be the first generation in this country, with another culture always looming over you, you are the ones who are born homeless, bedouins, not your immigrant parents. . . . You're torn in two. You get two looks at a world" (328, 330). And in Ariel Dorfman's autobiographical *Heading South, Looking North* (1998), the narrating "I" tells us about the resistance to "the madness of being double": "I instinctively chose to refuse the multiple, complex, in-between person I would someday become. . . . I refused to take a shortcut to the hybrid condition I have now embraced" (42).

I am not suggesting that the neither/nor territory I see revealed in these texts expresses a uniform diasporic experience that various characters share.[26] Although I draw attention to the multiplicity of national belongings, I do not intend to homogenize this location, as each needs to be analyzed in its specificity. What these voices collectively describe is an in-betweenness—a hyphenated Americanness—that threatens to rupture the nation's coherence, allowing for a critique of an exclusionary rhetoric surrounding the idea of rightful U.S. citizenry. This rupture is textually imagined in many of the narratives and certainly in *How the García Girls Lost Their Accents* as a space of nuanced resistance: to the binarized hierarchy of alien/native, as a protest against the elision of the foreigner's otherness, and as a defiance of the creation of a new "proper" subject that can successfully carry on in a new community once she moves through the trajectory of coercive assimilation. When I think about Yolanda's unbelonging, Said's words capture the conceptualization of this space: "Just beyond the perimeter of what nationalism constructs as the nation, at the frontier separating 'us' from what is alien, is the perilous territory of not-belonging" (1984, 51). It is ultimately the territory of not-belonging that discloses how the "hauntingly indeterminate" modality of transnational strangers works to "unmask the brittle artificiality of division" (Bauman 1990, 155) between the "I" rooted in nation and an exile who, by definition, is beyond nation.

Against Homogenizing Multiculturalism

Now that I have explicated the theoretical underpinnings of the exilic inbetweenness, the reader may wonder about the larger implications of these books

for studying American literature or why the category of Latina/o literature seems perhaps too narrow. Moreover, pushing this point further, I would suggest that other various alternative categories of ethnic, multicultural, or immigrant literatures that might—at a first glance—successfully classify a novel like *How the García Girls Lost Their Accents* appear insufficient and problematic as well. In situating my response, I again turn to Alvarez's words:

> And though I complain sometimes about the confusion resulting from being of neither world, and about *the marginalizations created on both sides*—the Americans considering me a writer of ethnic interests, a Latina writer (meaning a writer for Latinos and of sociological interest to mainstream Americans), or the Dominicans reaming me out, saying she's not one of us, she's not Dominican enough—though I complain about the confusion and rootlessness of being this mixed breed, I also think it's what confirmed me as a writer, particularly because I am a woman.
>
> (1998b, 174; my emphasis)

The notion that a writer like Alvarez, who does not comfortably fit in a single compartment, experiences marginalization "on both sides" shows us the importance of the double critique she submits. Both of these critiques energize resistance to the necessity of being claimed by one nation as an author. Alvarez's unease with the category of "a writer of ethnic interests" demonstrates the narrowness of a conceptualization of ethnicity as an external, exotic subcategory that becomes of interest to literary studies as Latina/o literature—hence, not quite American. Not opposed to being classified as a Latina writer or to the category of Latino literature in general, Alvarez nevertheless expresses her ambivalence about traditional literary divisions. On the other hand. In speaking out against monocultural reductive categories—what David Palumbo-Liu terms "homogenizing multiculturalism" (1995, 15), she draws our attention to the marginalization from her native circles that cast her as not adequately Dominican—a stranger whose national loyalty is suspect.[27]

In closing, Alvarez's point takes me back to Bauman's discussion of the ambivalent ontology of strangers who "gestate uncertainty." He writes that in postmodern times "the age of anthropophagic and anthropoemic strategies is over" and that "the question is no longer how to get rid of the strangers and the strange, but how to live with them—daily and permanently" (1997, 46, 55). As I explained in the introduction, the anthropophagic strategy (*devouring* the strangers) he refers to is the process of nullifying the stranger's ontological otherness by consuming his or her difference. In short, this is the process of often subtle coercive assimilation that smooths out the stranger's unsettling otherness, historically conducted in the name of cultural homogeneity. The anthropoemic strategy (*vomiting* the strangers), on the other hand, is one of ejection, a process that rests on ostracism and, ultimately, on banishing the stranger from the cultural space in question. In stating that the problem for contemporary cultures is figuring out the ways in which to live *with* the postmodern stranger, Bauman, on some level, echoes Julia Kristeva's sentiments when she writes that "the question [of foreignness] is again before us today as we confront an economic and political integration on the scale of the planet: shall we be, intimately and subjectively, able to live with the others, to live *as others,* without ostracism but also without leveling?" (Kristeva 1991, 1-2).

Bauman's and Kristeva's theoretical positions, at first glance somewhat similar, are nonetheless predicated on a crucial difference. Bauman, perhaps unconsciously, seems to maintain the "us" versus "them" division because he locates otherness and difference "somewhere else," in the space of "strangerhood." For Kristeva, however—at least the way I read it—something else is clearly at stake. Disrupting the binary logic of "I"-sanctioned native/"other"-unwanted intruder-stranger, she asks for a recognition of the foreigner's foreignness within the "I" itself. This is a much more difficult paradigm of thinking since it does not allow for the sublimation and purification of the "I," a paradigm that, in fact, allows us to question the shadow of discursive violence that envelops a privileged notion of the self. Hence, given the context of Alvarez's novel, I read Bauman's statement that "ours is a *heterophilic* age" as troubling. Foregrounding the notion of heterophilia, he means that contemporary societies, unlike during the period of modern nation-building, are generally more appreciative of difference: "postmodern times are marked by an almost universal agreement that difference is good, precious, and in need of protection and cultivation" (1997, 55). But, as we have seen in the case of Rudy Elmenhurst's parents, the idea that difference is good and precious is a form of discursive multiculturalism, that is, an abstract cultivation of diversity that ultimately serves to cohere the identity of the rightful American and stabilize the desirable homogeneous vision of a nation. Although *How the García Girls Lost Their Accents* critiques such a nonthreatening notion of difference, it does not reject the importance of multicultural consciousness. The consciousness that the novel posits is not necessarily heterophilic in Bauman's sense, but rather one that demands considering transnational locations through a lens of unresolvable tension that, while liberatory for some, for many remains the source of complex restrictions, curtailed mobility, and disenfranchisement. Certainly, the García girls occupy a posi-

tion of quivering ontologies that marks their Dominican American identities not as cosmopolitan, enviable hyphenated selves with the transnational passport in hand, but as exilic subjectivities who often painfully experience various shades of heterophilia on their very bodies.

Notes

1. See, e.g., Behdad 1993, 2000; Guarnizo and Smith 1998.

2. Even though the category of "immigrant literature" has a historically validated presence in the United States, its sanctioned deployment inadvertently creates a sense of marginalization, even ghettoization, and marks "immigrant" texts as if of special ethnic interests. I am thinking here, for example, about a 1999 anthology on immigrant writing, *The Immigrant Experience in North American Literature* (Payant and Rose 1999). The title of the book suggests the impulse I am discussing, that is, conceptualizing immigrant texts as worthy of being given a niche within the canon of American literature. In their introduction, the editors argue for this kind of literature in the following way: "First, our approach is thematic and we see no problem with discussing immigration as a theme in American literature. Second, we would argue that much of the literature discussed in these essays is of high aesthetic quality, fit to stand alongside writing by 'mainstream' American writers" (xxvi). What is troubling in these formulations is the way the immigrant texts are coded as second-class citizens for whom a special plea needs to be made based on their aesthetic literary merits.

3. Basch, Schiller, and Szanton Blanc 1994, 8. As many would point out, this is a debatable idea. For example, given the vast body of filmic work produced in the second half of the twentieth century within the category of what Hamid Naficy (2001) terms "transnational exilic cinema," this statement could be just as valid when we approach the analysis of "in-betweenness" in transnational filmmaking.

4. See Grewal and Kaplan 1994 as one of the important books in this area.

5. This is, of course, not an exhaustive list. I purposefully chose the authors whose narratives give a sense of the range of the heterogeneity of transnational identities in relation to American citizenry: Arab, Cuban, Dominican, Haitian, Indian, Korean, Polish, to name just a few. The issue of immigrant literature and its insufficient parameters to contain the work of the authors I am mentioning needs further clarification. While evaluating the positioning of the texts I am discussing in relation to American literature, the category of "immigrant writing" is the one typically evoked. For example, Alvarez, Danticat, Divakaruni, Garcia, Hoffman, Mukherjee have all been classified as immigrant authors. But such a rendition of these

writers and their work seems only partially fitting. Alvarez, Danticat, and Garcia, for example, were born outside U.S. borders, but were mainly raised and educated in the United States while maintaining connections with their respective originary places of belonging—Dominican Republic, Haiti, Cuba. Mukherjee, for instance, consciously rejects the label of an immigrant author, defiantly seeing herself as an American writer, a position for which she has been widely criticized: "I view myself as an American author in the tradition of other American authors whose ancestors arrived at Ellis Island" (Carb 1988, 650). Even though she is often classified as an Indian-American writer, she refuses the hyphen as well: "I choose to describe myself on my own terms, that is, as an American without hyphens. It is to sabotage the politics of hate and the campaigns of revenge spawned by Eurocentric patriots on the one hand and the professional multiculturalists on that other that I describe myself as an American rather than as an Asian-American" (Bharati Mukherjee, "Beyond Multiculturalism," *Des Moines Register,* October 2, 1994, 2C).

6. Carole Boyce Davies uses the interesting notion of migratory subjectivities to discuss "cross-cultural, transnational, translocal, diasporic perspectives" that allow for the redefinition of "identity away from exclusion and marginality." Her focus is the category of "black women's writing" (Davies 1998, 996).

7. In 1991, the novel won the PEN Oakland/Josephine Miles Book Award for works that present multicultural viewpoints. Reviewers and interviewers refer to *How the García Girls Lost Their Accents* as semiautobiographical, or loosely autobiographical. Given the history of Alvarez's family exile from the Dominican Republic to the United States as political refugees in flight from Rafael Trujillo's dictatorship, the connections between her life and the lives of the fictional characters in the novel seem obvious. Alvarez was brought up in the Dominican Republic and came to New York as a ten-year-old girl in 1960. In numerous interviews, she acknowledges that what she writes comes out of her experience, but it is also fictionalized, altered, expanded: "So I think definitely my story is part of that first novel. But not only my story, the stories of my people, Latinos who were also Americans, a hybrid. I was especially interested in Latinas who were also dealing with gender issues, issues about being 'nice girls' from Latino families who had to deal with the rough and tough new world to which they had come. This story, the story of women like us, was one I had never read before. That's why I felt it was necessary for me to put it down on paper." "Citizen of the World: An Interview with Julia Alvarez," in *Latina Self-Portraits: Interviews with Contemporary Women Writers,* ed. Bridget Kevane and Juanita Heredia (Albuquerque: University of New Mexico Press, 2000), 26.

8. See, e.g., Saadawi 1997, for a powerful explication of dominant "uses" of multiculturalism that become "an exhibition, a spectacle for the pleasure of others to see, to consume" (122).

9. Alvarez 1992, 160. Page numbers for further references to this novel appear in parentheses in the text.

10. For an important discussion on the way contemporary American nativism manifests itself in multiple efforts to regulate and restrict reproduction within the national boundaries, see Roberts 1997. She comments on laws that seek to control birthing of legal subjects-citizens: "Laws restricting the birth of citizens attempt concretely to control the demographics of the country. They are designed to reduce the actual numbers of disfavored groups in population, but their broader impact is mainly metaphysical. They send a powerful message about who is worthy to add their children to the future community of citizens. Denying dark-skinned immigrants the right to give birth to citizens perpetuates the racist ideal of a white American identity" (205).

11. Susan Miller, "Caught between Cultures," review of *How the García Girls Lost Their Accents,* by Julia Alvarez, *Newsweek,* April 20, 1992, 78.

12. Heather Rosario-Sievert, "Conversation with Julia Alvarez," *Review: Latin American Literature and Arts* 54 (spring 1997): 33. In *Something to Declare,* Alvarez, who now lives in Vermont, includes "A Vermont Writer from the Dominican Republic," a response to a query asking how she defines herself as a writer: "Jessica Peet, a high-school student, read my first novel, *How the García Girls Lost Their Accents,* in her Vermont Authors class and wanted to know if I considered myself a Vermonter" (xiv). In her essay, Alvarez stresses her doubleness: "So, yes, although I am from a tropical island, I am also a Vermont writer" (195). She mentions that, as a Vermont writer, she joins the company of such well-known authors as Jamaica Kincaid and Aleksandr Solzhenitsyn, among others, who, like her, defy the logic of monocultural belonging. She says, "Certainly none of us are Vermont writers in the way my old-time Vermont neighbor defines the term" (187). See also "Doña Aida, with Your Permission," in *Something to Declare,* an essay in which Alvarez further explains her hybridized identity that is "of neither world" (174) as a "pan-American, a gringa-dominicana, a synthesizing consciousness" (175).

13. Karen Castellucci Cox comments on the condition of the exilic in-betweenness explicated in the novel: "Thus, living between two cultures creates its own kind of 'dis-ease'—a discomforting consciousness of things missing, neither a language, nor a culture, nor an extended family within which to position oneself" (2001, 135).

14. Alvarez mentions that, although one could see *¡Yo!* as a continuation of the García family story, the novel is more about the process of writing and debunking

the myth of an artist as the sole source of the creation of the story: "[¡*Yo!*] suggests that the idea of the artist as an elite who has exclusive rights to the story is wrong. . . . And part of the novel is what price the people in an artist's life have to pay. We're always hearing about the anguish and the pain of the artist but not about the people who have to put up with the artist" (1998a, 141-42).

15. Roberta Rubenstein makes a good point in reading the significance of "Yoyo": "The narrator is 'Yoyo,' a nickname for the child Yolanda with a double meaning that encompasses her eventual predicament as an exile moving back and forth between two cultures" (2001, 75).

16. Donna Rifkind, "Speaking American," review of *How the García Girls Lost Their Accents,* by Julia Alvarez, *New York Times Book Review,* October 6, 1991, 14; Judith Freeman, "A Powerful Move Back to Ethnic Roots," review of *How the García Girls Lost Their Accents,* by Julia Alvarez, *Los Angeles Times,* June 7, 1991, 4.

17. For important critiques that interrogate the discourse of multiculturalism, see, e.g., Chicago Cultural Studies Group 1994; Goldberg 1994; Sharpe 2000; Shohat 1998; Wallace 1994; and Žižek 1997. Goldberg's essay is particularly valuable for sketching out the history of multiculturalism, which arose as a response to monoculturalism, understood as both an intellectual ideology and an institutional practice of the first half of the twentieth century. Of interest to my project is his discussion of the "homogenizing, assimilative thrust of conservative multiculturalism" (26). Other critical terms used are "corporate multiculturalism" (Chicago Cultural Studies Group critiques); "liberal multiculturalism" (Sharpe); "liberal-pluralist multiculturalism" (Shohat); multiculturalism based on "monological identities" (Wallace); and "Western liberal multiculturalism," or Eurocentrist "racism with a distance" (Žižek).

18. Some time ago my department discussed the need to hire a specialist in non-Western literature. The conversation emphasized how much we would profit from having a special person whose work would promote diversity. The unspoken assumption that underlined our discussion was that all the rest of us, the regular faculty, simply teach literature, and hence we do not need to be preoccupied with the issues of diversity. Diversity within this discourse is marked by specialness; an attractive bonus nowadays that, traditionally, is attached to scholars of color who are marked as multicultural specialists.

19. I discussed these ideas with my students in a world literature course, and my predominantly white students were interested to hear a black female student's comment that she routinely receives e-mail notes from the Office of Multicultural Affairs on our campus. The white students never received any notes from this office.

20. Ella Shohat and Robert Stam take up this issue in *Unthinking Eurocentrism*: "Eurocentric thinking, in our view, is fundamentally unrepresentative of a world which has long been multicultural. At times, even multiculturalists glimpse the issues through a narrowly national and exceptionalist grid, as when well-meaning curriculum committees call for courses about the 'contributions' of the world's diverse cultures to the 'development of *American* society,' unaware of the nationalistic teleology underlying such a formulation. 'Multiculturedness' is not a 'United Statesian' monopoly, nor is multiculturalism the 'handmaiden' of US identity politics. Virtually all countries and regions are multicultural" (1994, 4-5). My thinking on this subject is informed by my pedagogical experiences, especially when it comes to the formulation of world literature syllabi. The predominant assumptions made by curricula committees come from the idea that the literary texts placed on such syllabi should emphasize the benefits of learning about other cultures, supposing that students do not need to scrutinize their own cultural positions. Hence, my students are often surprised to see on my syllabus such American transnational novels as García's *Dreaming in Cuban* or Alvarez's *How the García Girls Lost Their Accents* because these texts, largely positioned within the American context, do not fit the traditional category of world texts.

21. I thank Donna Perry for drawing my attention to this point.

22. Ibis Gomez-Vega makes a similar point about Yolanda's encounter, suggesting that "having been raised on American television and the American fear of everything that is different, Yolanda learns to associate her own people with the negative stereotypes that she absorbs almost unconsciously as she becomes an adult in the United States" (1997, 238).

23. Deborah Sontag and Celia W. Dugger, "New Immigrant Tide: Shuttle between Worlds," *New York Times,* July 19, 1998, sec. 1, 1, 28A.

24. Ibid., 1.

25. Sontag and Dugger, "New Immigrant Tide," 30.

26. Jenny Sharpe's caution is pertinent here: "Instead of treating transnational diasporas as homogeneous groups, we need to exercise vigilance about locating their members within specific racial formations" (2000, 112).

27. I am indebted to Shohat's discussion on the inadequacy of "the single-hyphen boxes" when it comes to the delineation of hyphenated Americanism. See her introduction to *Talking Visions* (1998, 7).

Raphael Dalleo and Elena Machado Saez (essay date 2007)

SOURCE: Dalleo, Raphael, and Elena Machado Saez. "Writing in A Minor Key: Postcolonial and Post-Civil Rights Histories In The Novels Of Julia Alvarez." In

The Latino/a Canon and The Emergence of Post-Sixties Literature, pp. 134-57. New York: Palgrave Macmillan, 2007.

[*In this essay, Dalleo and Saez survey Alvarez's writing career to demonstrate how she has progressed from focusing on personal topics to tackling political and social issues in her novels.*]

Like Cristina Garcia, Julia Alvarez belongs to the generation of Latina writers who achieved remarkable critical and popular success during the 1990s. Alvarez is perhaps the most prolific of this group, publishing five novels, a book of essays, four collections of poetry, four children's books, and two works of adolescent fiction between 1991 and 2006. While writers from this generation—especially women whose work is not obviously ghetto-centric—have been criticized for achieving their market success at the expense of the political ideals of the Sixties generation, Alvarez engages that past directly, returning throughout her writing to the legacy of anticolonialism in order to thematize and think through the role of the contemporary writer in relation to politics and the market. Far from withdrawing from the messy world of politics, Alvarez's writing has progressively ventured further and further into that field. In this chapter, we will argue that Alvarez's work has evolved from an early desire for an autonomous art free of external demands to a richer conception of the author as a kind of public intellectual, positioning writing as a process intimately connected with history and social struggles. Beginning from Alvarez's hyper-personal first novel, *How the García Girls Lost Their Accents* (1991), to the later *In the Name of Salomé* (2000) and its exploration of the writer's ability to speak in the public sphere, we can see the novelist's growing awareness of her own position within the literary marketplace.[1] This trajectory develops from her first novel's depiction of the challenges the writer faces telling her personal story to the apparent exhaustion of that project in the face of the demands of the market that we see in *¡Yo!* (1997), to a consideration of political commitment as a new source of content and authority in *In the Time of the Butterflies* (1994) and *In the Name of Salomé.*

In the process of making that argument, we return to one of this book's premises: that post-Sixties Latino/a literature occupies overlapping territory between postcolonial and post-Civil Rights literatures, characterized as they are by entry into the culture industry and the crisis of the master narrative of liberation. Since postcolonial literature has essentially come to mean works written in English by writers born neither in Britain nor the United States, postcolonial studies is by definition distinct from U.S. ethnic studies, which takes as its subject groups within the United States that are not of white Anglo-Saxon Protestant descent. At the same time, the two fields share many overlaps and continuities. For example, some of the conceptual tools of postcolonial studies have been both inspired and appropriated by ethnic studies in the United States. The most noticeable efforts to connect those traditions have been to adapt some of the strategies and concepts of postcolonial studies to examining U.S. ethnic literatures, in such collections as *Beyond the Borders: American Literature and Post-colonial Theory* (Madsen) or *Postcolonial Theory and the United States* (Singh and Schmidt). The impulse exhibited in these cases is toward showing how postcolonial theorizing—for example, of the mutual implication of margin and center or of culture as a site of domination and resistance—can be imported into American studies.

In addition to this tendency to apply postcolonial theory to U.S. ethnic literatures, another more historically-minded trend has been to discuss the ways in which social movements in the United States cleared space for the ascendance of postcolonial studies in the academy. Fredric Jameson and John Carlos Rowe among others in American studies have written about this history, as well as Robert Young and Gayatri Spivak from postcolonial studies. That history forms an important backdrop to our argument. At the same time, our project positions the post-Civil Rights and postcolonial era as primarily a post-Sixties period, a simultaneous critique of and nostalgia for the politics made possible by that decade's struggles within and outside the United States. Rather than applying postcolonial concepts to a U.S. context, we will argue that looking at the transnational connections between the United States and the postcolonial world—in this case, examining a Latino/a-Caribbean literature that shows the interdependence of these spaces—we can see parallels or points of contact and overlap between the literary and cultural history of the United States and the rest of the Americas. In so doing, we can see that contemporary Latino/a literature is one of the postcolonial and U.S. ethnic literatures responding to a change from a modernist, anticolonial form of literature to a postmodern, postcolonial one.

POSTCOLONIALISM, U.S. ETHNIC STUDIES, AND THE POST-SIXTIES

Looking at Julia Alvarez's career as a whole, rather than focusing on an individual novel as representing either ethnic or postcolonial experience, allows us to see how her work continues to migrate between the categories of "ethnic" and "postcolonial." Because of this complex positioning, the novels become an especially productive occasion for placing these two approaches in dialogue in order to see the related contexts that have energized both intellectual fields. Born in New York City to Dominican parents and writing in English, Alvarez clearly fits the profile of a U.S. ethnic writer. Her novels trace the transnational route between Latin America and the United States, with her first novel, *How the García Girls Lost Their Accents,* focusing on the immigrant experience in the United States and the young girls' ambivalent acceptance of their acculturation. With this perspective in mind, critics have emphasized Alvarez's resemblance to such U.S. ethnic writers as Sandra Cisneros, Esmeralda Santiago, and Edwidge Danticat.[2] In the essay "On Finding a Latino Voice," Alvarez herself credits Maxine Hong Kingston's *Woman Warrior* as an inspiration (132). Moreover, essays about Alvarez have appeared in such anthologies of U.S. ethnic literature as *Beyond the Binary: Reconstructing Cultural Identity in a Multicultural Context* (Powell) or *Evolving Origins, Transplanting Cultures: Literary Legacies of the New Americans* (Alonso Gallo and Dominguez Miguela).

At the same time, Alvarez does not fit perfectly into the U.S. ethnic mold. Although she was born in the United States, she spent most of her early life in the Dominican Republic. Rather than this motherland becoming an idealized memory—as it does, for example, in Cristina Garcia's *Dreaming in Cuban*—the Dominican Republic remains a historically real and contested locale in Alvarez's work. In fact, while many of Alvarez's novels, beginning with *How the García Girls Lost Their Accents,* have been set primarily in the United States and focused on a U.S. ethnic experience, others have moved away from this setting. For example, *In the Time of the Butterflies* takes place entirely in the Dominican Republic. Alvarez consequently appears to be a prime candidate for a postcolonial approach; she is an English-language writer working through the inheritance of colonialism in the nations created by the end of the modern colonial era. Certain critics thus dub Alvarez a postcolonial writer and analyze her work as diasporic or Caribbean.[3] By downplaying her location in the United States, these approaches tend to frame Alvarez as a native informant or translator of her Third World history.

We argue that by casting her novels as neither purely American nor Other, Alvarez positions herself at the intersection of U.S. and Caribbean history, part of what we reference in chapter 3 as an "Other American" literature. Attending to Alvarez's hemispheric perspective emphasizes her most significant contributions to rethinking the relationships within the Americas. Many readings of Alvarez's fiction focus on the way in which she "write[s] making bridges that link margin and center" and "deftly connects two different cultures" (Bados Ciria 406). In emphasizing the "difference"

between the United States of America and the rest of the Americas, this celebratory multiculturalist reading—of the way in which "straddling two worlds" gives Alvarez a privileged vantage point (Jacques 22)—tends to obscure the historical inextricability of those "two different cultures." We suggest that Alvarez's novels return again and again to hemispheric history to undercut this understanding of the United States as separable from Latin America and the Caribbean. To highlight this context, Alvarez's early novels depict the effects of U.S. foreign policy and the ways in which decisions made in Washington are felt throughout the region. One recurring example of this connection appears in both *In the Time of the Butterflies* and *How the García Girls Lost Their Accents,* as the United States first supports and then cuts loose an anti-Trujillo underground movement, resulting in the massacre that the oldest Mirabal sister witnesses and that causes the García family to flee the island.

While this example still tends to figure the United States as an agent of history whose actions ripple throughout the Americas, an even more fundamental shift in the rethinking of hemispheric history appears in *In the Name of Salomé* through its contextualization of events in U.S. history as part of larger world-historical processes. Early in the novel, for example, Salomé positions the U.S. Civil War as part of the dismantling of the plantation system throughout the hemisphere, mentioning "Cuba and Puerto Rico about to fight for their independence, and [. . .] the United States just beginning to fight for the independence of its black people" (25). Placing U.S. history into this broader context contests the tendency toward American exceptionalism. A number of times, the novel's main characters, in looking at the United States with the eyes of outsiders, see resemblances to the so-called banana republics to the south. Camila notes that "in Washington, Senator McCarthy is launching a purge not unlike those of Batista's secret police" (69), while Salomé mentions an episode in which "American president Garfield was shot by a man who had been caught stealing stationery inside the White House. Mr. Garfield had been trying to reform his government, and this petty thief had been refused a job earlier" (184). In this way, the United States becomes a part of New World history, not only as its main protagonist but also as just another player with a history of corruption and turmoil not so different from those of its neighbors.

Because Alvarez's work calls attention to these contexts, it cannot be characterized as an uncritical celebration of a dehistoricized concept of cultural hybridity. At the same time, however, her writing cannot be identified with the opposite pole, because it refuses to reduce all cultural exchanges within the hemisphere to a totalizing cultural imperialism. The complex maneuvering of Alvarez's fiction speaks to Jean Franco's reservations about theories of cultural imperialism. These theories, as Franco notes, tend toward "considering media as uncontradictory expressions of the dominant ideology" (175), part and parcel of the "assumption that the effect of mass culture on the public is that which is intended by the emitter of the message" (176). Even though Franco urges the overcoming of this reductive assumption, she hesitates to entirely abandon the attention to hierarchies of production and reception enabled by the concept of cultural imperialism. She thus expresses some distrust of the critical movement in which "what was once designated 'cultural imperialism'—according to which Latin America was the passive recipient of Hollywood movies, Disney cartoons, and television serials—is now considered inventive cultural bricolage, whereby imported technologies and fashions are used to create new cultures" (199). She challenges us to construct an oppositional political project able to navigate between these two imperatives—to keep in mind the critique of unequal power positions undergirding the concept of cultural imperialism, while acknowledging the lesson of post-colonialism's deconstruction of margin and center, namely that hegemony is never total.

Alvarez's work is located precisely at the intersection of these demands. Just as *In the Name of Salomé* insists that the relationship between the United States and the Caribbean cannot be reduced to actions and reactions, the novel also represents how even those reactions remain unpredictable:

> Meanwhile, the present is being reported in dozens of recaps of the year's small and big news on television. Alaska and Hawaii have become states. The Barbie doll has been invented in imitation of dolls handed out to patrons of a West Berlin Brothel. Panty hose will now liberate women from girdles. In Cuba, the peasants are singing, "With Fidel, with Fidel, always with Fidel," to the tune of "Jingle Bells."

> (Alvarez, *Salomé* [*In the Name of Salomé*] 38)

In this case, the same U.S. foreign policy that supports Rafael Trujillo in the Dominican Republic and Fulgencio Batista in Cuba is connected to territorial expansion in the Pacific and the cultural imperialism of Barbie. The popularity of the song "Jingle Bells" in countries where snow and Santa Claus remain outside people's everyday experience appears to be a perfect illustration of the way in which the spread of U.S. culture colonizes Caribbean consciousness.[4] But in this case, the consequences of the spread of U.S. culture exceed the intentionality of its producers: while North American culture, represented by the song "Jingle Bells," may permeate the hemisphere, the purposes to which that song is put remain difficult to control and may even be deployed in the name of revolution.

Alvarez depicts the complicated relationship between the United States and the rest of the Americas from this hemispheric perspective. In addition, Alvarez's novels also call attention to the ways in which U.S. and Caribbean *literary* history overlap. The scope of her work points to the connections and fissures between the fields of U.S. ethnic and postcolonial studies, particularly the extent to which the experience of the Sixties has shaped both fields. What we have been abbreviating as the Sixties represents the height of an anticolonial struggle throughout the hemisphere, undertaken not only by the conscripts of modern colonialism in Latin America and the Caribbean but also by internally colonized populations within the United States. Furthermore, as our first chapter indicates, the movements both within and outside the United States were integrally connected with the anticolonial ideal of the intellectual as leader of the people, embodied in the United States by poet-warriors like Malcolm X, Amiri Baraka, Angela Davis, the Puerto Rican Young Lords, and the Nuyorican Poets, and internationally by intellectuals like Frantz Fanon, C. L. R. James, and Che Guevara. The social movements of decolonization gave these writers an instant source of authority to speak for their people and to wield literature as a weapon against injustice and oppression.

Alvarez's novels come from a post-Sixties historical period; she writes in an era where the anticolonial literature of action is in crisis. Her work displays ambivalence toward this loss of literary authority typical of what has come to be called both postmodern and postcolonial literatures. Postcolonial and U.S. ethnic literatures have been described as literatures of mourning, in particular mourning for the motherland or the mother tongue; the title of Alvarez's *How the García Girls Lost Their Accents* reflects this sense of loss.[5] Yet we contend being positioned in a post-Sixties moment leads both postcolonial and post-Civil Rights writers to mourn something else—a particular kind of literary vocation, a literary field in which the role of the writer is clearly defined and the writer's place assured. Alvarez offers a critique of this anticolonial ideal of the writer as spokesman and man of action; at the same time, however, she remains nostalgic for these social projects and the public voice that they offered the writer. In the rest of this chapter, we will look at the precise way in which that ambivalence is played out in her novels, and how her more recent work offers a measure of hope for a new role for the committed writer.

SELLING FAMILY SECRETS

As we have suggested, Alvarez's fiction can be grouped into two categories: the personal novels (*How the García Girls Lost Their Accents* and *¡Yo!*), which are transparently autobiographical works about the writer and her family; and the historical novels (*In the Time of the Butterflies* and *In the Name of Salomé*), which center on heroic figures from Dominican history. Alvarez's first novel reflects her pursuit of the personal; *How the García Girls Lost Their Accents* is an overtly autobiographical account of the private tribulations of an immigrant family in the United States.[6] With a large and mobile family as its collective protagonist, the novel includes multiple points of view and changing narrators to allow everyone's story to be told. What emerges as the novel's central interest is the tension between the stories of the ensemble and the individual figure of Yolanda García. As we learn that she is the sister who loves to tell stories and aspires to be a poet, we begin to see her as the author's double. The novel begins and ends with her perspective, and her struggles to establish and maintain her voice take center stage throughout. At the same time, Alvarez expresses anxiety within these personal novels that autobiographical fiction involves selling herself and her family—that the entry of these stories into the market involves an unacceptable commodification of the private sphere.

While the *bildungsroman* is often read as an allegory of the writer's struggle to establish his or her own voice, *How the García Girls Lost Their Accents* appears to depict a loss of voice for Yolanda or at least a submerging of her individual voice as we move forward in time.[7] It is a paradoxical loss because the plot's reverse chronology means that the novel begins with Yolanda's story being told in the third person and ends with her speaking directly to us in the first. Reading forward in time, however, the chapters from the young Yolanda's life are narrated in the first person, while the chapters from her adult life are told in the third person. The crucial moment for this loss of voice, the chapter in which Yolanda's narrative switches from first person to third, occurs when she suffers a nervous breakdown and has to be institutionalized. The breakdown manifests itself in Yolanda's losing her ability to communicate. Her collapse begins as a primarily verbal problem, with Yo hearing her husband speaking "babble babble" to her and being able to respond to him only with "babble babble babble babble" (Alvarez, *García Girls* [*How the García Girls Lost Their Accents*] 78). In trying to write a one-line note telling him she is leaving, she finds that the problem has seeped into her writing:

> *I'm going to my folks till my head-slash-heart clear.* She revised the note: *I'm needing some space, some time, until my head-slash-heart-slash-soul*—No, no, no, she didn't want to divide herself anymore, three persons in one Yo. *John,* she began, then she jotted a little triangle before *John. Dear,* she wrote on a slant. She had read in a handwriting analysis that this was not the

style of the self-assured. *Dear John, listen, we both know it's not working. "It's?"* he would ask. *"It's, meaning what?"* Yo crossed the vague pronoun out.

(78)

After this failed attempt at authorship, Yo returns to her parents but finds herself repeating what people around her say, as well as "quot[ing] famous lines of poetry and the opening sentences of the classics" (79). This lack of creativity and control clearly poses a problem for a writer. The chapter identifies the beginning of Yolanda's recovery as the moment when she comes up with something original to say. The recovery, we would like to suggest, is only partial: from the chapter describing this breakdown, set in 1972, to the novel's final sequential chapter, set in 1989, Yolanda's narrative never again appears in the first person, as though something has permanently stifled the author's creative voice.

The novel's final line, where Yo admits to a "violation that lies at the center of my art" (290), is a good place to begin to determine what stands in the way of her authorial voice. Coming in the novel's first sequential chapter, titled "The Drum," this admission points to her own discomfort with the competing responsibilities she feels to both her family and her craft. Within that chapter, her identification of what she terms this "violation" comes after a story involving a young cat and its family. In this story, Yo takes a newborn kitten away from its mother to make it into a pet, naming the black kitten Schwartz. Although Yo soon releases the kitten, the mother cat returns to haunt her dreams. In the mind of the older Yolanda remembering this episode, the cat is clearly associated with her writing life:

> The cat came back, on and off, for years [. . .] I began to write, the story of Pila, the story of my grandmother. I never saw Schwartz again [. . .] I grew up, a curious woman, a woman of story ghosts and story devils, a woman prone to bad dreams and bad insomnia. There are still times I wake up at three o'clock in the morning and peer into the darkness. At that hour and in that loneliness, I hear her, a black furred thing lurking in the corners of my life.

(290)

Two anxieties appear very clearly in this dream. Most obviously, the emphasis on the cat's blackness via its name and physical nature foregrounds the author's working through her conflicted relationship with the Dominican pueblo; from the first pages of the novel to the last, the interactions between the young García girls and the mostly black maids, cooks, and other servants of the household remain strained.[8] The story about the kitten also fits the novel's pattern of Yo's curiosity getting the best of her; she seems never to respect the boundaries of others and repeatedly underestimates the dangers of crossing them. Especially in the context of the surrounding chapters, then, we can also see how Yo's remorse for taking the kitten away from its mother stands in for the author's fear that she has transgressed something sacred in stealing her family's private stories and making them public. Yo is not the only one to violate this family privacy; it happens throughout the novel as other family members participate in gossip and storytelling about one another's secrets. What makes Yolanda's violation appear more serious and far-reaching is the entry of her stories into the marketplace via publication.

In the stories immediately preceding, "The Drum," the effect of publicity on art appears as an explicit subject. The chapter "Still Lives," also from the section "1960-1956," allows one of Yolanda's sisters, Sandi, to recount her own tentative entry into the world of cultural production as she takes painting lessons at the house of Doña Charito and Don José, a neighborhood couple who met while studying art in Europe. Sandi's access to those lessons is enabled by money in two distinct ways. First, Don José cannot make a living as an artist, meaning that "his wife was having to take in students in order to paya the bills" (243). But rather than a story of a starving artist unable to see his work, Don José's problem comes from his *success*: "Several years back, he had been commissioned to sculpt the statues for the new National Cathedral, but the dedication had taken place in an empty church. There were rumors. Don José had gone crazy and been unable to finish this colossal project" (243). With patronage having thus corrupted Don José's creativity, the couple is left in the paradoxical position of having to further prostrate themselves before the forces of the market when Sandi's parents are seeking a teacher for her: "As I understand it, at first Doña Charito was insulted at the de la Torre request: she was an *artiste*; she took on apprentices, not children. But paid in advance in American dollars, she made an exception in our case" (243). In this story—which ends with the surprisingly talented Sandi breaking her arm and, in a parallel to Yo's loss of voice, having to give up becoming a painter herself—we see the various ways in which money and the market are both necessary to the artist yet crippling to creativity at the same time.

Alvarez's third novel, *¡Yo!,* returns to the same set of characters and begins with the premise of the writer's silence. As the title suggests, *¡Yo!* moves away from telling the story of the family and focuses entirely on Yolanda. Yet despite becoming the novel's center, Yolanda's voice is completely absent from *¡Yo!* Each chapter is told from the point of view of someone around Yo, but we see nothing from Yo's own perspec-

tive. Various family members, friends, and acquaintances attest to the ways in which Yolanda's stories have affected them. The first and last chapters are narrated by Yo's mother and father respectively, each talking about the ways that Yo's stories have gotten them into nearly life-threatening trouble. Her mother tells of a visit by a social worker just after the family arrives in the United States, a visit occasioned by Yo's telling stories at school about her family life; the mother fears throughout the interview that the family will be deported. Yo's father recounts that Yo found his gun hidden beneath the floorboards of his closet while he was part of the anti-Trujillo underground and later mentioned her findings to a general, nearly forcing the family to flee the Dominican Republic. In each case, the parent implores Yolanda not to tell stories to outsiders because of the potential dangers involved.

In addition to this parental imperative, the novel identifies other sources of Yo's loss of voice. The first of these appears in the novel's preface, which begins with one of the sisters returning to the violation at the heart of *How the García Girls Lost Their Accents*— Yo's failure to keep family matters private: "Suddenly her face is all over the place in a promo picture that makes her look prettier than she is. I'm driving downtown for groceries with the kids in the back seat and there she is on *Fresh Air* talking about our family like everyone is some made-up character she can do with as she wants" (Alvarez, *¡Yo!* 3). The promotional picture and appearance on *Fresh Air* symbolize not only Yolanda's betrayal of her family's privacy but also the literary celebrity that this violation has allowed her to achieve. In Yolanda's conversations with her sister, we see her fears that as a crossover star, she is betraying her own community and becoming a sellout.

The entry into the market represented by the appearance on National Public Radio, along with the publication demands imposed by her new tenure-track job, combine with Yolanda's family's disapproval as the primary pressures on the writer's voice. The dangers of this authorial positioning become most palpable in the novel's penultimate chapter, narrated by a stalker who embodies the threatening and menacing side effects of mainstream success. The stalker initially appears as a parody of an overzealous literary critic. He works at the University of Chicago (although not as a faculty member, but in a "shelving job") and collects her books "which I have dismembered and reassembled so that not one page is the way you wrote it, sentences spliced into different stories [. . .] every word tampered with" (280). He is able to rearrange her words to suit his purpose—in this case, to make her "sound like the babelite you are, writing your gibberish and pretending there is any word of truth to it"

(280)—because once her books have entered the market, their meaning is thrown open to a wide audience unknown to the author. This market success places the author in this story in literal peril as this stranger develops an obsession with her. Later, the publicity machine that requires the author to promote her book puts her life in danger, as the stalker finds that she will be reading at a bookstore nearby. He even takes advantage of these market forces to get her alone, posing as an interviewer and playing on her sense of obligation to promote the book in order to arrange a meeting with her: "sorry to bother you, ms. garcía, but my secretary set this up with your publisher so I'm sorry to hear you didn't get word and I sure do hope you can squeeze me in as we've planned a big feature article for Sunday with color photos and we think this will sell lots and lots of your wonderful books" (281). The commodification of the personal is thus illustrated not merely as an abstract threat to creativity and artistic integrity, but in this case a very real danger to the writer's own physical safety.

CONJURING THE ANTICOLONIAL

Without an obvious source of literary authority—like the anticolonial master narrative of liberation—these powerful and contradictory external demands on the writer drown out her voice. Yolanda finds her private self already penetrated by the public world. The personal strand of Alvarez's fiction thus depicts the postmodern author running up against the exhaustion—or at least the extreme self-referentiality—of the writer's private struggles as a source of content. Almost as an antidote to this narrowing scope, Alvarez has repeatedly returned to grand historical themes in *In the Time of the Butterflies* and *In the Name of Salomé.* In these novels, confrontations with the difficult inheritance of the past become sources of new material for the storyteller. At the same time that the history of anticolonial struggle nourishes the writer, the novels also dramatize how these near-mythical figures cast daunting shadows over their potential heirs, demanding a heroism that seems only to reinforce the hopelessness of the postcolonial, post-Civil Rights present. Both *In the Time of the Butterflies* and *In the Name of Salomé* interpolate the stories of heroic women—the Butterflies in the first case and Salomé Ureña in the second—with the narratives of those who have inherited their stories—Dedé, the Mirabal sister who survives by declining to participate in her sisters' revolutionary activities, and Camila, Salomé's daughter, who moves to the United States and becomes a professor. Dedé and Camila, left behind to make sense of the legacies of the past and to tell these stories, regard the Butterflies and Salomé Ureña as pointed challenges. If the hopes and pos-

sibilities of epic social struggles for freedom and justice have been replaced by the commercial concerns of the literary marketplace, how can the contemporary writer live up to the standard set by these women? After anticolonial modernism's heroic roar, the decentered post-Sixties writer is hard-pressed to speak in that voice of authority. Yet what if that writer refuses to give up the grand social projects of earlier generations—for example, the project that the modernist José Martí called "Nuestra America," the progress toward freedom for the America of the oppressed and disenfranchised?

The concerns of U.S. ethnic and postcolonial literatures intersect at these questions of the writer's relationship to the collective and to the public sphere. *In the Time of the Butterflies* and *In the Name of Salomé* feature a number of characters expressing the modernist anticolonial ideology of the writer as cultural combatant in the struggle to create more just social structures. In *In the Time of the Butterflies,* that identity coheres primarily in Minerva Mirabal, the original Butterfly who gets her sisters involved in the movement to overthrow the dictator, Rafael Trujillo. Her anticolonialism is readily identifiable in both her notion of what a better world will look like, and her idea of the intellectual's role in bringing about that world. Minerva has a vision of liberation: before the underground has even gotten underway, she "suggested we just take off into the mountains like the *gavilleros* had done [a generation before] to fight off the Yanqui invaders" (Alvarez, *Butterflies* [*In the Time of the Butterflies*] 56). From a young age, she instinctively imagines a society in which the realm of power is open to all; one of Dedé's first memories of Minerva is her proclaiming, "It's about time we women had a voice in running our country" (10). And finally, she firmly opposes political or economic privileges based on birth or social connections: even in prison, she refuses to be pardoned while other political prisoners remain incarcerated, and she equally distributes the care packages that she and her sisters receive, because "she says we don't want to create a class system in our cell, the haves and have nots" (234).

Minerva articulates a set of beliefs clearly identifiable as the anticolonialism we describe in our first chapter as expressed by the program of the Young Lords, the early poetry of Pedro Pietri, and other works of their contemporaries. Minerva finds inspiration in some of the same symbols deployed by these groups. She recites the poetry of Martí, who has served as a model of the poet-warrior for anticolonial movements throughout the Americas over the course of the twentieth century. According to her sister's diary, Minerva moves rapidly from Martí's poetry, recorded in an entry dated December 31, 1954, to even more politically charged material on January 14, 1955: "There was a broadcast of a speech by this man Fidel, who is trying to overturn their dictator over in Cuba. Minerva has big parts memorized. Now, instead of her poetry, she's always reciting, *Condemn me, it does not matter. History will absolve me!*" (123). The early Castro here appears as another incarnation of the anticolonial intellectual whose words and deeds awaken his people, and who serves as a model for Minerva's own political and intellectual projects.

As an anticolonial intellectual, Minerva attends to both the political and aesthetic dimensions of her project. Her earliest foray into political protest is a theater piece that she and her friend Sinita compose and enact in front of Trujillo, a play "about a time when we were free" (26). Acting out this drama of bondage and freedom for the country's centennial clearly evokes the island's present situation, with Minerva as "bound Fatherland" reciting, "Over a century, languishing in chains, / Dare I now hope for freedom from my woes? / Oh, Liberty, unfold your brilliant bow" (28). The play nearly becomes more than just a rehearsal for political action when Sinita breaks from the script. Instead of unchaining Minerva, she points her bow and arrow at Trujillo, and his security forces have to intervene. The play that Minerva and Sinita craft intends to fuse art and action, calling into question the legitimacy of the dictatorship and inspiring their fellow citizens to action. As discussed in our first chapter, this kind of political art typifies the anticolonial ideology articulated by Jesús Colón in *A Puerto Rican in New York and Other Sketches* or by Pedro Pietri in "Puerto Rican Obituary."

Salomé Ureña combines her vocation as poet with commitment to her nation's independence even more explicitly, making *In the Name of Salomé* the novel in which Alvarez most fully confronts the legacy of anticolonial opposition in the postcolonial, post-Civil Rights era. Salomé, the nineteenth-century heroine of the Dominican Republic's struggle for independence from Spain, learns her role as anticolonial poet from her father, a less successful writer and political figure who instructs her in "what a poet is supposed to do" (Alvarez, *Salomé* 53). He gives her two pithy and memorable definitions of poetry: first, not to waste her tears, as "tears are the ink of the poet" (24); and second, that the poet "merely put[s] into words what everyone else in the whole capital [is] thinking" (53). These two maxims frame poetry as an activity with a strong ethical imperative, most importantly a responsibility to the collective. Salomé takes up the pen to fulfill her father's political and artistic dreams, to write lines like *"wake up from your sleep, my Patria, throw*

off your shroud" (63) or *"your patria still in chains [. . .] The tears you shed for her have never dried"* (62).

As Salomé develops her poetic gifts, she takes her responsibility to the patria very seriously. Reading Josefa Perdomo, a popular Dominican poet who writes "lovely verses" (56). Salomé determines that "I would never write verses out of politeness. Rather than write something pretty and useless, I would not write at all" (57). Josefa thus becomes a negative model of poetry that is too frilly, too uncommitted, and too womanly. Soon afterward, Salomé sees her poetry published in the newspaper under the pseudonym Herminia, and proudly thinks of her verses in such resonantly anticolonial terms as "waking up the body politic" and "bring[ing] down the regime with pen and paper" (62). Salomé's success is assured when she overhears her aunt comparing Herminia favorably to Josefa's "more sentimental, ingratiating style." "'This Herminia is a warrior,' my aunt said proudly. 'In fact, my theory is that Herminia is really a man, hiding behind a woman's skirt'" (63). This evaluation shows how successfully Salomé manages to live up to the anticolonial ideal of the masculine poet-warrior, an achievement that turns her into a Dominican hero in her own lifetime and beyond. Yet at the same time, the act of inhabiting this persona—a performance so successful that one of the reviewers of Alvarez's novel describes Salomé without any irony as "a sort of José Martí in skirts" (Ruta 24)—takes its toll on Salomé and eventually becomes more of a burden than inspiration for those who come after her.

POSTCOLONIAL MELANCHOLIA

While these novels thus illustrate the ways in which Minerva and Salomé embody the ideals of anticolonialism, the most compelling aspect of both *In the Name of Salomé* and *In the Time of the Butterflies* is the movement between those larger-than-life women and the chroniclers who are left behind to tell their stories. Through these figures, Alvarez's novels become not so much stories about the past but narratives about rethinking our relationship in the present to the ambiguous demands of that past. The questions of authorial voice in Alvarez's personal novels resurface here as the historical novels also experiment with different points of view. While Minerva and Salomé speak in the first person, both Dedé and Camila narrate in the third person, even though as the ones left behind, they are ostensibly also the ones telling the story. Dedé and Camila find themselves like Yolanda, unable to find their own voices, overshadowed and silenced by the enormous demands placed upon them. In *In the Time of the Butterflies* it is Dedé, the one Mirabal sister who didn't participate in the underground and didn't die with the others, speaking in 1994; in *In the Name of Salomé* it is Camila, the daughter who can never live up to her mythical mother, looking back on Salomé's legacy from 1973.

Both Camila and Dedé are thus located in a distinctly post-Sixties present. Curiously, both novels skip ahead from 1960, the year of Camila's return to Cuba and the Butterflies' death, to their respective presents of 1973 and 1994. The years between 1960 and 1973—years that in shorthand we might call the Sixties—are thus absent from both novels.⁹ This absence is especially pronounced in *In the Name of Salomé*. The novel covers many of the major events of U.S. and Dominican history from Salomé's birth in 1850 to Camila's death in 1973, yet has no scenes set in revolutionary Cuba or the United States in the Civil Rights era; its timeline jumps from Camila in Vermont in 1950 to her decision to leave the United States for Cuba in 1960 to her final arrival in the Dominican Republic to prepare for her death in 1973. While other events from U.S. history feature prominently in Camila's narrative—the renaming of the hamburger as the "liberty sandwich" and the dachshund as the "liberty pup" during World War I (238) or the segregated jazz clubs that Camila visits during the 1920s (201)—no event from the Civil Rights movement in the United States is mentioned. Furthermore, since none of the action in the novel actually takes place in revolutionary Cuba—events from that period appear only as flashbacks in the 1973 epilogue—the 1960s are narrated only as the past, an experience that Camila is still working through when the novel ends.

To add to this peculiarity of periodization, it is a remarkable historical coincidence that Camila Henríquez Ureña dies the day after the Pinochet coup in Chile, which overthrew Salvador Allende's socialist government with the aid of the U.S. Central Intelligence Agency (CIA). Allende had represented the possibility of a new kind of Latin American progressivism, steering away from the model offered by a Cuban revolution that had already become increasingly centralized and dictatorial by the early 1970s. September 11, 1973, the day of Pinochet's coup, thus marks a threshold in Our America, the moment when it becomes clear that the United States will not allow a socialist government to exist in the Americas—even one that is democratically elected and not aligned with the Soviet Union. Camila's last days coincide with the end of one of the great eras of hope for the Americas, the period set in motion by decolonization in the Caribbean and the Civil Rights movement in the United States. Her reflections on Cuba from this vantage point become an important voice for the post-

colonial, post-Civil Rights era, which in many ways begins in 1973. When Camila's niece wonders, "'What would Salomé say if she could see the place now,'" Camila speaks almost directly to us today: "What would she have said, except what she must have said to herself, time after time, when her dreams came tumbling down? Start over, start over, start over" (342).

Dedé also returns to narrate the Sixties from the perspective of memory in a brief epilogue that covers the actual events of the decade in one sentence: "The coup, the president thrown out before the year was over, the rebels up in the mountains, the civil war, the landing of the marines" (Alvarez, *Butterflies* 310). Rather than recounting these events, then, the epilogue rehearses the ways in which the period continues to reverberate for Dedé even after many years. She describes the decade with a wistful, melancholic nostalgia, located much further into our postcolonial present than Camila; Dedé speaks from 1994, the year when Trujillo's own puppet president, Joaquín Balaguer, won his sixth term as president of the Dominican Republic in elections so rife with fraud that he was forced to resign before completing his term. The history of the post-Trujillo Dominican Republic is enough to depress anyone; Dedé has watched an idealistic young poet named Juan Bosch overwhelmingly win a democratic election in 1962, only to have his presidency cut short. Dedé remembers meeting Bosch and the hope he represented:

> The president dropped in for a visit. He sat right there in Papá's old rocker, drinking a frozen *limonada*, telling me his story. He was going to do all sorts of things, he told me. He was going to get rid of the old generals with their hands still dirty with Mirabal blood. All those properties they had stolen he was going to distribute among the poor. He was going to make us a nation proud of ourselves, not run by the Yanqui imperialists [. . .] At the end, as he was leaving, the president recited a poem he'd composed on the ride up from the capital. It was something patriotic about how when you die for your country, you do not die in vain. He was a poet president, and from time to time, Manolo would say, "Ay, if Minerva had lived to see this." And I started to think, maybe it was for something that the girls had died.
>
> (310)

Dedé understands how Bosch, as a "poet president," means to establish himself as the inheritor of Martí, Minerva and Salomé, both in terms of his commitment to social justice and his aesthetic sensibility. His presence in office makes it "a manageable grief" for Dedé, allowing her to begin "hoping and planning," secure in the knowledge that the death of her sisters is something she can "make sense of" because their ideals are still alive (310). Within the year, though, a coup d'état deposes Bosch, leading Dedé to question whether her sisters' struggles will ever truly bear fruit.

Just as Bosch positions himself as heir to the legacy of the Butterflies, Minerva's husband Manolo becomes another proprietor of their memories and the anticolonial hope they represent. After he is released from prison, he becomes "our Fidel" and "drew adoring crowds" wherever he went (309). But that era of anticolonial possibility comes to a close after the overthrow of Bosch's government. Manolo attempts to rise up against the new military government, and Dedé's description emphasizes the delusion and hopelessness of Manolo's rebellion:

> "Fellow Dominicans!" he declaims in a grainy voice. "We must not let another dictatorship rule us [. . .] Rise up, take to the streets! Join my comrades and me in the mountains! When you die for your country, you do not die in vain!" But no one joined them. After forty days of bombing, they accepted the broadcast amnesty. They came down from the mountains with their hands up, and the generals gunned them down, every one.
>
> (311)

Manolo fails to recognize the futility of his form of anticolonial resistance against the post-Trujillo government. Dedé calls her brother-in-law's attempted uprising a "disgrace" (311) and loses faith entirely in the myth of the heroic individual leading the people to freedom.

The novel ends with Dedé wallowing in the depths of postcolonial despair. The failures of Bosch and Manolo as well as the release of her sisters' killers shortly after the beginning of their prison sentence lead Dedé to seriously doubt the possibility of any sort of social justice. The final chapter makes clear how heavily the past weighs upon her. She has become the official keeper of the story of the Butterflies, a story she obsessively tells others despite her friend imploring her to move beyond it. She recounts the tale of the Butterflies because, as she tells this friend, "after the fighting was over and we were a broken people [. . .] we had lost hope, and we needed a story to understand what had happened to us" (313). Yet the friend's criticism—that she is "still living in the past [. . .] in the same old house, surrounded by the same old things" (312)— makes Dedé question the usefulness of her coping strategy. Is she fulfilling the demands of the Butterflies by keeping their story alive, or would it be more in keeping with their legacy to bury the past and work to transform the present? How can Dedé honor that past without obsessively reliving it?

The present that Dedé inhabits has clearly not lived up to her expectations of what the anticolonial social movements would accomplish, yet she finds she has

no way of critiquing that present or imagining an alternative to it. She describes her situation as "living to see the end of so many things, including her own ideas" (316). Attending a ceremony in honor of her sisters, Dedé sees another painful reminder of the past; President Joaquín Balaguer, Trujillo's old ally, is also in attendance. When her old friend, Lío, tries to comfort her by reassuring her that "the nightmare is over, Dedé. Look at what the girls have done," Dedé begins to voice her dissatisfaction with the post-Trujillo world that her sisters helped to inaugurate:

> He means the free elections, bad presidents now put in power properly, not by army tanks. He means our country beginning to prosper, Free Zones going up everywhere, the coast a clutter of clubs and resorts. We are now the playground of the Caribbean, who were once its killing fields [. . .] The nightmare is over, we are free at last. But the one thing that is making me tremble, that I do not want to say out loud—I'll say it once only and it's done. Was it for this, the sacrifice of the butterflies?
>
> (318)

Dedé looks at her world and sees only the failure of anticolonial modernism to produce the utopias it promised: she even remembers with bitter irony Martin Luther King, Jr.'s promise of a world that would be "free at last." Instead of social justice, she sees the spread of unfettered capitalism in the form of trade agreements and the explosion of the tourist industry, the post-Sixties economic phenomenon we refer to in chapter 4 as globalization. In Dedé's refusal to read the newspapers, she disengages from that present as an historical moment. Instead of learning from the past or using its lessons to critique the present, she becomes completely paralyzed by retelling her sisters' stories. Dedé's melancholia arises not only from her disillusionment with the modernist anticolonial struggle but also from her inability to move beyond it to formulate any other source of hope.

REVITALIZING THE POST-SIXTIES PUBLIC SPHERE

While *In the Time of the Butterflies* ultimately ends with Dedé floundering in a postcolonial melancholia that cannot move beyond the past to engage the present, *In the Name of Salomé* offers a slightly more hopeful vision of the future by taking some distance from the past. While Camila finds the present nearly as depressing and overwhelming as Dedé does, she appears to develop more effective coping mechanisms. The epilogue of *In the Name of Salomé* hints at a tentative closure to her mourning process as she briefly escapes the pull of the past to point towards the future. Camila appears throughout the novel as a potential critic of the strand of anticolonial modernism that magnifies the role of the heroic man of action as leader of the people. In particular, the novel allows Camila to develop a critique of the anticolonial vision of the intellectual as spokesperson for the people, and the forms of hegemony that this move may reproduce. Instead of the Salomé that her sons and husband want to preserve, Salomé as the national poet and hero of the independence struggle, Camila points to another side of her mother's legacy.

As the novel develops, Camila and her brother Pedro provide competing visions of preserving and honoring Salomé's legacy. The different ways in which these siblings remember Salomé and imagine themselves as writers and intellectuals shed light on their different relationships to anticolonial modernism. The Pedro of the novel is, as scholars of Latin American literature know, one of the great critics of modernismo, Pedro Henríquez Ureña. In the novel, it is Pedro who as a child reads Martí's *La Edad de Oro* (226) and as an adult frequently references Martí, as when he opens a meeting of his friends by reciting Martí's poetry. Pedro's conception of his role as writer and intellectual is perhaps best expressed when he tells Camila:

> I am continuing the fight. I am defending the last outpost. [. . .] Poetry. [. . .] I am defending it with my pen. It is a small thing, I know, but those are the arms I was given. Defending it because it encodes our purest soul, the blueprint for the new man, the new woman. Defending it against the bought pens, the dictators, the impersonators, the well-meaning but lacking in talent.

(Alvarez, *Salomé* [*In the Name of Salomé*] 125)

In explicitly equating his vocation as intellectual with the armed decolonization struggles taking place around the world, Pedro expresses the anticolonial ideal of the writer's heroic role in the social movements of the twentieth century. By emphasizing the public and action-oriented potential of poetry, Pedro positions himself as Salomé's heir and casts as illegitimate Camila's poetry, which he labels as solely for private reflection.

Although the above passage comes from a private conversation with his sister, Camila notices that everything Pedro says or writes is marked by an awareness of its potential circulation as a public document. His preferred mode appears to be the essay, a genre well suited for turning personal reflections or observations into public proclamations. Camila notes that "in one of his essays that she found in a recent journal, she was surprised to read about 'the terrible moral disinheritance of exile'" (112). Her surprise comes from the fact that she had "to learn so impersonally of her brother's sadness" (112), which he has apparently not discussed with her privately. In addition to the essay, Pedro favors lectures and speeches as

other genres that lend themselves especially well to acts of heroic enunciation. He addresses one crowd by imploring them that "we must pledge ourselves to *our* America [. . .] the America our poor, little countries are struggling to create," while betraying his insecurity in insisting that "we cannot be mere bookworm redeemers" (121). Even his letters are written "as if he already knows that in the future his correspondence will be published (he *is* that famous)" (109).

As a counterpoint to Pedro's very public conception of writing, Camila emerges as a different kind of writer. Unlike Pedro's energizing speeches, calling his people to arms for their patria, Camila uses more personal forms of writing. After reading her poetry, Pedro advises Camila that she "should keep writing for her own pleasure" (124). This advice assumes that Camila's poems, written in what she calls a "minor key" (177), are not suited for circulation in the same way as Salomé's or Pedro's heroic proclamations. Even Camila's letters, although addressed to her closest friend, Marion, remain unsent and thus never find an audience or a public. These letters offer Camila a chance to "try out a new life by writing to Marion about it," so that "if nothing else, perhaps the story of what is happening will begin to make sense to her" (189). Writing as a way of making sense of the personal appears to be Camila's conception at this point in the novel of the role that writing can play in her life—a form detached from all external demands.

Pedro deliberately invokes Martí and Salomé in order to align himself with the specific notion of the anticolonial writer that they represent. Camila initially agrees with Pedro's interpretation of Salomé, calling Pedro "the one who received their mother's legacy" (122). As the novel develops, however, Camila's own voice emerges through her growing realization that Pedro's reading of Salomé, defining her accomplishments according to a particularly masculinist, anticolonial model, attends to only one portion of her legacy, and perhaps not the most useful one in a post-Sixties world. Like many of the events in Camila's story, her letters contain direct echoes in Salomé's story. Camila's resolution that writing can serve personal and private needs comes in a chapter directly following Salomé's loss of faith in public poetry as corruptible and unfaithful to her true voice. As early as the chapter "La fe en el porvenir," Salomé begins to wonder how the poet can balance politics with personal thoughts and feelings. Her first love poem is rejected by her father as apolitical, and derided by her sister as "the worst poem you ever wrote" for its "silly language" (95). In the fourth chapter, Salomé begins to express her sexuality in "Quejas," a poem that will become a source of controversy. Her sister recognizes right away that "you can't publish this. You're la musa de la patria, for heaven's sake [. . .] Nobody thinks you have a real body" (143-4).

Salomé comes to the conclusion that she is submerging her own voice in sounding the epic calls for the nation to throw off the shackles of Spanish rule. By allowing the nation to speak through her, her own self disappears. When her husband, Pancho, dismisses her poem "Vespertina" as "personal" and "tender" (176), she insists to him, "I am a woman as well as a poet" (177). She realizes that in these newer poems, "I had begun writing in a voice that came from deep inside me. It was not a public voice" (177). Because Salomé accepts the separation of poet from woman and public from private, she is never fully comfortable with expressing that inner voice in her poetry. In absorbing these absolute oppositions, she has trouble imagining a form of writing that would allow her to represent both at once. She finally agrees that the voice that comes from "deep inside" should not be made public and cannot be the source of poetry. As a result, she gradually shifts her energy away from poetic creation into raising her children and teaching at her school. When Pancho laments the erosion of her gift, she explicitly calls her children "the only immortality I want" (268).

Dissatisfied with her public role and discouraged by her husband from writing in her private voice, Salomé begins to withdraw from poetry. This dissatisfaction derives in large part from watching everyone around her appropriate her poetry and assign her a meaning that suits their ideological frameworks. "Vespertina" becomes the impetus for a real struggle between Salomé and Pancho over her poetic vocation. He tells her:

> You must not squander away your talent by singing in a minor key, Salomé. You must think of your future as bard of our nation. We want the songs of la patria, we need anthems to lead us out of the morass of our past and into our glorious destiny as the Athens of the Americas.
>
> (177)

In figuring the past as a "morass" to escape from, Pancho demands that Salomé fulfill her role as inspiration for and even leader of her people in overcoming that past. Pancho becomes something like Salomé's press agent, reminding her that "duty is the highest virtue" (176) and not to "shirk your duties" (177), as well as urging her to produce poems for national events. He commissions a painting of her that depicts her as "prettier, whiter" and closer to "the legend *he* was creating" (44). Pancho goes so far as to revise her older poems, to mold them to his image of a national poet. Suggesting changes to some of her early poems, he

tells her, "'Trust me, Salomé, I have your future in mind'" (170). Her son Pedro later joins Pancho's effort to remake Salomé to conform to their idea of the anticolonial writer as asexual and specifically not feminine. When publishing a posthumous edition of Salomé's collected works, Pedro omits entirely some of what he calls her "intimate verses" (161), including "Quejas."

Just as Pancho is pushing Salomé into this role, however, other forces are leading her to doubt the efficacy of poetry as a weapon in the anti-colonial struggle and her own ability to control the use of her poems. Her darkest moments come when she realizes that the dictator Lilís deploys her poetry to drum up nationalist sentiment for his regime: "Hadn't I heard that Lilís himself liked to recite passages of my patriotic poems to his troops before battle [. . .] The last thing our country needed was more poems" (187). Seeing the martial and epic poetry she had written in the spirit of anticolonial opposition claimed by diametrically opposed ideologies, Salomé witnesses within her lifetime what happened in death to Martí, who has become a symbol employed by both Havana and Miami since the Cuban revolution. Public poetry, by definition available to all, defies the poet's intentions once it begins to circulate and become a signifier anyone can use.

Camila comes to the same realization in her visit to the national cemetery in Santo Domingo, as she sees that in death the heroes of the nation become symbols available to anyone with the power to appropriate them. Reflecting on the cemetery where her parents and brother rest, Camila realizes that "depending on the president, the pantheon of heroes changes, one regime's villain is the next one's hero, until the word *hero,* like the word *patria,* begins to mean nothing. That is another reason why I do not want to be buried here among the great dead" (338). As Camila reaches the end of her life, she decides to be buried not in the cemetery reserved for national heroes where her mother, father, and brother lie, but in a private plot with her half-brother and "those of us in the family who aren't famous" (333). In choosing the resting place of her body, she is literally deciding the part of the ancestral legacy that she will affirm.

In choosing to define her relationship to her mother's inheritance—a choice deliberately opposed to Pedro's "dying wish" to lie next to Salomé (338)—Camila resolves to be, as she puts it, not the "clarion call," but the "chorus": "She, too, wants to be part of that national self-creation. Her mother's poems inspired a generation. Her own, she knows, are not clarion calls, but subdued oboes, background piano music, a groundswell of cellos bearing the burden of a melody. Every revolution surely needs a chorus" (121). Joining the chorus rather than the actors occupying center stage appears to be the reason that Camila tells her own story in the third person, while Salomé's story is told in the first person. Camila has decided that "there are other women she can be besides the heroine of a story" (126). Yet in the novel's epilogue, Camila's narration switches from third person to first, just as Dedé speaks in the first person for the first time in the epilogue to *In the Time of the Butterflies.* In these final chapters, narrating the stories of anticolonial struggles appears to give Dedé and Camila their own voices in a way that Yolanda García's personal stories can never sustain.

Camila chooses teaching, rather than Pedro's lecturing, as the activity best suited to fulfilling her mother's legacy. Camila becomes an educator not to lead the people forward but rather to participate in the everyday struggle to build a patria. As a teacher, Camila can keep the dreams of Salomé and Martí alive, and she does maintain a religious devotion to the cult of anticolonial modernism, praying to her own holy trinity "in the name of Hostos, Salomé, José Martí" (339). In this spirit, Camila initially perceives the Cuban revolution as the fulfillment of Salomé's dreams, noting that "at last I found her the only place we ever find the dead: among the living. Mamá was alive and well in Cuba, where I struggled with others to build the kind of country she had dreamed of" (335). It is tempting for Alvarez as a U.S. ethnic writer to flee from the bleak post-Civil Rights United States to redemption in the Third World. But as the epilogue unfolds, that optimism is gradually refined. By 1973 Castro's government had already lost the support of most Latin American intellectuals after Heberto Padilla was jailed for writing poems deemed counter-revolutionary. Yet Camila sides neither with Castro's regime nor with the critics of the revolution. When her half-brother bitterly calls Cuba "the experiment that has failed," Camila argues against giving up on the dream: "That is not the point [. . .] We have to keep trying to create a patria out of the land where we were born. Even when the experiment fails, especially when the experiment fails" (342). The revolution is not the final product, according to Camila, but the struggle to get there.

The novel ends with this lesson—that not only can Camila live in a minor key and still move our Americas closer to liberation, but in fact it may be only such mundane acts that can bring about the desired outcome. Unlike Dedé, trapped in telling and retelling her sisters' story, teaching offers Camila a post-utopian alternative. The great actors, like Salomé and Martí, have seen their dreams of transforming the world go awry. The novel's ultimate critique of

anticolonial modernism comes in Camila's response to her niece's comment, that she "[doesn't] think Castro is the answer." Camila responds: "It was wrong to think that there was an answer in the first place, dear. There are no answers [. . .] It's continuing to struggle to create the country we dream of that makes a patria out of the land under our feet. That much I learned from my mother" (350). Unlike the lecture format favored by Pedro, in which the lecturer processes reality for his followers and presents them with a coherent plan for action, Salomé offers the model of the teacher who values social justice and admits that the path cannot be predicted or dictated, but must be created as part of a common struggle to make meaning.[10]

At the end of her life, Camila comes to terms with the meaning of her mother's life, and decides that while she won't give up the struggle to remake the world, the struggle is also "to love the flawed thing we see" (339). While for Dedé, the flawed postcolonial world is a source of disillusionment, Camila refuses to succumb to despair. Although the revolutionary great leap forward that inspired anticolonialism no longer seems possible, Camila finally decides that it is through these fits and starts that Our America will be built, one person at a time. As she says, she "had never thought of the real revolution as the one Fidel was commanding" (347). The real revolution is not the change in leadership at the top; rather, it is found among the women sorting coffee beans who draw inspiration from Salomé's poems that Camila reads to them.

In the Name of Salomé ends with the hopeful scene of a blind Camila teaching a poor young Dominican boy to read her mother's name on her gravestone:

> The boy has guided my hand, and now I put my hand over his. "Your turn," I say to him. Together we trace the grooves in the stone, he repeating the name of each letter after me. "Very good," I tell him when he has done this several times. "Now you do it by yourself." He tries again and again, until he gets it right.
>
> (353)

Just as when she reads her mother's poetry to the coffee bean sorters, Camila is passing on her mother's heroic legacy to a new generation in having the boy trace Salomé's name; but just as importantly, she is passing on the quotidian triumph of literacy to the boy. The intellectual here is not the bearer of a transcendent and illuminating truth that only she can see, for the boy is leading Camila as much as she leads him, and eventually, the two will get it right together. Early in the novel, Camila mentions the "bad habit of writers, creating the world rather than inhabiting it" (113); she could be speaking to Minerva and Salomé as well as Malcolm and Che. In the end,

Camila offers an alternative to the anticolonial dictum that it is the duty of the writer to show the people how to create a better world. Composing in her minor key, she is one of the people, just one of the many who will work together to form a free and just society.

This ending of *In the Name of Salomé* connects to what has become another strand in Alvarez's writing. In addition to Alvarez's personal and historical novels, she has recently begun to write books for children and adolescents. In *The Secret Footprints* (2000), *A Cafecito Story* (2001), *How Tía Lola Came to Stay* (2001), *Before We Were Free* (2002), and *Finding Miracles* (2004), Alvarez is engaged in writing as an explicitly pedagogical vocation. The novels of the 1990s lamented the irrevocable loss of the utopian horizon—progressive hope offers no sustenance in either *How the García Girls Lost Their Accents* or *¡Yo!* and it appears only as something to be mourned in *In the Time of the Butterflies.* But Alvarez's new movement into children's literature resonates with Camila's final insight—that politics is a "minor," everyday, and collective activity. These latest works point toward Alvarez's contribution to the literature of the postcolonial, post-Civil Rights Americas, a literature in which politics takes place not only on the level of contests for national sovereignty but also in everyday struggles to build a better world.

Notes

1. Alvarez's novel *Saving the World* (2006) was published after this chapter had already been completed. It makes explicit the connections between the historical and personal strands that the earlier novels had only suggested. The latest novel uses the same alternating structure as *In the Name of Salomé,* but now the contemporary figure is a post-Sixties Dominican-American woman writer, suffering from writer's block explicitly derived from (a) a feeling of impotence about her ability to change the world; (b) the pressure put on by her agent and publisher; and (c) the attack on her authenticity at the hands of "Mario González-Echavarriga, the patrón of Latino critics," who labels her "a Machiavellian user of identity" who "undermine[s] the serious political writing by voices long kept silent" (Alvarez, *Saving* 20). This example shows Alvarez, more than perhaps any other writer we have discussed in this book, in direct conversation with her critics—in this case apparently referencing Roberto González Echevarría, whose review of *In the Time of the Butterflies* in the *New York Times Book Review* questioned Alvarez's ability as an "Americanized Dominican woman" to "really be able to understand" Dedé and the other Dominican women of the novel (28).

2. For example, see Carine Mardorossian's essay "From Literature of Exile to Migrant Literature" on Alvarez and Danticat, or Ellen Mayock's "The Bicultural Construction of Self in Cisneros, Alvarez, and Santiago."

3. For example, David Thomas Mitchell in his essay "The Accent of 'Loss': Cultural Crossings as Context in Julia Alvarez's *How the García Girls Lost Their Accents*" repeatedly refers to Alvarez as a "postcolonial writer."

4. Kamau Brathwaite is one of the Caribbean artists who talks about how his early poetry, about snow falling on cane fields, illustrates the influence of the Northern imaginary on the Caribbean mind. See *Three Caribbean Poets on Their Works: E. Kamau Brathwaite, Mervyn Morris, Lorna Goodison* (Chang).

5. The reader is again referred to "The Accent of 'Loss'" for a reading of *García Girls* as a melancholic novel.

6. We call Alvarez's first novel "overtly autobiographical" because in her personal essays, for example those collected in *Something to Declare,* Alvarez recounts many of the same anecdotes as episodes from her life that are attributed to her characters in *How the García Girls Lost Their Accents* and *¡Yo!*

7. Bakhtin discusses the *bildungsroman* in these terms in *The Dialogic Imagination.* Lisa Sánchez González invokes Bakhtin's theorization of genre in her chapter "The Boricua Novel: Civil Rights and 'New School' Nuyorican Narratives" (106).

8. Marta Caminero-Santangelo notes that "the dangers of speaking for/representing others are arguably the central theme of *¡Yo!*" (Caminero-Santangelo, "Speaking" 61), in making the broader case for Alvarez's novels as meditations on the relationship of the author to the people she represents.

9. As in Stavans's bookends or Alvarez's historical novels, the Sixties become a conspicuous absence in Cristina Garcia's *Dreaming in Cuban* as well. The main action in *Dreaming in Cuban* begins in 1972 and moves forward to 1980. Interspersed with this narrative, Celia's letters provide historical background beginning in 1935 and end at the beginning of 1959. The novel thus spans the period from 1935 to 1980, skipping only the years between 1959 and 1972.

10. One of the most famous theorists of the relationship between pedagogy and revolution, Paolo Freire, describes this form of lecturing as a two-stage process: "During the first, [the lecturer] cognizes a cognizable object while he prepares his lessons in his study or laboratory. During the second, he expounds to his students about that object" (67). As a result, the lecturer-intellectual speaks to the people with conclusions already drawn, trying only to persuade them to pursue this cause. By contrast, Camila eventually arrives at a view of pedagogy as a process of negotiation and dialogue.

Marta Caminero-Santangelo (essay date 2007)

SOURCE: Caminero-Santangelo, Marta. "Speaking for Others: Problems of Representation in the Writing of Julia Alvarez." In *On Latinidad,* pp. 73-92. Gainesville: University Press of Florida, 2007.

[*In the essay below, Caminero-Santangelo rejects the notion that writers own the authority to speak for their entire ethnic communities, and she commends Alvarez for highlighting the differences between her characters and the communities they represent.*]

The rise of ethnic literary studies, including Latino/a studies, is predicated, it would seem, on the given that groups must be allowed to speak for themselves, to represent themselves. And at face value, this seems an absolutely indisputable claim. Nevertheless, it hides some pressing difficulties—for example, those invoked by the two senses of "representing." As outlined by Gayatri Spivak in "Can the Subaltern Speak?" "representation" has two quite distinct senses: "representation as 'speaking for,' as in politics, and representation as 're-presentation,' as in art or philosophy" (275). Spivak insists that the two meanings must be considered separately when discussing the dynamics of speaking *for* a particular group, for "[t]he complicity [of these separate meanings] can only be appreciated if they are not conflated by a sleight of word" (277).

The "complicity" Spivak wants to highlight, by emphasizing the separate meanings of "to represent," lies in the assumption that a "representative" of a particular group can accurately and successfully "re-present" (reproduce) the needs, desires, and interests of the entire group. To conflate the two meanings of "represent" (what Spivak calls "proxy" and "portrait" [276]) is to assume as a given that any representative of a group can fully, faithfully re-present the group to others; thus the serious problems or risks of re-presentation go unexplored when a representative (someone positioned to "speak for" the group) is doing the re-presenting.

Writers are often called on to "represent" their ethnic groups in the slippery sense about which Spivak warns: that of colliding both meanings of "represent." It is not simply that an ethnic writer is viewed as *a* "representative" of a particular culture (in the simple sense of speaking from within that culture to a larger audience that lies, in part, outside of it), but that she is assumed to be *representative* of that culture. Take, for example, the comment by a writer for *New York Magazine,* printed as a selling point on the 1983 Signet paperback cover of Toni Morrison's *Tar Baby,* which proclaims Morrison to be "the D. H. Lawrence of the black psyche." Every time we invoke phrases such as

"the black psyche" or "the Latino/a experience," we reveal the presumption that this experience is fairly singular, homogeneous, and "knowable" by any representative, who can therefore "speak for" the group. Thus we are led to what Trinh T. Minh-ha has called the "automatic and arbitrary endowment of an insider with legitimized knowledge about her cultural heritage and environment": "An insider can speak with authority about her own culture, and she's referred to as the source of authority in this matter" (374). Representatives of a group, then, are assumed to have the "authority" to re-present the group accurately. The converse, of course, is that if you are not a "representative" (recognized proxy) of a particular group, then you cannot re-present it.

I have already discussed the deeply problematic assumption that a Latina/o from one national-origin group could in any sense be said to be "representative" of Latinos/as from another group—hence the fundamental problem with Latino/a panethnicity. Yet critics have often made such assumptions in practice. Roberto González Echevarría begins his essay on Julia Alvarez's second novel, *In the Time of the Butterflies,* by establishing what he sees as "the central concern of Hispanic writers in this country [the United States]": "the pains and pleasures of growing up in a culture and a language outside the mainstream." Based on this judgment of central experience for a (presumed) group, González Echevarría privileges Cristina García's *Dreaming in Cuban* and Julia Alvarez's first novel, *How the García Girls Lost Their Accents*; these novels are by recognized representatives of the Hispanic "group" who re-present that group accurately (according to González Echevarría) by writing about (his version of) U.S. Latino/a experience. In such an analysis, a Cuban American text and a Dominican American text are rendered fairly interchangeable, since both represent what has been designated as the essential Hispanic experience (linguistic and cultural marginality).

But the problem of representation arises in much more subtle and even unpredictable forms, as well. For instance, while González Echevarría seems not to have a problem placing Cuban Americans and Dominican Americans in the same group, he is apparently much more resistant to a transnational understanding of group identity which would include Dominican Americans and Dominican nationals. Julia Alvarez's *In the Time of the Butterflies* does not deal with the immigrant experience in the United States. Rather, this novel attempts to imaginatively re-create the stories of three sisters in the Dominican Republic who have become historical figures because of their efforts in the resistance movement against Rafael Leónidas Trujillo (dictator of the Dominican Republic from

1930 to 1961), for which they were killed. González Echevarría takes issue with the premise of **Butterflies** [*In the Time of the Butterflies*], suggesting that Alvarez writes "as if she needed to have her American self learn what it was really like in her native land, the Dominican Republic." Noting the metafictional figure in the narrative frame of **Butterflies** who is "a thinly disguised version of Ms. Alvarez, an Americanized Dominican woman who wants to write something about the Mirabals and is looking for information," González Echevarría maintains that Alvarez lacks "the realization that the *gringa dominicana* would never really be able to understand the other woman [i.e., the surviving Mirabal sister whom she interviews in the Dominican Republic], much less translate her." In other words, González Echevarría seems to be saying to Alvarez, "Speak for yourself."[1]

As Diane Elam observes of rhetorical situations like these, "in being told to speak, you are really being told *not* to speak. [. . .] In this case, 'speak for yourself' is tantamount to a faintly polite way of saying 'shut up'" (231). As an author raised largely in the United States, Alvarez has lost the right/ability to "represent" (in the conflated sense of the word) Dominicans who stayed in the Dominican Republic. Implicit in González Echevarría's review is the assumption that there is an unproblematic, fairly homogeneous, group—U.S. Latinos/as—for which Alvarez can speak, and a similarly homogeneous group—Dominican nationals—for which she cannot. González Echevarría insists, furthermore, on recognition of difference between Dominican Americans and "third world" Dominicans, but other differences within each group, such as class or race, go unarticulated.

Much more typical, in the U.S. popular imaginary, than González Echevarría's assumption of insurmountable difference between Dominicans and U.S. Latinas/os is the perception that Latinos/as continue to be essentially connected to their countries of origin. As Dalia Kandiyoti puts it, "One aspect of Latino identities as disseminated in media discourses is their assumed inherent transnationality—the seamlessness of the Latino—Latin American connection" (422). The stereotypical and uninformed understanding of Latino culture in the United States is that it is a fairly well-preserved carryover from the country of origin and that Latinos are fairly authoritative representatives of that culture. Indeed, the racist and xenophobic exhortation to "go back where you came from"—no matter for how long the recipients of such comments have been in the United States—is undergirded by the presumption that Latinos' real homes and proper places are "there" rather than "here." Further, as Rubén Rumbaut has written, "a language of kinship and of home—'homeland,' patria, 'fatherland,' 'mother

tongue,' 'blood ties,' a 'birth connection'—is often invoked [by immigrants themselves] to describe these attachments to an imagined common origin or ancestry" ("Severed" 44). Ilan Stavans writes, for instance, that Latinos are connected by an "umbilical cord [which] keeps us eternally tied" to our countries of origin (*Hispanic* 32).

This subjective rhetoric of intimate and biological connection is belied by objective measures of "transnationalism" even among first-generation immigrants. As Michael Jones-Correa has noted in *Between Two Nations,* for example, "[v]ery few Latin American immigrants are actively involved in the electoral politics of their home countries" (125). Immigrants, Jones-Correa argues, resist full political identification with their countries of origin as being "irreconcilable" with their present circumstances and their choice to reside in the United States (132). More markedly, Rumbaut's report on a ten-year longitudinal study of the children of immigrants notes that "the level of transnational attachments, both subjective and objective [. . .] is quite small[;] there is very little evidence that the kinds of attachments that are fundamental to pursuing a meaningful transnational project [. . .] are effectively sustained in the post-immigrant new second generation" ("Severed" 90-91).[2]

Silvio Torres-Saillant argues forcefully against the notion of the coextensiveness of U.S. Latino and Latin American identity, insisting that borders matter (436-37). In Alvarez's case, for example, the assumption of "seamlessness" obscures the ways in which her "first world" positioning gives her a particular *kind* of privilege unavailable to Dominicans. As a U.S. citizen, best-selling writer, and writer-in-residence at an American university in the Northeast, Alvarez is separated by far more than just miles from the Dominican Republic—even when, as recent book jackets attest, she "lives" there.[3] González Echevarría, as we can now see, stands at one end of a spectrum: Dominican Americans should not try to represent Dominicans. At the other end stands an equally problematic assumption: Dominican Americans are "essentially" connected to Dominicans.

Let us return to *In the Time of the Butterflies,* which González Echevarría condemns on the basis of insurmountable difference. (Alvarez could never understand a Dominican woman.) González Echevarría would apparently insist that the impossibility of "understanding much less translating" Dominicans renders any such effort futile if not downright imperialistic. But to reject his stance is neither to reaffirm that Alvarez has the authority as a Dominican American to speak for Dominicans (to widen the circumference of group identity which grants "authority" to speak), nor to claim that Alvarez is somehow able to imaginatively enter into, and represent, the subjectivity of Dominican women in some unproblematic, nonappropriative way. As Diane Elam (using Derrida's "Force of Law") forcefully asserts, "any attempt to do justice to the other, to speak of the condition of the other, necessarily involves appropriation of the other's discourse, involves, that is, a certain injustice." Yet Elam goes on to insist that "[t]he risk of speaking must still be taken, but it always remains a *risk*" (235). We might hypothesize that an early step in efforts toward cross-cultural understanding involves the effort to imaginatively engage in the experience of the "Other," such that the other is no longer viewed as an unintelligible, unreadable, or inscrutable category. Of course, the Other cannot be viewed "from the inside" in any real sense; no subject can ever escape his or her own limited subject position to "become" another. Yet, as Jean Wyatt puts it, "if one does not identify with the cultural other to some degree, does not make the conceptual leap to stand in her shoes, how can one be in a position to hear her point of view, to perceive things from her perspective?" ("Toward Cross-Race Dialogue" 880-81). An imaginative occupation of the Other's subject position (or something like what was once called "empathy"), with all its attendant problems and risks, is nevertheless potentially an initial stage in the process of coming to terms with, and taking ethical responsibility for, the conditions of others.[4]

Trinh T. Minh-ha, arguing along with Wyatt and Elam that "[a]wareness of the limits in which one works need not lead to [. . .] the narrow conclusion that it is impossible to understand anything about other peoples," goes on to explicate the position of a subject very much like Alvarez, writing both "inside" and "outside" the group identity "Dominican":

> The moment the insider steps out from the inside she's no longer a mere insider. She necessarily looks in from the outside while also looking out from the inside. Not quite the same, not quite the other, she stands in that undetermined threshold place where she constantly drifts in and out. Undercutting the inside/outside opposition [. . .] this inappropriate other or same [. . .] moves about with always at least two gestures: that of affirming "I am like you" while persisting in her difference[,] and that of reminding "I am different" while unsettling every definition of otherness arrived at."
>
> (374-75)

I would argue that, rather than treating the Dominican Other as a position for which she can speak with full authority, Alvarez continually risks speech about/for the Other while continuously resisting the guise of authority in her speech (whether the authority that comes with "identity" or the Western authority so often assumed when speaking about the Other).

As a writer, Alvarez is in fact quite aware of the difficulties of understanding differences, including those cultural differences which are a product of being Dominican American rather than Dominican, and she takes the problematics of cross-cultural understanding and translation (a project which inevitably involves "speaking for") explicitly as her subject matter. As González Echevarría observes, "*In the Time of the Butterflies* reads like the project the Americanized Dominican woman at the beginning of the novel [. . .] would have come up with after pondering the fate of the Mirabal sisters from her perspective as a teacher on a United States college campus today." And although he seems to think this a scathing criticism, it is clear that this is *precisely* the project of *In the Time of Butterflies*; the function of the "Americanized Dominican woman" in the novel is to investigate the problems of translation without abandoning the attempt.

The novel begins with an explicit reference to the imaginative perspective from which the stories of the Mirabal sisters will be re-created. Alvarez's persona is coming to interview the surviving sister for a book project about the Mirabals. The sister, Dedé, thinks to herself,

> The woman will never find the old house [. . .]. Not a *gringa dominicana* in a rented car with a road map asking for street names! Dedé had taken the call over at the little museum this morning.
>
> Could the woman please come over and talk to Dedé about the Mirabal sisters? She is originally from here but has lived many years in the States, for which she is sorry since her Spanish is not so good. The Mirabal sisters are not known there, for which she is also sorry for it is a crime that they should be forgotten.
>
> (3)

The barriers of language and of culture (Dedé must explain to the gringa that roads do not have names because "most of the *campesinos* around here can't read, so it wouldn't do us any good to put names on the roads" (4) create an enormous distance and potential for misunderstanding; the interviewer stumbles haltingly in Spanish, "I am so compromised [. . .] by the openness of your warm manner" (4). Alvarez's mocking treatment of her persona in the novel suggests the degree to which she is aware of the distance between herself and her subject matter. She knows, that is to say, that she shares only the most tenuous and fragile group identity with the Dominican national. Yet her own effort at storytelling works to reconstruct that larger group identity and testifies to her continuing sense of responsibility and commitment to Dominicans "at home."

Even when the *gringa dominicana* drops out of narrative view, Alvarez insists on calling repeated, self-conscious attention to the political imperative of speaking for others and the impossibility of ever doing so accurately. Within the main narrative of the novel, the surviving sister, Dedé, serves as a figure through whom Alvarez continues to investigate issues of representation and authority. Dedé is besieged by interviewers and journalists asking about her sisters at the same time every year, so she has developed mechanical responses which are already a warped distortion of the truth—she speaks in a "fixed, monolithic language around interviewers and mythologizers of her sisters" (7). Though as the surviving sister Dedé is granted by her country the authority to speak for the others, she is poignantly aware of the false claims of such authority; she has survived precisely because she was *not* actively involved in the resistance against Trujillo, as her sisters were. But if the act of speaking for another is dangerous, it is also potentially life-giving. Dedé is hyperaware of her role as the remaining reporter of her sisters' lives, and she receives the interviewers and responds to their questions, however imperfect her answers might be. Dedé knows that it is through her efforts that the story of her sisters is preserved, passed on, and she worries that "she doesn't want to be the only one left to tell their story" (10), so she continues to tell it to others, despite the inevitable distortions.

A third figure within the novel who tells others' stories—along with Dedé and the *gringa dominicana*—is Fela, who claims that the dead sisters literally speak through her:

> Possessed by the spirits of the girls, can you imagine! People were coming from as far away as Barahona to talk "through" this ebony black sibyl with the Mirabal sisters. [. . .] It gives Dedé goose bumps when Minou says, "I talked to Mamá at Fela's today, and she said . . ."
>
> Dedé shakes her head, but she always listens to what the old woman has to say.
>
> (63-64)

What is particularly disconcerting about Fela's version of the voices of the Mirabal sisters is that she claims that they are unmediated by her own interference and reconstruction. (She is what Spivak might call "transparent" ["Can the Subaltern Speak?" 275].) Fela, in other words, claims to be able to completely escape the limitations of perspective.

Dedé's reconstructions for the American writer are repeatedly likened to Fela's more mystical imaginings (and, tracing the chain of speakers back to the *gringa dominicana* who looms in the background, we can assume that Alvarez is implicating herself in this commentary, as well):

> "I'll tell you what I remember [. . .]," Dedé offers, stroking the lap of her skirt dreamily. She takes a deep breath, just the way Minou describes Fela doing right

before the sisters take over her body and use her old woman's voice to assign their errands. [. . .] Nonsense, so much nonsense the memory cooks up, mixing up facts, putting in a little of this and a little of that. She might as well hang out her shingle like Fela and pretend the girls are taking possession of her. Better them than the ghost of her own young self making up stories about the past!

> (66, 72)

The remainder of the novel is presented in the apparently unmediated "voices" of the dead sisters, speaking through Dedé as they would through Fela. Sections are named after the different sisters and narrated in alternating first-person points of view. The only disruption in the illusion of retrospective stories told by ghosts through their sister lies in the sections "narrated" by the youngest sister, María Teresa ("Mate"), which, because they are presented in the form of diary entries, create the impression of greater immediacy. (We are presumably reading what Mate actually wrote at different stages of her life, rather than hearing it retrospectively in a recalling which is always also a reconstruction and re-creation.)

Yet it is these diary entries, with their different quality of immediacy, which, ironically, begin to unravel the illusion of unmediated voice. As with the voices that speak through Fela, the danger is that we will mistake the diary for Mate's unmediated voice; to warn us against this mistake, moments in the diary call attention to its own artifice—its own impossibility. For example, in one entry, Mate notes that her sister Minerva scolds her about having abandoned her French studies, but "I decided to take English instead—as we are closer to the U.S.A. than France. [And then, in italics] *Hello, my name is Mary Mirabal. I speak a little English. Thank you very much*" (124). The italics that are meant to represent the change from Spanish to English remind us, as readers, that we have of course been reading English all along—this *cannot* be a verbatim transcription of Mate's diary; a "translator" has mediated between us and it. And, just in case we miss the point, the proximity of the Dominican Republic to the United States is invoked, to remind us that the real translator (the one "speaking for" the dead Mirabal sisters) is not Dedé but her after ego, Alvarez herself.

In some sense, of course, both Dedé (within the novel) and Alvarez *are* speaking for themselves; both of their projects of storytelling are informed by a desire to understand their relationship to a group of which they both are and are not a part. A story about another, this novel suggests, is always also a story about the relation between self and Other. Interestingly, the violent distortions of history associated with Dedé's packaged story for the journalists and interviewers are linked to her hesitation to explore this connection: "she is setting up her life as if it were an exhibit labeled neatly for those who can read: THE SISTER WHO SURVIVED. [. . .] [U]sually they leave, satisfied, without asking the prickly questions that have left Dedé lost in her memories for weeks at a time, searching for the answer. Why [. . .] are you the one who survived?" (5). The meaning of Dedé's life is fully implicated in the lives of her sisters. To understand herself, then, she must tell herself a story in which she wills herself across difference to understand her sisters, so that she may understand the things that separated her from them in life—even while she reminds herself, in little ways, that she will never fully know the answer, because she can never really speak her sisters' voices. Similarly, Alvarez tells the story of the Mirabal sisters' resistance in a way which points toward the distance between their positions and that of Alvarez, who left the Dominican Republic as a child and grew up in the nearby United States—speaking English, not Spanish.

Of course, there are others in the text of *Butterflies* whose "subject positions" are even further from Alvarez's own than that of the Mirabal sisters, namely, the lower-class, uneducated, illegitimate daughters of Enrique Mirabal. While class differences are an issue in *García Girls* [*How the García Girls Lost Their Accents*] as well, *García Girls* seems to be the least self-conscious of Alvarez's novels to date in its treatment of the possibility of representing "others"; as David Mitchell notes, Alvarez takes on the first-person perspective of Chucha, the García family's maid, only to give us a problematically reductive portrait in which Chucha bears a disturbing resemblance to the "clichéd role of the loyal domestic slave [. . .] left to mourn her kind keepers" ("Immigration" 35). In *Butterflies,* the issue of class difference is revisited with a greater degree of acknowledgment of the ways in which such difference can be an obstacle to understanding (much less to collective national—or even transnational—identity). The Mirabal sisters must learn to swallow their "pride" in order to rely on their illegitimate sisters for help in the struggle against Trujillo; the theme of coalition across class difference is repeated in the prison scenes, where Mate must overcome her initial revulsion toward the lower-class prisoners who share her cell.

Interestingly, Alvarez never attempts in this novel to speak from the "voice" of a lower-class Dominican (or even to create the illusion of such speech), suggesting an increased attention to the difficulties of bridging class division; we view the poorer illegitimate daughters of Enrique Mirabal only through the eyes of

their privileged sisters, who must learn to overcome prejudice but perhaps can never fully escape their upper-class perspectives.

Indeed, it is arguable that there are other ways—in addition to class and Americanized first world identity—in which Alvarez, in *Butterflies,* cannot fully escape her perspective. It is surely worth noting that, for all her attention to the divisions that impede understanding, Alvarez does not substantially take up the subject of a different transnational divide: the Haitian-Dominican conflict. During the Trujillo regime, this conflict had serious ramifications for a specific group of oppressed peoples within the Dominican Republic: those of Haitian descent.[5]

In *Americas* (1992), Peter Winn explains, "In most of the Americas, new nations forged a sense of their identity in opposition to the European colonial power from which they had separated. In the Dominican Republic, a national identity was created in opposition to Haiti: the independence day they celebrate is not their separation from Spain in 1865 but their liberation from twenty-two years of Haitian occupation in 1844" (287-88). Haiti had a history, Winn explains, of importing much larger numbers of African slaves than did the Dominican Republic in order to fuel a plantation economy; this would be a key factor in the construction of a Dominican national identity "defined in opposition to Haiti: If Haiti was black, African, and Voodooist, then the Dominican Republic would be white, Spanish, and Catholic" (288).

The history of what Ernesto Sagás terms "antihaitianismo" was not new to Trujillo's regime; rather, "[a]ntihaitianismo ideology is the manifestation of the *long-term evolution* of racial prejudices, the selective interpretation of historical facts, and the creation of a nationalist Dominican" collective identity (Sagás 21; emphasis added).[6] But it reached its nadir in 1937, with the massacre of thousands of Haitians—figures range from twelve thousand to thirty-five thousand—on the Dominican side of the border (Wucker 50-51; López-Calvo 12).[7] The massacre has been linked by scholars with the stirring up of racist fears about the "'Africanization' of the border" among Dominicans (López-Calvo 13; see also Winn 290). Sagás argues forcefully, however, that "[t]he Trujillo regime and its intellectuals did not invent antihaitianismo; it already was an integral part of Dominican culture. What the Trujillo regime did was to take antihaitianismo to new intellectual heights and convert it into a state-sponsored ideology" (46).

It is striking that, while Alvarez is very concerned to depict the evils of Trujillo's totalitarian regime in *Butterflies,* she gives virtually no attention to the broader issues of national identity and its aggressions which were a central aspect of the regime's repressive functions. Indeed, in ***Butterflies*** the racial issues implicit in Dominican nationalism, which rendered Dominican society complicit in the Haitian massacre, are largely suppressed. We can discern the outlines of this contrast in the single mention of the Haitian massacre in Alvarez's novel—a fact striking in itself, since the story narrated by the most "political" sister, Minerva, begins in 1938, only a year after the massacre. Yet Minerva does not mention the massacre, either at this point in her narrative or later; instead, the reference is put in the mouth of the sister named Patria (meaning "homeland"), almost ten years later, in 1946. Patria and Minerva look at side-by-side pictures of Jesus and Trujillo; Minerva scorns both figures, and Patria (who is represented as the more "religious" sister) narrates, "That moment, I understood her hatred. My family had not been personally hurt by Trujillo, just as before losing my baby, Jesus had not taken anything away from me. But others had been suffering great losses. There were the Perozos, not a man left in that family. And Martínez Reyna and his wife murdered in their bed, and thousands of Haitians massacred at the border, making the river, they say, still run red—*¡Ay, Díos santo!*" (53).

This passage is quite striking for its conflating of things that would seem to be of both different nature and different scope. The "disappearance" and murder of members of particular Dominican families, as a result of political oppression and silencing, are—while horrible in their own right—not parallel (in terms of causes or sheer numbers) to the nationalist killing, amounting to ethnic cleansing, of virtually an entire population within the borders of the Dominican Republic. One might argue, however, that since family is a dominant metaphor for, and way of understanding, ethnicity (Cornell and Hartmann 20), this represents a parallel structure for Patria—Haitians are simply another "family" that is separate and distinct from the Dominican "family." Also notable in the scene is the focus of culpability on the singular figure of Trujillo. Just as Jesus is ultimately seen as the giver and taker of life, whatever individual circumstances might have literally caused death, so Trujillo is the sole individual responsible for both the political oppression and the massacre of Haitians (whoever did the actual killing).

Patria's focus on Trujillo as the sole source of oppression is supported by the novel as a whole. Making the case for the horrors of Trujillo's regime, Alvarez depicts his crimes as political killings combined with lascivious womanizing (and perhaps rape). In this narrative, responsibility is contained, limited; while, clearly, those who commit the killings and tortures are also guilty, the only national culpability is silence, as

Dedé thinks at the novel's end: "People [. . .] kept their mouths shut when a little peep from everyone would have been a chorus the world couldn't have ignored" (317). Even the racial issues that, as Michele Wucker notes in *Why the Cocks Fight* (1999), drove Trujillo to lighten his complexion with pancake makeup in order to fit into the national narrative of Dominican whiteness (51) are reduced in ***Butterflies*** to his own personal whimsy—a vanity on a par with his collection of medals (Alvarez 95-96). In this sense, Alvarez's narrative can be read as *itself* a nationalist narrative, not only because she seeks to reimagine the "nation" (for example, along feminist lines),[8] but because the issues of nation-building that are so closely linked to the Haitian massacre are retold as the evils of an individual, though very powerful, man. (After all, "Patria" condemns the massacre.) As Dedé says at the end of the novel, trying to explain her need to tell her dead sisters' stories, "we were a broken people [. . .] and we needed a story to understand what had happened to us" (313). But the story—the collective fiction—that Alvarez tells through Dedé is one which in many ways exonerates the Dominican nation.

Indeed, a look at Alvarez's earlier novel, ***How the García Girls Lost Their Accents,*** suggests how the anti-Haitian construction of the Dominican nation is at times inadvertently reified in her narrative. The latter section of this backwards and multiple bildungsroman—the part of the novel set in the Dominican Republic during the García girls' childhood—also mentions the Haitian massacre: "It was the night of the massacre when Trujillo had decreed that all black Haitians on our side of the island would be executed by law. There's a river the bodies were finally thrown into that supposedly still runs red to this day, fifty years later"—that is, by rough calculation, in 1987 (218).

Chucha the maid, who survived the massacre, sought refuge with the de la Torre family and has been with them ever since. The introductory description of Chucha is as follows: "there was this old lady, Chucha, who [. . .] had this face like someone had wrung it out after washing it to try to get some of the black out. I mean, Chucha was super wrinkled and Haitian blue-black, not Dominican *café-con-leche* black. She was real Haitian too and that's why she couldn't say certain words like the word for parsley" (218). Two prominent symbolic identifiers used to distinguish between Dominicans and Haitians, race and language, are invoked in the description of Chucha: she is a *particular* kind of black ("blue-black," or dark skinned, that is, Haitian as opposed to Dominican); likewise, because she's "real Haitian" she can't say "parsley." This detail is itself a reference to the Haitian massacre; the pronunciation of the word "parsley" was the "test" given to Haitians to supposedly distinguish them accurately from Dominicans. As Wucker recounts,

> For Haitians [. . .]—in the streets or in the fields—the soldiers applied a simple test. They would accost any person with dark skin. Holding up sprigs of parsley, Trujillo's men would query their prospective victims: *"¿Cómo se llama ésto?"* What is this thing called? The terrified victim's fate lay in the pronunciation of the answer. Haitians, whose Kreyol uses a wide, flat *r,* find it difficult to pronounce the trilled *r* in the Spanish word for parsley, *perejil.* If the word came out as the Haitian *pe'sil* [. . .], the victim was condemned to die.
>
> (49)

Intriguingly, as Ana Celia Zentella has noted about Dominicans in the United States, "Dominicans, who are predominantly mulattoes, may hold on to Spanish more than other [U.S. Latino] groups because Spanish serves to identify them as non-Haitian in the Dominican Republic and as non-African American in the United States" (326)[9]—once again suggesting the pervasiveness of this collective construction of national identity, in which language and race are linked. Arguably, of course, the use of race and language as "keys" to national identity in the Alvarez passage cited above is that of the narrating García girls—and perhaps more broadly of upper-class Dominican society as a whole—rather than Alvarez's own; she is simply representing mimetically the culture of which she writes. But within the novel, these identifiers are not significantly challenged.[10]

In the only other mention of Haitianness in *García Girls,* the description of another maid, the "one-eyed" Pila, the signifiers are again reinscribed: "She had splashes of pinkish white all up and down her dark brown arms and legs. The face itself had been spared: it was uniformly brown [. . .]. She was Haitian, though obviously, only half. The light-skinned Dominican maids feared her, for Haiti was synonymous with voodoo" (279). Once again, the light-skinned are the Dominicans, while the "dark brown" maid is Haitian and therefore irredeemably "Other." The intriguing comment that she is "obviously, only half." Haitian is left without explication; what is "obvious" about this? If we read the obviousness in the mottling of her dark-brown skin with "pinkish white"—if, in the eyes of the young Yolanda, the pinkish white skin makes Pila obviously only *half* Haitian—then perhaps we can read the passage as poking fun at the absolutist equation of Haitianness with dark-skinned blackness (so that splotches of light skin obviously mean some other nationality), and as beginning in this way to unravel the strict construction of Dominicanness with whiteness.

Yet these correlations are not significantly undermined; much less is their collective force, and collective threat, exposed. That is, the text makes no particular link between the Haitian massacre, from which Chucha escaped, and the García girls' blithe equation of her blackness with her Haitianness, or the light-skinned maids' equation of Haitianness with fearful voodoo. The underlying causes—or at least the necessary preconditions—of the massacre, however, may well have been rooted in precisely such equations, which Dominican nationalist discourse on Haitians reproduced and reified. (In this alternative historical narrative, which takes account of the peculiar form of Dominican nationalism, Trujillo's orders *alone* do not hold sufficient explanatory power, whereas in both *García Girls* and *Butterflies* they are made to bear the burden of historical explanation by themselves.) For a fictional narrative of the massacre which *does* substantially thematize the complicity of Dominican society, we need to turn, tellingly, to a novel by a Haitian American: *The Farming of Bones* (1998), by Edwidge Danticat.[11] This contrast underscores, yet again, the fraught terrain of speaking for others—the inevitable blind spots, gaps, and silences—which Alvarez, to her credit, nevertheless refuses to shy away from.[12]

Though Alvarez's third novel, *¡Yo!* does not fill in this particular gap, it does take as its central theme the dangers of speaking for/representing others. The novel foregrounds the possibility that telling the story of another robs that Other of control over her own story—that is, of how she will represent herself. The prologue of *¡Yo!* introduces this theme through the resentment of the fictional sisters of Yolanda García, the main character and author-figure from *How the García Girls Lost Their Accents,* because Yolanda has written a novel loosely based on the events of their lives. (The self-conscious analogy to Alvarez's own novel *García Girls* is obvious.) As one of the sisters makes explicit in the opening paragraph of *¡Yo!* the issue is *control* ("[She is] talking about our family like everyone is some made-up character she can do with as she wants" [3]), suggesting that the act of representation of another might inevitably exercise a degree of power over that Other.

The project of the novel is apparently to "compensate" for this imbalance in textual control by having other characters from Yolanda's life tell their own stories about "Yo." The novel's title, referring overtly to Yolanda as the absent center around which this novel is constructed (unlike in *García Girls,* Yolanda's own voice is never heard in this novel except through the narration of others), is also the Spanish word for "I," suggesting the various subjects who will now, within the postulated world of the text, get to "speak for themselves." But the word "Yo" printed on a book jacket above the words "Julia Alvarez" cannot fail also to invoke the presence of Alvarez herself as author, emphasizing that all of these characters (like all the characters of *García Girls*) are her creations, described through her perspective. While the fictional characters offended by Yolanda's textual control can "take the mic" within the fictional world of *¡Yo!* this in no way corrects the problem of *Alvarez's* representation of others, and the potential violence of that representation. In this metafictional manner, Alvarez highlights once again her own presence as re-presenter, undermining the textual illusion of what Spivak might call "transparence" (i.e., the characters speak, "through" Alvarez, for themselves, in an unmediated way).

Alvarez extends the implications of this self-referential opening to the problems involved in representing the "less privileged" in two of the subsequent vignettes that constitute *¡Yo!*: "The Maid's Daughter" and "The Stranger." In "The Maid's Daughter," the narrator, Sarita, comes as a girl to the United States from the Dominican Republic in order to be with her mother, who is the García family's maid. Intriguingly, then, Sarita would seem to share an obvious group identity with Yolanda, who also came to the United States as a girl (just as, for González Echevarría, Alvarez and Cristina García share a group identity by virtue of being Latina immigrants). But Alvarez actually radically undermines even the more narrow group identity posited by a specifically Dominican immigration by emphasizing the ways in which class differences cut through this group. From the beginning, the García sisters—and particularly Yolanda—foster the illusion that Sarita is their "little sister" (56); but Sarita remains vividly aware of the class differences between them: "[Mamá] had spent her whole life working for the de la Torres [Mrs. García's family], and it showed. If you stood them side by side—Mrs. García with her pale skin kept moist with expensive creams and her hair fixed up in the beauty parlor every week; Mamá with her unraveling gray bun and maid's uniform and mouth still waiting for the winning lottery ticket to get replacement teeth—why Mamá looked ten years older than Mrs. García, though they were both the same age, forty-three" (66). Economic differences are not merely manifested through an unequal share of material possessions, but, rather, are engraved in the flesh itself, an inextricable part of identity. This understanding on Sarita's part makes her skeptical of the García girls' claims that they regard her as "family" (despite the ostensibly unimportant differences of class which separate them): "those girls treated me like a combination of favorite doll, baby sister, and goodwill project" (57).

Claims of kinship, of course, cannot fail to remind us of the ethnic ties which inevitably invoke them. As Stephen Cornell and Douglas Hartmann have insisted, ethnicity always involves a "claim to kinship, broadly defined" (19); "[e]thnic ties are blood ties" (16). Not only is dominant U.S. culture over-whelmingly likely to see Sarita and the García girls as "related" by virtue of their ethnicity, despite class differences, but Yolanda herself sees ethnicity as a close and intimate connection that overrides class. (More on this shortly.) Yet the physical differences occasioned by class seem to dismantle what might have been perceived racial similarities (which Cornell and Hartmann note may be one of the "potential bases of this belief in common descent" [17]).

While the privileged García girls repeatedly profess that Sarita is, so to speak, "one of us," Sarita knows better. Well-intentioned expressions of "familial" love by Yolanda, like a "dedication" of a school report to "Sarita y Primitiva, parte de mi familia" (part of my family), are rewritten by Sarita in her head to express her own resistance to such claims, which she knows are false: "I knew exactly what I wanted to do with that dedication. I wanted to write it over, using Mamá's rightful name. More than once, I had tried to get my mother to go back to her real name, María Trinidad. But Mamí refused. The de la Torres had given her that nickname when she was a young wild girl just hired out of the campo. 'I'm used to it now, m'ija'" (65-66). While Yolanda's dedication means to express her sense that the maid and her daughter are "parte de mi familia," and therefore regarded as "same" rather than "other," her wording reveals the extent to which class both determines and then occludes her vision: she has given the maid the name "Primitive" (Primitiva).

The crux of the story lies in this tug-of-war over representation. Yolanda wishes to write a "report" about Sarita for school: "What she proposed to do was observe my acculturation—I'd never heard of such a thing—as a way of understanding her own immigrant experience" (62). Once again, Yolanda convinces herself of identity while Sarita understands difference. Yolanda's report about Sarita is meant to be "a way of understanding" herself, but what Sarita feels is the way in which this report will be an attempt to capture and fix her: "I still felt as if something had been stolen from me. Later, in an anthropology course I took in college, we read about how certain primitive (how I hate that word!) tribes won't allow themselves to be photographed because they feel their spirits have been taken from them. Well, that's the way I felt. Those pages were [. . .] a part of me" (66). Like Yolanda's sisters, Sarita feels a lack of control over the way in which she will be represented. It is not *what* Yolanda writes about her that is at stake—it is not, that is, the accuracy of the representation ("Everything was set down more or less straight" [66]); rather, it is the simple fact that, in her textual representation of Sarita, Yolanda (like the "anthropologists" Sarita reads about in college) renders her an object of study. Sarita cannot speak, as a subject, out of the pages of Yolanda's report. Thus Sarita steals the report—an act of resistance in response to her sense that she is not in control of the text which represents her.

In "The Stranger" the dangers of theft through representation are even more pronounced, since in this story the inaccuracy of the text *is* an issue. Consuelo, an illiterate Dominican woman, receives a letter from her daughter Ruth (who has immigrated to the United States) seeking Consuelo's advice: the Puerto Rican man she married in order to obtain legal-resident status is now refusing to grant her a divorce. (In this "guest appearance" in the text by a Puerto Rican, it is worth noting that Alvarez again emphasizes difference over similarity: the Puerto Rican has advantages of citizenship that the Dominican immigrant lacks.) In a dream, the answer to her daughter's plea comes to Consuelo: "Consuelo was speaking wonderful words that flowed out of her mouth as if language were a stream filled with silver fish flashing in the water. Everything she said was so wise that Consuelo wept in her own dream to hear herself speak such true words" (99). But when she wakes up, she cannot remember the words from her dream. Nevertheless, she seeks the assistance of the American woman Yolanda—on a visit "home" to the Dominican Republic—to transcribe her words in a letter to her daughter.

The resulting scene enacts, at multiple levels, the struggle between and Yolanda for control over the text of the letter. Consuelo begins: "*My dear daughter Ruth [. . .] I have received your letter and in my dream came these words which this good lady is helping me to write down here with all due respect to el Gran Poder de Dios and gratitude to la Virgencita without whose aid nothing can be done'.* It was just as it had been in her dream: the words came tumbling from her tongue!" (105-6). But Yolanda responds that "[i]t's not a sentence [. . .] Let's say one thing at a time, okay?" (106), immediately moving beyond her role as transcriber to one of editor imposing a standard of order and correctness on Consuelo's words. When Consuelo dictates the message that her daughter must respect the "holy vow" of marriage and that "he will stop beating you if you do not provoke him" (106), Yolanda flatly refuses to transcribe Consuelo's words:

> "I'm sorry. I can't write that. [. . .] If I were you, I definitely would not advise her to stay with a man who abuses her [. . .] but, I mean, you write what you want."

> But Consuelo did not know how to write. [. . .] "You have reason," she said to the lady. "Let us say so to my Ruth."

> She had meant for the lady's words to be added to the ones that had already been written. But the lady crumbled the sheet in her hand and commenced a new letter. [. . .]

> *"My dear Ruth,"* the lady began, *"I have thought long and hard about what you have written to me."* Does that sound all right?" The lady looked up.

> "Si, Señora." Consuelo sat back in the soft chair. This indeed was a better start. [. . .]

> *"A man who strikes a woman does not deserve to be with her,"* the lady wrote.

(107-9)

By the end of this struggle over who will control representation, Consuelo's words have been literally obliterated under the pressure of Yolanda's authorial efforts.

The battle over textual control is further complicated by a series of ever-more-troubling questions, begged by the story's structure, which explore the problematics of representation. For the story surely represents Consuelo as unable to "speak for herself" in the sense that, by speaking in a manner which perpetuates gendered violence, she fails to accurately represent her own interests. But if we believe that Yolanda's advice to Consuelo's daughter is "correct" (or alternatively, if the text suggests that Yolanda's advice is correct) while Consuelo's advice is "wrong," are we then (is the text then) implicitly granting legitimacy to the position that Yolanda is *right* to wrest authorial control from Consuelo (that Yolanda, as first world, liberated, and educated American woman, can speak *for* her when she cannot speak for herself)?[13] The episode is even more disturbing, given that, when Consuelo was advising Ruth to stay with her husband, she "felt the words she was speaking were not the wonderful words of the dream" (107), while, when Yolanda wrote her own letter without input from Consuelo, Consuelo "could feel her dream rising to the surface of her memory. And it seemed to her that these were the very words she had spoken" (109). The text, in other words, opens itself up to the reading that Consuelo "authenticates" Yolanda's representation and appropriation through her sense that Yolanda's words are actually her own.

I would argue that, at a deeper level, the story works against such an interpretation, precisely by emphasizing the violence of Yolanda's appropriative act—for example, at the very moment where Yolanda substitutes, rather than supplements, Consuelo's words with her own, thus moving from textual manipulation or distortion to *destruction* of Consuelo's "text": "[Consuelo] had meant for the lady's words to be added to the ones that had already been written. But the lady crumbled the sheet in her hand and commenced a new letter" (108). Indeed, Consuelo's doubt about her own words being the inspirational words spoken in her dream, and her sense that in fact those words are Yolanda's rather than hers, suggests the almost violent force of Yolanda's will (ironically, since Yolanda's vigorous stance here is *against* violence), which discredits Consuelo's perspective even while attempting to represent it faithfully. (In other words, the story suggests the possibility that Consuelo discredits her own perspective because Yolanda does.) In "translating" Consuelo's words into writing, Yolanda does inevitable violence to them. I would argue, then, that the text does not work to endorse Yolanda's forceful appropriation of Consuelo's text (although it does not allow us simply to condemn Yolanda either, as I discuss below).

Nevertheless, the disturbing elements of the text (those elements which suggest the violence *of* the story, rather than the violence *within* it) are not fully eliminated by such a reading. We as readers cannot fail to be troubled by Consuelo's "endorsement" of Yolanda's substitution (which points beyond Yolanda's violence to Alvarez's, as the representer of a lower-class Dominican woman). Alvarez refuses to let herself off the hook by inscribing into the text a simple critique of Yolanda's textual violence; that violence is, indeed, arguably reproduced by Alvarez, who "represents" Consuelo as endorsing Yolanda's words. Stories such as "The Maid's Daughter" and "The Stranger" insist on the impossibility of representing the "Other"—in this case, the lower-class Dominicans—*without* doing violence. Indeed, we can see these stories not simply as attempts to "represent" or "understand" the lower class but, more significantly, as explorations of the class differences which render Alvarez's own position (as an American-raised, college-educated, upper-middle-class author) so precarious. Like Dedé's stories (in *In the Time of the Butterflies*) about her sisters, which are a means of grappling with her difference from them (they became politicized; she did not), Alvarez's fiction about "others" turns out to be in large part an exploration of the relationship of her own position vis-à-vis those others. The stories, in other words, call attention to the differences between Dominicans and U.S. Latinas (thus complicating the transnational model), as well as between privileged members of the upper- and upper-middle class and the working class who so often serve them.

And yet, in an ongoing project that *also* challenges the notion of unbridgeable difference, what is revealed is that the effort at understanding continues despite the obvious dangers—dangers which are neither preempted by empathetic identification (Yolanda "cares" about the working classes) nor vindicated by "ends" (Yolanda's letter contains better advice) nor even ameliorated by self-consciousness about the dangers (Yolanda herself is highly self-conscious of the dangers of appropriation). While Yolanda's representation efforts are marked by violence, the refusal to represent could be read as an abdication of responsibility, what Linda Martín Alcoff calls a "'retreat' response [. . .] in which a privileged person takes no responsibility whatsoever for her society (106-7). It is clear, of course, that Alvarez is still trying to understand Dominican society as in some sense "hers," at least to the degree that she must continue to take responsibility for it, even from a distance. As she writes to the concluding pages of her fourth novel, *In the Name of Salomé* (2000), "If continuing to struggle to create the country we dream of that makes a patria" (352). Alvarez's writings may sometimes be set in the United States but they invariably dream of the Dominican Republic.

In this sense Alvarez is indeed participating in a larger phenomenon of transnationalism: as Suárez-Orozco and Páez point out, "Dominican immigrants have developed political, economic and cultural adaptations that involve high levels of transnationalism. They remit large sums of money to their homeland, they remain substantially engaged in political processes there, and they return periodically with their children to nourish social and cultural ties" (6). We might connect Alvarez's decision to run a coffee plantation in the Dominican Republic to this larger cultural-economic phenomenon. In the afterword to *A Cafecito Story* (2001), a novella by Alvarez, her husband, Bill Eichner, explains the evolution of the coffee plantation:

> We met a group of farmers [in the Dominican Republic] trying to organize themselves around growing and finding markets for their organic, shade-grown coffee. We sensed that they were battling an agribusiness trend toward growing coffee in full sun, for better short-term yields, while deforesting the mountains and poisoning the rivers with pesticide and chemical fertilizers. We praised their efforts. They asked, would we like to join their struggle and buy some land before it was grabbed up by the big technified coffee plantations? Julia and I looked at each other [. . .] and said, why not?
>
> (40)

What is interesting about this particular depiction of transnationalism, however, is its emphasis on work and solidarity across lines of clear difference rather than on a presumed seamlessness of identity.

It is these lines of difference that Alvarez's work is increasingly attuned to, and her commitment to writing about them can surely be read as an expression of solidarity. By insisting on Yolanda's violence despite both her own best intentions and Consuelo's ultimate approval and agreement, Alvarez highlights the violence that attaches to *any* attempt to represent others (including those others that a mainstream U.S. culture might view as seamlessly connected to Alvarez herself, and as part of her own "group"). Nevertheless, Alvarez persists in her efforts. As Elam puts it,

> Responsibility to the other is excessive, although it is not simply paralyzing. Trying to do justice to the other, trying not to appropriate the other's discourse, is an unresolvable epistemological bind—which still does not mean that we stop trying to be just. Rather, the significance of this predicament lies in an *ethical* [. . .] recognition that there is no guilt-free speech. Injustice and appropriation are part of the violence of language; language can never be completely just, although we can continue to try to make it more so.
>
> (235)

If Alvarez's first representation of lower-class servants, Chucha from *García Girls,* enacts a particularly striking form of violence (Alvarez writes Chucha's first-person narrative—a narrative which creates the illusion that the working-class, Haitian maid "speaks for herself"—as one which "constructs" her only in terms of her employers), it is to Alvarez's credit that she returns to such representations in her third novel, in an attempt to make her language more just. Her self-consciousness does not mean innocence; while the acknowledgment that the servants in *¡Yo!* have lives of their own, never touched or even understood by their employers, is now clearly made (in stories like "The Maid's Daughter" and "The Caretakers"), other forms of violence continue to exist, Nonetheless, we can understand Alvarez's writing, at its best, as an expression of solidarity with those whose subject positions she represents, across lines of difference she acknowledges. As Kandiyoti has written, "notions of solidarity [. . .] based *primarily* on ideas of transethnic similarity may lead to [. . .] oppression, mutual misunderstanding and failure." Alternatively, "the recognition of unequal power relations [. . .] provide[s] a firmer ground for solidarity," allowing us "to continue imagining various forms and possibilities of mutual care and support in the contact zones of the Americas" (444). That is to say, when we (like Alvarez) recognize and explore difference, we can begin to imagine community.

Notes

1. In Alvarez's most recent novel to date, *Saving the World* (2006), she exacts hilarious revenge on González Echevarría by poking fun at a fictional "patrón of Latino critics," intriguingly named "Mario González-Echavarriga," for his over-the-top criticism of the novel's protagonist, a Dominican American writer like Alvarez herself (20).

2. The San Diego Children of Immigrants Longitudinal Study (CILS) sample, which Rumbaut discusses here, is composed of Mexicans, Filipinos, Vietnamese, Laotians, Cambodians, Chinese, and smaller groups of other national origin. Rumbaut qualifies the findings by noting that, despite the low levels of transnational attachment among the second generation (those displaying strong transnational behaviors were less than 10 percent of each ethnic group), there were differences among ethnic groups, with Mexicans and other Latin Americans "much more likely to maintain a level of fluent bilingualism [one of the 'objective' measures of transnationalism used in the study] into adulthood" than were other national-origin groups studied. He continues: [H]owever, "the fact that the Mexicans in this sample reside in a city that is situated right on the Mexican border [. . .] greatly facilitates their transnationality, especially the frequency. of visits across the border [another 'objective' measure]. Perhaps the surprise is that despite that advantage of nearness and familiarity, the level of binational and bicultural engagement is as low as it is" ("Severed" 90).

3. The biographical note for *In the Name of Salomé* reports that Alvarez "lives in Vermont and in the Dominican Republic, where she and her husband run a coffer plantation."

4. I do not mean to suggest that empathy is an unproblematic category, however. For more on this, see Chapter 7.

5. Among those killed were apparently substantial numbers of ethnic Haitians who were born in the Dominican Republic (Suárez, *Tears* 14).

6. Sagás notes that "the myth of the Dominican *indio* was the most important ethnic fabrication developed in the late nineteenth century—and remains influential to this day. [. . .] In order to varnish their common African past, the Dominican people essentially dropped the words *black* and *mulatto* from their vocabulary and replace them with the less traumatic and more socially desirable *indio*" (35). As in Piri Thomas *Down These Mean Streets,* "Indianness" became a way to avoid "blackness." Sagás also reports that in the early twentieth century—decades before Trujillo's rule—Dominican newspapers were "full of complaints about the immigration of black laborers," and that a law passed in 1912 limited immigration by black Haitians into the Dominican Republic (41).

7. Several scholars have discussed *In the Time of the Butterflies* in the context of Haitian American author Edwidge Danticat's *The Farming of Bones,* which represents the 1937 massacre from a Haitian woman's point of view. Kelli Johnson argues that both novels serve similar functions, commemorating a collective history otherwise "excluded from historical discourse" ("Both Sides" 76). In a slightly more critical

vein, Lynn Ink argues that Alvarez's novel attempts to offer a vision of nationalism that can counter the "masculinized [form of] nationalism [which] relegates women to the private sphere, establishing a gendered divide between the domestic and the political" (793)—but that, in its representation of the Mirabal sisters and the tensions between their "political" resistance and their private lives, it ultimately rein-scribes this gender divide. Most negatively, April Shemak—who mentions Alvarez's novel only briefly in a discussion of Danticat—contends that, "for all of [*Butterflies*'s] radicalism, it ends up reproducing a nationalistic history that ignores class and racial divisions within the nation" (84); Myriam Chancy adds that it is also silent on divisions symbolized by the Haitian-Dominican border (177). Lucía Suárez muses over whether Alvarez's representation of "Trujillo's despotism served to soften the extreme cruelty suffered under his reign" (21).

8. See Ink.

9. Zentella cites A. J. Toribio.

10. For a more positive reading of Alvarez's representation of Chucha, see Kelli Johnson, *Julia Alvarez,* 139-45.

11. In a climactic scene of racial violence which introduces the events of the massacre, Danticat's narrator describes how "[s]omeone threw a fist-sized rock, which bruised my lip and left cheek. My face hit the ground. Another rock was thrown at Yves. [. . .] The faces in the crowd were streaming in and out of my vision. A sharp blow to my side nearly stopped my breath. [. . .] Rolling myself into a ball, I tried to get away from the worst of the kicking horde. [. . .] The air vibrated with a twenty-one-gun salute. People applauded and stomped their feet and sang the Dominican national anthem" (194). In this scene, the emphasis is not on Trujillo but on the *collective* nature of the violence. Lucia Suárez reviews correspondence in which historian Bernardo Vega takes issue precisely with this aspect of Danticat's novel. According to Suárez, Vega "express[ed] consternation about her [Danticat's] representation of the Dominican people in her novel. He notes that one comes away from her story with the impression that civil society approved and participated in such a horrible genocide. He underlines the fact that it was a military order issued by Trujillo and executed by his army" (13). Danticat responded to Vega, in part, by pointing to the lingering manifestations of Dominican racial/national ideology which created the necessary condition for the killings (Suárez 13). This issue is also emphasized in *The Farming of Bones.* After the massacre, a survivor—a Haitian priest—parrots, in his own trauma-induced dementia, the Dominican nationalist discourse: "Our motherland is Spain; theirs is darkest Africa, you understand? [. . .] Those of us who love our country are taking measures to keep it our own" (260).

12. Indeed, as Kelli Johnson points out, Alvarez returns to the Haitian massacre once again in her fourth novel, *In the Name of Salomé.* One of the central characters, Camila Henríquez, a Dominican who is now a professor in the United States, is horrified by the massacre and eventually—in 1950—speaks of it publicly in what is intended to be a talk honoring her mother, famed Dominican poet Salomé Ureña. Johnson suggests that such repeated mentions "form a thread across Alvarez's work" that "reveals her commitment to exploring Haitians' role in Dominican collective memory" (*Julia Alvarez* 146). In fact, Alvarez explicitly discusses the racial component of the Haitian massacre in "A White Woman of Color." If she has yet to fully "explore" this issue in her fiction, it is certainly the case that she continues to revisit this particular, haunting gap.

13. In *Saving the World,* the thorny ethical issues raised by well-intentioned Americans imposing their will on the "third world"—even with the best of philanthropic intentions (e.g., developing a vaccine for AIDS)—are once again a subject of Alvarez's attention.

Marie-Elise Wheatwind (review date May-June 2008)

SOURCE: Wheatwind, Marie-Elise. "Quinceañera Barbie." *Women's Review of Books* 25, no. 3 (May-June 2008): 25-26.

[*In the following review, Wheatwind notes that* Once Upon a Quinceañera *strikes a balance between providing research-based facts and personal anecdotes about quinceañera celebrations. She also praises Alvarez for viewing this rite of passage with both a critical and a hopeful eye.*]

Rosie Molinary's *Hijas Americanas* is a collection of conversations that reminded me of 1970s feminist consciousness-raising sessions: women sitting in a circle, sharing significant passages from childhood to womanhood, finding common ground over issues such as menses, birth control, sexuality, motherhood, and men. But Molinary goes beyond the traditional CR model, expanding the conversation to a multicultural scale that is far more than a close-knit circle of twelve. Although she covers a lot of the same female milestones, she zeroes in on what many women seem powerless to overcome the expectation that we live up to an unattainable standard of beauty or perfection.

Her book began as a web-based survey, sent out to Latinas and Chicanas between February and June 2006. More than 500 women responded from all corners of the US. Molinary then solicited additional responses in a second, more detailed questionnaire, and conducted phone and in-person interviews with eighty of those women. Guided by Molinary's own revelations, the discussions among the *"hijas Americanas,"* [American daughters] in her book may sound familiar, especially if you've read Naomi Wolf's *The Beauty Myth* (2002) or Mary Pipher's *Reviving Ophelia* (2005). However, the cultural landscape and family influence in these women's lives adds complexity to their narratives, and their voices speak honestly from every page.

Poet, essayist, freelance writer, and teacher Rosie Molinary's Puerto Rican parents groomed her for college after she attended high school in Columbia, South Carolina, where her Latino family was one of only a few in their suburban community. Until recently, Molinary says, she had few Latina peers. She felt isolated and alone in a "sea of blondes" at the Ivy League college she attended as a scholarship student. In her twenties, she taught high school. The other young women who taught there "never mentioned their students calling them sexual nicknames or propositioning them" as some of her students had—despite her preference for "long skirts and baggy sweaters." After struggling in isolation with her ethnic identity, others' perceptions of her, and her own body image, she decided to find out how other Latinas faced these challenges. Among them, she found "comfort, solace, anguish, and, most important, understanding."

Molinary provides a lexicon upfront—even before her introduction—to set forth, among other things, how she defines "Latina," as well as why she painstakingly identifies each of her interviewees' country of origin.

> There is a range of truths and experiences among Latinas in America that is not often explored by the mainstream media and culture. My own story and the stories of the handful of Latinas I've come to know in my adulthood were not enough. I wanted a chorus of experiences. I wanted the volume to be loud and significant.

Indeed, the sheer number of contributing voices to *Hijas Americanas* assures its readers that they are hearing from a broad range of Latinas, of various beliefs and persuasions. Some lament or shrug off the inevitability of "turning gringa"; some justify and embrace, distance themselves from, or reject their religious origins; others examine, relive, and redefine the "double standards" of femininity and sexuality that are part of their "Latina mystique."

Then there are the ever-evolving standards of beauty that somehow change hues, but not shapes. While we may now see more Latinas in the media, the majority are light-skinned and thin. In her chapter "Maria de la Barbie," Molinary points out that a media-influenced standard of beauty affects most women's careers and can make breaking through the glass ceiling an impossible feat. "Beauty is so valued, it's become a commodity," she says. Many of her respondents attest to this: some must work to overcome feelings of inadequacy, while others ultimately "fit in" by subjecting themselves to plastic surgery. In fact, the rate of these surgeries among Latinas in the US leads that of all other minority groups: in 2004 they accounted for "6% of the 9.2 million cosmetic surgery procedures." While some Latinas have surgeries such as breast-size reductions to deflect attention, others are encouraged to have "nose jobs" by family members when they are scarcely in their teens.

If the tone of much of *Hijas Americanas* seems negative or worrisome, the final chapters are reassuring. Drawing from her teaching and counseling experience, Molinary knows that role models and mentors can "provide invaluable emotional, spiritual, intellectual, and social support," so she devotes one chapter, "Five Journeys to Success," to profiling successful Latinas who are not necessarily known for their beauty, but rather for their achievements in politics, business, the arts, and sports. She highlights their compassionate, intellectual, tenacious, and soulful qualities. In the final chapters, "Giving up Beauty" and "Raising Our Voices," the book's contributors offer to readers the wisdom they've gained from their experiences. Beginning by acknowledging that "scars show character." Molinary and the other *hijas* ask "what is beautiful?", express their "fearless duality" as women who also belong fully and equally to their cultures, and call on women to let go of negative stereotypes and to accept themselves "exactly how [they're] supposed to be." Finally, they "demand an end to the narrow beauty mystique":

> No matter where you have been on the journey to selfhood, start each day with the intention of championing yourself and others. It is never too late to claim yourself. The revolution—for all of us, of any upbringing—is about to crescendo.

With the voices of *Hijas Americanas* still resonating in my ears, I picked up Julia Alvarez's ***Once Upon a Quinceañera***—a girl's fifteenth birthday, celebrated by families in a number of Latino cultures—wondering if the younger generation was beginning to reject these wedding-like extravaganzas. Instead, I discovered that there is a growing *quinceañera* industry. "Given that we Latinos/Hispanics are the new booming minority," Alvarez explains in her opening chapter, "it seemed an apt moment to look at a ritual that marks a young Latina's coming of age." She spent a year talking to women from Cuba, Mexico, the Dominican Republic, Puerto Rico, and other countries. She also spoke with dozens of girls, their families, and members of their courts, with events providers and photographers, with parish priests, youth ministers, and choreographers. I talked to Latinas my age and older, Latinas in academia and in businesses catering to the *quinceañera* market, who observed that the *quinceañera* has become an even bigger deal stateside than it had ever been back home.

If you're wondering how an entire book can be devoted to answering the question "What exactly is a *quinceañera?*" think again. "The question might soon be rhetorical in our quickly Latinoizing American culture," reports Alvarez.

> Already, there is a *quinceañera* Barbie; *quinceañera* packages at Disney World and Las Vegas; an award-winning movie, *Quinceañera*; and for tots, *Dora the Explorer* has an episode about her cousin Daisy's *quinceañera.*

And it doesn't stop there. There are *quinceañera* cruises, *quinceañera* videographers, who for a price will document the day from early morning grooming rituals to midnight's final dance, and elaborate fifteen-tiered *quinceañera* cakes. Some parties feature private concerts, with bands and vocalists of international repute, and extravagant displays of fireworks, balloons, birds, and butterflies. It's no wonder that *quinceañeras* cost an average of about $5,000, with the price rising easily to $50,000 for some parents' ostentatious status statements.

I would be remiss if I were to describe **Once Upon a Quinceañera** as focused only on the elaborate preparations and expense of *quince* parties. Alvarez, the author of numerous works, including bestselling novels, poetry, and children's books, has given us only one book of nonfiction before this one: her collection of essays, **Something To Declare** (1998). In **Quinceañera** [**Once Upon a Quinceañera**], along with her research, interviews, and reportage, she offers autobiographical reminiscences about her own Latina angst, aspirations, and rites of passage into adulthood. These personal revelations are gifts: sometimes they are light-hearted and funny; other times they are bittersweet stories, honestly recollected. Although Alvarez becomes a "godmother" by default at the modest *quince* celebration she invites her readers to witness from start to finish, her book also includes a rebellious critique:

> Now into a second and third generation we are still celebrating *quinceañeras*! Is this a testament to the fact that in our struggle for rights, we have not forgotten our rites? Or, given the walloping expense and elaboration of the celebration stateside, is it a more sinister sign of a greedy market making *mucho dinero* by this oh-so-American supersizing of tradition? . . . In this post-September eleventh world, many of us feel a heightened need to provide our young people with ways to access deeper resources than can be found in a mall or purchased with a credit card.

Alvarez questions the "Cinderella fantasy" that is inherent in the pageantry of the *quince,* from the tuxedoed and gowned courtly processional of fourteen couples, who represent the fourteen years of childhood, to the father's removing his daughter's flat-heeled shoes (or soccer sneakers) and replacing them with the symbolic high heels. Alvarez admits to getting "tearful" at *quinceañeras,* but also to feeling "like a snake in the garden."

> [H]ere I sit in their living rooms or in their rented halls, eating their catered food, celebrating with *la familia,* and I am thinking, Why spend all this money enacting a fantasy that the hard numbers out there say is not going to come true?

The "hard numbers" include the percentage of Latina girls who become pregnant within one year of their *quince* celebration and the increasing violence at *quince* parties, because of snubbed, uninvited guests and party crashers. In fact, no prince is going to sweep these girls away to live happily ever after. After their evening of glory, they will enter the real world, for better or for worse.

Alvarez, like Molinary, does not end on a bitter note, however. Throughout her interviews with women—young and old—Alvarez hears a recurring refrain of change. Young women are adapting the *quince* tradition to express their independence. Family and community members form important bonds as they plan, design, and finance this gathering of friends and *la familia,* which celebrates, after all, a young girl's coming of age, not the giving of her hand in marriage. Alvarez offers information about the websites, helplines, and organizations that have sprung up to provide direction for young girls before and after their *quince* year.

"Our ongoing responsibility," Alvarez reasons, "is to revise and renew [traditions] so that they continue to fulfill their authentic purpose, to empower us." She concludes with a "gathering of wise women," truthsayers who provide "a kind of virtual *quinceañera,*" some of whom Alvarez introduced earlier in the book. These former teachers, ground-breaking writers, inspiring activists, and her mother—although their relationship was not easy—"served a guiding role" in her own life. "Wisdom is not a fixed quality," Alvarez muses. "It circulates among us." Despite her "once upon a time" title, we know better than to expect a fairy godmother waiting in the wings. Instead, Alvarez's circle of wise women offers a realistic promise of hope.

Sarika Chandra (essay date September 2008)

SOURCE: Chandra, Sarika. "Re-Producing a Nationalist Literature in the Age of Globalization: Reading (Im)migration in Julia Alvarez's *How the García Girls*

Lost Their Accents." *American Quarterly* 60, no. 3 (September 2008): 829-50.

[*In the following essay, Chandra analyzes* How the García Girls Lost Their Accents *to demonstrate the relationship between the globalization and the nationalization of American literature.*]

How should critics respond to the imperative to globalize the field of American literature?[1] Wai Chee Dimock and Lawrence Buell's edited volume *Shades of the Planet: American Literature as World Literature* is a useful contemporary example of how this is being attempted. It begins by taking up a by now familiar question, what is American literature in a global context?[2] The editors suggest de-linking the word *American* from its national and geographical boundaries. This question of de-linking has become especially important in a context of increasing U.S. military and economic aggression. But it is a difficult task indeed for a field with the name *American* in it.[3] *Shades of the Planet* is, in fact, one of a number of Americanist projects that have attempted to displace and decenter the field—projects that have helped to reinvigorate the discipline.[4] In their introduction, Dimock and Buell suggest treating American literature as a subset of, and a "taxonomically useful entity" within, the field of global literature (4). This invocation of the planetary allows them to "modularize the world into smaller entities able to stand provisionally and do analytical work, but not self-contained, not sovereign" (4). That is, the entity of American literature is not displaced entirely but is repositioned within the space of the "planet"—although Dimock and Buell are careful to argue that this "should not lure us into thinking that this entity is natural" (4).

SURVIVAL OF NATIONALIST PARADIGMS

Each of the essays in *Shades of the Planet* proposes its own particular way of decentering American literature, ranging from including literatures written in languages other than English to reimagining the spatial coordinates of America as beyond national boundaries. But I want to take a brief look at Jonathan Arac's essay, "Global and Babel: Language and Planet," since it serves as an especially good example of the difficulties encountered by scholars of American literature as they attempt to deal with issues of globalization.[5] The essay proposes a dyad: the "global," defined as "a movement of expansion that one imagines may homogenize the world," and "Babel," defined as a "movement of influx that diversifies our land, as in multiculturalism" (24). Parts of the essay make a case for displacing the English language from American literature by having graduate students learn three languages and also by helping students to learn the "value of imperfect speech" and "the capacity to speak on the street" (24). A major part of the essay deals with the reading of literary texts in a manner that unhooks them from national borders. Some of the authors whose work exemplifies the "global Babel" here are Emerson, Thoreau, Whitman, Henry Roth, and Ralph Ellison. Consider Arac's reading of Thoreau's *Walden,* which he cites as follows: "observe the forms which thawing sand and clay assume in flowing down the sides of a steep cut on the railroad" (25-26). Here Thoreau, says Arac, "feels as if he is in the 'laboratory of the Artist who made the world,' and 'nearer to the vitals of the global,'" which "'continually transcends and translates itself and becomes winged in its orbit'" (Arac's citations from *Walden,* 26). Arac interprets this for us, stating that "Thoreau's globalism at home provides the most morally reassuring babble" (26), and finds in Thoreau a guide for American literary critics to think globally. But here the focus is largely on language and the terminology of globalization and not on the sociohistorical conditions that might help us better understand the global context of Thoreau's work. Arac reads Ellison's *Invisible Man* in a similar way, citing the famous passage in which the narrator, looking at yams being sold in the streets of Harlem, proclaims: "I Yam what I am." The essay presents this as an example of heteroglossia, that is, Babel, as it "sets against each other radically different social registers of language," observing that the "root and its name aren't simply southern [that is, American] but also African" (27). Such connections indeed lead us to a broader interpretation of the text and Arac is careful to note what he calls the imperialist *thinking* of the authors in question. For example, while invoking the global dimension of Whitman, he also draws upon Edward Said, whose work, he says, "enables us to think openly, rather than defensively, about the imperialism that inescapably grids the planetary reach of Whitman's democratic idealism" (27). Arac cites Whitman's poem *A Broadway Pageant* as an example of this: "'Comrade Americanos!, to us then at last the Orient comes . . . Lithe and Silent the Hindoo appears, the Asiatic continent itself appears the past, the dead'" (27). The problematic aspect of this language, from the standpoint of the essay, is the imperialism of Whitman's "vision." However, globalization here remains primarily an issue of language, a linguistic globalism, as practiced by authors who already have a secure place in the American literary canon. In arguing for this kind of globalism, Arac thus allows the history of the U.S. imperialist economic and military policies to slide out of consideration.

It is true that the works of Melville, Emerson, and Whitman remain crucial for students of globalization today even as they must be critiqued as implicit apologies for imperialism. But it is notable here that despite the inclusion of Ralph Ellison, whose notion of America is often positioned against that of Thoreau or Whitman, the centrality of a traditional canon is left intact. In the very attempt to decenter American literature, there is a simultaneous move to shore up the canon to which such decentered works belong. In this respect "Global and Babel" has much in common with other moves in literary and cultural studies to "globalize" the field in such a way that the older curricular paradigms continue to exist unaffected and unthreatened.[6] I argue that this is a *rhetorical strategy* that critics employ to produce a larger transnational context for categories such as American literature—categories whose partial displacement is advocated only so as to resolidify the *nationalist* basis of the category per se. I would also insist on distinguishing between this rhetorical strategy and the historical processes of globalization themselves, processes that cannot be reduced to the former.

But, while critics such as Arac attempt to decenter nationalist paradigms and American literature itself by linking the established writer's work directly to the global in ways that nonetheless reinforce the national, other critics—especially those working in the field of immigrant/ethnic literary studies—have attempted to decenter American literature in what may appear to be a diametrically opposed move by displacing canonical works themselves so as to make room for other, less sanctioned writers within American literature. In this essay, I examine how the concepts of immigration and immigrant literatures—in ways subtly analogous to the rhetorical strategy described above—also assist American literary studies in reconstructing a nationalist paradigm even while attempting to "globalize" or update disciplinary practices. While the idea of immigration has long helped the United States to produce a national imaginary, the concept is now shifted in order to serve the same purpose in the "new era."

(IM)MIGRATION AND GLOBALIZATION

U.S. writers in the eighteenth and nineteenth centuries, including Benjamin Franklin and Ralph Waldo Emerson, took on the task of defining the "American" as the self-reliant and the self-sufficient. Their writings drew upon the notion of the "foreign" to define American-ness and positioned the United States as a nation of nations—an idea employed even today in chronicling the accomplishments of immigrants.[7] The image of immigrants who have nothing and yet are able to pull themselves up by the bootstraps has been fundamental for the way it suggests the rebirth of the

immigrant upon reaching the United States, repositioning the "foreignness" of the immigrants within domestic borders. This repositioning then provides the immigrants with their particular identities in relationship to the United States as a nation. In *The Next American Nation,* Michael Lind describes this phenomenon in a more contemporary context.[8] He suggests that many of the differences between groups of people that make up the population living within a nation are mitigated once they immigrate to the United States and are asked to join already existing, homogenized ethnic categories: "Mexicans and Cubans join Hispanic America; Chinese, Indians, and Filipinos join Asian and Pacific Islander America, and so on. Moreover each race, in addition to preserving its cultural unity and distinctness, is expected to act as a monolithic political bloc" (98). In effect, immigrants become localized ethnics in the United States. The term *immigrant* nevertheless continues to designate those who are different or "other" in some way. Unity is sought in diversity, but for such unity to exist, something, or someone, has to remain on the outside. A "unity" cannot simply be the sum of its parts. It must have an "other" as well.

Recent theories of globalization, moreover, have questioned the notion of stable and localized ethnic identities positioned as insider/outsider. In "Patriotism and Its Futures," Arjun Appadurai suggests that the "U.S. is not so much a nation of nations or immigrants but one node in a postnational network of diasporas."[9] While he may be a bit too quick to conclude that immigration has been supplanted by "migration," he appropriately suggests that the positioning of immigrants outside the dominant U.S. experience has become extremely complex. Though a significant number of earlier immigrant narratives such as Anzia Yezierska's *Bread Givers* (1925)[10] and Abraham Cahan's *The Rise of David Levinsky* (1917)[11] portrayed immigrants as negotiating their ethnicity and their status within this bounded space of the United States, more contemporary narratives such as Esmeralda Santiago's *América's Dream* (1997)[12] and Julia Alvarez's **How the García Girls Lost their Accents** (1991)[13] present immigrants who conduct similar negotiations but in a much more interconnected world. I examine Alvarez's novel below in some detail.

As literary critics undergo pressures to globalize their fields, they must do so in ways that prevent the complete dissolution of the discipline itself. In the contemporary, "globalized" context, critics present immigrant/ethnic literatures as cultural texts able to mediate current discussions of globalization because such literature has always produced an imaginary of displacement and made possible a connection between the United States and the rest of the world. Yet, might not the interest of critics in this broadening of literary scholarship be to *continue,* here in the name of the immigrant as marginal, the work that has always defined the field of American literature? In what follows, I will demonstrate how the figure of the marginal—here in the guise of the immigrant—is taken up in literary studies not simply out of an ethical opposition to the marginalizing of certain groups of people, but also to valorize this figure itself; not only for being outside the dominant, but also for the less obvious way in which it leaves what is inside the dominant intact. The figure of the immigrant comes to occupy the position of an "outsider" that helps make the "inside" seem more secure.

My critique takes aim at a domestic form of multiculturalism and politics of identity. I want it to be clear, however, that I am differentiating between identity as a politics of recognition and other ways of thinking and analyzing questions of identity that link culture to history, economics, and politics. By linking ethnic identity to a politics of recognition, decontextualized perspectives often position immigrants as necessarily in opposition to dominant groups. Such a notion of identity has been significant to immigrant/ethnic literatures. But analysis of identity need not remain within such a framework. A wide range of scholars, among them Anthony Appiah, Linda Alcoff, and E. San Juan Jr. have weighed in on the essentializing and liberal tendencies of identity politics and multiculturalism. Still others have noted that there has been a significant shift in what counts as politics both in and out of the university. Critics such as Jon Cruz, Paul Smith, Avery Gordon, Wahneema Lubiano, and Lisa Lowe have provided models for a scholarship that analyzes the dominant production and appropriation of identity categories within capitalist relations.[14] As Jodi Melamed has written:

> Race continues to permeate capitalism's economic and social processes, organizing the hyperextraction of surplus value from racialized bodies and naturalizing a system of capital accumulation that grossly favors the global North over the global South. Yet multiculturalism portrays neoliberal policy as the key to a postracist world of freedom and opportunity.[15]

Melamed argues that since the "1990s multiculturalism has become a policy rubric for business, government and education."[16] For instance, reading the 2002 Bush administration *National Security Strategy,* she notes its reference to the "opening" of "world markets" as a "multicultural imperative . . . opening societies to the diversity of the world."[17] In another example, Melamed reminds us that Bush has consistently used language of multiculturalism to justify the indefinite incarceration of Arab and Muslim prisoners at Guantánamo. His much publicized idea that the prison-

ers are given Korans and time to pray is supposed to work as a marker of racial sensitivity. This new racism uses the language of multiculturalism to at once change older racial binaries, such as Arab versus white, and also to obscure their continuation.[18] Questions of racial identity become in some ways even more salient in the global context outlined by Melamed. Analyses of identity that look at the uneven co-optation of groups of people in a globally structured economy must be distinguished from studies of identity as a politics of recognition and representation. Analytical frameworks that consider identity in its sociohistorical context are able to show how race, ethnicity, and gender-identity paradigms are part of the structural makeup of society.[19] Consider, for example, Lisa Lowe's argument in *Immigrant Acts* that the production of multiculturalism with a fetishized focus on identity as a positive force "'forgets' history, and in this forgetting exacerbates a contradiction between the concentration of capital within a dominant class group, and the unattended conditions of a working class increasingly made up of heterogeneous immigrant, racial and ethnic group."[20] These kinds of identity analyses have shown the problems that arise when positioning the categories of identity—easily appropriated by capital—as though they were themselves outside and critical of the dominant social relations. Multiculturalism then presupposes a politics of representation and recognition within a national frame that overlooks and even obscures the supranational power relations represented by international financial organizations such as the World Bank and the World Trade Organization (WTO). Even though there is disagreement in critical circles about whether the wars on Iraq, Afghanistan, and Lebanon are indications of the impending demise of the nation-state, there is a pervasive sense that politics and scholarship based on what are by some accounts the parochial domestic paradigms of multiculturalism and identity as a politics of recognition are inadequate or even out of date. In this context of pressure to move beyond previously accepted paradigms within immigrant/ethnic literary studies, there arises a countervailing pressure within the field to find new ways to consolidate the older paradigms. And, since immigration is often imagined as the movement from one nation into another—meaning that these paradigms are themselves predicated on the nation—we have in the process a consolidation of the nation and nationalist paradigms as well.

Identity politics' most prized notions—"multiculturalism," "diversity," and the generalized figure of the dominated "other"—are easily employed to move toward a global paradigm even while securing a nationalist one. As an argument for inclusion, identity politics has played an important and positive role in recent history. The question is, "inclusion" within *what*? I will show that identity politics and multiculturalism have sought to incorporate the figure of the immigrant into their own project of universality, and that this project remains, fundamentally, a nationalist one.

GLOBALIZING PRACTICES IN LITERARY
CRITICISM: READING *HOW THE GARCÍA GIRLS
LOST THEIR ACCENTS*

I will examine the move to "globalize" and at the same time renationalize practices in literary studies by focusing on the critical work produced in response to Julia Alvarez's novel *How the García Girls Lost Their Accents* (1991). Through an assessment of this critical material, I show how the curricular locus of immigrant/ ethnic fiction, counterposed to dominant literary categories, helps critics "globalize" while reproducing a nationalist imaginary within a domestic paradigm of race and gender politics. I have chosen to focus on this novel for several reasons. The scholarly reception of this text, which is widely taught in university classrooms, reflects how literary practitioners have produced a canon of immigrant/ethnic literatures with a heavy concentration of women writers, in part because women writers and their female protagonists allow for simultaneous conversations about race and gender. Moreover, since its publication in 1991, *The García Girls* [*How the García Girls Lost Their Accents*] has generated a significant amount of scholarship, work that reveals some of the changes that have been occurring within the field of literary studies in relationship to theories of globalization. For the remainder of this essay, I will show that, although Alvarez's text is in conversation with historical processes that complicate issues of localized immigrant identities, many critics have attempted to reappropriate those aspects of the novel, producing criticism in which "identity-thinking" is reintroduced, globalizing even while preserving the discipline of American literary study itself. Here, I emphasize the distinction between practices that at once displace and shore up the discipline of American literary study, and theories that scrutinize the United States as a historical entity with policies/practices that play a role in producing (im)migration.

The novel tells the story of the flight of the García family—father Carlos, wife Laura, and their four daughters, Yolanda, Sandi, Sophia, and Carla—from the Dominican Republic to the United States. In Santo Domingo they were a wealthy and prominent family, able to employ maids and servants. Carlos is implicated in a failed CIA plot to kill the dictator Trujillo and must flee with his family or face certain and violent retribution. The narrative itself begins in the 1980s

and chronicles the life of the family as the García girls grow up in New York City. The circumstances leading to the family's emigration from Santo Domingo are not related until the end of the novel, in a flashback to the 1950s. It is important to note, however, that these circumstances include the already widespread Americanizing influences on the island and that even after their emigration to New York—and the death of Trujillo in 1961—the family frequently returns to the Dominican Republic.[21] Critical scholarship on the novel for the most part consists of readings that focus on the negotiation of identity as part of the process the Garcías undergo as immigrants creating a space for themselves in the United States. In such critical work the identity of the Garcías is seen as dual or bicultural.[22] Other critical work attempts to place the novel in the context of conversations about globalization.[23] Such scholarship, attempting to displace identity-based readings, argues against dual/bicultural identity of the characters in favor of a transnational or global one. For example, Pauline Newton in *Transcultural Women* states:

> I do not wish to create a false binary relationship between the writers' new U.S. American culture and their old cultural differences or to delve into comparisons of various migrant generations or cultures, so instead I recognize their transcultural evolution within and outside of and across their cultural regions.
>
> (2)

However, this change, for the most part, remains one of terminology, because "transcultural evolution" keeps the emphasis on identity rather than the changed contexts of identity negotiation.

This strategy is common, but I will focus here on "From Third World Politics to First World Practices" by Maribel Otriz-Márquez, since it is a good example of the impetus to globalize/consolidate nationalist paradigms. The essay is part of a volume of critical feminist scholarship titled *Interventions: Feminist Dialogues on Third World Women's Literature and Film,* edited by Bishnupriya Ghosh and Brinda Bose (with a foreword by Chandra Talpade Mohanty). *Interventions,* according to Mohanty, is the first in a series called "Gender, Culture, and Global Politics," whose premise is based on the "the need for feminist engagement with global as well as local/situational, ideological, economic, and political process." Ortiz-Márquez's essay is an attempt to engage with such a global/local "political process." She speaks to issues of nationalism and displacement by asking:

> How could one successfully write about Latino/Latina writers in the United States without problematizing the categories which are at the core of our own definition of national literature? How could one engage in a

discussion of the 'politics of displacement' and cultural dislocation without, at least, questioning the notion of the Third World and those narratives?"

And she employs key words in the vocabulary of globalization studies: "dislocation," and "displacement." These are, according to the essay, notions that must be urgently considered if we are to understand current Latino/a literary production. Yet this exhortation to displacement further consolidates the very categories that she contends need to be displaced. Her questions are symptomatic of the way in which Latino/Latina narratives are employed to shore up the categories of American literature itself.

As I suggested earlier, immigrant fiction provides a ready narrative for resituating the study of American literature. For example, in thinking about **The García Girls,** Ortiz-Márquez certainly gives due attention to the ways in which travel between homelands and the United States is important to the construction of identities, but this is considered only in the context of how immigrants' cultural practices affect their position in the United States. It is only at one point that she gestures toward what she calls the "social reality" of the political turmoil that "lies at the margins of the text"—namely the escape from the Trujillo dictatorship (236). But apart from a cursory mention, hardly any attention is given to the ways in which historical processes of Americanization have influenced immigrants even before leaving the Dominican Republic. Ortiz-Márquez's essay is thus a good example of how, given "globalization," one now needs an "international" dimension within which to relocate the "national." Immigrant subjects are thus privileged in American literary studies because they serve as unique sites for that combination of the local and the global now required to reproduce the dominant imaginary of the United States itself as an "identity."

In addition to looking at Alvarez's writing, Ortiz-Márquez's essay also analyzes the work of Esmeralda Santiago and Christina Garcia. "Belonging," she says, "is the privileged feeling in all three narratives. It expresses the need to be somewhere where the boundaries of 'here' and 'there' can be easily defined, where the sense of estrangement can be easily defined" (233). Although she argues against easy definitions, Ortiz-Márquez casts the "negotiation" of belongingness for these characters in terms of gendered identities, concentrating on how female characters negotiate their place in the United States through their bodies. If, then, such gendered identities appear vexed, this is precisely because of issues of assimilation. Ortiz-Márquez thus states that "differences between male and female reproductive organs . . . translate . . . to differences in the way boys and girls are to behave once they enter puberty. The meaning of those differ-

ences is tied, in the novel, to Yolanda's understanding of language and language acquisition *in the United States*" (233; my emphasis). That is, the essay claims that assimilation in the form of language acquisition in the United States is "related to the configuration of sexual and gender identities" (233).

Analyzing gender politics is indeed crucial, but Ortiz-Márquez's reading, resting on a binary opposition between the two countries, implies that the United States is, a priori, less sexist than the Dominican Republic. This becomes clear if we consider how she reads the opening scene of the novel, in which Yolanda arrives on the island on one of her trips from the United States—the first of several chapters that cover (in reverse order) the time period stretching from 1989 back to 1972. Here is the description of Yolanda's entry, narrated from her own vantage point:

> The old aunts lounge in the white wicker armchairs, flipping open their fans, snapping them shut . . . [T]he aunts seem little changed since five years ago when Yolanda was last on the Island. Sitting amongst the aunts in less comfortable dining chairs, the cousins are flashes of color in turquoise jumpsuits and tight jersey dresses . . . Before anyone has turned to greet her in the entryway, Yolanda sees herself as they will, shabby in a black cotton skirt and jersey top, sandals on her feet, her wild black hair held back with a hairband. Like a missionary, her cousins will say, like one of those Peace Corps girls who have let themselves go so as to do dubious good in the world.
>
> (3-4)

While not citing this passage, Ortiz-Márquez writes about it as follows: "the opening scene is marked by Yolanda's subtle struggle to reject the norms established by her maternal family as proper 'woman's' behavior and her 'foreign' approach to issues such as clothes, makeup, traveling, and friends" (236). She interprets Yolanda's struggle as a challenge to the gender norms in the Dominican Republic and goes on to say that the "relative freedom she enjoys in the U.S. is clearly intertwined with the comfort she experiences in the familiarity of the surroundings in the Dominican Republic" (236). Though Ortiz-Márquez argues for reading this intertwining as a blurring of boundaries, she positions the familiar, comfortable, but, in matters of gender politics, less than ideal Dominican Republic against the unfamiliar, uncomfortable, but relatively free United States. This combining of experiences gestures at first toward blurring the boundaries, but only so as to redraw them in the end. And it is this blurring and preserving of boundaries that is read most pointedly through women's practices.

Here a politics of nationalism and displacement, inflected by issues of assimilation and dislocation, is equated with identity. **The García Girls** is read almost exclusively so as to reproduce arguments about race and gender identity negotiation and to bear the burden of representation that comes with such discussions. Although she wants to question what she calls the "ethnic reading" of these texts and even suggests that a "Latino" ethnicity is imposed on Alvarez's characters as a result of migration, Ortiz-Márquez nevertheless produces a reading of the novel that is in keeping with the U.S. rhetoric of individual identity as one that must be negotiated alone. She suggests that Alvarez's characters have taken on a fractured identity through mobility—which suggests in turn that somehow those not required to be "mobile" can have unfractured identities. Though the essay acknowledges that Latinas must struggle both in the United States and in their homelands, in the case of the García girls this struggle is also precisely what *gives* them identity. And there is an implicit argument here in *favor* of preserving this struggle indefinitely so as not to risk *losing* that identity. In fact, this narrative of displacement alongside "struggle" is not necessarily a narrative of dispossession and can just as well be understood as a narrative of cosmopolitanism in which the characters are presented as possessing a desirable perspective that *could only come* from being displaced. Displacement in such analyses is removed from the material realities in the lives of immigrants and becomes a kind of ethical privilege.

Other critical work on the ***The García Girls,*** such as Joan M. Hoffman's "She Wants to be Called Yolanda Now," concentrates, like many other readings of Latina texts, exclusively on how immigrants, in this case the Garcías, Manage their lives in the United States.[24] Hoffman says:

> All of these girls—Carla, Sandra, Yolanda and Sofia—do come to some trouble in the New World. . . . As the title of the novel suggests, not only words, but also the manner of speech is significant to the story of the García girls' coming-of-age in America. The struggle to master a second language is a constant reminder to these girls of their weakened position as strangers in a new land.
>
> (21-22)

On the one hand, Hoffman acknowledges that the girls suffer from a weakened position as a result of being immigrants; yet on the other hand, she champions that same identity. The article ends with the following remark about Yolanda:

> As troubled as it may be—by memory or failed love or fragmented identity or that precarious tightrope that is the immigrant's life—Yolanda still has spirit in her, she still has her art, her writing, her refuge. With that she will always be able to invent what she needs to survive.
>
> (26)

Hoffman makes a case for reading the novel almost exclusively along the lines of the U.S. rhetoric of individuality and individual immigrant spirit. She

concentrates on what is most typical about immigrant struggles and ends with the suggestion that even though Yolanda is in a precarious position as an immigrant, she has become sufficiently Americanized to realize that she can "invent" her own life. The foregrounding of Yolanda's "identity"—though neither Dominican nor U.S./American per se—serves to keep the novel well within the horizons of a U.S. nationalist paradigm.

This tendency to champion the tough, adaptive spirit of immigrants while defending their identity rights can be traced in sociohistorical scholarship on (im)migration as well. For instance, Mary Chamberlain in her introduction to the edited volume *Caribbean Migration,* a broad and instructive examination of the phenomenon of mobility from and through the Caribbean, states of the project that it "shifts the focus away from the causes of migration toward the nature and meaning of the migration experience, a shift that has radical implications for those concerned with the consequences of migration and its future."[25] It results in a form of analysis that attempts to capture what she calls the "vibrant culture of transnational and circular migration, in the home and the host countries" (10). In this shift, the focus on migrant *culture* can become celebratory—as signaled in the terms "vibrancy of culture." Take here as another example Peggy Levitt's cultural profile of Dominican (im)migrants in her book *The Transnational Villagers.*[26] While the latter places its findings within a global economic and social context, it nevertheless exhibits a tendency to rely on the descriptive language and metaphors of a more cosmopolitan narrative of (im)migration. Emphasizing the continuous contact between the residents of the Dominican city of Miraflores and Boston, Levitt writes:

> Though electricity goes off nightly for weeks at a stretch, nearly every household has a television, VCR, or compact disc player. And although it takes months to get a phone installed in Santo Domingo, the Dominican capital, Mirafloreños can get phone service in their homes almost immediately after they request it.
>
> (2)

"Because someone is always traveling between Boston and the Island," she goes on to say, "there is a continuous, circular flow of goods, news, and information. As a result when someone is ill, cheating on his or her spouse, or finally granted a visa, the news spreads as quickly in Jamaica Plain as it does on the streets of Miraflores" (3). There are a couple of points here that are especially worth considering. While Levitt does not state this, the mainland-island networks through which flow the goods, news, and information mentioned above are not unlike the financial networks connecting cities such as New York, London, and

Beijing—networks that appear to transcend unevenness within and across national boundaries so as to produce a culture of transnational cosmopolitanism. Invoking the gossip that travels faster between Boston and Miraflores than between Miraflores and Santo Domingo feeds into this same cosmopolitan narrative of mobility, even if unintentionally. Emphasis is placed on cosmopolitan interconnectedness rather than, say, on the uneven distribution of electricity.

Nevertheless, such metanarratives of (im)migration are still highly instructive when placed next to the critical neat narratives informing the scholarship on the *García Girls.* The details provided by Levitt show the extent to which the lives of Dominican immigrants in Boston are lived in continuous contact with the lives of those who remain on the island—a reality elided in the fetishized identity-based reading of immigrant culture and in narratives of assimilation within the United States. Chamberlain's edited volume, while tending to foreground the cultural and to celebrate the ways in which women adapt and change in the face of an obligatory mobility, nevertheless opens up new ways to consider the "links between subjectivity and material life" (11).[27] Take, for example, Elizabeth Thomas-Hope's "Globalization and the Development of Caribbean Migration," which situates the Caribbean colonies from the "outset as part of the wider global political economy."[28] Thomas-Hope analyzes the way that mercantilism, the trans-Atlantic slave trade, and the plantation were already signs of globalization. The essays in *Caribbean Migrations,* despite sharing with the identity-based work on U.S. (im)migrant literary fiction a focus on the *culture* of (im)migration, help to bring to light the *connections* between the material and the cultural.

One of the reasons that *The García Girls* has been so readily accepted into the canon of American literary studies can be inferred in the tendency of scholarship to emphasize the novel as a story about girls growing up in New York as "Latinas," trying to assimilate within the United States while still holding on to Dominican cultural practices. This is a real aspect of the novel—resulting perhaps from a need to keep up with a demand from publishers and readers for coming-to-the-U.S. (and finding-liberation) narratives—but their emphasis tends to be encouraged by scholarship that highlights identity-based readings. One can, to be sure, read certain aspects of *The García Girls* as reproducing dominant ideologies. For example, growing up in the United States, the girls rebel against what they see as their old world parents. In an effort to preserve their Dominican cultural practices, the parents send the girls to the Dominican Republic in the summers during their teenage years. Yet the girls experience their parents as overbearing and overprotective because of these very same cultural practices—a constant source of struggle in the family. The resolution of their scuffles is described as follows: "It was a regular revolution: constant skirmishes. Until the time we took open aim and won, and our summers—if not our lives—became our own" (111). The fact that their skirmishes are described as a "revolution" seems to resonate with the title of Ortiz-Márquez's essay "From Third World Politics to First World Practices." But the "revolution" in the Dominican Republic concerns the political situation that had implicated Carlos García (and by extension his family) in a plot to kill Trujillo, a situation from which they eventually had to flee. The "revolution" in the United States is about the girls being able to stay out late at night and go to school dances. It is precisely these teenage scuffles, presented within the context of an old/new world binary as the García girls try to figure out their place in their new environment, that become the focus of readings that emphasize women's identity formation and self-assertion as though outside the patriarchal old world, but also as though outside a dominant and oppressive *new* world.[29] Of course, one could also read such an episode, conveyed tongue in cheek, as a commentary on a U.S., metropolitan form of life in which the right to stay out could be even thought of as a "revolution."

What is most important here is how the concept of immigration itself allows critics to place *The García Girls* in a position to repudiate old world politics just as immigrants are seen to repudiate their homelands in search of a better life. Yet they are also expected to have the freedom in the United States to preserve those old world cultural practices. Furthermore, it is by staging the "revolution" of teenage rebellion that the urgency of cultural preservation—and women's need to be bearers of this preservation—is conveyed. That is, we have here a "critical" discourse that demands the preservation of Latino culture and yet at the same time is able to argue for the need for women to be outside of it. The revolution to overthrow Trujillo in the Dominican Republic turns into the revolution of keeping one's cultural identity in New York. Moreover, the old/new cultural practices dimension of the novel is best understood when read in connection with the rest of the novel, as well as its sociohistorical milieu; otherwise we can run the risk of decontextualizing the above characteristics.

To summarize, readings of *The García Girls* like the one proposed by Ortiz-Márquez appropriate the narrative's global frame of reference so as to make more credible and politically acceptable a localized situating of the novel as "U.S./American." Meanwhile, however, these approaches to the novel, in another move of displacement and consolidation, remain within the overarching framework of domestic multicultural identity issues. Either way, *The García Girls* is understood exclusively in the terms of a gendered and racialized identity effectively precluding other possible readings.

The New Context of (Im)migration

Notwithstanding how readily *The García Girls* has been appropriated by a domestic multiculturalism, however, I propose that the book *also* provides a place to examine some of the operative assumptions about (im)migration and how (im)migration as a rhetorical strategy often works to obscure the role of the United States in producing the phenomenon of immigration. That is, there may be ways in which the novel itself, in conversation with the (im)migration experience, refuses easy categorization within accepted U.S. literary paradigms of localized ethnic identity. I analyze some of these aspects of the novel below. I do not wish to produce a comprehensive reading here, but rather to merely point toward some ways in which we can see this recalcitrant aspect of Alvarez's narrative.

Local vs. Global

Insofar as *The García Girls* is ascribed to a "marginal literature" and counterposed to dominant literary categories, its characters are seen—or made—to fit the more U.S.-localized and "resistant" category of a Latina ethnicity. However, the book elides this easy localization of ethnicity at one level simply because the characters move back and forth and their lives are in continuous contact with Dominicans on the island itself. Recall that the girls' grandparents already live in New York because of their grandfather's post at the United Nations. But they also spend a lot of time in the Dominican Republic, bringing presents for the girls and thus prompting them to imagine a world beyond their hometown even before their own emigration. The girls' father, Carlos, also goes to New York often, and return visits to Santo Domingo remain frequent after emigration to the United States.

Moreover, the novel resists any positing of the local as a site of critical opposition—not only because the characters travel back and forth with such regularity, but also because the local itself varies in different contexts. To see what I mean here by the variation of the local, consider the following. Antiglobalization scholarship sometimes posits the nations of the "global South" as localities that can counter the forces of globalization. The Dominican Republic, as depicted in *The García Girls,* can be read on the surface as precisely that kind of locality in relationship to the globality of the United States. Thus, to return to the beginning of the novel, Yolanda's visit to the Dominican Republic becomes the opportunity for various characters to stress the "localism" of Santo Domingo in relationship to the global United States. Her aunts

greet her by saying, "Welcome to your little island." The cousins join in a chorus for her, singing, "Here she comes, Miss America." Yolanda, by the mere fact that she has been living in the United States, represents that country to her cousins. Her family encourages her to speak in Spanish, which she describes as her "native" tongue, thus choosing at least for the moment to assume an uncomplicated connection between herself, the Spanish language, and the Dominican Republic. But beneath the surface these easy connections and the sense of an uncomplicated locality rapidly fall apart. Recall the opening scene again:

> The old aunts lounge in the white wicker armchairs, flipping open their fans, snapping them shut . . . [T]he aunts seem little changed since five years ago when Yolanda was last on the Island. Sitting amongst the aunts in less comfortable dining chairs, the cousins are flashes of color in turquoise jumpsuits and tight jersey dresses. . . . Before anyone has turned to greet her in the entryway, Yolanda sees herself as they will, shabby in a black cotton skirt and jersey top, sandals on her feet, her wild black hair held back with a hairband. Like a missionary, her cousins will say, like one of those Peace Corps girls who have let themselves go so as to do dubious good in the world.

(3-4)

In addition to raising questions about behavioral norms and Yolanda's appearance, this passage suggests that the precise context in which the United States is seen as "global" is that of U.S. intervention in its various forms, including the Peace Corps. Note here as well that while those in the Dominican Republic come, for the moment, to occupy the "local" position (the aunts who "seem little changed") and Yolanda the global, when she is in the States, Yolanda is also part of a different kind of locality, that of a Hispanic woman or Latina. In addition, if the local can, in some sense, be said to represent accumulated cultural practices in the Dominican Republic, then how to account for Americanizing influences on the island? By the same logic, if we designate the U.S. "Latina" as the site of the local, then how to account for differences of class structure within this category, not to mention the differences of race/gender/language that give people within such categories varied access to the dominant sphere? Since the United States can claim Latino/a cultural practices as, in one sense, within its borders, it can posit itself as both a local and a global nation. The point of view according to which localized cultural practices are always a refuge from the global and in opposition to it thus becomes extremely complicated in relationship to the newer immigrant cultures and literatures. What then do we do with those aspects of the novel that complicate the equation of the local with an ethnically marginal position as construed by some identity-based readings?

Aside from telling the story of how its main characters become good U.S. subjects, complete with phases of teenage rebellion, the novel simultaneously points to the fact that such a negotiation of identity cannot necessarily be summoned to provide critical resistance to dominant cultures. Rather, the novel speaks to a condition in which, due to the U.S. presence in the Dominican Republic, one's identity shifts in relationship to the United States well before any physical act of immigration. We learn that Carlos is working with the U.S. State Department in the Dominican Republic in organizing against the dictator. Victor Hubbard, whom the girls call Tio Vic, a consul at the American embassy who is in fact a CIA agent, helps the family escape. Hubbard is presented as a good man who has followed through on his word to help get the failed anti-Trujillo conspirators out of the country should any problems arise. "It wasn't his fault that the State Department chickened out of the plot they had him organize" (202). His "orders changed midstream from organize the underground and get that SOB out to hold your horses, let's take a second look around and see what's best for us" (211). That is, caught in the turmoil of rapidly changing political events, the García family is sketched against a backdrop of what is already a complex historical account.

But this history is mentioned in much of the scholarship on the novel in a cursory way and often with little or no reference to the history of U.S. intervention. Perhaps inadvertently, this recalls what is often the downplaying of such intervention in much of the historiography produced about the Trujillo period, which, in a reflection of the lurid representations of Trujillo himself as evil incarnate, has tended to represent the actions of the United States (which installed the dictator in the 1930s) as exceptional, a necessary departure from the supposedly more benign parameters of the Good Neighbor Policy or the Alliance for Progress.[30] It is true, of course, that political events—especially the U.S. military invasion of the country in 1965 to overthrow the left-leaning Juan Bosch government and restore military rule—were the impetus for the first large waves of Dominican emigration to the United States.[31] But, although the phenomenon of (im)migration from the Dominican Republic and from the Caribbean in general cannot be truthfully represented without an understanding of this kind of political chronology, limiting oneself to chronological events alone runs the risk of obscuring the larger phenomenon of mobility in the context of the globalization of the region itself. I cannot adequately summarize here the breadth of the historical and economic research into the structural causes of the Dominican exodus to the United States, but work by scholars such James Ferguson, Eric Williams, Tom Barry, Peggy Levitt, Greg Grandin, Sherri Grasmuck, and Patricia Pessar allows us to see how the larger history of (im)migration from the island can be traced to the very socioeconomic conditions that have themselves

given rise to the history of U.S. occupation and intervention.[32] A careful study of the history of what has been, since the end of the ironically more nationalist and protectionist regime under Trujillo, the ever more merciless yoking of Dominican society to the needs of international (largely U.S.) capital, whether via IMF austerity programs or the forced conversion of the Dominican Republic into a tourism-based economy that has left the better part of the local population with little choice except to emigrate, helps to correct the limitations of American literary scholarship. This is a picture of suffering and hardship that is the unexceptional equivalent of the "exceptional" torture and brutality inflicted by Trujillo and by U.S. neocolonial aggression—and that Dominicans must contend with whether they leave the island or not.

While in some ways limited, too, by a more dramatic, "political" understanding of the causes of Dominican emigration, Alvarez's novel allows us to see not only the role of the United States in forcing the Garcías to flee the island, but also how their plight is symptomatic of interconnected economic, political, and cultural factors that produce (im)migration to the United States as a general phenomenon, and how these factors also affect those who will never (im)migrate. As James Ferguson has noted in *Far from Paradise*, U.S. popular culture in the form of television, films, and other media already fuels the desire of many Dominicans to reside in the United States. Even before emigration, the García girls are introduced to the world of New York through the gifts that their grandparents and father bring back with them. Given that the Garcías already have the money, the class status, and the family connections required to be quasi-"Americanized" before emigrating, it seems only natural for the family to do the logical thing and emigrate. However, even those who cannot and will probably never emigrate are also formed by this same kind of experience. Thus, for example, the U.S. magazines and television programs available in the Dominican Republic translate into Americanized cultural practices not only for the members of the prominent García family, but also for those who work for them as servants. The latter also contend with ideas of their own identity in relationship to the United States—a relationship that is again not indicative of critical resistance but rather of a desire to be part of the dominant order. Carla, the oldest sister, tells of how her mother, Laura, characterizes Gladys, one of their servants: "[she] was only a country girl who didn't know any better than to sing popular tunes in the house and wear her kinky hair in rollers all week long, then comb it out for Sunday mass in hairdos copied from American magazines my mother had thrown out" (258). Gladys, too, dreams of the metropolis: "'I wonder where I'll be in thirty two years,' Gladys mused. A glazed look came across her face; she smiled. 'New York,' she said dreamily and began to sing the refrain from the popular New York merengue that was on the radio night and day" (260). She is in some sense already practicing to be in New York before she gets there, and it does not fundamentally matter whether she ever gets there: her desires, too, are formed by the particular environment of transnational migration.

There is little here about fleeing from bad gender politics or poverty to the generous shores of a new country. Instead, the García family's immigration is portrayed in the novel itself as interconnected with the economic and political integration of the United States and the Dominican Republic. By not taking such conditions into account, and reading the novel—and immigration itself—exclusively in terms of a racialized and gendered identity, scholarship places itself in the position of regarding such interconnections, together with the current conditions that determine the experience of (im)migration, as secondary to a multiculturalist/identity politics framework—a framework that does not itself extend much, if at all, beyond U.S. borders. Or if it does, it is subordinated to and divorced from the historical and socioeconomic conditions of (im)migration.

The pressure on critics, readers, and teachers to rethink and update the field of immigrant/ethnic literatures in the face of globalization results in a displacement that is at the same time a reconsolidation of the U.S. nationalist tendencies underlying the field itself. Reading "(im)migration" as primarily a process affecting identity formation produces certain valid insights but leaves many questions unanswered. In the end, such "globalizing" practices, in an effort to resituate and re-secure scholars' own disciplinary loci, are unable to address and account for certain aspects of the texts themselves. But the question still remains: what are the implications for disciplinary practices as we engage the theories of globalization? Does the fact that categories such as the immigrant/ethnic have come under critical scrutiny mean that those categories ought to be displaced in favor of new ones? As I have shown, questioning nationalist paradigms, identities, and notions of immigration linked to these ideas does not necessarily mean that we should abandon them. We can certainly ask how it is that texts both produce and are produced by ideas of immigration, identity, nationalism, and globalization. But it is also fruitful to read the texts, especially contemporary narratives of (im)migration, for the ways that they discover contemporary historical and social processes on their own terms. Whatever else they show, newer immigrant/ethnic texts should dispel the notion that a culturalist identity politics can, on its own, become a refuge from and provide critical resistance to the contemporary forces of globalization.

Notes

1. The use of the term *American* to signify the United States is obviously problematic. My own usage of the term in this manner is restricted to accepted conventional categories of study such as "American literature." In some places, I have used "U.S./American" as a modifier. In addition, I have utilized the term *Americanization* since it has been historically employed to describe the political and economic influence wielded by the United States.

2. Wai Chi Dimock and Lawrence Buell, *Shades of the Planet: American Literature as World Literature* (Princeton, N.J.: Princeton University Press, 2007).

3. Janice Radway, in her 1998 presidential address to the American Studies Association, proposed changing the name of the association and possibly dropping the term *American.* "What's in a Name? Presidential Address to the American Studies Association, 20 November 1998," *American Quarterly* 51 no. 1 (March): 1-32.

4. See, for example, Carole Levander and Robert Levine, eds. *American Hemispheric Studies* (New Brunswick, N.J.: Rutgers University Press, 2008); John Carlos Rowe, *The New American Studies* (Minneapolis: University of Minnesota Press, 2002); Donald Pease and Robyn Wiegeman, eds. *The Futures of American Studies* (Durham, N.C.: Duke University Press, 2002).

5. Jonathan Arac, "Global and Babel: Language and Planet in American Literature," in *Shades of the Planet,* ed. Dimock and Buell (Princeton, N.J.: Princeton University Press, 2007).

6. This strategy is a broader phenomenon in the field of literary studies. Marjorie Perloff's 2006 MLA presidential address makes a case for a return to aesthetics and the "merely literary," advocating single author studies by positioning Samuel Beckett as a global writer because his work is globally read and celebrated. A further example of the attempt to globalize that consolidates nationalists paradigms can be found in Stephen Greenblatt's essay "Racial Memory and Literary History," published in the January 2001 special issue of the *PMLA* on "Globalizing Literary Studies." Greenblatt makes an argument similar to Perloff's about Shakespeare being a global writer. He argues that "Shakespeare may never have left England, yet his work is already global in its representational range" (59). Arguing that Shakespeare's works are read globally, he leaves the author's centrality in the canon intact.

7. Benjamin Franklin, *Autobiography,* ed. J. A. Leo Lemay and P. M. Zall (New York: W. W. Norton, 1986); Ralph Waldo Emerson, *Complete Essays and Other Writings* (New York: Modern Library, 1950).

8. Michael Lind, *The Next American Nation: The New Nationalism and the Fourth American Revolution* (New York: Free Press, 1995).

9. Arjun Appadurai, "Patriotism and Its Futures," *Public Culture* (Spring 1993): 423.

10. Anzia Yezierska, *Bread Givers* (Garden City, N.Y.: Doubleday, Page, 1925).

11. Abraham Cahan, *The Rise of David Levinsky* (New York: Harper, 1966).

12. Esmeralda Santiago, *América's Dream* (New York: Harper Perennial, 1997).

13. Julia Alvarez, *How the García Girls Lost their Accents* (Chapel Hill, N.C.: Algonquin Books, 1991).

14. See the following essays published in Avery Gordon and Christopher Newfield, eds. *Mapping Multiculturalism* (Minneapolis, MN: University of Minnesota Press, 1996): John Cruz, "From Farce to Tragedy: Reflections on the Reification of Race at Century's End," 19-39; Lisa Lowe, "Imagining Los Angeles in the Production of Multiculturalism," 413-23; Wanheema Lubiano, "Like Being Mugged by a Metaphor: Multiculturalism and State Narratives," 64-75; Avery Gordon and Christopher Newfield, Multiculturalism's Unfinished Business," 76-115.

15. Jodi Melamed, "The Spirit of Neoliberalism from Racial Liberalism to Neoliberal Multiculturalism," *Social Text 89,* 24.4 (Winter 2006): 1.

16. Ibid.

17. Ibid., 16.

18. Ibid.

19. See, for example, the work of E. San Juan Jr., Michael Omi, and Howard Winant, and Paul Smith.

20. Lisa Lowe, *Immigrant Acts: On Asian American Cultural Politics* (Durham, N.C.: Duke University Press, 1996), 86.

21. Although the earlier immigrant works also spoke about the way in which the United States encouraged immigration (Cahan's character, David Levinsky, says that in Russia, he was told that U.S. streets were paved with gold), the passage to the United States for these characters was characterized as very clear and definitive.

22. Much critical writing on Julia Alvarez's novel focuses on the aspects that speak to identity construction of the characters as they make adjustments and adapt to lives in the United States. See for example, Ellen Mayock, "The Bicultural Construction of Self in Cisneros, Alvarez, and Santiago," *Bilingual Review/La Revista Bilingue* 23.3 (September-December 1998): 223-29; William Luis, "A Search for Identity in Julia Alvarez's *How the García Girls Lost their Accents,*" *Callaloo* 23.3 (Summer, 2000): 839-49; Julie Barak, "'Turning and Turning in the Widening Gyre': A Second Coming into Language in Julia Alvarez's *How the García Girls Lost Their Accents,*" *MELUS* (Spring 1998): 159-76.

23. Lucía M. Suárez, "Julia Alvarez and the Anxiety of Latina Representation," *Meridians: Feminism, Race, Transnationalism* 5.1 (2004): 117-45; Pauline Newton, *Transcultural Women of Late-Twentieth-Century U.S. American Literature* (Burlington, Vt.: Ashgate, 2005); Maribel Ortíz-Márquez, "From Third World Politics to First World Practices: Contemporary Latina Writers in the United States," in *Interventions: Feminist Dialogues on Third World Women's Literature and Film,* ed. Bishnupriya Ghosh and Brinda Bose, 227-44 (New York: Garland, 1999).

24. Joan M. Hoffman, "'She Wants to Be Called Yolanda Now': Identity, Language, and the Third Sister in *How the García Girls Lost Their Accents,*" *Bilingual Review/La Revista Bilingue* (January-April 1998): 21-27.

25. Mary Chamberlain, ed., *Caribbean Migration: Globalized Identities* (New York: Routledge, 1998), 10.

26. Peggy Levitt, *The Transnational Villagers* (Berkeley: University of California Press, 2001).

27. See, for example, Helma Lutz's study of Surinamese mothers and daughters. Helma Lutz, "The Legacy of Migration: Immigrant Mothers and Daughters and the Process of Intergenerational Transmission," in *Caribbean Migration,* ed. Chamberlain, 95-108.

28. Elizabeth Thomas-Hope, "Globalization and the Development of a Caribbean Migration," in *Caribbean Migration,* ed. Chamberlain, 188-99.

29. Generational conflict is a rather old theme in immigrant narratives. For example, Anzia Yezierska's work in the 1920s depicts the parent's "old ways" as clearly a result of their experience in Eastern Europe, which is then placed against what is presented as the newer and more Americanized ways of the children.

30. See for example: Russell Crandell, *Gunboat Democracy U.S. Interventions in the Dominican Republic, Grenada and Panama* (New York: Rowan and Littlefield, 2006).

31. Lucía Suárez for instance cites the U.S. invasion in 1965 and the post-invasion period until 1970 that produced a major wave of emigration from the Dominican Republic (123).

32. Eric Williams, *From Columbus to Castro: The History of the Caribbean 1492-1969* (New York: Vintage, 1984); Sherri Grasmuck and Patricia Pessar, *Between Two Islands: Dominican International Migration* (Berkeley: University of California Press, 1991); Tom Barry and Beth Wood, et al., eds. *The Other Side of Paradise* (New York: Grove Press, 1984); James Ferguson, *Far from Paradise: Introduction to the Caribbean Development* (London: Latin America Bureau, 1990); Greg Grandin, *Empire's Workshop: Latin America, the United States and the Rise of the New Imperialism* (New York: Metropolitan Books, 2006).

FURTHER READING

Criticism

Alvarez, Julia, Bonnie Lyons, and Bill Oliver. "A Clean Windshield." *Passion and Craft: Conversations with Notable Writers,* edited by Bonnie Lyons and Bill Oliver, pp. 128-44. Chicago: University of Illinois Press, 1998.

Discusses Alvarez's short fiction.

Blackford, Holly. "The Spirit of a People: The Politicization of Spirituality in Julia Alvarez's *In the Time of the Butterflies,* Ntozake Shange's *sassafrass, cypress & indigo,* and Ana Castillo's *So Far from God.*" In *Things of the Spirit: Women Writers Constructing Spirituality,* edited by Kristina K. Groover, pp. 224-55. Notre Dame, Ind.: University of Notre Dame Press, 2004.

Blackford details how Alvarez's focus on Catholicism in *In the Time of the Butterflies* heals the community that serves as the subject of her novel.

Castelles, Ricardo. "The Silence of Exile in *How the García Girls Lost Their Accents.*" *Bilingual Review* 26, no. 1 (January-April 2001): 34-42.

Examines the nature and place of language and silence in *How the García Girls Lost Their Accents.*

Cox, Karen Castellucci. "Living in a Borderland: Cultural Expectations of Gender in Julia Alvarez's *How the García Girls Lost Their Accents.*" *Women in Literature: Reading through the Lens of Gender,* edited by Jerilyn Fisher, Ellen S. Silber, and David Sadker, pp. 144-46. Westport, Conn.: Greenwood Press, 2003.

Presents a synopsis of and study guide for *How the García Girls Lost Their Accents* aimed at young adult readers.

Ink, Lynn Chun. "Remaking Identity, Unmaking Nation: Historical Recovery and the Reconstruction of Community in *In the Time of the Butterflies* and *The Farming of Bones.*" *Callaloo: A Journal of African Diaspora Arts and Letters* 27, no. 3 (summer 2004): 788-807.

Reads *In the Time of the Butterflies* and Edwidge Danticat's *The Farming of Bones* from a postmodern perspective.

Jacques, Ben. "Julia Alvarez: Real Flights of Imagination." *Américas* 53, no. 1 (January-February 2001): 22-9.

Highlights Alvarez's life in Vermont and the collection *The Other Side/El Otro Lado.*

Patterson, Richard E. "Resurrecting Rafael: Fictional Incarnations of a Dominican Dictator." *Callaloo: A Journal of African Diaspora Arts and Letters* 29, no. 1 (winter 2006): 223-37.

Contrasts the fictional treatment of twentieth-century Dominican dictator Rafael L. Trujillo Molina by novelists Alavarez, Edwidge Danticat and Mario Vargas Llosa.

Stefanko, Jacqueline. "New Ways of Telling: Latinas' Narratives of Exile and Return." *Frontiers: A Journal of Women Studies* 17, no. 2 (July 1996): 50-69.

Assesses the hybrid nature of Latina writing, focusing on Alvarez among others.

Suárez, Luía M. "Julia Alvarez and the Anxiety of Latina Representation." *Meridians: Feminism, Race, Transnationalism* 5, no. 1 (autumn 2004): 117-45.

Analyzes the place and meaning of individual and national identities in Alvarez's work.

Tate, Julee. "Maternity and Mobility: The Search for Self in the Novels of Julia Alvarez." *Proceedings of the 23rd Louisiana Conference on Hispanic Languages and Literatures,* edited by Alejandro Cortazar and Christian Fernandez, pp. 195-200. Baton Rouge: Department of Foreign Languages and Literatures, Louisiana State University, 2003.

Explores themes of motherhood as they relate to personal identity in Alvarez's work.

Additional coverage of Alvarez's life and career is contained in the following sources published by Gale: *American Writers Supplement,* **Vol. 7;** *Authors and Artists for Young Adults,* **Vol. 25;** *Concise Major 21st-Century Writers,* **Ed. 1;** *Contemporary Authors,* **Vol. 147;** *Contemporary Authors New Revision Series,* **Vols. 69, 101, 133, 166;** *Contemporary Literary Criticism,* **Vol. 93;** *Dictionary of Literary Biography,* **Vol. 282;** *DISCovering Authors 3.0; Hispanic Literature Criticism Supplement,* **Ed. 1;** *Latino and Latina Writers; Literature and Its Times Supplement,* **Vol. 1:2;** *Literature Resource Center; Major 20th-Century Writers,* **Ed. 2;** *Major 21st-Century Writers,* **(eBook) 2005;** *Novels for Students,* **Vols. 5, 9;** *Something About the Author,* **Vol. 129; and** *World Literature and Its Times,* **Vol. 1.**

Thomas Kinsella
1928-

Irish poet, translator, essayist, and editor.

The following entry presents an overview of Kinsella's career through 2008. For further information on his life and works, see *CLC,* Volumes 4, 19, and 138.

INTRODUCTION

During a career spanning over fifty years, Kinsella has been consistently admired as one of Ireland's most significant poets. Speaking before a meeting of the Modern Languages Association in 1966, Kinsella conceded that the development of Irish poetry had been crippled by its "dual tradition"—English and Gaelic—and he concluded that the only course left open to a poet was the formation of a unique identity. In an effort to discover his own voice, Kinsella conducted extensive research into early Irish literature and mythology. He became widely respected for his translations of Old Irish poetry and, in his original work, for his insight into the endurance of the spirit in the face of natural and human destruction. Although Kinsella's technique has altered considerably over the years, moving from a preference for carefully ordered structures to a total rejection of traditional forms, his themes have remained constant: love, death, the creative process, loss, evil, time. Kinsella is closely identified with the Peppercanister Press, the publishing house he created in 1972 so that he might print his poetry regularly and cheaply in pamphlet fashion, sometimes referred to as "Peppercanisters." In 2007, along with artist Louis le Brocquy—the illustrator of Kinsella's English translation of the Old Irish *Táin* (1970)—Kinsella was conferred with the prestigious Freedom of the City of Dublin for his impressive poetic output and devotion to the city of his birth. Kinsella was also the subject of a major celebration that closed the 2007 Dublin Writers Festival.

BIOGRAPHICAL INFORMATION

Kinsella was born in Dublin on May 4, 1928. His father, a brewery worker, was a socialist and member of the Labour party and Left Book Club. Kinsella attended University College, Dublin, through a series of grants and scholarships. At first he studied physics and chemistry, but then later pursued a degree in public administration. Kinsella joined the Irish civil service in 1946, studying languages at night school. He lived on Baggot Street in Dublin—the subject of many of his poems—and became associated with a group of young intellectuals that included the composer Seán Ó Riada and the founder of the Dolman Press, Liam Miller. Kinsella married Eleanor Walsh in 1955; his wife's recurring health problems figured prominently in his poetic explorations of physical decay and human suffering, such as in the 1966 *Wormwood,* which describes his painful but enduring marriage. Beginning in 1952, Miller began publishing Kinsella's poems. Miller was responsible for encouraging Kinsella to start translating Old Irish literature into English, resulting in Dolman's publication of *The Breastplate of St. Patrick* (1954), *Longes Mac n-Usnig* (1954), *Thirty Three Triads* (1955), and the influential *Táin.* The Dolman Press also brought out Kinsella's first major collection, *Another September* (1958). Kinsella's work soon received attention in the United States, where Atheneum published the collection *Poems and Translations* in 1961. In 1965 Kinsella accepted an invitation to serve as poet-in-residence at Southern Illinois University. He transferred to Temple University in 1971, where he taught for almost twenty years. Kinsella established the Peppercanister Press—the name by which locals refer to Dublin's St. Stephen's Church—in 1972, running the press from his home. The press published limited printings of his works in progress and allowed him to indulge his habit for constant revision. In 1976 Kinsella founded Temple University's School of Irish Tradition in Dublin, enabling him to continue dividing his time between the United States and Ireland. Kinsella became a member of the Irish Academy of Letters in 1965 and is the recipient of three Guggenheim fellowships. He continues to publish and currently resides in Dublin.

MAJOR WORKS

Kinsella's earliest poems received attention for their technical virtuosity. These conventionally structured, lyrical verses invited comparisons with the poetry of W. H. Auden. The collections *Another September, Moralities* (1960), and *Downstream* (1962) established the themes with which Kinsella would come to be identified throughout his career, encapsulated in a single line from "Baggot Street Deserta": "endure and let the present punish" Kinsella depicts a world in which love, passion, and art face eventual loss and destruction, often through the agency of human corruption. "Old Harry," for example, examines the morality of Harry Truman's decision to unleash atomic bombs on Hiroshima and Nagasaki. The title poem of *Downstream* tells of a seeker's quest for "ancient Durrow," a center of learning and devotion; the downstream direction of the journey indicates the certainty of death. Other poems in this collection locate debilitation behind a peaceful facade of domesticity.

After moving to the United States, Kinsella came under the influence of the American modernists William Carlos Williams, Ezra Pound, Theodore Roethke, and Robert Lowell. Most critics recognize the meditative, loosely constructed *Nightwalker and Other Poems* (1968) as marking a formal departure in Kinsella's work. The title poem employs a poet-wanderer (a frequently occurring figure in Kinsella's poetry) who, under the influence of the moon, considers the modern profanation of art and religion as well as the dismal state of contemporary Irish politics. The poet Seamus Heaney wrote of Kinsella's break with formalism: "He has strenuously punished the lyricist in himself who carried off such stylistic performances in the early books. . . . [H]e has gradually evicted traces of Audenesque, iambic—strictly English—melody, in order to find a denser, more laconic, more indigenous way with the poetic line." As Heaney's remarks indicate, the transition in Kinsella's work also benefited from his study of early Irish history, literature, and mythology.

Kinsella's first four Peppercanister publications were occasional pieces: *Butcher's Dozen* (1972), a satiric response to the exoneration of British paratroopers who killed thirteen civil-rights activists on "Bloody Sunday"; two pamphlets commemorating the death of Sean Oriada, *A Selected Life* (1972) and *Vertical Man* (1973); and a poem written on the tenth anniversary of John F. Kennedy's assassination, *The Good Fight* (1973). Thereafter, the Peppercanister pamphlets began to evidence Kinsella's interest in the psychoanalytical theories of Carl Jung. Jung's concept of the Patriarch-Mother as a creative impulse is a recurring motif in Kinsella's poetry, recently appearing in the poem "A Morsel of Choice," from *Belief and Unbelief* (2007), where a woman appears to "unsettle his wandering purpose / and unfocus his old age." The psychological and historical direction taken by Kinsella resulted in poems that were increasingly obscure and fragmented, sometimes lacking clear beginnings and endings, such as many of those included in *Songs of the Psyche* (1985), *Out of Ireland: Metaphysical Love Sequence* (1987), and *St. Catherine's Clock* (1987), all of

which—like the later *Belief and Unbelief*—explore the possibility for a spiritual life in a morally bankrupt world. In Kinsella's more recent poetry, scholars have detected a trend toward a more public persona, as the poet seems increasingly intent on documenting the ills of contemporary society in precise, sometimes bitter, language. In *The Pen Shop* (1997), he walks through the streets of Dublin, naming specific streets and businesses and iconography of heroic figures, reflecting on Ireland's present woes in relation to its past. In *Man of War* (2007), the poetic voice hopes for the future abolition of war on a global scale.

CRITICAL RECEPTION

As many commentators note, Kinsella's perpetually evolving poetry—marked by frequent revisions and divergent stylistic approaches—is best understood as a continuous lifework, often compared to Ezra Pound's *Cantos*. His early volumes won acclaim for their well-crafted elegance, and by the mid-1960s he was considered Ireland's leading young poet. Kinsella's later volumes, while considered remarkable for their interior explorations of the psyche, often seemed to defy interpretation. In his important 2001 study of Kinsella's Peppercanister poems, Derval Tubridy described Kinsella's critical history as moving "from early celebration to muted appreciation as critics and readers responded to the increasingly allusive and complex poetry which has characterised his work since the early 1970s." In a similar vein, Ian Flanagan, in a 2008 essay, spoke to Kinsella's adoption of the formlessness of American modernism: "Given the evolutionary currents with the poetry, one could see Kinsella and [William Carlos] Williams sharing a Darwinian poetic, what might almost be called a poetry of 'natural selection,' in which a huge range of excerpts, fragments, and thematic strands coexist side by side on the page, fighting it out, as it were, for the reader's attention." The difficulty of Kinsella's poetry, combined with the small print runs of the Peppercanister poems, limited access to his work and diminished scholarly interest in his output. Tubridy credits a 1980 Ph.D. dissertation by Carolyn Rosenberg with uncovering new information essential to understanding Kinsella's poetic development. Still, it was not until the mid-1990s that a large number of full-length studies of Kinsella began to appear. The recent Oxford (2001) and Carcanet (2007) editions of Kinsella's collected poems have served to enhance his reputation as well.

One of the most frequent subjects of Kinsella scholarship is the progressive nature of his work. Critics often examine the effect of his changing outlooks on the development of his major themes. For example, they have addressed his different methods for creating order out of chaos, one of his lifelong preoccupations. In his early poetry, this impulse manifested in an obsession with formal structure, but in the poetry of his mature years, he sought to discover first principles and archetypal behaviors through his study of history and psychology. The graphic descriptions of corporeal decay in the later work have been viewed as an aspect of Kinsella's perpetual struggle to comprehend the cycle of life and death by cataloguing particularities of time and place, seen in the early poems in his attention to the minutiae of household activities. Not surprisingly, Kinsella's sophisticated themes and imagery have elicited a number of psychological, philosophical, and metaphysical readings. In addition, scholars have conducted influence studies charting Kinsella's poetic development. Kinsella's evocation of Ireland's ancient past, including the Gaelic verse he translated in *Táin* and *An Duanaire: 1600-1900: Poems of the Dispossessed* (1981), and his ongoing interest in Ireland's political strife have earned him great respect as a proponent for the recovery of a distinctly Irish culture. Most scholars agree that the rewards of reading Kinsella's works are worth the challenges they present. As Lilah Hegnauer remarked in a 2007 essay, "Kinsella's *Collected Poems* is a dense and difficult book. . . . [I]t's also a book of incredible pleasure, both intellectually and aurally. Kinsella confronts death, sickness, poverty, chaos, war and human dignity with writing that makes the page pulse."

PRINCIPAL WORKS

The Starlit Eye (poetry) 1952

Three Legendary Sonnets (poetry) 1952

Per Imaginem (poetry) 1953

The Breastplate of Saint Patrick [translator, republished as *Faeth Fiadha: The Breastplate of St. Patrick*] (poetry) 1954

Longes Mac n-Usnig, Being the Exile and Death of the Sons of Usnech [translator] (poetry) 1954

Thirty Three Triads, Translated from the XII Century Irish [translator] (poetry) 1955

Death of a Queen (poetry) 1956

Poems (poetry) 1956

Another September (poetry) 1958

Moralities (poetry) 1960

Poems and Translations (poetry) 1961

Downstream (poetry) 1962

Wormwood (poetry) 1966

Nightwalker (poetry) 1967

Nightwalker and Other Poems (poetry) 1968

Poems [with Douglas Livingstone and Anne Sexton] (poetry) 1968

Tear (poetry) 1969

The Táin [translator] (poetry) 1970

Finistere (poetry) 1971

Butcher's Dozen: A Lesson for the Octave of Widgery (poetry) 1972

A Selected Life (poetry) 1972

The Good Fight (poetry) 1973

New Poems, 1973 (poetry) 1973

Notes from the Land of the Dead and Other Poems (poetry) 1973

Selected Poems, 1956-1968 (poetry) 1973

Vertical Man (poetry) 1973

One (poetry) 1974

A Technical Supplement (poetry) 1975

The Messenger (poetry) 1978

Song of the Night and Other Poems (poetry) 1978

Fifteen Dead (poetry) 1979

One and Other Poems (poetry) 1979

Peppercanister Poems, 1972-1978 (poetry) 1979

Poems, 1956-1973 (poetry) 1979

Poems, 1956-1976 (poetry) 1980

Selected Poems of Austin Clarke [editor] (poetry) 1980

An Duanaire: 1600-1900: Poems of the Dispossessed [translator, with Seán Ó Tuama] (poetry) 1981

Her Vertical Smile (poetry) 1985

Songs of the Psyche (poetry) 1985

The New Oxford Book of Irish Verse [editor and translator] (poetry) 1986

Out of Ireland: Metaphysical Love Sequence (poetry) 1987

St. Catherine's Clock (poetry) 1987

One Fond Embrace (poetry) 1988

Blood and Family (poetry) 1989

Personal Places (poetry) 1990

Poems from Centre City (poetry) 1990

Madonna and Other Poems (poetry) 1991

Open Court (poetry) 1991

The Dual Tradition: An Essay on Poetry and Politics in Ireland (essay) 1995

The Collected Poems, 1956-1994 (poetry) 1996

The Pen Shop (poetry) 1997

The Familiar (poetry) 1999

Godhead (poetry) 1999

Citizen of the World (poetry) 2000

Littlebody (poetry) 2000

Collected Poems, 1956-2001 (poetry) 2001

Collected Poems, 1956-2001 (poetry) 2006

Marginal Economy (poetry) 2006

Belief and Unbelief (poetry) 2007

A Dublin Documentary (poetry and nonfiction) 2007

Man of War (poetry) 2007

Selected Poems (poetry) 2007

CRITICISM

Michael Scharf (review date 18 June 2001)

SOURCE: Scharf, Michael. Review of *Citizen of the World,* by Thomas Kinsella. *Publishers Weekly* 248, no. 25 (18 June 2001): 78.

[*In the following review, Scharf offers a brief overview of Kinsella's career and comments on the variety of topics covered in* Citizen of the World.]

Kinsella has spent several decades among Ireland's most difficult, strangest and most critically respected poets. The Dublin-based poet (no relation to Australia's John Kinsella) gained modest fame with elegant, if conventional, formal poems in the '50s and '60s; during the same years he translated many classic poems in the Irish language. After the "Bloody Sunday" killings of 1972, Kinsella responded with **Butcher's Dozen,** whose rough, angry couplets appeared as a pamphlet from Peppercanister Press, which Kinsella set up (with some help) himself. The death of an Irish composer prompted another poem and pamphlet; these in turn laid the foundation for the short, often bitter sequences—each a brief volume from Peppercanister—which have become Kinsella's life work. (**The Collected Poems** appeared from Oxford in 1996.) Some consider public events; others follow Kinsella on meditative walks through the Irish capital. Many pursue evasive memories or enunciate moral dicta—"Thou shalt not entertain, / charm or impress," one new short poem begins. Much of *Citizen of the World* (number 22 in the series) reimagines the 18th-century writer Oliver Goldsmith: its concluding sequence evokes instead dangerous women, from mermaids to Mary—"The Virgin is rising / to Her pale height, / feeding on our needs." *Littlebody* (number 23) becomes more contemporary and personal—in one poem, Kinsella refuses the "ghostly gold" of a demonic leprechaun; "I have all I need for the while I have left // without taking unnecessary risks." (July)

Forecast: *Kinsella will certainly gain critical attention in America sooner or later, whether or not these volumes prompt it. His acerbic, allusive verse may never command a broad following; it may, however, appeal to sophisticated fans of Geoffrey Hill or Peter Reading, both of whom Kinsella's cadences can recall. Derval Tubridy's hefty monograph* Thomas Kinsella: The Peppercanister Poems *offers readers everything they could want to know about Kinsella, from his complex publishing history to his intellectual obsessions: its chapters divide the Peppercanister series volume by volume, interpreting almost every poem and making careful observations throughout.*

Daniel T. O'Hara (review date summer 2001)

SOURCE: O'Hara, Daniel T. "*The Pen Shop* of Thomas Kinsella." *boundary 2* 28, no. 2 (summer 2001): 53-5.

[*In this review, O'Hara interprets* The Pen Shop, *concluding that the poem's main theme is the experience of writing poetry in old age.*]

The Pen Shop (1997) consists of two unequal, numbered sections—sections 1, "To the Coffee Shop," and section 2, "To the Pen Shop"—and a nine-line, untitled prelude that reads as if it forecasts the fate of the poem we are about to read:

> Under my signature, a final kiss.
> In fading ink. With added emphasis.
>
> That ought to tell her what she can do
> with her fierce forecasts:
>   Rage, affliction and outcry!
>
> —Wide awake at the faintest scent of trouble;
> contented, nosing around among the remains.
>
> I brought it over to the big letter box
> in the centre of the floor, and dropped it in.
>
> Another cool acquaintance.

The first part of the poem, "To the Coffee Shop," rehearses the poet's reflections on the statue of Cuchulain with the Irish harpy on his shoulder in the figure of the crow or raven. The ancient hero is in defeat, "sagging half covered off his upright, / looking down over one shoulder at his feet" (1). This is followed quickly by his reflections on the other heroes of Irish history, also enshrined in the Dublin Post Office, the site of the Easter Uprising in 1916, with their own statues, including Larkin, Sir John Gray, Smith O'Brien, and Daniel O'Connell. Into these mostly wry reflections, Joyce's Leopold Bloom makes his way, providing a comic send-up of the heroic principle itself: "when Mr. Bloom unclasped his hands in soft / acknowledgment. And clasped them. About here" (2). This spectral interpenetration of real and fictional figures prepares for a similar experience in the next section of this part of the poem.

Here, the poet sees the ghost of his dead father at work, loading his barge at the Guinness Brewery Gates, "starting downstream" and pausing to let another ship, "the Lady Patricia," dock. The scene stresses the deftness of touch in this spectral work:

> hogheads, swinging high up off the jetty,
> delivered down in their chains
>
> to a deaf ghost directing them to their places
>
> with the ghost touch of a palm.

(3)

The poet, perched on the bridge, now sees the father's ghostly barge "sliding in under my feet" as the Lady Patricia is temporarily moored "beyond Butt Bridge," "falling and lifting against the quay" (3). With this difference in class, for the first time, the father's clumsiness appears: "Family queen, / accept him, fumbling at your flank" (3). This epithet, presumably addressed to the Lady Patricia, recurs at the end of "To the Coffee Shop," when the poet shares a coffee with his family queen.

The poet in the next section stands ready to plunge over the parapet:

> Cold absence under the heart.
> Arrest of the will.
>
> My left hand distinct against the parapet.
> The parapet distinct, with my hand against it.
>
> It was over quickly. But something was indicated.
> Measured to the need. While not forgetting the capac-
> 　　ity.
>
> 　　　　　　　　　　　　　　　　　　　　(4)

The stoic comedy of this scene suggests that the poet would be willing to join the ghost of his father in his spectral work, and could choose to do so at any moment but chooses, for now, not to. The poet makes his way to Bewleys' Coffee Shop, famous in Dublin for its imported coffees and teas and fine cakes and breads. But the poet only consumes the two tablets he removes from their case, lifts "the coarse cup" in a salute to the family queen, "touching her glass, once, to mine" (5). It is as if the poet were seated with his ironic muse-figure who, in this instance, is not to be distinguished from the figures of Dublin and of death: "Her arm bare. A finger posed at her chin. / Attentive. Partly informed" (5). The final lines of this first part of the poem suggest a bitter renewal of imaginative response to life: "And the black draft / entered the system direct, / foreign and clay sharp" (5).

Section 2, "To the Pen Shop," reads more like a comic coda to the previous part of the poem, beginning as it does with the "organic blast" of bus "Number 21" (6) and the poet cursing this vehicle, and in this mood seeing then "The thick back of an enemy disappearing / in the side entrance of Trinity" (7). As the poet turns aside into the pen shop "for some of their best black refills" (8), he encounters, in the same narrow cell, "the same attendant / over alert all my life long / behind the same counter" (8). The poet is about to leave Dublin for good, moving to Wicklow in County Wexford, "and the company of women," (7) at the ends of the earth: "Finisterre" (8), which, in Irish legend, is also the place of rebirth.

I think *The Pen Shop* as a whole is about the renewal of the poetic career late in the poet's life. Just as he

needs "some of their best black refills" from the pen shop, so, too, he needs the black draft of medicinal inspiration to enter his system "direct" with its taste of death, "foreign and clay sharp"; for only in this way may he be jolted into imaginative life and become the grand instrument of his muse's spectral writing: "The long body sliding in / under my feet" (3). Only then may he no longer be, like the other old men in Bewleys', "Speechless" (4). Indeed, only then may he, like the first voices, "rising out of Europe," become "clear in calibre and professional, / self chosen, / rising beyond Jerusalem" (8).

Derval Tubridy (essay date 2001)

SOURCE: Tubridy, Derval. "Introduction." In *Thomas Kinsella: The Peppercanister Poems,* pp. 1-12. Dublin: University College Dublin Press, 2001.

[*In this essay, Tubridy focuses on the publishing history of Kinsella's career and explains the origins and development of Kinsella's Peppercanister Press.*]

The shape of Kinsella's career is distinctive among Irish poets, moving from early celebration to muted appreciation as critics and readers responded to the increasingly allusive and complex poetry which has characterised his work since the early 1970s. This study takes as its starting point Kinsella's decision to found his own press, The Peppercanister Press, from which all of his subsequent work has issued. Peppercanister is not simply a press: it is a series of distinctive and interconnected poetic sequences that build together to form a loosely structured whole, which links with Kinsella's early work to form a continuing project in which art, self and society are subjected to rigorous scrutiny. The power of Kinsella's work lies in its ability to avoid the generalisation or the grand gesture. By maintaining a fidelity to the minutiae of life the poet looks behind the constructs of history, society and the self to discover the rhythms and processes from which each arise.

Kinsella began as a lyricist in the manner of the early W. H. Auden and W. B. Yeats, writing finely crafted poems celebrating 'love, death and the artistic act'.[1] An example of work written 'specifically in Auden's manner' is **'A Lady of Quality'** from Kinsella's first collection, *Poems,* 1956[2]:

> In hospital where windows meet
> With sunlight in a pleasing feat
> 　　Of airy architecture
> My love has sweets and grapes to eat,
> The air is like a laundered sheet,
> 　　The world's a varnished picture.
>
> 　　　　　　　　　　　　　　　　　　　　(C 8)

For Kinsella, Auden provided an entry point into poetry: 'Reading Auden, it occurred to me that there was a need in myself, and that I could write poetry.'[3] Kinsella's early writing received wide acclaim, winning the Poetry Book Society recommendation on two occasions with *Another September* in 1958 and *Nightwalker and Other Poems* in 1967. *Another September,* for which he received the Guinness Poetry award, established Kinsella as 'the most distinguished younger poet writing in Ireland', displaying an increased confidence and ambition in work which acknowledged a debt to Ezra Pound and T. S. Eliot.[4] To these influences Dillon Johnston adds the mark of Keats in *Poems* and *Another September,* and Shelley and Austin Clarke in the 1962 volume *Downstream.*[5] Already, Kinsella's work was being compared with that of Robert Lowell, Richard Wilbur and Wallace Stevens.[6] The 1958 volume was followed in 1960 by *Moralities,* a collection which considers faith, love, death and song, and two years later by *Downstream,* in which Kinsella probes behind peaceful domesticity to find a world of death and decay, as in **'Chrysalides'**:

> To the unique succession of our youthful midnights,
> When by a window ablaze softly with the virgin moon
> Dry scones and jugs of milk awaited us in the dark,
>
> Or to lasting horror: a wedding flight of ants
> Spawning to its death, a mute perspiration
> Glistening like drops of copper, agonised, in our path.
>
> (C 52)

Kinsella's voice gains in strength and complexity as he moves towards looser and more open sequences of poems in which self-exploration plays a central role. The interim collection, *Wormwood,* which was incorporated two years later into *Nightwalker and Other Poems,* won him the Denis Devlin Memorial Award in 1967. The poems of *Nightwalker* operate in what he calls 'the violent zone, between the outer and the inner storms, where human life takes place'.[7] Within this zone, concerns of love and the artistic act mitigate the poet's increasing sense of life as ordeal. His address to the beloved with which *Wormwood* opens indicates the apocalyptic vision from which the collection takes its name[8]: 'Sensing a wider scope, a more penetrating harmony, we begin again in a higher innocence to grow toward the next ordeal' (C 62).

The language of these poems moves from what Edna Longley has called the 'mellifluous cadences' which characterised his earlier work, towards a free verse in which received forms and rhyme play a very minor part.[9] Yet still, Auden and Eliot make their mark through an 'echo from Auden's "Nones" and the persona of intellectual *noctambule*' which, in John Montague's opinion, 'is depressingly close to early Eliot'.[10] However, reviewing *Nightwalker and Other Poems,* Eavan Boland remarks on how the collection confirms Kinsella's change of direction towards a more abrupt, less lyrical line, and notes that:

> If there is at times a disquieting repression of lyricism in this volume, a banishing of the grace which one associated with Kinsella's early work, yet there is a new strength to replace it. One does not doubt that Kinsella has increased his own stature by exploring so relentlessly what, in his own lovely phrase, he calls "the stagger and recovery of spirit."[11]

Kinsella confirms his conscious decision to abandon traditional poetic structures of the well-made poem saying, 'Yes, I kicked the whole scheme asunder at a certain point, realizing that the modern poet has inherited wonderfully enabling free forms.'[12] An important influence on Kinsella's poetic development was his move in 1965 from his life in Dublin as a senior civil servant in the Department of Finance to a position as writer-in-residence in Southern Illinois University where he could devote himself full time to writing. Living in the US opened Kinsella's ear to the American voice, and in particular to the voice of William Carlos Williams. Auden's 'grace and eloquence, obeying the requirements of stanza form and rhyme with gaiety and expertise' joined with Yeats's 'carving of poems into a regular sequence of objects' to provided Kinsella with an exemplary poetic apprenticeship.[13] But both poets gave way to Williams's rangy line which provided Kinsella with a 'sort of leverage out of a rather clamped tradition—with very few exits for poetry—into a state of thinking, and attitude where anything is possible'.[14] Robert Lowell's *Life Studies* showed him how to develop a poetic sequence that 'develops a progressive experience shared with the audience.'[15] Ezra Pound's *Cantos* also provided Kinsella with an example of what is possible in poetry. He points to the 'revolutionary energy' in Pound's subject matter and technique and indicates three aspects of the *Cantos* which influenced his later work, especially the Peppercanister poems: 'their extraordinary scope, their reliability in local detail and their capacity to keep going'.[16]

The idea of keeping going is integral to Kinsella's writing. Part of the development of his poetry involves a move away from collections of discrete poems towards sequences of poems which are open-ended and interactive. As Kinsella puts it: 'I hope the echoes of one poem or sequence go on and get caught up by the next. The poems I'm writing now will, I hope, gather up previous work as well as move forward.'[17] The last poem of *Nightwalker and Other Poems,* **'Phoenix Park'**, incorporates this open-endedness into its structure. The last line of **'Phoenix Park'** ends with a comma—'Delicate distinct tissue begins to form,'—inviting the reader onward to the first line of

Kinsella's next sequence of poems, taken from **'Notes from the Land of the Dead'**, which begins in lower case with 'hesitate, cease to exist, glitter again (C 94-5). And, as Maurice Harmon points out, the epigraph to *Notes From the Land of the Dead* when it printed in the 1973 volume *New Poems* is taken directly from the last line of **'Phoenix Park'**:

> A snake out of the void moves in my mouth, sucks
> At triple darkness. A few ancient faces
> Detach and begin to circle. Deeper still,
> Delicate distinct tissue begins to form,
>
> (C 94)[18]

Reviewing Kinsella's 1996 *Collected Poems,* Floyd Skloot underlines the extent to which revision and incorporation are integral to Kinsella's poetry: 'At any given point—in the various editions of selected poems, in the assembling of smaller, privately published books into more comprehensive, larger books, or in this collected edition—poems mutate, adjacencies shift. These are not just cosmetic changes; they reflect new understandings of what his work means.'[19]

Kinsella's writing moves from what Longley calls the 'static pose'[20] of the contained lyric to a more fragmented form in which beginnings and endings are less easily defined, eschewing melody in favour of a shifting rhythm which lies closer to its subject matter. He explains the development of his style as a shift away from 'the notion of decorative language, of poetry as linguistic entertainment', which he terms 'facile rhetoric, or "music" or mimesis for its own sake', towards a 'totality of imaginative response with the merely linguistic characteristics deleted so that one is brought closer and closer to the data and to the form and unity embodied in the data.'[21] While praising *Notes from the Land of the Dead* for its ability to grapple 'with the complex plight and destructive energies of our society' John MacInerney criticises the occasional 'clotted phrasing' and 'obscure personification' of the poem.[22] Seamus Heaney, reviewing the anthology of Irish poetry *An Duanaire 1600-1900: Poems of the Dispossessed,* acknowledges the shift in tone and diction in Kinsella's poetry and attributes it partly to his work translating Middle Irish poetry:

> He has strenuously punished the lyricist in himself who carried off such stylish performances in the early books. As the influence of Pound and indeed of Ó Rathaille has taken hold, he has gradually evicted traces of Audenesque, iambic—strictly English—melody, in order to find a denser, more laconic, more indigenous way with the poetic line.[23]

Kinsella's work with Seán Ó Tuama on *An Duanaire* is part of a longstanding commitment to translation from Irish which began with *Longes Mac n-Usnig:*

Being the Exile and Death of the Sons of Usnech, and *The Breastplate of Saint Patrick,* both published in 1954, and followed by *Thirty-three Triads* the next year. Translation, for Kinsella, became both an act of commitment to a tradition of literature by giving it a 'new currency' in which it is made available to contemporary readers, and 'the best way', as he notes, 'of appreciating the work itself'.[24] One of Kinsella's great achievements of translation, and one with which he remains imaginatively involved, is his translation of the Old Irish epic Táin Bó Cuailnge, *The Táin.* Kinsella's work on *The Táin* involved extensive research in early Irish literature and mythology, the influence of which is evident particularly in the poetry such as *Notes from the Land of the Dead* and Peppercanister sequences such as *One,* which have as their backbone stories of Ireland's prehistory from the ninth century *Lebor Gabála Érenn* or *The Book of Invasions.* As he emphasises, the 'historical element' that the research for translations revealed became part of the subject matter of his own poetry.[25] However, Kinsella's increasing use of mythical material provided, for some, an obstacle to the understanding of his poetry. As Dillon Johnston explains, it was not always evident to critics that poems such as **'Survivor'** from *Notes from the Land of the Dead* were, what he calls, 'loose renditions' of episodes from Irish mythology.[26] **'Survivor',** for example, draws on an episode from the *Lebor Gabála Érenn* which tells of Fintan, last survivor of Cessair's people[27]:

> By twilight everything was destroyed,
> the only survivors a shoal of women
> spilled onto the shingle, and one man
> that soon—as they lifted themselves up
> and looked about them in the dusk—
> they silently surrounded.
>
> (C 115)

Kinsella's translation of the *Táin* arose through his involvement with Liam Miller's Dolmen Press, which had issued much of Kinsella's early poetry and all of his translations.[28] Miller prompted Kinsella to find and translate 'manuscripts of myths, legends, or stories in Irish which deserved publication in English'.[29] By founding Dolmen Press in 1951, Miller revived a tradition of Irish publishing that had ended with Maunsel & Roberts in 1926, and provided a vital publishing outlet for Irish writers.[30] Asked by Peter Lennon of *The Guardian* whether those who published with Dolmen had been refused by publishers abroad, Miller replied: 'Not at all. Several of them have had offers from England and America, but they continue to publish with us.'[31] Kinsella explains how,

> from the beginning the Press set itself the object of publishing work by Irish writers, and it soon found itself dealing with a new Irish poetry. For the next

three decades it provided professional primary publication in Ireland for poetry and drama, with commentary on Irish and Anglo-Irish literature.[32]

Dolmen focused on fine printing and good design and its editions of work by poets and playwrights including J. M. Synge, Brian Coffey, Austin Clarke and John Montague were often illustrated by artists such as Pauline Bewick, Harry Clarke and Louis le Brocquy (whose brush drawings for the *Táin* contributed to its success). A year after its foundation, Kinsella's *Three Legendary Sonnets* appeared under the Dolmen imprint. With the exception of *Notes from the Land of the Dead,* which was published by the Cuala Press in 1972, all of Kinsella's European editions of poetry came from Dolmen, with *Downstream, Nightwalker and Other Poems* and *Selected Poems 1956-1968* appearing also in association with Oxford University Press. His US editions at this time included *Poems and Translations* from Atheneum, New York in 1961, *Nightwalker and Other Poems* from Knopf in 1968, *Tear* from the Pym Randall Press in Cambridge, Mass. in 1969 and *Notes from the Land of the Dead* again with Knopf in 1973.

In 1964 the Dolmen Press was incorporated, and Kinsella, along with Liam Miller and Liam Browne, became one of its founding directors. This placed the poet in a difficult position since as a director he could not justify Dolmen publishing all of his work.[33] He needed to find another outlet for his poetry and, rather than moving to another publishing house, Kinsella decided to found his own imprint, the Peppercanister Press in 1972. There were other reasons for the establishment of Peppercanister. In his preface to Stephen Enniss's bibliography of Peppercanister, Kinsella expresses his frustration with magazine publications that do not always present work in the best way, and points to the need to publish work quickly and at regular intervals in order to get a sense of its progress. Kinsella explains how publishing with Peppercanister offers him the kind of interim publication usually provided by magazines and journals through which he can assess the progress of his work: 'Peppercanister became an alternative to the publication of poetry in literary journals. I had always found this unsatisfactory, with the poems placed between stories and articles and disappearing with a particular issue.'[34] By founding the Peppercanister Press, Kinsella follows in the tradition of small Irish presses such as Austin Clarke's Bridge Press, run from his home in Templeogue.

The Peppercanister Press takes its name from St Stephen's church on Upper Mount Street, Dublin, known locally as 'the Peppercanister'. The church is visible from Kinsella's home at the time on Percy Place, parallel to the Grand Canal, from where Peppercanister began issuing 'occasional special items'.[35] Kinsella explains the genesis of the press:

> The idea originated with *Butcher's Dozen,* written in April 1972 in response to the Widgery Report on the "Bloody Sunday" shootings in Derry. The poem was finished quickly and issued as a simple pamphlet at ten pence a copy; cheapness and coarseness were part of the effect, as with a ballad sheet.[36]

There followed two poems in commemoration of the Irish composer, Seán Ó Riada, *A Selected Life* and *Vertical Man,* the first of which raised funds for the Seán Ó Riada Foundation. The last of these occasional pamphlets was a poem called *The Good Fight* written for the tenth anniversary of the assassination of John F. Kennedy which was, like *A Butcher's Dozen,* issued as a small public pamphlet. Peppercanister retained a close connection with the Dolmen Press. *Butcher's Dozen* was printed at the Elo Press in Dublin and distributed by Dolmen, but the subsequent three pamphlets were both printed and distributed by Dolmen.

The character of the Peppercanister publications changed in 1974 with the publication of the fifth Peppercanister, *One.* For the next thirteen years the Peppercanister Press produced editions of poetry which matched the high standard of design and production notable in Dolmen editions. Kinsella acknowledges Miller's influence, saying 'I had admired Liam Miller's commitment to quality in materials and design, and for a while this was confused with the Peppercanister idea'.[37] *One* and *A Technical Supplement* contained illustrations, the first by Irish artist Anne Yeats and in the second plates were taken from Denis Diderot's eighteenth-century *Encyclopédie.* In all of the Peppercanisters great attention was paid to the covers, some of which, like *The Messenger,* display a virtuosity of design which contributes significantly to the understanding of the text inside. Peppercanisters five to twelve were each published in deluxe and trade editions, with some volumes also coming out in limited or library editions. The deluxe editions were printed on handmade paper, bound in calf, basil or vellum, and often presented in a slip case. Frequently, Kinsella included an additional verse written in the author's hand to the text of the deluxe editions. These lines then became part of the main text when the poem was reprinted in the larger collections issued by Oxford University Press or Wake Forest.

The two volumes of 1978, *Song of the Night and Other Poems* and *The Messenger,* were the last of the Peppercanisters to be printed at the Dolmen Press. The next four volumes, *Songs of the Psyche* and *Her Vertical Smile* of 1985, and *Out of Ireland* and *St. Catherine's Clock* of 1987 were set by Raymond and Nuala Gunn and printed by Reprint Ltd in Dublin for the Peppercanister Press. It was at this point that Kinsella took full control of the design and layout of the Peppercanisters, drawing on Liam Miller's expertise and advice to make sure that the 1985 volumes matched the high standards of the previous Peppercanisters. On 9 March 1984, Miller sent Kinsella 'notes towards a general specification for Peppercanister books', to help him plan the editions. These notes described the format of the Peppercanisters as US royal octavo, the type as Photoset Pilgrim Roman with Italic, printed on Artlaid Natural paper which was threadsewn in sections and then bound.[38]

Kinsella's publicity material for Peppercanister divides the editions into a number of series. The first series comprises the first four occasional poems, *Butcher's Dozen, A Selected Life, Vertical Man* and *The Good Fight.* The next three Peppercanisters, *One, A Technical Supplement* and *Song of the Night and Other Poems* form the second series; *The Messenger, Songs of the Psyche* and *Her Vertical Smile* the third.[39] There is a small discrepancy between the information included in the 1985 brochure, and that produced two years later. In 1985 Kinsella announces that the fourth series will begin with *One Fond Embrace* and *Out of Ireland.* By 1987 this information has been revised to read that the fourth series will open with *Out of Ireland* and *St. Catherine's Clock.* This change of plan is indicative of the more complicated publishing history of the Peppercanister Press at this time. In 1980, two years after the last editions to be printed at the Dolmen Press under Liam Miller's supervision had appeared, Kinsella was in correspondence with Peter Fallon of Gallery Press with a view to publish the poet's work.[40] In 1981 a version of *One Fond Embrace* was issued by Gallery Press, in association with the Deerfield Press of Massachusetts. However, Gallery did not assume the relationship with Peppercanister that Dolmen had in the past, preferring only to print those editions that would be published under Gallery's imprint.[41] When it seemed that the Peppercanister imprint was on less than secure ground, John F. Deane of Dedalus Press agreed to print and distribute Kinsella's work, which would continue to be published initially by the Peppercanister Press. Kinsella was careful to distinguish Peppercanister from Dedalus, refusing to be included in Deane's anthology of Dedalus poets and taking exception to the *Times Literary Supplement* review of *Personal Places* and *Poems from Centre City* which attributed the volumes to the Dedalus Press.[42] This misunderstanding no doubt arose

from the fact that neither volume contains the usual colophon giving publication details, and indeed the previous volume, *One Fond Embrace,* states in its colophon that 'Peppercanister 13, *One Fond Embrace,* has been printed by the Carlow Nationalist and published by The Dedalus Press.' In 1988 a revised version of *One Fond Embrace* was published as the thirteenth Peppercanister. A regular series of subsequent volumes followed, distributed by Dedalus: *Personal Places* and *Poems from Centre City* in 1990; *Madonna and Other Poems* and *Open Court* in 1991. After a break of five years during which Kinsella published an essay on poetry and politics in Ireland called *The Dual Tradition,* which was issued by Carcanet Press in Manchester as Peppercanister number 18, Kinsella returned with a volume of poetry called *The Pen shop,* which was published by Peppercanister in 1997. The two most recent Peppercanisters are *The Familiar* and *The Godhead,* which appeared in April 1999.

Though perhaps not initiated with this purpose directly in mind, Peppercanister quickly became an ideal format for the longer sequences of poems which are characteristic of Kinsella's writing. The loosening of stanzaic form and the introduction of narrative and dramatic passages into his writing suited the more adaptable format of Peppercanister. As Kinsella indicated, the Peppercanisters are a valuable form of interim publishing, allowing the poet to revise the work before it is published commercially. The initial four Peppercanister volumes were published together by Dolmen in association with Oxford University Press under the title *Fifteen Dead.* The next three were published similarly under the title *One and Other Poems.* Both of these editions were published in 1979. With the demise of the Dolmen press following Liam Miller's death in 1987, Peppercanister continued Dolmen's association with Oxford University Press issuing the volume *Blood and Family* in 1988, which gathered together *The Messenger, Songs of the Psyche Her Vertical Smile, Out of Ireland* and *St. Catherine's Clock.* In 1994 Oxford University Press published *From Centre City,* which brings together *One Fond Embrace, Personal Places, Poems from Centre City, Madonna and Other Poems* and *Open Court.* In each of these commercial editions Kinsella has revised the poetry, sometime extensively, especially with the later writing. In 1996 Oxford University Press produced a paperback volume, *Thomas Kinsella: Collected Poems 1956-1994,* in which the poet once again revises and reworks the poems, providing the reader with another version of the work-in-progress.[43] In his review of the *Collected Poems,* Floyd Skloot describes how Kinsella avails himself of the different forms in which his poems are published to constantly refer back to his earlier work, absorbing previous work into the current writing.[44] Skloot argues that while 'many critics since roughly 1968 have accused Kinsella of brooding himself to pieces, the presence here of the entire work shows how the pieces all fit':

> The impression is of a fully realized, cohesive endeavor that both concerns and enacts fragmentation, that mounts temporary incursions into chaos despite the futility of the undertaking, and that restlessly stalks peace.[45]

Thomas Kinsella's Peppercanister poems are vital to understanding how 'the pieces all fit'. With these slim volumes Kinsella develops the themes and references which link together apparently disparate works and provide an undertow to the surface movement of his poems. Until recently, criticism of Kinsella's poetry concentrated on the early writing, including **Notes from the Land of the Dead** and perhaps the first few Peppercanister pamphlets. Notable among early studies is Maurice Harmon's excellent study of 1974, **The Poetry of Thomas Kinsella,** which examines Kinsella's writings and translations from 1958 to 1974. The greater part of critical writing on Kinsella since this time has taken the form of journal articles or chapters in books such as Robert F. Garratt's paper on 'Fragilities and Structures: Poetic Strategy and Thomas Kinsella's **"NightWalker"** and **"Phoenix Park"'** published in *Irish University Review* in 1983, Dillon Johnston's (whose association with Kinsella arises through the Wake Forest Press which published Kinsella's early work in the US) part-chapter of Kinsella in *Irish Poetry after Joyce* in 1985, and Seamus Deane's chapter on Kinsella in *Celtic Revivals: Essays in Modern Irish Literature 1880-1980* of the same year. In 1987 John F. Deane produced a special issue of *Tracks* devoted to Kinsella, which included criticism, poetry and an interview with the poet. In 1980 Carolyn Rosenberg completed her compendious PhD dissertation 'Let Our Gaze Blaze: The Recent Poetry of Thomas Kinsella'. Rosenberg's research is exhaustive and comprehensive, providing invaluable information on Kinsella's family history and the influence of Jungian psychology and Irish mythology on his work. Her work has provided important groundwork for most subsequent scholars. Yet it was not until the latter part of the 1990s, forty-three years after Kinsella's first publication, **The Starlight Eye,** that complete critical surveys of Kinsella's work have been published. The first of these, Thomas H. Jackson's *The Whole Matter: The Poetic Evolution of Thomas Kinsella* pays particular attention to Kinsella's early writing, evaluating the Jungian and mythological basis of the poetry, and providing important local contextualisation for readers not familiar with Dublin. As part of Twayne's English Authors Series, Donatella Abbate Badin's *Thomas Kinsella,* published in 1996, is an ideal introduction to the reader unfamiliar with Kinsella's work. She plots out the main themes and approaches of his writing and provides a clear and comprehensive bibliography. Indispensable to Kinsella scholarship is Brian John's study of the same year, *Reading the Ground: The Poetry of Thomas Kinsella,* which meticulously draws together the key threads of the poet's work, and argues persuasively for Kinsella as an 'essential voice of our time'.[46]

These critical works provide a foundation for this present study of Kinsella's Peppercanister poems, which explains the genesis and development of the work and analyses each volume in detail within the context of the ongoing Peppercanister series. Drawing on material available in the Thomas Kinsella Papers held at Emory University, Atlanta, it sources the diversity of research which underpins Kinsella's poetry and explores how publication under the Peppercanister imprint has affected the direction and development of the poet's work. An informed reading of Kinsella's work requires an understanding of the scholarly framework in which it is written. This study hopes to make evident the breadth and richness of Kinsella's inquiry which enables him to write a poetry of great subtlety, rigour and engagement; and to provide a starting point for research into areas such as Kinsella's prosody and questions of how his handling of the poetic sequence compares with that of poets such as Ezra Pound or William Carlos Williams.

Adopting a chronological approach, the study examines the Peppercanister volumes under the general rubrics of tradition, subjectivity, history and politics. The chapters of this study do not adhere strictly to the sequences into which Kinsella arranged his writing since the structure that underpinned that arrangement was modified, and eventually dispensed with, as the writing developed. And indeed, as is pointed out above, practical circumstances on occasion intervened to change the planned order of publication. However, there are certain foci around which the Peppercanister volumes resolve. Chapter one reads the first four Peppercanisters, **Butcher's Dozen,** a satire on injustice, **A Selected Life, Vertical Man,** elegies for Seán Ó Riada, and **The Good Fight,** a commemoration of John F. Kennedy, through the lens of tradition. In each of these volumes Kinsella brings together visions of the past and of the future and explores the negotiations that the present must undergo in order to reconcile both. Chapter two examines the four volumes that continue Kinsella's inward turn begun in **Notes from the Land of the Dead.** Though quite distinct in context and tone, **One, A Technical Supplement, Song of the Night and Other Poems** and **The Messenger** each explore the idea of subjectivity in the context of family and society. It is here that we see Kinsella's attention to the visual aspect of his work at its most pronounced with, for example, deft arrangement of illustrations from Diderot's *Encyclopédie* interwoven with the text of *A Technical Supplement,* and visual puns on the cover of *The Messenger.* Chapter three opens with Kinsella's first Peppercanister volume after a seven-year period, *Songs of the Psyche.* This volume connects with the psychological exploration of the previous volumes and points toward Kinsella's greater engagement with larger historical contexts that inform the subsequent poems, *Her Vertical Smile, Out of Ireland* and *St. Catherine's Clock.* Once again the figure of Seán Ó Riada takes a pivotal position in Kinsella's poetry, here joined by another composer Gustav Mahler, the ninth-century philosopher Johannes Scotus Eriugena, and Robert Emmet in a juxtaposition which allows Kinsella to question the validity of historical narrative and the position of the individual within that narrative. The fourth chapter explores the shift in Kinsella's focus from the historical to the contemporary in *One Fond Embrace, Personal Places, Poems From Centre City, Madonna and Other Poems,* and *Open Court.* Situated in and around Dublin, these poems interweave the personal and the political in a poetry which is often darkly critical of contemporary Irish society. The study concludes with an examination of Kinsella's most recent Peppercanister volumes, *The Pen Shop, The Familiar* and *Godhead,* which signal a turning away from the sharp criticism of the early 1990s poetry towards a more lyrical meditation on the relationships that sustain the self.

Notes

1. *Poetry Book Society Bulletin* 17, Mar. (1958).

2. John Haffenden, *Viewpoints: Poets in Conversation with John Haffenden* (London: Faber & Faber, 1981), pp. 100-13 (p. 101).

3. Dennis O'Driscoll, 'Interview with Thomas Kinsella', *Poetry Ireland Review* 25: Spring (1989): 57-65 (p. 58).

4. Michael O'Higgins, 'Poets of the Fifties: Thomas Kinsella', *Oxford Opinion* May (1960): 21-2 (p. 21).

5. Dillon Johnston, *Irish Poetry after Joyce* (Indiana: U of Notre Dame P; Mountrath: Dolmen, 1985), p. 102.

6. O'Higgins, 'Poets of the Fifties', p. 21.

7. *Poetry Book Society Bulletin* 55: Dec. (1967).

8. Kinsella prefaces the collection with a quotation from Apocalypse 8: 10-11.

9. Edna Longley, 'Spinning through the Void', *Times Literary Supplement,* 19 Dec. 1980: 1446.

10. John Montague, 'And an Irishman', *The New York Times Book Review,* 18 Aug. 1968: 5.

11. Eavan Boland, 'Kinsella: A New Direction', *The Irish Times,* 6 Apr. 1968.

12. John Haffenden, *Viewpoints,* p. 108.

13. Daniel O'Hara, 'An Interview with Thomas Kinsella', *Contemporary Poetry* 4 (1981): 1-18 (p. 6).

14. Ibid.

15. Johnston, *Irish Poetry after Joyce,* p. 104.

16. O'Driscoll, 'Interview with Thomas Kinsella', p. 60.

17. Haffenden, *Viewpoints,* p. 105.

18. This connection no longer exists in the revised poems of *Collected Poems.* See Maurice Harmon, *The Poetry of Thomas Kinsella: 'With Darkness for a Nest'* (Dublin: Wolfhound, 1974), p. 81.

19. Floyd Skloot, 'The Evolving Poetry of Thomas Kinsella' *New England Review* 18: 4 (1997): 174-87 (pp. 174-5).

20. Edna Longley, 'The Heroic Agenda: The Poetry of Thomas Kinsella', *Dublin Magazine* 5: Summer (1966): 61-78.

21. O'Driscoll, 'Interview with Thomas Kinsella', p. 65.

22. John MacInerney, 'Searching for Structure: Kinsella's "Pause En Route"', *Hibernia,* 4 Aug. 1972.

23. Seamus Heaney, 'The Poems of the Dispossessed Repossessed', *The Government of the Tongue* (London: Faber & Faber, 1988), pp. 30-5 (p. 32).

24. Haffenden, *Viewpoints,* p. 112.

25. Philip Fried, '"Omphalos of Scraps": An Interview with Thomas Kinsella', *Manhattan Review* 4: Spring (1998): 3-25 (p. 12).

26. Johnston, *Irish Poetry after Joyce,* p. 98.

27. Brian John, 'Contemporary Irish Poetry and the Matter of Ireland—Thomas Kinsella, John Montague and Seamus Heaney', *Medieval and Modern Ireland,* ed. Richard Wall (Gerrards Cross: Colin Smythe, 1988), pp. 34-59 (p. 38).

28. Kinsella explains that the decision to do an edition of the *Táin* 'had to do with the Dolmen Press maturing to a certain point: we wanted to do a new kind of work. The first idea was the Deirdre story; it was a manageable length. Then I got interested in such things for their own sake.' Fried, 'Omphalos of Scraps"', p. 11.

29. Carolyn Rosenberg, 'Let Our Gaze Blaze: The Recent Poetry of Thomas Kinsella', unpublished PhD thesis (Kent State University, 1980), pp. 120-1.

30. For a history of Dolmen see Robin Skelton, 'Twentieth-century Irish Literature and the Private Press Tradition', *Irish Renaissance: A Gathering of Essays, Memoirs and Letters for the Massachusetts*

Review, ed. R. Skelton and D. Clarke (Amherst: U of Massachusetts, 1965), pp. 158-67; and Michael G. Freyer, 'The Dolmen Press', *The Private Library* (Apr. 1960). In 1976 Dolmen issued an illustrated bibliography of the first 25 years of the Press: Liam Miller, *Dolmen XXV: An Illustrated Bibliography of the Dolmen Press, 1951-1976* (Dublin: Dolmen Press, 1976).

31. Peter Lennon, 'Dolmen Dublin', *The Guardian,* 23 Oct. 1962.

32. Thomas Kinsella, 'A Note on Irish Publishing', *The Southern Review* 31: 3 (1995): 633-8 (p. 635). Also included in slightly revised form in Kinsella's *The Dual Tradition,* Peppercanister 18 (Manchester: Carcanet, 1995), pp. 107-10.

33. Rosenberg, 'Let Our Gaze Blaze', p. 209.

34. Kinsella, Preface to Stephen Enniss, *Peppercanister 1972-1997: Twenty-five Years of Poetry: A Bibliography* (Atlanta: Emory U, 1997), pp. 1-2. However, Kinsella did not abandon serial publication altogether. Certain poems in *Song of the Night and Other Poems,* published by Peppercanister in 1978, were first published in journals such as *Tracks, The Chowder Review,* and *The Sewanee Review.* Indeed this practice continues. Kinsella's recent journal publications include poems in *Agenda, Poetry* and *Ploughshares.*

35. Kinsella, Preface to *Peppercanister 1972-1997,* p. 1.

36. Ibid.

37. Ibid., p. 2.

38. Thomas Kinsella Papers, Woodruff Library, Emory University, box 24, folder 20.

39. For information on how Kinsella divides the editions into series, see the publicity pamphlets issued by Peppercanister in June 1978, 1985 and 1987.

40. Correspondence with Peter Fallon, 24 June and 12 Aug. 1980. Kinsella Papers, box 24, folder 1.

41. See Kinsella Papers, box 29, folder 10.

42. Ibid. See Dillon Johnston 'The Anthology Wars', *Times Literary Supplement,* 13 Sept. 1991 in which Peppercanisters 14 and 15 are listed under 'Dublin: Dedalus; distributed in the UK by Manchester: Password'.

43. Subsequent to the publication of the *Collected Poems,* OUP have ceased to publish their poetry list. Forthcoming commercial editions of Kinsella's work will be published by Carcanet Press, Manchester.

44. Skloot, 'The Evolving Poetry of Thomas Kinsella', p. 176.

45. Ibid.

46. Brian John, *Reading the Ground: The Poetry of Thomas Kinsella* (Washington: Catholic UP, 1996), p. 259.

Selected Bibliography

WORKS BY THOMAS KINSELLA

BOOKS OF POEMS

Three Legendary Sonnets. Dublin: Dolmen, 1952.

Poems. Dublin: Dolmen, 1956.

Another September. Dublin: Dolmen, 1958.

Moralities. Dublin. Dolmen, 1960.

Poems and Translations. New York: Atheneum, 1961.

Downstream. Dublin: Dolmen, and London: Oxford UP, 1962.

Wormwood. Dublin: Dolmen, 1966.

Nightwalker. Dublin: Dolmen, 1967.

Nightwalker and Other Poems. Dublin: Dolmen, and London: Oxford UP, 1968.

Nightwalker and Other Poems. New York: Knopf, 1968.

Poems: Thomas Kinsella, Douglas Livingstone, Anne Sexton. London: Oxford UP, 1968.

Nightwalker and Other Poems. New York: Knopf, 1968.

Tear. Cambridge, Mass: Pym-Randall Press, 1969.

Butcher's Dozen. Peppercanister 1, Dublin: Peppercanister Press, 1972.

A Selected Life. Peppercanister 2, Dublin: Peppercanister Press, 1972.

Notes from the Land of the Dead. Dublin: Cuala Press, 1972.

Notes from the Land of the Dead and Other Poems. New York: Knopf, 1973.

Selected Poems: 1956-1968. Dublin: Dolmen, and London: Oxford UP, 1973.

New Poems 1973. Dublin: Dolmen, 1973.

Vertical Man. Peppercanister 3, Dublin: Peppercanister Press, 1973.

The Good Fight. Peppercanister 4, Dublin: Peppercanister Press, 1973.

One. Peppercanister 5, Dublin: Peppercanister Press, 1974.

TRANSLATIONS, ANTHOLOGIES AND EDITIONS

Longes Mac n-Usnig: Being the Exile and Death of the Sons of Usnech. Dublin: Dolmen, 1954.

Thirty-three Triads, Translated from the XII Century Irish. Dublin: Dolmen, 1955.

Thirty-three Triads. Trans. Thomas Kinsella, illust. Pauline Bewick, Glenageary, Co. Dublin: Dolmen, 1955.

The Breastplate of St Patrick. Dublin: Dolmen, 1954; revised as *Faeth Fiadha: The Breastplate of St Patrick.* Dublin: Dolmen, 1957.

The Táin. Dublin: Dolmen, 1969 limited edn, reprinted in trade edn 1986.

An Duanaire 1600-1900: Poems of the Dispossessed. Ed. Seán Tuama and trans. Thomas Kinsella, Dublin: Dolmen with Bord na Gaeilge, 1981, reprinted 1994.

ESSAYS, NOTES AND EXCHANGES

'Note on *Another September'. Poetry Book Society Bulletin* 17: March (1958).

'Note on *Downstream'. Poetry Book Society Bulletin* 34: Sept. 1962.

Stephen Spender, Patrick Kavanagh, Thomas Kinsella, W. D. Snodgrass, 'Poetry Since Yeats: An Exchange of Views'. *Tri-Quarterly* 4 (1965): 100-11.

'The Irish Writer'. *Éire-Ireland* 2: 2 (1967): 8-15.

'Note on *Nightwalker and Other Poems'. Poetry Book Society Bulletin* 55: Dec. (1967).

'The Divided Mind'. *Irish Poets in English.* Ed. Seán Lucy. Cork: Mercier, 1973, pp. 208-18.

'Ancient Myth and Poetry: A Panel Discussion, David Greene, Thomas Kinsella, Jay MacPherson, Kevin Nowlan, Ann Saddlemyer'. *Myth and Reality in Irish Literature.* Ed. Joseph Ronsley. Waterloo, Ontario: Wilfred Laurier UP, 1977, pp. 8-15.

'W. B. Yeats, the British Empire, James Joyce and Mother Grogan'. *Irish University Review* 22: Spring-Summer (1992): 69-79. Also published in *PN Review* 19: 3 (1993): 10-14.

'Origins of Anglo-Irish'. *PN Review* 20: 1 (1993): 20-8.

The Dual Tradition: An Essay on Poetry and Politics in Ireland. Peppercanister 18. Manchester: Carcanet, 1995.

Thomas Kinsella, 'A Note on Irish Publishing'. *The Southern Review* 31: 3 (1995): 633-8.

SECONDARY SOURCES

Boland, Eavan. 'Kinsella: A New Direction' *The Irish Times,* 6 Apr. 1968.

Fried, Philip. '"Omphalos of Scraps": An Interview with Thomas Kinsella'. *Manhattan Review* 4: Spring (1988) 3-25.

Haffenden, John. *Viewpoints: Poets in Conversation with John Haffenden.* London, Boston: Faber & Faber, 1981.

Harmon, Maurice. *The Poetry of Thomas Kinsella: With Darkness for a Nest.* Dublin: Wolfhound, 1974.

Heaney, Seamus. 'Poems of the Dispossessed Repossessed'. *The Government of the Tongue: The 1986 T. S. Eliot Memorial Lectures and Other Critical Writings.* London: Faber & Faber, 1988, pp. 30-5.

John, Brian. *Reading the Ground: The Poetry of Thomas Kinsella.* Washington: Catholic UP, 1996.

———. 'Contemporary Irish Poetry and the Matter of Ireland—Thomas Kinsella, John Montague and Seamus Heaney'. *Medieval and Modern Ireland.* Ed. Richard Wall. Gerrards Cross: Colin Smythe, 1988, pp. 34-59.

Johnston, Dillon. 'The Anthology Wars'. *Times Literary Supplement,* 13 Sept. 1991, p. 26.

———. *Irish Poetry after Joyce.* Indiana: U of Notre Dame P/Mountrath: Dolmen, 1985.

Lennon, Peter. 'Dolmen Dublin'. *The Guardian,* 23 Oct. 1962.

Longley, Edna. 'Spinning through the Void'. *Times Literary Supplement,* 19 Dec. 1980, p. 1446.

———. 'The Heroic Agenda: The Poetry of Thomas Kinsella'. *The Dublin Magazine* 5: 2 (1966): 61-78.

MacInerney, John. 'Searching for Structure: Kinsella's Pause En Route'. *Hibernia,* 4 Aug. 1972.

Montague, John. 'And an Irishman'. *The New York Times Book Review,* 18 Aug. 1968, p. 5.

O'Driscoll, Dennis. 'Interview with Thomas Kinsella'. *Poetry Ireland Review* 25 (1989): 57-65.

O'Hara, Daniel. 'An Interview with Thomas Kinsella'. *Contemporary Poetry.* 4: 1 (1981): 1-18.

O'Higgins, Michael. 'Poets of the Fifties: Thomas Kinsella'. *Oxford Opinion,* May (1960): 21-2.

Skelton, Robin. 'Twentieth-Century Irish Literature and the Private Press Tradition: Dun Emer, Cuala, and Dolmen Presses: 1902-1963'. *Irish Renaissance: A Gathering of Essays, Memoirs, and Letters from The Massachusetts Review.* Ed. Robin Skelton and David R. Clarke, Amherst: U of Massachusetts, 1965, and Dublin: Dolmen, 1965.

Skloot, Floyd. 'The Evolving Poetry of Thomas Kinsella'. *New England Review* 18: 4 (1997): 174-87.

Maurice Harmon (essay date 2005)

SOURCE: Harmon, Maurice. "Thomas Kinsella: Jousting with Evil." *Yearbook of English Studies* (2005): 18-31.

[*In the essay below, Harmon studies the relationship between evil and art in Kinsella's poems, noting the influence of figures such as Gustav Mahler, Seán Ó Riada, and James Joyce.*]

At the beginning of his literary career Thomas Kinsella wrote poems about the precariousness of life and poems about love, eventually creating a style that incorporated the connection between them in language that embodied the idea of pain within love, loss within endurance. The language in which he describes mutability, various losses, pain, illness, violence, mutilation, death—what he terms 'evil'—gives his early work its distinctive texture. At the heart of his entire work, as he explores the presence of evil in increasingly more complex and more balanced poems, is the belief that art itself is the true answer to the power of evil. Through their creative energies, artists such as Sean O'Riada, Gustav Mahler, and Kinsella himself, provide a positive counter-force to its destructive activities.

While in the first two collections, *Poems* (1956) and *Another September* (1958), he emerges as a poet concerned with fragility in the nature of things, it is the epigrammatic poems in *Moralities* (1960) that define his outlook explicitly. The speaker in **'An Old Atheist Pauses by the Sea'** declares his shocked response to erosion:

> I choose at random, knowing less and less.
> The shambles of the seashore at my feet
> Yield a weathered spiral: I confess
> —Appalled at how the waves have polished it—
> I know that shores are eaten, rocks are split,
> Shells ghosted. Something hates unevenness.
> The skin turns porcelain, the nerves retreat,
> And then the will, and then the consciousness.[1]

'Something hates unevenness'. The last three lines summarize a point of view that is fundamental. Like a gambler, the speaker chooses at random. Lacking certainty he must yield to signs of weathering, must recognize not that process makes something beautiful but how the shell has been affected and must see it, paradoxically, within a movement that changes skin, nerves, will, and consciousness, the entire self into oblivion.

The frequency of oxymoron at this stage of Kinsella's development is worth noting. Even a random list from *Downstream* (1962) and *Nightwalker* (1968) shows its presence: 'with darkness for a nest'; 'a rack of leaves', 'a skull of light', 'both to horrify and instruct', 'crumbling place of growth', 'tender offals', 'the slithering pit', 'grim composure', 'a jewel made of pain'. These are signatures of Kinsella's imaginative faith, a linguistic mapping by which we trace the fundamentals of the work at this stage.

The clearest and most complex definition of paradox comes in the *Wormwood* sequence (1966). The title refers to the 'great star' that 'fell on the third part of

the rivers and upon the fountains of waters; [. . .] and the third part of the waters became wormwood; and many died of the waters, because they were made bitter' (*Revelations*, 8. 10-11). In an address to the **'Beloved'** Kinsella writes:

> It is certain that maturity and peace are to be sought through ordeal after ordeal, and it seems that the search continues until we fail. We reach out after each new beginning, penetrating our context to know ourselves, and our knowledge increases until we recognise again (more profoundly each time) our pain, indignity and triviality. This bitter cup is offered, heaped with curses, and we must drink or die. And even though we may drink we may also die, if every drop of bitterness—that rots the flesh—is not transmuted.
>
> (p. 62)

All of this—the search, the ordeal, the cup of bitterness, the need to absorb, the possibility of transmuting bitterness, the inevitability of death, and the importance of love—is fundamental to his work.

In a nightmare vision the 'I' figure strains after the echo of a blow that has left the trees 'stunned, minutely / Shuddering' and comes upon the symbolic tree.

> A black tree with a double trunk—two trees
> Grown into one—throws up its blurred branches.
>
> The two trunks in their infinitesimal dance of growth
> Have turned completely about one another, their join
> A slowly twisted scar, that I recognise.
>
> (p. 63)

The intertwined trees stand for a love that assimilates and transmutes the ordeal into a dance of growth. In Kinsella's mind creativity and love are inextricably linked. In **'Mask of Love'** the 'I' figure stresses the need to 'remember' that the marriage partners have 'climbed / the peaks of stress' and faced each other 'wearily' across the 'narrow abyss'. It is as though he fears their painful situation might be misrepresented, or minimized, its value not understood and therefore not made available to absorption and transmutation. For them there is no peace. The poem voices the feelings of a man doomed to utter his vision of the tragic nature of existence. He who has seen evil and understands both its destructive nature and its potential for growth calls upon her to grasp the interlocking truth of their doomed fruitful relationship.

'The Secret Garden' creates a balanced portrait of this truth, with dew as an image of fragile beauty in a threatening world. 'Tiny worlds, drop by drop, tremble / On thorns and leaves; they will melt away.' The withering is everywhere. The child is full of energy, 'light as light', but destined to absorb the necessary, inevitable 'first taint'. The wise father, in possession of insight, appreciates his son's 'pearl flesh', but knows he must release him 'towards the sour encounter'.

> Children's voices somewhere call his name.
> He runs glittering into the sun, and is gone
> [. . .] I cultivate my garden for the dew:
> A rasping boredom funnels into death!
> The sun climbs, a creature of one day,
> And the dew dries to dust.
> My hand strays out and picks off one sick leaf.
>
> (p. 65)

In these elegiac lines Kinsella voices his sadness at the nature of human existence, the presence of impermanence, suffering, death-in-life.

In the title poem of the next collection, *Nightwalker* (1968), the walker-narrator is a commuter who has to endure the journey from the depressing surroundings of Sandycove, a Dublin suburb, to the dispiriting routines of the Civil Service. He is the Civil Servant who reacts with scorn and anger to the First Economic Programme adopted by the Irish Government in 1958, his disappointment interfaced with the inscription on New York's Statue of Liberty. Also at the harbour mouth, Kathleen Ní Houlihan has become a debased figure called Productive Investment. The ironic tone is coloured by the clichés of the business world, the seductions of the new programme.

> Robed in spattered iron she stands
> At the harbour mouth, Productive Investment,
> And beckons the nations through our gold half-door:
> Lend me your wealth, your cunning and your drive,
> Your arrogant refuse. Let my people serve them
> Holy water in our new hotels,
> While native businessmen and managers
> Drift with them chatting over to the window
> To show them our growing city, give them a feeling
> Of what is possible; our labour pool,
> The tax concessions to foreign capital,
> How to get a nice estate though German.
> Even collect some of our better young artists.
>
> (p. 77)

At times his tale bristles with detail, as in the political fable of the Wedding Group which tells of a friendship that turned to enmity. The Groom, Best Man, the Fox, and their three ladies form the Wedding Group. Their sundering into violence and slaughter outlines what happened when former friends—the politicians Kevin O'Higgins, Rory O'Connor, and Eamon De Valera who had been at the wedding of Kevin O'Higgins—took opposing sides in the Civil War and the first two were killed.

> Look! The Wedding Group [. . .]

> The Groom, the Best Man, the Fox, and their three
>   ladies.
> A tragic tale. Soon, the story tells,
> Enmity sprang up between them, the Fox
> Took to the wilds. Then, to the Groom's sorrow,
> His dear friend left him also, vowing hatred.
> So they began destroying the Groom's substance
> And he sent out to hunt the Fox, but trapped
> His friend instead; mourning he slaughtered him.
> Shortly, in his turn, the Groom was savaged
> No one knows by whom. Though it's known the Fox
> Is a friend of death, and rues nothing.
>
> (pp. 78-79)

It is significant that as the walker approaches the martello tower in Sandycove he address the prose master (James Joyce) rather than the master poet (W. B. Yeats), the martello tower at Sandycove rather than the Norman tower at Thoor Ballylee. Kinsella is signalling the stance he has taken as a poet. On the one hand, sections of the poem resemble the stream of consciousness technique used in parts of *Ulysses*, having a similar fluidity of movement through incidents, memories, ideas, and images. On the other hand, in invoking his fellow Dubliner, Kinsella declares an allegiance to a writer who made his work out of the gritty and often unattractive reality of life in twentieth-century Dublin rather than to a writer who preferred to commemorate the fallen majesty of the Irish Ascendancy.

If the *Wormwood* sequence is realized in a straitjacket, the voice of the persona in *Nightwalker* is at once freer and more complex. Here the Tiresian consciousness in a sea of transient and changing circumstances seeks for structure and in the end finds it within. Its shifting scenes and changing voices convey the poet's anger at what has been done to a generation: the debasement of cultural values, the especial nationalistic pleading, all adumbrated in the phrase 'a dish of scalding tears [. . .] The food of dragons / And my own dragon self'. Juxtaposed with this ironical and angry summary is the elegiac voice of Amergin, the Old Irish poet, as a seamew lamenting what has happened to the country. 'Eire, Is there none to hear? Is all lost?' And with that voice goes a 'dying language'. In the face of this desolation, seeing his wife's shadow on the window blind, Kinsella states his belief in the value of love and expresses faith in a meaningful evolutionary process. Then in a dramatic change of mood and rhythm the self makes an imaginary flight to the Moon whose barren surface gives an unrestricted view of the depressive conditions that have reflected the walker's consciousness. The poem concludes:

> I think this is the Sea of Disappointment.
> If I stoop down, and touch the edge, it has
> A human taste, of massed human wills.
>
> (p. 84)

The psychological directions taken by the narrator in *Nightwalker* are deepened in *Notes from the Land of the Dead* (1972). If *Nightwalker* is politically challenging, the poems in the new collection mark a change—in the portrayal of the self, in the explicit autobiographical material, in the style that enables him to use language that is at one and the same time positive and negative. Kinsella dramatizes himself as a Faustian adventurer prepared to face abnormal states, one who has 'turned to things not right nor reasonable' as Faust did when he made his compact with the devil.

> Dear God, if I had known how far and deep,
> how long and cruel, I think my being
> would have blanched: appalled.

>   (p. 95)

In an exclamatory style the 'appalled' self remembers and recreates the extreme experience. The magician with his implements prepares to go out of his mind into the depths of the unconscious, to fall out of this world into the abyss, 'So far from the world and earth', where there is

> No bliss, no pain; dullness after pain.
> A cistern hiss [. . .] A thick tunnel stench
> rose to meet me. Frightful. Dark nutrient waves.
> And I knew no more.

>   (p. 96)

The loss of consciousness is followed by an embryonic state in which he drifts, seeking an empty shell in which to grow. The narrator remembers the ordeal, the fall and the search for a way back to the upper world.

This emblematic account prefigures what happens elsewhere in the collection, in particular in several poems that concentrate on the significance of a child's encounter with his grandmother, the one setting out on the road of life, innocent and untested, the other at the end of that road, shrivelling into death, the images associated with her those of blackness, decay, and fear. To the little boy she is a figure of dread, witchlike, predatory, mysterious, someone and something he is urged to visit, to kiss. The meeting is a conjunction of youth and age, innocence and experience, the pristine consciousness and the consciousness burdened with life's ordeals.

In these poems the 'I' narrator is a witness. In **'Hen Woman'** the tone is one of serious attention, alert, perceptive, reading the small event, the trivial scene, packing it with significance. The objective narrative freezes the moment, the figures and the event into a diagram: the woman hurries out, the egg falls and breaks but in slow motion. 'Nothing moved', 'time stood still', bird, woman, and child 'locked there [. . .]

gaping'. Then the dung beetle, bearer of life, advances, the egg falls, thunder sounds. This searching into the substance is presented as part of the way in which the imagination seizes experience and takes it in. 'I feed upon it still', he tells us:

> there is no end to that which, not understood,
> may yet be hoarded in the imagination,
> in the yolk of one's being, so to speak,
> there to undergo its (quite animal) growth,
>
> dividing blindly, twitching, packed with will,
> searching in its own tissue
> for the structure in which it may wake.
> Something that had—clenched in its cave—
> not been now was: an egg of being.

>   (p. 99)

When the boy encounters the woman, he receives some consolation. She represents the progress he must make, the evil he must absorb.

Throughout the Peppercanister publications (1972 to the present), Kinsella's handling of voice and persona is complex and varied, but on the whole is objective and rational. Instead of the diagrammatical tension of **'Hen Woman'** we have the separate portrayals of *The Good Fight* (1973): John F. Kennedy, Lee Harvey Oswald, Robert Frost, Plato. It is the interaction of these figures, their individual wills and values, and their interpretations of human psychology that gives the poem its particular force. Similarly, in other poems in the Peppercanister series, such as *Her Vertical Smile* (1985) and *Out of Ireland* (1987), the presence of contrasting figures is significant. We discover what the poem means by attending to distinct voices, each enunciating a particular point of view, no individual voice voicing the entire meaning.

In *The Good Fight* John F. Kennedy evokes the promise of New Frontier politics by his vigour and idealism, his ability to imbue a people with a vision of what is possible. It is based on the idea that 'All reasonable things are possible'. His final speech is juxtaposed with Plato's reflections on the dangers and pitfalls of leadership. The portrait of Lee Harvey Oswald begins with objective third-person narration as Kinsella describes him settling into the room from which he will shoot at the President, but this changes to the first-person voice of the alienated being who feels his isolation and loneliness. It is a moving threnody for what it feels like to be a nobody and how that feeling motivates him to do something to counter the negative state.

> I have seen very few
> cut so dull and driven a figure,
> masked in scorn or abrupt

impulse, knowing content
nowhere.

(p. 158)

Oswald is broodingly self-aware and at the centre of his own drama of changing response. He can decide to end this state through suicide or through reaching out and touching. The question then becomes 'Who was that! / What decision was this'? Again, Kinsella brings in Plato's reflections on the force of feelings that afflict the individual: passion, greed, reason submerged. He counters Oswald's mood with Plato's meditations on man's brutish propensity for evil.

The final voice is that of Robert Frost who has been stunned by the calamity of the assassination. His conclusion, 'That all *un*reasonable things / are possible. *Everything* / that can happen will happen' (p. 163), challenges Plato's philosophy of harmony, a balance between Body and Mind. Frost's view is post-Freudian. The twentieth-century poet knows what man is capable of, the evil that men do. The artist can cope with that.

It is we, letting things *be,*
who might come at understanding.
That is the source of our patience.

(p. 164)

The Good Fight works through a number of voices which are characterized at some length. In *Out of Ireland* the presentation of voices is more complex and more concise, and the expression of a final point of view, in effect, a resolution or working-out of the issues raised in the many voices, conveyed more through images than explicit statement. The setting is St Gobnait's cemetery in Ballyvourney where the composer Sean O'Riada is buried. The voices are several: a crow, the Black Robber which is a human head over the chancel of the church, a Sile na Gig on the south wall, and an open grave. As Irish scholars on the continent used to advertise their skills in the streets, so each figure here declares its particular values: the crow offers knowledge of flesh and blood; the Black Robber counters that deathly invitation with the fact that he is native born in our 'foul deeds', one with us in committing evil; Sile na Gig offers her vaginal orifice, source of life, superior to the other two; the grave offers redemption after death. Like instruments in an orchestra these conflicting appeals, sequential and contrapuntal, sound their values with accumulating force.

The poem shifts to selective appropriation of Eriugena's metaphor of instrumental harmony, the dance and fiery immolation, to express his philosophy of the return of all mankind to God. In the next section Kinsella takes up the idea of the dance to memorialize the dancing figure of O'Riada, his shifting rhythms, throaty piping, and dry taps on the drum skin. In the real world, however, Kinsella says in his own voice, drawing again from Eriugena,

it grows dark and we stumble
in gathering ignorance
in a land of loss
and unfulfillable desire.

(p. 266)

In the final section, called 'Exit', Kinsella expresses his own response, 'The dance is at our own feet': it is up to us to dance, putting the cemetery behind us. It is up to the poet to write: 'reach me my weapon / in the goat-grey light'. The conclusion suggests a dedication to art, but in the context of what has gone before.

The undefined 'us' in this poem connects with Kinsella's habit in several poems of moving from the 'I' persona to the general 'we'. It is particularly effective in the collection *One* (1974) where much of the material is drawn from *The Book of Invasions,* that work of pseudo-history that relates the coming of successive groups of people to Ireland in pre-historic times. **'Finistere'** celebrates the voyage of people from continental Europe to Ireland. The 'I' speaker is Amergin, the first Old Irish poet, it is he who responds creatively to the idea of voyaging, he who observes a 'point of light' on the horizon; it is in him that

A maggot of the possible
wriggled out of the spine
into the brain.

(p. 168)

The poem moves with rhythmic intensity and persistence, changing at once from 'I' to 'we', as the people set out: 'our heads sang with purpose / and predatory peace' (p. 168). They respond more to an excitement in the blood than to an idea in the head, but as they journey they bear within their minds the megalithic civilization they have already created in Finistere. The poem bears witness to the mystery that motivates them, asking unanswered questions about the source of their excitement and the origin of this 'ghostly hunger' that causes them to leave what they have and voyage into the unknown. The rhythms in this celebration of the human instinct for reaching forward carry the poem onward, mimicking the motions of the ocean. It becomes a womb journey as they move 'as one' through 'salt chaos', praying for peace to the moon, source of their 'unrest', whose power they have tried to depict on 'great uprights':

whose goggle gaze
and holy howl we have scraped

speechless on slabs of stone
poolspirals opening on
closing spiralpools
and dances drilled in the rock
in coil zigzag angle and curl.

                                                    (p. 169)

The 'I' speaker fuses naturally with the 'we' and 'us' of the poem. As they step ashore the speaker/narrator recites Amergins's famous 'Hymn to Creation', an affirmation of beginnings.

Several other poems in the collection *One* speak with this inclusive 'we' voice. The fluid interaction of 'I' and 'we' is perfectly adapted to the pervasive thrust of these poems, these explorations of Kinsella's past as percolating through recent generations, and the distant sources of beginnings. At the heart of this backward turning is the continuing idea of process, the ways in which things develop, a country's past, language and culture, the creative process itself both in evolutionary terms and in terms of the hidden ways in which works of art are processed: experience absorbed, acted upon within the psyche, brought forth as a work of art.

One of the significant strands in Kinsella's development has been the increasingly comprehensive manner in which he has written of opposing forces, the positive and the negative. The initial search for order has been deepened and extended. Universal patterns declared in the early poem **'Baggot Street Deserta'** or **'Downstream'** have become part of the imaginative life of later collections, such as *Out of Ireland* (1987), *Her Vertical Smile* (1985), or *The Pen Shop* (1997).

In *The Pen Shop* the 'I' figure walks through the centre of Dublin, from the GPO to Bewley's Café in Part I, from there to Hely's Pen Shop in Part II. The effect is of solidity, of a particular person in particular places, with his own memories and associations, observing his surroundings: the inside of the GPO, the statues in O'Connell Street, the bridge across the Liffey, the statues near Trinity College, directions west, east, and south from there, remembering the river's associations with his family, and referring to places associated with himself and his work.

The statues along O'Connell Street—of Jim Larkin, John Gray, Smith O'Brien, and Daniel O'Connell— are observed with partly critical, partly humorous comments. Kinsella remembers Leopold Bloom clasping and unclasping his hands in the vicinity of Gray's statue 'About here'. What Kinsella notes often corresponds to what Bloom sees. Although the lines are dense with detail, the poem, carried forward by the physical and mental movement of the walker, has a steady momentum. When he enters Bewley's Café the

effect of forward movement is maintained in parallel sentences, participial verbs, specific actions, and the arrival into the 'fellowship' of male elders, but the constant ingredient is concrete detail: 'grinder', 'bins', 'shelves', 'shoppers', 'scales'.

> I crossed over
> and as far as Bewleys'.
> By the great grinder, into the front shop;
>
> by the bins of coffee in their dark sorts
> on the high shelves; passing among the shoppers
> gathered at the scales, precise in their needs;
>
> to the women and the urns at the back counter.
> Carried my coffee among the tables
> through the inner room murmuring with crockery
>
> toward the few elders along the far wall.
> Set my tray down on the wiped marble
> with a nod of fellowship.
>
> And sat back against the plush.
> We were all males. There was no distraction.
> Speechless, ordering our cares.

The Pen Shop also opens outwards. The walker follows the impulses of his mind and invites us to engage with imaginative connections as they arise. Mind and imagination range beyond the immediate scenes. When Kinsella directs our attention to the Number 21 bus proceeding westwards, all the place names—the Fountain, the Forty Steps, Kilmainham, Inchicore— have associations with his family, his school, and the autobiographical poetry. But his mind proceeds further 'Toward the thought of places / beyond your terminus' to the west 'where I have seen / the light of cities under the far horizon'. In the west people believe in a city seen at times beneath the waters, but the reference to the New World also recalls people in *The Book of Invasions* led westwards by a speck of light on the horizon. That movement, too, connects powerfully with a large part of Kinsella's work. Indeed this section associates with so much of his work that it is impossible to make a full list; it includes many of the poems in *New Poems* (1973), most of *One* (1974), *The Messenger* (1978), all of the **'Settings'** in *Songs of the Psyche* (1985), all of *St. Catherine's Clock* (1987), and many of the early poems which have settings in the Basin Lane region.

When he looks south towards Grafton Street he draws in ancestors in County Wicklow, present in **'His Father's Hands',** his connections with Wexford through marriage, his poem **'A Country Walk'**; beyond Wicklow lies **'Finistere',** not only the place from which early ancestors set off but a reference to Kinsella's poem of the same title. When he looks eastwards he salutes 'voices' in Europe and beyond Jerusalem: 'clear in calibre and professional, / self chosen'. Such references remind us that his poetry reverberates with inner connections and associations. The figure of the walker recalls other walkers, adventurers, voyagers, explorers of physical, psychological, mental, and imaginative depths and the myriad indications of movement, advance, and liveliness. But the poem has a larger significance. As the spiritual 'cell' from which Kinsella has always bought refills, the Pen Shop itself is the source of his entire work, which explains and justifies the presence of intertextual elements. The specific allusions to different poems and the use of such metaphors and images as walker, woman, grill, black, river, cell, kiss, counter, journey reinforce its function as an echo-chamber for the work. A poet who has achieved so much can reject the Morrígan perched on the epic hero's shoulder in the GPO, can oppose her negative power with the creative force of this poem. The ending brings us back to the beginning which identifies the harpy as the Morrígan, the 'she' to whom he has written. With a 'final' kiss the walker rejects her 'fierce forecasts'. The poem itself counters the evil of violence and death in its measured rhythm, civilized responses, imaginative extensions, and the purposeful and confirming nature of the walker's journey.

In a further enlargement, *The Pen Shop* evokes a subliminal, archetypal myth. This, too, is the land of the dead, a descent into the lower regions past the bird of death. The souls in the GPO have come 'out of the light'; all those recalled are dead. The statues are from the past; the city is devoid of people; black is the dominant colour, in the crow, the brewery, the coffee bins, the coffee, the flats of the river, even in Bloom. Crossing the Liffey with the boatman underneath takes its place in the iconography of a journey to the Otherworld where the Lady Patricia is queen. Within the coffee shop the walker has the confirming contact with the elders and the coffee is appropriately 'foreign and clay sharp'. In Part II the poem lifts towards what has been confirmed: Kinsella's own work, its sources, and lights on the horizon. In *Ulysses* Bloom, too, emerged from the dead centre towards the glimmering gates.

Those lights animate **'Carraroe'** (*Song of the Night* (1978)), a poem exact in particulars, alive with descriptive detail and mimetic rhythms expressing movement and release, the force of water and light, the strong oceanic power working at the shore. The scene is described in terms of myriad movement, of wave and light, of the humans, the lamp, the light, the voices of the children, the cleansing of the utensils, the seething flight of the sand-eels.

> A cell of light hollowed around us
> out of the night. Splashes and clear voices echoed
> as the spoons and knives were dug down

and enamel plates scooped under water
into the sand, and scraped and rinsed.

(p. 215)

Against this emphatically physical reality comes the arresting moment of 'A new music', with Gustav Mahler's 'Song of the Night' providing a parallel imaginative treatment. The tone lifts to wondrous exclamation—music, bird, people, setting—in an act of contemplation and comprehension. Kinsella's handling of the material, an interweaving of themes, analogies, and commentary, resembles Mahler's arrangement of Hans Bethge's *'Der Abschied des Freundes'*. He inflates and intensifies the force of the lines, alternating between the music itself and lines of critical appraisal, repeating Mahler's ejaculatory style of musical rhetoric in the language of the poem. The common ground is the pressure of motion, in the ocean and in the behaviour of children and adults, which is then consummated and released in the charged, amplified finale where the rhapsody rises to fervent emotional heights.

> A new music came on the wind: string sounds hissing
> mixed with a soft inner-ear roar
> blown off the ocean; a persistent
> tympanum double-beat ('. . . darkly expressive,
> coming from innermost depths . . .') That old
> body music. *Schattenhaft.* SONG OF THE NIGHT.
> A long horn call, 'a single note
> that lingers, changing colour as it fades . . .'
>
> Overhead a curlew responded.
> 'poignant . . .' Yes.
> 'hauntingly beautiful . . .' Yes!

(p. 216)

Perhaps no single sequence so powerfully and so fluently reflects Kinsella's sense of the presence of evil as *Her Vertical Smile* (1985), a poem with an Overture, two movements divided by an Intermezzo, and a Coda. Set in Vienna at the time of the collapse of the Austrian Empire, the beautifully poignant **'Overture'** responds to the Earth Mother's song in Mahler's *Das Lied von der Erde*. The opening four stanzas interpret the song, ascribe tonal and emotional qualities to it, creating a portrait of a grieving woman, burdened by sorrow, looking inwards and withdrawing into the 'heavens' from whence she came. The poem delicately evokes the plaintive conclusion of *'Der Abschied'* where the voice of the grieving woman, slowly repeating the single word *ewig* ('eternal') nine times, becomes so inaudible that it seems gradually to come from beyond life. She sings for her son (both Mahler and O'Riada) but her lament is also an elegy for the end of the world ('that last lovely heartbeat'), the transition from the particular to the universal effected with ease in the fluid rhythm of the run-on lines.

As in Mahler's music where splendour and exceptional energy oppose the desolation of Li-Tai-Po's poem in Bethge's translation, *Her Vertical Smile,* in changing rhythms, abrupt transitions, changing tones, and connecting imagery, plays out incidents, metaphors, and occasions of hope and promise against those of disappointment and destruction.

In a change to a sturdier rhythm with interrupted, sometimes staccato lines, Kinsella begins the next section with a portrait of Mahler conducting the first performance of his Eighth Symphony. He is a model artist, committed to his work, theatrical, strong-willed, who never ceased to search for new ways in which to express his complex vision, his 'strange work', as Kinsella writes, characterized by 'the readiness to embrace risk':

> tedium, the ignoble,
>   to try anything ten times
> if so the excessive matter can be settled.
>
> (p. 249)

Although the excessive matter cannot be finally settled, not even in ten symphonies, the last incomplete, Mahler explores the Muse-Mother in the familiar Kinsellan rhythm of artistic response.

> every rhythm drained
>
> into nothing, the nothingness
>   adjusting toward
> a new readiness.
>
> (p. 249)

The excited young respond—Kinsella to O'Riada, the audience to Mahler—their naive enthusiasm 'there at the heart of old Vienna' expressing the optimism of the time. The association with *Der Rosenkavalier* is apt. No other opera captures so perfectly the mood of Europe on the verge of the First World War, the gaiety and splendour, the sense of time running out, the young in one another's arms, those vile bodies. The lines beginning the second part of the first movement recreate the mindless antics of privileged Viennese, the mechanical harmony of marching men, the fluttering of banneret and the racing pulses, heads filled with notions of 'glory'. The jaunty rhythm, deflating as it records, gives way to the journalistic flatness describing rivers as natural boundaries, marking a place of disaster. In a detached musing Kinsella grants that we 'might search for harmony there' among 'the tangled woebegone' but it would be in vain. We might listen to 'the logic of majesty' that makes music out of war ('drumroll', 'slow march'), aware of the emergence of destructive machines, the threat of war, and the litter of metaphorical pigs to which the Empire is about to give birth.

In a transition to the last years of the Austrian Empire, recreated in a combination of glorious surroundings and buffoonery, Kinsella uses exact detail to create yet another social setting. The tone is one of lament for the almost farcical nature of man's trust in and attraction to militaristic glory—the splendour of dress, the yearning for fame in battle—and the inevitable conclusion 'when the awful day is over'. There is no mistaking Kinsella's deep sense of lament at such recurrent instances of vainglory and loss. Giving imaginative life to this 'curse', Mahler's vision of a happy outcome creates in his listeners 'the pulse of order'. But that solution, expressed through a rapturous matriarchal litany in the symphony's jubilant, accelerating ascent as Faust is raised to an affirmative vision of '*Das Unbschreibliche*' (the indescribable), is startlingly juxtaposed in the poem with Michelangelo's patriarchal depiction of the Creation where, in Kinsella's view, the figures are a little ridiculous. Neither of these perceptions, as far as he is concerned, is fully satisfactory. The curse, he maintains, comes from within.

Considering these matters—Mahler's and Michelangelo's depictions, old Vienna destroyed, the collapse of the Austrian Empire, the pigs of war let loose—Kinsella asks the rhetorical question: what shall it profit an elder that civilization will be destroyed? The question extends over eight mocking, descriptive stanzas with brilliant detail and hypnotic rhythm: what is the value when we ourselves will turn to mud and gore, when the bannerets become bodies dangling on the barbed wire of trench warfare, when the rivers of blood are 'of our own making'? This vision of destructive behaviour counterpoints the brilliant, social activities of old Vienna and is effective because quietly made in contrast with the heightened rhetoric used for social and militaristic achievement. At the height of his powers Kinsella reiterates the vision of evil he had defined in more restricted fashion in **'Downstream'**, **'Old Harry'**, and other early poems.

Returning in the second movement to Mahler and the Eighth Symphony, the poem celebrates the maker and the music. Mahler's 'double beat' moves between creation and destruction, bringing new life out of nothingness. The poem, too, reiterates the idea of an art that draws upon the dark underside of existence. Mahler dissolves grief and death in transcendent music. Kinsella relies on the defusing corrective of ironic counterpoint.

Note

1. Thomas Kinsella, *Collected Poems 1956-1994* (Oxford; Oxford University Press, 1996), p. 26. Further references are given in the text.

Kit Fryatt (essay date winter 2006)

SOURCE: Fryatt, Kit. "Thomas Kinsella's 'Downstream' Revisions." *Irish University Review: A Journal of Irish Studies* 36, no. 2 (winter 2006): 321-34.

[*In this essay, Fryatt studies Kinsella's revisions to "Downstream," tracing the poem's development since its first publication in 1962.*]

In 1971, Thomas Dillon Redshaw published a magisterial account of Thomas Kinsella's poem-sequence *Wormwood* and the changes it underwent between its first Irish publication in 1966 and its inclusion in the American edition of *Nightwalker and Other Poems* (1968).[1] Redshaw's commentary is informed by a conviction that the 'experimental interlude' of *Wormwood* 'may [. . .] well indicate the sources' of what in 1971 was still an 'adventurous development'; that even minor and relatively unsuccessful poems might be read closely for their insights into the shape of a poet's career.[2] This essay, though somewhat narrower in scope than Redshaw's exhaustive treatment, shares his conviction about the value of noting even small variations and revisions. Although the original version of **'Downstream'** belongs to a period before Kinsella's experiments with open form and consciously modernist aesthetics, it is a poem which, even if only because of the poet's repeated revisiting of it, has a claim on the attention of any student of modern Irish poetry.

Since Redshaw wrote his article, Kinsella has emerged as a 'fanatic tinkerer'[3] who has developed a method of draft publication—the Peppercanister pamphlets—which precedes the compilation of his poetry into revised trade editions.[4] Kinsella's work rarely settles into final forms. The poet typically presents himself in interview and in his poems as a fastidious reviser, 'abolishing' frivolous and ornamental effects:

> It's not so much that I'm looking for anything laconic or lapidary, it's just that the notion of decorative language, of poetry as linguistic entertainment, seems to me a trivial exercise. I'm not talking about something necessarily elaborate, as with Rilke. What I mean is facile rhetoric, or 'music', or mimesis for its own sake.[5]

This painstaking persona gets a satirical treatment in the poems, such as **'Worker in Mirror, at his Bench'**:

> It is tedious, yes. The process is elaborate,
> And wasteful—a dangerous litter
> Of lacerating pieces collects.
> Let my rubbish stand witness.
> Smile, stirring it idly with a shoe.

> (*Collected Poems 1956-2001,* p. 124)

Nevertheless, there can be no doubt that Kinsella takes the business of revision seriously.

Both editions of his *Collected Poems,* the first published by Oxford in 1996, the second by Carcanet in 2001, incorporate substantial changes even to the early poetry. *Wormwood* is actually something of an exception to this pattern, hardly having altered since Redshaw wrote his article and, along with the never-revised **'Phoenix Park'**, constitutes one of the most stable features of the Kinsella canon. Other long poems which appeared in *Nightwalker and Other Poems* have proved far more volatile. The version of **'Nightwalker'** in that volume is a revision of a limited Dolmen edition of the poem, published in 1967. Further revisions to **'Nightwalker'** appear in both *Collected* editions [*Collected Poems 1956-2001 Collected Poems*]. Another poem that appeared in *Nightwalker and Other Poems* was **'Downstream II'**, in fact the third version of **'Downstream'** to appear in print, which is also revised both in the Oxford and Carcanet collections. The modifications to both these allegorical poems are highly suggestive of Kinsella's changing poetics, taking place as they do over five decades, but I have chosen here to focus on **'Downstream'**. Of the two poems, its revisions suggest more emphatically a changing attitude to poetic material and modality, where those to **'Nightwalker'** seem mainly concerned with eliminating hyperbole and other forms of what Kinsella terms 'bad material'.[6] It might be noted, however, that the 2001 version of **'Nightwalker'** ends with a picture of domestic peace, 'her dear shadow on the blind', and Kinsella's epigram 'I believe love is half persistence / A medium in which from change to change / Understanding may be gathered' (*Collected Poems 1956-2001,* p. 84), rather than **'The Sea of Disappointment'** which formed the closing image of its predecessors.[7] The latest revision's tentative final line notwithstanding—'Hesitant, cogitating, exit'—this represents a rare example of Kinsella revising a poem to make its end more consolatory. As we shall see, however, this tendency towards comforting rhetoric has its counterpart in the most recent **'Downstream'**. These revisions suggest growing ease with sentiment, and a turn away from irony and caution.

Simply, we can define **'Downstream'** as a progress allegory, and group it with Kinsella's other journey-poems of the 1960s, **'A Country Walk'** and **'Nightwalker'**. We are accustomed to thinking of allegory as a didactic mode, and all of these poems aim to teach, about corruption (both literal and figural), about the brutality of ancient and recent history, and the artist's proper response to these. A certain formal rigidity characterizes all the poems,[8] and they share a social conservatism which is often felt to typify allegorical expression. Joel Fineman, for example, notes that 'allegory is always a hierarchizing mode, indicative of timeless order, however subversively intended its contents may be'.[9] Allegory shows an intense interest in placing its signifying objects and persons within a chain of being, a hierarchical structure which Angus Fletcher calls 'kosmic order'.[10] The hierarchical nature of allegory also sanctions a great deal of violence towards the bodies and things with which it makes its meanings. Twentieth-century theories of allegory stress the real, material quality of allegory's signifiers—for Walter Benjamin in *The Origin of German Tragic Drama,* this materiality and propensity to decay make nature itself allegorical.[11] Equally, this materiality is something for which allegory has no concern, as it consumes lived particularity in order to produce ordered meaning.[12] In **'Downstream'**, Kinsella is concerned not only with the *portrayal* of violence, as the speaker remembers one man's death and imagines the death of thousands, but with the ways in which the allegorical mode *enacts* violence upon nature.

Fletcher notes the tendency of allegories to infinite extension and, as a result, 'arbitrary closure'.[13] Analogical correspondences are 'incomplete and incompletable' and have to be forcibly truncated.[14] Balanchandra Rajan, discussing the unfinished aesthetic of *The Faerie Queene,* remarks that 'closure is foreseen but deferred, with the poem remaining receptive to and even infiltrated by the finality it cannot attain.'[15] The deferred resolution of **'Downstream'**— 'Searching the darkness for a landing place' (***Collected Poems 1956-2001,*** p. 50)—is just about all that has remained unchanged over forty years of revisions. The changes register shifts in Kinsella's attitude to the 'poet's or artist's eliciting of order'.[16]

'Downstream' exists in five different versions. The first of these, a poem of 163 lines in *terza rima,* was published in the 1962 collection, also entitled ***Downstream.*** Kinsella revised this poem considerably, cutting almost half its length, removing ornamental *chiaroscuro* and local colour, and published the result in the *Massachusetts Review* in 1964. A finalized version of the *Massachusetts Review* revision, its imagery and diction tightened still further, appears in *Nightwalker and Other Poems* (as **'Downstream II'**), in *Selected Poems 1956-68,* and in *Poems 1956-73.* A further revision, published in the 1996 ***Collected Poems,*** abandons some of the *terza rima* patterning and shortens the poem still further, while the latest version, published in 2001, restores certain features of the 1962 text.

In its first, 1962 incarnation, **'Downstream'** is an intensely ornamented poem. Robin Skelton notes 'the almost decadent romanticism of the imagery'.[17] The reader finds that the demands of *terza rima* occasionally overwhelm narrative propulsion:

Past whispering sedge and river-flag that lined
The shallow marshlands wheeling on the furrow
And groups of alder moving like the blind;

By root and mud-bank, otter-slide and burrow
The river bore us, with a spinal cry
Of distant plover, to the woods of Durrow.[18]

Few critics have regretted the loss of such passages. Skelton welcomes Kinsella's 1964 and 1968 revisions as bringing rigour and discipline to the poem, while Brian John commends the 'universal relevance' afforded by the erasure of references to Durrow.[19] Jackson strikes a note of unease with Kinsella's revisions, finding **'Downstream II'** 'more limited in scope than the original', which is a 'compendium of the thematic concerns of Kinsella's earlier work'.[20] **'Downstream II'** is an oddly truncated poem compared with its precursor, which traces a progression in the speaker's attitude to nature and history that is analogous to the poet's response to allegory.

The first version of **'Downstream'** gradually implicates its speaker in an authoritarian, hierarchical cosmos with allegorical devices. These include Yeatsian emblematics: 'A ghost of whiteness broke into life, upheaved / On crest of wing and water out of hiding / And swanned into flight' (*Downstream,* p. 51), and more problematically, the pageantry of Ezra Pound's 'Chinese Cantos' (Cantos LII-LXI):

I chose the silken kings,

Luminous with crisis, epochal men
Waging among the primal clarities
Productive war. Spurred by the steely pen

To cleansing or didactic rages, these
Fed the stream in turn

(*Downstream,* p. 51)

'His choice might seem curious,' Alex Davis remarks in his essay on Kinsella's debt to Pound: the Chinese Cantos are 'among the driest', in which polyphony is replaced by 'monologic' listing.[21] Davis also finds the choice of these Cantos politically troubling, quoting Massimo Bacigalupo, who describes them as 'a glaring example of regime art, or [. . .] "fascist realism"'.[22] This overstates the case with regard to the 'Chinese Cantos' themselves—they are more than encomia to authoritarianism. It also risks losing sight of the implications of the speaker's *own* description of the Cantos in a debate about the fascistic nature of Pound's poetry. The pleasure Kinsella's speaker takes in these poems is pleasure in their allegorical structures, their cosmic orderliness. Attention to details of status and precedence establishes hierarchies which give the impression of 'primal clarities'. Within these allegorical structures 'men' may characterize epochs, and derive their epochal luminosity from violent crises whose human consequences have been suppressed, as allegory restrains the resistance of its signifying bodies to the imposition of meaning upon them. Such art, as Kinsella's speaker himself describes it, and without reference to Pound's biography or criticism on Pound, is certainly authoritarian, allegorical, and may be described as fascistic. In this case, intertextual reference to Pound is less important than the speaker's admission of a culpable pleasure in art that imagines violence as purifying or instructive.

Like intertexts in allegory generally, the Cantos literally involve themselves in the world of Kinsella's downstream journey: 'these / Fed the stream in turn'. As it grows too dark to read, 'The gathering shades beginning to deceive / Night stole the princely scene', the speaker is vouchsafed a vision of order, the importance of which is suggested by its use as an epigraph to **'Downstream II'**:

> Drifting to meet us on the darkening stage
> A pattern shivers; whorling in its place
> Another holds us in a living cage
>
> And drifts to its reordered phase of grace;
> Was it not so?
>
>   (*Downstream,* p. 51)[23]

Davis finds in these lines an 'interpretative crux [. . .] Do these shivering "phase[s] of grace" provide a natural correlative to the "epochal men" [. . .]? This question leaches into the central problematic of Kinsella's poetry, early and late: the relationship between poetic 'order' and the vagaries of lived experience.'[24]

The 'central problematic' of Kinsella's poetry in this account, then, is an allegorical one: can the 'hierarchizing mode' ever be other than hostile to human particularity; is it possible to wrest any kind of liberation from its ordering structures? Davis suggests that the question which immediately follows the revelation of pattern and grace ('Was it not so?') dispels or at least disrupts the illusion of timeless order and textual agency in the world (p. 41). But **'Downstream'** continues in the illusion for another thirty lines, bringing its speaker to a point of embarrassing intensity in his desire to control and order the cosmos:

> I stood on the strange earth and stared aloft,
>
> *Urmensch* and brute, in glassy unconcern,
> Where specks of alien light icily hung
> Sprinkled in countless silence—there to learn
>
> How the remote chaotic, far outflung
> In glittering waste, may shiver and become
> A mesh of order, every jewel strung!
>
>   (*Downstream,* pp. 52-3)

This revelation of order places the speaker in a chain of being: he partakes of demi-god ('*Urmensch*')[25] and 'brute', and thus occupies the place traditionally ascribed to humans in such cosmic arrangements. His 'glassy unconcern' is a device characteristic of allegory. As Teskey notes in *Allegory and Violence,* the mode presumes an intelligence below its coded discourse, and is anxious to present that intelligence as benign and reclusive, withdrawing before the probing of a reader it posits as aggressive. In fact, the presiding intelligence of allegory is seductive, ideologically coercive, and desires coincidence with the world,[26] something Kinsella's speaker finds it impossible to conceal beneath 'unconcern':

> Mind shifted in its seed; with ancient thumb
> I measured out above the Central Plain
>
> The named heavens' bright continuum,
>
> And, knowing the birth of soul again,
> The dim horizon uttered a word of thunder
> A soft flash of far Promethean pain
>
>   (*Downstream,* p. 53)

The second movement of the poem rebukes the desire to control and ultimately consume one's environment by presenting grim images of man coinciding with nature in decay: 'A man one night fell sick and left his shell / Collapsed, half-eaten, like a rotted thrush's' or in a Boschian phantasmagoria inspired by the speaker's recollection of first hearing about the Holocaust: 'the evil dream where rodents ply, / Man-rumped, sow-headed, busy with whip and maul // Among nude herds of the damned' (*Downstream,* p. 54). The deceptive 'glassy unconcern' of the speaker, secure in the hierarchy between god and beast, is juxtaposed to the corpse's gaze: 'It searched among the skies / Calmly encountering the starry host / Meeting their silver eyes with silver eyes' (*Downstream,* p. 55). '"**Downstream**" subjects to quizzical scrutiny the "pattern" after which it nonetheless hankers'[27] but its power to scrutinize is fatally damaged by the implications of its own allegorical making. The speaker claims that the anecdote of the corpse 'like a rotted thrush's' made him aware to some extent of the magnitude and enormity of the Holocaust. He previously imagined the Nazis' victims as a collective, 'a formal drift of the dead / Stretched calm as effigies on velvet dust / Scattered on starlit slopes with arms outspread', but comes to realize through his encounter with a more local death that each of them was particular, and each murder would leave 'actual mess' (*Downstream,* p. 55). By the end of the poem, this insight has been forgotten and allegorical order has taken possession of the speaker once again, in terms that recall his positioning of himself as '*Urmensch* and brute':

The phantoms of the overhanging sky
Occupied their stations and descended;
Another moment, to the starlit eye,

The slow, downstreaming dead, it seemed, were
    blended
One with those silver hordes, and briefly shared
Their order, glittering

(Downstream, p. 56)

Such a return to hierarchical allegory ('stations'), which legitimizes the desire of the self to order the other ('were blended / One') aids the poem's arbitrary closure, as in Rajan's account of allegorical ends. The permanent deferral of 'Searching the darkness for a landing place' is enabled by these infiltrations of hypostatized finality into the progress narrative. The shape of the original **'Downstream'** is distinct: it builds to a point of fixed allegorical order, attempts to dismantle that order, fails, starts to build again, but defers forever the consequences of that second attempt at making. It illustrates the political problems that allegory brings with it, suggesting that they are, unfortunately and uncomfortably, a function of the mode's appeal. It also points to the extreme difficulty, perhaps the impossibility, of disrupting allegorical hierarchy within the framework of an allegory.

'Downstream II', by omitting the first movement, in which the fascination of allegory is acknowledged through allusions to Pound's 'silken kings', foreshortens this allegorical shape. The poem now focuses roundly on the story of the corpse and the speaker's horror at the Nazi genocide. Between the 1964 and the 1968 versions we see a growing intolerance of personification and a commitment to plainer diction. Instead of 'the Wood's dark door / Opened and shut' (*Massachusetts Review*, p. 323), Kinsella writes 'Dark woods: a door / Opened and shut' (***Selected Poems 1956-1968,*** p. 56), instead of 'Night devoured' (*Massachusetts Review*, p. 324), 'night consumed' (***Selected Poems 1956-1968,*** p. 57). The opening of the poem is rearranged, to avoid anthropomorphism: 'The ripples scattered, dying, to their task' (*Massachusetts Review*, p. 323) becomes the simply descriptive 'The ripples widened to the ghostly bank' (***Selected Poems 1956-1968,*** p. 56). Where Kinsella allows a personification to stand, it is modified by homelier diction: 'hungry joy and sickening distress / Met in union by the brimming flood' (*Massachusetts Review*, p. 324) is altered to 'Fumbled together by the brimming flood' (***Selected Poems 1956-1968,*** p. 57). These changes should make for a more humane poem, one less acquiescent in the imposition of allegorical patterning upon the world, but they do not. 1968's **'Downstream II'** suppresses rather than avoids allegory's problematic textual interference in the real. We no longer have a sense of how the speaker's

pleasure in allegorical pageantry and his positioning of himself in allegorical terms permit and produce his vision of horror, and by inference, the 'calamity' itself (***Selected Poems 1956-1968,*** p. 54), but order and pattern still claim to function as benign instruments of a necessary and instructive revelation of death and violence. The rebuke which 'that story thrust [. . .] / Into my very face' (***Selected Poems 1956-1968,*** p. 57) is no longer set in a context of a present pleasure in hierarchical ordering and 'luminous crisis', but in one of past misperception and naïveté. The problem of allegorical making—its violent imposition on the world—is relegated to a boyish past, not impinging on the 'now' of the text. Instead of moving from hierarchical ordering to censure of such systems and back to hypostasis again, **'Downstream II'** develops from the particular to the general instance of death and decay, and thence to an ordered vision of '[t]he slow, downstreaming dead' (***Selected Poems 1956-1968,*** p. 59). It is a much more conventional essay into the heart of darkness than its antecedent.

In apparent recognition of these limitations, subsequent revisions reintroduce elements of the original poem. The Oxford **Collected Poems** restores the narrative of the first movement, the speaker reading from the *Cantos,* then getting out of the boat, 'Naming old signs above the Central Plain. / Distant light replied, a word of thunder' (***Collected Poems 1956-1994,*** p. 48). The form of this restored first movement is much freer, however: *terza rima* is only resumed with the anecdote of the corpse. The speaker of this version is less enchanted by Poundian pageantry, its heroes being 'silken kings / Luminous with crisis' but not 'epochal men', and there are no 'primal clarities' in which to wage 'productive war', no 'princely scene'. He also seems more aware of, and resistant to, its seductive power: 'I closed the book / The gathering shades beginning to deceive', though he is not impervious to the allegorical delusion that by naming, he can impose order upon nature, and reinscribe arbitrary events as a response to that imposition, an answering light or a 'word of thunder' (***Collected Poems 1956-1994,*** p. 48). The restoration of the first movement of the narrative refocuses **'Downstream'** on artistic problems, on the responsibility entailed by any claim to represent nature or the historical past. The change in its form and diction means that it is harder to draw instructive parallels, for instance between the speaker's gazing at the stars and the corpse's empty upward stare. The disappearance of distancing poetic diction[28] makes the speaker a more sympathetic and thoughtful figure; his implication in the problems of 'regime art' is less immediately perceptible but more effective when it is perceived.

The version of **'Downstream'** in *Collected Poems 1956-2001* restores more features of the original poem. The original opening line, 'The West a fiery complex, the East a pearl', returns. The boat becomes a 'skiff' again (*Collected Poems 1956-2001*, p. 47). Although the form of the first movement is still looser than the *terza rima* of the second, there is less of an attempt than in 1996 to form longer, independent stanzas. The first movement is now arranged as a kind of fragmented *terza rima* which develops coherence as the anecdote of the corpse approaches (*Collected Poems 1956-2001*, pp. 47-8). Most surprising of all, some of the speaker's enthusiasm for the 'silken kings' has been restored: 'Luminous with crisis, waging war / Among the primal clarities. Their names dying / Behind us in the dusk' (*Collected Poems 1956-2001*, p. 47). Kinsella emphasizes allegory's nostalgia and anteriority, its assaults upon the past for material with which to forge new meanings, which make appeals to 'primal clarities' probable, if not inevitable. There is a certain self-reflexivity in his emphasis; the most recent **'Downstream'** calls on forty years of alteration and revision. The speaker's naming of the stars is also embellished:

> Night voices: soft
> Lips of liquid, while the river swept
> Its spectral surface by.
>
> He coughed,
> Standing against the sky. I took my turn
> Standing on the earth, staring aloft
> At fields of light sprinkled in countless silence;
> I named their shapes, above the Central Plain,
> With primal thumb.
>
> Low on the horizon
> A shape of cloud answered with a soft flash
> And a low word of thunder
>
> (*Collected Poems 1956-2001*, p. 48)

A deliberately unshowy diction, with apparently artless repetitions of 'soft', 'Standing', 'shape', 'low', replaces the noisy rhetoric of '*Urmensch* and brute' so that the rhyme 'coughed / aloft' no longer seems bathetic. With regard to his political stance, however, this speaker positions himself exactly where his 1962 counterpart stood. He participates in the chain of being, '[s]tanding on the earth, staring aloft'. His vision is of the heavenly firmament laid out in passive silence, ready for him to name it. He orders the sky with an allegorical anteriority—'primal thumb'—and his reinscription of natural noise as acquiescence is now unmistakable. Where the Oxford edition had 'Distant light replied, a word of thunder' (*Collected Poems 1956-1994*, p. 48), which could be interpreted as a rebuke or warning, the response is now 'soft',

'low', a gentler sound which seems to endorse the speaker's posturing. The *Urmensch*, almost totally excluded from the Oxford version, makes a return in 2001.

The alterations to the second movement of the poem, which retains its *terza rima* throughout all the revisions, are less momentous. However, with a small excision, Kinsella alters the last six stanzas significantly. In the 1996 *Collected Poems,* the beginning of this passage reads as follows:

> the river bed
>
> Called to our flesh from under the watery skin.
> Breathless, our shell trembled across the abyss;
> I held my oar in fear. When deeper in
>
> Something shifted in sleep
>
> (*Collected Poems 1956-1994*, p. 50)

In 2001, this becomes:

> The river bed
>
> Called to our flesh, under the watery skin.
> Our shell trembled in answer.
> A quiet hiss
>
> Something shifted in sleep
>
> (*Collected Poems 1956-2001*, p. 50)

While the diction of the 2001 version is simpler, it does nothing to mitigate the sense of coincidence between water, boat, and speaker. He still places himself in a privileged position of communication with nature, assimilating the Other to the self in a characteristic allegorical manoeuvre. The latest version, in forsaking diction that might draw attention to it, naturalizes this authoritarian attitude to nature. The changes of lineation necessitated by the small alteration mean that the resonant final line, 'Searching the darkness for a landing place', no longer stands alone. Again, this works to de-emphasize the allegory, since the reader's eye is not drawn, as it was before, to the exceptional line. Its allegorical import is not lessened, but further integrated into the poem's fabric. Allegory, though it is fatal to the integrity of that which is not the self, becomes a natural way to encounter the world.

'Downstream' is an allegorical progress narrative which also describes the progression of allegory. The poem details the mode's aggregative ambition, gradually taking possession of a textual space, capturing the Other to make it signify within its system. Resistance to the signifying scheme is posited, in the form of objects like the corpse, which might appear to be radically Other and unable to signify.[29] Such resistance is ultimately captured in its turn, the 'slow, downstreaming dead' becoming a token of order to inspire the speaker's quest. The textual history of **'Downstream'**, incorporating revisions to show the development of thought across time, is also a form of progress allegory. Kinsella's other progress allegories of the 1960s, **'A Country Walk'** and **'Nightwalker'**, might also productively be considered in this way, though the revisions made to **'A Country Walk'** are less extensive and those to **'Nightwalker'** less clear in intention than to **'Downstream'**.

The Peppercanister publications are often considered to mark something of a turn away from progress allegories articulated as physical journeys, towards psychic quests. In Davis's words:

> Jung's discussion of the process of individuation draws its inspiration from the procedures of medieval and renaissance alchemy, and structurally speaking, constitutes a variety of questromance: the alchemist's decensus ad infernos and culminating hierogamos or chymical wedding afford a formal analogy for a wholeness of being attainable through the integration of consciousness and unconsciousness.[30]

While the influence of alchemy and Neoplatonic esoterica on Jung (and on Kinsella) is undeniable, this assertion is troubling. A psychoanalytic procedure is only a 'quest' insofar as it has already been allegorized, even if it is heavily dependent on the archetypal imagery or mythic narratives from which allegories typically draw their material. Although in his later work Kinsella uses quest narratives, he usually employs other metaphorical structures to represent intense psychic scrutiny: vivisection, consumption, digestion, and domestic scenery. The wandering, journeying persona in Kinsella often signifies the accommodation of the self in society, a theme which grows very prominent in his poems of the late 1980s and 1990s: the Peppercanister publications from *St. Catherine's Clock* (1987) to *The Pen Shop* (1997) feature journeys and quests to a greater extent than anything since **'Nightwalker'**. Kinsella's publications since *The Familiar* seem to be returning to more introverted and static concerns while maintaining a mobile lightness that we might associate with the kinetic, societal self. Some of these chapbooks read like digests of the dense psychic explorations of the late 1970s and early 1980s. The glosses which frame the chapbook *Godhead*, **'High Tide: Amagansett'** and **'Midnight, San Clemente: a gloss'** (*Collected Poems 1956-2001*, p. 335, p. 340), preserve a tension between the speaker inside his house and the world outside, which is reminiscent of *Song of the Night and Other Poems*. The poems in that collection, particularly **'Tao and Unfitness at Inistiogue on the River Nore'** (*Collected Poems 1956-2001*, p. 205)

explore in understated detail the contrast between physical journey and psychic 'quest'—precisely that which is elided in allegory. **'Migrants'**, from *Citizen of the World* (2000), records an instant of equilibrium between stasis and movement, 'Migrants. Of limited distribution' (*Collected Poems 1956-2001*, p. 343). This brings a light touch to a characteristically Kinsellan image of 'insistent animal life confronting unknown immensities, the language of a blind groping and twisting, and the expressed need to sacrifice the supports of the self in order to sustain an inward progress'.[31] The moment of rest depicted in **'Migrants'** is one in which the reader might find space to confront Kinsella's allegorical vocabulary of voracity.

Kinsella and his critics present his career as one in which growing confidence allows him to abandon, first, early influences (principally Auden), then constricting and artificial forms which encourage the production of 'bad material'. In some accounts the poet's development is made analogous with the processes of decolonization. For example, Ian Flanagan finds that Kinsella's later poetry reflects an 'uneasy recognition that his earlier urge to order replicates previous attempts at classification, all of which on some level served to sanction the categorization both of his own family ancestors and of Ireland itself, as racially inferior'.[32]

The revisions to **'Downstream'** complicate such accounts. Instead of moving smoothly away from elaboration and ornamented closed form to simplicity and open form, Kinsella incorporates old material into his most recent revisions, suggesting growing independence from the sarcasm which characterizes a 1970s poem like **'Worker in Mirror . . .'** ['Worker in Mirror, at his Bench'] and acceptance of early work as emotionally and politically honest. It may be that Kinsella's break with formal elaboration and discursive rhetoric is not after all decisive, and that his work is entering a period of second simplicity using modified and renewed versions of those old techniques. We should not, however, conclude from this that he has altogether repudiated irony. The latest rendering of **'Downstream'** restores political problems that were aired in the earliest and suppressed in intervening versions, but it does not move to resolve them. Indeed, the successive revisions add one more problem. In any version of **'Downstream'** we read a poem which rebukes the nostalgic belief in primal clarity and order even as it indulges it. In the five different versions of **'Downstream'** published to date, we see this nostalgia enacted as palimpsest.

Notes

1. Thomas Dillon Redshaw, 'The Wormwood Revisions', *Éire-Ireland* 6:2 (Summer 1971), 111-156.

2. Redshaw, pp. 155-56.

3. Floyd Skloot, 'The Evolving Poetry of Thomas Kinsella', review of *Collected Poems 1956-1994*, *New England Review* 18:4 (1997), 174-186, p. 174.

4. For Peppercanisters as drafts, see Thomas Kinsella, *Collected Poems 1956-2001* (Manchester: Carcanet, 2001), p. 365.

5. Dennis O'Driscoll, 'Interview with Thomas Kinsella', *Poetry Ireland Review* 25 (1989), 57-65, p. 65.

6. O'Driscoll, p. 63

7. See Thomas Kinsella, *Nightwalker* (Dublin: Dolmen, 1967), p. 17; *Nightwalker and Other Poems* (Dublin: Dolmen, 1968), p. 69; Kinsella, *Collected Poems 1956-1994* (Oxford: Oxford University Press, 1996), p. 84.

8. 'Nightwalker' is 'more closed than it looks' (O'Driscoll, p. 63).

9. Joel Fineman, 'The Structure of Allegorical Desire', in *Allegory and Representation,* edited by Stephen J. Greenblatt (Baltimore and London: Johns Hopkins, 1981), pp. 26-60, p. 32.

10. According to Angus Fletcher, the Greek word kosmos refers to small-scale signifiers of position and status as well as the universalized 'cosmic structures in which these have their meaning'. *Allegory: The Theory of a Symbolic Mode* (Ithaca, New York: Cornell University Press, 1964), pp. 70-146.

11. Walter Benjamin, *The Origin of German Tragic Drama,* translated by John Osborne (London: New Left Books, 1977), p. 166.

12. For a very full account of this process see Gordon Teskey, *Allegory and Violence* (Ithaca, New York: Columbia University Press, 1996).

13. Fletcher, p. 175.

14. Fletcher, p. 177.

15. Balanchandra Rajan, 'Closure', *The Spenser Encylopedia,* edited by A. C. Hamilton, *et al.* (Toronto, Buffalo and London: University of Toronto Press, 1990), pp. 169-70.

16. Philip Fried, '"Omphalos of Scraps": An Interview with Thomas Kinsella', *Manhattan Review* 4 (1988), 3-25, p. 15.

17. Robin Skelton, 'The Poetry of Thomas Kinsella', *Éire-Ireland* 4:1 (1969), 86-108; p. 101, p. 104.

18. Kinsella, *Downstream* (Dublin: Dolmen, 1962), p. 50.

19. Brian John, *Reading the Ground: The Poetry of Thomas Kinsella* (Washington: Catholic University Press, 1996), p. 68.

20. Thomas H. Jackson, *The Whole Matter: The Poetic Evolution of Thomas Kinsella* (Dublin and Syracuse: Syracuse University Press and Lilliput, 1995), p. 24.

21. Alex Davis, 'Thomas Kinsella and the Pound Legacy: His Jacket on the Cantos', *Irish University Review* 31:1 (2001), 38-53, p. 39.

22. Massimo Bacigalupo, *The Formèd Trace: The Later Poetry of Ezra Pound* (New York: Columbia University Press, 1980), p. 98.

23. Compare Kinsella, 'Downstream', *Massachusetts Review* 5 (1964), 323-325, p. 323; *Nightwalker and Other Poems,* p. 83; *Selected Poems 1956-1968* (Dublin: Dolmen, 1973), p. 56; *Selected Poems 1956-1973* (Mountrath, Portlaoise: Dolmen, 1979), p. 58. The words 'Was it not so?' appear only in *Downstream.*

24. Davis, p. 41

25. *Urmensch* is the term used by historians of Gnosis to signify the primal man who is the creator, saviour, and divine inner being of humans. See Kurt Rudolph, *Gnosis: The Nature and History of Gnosticism,* edited by Robert McLachlan Wilson, translated by P. W. Coxon, *et al.* (San Francisco: Harper and Row, 1987), pp. 92-4.

26. Teskey, p. 62

27. Davis, p. 42

28. For the distancing function of poetic diction in 'Downstream' and other early Kinsella, see Jackson pp. 27-8.

29. The corpse is 'that thing that no longer matches and no longer signifies anything'. Julia Kristeva, *Powers of Horror: An Essay on Abjection,* translated by Leon S. Roudiez (New York and Chichester: Columbia University Press, 1982), p. 4.

30. Davis, p. 51

31. Peter Denman, 'Significant Elements: *Songs of the Psyche* and *Her Vertical Smile*', *Irish University Review* 31:1 (Spring/Summer 2001), 95-109, p. 95.

32. Ian Flanagan, '"Tissues of Order": Kinsella and the Enlightenment Ethos', *Irish University Review* 31:1 (Spring/Summer 2001), 54-77, p. 56.

Robert Brazeau (essay date 2006)

SOURCE: Brazeau, Robert. "Thomas Kinsella's 'Local Knowledge.'" In *The Body and Desire in Contemporary Irish Poetry,* edited by Irene Gilsenan Nordin, pp. 55-75. Dublin: Irish Academic Press, 2006.

[*In this essay, Brazeau compares Kinsella's poetic representation of the human body—especially victims of social and political violence—to the work of philosopher Michel Foucault.*]

Many men refrain from reading Irish history as sensitive and selfish persons refrain from witnessing human suffering.

Charles Gavan Duffy, 1880

In an article on the 1985 Anglo-Irish Agreement, Tom Hadden jokes about the failure of politicians and academics to come to any kind of rapprochement regarding possible solutions to the internal political divisions in Ireland: 'There is a nice story about the relationship between political scientists and politicians in the early years of the current Northern Ireland crisis. Apparently the mandarins at the Northern Ireland Office summoned a select group of political scientists to advise them on what to do next. The meeting was not a success. The academics were appalled at the civil servants' ignorance of all the basic literature on divided societies. The civil servants were equally appalled by the fact that none of the academics seemed able to agree on what should be done, either in theory or practice.'[1] Hadden's academics and politicians seem, of course, clichéd; the academics talk about things such as internal colonialism, liminal identities, and partitioned states while befuddled politicians ask about the number of people who might sit on a committee designed to ensure fair housing or labour policies. Hadden's article on the accord hinges around these well-rehearsed assumptions: academics are incapable of actually 'doing' anything in the real world, and politicians are seemingly not interested in the theory that might contextualise, explain or invalidate the practical decisions that comprise their job. Whether or not we believe that such a non-meeting actually occurred does little to deflate the humour in the story, which seems all the more applicable since the 1985 Hillsborough Agreement evinces very little in the way of complex, subtle or sophisticated reasoning. The document simply recycles well-rehearsed rhetoric, and all but guarantees that no meaningful action would come of it because of how persistently it refuses to recognise the theoretical, psychological and even epistemological issues that lie at the heart of identity politics in Northern Ireland.

There is, however, an interesting insight about the Good Friday Agreement of 1998 to be gained from Hadden's probably apocryphal anecdote regarding the professors and the politicians. The latter, I would argue, exhibits an awareness of how contemporary theory and Irish political practice might profitably speak to each other in order to resolve sometimes seemingly intractable ideological problems. While there are a number of aspects of the recent agreement that suggest the kind of synthesis I am talking about (the importance accorded symbology, for example in the new Agreement, as well as its emphasis on the

rights and psychology of people instead of the possession of territory), I want to focus my remarks here on the changing attitudes towards political violence evinced in the latest accord and offered in striking contrast to the ethos of the 1985 Hillsborough Agreement.

The section of the Belfast Agreement that calls for 'A Review of the Criminal Justice System' repeatedly suggests that violence itself, long refused consideration as a legitimate political mode, is now something that falls under the legislative purview of both the accord and the various bodies to whom power could eventually devolve as the public sphere is reconstructed in Northern Ireland. For example, the Agreement calls for the 'release of prisoners, including transferred prisoners, convicted of scheduled offences in Northern Ireland, or, in the case of those sentenced outside Northern Ireland, similar offences'. In addition, and perhaps even more importantly, the Agreement extends this offer only to prisoners affiliated with paramilitary organisaions that agree to 'a complete and unequivocal ceasefire'. In terms of its conception of the role of violence in Irish politics, the Belfast Agreement clearly contrasts the stridency of the 1985 Anglo-Irish Agreement, which includes, among its introductory clauses, a call for 'the total rejection of any attempt to promote political objectives by violence or the threat of violence' and insists on the necessity that both the governments of England and Ireland 'work together to ensure that those who adopt or support [violent] methods do not succeed'.

There are a number of other sections in the more recent Agreement that emphasise the role that violence has played in contemporary Irish political and social life. For example, the sections on policing and security repeatedly assert or imply that the Royal Ulster Constabulary has failed to provide a service that is free from partisan influence on the community, and the RUC are characterised as a routinely violent and oppressive political vehicle. While the document offers most of its condemnation by implication, its reader must be struck by the sheer repetition, in different types of language, of calls that the police 'be constrained by, accountable to and act only within the law'. In fact, it seems at times that the Agreement becomes a catalogue of the human rights abuses and various types of violence that are practised in Northern Ireland under the aegis of security, and while there is very little that is certain about the actual political success of the Good Friday Agreement, there is every reason to believe that at least the parameters of the discussion have changed somewhat. The state is no longer assumed to be the impartial progressive political entity that will help the two communities settle their grievances; in fact, what might be called the state's complicity in prolonging the hostilities between Catholics and Protestants is in many ways assumed in the most recent accord. The Agreement is theoretically innovative in that it rejects a number of bedrock political assumptions that have held up the peace process in Ireland. Not only does it assume that social and political phenomena are open to a variety of interpretations, but it demonstrates an awareness of and explicit sympathy with what the French historian and philosopher Michel Foucault has termed 'local knowledges' that are mobilised strategically against the hegemony of the status quo. In fact, Foucault's work persistently depicts a status quo or dominant ideology that can become homogenous only as a result of a series of calculated exclusions that reify a certain ideology to the position of status quo. Rather than defend the status quo against political opposition, the Good Friday Agreement recognises the equally legitimate claims of those who have been systematically oppressed by this dominant ideology.

In this chapter, I shall offer a reading of the Irish poet Thomas Kinsella's thematising of this type of 'local knowledge' with a particular interest in the representation of the body in his poetry. This characterising aspect of Kinsella's poetics suggests an affinity between his poetry and the theoretical works of Michel Foucualt, whose installation of the figure of the body at the center of a post-structuralist ethics offers, in many ways, contemporary theory's most compelling criticism of ideology. Not only has Foucault's legacy of published works rendered him, however guardedly, the 'conscience' of French post-structuralist philosophy, it has placed his work at the epicentre of contemporary debates regarding the status of ethics in what is generally considered a post-humanist intellectual climate. Kinsella's poetry implicitly references a number of the debates that we find in Foucault's work, especially when the poet focuses attention on the embodied subject pitted against, and frequently victimised by, historical, political and even metaphysical forces beyond his or her control or understanding. In both Foucault's later works and Kinsella's poetry we see the body depicted as a site of contest, domination and counter-hegemonic or 'local' knowledge.

That Michel Foucault has emerged as the 'conscience' of post-structuralist theory is both predictable and paradoxical: predictable because Foucault's writings, especially after *The Archaeology of Knowledge* (1969), offer an exegesis of both the implicit and explicit ethical concerns that would come to dominate contemporary social and political theory; paradoxical because running alongside this discussion of contemporary ethics is a denunciation of rationality, morality, justice,

humanism—in short, the cornerstones of what we consider 'ethical' philosophy. It has proved difficult to appreciate the manifold opportunities that Foucault's theory might offer contemporary critics without also feeling un-Foucaultian in that the ends of such ethical critique would appear to valorise categories that Foucault consistently denounces. Foucault scholars have offered a number of sometimes unconvincing ways beyond this impasse, even while admitting its ostensibly intractable character. The limitations of space preclude me from enumerating the many contributions to this debate, but works by Susan Bordo, Kate Soper and Frances Bartkowski all reflect this tension in contemporary readings of Foucault. In short, even while feminism, queer theory and a number of other libratory or explicitly ethical modes of critique continue to draw on Foucault's texts as salient methodological precursors, and while they find in his various genealogies valuable pretexts for studies that question the formation of knowledge and power in any given historical context, they nevertheless reach a cul-de-sac in that Foucault himself denigrated the value of such emancipatory political agendas.

My own view is that Foucault's work does indeed evince this difficulty at times, and that disciples of Foucault have debated this difficulty to, as of yet at least, no convincing conclusion. Furthermore, none will be offered here. There is simply no way to reconcile the two Foucaults: the Foucault who, on the one hand, argues against power, painstakingly elaborating the manifold strategies and discourses it has used and could use in its totalising control of the subject, and the Foucault who would argue that there is no outside of this domination, and that all discourses of emancipation are ultimately co-opted and, in the end, simply and ironically confirm and even themselves become authoritarian strategies. This does not, however, mean that theorists coming after Foucault need simply throw up their hands in frustration regarding this perceived self-imprisoning tendency of liberationist political movements, but rather that such theorists need to remember that they are working with Foucault's texts, and not strictly within them. Put simply, if Foucault's principle hermeneutic contribution to contemporary theory is his willingness to work within contradictions that are potentially productive, then those wishing to engage with his texts need to see them, at least periodically, as problems rather than solutions to questions about history, alterity and the practices of power.

Rather than pursue this already well-trodden and daunting issue, I want to approach the question of the ethical subtext of Foucualt's writing somewhat obliquely, by tracing, in genealogical fashion, the notion of 'allegorical reading' that works its way into

Foucault's texts. The concept, which gains a dubious prominence in *The Archaeology of Knowledge,* survives its inauspicious introduction to become one of the characterising elements of Foucault's later thought. It no doubt runs counter to Foucault's well-known arguments about the death of the author to assert that the later work in some ways overcomes the problems in the earlier critique of history, but it is clear that *Discipline and Punish* calls for a strategy for the critical reading of historical texts and events that is explicitly abrogated in the earlier *Archaeology.*

What Foucault, in *The Archaeology,* calls 'allegory' is introduced as a kind of negativity, as a staple of hermeneutical activity that must be avoided:

> It is . . . clear that this description of discourses is in opposition to the history of thought. There too a system of thought can be reconstituted only on the basis of a definite discursive totality. But this totality is treated in such a way that one tries to rediscover beyond the statements themselves the intention of the speaking subject, his conscious activity, what he meant, or again, the unconscious activity that took place, despite himself, in what he said.[2]

Foucault adds that this 'analysis of thought is always *allegorical* in relation to the discourse that it employs. Its question is unfailingly: what was being said in what was said?'[3] Without specifically discrediting this hermeneutical enterprise at this point in the work, Foucault clearly asserts that his 'analysis of the discursive field is orientated in a quite different way'[4] since Foucault is concerned not with parsing out the unsaid beneath what is said in any utterance, but with grasping 'the statement in the exact specificity of its occurrence'.[5] Quite literally, for Foucault, the statement here is figured not as the harbinger or symptom of power, but only as a historical fact.

While he persistently separates himself from the allegorical method that he broaches on a number of occasions in *The Archaeology,* there is little doubt that Foucault nevertheless wants his readers to keep it in mind as the alternative to the reading practice he embarks on in this text. Midway through the work, Foucault asserts that: 'We know—and this has probably been the case ever since men began to speak—that one thing is often said in place of another; that one sentence may have two meanings at once; that an obvious meaning, understood without difficulty by everyone, may conceal a second esoteric or prophetic meaning that a more subtle deciphering, or perhaps only the erosion of time, will finally reveal; that beneath a visible formulation, there may reign another that controls it, disturbs it, and imposes on it an articulation of its own'.[6] From a less frequently cited essay from this period, 'Politics and the Study of

Discourse' (1968), Foucault describes a similar interpretive strategy that he is, again, not interested in putting into practice: 'The question which I ask is not about codes but about events . . . But I try to answer this question without referring to the consciousness, obscure or explicit, or speaking subjects; without referring the facts of discourse to the will—perhaps involuntary—of their authors; without having recourse to that intention of saying which always goes beyond what is actually said.'[7]

When viewed against the context of Foucault's later writing and the conclusion of *The Archaeology,* it is difficult not to read both of these assertions allegorically, as trying to reveal, even while explicitly abrogating, the centrality of the allegorical method in Foucault's 'ethical turn'. He hints at the nature of this later work in *The Archaeology,* giving a thorough prediction of his last writings: '[An archaeology of sexuality] would show, if it succeeded in its task, transgressions of sexuality, all its manifestations, verbal or otherwise, are linked to a particular discursive practice. It would reveal, not of course, as the ultimate truth of sexuality, but as one of the dimensions in accordance with which one can describe it, a certain "way of speaking": and one would show this way of speaking is invested not in scientific discourses, but in a system of prohibitions and values.'[8] Read together, these quotations, I would argue, reveal a substantive reorientation in Foucault's approach to historical data. The former passage elaborates a hermeneutical approach to texts that Foucault eschews in the early part of *The Archaeology of Knowledge,* where he insists on staying on the surface level of the sentence. In the latter passage, however, Foucault clears the way for an analysis of discourse that would be attentive to the operations of power as they are manifested in discursive acts. Foucault concludes the latter of these passages by calling this allegorical hermeneutics 'an analysis that would be carried out not in the direction of the episteme [as *The Archaeology* itself had been], but in the that of what we might call the ethical'.[9]

Clearly, this aversion to allegory separates Foucault's archaeological method not only from the history of ideas, which interrogates statements for the secret (or not so secret) content that they disclose, but also from the work of those who, coming after Foucault and working in a way that they perceive as consistent with the scholarly and politico-ethical programme outlined in his writing, traces in the statement the reserves of power, authority and knowledge that serve to discipline subjects. This mobilisation of Foucault's methodology represents his chief contribution to contemporary political and ethical theory. In fact, as we shall see, what Foucault saw as his explicit contribution to ethics has made far less of an impact on contemporary theory than has the more expansive ethical dimension that can be extracted from his work. My point is that Foucault's contribution might be more methodological than explanatory, since he provides in this 'allegorical turn' a way to investigate and chronicle power and its operations in explicitly ethical ways.

If, as I contend, the Foucault of *The Archaeology* resists this allegorical turn in his reading of historical material, the writer of *Discipline and Punish* came to recognise the value of such a strategy of reading. In the first section of *Discipline and Punish,* Foucault not only makes plain the organising theme of this work, which is directed towards unearthing the practices that constitute 'the political technology of the body,'[10] but also shows that he is able to do this only through a methodology that is explicitly allegorical. Take, for example, this lengthy exegesis:

> The public execution, then, has a juridico-political function. It is a ceremonial by which a momentarily injured sovereignty is reconstituted. It restores that sovereignty by manifesting it at its most spectacular. The public execution, however hasty and everyday, belongs to a whole series of great rituals in which power is eclipsed and restored (coronation, entry of the king into a conquered city, the submission of rebellious subjects); over and above the crime that has placed the sovereign in contempt, it deploys before all eyes and invincible force. Its aim is not so much to re-establish a balance as to bring into play, as its extreme point, the dissymmetry between the subject who has dared to violate the law and the all-powerful sovereign who displays his strength.[11]

This allegorical and counter-intuitive reading of historical data is familiar to readers of Foucault's work, but it still bears stating that this method of reading—of teasing out the latent content of power's operation that is anterior to the surface ritual of execution—represents a hermeneutical mode that is followed for the first time in *Discipline and Punish.* Furthermore, if this type of reading has come to characterise Foucault's work (and legacy), this owes more perhaps to how central this allegorical method has become to those critics who, following Foucault, see in it the outline of an ethical mode of reading that seeks to interrogate power not only in terms of what types of events, knowledges, objects or bodies that it makes possible, but rather for information about the ideology underlying it and the system of exclusions, repressions and disciplinary functions that it exerts on a population. This is an ethics that is told from the standpoint of those that are habitually excluded from the domain of power, and whose position is recognised within its discourse as a negativity. In addition, this ethics would trace the exercise of that power on the level of the body, asking such questions as how the body is codified, disciplined, divided and ultimately

mastered within the discourses that both bring it into being and attempt to stabilise its significance. It is hardly surprising that in the same work that Foucault introduces this method of reading he also explicitly equates power and knowledge in a way that would become characteristic with his ideological and political critique:

> Perhaps, too, we should abandon a whole tradition that allows us to imagine that knowledge can exist only where the power relations are suspended and that knowledge can develop only outside its injunctions, its demands and its interests. Perhaps we should abandon the belief that power makes mad and that, by the same token, the renunciation of power is one of the conditions of knowledge. We should admit rather that power produces knowledge . . . that there is no power relation without the correlative constitution of a field of knowledge, now any knowledge that does not presume and constitute at the same time power relations.[12]

It is sometimes difficult to differentiate between the ethics that Foucault enables with this method of reading and the ethics that he himself formulates in his final works. That ethics revolves around the preeminence of self-care and has very little in common with the use to which Foucault's interest in the politics of exclusion has been put. To take one example from a lengthy list, Kate Soper accurately characterises Foucault's *History of Sexuality* as offering 'an individualistic and even narcissistic conception of liberation,'[13] and goes on to suggest that this work evinces little of the type of ethics that has been periodically practiced, but more generally enabled, by Foucault's work. If Soper's generally helpful arguments reveal an instructive blindness, however, it is in her implicit assumption that *The History of Sexuality* and *The Care of the Self* represent a culmination of either Foucault's method of genealogical analysis or his ethical philosophy. This in no way is meant to excuse the sometimes problematic claims made in the volume,[14] but is intended only to draw attention to a frequently overlooked, although very important, difference between what Foucault himself sees as the culmination of his method as it is expressed in any particular analysis and the fuller force of that method as it is explored by scholars coming after Foucault. The point I am making is perhaps best demonstrated when we see critiques of Foucault's own work that use a distinctly Foucaultian method, Soper's essay included.

The critical strategy that Foucault makes possible in his work is directed against the foundational narratives of Western rationality and progress. In one of his most influential methodological statements, published under the generic title 'Two Lectures', he not only clarifies the allegorical approach to texts that characterises his post-archeological period, but also situates this critical practice within an ethical framework that most critics see as representative of the later Foucault's work. To put it simply, these later texts enable a mode of ideological and ethical critique that is independent of Foucault's specific genealogies. In fact, I have chosen the less familiar term 'allegorical' throughout the present chapter not only to distinguish the later work from the earlier archeological texts, but also to distinguish the method or technique (allegorical reading) from Foucault's specific employment of this method (his genealogies of the prison, sexuality, and so on). My point is, of course, that Foucault makes possible a critical approach that he does not always rigorously adopt in his own texts.

In 'Two Lectures' Foucault systematically lays out the critical strategy that has come to be most associated with his work and that has made it of perhaps singular relevance for contemporary theorists. Embarking from what he calls 'subjugated knowledges' Foucault ponders the question of how these knowledges, long dismissed, return to Western rationalism and historiography to unsettle its deepest assumptions about itself. Foucault argues persuasively for a local criticism that would function as 'an autonomous, non-centralised kind of theoretical production, one that is to say whose validity is not dependent on the approval of the established regimes of thought'.[15] This mode of criticism would pursue what Foucault calls 'the immediate emergence of historical contents'[16]—the latter phrase indicating the ostensibly counter-hegemonic character of these contents which do not crystallise into facts or events (although it is difficult to discuss such occurrences without using this terminology) because they refuse to be assimilated into dominant narratives that, after all, adjudicate the factual from its others. Stated simply, 'historical contents' resist the narratives that authorities use to explain events, and therefore remain outside of the text of history. As we will see, in his reading of the bombing of Hiroshima and Nagasaki and in his poetry that focuses on English colonial violence, Kinsella subscribes to Foucault's edict that 'one should try to locate power at the extreme points of its exercise, where it is always less legal in character'.[17]

In the remainder of this chapter, I investigate the status of the material body in Kinsella's poetry, arguing that the body is situated within a larger theoretical discussion regarding historiographic practice that works itself out in this poetics. More specifically, I contend that Kinsella 'reads' history upwards from its effects, usually on the body of the victims, and challenges its ethicality and 'rationality' from this perspective. Kinsella's poetry regards the body as the most immediate focus of the operation of power and, therefore, as the 'content' that best discloses its unethical use. Kinsella brings together material from ancient epic sources, the

bombing of Hiroshima and Nagasaki, the death of his own father, and, perhaps most comprehensively and controversially, Troubles-era Irish politics, in a poetics that seeks to redress, or even destabilise, received historical narratives. It is also worth pointing out that an interest in the body, and more specifically, in the body as it upsets conventional modes of historiography has infused itself into Kinsella's poetics from the very beginning. Kinsella's acclaimed translation of the Ulster epic *The Tain* is offered largely as a corrective to previous translations. Unlike Lady Gregory's Victorian version, Kinsella's translation retains the 'directness in bodily matters'[18] that seems to have been a characteristic of the culture that produced the document. Kinsella's translation languishes in the sometimes lurid and sensual details of the original: nits, urination, sexuality, grizzly murder are all included in Kinsella's translation. Moreover, the inclusion of graphic representations of bodily violence is central to understanding *The Tain* as a poem that revolves around what we would call class distinctions, given that Medbh is quick to send her own soldiers to their death, and even slaughter them herself, revealing the sometimes destructive relationship between the body and the grand forces of epic history that work against it.

The priority of the body and discourses of embodiment find their way into Kinsella's early original poetry as well. In **'Old Harry'** (1962), a poem about Truman's decision to bomb Hiroshima and Nagasaki, Kinsella looks at history from the perspective of an almost gothic metaphysics of the body. The poem's opening section, 'Death States the Theme' has the speaker trying to reconcile the contingency of individual existence with the sense of an eternal engine that governs it:

> 'Master Love' my grim instructor assured me,
> 'Moved already in the criminal darkness
> Before our dust was chosen, or choice began
>
> Devising—for spirits that would fall asunder
> At a touch—a flesh of thirst and pain, a blood
> Driven by onward self-torment and by desire.'[19]

The poem, then, is introduced and framed as a discussion about the eternal processes that subtend historical progress—a progress that also has a dubious value in Kinsella's poetry. By the end of this section, we have a clearer sense of the unethical imperatives that the poet sees as propelling history, politics and experience:

> *What of the guilty spirit* I inquired
> *Inviting darkness to the human womb?*
> 'The guilty will repay with flesh and blood.'

What of the innocent spirit, in pursuit
Of justice and the good? 'The innocent
Repay with flesh and blood.'[20]

Kinsella reveals himself to be an essentially humanist poet with a strong sense of the ethical, and there is, in all of his poetry, a sympathy for those who pay with flesh and blood. In **'Old Harry'** this ethical substructure comes through in his description of the victims of American military action. The middle section of the poem moves from an obviously critical description of Truman to the victims who absorb historical violence on a visceral level:

> A curb to the rash, a pupil to the wise.
> Until on a certain day he waved them out,
> Thoughtful before his maps. And chose at last
>
> The greater terror for the lesser number.
> With rounded cheeks he blew the moral blast
> And the two chosen cities on the plain
>
> Lost their flesh and blood—tiles, underwear, wild cries
> Stripped away in gales of light. Lascivious streets
> Heightened their rouge and welcomed baths of pure
>   flame.
>
> In broad daylight delicate creatures of love
> Opened their thighs. Their breasts melted shyly
> And bared the white bone.[21]

Analyses of right and wrong recede in the face of such visceral descriptions: there is no way we can consider Truman blowing a legitimately 'moral blast' in condemning the victims. In fact, the poem ironises the 'moral' here, even while sustaining an ethical argument. In **'Old Harry'** the poet intimates that there is a certain quotient of evil and violence that unfolds in history, and the only question remaining is how this violence gets expressed on the bodies of its victims. 'The white bone' becomes a kind of irreducible historical content—one that will not be explicable within the propaganda associated with delivering the greatest force on the fewest victims. That is, as world powers exert a murderous military violence on their victims, there remain inassimilable remnants of this unethical and barbaric power.

While space does not permit an extended reading of references to the body in other poems from roughly this era, *The Good Fight* (1973) and *The Messenger* (1978), it is nevertheless important to see these poems as drawing on this salient aspect of Kinsella's poetics. In the former poem, an elegy to John F. Kennedy, the subject is presented as, in some ways, Christ-like, and this connection is proffered in the register of the corporeal: 'One day in Philadelphia / His hand *burst* with blood.'[22] Furthermore, this strategy of referring to Kennedy as, first and foremost, an embodied subject, persists from the early stages of the poem until its

conclusion. Indeed, the poem's first reference to its subject is offered in the register of corporeality: 'He wiped his lips / And leaned tiredly against the window.'[23] Throughout the poem, excerpts from Kennedy's campaign speeches are juxtaposed against references to the body in order to represent Kennedy as both an agent of historical change and an embodied victim of it. It might seem reductive to suggest that Kinsella uses the language from these speeches to represent something like Kennedy's mind as exerting a force on history, while history, understood as animate and even monstrous, exerts a counter-force back against the body: 'He held out his inflamed right hand / for the Jaw to grip. The sinews winced.'[24] Kennedy is represented variously as mind and body, and the poem ultimately works to show that as much as history seems to move by large metaphysical or political currents, it is nevertheless the body that moves through this time and experiences its effects. The poem ultimately despairs about the resilience of the body in the face of these monstrous forces, and concludes with an image of the body giving up in the face of the overwhelming destructive power of history:

> Fumbling from doubt to doubt,
> One day we might knock
> Our papers together, and elevate them
> (with a certain self-abasement)
> —their gleaming razors
> mirroring a primary world
> where power also is a source of patience
> for a while before the just flesh
> falls back in black dissolution in its box.[25]

It is no doubt fitting that an elegy end with a burial, but 'the just flesh' does not refer to Kennedy's body; rather, it comes to represent, for Kinsella, the plight of all individuals, searching for an idealistic or ethical substure to history. The 'primary world' is an idealistic construction of the poet, and mirrors the idealistic assertions quoted from Kennedy earlier in the poem. Derval Tubridy is correct to assert that 'the dualism instigated by Plato's theory of forms is integral to the poem, and the notion of an unattainable ideal, matched with a flawed reality, characterizes Kinsella's portrayal of Kennedy'.[26] However, it is also worth stressing that this flawed reality is almost invariably represented in corporeal language, which suggests that Kinsella sees this intractable and irresistible historical force as exerting itself corporeally. We are, Kinsella seems to be saying with some pessimism, all finally victims of a monstrous history that will avenge itself on our bodies. Kinsella takes a similar approach to the figure of his father in the elegiac sequence *The Messenger,* ruminating on the manner in which the father's body was both his most memorable attribute and final undoing. While chronicling how his father was instrumental in unionising employees at the Guinness brewery, Kinsella notes, 'he brandished his solid body / thirty feet high above their heads' (219). However, this image of heroic physicality is quickly unwritten when the poem jumps ahead and records John Paul Kinsella's quick decline:

> And it befell that summer,
> after the experimental doses,
> that his bronchii wrecked him with coughs
>
> and the muffled inner
> heartstopping little
> hammerblows began.[27]

Both *The Good Fight* and *The Messenger,* then, depict the individual, embodied subject against the destructive capability of a time that erodes that body. In the latter poem, interestingly, this corporeal decay not only transpires within the body, but can also be felt as a bodily force within the survivors of the victim: 'A suspicion in the bones / as though they too could melt in filth.'[28] This is, I would argue, not merely a recitation of the cliché that death reminds us of our own mortality; rather, Kinsella is stressing that the body is capable of its own knowledge. That this knowledge must, perforce, become in some way cerebral before it can be transmitted in language certainly renders it suspicious, but Kinsella here is interested in suggesting that death is experienced not only psychologically, but, in some way, as a physical fact as well.

This important theme is also treated in Kinsella's poetic sequence *A Technical Supplement,* although here it is offered as part of a history that is explicitly Irish and colonial. The sequence opens with a reference to 'William Skullbullet', who is actually William Petty, the seventeenth-century cartographer who conducted the survey of County Down.[29] It is difficult to discuss *A Technical Supplement* without quoting the poems in full, especially because these generally brief but nuanced works sustain their inquiries across a number of poems in the sequence:

> Blessed William Skullbullet
> glaring from the furnace of your hair
> thou whose definitions—whose insane nets—
> plunge and convulse to hold thy furious catch
> let our gaze blaze, we pray,
> let us see how the whole thing works.[30]

There are a number of points to be made about this short, contextualising poem. First, the continuity that Kinsella draws between 'definitions' on the one hand and 'nets' on the other reveals the connection between intellectual or rational systems of domination and physical systems. 'The furious catch' is, here, an indigenous Irish Catholic population that is victimised by these various systems of control. In his writing, Foucault repeatedly refers to 'a microphysics of

power' or a system of overlapping strategies, agencies and institutions through which control and authority are exerted in any time and place. Kinsella's poem, however briefly, suggests to us such a microphysical deployment of power in its inquiry into the various methods, some constitutional and others physical,— that characterise English colonial violence. The point of this poem is to not only introduce us to the way in which this sequence is going to clarify the relationship between a historiography guided by themes such as 'the progress of reason' (that is, the state sanctioned justification for English colonial domination of Ireland) but also to connect these grand narratives to their somewhat baser or barbaric tactics.

The second poem in the sequence forges the link between reason and violence much more deliberately, and chronicles the association between truth, reason and a barbaric, because unethical, power. The final lines of the poem are indicative of its inquiry into this rationalist ideology:

> It would seem possible to peel the body asunder,
> to pick off the muscles and let them
> drop away one by one writhing
> until you had laid bare
> four or five simple bones at most.
> Except that at the first violation
> the body would rip into pieces and fly apart
> with terrible spasms.[31]

Here we see not only the distance between the clinical and rational application of power, but its inherent barbarism as well. As Foucault asserts, 'there can be no possible exercise of power without a certain economy of discourses of truth which operates through and on the basis of this association'.[32] Kinsella dramatizes the discursive operation of a colonizing power here; in fact, the word 'simple' calls attention to itself because it is clearly marked as a term of classification and division, and therefore as part of a rational or scientific approach to embodiment that cares little for the corporeal integrity of the patient/victim. It is also easy to read the final knowing assertion regarding the 'terrible spasms' as issuing from someone who has performed this kind of investigation. In fact, by linking the character of William Petty with the disembodied voice of a distant and pathological investigator, Kinsella characterises colonialism in Ireland as just such an autopsy on the living body of the nation. The body/nation resists the forces that would collude to dominate it, even if, ultimately, it is assailed on too many fronts to withstand this force.

A Technical Supplement is perhaps Kinsella's most challenging and thorough representation of how competing types of knowledge work to dominate the body and hold it in place within an architecture of discipline and control. Derval Tubridy correctly notes that 'Kinsella uses anatomical inquiry as a metaphor for understanding'[33] within the poetic sequence, but Tubridy fails to recognize the critical distance established in the poems between the poet (and his intentions) and the persona that he constructs. That persona, as I have been arguing, is steeped within an ideology of 'reason' and 'progress' and is unable to appreciate the nature of human suffering. The title of the sequence, is, of course, telling: this is a purely *technical* supplement to a political or ideological program of domination, by which I mean that it is presented as aloof from practical concerns. It is also a technical *supplement* in the Derridean sense of the term in that it is an addendum that does not complete the project as much as show that project's constant reliance on an outside to itself that it can neither include nor entirely exclude. Colonialism cannot admit its barbaric underpinnings—its unethical supplement— but nor can it dominate from above, intellectually, without controlling the land and destroying bodies. That is, it is an explicit discourse of modernity and progress that relies on an implicit violence that it can neither acknowledge nor abrogate.

What I now hope to show by this admittedly brief reading of embodiment and corporeality in Kinsella's poetry is that Kinsella's lengthiest and most incisive foray into this issue, offered in the much-maligned poem **'Butcher's Dozen'**, is not an aberration in Kinsella's career, and that the poem's representation of Troubles-era Northern Ireland can be readily situated within the larger ethical project of Kinsella's work. This might seem like a methodologically suspect gesture, in that it attempts to read selectively across a very diverse poetics in order to find a context for the somewhat troubling **'Butcher's Dozen.'** This criticism is, I think, a valid one, and it might seem a poor justification to say that I have worked in this way only to suggest that the critically accepted view that **'Butcher's Dozen'** is an aberration in Kinsella's poetry fails to read the poem as offering a response to political violence that emerges out of Kinsella's sustained rumination on the figure of the body. While this event may be too volatile for a number of critics to approach with anything like critical circumspection, it is nevertheless imperative to read the poem within the larger ethical concerns of Kinsella's work.

'Butcher's Dozen' is, indeed, a difficult poem for many of Kinsella's critics. For example, in **'Poetry and the Avoidance of Nationalism,'** Vincent Buckley remarks defensively that the poem, 'written in shock and protest . . . is extraneous to [Kinsella's] life work, and needs no further comment here'.[34] Donatella Badin also offers a scathing attack on the poem, calling it 'crudely sarcastic, embarrassing, even, in its

invective'.[35] Badin recognises only in passing that 'the narrator of the vision does not take sides, giving the last word to a more balanced victim',[36] and does not integrate the changing perspective towards violence offered in the poem within her overall reading of the work. While the poem may be uncomfortable to read at times, it must be admitted that this is partly to do with the atrocity itself, and not with Kinsella's handling of the material, which, while not even-handed, is still much more tempered than is often recognised in critiques of the poem. Finally, in perhaps the least generous response to the poem, Norman Vance asserts that 'the facile rhymes and rhythms of Kinsella's pamphleteer doggerel reduce everything to the primitive dogmatic clarity of unreconstructed nationalist rhetoric'.[37] If, as Vance argues, it is a mistake to look for 'simple answers in the emotive tangle of political aggravation',[38] then surely it is equally mistaken to reduce literary criticism to the level where it employs dismissive, uncritical and blatantly charged terminology in its interpretation and exegesis of literary works.

It is true that the tone of the poem does not obviously situate itself among Kinsella's other poems, as Kinsella suggests in the notes that accompany it: 'One changed one's standards, chose the doggerel route, and charged.'[39] However, this does not mean that the poem does not represent Kinsella's political views, only that overt politics does not often find its way into his poetry. It would seem all the more imperative for Buckley to focus on *Butcher's Dozen,* given that the stated aim of his paper is to research the prevalence of nationalist themes in contemporary Irish poetry. The difficulty for critics such as Buckley and Badin is to balance what Thomas Jackson refers to as 'the assertive public stance'[40] of the poem with Kinsella's generally introspective poetic practice. In fact, there is a tendency among Kinsella's critics either to ignore or devalue his public, socially engaged poetry, because his work frequently explores an interior psychological or personal space. The result is that psychoanalytic themes have tended to dominate the criticism of Kinsella's poetry, and this mode of inquiry is employed even where it seems least appropriate. For example, Jackson himself ultimately obfuscates **'Butcher's Dozen'** by viewing it through the lens of Jungian theory, but his assertions regarding the 'Jungian—not "Freudian"—symbolic sexual overtones of the unseen bullets and rifle shapes'[41] seems too abstract a reading of the poem to be of much explanatory value.

The bullets and rifles are 'unseen' in **'Butcher's Dozen'** because the poem is not only about the Bloody Sunday massacre in Derry on 30 January 1972. Instead, the poem, as Kinsella explains, is also about the whitewash of that massacre by a 'Tribunal of

Inquiry under the chairmanship of Lord Widgery'.[42] Set one month after Bloody Sunday, the poem uses the traditional form of the *aisling*[43] to present not only the victims' response to both the report and the massacre, but also to the state of English-Irish relations at the time. The poem's diction is jarring and uncompromising and evocatively mirrors the brutality of the massacre and the ensuing exoneration of the British soldiers. We see this, for example, early in the poem:[44]

> There in a ghostly pool of blood
> A crumpled phantom hugged the mud:
> 'Once there lived a hooligan.
> A pig came up, and away he ran.
> Here lies one in blood and bones,
> Who lost his life for throwing stones.'
> More voices rose. I turned and saw
> Three corpses forming, red and raw.[45]

There is a discernible continuity between the corpses, the inhumanity of the massacre and the poem itself. Phrases such as 'red and raw,' as well as references to 'mangled corpses, bleeding, lame, / Holding their wounds'[46] are troubling, and serve to inscribe the horror of the original violence of the event with their evocative diction. Given the preceding discussion, it is perhaps unnecessary for me to dwell at any length on the significance of references to corporeality and embodiment in this poem, but while critics of Kinsella's work do not write on the gruesome qualities of the previous poems I have looked at, they do condemn **'Butcher's Dozen'** for it. Edna Longley criticises the 'rather gruesomely evoked phantoms of the dead victims'[47] but it is difficult to imagine a pleasant way to represent the bloodshed that attends the shooting. However, Longley's point has to be conceded: the disconcerting, because too vivid, diction (as well as the stifled rhythm of the poem) make this a difficult work to read, and this difficulty is at least partly responsible for the predominantly negative response the poem has received among its critics.

Perhaps as culpable, however, are the final ghostly speeches presented in the work, two of which serve as an explicit response to the only extended gloss on the events provided by the narrator:

> The group was silent once again.
> It seemed the moment to explain
> That sympathetic politicians
> Say our violent traditions,
> Backward looks and bitterness
> Keep us in this dire distress.
> We must forget, and look ahead,
> Nurse the living, not the dead.[48]

These lines present a parody of the facile response to generations of colonial oppression that would not, in fact, end the violence in Northern Ireland. In fact, the suggestion that the victims of violence 'must forget' is especially egregious in the context of the poem, and this passage serves a kind of 'straight line' for the rejoinder by the eleventh victim:

> Here lies one who breathed his last
> Firmly reminded of the past.
> A trooper did it, on one knee,
> In tones of brute authority.[49]

The clichéd lesson here is that forgetting history dooms one to repeat it, but the passage also draws a connection between the history of colonisation, contemporary military violence, and the legislators (authorities) who called in the military to respond to the civil rights march. Foucault encourages us to see 'politics as sanctioning and upholding the disequilibrium of forces that was displayed in war',[50] by which he means that politics is an implicit war by other means. Similarly, **'Butcher's Dozen'** reads the events of Bloody Sunday allegorically, as pointing to the implicit war that politics has become in Troubles-era Northern Ireland. This is demonstrated when this victim goes on to espouse the doctrines of violent Republicanism:

> Persuasion, protest, arguments,
> The milder forms of violence,
> Earn nothing but polite neglect.
> England, the way to your respect
> Is via murderous force, it seems;
> You push us to your own extremes.[51]

The expression of this sentiment in the poem causes Buckley to assert that 'it is worth guessing . . . that this work and [Kinsella's] continued attitude to it are in part responsible for the weak reception Kinsella's poetry now receives in Britain'.[52] He is no doubt correct in this assumption, but within the overarching context of the poem these lines, as difficult as they seem, elaborate on the Foucaultian connection between politics, conflict and the body, and it is therefore surprising that in the most recently published version of the poem these lines are simply deleted.[53] The speech of the next victim expands the historical scope of the poem. For this victim, the massacre and the Widgery Report are connected with the ethos of 'Empire-building':

> The time has come to yield your place
> With condescending show of grace
> —An Empire-builder handing on.
> We reap the ruin when you've gone,
> All your errors heaped behind you:
> Promises that do not bind you,
> Hopes in conflict, cramped commissions,
> Faiths exploited, and traditions.[54]

The ideological terrain of the poem has shifted from the immanence of political violence as it is practised on both sides to some sense of the historical causes of that violence. The clearly Republican politics of the previous victim is replaced, even moderated, by the nationalist but non-violent politics of this speaker. The quick historicisation of the event is confirmed by the final speaking victim, who appears as a possible figure of rapprochement between the two nations even at a time when this seems impossible:

> They, even they, with other nations
> Have a place, if we can find it.
> Love our changeling![55]

Interestingly, then, **'Butcher's Dozen'** does not subscribe to the reading of history advocated by the eleventh victim: 'Simple lessons cut most deep.'[56] Instead, the poem develops a degree of complexity and distance from the event itself (and the report) to arrive at a guardedly optimistic view of the future: if both sides could honestly reflect on the things that they can legitimately change, and on their fundamental similarities ('we all are what we are, and that / Is mongrel pure'[57]) then there may be genuine progress made in English-Irish relations. When Edna Longley comments that 'it is alarming that Kinsella's search for meaning and an inspiring cause in contemporary Ireland should find expression in a backward—rather than forward-looking emotion',[58] it seems that she is ignoring both the speech of the final victim and the way in which the poem develops a more complex, future-oriented vision of the Troubles.

But this might be, ironically, the poem's chief failing. **'Butcher's Dozen'** ends on a note of what might seem half-hearted or misdirected reconciliation, and seems to subscribe to the belief that 'everyone's the same; everyone's to blame.' A critical reader cannot ignore how the scope of the poem changes from the immediate scene of violence in its opening lines to vague and macro-political (or world historical) themes like 'empire building' and the ostensible similarity of all human people at its conclusion, or how this shift in register mimics the narratives of historical progress and enlightened reason that Kinsella's poetics of embodiment, at times, rigorously critiques. This is not to say that historical change is not possible, or that political agendas that intransigently hold onto the past are the most legitimate. Rather, it is to assert that narratives that short-circuit our understanding of historical events by assimilating scenes of immanent and bodily violence to grand narratives are not likely to convince anyone, especially those who have lost loved ones as a result of political violence. Indeed, recent historical events have demonstrated how unconvincing the Widgery Report has become, even to the English government: British PM Tony Blair empanelled the Saville inquiry in January 1998 to review the conclusions of the Widgery tribunal. In this, we can appreci-

ate how the body of the victim can serve as a rejoinder to state sanctioned history, given that the sheer quantity of forensic evidence has forced the British government, reluctantly and only after thirty years, to examine the conduct of the 1st Parachute Battalion. Northern Catholics have long maintained that the corpses of the victims tell a more accurate history than did the Widgery tribunal. To take but two glaring examples, Patrick Doherty was shot while trying to crawl to safety, and Bernard McGuigan was shot in the back of the head while trying to help him. Not even the government now believes that either was armed, and neither could pose any threat to the soldiers. **'Butcher's Dozen'** does, uncannily, call for England to 'clear the air / And brood at home on her disgrace',[59] but uncharacteristically also calls for the Irish to understand colonial violence as part of a larger explicable historical movement; this comprehension of Bloody Sunday, I would argue, alienates the meaning of it within a narrative that conforms to very conventional and unconvincing models of historical progress. While the poem is criticised by some, such as Longley and Badin, for keeping an old wound open, the opposite is in fact true: the poem too quickly glosses events within a narrative cognisance of history that all but guarantees that their significance will be misconstrued within dominant and conventional notions of historical progress.

What is most striking about the conclusion of **'Butcher's Dozen',** then, is not its call for some kind of empathy for the colonizing power, but its rehearsal of a model of historical understanding that Kinsella eschews in his numerous poems on the status of the corporeal body. The body, for Kinsella, is precisely the entity that resists assimilation within these narratives that supplements them, as it were, and in doing so reveals how poorly this history speaks to or for the victims of violence. Perhaps more so than any contemporary Irish poet, Kinsella, in his visceral, engaging and frequently disquieting representations of corporeality, refuses to turn away from the scene of horrific, state-sanctioned brutality, and poems such as **'Old Harry'** and the sequence ***A Technical Supplement*** register the ways in which progress and brutality, as Walter Benjamin would assert, are conjoined. Surprisingly, however, in Kinsella's most comprehensive look at the repressive violence of English colonialism, he does turn away, however briefly, from the troubling and visceral body of the victim and confounds the Foucaultian ethics and sympathies that prevail in his wider poetic practice.

Notes

1. See T. Hadden, 'On the Internal Frontier', *Times Literary Supplement*, 6-12 January 1989, p. 7.

2. See M. Foucault, *The Archaeology of Knowledge,* trans. A. M. Sheridan Smith (New York: Pantheon, 1972), p. 27.

3. Ibid., p. 28.

4. Ibid.

5. Ibid.

6. Ibid., pp. 109-10.

7. See M. Foucault, 'Politics and the Study of Discourse', in G. Burchell, C. Gordon and P. Miller (eds), *The Foucault Effect,* (London: Harvester Wheatsheaf, 1991), p. 59.

8. See Foucault, *Archaeology,* p. 193.

9. Ibid.

10. See M. Foucault, *Discipline and Punish: The Birth of the Prison,* trans. A. Sheridan (New York: Random House, 1979), p. 26.

11. Ibid., p. 49.

12. Ibid., p. 27.

13. See K. Soper, 'Productive Contradictions', in C. Ramazanoglu (ed.), *Up Against Foucault: Explorations of Some Tensions Between Foucault and Feminism* (London: Routledge, 1993), pp. 35-6.

14. See especially Foucault's reading of the Lacourt case, and Soper's criticisms of it.

15. See M. Foucault, 'Two Lectures', in M. Foucault, *Power/Knowledge,* ed. C. Gordon (New York: Pantheon, 1980), p. 78.

16. Ibid., p. 81.

17. Ibid., p. 97.

18. See T. Kinsella, *The Tain* (London and New York: Oxford University Press, 1970), p. xiv.

19. See T. Kinsella, *Collected Poems: 1956-1994* (Oxford: Oxford University Press, 1996), p. 43.

20. Ibid.

21. Ibid., p. 44.

22. Ibid., p. 154.

23. Ibid., p. 153.

24. Ibid., p. 155.

25. Ibid., p. 164.

26. See D. Tubridy, *Thomas Kinsella: The Peppercanister Poems* (Dublin: University College Dublin Press, 2001), p. 45.

27. See Kinsella, *Collected Poems,* p. 219.

28. Ibid., p. 217.

29. See Tubridy, *Thomas Kinsella,* p. 77.

30. See Kinsella, *Collected Poems,* p. 184.

31. Ibid.

32. See Foucault, 'Two Lectures', p. 93.

33. See Turbidy, *Thomas Kinsella,* p. 78.

34. See V. Buckley, 'Poetry and the Avoidance of Nationalism', *Threshold,* 32 (1982), p. 28.

35. See D. Abbate Badin, *Thomas Kinsella* (New York: Twayne, 1996), p. 175.

36. See Badin, *Thomas Kinsella,* p. 177.

37. See N. Vance, *Irish Literature: A Social History; Tradition, Identity and Difference* (Oxford: Basil Blackwell, 1990), p. 220.

38. See Vance, *Irish Literature,* p. 220.

39. See T. Kinsella, *Fifteen Dead* (Dublin: Dolmen Press, 1979), p. 58.

40. See T. Jackson, *The Whole Matter: The Poetic Evolution of Thomas Kinsella* (Syracuse: Syracuse University Press, 1995), p. 112.

41. See Jackson, *Whole Matter,* p. 135.

42. See Kinsella, *Fifteen Dead,* p. 53.

43. Ibid., p. 57.

44. The problem of deciding which versions of Kinsella's poems to use is a difficult one, owing to the poet's habit of rewriting and republishing his poetry. Since I wish to use the notes that accompany the Peppercanister edition of 'Butcher's Dozen', and to call attention to an important revision to it, I have decided to quote from this edition here. When there is no pressing reason to favour one edition of a poem over another, I will cite the most recently collected version of that poem.

45. See Kinsella, *Fifteen Dead,* p. 13.

46. Ibid., p. 14.

47. See E. Longley, 'Searching the Darkness: The Poetry of Richard Murphy Thomas Kinsella, John Montague and James Simmons', in D. Dunne (ed.), *Two Decades of Irish Writing: A Critical Survey* (Cheshire: Carcanet Press, 1975), p. 136.

48. See Kinsella, *Fifteen Dead,* p. 16.

49. Ibid.

50. See Foucault, 'Two Lectures', p. 90.

51. See Kinsella, *Fifteen Dead,* p. 17.

52. See Buckley, 'Poetry and the Avoidance of Nationalism', p. 28.

53. See Kinsella's *Collected Poems*: 1956-1994, pp. 137-42.

54. See Kinsella, *Fifteen Dead,* p. 18.

55. Ibid., p. 19.

56. Ibid., p. 16.

57. Ibid., p. 19.

58. See Longley, *Searching the Darkness,* p. 137.

59. See Kinsella, *Fifteen Dead,* p. 19.

References

The Agreement Reached in Multi-party Negotiations (1998).

The Anglo-Irish Agreement (1985).

Badin, D. Abbate, *Thomas Kinsella* (New York: Twayne, 1996).

Bartkowski, F., 'Speculations on the Flesh: Foucault and the French Feminists', in J. Genova (ed.), *Power, Gender, Value* (Edmonton: Academic Printing and Publishing, 1987) pp. 69-80.

Bordo, S., 'Feminism, Foucault, and the Politics of the Body', in C. Ramazanoglu (ed.), *Up Against Foucault: Explorations of Some Tensions Between Foucault and Feminism* (London: Routledge, 1993), pp. 179-202.

Buckley, V., 'Poetry and the Avoidance of Nationalism', *Threshold,* 32 (1982), pp. 8-34.

Foucault, M., 'Politics and the Study of Discourse', in G. Burchell, C. Gordon and P. Miller (eds), *The Foucault Effect* (London: Harvester Wheatsheaf, 1991), pp. 53-72.

———— *The Archaeology of Knowledge,* trans. A. M. Sheridan Smith (New York, Pantheon, 1972).

———— *Discipline and Punish: The Birth of the Prison,* trans. A. Sheridan (New York: Random House, 1979).

———— 'Two Lectures', in M. Foucault, *Power/ Knowledge,* ed. C. Gordon (New York: Pantheon, 1980), pp. 78-108.

Hadden, T., 'On the Internal Frontier', *Times Literary Supplement* (6-12 January 1989), p. 7.

Jackson, T., *The Whole Matter: The Poetic Evolution of Thomas Kinsella* (Syracuse, NY: Syracuse University Press, 1995).

Kinsella, T., *The Táin* (London and New York: Oxford University Press, 1970).

———— 'Butcher's Dozen', in T. Kinsella, *Fifteen Dead* (Dublin: Dolmen Press, 1979), pp. 13-20.

———— *Collected Poems: 1956-1994* (Oxford: Oxford University Press, 1996).

Longley, E., 'Searching the Darkness: The Poetry of Richard Murphy Thomas Kinsella, John Montague and James Simmons', in D. Dunne (ed.), *Two Decades of Irish Writing: A Critical Survey* (Cheshire: Carcanet Press, 1975), pp. 118-53.

Soper, K., 'Productive Contradictions', in C. Ramazanoglu (ed.), *Up Against Foucault: Explorations of Some Tensions Between Foucault and Feminism* (London: Routledge, 1993), pp. 29-50.

Tubridy, D., *Thomas Kinsella: The Peppercanister Poems* (Dublin: University College Dublin Press, 2001).

Vance, N., *Irish Literature: A Social History; Tradition, Identity and Difference* (Oxford: Basil Blackwell, 1990).

Lucy Collins (essay date 2006)

SOURCE: Collins, Lucy. "Enough is Enough: Suffering and Desire in the Poetry of Thomas Kinsella." In *The Body and Desire in Contemporary Irish Poetry,* edited by Irene Gilsenan Nordin, pp. 182-94. Dublin: Irish Academic Press, 2006.

[*In the following essay, Collins explains how Kinsella's poetry makes a connection between suffering and desire in relation to the body, and notes that this impacts the relationship between the self and others.*]

> Suffering as the place of the subject. Where it emerges, where it is differentiated from chaos. An incandescent, unbearable limit between inside and outside, ego and other.
>
> Julia Kristeva, *Powers of Horror*

The poetry of Thomas Kinsella conducts an ongoing enquiry into the meaning of human experience and our desire to reach self-understanding. In his interrogation of the relationship between individual and collective experience, and its representation in the creative act, Kinsella explores the body as the nexus of physical and cultural impulses and thus accords it a mediating role in the journey towards knowledge. Suffering and desire have a close and complex relationship in this scheme, as the body is explored as the site of desire and of denial. In this chapter I shall be concerned chiefly with how these states influence the construction of the subject position in poetry, since Kinsella is at once concerned to explore the implications of the speaking subject for the testing of intellect and emotion, and to avoid fixed forms of identity. Both suffering and desire draw attention to the relationship between self and other and in particular to the ways in which experience and emotion can be made meaningful in both individual and more broadly cultural contexts.

The need to progress or to die is a driving force of Kinsella's poetry and the reflection on this dynamic informs both the structure and themes of his oeuvre, as well as of individual poems. Both suffering and desire are states of being that bring the individual to acute awareness of his or her own selfhood by problematising its very existence. Arthur E. McGuinness sees in Kinsella's poetry 'an unbridgeable gap between the subject and object, between the knower and the known',[1] and it is this 'gap' that Kinsella must attempt to map in his exploration of our search for meaning. Desire posits a form of relationship: it must have an Other, we must be aware of what we lack in order to desire it. It therefore suggests a dynamic state of being, a projection forward in time, a refusal to accept things as they are. Suffering by contrast turns us inward, making us sensitive to our own pain, forcing us into states of reflection. The dialectic between these two positions is essential to an understanding of Kinsella's work: the need to endure amid self-reflection that is often demanding and painful. It centres too on the quest for knowledge and meaning that itself is always other, always just beyond our grasp, or when partially attained can be troubling rather than consoling. The acquisition of meaning is a cumulative one for Kinsella, there is always the need to turn back, to recollect in order to understand more fully.

The idea of transition is highlighted by these processes: first by the dynamic nature of desire; then by the role of change in the production and understanding of meaning. Transition indicates Kinsella's desire to seek new forms and contexts to facilitate complex exploration of the relationship between individual experience and the human condition. This territory is resistant to ordering principles but the resulting tension has proved a productive one for Kinsella in allowing him to encompass the worlds of dream and myth within an intellectual framework. Jefferson Holdridge sees Kinsella using history and myth 'as correlatives for more personal modes of being' thus facilitating the blending of private and public in his work.[2] Yet the control to which myth in particular is subject in his work has resulted in a critical emphasis on the oblique nature of Kinsella's emotional expression, as Guinn Batten writes: 'Kinsella's lifework typically has been judged to be an act of "structuring" that separates the poet from the psychic shattering that might have ensued had he remained within the matriarchal imaginary.'[3] Kinsella's early work often presents the dilemma of reconciling an instant of illumination with an unending philosophical enquiry; we see the speaker pausing, on the brink of discovery or statement, self-consciously aware of his position as witness. This self-consciousness shapes Kinsella's handling of the subject position in important ways. By exploring the self in relation to the other, often a woman, Kinsella shows that relationship not only to be inherently unstable but to be rendered more so through the act of representation. His attempts to portray the fluidity of

the relationship between self and Other often result in poems that resist the act of centring itself and deny the comforts offered by a certainty of focus.

An important way in which Kinsella articulates issues of the subject position is through the representation of illness in his poetry. This has both a personal and symbolic resonance for the poet as his wife's regular hospitalisation renders him a passive observer of her suffering and endurance. The emotional responses of sympathy, frustration and fear, as well as the closeness of the marriage relationship, complicate the boundary between self and Other in some of these poems—a boundary already troubled by the body's vulnerability in illness. Yet this experience also marks the singularity of being, the inability of others to feel exactly as the sufferer does at a given moment. The frailty of the body in many of Kinsella's poems allows him to explore the drive to discover the self at the same time as it renders the ability to do so problematic. Thus the physical debility signified by illness may draw lived identity closer to the abstract realm. Kristeva has argued that this drive towards self-identity is a mistaken one and that the recognition of this comes as a relief to the subject. Yet for Kinsella it seems that this kind of recognition can be at best temporary, so closely is the journey of self-discovery linked to the desire to find meaning in human existence. It is belief in the elusiveness of meaning, rather than optimism concerning the outcome of the search that often seems to govern Kinsella's aesthetic.

Problems of representation necessarily attend the theme of illness as Elaine Scarry claims: 'Physical pain is not only itself resistant to language but also actively destroys language, deconstructing it into the pre-language of cries and groans.'[4] Yet while the loved one suffers physically, the emotional impact on the witness of such suffering can also place extreme demands on the function of language. The speech of the depressed is 'repetitive and monotonous', Kristeva asserts: '[f]aced with the impossibility of concatenating, they utter sentences that are interrupted, exhausted, come to a standstill'.[5] Often we may hear the voice in Kinsella's poetry faltering or hesitating, uncertain as to what—if anything—he seeks to express. A number of early poems, especially those from *Poems* (1956), *Another September* (1958) and *Downstream* (1962) exemplify this occlusion. **'A Lady of Quality'** marks the first overt statement of the body's frailty: set in a hospital where the speaker's 'love lies down for healing' (line 20), it weighs the endurance of emotion against the struggle on which his beloved has embarked.[6] In this testing atmosphere his love may indeed need healing and the other emotions that emerge in the text—terror, sorrow, grief—demonstrate how layered and uncertain his feelings are. The much later

'Visiting Hour' from *Madonna and Other Poems* (1991) reverses the position: here the speaker is the patient, whose body is rendered passive and at the whim of medicine 'The pale inner left arm pierced and withdrawn' (1). The female figure who enters this world is not the expected figure of the nurse but the self-contradicting woman of myth, a supplicating yet sexual being to which the speaker longs to return:

> One thin hand out, denying,
>
> the other pulling the lace back from her thigh
> and the dark stocking with the darker border
> toward the pale motherly places:
>
> . . .
>
> take my love back, into the medicine dark
>
> (18-21; 27)

The woman who becomes at once mother, martyr and seductress is by this stage a familiar image in Kinsella's work. Earlier this cycle of decay and re-birth is demonstrated in ways that reach more comprehensively into the archetypal past. In *Notes from the Land of the Dead,* the journey to the underworld becomes both an exploration of the deepest recesses of the self and of Ireland's history of endurance and renewal.[7] Kinsella often associates bodily decay with cultural and social decline, so that the individual, fighting extinction, is part of the community also struggling to seize life and value from overwhelming forces. Poems such as **'Survivor'** depict just this struggle, in ways that display hunger, lust and sickness in vivid, hallucinatory images: 'Everyone falling sick, after a time. / Thin voices, thin threads of some kind of sweetness / dissolving one by one in the blood' (3.26-8). Lack is prominent here too, as paradise is defined negatively and the actions of the figures are determined by need: 'Paradise. No serpents. No noxious beasts. / No lions. No toads' (3.20-1). Amid representations of the body that are both sexual and violent, any sense of clear individual identity is obscured, yet the speaker occasionally—as in **'Sacrifice'**—records deep emotional involvement: 'I've never felt / So terribly alive, so ready, so gripped by love' (2.1-2). This is one of the most disconcerting and moving aspects of Kinsella's work: his ability to draw the reader through bizarre and often incomprehensible scenes towards sudden emotional experience.[8]

The tendency of Kinsella's work to fragment—as it increasingly begins to do from the late 1960s onwards—and for the speaker's position to become ever more indistinct impacts greatly on the subject-object relation in the poetry. This in turn alters Kinsella's explorations of suffering. In the relationship with the Other, both suffering and desire involve a dismantling of unity, an awareness of loss and temporal instability, yet the experience of pain can also bring with it a kind of passivity, an endless objecthood that can only be overcome through some form of representation:

> in isolation, pain 'intends' nothing; it is wholly passive; it is suffered rather than willed or directed. To be more precise, one can say that pain only becomes an intentional state once it is brought into relation with the objectifying power of the imagination: through that relation, pain will be transformed from a wholly passive and helpless occurrence into a self-modifying and, when most successful, self-eliminating one.[9]

Thus the representation of pain is crucial in changing its relationship to the sufferer. The role of the imagination in the transcendence of suffering is a more difficult issue for Kinsella, due in part to the cyclical nature of his work. While he may be capable of depicting pain and thus implicitly of moving beyond it, this is a form of resolution that will always be provisional since his understanding of growth involves endless return to the emotionally formative experiences of life.

This endless return is part of the compulsion to gain knowledge that is a driving force of Kinsella's poetic life. It is an approach to knowledge that may more accurately be seen as understanding; understanding that encompasses the spiritual, emotional and intellectual while also reading the individual not only as a being anchored in time but simultaneously encountering a range of personal and historical contexts. By refusing to read history as a fixed or controlling framework for imaginative discovery, Kinsella allows temporal shifts to offer new ways of viewing the human predicament and of essaying psychic development.

To represent bodily experience as a means to understanding Kinsella often uses the process of dissection to explore both the power of sensation and the relationship of the part to the whole. One of the most interesting approaches to this idea occurs in *A Technical Supplement* (1976) where the speaker is firstly dissociated from the abject body, being lecturer, scientist, demonstrator: 'You will note firstly that there is no containing skin / as we understand it, but "contained" muscles—separate entities, interwound and overlaid' (2.1-3). The act of dissection is one that must be viewed—the inner body must be exposed twice, once physically and once in language. The muscular structure that is laid bare is both vulnerable and strong, each dependent on the other, a unified whole. That the skeleton seems fragile beneath this shows a fear of the disintegration of the body, its ultimate resistance to further classification.

This clinical emphasis quickly moves to a scene where the violence against the body is multiplied; no longer a controlled exercise but an endless routine procedure.

It is captured memorably in Poem 6 in the image of the 'dripping groves' of the slaughterhouse where the evisceration of animals is graphically depicted. Kinsella relies on gruesome sensory detail—'the scream-rasp of the saw', 'the pool of steaming spiceblood' (2-6)—assaulting the reader with the sound, smell and sight of the crowded scene. The violence is abrupt and economical: we witness creatures divested of their skin: 'a man . . . loosens the skin around their tails / with deep cuts in unexpected directions; / the tail springs back; the hide pulls down to the jaws' (16-18). Yet in this poem human response to these events is withheld; it is in the following poem he finally asks:

> Is it all right to do this?
> Is it an offence against justice
> when someone stumbles away helplessly
> and has to sit down
> until her sobbing stops?
>
> (7.6-10)

The introduction of the witness in the poem is crucial in Kinsella's use of the bodies of animals to interrogate human instincts. Yet by separating the response from the dynamic scene of slaughter, Kinsella ensures that it acquires if anything a greater significance in recording human despair at excesses of violence. That the witness should be female allows the emotional expression here to be distanced from the analytical precision of the speaker, indeed it is clear that the tears of his female figure do not exonerate the poet from identification with both the creature and the slaughterers here: the artist or writer, in gazing into the object and penetrating beneath its surface, performs an analogous act of incision. This is rendered powerfully in the fourth poem of the series, which also echoes Kinsella's earlier use of the imagery of cells and microscopic observation to approach the most minute alteration of the living organism. Depth becomes a significant aspect of this poem: the 'deepening damage' after the first rupture and the blood that wells up 'bathing the point as it went deeper' (6-10). The instrument of incision takes on the life-force of this body:

> Persist.
>   Beyond a certain depth
> it stands upright by itself
> and quivers with borrowed life.
>
> Persist.
>   And you may find
>
> the buried well. And take on
> the stillness of a root.
>
> (11-18)

The collection marks an increasing concern on Kinsella's part with probing to the depths of being, with taking new imaginative risks to reach a more profound understanding of the human condition. And, of course, for Kinsella the instrument is language; it is language that is vivified by being tested and pushed to its limits, as Poem 15 records: 'The pen writhed / It moved under my thumb' (1-2). It becomes clear with the shift at Poem 10 that this enquiry is about the nature of the creative process, and in particular about the ways in which the artist mediates between imaginative and real worlds; between the field of abstract ideas and the ways in which these ideas have shaped his being. The scrutiny within the early poems in the sequence—instructive, voyeuristic, analytical—becomes in the remainder a form of self-scrutiny that allows the physicality of experience to be linked more forcefully to creative meaning.

From his earliest work Kinsella has been preoccupied with the interrelationship between the speaking voice within the poem and the man who is the object of its scrutiny. For him the split self is both a testament to a complex and often contradictory response to human desire and suffering and a result of the inevitable self-consciousness of representation; the deliberate nature of language. It seems that for Kinsella, language is both a powerful instrument for the expression of isolation and pain and the means by which those experiences can be named and understood by the sufferer. Seeing ourselves at second-hand, through another's eyes or through a mirror or a static image, splits the self into observer and observed and causes Otherness to be associated with the observing mind: 'The beginning / must be inward. Turn inward. Divide' (16.6-7). The disintegration that marks this severance of self from self is destructive of any clear sense of identity and affirms the pain and disorientation of the speaker: when, in Poem 22 the face divides and becomes two faces—'each whole yet neither quite "itself"'—the acknowledgement of the impossibility of definition, or even unified meaning deepens: '(But then the original could not / have been called "itself" either. / What but some uneasiness made it divide?)' (18-21). What changes fundamentally is the relationship between the staring figure (the self gazing into the mirror) and the object of the gaze (the self gazing back).

The moment represents doubleness being discerned and the relationship between the two selves—ostensibly the bifurcating image yet also the living face and the representation of the face—being acknowledged. The 'uneasiness' here belongs to the speaker, who cannot properly maintain the gaze. To see, in these circumstances, is also to be aware of the questionable nature of the act of witnessing and of its subjective cast. The surgical illustration of an eye operation, scalpel poised before the eyeball, suggests the unique aspect of visual representation—imperfections of the eye determine our view of the world.

In the following poem the self is further divided 'by a great private blade'—private in a sense that blurs and troubles the relationship between 'real' bodily experience and a psychic state that yet tells the speaker something of his physical predicament. Here the division of the self is also the tyranny of multiple sensation:

> From that day forth I knew
> what it was to taste reality
> and not to; to suffer tedium or pain
> and not to; to eat, swallowing with pleasure
> and not to; to yield and fail,
> to note this or that withering in me,
> and not to

(23.8-14)

That the lines break on this duality of experience also emphasises the momentary or tenuous quality of physical sensation itself, and the sense that this momentary quality can both affirm and negate the reality of that experience.

Hanging in the balance is also the act of representation itself that must now strive to express apparently opposing concepts within the same frame of language. At the boundaries of **A Technical Supplement** is always the infliction of pain in the search for knowledge. It is clear also that language and form must undergo the same rigorous process to achieve the poet's most precise ends; as Trinh T. Minh-ha writes: 'To write "clearly" one must incessantly prune, eliminate, forbid, purge, purify; in other words, practice what may be called an "ablution of language".'[10] The rendering of pain in poetic form, therefore, not only pushes poetry to the limits of its aesthetic capabilities, it also bridges that important gap between private and public realms, between past and present, between the body and the imagination, between nature and culture.

Nine years later Kinsella published **Songs of the Psyche** (1985), a collection that again foregrounded the importance of origins—in particular of Kinsella's Dublin upbringing—in the formation of his adult self. This combination of the detailed evocation of the child and the abstract musing of the adult poet are increasingly typical of the development of his work and will shape the obscure simplicity of the most recent poetry. Yet this is not an impulse towards nostalgia: as W. J. McCormack argues, 'Kinsella's uncanny "preservation" of Dublin idiom, what seems at times ink running through a gravelly accent, should . . . be distinguished from any vanished working-class potential which might be ghosted by the seeming survival of a speaking voice.'[11] The voice mediates between the body, which is often debilitated here, and

an imagination that maintains a youthful energy and power. Desire for knowledge again lies at the heart of the work, but this time it is more heavily interiorised and less reliant on the world of objects to display and define it. In this way it moves from the visceral world into a realm often primal or ghostly. Here the desire for knowledge necessitates a return to the past that is, as is so common in Kinsella's work, at once personal and mythical. In the opening section, named 'Settings', this return is made explicitly. The sequence which follows creates an observing 'character' later to merge with a figure we may assume to be the poet. The need for clarity is signalled from the start:

> Why had I to wait until I am graceless,
> unsightly, and a little nervous of stooping
> until I could see
> through those clear eyes I had once?

(1.3-6)

To become what he once was the character must return to 'stupid youth', thus simultaneously occupying the present and the past, the developed and the still-to-be-formed. The desire for wisdom finds mythical form here in the *imbas forosnai*, a Celtic ritual whereby knowledge is acquired through mantic sleep.[12] The 'ill-chosen spirits' of the fourth poem are part of this ritual; hoarders of knowledge, possessing an appetite that at once unites them and keeps them apart: 'Their need binds them / and hangs between them . . . They have eaten / and must eat' (7-8; 13-14). That desire for knowledge should be figured as appetite is an allusion to the Fall of Man—'the serpent beguiled me, and I ate' (1 Gen. 3.13)—and a reading of desire that is laden with sexual meaning. Here desire is represented both spatially and temporally, a significant feature for a poet so testing of form and conscious of continuity. The desire for wisdom that has turned the poet inward may also be a destructive one, turning self against self. To endure is also to perpetuate this ruthless desire: 'A monster bore me / and I bear / a monster with me' (5.7-9). Even the element of romance that enters the sequence in Poems 7 and 11 does so in ways that are at once old-fashioned ('Come with me / o'er the crystal stream' (11.1)), and eerily dark:

> Your feathery flesh
>   I will kneel and kiss.
> Your slender bones
>   I will take in mine.
>
> . . .
>
> and so retire
>   while the grasses whisper
>
> and leeches wrinkle
>   black in the water

(11.9-12;1 5-18)

In this poem, Kinsella employs a form that may be at once traditional and suggestive of such intermediaries as Austin Clarke, himself a poet who re-used archaic forms to precise effect. More striking perhaps is the way in which corporeal form becomes attenuated or mutable here: flesh is 'feathery' and the body is reduced to a skeleton; the other almost subsumed by the self in the moment of embrace.

The journey towards knowledge is not about the discovery of a unitary self but rather about the formation of the self through intellectual investigation: the quest for identity does not reveal it but helps it to form through intellectual and spiritual testing and discovery. Thus desire for, and fear of, what is Other than the self is not only represented in language but is constitutive of expression. At the close of *Songs of the Psyche* two poems, **'Self-Release'** and **'Self-Renewal',** explore this idea in more focused and explicit ways. Violence against the self takes sensory form in the first of these poems: curses, the sound of nails dragged down the wall, the speaker 'dashing [him]self to pieces' (1-5). To calm this situation, Kinsella resorts again to the connections between dissection and writing to demonstrate how the personality can be toyed with, adjusted:

> I could pull down a clean knife-shaft
> two-handed into the brain and worry it
> minutely about until there is
> glaze and numbness in 'that' area.
>
> Then you would see how charming
> it is possible to be
>
> (7-12)[13]

Likewise in **'Self-Renewal'** Kinsella returns to familiar imagery, first rendered memorably nearly twenty-five years earlier in **'Mirror in February'** (1962). There the speaker was 'not young and not renewable' (21); here, much older still, he scrutinises the face not as a key to the individual man but as a link to 'all / the lonely that had ever sat by their lonely mirrors' (9-10). In this later poem the mirror is in the form of a triptych, 'reveal[ing] everywhere' (2-3) rather than providing speaker, and reader, with a limited or traditional representation. Moving beyond the binary aspect of the reflection depicted in *A Technical Supplement* Kinsella sees the ageing and suffering self not locked in a tension of opposites but in an act of opening outward to past and future, a fleeting moment in an objectless world.

'Writing expresses and testifies to a life that cannot be truly lived or can be lived only at great peril'.[14] The partial life—the suffering entailed not in living too fully but in failing to live fully enough—is a concern

for Kinsella; the speaker as observer exemplifies this distance. The visual emphasis of sexual desire takes precedence and implicates the (typically male) gaze in demarcating the relationship between subject and object, yet desire, no matter what its object, is predicated on knowing that the Other, the desired thing, exists. So that desire may at once posit a connection that it at the same time impedes. We can approach but never reach the desired object as the moment of reaching is the same in which desire is transferred to another distant object. The expression of desire is both a part of understanding it and an articulation of its dangers. For Kinsella it confirms the circular nature of life's processes; the compulsion towards the object that is yet an acknowledgement of the emptiness of that attainment.

From the beginning of his career, sexual longing in particular is marked by uncertainty, by a kind of drawing back that enacts the impossibility of ultimate satisfaction. It is a longing that is always qualified by emotional complexities, by uncertainties concerning the articulation of desire that are as much related to Kinsella's fear of language's simultaneous power and inadequacy as to his personal feelings. Later the ways in which he articulates desire connects his attachment to the material world—the world of the flesh and the senses—to his pursuit of complex philosophical issues, especially those relating to creative acts. Increasingly, the resistance to emotional closure that has been a feature of Kinsella's work begins to be reflected in the texture of the writing itself. Sex becomes a destabilising force, bringing physicality to bear on delicate inner states. **'Madonna',** from the 1991 collection *Madonna and Other Poems,* first evokes woman's presence in indefinite, sensory terms: the sound of her feet approaching through the church and the smell of her flesh—'her meat sweet' (1.6). Her footsteps are both a distraction from prayer and an indication of the disturbing nature of female presence with its power to shift language in unexpected ways, as evidenced by the suddenly glimpsed animal response beneath the religious pose. Interiors and exteriors become important here as we next see woman standing at the border between public and private, motionless and watchful (2.1-6). Then there is a movement towards completion, sexually and poetically, the post-coital moment framing a unity—'two awarenesses / narrowed into one point' (3.2-3)—but one which struggles to contain tensions: strangeness and familiarity altering the speaker's representation and understanding of desire.

> Our senses tired
> and turning toward sleep,
> our thoughts disordered
> and lapped in fur,

your shoulder sleeping
distinct in my hand,
the tally of our remaining encounters
reduced by one.

(3.6-13)

Fragmentation is a disturbing impulse here: senses no longer alert; thoughts 'disordered'. The body too is dissected by language, not only lover from lover but from parts of itself—her 'shoulder sleeping / distinct in my hand'. The repeated rhythm of the lines enacts a relentless separation of one moment from the next, so that the dissociative impulse proves both temporal and spatial and deepens the alienation of the moment. The disturbing severance within the subject implies that the troubled perspective of the speaker relates not only to the relationship with the other, but to that with the self. To see the self as whole, of body, of spirit, of mind, is a fleeting illusion. That completeness is seen to exist, yet to resist prolonged understanding creates the painful tension evident in the poem and central to human experience. The orange of the final section, a contained and unified object, is cut open. The perfection of its wholeness is sundered; we glimpse a space that is intimate (perhaps female) and discern a taste—encompassing rich yet delicate flavours and subtle differences of texture—that invokes the insatiable human appetite. Memory also plays a key role here, in keeping sensory experience alive in the present and in exploring just how elusive the past may be. To return endlessly to the past is not to render that past explicable but to alert the reader to the inseparable nature of moments of intense experience. It is, in a sense, to elide the sequential meaning of time and to emphasise instead its role in establishing depth of understanding and of emotion.

'The Familiar' is another late poem that links sensory and emotional experience to mythical or symbolic structures, probing the ways in which the desires of the individual become implicated in larger human urges. The opening epigraph, with its image of Cupid as Love, also invokes Wisdom in female form as Kinsella turns again to the figure of woman as one laden with personal, literary and mythical associations. What follows is a sequence of seven poems that deal with love and with the appetites of body and intellect. The muse or lover is welcomed into the speaker's neglected space: 'I lifted in her case / It was light, but I could tell / She was going to stay' (1.12-14). The unencumbered state does not make for simplicity or directness, however: the fragmentation of the poem ensures a strange co-existence of sensual experience and troubling mental states. The bare-eyed muse is both erotic and disturbing in ways that again show the destabilising influence that sexual desire has on form and language in Kinsella's work. Her movement from

hallway to bed is marked by uncanny changes that also challenge the notion of singular identity. She becomes first a devouring figure 'bending above me' (3.9), 'feeding' (4.2); then she is a reassuring presence: 'Her voice whispering in my ear: It is all / right. It is all right' (4.7-8). The sequence charts the course of a night and moves between conscious and semiconscious states, permitting the events to move from the personal to the archetypal with case: 'The demons over the door' (2.1); 'The three graces above the tank' (5.5) invoke spaces or thresholds marked by supernatural figures both civilised and primitive. Kinsella's treatment of desire is often marked by these contradictory impulses: towards the decorative as well as towards the animalistic; the expected trope alongside stark and challenging forms of expression. It allows him to acknowledge precursors—desire as the expressed lot of the poet and of his former self—as well as to explore pain and growth as an important legacy of unfulfilled desire. The preparation of breakfast recalls Bloom's attentive housekeeping in *Ulysses*,[15] as well as Kinsella's earlier **'Madonna'**.[16] The orange is replaced by a grapefruit here and the poet—rather than the woman—occupies the liminal space between inner and outer worlds: 'looking out through the frost on the window', 'looking up along the edge of the wood' (7.2; 9).

Again in Kinsella's work to look away to the distance is in fact to look inward; to detach the self from close and demanding relationships. Yet this looking inward is a reflective act that enables the speaker to encounter experience to its fullest extent and to acknowledge temporality as formative of human meaning. The suffering body, in prefiguring death, is emblematic both of human desire for the inhuman—what is beyond experience and understanding—and of the totality of change in human life. In Kinsella's work it signals the need for humankind to participate in and to understand these changes.

Notes

1. See A. E. McGuinness, '"Bright Quincunx Newly Risen": Thomas Kinsella's Inward "I"', *Eire-Ireland,* 15 (1980), pp. 106-25, p. 110.

2. See J. Holdridge, 'Homeward, Abandoned: The Aesthetics of Family and Home in Thomas Kinsella', *Irish University Review,* 31, 1 (Spring/Summer 2001), pp. 116-34, p. 122.

3. See G. Batten, '"The More with Which We Are Connected": The Muse of the Minus in the Poetry of McGuckian and Kinsella', in A. Bradley and M. Valiulis (eds), *Gender and Sexuality in Modern Ireland* (Amherst: University of Massachusetts Press, 1997), pp. 212-44, p. 214.

4. See E. Scarry, *The Body in Pain: The Making and Unmaking of the World* (New York: Oxford University Press, 1985), p. 172.

5. See J. Kristeva, *Black Sun: Depression and Melancholia,* trans. L. S. Roudiez, (New York/Oxford: Columbia University Press, 1989), p. 3.

6. This poem is reprinted in the first section of *Collected Poems*—'Poems' (1956); 'Another September' (1958).

7. This series of poems, revised to become 'From the Land of the Dead' in the 1996 *Collected Poems,* underwent significant changes from the time of its first publication. The versions referred to here are those from the Carcanet *Collected Poems* (2001).

8. Eamon Grennan describes coming to terms with Kinsella's work as learning to experience rather than understand the poems. This runs counter to most critical responses to the work which view its complexity as requiring an analytical approach. It is the combination of intellectual and emotional challenge that this work offers that makes fixed interpretations especially limiting.

9. See Scarry, *The Body in Pain,* p. 164.

10. See L. Heywood, *Dedication to Hunger: The Anorexic Aesthetic in Modern Culture* (Berkeley: University of California Press, 1996), p. 1.

11. See W. J. McCormack, 'Politics or Community: The Crux of Thomas Kinsella's Aesthetic Development', *Tracks,* 7 (1987), pp. 61-77, p. 76.

12. See D. Tubridy, *Thomas Kinsella: The Peppercanister Poems* (Dublin: University College Dublin Press, 2001), p. 125.

13. This imagery forms an important pattern in Kinsella's work and can be muted, as in the later 'Visiting Hour', where it becomes sexually suggestive—'I lay and fingered my mental parts' (3).

14. See E. Goodheart, 'Desire and its Discontents', in *Desire and its Discontents* (New York: Columbia University Press, 1991), pp. 113-41, p. 113.

15. 'Another slice of bread and butter: three, four: right. She didn't like her plate full. Right. He turned from the tray, lifted the kettle off the hob and set it sideways on the fire.' See *Ulysses,* trans. H. Gabler (London: Penguin Books, 1986), ch. 4.

16. There are many similarities between these two poems, extending from their structure (discrete sections depicting the meeting with the woman, sexual intimacy, breakfasting) to details in the text: 'her meat sweet' becoming 'her body / in an oxtail odour'; the woman 'minding her hair / at the window' envisioned again in the second of the graces 'settling her hair'. Familiarity is an idea acknowledged in 'Madonna' but central to the later poem.

References

Batten, G., '"The More with Which We Are Connected": The Muse of the Minus in the Poetry of McGuckian and Kinsella', in A. Bradley and M. Valiulis (eds), *Gender and Sexuality in Modern Ireland* (Amherst: University of Massachusetts Press, 1997), pp. 212-44.

Goodheart, E., 'Desire and its Discontents', in E. Goodheart, *Desire and its Discontents* (New York: Columbia University Press, 1991), pp. 113-41.

Grennan, E., '"Random Pursuit": Mining Kinsella's *One* and *A Technical Supplement*', in E. Grennan, *Facing the Music: Irish Poetry in the Twentieth Century* (Omaha, NE: Creighton University Press, 1999), pp. 218-28.

Heywood, L., *Dedication to Hunger: The Anorexic Aesthetic in Modern Culture* (Berkeley: University of California Press, 1996).

Holdridge, J., 'Homeward, Abandoned: The Aesthetics of Family and Home in Thomas Kinsella', *Irish University Review,* 31, 1 (Spring/Summer 2001), pp. 116-34.

Kristeva, J., *Powers of Horror: An Essay on Abjection,* trans. L. S. Roudiez (New York: Columbia University Press, 1982).

———— *Black Sun: Depression and Melancholia,* trans. L. S. Roudiez (New York/Oxford: Columbia University Press, 1989).

McCormack, W. J., 'Politics or Community: The Crux of Thomas Kinsella's Aesthetic Development', *Tracks,* 7 (1987), pp. 61-77.

McGuinness, A. E., '"Bright Quincunx Newly Risen": Thomas Kinsella's Inward "I"', *Eire-Ireland,* 15 (1980), pp. 106-25.

Scarry, E., *The Body in Pain: The Making and Unmaking of the World* (New York: Oxford University Press, 1985).

Tubridy, D., *Thomas Kinsella: The Peppercanister Poems* (Dublin: University College Dublin Press, 2001).

Lilah Hegnauer (review date winter 2007)

SOURCE: Hegnauer, Lilah. Review of *Collected Poems: 1956-2001,* by Thomas Kinsella. *Virginia Quarterly Review* 83, no. 1 (winter 2007): 299-300.

[*In the following review, Hegnauer praises* Collected Poems: 1956-2001, *calling it a challenging but rewarding book.*]

[In *Collected Poems: 1956-2001*] Kinsella writes in **"Dura Mater,"** "She came along the passage in her slippers / with a fuzz of navy hair, and her long nails / held out wet out of the washing water. // Come here to me. Come here to me, my own son." Kinsella's poems never fail to be that mother, slipper-footed and wet-handed, waiting for her son to embrace her. The poems move from Kinsella's early form Kinsella's early formalist years—*Another September* (1958)—to the more modernist poetics of *Poems from Centre City* (1990); throughout his epic body of work, the poems are "eliciting order from significant experience," leaving no doubt that Kinsella is a poet of major literary significance, both in and out of Ireland.

In **"An Ancient Ballet"** (1956), Kinsella writes, "All about her lit as though / Blood rang, marvels toiled. / Close at heart there sailed / A stately vast plateau." The kind of formalism Kinsella was writing early in his career was not stodgy or simplifying; it was fully engaged in the embodied reality of his world: "Domestic Autumn, like an animal / Long used to handling by those countrymen, / Rubs her kind hide against the bedroom wall." Later, in **"Madonna"** (1991), Kinsella writes, "the thick orange, honey-coarse. / First blood: a saturated essence / tasted between the teeth."

Kinsella's **Collected Poems** is a dense and difficult book. It's not one to be taken to bed, but one to sit with while drinking a hearty cup of coffee, one to give a finely tuned attention. That said, it's also a book of incredible pleasure, both intellectually and aurally. Kinsella confronts death, sickness, poverty, chaos, war, and human dignity with writing that makes the page pulse: "Love bent the sinewy bow / against His knee, / saying: *Husband, here is a friend / beseeming thee.* // Comely Wisdom wearing / a scarf around Her throat."

John Fanning (essay date 2007)

SOURCE: Fanning, John. "What Business Can Learn from the Poetry of Thomas Kinsella." *Irish Marketing Review* 19, nos. 1-2 (2007): 46-53.

[*In the essay below, Fanning urges business people to look to Kinsella's poetry for insight into improving their companies' marketing functions and increasing creativity.*]

INTRODUCTION

During the past decade businesses have been harangued from all sides on the need to become more innovative and creative if they are to have any hope of surviving in an increasingly competitive world. From

Michael Porter: 'innovation is the central issue in economic prosperity', to Gary Hamel: 'radical non-linear innovation is the only way to escape the ruthless hypercompetition that has been hammering down margins in industry after industry', all of the 'big beasts' of the business academic world have been singing the same tune. In the past business has never been shy of ransacking other disciplines for any insights they may have to offer, so it should come as no surprise that the humanities have now become a particular target.

'Creative writers can better articulate the essence of everyday experience, the consumer condition if you will, than any number of questionnaires, surveys, focus groups or ethnographic safaris into the precast canyons of the concrete jungle—culture makes the invisible visible and brings into material form the unexpressed conditions of being.'[1] Even the prestigious *Harvard Business Review* has succumbed to the lure of literary criticism, prompting one business academic to declare that 'art for mart's sake is the order of the day'.[2] 'Pragmatic and powerful insights can be found in the works of Sophocles, Shakespeare, Conrad and others. But you've got to know where to look and how to understand what they're saying.'[3]

Six years earlier a leading Irish management consultant made the same point: 'At the heart of the enlightenment project was the notion that a scientifically enlightened elite could map all knowledge and make all social and economic reality predictable and controllable. All this was rooted in a morbid anxiety, fear and dread of the essentially uncertain and messy nature of human existence. A degree of scepticism with rational planning has now become commonplace; it is [therefore] not surprising to see leading edge management thinking and practice move away from natural and social scientism and increasingly seek to recapture insights from literature and the humanities.'[4]

More predictably, perhaps, the former 1960s *enfant terrible*, Richard Neville, now a respected business consultant in Australia, weighed in with: 'To transform information into knowledge and knowledge into something useful, original and marketable, you need the alchemy of creativity. To be fast and agile in a volatile world, you need an endless fount of this magic elixir. You need it to out-innovate your competitors, to respond to fluid markets, to read the footprints of the future in the sand. In the twenty-first century creativity will became the interface between commerce and art.'[5]

If as a result of this new consensus about the importance of art, literature and the humanities in general, businesses were tempted to examine what contemporary Irish literature had to offer, Thomas Kinsella would probably represent the most fruitful starting point. Kinsella's poetic career has now spanned over half a century and he has long been preoccupied with the nature and vagaries of the creative process. He has also been associated with the concept of 'quincunx' which, apart from reflecting a 'new self', has often been used in connection with the ancient division of Ireland into five provinces and 'can be observed on the cover of [Kinsella's] *Fifteen Dead,* where the roman numerals for fifteen (XV) can also be read as quincunx and vertical man.'[6] It seems appropriate, therefore, to try to distil his potential relevance for the business world, and particularly marketing communications, into five key insights.

PERSISTENCE, PATIENCE AND PRESCIENCE

Achieving creative breakthroughs involves time, effort and failure. You can't order it on demand; you can't even specify what it is you want, you must gather as much experience and information as possible and keep trawling through it until some order can be established:

> It is tedious, yes the process is elaborate
> and wasteful—a dangerous litter
> of lacerating pieces collects
> let my rubbish stand witness
> smile stirring it idly by with a shoe.

(p. 124)[7]

Kinsella himself describes how it works: 'the whole process of note-taking, drafting, exploration and the absorption or dismissal of material continues, mining away until the poem shows its proper direction and whether or not the data are going to cohere'.[8] It has been pointed out that a fundamental element of his art is the 'dual technique-cum-ethic of eliciting order *from* experience rather than imposing order upon it'.[9] He doesn't set out with a grand plan, he assembles the material, allows it to intermingle and although ultimately exercising the artist's authority over it he also respects that it has a life of its own.

Kinsella feeds his ambition to come to a creative understanding of our lives today by absorbing information about our immediate and ancient past in an effort to come to terms with who we are now. He allows all of this information to be absorbed and digested in the hope that it will in its own good time yield results:

> I feed upon it still, as you see
> there is no end to that which, not understood,
> may yet be hoarded in the imagination
> in the yolk of one's being, so to speak,
> there to undergo its (quite animal) growth,

(p. 99)

It is interesting to note that Kinsella wrote this in the early 1970s and over twenty years later developments in neuroscience provided proof of the brain's capacity

for absorbing infinitely more information than had hitherto been realised: 'Unconscious processing of external stimuli takes place and influences our actions without our conscious awareness—the vast bulk of the information that we need to function must be processed in the unconscious part of the brain—95 per cent of our actions are unconsciously determined.'[10]

One of the most ambitious attempts to define the nature of creativity was Arthur Koestler's *The Act of Creation*: 'The creative act is not an act of creation in the sense of the Old Testament. It does not create something out of nothing; it uncovers, selects, reshuffles, combines, synthesises already existing facts, ideas, faculties, skills.'[11] This led Koestler to his creative theory of 'bisociation' in order to distinguish between routine thinking on a single plane and creative thinking that always occurs on more than one plane. 'The bisociative act connects previously unconnected matrices of experience—the essence of discovery is that unlikely marriage of cabbages and kings, of previously unrelated frames of reference or universes of discourse whose union will solve previously unsolvable problems'.[12] Koestler also believed that we are conscious of only a fraction of what may be 'hoarded in the imagination' and he addressed the problems of Cartesian thinking long before *Descartes' Error*[13] was more widely published. It should follow therefore that when trying to arrive at creative solutions the more we know about the background to the problem under review the more likely we are to make the necessary connections and, as Kinsella advises, we need to keep stirring the pot:

> We have to dig down
> sieve, scour and roughen
> make it all fertile and vigorous
> get the fresh rain down.

(p. 184)

The more we 'let our gaze blaze' the more likely we are to be successful. Concentrated thinking about the material is one method of making the necessary connections but both Koestler and Kinsella also emphasise the creative possibilities of the unconscious: 'The creative act, in so far as it depends on unconscious resources, presupposes a relaxing of the controls and a regression to modes of ideation which are indifferent to the rules of verbal logic, unperturbed by contradiction, untouched by the dogmas and taboos of so-called commonsense'.[14] Both writers are influenced by the thinking of Carl Jung, whose theory of the Active Imagination involved 'going down a steep descent akin to entering a trance during which unconscious personalities emerged with sufficient clarity to hold conversations with them—conversations with them brought him the critical insight that things happen in the psyche that are not produced by conscious intention'.[15] Henri Poincare, another writer who has considered the nature of creativity, came to a similar conclusion: 'preparatory thinking activates potentially relevant ideas in the unconscious which are there unknowingly combined'.[16]

Perhaps the most important lesson we can learn from Kinsella's approach to creativity and the creative process is that real breakthroughs are unlikely to occur as a result of hastily convened 'brainstorming' sessions or even more carefully planned 'away-days'. A second lesson is that inexperienced executives with limited knowledge of the market are unlikely to be equipped to contribute much in the way of real innovation. Continuous absorption of all available product or service knowledge and of the behaviour and attitudes of the type of consumers under review is the best guarantee of making the unlikely connections that are invariably at the heart of new thinking. It should be a regular process which can be induced from time to time by complete immersion designed to dredge up all our unconscious as well as conscious knowledge. The implication that the process cannot be subject to the same degree of logistical control as other elements in the business supply chain will not be popular with senior management and in particular the accountancy function, but it is better that they are aware of the reality of the creative and innovative process than that they imagine they can impose their own logic.

Discussions with creative people in advertising agencies will confirm that the best ideas often emerge from unconscious moments of reflection rather than during the time strictly allotted to solving the problem. But whether the such moments of reflection are conscious or unconscious, the entire process would be more productive if we ensured that anyone with responsibility for a brand is thoroughly familiar with: (i) the entire history of the brand—with every aspect of its origins, changes in its composition, its ups and downs and how it has arrived at its present position; (ii) the attitudes and behaviour, the lives and loves, the fears and hopes and the dreams and aspirations of the target group for the brand; and (iii) all relevant published case histories. Only when people's heads are immersed in this knowledge will genuine creative breakthroughs emerge. The fact that we work in an area which is not conducive to what Stephen Brown refers to as the APIC (analysis, planning, implementation, control) paradigm[17] is no excuse for a sloppy, unprofessional attitude to the creative process. Thomas Kinsella's painstakingly dedicated approach should be our goal.

BEWARE ALL TOTALISING SYSTEMS

The understandable desire for strict accountability in the business world can often lead to hugely ambitious but ultimately doomed attempts to exert a totalising level of control over one's consumers. Classic examples from the world of marketing are the regular announcements of techniques which claim to measure the precise effects of marketing communications campaigns, especially advertising. An industry perpetually smarting from the oft repeated jibe 'half of my advertising works but I don't know which half' is reluctantly forced to cooperate with these exercises while secretly regarding them as futile.

A recent book on this subject is enthusiastically gushing about what the author regards as the imminent arrival of technology which will enable advertisers to define precisely what and how different pieces of marketing communication work. 'In a few years time we should be able to measure brand communication exposure from all sorts of sources—from a logo on a T-shirt to an ad on the back of a bus, to a gondola end promotion in a supermarket, even to a branded lounge tent at a music festival. That's because all these things will be equipped with short range transponders that will register on receivers worn by volunteers on watches or spectacles or even embedded in their mobile phones or cars'.[18] The fact that this futuristic nightmare will never see the light of day won't stop the management consultancies, the market research companies and the media planning agencies from peddling 'comfort blankets for incontinent executives' to the masters of the universe in corporate head offices.

Kinsella has commented on the ultimate futility of this type of imperialism and although he was thinking more of attempts by British administrators in the seventeenth century to subdue Ireland by accurate mapping and categorising, the fact that the business world would merely substitute the words 'market surveying' and 'segmentation' shows that they are engaged in precisely the same activity in relation to twenty-first-century consumers. His most famous target is William Petty, the seventeenth-century cartographer whose Down Survey of Ireland is taken by the poet as 'an example of the difficulty encountered if a system or structure is imposed upon the details of experience rather than being elicited from them'.[19] The fact that Kinsella changes the name of the unfortunate mapmaker to Skullbullet should be enough to alert readers to his attitude:

> Blessed William Skullbullet
> glaring from the furnace of your hair
> thou whose definitions—whose insane nets
> plunge and convulse to hold your furious catch

let our gaze blaze, we pray
let us see how the whole thing works.

(p. 177)

Flanagan argues that Kinsella's intentions are twofold; 'to explore and reveal how the original classifying gaze quickly follows cultural generalisations to acquire the armour of scientific statement', and how inexorably the textual and contemplative awareness gradually becomes 'administrative, economic and even military.'[20] In a business context it is the 'armour of scientific statement' that tends to create the most serious problems. The fact that the measuring devices are faulty is ignored once the ever-seductive figures are available. But some management theorists are now sounding a warning. 'We should abandon the search for the Single Criterion—the feeling that quantification is the ultimate source of unerring certainty and oracular wisdom and that the evaluation process is "nothing but" the one or two figures that result'.[21]

Later in the same poem Kinsella goes further by pointing out that the very act of measurement causes the subject to change, thus immediately rendering the whole exercise invalid ('Except that at the first violation / the body would rip into pieces and fly apart / with terrible spasms'). Here he is alluding to Heisenberg's Uncertainty Principle from quantum mechanics which casts doubt on the assumption that if we can calculate the present exactly we can calculate the future. In a quantum world it is our ability to 'calculate the present exactly' that is in doubt. Unfortunately, these earth-shattering developments were conveniently ignored by the business world, where managers are continually being told that 'you can't manage what you can't measure.'[22]

The world of marketing communications has always had reservations and is more instinctively in tune with the 'uncertainty principle' but rarely has the self-confidence to raise its head above the parapet, although there have been exceptions: 'You could say if you felt like being cynical that peddling statistics of dubious value to the profoundly unimaginative and unselfconfident would provide a pretty good living for a lot of clever people even though it may not help very much to create successful new brands or revive sad old declining ones. But numbers are the talisman of our age, they justify everything, it must be true because the numbers say so. I've always been amused and sometimes amazed by the way in which numbers, sometimes tendentious, sometimes torn out of context, occasionally quite meaningless and arbitrary are used to give a false, but nevertheless a comfortable air of verisimilitude to even the most evident rubbish.'[23] But there are now signs of a wider revolt against the obsessive application of dubious mathematical models and

two leading US business academics have recently argued that 'business schools have lost their way because of the scientific model that dominates business research and teaching.'[24] They go on to argue that business students should all take a course in literature, which would teach them more about human nature and the real world than any business case study.

Beware the Ease of the Spurious

Creativity and innovation involve risk. In the business world market research can reduce but never eliminate risk, as evidenced by the alarmingly high failure rate for new product development launches. The main reason for this failure is that the products or services were not sufficiently different from what was already in the market. Not enough risks were taken because managers settled for products or services which could be safely evaluated within consumers' existing conceptual framework and therefore weren't really all that new. Kinsella has obviously studied not only the nature of the creative process, but the working methods of the fellow artists he admires:

we find everywhere
in his strange work
the readiness to take risks
tedium, the ignoble,
to try anything ten times
if so the excessive matter can be settled.

(p. 240)

Here he is referring to Mahler, who was a particular inspiration ('if only we could wring our talent out / wring it and wring it out to dry like that'). His triple use of the work 'wring' in two lines shows how much effort Kinsella believes must go into creative work. He makes frequent reference to the sheer 'ordeal' involved and to the constant failure before some kind of result is achieved. By definition, therefore, success is rare and most of the time:

it grows dark and we stumble
in gathering ignorance
in a land of loss
and unfulfillable desire.

(p. 259)

But a willingness to face the ordeal, to accept the inevitable failure will eventually be rewarded:

a few times in a lifetime, with luck,
the actual substance alters: fills with
expectation, beats with a molten glow
a change occurs; grows cool; resumes.

(p. 187)

But it may be that Kinsella's most important lesson under this heading is to avoid the easy, often crowd-pleasing solution. Writing about Thomas Moore, he damns the eponymous melodies with faint praise ('some of these songs established the imagery of harp, heartbreak and vague patriotism that passes for Irish still in England and the United States')[25] and dismisses his poetry as 'commonplace ideas with verbal ingenuity and charm, always a marketable combination'.[26] He himself was determined to avoid what he often referred to as 'the ease of the spurious':

> I have known the hissing assemblies.
> The preference for the ease of the spurious
> the measured poses and stupidities.

(p. 352)

The number of 'me-too' product and service offerings that are still being launched into the market and doomed to early failure, not to mention the number of mind-numbingly boring advertisements unleashed on the public, is testament to the fact that we are all too inclined to settle for the 'ease of the spurious'.

WALK, DON'T RUN

The runner reaches the destination first but the walker observes more and therefore understands more along the way. Creative breakthroughs are more likely to occur to the walker because of the ability to focus on the concrete or specific in order to understand the wider world:

> emotion expelled, to free the structure of a thing
> or indulged to free the structure of an idea.
> The entirety of one's being
> crowded for everlasting shelter
> into the memory of one crust of bread.
> Granting it everlasting life.
> Eating it absolutely.

(p. 171)

Kinsella has always been a great walker, from **'A Country Walk'** in the early 1960s, where each step represents 'a drop of peace returning', to **'The Pen Shop'** in the late 1990s, where he indulges in a Leopold Bloom-like perambulation around the streets of central Dublin, and to his prescient observations on the embryonic Celtic Tiger prompted by a walk around the newly emerging Dublin suburbs in *Nightwalker.* Tubridy has argued that 'the degree of precision afforded to the walker acts as a stimulus to creative insights' and has drawn our attention to the connection that Michel de Certeau makes 'between the act of walking and the process of understanding as it relates to systems of totalisation and power'.[27] She goes on to comment on Kinsella's creative use of walking to substitute a synchronic view of a particular place, people or society with a more diachronic perspective: 'Kinsella's trajectory through the city disrupts the stable, isolatable and interconnected properties through which the urban space is conceived introducing an irreducible diachronicity that troubles personal as well as public history.'[28]

Kinsella's message for us under this heading is that we are more likely to achieve real insights through direct observation than relying on outsourced market research. Research is essential for an overview and accurate structure of a market, but if we accept the fact that genuine innovation occurs at some point between expert knowledge of a particular market and acute understanding of consumers in that market then there's no alternative to combining both sets of expertise in the one person. This could account for the fact that smaller businesses that can't afford to divide these functions have a better track record in developing and launching new initiatives than the large corporations. But the one large corporation that is recognised as genuinely innovative, Procter & Gamble, is acutely aware of the need for the 'walker approach' to new product development. Its chief executive was recently quoted as advising: 'if you want to understand the lions go to the jungle not the zoo'. The same advice was proffered by Thomas Kinsella twenty years ago in *St. Catherine's Clock,* where he takes the reader on a walk through time around the historic lanes and alleyways that stretch out from Thomas Street:

> I inhaled the granite lamplight
> divining the energies of the prowler.

(p. 261)

Thus the walker/prowler sets out to 'divine', which can be defined as 'discovering by intuition', and in another memorable line from the same poem 'reading the ground' provides an inspirational metaphor for market research. The poet points business in the direction of minute observation of the particular as the most likely and rewarding path to innovation. This is an area where we have made rapid progress in recent years as semiotic and ethnographic techniques are introduced into mainstream market research. 'Semiotic analysis (of communications) concerns reading the hidden meanings of marketing messages, exploring the discourse, decoding the conscious signals the brand is sending out, revealing and retuning the brand's conscious beliefs about its consumers. Observational interviewing is literally living with people in the real time of their use of products and brands, sharing the minutiae of behaviour and relationships that constitute usage and attitudes, widening the perception to the reality of the consumer's whole world.'[29]

AN UNDERSTANDING OF THE PRESENT IS DEPENDENT ON AN UNDERSTANDING OF THE PAST

Kinsella was always conscious of history. He was born and raised in Inchicore in Dublin, close to Kilmainham Gaol. Both his grandmothers ran small shops from their homes in the Liberties, an area rich in historical associations and at a time, only a few decades after the War of Independence and the Civil War, when these recent events weighed heavily on all sections of the population. The reference in an early poem ('ourselves though seven hundred years accurst') is testament to an early endorsement of the official Irish historical line, though young Thomas was the recipient of extra-curricular tuition in the home:

> Your family, Thomas, met with and helped
> many of the Croppies in hiding from the Yeos
> on their way home after the defeat
> in South Wexford. They sheltered the Laceys
> who were later hanged on the Bridge in Ballinglen
> between Tinahely and Anacorra.

(p. 172)

However, it was his later exposure to the works of Carl Jung that provided a more intellectual basis for the poet's subsequent immersion in his country's immediate and ancient past. Jung believed that for man to attain complete fulfilment, which he referred to as a state of individuation, akin to Maslow's better known 'self-actualisation', it was first necessary to come to an understanding of our 'collective unconscious'. Jung believed that the collective unconscious was 'composed of functional units, archetypes, identical psychic structures common to all which together constitute the archaic heritage of humanity'.[30] He believed we have all allowed ourselves to become too far removed from our psychic roots and this hinders our ability to operate at full capacity in today's world.

Kinsella's reaction was twofold: first, to delve deep into his own family background, being prepared to confront any dark secrets that may have been repressed; and second, to reconstruct the original foundations of his society. In successive poems from *New Poems* in 1972 to *St. Catherine's Clock* in 1987 Kinsella explores, examines and exhumes his immediate family, especially his father and grandmother, and creates an imaginative reconstruction of the origins of life on the island of Ireland. With these descriptions of childhood and the forces which shaped the society in which he lived, Kinsella comes to a better understanding of himself and the world that surrounds him. Like most intellectuals of the second half of the twentieth century he may still be alienated from the modern world, but by reconnecting with his psychic heritage he is in much better shape to confront it.

Many business organisations are unable to confront the challenges of today's marketplace because of their inbuilt historical provincialism. Since the late 1970s when the Irish Marketing Society ran a conference for its members under the title 'The Challenge of Change', no sector of the business world has remained free from a conference, a seminar or a 'think-in' devoted to the same topic. A rain forest of books, a slew of MBA modules and a swarm of management consultants and celebrity business gurus have dedicated themselves to the subject of change management; all to very little avail. The general consensus is that change management programmes change very little. The generally accepted reason is that senior management are not fully committed to the process and therefore those under them see no reason to make the effort to change.

Kinsella's quest for 'wholeness' suggests a different reason—that if you are not fully aware of what you are then by definition you can't change, and you can't fully comprehend what you are unless you know where you came from. Professor Tim Ambler of the London Business School describes the problem well: 'Institutional memory loss is exacerbated by rotating marketing directors who regard an eighteen month tenure as the norm. They demand new insights from new research ignorant of the similar research piled up by predecessors. The modern marketers life is a whirl of meetings. These leave little time for field visits, consulting back files, or sitting with long-serving managers still less company pensioners to absorb the history of trials, what worked and what didn't in the past.'[31] The importance of understanding business organisations by studying their history is now becoming more acceptable and a recent influential book on brand innovation included the following recommendation. 'Who are we? The underlying premise here is that the identity of the company already exists—that is there's a lot of potentially valuable components of the brand's past stored away in a metaphorical vault—we just need to find the most relevant dimensions of these facts, equities or ideas.'[32]

Conclusions

Businesses are constantly being urged to adapt to a rapidly changing world by becoming more creative and innovative. A feature of all this pressure is the belated recognition that this change, if it is to have any change of success, must involve everyone in the organisation and not just senior management. But too often there is a complete disconnection between this aspiration and the reality of how the business world is managed. This is particularly marked in terms of the language used in business, or more accurately the impoverishment of that language whose empirical nature is simply not commensurate with the complexity of the real world its seeks to understand and influence.

The precision of poetry, and the need for those who engage with it to concentrate in order to 'ease the particular of its litter' makes it a potentially invaluable resource for business. Long-term labourers in the Lit Crit vineyards may feel aggrieved, but shouldn't be all that surprised. Terry Eagleton explains: 'Capitalism is impeccably inclusive—in its hunt for profit it will travel any distance, endure any hardship, shack up with the most obnoxious of companions, suffer the most abominable humiliations, tolerate the most tasteless wallpaper and cheerfully betray its next of kin.'[33]

In their quest for innovation and creativity businesses spend very large sums of money every year organising away-days, think-ins, brainstorming sessions and sometimes even more bizarre practices like walking over hot coals in an effort to squeeze insights from hard-pressed executives. If a close reading of the poetry of Thomas Kinsella could be positioned as a more civilised way to release these insights, then there would appear to be no harm in the poet benefiting from the increased sales and his interpreters and critics from the resulting consultancy fees.

Notes

1. Brown, S. (2005), *Writing Marketing: Literary Lessons from Academic Authorities,* Sage Publications, London.

2. Ibid.

3. Badaracco, J. (2006), 'Leadership in literature', *Harvard Business Review,* March 2006.

4. Carroll, C. (2000), 'The end of modernity', *Management,* April/May.

5. Neville, R. (2000), 'The art of work and the work of art in the 21st century', an address to international business leaders given at the art gallery of New South Wales to celebrate Korn/Ferry's 20 years in Australia, June.

6. McGuinness, A. (1980), 'Bright quincunx newly risen', *Éire-Ireland,* vol. 15, winter.

7. All quotations are referenced from the Carcanet Press, Manchester, edition of Kinsella's *Collected Poems,* published in 2001.

8. John, B. (1996) 'Reading the ground: the poetry of Thomas Kinsella', CUA Press, Washington, DC.

9. Clutterbuck, C. (2005), 'Thomas Kinsella', in A. Roche et al. (eds.), *The UCD Aesthetic: Celebrating 150 Years of UCD Writers,* New Island, Dublin.

10. Bargh, J. and T. Chartrand (1999), 'The unbearable automaticity of being', *American Psychologist,* issue 54.

11. Koestler, A. (1975), *The Act of Creation,* Pan Books, London.

12. Ibid.

13. Damasio, A. (1994), *Descartes' Error: Emotion, Reason and the Human Brain,* Putnam Berkley Group, New York, NY.

14. Koestler, A. (1975), op. cit.

15. Stevens, A. (2001), *Jung: A Very Short Introduction,* Oxford University Press, Oxford.

16. Boden, M. (2004), *The Creative Mind: Myths and Mechanisms,* Routledge, London.

17. Brown, S. (2001), *Marketing—The Retro Revolution,* Sage Publications, London.

18. Taylor, J. (2005), *The Space Race,* Wiley, Chichester.

19. Tubridy, D. (2001), *Thomas Kinsella: The Peppercanister Poems,* University College Dublin Press, Dublin.

20. Flanagan, I. (2001), 'Tissues of order: Kinsella and the Enlightenment ethos', in C. Clutterbuck (ed.), *Irish University Review* special issue on Thomas Kinsella, spring/summer.

21. Tasgal, A. (2003), 'The Science of Brand', Market Research Society Annual Conference, London.

22. Karplan, R. and D. Norton (1996), *The Balanced Scorecard,* Harvard University Press, Cambridge, MA.

23. Olins, W. (2003), *On Brand,* Thames and Hudson, London.

24. Bennis, W. and J. O'Toole (2005), 'How business schools lost their way', *Harvard Business Review,* May.

25. Kinsella, T. (1995), *The Dual Tradition: An Essay on Poetry and Politics in Ireland,* Carcanet Press, Manchester.

26. Ibid.

27. Tubridy, D. (2001), 'Difficult migrations: the Dinnseanchas of Thomas Kinsella's later poetry', *Irish University Review,* vol. 31, no. 1, spring/summer.

28. Ibid.

29. Gordon, W. and V. Valentine (2000), 'The 21st century consumer: an endlessly moving target', *Market Leader,* issue 11, winter.

30. Stevens, A. (2001), *Jung: A Very Short Introduction,* Oxford University Press, Oxford.

31. Ambler, T. (2004), 'Innocents and experience', *Financial Times,* 30 November.

32. Morgan, A. (1999), *Eating the Big Fish,* Wiley, Chichester.

33. Eagleton, T. (2004), *After Theory,* Penguin, London.

Andrew Fitzsimons (essay date August 2008)

SOURCE: Fitzsimons, Andrew. "'Let the Fall Begin': Thomas Kinsella's European Dimension." *Irish Studies Review* 16, no. 3 (August 2008): 267-81.

[In the essay below, Fitzsimons highlights Kinsella's European influences, referencing figures such as writers

Goethe and Thomas Mann and psychiatrist Carl Jung.
Fitzsimons also draws a connection between Kinsella's
work and the writing of Czeslaw Milosz.]

It takes no great imagination to see in Thomas Kinsella's first review the outline of his own subsequent work: 'The great poem of *Faust* occupied Goethe during his entire life', Kinsella wrote, remarking upon Faust's 'restless striving [. . .] and his titanic urge to comprehend the harmony of the universe and to take upon himself the whole of human experience'.[1] In the inaugurating work of his own decades-long attempt to 'see how the whole thing / works' (**'One'**, 33), *Notes from the Land of the Dead* (1972), Faust is emblematic of the near-madness of artistic toil and is almost indistinguishable from the speaker of the introductory poem of that sequence, *'hesitate, cease to exist'*:

> Many a time
> I have risen from my gnawed books
> and prowled about, wrapped in a long grey robe,
> and rubbed my forehead; reached for my instruments
> —canister and kettle, the long handled spoon,
> metal vessels and delph; settled the flame,
> blue and yellow; and, in abstracted hunger,
> my book propped before me, eaten forkfulls
> of scrambled egg and buttered fresh bread
> and taken hot tea until the sweat stood out
> at the roots of my hair!
>
> (*New Poems 1973,* 9; henceforth *NP* 1973)

In early poems such as **'Baggot Street Deserta'** (1958), with the 'mathematic / Passion' (*Another September,* 29; henceforth *AS*) of its Bach cello suite, and in *Notes from the Land of the Dead* and the Peppercanister series, the cycle which has occupied Kinsella since 1972, there is a consistent and constant German influence. This can be seen most prominently in the frequent references that Kinsella makes to the writings of Thomas Mann and to the music and artistic example of Gustav Mahler. When asked about his initial attraction to German literature, Kinsella replied:

> It was only a student interest. I was interested in Goethe and Kafka and Rilke, above all in Thomas Mann. All in translation. There was an opportunity once, to study the German language—in UCD; but there weren't enough students and it faded, and my studies in German faded. So I have only the slightest acquaintance with the language.[2]

In this same interview, Kinsella discounted a historical derivation for this interest, ascribing it mostly to an abiding interest in German music, and connecting the reasons for his attraction to Bach with the effect that reading Thomas Mann (and James Joyce) had on his own work:

> The manipulation of maximum detail, immense quantities of material in radiant order as in the great *Passions* and *Masses.* With the same skill in miniature, the power

in delicacy, as in the cello suites. Similarly—although I have to allow for the fact of translation—with Thomas Mann, where you have the great structures, with control over detail. I was reading the Joseph stories, and Joyce, for the first time, and at the same time, with the same enthusiasm.[3]

Concerning his use of the Faust story in *Notes from the Land of the Dead,* Kinsella indicated in this interview that for him the significance of the story derived less from Goethe than from Carl Jung. Though Kinsella's knowledge of Goethe's masterpiece stretched back to his earliest critical writings, what he required of the poem for his own work arrived via Jung, with an influence that was fundamental in the development of his mature aesthetic. *Notes from the Land of the Dead* signalled a definitive move away from the 'mathematic' formal procedures of Kinsella's verse of the 1950s, but it also enacted a return to the imaginative realm that this earlier poetry had discovered. In *'hesitate, cease to exist'* Kinsella blends a version of himself as a young poet and Goethe's Faust in the figure of a writer/alchemist/insomniac 'getting quietly ready / to go down quietly out of [his] mind' in deliberate and methodical derangement in a room which has the aura of both alchemical chamber and domestic scullery. Kinsella returns here to the act of creating his poetry of the 1950s, in which images welled-up unconsciously, discoveries out of the 'God knows what hole' of the imagination. The 'narrow room' of the Baggot Street flat in which Kinsella lived for most of that decade is a crucial reference point in his personal and poetic development, and will become associated in *The Pen Shop* (1997) with the 'narrow cell' of the ancient Irish scribes:

> It was a room where I did a tremendous amount of reading, writing and growing up. I think I was growing imaginatively then more than ever before or since, coming in contact with many important things for the first time. You come in contact with important things for the first time right through your life, but at that point, in my early twenties, a whole deluge, poured in.[4]

Kinsella's poetry of the 1950s revolves around the problematic of classicist form. Traditional form offers, he says in **'Writer at Work'** (1961), an existential consolation in the encounter with formlessness, but Kinsella's art even at its earliest stage is one in which accomplished form is only a temporary salve before the (inevitable) unravelling of accomplished shape. At this time Kinsella's main reading was in Blake, Joyce and Thomas Mann,[5] and it was Mann's sense of the consolations derived from language and form which provided a potential solution to Kinsella's intimations about the futility of writing:

> But his love of the Word kept growing sweeter and sweeter, and his love of form; for he used to say (and

had already said it in writing) that knowledge of the soul would unfailingly make us melancholy if the pleasures of expression did not keep us alert and of good cheer.[6]

The introduction to *Notes from the Land of the Dead* returns to the setting of **'Baggot Street Deserta'**, a poem of formal poise which expresses dissatisfaction with the formal idea of poetry itself. The 'key', the prize that the speaker holds 'glowing' in his hand at the end of his terrifying descent is an emblem of Kinsella's turn inward into his own sources and away from inherited aesthetic conventions, with the connotations Jung finds in its Faustian template: '[t]he insignificant looking tool in Faust's hand is the dark creative power of the unconscious, which reveals itself to those who follow its dictates'.[7] Only at the end of his journey does Kinsella's speaker realise that this power had been in his possession all along: 'The key, though I hardly knew it, / already in my fist' (*NP* 1973, 10). The creative power of the key is phallic, yet also has the qualities of a pen, which like the pen in Seamus Heaney's well-known poem 'Digging' is a tool for an almost archaeological excavation of self.[8] In a sense what we are seeing in this return to an earlier stage of his development is Kinsella re-making his work, finding in early discoveries enlarged implications.

In *A Technical Supplement* (1976) the pen resembles a tool for self-laceration. Already in **'Clarence Mangan'** (1958) Kinsella had presented artistic endeavour in such terms: 'Ultimate, pitiless, again I ply the knife' (*AS,* 24). In the draft versions of The 'Prologue' to *Downstream* (1962) we see this aspect of Kinsella's work reach its direst, yet most comical, pitch. This introductory poem to the volume was at one stage in its composition called **'Good Morning'**.[9] As well as being a testament and a farewell to his twenties, the poem in draft form looks forward ten years, to '1968'. The poet plans to get rid of old habits and expresses the wish to 'start my thirties sweet and clean. / To tidy my twenties for the bin'. Physically, he is 'well-enough', but cautions that 'The psyche is another matter':

> Hands that twitch & nerves that shatter
> Sometimes seem to show the cracks,
> The choppings of the inner axe.[10]

The violence of the metaphors reaches a comic climax when he names his indefatigable psychic demon 'the inner Lizzie Borden'. There is, of course, self-deprecation in all of this. The poem in this draft, and in its final form, is wry in its reflections on self and social position: 'I have stayed a poet / Though, honestly, you'd scarcely know it'. The everyday grind the speaker faces is full of *ennui*, but most significantly there is boredom with the resources and machinery of poetry itself: 'Three steps on, two back, we come / Beating the iambic drum'. The frustrations with form in **'Baggot Street Deserta'** had been for the most part connected to the depredations of time and the difficulty of the attempt to establish a satisfying relationship between form and the past; in *Downstream* the frustrations are more markedly connected to the habits and rhetoric of poetry. In **'The Force of Eloquence'**, words are (and the violence of the verb indicates the suspicion in which the act is held) 'constricted into other terms' to create 'eternal breathless appearance' (*Downstream,* 62; henceforth *D*). This frustration is accompanied by an awareness of the need to move on from the provisional achievement of form: 'He must progress / Who fabricates a path' (*D,* 32).[11]

Kinsella's move to America in 1965, to take up a position as Artist in Residence at Southern Illinois University, is often seen as crucial to his poetic development, yet even before the publication of *Another September,* Kinsella had in 1956, almost ten years before his move, written in praise of Stevens and Pound in reviews in the *Irish Press*.[12] In an interview with Dennis O'Driscoll, Kinsella says that he 'was excited about the poetry of Pound long before going to America'.[13] It is from Pound that another influence makes its presence felt in the 'Prologue', that of François Villon's 'Le Testament', written like Kinsella's poem 'En l'an de mon trentiesme aage' (In the thirtieth year of my age) when the poet admits to being 'Ne du tout fol, ne tout sage' (not wholly foolish, nor yet a sage).[14] The drafts confirm this source: Kinsella adopts the 'Item' refrain that Villon uses in his long poem of final bequest.[15] Villon's influence has been unremarked upon, though Kinsella, in **'Time and the Poet'** (1959), sees Villon as having written perhaps 'the most beautiful and illustrative' poem on the 'sorrow caused by the plunder of time'.[16] Villon's significance in terms of Kinsella's later work can be seen here, particularly in relation to the light the comments throw on the mix of anger and ruefulness in **'Nightwalker'**:

> Everything that he considered reality is mentioned in his huge tomes, with malice but also with regret, e.g. the bourgeois mind and the church [. . .] in a way that seems to say that they (the poet and his enemies) are all children of the one mother.[17]

Villon's poems derive their origin and their theme, Kinsella writes, from the 'ever active image of Death and separation'.[18] He relates that in Villon's Paris there was a painting of the *danse macabre* along one wall of Les Invalides, and that Montfaucon, the haunt of courting couples, was festooned with the rotting carcasses of the hanged. With this mind it is clear that the medieval mode of *Moralities* (1960), which Kinsella was working on at the time of this lecture, was undoubtedly influenced by Villon.

The temporary appeasing of the inner demon is a constant temptation. The pleasures of form, as in Mann's *Tonio Kröger,* keep the artist in good cheer, but, as in **'Baggot Street Deserta,'** also 'risk the spurious'. In *Downstream* Kinsella evokes a different conception of 'risk'. In **'Into Thy Hands'** (*Moralities*), the speaker proclaims: 'let accident / Complete our dreadful journey into being' (*D,* 28). The original title of this poem, **'Savour of Desperation',**[19] captures well what becomes the characteristic Kinsellian note, the embracing of adversity in pursuit of increased understanding, and as an opportunity for growth. The diver preparing to jump in **'Into Thy Hands'** prefigures the recurrent emergence of tropes of falling in Kinsella: in *Notes from the Land of the Dead,* as I have shown, and in *Her Vertical Smile,* as I will show below, this trope occurs often in contexts and occasions with German influences. Falling as necessary to increased understanding, the appraisal of the negative in positive terms, and its use for positive ends, informs Kinsella's aesthetic change. Disappointment, which like futility could cripple the creative act, is transformed into a creative force. Kinsella's disparagement of poetry's 'unreality' when faced with time, death, natural process and the forces of industrial might (**'A Portrait of the Engineer'**, *D,* 15), provokes him into change, just as disappointment with the 'elaborately prepared solutions'[20] of religion, and of 'classicist' forms, spurs the discovery of alternative organising principles for his experience.

The self-critical element in Kinsella, the 'inner Lizzie Borden', is prominent in **'Downstream'**. The self-accusation centres mainly on the innocence of the speaker. However, in referring to himself in Nietzschean terms as 'Urmensch and brute', and thereby implicating himself in the European horror, the speaker reveals that the self-accusation also concerns a fundamental human baseness. **'Downstream'** takes its place, in this context, with **'Nightwalker'** and **'A Country Walk',** as a poem in which the instability of the present derives from violence in the past. **'Baggot Street Deserta'** noted the consequences for the artist of the 'shreds of disappointment'[21] of the present; but in *Nightwalker and Other Poems* (1968) and in the later work, Kinsella accounts for how the decrepit present had originated. The effect on Samuel Beckett of his experience at the Irish hospital at Saint-Lô in 1945-46 is appropriate in this context: the vision, Beckett wrote, of 'humanity in ruins' provided 'an inkling of the terms in which our condition is to be thought again'.[22]

In a conversation with Tom Driver in 1961, Beckett, according to Driver's account, returned frequently to what he called 'the mess', and said 'the only chance of renovation is to open our eyes and see the mess'.[23] In the vocabulary used and in connecting aesthetic form with obligations towards a reality felt to be disintegrative, Beckett's 'mess' bears a striking resemblance to Kinsella's formulation of this same problem in **'Downstream'**, a poem first published at roughly the same time as the conversation with Driver: 'that story thrust / Pungent horror and an actual mess / Into my very face, and taste I must!' (*D,* 54). **'Downstream'** dramatises a conflict between poetic order and the disruptive capacities of the actual. The story of the dead body found in Durrow Wood is an irruptive force which causes a re-assessment of the ultimate basis of 'reality' as the speaker acknowledges the necessity that the horror be integrated into a revised pattern of the actual. Beckett offers a succinct formulation of the problem in its historical moment:

> Until recently, art has withstood the pressure of chaotic things. It has held them at bay. It realized that to admit them was to jeopardize form. 'How could the mess be admitted, because it appears to be the very opposite of form and therefore destructive of the very thing that art holds itself to be?' But now we can keep it out no longer, because we have come into a time when 'it invades our experience at every moment. It is there and it must be allowed in.'[24]

Kinsella's aesthetic renovation has origins in this impulse to respond to the consequences of historical 'mess', a response complicated by the loss of coherent social structures and controlling perspectives.

'Ballydavid Pier' associates the problematic of aesthetic form with the loss of religious conviction, and evokes a stage in the attempt to find forms to accommodate meaning more amply and adequately. Like **'The Shoals Returning'** and **'Seventeenth Century Landscape: near Ballyferriter'** the poem is set in the Dingle Peninsula. The coastal setting and the movement from neutral observation to implication carries traces of the influence of Elizabeth Bishop's 'At the Fishhouses'.[25] From the eponymous pier an observer follows the movement of a 'film of scum' through a wash of detritus, and through stony shallows which cover the silent traces and shardlike remains of marine life. The line of vision moves out to 'a bag of flesh, / Foetus of goat or sheep'. The second stanza presents a reckoning of what has been observed:

> Allegory forms of itself:
> The line of life creeps upward
> Replacing one world with another,
> The welter of its advance
> Sinks down into clarity,
> Slowly the more foul
> Monsters of loss digest . . .

Small monster of true flesh
Brought forth somewhere
In bloody confusion and error
And flung into bitterness,
Blood washed white:
Does that structure satisfy?

(*Nightwalker and Other Poems,* 14; henceforth *N*)

A note on the side of an early typescript of the poem reads 'of fruitful incompleteness contemplation of own incompleteness'.[26] In **'Baggot Street Deserta'** incompleteness of self is a debilitating negative; here, Kinsella re-positions himself with regard to his earlier insights. As in Bishop's poem, meaning tempts with its availability, and is continually on the point of emerging, 'as if considering spilling over'.[27] In Kinsella's poem 'The ghost tissue hangs unresisting / In allegorical waters', but at the same time maintains an inward-looking autonomy, 'Lost in self-search' (*N,* 15). The liminal, 'half-formed', yet potential, meaning is disquietingly rendered by the foetus 'unshaken / By the spasms of birth or death', just as it is also emphasised by the liminal setting: **'Noon'.** Around the time of this poem's composition, in the Yeats Centenary symposium held at Northwestern University in 1965, Kinsella described the poetic image as a 'mediator between man and his experience'.[28] The foetus as mediator exists in a state the meaning of which is, and at the same time is not, co-opted by the 'order-imposing victim',[29] Kinsella's term for the human observer. The attributes of the actual and evolutionary process are inviolable. The scene shifts to 'some church in the distance', and both the vague determining pronoun and the geographical remove emphasise how little the religious reckoning of the process has to offer:

The Angelus. Faint bell-notes
From some church in the distance
Tremble over the water.
It is nothing. The vacant harbour
Is filling; it will empty.

(*N,* 15)

The final image is one which out of brutal fact both offers and resists transmutation: 'The misbirth touches the surface / And glistens like quicksilver' (*N,* 15). **'Ballydavid Pier'** evokes the coming to consciousness of the kind of poetic meaning Kinsella in his poetry now aimed for, a meaning which resulted from the absorption of what Samuel Beckett called, in another context, 'the new thing that has happened',[30] and what Kinsella calls man's 'recent new experience of himself'.[31]

In the Yeats Centenary symposium Kinsella gave, 'with grave reservations', the name Teilhard de Chardin in connection with the search for a new kind of poetry:

As mediator between man and his experience the new image, or whatever is to perform the crystallizing function for a new poetry, must possess new characteristics and must also continue to have some of the characteristics of the Romantic image, but transformed.[32]

In his presentation at the symposium Kinsella related the need for renovation of the poetic image to 'the experience of history as treadmill, a nightmare of returning disappointments'. The Romantic image, he said, was 'hitherto the hypnotic focus of the poet's stare, an entity with an independent "other" vitality, which it is the poet's function to find and make concrete in our terms'.[33] Kinsella was not sure what form the image which might arise out of man's absorption of the nightmare would take, but in **'Ballydavid Pier'** he discloses an image which, in Seamus Deane's words, 'remains itself, just beyond the range of structuring's good intentions'.[34]

There is in *Nightwalker* the collection, as in **'Nightwalker'** the poem, an attempt at a creative engagement with energy as a reality principle with origins in darkness. Kinsella recognised the need for his potentially overblown poetry to have a basis in experience: 'To put reality in such ideas it is necy [necessary] to have expd [experienced]—to be convinced is the being & the meaning.'[35] How Kinsella went about this is instructive, and once again reveals the influence of German literature.

Just as he made personal connections to the story of *Faust* via the associations between the names Helen and Eleanor, Kinsella found in Rilke's, *Letters to a Young Poet* a corroboration for the goal of 'making real' the obsessions of his imaginative life: 'Art too is only a way of living, and, however one lives, one can unwittingly, prepare oneself for it; in all that is real one is closer to it.'[36] Kinsella took notes from this passage[37] and, as the final part of his paragraph of notes, quotes from an earlier line in Rilke's tenth and final letter to Franz Xaver Kappus: 'To be among conditions that work at us, that set us before big natural things from time to time, is all we need.'[38]

Wormwood (1966) begins Kinsella's active engagement with the darker energies of his own imagination in order to create what he calls **'Heaven—the Paradise of Art: paradox flux in stasis'.**[39] Energy, of whatever kind, becomes its own value. In his notes on Blake, Kinsella emphasises process, flux instead of stasis: 'Everything that lives is holy (not "that *is*")'. The 'conditions that work at' Kinsella, the 'hells of circumstance' as he calls them in *Wormwood,* set before him the question of where the imagination lies in this struggle between light and dark: 'All deities reside in the human breast;—Good and Evil, Messiah and Devil: they spring from Contraries without wh[ich] is no progression.'[40]

'**Phoenix Park**' is Kinsella's most significant and ambitious love poem, and as well as drawing together many of the strands of *Nightwalker* it points directly towards *Notes from the Land of the Dead* in that the final four lines become the epigraph to that sequence. Echoes and quotations from '**Phoenix Park**' continue in the Peppercanister series, most notably in *Out of Ireland*. The poem's form mirrors the attenuated 'structure / Without substance' that the speaker finds 'all about us, in the air, / [. . .] insinuating itself / Into being' (*N*, 79). It is written to a strict count of 11 syllables (of the 225 lines in the poem only five deviate). Kinsella's interest in numerology may have inspired this count of 'one plus one' to reflect the marriage relationship in the poem. Though '**Phoenix Park**' is as aware of disease and decay as other Kinsella poems, it also has an air of new beginnings. It is informed by that mix of optimism and knowledge of limit expressed by Teilhard de Chardin when he writes that 'the earth is veiled in geometry as far back as we can see. It crystallizes. But not completely.'[41] Kinsella's aesthetic is an elaborate process of adjustment to the incomplete and the flawed, and '**Phoenix Park**' provides an eloquent account of how this process informs Kinsella's move away from the traditional paradigms of poetic form:

> let the crystal crack
> On some insoluble matter, then its heart
> Shudders and accepts the flaw, adjusts on it
> Taking new strength[.]
>
> (*N*, 77)

The negative is to Kinsella the means of potential aesthetic and existential redemption, as evoked in *Faust*: 'You send me to emptiness / That there my arts and powers may both increase; / . . . So be it. We will fathom it or fall, / And in your Nothing may I find the All!'[42] Kinsella's aesthetic gradually discards inherited form, the traditional solution of the well-made lyric, and begins again. This time the solution to isolation is archetypal experience. Kinsella bases the foundation for communication on mythical process because basic experiences 'are *not* eccentric—they are shared'.[43] The journey into private areas of experience is bolstered by this sense of suprapersonal concern, and by a belief that, though specific references may elude him, the reader 'will, in completing the act of communication, undergo in his turn a primary mythical experience'.[44]

Though the narrative and imagery in '*hesitate, cease to exist*' derive directly from Goethe,[45] Kinsella, as I have indicated, drew the psychic import of the Faustian journey to the place of the '**Mothers**' from Jung's *Symbols of Transformation*. The journey portrayed in *Faust* parallels Kinsella's own aesthetic transforma-

tion in its demonstration of what Jung calls the 'unquenched and unquenchable desire for the light of consciousness'.[46] To bring repressed/hidden contents of the unconscious to light is an act of completion of the personality, and an increased encounter with reality. The return to childhood memories in *Notes from the Land of the Dead* derives its impetus from the Jungian imperative for those approaching middle age to 'confront the shadow', which entailed as Kinsella noted 'a[n] insular look at one's own nature'.[47] According to Jolande Jacobi, '[t]o confront the shadow . . . means to take a mercilessly critical attitude towards one's own nature'.[48] Jacobi's elucidation of the 'shadow' gives a further indication of the significance of the speaker's descent to the place of the '**Mothers**':

> The shadow stands, as it were, on the threshold of the realm of the '**Mothers**', the unconscious. It is the counterpart of our conscious ego, growing and crystallizing in pace with it. This dark mass of experience that is seldom or never admitted to our conscious lives bars the way to the creative depths of our unconscious.[49]

Recognising the dark side of the personality as 'present and real' is in Jungian terms a creative act, which 'often coincides with the individual's conscious realization of the functional and attitudinal type to which he belongs'.[50] Kinsella saw himself as an 'intuitive', one in whom the dominant function is to see the 'inherent potentialities of things'.[51] In recognising his functional type, Kinsella also brings to conscious realisation the inner workings of his own creative drive: 'the neglected sensation function of the one-sided intuitive type will compel him, often by seemingly incomprehensible onslaughts, to take account of hard reality'.[52] Kinsella's aesthetic adjustments take place as a result of the 'onslaughts of hard reality'. Through Jung he decides that to confront the actual requires him to get beyond the distortions of the ego and the distortions of personality type or risk the consequences in a distorted view of reality: 'The result of continued imbalance—the inferior function will start to claim its rights, & must be confronted. i.e. I must accept the actual: try to see things as they are and not otherwise.'[53]

In this new process he admonishes himself to '(i) discipline the psyche to be open: to receive (ii) actively permit the archetypes to irrupt'.[54] Like the '**Mothers**' themselves, the cauldron that the speaker approaches is Faustian in origin and Jungian in import. It is an image of the matrix within which the archetypes form and irrupt. Kinsella's notes for *Notes from the Land of the Dead* contain a large section on *Faust*, which includes what he refers to as the thesis of the poem: Thesis '→ (via pain) → ambivalence → (pain) → ecstasy]'.[55] Kinsella quotes the reaction of Faust and

Helen to the death of their son Euphorion: 'Joy is but throned for pain to dethrone.'[56] This is part of the 'thesis' of *Notes from the Land of the Dead*. Pain is both terrible, but also a source of potential joy. In **'Sacrifice',** and in his notes to Faust's claim that '[t]o feel appalled is the greatest gift of man', the active acceptance of the negative is a source of strength.[57]

Growth is achieved and redemption found through the psychic and the actual forms of the feminine. Kinsella associates Faust's Helen with his wife's name 'Eleanor': 'Faust's Helena Eleanor confused with Selene—moon—& mother-goddess—connects erotic with redemption'.[58] Eleanor is, in Jungian terms, Kinsella's 'soul-image', and source of redemptive contact with the actuality of the feminine archetype. Kinsella is here following the Jungian imperative to remember the 'living reality' of the archetype.[59] In the notes we see him recognising intuitions from his earlier poetry, which read in the light of Jungian analysis urge him towards the goal to 'release from the unconscious the power to grasp actuality directly (Eleanor, as my opposite, shd. [should] be the ideal "clasp directly, qn. [question] fiercely")'.[60] The self-quotation, from **'Phoenix Park',** shows the importance of the erotic and love in the achievement of totality:

> in the second [half of life] the essential becomes the psychic *coniunctio,* a union with the contrasexual both in the area of one's own inner world and through the carrier of its image in the outer world.[61]

In *Notes from the Land of the Dead* the speaker makes a journey to the **'Land of the Dead',** which is also the place of the **'Mothers',** a link derived in part from Goethe's *Faust Part Two,* and from Jung.[62] The journey that Kinsella presents, mixing Faustian alchemical phantasmagoria and colloquial idiom, parallels Jung's own attempts to bring to conscious awareness the contents of his unconscious. Indeed, Jung's description of the process resembles both the lunar trajectory of **'Nightwalker'** and the subsequent descent portrayed in *Notes from the Land of the Dead*:

> In order to seize hold of the fantasies, I frequently imagined a steep descent. I even made several attempts to get to the very bottom. The first time I reached, as it were, a depth of about a thousand feet; the next time I found myself at the edge of a cosmic abyss. It was like a voyage to the moon, or a descent into empty space. First came the image of a crater, and I had the feeling that I was in the land of the dead.[63]

The deliberate nature and goal of Jung's descent is reflected in Kinsella's own version of this imaginative adventure. In *'hesitate, cease to exist',* as the speaker approaches 'the heart of the pit', he sees 'through the gloom' the foaming cauldron. Within its 'vapour of forms' he makes out 'a ring of mountainous beings

staring upward / with open mouths—naked ancient women'. These Faustian 'Mothers' are images of frightening sterility, 'Nothingness silted under their thighs / and over their limp talons.' The fearful speaker continues towards his goal, and in an image which prefigures and reverses the perspective of the egg's fall through the sewer grill in **'Hen Woman',** raises his 'eyes / to that seemingly unattainable grill / through which I must return, carrying my prize'. Intermittent rhyme (the endings of the last seven lines are: thighs / confess / enterprise / fear / eyes / grill / prize) gives a sense of urgency and momentum to this passage, and demonstrates Kinsella's continued commitment to elements of conventional measure and literary effects.

Eavan Boland recognised that in *Notes from the Land of the Dead* Kinsella's change was a 'profound reworking of themes in a new light or darkness'.[64] In her review of *New Poems 1973* she saw Kinsella returning to the image 'of the poet himself, on the edge of his journey inwards'.[65] Boland cites **'Baggot Street Deserta'**[66] as an early example of this image. Boland's remarks and reference to **'Baggot Street Deserta'** are perceptive. In the drafts for this section of *Notes from the Land of the Dead* Kinsella refers directly to the Baggot Street period of his life,[67] and in the published version he writes of 'The excitement, / underlining and underlining in that narrow room!' (*NP* 1973, 9).

Her Vertical Smile is Kinsella's most mature reworking of the themes and images I have been discussing and offers an example, through the musical achievement of Gustav Mahler, of an art cognisant of discouraging realities but capable of harnessing disappointment to creative ends. In notes on Mahler for *Her Vertical Smile* Kinsella writes: 'Why am I the one? How come I am so driven? Single-minded, single-bodied. Out of where? Into where? That *this* direction was chosen, into close pursuit of which it appears I am fated, and born'.[68] *Her Vertical Smile* answers some of these questions. The artistic drive emerges 'out of nothing' and moves 'into' nothing; the artistic task is adjustment towards this nothingness. That Kinsella uses the figure of Mahler to explore his own position as artist can be seen in the early drafts of **'Das Lied Von Der Mahler'** which contained a quotation from Schoenberg on Mahler's *Ninth Symphony*: 'It almost seems as though this work had another, concealed author, who was merely using it as a mouthpiece . . .'[69]

The two main sections are prefaced by an Overture, and the poem also contains an Intermezzo, which versifies a December 1914 letter from Thomas Mann to the Berlin poet Richard Dehmel, and a bathetic Coda, which places the theme of artistic response to calamity within comic and perspective-enhancing parentheses. The 'she' of the Overture, the 'great contralto', is another of Kinsella's self-engendering creatives, 'dwelling upon herself' (***Blood and Family***, 43; henceforth ***BF***). To the self-absorption, which again recalls the Kinsella of **'Baggot Street Deserta'**, the poem adds a recognition of art's ultimate ground-lessness:

> A butt flung into a dirty grate.
>   Elbows on knees, head bowed
> devouring an echo out of nothing.
>
>   (***BF***, 43)

In the **'Prologue'** to ***Downstream*** the poet looked at himself at thirty, in ***Notes from the Land of the Dead*** at forty, so in ***Her Vertical Smile*** Kinsella at fifty examines himself as artist through the prism of Mahler ('aetat fünfzig') conducting the first performance of his Eighth symphony (the 'Symphony of a Thousand', which incorporates a setting of the final scene of *Faust Part Two*) in 1910. Mahler is as daemonic, and driven an artist as the Kinsella of **'Baggot Street Deserta'**[70]:

>   the force of will
>
> we find everywhere
>   in his strange work:
> the readiness to embrace risk,
>
> tedium, the ignoble,
>   to try anything ten times
> if so the excessive matter can be settled.
>
>   (***BF***, 44)

The void out of which creation emerges and into which it returns is evoked in sexual/musical imagery: 'every rhythm drained // into nothing, the nothingness / adjusting toward / a new readiness' (***BF***, 44-5). The readiness is required to confront the awful ordeals of life, the dark matter of war, and violence from which 'our most significant utterances // have been elicited' (***BF***, 46). Artistic order may be temporary, but valuable for all that, if the artist can 'fold the terms of the curse / back upon itself' (***BF***, 47).

In part II Kinsella re-figures the terms of aesthetic advance with a picture of Mahler on the conducting podium: 'A step forward and a lesser / step back' (***BF***, 51), an echo of the formulation in the notes to the **'Prologue'.** Yet even major artistic achievement offers no peace:

'But why is there no ease? / For something magnuscule has been accomplished' (***BF***, 51). The creative impulse is instinctual, with mysterious motivations and impulses of its own:

> —teeming everywhere
> with your aches and needs

> along our bloody passageways,
>   knocking against one another
> in never ending fuss[.]
>
>   (***BF***, 52)

This 'never ending fuss' is 'propped upon promise / implying purpose' (***BF***, 53), but Kinsella, in a comic gesture, 'wag[ging] his pale finger', warns that this inward impulse and fuss which makes of hope a potential index of meaning is shadowed by an 'outer carrion', as uncooperative and distant as the Real in **'Baggot Street Deserta'**:

> bone-walking in a dream bedlam,
> half lit, idling
>
> in foul units,
>   circling our furthest reach
> with a refusing snarl[.]
>
>   (***BF***, 53)

The problem of art is twofold: adequate response to events such as the 'muttonchop slaughter' (***BF***, 45) of the First World War; and 'how to admire the solid beloved' (***BF***, 54). Kinsella recapitulates his entire enterprise, once again in the context of a **'Fall'** welcomed for the comprehensive perspective it offers:

> Let the Fall begin,
>   the whole wide
> landscape descend gently [. . .]
>
> And there ought to be
>   a good deal of wandering
> and seeking for peace
>
> and desire of one kind and another,
>   with the throat employed
> for its own lovely sake
>
> in moving utterances
>   made of the simplest poetry.
>
>   (***BF***, 54-5)

The 'design' that would fulfil this should be composed of 'Good man-made matter', and Kinsella evokes *Das Lied von der Erde* as the ultimate expression of Mahler's artistic goal, which is also his own, in language of serene and beautiful simplicity:

> forest murmurs; a tired horseman
> drinking in friendship and farewell;
>
> voices blurred in longing;
>   renewal in Beauty;
> Earth's pale flowers blossoming
>
> in a distance turning to pure light
>   shining blue
> for ever and for ever.
>
>   (***BF***, 55)

In an essay entitled 'Poets and the Human Family', Czeslaw Milosz argues against a 'pure poetry' which would isolate itself from History, from 'Movement', which, quoting his French cousin Oscar Milosz, 'would remove religion, philosophy, science, politics from its domain'.[71]

The similarities with Kinsella's transformation are striking. Kinsella moves from a 'pure poetry' consoled by its own formal procedures, to a position which shares the 'openness' of the poetics outlined by Milosz. Milosz's discussion of the term 'Movement' also offers an insight into the philosophical orientation that Kinsella displays in the Peppercanister poems: 'It is worth noting that it is not the word Progress but Movement (capitalized) that is used, and this has manifold implications, for Progress denotes a linear ascension while Movement stresses incessant change and a dialectical play of opposites'.[72] Both Kinsella and Milosz are acutely conscious of the history of their art, and of their own historical moment, and this awareness brings to bear on their work the imperative to forge a poetics rinsed of lyrical delusion. Yet Kinsella's **Her Vertical Smile** and Milosz's 'No More' (*New and Collected Poems*, 158) shows that both also remain faithful to the capacity of the poetic voice to create out of diminished circumstance, beauty; chastened though it be by the treadmill of historical experience, but beauty nonetheless.

ACKNOWLEDGEMENTS

Parts of this essay are adapted from *The Sea of Disappointment: Thomas Kinsella's Pursuit of the Real* (UCD Press, 2008).

Notes

1. Kinsella, review of *Urfaust*, 19.

2. Fitzsimons, 'An Interview with Thomas Kinsella', 90.

3. Ibid., 91.

4. Kinsella Papers, Emory University, box 12, folder 35.

5. Thomas Kinsella, letter to author, 28 August 2003.

6. Mann, *Death in Venice*, 147. For the identification between Kinsella and Tonio Kröger see 'Brothers in the Craft': 'Tonio Kroeger, malodorous, prowled Inchicore' (*From Centre City*, 19). See also Tubridy, *Thomas Kinsella*, 181; John, 252.

7. Jung, *Symbols of Transformation*, 126.

8. 'the *phallus*, . . . working in darkness, begets a living being; and the *key* unlocks the mysterious forbidden door behind which some wonderful thing awaits discovery' (Jung, *Symbols of Transformation*, 124).

9. Kinsella Papers, box 3, folder 3. Subsequent quotations of the poem come from this box and folder.

10. Ibid.

11. For a suggestive explication of the stanza in 'Interlude: Time's Mischief' (in *Moralities*) from which this line comes, see Heaney, 'Cornucopia and Empty Shell', 57-9; and Heaney, *Finders Keepers*, 240-1.

12. See Kinsella, 'Major American Poet'; and Kinsella, 'The Hundred Cantos of Ezra Pound'. These reviews are interesting for the light they throw on Kinsella's ambitions for his own poetry. Kinsella expressed admiration for Stevens's 'disturbingly precise sensibility, as fit to paint a shading of light or colour as to sculpt an idea'. His review emphasises the idea that 'good poems [. . .] do not ignore the intellect', but also that Stevens's poems 'see things whole—as they are—and not with the intellectual faculty, which would see things as they "ought to be"'. Good poems, Kinsella says, 'direct their effect towards [. . .] the whole mind and not to one part only'. The review of Pound provides an intriguing early insight into Kinsella's thoughts on waste, and his interest in a poetry that goes beyond the confines of 'the lovely short poem': 'believers in Mr. Pound's method are tired of the view that the cantos consist of a series of lovely short poems embedded in a waste of poetical and syntactical error. But their counter-praise seems as extravagant as that view is stupid'. Kinsella's first visit to America occurred in 1963, on an exchange scholarship visiting and lecturing at 'centres concerned with poetry', including Harvard, Berkeley, the University of Washington, and the University of Chicago. Kinsella Papers, box 71, folder 20.

13. O'Driscoll, 'Interview with Thomas Kinsella', 60.

14. Villon, *Selected Poems*, 41. Pound adapted Villon's opening line in the 'E.P. Ode Pour L'Election De Son Sepulchre' section of *Hugh Selwyn Mauberley*: 'Unaffected by the "march of events", / He passed from men's memory in *l'an trentuniesme / De son eage*' (Pound, *Collected Shorter Poems*, 187).

15. The refrain is also used in Villon's 'Le Lais' [The Legacy] which Kinsella quotes from in 'Time and the Poet' (718). See Villon, *Selected Poems*, 26-8.

16. Kinsella, 'Time and the Poet', 718. The poem that Kinsella is referring to is 'Ballade: Des Dames du Temps Jadis', the famous refrain of which can be rendered into English as 'Where are the snows of yesteryear?'.

17. Kinsella, 'Time and the Poet', 717; parentheses in original.

18. Ibid., 718.

19. Kinsella Papers, box 3, folder 42.

20. Haffenden, 'Thomas Kinsella', 100. Asked whether he regretted the loss of the religious framework, Kinsella replied: 'No, the supports that one might think of finding in organized religion I found elsewhere.'

21. Kinsella Papers, box 4, folder 10.

22. Beckett, 'The Capital of the Ruins', in *As the Story was Told,* 27-8; written for a Radio Éireann broadcast in June 1946. Beckett worked as an interpreter and store keeper from August 1945 to January 1946. See also Knowlson, *Damned to Fame,* 345-51.

23. Driver, Interview with Samuel Beckett, 218. Beckett's words were reconstructed from notes that Driver made shortly after his conversation with Beckett in 1961.

24. Ibid., 218.

25. Kinsella reviewed, and praised, Bishop's *Poems* in *Irish Writing* 36 (late Autumn 1956). In the review he agrees with the writer in the New York *Sunday Herald Tribune* who believed, Kinsella says, that some of Bishop's poems would 'become a permanent part of the poetry of our time' (186).

26. Kinsella Papers, box 5, folder 1.

27. Bishop, *Complete* Poems, 64.

28. Kinsella, 'Poetry since Yeats', 109.

29. Ibid.

30. Beckett, 'Recent Irish Poetry', 70.

31. Kinsella, 'Poetry since Yeats', 109.

32. Ibid.

33. Ibid., 108.

34. Deane, *Celtic Revivals,* 139.

35. Kinsella Papers, box 71, folder 13.

36. Rilke, *Letters to a Young Poet,* 78.

37. Kinsella Papers, box 71, folder 13.

38. Ibid.; Rilke, *Letters to a Young Poet,* 77.

39. Kinsella Papers, box 71, folder 13.

40. Ibid.

41. Teilhard de Chardin, *The Phenomenon of Man,* 69.

42. Goethe, *Faust Parts 1 and 2,* 167.

43. Kinsella, 'Ancient Myth and Poetry', 10; Kinsella's emphasis.

44. Ibid. The consistency and sustaining longevity of the ideas that Kinsella developed in the late 1960s can be illustrated with reference to the idea of communication he expressed at the 1973 Montreal panel discussion. In an interview with the present author in 2004 Kinsella said: 'The embodiment [of poetic material] needs to stand by itself, with the significant contents functioning in detail and form so that a reader can repeat the experience' (Fitzsimons, 'Interview', 80).

45. 'Faust gets a little key from Mephisto. It glows in his hand. He follows it down to the Mothers, to desolate loneliness. He feels appalled at the prospect/visit, but recognises that to feel appalled is the greatest gift of man (!) (he feels in his core, immensity.) He goes from created things into the realm of forms: drifting clouds of energy. Down to a glowing tripod (make it floating, or a monopod?)[.] The Mothers cannot see him: they are wreathed with all floating forms of what may be & see only shadows[.] He touches the tripod with the key & it comes with him (the Prize) back to the Hall where he will summon Paris and Helen from it' (Kinsella Papers, box 10, folder 16).

46. Jung, *Symbols of Transformation,* 205.

47. Kinsella Papers, box 5, folder 29.

48. Jacobi, *The Psychology of C. G. Jung,* 113.

49. Ibid., 112. Kinsella's notes on the shadow elaborate on this passage from Jacobi: 'my dark side, wh. [which] I reject . . . / it is in opposition to my conscious principles, or attitudes / (wicked meanness, / hypocrisy / scrupulous polishing of the shallow, the empty / [my own repressed tendencies] / [—barring the way to the creative depths' (Kinsella Papers, box 10, folder 21).

50. Jacobi, *The Psychology of C. G. Jung,* 110.

51. Kinsella Papers, box 10, folder 21.

52. Jacobi, *The Psychology of C. G. Jung,* 18. Kinsella quotes these lines in box 10, folder 21, a page on which he charts his own personality, '(me), (if normal)', in Jungian terms.

53. Kinsella Papers, box 10, folder 21.

54. Kinsella Papers, box 10, folder 17.

55. Kinsella Papers, box 10, folder 16.

56. Ibid. Kinsella's notes are from Louis MacNeice's 1949 translation of *Faust Parts 1 and 2,* 237.

57. Faust says 'My welfare rests upon no rigid plan, / To feel appalled is the greatest gift of man; / Whatever the world impose as penalty, / His core is moved to feel immensity' (*Faust Parts 1 and 2,* 168).

58. Kinsella Papers, box 10, folder 16.

59. Jung, 'Approaching the Unconscious', in *Man and His Symbols,* 90.

60. Kinsella Papers, box 10, folder 17.

61. Jacobi, *The Psychology of C. G. Jung,* 123. Jacobi sees Goethe's *Faust* as the quintessential imaginative expression of this process: 'In the first half Gretchen carries the projection of Faust's anima. But the tragic end of this relationship compels him to withdraw the projection from the outside world and to seek this part of his psyche in himself. He finds it in another world, in the "underworld" of his unconscious,

symbolized by Helen of Troy. The second part of *Faust* portrays an individuation process with all its archetypal figures; Helen is the typical anima figure, Faust's soul-image' (Jacobi, *The Psychology of C. G. Jung,* 124).

62. Jung, *Symbols of Transformation,* 204-6. The speaker's 'dive' or 'drop' is also reminiscent of Jung's description of his own discovery of the inner world: 'It was during the Advent of the year 1913— December 12, to be exact—that I resolved upon the decisive step. I was sitting at my desk once more, thinking over my fears. 'Then I let myself drop. Suddenly it was as though the ground literally gave way beneath my feet, and I plunged down into the dark depths.' On his descent Jung encounters a 'black scarab', and recognises that his vision is a 'hero and solar myth, a drama of death and renewal, the rebirth symbolized by the Egyptian scarab' (Jung, *Memories, Dreams, Reflections,* 179). The speaker in 'Hen Woman' also encounters the scarab beetle.

63. Jung, *Memories, Dreams, Reflections,* 181.

64. Boland, 'The New Kinsella'.

65. Ibid.

66. Boland mistakenly says the poem comes from *Downstream.*

67. Kinsella Papers, box 9, folder 16.

68. Kinsella Papers, box 20, folder 12.

69. Kinsella Papers, box 18, folder 8.

70. Recall the lines 'We fly into our risk, the spurious' (AS, 29), and 'I nonetheless inflict, endure, / Tedium, intracordal hurt' (AS, 31).

71. Milosz, *The Witness of Poetry,* 29, which collected the Charles Eliot Norton Lectures that Milosz delivered at Harvard University in 1981-82. Milosz's discussion of the term 'Movement' also offers an insight into the philosophical orientation Kinsella displays in the Peppercanister poems: 'It is worth noting that it is not the word Progress but Movement (capitalized) that is used, and this has manifold implications, for Progress denotes a linear ascension while Movement stresses incessant change and a dialectical play of opposites' (35).

72. Milosz, *The Witness of Poetry,* 35.

Bibliography

The archive material in this essay can be found in the Thomas Kinsella Papers (MSS 774), Special Collections and Archives Division, Robert W. Woodruff Library, Emory University, Atlanta, Georgia, USA.

Beckett, Samuel. *As the Story was Told.* London: Calder, 1990.

———. 'Recent Irish Poetry'. In *Disjecta: Miscellaneous Writings and a Dramatic* Fragment, 70-6. London: John Calder, 1983.

Bishop, Elizabeth. *Complete Poems.* 1983. London: Chatto & Windus, 1991.

Boland, Eavan. 'The New Kinsella'. Review of *New Poems 1973. Irish Times,* 28 July 1973, 12.

John, Brian. *Beading the Ground: The Poetry of Thomas Kinsella.* Washington D.C.: Catholic University of America Press, 1996.

Deane, Seamus. *Celtic Revivals: Essays in Modern Irish Literature 1880-1980.* Winston-Salem, NC: Wake Forest University Press, 1985; London: Faber & Faber, 1985, 1987.

Driver, Tom. 'Interview with Samuel Beckett'. In *Samuel Beckett: The Critical Heritage,* ed. Lawrence Graver and Raymond Federman, 217-23. London: Routledge & Kegan Paul, 1979.

Fitzsimons, Andrew. 'An Interview with Thomas Kinsella'. *Poetry Ireland Review* 82 (March 2005): 84-94.

Goethe, Johann Wolfgang von. *Faust Parts 1 and 2.* Trans. Louis MacNeice. 1949. New York: Continuum, 1994.

———. *Faust Part Two.* Trans. Philip Wayne. London: Penguin, 1959.

Haffenden, John. 'Thomas Kinsella'. In *Viewpoints: Poets in Conversation with John Haffenden,* 100-13. London: Faber & Faber, 1981.

Heaney, Seamus. 'Cornucopia and Empty Shell: Variations on a Theme from Ellmann'. In *The Place of Writing,* 57-9. Atlanta, GA: Scholars Press, 2002. Partially reprinted as 'Thomas Kinsella'. In *Finders Keepers: Selected Prose 1971-2001,* 240-1. London: Faber & Faber, 2002.

Jacobi, Jolande. *The Psychology of C. G. Jung.* 1942. New Haven and London: Yale University Press, 1973.

Jung, Carl Gustav, ed. *Man and his Symbols.* 1964, London: Picador, 1978.

———. *Memories, Dreams, Reflections,* 1973, Rev. ed. Recorded and edited by Aniela Jaffé. Trans. Richard Winston and Clara Winston. New York: Vintage, 1989.

———. *The Spirit of Man in Art, and Literature. The Collected Works of C. G. Jung.* Vol. 15. Trans. R. F. C. Hull. Bollingen Series XX. 1966. Princeton: Princeton University Press, 1972.

———. *Symbols of Transformation. The Collected Works of C. G. Jung.* Vol. 5. Trans. R. F. C. Hull. Bollingen Series XX. 1956. Princeton: Princeton University Press, 1967.

Kinsella, Thomas. 'Ancient Myth and Poetry: A Panel Discussion'. In *Myth and Reality in Irish Literature,* ed. Joseph Ronsley, 1-16. Waterloo, Ontario: Wilfrid Laurier University Press, 1977.

———. *Another September.* Dublin: Dolmen Press, 1958.

———. *Blood and Family.* Oxford: Oxford University Press, 1988.

———. *Downstream.* Dublin: Dolmen Press, London: Oxford University Press 1962.

———. *From Centre City.* Oxford: Oxford University Press, 1994.

———. 'The Hundred Cantos of Ezra Pound'. Review of *Section: Rock-Drill 85-95 de los cantares. Irish Press,* 26 October 1957, 4.

———. 'Major American Poet'. Review of *Collected Poems,* by Wallace Stevens'. *Irish Press,* 23 June 1956, 4.

———. *Moralities.* Dolmen Chapbook, Pt 12. Dublin: Dolmen Press, 1960.

———. *New Poems 1973.* Dublin: Dolmen Press, 1973.

———. *Nightwalker and Other Poems.* Dublin: Dolmen Press, 1968.

———. *Out of Ireland.* Peppercanister 11. Dublin: Peppercanister, 1987.

———. *The Pen Shop.* Peppercanister 19. Dublin: Peppercanister, Dedalus Press 1997.

———. 'Poetry since Yeats: An Exchange of Views'. Transcript of panel discussion featuring Stephen Spender, Patrick Kavanagh, Kinsella and W. D. Snodgrass, Northwestern University Yeats Centenary Festival, 29 April 1965'. *Tri-Quarterly* 4 (1965): 100-11.

———. Review of *Urfaust,* by Johann Wolfgang von Goethe, ed. Dr. R. H. Samuel (Allen & Unwin). Signed Th. K. *National Student* 112 (October 1951): 19.

———. *A Technical Supplement.* Peppercanister 6. Dublin: Peppercanister, 1976.

———. 'Time and the Poet'. Paper originally published as *An File agus an tAm.* Signed Tomás Ó Cinnseallaigh. *Comhar,* 18 June 1959, 24-6. and 18 July 1959, 23-6. English translation by Máire Ní Chinnéide. Reprinted in Rosenberg, Carolyn. 'Let Our Gaze Blaze: The Recent Poetry of Thomas Kinsella'. Diss., Kent State University', 1980: 711-21.

———. *Wormwood.* Dolmen Editions 1. Dublin: Dolmen Press, 1966.

———. 'Writer at Work: Thomas Kinsella'. *St. Stephen's* (U.C.D) Series II, no. 3 (Trinity Term Spring 1961): 29-31.

Knowlson, James. *Damned to Fame: The Life of Samuel Beckett.* London: Bloomsbury, 1996.

Mann, Thomas. *Death in Venice: Tristan: Tonio Kröger.* Trans. H. T. Lowe-Porter. 1928. London: Penguin, 1955.

Milosz, Czeslaw. *New and Collected Poems 1931-2001.* New York: Ecco, 2001.

———. *The Witness of Poetry.* Cambridge, MA: Harvard University Press, 1983.

Newmann, Erich. *The Origins and History of Consciousness.* Trans. R. F. C. Hull. Bollingen Series XLII. 1954. Princeton: Princeton University Press, 1970.

O'Driscoll, Dennis. 'Interview with Thomas Kinsella'. *Poetry Ireland Review* 25 (1989): 57-65.

Pound, Ezra. *Collected Shorter Poems.* London: Faber & Faber, 1984.

Rilke, Rainer Maria. *Letters to a Young Poet.* 1954. Rev. ed. Trans. M. D. Herter Norton. New York: W.W. Norton, 1993.

Teilhard de Chardin, Pierre. *The Phenomenon of Man.* Trans. Bernard Wall et al. Intro. Julian Huxley. Rev. ed. New York: Harper & Row, 1975.

Tubridy, Derval. *Thomas Kinsella: The Peppercanister Poems.* Dublin: University College Dublin Press, 2001.

Villon, François. *Selected Poems.* Trans. Peter Dale. London: Penguin, 1978.

FURTHER READING

Criticism

Clutterbuck, Catriona. "Scepticism, Faith and The Recognition of the 'Patriarch-Mother' in the Poetry of Thomas Kinsella." *Irish Studies Review* 16, no. 3 (August 2008): 245-65.

> Clutterbuck interprets the figure of the Patriarch-Mother in Kinsella's poetry, focusing on the poet's aesthetic juxtaposition of belief and scepticism.

Collins, Lucy. "'Never altogether the same. But the same': Strategies of Revision in Thomas Kinsella's *Notes from the Land of the Dead.*" *Irish Studies Review* 16, no. 3 (August 2008): 283-93.

> Analyzes the evolution of Kinsella's creative process.

Fitzsimons, Andrew. "The Sea of Disappointment: Thomas Kinsella's *Nightwalker* and the New Ireland." *Irish University Review* 36, no. 2 (winter 2006): 335-52.

Discusses the poem "Nightwalker," focusing on the themes and intent of the poetry and asserting that while Kinsella's verse acknowledges disappointment, despair, and "moral and political squalor," it also seeks to reaffirm, rebuild, and "bring new order."

Flanagan, Ian. "Hearing American Voice': Thomas Kinsella and William Carlos Williams." *Irish Studies Review* 16, no. 3 (August 2008): 305-27.

Flanagan compares Kinsella's poetry to William Carlos Williams's *Paterson.*

Johnston, Dillon. "Kinsella's Dublins and the Stone Mother." *Irish Studies Review* 16, no. 3 (August 2008): 295-303.

Assesses the place and meaning of female figures in Kinsella's poetry about the city of Dublin.

Lyden, Jacki. "An Ireland of Legend." *Atlantic Monthly* 289, no. 3 (March 2002): 90-5.

Presents Lyden's experiences on a trip to Ireland in search of the history that informs Kinsella's *The Táin.*

Newman, Neville F. "Kinsella's *Butcher's Dozen.*" *Explicator* 57, no. 3 (spring 1999): 173-76.

Offers an historical analysis of the poem "Butcher's Dozen: A Lesson for the Octave of Widgery."

O'Connor, Laura. "Between Two Languages." *Sewanee Review* 114, no. 3 (summer 2006): 433-42.

Explores Kinsella's Gaelic- and English-language collection titled *An Duanaire, 1600-1900: Poems of the Dispossessed.*

Skloot, Floyd. "Airy Architecture." *Sewanee Review* 114, no. 3 (summer 2006): lv-lvii.

Praises Kinsella's later poetic output, calling it "essential reading."

Tubridy, Derval. "'Keep us alert / for the while remaining': Kinsella at Eighty." *Irish Studies Review* 16, no. 3 (August 2008): 231-34.

Focuses on Kinsella's writing career and accomplishments

———. "Thomas Kinsella: A Selected Bibliography, 2008." *Irish Studies Review* 16, no. 3 (August 2008): 235-43.

Lists sources relevant to a special issue devoted to Kinsella.

Wheatley, David. "'All is emptiness / and I must spin': Thomas Kinsella and the Romance of Decay." *Irish Studies Review* 16, no. 3 (August 2008): 329-33.

Considers Kinsella's cultural dismay, his juxtaposition of past with present, and use of allegory.

Additional coverage of Kinsella's life and career is contained in the following sources published by Gale: *British Writers Supplement,* **Vol. 5;** *Concise Major 21st-Century Writers,* **Ed. 1;** *Contemporary Authors,* **Vol. 17-20R;** *Contemporary Authors New Revision Series,* **Vols. 15, 122;** *Contemporary Literary Criticism,* **Vols. 4, 19, 138;** *Contemporary Poets,* **Eds. 1, 2, 3, 4, 5, 6, 7;** *Dictionary of Literary Biography,* **Vol. 27;** *Encyclopedia of World Literature in the 20th Century,* **Ed. 3;** *Literature Resource Center;* *Major 20th-Century Writers,* **Eds. 1, 2;** *Major 21st-Century Writers,* **(eBook) 2005;** *Modern British Literature,* **Ed. 2;** *Poetry Criticism,* **Vol. 69;** *Reference Guide to English Literature,* **Ed. 2; and** *Twayne's English Authors.*

Native Speaker

Chang-rae Lee

The following entry presents criticism on *Native Speaker* (1995), a novel examining personal, racial, and ethnic identity. For further information on Lee's life and works, see *CLC*, Volumes 91 and 268.

INTRODUCTION

Lee became a literary celebrity almost overnight with the appearance of *Native Speaker*, an experimental novel that defied expectations for Asian American fiction by allegorizing its Korean American hero's identity crisis in his occupation as a professional spy. The winner of several literary prizes, including the American Book Award and the Hemingway/PEN Award for First Fiction, *Native Speaker* is frequently compared to Ralph Ellison's *Invisible Man* for its penetrating examination of personal, racial, and ethnic identity set against a backdrop of New York City politics. *Native Speaker* has been widely praised for its complicated portrayal of the role of language in identity formation and atypical articulation of themes commonly associated with Asian American literature: alienation, assimilation, cultural hybridity, racial and generational conflict, cultural hegemony and the marginalization of minorities. The first entry in G. P. Putnam's Riverhead series devoted to "multicultural" books, *Native Speaker* went on to disrupt prevailing notions of cultural plurality as well as the status of ethnic literatures in the American marketplace and literary canon.

PLOT AND MAJOR CHARACTERS

Although not particularly autobiographical, *Native Speaker* profits from Lee's experiences as a Korean immigrant. Like Henry Park, who is the main character in *Native Speaker*, Lee grew up in an affluent suburb of New York City, attending elite schools and struggling to conform to middle-class American values. As an author whose avowed purpose is to answer the question "Who am I?" Lee infuses Park's story with firsthand knowledge of the alienation that results from trying to balance two cultures. The story of *Native Speaker* is narrated by Park in retrospect, as he

formulates the competing influences in his fractured self: his widowed father, a successful first-generation Korean-American grocer who clings to traditional Korean customs; his Caucasian wife, Lelia, a children's speech therapist; John Kwang, an idealistic but flawed Korean-American politician who speaks for New York City's minority interests; and his own role-playing as a spy.

During the first few pages of *Native Speaker*, Park confesses that his wife has initiated a trial separation, saying goodbye with only a note listing the "difficult truth" of Park's fake life: "a B+ student of life," "Yellow peril: neo-American," "traitor," "spy." Park's narrative then drifts back in time, detailing his prior history as he finally confronts the disastrous consequences of his false existence: privately, a "white manqué"; publicly, an "ethnic consultant" for Glimmer & Associates, an independent detective agency specializing in the profiling of "foreign workers, immigrants, and first generations." Shifting from the private to the public sphere and back again, Park's story reveals that he has tried to divest himself of several Korean aspects of his personality at Lelia's urging. Among the many "Korean" things that Park tries to forget are the following: that his seven-year-old son with Lelia died as the result of being suffocated on the playground in a "dog pile" of white children; that one of Park's undercover assignments was to investigate a Filipino psychoanalyst and Marcos supporter, Emile Luzan; and that Park's most recent work detail involved the infiltration of the mayoral campaign of John Kwang.

Park's purpose at Glimmer & Associates is to gather intelligence by creating what Lee calls "a string of serial identity." Park's facade had begun to crack before Lelia's departure. Having become comfortable with Luzan in the course of his assignment, Park suffers an episode of remorse in his office, warning the doctor of possible danger and revealing certain facts of his real life. When Park's boss, Dennis Hoagland, learns of his meltdown, Luzan is mysteriously killed in a boating accident. Assigned to Kwang as a test of his "emotional neutrality," Park uncovers information about Kwang's fundraising apparatus that leads to the deportation of many illegal aliens and the public disgrace of Kwang. In the end, Park can no longer contain his guilt for betraying Lelia and persons of ethnic identity—his own kind—in the course of his work. He quits his job and attempts to establish a coherent identity by confronting his penchant for disguise. He eventually reunites with Lelia; together, they try to reach an understanding of their mutual responsibility in the disintegration of Park's selfhood and their marriage.

MAJOR THEMES

The title of *Native Speaker* announces the controlling theme of the novel: language. Park is not a native speaker in either English or Korean. However, he has spent his whole life trying to perfect his English, emblematic of the identity to which he aspires. He has never forgotten being called "Marble Mouth" in remedial speech classes as a child, and he is unable to converse without feeling self-conscious. After attending a crowded party with his wife, Lelia remarks, "You look like someone listening to himself." It appears that Park connects the ultimate success of his assimilation with Lelia, the white teacher of English. Accordingly, he accepts without question Lelia's suggestions about how he should talk and comport himself, viewing her as the standard bearer of middle-class American values.

Park grows attached to Kwang, largely because he speaks the "perfect English" of the dominant culture but is nonetheless able to deliver rousing speeches to his large following of minority constituents in Queens. The meaning of the novel's title remains unresolved. The reader is left to question whether the "native speaker" is Park, a second-generation Korean American who has learned proper English; Lelia, a white American; Lee, the author; or Kwang, who seeks to become "the living voice of the city, . . . unafraid to speak the language like a Puritan and like a Chinaman and like every boat person in between."

Closely connected to the theme of language in the novel is the idea of silence. Growing up in a home where Korean values prevailed, Park is naturally reticent to speak about his feelings. His success as a spy derives in part from his ability to keep secrets and to interpret subtle facial expressions and body gestures, the modes by which Koreans traditionally express feelings. Lelia becomes exasperated by the lack of intimacy in their marriage, calling Park an "emotional alien," particularly because he is unable to vocalize the loss of their dead son, Mitt.

The motif of spying operates as a metaphor for Park's fractured self, his condition of existing between two cultures. Park is attracted to the job because it seemed "the perfect vocation for the person I was, someone who could reside in one place and take half steps out whenever he wished. . . ." Park creates "legends" about himself in order to enter the confidence of his clients. Lee presents Park's skill at impersonation as an extension of his bicultural childhood, during which he learned to don masks in his constant quest for social acceptance, his Korean identity at home differing markedly from his American identity at school.

CRITICAL RECEPTION

The critical reception of *Native Speaker* is characterized by serious discussion about ethnic discourse as it pertains to multicultural literature in general, and to Lee's formal experimentation in particular. Scholars have focused on the interplay between Park's private and public lives as an innovative technique that allowed Lee to challenge theories equating cultural identity with ethnicity and race. Lee's examination of the powers and limitations of language to define identity has garnered particular attention.

Some scholars question whether Park ever really achieves a viable cultural hybridity, likening his employment as a spy—typically the purview of patriotic, white males—to Kwang's status as a token ethnic politician. Critics also note that, even after his reconciliation with Lelia, Park hides his foreignness behind a "Green Monster" face mask in his role as a comic sidekick in her English classes. Critics have argued that Park's fake existence is an indictment of the plasticity of American society, where white hegemony masquerades behind lip service promising enfranchisement for Asian Americans. They cite as evidence the silencing of Kwang, whose aspirations of becoming more than "just another ethnic pol" pose a threat to the racially insular New York political establishment. As Betsy Huang remarked, "If the ideals of American democratic liberalism . . . can be spoken, and thus represented, by an ethnic, then the unspoken whiteness of Americanism can be easily unraveled." In another reading of *Native Speaker* as an example of identity politics, Klara Szmańko argued, "[I]mmigrants . . . are often forced to play by the rules of whites to survive. Whenever someone from the marginalized group tries to step out of their place and inch closer to the foreground, people from the mainstream do their best to clip their wings. Most often they use other immigrants to keep the insubordinate in their place." Crystal Parikh describes a similar "catch-22" situation for educated Korean Americans such as Park and Kwang: "[T]he ethnic intellectual antagonizes both the dominant and minority formations in the difficulties of his or her positioning."

Although the response to *Native Speaker* has been overwhelmingly positive, some Korean Americans complain that the novel perpetuates cultural stereotypes. Critic Yung-Hsing Wu articulated this position, stating that members of the Korean-American community "targeted Lee's choice of profession for his protagonist, arguing that the novel reinforced the cliché of Asian inscrutability by casting Park as a spy." Still, most readers applaud *Native Speaker* as a much-needed corrective to the saccharine stories of successful assimilation that have dominated the marketplace. *Native Speaker* continues to elicit strong praise and thoughtful discussion of Lee's use of the spy motif to portray the realities of the Korean-American experience.

PRINCIPAL WORKS

Native Speaker (novel) 1995
A Gesture Life (novel) 1999
Aloft (novel) 2004
The Surrender (audio novel) 2008

CRITICISM

Crystal Parikh (essay date summer 2002)

SOURCE: Parikh, Crystal. "Ethnic America Undercover: The Intellectual and Minority Discourse." *Contemporary Literature* 43, no. 2 (summer 2002): 249-84.

[*In this essay, Parikh compares the roles of the "ethnic intellectual" in* Native Speaker *and Mexican American writer Américo Paredes's novel* George Washington Gómez.]

> Always . . . the intellectual is beset and remorselessly challenged by the problem of loyalty. All of us without exception belong to some sort of national, religious or ethnic community: no one, no matter the volume of protestations, is above the organic ties that bind the individual to family, community, and of course nationality.
>
> Edward Said, *Representations of the Intellectual*

> We live in an institution, and we live outside it. We work there, and we work with what we have at hand. The University is not going to save the world by making the world more true, nor is the world going to save the University by making the University more

> real. . . . Change comes neither from within nor from without, but from the difficult space—neither inside nor outside—where one is.
>
> Bill Readings, *The University in Ruins*

The anxiety that the minority insider might come to serve as a traitorous informant on his or her community is one commonly found in the texts of writers of color and often comes accompanied with a mandate to "not tell." For example, Maxine Hong Kingston's *The Woman Warrior* explores this instruction toward silence and the conditions in which speech is possible throughout her text, most memorably in the sections "No Name Woman" and "White Tigers."[1] Similarly, Richard Rodriguez's memoir *Hunger of Memory* describes his mother's aversion to his autobiographical works: "Just keep one thing in mind. Writing is one thing, the family is another. I don't want *tus hermanos* hurt by your writings. . . . Especially I don't want the *gringos* knowing about our private affairs. Why should they?" (178).[2] The often unwanted attention of "outsiders" haunts minority discourse, constituting the grounds for the possibility of duplicity and betrayal, and requires us to go beyond the fact of cultural representation itself. That is, cultural workers cannot be satisfied with the production of narratives of minority lives but must inquire into the conditions of the production of those narratives, in order to understand the way in which the knowledge offered in this process might at once authorize and betray the subjects it is meant to represent.

By pointing to "conditions of production," I mean to emphasize that the cultural work of representation cannot be understood to occur in a social and historical vacuum. The narratives, identities, and knowledge about ethnic subjects that minority discourse struggles to create and legitimate must be structurally located within institutional, national, and global networks of power. Most immediately, this means situating ourselves—as writers, readers, and critics—within these relations in order to examine more fully the extent to which a dominant national culture, one which is often privileged within a *trans*national field of cultural and economic exchange, and academic and institutional pressures overdetermine the responsibilities of representation to which ethnic studies is obligated. For those located in the ethnic studies of American literature, it is only through this self-reflexive mode of accountability that one can respond critically to the prevalent charges that institutionalization and professionalization have superseded ethnic studies' prior and primary activist, practical, and "real" impulses and agendas.

In this essay, I argue that the fear of being "sold out" and given away by one's own is concretely realized in the troubled figure of the minority spy, a figure that allegorizes the crisis of the "ethnic intellectual" as a self-representing agent within minority discourse. The two novels I discuss, Américo Paredes's *George Washington Gómez* (1990) and Chang-Rae Lee's *Native Speaker* (1995), not only illustrate the heterogeneities through which the "betrayal" of the knowledge worker is enacted, but also imagine alternative articulations for the intellectual with respect to the responsibilities and politics of minority representations, especially within ethnic studies. The figure of the ethnic spy, like the minority intellectual, challenges conventional models of knowledge-power relationships by calling into question the extent to which the material processes of race mediate the class and professional affiliations of intellectual and institutional power. Conventional spy narratives have been predominantly concerned with the adventures of the white, usually male, patriotic spy. His agency is linked to the nation-state formation, whose politico-military dominance he is meant to secure.[3] Paredes and Lee offer, instead, a markedly different type of agent. Their novels attest to Edward Said's observation that "the intellectual is beset and remorselessly challenged by the problem of loyalty" to national, religious, or ethnic communities. Knowledge production occurs within and against these ties, at once constituting and compromising them.

Minority discourse attempts to achieve representation on a multiracial, multicultural terrain, engaging and negotiating the minority and dominant cultures simultaneously. This double-speak gives voice to the minority subject but also cannot but compromise it. The relevance of Said's remark to my argument, then, is double. First, Said suggests that the intellectual does not form an entirely separate "knowledge class." Rather the critical function of the intellectual is imbricated in and contested by the social formations to which he or she is subject. Second, the concept of loyalty to these "communities" also implies the possibility of the intellectual "failing" the community, a failure that amounts to betrayal. Paredes's and Lee's novels challenge us to ask to what degree intellectual work is actually "intelligence work." What does it mean to "betray," and what is it that is betrayed? These authors, I contend, attempt to reenvision agency in relation to and in excess of racial and national totalities.

I turn here to these questions of knowledge production and the "treasonous" character of intellectual identities within the contexts of minority discourse and the academic institutional setting. In the first part of this essay, I consider the debates surrounding the sociopolitical formation and ethical responsibilities of the intellectual and the impact of these debates upon the specific site of the university and academic ethnic

studies programs. The second part then examines Paredes's and Lee's novels as critical interventions in these debates, texts that narratively imagine and thus create, through the trope of the spy-traitor, the "difficult space," as Bill Readings has called it, of the minority intellectual, in order to reread the terms of knowledge-power and betrayal in minority discourse.

To define an intellectual is in itself a difficult task, and certainly there is no consensus among the many critics who have taken up the challenge.[4] Much of this deliberation has been framed around two issues: the social function of the intellectual and the intellectual's social positioning. That is to say, discussions about the intellectual either ask about the moral or political responsibility of the intellectual and the processes by which one "proves" one's status as an intellectual, or they consider whether or not intellectuals, from a sociohistorical framework, constitute an autonomous class. The difficulty in formulating a definition from either of these approaches is that it is almost impossible to do so without involving the other (Leonard 10-11). Furthermore, intellectuals themselves, like other objects of discursive contention, have been shaped by these debates. They are created and being re-created by what, in this case, is always to some degree self-reflexive debates about who can or must claim this name.[5]

Said suggests:

> [T]he intellectual is an individual endowed with a faculty for representing, embodying, articulating a message . . . to, as well as for, a public. And this role has an edge to it, and cannot be played without a sense of being someone whose place it is publicly to raise embarrassing questions, to confront orthodoxy and dogma (rather than to produce them), to be someone who cannot easily be co-opted by governments or corporations, and whose *raison d'être* is to represent all those people and issues that are routinely forgotten or swept under the rug.
>
> (11)

The emphasis here is on the *critical* and *oppositional* consciousness of the intellectual and the intellectual's production and dissemination of a kind of public knowledge.[6] Nevertheless, the insistence on this function of the intellectual's identity belies a less explicit point, that the line between an "intelligentsia" or the "experts" and "intellectuals" is not always a very clear one, and from many perspectives does not exist at all. If the intellectual should be conceived as one who works both against and with a degree of independence from structures of power, it must also be admitted that their "intelligence" and other forms of cultural capital render them a narrower subset of the technologically proficient or knowledge-rich intelligentsia. In other words, underlying the emphasis on the critical nature of the intellectual's activity is the recognition that the intellectual might "slip" or be co-opted from his or her responsibility of oppositional representation into this latter, less noble, merely "academic" position.[7]

The spaces of fact management, knowledge production, and value critique are tricky, overlapping ones. The *self*-consciousness demanded of the intellectual must be qualified by the material conditions and structural limits of subject formation. Thus, as Andrew Ross explains, "Increasingly positioned by the contractual discourses of their institutions and professions, [traditional intellectuals] have had to forsake the high ground and recognize the professional conditions they share, for the most part, with millions of other knowledge workers" (229). The emergence of such a professional-managerial intelligentsia is grounded most immediately in the institutionalization of knowledge-power as part of the larger development of a rationalized, technocratic society (Ross 225-26). Within this social structure, the concept of the "public intellectual"—much romanticized and eulogized—has been replaced with a variety of "specialists," located in a range of institutions, such as state agencies, corporations, nongovernmental organizations, publishing houses, print and broadcast media, think tanks, advertising firms, and universities. The coherence of this bloc as a "new class" is debatable insofar as there is little agreement over whether this group recognizes and reproduces its own self-interests or whether it works in the interest of older capitalist classes, and to what extent the emergence of knowledge as a crucial productive force transforms conditions of class formation itself.[8]

But what is clear, as Pierre Bourdieu convincingly argues, is that this cadre of professionals is as beholden to the rules and stratagems of the autonomous, professionalized fields in which they operate as to the "mandators" whom they claim to represent.[9] However, Bourdieu also emphasizes that representation is "always doubly determined," although the intellectual agent may very well be unconscious of this. On the one hand, in order for the representative agent to identify fully with the group being represented, the delegate abolishes the self in the group, "make[s] a gift of his person to the group": "There is a sort of structural bad faith attached to the delegate who, in order to appropriate for himself the authority of the group, must . . . reduce himself to the group which authorizes him" (Bourdieu, *Language* 209). Yet it is a mistake to see this "bad faith" as an *individually* motivated one, as the emphasis is on the *structural* implications of representation.

On the other hand, the agent's position is determined *within* the institutional or professional field of representation. As the agent establishes him- or herself in the field (by participating in the activities and language of the profession or institution), in the name of the represented, the represented is unable to recognize itself in that field and is dispossessed of it. The political or cultural alienation of those who are purportedly represented is an effect of this duality. In other words, Bourdieu suggests that the social formation and practices of the intellectual agent necessarily coalesce around a duality (or even multiplicity) of subjectivity. If this is the case, I would then like to argue that this "reduction" or identification is never complete and total, but rather that there are subjective excesses that escape the reduction of the agent to the group, on the one hand, and to the field on the other. Moreover, as my readings of *George Washington Gómez* and *Native Speaker* will demonstrate, these subjective excesses can reemerge as critical antagonisms to both the professionalized or institutional field and the formation of the represented group.

How then might we account for the position of the intellectual, particularly the professionalized intellectual, in the (re)production of minority discourse? The formation of ethnic studies programs not only offers us a material site to think through this model of social reproduction but also requires such a theorization if it is to remain a space of critical engagement in cultural politics.[10] Begun as grassroots and student-driven initiatives, cultural nationalist movements were considerably successful, especially on the West Coast, at establishing themselves within academic institutions, namely in the form of ethnic studies programs.[11] This success, however, did not come without considerable ideological and political tension and compromise. While ethnic studies produces a tremendous amount of knowledge on racial minorities, there has been a concurrently growing sense since the 1970s among cultural workers that these programs have failed to provide for direct, relevant community initiatives and efforts.[12]

Despite the growing number of minorities on university campuses (even in the face of affirmative action rollbacks), academic ethnic studies programs are labeled as separated from and out of touch with "the community" that constitutes ethnic America. Its critics charge that this separation in turn bears the blame for the ineffectiveness of academics in initiating real— that is, practical—political and social change. This division between the theoretical abstractness of academic study and practical, community-oriented work is, of course, hardly unique to ethnic studies. It is a version of the opposition of the "ivory tower" and the "real world" which so extensively plagues the university. But this charge is acutely wrenching in this context insofar as the very formation of ethnic studies programs has been understood by many as organically tied to the material histories of minority communities.[13]

I would like to argue, however, that this construction of ethnic collectivity along the lines of an institution versus community binary veils the way in which the university itself is a hegemonic site of political and cultural articulation, subject to the same local, national, and transnational pressures as resistance movements located elsewhere. If, on the one hand, we should challenge the short-circuiting of cultural criticism through the professionalization of the minority intellectual, we must also wonder that ethnic studies programs (and the sometimes very radical critiques that they involve) have been able or allowed to endure at all within the conservative institutional structure of the university. By insisting on the university as both a hegemonic and a contested site, we can begin to understand both of these processes. This perspective has what I consider to be far-reaching implications for students and academics, like myself, who intend to engage in a form of political activism vis-à-vis the production of new—and, we hope, oppositional—knowledges within these very institutions.

Institutional directives cut across various axes of identification and often mitigate the efficacy of oppositional discourse. For example, the demand for academics in the field of ethnic studies can be read as a product of the confluence of a benign multiculturalism and the market pressures to which the academy responds. Increasing rates of minority enrollment in colleges and universities produce individuals who perform within the strictures of global capitalism, often "exploiting" their own cultural insidership and familiarity in order to facilitate transnational exchange and "development." These critiques of the construction and institutionalization of minority discourse as an object of study and knowledge highlight important points about the educational and academic sites of cultural representation and resistance. The questions that they pose and that must be repeatedly asked with respect to particular cultural representations are many: What are the material and historical contexts of minority representations? Who authorizes such representations, and what is the process through which they are legitimized? What types of subject positions are being enunciated, and, as importantly, do we recognize that there are differences and positionalities that exceed these categories and thus remain unarticulated? What are the multiple effects of the deployment of these representations? The sites from which ethnic identities are being constructed are multiple and wide-ranging, including churches, local "cultural" associations, social service agencies, and cyberspace sites. And throughout these sites there exist variant conditions for identity

formation. For this reason, I feel it to be of equal and crucial necessity to resist binarizing the academic and the community and consequently naming an academic "we" who attempts to speak about without really speaking as, for, or to the objects of knowledge. Rather, I would like us to conceive of the "difficult space" of the university as one of the many sites from which racial formations are made and unmade.

Toward this end, Bill Readings's *The University in Ruins* proves an impressive and relevant study that traces the "idea of the University" as a project of Enlightenment rationalism and of statist constructions of the nation to its present "ruin," the moment of transnational capital. Readings argues that the university must be understood as a "ruined" institution insofar as it no longer serves the national function of producing culture and citizen-subjects within the economy of the nation-state, because the nation-state itself no longer serves an essential purpose in a system of global capital. Without the unifying narrative of a liberal, national culture, the university has become a corporation, managing information and knowledge in order to extract a surplus value in this administration. This analysis goes a long way toward answering the question of how the radical critiques made within ethnic studies have managed to persevere. Because it is no longer in the service of reproducing national culture, the university "does not carry with it an automatic political or cultural orientation," whether conservative or radical:

> This is one of the reasons why the success of a left-wing criticism . . . is turning out to fit so well with institutional protocols. . . . It is not that radical critics are "sell-outs," or that their critiques are "insufficiently radical" and hence recoverable by the institution. Rather, the problem is that the stakes of the University's functioning are no longer essentially ideological, because they are no longer tied to the self-reproduction of the nation-state.
>
> (13-14)

While Readings's argument seems to me to overstate the irrelevance of the nation-state and the institution as ideological apparatus—certainly changes in state programs and agencies such as immigration and welfare continue to have immense meaning in the lives of people of color—his description of the "decentered" university is convincing.[14] For Readings, the "culture wars" that have troubled the university for the past two decades are themselves symptomatic of the lack of any central, unifying teleology that defines the university's role and the meaning of culture more generally: "The University as an institution can deal with all kinds of knowledges, even oppositional ones, so as to make them circulate to the benefit of the system as a whole" (163).

The situation for the academic, then, is perhaps best described as an uncomfortable and troubled one, where neither nostalgia for a lost tradition of culture or political radicalism nor capitulation to economic pressures of "accounting" suffices in the face of our ethical and pedagogical obligations to others. Readings specifies a notion of ethical work in the context of the university, suggesting that the pedagogical relationship can resist the rationalized "accounting" of the contemporary university by attending to the question of accountability and justice—the obligation of the self to the other. This ethical, pedagogic relationship is perhaps best articulated in the "amateur," or nonprofessional and nonauthoritative, status of the student. The ruins of the university make visible—as Readings's analysis of the student movements of 1968 demonstrates—the "excess of the subject": "[The students'] militancy challenges the representational claim of democracy, the claim that liberal democracy achieves exhaustive representation, reflects itself to itself" (147). If the university serves as one institutional face of the national culture, then the challenge embodied in the student demystifies the nation's attempts to assimilate its many differences into a totalized unity.

The implications of this argument are substantial for ethnic studies. University-based identities and knowledges cannot simply be understood as second-level reflections of "real" identities and experiences that take place off campus. To the extent that ethnic studies has taken the "ethnic subject" and "ethnic culture" as its grounds of analysis, it continues to insist upon a discursive unity that has become increasingly untenable. Ethnic studies must not invoke the "alibis" that Readings suggests continue to mystify academic work as a search for truth in the production of knowledge and representation. The minority intellectual must not look to an "outside" referent who legitimates by authenticating the truth of representation. Ethnic studies must not participate in the drawing up of new, restrictive disciplinary boundaries according to such legitimate(d) identities. The key for cultural workers, then, is to resist seeing the articulatory acts of the minority agent within the binary of "resistant" and "accommodationist," and to understand that these categories themselves are not mutually exclusive. As Ross has written of the "new intellectuals," these subjects are "uneven participants on several fronts. They are likely to belong to different social groups and have loyalties to different social movements" (230). The minority intellectual personally participates in the politics of resistance *and* accommodation, loyalty *and* betrayal, in his or her knowledge production.

The construction of racial and ethnic identities themselves is actively performed—unevenly, temporarily, and contingently, but also historically and substantively—on campus as well as off. The minority intellectual, whom I am recasting here as the student of ethnic studies, both occupies the space of racial identity and exceeds it, gives voice to the racial minority but also gives it away. Minority intellectuals, in gaining access to the mechanisms of cultural and political representation, no longer speak from a marginalized position. They have "gained position" and thus wield a symbolic power that alienates them from those whom they purport to represent.

Yet for the minority subject, living, working, and thinking in the university also generates an anxiety that stems from a fear of loss, a fear, that is, of homogenization and integration into the structure of the field that Bourdieu describes.[15] We might conceive of the encounter between the minority subject and this anxiety as an encounter with an alienating separatedness from the institutional structure—a ghostly existence disarticulated from both "here" and "there," never successfully being incorporated into the institutional structure, but also no longer unself-consciously identifying with one's "original" home. For many, this anxiety manifests itself as a sort of anger, mostly directed at the university as a cultural center. But I want to suggest too that there is a certain critical pleasure in the performance of the professional identity within the institutional context, a pleasure that the performance affords and even justifies. This pleasure cannot guarantee the transformation of the structure itself, but the performance, in its parodic imitation and in its slippages, is revelatory of the naturalized assumptions that generate the citizen-subject of national(ist) cultures within the institutional context. In the next section of this essay, then, I would like to argue that *George Washington Gómez* and **Native Speaker,** in both their literal representations of education and their symbolic portrayals of knowledge production, and in the places where these two levels of the narratives intersect, conceive of this performance of professional identity and, in doing so, offer a way of thinking through what has become an otherwise stalemated issue in ethnic studies: the academic/community divide in minority discourse and cultural formations.

An investigation of the minority agent thus brings to bear the question of "excess" on Bourdieu's model in its positing of the fields of cultural and political representation. Paredes's and Lee's novels offer sophisticated accounts of the intersections, as well as divergences, between social/racial and cultural/economic positionings. As the novels' protagonists Gualinto/George and Henry demonstrate, "gaining position" is hardly a simple game of self-interest, insofar as for these agents, self-interest is itself heterogeneous and contradictory. On the one hand, it is through their positions as racially marked subjects, who are recognized by both the dominant culture and by the ethnic community to be racial minorities, that the knowledge produced by the informant is legitimized. On the other hand, the minority spies of Lee's and Paredes's novels critically foreground the distance between the economically dominated and culturally dominant classes, illustrating that it is this very distance that allows for the betrayal of the dominated groups. The minority spies in the novels can be identified with specialist intellectuals insofar as they undertake the representational work of identification through a process of recognition and naming of the singularities of race and ethnicity. Yet Lee and Paredes demonstrate the degree to which intelligence work through the acquirement of knowledge and the representation of the subject can be only partial. The narratives imagine the ways in which the discourse produced for the dominant culture about the minority object is antagonized by the agents' position within the ethnic collectivity, a position whose articulation subverts any suturing of the dominant national formation.

While much has been written about Américo Paredes's exploration of identity and hybridity in the Texan borderlands in his bildungsroman *George Washington Gómez,* critics have generally not commented on the significance of the protagonist's decision to become a spy at the novel's end. The novel opens in 1915, the year that sees the rise of an insurgency movement by Mexican Americans, *los sediciosos,* against the Texas Rangers, and ends with the onset of World War II. Within this historical context, it traces the birth, youth, and education of George—whose nickname Gualinto encapsulates Paredes's central thematic concern, George's conflicted subjectivity as he struggles between a romanticized American ethos of egalitarianism and progress and his sense of himself rendered a "foreigner in his native land" and accompanying pride in a Mexican heritage. His father is murdered by Texas Rangers when George is an infant, and he comes of age under the care of his mother and uncle Feliciano. Paredes's depiction of George centers largely on his education. It is one limited by the racial and economic hierarchies that make the classroom a "kind of hell" but motivated by his parents' and uncle's overriding desire to see him become "a leader of his people."

Gualinto's struggles with the contradictory implications of schooling and formal education and with his own divided self are seemingly resolved at the end of part 4 of the novel, where, upon his graduation from high school, Gualinto finally commits to attending college. This decision implicitly signals the character's agreement that he is needed as a representative of his

people. Two main points support this reading of Gualinto's commitment to his own education and to the Mexican American collectivity. First, Gualinto's decision is shown to be the result of his learning about his uncle Feliciano's involvement as a *sedicioso*—a role that Feliciano has kept secret. Thus Gualinto's decision can be seen as following in his father figure's footsteps, a predetermined path, one that he has questioned in the past but now sees as necessary. Motivated by the death of Gualinto's father Gumersindo, Feliciano saw his role as revolutionary to be in the interest of his people, in the need to defend their political rights and national interests, and George assumes this responsibility as well.

Secondly, Paredes further impels Gualinto's decision by offering an illustration of the already existing representative of the Mexican American, through the character of K. Hank Harvey, the graduation speaker who, despite his lack of fluency in Spanish, is considered "the foremost of authorities on the Mexicans of Texas" (270). In introducing what otherwise seems an extraneous figure to the narrative, Paredes parodies the legitimized "expert" on this minority culture: "K. Hank Harvey filled a very urgent need; men like him were badly in demand in Texas. They were needed to point out the local color, and in the process made the general public see that starving Mexicans were not an ugly, pitiful sight but something very picturesque and quaint, something tourists from the North would pay money to come and see" (271). Clearly, Harvey's studies only further a discourse that casts Mexican Americans as the premodern others of the modern, progressive nation. This type of knowledge production might be best understood as what Trinh T. Minh-ha has described as a form of anthropological "gossip," a "conversation of 'us' with 'us' about 'them' . . . in which 'them' is silenced," a "chatty talk" where "we speak together about others" (67-68). Gualinto's decision, then, to become educated in order to represent the interests of his community can be read as an act of self-authorization by the minority subject.

Yet in a complicating narrative move, Paredes progresses from this decision at the end of part 4 to a surprisingly different and seemingly discontinuous conclusion. Part 5 presents an adult George—who has served as a spy in Europe until the onset of World War II—returning to the Texas borderlands, where he works to maintain security along the U.S.-Mexico border. Now married to a white woman (a sociologist who, like Harvey, has studied Mexicans in the American Southwest, albeit with more tact and sympathy, but who, again like Harvey, does not speak Spanish), George disappoints his former classmates and friends when they urge him to join their political coalition. He admits to them that not only does his "company" prohibit him from becoming involved in politics, but that he would be more likely anyway to back the incumbent. As for "our people," he argues that they will continue "clearing more brush" and "digging more ditches," "if that's all they can do" (292-94).

When Feliciano surmises that his nephew's true job is as a government agent, George confides, "If any spying or sabotage takes place it will be by some of our own people" (299). In addition to explaining that he will not teach his children to speak Spanish, he bluntly expresses his scorn for the Mexican American activists:

> "The leader of his people," Feliciano said.
>
> "What do you mean?"
>
> "That was what you were going to be, have you forgotten? The Prietos will be disappointed when they hear you have changed your mind."
>
> His nephew snorted disdainfully. "I had a meeting with them before I came out here. They're a bunch of clowns playing at politics. And they're trying to organize yokels who don't know anything but getting drunk and yelling and fighting."
>
> "Then you see no future for us."
>
> "I'm afraid not. Mexicans will always be Mexicans. A few of them, like some of those would-be politicos, could make something of themselves if they would just do like I did. Get out of this filthy Delta, as far away as they can, and get rid of their Mexican Greaser attitudes."
>
> "Do like you did," Feliciano said.
>
> "Oh, I know I didn't do it alone. I am grateful for your help. I couldn't have done it otherwise."
>
> (300)

To all appearances, then, the Anglo-American George seems to have emerged triumphantly, easily earning him the affront his former classmate Eloida intends in calling him *Vendido sanavabiche!* (294). George seems to have clearly betrayed, "sold out" his people, exploiting his intimate knowledge of the community in order to maintain the surveillance, control, and, ultimately, suppression of their politicization.

Yet while ostensibly securing the totalized formation of the nation, this section of the novel also opens with George daydreaming about living during the time of the Mexican-American War. In his fantasy, he builds his own armed militia, populated by minorities, that valiantly defends itself against the U.S.:

> He would imagine he was living in his great-grandfather's time, when the Americans first began to encroach on the northern provinces of the new Republic of Mexico. Reacting against the central government's inefficiency and corruption, he would organize *rancheros* into a fighting militia and train them by using them to exterminate the Comanches. Then, with the aid of generals like Urrea, he would extend his influence to the Mexican army. He would discover the revolver before Samuel Colt, as well as the hand grenade and a modern style of portable mortar. In his daydreams he built a modern arms factory at Laredo, doing it all in great detail, until he had an enormous, well-trained army that included Irishmen and escaped American Negro slaves. Finally, he would defeat not only the army of the United States but its navy as well. He would reconquer all the territory west of the Mississippi River and recover Florida as well.
>
> (282)

The fantasy itself undermines George's claim that "I am doing what I do in the service of my country" (302). José David Saldívar has argued that even as George attempts to constitute himself into the bourgeois American subject, the phantasm of the American racial minority haunts and ruptures the parallel suturing of the nation-state. The intelligence agent finds himself actively involved in this rupturing as he comes to account for his own positioning within and without ethnic America. The duality of George/Gualinto's subjectivity emerges to undermine the nationalist identifications he has attempted to consolidate. In fact, the opportunity and decision to become an intelligence officer in themselves symbolize the extent to which the nation is highly vulnerable to invasion and subversion from both "within" and "without," as well as the state's paradoxical willingness to undermine its own principles of democratic openness in the name of securing the nation.

Bradley A. Levinson and Dorothy C. Holland have suggested that while schools supplement the education of the home and one's immediate locality with "an educational mission of extra-local proportions," they are also the sites of "intense cultural politics" between the local (in this case, the minority) and the national. Schools are a "contradictory resource" where students are taught to think of themselves as "somebody" within the systems of class, race, and gender that undergird national formations while simultaneously effecting a sense of loss of self, insofar as "[e]ncounters with formal education can result in a feeling of responsibility for one's lowly social standing" (1). Whereas, on the one hand, the educated person is produced through the cultural transmissions that education mediates, the student also employs his or her own interests in resisting and creatively incorporating that education. Paredes's depiction of Gualinto/George rests upon this tension.

There is a recognition by all those of his community that Gualinto must attain the symbolic and cultural capital that will legitimize him as a "leader of his people," but the process by which he will secure these privileges, which are in turn meant to be reinvested into the community, also gives birth to the "traitorous" Anglo-American George. Paredes portrays the fear that haunts the racial minority as it seeks cultural and political representation, that the "insider," given the responsibility to represent, will use and betray the community rather than work in its interest. Yet in carefully and consistently insisting on George as a fragmented subject, Paredes advises that this betrayal is itself complicated. Thus on the last page of the novel, Feliciano challenges George's defense of his choice of profession as a matter of "service [to] my country" by asking, "Does 'your country' include the Mexicans living in it?" It is a question that George would "rather not go into" because it exposes the plenitude that escapes and transgresses nationalist identifications. To what extent do George and the nation admit the racial minority as a constitutive element without insisting upon its assimilation to the dominant culture? It is a question that George refuses, because there are no easy answers, but only relational negotiations of personal and collective interests, rights, and histories.

Paredes's novel pictures alternative types of "experts" on the American racial minority. Most familiar is the one represented in the character of Harvey. In his portrayal of the benevolent and affectionate racism that underpins Harvey's expertise, Paredes affirms that while there was certainly no lack of earlier scholarly knowledge of these groups, these discourses worked mainly to reproduce the social, political, and economic hierarchies already in place. In contrast, the figure of George as the bearer of a more "authentic" expert knowledge is at once more prophetic and more troubling as it predicts the multiplicitous character of the self-knowledge produced by minority "insiders." The narrative suggests the need to theorize, and thus account for, the relationship between intellectual transformations and higher education on the one hand and class and professional status on the other, as well as the antagonisms that these pose for collective organization of racial identity and minority discourse.

Temporally located between Gualinto's self-inscription as a leader of his people and George's emergence as the traitor of them is a period in the narrative left unspoken and, thus, unimagined—his time at the university. As such, the literal and figurative dimensions of betrayals that I have outlined, that of the spy and of the intellectual, are explicitly coupled and equated. The novel suggests that George is interpellated by the nation-state and emerges as a subject assimilated to it. Thus his betrayal is actuated in his symbolic and literal separation and distance from Chicano/as while at the university. This narrative,

conceived during a moment in which minorities were by and large barred from access to the institutions of higher education, accordingly imagines the university as a site wherein the minority subject is inculcated into the dominant national culture. The negotiations and oppositional discourse that Gualinto engaged in during high school are therefore left behind and unvoiced here. It is, in many ways, a story that does not need telling—as the novel's silence intimates— because it is a story familiar to the minority subject: only through assimilative processes can one become equal.

As the conclusion of *George Washington Gómez* suggests, at this historical moment political and cultural equality is difficult to envision as anything but a salutary acceptance of the dominant culture. Yet the conflict set out in the closing of this novel also gestures toward the predicament of minority discourse following the success of the civil rights and cultural nationalist movements' demands for political representation of cultural difference. As Michael Omi and Howard Winant have contended, these movements effected a paradigm shift on a national scale in which the nature of racial politics and the meaning of racial identity itself were altered. A burgeoning sense of a collective subjectivity based on race allowed for an oppositional articulation of racial identity that critiqued the dominance of Eurocentric (that is, white) and often biological conceptualizations of race. With this shift, self-representation became both possible and treacherous, as the minority cultural worker attempted to enter a social terrain that remained highly uneven despite claims by the dominant culture of an already accomplished equality.

Paredes's intimation that the subject of minority discourse remains conflicted by different sets of interests seems remarkable in its ability to suggest the contesting claims that class positions (or any of the host of other differences that cultural critics have explored) effect upon racial identifications. Ramón Saldívar has written of Paredes's works in general: "Given the modernity of their concerns, it is startling to learn that Paredes' literary creations are not contemporary pieces, nor even products of the fifties and sixties. . . . As products of an era and of literary formations different from those currently in vogue, the literary texts belie their postmodern, post-Chicano Movement thematics and publication dates" ("Border Subjects" 373). Moreover, as Saldívar has argued about *George Washington Gómez* specifically, it is a "curious polytemporal text" ("Borderlands" 274). Written between 1935 and 1940, set during the first half of the twentieth century, and published in 1990, it provides "a prefigurative instance of the state of Chicano literature and the Chicano subject at the end of the twentieth century" (274).[16]

Paredes wrote this novel after the mass deportations of Chicanos during the Great Depression and just before the onset of World War II, in which unprecedented (and disproportionate) numbers of Mexican Americans participated. After World War II, many Mexican Americans were able to avail themselves of the provisions of the G.I. Bill. Because of this newly available access to higher education, Mexican Americans (especially in contrast to more recently arrived Mexican immigrants and *braceros* [manual laborers]) found themselves moving into the middle class, but also becoming politically mobilized around civil rights discourses and later in El Movimiento, the Chicano cultural nationalist movement that allied itself with the mobilization of other people of color in the U.S. and decolonization campaigns in the third world. The historical moment of the narrative's production and narration is also significant in light of Gilbert G. Gonzalez's compelling argument that U.S. foreign policy "aimed at preventing Mexican political and social organizations from 'becoming disruptive or divisive factors'" and that promoting "inter-American political solidarity" was partly responsible for the implementation of education reform in Mexican American communities, effectively ending segregation and introducing some curricular changes (75). In the fragmentations and transformations that Gualinto/ George undergoes, Paredes's novel traces these momentous changes, of which Chicanos were both subjects and objects. Poised as it is just prior to the onset of World War II, the narrative considers what possibilities face a community which had articulated its collective interest in the more singularly heroic oppositional forms of the border ballad. The novel itself predates the collectivist articulations of race of El Movimiento and the theorization of difference that postmodernist, poststructuralist, and feminist thought has brought to minority discourse, but its seemingly "modern" (post—civil rights, post—cultural nationalist) positioning and perspective with respect to Chicano history denotes the extent to which racial identity has been lived and understood through multiple axes of difference.

It is a multiplicity that Chang-Rae Lee likewise attends to in his novel *Native Speaker.* Whereas Paredes's novel concludes with George's decision to become a spy among his own people, Lee takes a similar situation as a point of departure for his novel. Published in 1995, *Native Speaker* focuses on a multicultural New York City, nearly three decades after the race-based movements of civil rights and cultural nationalism began. My reading of *Native Speaker* in conjunction with *George Washington Gómez* is framed so as to take up the question with which Paredes ends: What is the nature and content of the betrayal that the ethnic intelligence worker enacts? Who is the subject and object of this betrayal, and how are we to understand interests, both self-interest and interest groups, as they play out in these treasonous acts? What replaces national interest, the "in the service of my country," when it no longer serves as the ideological alibi of the minority spy? In this case, as Lee's novel illustrates, "self-interest" is constituted through the multiple axes of race, class, nation, gender, and sexuality, and representation becomes an even more difficult thing to control.

At the beginning of this novel, the wife of the narrative's Korean American protagonist Henry initiates a trial separation, leaving him with a partial, haphazard list of adjectives that he recognizes is a description of the way in which he has come to see himself. Lelia's list (what Henry initially thinks to be a "love letter") portrays him as an "illegal alien" and an "emotional alien," as a "traitor" and a "neo-American." Because elsewhere in the novel Lelia's figurative role as a cultural "standard bearer" and her "whiteness" are both stressed, Lelia's articulation of Henry's identity— especially as it reinscribes the alien status of the Asian American—are crucial to the development of Henry's narrative. Standing in as the dominant culture's arbiter of legitimacy and normativity, Lelia's catalogue of descriptors for Henry installs him as the duplicitous and illegitimate subject of American history.

This sense of himself as a "fake" is further concretized in Henry's professional identity as a spy. The intelligence agency for which Henry works is not a governmental division but rather Dennis Hoagland's independent agency, which specializes in "ethnic coverage," and whose clients vary but include multinational corporations and foreign governments. Lee thus sets his narrative squarely in a post—cold war moment, in which nation-states no longer constitute the only or primary actors in political contests. In contrast to the task of the agent in many works of the spy genre, where intelligence work is to lead to state control over the object of scrutiny through the secret securing of knowledge about it, Hoagland already recognizes that all knowledge and the consequent power it produces are partial, never totalized, and that no one can see the entire "game": "[Y]ou know that no matter how smart you are, no one is smart enough to see the whole world. There's always a picture too big to see. No one is safe. . . . There's no real evil in the world. It's just the world. Full of people like us. Your immigrant mother and father taught you that, I hope. Mine did" (41-42).

Consequently, without the alibi of nationalist service, Lee refuses to romanticize Henry's profession, instead depicting him as rather self-deprecating and self-aware:

> We casually spoke of ourselves as business people. Domestic travelers. We went wherever there was a need. The urgency of that need, like much of everything else, was determined by some calculus of power and money. Political force, the fluid motion of capital. Influence on your fellow man. These basics drove our livelihood. . . .
>
> We pledged allegiance to no government. We weren't ourselves political creatures. We weren't patriots. Even less, heroes.
>
> (15)

As spies, Hoagland's employees engage their subjects in casual relationships and take the material of everyday life to formulate narratives about themselves. The reports they produce for their clients are meant to be objective, impersonal accounts of these details, "unauthorized biographies" (16). As Henry explains, the spies begin this process by creating "legends" of their own, "extraordinarily extensive 'stor[ies]' of who we were, an autobiography as such, often evolving to develop even the minutiae of life experience, countless facts and figures, though [they] also required a truthful ontological bearing, a certain presence of character" (20). These performances, then, are stronger the more closely they ride the unstable line between fact and fiction, articulating but also reimagining the various subject positions of family, profession, ethnicity, and sexuality that the spy already inhabits.

Henry's story is told in retrospect, and his feelings of guilt emerge when he becomes personally attached to one of his subjects, a Filipino psychoanalyst, Emile Luzan. Henry begins introducing into his legend for Luzan the facts of his real life, but "no longer extrapolating; I was looping it through the core" (20). Thus he finds himself trying to account for his own losses—his mother's death to cancer while he was still a boy, his struggles with his own masculinity against and alongside the model offered to him in the figure of his immigrant father, his sense of racial and cultural dispossession, his marriage to a white woman and the death of their son. When Henry attempts to warn Luzan about possible dangers the doctor might face, Hoagland pulls him off the case. Luzan thereafter dies in a boating wreck that is declared accidental but which Henry suspects is the result of political machinations. Henry's likely betrayal of Luzan initiates his sense that his own encounters with traumatic loss and epistemic violence become symptomatic of his part in the "selling-out" of those around him, his sense that he is responsible, because of something lacking in

him, for the pain he finds in others. This sense of responsibility, and the accompanying guilt, deviates from the emotional neutrality and distance that the spy must maintain, as Hoagland and his colleagues repeatedly remind him.

Henry's assignment to John Kwang is meant as an easy and gradual reintroduction to the job and a test of his ability to carry it out. As the novel narrates his "infiltration" of the campaign and party structures of this rising New York City political star, Henry grows increasingly attached to and identifies with his subject. He finds that he is no longer able to represent Kwang, with whom he has begun to identify, in any "neutral" or nonself-interested manner but wishes instead to know him more intimately, familiarly: "I believed I had a grasp of his identity, not only the many things he was to the public and to his family and to his staff and to me, but who he was to himself, the man he beheld in his most private mirror" (130). Yet by the end of the novel, the fiction of this understanding is revealed as a circuit of betrayed trusts and interests.

Two key moments in the novel demonstrate this critical recognition. A firebombing of the campaign headquarters, which results in the death of one of Kwang's most trusted volunteers, Eduardo, ultimately leads to the revelation that Eduardo was in fact working undercover for a rival candidate. The attack is also revealed to be not the work of Hoagland and Henry's colleagues (a suspicion which has left Henry feeling utterly responsible) but of Kwang's own affiliates. Kwang tries to explain to Henry his own reasoning: "[H]e was betraying us, Henry. Betraying everything we were doing. . . . I loved him, Henry, I grieve for him, but he was disloyal, the most terrible thing, a traitor" (289-90). The second instance occurs in the exposure of the *ggeh* (Korean "money-club") formation of Kwang's fund-raising apparatus, which results in the arrests and deportation of numerous undocumented immigrants by the INS. Henry comes to understand his role as an intelligence and social agent in both of these instances as only partial; he has only partial claim to, control over, and responsibility for the knowledge he has produced, the identity he has performed, and the consequences it has effected. But he does indeed have partial control and responsibility—in other words, Lee does not exonerate Henry in the game of interests and intelligence.

The novel's ultimate revelation that it is the INS that has commissioned Henry's collection of data on the *ggeh* members in order to deport the undocumented immigrants associated with Kwang's campaign offers a significant recognition of the complex interrelations between transnational and nationalist politics, demonstrating that the nation-state, although increasingly subject to and transgressed by transnational flows of peoples and capital, is hardly a defunct category. The swift roundup and deportation of Henry's subjects and Henry's sense of responsibility in the betrayal of these subjects point to the material regulation of the nation by the state. Henry recognizes the betrayal of these immigrants as a betrayal of himself:

> Whether I wish it or not, I possess them, their spouses and children, their jobs and money and life. And the more I see and remember the more their story is the same. The story is mine. How I come by plane, come by boat. Come climbing over a fence. When I get here, I work. I work for the day I will finally work for myself. I work so hard that one day I end up forgetting the person I am.
>
> (260)

Set against the narrative of political and intelligence intrigue, Lee unfolds the stories of Henry's personal life, including a recounting of his fraught relationships with his parents and his attempt to reconcile with Lelia after the tragedy of their son's death and her discovery that he is a spy. As in *George Washington Gómez,* this novel focuses closely on the cultural production of Henry as an object of education and reinforces the point that, as some critics of globalization have emphasized, it is a mistake to "confuse a loss of [the nation-state's] sovereignty with a loss of power" (Morrow and Torres 37). But *Native Speaker,* as the title suggests, approaches this process through the question of language. Like Gualinto/George, school provides for Henry the locus of the intense cultural politics of language, and, as with Gualinto/George again, Henry finds the opportunity for his own assimilative survival and success embodied in the figure of the white teacher, in particular the speech therapist. Henry describes himself as having been "raised by language experts, saved from the wild" (216):

> [Miss Haven would] give each of us a small hand mirror so that we might examine our mouths as we spoke, and then she'd come around and practice with us. She would go from one student to the next, sit herself squarely before him or her, and say, *Now put your hand on my throat.* She wanted us to understand the vibration certain sounds required. If the kid wouldn't do it—most of us would automatically reach for her neck—she'd take the hand and move it up there herself and say something deep and thrilling like *vampire,* and you thought, this is a teacher, a person who can show, her mottled milky skin still damp with the sweat of other palms, her breath sweet.
>
> (219)

The teacher offers up her very body to the students as an instrument through which they might be domesticated, made no longer wild or foreign, and thus made part of the nation. Throughout the novel, as in this scene, Lee conceives of the execution of language as literally a bodily act. It is an act that is meant to be a seamless performance of the continuities of body, identity, and culture, but it often instead exposes the construction of these connections through the processes of education and cultural negotiations.

Lelia, too, is occupied as a speech therapist, a trait that Henry explains immediately drew him to her: "At first I took her as being exceedingly proper, but I soon realized that she was simply executing the language. She went word by word. Every letter had a border. I watched her wide full mouth sweep through her sentences like a figure touring a dark house, flipping on spots and banks of perfectly drawn light" (9). In this first meeting, Lelia surmises that Henry himself is not a "native speaker" (11), despite his rather perfect approximation of English, suggesting that his body betrays the self-consciousness with which he performs the language. In contrast, English "fills" Lelia's voice, and conversely her body inhabits the language with a natural(ized) continuity that makes her "an average white girl [who] has no mystery" and whose "job" is to serve as the "standard-bearer" (9, 11). Henry's desire for Lelia is explicitly tied to the racial (her whiteness) and cultural (her perfect English) privilege that she embodies. In contrast, it is the tension between his face and his voice—that is, the markers of his race and his education—that affords Henry his profession as a spy among his "own kind." While his face registers him as the other of the national body that is the minority immigrant, his voice links him to a class that has "made it," has successfully assimilated to the dominant language and culture.

Henry's attraction to Kwang also rests, in part, on this shared trait—that Kwang can speak both for his constituency, the racial minority groups of Queens, and to a dominant culture. Thus Kwang is pictured as a nodal point in a Rainbow Coalition-like alliance of minority interests that are translated into the language of "Americans" and political rights. Lee hardly portrays this coalition as a harmonious coming together of racial minorities; Kwang labors to manage the difficult relations of his constituents, most notably tensions between African Americans and immigrant communities. Yet the narrative suggests a remaking of American electoral politics, where canvassers offer the residents a remarkable message: "In ten different languages you say *Kwang is like you. You will be an American*" (143). Among the "scores and scores of his versions" that Henry records (196), he is most drawn to this story, the one by which Kwang becomes an American, and further, an American representative of ethnic and immigrant minorities:

> [H]ere is a man named John Kwang, born in Seoul before the last world war, a boy during the Korean one,

his family not mercifully sundered or refugeed but obliterated, the coordinates of his home village twice removed from the maps . . . he stole away to America as the houseboy of a retiring two-star general. Where he saved enough money to leave the general's house in Ohio and go to New York. Where he named himself John. Where he was beaten nearly to death and robbed of all his savings. Where he worked in a Chinatown noodle shop and slept outside next to the steam vent and awoke one morning to see that his feet had turned almost black with the cold. Where he knew hunger again, the unforgettable taste of his other country. Where, desperate as he was, he took to stealing from others, one of them a young priest who saw something to salvage and took him to a Catholic orphanage. Where he first went to a real school and learned to read and write and speak his new home language. And where he began to think of America as a part of him, maybe even his, and this for me was the crucial leap of his character, deep flaw or not, the leap of his identity no one in our work would find valuable but me.

(196)

Henry attempts to separate emotionally the reports that he produces for Hoagland of Kwang from what he sees as the ethical impulse underlying the political work that Kwang's campaign espouses, the representation of the disempowered whom Kwang embodies in his own history. Yet Kwang himself confirms for Henry the impossibility of such a separation between the narrative and the political: "When you are someone like me, you will be many people all at once. You are a father, a dictator, a servant, the most agile actor this land has ever known. And all throughout you must be the favorite chaste love of the people" (273).

The series of identifications produced by Henry's attraction to Kwang and his desire to see in Kwang a fatherly figure who articulates the dispersed interests of minorities is completed by his comparisons of Kwang to his own father. Henry's assessment of his own father tends to be rather harsh, a testament to both his disdain for his father's immigrant work ethic and apolitical presence in the American landscape and the pain he harbors from his father's ability to convince him of his own fundamental unassimilability. Yet the narrative ultimately comes to a different understanding of Henry's father's position, aligning it explicitly with both Henry and Kwang through the language of betrayal. Lee characterizes the affinities between Kwang and Henry's father and between Henry's father and Henry himself through their shared relationships of difference and distance from others of their "own kind":

> If anything, I think my father would choose to see my deceptions in a rigidly practical light, as if they were similar to that daily survival he came to endure, the need to adapt, assume an advantageous shape.
>
> My ugly immigrant's truth, as was his, is that I have exploited my own, and those others who can be exploited. This forever is my burden to bear. But I and

my kind possess another dimension. We will learn every lesson of accent and idiom, we will dismantle every last pretense and practice you hold, noble as well as ruinous. You can keep nothing safe from our eyes and ears. This is your own history. We are your most perilous and dutiful brethren, the song of our hearts at once furious and sad. For only you could grant me these lyrical modes. I call them back to you. Here is the sole talent I ever dared nurture. Here is all of my American education.

(297)

For Henry, the truest "burden" that links him to his father and to Kwang is not in their ability to represent through sameness but to betray through distance and difference their own kind. Paradoxically, however, if this is the "immigrant's truth," it is one engendered in their inhabiting the space between native and foreign alien. In this passage, the difference marked by the "we," at first suggesting the spy, shifts with the introduction of a rather indeterminate "you," an interpellation of the audience as American, the disseminators of the "lyrical modes" and "American education" through which the betrayal is enacted. The betrayal that the spy carries out is shown as only one instance of the perfidious character of representation within the multicultural terrain.

Both Lee and Paredes foreground descriptions of the difficulties the protagonists face in learning English and interacting with white Americans, and in their troublesome relationships as "insiders" of a particular minority community. This foregrounding suggests that it is these experiences of race, of the material processes and modes through which racial identities are constructed, that make them expert spies. As adults, they both continue to face racist exclusions in the most intimate of settings, the family. For example, both authors depict their protagonists as resented by and resentful of their fathers-in-law, white men who enact an othering by articulating their own ethnic chauvinism. These material experiences of the psychic and bodily markers of race, then, are what authorize George and Henry as minority subjects. And like the minority intellectual, the minority intelligence worker's expertise lies in his or her ability to produce authoritative knowledge about this racial identity and its cultural contexts.

Rather than being wholly disarticulated from racial formations, the novels suggest that the ethnic intellectual antagonizes both dominant and minority formations in the difficulties of his or her positioning. Michael Denning has suggested that the conventional spy novel mediates between the political conditions of social relations and individual experience: "[The genre] kept a fairly traditional plot by making the spy the link between the actions of an individual—often an 'ordinary person'—and the world historical fate of nations and empires. History is displaced to secret conspiracies and secret agents, from politics to ethics. The secret *agent* returns human *agency* to a world which seems less and less the product of human action" (14). The narrative of the ethnic secret agent, however, like that of the minority intellectual, must grapple with both the historical conditions that produce racial meanings and the ethical responsibilities of personal agency and accountability. Rather than the ethical binaries that both conventional spy narratives and assertions of the responsibility of the intellectual seek to impose, these narratives suggest, as Lee's Hoagland suspects, that "it's just the world," brought into being in the negotiations, whether profound or absurd, between the personal and the historical-political.

By way of a conclusion to this essay, but of course in no way a complete resolution to the problems I have set out in it, I would like to argue that minority intellectuals—academics, critics, and artists—should actively revisit and reconceive of the position of "student" in order to more precisely (and rather paradoxically) articulate the indeterminacy of the minority subject. Such a reconceptualization has several implications. We must think of the student neither as the liberalist citizen whose engagement with higher education is a process of "self-discovery," of learning, that is, who he or she already essentially is, nor as a consumer interested only in the purchase of a commodified object of pedagogy, credentials, as a "shopping mall" model of educational curriculum promotes. Instead, my reconceptualization of "student" within the context of the university and ethnic studies means to highlight the way in which this subject embodies the heterogeneities that are inherent in cultural production but not exhausted by this process. Thus the ethnic studies "student" names at once, but always incompletely, the self and its others.

Native Speaker imagines the ethnic studies student's critical pleasure in detail in its closing with what Readings describes as a "scene of teaching." Henry, now "between jobs" (321), assists Lelia in her speech therapy practice, working with immigrant children. As they visit low-income schools, Henry plays the role of the "Speech Monster": "I gobble up kids but I cower when anyone repeats the day's secret phrase" (323). In this case, where most of the students are foreign-language speakers, Henry describes Lelia's focus to be less on the actual words and utterances of the language itself and more on a welcoming to the language as a whole: "She wants them to know that there is nothing to fear, she wants to offer up a pale white woman horsing with the language to show them it's fine to mess it all up" (324). This closing offers a moment of both astonishment and acceptance. The children

wonder at the way in which Henry's voice, when unmasked, both succeeds and fails to "match his face": "they check again that my voice moves in time with my mouth, truly belongs to my face." Then Lelia awards the students with badges, symbols of everyone having "been a good citizen": "Now, she calls out each one as best as she can, taking care of every last pitch and accent, and I hear her speaking a dozen lovely and native languages, calling all the difficult names of who we are" (324).

In this scene, the value of teaching itself, and the discontinuities between the speaker, the listener, and that which is spoken, is foregrounded. Within this context, teaching could be reduced to the management of subjects, facts, and bodies—Henry suggests that the speech-therapy class is, in fact, considered by many in the school as a "form of day care, ESL-style" (323).[17] Yet the participants attempt to displace the privilege of authority and autonomy in light of a network of ethical obligations. In Lelia's calling the many "difficult names of who we are," there occurs an interpellation of the students as American in the name of a radically democratic impulse. As in *George Washington Gómez*, the classroom serves as the site for a utopian articulation of citizen-subjecthood within the democratic project. But again, as in Paredes's novel, this scene is conditioned by the restrictions of class and race. It is one moment in the institutional context of education, especially vulnerable to the violence and lack of resources and funds that threaten the development of these minority voices. As Henry explains, there are too many students for them to each receive individual attention, and Lelia's interaction with them is on a freelance basis, haphazard and infrequent.

Moreover, Henry's performance and disrobing as the Speech Monster and the children's surprise at the presence of a racial minority who inhabits the dominant language so "invisibly" exposes the heterogeneities that exist *within* the moment of articulation. Henry's Speech Monster is a disruptive ghost in a narrative about intelligence and power, haunting and refusing a full identification with either the children or Lelia. Rather than a one-directional portrayal of the transfer of knowledge and power—where either the children are being domesticated by the teaching of the language or they gain unassailable power in being able to represent themselves in the language of the dominant culture—the scene of teaching insists on a radical uncertainty over who it is that embodies privilege through knowledge and knowledge through privilege. If multiculturalism has been "a form of disciplinarity of difference in which the matter of alterity has been effectively displaced as a supplement" (McCarthy and Dimitriades 187), and if there is no giving of "voice" to marginalized groups in school that is not always already "the historical effects of multiple discourses through which power is effected" (Popkewitz 174), then the haunted scene of teaching nevertheless maps the productive agency of desire, the excesses that cannot be integrated into liberalist and consumerist models of citizenhood, but that circulate and produce new possibilities for articulating discursive positioning, subjective relationality, local and national imaginaries, and ethical action.

The meaning and consequences of the students engaging in knowledge production in Lee's novel are certainly quite distinct from those in which undergraduate students, graduate students, and faculty participate. To this extent, primary and secondary schools serve as one of the many alternative sites in and through which racial identity is constructed, and the formation of these identities can complement and contradict those articulated elsewhere. Yet the self-critical mode of this scene provides a conceptual structure for the problematic of the minority intellectual as he or she engages in the production and dissemination of knowledge about his or her "own selves." If, as I have noted, the minority intellectual's experience of the university is a ghostly one, this existence is in fact the product of extensive curricular reforms on a global level that, as Thomas S. Popkewitz contends, "are concerned less with the specific content of school subjects and more with making the child feel 'at home' in a cosmopolitan identity that embodies a pragmatic flexibility and 'problem-solving' disposition" (171).

As these reforms introduce local, decentered epistemologies, the different conceptions of "home" emerge as ambiguities, conflicts, and tensions, such that competing social memories and "forgettings" are lived as institutional and personal anxiety. However, as *Native Speaker* surmises, surprise and pleasure attend such anxiety as well; the ethical obligation of the self to the other opens out onto new, unimagined terrains for identification and articulation. To acknowledge alternative agencies, generated by the subject's location at the intersections of racial dispossession and symbolic privilege, is to understand ethnic studies not as a site where the work of self-discovery goes on, but rather as one place among many from which racial identifications are *made* and *unmade* and as a site of a radical, critical pedagogy that insists on opening up the question of "the possibility of justice" in knowledge production and representation.

Notes

1. For a detailed discussion of Kingston's use of "provocative silences" in *The Woman Warrior,* see Cheung.

2. Doris Sommer convincingly argues that these refusals to reveal are in themselves strategies by which insider and outsider positions are created; writers like Rodriguez who use such a strategy affirm their cultural identity by calling attention to an object of knowledge unknowable "from the outside."

3. Even a complex novel such as Rudyard Kipling's *Kim* that explores the colonist/native dialectic through the act of "passing" nonetheless forecloses the question of betrayal by positing Kim as a true, white, British citizen-subject, whose allegiance is founded in this organic tie. For studies that explore the national, class, and international politics of the genre of the conventional spy-thriller novel, see Bloom, Denning, Sauerberg, and Stafford. These investigations, and others like them, focus primarily on the spy genre as a peculiarly British form and, as such, on British spy novels. As Michael Denning maintains, "The spy thriller has been, for most of its history, a British genre, indeed a major cultural export" (6). It is not my intent to make an argument for *George Washington Gómez* or *Native Speaker* as part of this genre, but these studies do elucidate Paredes's and Lee's novels, especially as they suggest the paradigms of spy narratives that these authors both incorporate and rework in their texts.

4. Andrew Ross and Stephen Leonard provide helpful genealogies on the concept of the intellectual. Stanley Aronowitz discusses the social position of intellectuals as an emergent class.

5. This is true even if individuals are unwilling to take on the name of "intellectual." Despite their often privileged positions, intellectuals have also been subject to a long history of disparagement and anti-intellectualism—a phenomenon especially evident in American political and cultural history. Political and cultural workers and elites have thus often tried to distance themselves from those they see as "true intellectuals," for example, academicians. This question of defining the role of the intellectual was taken up in the "Forum" section of a recent *PMLA*. The very fact that this leading journal in the field of literary studies felt pressed to address this issue—and that those who participated in the debate are themselves leading intellectuals and scholars in the field—further underlines the extent to which the formation of the intellectual subject occurs within a (self-)critical discursive practice. Tzvetan Todorov, for example, argues that the intellectual "is engaged in an activity of the mind resulting in the production of a work. . . . [and] is also concerned about the state of society and participates in public debate." For Todorov, "the intellectual cannot be replaced by the expert: the latter knows facts; the former discusses values. . . . there is a difference in their positions."

6. Interestingly, one crucial moment to which this particular definition can be traced, the Dreyfus affair of the 1890s and Emile Zola's condemnation of the

French government in his famous *"J'accuse"* article, also invoked the specter of the spy-traitor and pitted racial (in the form of a virulent anti-Semitism) and national loyalties against each other.

7. Margaret Soltan, for example, dramatically explains: "[A]ttentiveness, passion, and lack of compromise are the attributes that an advanced technical, managerial, consumer society confounds. Concentration disperses when the object world thins to images; passion goes when, after sufficient betrayal and confusion, people become affectless and paranoid; conviction falters when everyone self-protectively refuses to make judgments."

8. Again, for further detail on this debate, see Aronowitz.

9. Bourdieu has offered a detailed analysis of how these conditions reproduce social and economic hierarchies. For Bourdieu, social and cultural representations are tied to social power relations, which underwrite "the game" of social practice. In this sense, all intellectuals, that is, cultural producers—even those without access to material capital or any control over *economic* modes of production—occupy positions of power, have "gained position," through their accumulation of cultural capital. The cultural producer, Bourdieu contends, is a symbolically empowered yet economically dominated subject who positions himor herself oppositionally by identifying with those who are both economically and culturally dominated (*Field* 44). For Bourdieu, cultural producers, those whom I refer to as intellectuals, who make easy identifications with the economically disenfranchised, especially in their claims to represent these dominated classes, fail to recognize that their access to the means of representation distances and differentiates them from these very classes.

10. The parameters that mark my discussion of minority intellectuals and ethnic studies need to be noted. Most importantly, I must acknowledge that my discussion of the minority intellectual has been restricted to a certain group. First, these are individuals, whether artists or critics, working within ethnic studies, primarily in an academic setting. Of course, a large number of minorities work in fields other than ethnic studies and the humanities and social sciences from which these academic fields are drawn, especially, for example, in the sciences. Yet one might contend that these individuals, despite their amassing of cultural capital, are not "minority intellectuals" insofar as they have not, at least within their own scholarly production, committed to the work of cultural and political *self*-representation. While those people of color who work outside of ethnic studies certainly play an important role simply in their presence and visibility on campus (a presence which in turn is often the consequence of the racial politics most clearly articulated on campus in the formation of ethnic studies), and while many of

my arguments might be extended and applied to include these individuals, their own knowledge production is less straightforwardly tied to the value critiques or the ethical commitments of ethnic studies. Secondly, the intellectuals I consider are themselves people of color. As my argument below suggests, a certain notion of a "true" minority subject has also posited a conception of the most "appropriate" type of intellectual in ethnic studies. Accordingly, it becomes difficult for a non-"insider," especially white academics, to "justify" or "legitimate" their work in ethnic studies and defend themselves against charges of orientalism or a racist othering that is portrayed, as I describe below, in Paredes's "experts." In other words, they are rather "imperfect" spies because they clearly cannot claim a transparent identification with their objects of study. Ultimately, this essay implicitly argues against such constructions of racial authority, contending that the possibilities of betrayal reveal the problems with "authenticity" and transparency on the part of minority intellectuals. Finally, the focus of my argument is the production of knowledge by and about minority subjects, and ethnic studies seems to offer the most formalized version of this process. But I mean to include in this category those individuals working in traditional academic departments and disciplines whose scholarship nevertheless includes the subject of race and ethnicity.

11. For historical accounts of these movements and the establishment of ethnic studies programs, see Wei and Muñoz.

12. Most minority activists and critics saw the goal of these programs to be multiple: they were intended to raise the consciousness of students in terms of racial and ethnic identities, produce and disseminate historical and cultural knowledge about ethnic minorities in the United States, and provide culturally specific and sensitive services to both minority students and communities.

13. For examples of such critiques in Chicano/Latino studies and Asian American studies, see García, and Hirabayashi and Alquizola.

14. See also Dominick LaCapra's critique of Readings, in which LaCapra explains that such contentions about "self-awareness" regarding one's actions in the interests of the reproduction of capital and social relations do not address the model of ideology asserted by Slavoj Žižek, whereby "a subject sees through or recognizes the baselessness of an ideological perspective but affirms or follows its injunctions anyway" (48).

15. Several anthologies provide a range of compelling narrative and critical essays attesting to the experiences of the marginalized subject in the university context; pedagogical strategies; and the departmental, disciplinary, and institutional politics of difference.

See, for example, Dews and Law, Mayberry, Lim and Herrera-Sobek.

16. Christopher Schedler's reading of *George Washington Gómez* as an inscription of border modernism—a deconstruction of the epic tradition of *corridos* that responds to both the experimental aesthetics of high modernism and the uneven process of social and cultural development in the U.S. borderlands in the twentieth century—brings our attention to the historical situatedness of this novel as well.

17. For a helpful discussion of the impact of the scarcity of resources on racial formations and the competition for such resources by minority groups in the U.S., see McCarthy and Dimitriades.

Works Cited

Aronowitz, Stanley. *The Politics of Identity: Class, Culture, Social Movements*. New York: Routledge, 1992.

Bloom, Clive, ed. *Spy Thrillers: From Buchan to le Carré*. New York: St. Martin's, 1990.

Bourdieu, Pierre. *The Field of Cultural Reproduction: Essays on Art and Literature*. Ed. Randal Johnson. New York: Columbia UP, 1993.

———. *Language and Symbolic Power*. Ed. John B. Thompson. Trans. Gino Raymond and Matthew Adamson. Cambridge, MA: Harvard UP, 1991.

Burbules, Nicholas C., and Carlos Alberto Torres, eds. *Globalization and Education: Critical Perspectives*. New York: Routledge, 2000.

Cheung, King-kok. *Articulate Silences: Hisaye Yamamoto, Maxine Hong Kingston, Joy Kogawa*. Ithaca, NY: Cornell UP, 1993.

Denning, Michael. *Cover Stories: Narrative and Ideology in the British Spy Thriller*. New York: Routledge, 1987.

Dews, C. L. Barney, and Carolyn Leste Law, ed. *This Fine Place So Far from Home: Voices of Academics from the Working Class*. Philadelphia: Temple UP, 1995.

García, Ignacio M. "Juncture in the Road: Chicano Studies since 'El Plan de Santa Barbara.'" *Chicanas/Chicanos at the Crossroads: Social, Economic and Political Change*. Ed. David R. Maciel and Isidro D. Ortiz. Tucson: U of Arizona P, 1996. 181-203.

Gonzalez, Gilbert G. "Segregation of Mexican Children in a Southern California City: The Legacy of Expansionism and the American Southwest." *Western Historical Quarterly* 16 (1985): 55-76.

Hirabayashi, Lane Ryo, and Marilyn C. Alquizola. "Asian American Studies: Reevaluating for the 1990s." *The State of Asian America: Activism and Resistance in the 1990s*. Ed. Karin Aguilar-San Juan. Boston: South End, 1994. 351-64.

LaCapra, Dominick. "The University in Ruins?" *Critical Inquiry* 25 (1998): 32-55.

Lee, Chang-Rae. *Native Speaker*. New York: Riverhead, 1995.

Leonard, Stephen T. "Introduction: A Genealogy of the Politicized Intellectual." *Intellectuals and Public Life: Between Radicalism and Reform*. Ed. Leon Fink, et al. Ithaca, NY: Cornell UP, 1996. 1-25.

Levinson, Bradley A., Douglas E. Foley, and Dorothy C. Holland, eds. *The Cultural Production of the Educated Person: Critical Ethnographies of Schooling and Local Practice*. Albany: State U of New York P, 1996.

Lim, Shirley Geok-lin, and María Herrera-Sobek, eds. *Power, Race, and Gender in Academe: Strangers in the Tower?* New York: MLA, 2000.

Mayberry, Katherine J., ed. *Teaching What You're Not: Identity Politics in Higher Education*. New York: New York UP, 1996.

McCarthy, Cameron, and Greg Dimitriades, "Globalizing Pedagogies: Power, Resentment, and the Re-Narration of Difference." Burbules and Torres 187-204.

Morrow, Raymond A., and Carlos Alberto Torres. "The State, Globalization, and Educational Policy." Burbules and Torres 27-56.

Muñoz, Carlos, Jr. *Youth, Identity, Power: The Chicano Movement*. London: Verso, 1989.

Omi, Michael, and Howard Winant. *Racial Formation in the United States from the 1960s to the 1980s*. New York: Routledge, 1986.

Paredes, Américo. *George Washington Gómez: A Mexicotexan Novel*. Houston: Arte Público, 1990.

Popkewitz, Thomas S. "Reform as the Social Administration of the Child: Globalization of Knowledge and Power." Burbules and Torres 157-86.

Readings, Bill. *The University in Ruins*. Cambridge, MA: Harvard UP, 1996.

Rodriguez, Richard. *Hunger of Memory: The Education of Richard Rodriguez*. Boston: Godine, 1982.

Ross, Andrew. *No Respect: Intellectuals and Popular Culture*. New York: Routledge, 1989.

Said, Edward W. *Representations of the Intellectual: The 1993 Reith Lectures*. New York: Pantheon, 1994.

Saldívar, José David. *The Dialectics of Our America: Genealogy, Cultural Critique, and Literary History*. Durham, NC: Duke UP, 1991.

Saldívar, Ramón. "Border Subjects and Transnational Sites: Américo Paredes's *The Hammon and the Beans and Other Stories*." *Subjects and Citizens: Nation,*

Race, and Gender from Oroonoko to Anita Hill. Ed. Michael Moon and Cathy Davidson. Durham, NC: Duke UP, 1995. 373-94.

———. "The Borderlands of Culture: Américo Paredes's *George Washington Gómez* and Chicano Literature at the End of the Twentieth Century." *American Literary History* 25 (1993): 272-93.

Sauerberg, Lars Ole. *Secret Agents in Fiction: Ian Fleming, John le Carré and Len Deighton.* London: Macmillan, 1984.

Schedler, Christopher. "Inscribing Mexican-American Modernism in Américo Paredes' *George Washington Gómez.*" *Texas Studies in Literature and Language* 42 (2000): 154-76.

Soltan, Margaret. Letter. "Forum." *PMLA* 112 (1997): 1131-32.

Sommer, Doris. "Resisting the Heat: Menchú, Morrison, and Incompetent Readers." *Cultures of U.S. Imperialism.* Ed. Amy Kaplan and Donald E. Pease. Durham, NC: Duke UP, 1993. 407-32.

Stafford, David. *The Silent Game: The Real World of Imaginary Spies.* Athens: U of Georgia P, 1991.

Todorov, Tzvetan. Letter. "Forum." Trans. Martha Noel Evans. *PMLA* 112 (1997): 1121-22.

Trinh, T. Minh-ha. *Woman, Native, Other: Writing Postcoloniality and Feminism.* Bloomington: Indiana UP, 1989.

Wei, William. *The Asian American Movement.* Philadelphia: Temple UP, 1993.

Liam Corley (essay date spring 2004)

SOURCE: Corley, Liam. "'Just Another Ethnic Pol': Literary Citizenship in Chang Rae-Lee's *Native Speaker.*" *Studies in the Literary Imagination* 37, no. 1 (spring 2004): 61-81.

[*In the following essay, Corley shows how* Native Speaker *traces the role of immigrants throughout the history of the United States.*]

> It is ridiculous to set a detective story in New York City. New York City is itself a detective story.
>
> —Agatha Christie (qtd. in Wertsman)

> The political importance attaching to languages derives from their being regarded as signs of race. Nothing could be more false.
>
> —Ernest Renan, "What is a Nation?" (16)

On 6 June 1993, the *Golden Venture*, a freighter carrying nearly three hundred illegal Chinese immigrants, ran aground only a few miles away from downtown New York City. Aware that the vessel was taking on water, crew members ordered the passengers to swim ashore in the choppy, cold waters. Of the two hundred or so who complied, at least eight drowned before reaching the shore. The remaining passengers were rescued by Coast Guard cutters and subsequently arrested and imprisoned by the United States government. Major television networks provided live coverage of the rescue and arrest operations, and thousands of American citizens watched the Chinese immigrants splash to shore or be plucked from the water with gaffs and ropes.[1] Literally and figuratively, the *Golden Venture* of these hopeful emigrants was broken upon the forbidding shore of New York City, and their journey toward freedom and prosperity was interpreted to the American public through a media spectacle of abjection.

Written around the time of the *Golden Venture* and published in 1995, Chang-rae Lee's **Native Speaker** includes a version of the incident at the novel's crucial transition point. **Native Speaker** charts the rise and fall of a mayoral challenger who is racially marked as an immigrant in the turbulent New York political scene of the mid-1990s. John Kwang, a Korean American businessman and city council member, runs a permanent campaign for mayor in his attempt to become part of the political "vernacular . . . a larger public figure who was willing to speak and act outside the tight sphere of his family" (139). Kwang's challenge to the racially insular New York political establishment leads to his eventual disgrace and exile to Korea. By depicting the infiltration of Kwang's political organization and deportation of his key supporters as illegal immigrants, Lee demonstrates the powerful array of forces brought to bear against the full political enfranchisement of New Yorkers who can be constructed as both racially minoritized and foreign. However, Lee complicates this reading of Kwang by framing the story of his destruction against the anti-Bildungsroman of another Korean American, Henry Park, the narrator of the novel and corporate spy who infiltrates Kwang's campaign. The self-doubts and tensions resulting from Henry's infiltration of Kwang's political organization and concurrent attempts at rapprochement with his white American wife Lelia restate on a micro level the questions of political and social enfranchisement posed by Kwang's sabotaged campaign for mayor. The interplay of the domestic and political plotlines allows Lee to critique the dominant paradigms of racial enfranchisement in the United States and the status of "ethnic" literatures within the American publishing industry and literary canon. The book's title draws attention to Lee's self-conscious complicity in the racial marketing of his book, and the ambiguity surrounding the identity of the novel's "native speaker" (Park? Lelia? Kwang? Lee the author?) sharpens the edge of the novel's paratextual critique. Ultimately, the novel moves beyond New York and its political/publishing establishment to address the roles that immigrants have played historically in the literature and politics of the United States, a trajectory that Lee traces from the colonial era through the democratic vision of Walt Whitman and into the dystopic world of twentieth-century media culture.

The *Golden Venture* incident contributed to fears among the American populace of an "Asian invasion" facilitated by unscrupulous smugglers and international networks of organized criminal syndicates (P. Smith 2). The exceptionally harsh treatment meted out to the Chinese immigrants on the *Golden Venture* was meant to serve as a warning to aspiring immigrants around the world that they were not welcome in the United States. Most of the passengers on the *Golden Venture* were imprisoned for periods extending into years, and the last of the *Golden Venture* detainees were not released until fifty-three of them were pardoned by President Clinton in March of 1997, nearly four years after their disastrous entry into the country. The White House press secretary's comments on the occasion of the pardon give a clear summary of the reasons for their long imprisonment:

> The Administration's policy of detaining smuggled aliens has deterred smuggling by organized criminal syndicates, resulting in a sharp decrease in the number of alien smuggling vessels that have reached U.S. shores. Moreover, the newly enacted immigration bill's provisions that permit the expeditious exclusion of smuggled aliens has significantly strengthened our ability to deter alien smuggling.

While the insistent repetition of "alien" is meant to distinguish the government's policy from the reception given to legal immigrants, the treatment of the *Golden Venture* detainees is only a more extreme version of the exclusionary attitude faced by other racially marked minorities within the national culture of the United States. Lisa Lowe describes the exclusion of Asian immigrants from full participation in modern American society as the result of a

> national memory [that] haunts the conception of Asian American, persisting beyond the repeal of actual laws prohibiting Asians from citizenship and sustained by the wars in Asia, in which the Asian is always seen as an immigrant, as the "foreigner-within," even when born in the United States and the descendant of generations born here before.
>
> (5-6)

Due to the *a priori* construction of Asians as inescapably foreign within a domestic visual economy brokered by the mass media and popular culture, Asian

Americans are not fully naturalized into American national culture. Thus, the threat of detention and expulsion aimed at "smuggled aliens" can also be used against Asian Americans who threaten in some way the economic or political dominance of citizens who are visually constructed as "native." Like all citizens of non-Anglo-European descent, Asian Americans undergo a double scrutiny when attempting to enjoy the full spectrum of rights guaranteed to Americans, regardless of race. Lee invokes this experience of containment, exclusion, and potential expulsion throughout his novel.

Lee prefigures the significance of the *Golden Venture* incident to the Kwang subplot by incorporating the image of a shipwreck into the narrative fulcrum of Henry and Lelia's relationship. Separated previously by their culturally disparate responses to the death of Henry's mother and the accidental smothering of their biracial son, Henry and Lelia undergo an emotional journey of reconstruction after the death of Henry's father. This journey leads eventually to Henry's reconciliation with both Lelia and the ambivalent effects of the cultural heritage passed on to him through his familial relationships. Henry and Lelia's restored physical intimacy represents the turning point in the subplot of marital accommodation. Lee connects the scene of conjugal intimacy with the crisis of political visibility through a careful use of descriptive language that associates sex with the arrival of smuggled immigrants:

> She wanted me to push down on her harder. I couldn't, so then she turned us around and pushed down on me, the slightest grimace stealing across her face. Her body yawed above me, buoyed and restless. I held on by her flat hips, angling her and helping her to let me in. Mixed-up memories, hunger. It was like lonesome old dogs, all wags and tongues and worn eyes. This was the woman I promised to love. This is my wife.
>
> (230)

Initially, Henry is in a traditional posture of male dominance, but Lelia demands that Henry exert more leverage—more dominance—than he is capable of in order to consummate her physical pleasure and his full penetration of her body. She therefore inverts their sexual/political roles and uses the greater (social) force afforded to white bodies to facilitate Henry's sexual penetration of her body and the consummation of her pleasure. In the moment of reversal, Lelia's body is figured as a seafaring vessel, associating her with the immigrants of the *Golden Venture* and also invoking the memory of Puritan immigration. Henry is pushed down into the floor as Lelia's body "yawed above." Buoys and angling (tacking) continue the maritime imagery as Henry "help[s] her to let [him] in." The crossing of boundaries is here described as a consensual act in which the pilgrim Lelia is nonetheless a gatekeeper who must initiate a more aggressive form of hospitality in order to achieve sexual union. Lee returns to this metaphor at the novel's close when Henry and Lelia ironically agree to call Henry a "long-term guest. Permanently visiting" in Lelia's apartment (347). Lelia's contractual claim to her apartment can be understood as a legal fiction that requires her to undercut her own "natural" rights in order to live with her husband, another instance in which she must acknowledge the superior status afforded to her as a white American and the concomitant need for her to restore the historical equivalence between immigrants like her and Henry within America's political and economic worlds. The definitive shift in the novel is signaled by the transition from past tense into present. Henry declares, "This is my wife," and for the rest of the novel the use of the present tense indicates the un-fixed possibilities of narrative development, a syntactic expression of hope in contrast to the narration of past events that heretofore gave the novel its determined atmosphere of helplessness and despair.

Upon this transition, Henry and Lelia reminisce freely about their past and speculate about its effects on the course of their lives. A barrage of past events, landmarks, and cultural icons serves to illustrate the political and historical currents that have affected Henry and Lelia's sense of themselves: World War II, the Korean War, the Statue of Liberty, Ellis Island, a ferry ride, spy thriller movies, racial slurs. In a redoubling of their physical union, they make love again. Afterward, they watch the local news. The first report they watch involves the most recent in a string of cabby murders. New York cab drivers are drawn from all nations, "recently arrived Latvians and Jamaicans, Pakistanis, Hmong" (246). The cabbies are an exploited immigrant labor pool, perpetually in motion as they fulfill their instrumentality as a means of transporting white subjects from work to home, and from home to work and play. The vulnerability of these immigrants to economic violence is emphasized by the physical violence that circumscribes their lives. Linguistic barriers, a theme I will treat at some length, exacerbate the problem. Henry muses, "I wonder if the Cuban [cabby] could even beg for his life so that the killer might understand. What could he do? *Have mercy,* should be the first lesson in this city, how to say the phrase instantly in forty signs and tongues" (246, Lee's emphasis). An appeal to mercy is the most urgent lesson for immigrants to America, and tellingly, the linguistic barriers indigenous to the city require facility in "forty signs and tongues." Like the *Golden Venture* incident, Lee adapts the story of cabby

murders from readily available news sources. Since 1990, two hundred and forty-three cabbies have been murdered in New York City, and the tragedies emerge in the media as "news" whenever a sufficiently large number of murders occurs close enough together in time to constitute a "string." In addition to dramatizing the spectacular nature of violence against immigrants, the narration of the cabby murders also suggests the existence of pan-ethnic coalitions constructed by the negative force of that violence. Other instances of pan-ethnic grouping appear in *Native Speaker,* most notably the money club managed by Kwang and Hoagland's Glimmer & Co., but these groupings are also the result of economic expediency and political contingency, negative origins that Lee appears to portray as teleologically bounded by the logic of racial exclusivism.[2]

Following the cabby story is the fictionalized version of the *Golden Venture* incident, a "small freighter that runs aground" with fifty smuggled Chinese men who leap from the sides of the boat into the choppy waters. Lee's fictional Chinese immigrants face the same treatment as their historical models: "The drowned are lined up on the docks beneath canvas tarps. The ones who make it, dazed, soaked, unspeaking, are led off in a line into police vans" (246-47). The spectacle of shipwreck recapitulates the theme of immigrant experiences in America already associated with Henry and Lelia through Lee's description of their initial sexual rapprochement. At this point in the novel, the narrative tension flows from Henry and Lelia's sexual union into the rising subplot of Kwang's political demise. Henry and Lelia's restored intimacy is punctuated by the next news report, footage and interviews describing a bombing and double murder at Kwang's campaign headquarters. The refusal of John Kwang's staffers to comment in the news story on the bombing of his main office thematically repeats the cabbies' silencing and the unspeaking Chinese immigrants. Through this litany of spectacles involving the death, silencing, and imprisonment of immigrants, the private space of rapprochement in Henry's marriage becomes linked to the public crisis of John Kwang's political fortunes. This oscillation between the personal and the private, the physical and the political, is a part of a larger strategy of articulation in which Lee's novel stands in as a commentary on New York and the fate of immigrants in the no-less-violent world of fact. The competition between fact and fiction, political commentary and plot development, dramatized in Lee's narrative indicates how the novel is embedded within the literary and literal context of New York. Attention to the historical context of New York in the 1990s is needed for a fuller explication of Lee's realist and subversive technique.

De Roos, New Amsterdam, and the Permanence of Racial Struggle

In early 1994, Rudolph Giuliani took over from David Dinkins as mayor of New York City. This signal transition in New York politics ushered in "Giuliani time, not Dinkins time," a phrase reportedly chanted by New York City police officers as they assaulted Abner Louima and repeatedly sodomized him with a broken-off broomstick. According to Neil Smith, the beating of Louima, a Haitian immigrant, expressed succinctly the mood of *revanchist* New York politics in the mid-1990s: "Revanchism is in every respect the ugly cultural politics of neoliberal globalization. On different scales, it represents a response spearheaded from the standpoint of white and middle-class interests against those people who, they believe, stole their world (and their power)" (196).[3] The attack on Louima in 1997 expressed symbolically the consummation of a politics of nativism and blame that helped determine the 1993 mayoral election. Louima's tortured body gave lurid expression in a physical register to the political climate for racially constructed immigrants. "Giuliani time" thus describes both an eruption into public discourse of violence against racially marked immigrants and a particular historical moment in which a majority of New Yorkers expressed their political and racial allegiances.

Although Rudolph Giuliani is mentioned by name only once in **Native Speaker,** "Giuliani time" is an important concept in the novel's implicit world. Henry and his co-worker Jack speculate that their employer, Dennis Hoagland, treasures a signed photograph from Giuliani in his office—a sign of Hoagland's political and cultural allegiances (32). Glimmer & Co., founded by Hoagland in the 1970s, is an espionage firm that focuses on immigrant populations who threaten in some way the economic or political interests of "multinational corporations, bureaus of foreign governments, [and] individuals of resource and connection" (18). Henry eventually learns that the Immigration and Naturalization Service is the client who has hired Glimmer & Co. to infiltrate John Kwang's campaign, and the INS uses the information provided through Henry's espionage to fulfill the general pattern of immigrant containment, brutalization, and expulsion characteristic of "Giuliani time." Instead of dealing more extensively with Giuliani, Lee establishes a ruse character who functions as Giuliani's stand-in. By giving the incumbent mayor a Dutch name, "De Roos," Lee invokes New York's historical nature as a long-contested site of political and linguistic allegiances as well as the apartheid-era government of South Africa. Founded as New Amsterdam in 1626, New York has long been the most visible site of the struggle over American identity as it has been domestically and

transnationally constructed. Linguistically and ethnically diverse from its founding, the colony was held together by a common desire for profit. Conquered by the English in 1664, New York became a royal colony and grew rapidly through an influx of English settlers, but the Dutch influence persists today, making the choice of "De Roos" as a character name a subtle indicator of both the permanence of ethnic difference and the dynamic of assimilation that hides the social, economic, and political value accruing to whiteness.

Like De Roos, John Kwang makes a claim for legitimacy as the inheritor of New York's political tradition. Henry describes him as someone who didn't want to be "just another ethnic pol[itician] from the outer boroughs" (303). Instead, he would become "the living voice of the city, which must always be renewed. . . . He would stride the daises and the stages with his voice strong and clear, unafraid to speak the language like a Puritan and like a Chinaman and like every boat person in between" (304). Kwang's mark of success is his ability to give voice to the city as a native speaker. Language becomes the figure that equates both Puritans and Chinese as "boat person[s]," immigrants from other lands with equal claims upon the privileges of citizenship. Kwang's optimism in this regard runs up against the vested interests of Glimmer & Co.'s clients. Kwang sinks into a depression after the bombing at his headquarters, and he goes on a drinking binge that ends with a car wreck in which an underage illegal immigrant bar girl is killed. Henry's research revealing that John Kwang ran a Korean-style money club with hundreds of illegal immigrants is then leaked to the press, and Kwang's destruction is complete. In place of his dream of full political inclusion as mayor, Kwang is assaulted at his home by a crowd carrying banners reading "Smuggler Kwang" and "AMERICA FOR AMERICANS." One of them shouts, "We want our fucking future back" (331-32). Kwang's fate is thus the result of both his racial exclusion from full enfranchisement and the revanchist features of New York politics at the time.[4]

Yet despite his failure, Kwang's vision of New York is truer to the city than the protests of the (presumably) white Americans who want to claim it and America exclusively as their own. As a symbol for the country, New York is a site of contestation and cultural pluralism. Home of the Statue of Liberty, Ellis Island, the Empire State Building, Wall Street, Broadway, Madison Avenue, and the United Nations, New York is used as an important symbol in both the domestic and transnational imaginary construction of nation. Each of these national and international icons maintains a dual life as representative instances of material and political connections between New York and a global urban community. New York's economic success and growth in the late eighteenth and early nineteenth centuries depended upon its participation in world systems of trade, most notably as an intermediary with China. Then, as now, New York existed not solely in the domestic imagination but also as a projection of world expectations and desires. France's gift of the Statue of Liberty is a representative instance of such exchange of approbation and obligation. Although few would go as far as Ford Madox Ford, who claims in the title of his 1927 travelogue that "New York Is Not America," New York is an undeniably transitional space between the domestic and the foreign and, as such, symbolizes the hybridity of American identity through its cultural centrality within the American national consciousness.

The novel's ultimate display of revanchism at Kwang's home emphasizes the national fantasies that would deny American identity's historical and contemporary hybridity. The demonstrators' impassioned declarations of American purity ("America for Americans") enact what Homi Bhabha describes as the pedagogic function of the nation-state in contrast to the performative challenge brought by Kwang. In "DissemiNation: Time, Narrative, and the Margins of the Modern Nation," Bhabha analyzes modern concepts of the state as an affective and delimited unity, a homogeneity determined by its valorized history and symbols. Bhabha questions the primacy accorded to national narratives that exclude the presence of the marginal, countering their spurious portrait of domestic uniformity and tranquility with the agonistic tensions of the performative and the pedagogical. Because of the "powerful master discourse" of the pedagogical State that busily constructs a homogenous (and wholly imagined) national origin, migrants are excluded from the cultural discourse of national construction (306).

Bhabha ultimately asks how we can recast the formative myths (narratives) of nations in a manner that accounts for the presence of marginal peoples. As the ordering principle of the nation replaces the affective ties of kin, culture, and geography, pedagogical theorists make enunciative attempts to clarify "the other" and "the insider," much in the way that Mayor De Roos attempts to paint John Kwang as "just another ethnic pol." In the heterogeneous nation-state, dominance has been accorded to declarative and arbitrary national symbols that exclude or ignore marginal, migrant voices, which in turn leads to a despotic and imagined homogeneity. In a remarkable gloss of Ernest Renan's aphoristic claim that a "nation's existence is . . . a daily plebiscite" (19), Bhabha argues that contemporaneity and locality are more important to a nation than affective (read: temporally constructed and ultimately arbitrary) ties to an envisioned or imagined past. If we construe the construction of the nation-

state as iterative, liminal, and essentially performative in its contemporaneous construction, then "no political ideologies could claim transcendent or metaphysical authority for themselves" (299). "America for Americans" would be clearly exposed as a racist ideology of exploitation and exclusion. The Statue of Liberty could be acknowledged as oscillating in the symbolic realm between the domestic matron of unifying (and homogenizing) liberty and the immigrant as naturalized foreign gift. However, before engaging in a more detailed reading of the novel as an enactment of pedagogic and performative tensions in the narration of New York as an American zone of linguistic fluency and racial homogeneity, I want to explore how Lee uses the novel to interrogate the status of "ethnic" literatures within the American publishing industry and academic canon.

New York as the Capitol of the U.S. Publishing Industry: Lee as Native Speaker

Native Speaker was published in 1995 as the first title under a new imprint launched by the international publishing conglomerate that became Penguin Putnam. Susan Petersen, the founding editor, and four others formed Riverhead Books with "the goal of publishing quality books in hardcover and then in trade paperback—both fiction and nonfiction, including significant religious and spiritual titles—that would open readers up to new ideas and points of view."[5] Riverhead Books was formed, then, in response to the economic imperative to incorporate potentially subaltern multicultural aesthetic and spiritual productions into the dominant national economy of entertainment commodities. Part of the salability of Riverhead's offerings required a grounding of "new ideas and points of view" in the recognizably other bodies of racially constructed minorities. Lee's ***Native Speaker*** played a significant role in the success of the Riverhead imprint and, consequently, in the promulgation of its particular ideology of multiculturalism, which required the commodification of minority subjects as aesthetic exemplars. Another early commercial success was James McBride's *The Color of Water,* "a poignant memoir" that relates how a Jewish woman raised her twelve mixed-race children in predominantly black neighborhoods before seeing all of them through college. In addition to Kathleen Norris's books on monastic Christianity, Riverhead's religious offerings emphasize Asian spirituality, including two books by the Dalai Lama and Thich Nhat Hanh's *Living Buddha, Living Christ.* However, Riverhead's most successful hardcover offering to date is Suze Orman's *The Courage to be Rich.* The title and cover of the book, which features a large color photograph of a blonde-haired, white, smiling Orman, suggest again the publisher's priorities and the financial grounds for its promulgation of this particular brand of editorial difference.

Given *Native Speaker*'s seminal role in Riverhead Books's establishment and in Chang-rae Lee's writing career, the marketing strategies engaged to bring about this success merit close attention. How does the literary "immigrant" fare in the publishing—and, arguably, the cultural—capitol of the United States? The cover of the book features three images of recognizably Asian subjects. The front cover contains a montage in which the mouth of a two-toned, gray-and-black image of an almost featureless and indistinct adult Asian male face is overlaid with a small photograph of an Asian child dressed in festive cowboy attire. The mixture of images suggests both the dynamics of assimilation and the effects of a childhood spent immersed in American culture on the tendency of an adult Asian American toward speech or silence. The image montage also suggests how the death of Mitt, Henry and Lelia's biracial child, has affected Henry in his relationship with Lelia. The book's back cover is almost completely covered with a black-and-white portrait of a debonair-looking Chang-rae Lee, clad in a stylish turtleneck and sweater ensemble, his hair rakishly tousled. His mouth is closed, and his eyes look off into the distance. The effect of the portrait is to convey an impression of Lee as a youthful (he was twenty-eight at the time of the portrait) and suave standard-bearer of a distinctly Asian American literary tradition. The white turtleneck peeping up from the dark-toned sweater provides the necessary element of contrast in the photograph: whiteness held close to the skin, yet obviously distinct. The mirroring effect of the images, front and back, emphasizes the consonance between Lee and the novel's Korean American characters. The prominence of Asian faces on the cover further serves as a guarantee of the "difference" in the contents—visual evidence that the novel will contain "new ideas" from a "new point of view."

The book's title also contains a dual signification in that it refers both to the linguistic facility of John Kwang the character and the luminous prose of Chang-rae Lee the author. Kwang's tragedy lies in the fact that his English fluency cannot erase in Mayor de Roos and the INS's eyes—and ultimately in the eyes of the mob that assails him—the interpretation that his face connotes foreignness, not nativity. Likewise, Lee's lyrical writing and mastery of craft take a back seat to the predictable marketing of the book as "Asian American" fiction, treating customary themes of immigration, "biculturalism, racial conflict, generational conflict, and resistance to U.S. hegemony" (R. Lee 107). However, following Dorinne Kondo's notions of complicitous critique, Lee's title and choice of genre can also be seen as performing an opposition which is "both contestatory and complicit and yet still constitute[s] a subversion that matters" (11). Kondo distinguishes between western forms of orientalism, autoexoticisms by Asian subjects, and counter-orientalisms that subvert western modes of apprehending discursively produced Asian identities. The blurred lines of significance in the different uses of stereotypes define what is potentially a very muddy project: the differentiation of subversions that succeed from those that fail. Lee's commodification as an author within the publishing industry's code of orientalism does not, in this view, eliminate the contestatory value that may result from the counter-orientalisms deployed in his text, even as certain autoexoticisms within the text insure that *Native Speaker* is read as a novel with a commodifiable difference. Although Lee's sea passage into print occurs at a price, the characters in the text remain as evidence of a repressed reality within the national culture.

Lee has stated in interviews that, while "he does not define himself as an Asian-American writer, he acknowledges that he has used the Asian-American experience for his inspiration so far" ("Chang-rae Lee"). *Native Speaker* enunciates this tension in its choice of genre and its sustained engagement with Walt Whitman's poem, "The Sleepers," from which the novel's epigraph is taken. *Native Speaker* can be characterized as a spy/thriller novel, described by many reviewers as a "page-turner"—a standard term of praise in this genre.[6] In contrast to immigrant literature, which is often read as following the pattern of Bildungsroman, Lee's novel moves from unity to dissolution in the Kwang subplot, the portion of the novel in which the espionage genre is prevalent. Lee maintains the tension in this plot through the clever construction of the novel's audience as white and, therefore, invested in the exclusion of Asian Americans from full participation in American national culture because they are visibly "foreign" and not "native." To the degree the espionage plot engages the reader, the novel interpellates its audience into the subject position of the INS agents who hire Glimmer & Co. to investigate Kwang's campaign (R. Lee, in conversation). The assumption that Kwang has something to hide, that his success in the New York political scene masks some dirty secret that makes him a threat to the city's tranquility, reveals both reader and revanchist government agents as invested in constructions of Asian Americans as ineradicably foreign and hence a threat to the tranquility of American society. In fact, the novel is framed by a confessional second-person narrative in which Henry Park addresses the reader as the target of his infiltration: "I won't speak untruths to you . . . I make do with on-hand materials, what I can chip out of you, your natural ore. Then I fuel the fire of your most secret vanity" (7). "You" in this case, and in the asides throughout the novel, is not primarily the immigrant subject to whom Henry would normally be assigned by Glimmer & Co. Instead, it is the representative white American who constructs his or her national identity as one that excludes racially differentiated immigrants, whose "natural ore" is a hermeneutic of suspicion toward political or social accomplishment when unaccompanied by a white face. It is this discursively produced subject that Park targets in his narrative.

Lee performs here the same inversion charged against Henry Park by his estranged wife—that of being a "genre bug" (5). In the act of refusing to conform to expectations of commodifiably multicultural Asian American writers who are expected to write autobiographies or tortured tales of assimilation, Lee presents his spy anti-hero as the "most prodigal and mundane of historians" churning out "remote, unauthorized biographies" (18). Henry is here figured as a stand-in for the writers of biographical and autobiographical Asian American works that can be commodified as "simple" immigrant literature. This counter-orientalist maneuver contends that the role of a writer in the employ of the late capitalist state is that of a hack, alienated from his subject material and constrained to produce the portrait already determined by those who commission the investigation. As the commodifiable Asian American writer, Henry Park expresses his ambivalent relationship to the repressive work of Glimmer & Co. through an uneasy acquiescence to a profession that seems to suit him perfectly and yet is used against him and others with whom he comes to identify, most notably the psychiatrist Emile Luzan and John Kwang himself. Henry's eventual break with Glimmer & Co. and his refusal to reveal the most damning evidence against John Kwang represent his limited agency in a profession that can mean death to leave. Likewise, Lee's attempt to "turn" from the spectacle of Asian immigrant exploitation and its eventual literary recuperation within late capitalism does not succeed in allowing him to fully "extricate himself" from the "confused, the past-reading" (vii), that constructs him as a literary outsider regardless of his linguistic fluency. To fully understand, however, Lee's engagement with the American literary tradition, we must look more carefully at the novel's epigraph, from which the quotations expressing Lee's authorial strategy in the previous sentence are taken.

Chang-rae Lee grew up in New York City, and that may be reason enough for his choice of setting. However, New York's status as the capitol of the United States publishing industry inflects that choice in a way that Lee's invocation of "Walt Whitman, a kosmos, of Manhattan the son" makes explicit. Walt Whitman, poet of America, boldly claimed a universal perspective that subsumed all differences within its capacious vision. Whitman was also a rough, a dandy, a man of the city. Whitman's literary star has brought him from the margins of American literary studies to the center. Throughout *Native Speaker,* Lee performs an equivalent claim to universality that depends, as Whitman's did, upon a narcissistic focus on the embodied self as the representative figure of humanity. Instead of escaping from the particularity of a "wide immigrant face" (343), Lee focuses upon it and the contradictions it presents to an American national culture that has repressed knowledge of its hybridity and the racially based categories subsumed within the concept of abstract citizenship. Through his narrative, Lee revises Whitman's heritage of representative Americanness to include the immigrant experience as central.

The epigraph, taken from the fourth poem in "The Sleepers," is worth considering as a whole and in context to better understand how Lee accomplishes this revision: "I turn but do not extricate myself, / Confused, a past-reading, another, / but with darkness yet" (546). The spectacle from which Whitman turns here is a shipwreck. The image of a "beautiful gigantic swimmer swimming naked through the eddies of the sea" (545) and battered to death by the waves against the rocks on the shore in the third poem of the cycle has been transformed in the fourth poem into the more representative tragedy of a shipwreck. The poet can "hear the howls of dismay" (546) as the passengers are cast into the waters, but he is powerless "to aid with [his] wringing fingers." Though he turns away from this horrific scene of death and destruction, he is unable to escape it. In the morning, the poet is drawn back to the shore and helps to "pick up the dead and lay them in rows in a barn."

Lee charges this poetic scene with multiple meanings through his numerous visual and conceptual citations of it in *Native Speaker.* The starting point for any explication of the poem's meaning within *Native Speaker* is the spectacle with which this paper began: the wreck of the *Golden Venture* as it is fictionalized in the novel. Even as John Kwang claims a continuity with the Puritans as "boat people," so is the traumatic experience of immigration into a nativist and exclusionary society here associated with Whitman's vision of a shipwreck, a searing, inescapable vision. The immigration tragedy Henry views on television ends when "the drowned are lined up on the dock beneath canvas tarps" (246-47). Order is imposed on both Whitman's and Lee's spectacles of suffering by the organization of the dead into uniform spaces. Within the novel, the comparison of the *Golden Venture* scene to Whitman's poem serves to link the spectacle of immigration to universal experiences of human suffering such as those Whitman explores in "The Sleepers."[7] For Henry, this scene also links his nautically described rapprochement with his wife to John Kwang's political destruction. As an epigraph, the passage also serves to explain how Lee, who has "turn[ed] away" from a self-definition of Asian American that he deems limiting, cannot extricate himself from the market pressures that force him to collaborate in his own commodification as an Asian American author. Nonetheless, Lee's "wringing fingers" create a story of considerable power and beauty.

In spite of the double-bind experienced by both Kwang and Lee—of being fluent and acculturated yet also constructed as foreign and other—Lee is able to contest the interpellation of racially marked immigrant subjects as always already excluded from the category of "American" by making the more controversial claim that terrorizing and exploiting immigrants is quintessentially American:

> My ugly immigrant's truth . . . is that I have exploited my own, and those others who can be exploited. This forever is my burden to bear. But I and my kind possess another dimension. We will learn every lesson of accent and idiom, we will dismantle every last pretense and practice you hold. . . . This is your own history. We are your most perilous and dutiful brethren, the song of our hearts at once furious and sad. For only you could grant me these lyrical modes. I call them back to you. Here is the sole talent I ever dared nurture. Here is all of my American education.
>
> (319-20)

Here, Henry returns to the second-person form of address in order to more clearly label and indict his audience. Henry's "ugly immigrant truth" is America's, and his memoir of complicity with John Kwang's investigation and destruction is "your own history," the legacy of immigrant and racial minority scapegoating that is instantiated in "Giuliani time." The "lyrical modes" of Lee's novel participate in and subvert the circulation of orientalist marginalizations of Asian American writers as "ethnic authors" cut off from the mainstream of American literary creation in much the same way that Henry Park participates in and resists the destruction of John Kwang. Or, in the words of Walt Whitman at the end of the seventh movement of "The Sleepers," "the diverse shall be no less diverse, but they shall flow and unite—they unite now" (549).

The diverse facets of American national culture that flow and unite in Whitman's poem are no less diverse for being ignored by homogenizing constructions of national identity that achieve unity through the erasure in popular memory of historically vibrant instances of diversity and exchange. In this vein, Traise Yamamoto has argued that "the private contains all things that exceed normative categories. To bring these things into public culture affects the construction of the national imaginary." Earlier in my discussion of revanchist New York politics and the repression of material history it entailed, I alluded to the question of performative American identities and how they reveal in the private realm historical truths that exceed the normative categories of public culture. It is to this mode of theoretical explication that I wish to return in conclusion as a means of illustrating Lee's argument in *Native Speaker* that American history is repressed history.

The average citizen knows very little about American history, and this ignorance is perpetuated largely because the past exists for us only as it can be strategically deployed in contemporary arguments in which it is useful to "claim transcendent or metaphysical authority" (Bhabha 299). When Lelia complains that the "average white girl has no mystery any more, if she ever did. Literally nothing to her name," Henry correctly replies, "There's always a mystery. . . . You just have to know where to look" (10). Mystery, as Lee's choice of genre emphasizes, has been displaced in American national culture onto racialized others who can then be constructed as spectacle, interrogated as foreign, and treated like aliens.[8] If, in contrast to the orientalist assumption that Lee invites by his choice of genre, the mystery at the heart of *Native Speaker* is not the legitimacy of John Kwang's campaign for mayor, then where else might we look for the target of Lee's investigation? Rejecting the standard immigrant's tale in which interracial marriage represents the plot's consummation, Lee instead begins *Native Speaker* with the rupture of Henry and Lelia's relationship, displacing the story of their romance into the narrative past. More private history is also encapsulated in Mitt, the fruit of their relationship, and the details of his life and death are slowly and tantalizingly revealed through hints and indirections. The exploration of Henry, Lelia, and Mitt's mysterious and repressed past together provides most of the narrative tension in the first portion of the novel; the suspenseful unraveling of their private history thus stands in for the pressing critical interrogation of the originary American family unit they corporately represent. In such an interrogation, the symbolic role Lelia plays as a "pure" American native speaker can be analyzed in a manner that reveals her repressed cultural and racial heterogeneity.

Lelia's complaint about mystery and white identity is prompted by Henry's ethnographic interpretation of her surname. Her given name, however, receives less scrutiny, despite Henry's assurance that "there's always a mystery." In this case, a second look at the first syllable of Lelia's awkward given name suggests that Lee accomplishes more in this name choice than merely a parodic redoubling of consonants that are stereotypically difficult for many non-native English speakers to pronounce. Encoded in Lelia's name is a syllabic evocation of the author's name, an association also suggested by Lelia's aspiration to be a writer, her vocation of teacher, and the beauty of her linguistic ability, all characteristics shared by Chang-rae Lee. But "Lee" is only part of Lelia's mysterious derivation and identity. Tim Engles's discussion of Lelia as the novel's symbol of doxic whiteness emphasizes her role in Henry's refashioning of himself according to white middle-class norms. According to Engles's reading of the novel, Henry "resolve[s] his identity crisis by unwittingly casting himself as a white manque" (45). Engles's detailed analysis of Henry and Lelia's interactions highlights the ways in which Henry comes to accept many of Lelia's judgments about him as encapsulated in the list she gives him at the beginning of the novel: "visions of me in the whitest raw light" (1). Engles chooses to focus his reading of the novel on the "whiteness" of the light cast upon Henry throughout the book, as though Lelia represented a pure space of white, middle-class American identity—as if, in fact, there were such a thing at all. Although Engles's interpretation is compelling to a point, he fails to account for the significant evidence throughout the novel that the most careful performer of American identity, in pursuit of the perfection that June Dwyer describes as the "greenhorn desire to fit in" (78), is Lelia herself. Far from fulfilling the role of "standard bearer" (12) she claims for herself at the beginning of the novel, Lelia, as Henry observes, succeeds by "executing the language" (10), a figure of speech that associates both death and formality with her verbal abilities.

At the point when Henry capitulates to Lelia's demand that he abandon his Korean reserve and speak openly about his fears for himself and Kwang, Lelia begins to exhibit signs of cultural and racial heterogeneity. When Henry and Lelia clean out Henry's boyhood home during the last stage of their journey toward rapprochement, surrounded by pictures and mementos of Henry's Korean family and past, Lelia expresses her frustration at the effects of Henry's espionage work on their relationship. Swinging her arms in emphasis, Lelia "accidentally knocked over the rest of her coffee onto the white carpet rug" (226). As the brown stain spreads over the rug, "suddenly she looked exhausted, sodden in the face. 'As long as you don't get hurt, I won't care. . . . I won't say a word to you. I won't even think it'" (226). The staining of the white carpet

becomes an image of Lelia's transformation as the coffee-soaked carpet is refigured in Lelia's "sodden" face. At this point, Henry reveals the name of his mark: John Kwang. "I could see her turning the words inside her head. . . . She didn't say anything, though, and I could see that she was trying her very best to stay quiet" (227). Henry recognizes her behavior as reflective of his own as a Korean man, the reserve Lelia has decried up to this point in the novel: "Ten years with me and now she was the one with the ready method" (277). Finally, "in a voice [he] hardly recognize[s]," Lelia surrenders, both to Henry's will as her husband and to his manner of speaking: "You just say what you want. Please say what you want" (277). By the end of the novel, Lelia is depicted as "horsing with the language to show [her students] that it's fine to mess it all up" (349). The novel ends with Lelia's vaunted linguistic facility challenged by the diversity acknowledged as belonging to the city. Dismissing her students by name at the end of the day, "she calls out each one as best as she can, taking care of every last pitch and accent, and I hear her speak a dozen lovely and native languages, calling all the difficult names of who we are" (349). In a "difficult" sea voyage in which she must take "care of every last pitch," Lelia finally discovers who "we" really are.

For Chang-rae Lee, who toyed at an early age with changing his own first name to something more typically American, like "Tom" or "Chuck," foreign names are no barrier to an American identity. As an authorial calling card, "Chang-rae" indicates a much different trajectory of social incorporation than "Amy," "Frank," or "Maxine." June Dwyer, among many reviewers of **Native Speaker,** recognizes the importance of language in the novel's schema and denouement, but the significance of John Kwang's becoming "a part of the vernacular" lies in his ability, for as long as it lasts, to bring his Korean identity along with him (139). Jack Kalantzakos, Henry's mentor in surveillance, describes the constitutive function of Kwang's speech this way: "'He is in the language now. The buildings and streets there are written with him. In this sense he exists'" (169). Yet this movement from existence in the material world to constitution in language reveals troubling contradictions within America's national culture. Kwang's existence in language "helplessly heads end on" (vii) into his construction within the visual economies of race in the United States. The novel's conclusion does not, as Dwyer claims, ask us to "listen to immigrants' incorrect but highly expressive English" (82). It points out instead in a dual movement that *native speakers,* like Lelia, cannot equate their whiteness with ownership of the language unless they repress the material histories of *other native speakers,* like John Kwang. Being Korean and being a *native speaker* embodies a contradiction that requires the deconstruction of white English speakers as native. Lee does this by including Henry in Lelia's work at the end of the novel and recording the "wonder in [the immigrant children's] looks as they check again that my voice moves in time with my mouth, truly belongs to my face" (349). Henry challenges prevailing constructions of American identity in the same way Chang-rae Lee does in choosing to allow his book to be marketed with a picture of himself alongside the polysemic title *Native Speaker.*

The claim that American identities are performative through language carries many consequences for contemporary debates within Asian American cultural studies about the status of Asian Americans within American national culture. Imperatives to "claim the language" and thereby claim a place within the American polity, which have impelled the enterprise of Asian American cultural nationalism, are valuable and yet incomplete. More recent emphases on the diasporic components of Asian American identity, in which private memory is used to link public contradictions with material histories of imperialism, hybridity, and exploitation, enable a broader venue for critiques of American national culture as it has been constituted through repressed transnational exchanges. Vital, however, to both enterprises is the public recuperation of what Chang-rae Lee calls America's "ugly immigrant's truth": the material success and social structuring of the United States that has depended from its earliest days upon the exploitation and alien/nation of racially marked others. From Peter Minuit's founding of New Amsterdam on the backs of swindled Native Americans to the harsh treatment of immigrants such as those smuggled in the *Golden Venture,* "boat people" have always been a part of the American vernacular.

In the first movement of "The Sleepers," Walt Whitman calls out what he views as the constitutive elements of American identity:

> I am the actor, the actress, the voter, the politician, The emigrant and the exile, the criminal that stood in the box, He who has been famous and he who shall be famous after to-day, The stammerer, the well-form'd person, the wasted or feeble person.
>
> (544)

By means of the universal "I," Whitman brings the concepts of performance and political involvement into apposition with the categories of immigrant, exile, and criminal. He associates fame with speech and the body in a shrewd evocation of the marginality that defines the performative center stage of American

identity. Homi Bhabha describes how "minority discourse . . . contests genealogies of 'origin' that lead to claims for cultural supremacy and historical priority" (307). In the place of definitions of American society or literary canon that argue for the primacy and centrality of doxically white Americans, "minority discourse acknowledges the status of national culture—and the people—as a contentious, performative space." The actor and the politician, the politician and the emigrant, the emigrant and the criminal—all combine in Chang-rae Lee's evocation of the "contentious, performative space" in American literary and political citizenship.

Notes

1. See Paul Smith, *Chinese Migrant Trafficking* 1-4, for a complete description of the *Golden Venture* incident, including responses in national media.

2. Caroline Rody further discusses Lee's ambivalent portrayal of interethnic collaboration in a paper given at the 2004 Modern Language Association convention entitled, "The Interethnic Imagination in Contemporary Asian American Fiction." Rody associates interethnic coalitions in *Native Speaker* with similar instances of interethnic imagination in works by, among others, Gish Jen and Karen Tei Yamashita, and suggests that such groupings may grow in importance as contemporary Asian American writers grapple with the distinctive future of Asian America within an increasingly multicultural United States.

3. N. Smith uses *revanche,* the French word for *revenge,* to reference an 1890s French movement of reactionary populists known as the *Ligue des Patriotes.* These revanchists "mixed militarism and moralism with claims about public order on the streets as they flailed around for enemies" (185).

4. Lee is careful not to paint Kwang as an unequivocal victim of New York racism. The closing pages of the book reveal that the trigger event for Kwang's decline, the bombing and deaths at his headquarters, is ordered by Kwang himself in a fit of rage when he learns that his closest associate—another Glimmer & Co. operative—has been collecting evidence against him. While Kwang's personal failings of rage, alcoholism, and philandering played a role in his political destruction, they would not have had such a prominent effect if the INS had not hired Glimmer & Co. to infiltrate his campaign. In his failings, Kwang is not unlike many of New York's and the United States' most successful political leaders.

5. All quotations regarding Riverhead Books's history and editorial policies are taken from the Penguin Putnam website, www.penguinputnam.com.

6. Taken from editorial endorsements included in the trade paperback edition.

7. Universality and Whitman is an extremely vexed subject in Whitman scholarship. While the suspect foundation of Whitman's use of himself as a representative figure is rightly interrogated by many scholars, Lee is not here invoking Whitman as an example of how an all-seeing eye colonizes the subjects it surveys. Likewise, Whitman's role in my argument about *Native Speaker* and literary citizenship should not be construed as casting Whitman into the role of unproblematic touchstone of American literature and identity. This is, however, very nearly the way that Lee uses Whitman, but only, I think, in order to link Whitman to a revised understanding of American identity as inclusive of Asian American immigrants.

8. Another, more poignant, symbolic evocation of this theme is the death of Mitt, Henry and Lelia's biracial son, who is crushed to death by his white neighbors in a game of dog pile. Since the game occurs during Mitt's birthday party, his nativity is highlighted. Mitt is the physical representation of American hybridity that the collective weight of (perhaps) unthinking White America definitively removes. This crushing moment can also be contrasted with Lelia's desire to push down harder on Henry during their initial sexual rapprochement.

Works Cited

Bhabha, Homi K. "DissemiNation: Time, Narrative, and the Margins of the Modern Nation." *Nation and Narration.* London: Routledge, 1993. 291-322.

"Chang-rae Lee, Writer on the Rise, Inspired by Questions of Belonging." Reuters News Service. 1 Nov. 2000.

Dwyer, June. "Speaking and Listening: The Immigrant as Spy Who Comes in from the Cold." *The Immigrant Experience in North American Literature: Carving Out a Niche,* Ed. Katherine B. Payant and Toby Rose. Westport, CT: Greenwood P, 1999.

Engles, Tim. "'Visions of Me in the Whitest Raw Light': Assimilation and Doxic Whiteness in Chang-rae Lee's *Native Speaker." Hitting Critical Mass* 4.2 (1997): 27-48.

Ford, Ford Madox. *New York Is Not America.* London: Duckworth, 1927.

Kondo, Dorinne. *About Face: Performing Race in Fashion and Theater.* New York: Routledge, 1997.

Lee, Chang-rae. *Native Speaker.* New York: Riverhead Books, 1995.

Lee, Rachel C. *The Americas of Asian American Literature: Gendered Fictions of Nation and Transnation.* Princeton: Princeton UP, 1999.

————. Personal interview. 2 November 2000.

Lowe, Lisa. *Immigrant Acts: On Asian American Cultural Politics.* Durham: Duke UP, 1996.

Renan, Ernest. "What is a Nation?" *Nation and Narration.* London: Routledge, 1993. 8-22.

Rody, Caroline. "The Interethnic Imagination of Contemporary Asian American Fiction." "The Future of Asian American Literary Studies" panel. MLA Convention, Grand Hyatt Hotel, San Diego, CA, 29 Dec. 2003.

Smith, Neil. "Which New Urbanism? New York City and the Revanchist 1990s." *The Urban Moment: Cosmopolitan Essays on the Late-20th-Century City.* Ed. Robert A. Beauregard and Sophie Body-Gendrot. Urban Affairs Annual Reviews 49. Thousand Oaks, CA: Sage P, 1999. 185-208.

Smith, Paul J. "Chinese Migrant Trafficking: A Global Challenge." *Human Smuggling: Chinese Migrant Trafficking and the Challenge to America's Immigration Tradition.* Ed. Paul J. Smith. Significant Issues Series 19.2. Washington, DC: Center for Strategic and International Studies, 1997. 1-22.

Wertsman, Vladimir F. ed. *New York, the City in More Than 500 Memorable Quotations.* Lanham, MD: Scarecrow P, 1997. 29.

White House press statement. 14 Feb. 1997.

Whitman, Walt. *Leaves of Grass.* 1891-92 edition. Ed. John Hollander. The Library of America. New York: Vintage, 1992.

Yamamoto, Traise. Personal interview. 7 December 2000.

Jane Yoo (review date 2005)

SOURCE: Yoo, Jane. "Cultural Alienation and the Asian American: Chang-rae Lee, Native Speaker." *Asian American Policy Review* 14 (2005): 57-9.

[*In this review, Yoo declares that although* Native Speaker *excels in revealing how generations of immigrants assimilate into U.S. culture, the novel fails to present an accurate depiction of the Korean American experience.*]

> "I turn but do not extricate myself, Confused, a past-reading, another, but with darkness yet."
>
> —Walt Whitman

Chang-rae Lee's epigraph from Whitman serves as a fitting introduction to his work [*Native Speaker*], a story that centers around a second-generation Korean

American searching to define himself and elucidate the relationships in his professional and private life. As the novel begins, Chang-rae Lee introduces us to Henry Park, the son of Korean immigrants and husband of Lelia, a fiery New England Caucasian woman. In the opening scene, Henry's wife hands him a list just as she is about to board a plane to take a trip to the Mediterranean. Although Henry is aware that his marriage is encountering difficulties, he is surprised to see the list containing phrases such as "You are surreptitious/B+ student of life/emotional alien/Yellow peril: neo-America/stranger/traitor." Henry, who cannot resist the idea of considering the list as a cheap parting shot, is left to ponder the implications of Lelia's stinging words and thus brings the reader closer into his peculiar and rather unconventional life.

We quickly learn that Henry does not hold the typical 9-to-5 job bagging groceries or working in the corner office. He is a spy for Glimmer and Associates, a private intelligence agency specializing in gathering information on non-white subjects for its clients. As Henry's adroit ability to remain tight-lipped and expressionless has engendered him much success in his career, it has created many problems for him at home. His past includes the recent loss of seven-year-old son Mitt, who died while being suffocated under a pile of neighborhood White children. Henry's detachment from his son's death has made Lelia retreat from her husband and struggle to understand his cold-hearted demeanor.

As Henry begins to contemplate his own reaction and reconsider who he is, his work brings him to shadow New York City councilman, John Kwang, a Korean American contender for New York's mayoral seat and the favorite son of thousands of immigrant voters in his home district of Queens. Henry's professional demeanor soon fades as he views Kwang as a father figure and becomes personally involved in the case.

In moving between the past and the present through flashbacks, Chang-rae Lee brings to bear the troubling relationships that Henry exhibits with his traditional Korean father and his American wife, however, there are some striking similarities in Park's interactions with his father and wife: the inability to express love and incomplete understanding of both cultures.

As a speech therapist, Lelia acts as a window for Henry to reflect on the lives of struggling immigrant laborers and their children. When two Laotian boys visit the apartment for speech therapy, Henry learns that the boys are first cousins and have fathers who run a business selling merchandise from the back of a

Ford van. As Henry listens to father and son communicating with customers in broken English, he knows all too well that the boys will soon break their association with their native language in hopes of adopting and assimilating the new language.

As a result, Lee weaves a poignant story of how assimilation occurs between generations of immigrants. While second-generation children are quick to embrace the new language and culture, parents are more reluctant to fully immerse themselves—instead choosing to hold fast to their native roots. Although Henry's father holds a college degree in engineering, his father is forced to earn a living as a grocery store owner because his difficulty with English is too great an obstacle to finding employment in a technical field. His father's hard work and success as a grocer has resulted in a nice suburban home for Henry. Although never wanting to sell fruits and vegetables for a living, his father desires a better life for his son; we feel empathy for Henry's father for making sacrifices for his only child, only to find his son all too eager to reject his Korean heritage.

Yet, ironically enough, we realize that Henry will never be a "native speaker," either from the viewpoint of his Korean roots or American upbringing. He will serve as a bridge between both worlds and continue to examine his life through the eyes of Lelia, his father, and a spy. His latter role highlights the fact that he will always be considered an outsider, despite his valiant efforts to mask reality.

In this rich tapestry, Chang-rae Lee confronts not only issues of identity but also the various aspects of the immigrant and minority experience, including the complexity of racial tensions that exist among Blacks and Koreans. The aspirations of a minority politician struggling for higher office dwindle when it is learned that Kwang has engaged in behavior that is largely unethical by American standards.

Nevertheless, the theme of espionage is difficult to apply to second-generation Korean Americans. The realities of Korean American life do not conform to that of spy Henry Park. Lee neglects to reflect on important features of Korean American culture that include socioeconomic status and hierarchy. Sprinkled with Korean phrases that appear awkwardly placed, the novel depicts an incomplete and distorted portrayal of Korean American lives. For the Korean American reader, it leaves one with the sense that we can all be characterized as traitors to our roots and that our inner tensions cannot easily be resolved. Wherein there are varying degrees and circumstances that comprise of the pressures felt by Korean Americans, this work only highlights certain facets. Chang-rae Lee's *Native Speaker,* while providing insight and reflection about broad themes engaging culture, still leaves much to be desired.

Betsy Huang (essay date October 2006)

SOURCE: Huang, Betsy. "Citizen Kwang: Chang-rae Lee's *Native Speaker* and the Politics of Consent." *Journal of Asian American Studies* 9, no. 3 (October 2006): 243-69.

[*In the essay below, Huang focuses on the subject of political representation through the character John Kwang, the Asian American politician in* Native Speaker.]

On January 28, 2003, Governor Gary Locke of Washington[1] began his Democratic response to President George W. Bush's State of the Union Address with an anecdotal history of his humble immigrant beginnings: "My grandfather came to this country from China nearly a century ago and worked as a servant. Now I serve as governor just one mile from where my grandfather worked. It took our family 100 years to travel that mile. It was a voyage we could only make in America."[2] Of note in this brief account of his family history was his effective combination of the familiar American Dream immigrant tale with the less familiar narrative of a political ascendancy. The latter is particularly alien to the macrotext of Asian American and immigrant fiction, which has been primarily concerned with cultural and generational conflicts within the domestic setting. Locke's political accomplishment is not what we've come to expect from Asian American immigrant narratives, in which the "success" of assimilation is typically measured in terms of cultural belonging or financial gains. Rather, his particular immigrant tale had culminated with his entrance into an arena in which Asian Americans have yet to make their presence felt—U.S. electoral politics.[3] Another striking aspect of Locke's speech is his claim that this is "a voyage we could only make in America"—an avowal of the Dream made all the more powerful in its utterance by someone who would have reasons to question its validity. In other words, the idea of "only in America" acquires particular incontrovertible power when it is validated by someone of political legitimacy but of ethnic or immigrant ilk—a validation that implicitly de-legitimizes contestations by those who are less "successful" and potentially neutralizes complaints lodged against the validity of the American Dream and the U.S. as a promised land for immigrants.

That Locke had been entrusted with the job of delivering the democratic response to a highly popular Republican president's State of the Union Address might have come as a surprise to some. John Mercurio of *CNN.com* saw the choice as a "curious" one, describing Locke as "an obscure, two-term executive" who was "not known as an accomplished speaker."[4] The Asian American community, however, saw the choice as a positive indication of the growing recognition, visibility, and influence of Asian American elected officials in national politics. Locke had been given the mantle of representation by the Democratic Party to speak for not just the constituency with which he was racially associated, nor the state of Washington over which he presided as Governor, but the broader demographics, interests, and views of the Democratic Party as a whole. Though brief (the role having run its course at the end of the ten-minute response), this level of spokesmanship is arguably one of the highest achieved by an Asian American in U.S. history. Locke's response also signaled an important step for Asian American politics and perhaps even an end to the common perception that Asian Americans are politically disengaged or apathetic.

The absence of Asian Americans in American political systems and institutions is reflected in literary representations of Asian immigrant and Asian American experiences. Public service and political participation have been elusive subject matters in Asian American literature, a phenomenon that seems to bear out the longstanding view of the apolitical nature of Asian immigrants and Asian Americans.[5] Gordon H. Chang has observed that "despite the highly political circumstances under which the term *Asian American* emerged in the late 1960s and despite the politicized field of academic work known as Asian American studies, the work on Asian Americans and politics has attracted relatively little attention compared with other fields of study about Asian Americans."[6] Don T. Nakanishi's study of Asian American electoral politics notes that while interest in electoral political access, representation, and influence has been on a continual increase over the recent decades, Asian American political participation remains low, largely due to the strategies of exclusion and discrimination successfully enacted by American political institutions against Asian Americans over the last century.[7] Indeed, interrogations of how American "citizenship"—in terms of its political, legal, and cultural definitions—contributes to the formation of the Asian American subject eluded Asian American literature and scholarship until Lisa Lowe's 1996 landmark study, *Immigrant Acts,*[8] spawned a spate of studies along the nation-citizenship axis from 1998 onward.[9] Until recently, Asian American fiction has largely adhered to the tried-and-true formula of family dramas that deal with issues concerning cultural conflicts and ambivalences, focusing on the effects wrought on individuals and families within the domestic sphere. Rachel Lee has noted that "reading ethnic literature in terms of the nation frequently leads to a reduction of the role of the family to that of a resistant ethnic enclave vis-à-vis dominant U.S. culture."[10] The critical scope of the literature, then, has been delimited by the twin oppositions of home vs. society and immigrant vs. U.S.-born generations—limitations symptomatic of the fact that such problems and struggles are ongoing.

It is within the context of political representation that I situate Chang-rae Lee's 1995 debut novel, *Native Speaker,* now much read and written about for the novel's incisive examinations of the instabilities and performativity of identity.[11] What has escaped critical attention is Lee's portrayal of an Asian American politician, a figure previously unseen in the Asian American literary imagination. Tracing the connections between the public and private lives of this very public figure, Lee stages the examination of the politics of ethnic identity and representation in the dynamic public theater of electoral politics, exposing the representational predicaments faced by Asian American politicians, and by ethnic politicians more generally. Lee's characterization of an Asian American elected official performs a double-layered critique of the politics of citizenship and the crisis of representation. At issue in this fictional case study is not only how Lee represents, via literary strategies, the trials and tribulations of an Asian American politician with high political ambitions, but also how *John Kwang,* the politician in question, represents—that is, speaks for and acts on behalf of—his actual and potential constituencies. *Native Speaker* interrogates the expectations that American citizenship explicitly and implicitly imposes on its immigrant and ethnic constituents, and Lee's figuration of Kwang uncovers the possibilities and limitations of participatory citizenship for ethnic subjects. As William Boelhower has noted, "the issue of ethnicity in the United States inevitably surfaces at the national level whenever the ideology of the American Dream or of Americanism *tout court* malfunctions or hyperfunctions or simply comes in for such routine scrutiny as the presidential elections."[12] This drama of an immigrant who climbs not the socio-economic but the political ladder reveals the relentless circumscription of minority voices, even as the nation extols the assertion of voice as an essential form of participatory citizenship.

My aim in this paper is to show the ways in which Lee's portrayal of John Kwang and his brief political career exposes the ideological and material imperatives of U.S. citizenship for its ethnic and immigrant

subjects, and the kind of cultural consent, to use David Leiwei Li's term, it uncompromisingly demands of them.[13] Kwang's political rise and fall aptly dramatizes Li's notion of Asian abjection, a state concomitant with Asian Americans' designation as the nation's "model minority." "Model minority" discourse, authored by the Anglo-dominated institutions of the dominant culture and often carefully cultivated by the minority group that bears the designation, is a discourse of control that delineates in clear terms acceptable and unacceptable types of ethnics—terms that the "model minorities" in question often internalize and strive to fulfill. Li calls it "a classificatory wonder of the dominant social strategy [that] detaches Asians from their association with other racial 'minorities' by hailing them as a white-appointed 'model,' while it distinguishes them from the unmarked 'true' nationals by calling Asians their 'minor.'"[14] In the political arena, the growing number of Asian American public officials year after year, along with the rising level of public offices held, indicates an increase in Asian American political participation as well as their acceptance by the political mainstream. But such political participation, in Li's view, also constitutes a kind of Asian American inclusion that may be "a strategy of the dominant culture to maintain its continuing 'positional superiority' by reforming alliances and managing ethnic consent."[15] Such forms of inclusion, Li suggests, risk engendering not a constitutive Asian American subject but an "abject," an entity "neither radical enough for institutional enjoinment . . . nor competent enough to enjoy the subject status of citizens in a registered and recognized participation of American democracy."[16] Li elaborates further on this point:

> On the one hand, it works as a form of sanctioned articulation—Asian Americans are to speak in the official voice of the nation. On the other hand, it works as a form of substituted articulation—Asian Americans are to be spoken for by a delegated dominant authority. In both instances, however, abjection is a form of denied Asian American articulation that serves to immobilize the race- and culture-specific national embodiment of the Asian American.[17]

Asian American elected officials, and ethnic American officials more generally, are perpetually confronted by the potential for such abjection. As Lowe observes, "If the notion of citizenship proposes the state as the unified body in which all subjects are granted membership, it simultaneously asks that individual differences (of race, ethnicity, class, gender, and locality) be subordinated to the general will of the collective polity."[18] The subordination, Lowe explains, is a transparent and accepted aspect of American democracy because "it is under its ideology of pluralism that the notion of 'equal citizenship' and of the subordination of private interests to the will of the majority in exchange for political representation make the most sense."[19] Such idealized notions of democracy, when invoked, are powerful enough for the state to impose its "requirement for uniformity" and secure the consent of subjects who wish to become citizens or to fully enjoy the rights and privileges of U.S. citizenship. In other words, ideological consent is a prerequisite for an ethnic minority's political candidacy and electability, particularly for public offices on state and federal levels. Yet, while Lee's John Kwang—a gifted speaker whose politics of inclusion calls to mind the likes of Illinois Senator Barack Obama and Antonio Villaraigosa, the Latino mayor of Los Angeles—speaks the language of cultural consent beautifully, his eventual failure to rise higher on the political ladder suggests that consent may be, in reality, a set of limitations cloaked in the rhetoric of possibilities. Thus, *Native Speaker* reveals the ways in which ideological, cultural, and political consent disguise the strict parameters marked by the dominant culture, and produce "Asian abjection" rather than speaking Asian American subjects.

Lee explores the tropes of ideological consent and voiceless abjection in *Native Speaker* via the relationships between the novel's three principal male characters, John Kwang, Henry Park, and Henry's father. Henry, from whose perspective *Native Speaker* is narrated, is a private investigator assigned to trail and gather information on Kwang, a New York City councilman with his sights set on the mayorship. Henry is beset with an inarticulateness that he prefers to characterize as a choice not to speak. He attributes his lifelong struggle with his voice—or lack thereof—to what he perceives to be his immigrant father's difficulties with the English language and strict adherence to Korean cultural customs. Henry's father is stubbornly taciturn, a manner interpreted by his son as essentially Korean and, by implication, un-American. Against American cultural standards, to which Henry subscribes uncritically, his father's reticence and hermetic lifestyle appear as a lamentable inability to assimilate. Henry interprets the reticence as a form of self-silencing; he recalls his father's exhortation to keep their grievances to themselves: "Nobody give two damn about your problem or pain. You just take care yourself. Keep it quiet" (182). Yet, Henry has inherited, as his wife Lelia theorizes, the same unwillingness to make use of his voice. A self-proclaimed celebrator of "every order of silence borne of the tongue and the heart and the mind" (171), he has been accused by Lelia to be "surreptitious" and an "emotional alien" (5).

Situated against these two figures of abjection, John Kwang immediately strikes the reader as a different kind of Asian American, as well as a different kind of *American*. He is a clear foil to Henry's father, who, in many ways, typifies the stock "old-world" parent figures that have populated countless immigrant narratives. While Henry's father never ventures far from the safe confines of his home and his grocery stores, Kwang has stepped boldly into the public arena. In Henry's eyes, Kwang is the very image of successful assimilation, thriving in cultural spaces where his father would never dare to tread. Newly elected to the city council in New York City, Kwang is the first Asian American to hold such an office. Henry's initial descriptions of Kwang barely conceal his admiration for the rising politician. He remarks on Kwang's "beautiful, almost formal English" (23) and on his impressive ability to be "effortlessly Korean" and "effortlessly American" (238) at the same time. In his eyes, Kwang is a combination of a model minority and a self-made man, the very embodiment of the American Dream: "He had a JD-MBA from Fordham. He was a self-made millionaire. The pundits spoke of his integrity, his intelligence. His party was pressuring him for the mayoral race. He looked impressive on television. Handsome, irreproachable. Silver around the edges. A little unbeatable" (23). If Henry's father is a model of repudiation against the dominant culture's demand for cultural consent, then Kwang has wholeheartedly embraced all that Henry's father has resisted. As a kind of Asian American wish fulfillment for Henry, and perhaps for Lee and for the Asian American community, Kwang appears to be someone who can play the double role of the American and the ethnic, to be "self-made," and "impressive," *and* Korean at the same time with impunity, to be so "irreproachably" and "unbeatably" perfect a combination of both.

To paint a realistic portrait of an exemplary politician, Lee bestows Kwang with superior oratorical talent—arguably one of the most important skills a politician must possess. Kwang's outspokenness and eloquence, the defining factors of his political success, reflect Lee's recognition of the importance of speech and the assertion of voice as the most fundamental means by which citizens and subjects claim and express their membership in American society. America has never looked kindly upon silence. Socially, politically, and historically, voice—specifically the act of speaking out—has been associated with power, participation, recognition, and enfranchisement; in America, King-kok Cheung asserts, "voice is tantamount to power."[20] Silence, by contrast, often is perceived as voicelessness, which in turn signifies social invisibility and political disenfranchisement. While silence can suggest agency, a choice made by the subject not to speak, it is more often interpreted as complicity, apathy, political quietism, lack of intelligence, or even guilt. Henry's fixation on Kwang's verbal skills is therefore not surprising, since Kwang's "strong and clear" voice is, in his view, a positive obverse of not only his father's but also his own awkward and inarticulate silences. Lee romanticizes Kwang through Henry's eyes:

> He was how I imagined a Korean would be, at least one living in any renown. He would stride the daises, and the stages, with his voice strong and clear, unafraid to speak the language like a Puritan, and like a China-man, and like every boat person in between. I found him most moving and beautiful in these moments. [. . .] He has sung whole love songs to the cynical crowds, told tall stories of courage and honor, doing all this without any mythic display, without savvy, almost embarrassing the urban throng. They would look up at him from their seats, and see he was serious, and then quietly make certain to themselves that this was still the country they grew up in. They had never imagined a man like him, an American like him. But no one ever left.
>
> (304)

Kwang's voice provides a much-desired outlet for Henry's own inability to verbalize his feelings toward his estranged wife and dead son, but also his confusion and anxiety about his identity and his "place in the culture" (127).

Lee, however, envisions Kwang as more than just a panacea for Henry's private struggles with his voice. As a member of the city council representing a district with a high immigrant population, Kwang gives voice to a much-neglected segment of New York's populace, providing representation for the grossly underrepresented immigrants that make up his constituency. The political invisibility and voicelessness of this population is largely an effect of the language barrier, a fact Lee addresses anecdotally in *Native Speaker.* When cab drivers around the city were being serially murdered, Henry notes that the fears and concerns of the cab drivers remain largely unheard and unaddressed because "there's nobody who can speak for the drivers as a group, who even wants to, they're too different from one another, they're recently arrived Latvians and Jamaicans, Pakistanis, Hmong" (246). These recent immigrants remain voiceless because they register each other's differences over affinities, they feel no sense of a shared fate with one another, and they possess little or no political knowledge. What they *do* share is their commitment to their families and their nostalgia for their cultures of origin, expressed through "the trinkets from their homelands swaying from the rearview mirror, the strings of beads, shells, the brass letters, the blurry snapshots of their small children, the night-worn eyes" (246). From the perspective of the dominant culture, they have not

shed their ethnic pasts to re-invent themselves as Americans. Their lives are primarily governed by attending to the needs of their private lives and daily survival, and seeking redress through political means in the public sphere is rarely considered a viable option. Their silent endurance is understandable when facility with English is often regarded as a necessary requirement for exercising one's voice and rights in the sociopolitical arena. Because non-English-speaking immigrants rarely make the attempt to demand their rights, a figure like Kwang carries out an essential representative function for groups whose voicelessness is as much the result of verbal diffidence from within as an imposed silence from without.

The spokesmanship that Kwang provides for this constituency also enacts what Anne Cheng describes in *The Melancholy of Race* as "transforming the marginalized, racialized person from being an object bearing *grief* to being a subject speaking *grievance.*"[21] If Henry, his father, and all the voiceless immigrants of New York are figures silently bearing *grief*, Kwang's distinguishing feature is that, unlike them, he is a speaking subject who is able to transform their grief into articulated *grievances*. Werner Sollors has observed that ethnicity and ethnic groups often "exist as abstract, complex, unfathomable units in constant need of symbolic representation."[22] At the height of his popularity, Kwang is described by Henry in Whitmanian terms, as a figure aspiring to represent synecdochally all of the disparate ethnic groups that make up his constituency. Brook Thomas has noted that, "Within the American literary tradition, the most prominent attempt to represent the interaction of a diverse citizenry is Walt Whitman's embrace of it through an expansion of the self. But this expansion depends upon the ability of a part to represent the whole, as Whitman takes on the task of speaking for others, especially those who have often been silenced."[23] Kwang thus appears as a kind of Whitmanian figure whose image consolidates the fragmented immigrant population into an amalgamated whole and coalesces faces of difference into one identifiable shape. As a sign of the invisible made visible as well as the fragmented made coherent, Kwang is able to represent a universality that is achieved through the incorporation of the seemingly irreconcilable particularized interests of a polyethnic constituency.

But, it is precisely through Kwang's politics of polyethnicity that Lee exposes the fine line that separates the languages of consent and dissent. Kwang's politics redefines Americanness as essentially and fundamentally multiethnic; thus, his political vision offers an alternative model to the "paradigm of cultural rebirth" described by Thomas Ferraro to be definitive of most U.S. immigrant experiences, which is always based on the conversion "from alien to American."[24] Kwang, according to Henry, has set his sights on being more than just "another ethnic pol from the outerboroughs, content and provincial;" rather,

> he was going to be somebody who counted, who would stand up like a first citizen of these lands in every quarter of the city, in Flushing and Brownsville and Spanish Harlem and Clinton. He would be the one to bring all the various peoples to the steps of Gracie Mansion, bear them with him not as trophies, or the subdued, but as the living voice of the city, which must always be renewed.
>
> (304)

In Kwang's vision of citizenship, Lee rejects the "straight-line theory" of assimilation,[25] which hypothesized the eventual disappearance of "ethnic traces" of the immigrant generation with each successive generation. Instead, Kwang's model equates ethnicity with Americanness and vows to "renew" the "primary Latin" of the dominant culture with a multilinguistic and heteroglossic one. Instead of "subduing" ethnic voices, he seeks to integrate them into the American *parole* as well as the *langue,* the *lingua franca* of the nation. Lee also emphasizes Kwang's ability to literally and figuratively speak the languages of his ethnic constituents: "In the afternoons, we heard him greet his citizens in Spanish, Hindi, Mandarin, Thai, Portuguese, with a perfection unborrowed and unstudied: *Keep on, keep faith, we know how you feel, you are not alone*" (268). It is Kwang's multilingual capacities and, more importantly, and his mastery of the language of both grievance and hope, that account for the rapid rise of his popularity among communities that have long born the grief of social and political invisibility.

Among other forms of grief that have long gone unarticulated, though at times expressed violently and emotionally through other channels, are the ongoing clashes between neighboring ethnic communities. Lee reveals through Kwang's speeches a mediatory stance that reflects the delicate balance that ethnic politicians must strike between expressions of hope and grievance, between consent and dissent. In a scene that bears particular significance because it is based on the real and ongoing conflicts between the Korean and black communities in New York City,[26] Kwang speaks across ethnic and racial lines in hopes of bridging the explosive rift between the two communities. He invokes their common histories as victims of racism and oppression and exposes their faulty presumptions about one another. Speaking explicitly to the Korean American community and implicitly to the African American community, he tells what they have not been able to tell one another:

> If you are listening to me now and you are Korean, and you pridefully own your own store, your *yah-cheh-ga-*

> *geh* that you have built up from nothing, know these facts. Know that the blacks who spend money in your store and help put food on your table and send your children to college cannot open their own stores. Why? Why can't they? Why don't they even try? Because banks will not lend to them because they are black. Because these neighborhoods are *troubled, high risk.* Because if they did open stores, no one would insure them. . . .
>
> We Koreans know something of this tragedy. Recall the days over fifty years ago, when Koreans were made servants and slaves in their own country by the Imperial Japanese Army.
>
> (153)

This speech provides vicarious expression of injustices endured by both Korean Americans and African Americans, uncovering the sociopolitical circumstances that have brought the two groups to their uneasy coexistence in New York City. He tells them that he is "speaking of histories that all of us should know," and entreats them to "know that what we have in common, the sadness and pain and injustice, will always be stronger than our differences" (153).

Kwang's speech is modeled after the rhetoric of unity employed in many campaign speeches of electoral candidates, particularly those of a moderate or centrist persuasion.[27] Because the very sign of the ethnic's visage is one that bespeaks "special interest" and cultural particularity, an ethnic politician must sing the tune of the broadest, and oftentimes the most abstract and idealistic versions of liberal humanism to overcome the typecast of the "ethnic pol." Thus, every expression of grievance must be counterbalanced with an expression of hope, every expression of difference balanced with a recognition of resemblance. And, Kwang indeed concludes his speech on a conciliatory note: "This person, this person, she, that person, he, that person, they those them, they're like us, they are us, they're just like you! They want to live with dignity and respect! [. . .] I ask that you remember these things, or know them now. Know that what we have in common, the sadness and pain and injustice, will always be stronger than our differences." (152-153).

Everything Kwang says is decidedly in the American grain. His public speeches as well as his private conversations with Henry reflect his full subscription to the founding philosophies of American citizenship and democracy. But, it matters *who* speaks this language of unity. If the ideals of American democratic liberalism—the ideological underpinnings of the rhetoric of "unity in diversity"—can be spoken, and thus represented, by an ethnic, then the unspoken whiteness of Americanism can be easily unraveled. Thus, Kwang poses a threat precisely because he speaks the language of cultural consent fluently—

perhaps *too* fluently and convincingly. The believ-ability is the threat, for it makes possible the closing of the gap between the ethnic and the American, a fusion for which many are unprepared. The *punctum* of this image of an otherwise all-American elected official, to borrow Roland Barthes' term, is Kwang's face.[28] For many, his *look* trumps his *talk*; his *look,* a physical marker that cannot be shaped or morphed to perform the expected whiteness that most still insistently associate with Americanness, becomes even more visibly different. This difference also neutralizes the promises of egalitarianism in the American political process. While someone like Kwang has every right to run for office, his electability is not an issue of access to public office but an issue of whether he will be accepted by the constituency as a representative of their collective identity and interests. Li points out the significance of such identification:

> Although the law necessarily ensures the contractual terms of citizenship in abstraction, it can hardly change the cultural condition of Asian American abjection. This is because the law cannot—even if it is willing to try—possibly adjudicate the psychocultural aspects of subject constitution; neither can it undo the historically saturated epistemological structures of feeling, which continue to undermine the claims of Asian American subjectivity.[29]

If the law cannot adjudicate cultural perceptions of Asian Americans as perpetually "other," then it becomes nothing more than a hollow gesture of granting equal access only in letter but not in spirit. And, the fact that Kwang will never be able to run for the presidency, much less occupy it, reveals the highest level an ethnic can "represent" to be at the state level or below.[30]

Kwang's fall and eventual expulsion from the political arena reflect Lee's cynical view of the capriciousness of public opinion, a veritable force no politician would be foolish enough to dismiss. But, Lee also uncovers the power of institutional forces, often operating below the radar of public awareness, to discredit and malign those regarded as a threat to the dominance of the Anglo-conformity model.[31] The most serious threat that Kwang poses is the potential for a successful polyethnic and pluralistic New York, for which Kwang has become a posterboy. It is the possibility of this future, one that some are unwilling to accept, that sets in motion the machinations by those who seek to put an end to Kwang's political rise. Throughout the course of the novel, his shadowy opponents are revealed to be individuals and institutions with nativist agendas: Mayor De Roos, the incumbent whom Kwang would run against if he sought the mayorship; Dennis Hoagland, the owner of Glimmer & Co, the private investigation firm for whom Henry works; and, in a

final, stunning revelation at the end of the novel, the Immigration and Naturalization Service (INS), for whom Hoagland provides agents like Henry to tail potential immigrant and ethnic "menaces." These agents and agencies dramatize a kind of tacit institutional collaboration against the would-be ethnic upstart to prevent the ethnic from becoming American, or, to be more precise, from becoming a representation of Americanness, symbolic, material, or otherwise.

The political battle waged between Kwang and his opponents is thus waged on the grounds of the politics of consent, in which Kwang's detractors discredit him by strategically turning his language of consent into dissent. In the end, Kwang's language of consent proves inadequate for safeguarding him from charges of special-interest agendas, racial bias, and provincial vision typically associated with minority politics. Mayor De Roos engages in veiled attacks against Kwang around the city to hold his popularity in check, targeting Kwang's efforts to work with all ethnic groups in the city and criticizing the fact that Kwang is "trying too hard to be all things to all people" (36). De Roos, according to Henry, "was a careerist, a consummate professional, and he knew how the game should be run against an ethnic challenger: marginalize him, isolate him, acknowledge his passion but color it radical, name it zealotry" (36). De Roos strategically narrows Kwang's representational scope, which in turn highlights his own status as the white man whose universal spokesmanship can never be assumed by an ethnic. His tactics succeed in undermining Kwang's endeavors to build cross-ethnic relationships, by making Kwang's integrationist rhetoric sound blindly optimistic and out of touch with the reality on the streets: "The press was having a field day. They had multiple boycotts to cover. Vandalism. Street-filling crowds of chanting blacks. Heavily armed Koreans. . . . Nothing John Kwang could say or do would win him praise. His sympathy for either side was a bias for one" (192-193). Ultimately, three deciding factors seal Kwang's defeat: the successful effort mounted by his opponents to convert Kwang's language of consent into an act of non-compliance; Kwang's inability to defend himself against these smear campaigns and his failure to control the political and media discourses surrounding his tarnished public image; and the public's final analysis of Kwang as someone who strayed from the only approved model of consent for non-Anglo immigrants: the financially-driven but politically silent model minority.

To survive smear campaigns and underhanded political tactics, politicians must continually stay one step ahead of opponents' attacks and media spin, and in many ways participate in the very game itself. The detailed descriptions of Kwang's public persona as a media production attest to Lee's clear understanding of the relationship between the medium and the message in the world of high-stakes politics. Kwang's scheduling manager, Janice Pawlowsky, carefully scripts his speeches and frames his photo ops, arranging the "color" of Kwang's audience for the media and "figuring in her head the positions of . . . the crowd, Kwang, paletting their various skin tones into an ambient mix for the media" (93). She tells Henry that "it's like flower arranging," and that "too much color and it begins looking crass'" (93). She also dictates Kwang's speaking appearances, even the cameo-length ones, in order to minimize the potential for the manipulation of his words by the media:

> She tried to measure all his talking and stops in that same interval, so if they ran a clip of him on the news they'd be pressed to play the whole thing. If she let him talk for minutes and minutes whenever he wanted they'd just pick and choose quotes to suit their story, and not necessarily his. She made him speak in lines that were difficult to sound-bite, discrete units of ideas, notions. You have to control the raw material, she said, or they'll make you into a clown.
>
> (87)

Kwang's image suffers its first major breach when he suspects one of his staffers, Eduardo Fermin, of being a mole planted by his political opponents, and arranges to have some shady acquaintances "take care" of him. The campaign office is bombed, and Eduardo is killed along with Helga, the office janitor who is also a family friend of Kwang (Henry finds out later, after he has resigned from Glimmer & Company, that Eduardo was actually a Glimmer & Company spy). Claiming to Henry that he did not anticipate death as a possible outcome, a guilt-ridden Kwang falters in the ensuing media coverage of the investigation. Henry begins to detect "cracks" in his façade:

> Perhaps for the first time in his public life he mumbles, his voice cracks, and even an accent sneaks through. He doesn't seem to be occupying the office, the position. He gazes listlessly at the cameras and responds like a man stopped on the street, dutifully answering each part of each question, answering the follow-ups, searching through the mess of his emotions for reasons this could happen.
>
> (294)

Janice calls Kwang's debilitation "total amateur hour" (294). It is interesting to note, too, that Henry points to Kwang's voice and speech "flaws"—insofar as an accent is perceived as a speech flaw by the dominant culture—as the principle evidence that he has finally shown his "true colors." The tragic lesson to be learned here, Lee seems to say, is that one must maintain control over the medium in order to control the message. Kwang's eventual failure to "control the raw

material" secured his political demise, for when he fell silent during the news coverage of the bombing, he ceded that control to the speculative excesses of the media.

Lee's dramatization of Mayor De Roos's tactic of "coloring" Kwang's politics brings to light a potent weapon that can be wielded against unwanted civic participation by ethnic minorities. This reality was most troublingly borne out by the discourse surrounding the campaign financing scandal during the actual 1996 presidential election, in which contributions (some allegedly illegal) made by Asian Americans to the Democratic National Committee (DNC) were painted by conservative pundits and the news media as nefarious infiltrations of "foreign influence" on domestic politics.[32] As Frank H. Wu and Francey Lim Youngberg so aptly put it, the scandal "transformed [Asian Americans] from invisible to infamous."[33] Fanning the flames of nativism, the media cast the incident as a drama of the "native" versus the "foreign" and effectively relegated Asian Americans to the purview of the latter—this despite the fact that many of the parties involved were American citizens exercising their right to participate in the electoral process. When the story broke, it was their faces, and not their citizenship status, that registered with the public. As Wu and Lim Youngberg describe, "a parade of Asian faces showed up on the television news and a lengthy list of Asian names appeared in the newspaper headlines," and the entire scandal was dubbed the "Asian Connection" by the press.[34] These faces, operating as the *punctum* of the presidential election landscape and eliciting some of the most egregiously racist representations of Asians by the media in recent years, all too perfectly exemplify the abjection of Asian American subjects described by Li, as well as what Neil T. Gotanda has called "citizenship nullification."[35]

In addition to exposing the nativist forces that persistently ethnicize and make foreign Americans of Asian descent, Lee also places responsibility on Asian Americans who fail to deploy effective damage control. Kwang's failure to maintain authorship over his own self-fashioning leads to a loss of control over the entire discourse surrounding his legitimacy as a citizen, civil servant, and elected official. When the press demands explanations from Kwang, Kwang turns mulishly silent, refusing to provide explanations, interviews, and public statements altogether. "What they want from me is a statement about color," Kwang tells Henry. "Whatever I say they'll make into a matter of race" (274). But his assessment is flawed, for if he believes that talk is difficult to control, he fails to see that silence is even more so. His silence is read as a tacit admission of guilt rather than as a means to prevent self-incrimination. Henry notes that it generates a plethora of wild speculations:

> I hear the talk from all his people. They offer each other the spectrum of notions; the bombers are North Korean terrorists, or the growing white-separatist cell based on eastern Long Island, or even the worldwide agents of the Mossad—you can always lay blame on them—who will never forget Kwang's verbal support of the children of the Intifada. The late money says it's the Indians, who so despise Korean competition, it's the Jews envious of new Korean money, Chinese hateful of Korean communality, blacks who want something, anything of justice, it's the uneasy coalition of our colors, that oldest strife of city and alley and schoolyard.
>
> (260)

The talk of ethnic conflict begins to fill the void left by Kwang's silence. Moreover, his refusal to speak is translated into an inability to take sides, a flaw immediately pounced upon by his opposition and the public alike.

Even more damaging to his tarnished public image is what the public, and even Henry, perceive as Kwang's eroding Americanness in the wake of the scandal. When the media speculations and recriminations cause Kwang to retreat from the public eye, Henry observes that Kwang begins to speak Korean more than English, alienates his non-Korean staffers, and keeps Henry, the only Korean staffer, by his side. Henry, too, racializes Kwang's silence and reads it as evidence of Kwang's "reversion" to his Korean self. He interprets Kwang's coping strategy as a manifestation of an essential Korean trait:

> My mother said to me once that suffering is the noblest art, the quieter the better. If you bite your lip and understand that this is the only world, you will perhaps persist and endure. What she meant, too was that we can not change anything, that if a person wants things like money or comfort or respect he has to change himself to make them possible, because the world will always work to foil you."
>
> (333)

While such silence might be perceived within Korean cultural customs as a "mask of serenity and repose" (296), an expected, even respected manner for public figures to adopt, it is perceived as a sign of vulnerability in the United States. Here, such silence only exposes Kwang to the inscriptive power of the media, whose propensity to interpret silence as evasion and guilt is all too familiar. It is in such moments when Lee makes most plain the limitations of the minority voice. Ethnic politicians are perpetually caught between the often competing interests of the ethnic group with which they identify and the wider populace they seek to represent—a political dilemma that few ethnic politicians have been able to negotiate successfully.

As all of Kwang's activities and operations come under public scrutiny, each is subject to the trappings of binaristic thinking pervasive in political discourse. Take, for instance, the ways in which Kwang's *ggeh* is characterized as both un-American and un-Korean. As Henry explains, Kwang's vision of the *ggeh,* a "Korean money club in which members contributed to a pool that was given out on a rotating basis" (51), is a system based on social responsibility and active participation, in which every member has a stake in its survival: "In this sense we are all related. The larger *ggeh* depend solely on this notion, that the lesson of the culture will be stronger than a momentary lack, can subdue any individual weakness or want. This is the power lovely and terrible, what we try to engender in Kwang's giant money club, our huge *ggeh* for all" (279-280). Kwang's *ggeh,* however, departs from the traditional Korean-only model by allowing members of other ethnic groups to participate. Thus, the inclusionary principles that inform Kwang's multi-ethnic *ggeh* make it vulnerable to not only charges of illegality by the state (for it operates outside of legitimate systems of banking), but also to charges of un-Koreanness by the Korean immigrant community by dint of its multi-ethnic membership. Moreover, when the media gets wind of the *ggeh,* it paints the *ggeh* as an operation that smuggles illegal immigrants into the country. While Henry is able to see the *ggeh* as an essentially democratic enterprise, one that encourages active participation and strives for equal distribution of wealth, the INS sees it only as an illegitimate "private bank that pays revolving interest and principle to its members, many of whom are Korean, lending activities that aren't registered with any banking commission and haven't reported to tax authorities" (328-329). To Hoagland and the media, it is perceived as the illegal activities of the likes of the mafia and other "public enemy" types who have refused to play by the rule of law:

> To Dennis, and to the reporters that are here, I could explain forever Kwang's particular thinking, how the idea of the *ggeh* occurred as second nature to him. He didn't know who was an 'illegal' and who was not, for he would never come to see that fact as something vital. . . . He wasn't a warlord or a don, he had no real power over any of them save their trust in his wisdom. He was merely giving to them just the start, like other people get an inheritance, a hope chest of what they would work hard for in the rest of their lives.
>
> (334)

The threat of Kwang was his potential "Koreanizing" of American culture, and his revision of American citizenship based on, of all things, a system of Korean origin. Despite Kwang's good intentions, the *ggeh* is perceived as a legal *and* a social violation. The economic assistance that he has provided to immigrants, particularly the illegal ones, is unpalatable to a society already skeptical about the nation's "open-door" immigration policies.

Barefaced nativism is most emboldened and openly expressed when an ethnic is publicly branded by institutions of power as a potential threat to the national identity. Henry has always imagined the unnamed client who commissioned his services as "a vastly wealthy voyeur, a decrepit, shut-away xenophobe who keeps a national vigilance on eminent agitators and ethnics" (295). As it turns out, he is not too far off in his speculation; the client is finally revealed to be the INS, the legislator and enforcer of the laws that, in Angelo Ancheta's view, "most powerfully reflect American nativism."[36] Among those who picket outside of Kwang's house to protest his alleged malfeasance is a group of "generally younger, white male" individuals, carrying a banner with the slogan, "AMERICA FOR AMERICANS," and chanting, "We want our fucking future back" (332). This image carries multiple messages: that to these folks, Kwang was never considered an American; that his multi-ethnic "family," his *ggeh,* will not be accepted as the "future" of America; and that with every ostensible failure of the minority to keep up the good performance, the sentiment of the people turns against him in favor of the old notion of a white, eurocentric America. They succeed in ousting Kwang, too, not just from the city council, but from the country. Posing as a potential buyer, Henry visits Kwang's vacated house a few months after the protest; when he asks the realtor to whom the house had belonged, she replies: "Foreigners. They went back to their country" (347).

Lee's portrayal of the fall of John Kwang suggests that America, in Lee's eyes, is as yet unable to consider an ethnic as a representative of America. David Palumbo-Liu has noted that *Native Speaker* "outlines a utopian vision of overcoming and subverting dualistic (that is, hyphenated) thinking, but ultimately declares that that moment is not yet ripe."[37] The speech Kwang delivers on the steps of City Hall is filled with such seductively idealistic rhetoric of democratic pluralism that for a brief moment, everyone in the crowd—and perhaps the reader included—is won over. This moment of shared idealism, however, is violently punctuated with a gun shot, a voluble symbolic statement that aims to put a stop to the polyethnic utopian politics that Kwang represents. The gunshot, which scatters the crowd and sends Kwang fleeing for his limousine, potently expresses Lee's realistic understanding of the hazards of ethnic politics

and the cynicism of a citizenry that is as yet unprepared to elect an Asian immigrant to the city's highest office. In Lee's pessimistic vision, Kwang's attempts to "bring all the various peoples to the steps of Gracie Mansion," and to be "the living voice of the city" (304), are thwarted by nativist agents invested in preserving the dominance of the "primary Latin" and containing the growing visibility and power of ethnic minorities. His seemingly impeccable performance as a "native speaker," with all the requisite recitations of ideological consent, and his subsequent turn to silence, attest to the sluggish pace at which recognition of immigrant and ethnic voices is won. Faced with the problem of having to speak from too many different cultural and ideological positions, Kwang asks Henry if there is "a way to speak truthfully and not be demonized or made a traitor" (196-197). Henry replies with what he calls "the steady answer of [his] life," an answer that attests to his lack of faith in the minority voice: "Very softly, and to yourself" (197).

Through the various personal and political dilemmas faced by Henry Park and John Kwang, Lee brings to light the difficulties of negotiating the competing demands of consent or descent, in Sollors's terms,[38] or "[conceding] to the European American cultural exclusivity of the nation" and "being co-opted into orientalism and displacing Asian Americans once more onto their 'immutable' ancestral origins," in Li's analogous distinction. No matter what they do, the choice is always diminished to these reductive binary terms. Kwang expresses his frustration with this double bind when he confesses to complying with stereotypes in order to win public favor. "When others construct and model you favorably," he tells Henry, "it's easy to let them keep at it, even if they start going off in ways that aren't immediately comfortable or right. This is the challenge for us Asians in America. How do you say no to what seems like a compliment? From the very start we don't wish to be rude or inconsiderate. So we stay silent in our guises" (193). However, mimicries and masquerades are inadequate and imperfect means of securing cultural membership, since, as Li explains, "The assimilable Asian cannot belong but must be measured by his *proximity* to the center/same, which welcomes copies, imitations, and mimicries for the security of its own value while insisting on their inauthenticity and their illegitimacy."[39] Nevertheless, romanced by discourses of the American Dream, many Asian Americans continue to reify the model minority myth. Such are the costs exacted by cultural consent, for consent is always an agreement to abide by the rules and roles authored by others. As such, consent is essentially a form of silence, and the demand for consent a form of silencing.

The problems surrounding citizenship status and participatory politics for Asian Americans has generated numerous disagreements and conflicting propositions for the Asian American's "truest place in the culture." Lowe, in *Immigrant Acts,* advocates a politics of resistance by Asian Americanists, to make use of their "distance from the national culture . . . as an alternative formation that produces cultural expressions materially and aesthetically at odds with the resolution of the citizen in the nation."[40] Lowe sees Asian American citizenship as a radical destabilizing force in reimagining and redefining American citizenship and suggests that "rather than expressing a 'failed' integration of Asians into the American cultural sphere, this distance preserves Asian American culture as an alternative site where the palimpsest of lost memories is reinvented, histories are fractured and retraced, and the unlike varieties of silence emerge into articulacy."[41] Li, however, believes in "neither [Lowe's] conclusion that Asian American culture is an autonomous alternative of resistance to the dominant formation of the nation, nor her postulation of an Asian American subject who is able to supercede the narrative of the nation and the 'discourse of citizenship.'"[42] To Li, "the Asian American formation is not necessarily a solution to but a problem in and of the contradictions of American citizenship, which can only be resolved through a radical divorce of racial inheritance and national competence."[43] Kandice Chuh, taking the idea of radical rejection further, calls for a "disowning" of an idealized America by "[disarticulating] 'nation' from 'home,'" and by "radically [destabilizing] the kind of subjective, nation-oriented politics that have historically anchored Asian American studies" through the methodologies of postcolonial theory.[44] E. San Juan, Jr. goes even further in a not-so-subtle jab at both Li and Lowe, describing their work as "vacuous texts on citizenship within the U.S. nation-state immigrant acts of representation, consent, and so on, that litter the archives of Asian American scholarship."[45] San Juan argues for a rejection of liberal democracy altogether because it, in his view, "thrives on the spoils of wage-slavery" and contends that "the mutual recognition of rights to property and the formal equality of individual citizens are the key precondition for economic exploitation regulated and supervised by the liberal democratic state."[46] But, the problem faced by Lowe, et al. is still the tenacious inextricability of racial inheritance from the discourse of citizenship and measurements of "national competence," whether it be for the purpose of changing the terms of citizenship from within (as Li and many Asian American political scientists would have it), or constructing an alternative and oppositional citizenship from without (as Lowe, Chuh, and San Juan would have it). We return to what is becoming a *reductio ad absurdum* time and again:

is racial and/or ethnic "inheritance" a constitutive or an oppositional aspect of citizenship? Lee's John Kwang, who fails spectacularly despite his ability to be "effortlessly Korean" and "effortlessly American," suggests that the real problem is our inability to imagine a solution somewhere in between.

Notes

1. Gary Locke was governor of Washington from 1997 to 2004. For a biography of Locke, see http://www.digitalarchives.wa.gov/governorlocke/bios/bio.htm.

2. "Democrats' Response to the State of the Union Message," Transcript of Governor Gary Locke's Response, *CNN.com,* Feb. 14, 2003, Politics Section. http://www.cnn.com/2003/ALLPOLITICS/01/28/dems.transcript/

3. An exemplar of a "political" immigrant success story is that of the Kennedy family. The Kennedys built a political dynasty in spite of its Irish Catholic roots, which, at the time of John F. Kennedy's election, was still seen as an "ethnic" liability. John F. Kennedy's *A Nation of Immigrants,* written in the late '50s as he pushed for Congressional revisions of immigration laws and published posthumously in 1964, was a personal as well as a public appeal to the nation to adopt a more embracing attitude towards its immigrants. But for the generations of Asian immigrants who came before and after JFK's appeal and the Immigration Act of 1965, public service has not been a part of their narratives of success. While "ethnic" faces, and Asian American faces more specifically, are more familiar in local and state politics and on the increase in national politics, they remain few and far between in the latter when compared with the number of public officials of white-European descent.

4. John Mercurio, "GOP Sees Easy Target in Democratic Responder," *CNN. com,* Jan. 28, 2003, Politics Section. http://www.cnn.com/2003/ALLPOLITICS/01/28/locke.democrats/.

5. There is undoubtedly a growing presence of Asian Americans in American political arenas, particularly in recent decades. While Asian Americans have held seats in the House of Representatives and in city and state legislatures, there has been a glaring absence of Asian Americans in the higher offices, from governorships to Senate seats, cabinet posts, and, of course, the highest representative role in the nation—the presidency. The last few decades have seen some increase in that presence, from Gary Locke's successful bid for the Washington governorship to President Clinton's appointment of Norman Mineta to the post of Secretary of Commerce, making Mineta the first Asian American to hold a cabinet post. For more complete and in-depth accounts of Asian American political activities past and present, see the

essays collected in Gordon H. Chang's *Asian Americans and Politics: Perspectives, Experiences, Prospects* (Stanford, CA: Stanford UP, 2001). Closer to Lee's fictional account of New York City Councilman John Kwang in *Native Speaker* is the election of John Liu to the New York City Council in 2001. Liu, the first Asian American to serve on the City Council, represents both a significant milestone for New York-based Asian American political involvement and an overdue step in the city's recognition of its long-established Asian and Asian American communities, particularly Chinese Americans who have been part of the city's citizenry (if not "citizens" in the legal sense) since the mid-1800s.

6. Gordon H. Chang, "Asian Americans and Politics: Some Perspectives From History," *Asian Americans and Politics: Perspectives, Experiences, Prospects* (Stanford, CA: Stanford UP, 2001), 31.

7. Don T. Nakanishi, "Beyond Electoral Politics: Renewing a Search for a Paradigm of Asian Pacific American Politics," in *Asian Americans and Politics: Perspectives, Experiences, Prospects,* ed. Gordon H. Chang (Stanford, CA: Stanford UP, 2001).

8. Lisa Lowe, *Immigrant Acts: On Asian American Cultural Politics* (Durham, NC: Duke UP, 1996).

9. See, for instance, David Leiwei Li, *Imagining the Nation: Asian American Literature and Cultural Consent* (Stanford: Stanford UP, 1998); Rachel Lee, *The Americas of Asian American Literature* (Princeton: Princeton UP, 1999); David Palumbo-Liu, *Asian/American: Historical Crossings of a Racial Frontier* (Stanford: Stanford UP, 1999); Patricia Chu, *Assimilating Asians: Gendered Strategies of Authorship in Asian America* (Durham: Duke University Press, 2000); Kandice Chuh, *Imagine Otherwise: On Asian Americanist Critique* (Durham: Duke UP, 2003).

10. Rachel Lee, *The Americas of Asian American Literature* (Princeton: Princeton UP, 1999), 13.

11. Chang-rae Lee, *Native Speaker* (New York: Riverhead Books, 1995). All subsequent citations from this text are noted parenthetically. Astute readings of the identity politics of the novel have been done by Patricia Chu, David Palumbo-Liu, Tim Engles, among others, and so I will not rehearse them here. See Tim Engles, "'Visions of me in the whitest raw light': Assimilation and Doxic Whiteness in Chang-rae Lee's *Native Speaker*," *Hitting Critical Mass: A Journal of Asian American Cultural Studies,* 4.2 (Summer 1997): 27-48; Patricia Chu, "Introduction: City of Words," in *Assimilating Asians: Gendered Strategies of Authorship in Asian America* (Durham: Duke University Press, 2000); and David Palumbo-Liu, "Double Trouble: The Pathology of Ethnicity Meets White Schizophrenia," in *Asian/American: Historical Crossings of a Racial Frontier,* 295-336.

12. William Boelhower, "A Modest Ethnic Proposal," in *American Literature, American Culture,* ed. Gordon Hutner (New York: Oxford UP, 1998), 443-454.

13. Li, *Imagining the Nation,* 1-10.

14. Ibid., 10. Also see David Palumbo-Liu's appendix on model minority discourse in his *Asian/American: Historical Crossings of a Racial Frontier* (Stanford: Stanford University Press, 1999), and Vijay Prashad's "Ethnic Studies Inside Out," *JAAS* 9.2 (2006), pp. 163-170. Prashad argues that the term "model minority," which functions as "a useful bludgeon against 'problem minorities,'" is cultivated by segments of Asian American communities because the idea appeals to those who are upwardly mobile. Prashad uncovers the ill effects of this acceptance, arguing that valuing the stereotype creates a "cage of the model minority" by transforming "Asian Americans" into a class category and leaving "little room within it to account for the experiences of working-class Asian Americans" (167-168).

15. Ibid., 8.

16. Ibid., 6.

17. Ibid., 8.

18. Lowe, *Immigrant Acts,* 144.

19. Ibid., 144.

20. King-kok Cheung, *Articulate Silences* (Ithaca: Cornell UP, 1993), 2.

21. Anne Anlin Cheng, *Melancholy of Race* (New York: Oxford UP, 2000), 174.

22. Werner Sollors, *Beyond Ethnicity: Consent and Descent in American Literature* (New York: Oxford UP, 1986), 15.

23. Brook Thomas, "*China Men,* United States v. Wong Kim Ark, and the Question of Citizenship," *American Quarterly* 50.4 (1998): 712-713.

24. Thomas J. Ferraro, *Ethnic Passages: Literary Immigrants in Twentieth-Century America* (Chicago: University of Chicago Press, 1993), 1.

25. Herbert Gans, "Symbolic Ethnicity: The Future of Ethnic Groups and Cultures in America" (1979), in *Theories of Ethnicity: A Classical Reader,* ed. Werner Sollors (New York: New York UP, 1996), 425-459. "Straight-line theory" is now understood as a model applicable only to immigrants of Anglo or white-European descent.

26. Elaine H. Kim had made a similar appeal to the American public in the wake of the uprising that followed the acquittal of four police officers in the Rodney King beating case. In her essay, "Home is Where the *Han* Is: A Korean-American Perspective on the Los Angeles Upheavals," published in the collection *Reading Rodney King/Reading Urban Uprising,* ed. Robert Gooding-Williams (New York: Routledge, 1993), she underscores the common histories between African Americans and Korean Americans, suggesting that both groups "were kept ignorant about each

other by educational and media institutions that erase or distort their experiences and perspectives." She also pointed to the uneven economic conditions that contribute to the hostilities. Interestingly, Kim also discussed the considerable amount of hate mail she received for her *Newsweek* column, in which she held corporate and government institutions accountable for the conflict between Korean Americans and African Americans. The hate mail revealed a remarkable emphasis on how Kim should speak, how she should use her voice: "Even though my essay revealed that I was born in the U.S. and that my parents had lived in the U.S. for more than six decades, I was viewed as a foreigner without the right to say anything except words of gratitude and praise about America" (527). Many letters she quoted also called her critical voice "whining."

27. The familiar theme of "unity in diversity" is one that is often invoked by moderates on both sides of the aisle. Kwang's speech, while addressed to an ethnically diverse audience, is modeled on the tradition of speeches given by American statesmen at times of serious internal divisions in domestic politics. The casting of divisive politics as a test of the soundness and strength of a national body, and the appeal for unification as proof of that strength, are rhetorical strategies widely employed by presidents, generals, and civic leaders. Illinois Senator Barack Obama, whose keynote address for the Democratic National Convention in July 2004 resonated with Abraham Lincoln's famed speeches, consciously invoked unity as a key theme for his party's ideological positioning. He also invoked the beloved narrative of how a racial Other became a representative American—a variation of the same narrative employed by Gary Locke in his response to President Bush's SoTU address. Most significant about the two men's variations on this narrative theme is their implicit concession that racialized or ethnicized subjects such as themselves who seek representative status must first prove that they have "evolved" from an ethnic to an American, thereby abiding by, however unconsciously, the Anglo conformity paradigm.

28. Roland Barthes, *Camera Lucida,* trans. Richard Howard (New York: Hill and Wang, 1982). Barthes's idea of the *punctum* is that "stray" element in a picture that "pricks" or "wounds" him.

29. Li, *Imagining the Nation,* 11.

30. The ceiling of the political ladder for ethnic minorities is clearly and firmly exemplified by the inaccessibility of the nation's highest office—the presidency. The discourse of presidential elections articulates, in often startlingly nativist language, the nation's institutional denial of an ethnic minority's capacity to represent the identity and the interests of the nation as a whole. Naturalization as the primary requirement for candidacy clearly delineates the native from the foreign, but naturalization itself relies on a questionable combination of geographic genealogy and birthright.

31. Will Kymlicka, "Multination States and Polyethnic States," *Multicultural Citizenship* (Oxford: Oxford UP, 1995), 14. The Anglo-conformity model of immigration, widely known as a fundamental part of U.S. immigration policies prior to the 1960s, made it clear that immigrants entering the U.S. and Canada were expected to shed the cultural beliefs and practices of their cultures of origin and assimilate fully into the existing cultural norms of their newly adopted countries. "Assimilation," Kymlicka explains, "was seen as essential for political stability, and was further rationalized through ethnocentric denigration of other cultures" (14). Though the Anglo-conformity model is now seen as a policy of the past in official immigration discourse, Kymlicka points out that "the rejection of Anglo-conformity has not meant a slackening in this commitment to ensuring that immigrants become Anglophones, which is seen as essential if they are to be included in the mainstream of economic, academic, and political life of the country" (15).

32. For a complete account of the scandal, see Frank H. Wu and Francey Lim Youngberg's "People From China Crossing the River: Asian American Political Empowerment and Foreign Influence," in *Asian Americans and Politics: Perspectives, Experiences, Prospects,* ed. Gordon H. Chang (Stanford, CA: Stanford UP, 2001), 311-353.

33. Wu and Youngberg, "People From China," 311.

34. Ibid.

35. Neil T. Gotanda, "Citizenship Nullification: The Impossibility of Asian American Politics," in *Asian Americans and Politics* [Full citation is in n. 32.]), 79-101.

36. Angelo Ancheta, *Race, Rights, and the Asian American Experience* (New Brunswick: Rutgers UP, 1998), 114. The salience of Ancheta's observation became all the more striking when, in response to 9/11, a series of legislation to "secure" America's borders from foreign threats resulted in the Homeland Security Act of 2002, which transferred INS jurisdiction to the newly formed Department of Homeland Security.

37. David Palumbo-Liu, *Asian/American: Historical Crossings of a Racial Frontier,* 317.

38. Wernor Sollors, *Beyond Ethnicity: Consent and Descent in American Literature* (New York: Oxford UP, 1986). Sollors defines descent language as "our positions as heirs, our hereditary qualities, liabilities, and entitlements," and consent language as "our abilities as mature free agents and 'architects of our fates' to choose our spouses, our destinies, and our political systems" (6). The central questions concerning consent and descent that Sollors poses in terms of

ethnicity are: "How can consent (and consensus) be achieved in a country whose citizens are of such heterogeneous descent? And how can dissent be articulated without falling back on myths of descent?" (6)

39. Li, *Imagining the Nation,* 10.

40. Lowe, *Immigrant Acts: On Asian American Cultural Politics,* 6.

41. Ibid., 6.

42. Li, *Imagining the Nation: Asian American Literature and Cultural Consent,* 15.

43. Ibid., 15.

44. Chuh, *Imagine Otherwise,* 124; 114.

45. E. San Juan, Jr., *Racism and Cultural Studies: Critiques of Multiculturalist Ideology and the Politics of Difference* (Durham: Duke UP, 2002), 161.

46. Ibid., 161.

Yung-Hsing Wu (essay date October 2006)

SOURCE: Wu, Yung-Hsing. "Native Sons and Native Speakers: On the Eth(n)ics of Comparison." *PMLA: Publications of the Modern Language Association of America* 121, no. 5 (October 2006): 1460-474.

[*In the following essay, Wu examines representations of ethnicity in* Native Speaker *and African American author Richard Wright's* Native Son.]

[Comparison] *brings with it new problems: descriptivism, summary, anthologism—a certain analogical logic. [O]ne compares A to B according to a model.*

—Alice Jardine, *Gynesis: Configurations of Woman and Modernity*

Chang-Rae Lee's **Native Speaker** was published in 1995 to almost immediate acclaim—the novel, Lee's first, garnered glowing reviews, several awards, and prestige for its author. The tale of a Korean American "ethnic consultant" impressed critics with its witty, sly evocation of an American identity politics that transforms the model minority employee into the model corporate spy. Reviewers saw in the novel's protagonist, Henry Park, a postmodern figure for the trials constitutive of ethnic identity. An expert in profiling "foreign workers, immigrants, first-generationals, neo-Americans" and a specialist in Asian immigrants, Park provides his firm's clientele—"multinational corporations, bureaus of foreign governments, [and] individuals of resource and connection"—that most crucial of services, the acquisition of usable information (17). Ethnicity marks Park's difference and is his greatest occupational asset. In offering this view, **Native Speaker** was said to register the complex identifications attending ethnicity in the United States.

Such approbation dissipated seven years later, when a selection committee nominated **Native Speaker** as a finalist for a New York City reading campaign. The committee commended the novel for its deft urban characterization, praising Lee's exploration of the relations among the city's diverse populations.[1] Dissent emerged, however, when members of the Korean American community insisted that the selection committee retract its nomination, claiming the novel shed stereotypical light on Korean American culture.[2] These readers targeted Lee's choice of profession for his protagonist, arguing that the novel reinforced the cliché of Asian inscrutability by casting Park as a spy. Far from correcting or commenting on that typical identity, Park's position as an "ethnic consultant" had fallen prey to it. Park had failed, in other words, his task as a representative of ethnicity.

For those involved in the reading-campaign controversy, the logic of stereotyping marks ethnic representation at its most reductive and therefore, its worst. Meanwhile, in the criticism of **Native Speaker,** the stereotype leads some to the different conclusion that the conflation of Park's occupation with his ethnicity is all but inevitable. For June Dwyer, the matter is as simple as a good match: Park's job is "a strikingly unusual, but altogether *appropriate* job for an immigrant" (74; my emphasis). Or, as James Kyung-Jin Lee puts it, "[T]he assimilated Henry is crucial to his capacity to work as a spy, and thus *serves perfectly* as Lee's emblem of a self-conscious, self-aware model minority" (247; my emphasis). Tim Engles argues that Park's profession, while taking advantage of his heritage, offers a mirror image of his biography. "Henry's vocation acquires nuanced significance," Engels remarks, "when read as a more precise representation of Korean American experience" (43). The connection is even more direct for Tina Chen, who focuses in large part on Lee's racialized revision of the spy thriller genre. While Chen claims that invoking the spy thriller allows Lee to "redress the popular stereotypes of Asian secret agents created by Anglo-American writers," she nonetheless describes Park's occupation as "a *logical* extension of his personal history as a Korean American" (656, 638; my emphasis). Figuring Park through a type makes in these accounts a kind of interesting sense. What is more, such figuration enables the novel's work as cultural analysis. Espionage "metaphorically adds a new level to our understanding of what immigrants do for their adopted country" (Dwyer 74), depicts "a representative Korean American's cultural self-evisceration" (Engles 46), and even provides "a provocative thematization of racial in/visibility" that "alludes to the structural role Asian Americans have served" (Chen 656; J. Lee 247). *Native Speaker* speaks, in other words, to its protagonist's signification.

The trouble (or fascination) with typing lies, then, in its effect on the singularity ethnicity is said to embody. A typecast Park means that his ethnicity is not only scripted but indeed the script by which his narrative proceeds. Perhaps less obviously, the logic of the type renders Park's ethnicity recognizable in another sense—that is, recognizable in relation to another ethnic type. For reviewers and critics alike, Park's significance as an ethnic character registers him as an "invisible man" whose resemblance to "the nameless protagonist of Ralph Ellison's *Invisible Man*" lies in "the refusal of others to see him" (Chen 638) as well as in the "racial identity search" on which he embarks (Engles 32). As one reviewer puts it, "With echoes of Ralph Ellison, Chang-rae Lee's extraordinary debut speaks for another kind of invisible man: the Asian immigrant in America."[3] These comparisons attribute invisibility specifically to Asian Americans, the model minority that does not require tracking.[4] Yet they also conflate ethnicity with invisibility and in so doing name invisibility as a shared trope, a shared difference. Linking *Native Speaker* with *Invisible Man,* not despite, but through ethnic difference, they suggest an intertextual association that emerges out of the relation between the novels' protagonists. The interethnic makes it possible to imagine an ethnic intertextuality.

Long deployed in efforts to claim the legitimacy of individual ethnic literary traditions, intertextuality here provides the basis for reading affinities between specific ethnic literatures. When Henry Louis Gates, Jr., in *The Signifying Monkey* names Signifyin(g) as "a metaphor for formal revision, or intertextuality," he defines a specific African American literary practice that in turn defines the literature through that practice (xix-xxi). Indeed, the textual persona for this dynamic, Esu-Elegbara, has become a figure for intertextuality, and his critical counterparts—including, for instance, the Monkey King and the Chippewa trickster Nanabozho—have followed him in performing similar feats of legitimation for their literatures.[5] Intertextuality thus shores up what Sau-ling Cynthia Wong calls "a sense of an *internally meaningful* literary tradition" (11; my emphasis).[6] At the same time, the political urgency of such thinking cannot contain the impulse of intertextuality to seek out new relations. Despite the priority she places on establishing an Asian American literary tradition, Wong in *Reading Asian American Literature* finds herself drawn to the prospect of reading across ethnic literatures. In one striking instance, Wong ends a discussion of the "racial shadow" in Asian American literature—one in which she estab-

lishes carefully this shadow's relation to the classic psychoanalytic figure of the double—by remarking that African, Native American, and Chicano and Chicana literary histories yield a similar troping.[7] "The possibilities for comparative study," she writes, "appear numerous and promising" (117).

This essay cultivates the promise scholars like Wong have identified but not pursued.[8] Following a series of contexts that spans disciplinary, metatextual, and critical discourse, I argue for an intertextuality made possible by the ethical limit posed by ethnic difference. More specifically, this intertextuality faces the obligation to foreground ethnicity as a specific textual presence. Thus an attentiveness to the representation of ethnicity—its embodiment through characterization, its formal or generic manifestations—comprises the effort to honor its difference. At the same time, the limiting force of such obligation sustains ethnic intertextuality. Far from prohibiting, for instance, a comparison of distinct ethnic literatures, the injunction to pay heed to ethnicity produces a specific reading motion, a perpetual rotation of the intertextual engine for which another comparison is just a turn away. The prospect always exists for having missed the ethnic mark. That missed encounter, however, yields the imperative to continue reading without knowing how difference will emerge. Heeding this imperative not only results in an altered sense of *Native Speaker* and its rendering of Henry Park. It also alters what it means to read ethnic literature.

DISCIPLINING COMPARISON

Gayatri Spivak's recent *Death of a Discipline* opens with a tale of rebuilding: "Since 1992," she writes, "three years after the fall of the Berlin Wall, the discipline of comparative literature has been looking to renovate itself." The fate of the Berlin Wall enjoins comparative literature to rethink its mapping of literary borders. For Spivak, Charles Bernheimer's *Comparative Literature in the Age of Multiculturalism* indexes this impulse as a preoccupation with ethnic difference, or what she calls "the rising tide of multiculturalism and cultural studies" (1). Awash in this tide, comparative literature calls for its own reformation even as it faces internal critique—it faces, in other words, the difficult conditions of its possibility. Difference, embodied in this historical moment by ethnicity, constitutes an edge to comparative literature that is simultaneously the discipline's raison d'être.

In the essays collected in *Comparative Literature in the Age of Multiculturalism,* ethnic difference is singular not only for its aesthetic, political, or ethical relevance but also—and perhaps even more forcefully—for its disciplinary significance, as is evident in

Bernheimer's history of reports made to the American Comparative Literature Association (ACLA) since 1975. The Bernheimer Report, presented to the ACLA in the spring of 1993, as well as its two predecessors—known familiarly as the Levin Report (1965) and the Greene Report (1975)—seeks to hold a mirror to the discipline: its vision of literature (as distinct from the one endorsed in national literature departments), its account of current standards and methodologies, its sense of pressing questions straining and potentially redefining comparative practice.[9] Not unlike a State of the Union address, each ACLA report describes and assesses disciplinary conditions and by extension, the state of literature itself. In Bernheimer's genealogy, however, this function is interrupted when the report written to follow the Greene Report goes unsubmitted because "the chair of that committee was so dissatisfied with the document that he exercised a pocket veto" (Bernheimer, Preface ix). The aberration testifies to the reports' institutional weight: in noting the gap, Bernheimer underscores the existence of the tradition, and in inheriting this gap from its forebears, his report is in turn defined by it. Yet Bernheimer's reference calls attention to the ghostly 1985 report and the conditions that surrounded its demise. What disciplinary vision warranted the executive veto? A clue lies in the belligerent conservatism the Bernheimer Report attributes to its immediate predecessor. Of the 1975 Greene Report, Bernheimer and the members of his committee say that it "does not so much articulate new goals and possibilities for comparative literature as it *defends* the standards proposed by Levin against perceived challenges" (Bernheimer et al. 39; my emphasis). Specifically, the Bernheimer committee recalls three such "perceived challenges" named as threats to the discipline's high standards of excellence—the use of translations in research and teaching, the growth of interdisciplinary programs, and the presence of literary theory, whose synchronic view of interpretation receives from the Greene Report an "implicit rebuke" (41). Retrospection yields introspection: the review of the Greene Report reveals that contention has driven the discipline's self-portraits.

The Bernheimer Report's attentiveness to this history of divisive concerns provides a context for the ellipsis that follows ten years after the Greene Report. Indeed, the Bernheimer Report makes it possible to imagine how ethnic difference might have been at stake in the 1985 report's demise. By the time of that report's drafting, the academy had witnessed the explosive entry of "minority literatures" into departments of English, comparative literature, and a host of national language and area studies programs. Postcolonial studies hit American shores in the early 1980s, bringing a gaze that criticized the production and maintenance of cultural epistemologies forged in the name of the West and that exposed literature as a privileged and therefore unquestioned site of such historical constructions. Similarly, the presence of the ethnic in American literary studies compelled a reconfiguration of canons and literary histories such that the field could no longer easily assume "canon" and "literary history" as precepts. Finally, as a synonym for singularity, specificity, and particularity, ethnic difference in this moment began to acquire the kind of exemplarity previously attributed to gender, race, and sexuality. This moment rendered ethnicity the redeeming difference. Its force occurred through its identity as difference.

For comparative literature, historically a discipline invested in crossing the borders of literary and disciplinary nationalisms, these developments have cast ethnic difference as an object of interest, preoccupation, and even anxiety. My speculations about the missing ACLA report have less to do, therefore, with exposing shady institutional dealings than with positing a connection between the literary political significance of ethnicity and current discussions in comparative literature about the health of the discipline and what its defining activity, comparison, signifies. Reading *Comparative Literature in the Age of Multiculturalism* makes clear that ethnic difference stands simultaneously at opposite ends of this discussion. It embodies for some contributors a predicament facing contemporary comparative practice: the spectral other, the index of Eurocentric privilege and guilt, the limit case of a discipline already on the edge. For others, however, ethnic difference characterizes and explains the discipline at its most visionary—its approach to historicist thinking, its insistence that nationalism affords an insufficient picture of the cultures of literature. Ethnic difference would appear crucial to the disciplinary silhouette comparative literature projects for its present as well as its future.

In the first view, ethnic difference marks what Mary Louise Pratt calls "crises of accountability and expertise" for the discipline (62-63). The emphasis on cultural specificity enjoins comparatists not only to include ethnicity but also to address how it alters their critical practice—and even whether their practice adequately attends to its handling. Pratt welcomes this doubled crisis, arguing that it exposes the discipline's conservative bent. She laments the resistance to dislodging Europe from the center of comparative study, remarking that "one continues to be haunted by a specter that surged forth at the height of the so-called Western culture debates," and urges her colleagues to continue exorcising the demon of Eurocentrism (62). Yet such purification rites trouble other scholars, who see in the privileging of ethnic difference the source of a restrictive disciplinary identity politics. Bernheimer imagines how the reification of ethnicity consigns any comparatist endeavor to inadequacy; any critic "who ventures beyond the European area or gets involved with ethnic cultures at home . . . will always . . . be found lacking in some quality of authenticity" ("Anxieties" 9). In the meantime, David Damrosch claims that the distinctiveness of comparative literature is at risk. For him, ironically, "the new emphasis on cultural context" has not broadened but constrained the sphere of comparative activity by "increas[ing] the nationalism of much study" (123). In the guise of "cultural context," ethnic difference intensifies a disquieting separatism—an isolationist view that may preclude the connections on which comparative literature thrives.

These arguments cite ethnic difference for the trouble it has caused comparative literature. Yet a discourse also exists that articulates how ethnicity resides productively in the field. Thus the Bernheimer Report describes comparative literature "as a privileged locus for cross-cultural reflection" (45), emphasizing that the discipline values encounters with difference and declaring its "inherently pluralist" nature, as Ed Ahearn and Arnold Weinstein put it (78). "Cross-cultural reflection" also inflects Emily Apter's sense that an "exilic consciousness" has enabled "comparative literature's very disciplinarity" (94). The flight of scholars from World War II-torn Europe to American universities; the postcolonial version of that intellectual diaspora—here experiences of displacement ground the discipline's theoretical predispositions. In rejecting literary nationalism, in foregrounding ambiguity as a cultural dynamic and melancholy as a psychic manifestation of social upheavals, this comparative literature attends to the wrenching disidentifications of history. Or, as Ahearn and Weinstein write, this comparative literature proceeds "aware of but not defined by Difference in all its powerful forms" (78).

In short, ethnic difference is for comparative literature both limit and inherent principle. Here Rey Chow's ascription of a "fundamental ambivalence" to the discipline offers a useful perspective on the institutional construction of ethnic difference (108). Chow suggests that comparative practice can draw no certain path from this ambivalence. But it can, I suggest, draw on ambivalence to sustain a perspective Damrosch calls "inherently elliptical" (128). To do so is, first, to follow Damrosch's lead, refuse the comparative act a fixed point on which to center its operations, and posit instead "a new literary geometry" in which the ellipse—"that geometric form generated from two foci"—propels comparison into action. Generated in this way, comparison clears ground for difference by

redefining the discipline and its object and adapting disciplinary practices to previously "marginal subjects" (122). Modeled on the ellipse, comparison yields more attentiveness to difference. Yet second, and more significant for the purposes of this argument, Damrosch's sense of the elliptical makes room for reconstructing the place of difference in comparison. In the elliptical dispersion of terms, the potential exists for difference to be always variable, instead of a point of permanence. Difference remains perpetually on the verge of its own displacement. Or, to put it another way: in the ellipse of comparison, difference slips into *différance*.

BIGGER THOMASES EVERYWHERE

If Damrosch's ellipse plots comparison around difference—or what Damrosch might call unforeseeable pivot points—his view of comparison discovers a pivot in Bigger Thomas, whose biography Richard Wright reconstructs in "How 'Bigger' Was Born." The novel's critical history offers at least two contexts for this comparative thinking. *Native Son* has been taken up as a naturalist work, a precursor to the more explicitly existentialist *The Outsider,* and a protest novel. Often biographically based in Wright's involvements with Communism, French existentialism, as well as the negritude movement, these readings turn on a comparative gesture situating Wright's work in a dynamic of influence. The early reception of *Native Son* thus repeats the filiation described by the novel's title. By contrast, when, thirty-odd years later, a newly emerging African American literary studies turned to *Native Son,* it did so also by playing a comparative hand. Thus Houston A. Baker concedes the validity of prior interpretations of the novel but insists on defining *Native Son* as "the first black novel that captured [the] full scope and dimension of African American 'folk heritage'" (13). Against the intertextual comparisons in which *Native Son* travels between European and American literary traditions, Baker urges readers to consider the novel in its indigenous context. In so doing, he places Wright in a literary tradition that includes James Weldon Johnson's *The Autobiography of an Ex-Colored Man,* Jean Toomer's *Cane,* Langston Hughes's *Not without Laughter,* and Arna Bontemps's *Black Thunder.* He secures the novel's textuality through its expression of nativity.

Baker's insistence on a native textuality emphasizes that comparative arguments proceed too often blind to their own logic. His challenge to such blinkered thinking echoes Frantz Fanon's scathing assessment of the function the black performance of alterity serves: "the Negro," Fanon writes; "is comparison."[10] For Fanon, this comparison elevates whiteness because "the world always expects something of the Negro" (139)—that is, because the world consigns blackness to failure. Yet Fanon's syntax also identifies blackness with comparison in a way that exposes the operations of the latter. This is the double rhetoric driving "How 'Bigger' Was Born," in which Wright both follows Fanon in critiquing the comparative act and refuses the rigidity of Fanon's despair. Wright's essay conjures a peculiar existence for Thomas—one in which he shuttles between being a specific classification and a global type—that renders comparison the ceaseless process of management, negotiation, and evaluation. In so doing, the essay suggests that comparison accommodates (ethnic) difference by repeatedly suspending it.

Comparison underlies "How 'Bigger' Was Born" from the outset. If the essay does not begin with Bigger Thomas, its discussion of genre—in which perpetual exclusions establish and maintain a literary taxonomy—catapults the essay into comparative action.[11] Of the genre, Wright observes:

> In a fundamental sense, an imaginative novel represents the merging of two extremes; it is an intensely intimate expression on the part of a consciousness couched in terms of the most objective and commonly known events. It is at once something private and public by its very nature and texture. Confounding the author who is trying to lay his cards on the table is the dogging knowledge that his imagination is a kind of community medium of exchange: what he has read, felt, thought, seen, and remembered is translated into extensions as impersonal as a worn dollar bill.
>
> (vii)

Claiming *Native Son*'s generic uniqueness, Wright also acknowledges that the novel's singularity puts his authorship at risk. Thus while he describes the imaginative novel as the "merging of two extremes," he speaks of the toll the blending takes on his status as the novel's originating voice. The ability of the imaginative novel to straddle intimacy and objectivity, to strike the private and the public in one blow, produces the author's imagination as common coin, "a kind of community medium of exchange." The distinctiveness of the genre lies in its repudiation of authorial centrality. Or, to follow Wright's logic to its end, *Native Son* accomplishes its uniqueness by making its author fit a type—comparable to others.

That the passage registers Wright's unease through a trope of currency underscores the significance of conceding authorial comparability. Wright admits his distaste for viewing his work as "a kind of community medium of exchange," going so far as to suggest that having an audience, because it involves exchange as readerly consumption, means chancing the imagination that has enabled the exchange in the first place.

To be read is to have had that imagination "translated" and thereby to have entered into relations "as impersonal as a *worn* dollar bill" (my emphasis). Significantly, the passage critiques authorial originality through a mixed metaphor compounding the linguistic with the economic. Mingling translation with the image of a dollar bill faded by countless hands effects a view of usage not so much as an index of value but as a lessening by dilution. This is a fate to which Wright seems both resigned and resistant. His description of writing as a gamble only heightens the sense that fate is on the line. An effort "to lay his cards on the table," writing necessarily risks exposure. Or, more pointedly, writing is sustained by the exposure by which it can also be undone.

Yet Wright's discomfort regarding his authorship does not extend to the portrait of his character. If the challenges inherent in preserving ethnic difference against absorption or assimilation worry today's comparatists, they pose no such qualms for Wright. He veers, instead, in the opposite direction, insisting on Bigger's typicality as well as the political necessity of such characterization. One might even go so far as to say that Wright's comparative thinking in his analysis of "the imaginative novel" anticipates his discussion of his protagonist's functional typicality. Thus, when Wright concludes his discussion of genre and authorship, he proceeds with an account of the Bigger type that then propels his vision of a global politics. From a description of the five-Bigger spectrum to the contention that Bigger embodies a metaphoric alliance between oppressed populations: in Wright's hands, typology marks a comparative rhetoric structuring "How 'Bigger' Was Born." Comparison moves the essay, simultaneously shoring up and complicating Bigger's status as a representative African American.

The idea of a Bigger type first appears with an autobiographical claim—"the birth of Bigger goes back to my childhood"—which soon gives way to the complications of a multiple "birth." "There was not just one Bigger," Wright insists, "but many of them, more than I could count and more than you suspect" (viii). Multiply conceived, the construction of the type progresses through a sequence of five portraits. An escalation of social defiance marks how Biggers number 1 and 3, in bullying and taking advantage of fellow African Americans, anticipate the behavior of later Biggers, including that of Bigger number 5, who reserves his far more open rebellion for white authority—sitting, for instance, in the white section of streetcars and challenging conductors to move him to his "proper" place (ix-x).[12] The lives of African Americans writ large through this serialized type drop out, however, within pages of the classification scheme. Bigger's typicality undergoes a radical shift when Wright makes the provocative claim that "Bigger Thomas was not black all the time"—that he numbers in the "millions" and appears "everywhere" (xiv). Indeed, describing how his new understanding of Bigger has rendered him more sensitive to the machinery of oppression worldwide, Wright declares that he "began to feel far-flung kinships, and sense, with fright and abashment, the possibilities of alliances between the American Negro and other people possessing a kindred consciousness" (xv). A vision for unity, the passage nominates Bigger as a representative "American Negro," placing him as an equal alongside potential comrades in the larger, global realm of political transformation. Yet so does it imply that Bigger is not simply a comrade but also the unlikely touchstone for an oppressed subjectivity around which "alliances," based in a sense of "far-flung kinships," can be built. In this moment of revolutionary imagination, the extended family models politics.

What to make of this transformation? How can Bigger live doubly in the essay, as both a type based in particularity and a figure of general proportions, without having his ethnic specificity compromised?[13] I suggest that the tension between the two turns "How 'Bigger' Was Born" into a restaging of the act of comparison. Early in the essay, the comparative act both yokes and specifies, producing the representative African American man and the inevitable narrative that scripts his American fate. The Bigger type proceeds serially, each of the five Biggers reinforcing it through an implied comparison with his counterparts. Each of the five Biggers, in other words, is himself Bigger by virtue of his difference: "If I had known *only one* Bigger," Wright observes, "I would not have written *Native Son*" (ix; my emphasis). Meanwhile, when the vision of revolution takes center stage, a comparative turn redraws Bigger's silhouette as that of Everyman. Here Bigger exceeds the ethnic type he has earlier defined: Wright's account of an "*extension* of my sense of the personality of Bigger" means the character has grown "Bigger" than the initial portrait that gave him life (xiv; my emphasis). At the same time, the force of this generalization depends on Bigger-the-specific-type as the ground from which it derives. Without Bigger—the representative of the African American experience—as a point of comparison, the Bigger Everyman could not exist.

"How 'Bigger' Was Born" thus locates an understanding of Bigger Thomas with the comparative complexities I have been describing. In Wright's hands, Bigger shifts from position to position, serving as a representative of ethnic difference and a generalized human condition. Readers uncomfortable with the universalizing gesture have sought to explain it through

Wright's political affiliations; the alliance he envisions, as more than one critic has argued, manifests a Communist ideology of unified revolution in which the novelist imagines African Americans playing a part.[14] In this familiar account, Bigger's difference is assumed into (and that assimilation justified by) the putatively larger, transcendent view of humanity in the throes of an emergent political consciousness. Thus Wright's essay, ostensibly concerned with the character's evolution, rhetorically produces Bigger through multiple comparisons—in particular, through the implicit comparison that emerges when Wright moves Bigger from one typology to another. In that instance, in the shift from racialized specificity to an extended familial type, the essay leaves Bigger suspended. In that instance, Bigger enacts that sense of hovering any act of comparison must at some point face, becoming, in effect, a figure for comparison.

"How 'Bigger' Was Born" defines comparison by insisting on and deferring (Bigger's) difference. This double action allows Wright to sustain contradictory analyses: thus an account of the ways in which American racism creates, only to repudiate, African American subjectivity can coexist with a universalist vision that foregoes ethnic and national differences in the name of political alliances. The essay's production of Bigger points out and troubles that political reduction of ethnicity that would make comparison prohibitive. And more: it describes a comparative practice that, by performing the dilemma of accommodating difference, also retains difference as a necessary and invigorating limit. As premise and subject, difference provides the basis for an intertextuality in which the terms of comparison are neither fixed nor left untouched. Difference ensures that another comparison is always on the horizon.

RESTLESS NATIVITY

I approached all of these new revelations in the light of Bigger Thomas, his hopes, fears, and despairs; and I began to feel far-flung kinships, and sense, with fright and abashment, the possibilities of alliances between the American Negro and other people possessing a kindred consciousness.

(Wright, "How 'Bigger' Was Born" xv)

But can you really make a family of thousands? One that will last? I know he never sought to be an ethnic politician. He didn't want them to vote for him solely because he was colored or Asian. He knew he'd never win anything that way. There aren't enough of our own. So you make them into a part of you . . . all this because you are such a natural American, first thing and last, if something other in between.

(C. Lee 326)

Fifty years after Wright "sense[s]" in Bigger Thomas the viability of global "alliances," Chang-rae Lee imagines John Kwang, a Korean American borough councilman who speaks across ethnic populations and creates a constituency despite—or out of—interethnic tensions. At press conferences and rallies, in formal speeches as well as informal dinners with volunteers, Kwang calls for what Wright might have viewed as an example of kindred consciousness. In one such instance, Kwang addresses a crowd after hostilities between African Americans and Korean Americans have left two people dead and several stores firebombed. Drawing on a rhetoric of psychic interiority, Kwang implores his audience to understand the incidents not as "a black problem or a brown and yellow problem" but as the product of "self-hate." He urges those in the crowd to "think of yourself, think of your close ones, whom no one else loves, and then you will be thinking of them, whom you believe to be other, the enemy and the cause of the problems in your life" (151-52). He proposes using self-reflection to engage empathy and affiliation. If Wright turns Bigger into a figure for a politics based in alliances, Lee figures Kwang as the voice for such a politics.

Yet both Wright and the protagonist Henry Park know that realizing this vision is no easy feat. Despite characterizing politics as a family affair, Wright acknowledges the "fright and abashment" that accompany his sense of "far-flung kinships"; meanwhile, Park suspects that the unity of "a family of thousands" can only be fleeting. Further, both address how unlikely a springboard ethnic difference is for movements broader in scope. Thus Wright anticipates in "How 'Bigger' Was Born" that turning his character into a global rallying call will incur skepticism and anger from certain readers. And when Park observes that Kwang "didn't want them to vote for him solely because he was colored or Asian," he articulates the dynamic that will inevitably cast the councilman—however thoughtful his platforms—as a token, the ethnic politician. A global type for the countless oppressed, Bigger jeopardizes his specificity. A politician who endorses the strategic value of coalition building for ethnic groups, Kwang faces being reduced to a type. The risk boils down to the status accorded to their acts of ethnic representation.

Bigger Thomas and John Kwang embody, in other words, the difficulty of interethnic politics. And their fates—when Kwang suffers a political scandal the public turns against this upstart immigrant, and Bigger's actions only confirm what the public believes it knows about African Americans—demonstrate that accomplishing this politics is far from certain. Yet I want to take both characters seriously and argue for a textual version of the interethnic relations they propose. What happens, then, to the difference of ethnicity when it is read across texts, when an act of reading places *Native Son* and **Native Speaker** alongside each other? Even a quick consideration of the chiasmus of the novels' titles makes the intertextual relation seem inevitable. If *Native Son* foregrounds the filiation structuring Bigger Thomas's relations to family, culture, nation, and the world, it also insists that speaking these relations contributes to their significance. Meanwhile, **Native Speaker** places language at the heart of Henry Park's narrative but asserts that the character cannot avoid filiation in what he will have to say. In this crossing, ethnic difference is not simply a construction but indeed constructed by the imbrication of filiation with speech.

Indeed, further unraveling the titular thread reveals how nativity functions as a decisive and troubled factor in the intertextual construction of ethnic difference. Nativity links filiation and speech as conditions of the protagonists' subjectivity: native sons by virtue of their birth, Bigger Thomas and Henry Park are also native speakers. Both speak to the effects of nativity, indicting the pretense with which it confers legitimacy on their ethnic differences only to find them wanting. Nativity is also, however, the site at which the intertextual relation encounters its own ethical complicity in the ethnic femininity both novels exploit. To the extent that the erasure of women of color enables the novels' analysis of nativity, a comfortable resolution to this problem may not exist. Rather, this discomfort marks a necessary condition for an intertextuality invested in the honoring of difference.

The novels' critique of nativity is most pointed when the texts take two all-American institutions—the legal system and private sector capitalism—as targets. Thus *Native Son* articulates how the law can preserve the maxim "innocent until proven guilty" and simultaneously find Bigger Thomas guilty by calling him a native son. Bigger's attorney, Max, makes this point clear in his closing speech, asserting that Thomas represents "a mode of life in our midst . . . plowed and sown by our own hands" (359). The figure of "life" in native soil describes African American history as an organic process, one in which "life new and strange" arises from surrounding conditions. "So old" is this cultivation that it precedes Thomas as "an order of nature" (368); the result, Max observes, is that Thomas's way of life could only be "a way of guilt," his "crime exist[ing] long before the murder of Mary Dalton" (361). Racism enables the proleptic cultivation of African American nativity. These are terms that earlier, during the inquest, Thomas himself anticipates—as he has known them all his life. When the coroner exhibits Bessie Mears's body to prove Mary Dalton's rape, Thomas recognizes the ploy and its possession of him as the native ethnic subject: "even after obeying, after killing, they still ruled him. He was their property, heart and soul, body and blood;

what they did claimed every atom of him, sleeping and waking; it colored his life and dictated the terms of his death" (307). Power ("they still ruled him") and possession ("he was their property") converge in a lifelong association in which his nativity is inescapable.

Native Son demonstrates that Thomas's value stems not from what his body can do but from the fact that his difference—bodily inscribed in his crime—can be claimed and thereby judged. Thomas is claimed for his difference and then abandoned because of it. This dynamic acquires even more force when its inverse illustrates the eager embrace with which a multiculturalist capitalism commodifies Henry Park's nativity. The thinking that makes Bigger Thomas both native and a default criminal finds a telling counterpart in the strategies of Glimmer and Company, a private sector firm for which Park works as an ethnic consultant. Founded by Dennis Hoagland—who realizes that the mid-seventies influx of immigrants will create a "growth industry"—Glimmer and Company provides "ethnic coverage" in the guise of information. The firm proceeds from no national agenda, pledging "allegiance to no government" but "dealing" in people instead and valuing Park because of his ability to facilitate such dealing. As an ethnic consultant, Park profiles Asians and Asian Americans who have drawn the attention of businesses and government units anxious to protect their own interests. His ethnicity marks his first qualification: in a telling slippage, the firm deems Park a *fellow* native by presuming that he shares with his assignments common heritage—enough to win their confidence and elicit the information they reputedly possess (17-18).

This is not to say that American nativism does not value its subjects but to emphasize the uses to which such value is put. In his fantasy of "running a big house like the CIA," Hoagland describes a plan by which he would "breed agents by raising white kids in your standard Asian household" (173). This thinking regards Asian discipline in much the same way that it damns Thomas's "Negro" criminality—by casting Asian discipline as a supplement to an American nativity that then absorbs the ethnic native for its own convenience and profit. Park's hybrid identity makes him the exemplary spy, distinct and heads above "white" Americans who, "even with methodical training were inclined to run off at the mouth" (172). *Native Speaker* affords Park the status of a subject—he does the profiling, while *Native Son* addresses how Thomas is the object of profiling—but that status is overdetermined. Perhaps more important, the brazenness with which the firm treasures Park reveals not

only how it serves this nativist American ideology but also the ideological zeal with which district attorney Buckley relies on profiling to prosecute Bigger Thomas.

Driven by fantasy, neither Hoagland's nor Buckley's nativism can move forward without women: Hoagland's house of hybrid agents presumes the existence of mothers, while Buckley cannot do without Bessie Mears in arguing the case against Thomas. The novels (whose narratives otherwise center on male protagonists) cannot do without femininity: the murder and supposed rape of Mary Dalton propels Thomas into public consciousness, and Park's narrative begins when his wife Lelia leaves him. Yet the textual gesture locating femininity as a narrative crux, as the linchpin of the protagonists' troubles, raises questions about the analysis of nativity the novels advance. Femininity leaves both novels vulnerable to the critique that their analysis of nativity is not innocent. What does it mean that the novels proceed at the cost of their depictions of women? How does paying heed to femininity contribute to, complicate, or even impede the argument that an intertextual dynamic constitutes ethnic difference?

One feminist response to these questions might begin with the placement of women of color as guarantors of (male) ethnic subjectivity. You-me Park and Gayle Wald thus explain that Ahjuhma, the sole Korean woman in *Native Speaker,* shoulders weight crucial to the novel's narration of Park's past. Brought to the United States after the death of Park's mother, Ahjuhma confirms the Parks' accomplishment of the American dream (their domesticity is sustained by the labor of an other) even as she embodies Korean authenticity (in cuisine, for instance). As such she sustains the adolescent Park's self-loathing—his revulsion at her appearance displaces hatred "towards the part of [his] Koreanness that refuses to yield to 'real' Americanness" (621). Trudier Harris discovers much the same situation in *Native Son,* where the narrative pits Bigger Thomas against the black women (his mother and Bessie Mears). *Native Son* views black women's subservience as complicity and in so doing turns black women's work into collaboration or "being in league with the oppressors of black men." Calling this representation a kind of double-standard nativism, Harris remarks that black women function as "native" to "what whites want for blacks" and "foreign . . . to individual black development" while the novel casts Thomas's desires as "native" to "the best of American traditions" and "foreign" to such "Afro-American subservience" (63). Thomas emerges the exemplary American hero, his disenfranchisement the source of his heroism. Had Harris known of Henry Park, she might have put him on Thomas's case.

For these readers, *Native Son* and **Native Speaker** regress through the representation of women of color: the textual violence wrought on ethnic femininity diminishes any analysis of nativity the novels might pose. Yet I want to suggest that the novels' construction of ethnic femininity emerges out of a view of ethics distinct from that which such criticisms assume. To make this argument is to shift away from the ethical positions that have come to dominate ethnic literary study: that reading literature entails holding representation responsible, that reading literature means holding out for more or more responsible representations, and that reading ethnic literature means attributing ethical force to ethnicity. Rather than proceed only with these formulations in mind, I suggest that an intertextuality produces ethnic femininity across *Native Son* and *Native Speaker* by enacting the risk of diluting ethnic difference. Moving between the bodies of Ahjuhma, Mrs. Thomas, and Bessie Mears, this intertextuality foregrounds the ethical difficulty of writing women of color even as it insists on the necessity of doing so.

I begin this case for an intertextual construction of ethnic femininity by observing that **Native Speaker** and *Native Son* depict the charges leveled at them by feminist readers. In **Native Speaker,** this is to recall, as the novel does in flashback, a family visit during which Lelia accuses Henry and his father of exploiting Ahjuhma. When she learns that "Ahjuhma" is a formal title and not a name, Lelia refuses to imagine that the woman's life could remain so unacknowledged. "This woman has given twenty years of her life to you and your father," she says to Henry, "and it still seems like she could be anyone to you" (69-70). In this way, Lelia critiques the coincidence of anonymity with femininity and anticipates the unease Park and Wald articulate (623-24). Meanwhile, Harris's claim that *Native Son* relegates black women to complicit subservience finds articulation in Bigger's identification with Bessie at the inquest. There Bigger not only understands the coroner's spectacular and strategic use of Bessie's body but through that understanding can voice her anger at the subservience trapping her: "Anger quickened in him: an old feeling that Bessie had often described to him . . . a feeling of being forever commanded by others so much that thinking and feeling for one's self was impossible" (307). Bessie's consciousness dictates the terms of Bigger's response. The anger quickening in Bigger has its source in "an old feeling" of Bessie's; his experience of anger, while a product of his frustrations, nonetheless derives from hers.[15] Lelia's accusation and Bigger's identification: both acts make acknowledging ethnic femininity a textual imperative.

My point is not to defend either novel for its representation of women of color. Readings that pinpoint Bess-

ie's depiction or Ahjuhma's relative absence turn to the two as representatives of ethnic difference, indexing what *Native Son* and **Native Speaker** have to say about African and Korean American women.[16] Their terms—the realistic, the ideal, or even the authentic—presume that representation can be judged on some success-or-failure rate. I argue instead that ethnicity demands and profits from intertextual reading. The juxtaposition of Bessie and Ahjuhma, because it must keep in mind the "other" woman of color, can begin to account for the turns by which femininity figures ethnicity. Thus Ahjuhma's silent preservation of Korean cultural traditions in the Parks' Korean American home acquires critical force through Bessie's articulation of her place in white domesticity; thus the futility of Bessie's speech is confirmed by Ahjuhma's insistent refusal of speech. Invested in their protagonists, the novels may speak only indirectly, if at all, to the textual deployment of femininity as the material ground for ethnicity. But that ground cannot be avoided in their juxtaposition.

The novels in fact enact this juxtaposition in their negotiation of interethnic relations between women. When, for instance, Lelia solicits Ahjuhma's speech, Park's narration implies that she does so hoping that conversation will induce cross-cultural understanding (70). And yet these good intentions only meet hostility: Ahjuhma tells Henry that there exists "nothing for your American wife and me to talk about" (71). While Lelia's advances seek to bridge difference, Ahjuhma's response reinforces it. Ahjuhma speaks through Henry what Bessie Mears might have said to Mary Dalton: that womanly bonds of identification are difficult to make, or, more pointedly, that the American (or white feminist) presumption that no difference will remain a difference is ill conceived. Only ever mediated by Park, Lelia and Ahjuhma's conversations emphasize that the relations between Bessie and Mary are little more than a missed encounter. On the night of her death, Mary says to Bigger that she would like to meet his "girl," never knowing that the two have already not met at Ernie's Kitchen Shack and that Bessie was the one to foil that encounter (73-75). When Ahjuhma insists that she and Lelia share no common ground, she puts into words what Bessie performs. To call these incidents "missed encounters" is to underscore their necessary elusiveness. If *Native Son* does not imagine any affiliation between Bessie Mears and Mary Dalton, **Native Speaker** confirms the impossibility of such affiliation by imagining it only to refute it.

Through their juxtaposition Bessie and Ahjuhma argue against their placement in relation to one another. That juxtaposition asserts, ironically, the implausibility of interethnic relations as well as that intertextuality that brings them together. What does it mean that ethnic intertextuality should post warnings against the crossing its presence implies? I have argued that this irony does not signal the futility of ethnic intertextuality but rather that its limits will always be felt and must be made manifest. At times such limitation must be spoken through that intertextual association it critiques. Unlike a model of multiculturalist reading that turns to the promise of otherness shared by ethnic literatures (a transcendent ethnic commonality), ethnic intertextuality promises only that textual affinities are as viable as they are provisional. The balance lies between a double insistence on possibility and responsibility: a balance struck, for instance, by Bigger Thomas's comparative figure. If the problem is one of ethics—of not skirting the obligation to account for ethnic difference—then I am suggesting that intertextuality renews this obligation by defining ethnicity as difference never fixed but always suspended. In intertextuality, ethnic literature renews itself as a project capable of exceeding—indeed, risking—its own bounds in its willingness to view difference not separately but crosswise.

Notes

1. The One Book, One New York campaign featured a sponsorship of businesses and organizations, including *Publishers Weekly, Library Journal,* the *New York Times,* and the New York Public Library ("NYC").

2. The New York Women's Agenda expressed similar concerns (Kirkpatrick). Of this dispute Rachel Lee notes the assumption "that positive portraiture of Korean Americans equals further representational progress for Korean Americans" (343).

3. Catherine Hong's review of the novel is among four of the twenty-three reviews excerpted on the book jacket that read the novel alongside an African American tradition of cultural expression. Hong makes explicit reference to Ellison. Meanwhile, the back cover jacket quotes Frederick Busch's remark that the novel composes "the wounded love of Asian Americans for their nation" as a "moving, edgy new *blues*" (my emphasis).

4. At the same time, this invisibility becomes a reason to keep a watchful eye on Asian Americans. Consider here the FBI's pursuit of the Los Alamos scientist Wen Ho Lee in November 1999 (Persico).

5. For a sustained account of the trickster figure, see Jeanne Rosier Smith.

6. Wong's *Reading Asian American Literature: From Necessity to Extravagance* (1993) was one of the first full-length studies of Asian American literature.

7. Wong describes "counterparts to the Asian American racial shadow": the "tragic mulatto/mulatta" in Nella Larsen's *Passing* and the "mixed-blood Pauline/Sister Leopolda" of Louise Erdrich's *Love Medicine* (115-16).

8. See also King-Kok Cheung. This status quo remains, even when cross-cultural work begins to emerge. Thus Smith in *Writing Tricksters* calls for "models of successful cross-cultural negotiation, which allow for points of exchange and intersection across racial, cultural, and ethnic divides, without obliterating or oversimplifying differences" (xii-xiii). Her book, however, repeats these divides, with individual chapters on Asian American, Native American, and African American literatures.

9. The Levin, Greene, and Bernheimer Reports appear in full in Bernheimer's volume.

10. See Fanon 211, 139. As Diana Fuss argues in *Identification Papers,* for Fanon the Negro is not even afforded the realization of alterity, since that would imply access to subjectivity. Fanon's reference to Bigger Thomas is well known.

11. Consider how Derrida's argument in "The Law of Genre" presumes a comparative logic.

12. I number these Biggers for clarity of reading, not in any attempt to describe a progression in Bigger's characterization.

13. One of this essay's readers suggests that Wright's yoking of the global and the political is fraught with broader complications. Postcolonial and transnational thinking have interrogated appeals to the global as some exemplary site of politics for their unquestioning universalism. Yet appeals to particularity as political ground are no less untroubled. My reading emphasizes that Wright's rhetoric places Bigger in both positions: potentially guilty of universalist politics or of identity politics or both. But so is his figure suspended between the two.

14. Wright's tangled relationship to Communism is outside the scope of this argument. It is worth noting, however, that the Communist Party took *Native Son* to task for what it deemed its excessive turn to individualism.

15. For Barbara Johnson, this intimacy of consciousness means that Bessie, "the silent presence in the scene in which Bigger Thomas writes," is Bigger's best reader (69).

16. Calling Ahjuhma a Korean American woman raises a number of questions that I have not the space to address here. What, if anything, makes Ahjuhma American? Her arrival at the Park home? The period of her residence?

Works Cited

Ahearn, Ed, and Arnold Weinstein. "The Function of Criticism at the Present Time: The Promise of Comparative Literature." Bernheimer, *Comparative Literature* 77-85.

Apter, Emily. "Comparative Exile: Competing Margins in the History of Comparative Literature." Bernheimer, *Comparative Literature* 86-96.

Baker, Houston A. Introduction. *Twentieth Century Interpretations of* Native Son. Englewood Cliffs: Prentice, 1972. 1-20.

Bernheimer, Charles. "The Anxieties of Comparison." Introduction. Bernheimer, *Comparative Literature* 1-17.

———, ed. *Comparative Literature in the Age of Multiculturalism.* Baltimore: Johns Hopkins UP, 1995.

———. Preface. Bernheimer, *Comparative Literature* ix-xi.

Bernheimer, Charles, et al. "The Bernheimer Report, 1993." Bernheimer, *Comparative Literature* 39-48.

Chen, Tina. "Impersonation and Other Disappearing Acts in *Native Speaker* by Chang-rae Lee." *MFS* 48 (2002): 637-67.

Cheung, King-Kok. *Articulate Silences: Hisaye Yamamoto, Maxine Hong Kingston, Joy Kogawa.* Ithaca: Cornell UP, 1993.

Chow, Rey. "In the Name of Comparative Literature." Bernheimer, *Comparative Literature* 107-16.

Damrosch, David. "Literary Study in an Elliptical Age." Bernheimer, *Comparative Literature* 122-33.

Derrida, Jacques. "The Law of Genre." *Acts of Literature.* Ed. Derek Attridge. New York: Routledge, 1991. 221-52.

Dwyer, June. "Speaking and Listening: The Immigrant as Spy Who Comes in from the Cold." *The Immigrant Experience in North American Literature.* Ed. Katherine B. Payant and Toby Rose. Westport: Greenwood, 1999. 73-82.

Engles, Tim. "'Visions of Me in the Whitest Raw Light': Assimilation and Doxic Whiteness in Chang-rae Lee's *Native Speaker.*" *Hitting Critical Mass* 4.2 (1997): 27-48.

Fanon, Frantz. *Black Skin, White Masks.* New York: Grove, 1967.

Fuss, Diana. *Identification Papers.* New York: Routledge, 1995.

Gates, Henry Louis, Jr. *The Signifying Monkey: A Theory of African-American Literary Criticism.* New York: Oxford UP, 1988.

Harris, Trudier. "Native Sons and Foreign Daughters." *New Essays on* Native Son. Ed. Keneth Kinnamon. Cambridge: Cambridge UP, 1990. 63-84.

Hong, Catherine. Rev. of *Native Speaker* by Chang-rae Lee. *Vogue* Apr. 1995: 236.

Johnson, Barbara. "The Re(a)d and the Black: Richard Wright's Blueprint." *The Feminist Difference.* Cambridge: Harvard UP, 1998. 61-73.

Kirkpatrick, David. "Want a Fight? Pick One Book for All New Yorkers." *New York Times* 19 Feb. 2002: B1. Lexis-Nexis. Dupré Lib., U of Louisiana, Lafayette. 16 July 2004 <http://web.lexis-nexis.com/.

Lee, Chang-rae. *Native Speaker.* New York: Riverhead, 1995.

Lee, James Kyung-Jin. "Where the Talented Tenth Meets the Model Minority: The Price of Privilege in Wideman's *Philadelphia Fire* and Lee's *Native Speaker.*" *Novel* 35 (2002): 231-57.

Lee, Rachel. "Reading Contests and Contesting Reading: Chang-rae Lee's *Native Speaker* and Ethnic New York." *MELUS* 29.3-4 (2004): 341-52.

"NYC to Read *Native Speaker.*" *Publishers Weekly* 18 Feb. 2002: 16. *Cahiers Business Information.* Lexis-Nexis. Dupré Lib., U of Louisiana, Lafayette. 16 July 2004 <http://web.lexis-nexis.com/.

Park, You-me, and Gayle Wald. "Native Daughters in the Promised Land: Gender, Race, and the Question of Separate Spheres." *American Literature* 70 (1998): 607-33.

Persico, Joseph E. "Life under Suspicion." *New York Times* 17 Feb. 2002, sec. 7: 9.

Pratt, Mary Louise. "Comparative Literature and Global Citizenship." Bernheimer, *Comparative Literature* 58-65.

Smith, Jeanne Rosier. *Writing Tricksters: Mythic Gambols in American Ethnic Literature.* Los Angeles: U of California P, 1997.

Spivak, Gayatri. *Death of a Discipline.* New York: Columbia UP, 2003.

Wong, Sau-ling Cynthia. *Reading Asian American Literature: From Necessity to Extravagance.* Princeton: Princeton UP, 1993.

Wright, Richard. "How 'Bigger' Was Born." Introduction. Wright, *Native Son* vii-xxxiv.

———. *Native Son.* New York: Harper, 1940.

Lou Freitas Caton (essay date 2008)

SOURCE: Caton, Lou Freitas. "A Korean American Perspective: Tolerating Truth and Knowledge in Chang-Rae Lee's *Native Speaker.*" In *Reading American Novels and Multicultural Aesthetics: Romancing the Postmodern Novel,* pp. 121-37. New York: Palgrave Macmillan, 2008.

[*In the essay below, Caton traces the relationship between tolerance and truth in* Native Speaker *through Henry Park's experience.*]

Henry Park, the viewpoint character of *Native Speaker,* begins his story like one of the many walking wounded of contemporary American literature. Exhibiting the inward illness of repressed anger and despondency, Henry's pain derives from a largely unarticulated awareness that the deepest philosophical questions, those having to do with the seemingly arbitrary nature of experience, are burdened by confusion, incoherence, and simulation. These ontological and epistemological uncertainties turn into a physical injury when, in a supreme moment of incomprehensible injustice, his only son dies in an accident. Because the world— unfairly imperfect—allowed his son to die in a foolish schoolyard catastrophe, Henry feels life has little meaning or joy. This bitterness of being unjustly singled out by fate is further compounded both by misrepresentations related to his ethnicity and the duplicity associated with his job. That is, Henry lives an unrecognized, uncertain American life in at least three distinct ways: the world refuses to recognize him, he works as a spy, and he is Asian. Serving as a type of psychological paralysis, such a triple whammy produces in him a sorrowful desire for authenticity and acceptance.

And that desire does bear fruit; as his story unfolds, this ethnic outsider becomes healthy. He learns how tolerance, defined here as an openness to unintelligibility and difference, arises necessarily and unwilled. Stated differently, Henry heals himself when he discovers that a tolerant acceptance of an impure knowing leads to self-forgiveness, a compassionate response that arises as a necessary consequence of that very imperfect world that had earlier troubled him. The novel, after all, is an effort at finding truth as self-forgiveness through confession. Henry states early on: "I lied to Lelia. For as long as I could I lied. I will speak the evidence now" (6).[1] Henry's eventual realization of tolerance enables him to acknowledge this "lying" self and the arbitrary consequences of an unfair world.[2]

This approving partnership of self and world forms a phenomenon I call "romantic negative tolerance." I enlist the term "romantic" in the William Blake or Walt Whitman sense of an embracing of contradictions, uncertainties, and confusions.[3] Whitman's ranging recognition that opposites form dialectical relationships, reason fails to fully explain experience, and personal authenticity arrives through an acceptance of global differences, all of this—the spirit of romanticism—underlies Henry's eventual ability to gain self-understanding. Specifically, my Whitmanesque point is that because experience is ultimately unknowable, one must accept the various forms of diversity and uncertainty that compose the phenomenon of knowledge and truth in an unfair world. Since this is a

generalized principle, not dependent on individual will or agency, I label it as a negative force.[4] Through this romantic interpretation, *Native Speaker* offers tolerance as an inherent, universal quality of consciousness, one based on what we do *not* know rather than what we *do* know.[5] It arises as a radical principle of doubt to liberate Henry toward a full reception of his actions in a seemingly uncaring world. Such tolerance grows into a bridge toward others as it reminds Henry of how difference and unknowing can combine to create an introductory, open acceptance of blind experience.[6] How does this occur? I begin with the specifics of Henry's ailment and later locate the insights that prepare him for possible healing through this negative romantic tolerance.

On the very first page Lee reveals Henry as a character seeking but unable to find his authentic voice; Henry wants to be a "native speaker" of his real self but continually stumbles, as the opening episode regarding the "list" suggests. The first sentence of the novel states: "The day my wife left she gave me a list of who I was." Will the list provide the necessary ingredients of who Henry is? Such an inventory no doubt contains valuable information, yet the reader is denied immediate access to it. Lee defers revealing the items on the list for several pages. In fact, before presenting this initial information to the reader, Henry tells us that he threw away the original and only kept photocopies; hence, when the reader eventually *does* hear of the particulars, they come from a copy not an original. Henry does, in fact, directly refer to this list in a general fashion: he comments on it and even anticipates its possibilities, but he does not actually report on the contents until page five. The repeated references to the note, but not the actual information, create other "copies" that continue the occurrences of postponement and deferral rather than what one would expect: lines of revelation or discovery. And then just before the note is finally disclosed, after pages of anticipation, its status and significance are thoroughly disputed.

Henry, after all, expects the note will at least be affectionate and personal: he wants "a love poem." He knows, however, that the list could just as easily be considered "a cheap parting shot, a last-ditch lob between our spoiling trenches" (5). The note, then, becomes important only for its uncertain, fragmentary, belated, and simulated status rather than for its ability to reveal information. A communiqué that might hold insights into authentic self-discovery turns into reiterated displacements or duplications that are continually postponed until they eventually surface as a list of severed, ambiguous fragments. This emphasis on *incompletion* inaugurates the central force of the psychological thesis of the novel: feeling frustration over the disjointed inscrutability of the world, Henry suffers and seeks healing.

Lee's narrative continues to underscore this theme of dissatisfaction at self-discovery due to much of this same interference from substitutions, displacements, and ambiguous fragments of information. One could call this a variant of the "postmodern condition"; it serves as the opening gambit for what will develop into even deeper psychological illnesses for Henry. Of course, one could claim that the major contributor to Henry's inability at self-discovery derives not from the inchoate quality of this note and his interpretations of experience but, instead, from his first-generation Asian American status. And, indeed, sections of the story do show him to be very similar to the "invisible" Korean stereotype that Lee portrays at various times: dispassionate, stoic, quiet.[7] For instance, when his wife complains that she does not "know how [Henry] felt about anything, our marriage. Me. You," Henry cannot respond: "[O]nce again I had nothing to offer" (127). Henry does, indeed, appear to be someone like his parents who, as he says, tend to "lock up" (158) just when personal revelation is needed. What complicates this commonsense observation, though, is that Henry *can* reveal himself under the care of Dr. Luzan, the psychiatrist Henry is investigating in his job as a spy. He is able to move beyond his inhibitions or psychological blocks in this specific situation of doctor/patient. But that satisfaction occurs only when he is in the disguise required for his job, when he is technically someone else.

Under these occupational conditions of *in*authenticity, then, he is able to achieve the public facade *of* authenticity. Complicating this situation even more is the fact that Henry seems to be able to talk about his real life only while playing this role of someone else. His "mask" or legend belies his true self, and Luzan is proven clairvoyant when he tells Henry, "You'll be fine." "You'll be your self again, I promise" (22). Henry, in fact, is so adept at confessing his real life while in the disguise of someone else that his employer must pull him off the case. Knowing he has divulged too much about himself, Henry admits that his "legend" or false identity was actually turning into his real identity: "I was looping it through the core, freely talking about my life, suddenly breaching the confidences of my father and my mother and my wife" (22). This leads eventually to Henry wanting to reveal the whole truth, "whatever was required for him [Luzan] to take me seriously" (209). But before that can happen, Henry is ushered out the door and Dr. Luzan dies in the so-called boating accident.

This loss of human connection and redemption through confession matches that loss of communication discussed in the fragmentary personal note of the open-

ing pages. In this case, the promise offered by the humanism of psychoanalysis is perverted by Henry's obligation to work as a spy; deception and mendacity take precedence over his efforts to achieve self-discovery. Contrasting sharply with Dr. Luzan's psychology of hope, then, is the spy's realization that telling the truth endangers one; it joins my other examples of disillusionment and frustration when one tries to find the truth of knowledge and authenticity in an arbitrary world. That is, Henry's early emphasis on "copies" and the deferred experience of the note matches his squandering here of an opportunity to narrate an original, immediate, holistic story, one that might have moved him toward self-knowledge and principled truths. For after all, Luzan counsels Henry to reveal himself through the wholeness of a story; his psychologist wanted direct, unified narratives: "Luzan always preferred that I speak to him in skeins such as this; he urged me to take up story-forms, even prepare something for our sessions" (206). In other words, Luzan believes that the originality and organicism of a personal story represents the nature of an individual "although the crucible of a larger narrative" (206). But, as before, instead of the satisfaction of originality, immediacy, and knowledge that arises from a personally told-story narrated to an insightful audience, Henry is left, as before, with only clouded thoughts, past images, and scattered experiences. In order to realistically and metaphorically emphasize this insensibility, Henry is physically drugged and taken out of Luzan's office, the location of potential truth, by thugs who were hired by his employer, Dennis, to guarantee that Henry not reveal such knowledge. Hence, it is at the moment of possible redemption, confession, and revealed selfhood that the strongest evidence yet of an arbitrary world of power sabotages the chances for healthy self-knowledge.

The novel continually complicates these problems of authenticity and instability through other characters and incidents, as well. We see it in Dennis Hoagland, the boss and "director" who is "of course . . . a sick man" (31). He is responsible for Henry's employment and contributes to the pessimism and depression surrounding him. For example, Hoagland's pervasive cynicism comes forth in his introductory comments about how "[t]he fucking sun must have died" (38). He is a "dyspeptic," "fitful," "freak of a man," also known as "the human black cloud" (32-3). Not as morbid but finally regarded with similar displeasure, the politician John Kwang devolves into an untrustworthy and deceptive person, someone who early in the story is a character of promise and principle. But perhaps the most powerful incident to register the notion of an uncaring, hurtful world for Henry is the accidental death of his son, Mitt. Mitt dies in a playground, a specifically designated area of innocent fun and joy where children should be able to play harmlessly with each other. Instead of experiencing such mirth, Mitt suffocates at the bottom of a "dog pile." That is, Mitt dies without reason in a place foreign to death, in a moment of supposed innocence and purity. The haphazard nature of the incident and its inhumanity is borne out by the continuing declaration of one of the children, *"It was just a stupid dog pile"* (emphasis in original, 105). The incident leads Henry to a comatose-like existence. He loses caring for much of anything, but he especially loses emotional contact with Lelia, his wife: ". . . it was about what must happen between people who lose forever the truest moment of their union." Henry describes it as "living, remaining on the ground, and what we know as the narrow and the broken" (106). Lelia tells him, "You live in one tiny part of your life at a time" (224). It is as if he cannot take Luzan's advice to see himself in the larger narrative that world-acceptance might offer him. He, instead, becomes as "serene as Siberia" (248).

But Henry does come back to life. Through an accepting tolerance of this exact same pain, he reaches a point where he can no longer resist and indict hurtful experiences, especially those he cannot completely govern or prevent. For example, near the end of the novel when John Kwang has been exposed as a corrupt politician and must face a crowd composed of the hateful and violent, Henry chooses not to be a passive observer. Pushing his way through the crowd in an effort to join and, ultimately, defend Kwang, Henry "strike[s] at everything that shouts and calls." In the end, they are both knocked to the ground, and Henry sees Kwang "like a broken child; shielding from me his wide immigrant face" (343). In that instant of solidarity with this symbol of abused authority and shocking duplicity, Henry reveals a tolerance and forgiveness for others who have been damaged in this same arbitrary, enigmatic world. His momentary joining with Kwang is a joining with the entire world's guilty. It gives Henry the symbolic redemption and unity he has unconsciously desired throughout the novel. This climatic event prepares the reader for the conclusion when Lee, making a more complicated use of masks and impostures, has Henry helping Lelia in her job as a speech therapist. No longer deferred, separated, or fragmented in the world (signaled by Lee's use of the present tense), Henry, possibly for the first time, feels as if his "voice moves in time with [his] mouth, truly belong[ing] to [his] face" (349). And as "the difficult names" of the children are called, they sound "lovely and native," no longer foreign and alienated. I will discuss this scene in more detail soon. For now, though, I simply want to posit that the novel does end with affirmation and hope.

Is such an ending earned? In other words, has Lee provided adequate cause for Henry to declare these differences as "lovely and native," differences that earlier might have separated him from others and/or been considered by him to be random, hurtful, and fragmentary? Most critics affirm and applaud the positive autonomy suggested in this conclusion; however, none has read it as a philosophical statement of tolerance and self-forgiveness.[8] To begin in that regard, it is important to remember that Henry does fully embrace difference for the first time at the end of the novel, but he does so as one who remembers a forgotten friend. The acceptance of others, which includes an implicit reception of difference, had partially composed his character before his son died, as was evidenced by his ability to accept and withstand racial slurs (103) or his father's immigrant behaviors (185). Revisiting that tolerance now with a fullness of being and an apparent awareness not displayed previously, Henry is alive again. Only this time he recognizes that the same notions of arbitrary difference that had prevented him from an experience of authenticity after his son died can now be used to unify him. For instance, in that moment cited above of Henry aiding the corrupt John Kwang against the hatred of the crowd, Henry acts in spite of the uncaring quality of the world. Rather than violently fighting and joining a crowd that constructs a reductive and melodramatic scene of goodness over evil, Henry, for no apparent reason, joins the side of the beleaguered and tries to protect John Kwang. And Lee suggests that it is not only Henry who has the potential to rise above the reductive and hubristic reaction of "good over evil." Lee hints that even the crowd displays a latent ability for Henry's type of undifferentiated compassion and acceptance. Early in the scene "they [the crowd] gaze at [Kwang] as if he were their son . . ." (342). And, in fact, Lee had earlier suggested that a "messianic" mood had, indeed, enveloped the Kwang organization (143). The notion here that Kwang might be a Christ-like figure reckoned in conjunction with the reader's awareness of Mitt's martyr-like death turns the climax into a portrait of love without reason. Granting Kwang a charismatic, spiritual aura, Henry struggles to perceive and "see" Kwang as the crowd thickens: "Suddenly I can't see him any longer. I can bear anything but I will not bear this" (342). Henry must "see" or perceive Kwang as a full, substantial person, not the one-dimensional monster that the crowd constructs. This effort by Henry to fully "see" Kwang, in fact, turns into a kind of love or compassion for what Kwang represents: the misguided, the corrupted, the lost promise of anyone facing violence and possible harm. The scene ends with the two of them together, almost in each other's arms.

A quick review. Forgiveness and sympathy for those who have fallen compose this climatic scene due to Henry's accepting tolerance for the corrupted Kwang. Henry begins the story, as I mentioned earlier, with an array of contextual and psychological confusions, all of which lead to his loneliness, sadness, and anger at an unknowable world. But he later realizes that it is precisely the ability of these uncertainties to underpin how we are different, how we cannot be sure of what constitutes our differences, that obliges us to maintain an acceptance and/or tolerance of our inability to know the other.[9] Consequently, then, acceptance cannot be generated by positive knowledge or what one knows about the other, but just the opposite: what one cannot know generates compassion. As a further indication of Lee's interest in this matter, I would like to turn now to the Walt Whitman epigraph that begins this novel.

As I mentioned earlier, Whitman's romanticism haunts this novel. Lee uses two lines from the start of stanza four of Walt Whitman's poem "The Sleepers" as his epigraph: "I turn but do not extricate myself, / Confused, a past-reading, another, but with darkness yet" (Whitman 428). One might critique these lines as generally representative of Whitman's desire to embrace and comprehensively embody as many of the contradictions and uncertainties of the past as possible. These words, and the poem generally, show an interest in historical experience that is not dependent on intellect or reason. Hence, an early biographer of Whitman noted that "The Sleepers" presents emotions, thoughts, and images as "they actually occur, apart from any idea—the words having in the intellectual sense no meaning, but arousing, as music does, the state of feeling intended" (Bucke 5). Typical for Whitman, such expressions of the world may confuse or contradict but that should not encourage one to "extricate" oneself from history or relationships. Grasping history—our "past-reading[s]"—includes not only this uncertainty but even, as the last line indicates, the more generalized "darkness" of unknowing. That is, the compromised clarity of one's insights must not prevent one from accepting or tolerating the past; the full spectrum of such perceptions, distorted and unclear as many of them are, still offers a fuller comprehension of what it means to be alive than simply the enlightened notions of rationalizations and reasoned facts.[10] With this epigraph Lee begins his thesis on negative tolerance, negative in the inability of individual reason to adequately define the identity of oneself and others in an ultimately unknowable world.

The foundation for my approach to tolerance comes from writers such as Milton, Locke, and Mill who, in their assorted arguments on diversity and difference, variously suggest that an aspect of sympathy arises from reason's inability to perfectly comprehend an inscrutable world.[11] Their ideas arose in an era of religious oppression but eventually expanded to the larger areas of morals, ethics, and societal behavior in general.[12] Milton's *Areopagitica,* Locke's *A Letter Concerning Toleration,* and Mill's *On Liberty* all argue that people need to be released from unnecessary state restrictions in order to freely form a more prosperous community. Locke especially makes the case that compassion for others develops when those in authority realize that no amount of outward force will change a person's convictions. Because logic, facts, or persuasion is not likely to change beliefs, individuals must be allowed to differ in ethical, moral ways. The concern that begins over religious freedom, then, almost naturally finds its way into the realm of philosophy.[13] Underneath these forms and recognitions of "live and let live," in other words, there exists an unassuming hesitation to see reason leading to ultimate truth. Of course, such humility around rationality is typical for the Enlightenment poet or philosopher who cautioned that claiming too large a domain for the mind's abilities caused disappointment and hubris. One should only pursue truth with limitations and discretion. Hence, Alexander Pope notably wrote in the first epistle of his *Essay on Man* that we humans might, indeed, get close to the truth; however, "'Tis but a part we see, and not a whole." That is, since all people agree that reason's abilities are finite, there must remain crucial concerns that will never be fully understood. With that in mind, the only humane response to seemingly mysterious arbitrary occurrences and strange radical differences is to accept rather than censor or resist.[14] A respect for rationality's limits requires such a forgiving initial response.[15]

This romantic skepticism about reason's powers led transcendental philosophers such as Coleridge, Kant, and Schelling to concentrate more on the conditions rather than the content of experience. As Kant famously stated: "I have therefore found it necessary to deny *knowledge,* in order to make room for *faith*" (emphasis in original, *Reason* 29). These writers emphasize what I am calling the romantic element of tolerance because they recognize a crucial significance in one's inability to know. But, of course, there are problems with this linkage of tolerance and uncertainty. For example, losing a sense of the promise or confidence in reason might encourage one to believe in counter-forms of intelligence. That is, theorizing about why human reason is limited could lead to beliefs in extreme forms of mysticism, religion, and the supernatural. This may be true; however, nothing entails it. In actuality, this type of tolerance more frequently generates useful principles of behavior. For instance, the romantic critic interprets the Enlightenment philosopher's cautious skeptical reason to mean that one must be respectful of what one cannot know. The romantic's preference for transcendental proofs (the preference of Kant, Coleridge, and Hegel, for instance) occurs as a method of deciding where common (knowable) reason ends and uncommon (unknowable) difference begins. Tolerance as a principle or condition of knowing, then, remains reasonable while acts of toleration move beyond reason. This is the insight of acceptance that Henry, through most of the story, cannot comprehend. For my purposes, I am not suggesting here that Henry, or anyone, subscribe to a romantic philosophy in order to accept these ideas; rather, I am proposing that Lee's novel denies a strong form of knowledge (conceptual or discursive reason leading to truth) in order to make room for a strong form of acceptance (aesthetic or poetic reason leading to tolerance).[16] And I do not mean to imply that the non-rational base of this romantic tolerance allows one to become healthy by returning to an "ignorance is bliss" type of existence. My negative tolerance does not encourage naïveté, anti-intellectualism, or complacency. It encourages knowledge but recognizes such a project as always unfinished, insufficient, and inadequately realized. Of course, this kind of tolerance only works if all parties have a collective faith in at least a minimal model of rationality. And it implies the eventual strength of an autonomous subjectivity. These are disputable positions, and both of them, in fact, were famously rejected by Herbert Marcuse in his lecture "A Critique of Pure Tolerance." In it, Marcuse resists the notions of tolerance that I have put forth thus far because, for him, reason *can* achieve objective truth. Since truth, for Marcuse, is knowable, intellectuals should practice "a liberating tolerance" (*Repressive* 109) rather than a humanistic one. Marcuse's tolerance amounts to an intolerance for those groups and individuals who do not promote this objective truth.[17] Because his position squarely opposes mine and is buttressed by a similar distrust of conventional definitions of reason, I want to consider its strengths in light of my interpretation thus far of Lee's novel.

Herbert Marcuse's pessimistic appraisal of the history of toleration as a progressive social policy relies generally on Max Weber's research regarding rationality. According to Weber, reason fails to generate a forward-looking tolerance, one that might provide social liberation, because the material interests of the culture wholly determine reason's manifestations. Rationality does follow formal principles—logic, sequence, coherence, and the like—but it has no inherent qualities that might override culture to necessarily serve "goodness" or "justice." Reason can just as easily serve evil, oppression, and violence. This is why

reasonable people freely lead other reasonable people into massacres, wars, genocides: any action can be "rationalized" by reason. Thus, reason is best described as instrumental or a form of rationalization rather than emancipatory or liberatory.[18] Moreover, ever since the nineteenth century, the demands of advanced industry and technology have significantly changed consciousness. In a "one-dimensional" society, a society that is structured to serve the needs of the powerful and to resist all undermining forces, the resources needed for change will be in the hands of the authorities. Today's "totally administered" societies have become effective "machines" that manipulate reason's potential independence: "The brute fact that the machine's physical (only physical?) power surpasses that of the individual, and of any particular group of individuals, makes the machine the most effective political instrument in any society whose basic organization is that of the machine process" (Marcuse, *One* 3). This late-stage capitalist society so suppresses individuals ability to reason in a deeply oppositional manner that most are incapable of being autonomous subjects (*One* 22). Additionally, consumerism has transformed reason to the point that many people can reflect and reproduce only what the current economic forces dictate: "a mentality is created for which right or wrong, true and false are predefined whenever they affect the vital interests of society" (*Repressive* 95). Individuals "parrot, as their own, the opinions of their masters" (*Repressive* 90). As a consequence, not all individuals can be trusted or expected to know what the truth is. This is a pivotal problem because, after all, "there *is* an objective truth which can be discovered . . ." (emphasis in original, *Repressive* 89). It is, therefore, the responsibility of the strong intellectual, who *does* know this truth, to show the masses what it is. Although toleration may be a virtuous ideal, it must be seen as less important than improving the welfare and economic standards of the majority of people: Truth, according to Marcuse, only emerges via concrete, historical, and material improvements. Intolerance for those who prevent this progress, then, becomes the virtue that conventional forms of tolerance cannot provide.

Many of these points have merit. That is, although I disagree with his thesis, especially his emphasis on defining truth as *only* the material conditions of culture, his argument does thoughtfully highlight key issues in my discussion. He underscores, for example, the importance of tolerance creating space for diversity. In some ways, Henry *is* searching for meaning about the diversity of life. In addition, Marcuse recognizes, and most critics would agree, that those in power do everything they can to stay in power. And if that means controlling an individual's access to the institutions of media, communication, and so on, so much the better.

Again, as the corruption and duplicity in *Native Speaker* seem to indicate, ruling forces mostly operate absent of conventional notions of ethics and morality. Where Marcuse errs, however, is in objectifying truth in conjunction with tolerance. His vivid sense that truth emerges historically when the social conditions have evolved devalues the process of determining what that truth, or truths, might be. In other words, tolerance, for Marcuse, must be "repressive" since truth is an objective reality that one creates. Those who interfere with this material creation cannot be tolerated. *Native Speaker* rejects that notion of tolerance. According to Lee, by contrast, tolerance instead demands a forgiving consciousness because truth consists in the process by which one determines it. Everyone in the novel is involved in the creation of truth so all (except, of course, those who consciously harm others, as Mill stated) should be tolerated. A useful way to see this crucial difference is through dialectical or, what I am calling, romantic examples of not only tolerance but self-knowledge, as well. Dialectic underpins my form of tolerance because it emphasizes an ahistorical idealism that situates important historical, cultural realities in terms of broader, metaphysical concerns. I will come back to this notion soon when I revisit the climax of *Native Speaker* in more detail. But for now I want to briefly outline an example of how a romantic dialectic generally structures our understandings of tolerance. Using Coleridge (a choice that Whitman no doubt would endorse), I present the process of perception as demanding a humanistic tolerance, one that rebuts Marcuse's approach.

When one embraces the liberating significance of unknowing, one participates in a romantic dialectic. My continual use of a romantic discourse, then, specifies how an incomplete knowledge of self and world create just such an interdependent organic enterprise. Although this relationship is complex and oftentimes unsatisfying, it still does advance my argument in useful directions: that is, invoking romanticism moves my argument toward a metaphysical discussion of how knowing is linked to unknowing, self to other, and, still more globally, truth to deception.[19] Much of this may seem elementary; however, it is worth remembering that before the surge of romantic ideas (at least in the Western world), many writers were generally content to conceive of the individual as more or less independent of the world. Coleridge, along with many of the intellectuals of his generation (especially Fichte), challenged that dualism by recognizing the revolutionary implications of transhistorical theories that linked self and world. And those understandings continue today. Indeed, my choice of Coleridge as a spokesperson for this type of romanticism continues his remarkable presence in all manner of contemporary academic and philosophical concerns. Coleridge was, after all, particularly concerned with how self-knowledge affects the politics of a society.[20] Hence, I disagree with those critics who consider English or German romanticism to be a mystifying and conservative political strategy intended to screen the truth of social conditions.[21] Instead, romantics like Coleridge help one see how self-grounding, universal concepts of personhood provide strong political positions for claims of equality and social justice.[22] Further, I do not read Coleridge in order to claim him as an *avantgardist* or someone who anticipated current academic positions. I read him, instead, as a conversation participant, much in the spirit of Hans-George Gadamer's hermeneutic conversations. Finally, because Coleridge synthesizes so many romanticisms of selfhood (Schelling, Kant, Fichte, etc.), he brings an exciting mixture of perspectives into our discussion of knowledge and self-understanding.

Certainly in many ways, a romantic mood could be said to broadly prefigure the compassionate tolerance and self-forgiveness referenced above in my critique of *Native Speaker,* but in at least one important way it indirectly arises out of a major part of Coleridge's explanation of subject/object perception, again, in chapter twelve of his *Biographia Literaria.*[23] As I have mentioned in other chapters, there one sees that the identity of the other "is unconsciously involved" in the identity of one's selfhood (*BL* [*Biographia Literaria*] 1: 260). Similar to the writings of many current philosophers of alterity, the "other" as perceptive object theoretically resides within the subject.[24] This shared otherness, then, is "one and the same thing with our own immediate self-consciousness" (*BL* 1: 260). Such thinking has obviously led many critics to accuse Coleridge, and transhistorical critics generally, of leveling difference and history to make room for a universalist vocabulary of humanism that hides the "real" material relations between people.[25] A close reading, though, indicates otherwise. Recall that Coleridge earlier states that otherness always retains its "extrinsic and alien" quality. In a dialectical operation, though, he also theorizes that simply to recognize otherness means that it is not wholly foreign to our consciousness. And, in fact, every such acknowledgment "modifies" our "being" (*BL* 1: 259); that is, our contact with otherness transforms us. But we can only experience such an alteration if we admit to our *inability* to understand it. This, then, opens to a profound paradox: the unknowable world of otherness becomes part of our consciousness and yet remains unknowable, remains historically different. Or stated in another way, otherness, by definition outside our consciousness, is brought *into* our consciousness but forever retains its alien quality. Coleridge claims this as a proposition of existence and perception that is both unassailable and yet remains "inconceivable" (*BL* 1:259). The implication here is that recognizing such an inability to knowledge opens up a space for tolerance and acceptance, an acceptance not based on what the other is but on one's inability to know that other.[26]

We see such nonrational but inclusive and dialectical moments in the closing scenes of **Native Speaker**. Although Lee should not be classed as a "romantic" writer, he does present somewhat romantic transhistorical, nonrational subjectivities in these closing pages. In Lee's last chapter, for example, he has Lilia face a classroom full of non-English speakers, but she does not teach a strongly structured, highly rational lesson. Instead, "she wants [the children] to know that there is nothing to fear . . ., [that] it's fine to mess [the language] all up" (349). And, in fact, Henry recognizes that with these "foreign language speakers," these small representatives of otherness, what is best is to simply "give them some laughs" (349). In responding to the differences and uncertainties of these children, Henry suggests that it "doesn't matter what they understand" (349). Even without knowing who they are, indeed, perhaps because he cannot understand who they are, Henry thinks of these children as awe inspiring and "wondrous" (349). In the middle of this doubtful landscape, though, Lelia is still able to call out their names in their own language "taking care of every last pitch and accent" (349). By only carefully repeating their names, she speaks "a dozen lovely and native languages, calling all the difficult names of who we are" (349). In other words, Henry and Lelia's inability to arbitrate the various and arbitrary differences represented by the children does not translate into psychological separatism or alienation. As Coleridge suggested above, the children's strangeness, their historical and cultural differences, unconsciously and irrationally enter Lelia and Henry. Indeed, it is through an acceptance of the children that is not dependent on a conventional knowledge of them that Henry frees himself for self-love and an accepting tolerance of their difference. When he embraces them, he declares to himself that his "voice moves in time with [his] mouth, [it] truly belongs to [his] face" (349). He has discovered a form of self-awareness that can unite with others; a unity forms now that was seemingly unavailable to him earlier.

Somehow the otherness of the children, their "extrinsic and alien" identity, as Coleridge calls it, remains distinct and manages to transform Henry. This is, the very dialectical operation of perception itself carries with it the implied structures that necessitate an initial acceptance or tolerance of what we perceive. Henry seems to learn that since *what* we perceive is intimately

linked with *how* we perceive, one must accept the world. Subject and object positions are so intimately related that the sensation of separateness can only be an initially seductive but ultimately incomplete articulation of our experience of the world.[27] One could say, then, that Henry's illness of alienation and inability to love was based on an inaccurate understanding of perception. As Coleridge comments, ". . . object and subject, being and knowing are identical, each involving, and supposing the other" (*BL* 1: 273). In the act of perceiving, one recognizes that the world will not be completely knowable; however, the dialectical structure of perception, not the information it provides, forms a truth of connection that becomes a substantial part of our being. The world remains sharply distinct and foreign while the act of recognizing its particular otherness draws us to it. Henry learns, then, that perception so intimately relies upon an arbitrary world that self-love and tolerance are necessary.

Although almost all critics have acknowledged that Henry finds his own voice at the close of the novel,[28] none has pointed to this dialectic of tolerance and unknowing as the central element. And yet more close readings of several sections suggest that Lee desires this interpretation. We saw it earlier with the dialectic of truth and falsehood in the Luzan sessions. In addition, the overarching spy metaphor, for example, broadly indicates that truth participates in a similar relational operation with its opposite, with deception. When Henry helps Pete Ichibata "break" Wen Zhou— "[Wen] opened like the great gates of the Forbidden City" (174-5)—"he [Henry] was thrilled with what [they] were doing, as with a discovery, like finding a new place you like, or a good book" (175). Henry is "thrilled" because he unconsciously senses at that moment how the dishonesty of his life, "that secret living [he'd] known throughout [his] life," turns out to be a part of what makes for a more complete truth of the world. At other times, Henry believes truth to be less global and more a reductive, transparent event. The reigning illustration for this is Henry's ongoing desire to satisfactorily know why Mitt had to die. But, additionally, he also thought at one point that he might easily "peg" John Kwang (139). Early in the novel, Henry felt he could infiltrate Kwang's organization, "tick off each staging of the narrative" (139), and then simply "tell a familiar story" (140). He would remove the masks, layers, and faces of Kwang "until he revealed . . . a final level that would not strip off" (141). This is the utopian dream of truth and one that Henry, perhaps unawares, discards at the conclusion. For at the close of this novel, Lee gives the reader one final scene of masks; only there, instead of sadly observing that the mask removal does not unveil a single, knowable, Marcuse-like truth, Lee accepts, integrates, and almost celebrates the masks' participation in the community.

The end of the story is upbeat and lighthearted; Lelia wants to give her students "some laughs" (349). She "uses buck-toothed puppets with big mouths [and] scary masks" while Henry wears "a green rubber hood" (348). The masks help make "the talk unserious and fun" (348). For Henry, it helps turn the difficult phrase that the children must learn into "the melody" that they can "singsong" (343). In other words, through both an easing of the role of intelligibility and an acceptance of duplicity, the substitutions, deceptions, and displacements that had so wounded Henry throughout the novel finally become bearable in their final scene. The children, after all, are loved even though confused: "They don't quite know how to respond" (349). Lee offers a relaxation of knowing that brings Lelia and Henry closer to the children and to themselves. And, as a crowning ironic reference to the dialectic of truth and deception, the "truest" advice Henry receives regarding his illness comes from the most deceptive character, Dennis Hoagland, who tells Henry: ". . . no matter how smart you are, no one is smart enough to see the whole world" (46).

Finally, this effort to accept the fact that the complete truth is always unintelligible also occurs in the touching scene of the twig house. As she considers a life without their son, Lelia gathers rocks, twigs, and leaves in order to build a miniature house. She constructs it slowly, a simple analogy for building a life. When she's done, Lelia "peers inside, expressionless" (249). Henry "kneels down before it" as one might in front of a sacred icon (249). It is the transparent metaphor of creation, bonding, and beginnings. Although crucial and satisfying, this is still only a part of the dialectics of a life; existence demands unintelligible destruction and loss, as well. Thus, after Lelia has departed, Henry deconstructs the house, piece by piece. Before beginning the orderly dismantlement process, though, he shouts his son's name "as loud as [his] meager voice can" (249). Finally, he collects the pieces and "fling[s] it all in the woods" (249). The idea here is that the immensity of Henry's experience cannot be indexed adequately by reason, and this recognition begins to release him from the bonds of suffering and toward the purification of cathartic healing. Without this release, Henry is left with Lelia's tragic observation about Mitt's death: "I go crazy thinking about it" (129).

I want to end with a few observations about how my sense of tolerance in literary theory relates to historicity in literature. Merging literary theory with social theory, I maintain that how one sees, the aesthetics of our perception, needs to be understood in terms of social tolerance for difference in an arbitrary world that is not dependent on particular historical differences. That mixture often baffles critics. That is, social theories of tolerance, which are perhaps more frequently discussed in local and historical ways, are often thought to conflict with transhistorical theoretical appreciations. Or, stated differently, the social interpretations of tolerance are seldom presented as universal; most critics claim that social concerns such as tolerance need to arise directly from the specific local, historical structures of the literary work under review.[29] Transcultural interpretations of tolerance, so the argument might go for something like a Korean American novel, devalue the particular political realities of the narrative. Min Hyoung Song declares, for example, that *Native Speaker* should not be read as "a novel about deracinated themes that refer in equal proportion to everyone who might read the book" (80).

But is it that easy? Even when a critic attempts to evaluate a work on its own cultural turf, she still must consider it through certain aesthetic and textual procedures. Do not all of these restructuring efforts, those from within and those from without, change the work in profound ways? James Clifford asks "[h]ow can one ultimately escape procedures of dichotomization, restructuring, and textualizing in the making of interpretive statements about foreign cultures and traditions?" (261). My desire to impose a discussion of transhistorical tolerance onto *Native Speaker* is a move toward a more "tolerant" inclusivity that need not erase historical differences. Finding overarching themes of social bonding does not replace an appreciation for a specifically local, often ethnic, aesthetic that might also be present. Large sections of *Native Speaker* signal interests in specifically Korean expressions, relations, features, characteristics, traits, and so on.[30] And yet such aesthetic and local appreciations appear lost on the uninformed and uninitiated. That exclusion, however, amounts to a loss only when the effort and desire to understand such sections expire. That is, simply our attempt at intelligibility places us inside that culture, if only modestly. The contrary position, that only experts of a culture can profitably explain the text, would force us to only read what we presumably already know. In fact, my emphasis on the incomplete "universal" quality of finite consciousness reminds one that unintelligibility is not the same as an absence of meaning. My position suggests that when one accepts the limits of rationality and experience, as Henry finally does, one is open to new realities, new local understandings of truth. Because I do not sufficiently or completely know the Korean American experience of Henry Parker, for example, does not mean I have squandered my understandings. As I hope this chapter demonstrates, there are recognitions that arrive separate from the ideological cultures of knowledge. Forms of meaning develop when one simply struggles with that which is unintelligible. Moreover, too much comprehension of a subject can conversely keep one only involved in what one already knows—or thinks one knows. Hence, Henry's implicit recognition at the conclusion of *Native Speaker* that certain truths arise out of insufficient knowledge acts as a lesson for all readers of sharply ethnic "foreign" works. Twenty years ago. Reed Way Dasenbrock noted this problem and commented: "A full or even adequate understanding of another culture is never to be gained by translating it entirely into one's own terms" (18).[31] When we fail to see that there is meaning in *not* knowing, we inevitably turn another's cultural categories into our own. Finally, and most importantly, this does not imply that one needs to evacuate historical difference by seizing on "human nature" or "universal" meaning; history, difference, and local recognitions of truth exist in relation to transcultural understandings. Each in dialectical form makes the other understandable. And that helps create respect for an ultimately unknowable world.

Notes

1. Like this one, all references to Lee's novel will be cited in the text via parenthetical page number.

2. Discussions regarding the concept of tolerance are voluminous. I can only hope to suggest a few applications and workable definitions in this essay. My central concern internalizes J. S. Mill's "one very simple principle" for society—that individuals must tolerate various notions of "the good" as long as it does no harm to others (68)—to a toleration of the "goodness" in each individual's imperfection. In other words, I seek to turn Mill's social issue into a psychological issue. This internalization of the concept retains a core principle of toleration: one should not condemn or rebuke experiences of alterity, difference, or arbitrary consequence since one cannot fully understand them.

3. This recognition also duly belongs to the German romantic tradition, one that Whitman favored. Schelling, for example, comments: "For it will be presupposed as undeniable that the representation of a succession of causes and effects outside us is as necessary to our spirit as if it belonged to its being and nature" (qtd. in Snow 77).

4. Negativity here is, among other things, the realization that the complete truth is never available to anyone at any one particular time. The commonsense information that "facts" provide is always partial. Moreover, truth has within itself its own negativity, its own opposition. Hence, the famous Hegelian notion (one that Whitman endorsed and Henry will come to implicitly understand) that "all things are contradictory in themselves" underlies my use of negativity as an unwilled acceptance of the world.

5. My use of tolerance should not suggest the conventional definition of enduring something while repressing a more forceful repugnance or distaste. What I am calling negative tolerance, in contrast, is a somewhat subconscious or implicit recognition and acceptance of another due to the mental and physical limitations we share with all humanity. Although it could devolve into a form of indifference or neutrality, I will use it as a first step toward authentic self-awareness in an arbitrary world.

6. The key rationale here is that the human is primarily imperfect and must tolerate the uncertain. By understanding tolerance in this way I continue some of the ideas of philosophers like Immanuel Kant who investigated the concept of tolerance and tried to move Voltaire and Locke's emphases on "rational-natural law" into a more progressive liberalism that recognized the limits of reason rather than reason's potentiality. For instance, Kant's "indeterminate concepts"—which help show the impossibility of complete understanding—reassert the need for public toleration. I will write much more on uncertainty and tolerance shortly. For more on tolerance as this type of skepticism, see Fotion and Elfstrom (32-5) and Mendus (75-9). For more on how Kant's "indeterminate concepts" are related to tolerance, see Benjamin, especially (36-7).

7. For more on how the theme of invisibility and ethnic marginalization fits closely with the detective or spy elements of this novel, see Chen.

8. Most critics have been rather straightforward and unapologetic in their blanket approval of Henry's ability to "find himself." Kim represents the majority when she compliments Lee for giving the reader a Korean (Henry) who is able to create a composite personality "according to the truth" (147).

9. Literary and social critics frequently struggle to define the importance of unknowing and difference in asserting values. One would think, then, that the concerns over tolerance that I am outlining here might arise in these conversations. After all, the liberal mandate of the Enlightenment (according to Mill) suggested that tolerance would encourage diversity and difference. And Walzer reminds us "toleration makes difference possible; difference makes toleration necessary" (xii). Surprisingly, though, tolerance rarely receives much philosophic attention in these literary, cultural debates. Perhaps like generosity, respect, and acceptance, toleration appears to many to be a simple, unambiguous virtue. Yet a close look at the issues around this word, as I hope this essay provides, demonstrates that complexity not complacency underlies its usage.

10. My emphasis on linking one's inability to know with an acceptance of an imperfect world in *Native Speaker* is in contradistinction to critics such as

Engles who tend to see the Whitman influence representing an erasure of history. For Engles, Henry's self-forgiveness and toleration of an unfair world promotes "a warm, fuzzy White-man-ian [read Whitman as a white man] embrace of immigrant masses [that overlooks] the historical and contemporary density of . . . the struggles of various immigrant groups" (45). This is, of course, the traditional complaint against Whitman, Coleridge, and almost all metaphysical philosophers. And Engles is right to point to this complication; however, I believe one can be globally forgiving *and* historically sensitive, aware of a transcendent unity of tolerance *and* politically astute. That said, it does seem that Lee uses Whitman to indicate how Henry needs more of an oceanic appreciation of the world of woe rather than a specific history lesson in ethnic relations. For a theoretical approach similar to Engles, see the historical reading of Song.

11. I do not want to imply that these writers were relativists or in favor of the irrational over the rational. They all knew that one needed to be rational in order to be tolerant; however, their views also romantically implied that truth is served in the *process* of toleration, rather than in the embracing of one specific view. For instance, Mill's theories have been called romantic for their sweeping endorsement of the different, the marginal, and the minority among us (Dunn 53).

12. "Thus, the debate on toleration moved over the centuries from religion to politics to society" (Fotion and Elfstrom 80). In this regard, Mill is famously known for pushing tolerance toward an acceptance of the alterity implied in "eccentricity," "genius," and "diversity" (132-3).

13. For a view that counters this notion of toleration's steady evolution from a religious virtue to a philosophical concept, see Wolfson.

14. I am, again, indebted here to some of McGowan's comments on Kant's *Critique of Pure Reason.* McGowan states: "While reason will inevitably lead all who employ it properly to the same conclusions, one of those crucial conclusions is that large areas of human concern actually lie outside reason's purlieu. In such cases, the only rational response is to respect different preferences, since no legitimate grounds exist for asserting the superiority of one preference to another" (34). This epistemological predicament, the *via negativa* approach, necessitates an unwilled tolerance.

15. My modulation here from intellectual uncertainty to a liberal pluralism generally follows the philosophical path that Mendus details in sections from her *Toleration and the Limits of Liberalism.* My negative romantic tolerance does tend to grow out of the broader skeptical position that she notes: "there is no moral truth and therefore no one can properly presume to impose it" (76). My more careful articulation, though, emphasizes the uncertainty aspect. That is, there may indeed be moral truths; however, they are impossible to prove with a finite mind. Thus, the best strategy is to initially accept whatever is not immediately harmful or understood.

16. I use reason and understanding in a conventional manner throughout this essay. I do not mean to suggest Coleridgian definitions.

17. "[U]niversal tolerance is possible only when no real or alleged enemy requires in the national interest the education and training of people in military violence and destruction. As long as these conditions do not prevail, the conditions of tolerance are 'loaded'" (*Repressive* 84). For Marcuse, the reality of an authoritative state apparatus (police, national guard, "swat" teams, state troopers, etc.) that, when necessary, can crush any opposition that opposes the current order means that forms of negative Romantic toleration will be counterproductive of any "real" liberation.

18. For more on this, see Webber (24-5, 36-7). Also, useful here is Horkheimer, especially his "The Concept of Man" (1-33).

19. On why this overarching organic dialectic best exemplifies a romantic approach to world-knowledge and self-knowledge (and why it can often disappoint), see Haney's chapter "Oneself as Another: Coleridgian Subjectivity" (173-226) and Thorslev. That said, the notion of an organic dialectic should not be understated as a principle of romanticism. My desire to theorize on how unknowability liberates does not eliminate the core romantic realization that "human beings and natural objects interpenetrate in an 'interactive responsiveness'" (Peer 2). That is, seeing the world as ultimately unintelligible only highlights the imperfection of the human observer. One is still intimately connected to that same incomprehensible world. The two ideas, finite limitations and organic relationships, can and must exist harmoniously in romantic theory.

20. For a brief cross section of just a few of the notable writers who have used Coleridge in this way, see Haney, Lockridge, and Perkins.

21. A well-known advocate of this position is McGann (see chapter 5 in this book). According to him, the romantic's reliance on a miraculous theological aesthetic is no more than a mystified "particular socio-historical position" (1-2). Romantic theories simply shield "the truth about social relations: that the rich and the ruling classes dominate the poor and the exploited" (8).

22. For more on how romantic concepts offer political and social liberation today (played out in terms of Kant's universalism and poststructuralism), see Mohanty's book (199) and my review.

23. Future references to this book will be as follows: *BL.*

24. See Kristeva and Levinas for two representative examples.

25. In general terms, this romantic approach to relationship theory anticipates Whitman and the above-mentioned criticism of Engles. In addition, see Song's worries over the "typical liberal-humanist habit of reading" that only finds "deracinated themes." For Song, such an approach may, intentionally or unintentionally, replace Lee's "unique" concerns for "Korean American self-representation" (80). I am not convinced, however, that transhistorical theories must always erase or replace historical theories. For some examples and explanations of why some critics feel otherwise, see chapter 2 in this book.

26. My reader may want me to fret a bit more on this point. My emphasis on perceptive and rational limitations perhaps links Coleridge too easily with contemporary notions of uncertainty and relativity. Is not this the same Coleridge who had periods of close adherence to Christian values and doctrine that would seem to be anything but relative and uncertain? My response is to point toward the questioning "Coleridge" of Kathleen Coburn's edited *Inquiring Spirit* rather than the more sermonizing one projected within *On the Constitution of the Church and State* and other more dogmatic writings. My "Coleridge" is the one who Coburn in her introduction to *Inquiring Spirit* calls "a questioner rather than a systematizer, provocative rather than dogmatic." He has "the kind of not-rigidly-compartmentalized mind that asks questions that are more important than the answers" (20).

27. By calling on these speculative structures, I suggest that dialectic defines large areas of romantic theory and is useful in understanding how the idealism of tolerance and self-forgiveness arise. I consider the term not only helpful in sensing a "subject-in-process," but also reflective of a broad collection of interdependent relations that unify the world and the subject. It is a concise way to speak of the organic nature of knowing and unknowing. Bowie, commenting on Schelling's thoughts, phrases this Romantic dialectic between the mind and the world as follows: "The basic structures of the world . . . are nothing but a lower form of structures of the mind." Without this modest but essential idealism, one might wrongly believe that one is isolated, alienated, and apart from all others. Without this relational dynamic "the world [comes] to be felt and thought of as [only] other . . ." (48), that is, as separate and essentially unavailable to us. This was Henry's ailment.

28. An important exception, Engles claims Henry fails to achieve autonomy because the "resolution of his identity crisis" culminates in his assimilation into America's pervasive white culture (29). In some

ways reflective of Marcuse's analysis, Engles portrays Henry as more or less trapped by "the effects middle-class white culture has had on him" (28). Perhaps given that, as Engles admits, Henry, like all Americans, is "[i]mmersed . . . in a sea of undeclared whiteness" (28), he obtains about as much autonomy as any Korean American is allowed. But also given that Henry does suffer such extreme emotional hurt throughout the novel, even Engles's qualified autonomy must still at least minimally satisfy one's desire to see Henry as uplifted at the end of the story.

29. This is the "standpoint" criticism that cautions one from maintaining a "view from nowhere" interpretation. The "wall-to-wall" ideological critics who follow such warnings do not allow a discussion of, say, selfhood that is distinct from the local political and social representations of that same self. By contrast, romantic critics maintain that selfhood can be discussed, as can consciousness, as an autonomous idea that generates a philosophical appreciation of the world.

30. Engles is quite useful here in his discussions of Korean realities such as social silences, *nunch'i,* and Ahjuhma (see especially 43-4).

31. I would like to cite my appreciation of Dasenbrock's article. Many of my closing thoughts are closely tied to his.

Works Cited

Bucke, Richard Maurice. *Walt Whitman.* Philadelphia: David McKay, 1883.

Coburn, Kathern, ed. *Inquiring Spirit: A New Presentation of Coleridge from His Published and Unpublished Prose Writings.* New York: Pantheon Books, 1951.

———. *Biographia Literaria.* Ed. James Engell and W. Jackson Bate. 2 vols. Princeton: Princeton UP, 1983

Dasenbrock, Reed Way. "Intelligibility and Meaningfulness in Multicultural Literature in English" *PMLA* 102 (1987): 10-19.

Engles, Tim. "'Visions of Me in the Whitest Raw Light': Assimilation and Doxic Whiteness in Chang-Rae Lee's *Native Speaker.*" *Hitting Critical Mass: A Journal of Asian American Cultural Studies* 4.2 (1997): 27-48.

Kant Immanuel. *Critique of Pure Reason.* Trans. Norman Kemp Smith. New York: St. Martin's Press, 1965.

Lee, Chang-Rae. *Native Speaker.* New York: Riverhead Books, 1995.

Marcuse, Herbert. *One Dimensional Man Studies in the Ideology of Advanced Industrial Society.* New York: Beacon Press, 1964.

———. "Repressive Tolerance." *A Critique of Pure Tolerance.* Wolff et al. New York: Beacon Press, 1965.

———. *The Ticklish Subject: The Absent Centre of Political Ontology.* London: Verso, 1999.

FURTHER READING

Criticism

Carroll, Hamilton. "Traumatic Patriarchy: Reading Gendered Nationalisms in Chang-rae Lee's *A Gesture Life.*" *MFS: Modern Fiction Studies* 51, no. 3 (fall 2005): 592-616.

> Argues that *A Gesture Life* contains a dual narrative, in the form of a tale recounting Doc Hata's assimilation and the story of Kkutaeh and Sunny.

Chen, Tina Y. "Recasting the Spy, Rewriting the Story: The Politics of Genre in *Native Speaker* by Chang-Rae Lee." In *Form and Transformation in Asian American Literature,* edited by Xiaojing Zhou and Samina Najmi, pp. 249-67. Seattle: University of Washington Press, 2005.

> Argues that Lee rewrites the conventions of the spy novel in *Native Speaker* to both formal and thematic consequences.

Cheng, Anne Anlin. "Passing, Natural Selection, and Love's Failure: Ethics of Survival from Chang-rae Lee to Jacques Lacan." *American Literary History* 17, no. 3 (2005): 553-74.

> Explores literary representations of racial minorities in the United States.

Cowart, David. "Korean Connection: Chang-rae Lee and Company." In *Trailing Clouds: Immigrant Fiction in Contemporary America,* pp. 101-25. Ithaca, N.Y.: Cornell University Press, 2006.

> Studies literary influences, politics, and personal and political identity in *Native Speaker.*

Engles, Tim. "'Visions of Me in the Whitest Raw Light': Assimilation and Doxic Whiteness in Chang-Rae Lee's *Native Speaker.*" *Hitting Critical Mass: A Journal of Asian American Cultural Criticism* 4, no. 2 (summer 1997): 27-48.

> Engles examines the influence of white, middle-class culture on protagonist Henry Park in *Native Speaker.*

Eoyang, Eugene Chen. "English as a Postcolonial Tool." *English Today: The International Review of the English Language* 19, no. 4 (October 2003): 23-9.

> Eoyang interprets *Native Speaker* as a bicultural novel, comparing the text to John Okada's *No-No Boy* and Frank Chin's *Donald Duk.*

Huang, Joan. "Oral Fixations: An Exploration of *Native Speaker.*" *Hitting Critical Mass: A Journal of Asian American Cultural Criticism* 6, no. 1 (fall 1999): 79-87.

> Huang focuses on Henry Park's obsession with how others utilize their mouths, as well as his insecurities with his own oral functions.

Jerng, Mark C. "Recognizing the Transracial Adoptee: Adoption Life Stories and Chang-rae Lee's *A Gesture Life.*" *MELUS: The Journal of the Society for the Study of the Multi-Ethnic Literature of the United States* 31, no. 2 (summer 2006): 41-67.

> Characterizes *A Gesture Life* as one of the more successful works among a growing body of literature on transracial adoption.

Kim, Daniel Y. "Do I, Too, Sing America? Vernacular Representations and Chang-rae Lee's *Native Speaker.*" *Journal of Asian American Studies* 6, no. 3 (October 2003): 231-60.

> Contrasts *Native Speaker* with Ralph Ellison's *Invisible Man.*

Lee, Chang-rae, and Sarah Anne Johnson. "Chang-rae Lee: The Drama of Consciousness." In *The Very Telling: Conversations with American Writers,* edited by Sarah Anne Johnson, pp. 105-20. Lebanon, N.H.:, 2006.

> Discusses plot choices and characterization in Lee's work.

Lee, James Kyung-Jin. "Where the Talented Tenth Meets the Model Minority: The Price of Privilege in Wideman's *Philadelphia Fire* and Lee's *Native Speaker.*" *Novel: A Forum on Fiction* 35, no. 2 (spring-summer 2002): 231-57.

> Compares the ways in which Lee and novelist John Edgar Wideman explore postmodern language, politics, and identity.

Lee, Rachel C. "Reading Contests and Contesting Reading: Chang-rae Lee's *Native Speaker* and Ethnic New York." *MELUS: The Journal of the Society for the Study of the Multi-Ethnic Literature of the United States* 29, no. 3-4 (fall-winter 2004): 341-52.

> Describes the controversy surrounding the selection of *Native Speaker* for New York City's 2002 One Book, One City program.

Lee, So-Hee. "Cultural Citizenship as Subject-Making in *Comfort Woman* and *A Gesture Life.*" *Feminist Studies in English Literature* 14, no. 2 (winter 2006): 91-123.

> Applies Aihwa Onge's concept of "cultural citizenship" in examining the role of gender politics in everyday assimilation practices in *A Gesture Life* and Nora Okja Keller's novel *Comfort Woman.*

Lee, Young-Oak. "Gender, Race, and the Nation in *A Gesture Life*." *Critique: Studies in Contemporary Fiction* 46, no. 2 (winter 2005): 146-59.

> Demonstrates that conflicting ideologies of colonization, patriarchalism, nationalism, and racism interfere with the central character's attainment of a single coherent national identity in *A Gesture Life*.

Ludwig, Sämi. "Ethnicity as Cognitive Identity: Private and Public Negotiations in Chang-rae Lee's *Native Speaker*." *Journal of Asian American Studies* 10, no. 3 (October 2007): 221-42.

> Credits Lee with inaugurating a "major paradigm shift" in ethnic identity theory by changing the focus to the personal dimension of language.

Narkunas, Paul. "Surfing The Long Waves of Global Capital With Chang Rae-Lee's 'Native Speaker': Ethnic Branding And The Humanization Of Capital." *Modern Fiction Studies* 54, no. 2 (Summer 2008): 327-352.

> Analyzes the use of ethnic informants as represented in *Native Speaker*.

Reese, Jennifer. "Flight For Glory: A Father Tries to Connect With His Scattered Family in Chang-rae Lee's Sparkling *Aloft*." *Entertainment Weekly* 755 (12 March 2004): 117.

> Offers a reserved though positive appraisal of *Aloft*.

Russell, Keith A., II. "Colonial Naming and Renaming in *A Gesture Life* by Chang-rae Lee." *Notes on Contemporary Literature* 36, no. 4 (September 2006): 7-9.

> Examines allegorical renderings of the names Kkutaeh and Franklin in *A Gesture Life*.

Seaman, Donna. Review of *A Gesture Life,* by Chang-rae Lee. *Booklist* 95, no. 21 (July 1999): 1894.

> Notes the apt descriptions of the book's main character, Doc Hata, who leads a proper, but emotionally scarred, existence.

Song, Min Hyoung. "A Diasporic Future? *Native Speaker* and Historical Trauma." *Lit: Literature Interpretation Theory* 12, no. 1 (April 2001): 79-98.

> Examines how Henry Park represents himself as a Korean American.

Szmańko, Klara. "Beyond Black and White: Striving for Visibility in *Tripmaster Monkey* by Maxine Hong Kingston and *Native Speaker* by Chang-rae Lee." In *Close Encounters of an Other Kind: New Perspectives on Race, Ethnicity, and American Studies,* Roy Goldblatt, Jopi Nyman, John A. Stotesbury, and Amritjit Singh, pp. 26-31. Joensuu, Finland:, 2005.

> This essay was originally presented June 6, 2003, at the "Close Encounters of An Other Kind: New Perspectives on Race, Ethnicity, and American Studies" at Joensuu University, Finland. Szmańko analyzes *Native Speaker* and Maxine Hong Kingston's *Tripmaster Monkey,* noting that both novels reveal how mainstream society overlooks and exploits minority groups—especially Asian Americans.

Additional information about Lee's life and works is available in the following sources published by Gale: *Asian American Literature*; *Contemporary Authors,* **Vol. 148;** *Contemporary Authors New Revision Series,* **Vol. 89;** *Contemporary Literary Criticism,* **Vols. 91, 268;** *Contemporary Novelists,* **Ed. 7;** *Dictionary of Literary Biography,* **Vol. 312;** *Literature and Its Times Supplement,* **Vol. 1:2;** **and** *Literature Resource Center.*

Haruki Murakami
1949-

Japanese novelist, short story writer, translator, and nonfiction writer.

The following entry presents an overview of Murakami's career through 2008. For further information on his life and works, see *CLC*, Volume 150.

INTRODUCTION

Murakami is a best-selling novelist and short story writer whose works have been translated into forty languages. His unusual style, which combines elements of surrealism, science fiction, fantasy, and high and low culture—all relayed with deadpan irony—has consistently appealed to readers of diverse backgrounds for its evocation of modern detachment and the alienating effects of technology-based societies. Murakami's writings are highly evocative of popular culture in the United States, displaying an encyclopedic knowledge of American music, movies, television, brand names, and popular fiction, particularly the hard-boiled detective stories of Dashiell Hammett and Raymond Carver, whom he cites as his earliest and most enduring influences. Murakami has also extensively translated works of modern American fiction into Japanese, including those of Carver, F. Scott Fitzgerald, Truman Capote, John Irving, and Ursula K. Le Guin. Murakami's eclectic technique, while enthusiastically greeted by Western critics, was harshly judged at first by Japan's literary elite, the *bundan,* who since World War II had advocated a serious literature grounded in history, politics, and authentic Japanese themes. Their unease with Murakami was compounded by his enormous appeal to the *shin-jinrui* ("new human beings")—the affluent postwar generation who shunned Japanese values in favor of all things American, and who brought Murakami to the attention of a global audience. Some of Murakami's later works have directly addressed subjects of historical and political concern to the Japanese, thus containing the element of social consciousness considered so vital to the old guard of Japan's literary establishment. One of the harshest critics of Murakami's earlier writings, Nobel Prize-winner Kenzaburō Ōe, was among the committee who selected his *Nejimaki-dori kuronikuru* (1994-95, *The Wind-Up Bird Chronicle*), an investigation of Japan's role in World War II, for the prestigious Yomiuri Prize.

In 2006 Murakami was awarded the Kafka Prize for his 2002 novel *Umibe no Kafuka* (*Kafka on the Shore*).

BIOGRAPHICAL INFORMATION

Murakami grew up in Ashiya City, Japan, a suburb of Kōbe. His grandfather was a Buddhist priest and his parents, both of whom taught Japanese literature, encouraged a reverence for traditional Japanese values. However, Murakami rejected the classics of Japanese literature, first turning to European writers of the nineteenth century and then later, as a teenager, to American detective stories he acquired in Japanese paperback editions. Equipped with an American dictionary, Murakami began to read the stories of Hammett, Carver, Kurt Vonnegut, and Ed McBain in English, becoming increasingly fascinated with American popular culture. He acquired a prodigious knowledge of jazz by spending his school lunch hours at record stores, and his transistor radio introduced him to the music of Elvis Presley, the Beatles, and the Beach Boys, whose songs provided the inspiration for the titles of some of his works. In interviews, Murakami has linked his distinctive style—a rhythm of short sentences—to his habit of translating into Japanese from his original, somewhat choppy, English, a language in which he was not proficient until later in life. In 1968 Murakami entered Tokyo's Waseda University, where he studied theater arts. When student uprisings caused classes to be dismissed, Murakami used the extra time to indulge his taste for American film. He married fellow student Yoko Takahashi in 1971; together, they operated a Tokyo jazz bar called Peter Cat for several years until 1981.

Murakami traces his decision to write fiction to an epiphany that occurred while he was watching a baseball game in 1978. His first effort was *Kaze no uta o kike* (1979; *Hear the Wind Sing,* which won the *Gunzo* journal's New Writer's Award. The book—its title borrowed from a Truman Capote short story and featuring Beach Boys lyrics on the back cover—became an instant success among young Japanese readers with its coming-of-age theme, detached sensibility, and oddball sense of humor. The protagonist of *Hear the Wind Sing*—like those of Murakami's other novels—is, significantly, both nameless and referred to as "Boku," the colloquial form of the

251

Japanese pronoun for "I," rendered by old-school establishment writers with the more formal *watashi* or *watakashi*. In 1981 Murakami published his first work in a continuous series of Japanese translations of modern American fiction. With the enormous success of *Noruwei no mori* (1987; *Norwegian Wood*), Murakami became a pop icon in Japan. He achieved international celebrity with his first translated novel, *A Wild Sheep Chase*, the 1989 English-language version of *Hitsuji o meguru bōken* (1982). After traveling in Greece and Italy, Murakami settled for a time in the United States, serving as a visiting scholar at Princeton University (1991 to 1993) and as a writer-in-residence at Tufts University (1993 to 1995). His return to Japan coincided with the horrific aftermath of 1995's Kōbe earthquake and Tokyo subway gas attack. In 1982, at the age of thirty-three, Murakami began training to run marathons, giving up the smoking and drinking habits he had acquired while managing Peter Cat. He has since completed twenty-five marathons and several triathlons; his physical workouts and their effects on his writing are recorded in his *What I Talk About When I Talk About Running* (2007).

MAJOR WORKS

The protagonist in a Murakami novel is typically an apathetic young man—either school age or newly entered into the workforce—who commonly aspires to a career in advertising, journalism, publishing, or music. He is generally called on to aid in the unscrambling of a mystery that takes him in unexpected—and bizarre—directions. Murakami's typical protagonist has been viewed by critics as a bookish parody of the cynical, tough-guy American detective. He reports the supernatural occurrences he witnesses with the same frankness and deadpan understatement he brings to the minutiae of daily activity, making the abnormal seem perfectly normal. With the exception of the anonymous narrators, all of Murakami's characters have Japanese names, and the stories all take place in Japan. Yet, because of the profusion of references to Western culture, the novels might be imagined to take place anywhere in the world.

Hear the Wind Sing is the first novel in a trilogy that also includes *1973-nen no pinbōru* (1980; *Pinball, 1973*) and *A Wild Sheep Chase*. The story unfolds in flashbacks, as the twenty-nine-year-old narrator of *Hear the Wind Sing,* an author and divorced upwardly-mobile urban professional man, recalls how it took him eight years to write his first book, a fictional account of the Japanese government's silencing of student unrest in the early 1970s. At the time of the uprisings, the narrator was a self-absorbed biology student obsessed with pop trivia. His political consciousness is awakened by a friend, known as the "Rat," a disillusioned activist. The third novel in the trilogy finds the narrator in search of a mystical sheep, who embodies the persona of the Rat, at the behest of a right-wing power broker. The novel *Dansu, dansu, dansu* (1988; *Dance, Dance, Dance*) continues the adventures of this same protagonist when he uncovers information leading to his discovery that an old girlfriend has been murdered by a famous movie star. The student uprisings of Murakami's college days also provide the backdrop for *Norwegian Wood,* which, like *Kokkyō no minami, taiyō no nishi* (1992; *South of the Border, West of the Sun*), is a more realistic treatment of Murakami's familiar themes of alienation and loss.

Sekai no owari to hādoboirudo wandārando (1985; *Hard-Boiled Wonderland and the End of the World*) is more representative of Murakami's stories with its alternating chapters describing two separate, but equally surreal, worlds—one set in near-contemporary Tokyo describing an information war between rival data-processing gangs and the other set in a timeless realm of the unconscious populated by unicorns and surrounded by a mysterious, threatening wall. In *Kafka on the Shore,* alternate chapters are narrated by the protagonist, a fifteen-year-old Tokyo runaway who lands in the faraway town of Takarnatsu, and the half-witted old man Nakata, possessed of supernatural powers that direct the boy's destiny.

Many of Murakami's short stories also portray the loss of borders between the real and the imaginary. Like his novels, they suggest a hyper-reality made possible by technology and indescribable in linear time, but they also express nostalgia for a less hectic, not-too-distant past: the same characters who take quantum leaps forward and backward in time to the other side of consciousness also quietly sip coffee in twenty-four-hour Denny's restaurants, listening to Bob Dylan and discussing Woody Allen movies. One of Murakami's most famous short stories is "TV People," included in the collection *The Elephant Vanishes* (1993), in which little men from inside the television set invade the protagonist's living room. A reversal of this motif occurs in the novel *Afuta daku* (2004; *After Dark*), in which a sleeping woman is literally sucked into a flashing television screen. "The Rise and Fall of Sharpie Cakes," from the short-story collection *Blind Willow, Sleeping Woman* (2006), is a metaphoric account of Murakami's falling out with Japan's literary elite. In this story, the narrator enters into a contest to invent a new recipe for a popular snack food, but the judges—the "Sharpie Crows"—consider his innovation, though more palatable to younger consumers, far too radical.

The Wind-Up Bird Chronicle and the two-volume *Andaguraundo* (1997-98; *Underground: The Tokyo Gas Attack and the Japanese Psyche*) are distinguished among Murakami's output by their focus on historical and political events. In the first, a rootless young man descends into a dry well in Tokyo, where he is transported to wartime Manchuria through the voice of Mamiya, a survivor of the battle of Nomonhan. Though fantastical, *The Wind-Up Bird Chronicle* is based on extensive research; Murakami sought to confront Japan's legacy of aggression during World War II as a corrective to the popular Japanese image of its citizens as victims of the war. The first volume of *Underground* is a collection of interviews with victims of a sarin gas attack on a Tokyo subway that occurred in March 1995, perpetuated by a radical cult group called "Aum Supreme Truth." The second volume is a collection of interviews between Murakami and members of the cult. *Supuutoniku no koibito* (1999; *The Sputnik Sweetheart*) was inspired by Murakami's sense of the inadequacies of language to describe the horror of such traumatic events as the Kōbe earthquake and the Tokyo subway attack. The Russian Sputnik—the forerunner of modern communications satellites—is used as a vehicle for ironic commentary on the limitations of information technology.

CRITICAL RECEPTION

Critical studies of Murakami rarely fail to address the subject of his attitude towards Japan and the West, especially the United States. These discussions invariably generate questions about his relationship to modern and postmodern trends in literature. As Rebecca Suter notes, first-generation postwar *bundan*—self-appointed defenders of quality literature in the face of pop and pulp—denounced the decadence of Murakami's early writings, considering him postmodernist in his rejection of Japanese themes and identity. Yet, as Steffen Hantke points out, Murakami simply presents his own reality: "Postwar Japanese culture as Murakami has experienced it and as he describes it in his fiction has embraced American cultural imports for so long that they are virtually taken for granted." Noting the tendency of Murakami's narrators to search for life's meaning in their memories of youth—nostalgia that Suter traces to the influence of American modernists F. Scott Fitzgerald and Ernest Hemingway—some critics aver that Murakami believes corporate greed has caused technology to run awry in present-day Japan, resulting in the alienation of its citizens. Matthew Carl Strecher writes, "Murakami Haruki's *raison d'être* as a writer lies in certain key questions he raises about the nature (and ultimate fate) of individual identity in contemporary Japan. . . . [A]s a result of the hyper-commodification of late-model capitalism, the total focus on economic prosperity, and the need in such an economy to control the desire of the consumer, individual identity has been gradually lost, replaced by what might be termed a 'manufactured' subjectivity."

Strecher also underscores the ambiguity of Murakami's position relative to literary practice, calling him a "reluctant postmodernist"—engaged in a struggle to generate new insights about the human condition through the blurring of boundaries between real and magical worlds but aware of the limitations of language to express the inner feelings of his characters as they search the depths of their unconscious. Many critics have viewed Murakami's absurd, illogical plots as commentary on the fragmentation of modern life. On the other hand, Hantke argues that Murakami's disillusionment with society is expressed through the atmosphere of *noir* he creates: "A psychological reading of Murakami's central characters suggests that hard-boiled weariness functions as a mechanism against the trauma of modernity."

Despite the objections of Japan's literary and intellectual elite, Murakami has been widely embraced in his native country for his introduction of a new type of *jun-bungaku* ("serious literature") hero, one who reflects the confluence of East and West in Japan. According to Chloë Schama, it is this sense of Murakami as an agitator for change that accounts for his worldwide appeal: "Murakami's protest speaks not only to his own generation, but to generations younger and older; and not only to the Japanese, but to people scattered across the globe. . . . The rebel figure, set against conformity and commodity, appears throughout Murakami's work. . . ."

PRINCIPAL WORKS

Kaze no uta o kike [Hear the Wind Sing] (novel) 1979
1973-nen no pinbōru [Pinball, 1973] (novel) 1980
Hitsuji o meguru bōken [A Wild Sheep Chase] (novel) 1982
Sekai no owari to hādoboirudo wandārando [Hard-Boiled Wonderland and the End of the World] (novel) 1985
Noruwei no mori [Norwegian Wood] (novel) 1987
Dansu, dansu, dansu [Dance, Dance, Dance] (novel) 1988
Murakami Haruki zensakuhin, 1979-1989. [Complete Works of Murakami Haruki, 1979-1989] (novels and short stories) 1990-91

Kokkyō no minami, taiyō no nishi [*South of the Border, West of the Sun*] (novel) 1992

The Elephant Vanishes (short stories) 1993

Nejimaki-dori kuronikuru. 3 vols. [*The Wind-Up Bird Chronicle*] (novel) 1994-95

†*Andaguraundo* 2 vols. [*Underground: The Tokyo Gas Attack and the Japanese Psyche*] (nonfiction) 1997-1998

Supuutoniku no koibito [*The Sputnik Sweetheart*] (novel) 1999

All God's Children Can Dance (short stories) 2000

Sydney! [2 volumes] (nonfiction) 2001

Kami no kodomo-tachi wa mina odoru [*After the Quake: Stories*] (short stories) 2002

Umibe no Kafuka [*Kafka on the Shore*] (novel) 2002

Afuta daku [*After Dark*] (novel) 2004

Birthday Stories (short stories) 2004

Blind Willow, Sleeping Woman (short stories) 2006

What I Talk About When I Talk About Running (nonfiction) 2007

*Hear the Wind Sing, Pinball, 1973, and *A Wild Sheep Chase* comprise the *Trilogy of the Rat.*

†Part Two of this two-part work was published in Japan as *Yakusoku sareta basho de* in 1998. The English-language translation of *Underground* was published in 2001 and combined the two volumes into a single work.

CRITICISM

Phoebe-Lou Adams (review date November 1997)

SOURCE: Adams, Phoebe-Lou. Review of *The Wind-Up Bird Chronicle*, by Haruki Murakami. *Atlantic Monthly* 280, no. 5 (November 1997): 165-66.

[*In the following review, Adams concludes that* The Wind-Up Bird Chronicle *is an enjoyable and valuable book, despite being difficult to read.*]

Mr. Murakami's long and devious novel [*The Wind-Up Bird Chronicle*] opens in a resolutely mundane way, with the narrator cooking spaghetti. The significant items in the ensuing phantasmagoria soon appear, however—a dry well, a house abandoned because of a series of tragedies, a so-called alley blocked at both ends, the statue of a bird looking sadly unable to fly, and the unidentified wind-up bird that creaks invisibly in a nearby tree. "Wind-up" can mean either an end or a preparation for action. Whether his target is Japan or the world, Mr. Murakami's work sums up a bad century and envisions an uncertain future. His protagonist is a harmless fellow who merely wants to recover his cat and his wife. The troubles, real and

delusional, that he encounters can be seen as extravagant metaphors for every ill from personal isolation to mass murder. The novel is a deliberately confusing, illogical image of a confusing, illogical world. It is not easy reading, but it is never less than absorbing.

Susan Fisher (essay date 2000)

SOURCE: Fisher, Susan. "An Allegory of Return: Murakami Haruki's *The Wind-Up Bird Chronicle*." *Comparative Literature Studies* 37, no. 2 (2000): 155-70.

[*In the following essay, Fisher proposes that the plot of* The Wind-Up Bird Chronicle *mirrors Murakami's change in focus in his work from concentrating on the West to writing about Japan.*]

Murakami Haruki (1949-) has made no secret of his fascination with the West and his admiration for Western things. His fiction abounds in references to jazz, rock and roll, European authors, and American brand names. For ten years, he lived abroad, first in Greece and Italy, and then in the United States. He even claims to have developed his distinctive style by writing first in English, and then translating into Japanese.[1] His deadpan fantasies, with their parodic echoes of American authors such as Raymond Chandler, have earned him considerable success in the West; he is, for example, one of the few foreign contributors to the *New Yorker.*

But in 1995, Murakami decided to return to Japan, and to judge from *The Wind-Up Bird Chronicle* (*Nejimaki-dori kuronikuru,* 1994-1995; tr. 1997), his return coincided with a new direction in his career.[2] For the first time, Murakami has written a novel that deals explicitly with Japanese history and culture. The novel's protagonist, a rootless man with tastes and habits like Murakami's own, descends into a dry well in Tokyo; there, he enters a parallel world where he must do battle with the demons of Japan's recent history—the horrors of the war in China, and the corruption of the modern state. This descent can be seen as an allegory of Murakami's own return to Japan, of his attempt to understand and reenter the world he left behind.

This brief outline suggests that Murakami's career resembles that of many modern Japanese writers: after studying and admiring Western things from afar, he went to live in the West; when disillusion set in, he returned home in order to re-discover and embrace his own tradition. But closer inspection reveals that his relationship with the West is rather more complicated.

To the Japanese writers of earlier generations, the West represented modernity—with all the promise of individual freedom and release from tradition that modernity once seemed to hold. But for a writer of Murakami's generation, modernity is no longer the exclusive property of the West, nor is it so attractive a condition. In order to understand Murakami's relationship to the West, it is necessary to consider him a writer of the postmodern world, of a world in which the "West" and "Japan" are problematic entities, and in which the objects and cultural practices that once defined the West can also be found in Japan. A second complication derives from tensions within Murakami's work. Murakami's early fiction is indeed pervaded by references to Western things and even by Western literary styles; one critic has called it "American fiction translated into Japanese."[3] It is nonetheless fiction about Japan, set in Japan, with Japanese protagonists, and even occasional allusions to Japanese myth and history.

Moreover, can we assume that Murakami's decision to return to Japan was motivated by disillusion? Murakami's references to Western things have from the outset been tinged with irony, and irony is the great solvent of illusion. Of course, someone who knows his subject so well—Murakami's knowledge of jazz and American popular fiction and pop music is encyclopedic—is doubtless half in love with it, but it would be a disservice to Murakami to assume that he thought the West would be somehow better, more magical, more liberating that it actually was.

And what are we to make of the turn to Japan in Murakami's recent writings? First, it is not so radical a change of direction: many themes he explores in *The Wind-Up Bird Chronicle* are also present in his earlier "American" fiction. Moreover, Murakami's return to Japan has not initiated a phase of homage to an idealized, traditional Japan. On the contrary, he seems determined to examine the darkest aspects of recent Japanese history. In this paper, I examine Murakami's relationship to the West and to Japan, with particular reference to *The Wind-Up Bird Chronicle*. I begin, however, by looking at his early fiction in order to demonstrate the tension between the West and Japan that has always characterized his work.

THE BEGINNINGS OF "AMERIKA SHOSETSU"

Murakami, who was born in Kyoto in 1949, was brought up in a household where Japanese literature was important. His parents were teachers of Japanese, and he recollects that "at the dinner table we talked about the *Manyoshu*."[4] As a child, he was made to read classics such as *Makura no soshi* and *Heike monogatari*, but he did not enjoy them. What he did enjoy was Western classics: by the time he was in middle school, Murakami was reading Stendhal, Tolstoy, and Dostoevsky. He was also beginning to acquire his

prodigious knowledge of jazz: he went without lunch in order to buy records.[5] Then at age fifteen, he discovered American popular fiction. With the aid of a dictionary, he made his way through paperback novels: "The first thing I read in paperback was Ross McDonald's *My Name Is Archer.*" While he was still in high school, he also read Ed McBain, Raymond Chandler, F. Scott Fitzgerald, and Kurt Vonnegut: "those sorts of popular novels were the only works I was reading."[6]

After one year as a *ronin,* Murakami entered the drama department of Waseda University. When the student unrest of the late sixties disrupted campus life, Murakami's response was to go to the movies: "I was bored so all I did was watch movies; in one year I think I saw at least two hundred movies."[7] It took Murakami seven years to graduate from Waseda. His graduating essay, "The Idea of Travel in American Cinema," examined movies from *Wagon Train* to *2001: A Space Odyssey.*[8]

Thus, quite early in his life, long before he contemplated becoming a novelist, Murakami was well informed about Western culture, both "high" and popular. His knowledge of the West, untempered by experience, was to give him the raw material to create what Ian Buruma has called Murakami's "virtual reality of America"[9]—that world of his novels where, despite Japanese names, the characters behave, eat, dress, talk, and shop as if they were living in Manhattan.

Take, for example, Murakami's protagonist in *Hard-Boiled Wonderland and the End of the World (Sekai no owari to haadoboirudo wandarando,* 1985; tr. 1991), fantasizing about a night on the town.[10] First the setting: "A quiet bar, MJQ [Modern Jazz Quarter]'s *Vendome,* playing low, a bowl of nuts, a double whiskey on the rocks." Then he imagines the perfect outfit for such an occasion: "A dark blue tweed suit. Three buttons, natural shoulder, no taper, old-fashioned cut. A George Peppard number from the early sixties. The shirt, a lighter shade of blue, Oxford broadcloth, regular collar. The necktie, a two-color stripe. . . ."[11]

While proper nouns that evoke American pop culture are the most noticeable "Western" feature of Murakami's fiction, there are also many references to Western "high" culture. For example, in *Hard-Boiled Wonderland [Hard-Boiled Wonderland and the End of the World]* there are explicit allusions to Bruckner, Bach, Proust, H. G. Wells, Conan Doyle, Lewis Carroll, Borges, Balzac, Stendhal, Turgenev, Dostoevsky, Conrad, Camus, and Somerset Maugham. These allusions, it should be noted, are usually delivered in an ironic manner: for example, the protagonist complains of his Turgenevo-Stendhalian gloom,[12] and prides himself on being one of the few Tokyo residents who can remember the names of all of the brothers Karamazov.[13] In *Hear the Wind Sing* (*Kaze no uta o kike,* 1979; tr. 1987), the protagonist's old friend, known only as the Rat, is writing a novel "about a comedy team loosely based on *The Brothers Karamazov.*"[14] Throughout *A Wild Sheep Chase* (*Hitsuji o meguru boken,* 1982; tr. 1989), a mock-detective story, the protagonist is reading *The Adventures of Sherlock Holmes.*[15]

The Western qualities in Murakami's fiction are not restricted to proper nouns or literary allusions; even his style is perceived as "un-Japanese." Naomi Matsuoka, discussing the links between Murakami's *A Wild Sheep Chase* and Raymond Carver's "Blackbird Pie" (a short story which Murakami has translated into Japanese), demonstrates how Murakami's Japanese emulates the everyday American speech in Carver's fiction. Indeed, she gives examples of how Murakami's characters sometimes use non-idiomatic Japanese phrases that are literal translations of American idioms. Matsuoka quotes critic Inoue Ken, who describes this style as "translation Japanese"; he maintains that writers such as Murakami, who write Japanese but with the syntax of English, have renewed Japanese literature. Indeed, according to Matsuoka, "the American English-like Japanese of such writers as Murakami is also authentic Japanese at the present time."[16]

In an interview with the American writer Jay McInerney, Murakami makes it clear that writing English-like Japanese is exactly what he set out to do:

> When I was a teenager, I thought how great it would be if only I could write novels in English. I had the feeling that I would be able to express my emotions so much more directly than if I wrote in Japanese. But with my limited proficiency in English, that was impossible. It took a very long time before I could somehow write a novel in Japanese . . . because I had to create, all on my own, a new Japanese language for my novels.[17]

Murakami created this "new Japanese language" by writing in English:

> I began by writing in a kind of realistic style. But when I tried to re-read my work, I could hardly bear it. So I re-thought things, and tried writing the first draft in English. When I translated it into Japanese, it had a slightly different form. If I wrote in English, I didn't know very much vocabulary, and I couldn't write long sentences. So the result was a rhythm of writing in short sentences with relatively few words.[18]

This aspect of Murakami's formation as a writer is well known. Added to his reputation as a translator of American fiction, it has contributed to the general view that he is somehow non-Japanese:

> Murakami's novels are like American literature translated into Japanese . . . This impression has been reinforced more than anything by the fact that Murakami himself has said that when he began writing novels, he on one occasion re-worked his style by translating into Japanese what he had written in English; moreover, the impression of the style of the "Murakami editions" of writers he has translated such as [F. Scott] Fitzgerald and [John] Irving has presumably also contributed to the formation of Murakami's public image as a faithful translator of American literature.[19]

Murakami's style, however, is not the accidental product of his limited English vocabulary or of his over-exposure to American writers. It is in fact a deliberate imitation of the hard-boiled detective style developed by Dashiell Hammett (who modelled himself on Hemingway). In her study of American hard-boiled fiction, Cynthia S. Hamilton lists its key ingredients: "the use of simple, stripped-down sentences, the portrayal of actions as a series of component movements, the use of understatement, and the practice of giving descriptively equal treatment to human beings and to inanimate objects."[20] These stratagems are also central to Murakami's trademark deadpan style. For example, the following passage from *A Wild Sheep Chase* devotes more attention to making coffee than to the narrator's estranged wife:

> . . . I got up and went over to grind coffee for two cups. It occurred to me after I ground the coffee that what I really wanted was ice tea. I'm forever realizing things too late.
>
> The transistor radio played a succession of innocuous pop songs. A perfect morning sound track. The world had barely changed in ten years. Only the singers and song title. And my age.
>
> The water came to a boil. I shut off the gas, let the water cool thirty seconds, poured it over the coffee. The grounds absorbed all they could and slowly swelled, filling the room with aroma.
>
> "Been here since last night?" I asked, kettle in hand.
>
> An ever so slight nod of her head.
>
> "You've been waiting all this time?"
>
> No answer.
>
> The room had steamed up from the boiling water and strong sun. I shut the window and switched on the air conditioner, then set the two mugs of coffee on the table.[21]

Like Murakami's allusions to Western culture, his imitation of the hardboiled style is ironic. Murakami is not attempting to write detective novels; rather, he is parodying their stylistic conventions, using an American tough-guy style to recount the misadventures of his bookish, melancholy Japanese protagonists. If earlier generations of Japanese writers aspired to write like Goethe or Zola, Murakami has set his sights somewhat lower: he claims that F. Scott Fitzgerald, Raymond Chandler, and Truman Capote are his favourite writers.[22] Murakami indiscriminately mixes references to high and pop culture: the Beach Boys and Vivaldi, Dostoevsky and Elvis Presley, Sam Peckinpah and Michelet. On the one hand, he is genuinely knowledgeable about the names he drops; on the other hand, he seems to be treating the products of both high and low culture as commodities, brand names that can be flourished to signal one's lifestyle and consumer preferences.

Coupled with Murakami's conspicuous though ironic attention to Western culture are motifs and themes related to Japanese literature. Upon close examination, one might conclude, as Ted Goossen does, that even Murakami still has echoes of that "old legacy no one wants to do away with."[23] Perhaps Murakami admits as much through his protagonist in *Hard-Boiled Wonderland*:

> I read *The Greening of America,* and I saw *Easy Rider* three times. But like a boat with a twisted rudder, I kept coming back to the same place. I wasn't going anywhere. I was myself, waiting on the shore for me to return.[24]

As early as 1983, in an interview with Itsuki Hiroyuki, Murakami explicitly acknowledged this turning towards Japan:

> When I myself first started writing, I began from a place where I was converting into Japanese the techniques of Americans like [Kurt] Vonnegut, [Richard] Brautigan, and [Raymond] Chandler, but now I have the very strong feeling that I myself am turning very much towards Japanese things.[25]

How does this turning towards "Japanese things" (*nihonteki na mono*) manifest itself in his fiction? One way is intertextual connections to Japanese literature. For example, *Hard-Boiled Wonderland* has strong parallels with Abe Kobo's *Inter-Ice Age 4* (Dai yon kanpyo-ki, 1951; tr. 1971): both novels feature a detective story subtext, the invention of a machine to alter consciousness, and a watery underground world.[26] And while *Hard-Boiled Wonderland* contains explicit references to the Greek myth of the poet/musician Orpheus—indeed, Suzumura Kazunari asserts that "[i]t certainly might be possible to interpret *Hard-Boiled Wonderland* in terms of the structure of the Orpheus myth"[27]—it also has echoes of the underworld encounter of Izanami and Izanagi. For example, the leeches that infest the underground sanctuary in *Hard-Boiled Wonderland* recall the squirming maggots in Izanami's putrefying body. Lest it seem far-fetched to link this postmodern novel to an ancient Japanese myth,

Izanami and the maggots make an unmistakable appearance in Murakami's short story **"The Dancing Dwarf"** (**"Odoru kobito,"** 1984; tr. 1993). The hero of this story enters into a Faustian bargain with a mysterious dwarf. The dwarf will give him the power to dance and thus attract a beautiful woman, but if the hero speaks, the dwarf will take over his body. The hero successfully uses his dancing ability to seduce the woman he desires without having to say a word:

> I kissed her on the lips and drew back from her, looking at her face once again. She was beautiful, as beautiful as a dream. I still could not believe I had her in my arms like this. She closed her eyes, waiting for me to kiss her again.
>
> That was when her face began to change. A fleshy white thing crept out of one nostril. It was a maggot, an enormous maggot . . . Then came another and another, emerging from both her nostrils, and suddenly the stench of death was all around us.[28]

A Wild Sheep Chase offers a different example of how Murakami's fiction, despite its crypto-American gloss, is concerned with Japan. In the novel, a right-wing power broker, the Boss, wants a particular sheep eliminated; he hires the central character (known only as Boku) to do the job. When the Boss's secretary first briefs Boku on the sheep, his comments hint at its symbolic meaning:

> . . . sheep as an animal have no historical connection with the daily life of the Japanese. Sheep were imported at the state level from America, raised briefly, then promptly ignored. That's your sheep. After the war, when importation of wool and mutton from Australia and New Zealand was liberalized, the merits of sheep raising in Japan plummeted to zero. A tragic animal, do you not think? Here, then, is the very image of modern Japan.[29]

Since the entire novel is devoted to the somewhat ludicrous search for a sheep, one can perhaps assume that the real target of the quest is "modern Japan" itself. There is some justification for this view in what Murakami has said about the "Western" atmosphere of his novels:

> . . . it's not as though I am after a sense of non-nationality. If that were really what I was after, I think maybe I would have set my novels in America. It would be easy if I were really to have them take place in New York or San Francisco. But, you see, what I wanted was first to depict Japanese society through that aspect of it that could just as well take place in New York or San Francisco. You might call it the Japanese nature that remains only after you have thrown out, one after another, all those parts that are altogether too "Japanese." That is what I really want to express.[30]

In part, he is merely representing Japanese urban life as it is at the present time—thoroughly permeated by the popular culture of the West. As Glynne Walley points out in describing Murakami's *Hear the Wind Sing,* American pop culture "is part of Japanese contemporary culture. Any faithful representation of Japan in the 1970s and 1980s must include it."[31] But Murakami is also attempting to write about Japan without falling back on any precious details about traditional life or attitudes. This stance is not merely an attempt to be a transparent recorder, a mere camera. His style and his use of Americanisms are specifically designed to repel sentimental clichés about Japan and the Japanese.

DESCENT INTO THE WELL

If Japan and its modern condition hover in the background of Murakami's early fiction, they erupt into the foreground of *The Wind-Up Bird Chronicle.* It begins in Murakami's familiar vein. The opening chapters present a narrator, Boku, who is an obvious descendant of the narrators of the previous novels: a loner who likes jazz, opera, and pasta. As the central narrative begins to unfold, it appears to focus on Boku's attempts to locate his missing wife and his missing cat. But gradually a darker story comes to dominate the novel: the Japanese experience in Manchuria, the fifteen-year war.

Early in volume 1, Boku visits a man named Honda, a veteran of the Nomonhan Incident. Honda, who is greatly esteemed by Boku's wife's family as a fortuneteller (1:88), has a significant message for Boku:

> When it is time to go up, climb to the top of the tallest tower; when it is time to go down, find the deepest well and go to the bottom of it. If there is no flow [*nagare*], it is best to sit still and do nothing. If you oppose the flow, everything dries up. If everything dries up, this world turns to darkness.
>
> (1:94)[32]

Honda also foreshadows the troubles that lie ahead for Boku: "It is hard to wait for the flow to come out, but you must wait. While you are waiting, it would be better to be dead" (1:96). This flow or *nagare* is Boku's connection to the past, to his own Japanese identity.

In the course of the first volume, Boku discovers a dry well in his Tokyo neighbourhood. He feels compelled to descend it; at the bottom, he finds himself slipping through the walls of the well into a nightmarish realm of depravity, corruption, and violence. In a strangely distorted form, what happens to Boku in this underground world mirrors the experiences of various secondary characters in Manchuria. *The Wind-Up Bird Chronicle* is set in Tokyo in 1984, but the real world of the novel, as Boku comes to understand, is somewhere, sometime else:

> Everything was connected in a kind of circle and the thing in the middle of this circle was the Battle of Nomonhan, Showa 14, in Manchuria, in Asia, before the war. But why Kumiko and I were being dragged into the middle of this kind of historical karma, I couldn't understand. It was something that had happened long before Kumiko and I were even born.
>
> (3:275)

Murakami seems deliberately intent on making his young readership rediscover the truth (or truths) about Japan's war—to understand how this "historical karma" still affects them. Lieutenant Mamiya, a geographer who served in Mongolia with Honda, tells Boku, "Young people like you, Okadasan, probably find this kind of old story boring. But one thing I want to tell you, we were ordinary young men like you once too. I never once thought I wanted to be a soldier. I wanted to be a teacher . . ." (1:243).

Another character who brings into the novel the events of forty years earlier is a psychic healer named Nutmeg (her son is called Cinnamon). Encountering Boku on a Tokyo street, she for unexplained reasons takes him on as an apprentice. (Nutmeg was a child during the war, but she is able to act as a conduit for her father's experiences; Murakami never bothers to explain how Nutmeg, who fled Manchuria with her mother at the end of the war and never saw her father again, is able to recount to Boku what her father witnessed.) Nutmeg's father was the veterinarian in charge of the zoo in Shinkyo, the capital of Manchukuo. At the end of the war, as Soviet troops approached the city, Japanese soldiers were ordered to execute the zoo animals, since they could not be fed during the coming battle. Murakami's description of their slaughter succeeds in making the animals sacrificial victims, emblematic of the uncountable, unnamed human casualties of the war.[33]

A second event witnessed by Nutmeg's father also has a key role in Murakami's reconstruction of the past. A Chinese prisoner of war who attacked his guards with a baseball bat is to be executed with the same weapon. The unhappy Japanese lieutenant who must carry out this order explains it to Nutmeg's father:

> "I've received orders from above that this man is to be beaten to death with the same weapon," the lieutenant said in a dry voice, lightly tapping the ground at his feet with the tip of the bat. "An eye for an eye, a tooth for a tooth, eh. With you, I can speak frankly, but it's a senseless order. Killing these men now, what on earth is the point? We don't have any more planes, we don't have any more battleships, most of the good soldiers are already dead. With a new type of special bomb, Hiroshima was wiped out in the twinkling of an eye. Soon we will be driven out of Manchuria, or else we'll be killed; whatever happens, China will belong to the

Chinese again. We've already killed a lot of Chinese. It is meaningless now to increase the number of corpses. But an order is an order. I'm a soldier and I have to follow orders no matter what they are. Just like we killed the tigers and the leopards yesterday, today we have to kill these men. Please watch, sir. This is another way for a man to die. You're a doctor. You must be used to knives and blood and guts, but you've probably never seen anyone clubbed to death with a baseball bat."

(3:320)

Although the novel is based on considerable research, its key events, such as this execution and the zoo slaughter, are Murakami's inventions.[34] The war recollections are presented in sober, realistic detail. But in a disquieting juxtaposition of fantasy and history, Murakami reworks key images of the war into Boku's dream-like adventures in the well. The baseball bat incident, for example, reasserts itself when Boku finds himself on a street in Tokyo attacking a man with a baseball bat.

The well itself is a re-working of a motif first introduced in the recollections of Lieutenant Mamiya. As a geographer with the Kwantung Army in Northern Manchuria, Mamiya was doing reconnaissance work on the frontier when he and an assistant were captured by Mongolian soldiers. On the orders of the Russian intelligence officer commanding the Mongolians, the assistant, a man named Yamamoto, was flayed alive. Mamiya was forced to watch this most hideous death (described in excruciating detail by Murakami). He then had to choose his own fate: be shot and die instantly, or jump into a well. One of the Mongol soldiers tossed a stone down the well: "To judge from the time the stone travelled until it reached the bottom, the depth seemed considerable" (1:291). Mamiya chose the well, expecting to die there of starvation or exposure. But, miraculously, Honda, who had escaped the Mongolians, rescues Mamiya. In the well, Mamiya had a strange vision:

When I was abandoned by the Outer Mongolian soldiers in the middle of the Mongolian steppes at the bottom of a deep dark well, my legs and shoulders injured, without food or water, I simply waited to die. Before this, I had seen a man flayed alive. Under such unusual circumstances, my awareness was extremely heightened, so perhaps that is why when, for a moment, a brilliant light came shining down on me, I was able to go directly to the very kernel of my own consciousness. In any case, I saw the shape of something there. My surroundings were covered by that intense light. I was in the midst of that flood of light. My eyes could see nothing. I was completely covered in nothing but light. But I could see something [*nanika*] there. In my temporarily blinded eyes, something was trying to take shape. It was *something*. It was something alive. In the middle of the light, just like a solar eclipse,

something seemed to be floating upwards blackly. But I couldn't clearly define its form. It was trying to come towards me. It was trying to offer me something that was like a kind of grace. As I trembled, I waited for it. But that "something," whether it ran out of time or changed its mind, in the end it didn't come to where I was.

(2: 65-66)

Soon after reading this description in a letter he has received from Mamiya, Boku, equipped with an earthquake emergency backpack (2:83) and a rope ladder, descends into the well in his neighbourhood. For reasons he cannot explain, the bottom of the well seems the right place to "think about things" (2:150). After spending the night there, Boku has a dream:

Before dawn, at the bottom of the well I had a dream. But it wasn't a dream. It was something [*nanika*] that happened to take the form of a dream.

(2:130)

Entering the well seems to enable Boku to experience for himself the horrors that Mamiya and others recount. His assaults with a baseball bat mirror the execution of the prisoner. He also sees a man cut away his own skin like the peel of an apple, just as Mamiya witnessed the flaying of his junior officer. Born in 1949, Murakami did not experience the war, but Boku's descent into the well represents Murakami's attempt to enter imaginatively into the suffering of that time.

The well also reveals to Boku the evil of the present. When he slips through the wall of the well, he finds himself in a hotel lobby where, on a giant television screen, his brother-in-law Wataya Noboru, economist and media pundit, is holding forth. In Boku's view, Wataya Noboru is a "chameleon . . . [who] changes his colours according to his opponent's colors" (1:140). He is also a rapist and sadist, who has driven one of his sisters to suicide and has now spirited away his other sister, Boku's wife. Wataya Noboru aspires to the Diet seat vacated by his deceased uncle; in pursuit of his political ambitions, he employs a thug named Ushikawa to ensure that no scandal will emerge about his dark and secret side. With his hidden evil and public prominence, Wataya Norobu seems to symbolize a kind of corruption in the Japanese political system.

As a symbolic device, the well could be connected to Murakami's persistent interest in the myth of Orpheus: after all, Boku goes down into the well in order to find his lost wife whom, ultimately, he cannot regain. But the well also has intriguing connections to ritual patterns in Japanese folk religion. In her famous study of Japanese shamanism, *The Catalpa Bow*, Carmen

Blacker describes two types of shaman. One is the oracle, the receiver of messages from the spirits. The other is the ascetic:

> He is primarily a healer, one who is capable of banishing the malevolent spirits responsible for sickness and madness and transforming them into powers for good. To acquire the powers necessary for this feat, he must accomplish a severe regime of ascetic practice, which should properly include . . . a journey to the other world. . . . [He] must leave our world and make his way through the barrier to visit [the world of the spiritual beings]. This journey he may accomplish in ecstatic, visionary form; his soul alone travels, his body left behind meanwhile in a state of suspended animation.[35]

Clearly, Boku makes a journey, via the barrier of the well wall, into another world. Like the ascetic shaman Blacker describes, Boku becomes a healer: Nutmeg trains him in special psychic therapies. Blacker mentions an "ecstatic interior heat" that the shaman experiences as "proof that he has risen above the ordinary human condition."[36] When Boku returns through the wall of the well, he spontaneously acquires a birthmark that glows with a mysterious heat. The shaman receives help from "a retinue of assistant spirits" and "a panoply of magic clothes."[37] Boku's assistant spirits are the "wind-up bird" (which no one ever sees) and a missing cat (which mysteriously reappears after its long absence); his magic clothes are the earthquake emergency backpack and his rubber-soled shoes, familiar from the "gumshoe" activities of earlier Murakami protagonists. In order to prepare for the mantic journey to the other world, the initiate may undergo *komori,* the practice of "seclusion, preferably in the darkness of a cave," and "in this womb-like stillness he undergoes his fasts and recites his words of power, emerging only to stand beneath his waterfall."[38] Avoiding human contact can be another aspect of training.[39] During the winter after his wife Kumiko leaves him, Boku becomes a hermit, seeing no one. The well he enters is a dark, secluded enclosure. In his first stay in the well, Boku fasts: he has only water and lemondrop candies with him and these soon run out. When he emerges from the well, he takes a shower. Blacker also notes that many ascetics experience an initiatory dream, the "distinctive feature" of which is that "the figure who appears to the sleeper is a spiritual being who afterwards functions as his guardian numen."[40] Kano Crete, one of two psychic sisters whom Boku encounters, appears to him in a dream; she ultimately rescues him from the well. Set against this description of the "other world" journey in Japanese folk religion, Boku's experiences seem less like wild invention, and more like a deliberate re-casting of ancient folk tradition.

The constant associations with water and flow (*nagare*) point also to a Shinto or folk religion context. When Boku returns from his last journey to the other world of the hotel, he is covered in blood; blood and association with death are forms of pollution. The magical re-appearance of water in the well at the end of the novel is a kind of *misogi,* a cleansing of body and mind that enables Boku to return to the ordinary world.

The image of the well has a long history in Murakami's work. In the foreword to *A Distant Drum* (*Tooi Taiko,* 1990), an account of living abroad, Murakami describes what it was like to write Japanese novels while living in Greece and Italy: "Somehow, it felt exactly as if I was writing novels at a desk that was at the bottom of a deep well."[41] In his first novel, *Hear the Wind Sing,* the narrator recounts the plot of a science fiction novel by a writer he admires, the American Derek Heartfield (an invention of Murakami's). This novel, entitled *The Wells of Mars,* describes how "a youth goes down in one of the myriad bottomless wells sunk into the surface of Mars."[42] No other explorer has ever survived descent into the wells, but after many hours of wandering through side tunnels, the youth emerges onto the surface again. He is astonished to discover that fifteen billion years have elapsed while he was in the well. The dying sun explains that "the well passages you came through were dug to curve along the warp of time"[43]—just as the well in *The Wind-Up Bird Chronicle* leads to a world outside time. In *Pinball 1973* (*1973 Nen no pinboru,* 1980; tr. 1985), the narrator tells a brief story about a welldigger, "a bona fide folk genius" who could sniff out the presence of water. The wells he found yielded such sweet water that "some folks claimed [it] came from the melting snow of Mt. Fuji."[44] Before Murakami gets too deep into sentimental folkloric territory, he brings the story to an abrupt end: the well-digger is hit by a train and "several thousand chunks of his body . . . [are] strewn over the fields."[45] Murakami's narrator concludes the episode by cheerily noting that "I like wells, though. Ever time I see a well, I can't resist tossing a rock in. There's nothing as soothing as the sound of a pebble hitting the water in a deep well."

The well serves as Murakami's image for the exploration of the past and of memory. More explicitly, descending into the well represents his effort to understand himself as a Japanese person of the present time—cosmopolitan, fully aware of the literature, music, and popular culture of the West, but grounded in the history and literature of his own society. In 1994, Murakami visited the plain of Nomonhan, and there he had a revelation that changed his life: "in that arid Mongolian borderland, he felt that he could no longer escape from something he had always feared: the capacity for irrational violence in Japanese society."[46] He was already at work on **The Wind-Up Bird Chronicle,** and its focus on strange and gruesome events—the slaughter of the zoo animals, the baseball bat execution of the prisoner—seems to signal Murakami's preoccupation with this fear. In 1996, while Murakami was still working on the novel, the sarin gas attacks took place in the Tokyo Subway. The attacks were a real-life, present-day example of "irrational violence" erupting at the heart of Japanese society; some of the Aum Shinrikyo adherents were (like Wataya Noboru) members of Japan's "superelite" who, despite their education and privilege, had abandoned reason and chosen a murderous and self-destructive course. Moreover, as if to echo Murakami's own symbol system, the attack took place in a literal underworld. His latest major work, **Underground (Andaaguraundo,** 1996), is a non-fiction study of the sarin gas incident, consisting largely of interviews with survivors.[47] Clearly, Murakami's return to Japan initiated a new phase in his career, one in which he seems gradually to be turning away from the West, and reinvesting himself in the study and contemplation of the society that formed him.

Quotations from *Hear the Wind Sing, Pinball 1973,* "The Dancing Dwarf," *A Wild Sheep Cheese,* and *Hard-Boiled Wonderland and End of the World* are taken from the published translations. All other translations are my own.

Notes

1. Murakami Ryu et al., *Shiku & faindo: Murakami Haruki* (Tokyo: Seido, 1986) 246-7.

2. Murakami Haruki, *Nejimakidori kuronikuru,* 3 vols (Tokyo: Shinchosha, 1994-95). Published in English as *The Wind-Up Bird Chronicle,* trans. Jay Rubin (New York: Knopf, 1997).

3. Otsuka Eishi, "Murakami Haruki no tsukinamisa," *Bungakkai* (June 1998): 265.

4. Murakami Ryu 244.

5. Murakami Ryu 244.

6. Murakami Ryu 244.

7. Murakami Ryu 245.

8. Murakami Ryu 246.

9. Ian Buruma, "Becoming Japanese," *New Yorker* (23-30 Dec. 1996): 62.

10. Murakami Haruki, *Sekai no owari to haadoboirudo wandarando.* Vol. 4 of *Murakami Haruki zensakuhin* (Tokyo: Kodansha, 1990). Published in English as *Hard-Boiled Wonderland and End of the World,* trans. Alfred Birnbaum (Tokyo: Kodansha International, 1991).

11. *Hard-Boiled Wonderland* 240.

12. *Hard-Boiled Wonderland* 165.

13. *Hard-Boiled Wonderland* 390.

14. *Kaze no uta o kike,* vol. 1 of *Murakami Haruki zensakuhin* (Tokyo: Kodansha, 1990). Published in English as *Hear the Wind Sing,* trans. Alfred Birnbaum (Tokyo: Kodansha International-Kodansha English Library, 1987) 125.

15. Murakami Haruki, *Hitsuji o meguru boken,* vol. 2 of *Murakami Haruki zensakuhin* (Tokyo: Kodansha, 1990). Published in English as *A Wild Sheep Chase.* Trans. Alfred Birnbaum (Tokyo: Kodansha International, 1989).

16. Matsuoka Naomi, "Murakami Haruki and Raymond Carver: The American Scene," *Comparative Literature Studies* 30 (1993): 435.

17. Jay McInerney, "Roll Over Basho: Who Japan Is Reading, and Why" (Interview with Murakami Haruki), *New York Times Book Review* (27 Sep. 1992): 29.

18. Murakami Ryu 246-7.

19. Otsuka 264-5.

20. Cynthia S. Hamilton, *Western and Hard-Boiled Detective Fiction in America: From High Noon to Midnight* (London: Macmillan, 1987) 139-40.

21. *Wild Sheep Chase* 15.

22. Murakami Haruki, *Haiho!* (Tokyo: Shinchosha, 1989) 123.

23. Ted Goossen, "After the Cherry Blossoms: Writing Today's Japan," *Descant* 26 (1995): 17.

24. *Hard-Boiled Wonderland* 341.

25. Quoted in Inoue Yoshio, "Kioku no uzumibi: Murakami Haruki no Uchu," *Shincho* (June 1998): 232.

26. Abe Kobo, *Inter-Ice Age 4,* trans. E. Dale Saunders (London: Jonathan Cape, 1971). Translation of *Dai yon kanpyo-ki* (Tokyo: Kodansha, 1959; Shinchosha, 1970).

27. Suzumura Kazunari, *Murakami Haruki kuronikuru 1983-1995* (Tokyo: Yosensha, 1994) 119.

28. "Odoru kobito." *Hotaru, Naya o yaku, sono ta no tanpen* (Tokyo: Shinchobunko, 1984). Published in English as "The Dancing Dwarf" in *The Elephant Vanishes,* trans. Alfred Birnbaum and Jay Rubin (New York: Knopf-Borzoi, 1993) 262-3.

29. *Wild Sheep Chase* 111.

30. McInerney 28.

31. Glynne Walley, "Two Murakamis and Their American Influence," *Japan Quarterly* (1997): 43.

32. References to *Nejimakidori kuronikuru* (*The Wind-up Bird Chronicle*) are represented henceforth by volume number and page number in parentheses. All translations are my own.

33. This incident is presumably based on what happened at Ueno Zoo during the war when zoo attendants reluctantly killed the elephants to prevent a stampede during bombing raids. See Norma Field, *From My Grandmother's Bedside: Sketches of Postwar Tokyo* (Berkeley: U of California P, 1997) 30.

34. Murakami lists nine books as sources at the end of Volume 1 and two more at the end of Volume 3. Kawamura Minato's essay "*Nejimakidori kuronikuru* no bunseki: Gendaishi to shite no monogatari—Nomonhan jihen o megutte" [Analysis of *The Wind-up Bird Chronicle*: The novel as modern history—about the Nomonhan Incident] (*Kokubungaku* 40 [March 1995]: 57-63) discusses the extent to which specific incidents described in these works might have influenced Murakami's novel.

35. Carmen Blacker, *The Catalpa Bow: A Study of Shamanistic Practices in Japan* (London: George Allen and Unwin, 1975) 22.

36. Blacker 93.

37. Blacker 25.

38. Blacker 98-9.

39. Blacker 164.

40. Blacker 169.

41. Murakami Haruki, *Tooi taiko* [A Distant Drum] (Tokyo: Kodansha, 1990) 17.

42. *Hear the Wind Sing* 101.

43. *Hear the Wind Sing* 103.

44. Murakami Haruki, *1973 Nen no pinboru* (Vol. 1 of *Murakami Haruki zensakuhin,* Tokyo: Kodansha, 1990). Published in English as *Pinball, 1973*. Trans. Alfred Birnbaum (Tokyo: Kodansha International-Kodansha English Library, 1985) 17-18.

45. *Pinball, 1973* 18.

46. Buruma 61.

47. Murakami Haruki *Andaaguraundo* [*Underground*] (Tokyo: Kodansha, 1997).

Matthew Carl Strecher (essay date 2002)

SOURCE: Strecher, Matthew Carl. "The Reluctant Postmodernist." In *Dances With Sheep: The Quest for Identity in the Fiction of Murakami Haruki,* pp. 206-15. Ann Arbor: Center for Japanese Studies, University of Michigan, 2002.

[*In this essay, Strecher considers Murakami's literary identity, arguing that although his writing demonstrates postmodernist themes, Murakami himself rejects the postmodernist label.*]

People can read my books, or books by my contemporaries, and they can say, "Hey! I could do this!" That's my role, what I want my readers to learn from me. Not theories and rules, just an example to follow.

—Murakami Haruki

Throughout this book, I have sought above all to demonstrate my contention that Murakami Haruki's *raison d'être* as a writer lies in certain key questions he raises about the nature (and ultimate fate) of individual identity in contemporary Japan. As we have seen, his basic thesis, perhaps more accurately termed his fundamental ideological principle, is that under the best of circumstances individual identity emerges on its own through a process of discursive engagement with other people, through the pursuit of goals, and through a process of overcoming hardship; in contemporary Japan, however, as a result of the hyper-commodification of late-model capitalism, the total focus on economic prosperity, and the need in such an economy to control the desire of the consumer, individual identity has been gradually lost, replaced by what might be termed a "manufactured" subjectivity, a "ready-made" identity. This "manufactured" identity, according to my reading of Murakami's fiction, is created and imposed by a consortium of major power groups in Japan: political, industrial, financial, and the mass media. As has been noted by a variety of commentators, from academics (Ivy, Treat, Karatani, and Jameson among many others) to journalists (Honda, Hidaka, Kawamoto, van Wolferen), this system of controlled desire is very much consonant with the parameters of postmodernism, particularly in its tendency to seek out new markets, its gradual assumption of control over the collective unconscious, and its reliance on a complex web of power structures, all of which combine to form the so-called "empty center" of power in Japan.

Because of this, it has been necessary to cast the author's search for identity into the terms and the historical moment of the postmodern, despite some interesting dilemmas to which this has led. Among the more perplexing questions is that of the author's own attitude toward the postmodern tendencies that so frequently show up in his writing. What is revealed there, I think, is a highly ambivalent stance toward the postmodern on the author's part, one we might even choose to term "opportunistic." In short, while Murakami frequently borrows from the trappings of postmodernism, if he is himself "postmodern" in any respect, he is so reluctantly, with reserve. In fact, in terms of narrative content, Murakami finds the postmodern useful for presenting his message; in cultural terms—particularly but not exclusively the economic—he sees the postmodern as a harmful factor, suppressing the impulse to establish meaningful identity. Similar to Jameson and Althusser, he sees real-world manifestations such as "late-model capitalism," and his own "rapid capitalism," as dictatorial and intrusive—perhaps even as the result of a kind of ideological "class struggle" between materialism and idealism. As we have seen, this argument can be cast in Marxist terms as a kind of induced fetishism, one that replaces individual desires with those supported by the needs of the market; it can also be presented in Lacanian terms as the suppression of the desire for the individual, internal self (the Other) in favor of the terms and conditions of the symbolic, now almost wholly given over to powering the economic needs of the state.

The issue can also be presented as an expression of artistic resistance, however, and this is what I have attempted to show in the first chapter of this book, where, as we have seen, Murakami tests the limits of literary identity. His play with the literary formula, and more importantly, his subversion of the very expectations that define the formula, are themselves challenges to the fixed identity of literary forms, most particularly the traditional distinctions that have existed between "pure" and "mass" literature. It is unlikely, however, that Murakami involves himself in this debate for the sake of aesthetics in and of themselves; rather, his hostility is inevitably directed toward all attempts to fix identity in any uniform or predetermined way. If the above examinations of Murakami's fiction tell us anything, it is that the author is committed to the preservation of a uniquely constituted identity, one developed through a discursive process, through action, reaction, and interaction of distinctly determined units. In the case of the literary formula, this amounts to the interaction of literary elements previously thought to be incompatible with one another: the inventive and the formulaic.

We have seen a similar impulse in the production of works like **Underground** and **Underground 2,** which are clearly journalistic in their efforts to discuss an event that is more or less "current," recent enough to remain imprinted on the collective consciousness of Japanese society, yet that is also "historical" in the far-reaching implications of the event—one that dispelled in part the myth of Japan as a society that miraculously combines spectacular economic dominance with a happy, stable, controlled society. But in approaching this event through these two texts, Murakami has again disrupted not only the methodology of orthodox journalism, but indeed that of nonorthodox journalism, by combining together the tropes of the politically resistant "New Journalism" and the equally subjective, but decidedly more humanistic (if anachronistic) "literary journalism." In both cases he succeeds in producing texts that are at once "true" (the events happened),

subjective (each "voice" is but one tiny part of a very large whole), and interpretive (the author plays an active role in guiding the discussion, and occasionally adding his own comments). In so doing, Murakami implicitly attacks the binary opposition of "fact versus fiction," "journalism versus fiction/literature," "subjectivity versus objectivity," and even that of the center (mainstream journalism) versus the periphery (subjective journalistic accounts). In other words, his approach is again "postmodern" in its methodology, if not in its agenda of expressing his contention that both victims and perpetrators alike of the sarin incident have been abstracted, reduced to mere symbols ("good" and "evil"; "purity" and "defilement").

This, as noted above, is part of the reason certain elements of the literary establishment have judged Murakami's fiction to bode ill for the future of Japanese literature in general. Such concerns are reasonably well founded, for certainly Murakami's writing does not necessarily conform to what we would normally consider *belles lettres*; nor, in fact, does it even aspire to produce the sense of "newness" or "differentiation" that the For Malists and the avantgarde hold in such high regard. For Murakami and many of his fellow contemporary writers, the story is everything, and all aspirations to Art must be subordinate to this. At the same time—and the analyses in this book support this—there can be no question of Murakami commitment to the potential of the story to share new insights about the nature of reality and the need for change. In this sense, Murakami's fiction demonstrates the same didactic potential as other writing of the postwar. It is, then, the lack of an active aesthetic, of an aspiration to create Art, in the author's work to which the literary establishment—I am still thinking primarily of Ōe here—will object.

It is, of course, also an issue of recent postmodern writing in general, for many of the writers mentioned in the analyses above share Murakami's rejection of fiction as Art (literature). But then the issue arises again, how are we to characterize the postmodernism of Murakami Haruki? More to the point, his rejection of fiction as Art aside, can one who views so negatively late-model capitalism, who so obviously sees the contemporary moment as less free rather than *more* free, be termed a postmodern writer at all? Murakami unquestionably embodies many of the attributes most commonly associated with postmodern expression: his writing crosses boundaries between genres and styles; he works in an ever-changing "no man's land" between the real and magical; his settings are always marked by shifting boundaries between real and unreal; his thematics is constantly aware of the limitations of language in the representation of those realities and unrealities; he is concerned with offering new perspectives, new ways in which to look at the world already around us.

And yet, he is no apologist for the postmodern. Unlike Hutcheon, who sees the postmodern as liberating, an opportunity for the recovery of a lost periphery, Murakami seems perfectly willing to explore these possibilities, but not to follow them through to their logical conclusions. In other words, his protagonists *fail* in their quests to rediscover what has been lost or peripheralized. For them, the peripheral is always hidden in the dark recesses of the unconscious, always in the mode of memories, represented through language—a chain of metonymical signification—that permits the protagonist a certain freedom of interpretation (which is to say, the invention of nostalgic images), but prevents direct contact with the object of desire. Thus, Murakami offers a "reading" of the unconscious that is consonant with the Lacanian understanding of the inner and outer minds as connected always by language, chains of signification, the displacement of desire by the Symbolic Order (or, in Murakami's terms, the state, authority), and thus always marked by the inevitable frustration of the quest for the other. Unlike Lacan, however, as noted earlier, Murakami is unprepared to view the intervention of the symbolic as "neutral," preferring instead to assign a persona to this authority in the form of the state.

Murakami's fiction suggests a determination to view this intervention as a willful, calculated attempt to subvert the "free" development of the self in order to transplant a more easily controlled version of identity into each individual subject, transforming them from *thinking* subjects into *consuming* subjects. Moreover, as the allegory we have already outlined in *A Wild Sheep Chase* would seem to suggest, this authority, this intervention on both an individual and a collective scale, is represented in the confrontation between materialism (mainstream) and idealism (counterculture) in the 1950s and 1960s. This is admittedly an oversimplification, but Murakami's allegories *are* simple—they do not reflect the true complexity of what Zenkyōtō was or was not, but rather seek to reduce the conflict down to individual entities—entities we can comprehend, like, dislike, and so forth. (We cannot help noting then, perhaps, that *A Wild Sheep Chase,* from one point of view, does what Murakami seems to reject in *Underground* and *Underground 2*—the reduction of the conflict into simplified binaries of "good" and "evil." There is no denying this, but Murakami's purpose in *A Wild Sheep Chase* is clearly to make Zenkyōtō *more* human through its identification with Rat, whereas in the case of the

sarin incident, the mass media's approach to the victims and perpetrators as a thing of the moment—as *disposable*—has the opposite effect of dehumanizing them.)

This conflict can certainly be read in terms of a kind of class struggle; if not the classic Marxist model of capital versus the proletariat, then at least the conservative right against a reformist-minded left. This is the link, not so tenuous, between Althusser and Murakami, for while Murakami is by no means a Marxist in the common sense of the term (despite his baleful view of fetish consumerism), he does seem to view the ascendancy of the conservative right, and the attendant growth of "rapid" capitalism, as the result of a kind of class struggle—one that ended in the defeat of the left, and the rise of the conditions of the postmodern I have described above.

In terms of the postmodern as it is manifested in social conditions, then, Murakami's work demonstrates a greater affinity with the thinking of Althusser, and even Fredric Jameson, than with that of Linda Hutcheon (even though his experiments with different literary methodologies could almost be read as a summary of Hutcheon's *Poetics of Postmodernism!*) While Murakami does not necessarily share Jameson's belief that the postmodern moment poses a threat to a stable identity—his work suggests more the concern that the state replaces individual identity with an equally stable, but more "ready-made" variety—he *does* echo Jameson's contention that the previously autonomous realm of the cultural has been infiltrated by capitalism, and that this has resulted in the commodification of areas of our personal lives that had hitherto been considered sacrosanct.

Indeed, we may be forced to conclude that, but for the determinism of the dialectical model of historical progress, the author does in fact seem to have a greater affinity with the Marxist camp than with those who celebrate the postmodern as ushering in a period of previously unimagined awareness of the realities that surround us. His texts are filled with nostalgia, but for Murakami the nostalgia of the present for the past is not couched in terms of pleasure and rediscovery, but of crushing sadness and loss. His characters do not express their nostalgia through "retro" fetishism but by their stubborn refusal to engage in the commodity fetishism that surrounds them. Pressed to join this economy, they retreat to the unique, private space of the unconscious, where they (partially) satisfy their desire by "consuming" their own memories, only to find, however, that there can be no true satisfaction from such recourse, nor is there to be any permanent escape from the system that surrounds them.

NEW DIRECTIONS

These characters represent, of course, the contemporary Japanese subject. At various points in the text above it has become clear, I believe, that Murakami's commitment as a writer lies in a project to break down some of the walls that isolate this subject, to resuscitate it through a sense of humanity, and induce others to recognize it as such. This is an impulse that appears as early as *A Wild Sheep Chase,* and comes to full fruition in *The Wind-Up Bird Chronicle.* As the chapters above have hopefully shown, Murakami's expression of this agenda has varied over the course of his first twenty years as writer, from focus on his protagonist's attempts to rediscover himself early on, to later attempts to save others. The methodologies taken to this end have also varied over time (formulaic fiction, magical realism, historiography, literary journalism, etc.). The central *raison d'être* of Murakami, however, has not in itself altered much.

This book has been admittedly limited in the breadth of texts it is to cover; for the most part I have deliberately looked only at the first twenty years of Murakami fiction, 1979 to 1999, partly out of a need to bind the scope of my work somehow, but also because Murakami himself seems ready, with the recent *fin de siècle,* to look at different modes of expression. To look very closely at his work since *The Sputnik Sweetheart,* in my opinion, is to open a whole new study. It is my intention to avoid this. I have also held myself, with just a couple of exceptions, to examining Murakami's fiction, because I sense that the surest way to the heart of the author's most critical agenda is through his purely imaginative writing. This is not to say, however, that studies of Murakami's translations of Carver or Fitzgerald, or indeed his numerous travelogues, or his "guides" to reading modern Japanese fiction, will not yield interesting results that may corroborate or refute the observations made in the present text. Indeed, I hope that such studies will be forthcoming in the near future.

Readers will perhaps have noticed that my methodology in writing this study has been historical and theoretical rather than aesthetic. In fact, this is not even what might be termed in Japanese a *sakka-ron,* a study of Murakami Haruki and his works first and foremost. Instead, I have tried to walk a fine line between a text that approaches the complexities of the Murakami fictional universe, while at the same time maintaining a level of accessibility that the casual reader will find comfortable. For this reason I have elected to deal with challenging concepts, yet to focus on texts by Murakami that are exemplary of the questions and ideas I have raised above, and at the same time available to readers in translation.

Some readers may object to the limited number of texts discussed in the pages above; indeed, several of the novels are covered in more than one chapter, while many of the short stories have been left out altogether. But my methodology throughout this book has been to focus on the major thematic and methodological points of interest in the author's writing, and these appear with the most clarity and profundity in the novels. The short stories, on the other hand, while often containing single images or concepts that appear more fully in other texts (the image of the worlds reflected in **"The Mirror"** comes to mind, or that of water in **"Kanō Crete"**), taken singly do not impart the same sense of development in the author's writing and worldview as we see in the longer fiction. One might say that Murakami experiments with individual images and ideas in his short stories, which are then given much more critical and considered treatment in the expanded versions.[1]

My focus on the historical and theoretical rather than the aesthetic may also call for a comment or two. If my attention has been more focused on the historical and theoretical parameters that shape Murakami than on examining each of his hundreds of works individually, this is because, in my opinion, Murakami's value as a writer (if we seek this) does not lie in his variety. While prolific and skillful, Murakami's fictional output does not demonstrate much diversity. His plots, in fact, are remarkably similar, and his characters are even more so. If one has encountered the Murakami hero in one novel, one knows something about most other Murakami protagonists, as well.

Yet there is inventiveness to Murakami as well; one feels he has grasped intuitively the tropes of postmodern expression, and chosen to explore these within the fictional world he envisions. That world itself, once established, has remained more or less regular and predictable. Murakami's inventiveness lies in the subtle, often difficult to discern variations he introduces, a talent he shares with the better formulaic writers. But Murakami is no formulaic writer, as I have demonstrated above. A more appropriate analogy might be found in the terminology of music; Murakami's strength lies in his ability to compose variations on a theme. This is by no means a negative reflection on his talent; indeed, among the great composers, Bach, Schubert, Tchaikovsky, and particularly Mozart, are known for their innovative variations.

It would not be inaccurate, however, to suggest that the relative lack of variety in Murakami fiction is a reflection on the author's worldview, his perspective as an individual looking outward. Most of his protagonists, for instance, are merely variations on the author himself, who is less interested in external human nature than how he himself might internally respond to specific circumstances. At times these circumstances are absurdly prosaic; as Murakami struggled to give up cigarettes in 1982, for instance, his sheep-chasing protagonist was also compelled to quit smoking. But these changes also occur on a more life-altering scale. We certainly notice that as Murakami matures, so, also, do his protagonists grow up. Murakami's reaction to the 1995 Kobe earthquake was real—its epicenter, in fact, was directly under his neighborhood in Ashiya—and the AUM Shinrikyō incident later that year struck him equally hard. When the author returned to Japan from his years of travel abroad shortly thereafter, he did so with a newfound desire to explore the potential for a more active stance toward the world—more or less as Ōe once wished he would do—and at the same time his protagonists became more militant, more demanding, more insistent on having answers to the pressing questions in their lives.

As the text above has shown, the question that most often concerns him is one of identity—how it is formed, how it may be maintained, how it can be lost due to traumatic circumstances, and what its loss might mean to contemporary society. Indeed, to judge from the analyses of his literature above, I think one would have to conclude that Murakami's interest in the near total focus on economic interests in Japanese society during the past two decades stems directly from the supposed and real effects he believes this has had on individual Japanese. Certainly works such as ***Underground, The Wind-Up Bird Chronicle, The Sputnik Sweetheart,*** and ***All God's Children Can Dance*** leave us in no doubt about Murakami's increasing conviction that major traumatic events, as well as the general malaise of the era, are closely connected to the loss or radical transformation of identity among contemporary Japanese.

Where, exactly, the author's work will take him in the years to come is anyone's guess, and I will not hazard to do so at this stage. I will make a mild objection to Ōsugi Shigeo's assertion not long ago that a new Japanese "political correctness" in the 1990s has brought an end to Murakami's importance in contemporary writing. The new focus of Japanese postcolonial studies on other Asian cultures rather than on "things American," he argues, means that the age of writers like Murakami Haruki, and perhaps more especially, Murakami Ryū, has passed.

> This has been the time to be working on "the Korean problem," or on "the Asian problem." This is also part of a trend, but I think very few people were really conscious of America during the 1990s. Instead everyone turned to postcolonialism, to culture studies.
>
> In that sense, this is no longer the age of Murakami Haruki or Murakami Ryū. . . . It is the age of "political correctness" . . . an age when you have to adopt a

certain political stance or you won't make it as a writer. So how are we supposed to explain the continued vitality of these two?

(Kawamura and Ōsugi 2000, 133)

But this is too narrow a view of either Haruki or Ryū as a writer. To sum up Murakami Haruki's entire career in terms of some kind of era-bound longing for things American is absurd, as the analyses above should make quite clear. In fact, if the existence of works like ***Underground, Underground 2,*** or for that matter ***All God's Children Can Dance*** tell us anything, it is that Murakami Haruki has shown himself capable of moving on with the times. Rather, one cannot help feeling that Ōsugi, among others, has critically missed the point of the last six years of Murakami fiction, has failed to grasp that behind the hard-boiled "American" flavor of Murakami's prose style (though this has changed too!), the author's sights are squarely on Japan and have been for quite some time.

As I have striven to show repeatedly above, the most important thing we should "get" from Murakami Haruki and his fiction is that the face and expression of Japanese literature have changed, and Murakami has spearheaded that change. Kawamoto Saburō said in 1985 that Murakami was a "totally *un*-political" writer whose works nevertheless always made us think of politics. This is one way to phrase the matter. Another would be to say that Murakami is a totally political writer who always pretends he is not. In that regard his literary style is capable of obscuring the political content of his work, but only so far; his political agenda never fails to emerge at some point. Thus, if Ōsugi is correct that no writer can survive without a political angle, herein may well lie the secret of Murakami's continued success (even Ōsugi grants him this): that he is capable of combining the political, the formulaic, the magical, and the deeply psychological, with a style of expression so entertaining as to make the dull seem fresh, the serious seem fun, and the frightening seem a little more familiar.

Note

1. At least two of the author's novels began this way: *Norwegian Wood* was based on an earlier story called "Hotaru" (Fireflies, 1983); *The Wind-Up Bird Chronicle* grew out of "Nejimakidori to Kayōbi no Onnatachi" (1986; trans. Jay Rubin as "Wind-Up Bird and Tuesday's Women"), and the characters Kanō Malta and Kanō Crete appear in the story "Kanō Kureta" in *TV People*.

Bibliography

Hutcheon, Linda. 1988. *A poetics of postmodernism: history, theory, fiction.* New York: Routledge.

Kawamura Minato. 2000. With Ōsugi Shigeo. Murakami Ryū to Murakami Haruki: 25-nen no bungaku Kūkan (Murakami Ryū and Murakami Haruki: 25 years of literary space). *Gunzō* 55.7 (July).

———. 1999b. *Supūtoniku no koibito (The Sputnik Sweetheart)*. Tokyo: Kōdansha.

———. 1998. *Yakusoku sareta basho de: Underground 2 (The Place That Was Promised: Underground 2)*. Tokyo: Bungei Shunjū.

———. 1997a. *Andāguraundo (Underground)*. Tokyo: Kōdansha.

———. 1997b. *The Wind-Up Bird Chronicle*. Translated by Jay Rubin. New York: Knopf.

———. 1994-96. *Nejimakidori kuronikuru (Wind-Up Bird Chronicle)*. Tokyo: Shinchōsha.

———. 1991. *Hard-Boiled Wonderland and the End Of The World* Translated by Alfred Birnbaum. New York: Vintage.

———. 1989. *A Wild Sheep Chase*. Translated by Alfred Birnbaum. New York: Plume.

Yoshiko Fukushima (essay date April-June 2003)

SOURCE: Fukushima, Yoshiko. "Japanese Literature, or 'J-Literature' in the 1990s." *World Literature Today* 77, no. 1 (April-June 2003): 40-4.

[*In the following essay, Fukushima reveals how Murakami and other contemporary Japanese writers have explored the social and political crises that plagued Japan in the 1990s.*]

The 1990s ended just three years ago yet as I gather my thoughts on Japanese literature in the 1990s, I feel as if I am writing about the remote past. Japanese postwar literature, as with literature elsewhere, continues to lose its readership under the pressure of multiple media—film, television, and comic books—even though some writers in the 1980s successfully established a class of commodified "pure" literature. To refer to Japanese literature of the 1990s, the editorial staff of Kawade Shobō's literary journal *Bungei*, hoping to attract a young readership, created the neologism "J-Literature," inspired by J-Pop (Japanese popular music) and J-Comic (Japanese comic books). The decade of the 1990s marked a period during which the distinction of two types of Japanese literature— pure literature as serious, elite, and political and popular literature as light, common, and entertaining—became radically blurred. New writers and works, representing diversified styles and themes,

surged into literary culture. The list I propose introduces a palette of ten different—as distinguished from *best*—novelists, five men and five women.

The death of the Shōwa emperor Hirohito in 1989 represents a significant marker dividing the decades of the 1980s and 1990s. His passing meant that Japan could no longer interrogate the emperor's wartime responsibility, and it gave the Japanese people an opportunity to question the existence of the emperor system. Once the emperor's sickness was reported, the entire nation could participate in the national project of self-restraint, or *jishuku,* canceling festivals and weddings. The decade of the 1990s following his death, with the burst of the economic bubble, was not a particularly joyous period for Japan. Economic and political turmoil continued unabated. Political corruption came to the public's attention, beginning in the late 1980s with the bribery scandal of the information services company Recruit. The media reported the daily arrests of politicians and bureaucrats who had received bribes from private firms and brokers. Meanwhile, Japan experienced two catastrophes. The Hanshin/Awaji earthquake that struck the Kobe area in January 1995 killed more than five thousand people and damaged highways, railways, and major utility pipelines. In March of the same year, a member of the religious cult Aum Shinrikyō released a nerve gas, sarin, in the subway system of Tokyo. Twelve people were killed and nearly four thousand were injured. In short, Japanese writers were confronted with a groundswell of problems from Japan's past and present during the era of the 1990s.

Two Murakamis—Haruki Murakami and Ryū Murakami—and Banana Yoshimoto, the best-selling writers of the 1980s, continued to write throughout the 1990s. Haruki Murakami completed three volumes of **The Wind-Up Bird Chronicle** in the mid-1990s. Murakami presents the main character—Tōru—in search of his missing wife, his own identity, and the forgotten past of the nation, exploiting a variety of styles— surreal, fantastic, mysterious, and hard-boiled. The enigmatic psychic sisters, Malta and Crete, and the mother and son with healing powers, Nutmeg and Cinnamon, aid him in his search. His fatal enemy, Noboru—the vulgar, egoistic, yet talented university professor, postmodern critic, and politician—represents the systems of Japanese society that Murakami has criticized in many works. Tōru regains communication with his wife in an Internet chat and learns that she plans to kill her brother, who had defiled her and her sister.

Tōru makes a quantum leap to wartime Manchuria and uncovers the repressed memory of the war through the voice of an old veteran, Mamiya. He is a survivor of the cruel and meaningless battle of Nomonhan at the Siberia-Manchuria border during World War II. Tōru, caught up in Mamiya's story about his superior who was skinned alive and his confinement in a dried-up well, inters *himself* in a neighborhood well, where he experiences a spiritual journey to the depths of his consciousness—his own past. Nutmeg, finding the same blue-black stigma that her father has, tells him another war story about her father, who attended the killing of animals and the massacre of Chinese prisoners by Japanese soldiers at the zoo in Manchuria. Tōru, like the wind-up bird that appears in Nutmeg's story (written by Cinnamon), witnesses the darker side of Japanese society—the corruption of political systems and repeated atrocities of the war years. Murakami successfully "winds up" the chaotic history of postwar Japan, culminating in the present.

The political tenor of Ryū Murakami's novels never receded in the 1990s. *Love & Pop/Topaz II* portrays the phenomenon among high-school girls in the mid-1990s called *enjo kōsai*—having dates or sometimes sexual intercourse with middle-aged men in exchange for expensive brand-name clothes and accessories. Murakami presents the solitude of the girls, who wander through the busy streets of Shibuya in the cold metropolis of Tokyo. Their dialogues intersect with various noises—sounds from television and radio, the voices of strangers, routine dialogues from fast-food restaurants, and loud commercial ads from the stores. In order to write this novel, Murakami visited telephone clubs and "love hotels" (hotels for lovers to have sex), listened to the girls' messages left on the voice mail of the sex club, and conducted interviews with the girls.

The heroine, Hiromi, is a seventeen-year-old high-school student living in a suburb of Tokyo. Her father is a trading-company employee and her mother an official in an art museum. Hiromi finds an imperial topaz ring at a jewelry store in Shibuya and decides to take part in *enjo kōsai* for the first time to buy the ring, which costs $1,000. Using a cell phone that her friend has borrowed from a stranger, she chooses two clients from the message box. She helps her first client masturbate inside the convenience store, then goes to a "love hotel" with her second client, Captain EO. Captain EO, who talks to girls with his shabby stuffed Fuzzy Ball carried in his knapsack, is a psychopathic thief who steals the girls' money. Instead of having sex, Hiromi has a chat with him, and sews up his Fuzzy Ball's tail. Murakami examines the problems of the social evil of *enjo kōsai* from Hiromi's perspective. What she misses is contact with other people. She cannot communicate well with her busy parents and feels some hatred toward them. Although she cannot buy the ring, she receives a measure of warmth

from her psychopathic client, who criticizes her attempt at prostitution and gives her the secret name of his Fuzzy Ball—"Mr. Love & Pop."

Banana Yoshimoto, who made her debut with the award-winning short story "Kitchen" in 1987, subsequently created the "Banana" boom in Japan. *Lizard* is a collection of six short stories about lovers facing an uncommon circumstance. Using her elaborate, mysterious lyricism, Yoshimoto portrays the relationships of Japanese couples found in every corner of the urbanized towns. Lovers in her stories achieve a moment of clarity after solving their emotional struggles regarding the past and present.

The narrator of the first story, "Newlywed" (first serialized on posters on Japan Railway's commuter trains in Tokyo), heavily drunk, is reluctant to go home to see his newlywed wife. With the help of a homeless man, who transforms himself into an attractive young woman to talk with him, he becomes aware of his wife's magical power. The second, eponymous story depicts a man who works as a doctor for autistic children and a lizard-looking woman who works as an acupuncturist. Each confesses to the other the traumatic incidents of childhood, affirming their strong bond and fate of becoming healers for their patients. A writer's girlfriend in "Helix" is planning to attend a brainwashing seminar to forget the past. Witnessing an explosion on the street together, the couple reaffirm their love, feeling their souls dancing together like the infinite helix of DNA. A woman in "Dreaming of Kimchee" has an affair with a married man, whom she eventually marries. She now suspects a new affair, but their love is proved real after both have a similar dream of kimchee, a spicy Korean condiment, while sleeping in a room filled with its strong smell. In "Blood and Water," Chikako flees the religious commune where her parents live and joins Akira, maker of healing amulets. Surrounded by the love of Akira and her father, she learns the true meaning of independence and solitude. In the final story, titled "A Strange Tale from Down by the Big River," Akemi, a former member of a sex club, plans to marry the son of a rich family. After learning that her mother tried to kill her by throwing her into a river when she was a baby, she becomes aware of her spiritual power to survive and feels hope for a new life with her future husband, overcoming her strange past. All six stories are linked to one another and share similar elements—fear and healing in the present, memories from the past, and hope for the future.

Yoriko Shōno, who made her debut earlier than Yoshimoto, became known to the public in 1991 when she received the Noma Prize for New Writers for her work *I Did Nothing. Restless Dream,* published between 1992 and 1994 in four stories—"Restless Dream," "Restless Game," "Restless World," and "Restless End"—depicts the dual world of reality and fantasy, deploying inexhaustible imagination and adventurous wordplay—puns, jargon, and nonsensical yet rhythmical dialogues. The first-person narrator relates her Dragon Quest-like nightmare of using the word processor. In the nightmare, she is the cyborg fighter Momoki Tobihebi who lives in Splatter City, the magic town under the control of the male-centered Big Temple. Momoki, fighting against zombies and crow cyborgs, finally reaches the magic mirror, Mandala, and destroys Splatter City.

What Shōno criticizes is the nightmare of fin-de-siècle gender hierarchy in Japan: deploying language and metaphor as her weapons, she fights against the male-centered Japanese society. Momoki, Japanese gender, confronts female zombies and other woman in the language of men. The original Cinderella-like plot—with a prince and two sisters, one ugly and the other beautiful, and the marriage of the prince and beautiful sister—is rewritten by Momoki. Unlike the knight in Dragon Quest, who sets off on a journey to save the princess, Shōno's princess, transforming herself into a snake, devours the prince at the end of the story.

Yoshimoto's and Shōno's fantastic style and the motif of transformation are commonly found in the Akutagawa Prize-winning female novelists Hiromi Kawakami and Tawada Yōko. Kawakami was a secondary-school science teacher for four years before embarking on her creative-writing career. *Tread on a Snake* presents a contemporary folktale about the erotic supernatural world where the characters live without the ordinary boundary between humans and snakes. The narrator of the story, Hiwako, working at a store selling Pure Land rosaries, steps on a snake on her way to work. The snake transforms herself into a fifty-ish woman and disappears. When Hiwako returns home, the snake/woman has prepared a dinner and is waiting for her. The woman claiming she is her mother (although the narrator's mother is still alive somewhere else), knows everything about her private life and begins living in her house. Gradually, Hiwako becomes comfortable eating dinner with her and finds that all her friends are actually snakes. Rejecting the snake's invitation to their homey world she accepts the fatal battle with the snake. Snakes in her story, unlike their symbolism of evil in the Judeo-Christian tradition, are very humane and remind us of ancient deities worshipped by Japanese people. Hiwako draws the reader into the mythological, chaotic space where humans and animals used to coexist.

Tawada Yōko moved to Hamburg, Germany, to work for a book export and distribution company in her early twenties. Five years later, she published her first collection of poetry and a novel, *Nur da wo du bist da ist nichts,* in Hamburg. In the 1990s she won many literary awards in both Germany and Japan, including the Förderpreis für Literatur des Freien und Hansestadt Hamburg (1990), the Albert-con-Chamisso Prize (1996), the Gunzō Prize for New Writers (1991), and the Akutagawa Prize (1993). Tawada, like Kawakami, presents the reader with another supernatural world, employing an absurd, imaginative, and unconventional narrative in both Japanese and German. *The Bridegroom Was a Dog,* inspired by Japanese folktales about human-animal marriages, portrays the bizarre relationship between an eccentric after-school teacher, Mitsuko, and a doglike man, Taro. Mitsuko, popular among children, tells them bizarre folktales, including a tale about a dog marrying a princess after licking her bottom clean. Like a stray dog one day Taro suddenly appears and begins to help her with canine devotion. Taro, nervous in the presence of cats and dogs, sniffs her body inexhaustibly and sleeps during the day. Behind this odd incident, the reader finds Tawada's criticism of the conservative mores of Japanese suburban communities, which reject the outsiders of society. Not only Mitsuko but also his wife, his gay friend Matsubara, and Matsubara's bullied daughter, Fukiko, are different from ordinary people and easily become fodder for the neighborhood gossips. Tawada saves them by sending them off on a meandering trip.

The works by three multitalented authors—former punk rocker Kō Machida, novelist and film critic Kazushige Abe, and former theater director Miri Yū—represent the Japanese style of avant-pop or postpunk novels. Their originality and creative, experimental, yet legitimate approaches shocked readers and critics in the 1990s. Kō Machida who started out as the vocalist and songwriter of a punk-rock group in the 1970s, began writing poems in the early 1990s. His work, strongly influenced by forms in the Japanese oral tradition—especially the comic monologue in Osaka and Tokyo called *rakugo* and storytelling from Osaka called *naniwabuslu*—reassembles their rhythms and language techniques in his work. Mixing them with the Osaka dialect and the literary (nonspoken) language, he creates a melodious, entertaining, and humorous writing style. *Kussun daikoku,* his first novel, is about a man, formerly a musician, who quits his job to assume the lazy life of a drunkard. After his wife leaves him, only a well-balanced statue of the ancient god of wealth and farmers, Daikoku, is left to him. Annoyed by the statue—incessantly smiling even if it falls—Kusunoki wants to throw it away, but he cannot. Observing him lying down on the beach, totally broke, his friend points out that he resembles the statue. Behind the meaningless plot about a nonproductive outsider of the society and his buffoonish attitude toward that society, Machida presents his nihilistic criticism against a contemporary Japan controlled by hyperconsumer capitalism.

Kazushige Abe studied cinema and began making private films while writing fiction in the late 1980s. *Individual Projection,* similar to the Hollywood film *Fight Club,* is a murder mystery written in a diary format. For this work, Abe was recognized as the leader of J-Literature among Japanese literary circles. Onuma, the writer of the diary (a fictional report written for the spy school) as well as one of the kidnappers of the gangster boss, works as a projectionist at the movie theater in Shibuya (where Ryū Murakami's heroine, Hiromi, is negotiating for prostitution with her clients). After experiencing violent fights with gangsters and witnessing murders over the disappearance of a nuclear explosive during the kidnapping, Onuma begins projecting his alter ego onto his violent and cruel classmate from spy school, Inoue. Abe, exploiting this fictional setting, portrays the empty and callous landscape of noisy Shibuya, flooded by people who are indifferent and cruel to one another.

Korean-Japanese Miri Yū formed her own theater group at the age of twenty in 1988. Yū received the Kishida Drama Award for her eighth play, *Festival for the Fish* (1992), then shifted to writing novels. Her parents, both born in South Korea, migrated to Japan during their early childhood, shortly before the outbreak of the Korean War. Her work has no political or critical undertones like other Korean-Japanese works treating the problems of colonial history and discrimination against Koreans.

Family Cinema is a story about a family similar to Yū's estranged family, which broke up after frequent violent confrontations when she was a teenager. The family, at the filmmaker's request, is making a film about their reunion. The family members, who were separated twenty years ago, reunite for the first time. Whereas the mother and father are enthusiastic about reenacting the family's old days in front of the camera, their children gradually remember their pain and hatred for the father's violence and their mother's sexual flirtatiousness. They also learn that they are about to lose the only tie for the family, health insurance, because the father is losing his job. While maintaining a humorous tone throughout, the novel depicts the figure of a family whose reality can easily turn fictitious. Their egotistical behaviors and emotional struggles can, in reality, be found within any family. The Korean film director Park Chul-soo created the film version of the novel in 1998, which was coproduced in Korea and Japan. In the film, Yū's sister plays the role of the small sister. Yū received the 116th Akutagawa Award for this work in 1996.

In 1994 Kenzaburō Ōe became the second Japanese author to receive the Nobel Prize in Literature. *The Burning Green Tree,* written between 1993 and 1995, is a trilogy about atonement and salvation, comprising *Until the "Savior" Gets Socked, Vacillating,* and *On the Great Day.* The phrase "burning green tree" derives from a stanza of William Butler Yeats's poem "Vacillation," in which Yeats sings about a tree whose topmost bough is "half all glittering flame and half all green abounding foliage moistened with the dew." Responding to Yeats's concept, Ōe questions how human beings live by vacillating between two extremities—the body and the soul—and how human beings live and die, relating them to society and the world. Ōe replicates the world of Yeats in the village and forest of his homeland, Shikoku—the smallest of the four major islands in Japan—and its ritual for the spirits of the dead (in which villagers lead the spirit to the forest of the mountain and help it settle at the root of a tree). The tree in the ritual, as a metaphor connecting life and death, symbolizes the cycle of death and rebirth.

The narrator of the story, Sacchan, is an androgyne who has recently undergone a sex-change operation; although she has been reborn as a female, she still has both sexual organs. Sacchan, at the request of Uncle K, is writing a story about Brother Gü. Granny, the dying healer, selects the elite foreign ambassador's American-born son as Brother Gü, the "savior" of the village. He is a survivor of a revolutionary sect from the student movement of the 1960s. Brother Gü, reluctantly plays the role of the healer and builds his church, called Burning Green Tree, in the village, Villagers, hostile toward Brother Gü's religious activities, stone him to death. Nevertheless, the story ends in rejoicing, celebrating the rebirth of Brother Gü's spirit.

Although Ōe criticized the subcultural nature and the economic success of such young writers as Haruki Murakami and Banana Yoshimoto in the 1980s, his works joined the list of best-sellers for the first time in his writing career after the received the Nobel Prize. J-Literature in the 1990s may not be what Ōe would term "serious" literature. The tone of the nine works (except for Ōe's work) introduced here overlaps with that of pop-cultural forms. Still, it is also undeniable that many elements consisting of Ōe's experimental spirit can be found in them—attention to the margins of society, the political and social functions of literature, creation of a new "I-novel," and verbal theatrics mixed with fantasy or illusion. Japanese postwar writers still seem to be working on a big project—how to go "beyond Ōe," regardless of the outcome.

Michael Fisch (essay date 2004)

SOURCE: Fisch, Michael. "In Search of the Real: Technology, Shock and Language in Murakami Haruki's *Sputnik Sweetheart*." *Japan Forum* 16, no. 3 (2004): 361-83.

[*In the essay below, Fisch sees* The Sputnik Sweetheart *as concerned with recovering and restoring language—which he contends was weakened for Murakami and other intellectuals—as a result of the poor Japanese economy in 1995 and the earthquake and subway gas attack in Japan that year.*]

In December 2000, a 17-year-old high school student from Tochigi-ken in Japan was arrested for throwing a small home-made bomb packed with nuts, bolts and box-cutter blades into a crowded video store in Tokyo's Kabuki-cho area. Upon questioning, the youth expressed remorse only over the fact that he had not been able to execute his full plan, which involved firing a shotgun at the survivors. The youth told police that he had wanted to 'hear what people's screams would be like and to see people broken into pieces, to see their bones and internal organs' (*hito wo barabara ni kowashite hone ya naizō wo mitakatta*) (*Mainichi shinbun* 6 December 2000). He explained that he felt there was nothing behind people's superficiality so he wanted to be able to 'see inside people'. The youth's confession evokes an association with the now infamous murders committed by another child, known in the media as '*Shōnen A*' (Youth A). Similar to the Tochigiken youth, 'anxiety about the artificiality of the world' and an obsession to 'destroy it in order to reveal the Real' is cited as a compelling force behind *Shōnen A*'s gruesome decapitation of a local child—a sacrifice for his invented god (Iida 2002: 446). Is there a hidden logic behind these desperate and bloody acts What is it that binds the spilling of blood, moreover innocent blood, with angst over the artificiality of the world

The sense of artificiality that troubled these youths bespeaks a crisis in representation, where referents are perceived as failing to mark a concrete real and appear instead to cascade precipitously in a chain of semantic displacement that renders language for ever a process of misapprehension. It is tempting to interpret their violence as a desire to resuscitate a semiotic veracity via the magic of sacrifice, in which, as Henri Hubert and Marcel Mauss tell us, the slaughter of the sacred victim produced real affects (Hubert and Mauss 1964). The mimetic logic of sympathetic magic induced through sacrifice bound the *thing* to its representation so that 'what happens to the enemy's spear, hair or name, also happens to the individual' (Horkheimer and Adorno 1988: 10). Yet, as Horkheimer and Adorno

point out, since the principle of substitution in sacrifice contradicts the representational specificity upon which the efficacy of the ritual rests, it signals a future unraveling of its effects—the semiotic fix it offers is at best temporary (1988: 10).

Concern for the condition of language and its restoration is also at the heart of Murakami Haruki's novel **Sputnik Sweetheart** (2001). For Murakami, as well as other contemporary Japanese thinkers, anxiety over the condition of language and communication was brought to the fore by the nearly consecutive occurrence of two excessively violent events: the 1 January 1995 Hanshin earthquake and the 20 March 1995 *Aum Shinrikyō* sarin gas attack in Tokyo's subway. The shock of these events was compounded by the already weakened state of national confidence resulting from economic collapse (Murakami 1999: 746-5).[1] In a manner that brings to mind the two incidents of juvenile crime cited above, the restoration of language in **Sputnik Sweetheart** is initially allegorized in terms of a sacrificial ritual that will recuperate the force of language by facilitating a proximity to a real, conceptualized as *achiragawa* (another world or the other side). The allegory proves insufficient however, and the image of blood in sacrifice is instead appropriated as a metaphor for shock and a confrontation with a repressed awareness of the conditions of existence in contemporary late-capitalist Japan. The following argument traces this development in the narrative while attempting to explicate the status of the real *vis-à-vis* Murakami's notion of *achiragawa*.

The transformation and recovery of language in **Sputnik Sweetheart** is predicated on an encounter with *achiragawa*. I argue that Murakami's depiction of this encounter draws on a certain psychology of shock as a condition whereby mechanisms of disavowal are short-circuited and that which has been repressed in the unconscious, or split off from awareness, is allowed to surface momentarily. In this theorization, which will be explained in greater detail below, shock is a particularly modern phenomenon born of the effects of a technologically mediated existence. In its capacity to reveal that which has been obscured by habituation and adaptation to the conditions of everyday life, shock is a dangerous yet liberating moment of encounter with a real.

Achiragawa and the real that it designates in **Sputnik Sweetheart** undergo several permutations before the relation to shock becomes clear. In its initial evocation within an allegory of sacrifice, the real that *achiragawa* specifies is a condition of greater authenticity. It is simply a space not colonized by modern reason and its bifurcating logic: a space without contradictions in which magic is still instrumental—a place of pre-modern origins, so to speak. But *achiragawa* is also depicted as accessible via mundane technologies (phones, computers, binoculars) or 'inner-medium' spaces at the edge of society, even while it is characterized as a time and space outside technological mediation.[2] In this sense, it is consistent with fantasies of occult spaces that have surrounded such technologies since their emergence, and the real toward which it gestures can be seen as modernity's remainder, the excess of a split consciousness of a subject constituted in mediation.[3] *Achiragawa* is thus decisively sheered of its exterior spatial component and situated as a corollary of the unconscious. In this capacity, it begins to take on the function of a real that is the effect of the stripping away of the illusory framework constituting the consciousness of the everyday and marks an uncanny recognition of a sustained commitment to disavowal. Although this sense of the real in *Sputnik Sweetheart* slides at moments toward the terminality of a Lacanian Real—that empty space from which the subject emerges in the symbolic and which cannot be represented or faced but only experienced in the form of its symptoms (Lacan 1977)—it is never capable of reaching that point.[4]

My reading of *Sputnik Sweetheart* negotiates these various configurations of *achiragawa* by identifying it as a hyper-real, or para-space, similar to what one finds in the science fiction genre. The decision to do so is, in part, a strategic consideration aimed against an interpretation of Murakami as participating in a specifically Japanese literary tradition. The hyper-real is a phenomenon that is decisively modern as well as not restricted by discursively constituted national literary boundaries. Furthermore, the hyper-real accessed through, yet beyond, technology is read as an attempt to push the print medium to its limits by harnessing technology's potential for generating the phantasmagoric.[5] Yet, by depicting the actual experience once inside the hyper-real as entirely unmediated, Murakami signals a desire to erase the technological apparatus through which the hyper-real is ultimately generated, and to recover a pure and radically empowered new language.

The Japan of *Sputnik Sweetheart*

The appearance of some of Murakami's motifs and narrative devices in *Sputnik Sweetheart,* such as the encounter with *achiragawa* and the search for a vanished mysterious woman, render it similar to his previous novels. As in all his works, these devices are employed toward a depiction of a crisis of representation as a critique of the condition of language (and by extension human relations) in the mass-mediated culture of late-capitalist Japan. However, *Sputnik*

Sweetheart delivers an important departure from Murakami's previous novels in its depiction of a return from the *achiragawa* and the subsequent transformation of language and communication. Such a transformation allows for imagining a new form of contemporary subject capable of authentic communication (Takushoku 1999a: 35-6; Yoshikawa 2000).[6]

Sputnik Sweetheart emerges from Murakami's impressions of the media coverage of the *Aum Shinrikyō* cult's sarin gas attack on the Tokyo subway and his experience recording the victims' stories in his work *Underground* (1999). In the epilogue to *Underground,* Murakami criticizes the reporting of the incident in the Japanese media, claiming that the media built a bandwagon of consensus with exhausted, systematic and banal words (*riyō shitsukusareta, seidoteki ni natte shimatta, teaka ni mamireta kotoba*) (Murakami 1999: 739). The critique, however, is less a criticism of the media *per se* and more a comment on the inadequacy of contemporary language in relating the true sense of the event. Following the statement concerning the media, Murakami suggests that 'what we need now, I'm afraid, are words that work in a new direction and an absolutely new story that will be told in those words (another story in order to purify the story)' (ibid.: 739).[7] What Murakami is confronting here is the difficulty of articulating an experience so overwhelming that it exceeds the available economy of signification. Language has reached the limits of its expressive capacity and is unable to convey a subjective sense of a lived reality. Consequently, dialogue between people is either eclipsed by silence in the face of the ineffable or filled with words void of affect. This sense of frustration with the inadequacy of language to relay the experience of the gas attack echoes Walter Benjamin's disquiet regarding the end of storytelling that he perceived in the incapacity of language to relate the traumatic experience of modern warfare in World War I.[8] Benjamin writes that the 'art of storytelling is coming to an end':

> Less and less frequently do we encounter people with the ability to tell a tale properly. More and more often there is embarrassment all around when the wish to hear a story is expressed. It is as if something that seemed inalienable to us, the securest among our possessions, were taken from us: the ability to exchange experiences.
>
> (Benjamin 1968: 83)

In view of the motif of solitude that dominates Murakami's works, one senses that for Murakami, as with Benjamin, the crisis of storytelling is an accumulated effect that has worsened over the course of modernity rather than a recent and sudden phenomenon. But it is the arrival of shock that brings awareness of this condition into consciousness. For Benjamin, the senseless mechanized slaughter of World War I provided the necessary shock; the definitive presentation of a crisis in language (more than in any previous novel) that emerges in **Sputnik Sweetheart** suggests that for Murakami the events of the 1990s (including the Great Hanshin earthquake and Japan's economic collapse) function metaphorically as examples of what will be discussed below as technological accidents of modernity.

SHOCK

Shock, as described by Wolfgang Schivelbusch in connection with the modern technological accident, is a 'kind of sudden and powerful event of violence that disrupts the continuity of an artificially/mechanically created motion or situation, and also the subsequent state of derangement' (Schivelbusch 1986: 157-8). The technological accident and economic crisis, which are inherently related by the 'management of industry through capitalist principle' (ibid.: 132), are also similar forms of a systemic breakdown with corresponding effects of shock and trauma. The modern technological accident, which was perceived as the result of the loss of structural integrity maintained by containing the mechanical production of energy within safe parameters of operation, parallels the manner in which Marx defined economic crisis as a loss of equilibrium between the functions of buying and selling in the circulation of commodities (ibid.: 132). The 'state of derangement' resulting from the accident or crisis is a condition arising from an assault on mechanisms of repression produced by the modern (urban) individual as part of the imperative to negotiate a daily interface with constructed environments:

> The technology has created an artificial environment which people become used to as second nature. If the technological base collapses, the feeling of habituation and security collapses with it. What we called the 'falling height' of technological constructs (destructivity of accident proportionate to technical level of construct) can also be applied to the human consequences of the technological accident. The web of perceptual and behavioral forms that came into being due to the technological construct is torn to the degree that the construct itself collapses. The higher its technological level, the more denaturalized the consciousness that has become used to it, and the more destructive the collapse of both.
>
> (Schivelbusch 1986: 162)

The notion of habituation to which Schivelbusch refers is the structure of repetition that allows one to become accustomed to technology while repressing the initial fears that marked the first encounter with the technol-

ogy. It is the mechanism that enables, or rather demands, that one become absorbed in reading on the train or the in-flight movie on the plane in order to preclude the possibility of cognizing a potential disaster. Habituation thus points to what psychoanalysis calls the mechanism of disavowal, a form of dissociated altered state of consciousness, in which a part of the consciousness is circumscribed from the working memory. It is the same principle that drives the logic of the fetish, where one constructs a wall between what one knows and what one supposedly does not know, or can no longer remember.[9] One becomes absorbed in the technologically constituted space of in-between-ness with the certain expectation that there will be a safer and more certain world waiting at the point of disembarkation. Hence habituation operates toward the construction of an illusionist framework, a certain politics of representation that enforces the notion of a real existing immediately outside the space of the artificially produced in-between. In the contemporary illusionist framework driven by an interlocking global net of electric information technology and media-driven consumer desire, in which (to borrow a phrase from pop-culture) 'resistance is futile', it is the idea that one still maintains some semblance of control that has been displaced into the forever waiting, forever insistent and forever deferred destination of the real. The real is thus that imagined space outside the forever in-between world of mass-mediated culture, where we believe we can turn the technology off and separate ourselves from its all encompassing web. And yet, as the real is itself constituted by technology, we are secretly aware of the truth that there is no alternative; once technology has been switched on we can never step outside its effects.

Shock, then, is the condition in which the continued deferral of the contradiction in our mode of being is made untenable. In other words, the shock that results from the technological accident, the economic crisis or the systems crash is the moment when the politics of representation supporting the illusion to which we are committed becomes impossible. A breach opens between the designated spaces of the real and artificial to reveal the constructed nature of both. When the instinct for self-preservation, which is a preservation of the *status quo,* is strong, we respond to shock by attempting to defer the realization that what is being recalled is not just the initial repression from which the illusionary framework emerged, but rather something that is more frightening than death: the systematic nature of everyday life and the correlative mechanism of repression instantiated in order to live.[10] If there is a potential to be realized from the shock of the accident, it is in a momentary lapse of the dissociated/disavowed condition, the tearing down of the wall between what we know and do not know and an intensely physical encounter, unmediated by mechanisms of repression, with the material world.

UNCONNECTED

The Russian forerunner of all communication satellites and symbol of a new phase in the Cold War and information technology, 'Sputnik', which also means 'companion,' operates on an ironic level as the central metaphor for the impossibility of communication and absolute solitude in *Sputnik Sweetheart.* The image of the satellite orbiting against the emptiness of space comes to signify utter futility in the aspiration for intimacy between two people. Meditating on the hopelessness of this solitude, Murakami's quintessential first-person narrator, Boku (I),[11] remarks that individuals are no more than 'lonely metal souls in the unimpeded darkness of space, they meet, pass each other and part, never to meet again. No words passing between them. No promises to keep' (Murakami 2002: 179).[12] His use of the Sputnik metaphor at this point in the story appears as an unconscious echo of a sentiment expressed earlier by Miu, a Korean Japanese woman whom Boku has joined on a small Greek island to help look for Sumire. In yet another instance of this sort of unconscious echo that moves from one character to another, in telling Boku about Sumire's vanishing, Miu appropriates the metaphor, 'like smoke', from Sumire, who employs it in describing to Miu the disappearance of a cat during her childhood. Finally, the metaphor makes its way into Boku's explanation of Sumire's disappearance. For Murakami this is a media model of communication rather than a model for an authentic communication between individuals; it is communication via contagion where the individual is transformed into a relay that simply receives and transmits within a network. Such a mode of communication precludes the necessary reflective intervention of a thinking subject, a subject that can perceive, interpret and articulate the 'new story'. Yet, the essentially perfect transmission of a phrase gestures toward the possibility of perfect communication, that is, communication that occurs at a telepathic subconscious or perhaps extra-linguistic level, free from the specter of semiotic slippage and miscommunication. As we shall see throughout the following argument, Murakami's attempt to develop a new (pure) story and language appears trapped between the media and an authentic model of communication as he is bound by the materiality of the print medium and associated technologies of distribution.

When individuals do attempt to communicate in *Sputnik Sweetheart,* it is misunderstanding and imperfect communication rather than perfect communication that characterizes their interaction and serves as the grounds for incomprehensible alienation and loneliness. The notion that this miscommunication is a result of a crisis in signification emerges most explicitly in the conversations between Boku and Sumire concerning semiotics and writing. Sumire is a 22-year-old woman with a penchant for a bohemian lifestyle and American beatnik literature who is herself struggling to become a writer. Boku is in love with Sumire but she is completely without sexual desire for men. Thus their relationship remains confined to a strained platonic affair maintained mostly through inconvenient (for Boku) late-night telephone conversations as a result of Sumire's insomnia. In one of the initial dialogues between the two, a telephone conversation at 4:30 in the morning, the extent of the moribund condition of signification is revealed in Sumire's confusion over the functional difference between a sign (*kigō*) and a symbol (*shōchō*). Boku, as the forever pragmatic and rationally minded character that he is, attempts to explain the difference between the two via an example of a symbol that one could assume would be common sense for anyone with knowledge of Japan, especially a citizen: 'The emperor is a symbol of Japan. Do you follow that' (Murakami 2002: 28) Sumire does not, however, and responds with an ambiguous, 'sort of' (*nantoka*). Pressing the fact that the currency of this symbol is reified by the Japanese constitution and thus not a point for ambiguity, Boku insists that Sumire acknowledge it unequivocally for the conversation to continue. Sumire accepts, reluctantly, and Boku attempts to explain the critical difference in the quality of reciprocation that distinguishes a sign from a symbol. The concept, however, remains elusive for Sumire. It would be wrong to interpret Murakami's choice of this specific symbolic equation, which is currently the focus of numerous anxieties and debates as a result of what is seen as the threat of a resurgent nationalism, as a statement regarding the condition of nationalism among Japanese youth. Instead, by using what should be an obvious symbol and yet presenting it as devoid of rhetorical force, Murakami is suggesting a lack of vitality in contemporary language, which is needed to either establish or represent a physical reality.

Sumire's failure as a writer is the result of the moribund condition of language that Murakami belabors. She desires to create a great work that will 'capture the soul and human destiny' (Murakami 2002: 14) yet senses that her writing lacks some essential element. In an attempt to explain the art of literature, Boku allegorizes writing novels with an ancient Chinese gate-building ritual according to which the gates for walled cities in ancient China were constructed from the bones of fallen soldiers. It was only after the bones had been doused with the blood of a freshly killed dog that the 'ancient souls of the dead [would] magically revive' (Murakami 2002: 16). Boku explains:

> Writing novels is much the same. You gather up bones and make your gate, but no matter how wonderful the gate might be, that alone doesn't make it a living, breathing novel. A story is not something of this world. A real story requires a kind of magical baptism to link the world on this side with the world on the *other side*.
>
> (Murakami 2002: 16, emphasis in original)

The allegory evokes the ancient magic of sacrificial ritual and suggests an analogical equation in which blood is to bones as meaning is to signifier. Accordingly, 'magical baptism' (*jujutsu teki na senrei*) in the blood of the sacrificial victim promises to restore meaning to the semiotic structure of language just as spirits of fallen soldiers are restored to weathered bones. This logic draws on a modern anthropological interpretation of sacrifice as a sacred ritual that restores meaning to its proper place by fastening the symbolic to a material referent, thus restoring order to the realm of the profane . . . (see Hubert and Mauss 1964). The efficacy of sacrifice lies in the process of a literal identification within the mimesis of sympathetic magic ('what happens to the enemy's spear, hair or name, also happens to the individual'). Thus the *other side* (*achiragawa*) in this instance specifies both the pre-modern condition in which sacrifice was possible, and a sacred realm beyond the contemporary environment of the modern. In either case, it is a circumscribed space inhabited by a semiotic authenticity that Boku feels is absent in the present. Based on this reading, Murakami's longing for a new kind of story seems little more than cliched nostalgia for an imagined purity and simplicity of a pre-modern era. What challenges such an interpretation, however, is that despite Boku's pedantic stance toward Sumire, it is not at all clear which of the two is in need of the 'magical baptism' or whether such magic is indeed the solution. This becomes apparent from Sumire's literal understanding of Boku's allegory. The idea that a word or phrase could succumb to a doubling that troubles the literal meaning by suggesting a secondary, abstract, interpretation does not occur to her and she responds to Boku, 'I really don't want to kill an animal if I can help it' (Murakami 2002: 16). Boku reassures her that he is only speaking 'metaphorically' and there is no need actually to kill anything. But to speak metaphorically of sacrifice is to displace via abstraction an act that by the virtue of its literal mimetic logic is antithetical to metaphor. That is, in the Chinese gate building ritual, the blood of the dogs *is* the life of the animal that will restore the life to the bones. That Sumire understands this (albeit intuitively) while Boku

does not is the first indication that the central transformation in language that will occur over the course of the narrative (the emergence of the pure story) will be mediated through Boku while Sumire will be the catalyst in this process. How does the transformation happen?

The transformation of language occurs not, as Boku first imagines, by virtue of magic but rather its absence. It is the result of a brutal stripping away of the illusory framework, the padding between the self and world produced in the process of habitualization. In connection with this thematic shift, Boku's allegorical use of sacrifice and magical baptism is detached from its anthropological context and re-appropriated as a metaphor for shock. In its modified designation, the analogy equating blood and reanimation of bones with the recuperation of words comes to reference the capacity to recognize a relation between phenomena, stated as the realization that 'when people get shot, they bleed' (Murakami 2002: 136).[13] In other words, to recognize blood is to be aware of the material conditions of existence—an effect of being unable to sustain a state of disavowal. *Achiragawa,* in this sense, induces or is induced by a state of shock in which the mind is exposed to that which it has deferred into the unconscious. In the journey to the 'other side', the writer, or rather new storyteller, slips outside the 'fictional framework' of the everyday and engages the real by disengaging what Freud called a stimulus barrier, and which Boku describes in terms of the mechanics of a car's transmission:

> I think most people live in a fiction. I'm no exception. Think of it in terms of a car's transmission. It's like a transmission that stands between you and the harsh realities of life. You take the raw power from outside and use gears to adjust it so everything is in sync. That's how you keep your fragile body intact.
>
> (Murakami 2002: 62-3)[14]

Boku's mechanical metaphor clearly situates the contemporary fictional framework within the effects of technological mediation. *Achiragawa* is thus definitively not outside technology but is rather its symptom. The encounter with *achiragawa* suggests a situation in which one is able to inhabit modernity while maintaining an awareness of its effects. Hence, the art of storytelling, for Murakami, is the capacity to capture in narration the 'raw power' that shapes and controls our lives in a manner that is often too terrifying to acknowledge.

Murakami's depiction of *achiragawa* as a place that is accessed through the liminal spaces in society has been associated with a traditional narrative device in Japanese literature and culture. For example, citing the ethnologist Origuchi Nobuo's (1883-1953) research into the Japanese folk belief concerning passages to parallel worlds, Takushoku Mitsuhiko (1999a: 24-7) suggests that Murakami works within this tradition. Certainly one can find similarities between the other worlds depicted in Murakami's novels and those other spaces described in Origuchi's work. But to relegate Murakami to a specifically (traditional) Japanese context is to disregard the centrality of the struggle with the decisively modern condition of a dissociative state for which the technology of a mass-mediated culture is its condition of possibility. In other words, it is this condition that establishes both the possibility of and the need for the encounter with the *achiragawa*. Moreover, the displacement of the modern by the traditional that is required to consign Murakami's work to the status of traditional expression, signals yet another instance of disavowal (of the modern in Japan) and of split consciousness—'I know but I do not know'—that is part of the same modern phenomenon Murakami is attempting to confront through *achiragawa*. Hence, I would argue that, if there is anything traditional or pre-modern about Murakami's other worlds, that traditional or depiction of a pre-modern milieu is entirely embedded within the desires and logic of modernity.

In order to avoid any association with attempts to locate in Japan an intact and irreducible manifestation of tradition *despite* modernity, I read Murakami's depiction of *achiragawa* as similar to what Samuel Delany defines as the para-space found in cyber-punk fiction. According to Delany, the para-space is an alternate space that 'exists parallel to the normal space of the diegesis—a rhetorically heightened other realm' (cited in Bukatman 1993: 157). While the para-space is often inaugurated through cognition it is always a 'materially manifested' and 'linguistically intensified' space in which 'conflicts that begin in ordinary space are resolved' (Murakami 2002: 157). Yoshikawa Yasuhisa notes that, when writing about the regular world, Murakami frequently employs allegory and metaphor, and in the moment of transition between this world and the 'other world' the technique is drastically intensified. However, following the transition into the other world, allegory and metaphor vanish into simple narration (Yoshikawa 1999: 41-2). Such a mode of description clearly designates *achiragawa* as a space that is accessed via and at the same time beyond mediating technologies, of which language is the most fundamental. More importantly, the simplification of language announces a desire to retreat from the mechanism of disavowal actualized in the symbolic function of language. That is, it is through entrance into language and its corresponding capacity to displace meaning in signification that the mechanism

of disavowal in the logic of the fetish is made operative. Stripping away metaphor announces an intent to re-experience the moment of shock, the moment before what is revealed in that shock is lost in a dissociative reaction that splits the consciousness and separates the realization from the working memory. The journey to *achiragawa* thus expresses a movement back from the symbolic to the imaginary *toward* the Real and a confrontation, or, as Sumire will call it, 'collision' (*shōtotsu*), where the realization that 'when someone gets shot they bleed' cannot be deferred.

In an attempt to re-experience the moment of shock, Murakami's work harbors the possibility for the kind of 'traumatic realism' that Hal Foster finds enabled through the strategy of repetition in the work of Andy Warhol, especially *Death in America,* which focuses on images of accidents (Foster 1996). According to Foster, the repeated images of accidents in Warhol's work can be read as an attempt to 'repeat a traumatic event (in actions, in dreams, in images) in order to integrate it into a psychic economy, a symbolic order' (1996: 42). However, Foster suggests that this repetition is not so much 'restorative' or an attempt to 'reproduce traumatic effects', but rather 'to produce them as well' (1996: 42). Foster's theoretical model here regarding trauma is the Lacanian definition of trauma as a 'missed encounter with the real' that cannot be represented but only repeated. Hence, according to Foster, 'repetition in Warhol is not representation':

> Repetition serves to *screen* the real understood as traumatic. But this very need *points* to the real, and it is at this point that the real *ruptures* the screen of repetition. It is a rupture not in the world but in the subject; or rather it is a rupture between perception and consciousness of a subject *touched* by an image.
>
> (Foster 1996: 42)

Foster suggests that the effect produced echoes both Roland Barthes' notion of *punctum* as the moment when the screen is popped and the real pokes through and Walter Benjamin's concept of 'optical unconscious' that 'describes the subliminal effects of modern technologies of the image' (Foster 1996: 42-5). Although Barthes' and Benjamin's concepts are similarly aligned *vis-à-vis* what I have been referring to as an effect of shock, the 'real' to which they refer is the product of separate theoretical moments in a history guided by a different set of problematics. Benjamin's real is rooted in a Marxian critique of ideology as that which obfuscates an awareness of the true nature of the relations of production while Barthes' sense of the real is, as Foster points out, closer to the Lacanian Real. Foster's conflation of these two conceptualizations of a real is appropriate for the analysis of *Sputnik Sweetheart,* as Murakami's real also vacillates between similar conceptual poles.

What unites *punctum* and 'optical unconscious' is their reference to a critical point at which the mechanism that defers shock into trauma (the missed encounter with the real) is disabled and shock is revisited. It is a moment of radical disjuncture and instability but also a moment that carries the possibility of the recuperation of the subject, in the sense that it provides a tentative suturing of a split psyche and subsequent flash of anamnesis. In the encounter with *achiragawa* that will occur on the small Greek island, each of the three central characters in **Sputnik Sweetheart** is forced to confront a memory or realization that has been repressed. For Miu and Sumire the nature of the repressed memory and experience comprise a more personal psychological drama. For Boku the encounter will be nothing less than a collision with the illusionary framework of the everyday and the systematic nature of repression demanded by life in late capitalist Japan. While Miu will defer what is revealed for a life of further disenchantment, and Sumire's fate is left ambiguous, Boku will discover a new self-awareness and emerge from a lifetime of alienation.

TOWARD *ACHIRAGAWA*

Sumire's journey toward *achiragawa* and initiation into the art of storytelling begins when she falls in love with Miu, a Korean Japanese woman who is an independently employed wine importer and seventeen years Sumire's senior. She starts working for Miu and the two of them travel to Europe together for business. Declaring finally that 'blood must be shed', Sumire confesses her love and sexual attraction toward Miu while the two of them are vacationing on a small Greek Island. Miu, however, rejects her and Sumire disappears the next morning. The only traces of her that remain are two documents on a computer disk. The disk is left for Boku to find locked inside a suitcase that will open to the combination of Boku's telephone number area code. The cryptography is eminently appropriate as even in Japan it was the phone line that connected Boku's and Sumire's worlds. It is also another late night phone call that summons Boku across the world to the small island in the Aegean Sea that is so far beyond contemporary civilization that its 'communications are a bit backward' and 'there aren't any faxes or the internet' (Murakami 2002: 98).

The summons to the island is also Boku's call to *achiragawa* and it is initiated in a moment of misrecognition—'it didn't sound like my name, but there it was'—over a phone line 'distorted by some far-off inorganic substance' (Murakami 2002: 79). In an era in which instantaneous communication obfuscates an awareness of the distance mediated by the networks connecting talking heads, the delay and distortion that

marks this summons is an indication of the impossible distance whence it originates and subsequently manifests its meaning as a call from the *achiragawa*. Similarly, the materiality of the connection—the phone line—signifies the call from the 'other side' as a summons from Boku's unconscious, which is never so far as it is near: 'Only an apparatus such as the telephone can transmit its [the unconscious'] frequencies, because each encoding in the bureaucratic medium of writing would be subject to the filtering and censoring effects of a consciousness' (Kittler 1999: 89).[15]

At last it is Miu's voice that traverses the distance to inform Boku that Sumire has disappeared and to ask him to come to the island and help her look for her. She gives Boku the name of the island, which is never revealed to the reader. Boku has never been to the island. Yet, as in the Freudian notion of the uncanny as something that is both familiar and unfamiliar (Freud 1997), it is a place that sounds to him 'vaguely familiar' (Murakami 2002: 80). To get there, Boku must take a train to Tokyo's Narita airport, a flight to Athens that connects through Amsterdam, catch another plane to Rhodes and then a ferry to the island. Even before departure, however, there is a moment of radical disorientation in the form of an 'illogical dream—or uncertain wakefulness' in which '[t]he world had lost all sense of reality. Colors were unnatural, details crude. The background was papiermache, the stars made of aluminum foil. You could see the glue and the heads of the nails holding it all together' (Murakami 2002: 84).

The Boku who is summoned to *achiragawa* manifests symptoms that Weber associated with the process of disenchantment in a capitalist society. He is a man who, in his desire to know more about 'the objective reality of things outside' himself and how he maintains 'a sense of equilibrium by coming to terms with it' (Murakami 2002: 55), remains tormented by isolation and plagued by the inability to answer the question, 'who am I' (Murakami 2002: 54).[16] He is a man who attempts to contain mystery within the rational universe of equations, as witnessed in his reaction to Miu's summons. After hanging up the phone he writes:

> 1. Something has happened to Sumire. But what happened, Miu doesn't know.
>
> 2. I have to get there as soon as possible. Sumire, too, Miu thinks, wants me to do that.
>
> I stared at the memo pad. And I underlined two phrases.
>
> (Murakami 2002: 82)

Boku's encounter with the *achiragawa* holds the promise of shock and transformation thematized in the language of death and rebirth.

Once on the island, Boku's first genuine experience with *achiragawa* is mediated by the documents Sumire has tactfully hidden in anticipation of his arrival. By mimicking the reader's engagement with Murakami's fiction as another world in itself, the mode of Boku's textual encounter with this *achiragawa* serves as a doubling that both reveals and emphasizes the potential for the novel to operate on a performative level as traumatic realism; Murakami's aim is to reproduce in the mind of the reader the transformation that Boku will undergo as a result of his experience. In other words, Murakami intends for Boku's encounter with *achiragawa* via Sumire to act in the capacity as a fictional 'other world' and potential catalyst for transformation of the reader.

Sumire's message to Boku contains two documents. The first document is written in a self-reflective diary form in which Sumire attempts to analyze her desire to write. Through a mode of metonymic progression she discovers that her 'basic rule of thumb in writing has always been to write about things as if I *didn't* know them—and this would include things that I did know or thought I knew about' (Murakami 2002: 133). This practice for producing literary description almost immediately evolves into an understanding that:

> inside of us what we know and what we don't know share the same abode. For convenience' sake most people erect a wall between them. It makes life easier. But I just swept that wall away. I had to. I hate walls. That's just the kind of person I am.
>
> (Murakami 2002: 135)

In describing the simultaneous harboring of 'what we know' and 'what we don't know', Sumire is pointing to nothing other than the logic of the fetish and corresponding mechanism of disavowal: the wall constructed out of 'convenience'. Without this wall, Sumire realizes, there is no way to avoid 'collision' (*shōtotsu*). While 'collision' carries the threat of a permanent destabilization of the psyche, in its promise of an engagement with the real, which is announced here in the realization that 'when someone is shot they bleed', it also harbors the potential for revelation. Sumire is tempted to defer, yet again, this promise of revelation by escaping into dreams. In dreams, according to Sumire, 'boundaries don't exist. So in dreams there are hardly ever collisions. Even if there are, they don't hurt. Reality is different. Reality bites' (Murakami 2002: 136). Dreams, however, are the territory of the unconscious and hence for Murakami the gateway to *achiragawa,* where confrontation ('collision') cannot be avoided. No sooner has Sumire determined that dreams promise a refuge from collision than she begins to recount a recurring dream by prefacing it with a metaphor announcing the impending derailment and collision: 'A single theme is repeated [in the dream] over and over, like a train blowing its whistle at the same blind curve night after night' (Murakami 2002: 138). Sumire's recurring dream involves a missed encounter with a mother who died when Sumire was 3 and whom she knows only through a few photos in an album her father showed her. In the dream, when Sumire is not able to recognize the woman as her mother from her memory of the pictures in the album, she 'feels a wall of sorts melt away inside her' (Murakami 2002: 139) and concludes that her father tricked her. Her mother tries to speak to her but Sumire is unable to hear her words. When she awakes she is also unable to remember her mother's face from the dream. Sumire's dream ultimately points to a history of repressed animosity toward her father as the obstacle inhibiting a proper memory of her mother. He is the cause of her inability to mourn and the root of Sumire's alienation. Having faced this first encounter, Sumire's confidence is strengthened and she determines 'I want to make love to Miu, and be held by her.' With that she declares that '[b]lood must be shed. I'll sharpen my knife, ready to slit a dog's throat somewhere' (Murakami 2002: 141).

Despite the expectation that the second document will recount what happens when Sumire acts upon this resolve, the document tells the story rather of Miu's experience fourteen years earlier, as narrated by Sumire-cum-storyteller. As the climax of the novel, the story of Miu's experience clinches the theme Murakami has been building concerning the confrontation with the real as the condition of possibility for the emergence of the new story. Miu's story demonstrates unequivocally that the encounter with *achiragawa* inaugurates a shock in which the mechanism of repression is disabled and anamnesis is actualized. Murakami makes it clear that to grasp this moment is to re-emerge from the encounter with the new story, or in Miu's case the potential to become a great pianist. To defer the encounter again is to re-immerse oneself into empty signification and isolation, which is demonstrated in Miu's quitting piano for a profession in trade and commerce and her estrangement from all intimate relations.

In Sumire's narration, Miu (unintentionally) frames her story of the encounter with *achiragawa* between the narrations of two experiences of racial/national discrimination: the first in Europe and the second in Japan as a Korean-Japanese. In the first instance Miu describes a sudden awareness of a 'prejudice against her as an Asian' (Murakami 2002: 146) while spending a summer in a small Swiss town when she was 25 and attending music school in Paris. In this town, Miu makes the acquaintance of a 'handsome fiftyish Latin type' man named Ferdinando, whom Miu meets once for coffee but then attempts to avoid after feeling suspicious about his motives toward her (Murakami 2002: 145). The uncanny, however, is already in motion, and just as Freud, outside his native Germany, wanders the streets of a provincial town in Italy only to find himself returning again and again to the same sexually charged street with 'painted women' lurking in the shadows (Freud 1997: 213), Miu—doubly displaced from her 'native land' as a Korean-Japanese—finds herself (accidentally) running across Ferdinando 'often enough to make her feel he was following her' (Murakami 2002: 146). She begins to feel 'irritated and uneasy' and views 'Ferdinando as a threat to her peaceful life' (Murakami 2002: 146). Moreover, the mechanism that will take her to *achiragawa* has begun to summon her through phone calls in the middle of the night that go dead the moment she answers—which she mistakes for Ferdinando. Since 'the phone was an old model' that 'she couldn't just unplug' (Murakami 2002: 147) she has no choice but to go along for the ride pretending not to hear the 'train blowing its whistle at the same blind curve night after night' until the jolt of the accident will throw her into a direct confrontation with the real and her state of disavowal.

The jolt occurs when nostalgia for her father draws her toward a Ferris wheel at a local amusement park one evening. It is near closing time but she manages to buy a ticket for the last spin of the wheel with the hope that from the top of the wheel she will be able to view her own apartment across town through a small pair of binoculars she carries in her bag. Unfortunately, she has time only to locate her apartment window before the wheel finishes its spin. But the logic of repetition and desire that drives the uncanny never really kicks in until the second time around and thus Miu finds herself unexpectedly locked in the gondola starting a second spin. This time around, despite feeling an illogical sense of guilt over her voyeuristic intent, she is able to peer into her own apartment as the wheel rounds the top and she wishes that she could place a call to the phone in her room or read the letter she left on the table (Murakami 2002: 150). Just as it is a 'more unusually violent jolt of the train' that precedes the uncanny appearance of Freud's double,[17] Miu's encounter with her *doppelgänger* occurs as the Ferris wheel comes to a sudden halt and she is 'thrown against the side of the car, banging her shoulder and nearly dropping the binoculars on the floor' (Murakami 2002: 150). She has been abandoned for the night locked inside the now motionless wheel and when she peers through her binoculars into her apartment again

she confronts her darkest fears and desires in the form of her double engaging in tempestuous sex with the hairy, animal-like Ferdinando (Murakami 2002: 154). Miu is both horrified and captivated by the sight, nauseated and yet unable to 'drag her gaze away' (Murakami 2002: 155). She feels outraged by the sense that what she is watching is being performed especially for her and that she is unable to control this 'meaningless and obscene' violation of her body that will leave her 'polluted' (Murakami 2002: 156). At last, the man who is ravaging her double is not 'even Ferdinando anymore' but a face that she will be unable to recall after she eventually loses consciousness. She is found the next morning by the amusement park employees and when she awakes in the hospital her hair has turned pure white, visually inscribing both the memory of the event and the radical transformation of her body and mind:

> I was still on *this* side, here. But *another* me, maybe half of me, had gone over to the *other* side. Taking with it my black hair, my sexual desire, my periods, my ovulation, perhaps even the will to live. . . . I was split in two forever.
>
> (Murakami 2002: 157)

Miu is forever plagued by the question of which is her authentic self. 'Is the real me the one who held Ferdinando Or the one who detested him' (Murakami 2002: 157).

Miu's uncanny encounter carried the potential for securing her link with *achiragawa*, which Boku situated earlier as the essential element for the real story. Instead, she withdraws, confessing that she does not have the confidence to face the experience (Murakami 2002: 157), while attempting to dismiss it as a figment of her imagination: 'What happened in Switzerland fourteen years ago may well have been something I created myself' (Murakami 2002: 160). Without that link, something is missing from her (Murakami 2002: 158) and her piano playing fails to move an audience. Moreover, she finds herself unable to compete even with pianists of less refined technique.

Miu closes her story by attributing the strength she had to continue life after the event to her parent's insistence that she recognize that she must always live as a foreigner in Japan despite her perfect identification with the culture. This very strength, which is nothing less than the strength to construct a wall for sake of convenience between 'what you know and what you don't know', is thus the same force driving the mechanism of repression behind the illusory framework of the everyday.

Following the vicarious exposure to *achiragawa* via Sumire's documents, Boku experiences the realm for himself when he is awakened late at night by 'far-off music, barely audible' (Murakami 2002: 168). The music lures him out of bed into a bright moonlit night toward a hilltop in the woods. Sensing danger, Boku feels that he should 'keep his distance' and at the same time he feels that he has to go forward: 'I felt like I was in a dream. The principle that made other choices possible was missing' (Murakami 2002: 169). At once, Boku feels himself separated from his body and the moment before the final transition to the *achiragawa* he declares that 'the spark of life had vanished. My real life had fallen asleep somewhere, and a faceless someone was stuffing it in a suitcase, about to leave' (Murakami 2002: 170). What he mistakenly refers to here as his 'real life' is in fact the life that was subdued in habituation, the life that had 'fallen asleep'. Once the transition is complete, we are in the space of the hyper-real where the process of abstraction in signification ceases and words are imbued with the power to invoke an immediate physical consequence; it is an experience of virtual reality encountered through print where, similar to those computer-generated realities of science fiction, the 'mind makes it real'.[18] Feeling overwhelmed, Boku takes a breath and literally sinks in the 'sea of consciousness to the very bottom' (Murakami 2002: 170):

> Pushing aside the heavy water I plunged down quickly and grabbed a huge rock there with both arms. The water crushed my eardrums. I squeezed my eyes tightly closed, held my breath, resisting. Once I made up my mind, it wasn't that difficult. I grew used to it all—the pressure, the lack of air, the freezing darkness, the signals the chaos emitted.
>
> (Murakami 2002: 170)

When Boku resurfaces the music is gone and the transformation that will result from this encounter with the *achiragawa* has begun. He returns to his bed and, unable to sleep, realizes that the real Boku is dying somewhere while starving kittens are consuming his brain (Murakami 2002: 172).

The night before Boku returns to Japan he realizes that the process of transformation and rebirth is nearly complete: 'When dawn comes, the person I am won't be here anymore. Someone else will occupy this body' (Murakami 2002: 179). Immediately following this declaration, Boku is suddenly able to articulate the heretofore ineffable sensation of loneliness that has plagued his life. But the real marker of a transformation having occurred appears when he is back in Japan and is able to reach out and build rapport with a troubled grade school student from the class he teaches. The student, whom Boku calls 'Carrot' after the nickname given to him by his classmates, also

happens to be the son of a woman with whom Boku is having an affair. Carrot is no doubt aware of and troubled on an intuitive level by his mother's infidelity, and yet he is unable to either articulate or understand his feelings. Instead, he becomes an obsessive shoplifter and, when he is caught for the third time, Boku and the mother are summoned to the store's security office for a conference. The serial nature of the items Carrot steals from the same store despite being caught each time—eight identical staplers in the third instance, fifteen mechanical pencils in the second and eight compasses in the first—is at once a parody of the serial nature of the institutional pedagogic apparatus producing endless ranks of salarymen and the culture of late-capitalism in which the commodity fetish is intentionally cultivated in children. Concurrently, the profound sense of alienation and confusion that drives Carrot to reject, by stealing, the proper relations of exchange fundamental to this culture, prefigures his potential future as the serial killer—the next *Shonen A*—the next kid to throw a bomb into a crowded video store or the next Asahara Shoko.[19] Boku saves Carrot not through reproach or re-establishing the institutional moral pedagogy, but by opening his heart to him and sharing with him the story of his unsuccessful search for a lost friend on the Greek island. He tells Carrot also of the estrangement he always felt from his family, of the dog he loved when he was a child that was killed in an accident and of his years of social alienation during university. In a final moment of empathy Boku tells Carrot: 'being alone is like the feeling you get when you stand at the mouth of a large river on a rainy evening and watch the water flow into the sea' (Murakami 2002: 195).

While the final pages of **Sputnik Sweetheart** leave the matter of Sumire's return from *achiragawa* an open question, the scene between Boku and Carrot renders the question essentially unimportant.[20] The significance of the novel lies in what this poignant moment of bonding between Boku and the child suggests—which is something that has remained entirely ambiguous in Murakami's previous novels. What emerges here is finally the suggestion of a resolution of the crisis in language, the rebirth of the storyteller and story, and the subsequent condition of possibility for authentic communication and understanding between individuals. This is the culmination of a long process of maturation and self-exploration over the course of Murakami's work, of the first-person narrator, 'Boku', who made his debut in Murakami's first book, **Hear the Wind Sing** (1979). by announcing a commitment to the art of story telling:

> All sorts of people have come my way telling their tales, trudged over me as if I were a bridge, then never

come back. All the while I kept my mouth tight shut and refused to tell my own tales. That's how I came to the final year of my twenties.

Now I am ready to tell.

(Murakami, in Rubin 2002: 42)

Even from that initial moment, the process of telling one's story was more than simple fiction. It was a gesture toward recovery from the malaise of modernity through a practice of the Freudian talking cure. Only for Murakami, the therapy is exercised via the most basic technology of recording, namely, print. In the sentence that follows his declaration of intent to begin writing in **Hear the Wind Sing,** Boku states: 'When you get right down to it, writing is not a method of self-therapy. It's just the slightest attempt to a move in the direction of self-therapy' (Murakami 2002: 42). In structuring an encounter with *achiragawa* as a bridge to the unconscious, the print medium imitates those other media (telephone, phonograph, film). These technological apparatuses appear incessantly in Murakami's work as narrative devices that, by linking the characters to another world, manifest a function they have been perceived to perform since their emergence. That is to say, they connect the here and now with those imagined spaces of the occult and the deeper recesses of the mind.

CONCLUSION

I began with a discussion of instances in which individuals, driven by a desire to recover a vanishing real and break out of what they perceived as the overwhelming artifice of the social facade, attempted to disassemble actual or institutional bodies. In either case, these misguided attempts to reveal a material form of something that can exist only in abstraction led to the shedding of blood and death of innocent people without making perhaps even a dent in the social facade. While such events may have failed to reveal the illusive *real,* for Murakami, the shocking nature of the violence and subsequent failure of language to represent adequately its emotional impact was indicative of the complicity of modern technologies of mediation in the production of a dissociated state in individuals and a prevailing sense of social alienation. In this respect, it seems ironic, then, that Murakami's attempt to find 'words that work in a new direction and an absolutely new story that will be told in those words (another story in order to purify the story)' insists on a primary interface with technology before a secondary unmediated experience in the hyper-real. Although the narrative of **Sputnik Sweetheart** concludes with the possibility of the new

language and story, the reader is ultimately left to wonder whether the novel (or, in that case, any novel today) is capable of the promise Murakami assigns to it.

In designating the phrase 'blood must be shed' as a metaphor for shock and an engagement with the real that occurs entirely within the doubly abstracted realm of signification—the hyper-real literary construct— Murakami gestures to the unrepresentable and intangible nature of the real. Also, by situating shock as the crucial moment in which something approaching a movement toward a Real is sensed, Murakami implicates the role of the unconscious in creating both the sense of a loss of the real and a desire for its recovery. The unconscious is ultimately burdened with the responsibility of producing a stable relationship between the individual and his or her surroundings by concealing that which the individual is unable to assimilate into the everyday without dire consequences for the stability of the psyche. In other words, it is the central mechanism behind the process of habitualization. For Murakami, recovering something of the real does not involve ripping apart bodies but rather a foraging through the unconscious via a ripping apart of language and the subsequent de-familiarization of one's self and surroundings that this involves. It is also more about remembering what language prevented one from remembering than it is about assimilating new knowledge from an external experience. Thus, while the technological accident remains the metaphor in Murakami's work for the experience of a radical de-familiarization that occurs through shock, the idea of an encounter with the real is realizable through those technologies that are seen to access the unconscious by working through and beyond language. The primary medium in this case, for Murakami, is the technology of mass printing that has made his novels available in Japan in pocket-size segments called *bunkō bon,* the main consumers of which are the masses of workers whose long commute by train each day provides ample time for reading. In this inversed schema, even the book on the train no longer offers the sense of safety it once did.

Finally, it can be suggested that shock, in Murakami's work, establishes the potential for the emergence of a new subject in the anticipation that what is not known is not something that was not encountered and recorded into memory, but rather something that is there but simply cannot be accessed. Such a schema however, produces incongruent notions of the nature of the subject who is in command of such knowledge. On one hand, this relation between memory and the subject assumes the *a priori* existence of an autonomous individual/subject who is able to re-establish subjecthood by reclaiming memory. On the other hand, the automaticity of the recording function that is memory here suggests a recording apparatus that resembles the operation of an electric recording medium absorbing all data. In this case, the subject emerges not by reclaiming memory but by reorganizing and censoring memory.

Notes

1. See also *Shinseiki no Riaru* (Miyadai *et al.* 1997) for a discussion of the impotent condition of language in contemporary (post-bubble) Japan.

2. Takushoku Mitsuhiko uses the term 'inner-medium' to describe those spaces in Murakami's works from which the character moves into the 'other world' (see Takushoku 1999a: 22-3). He also draws a correlation between Murakami's use of a well, called *ido* in Japanese, as an inner-medium and the Freudian notion of the Id (see Takushoku 1999b: 125-6).

3. Friedich Kittler argues that the invention of media technologies capable of storing image and sound and Freud's discovery of the structured unconscious must be seen as concurrent and integrally related phenomena. The ability to store image and sound in a space outside the immediate access of the human mind as well as the potential for this technology to make visible or audible things that were not apparent via an unmediated interface with reality no doubt propelled the imagining of another space in the human mind, circumscribed from the working memory, in which excess image and sound data were stored. On the question of the connection between electronic media, the unconscious and imagined 'other worlds', see Kittler (1990, 1999).

4. Of course, since an encounter with the Lacanian Real can end only in insanity or annihilation, this is a condition to which Murakami only gestures throughout his works. Perhaps a good example of what the symptoms of such an encounter might look like can be found in the film *Ringu* (1998), where even a glimpse into the eye of the Real results in a terminal catatonic state; another example can be found in the Edogawa Rampo short story, 'The Hell of Mirrors', in which the protagonist is driven to insanity after locking himself into a giant ball lined with a seamless mirror (Edogawa 1956).

5. Kittler explains that the potential to store sound and image in the new technologies of phonograph and film allowed these devices to appropriate all of the fantastic or the imaginary that had theretofore been the exclusive property of literature (1999: 154).

6. While it is tempting to qualify this imagined new subject as Japanese, to do so would be to disregard what I strongly believe is Murakami's attempt to address a condition of late capitalist modernity rather than a specifically national cultural issue.

7. The Japanese is *'monogatari wo jyōka suru tame no betsu no monogatari'*.

8. It should be noted here that, although Benjamin does not unequivocally conflate the end of storytelling with the advent of the modern, he does state that the end of storytelling is a process that has become apparent since the First World War (Benjamin 1968: 84).

9. This applies to both the Freudian and Marxian notion of fetish.

10. I am in debt to John Pemberton for these insights.

11. Although Murakami does name his character in one sentence of the novel as 'K—', I chose to refer to him as 'Boku' in order to maintain the tentative connection with the first-person narrator in Murakami's other novels. Furthermore, the one instant in which Boku is properly named is due to the structure of the sentence that precludes the possibility of using the first person.

12. Except where noted otherwise I am relying on Philip Gabriel's excellent translation of *Sputnik Sweetheart* for citations from the work.

13. This is my translation of *'hito ga utaretara, chi wa nagareru mono da'* (Murakami 2001: 197). Gabriel, however, translates it as 'Did you ever see anyone shot by a gun without bleeding'

14. It is worth mentioning that sense of a 'real' evoked here bears similarities with the notion of a *riaru* (real) that emerges in the dialogue between Miyadai Shinji, Fujii Yoshiki and Nakamori Akio in *Shinseiki no Riaru* (Miyadai *et al.* 1997). The 'real' for these three is a condition devoid of the illusions (such as the value of the family and education) to which an adherence defers awareness of the constructed nature of values and social cohesion. Such illusions operate in a manner similar to the 'fictions' to which Boku refers. They shield one from the 'harsh realities' in life.

15. Kittler writes that Freud's description of the psychiatric practice in terms of 'telephony' manifests the perception that the 'unconscious coincides with electric oscillations' (Kittler 1999: 89).

16. Weber declares in his thesis on disenchantment that science and its corresponding process of rationalization and intellectualization still 'gives no answer to our question, the only question that is important for us: What shall we do and how shall we live' (1946).

17. In a footnote in his paper 'The Uncanny', Freud relates that 'a more than usually violent jolt of the train' caused the door of his compartment to swing back and his own reflection in the glass of the door to appear before him, which his initially mistook for another person (Freud 1997: 225, fn. 1).

18. I borrow this expression from the quintessential portrayal of such a space in the film *The Matrix* (1999).

19. Asahara Shoko is the founder and leader of the *Aum Shinrikyō* cult who is currently serving a jail sentence.

20. A number of critics insist on reading the phone call from Sumire in the last page of the novel as her return from the other side; see, for example, Takushoku (1999a). However, Murakami offers no substantial support of this reading or any other and instead leaves the matter entirely ambiguous.

References

Benjamin, W. (1968) *Illuminations,* New York: Harcourt Brace World.

Bukatman, S. (1993) *Terminal Identity: The Virtual Subject in Postmodern Science Fiction,* Durham, NC: Duke University Press.

Edogawa, R. (1956) *Japanese Tales of Mystery & Imagination,* trans. J. B. Harris, Singapore: Tuttle.

Foster, H. (1996) 'Death in America', *October* 75: 37-59.

Freud, S. (1997) *Writings on Art and Literature,* Stanford, CA: Stanford University Press, pp. 192-233.

Horkheimer, M. and Adorno, T. W. (1988) *Dialectic of Enlightenment,* New York: Continuum.

Hubert, H. and Mauss, M. (1964) *Sacrifice: Its Nature and Function,* Chicago, IL: University of Chicago Press.

Iida, Y. (2002) *Rethinking Identity in Modern Japan: Nationalism as Aesthetics,* London: Routledge.

Kittler, F. A. (1990) *Discourse Networks 1800/1900,* Stanford, CA: Stanford University Press.

—— (1999) *Gramophone, Film, Typewriter,* Stanford, CA: Stanford University Press.

Lacan, J. (1977) *Ecrits: A Selection,* New York: Norton.

Miyadai, S., Fujii, Y. and Nakamori, A. (1997) *Shinseiki no riaru,* Tokyo: Asuka Shinsha.

Murakami, H. (1999) *Andaguraumdo,* Tokyo: Kodansha bunko.

—— (2001) *Suputoniku no koibito,* Tokyo: Kodansha bunko.

—— (2002) *Sputnik Sweetheart,* trans. P. Gabriel, New York: Vintage International.

Rubin, J. (2002) *Haruki Murakami and the Music of Words,* London: Harvill.

Schivelbusch, W. (1986) *The Railway Journey: The Industrialization of Time and Space in the 19th Century,* Berkeley, CA: University of California Press.

Takushoku, M. (1999a) in H. Murakami, Y. Kuritsubo, and T. Tsuge (eds) *Murakami Haruki sutadizu,* Vol. 5, Tokyo: Wakakusa Shobo.

—— (1999b) in H. Murakami, Y. Kuritsubo, and T. Tsuge (eds) *Murakami Haruki sutadizu,* Vol. 5, Tokyo: Wakakusa Shobo, pp. 124-32.

Weber, M. (1946) *Max Weber: Essays in Sociology,* trans. H. H. G. Mills and C. W. Mills, Oxford: Oxford University Press.

Yoshikawa, Y. (1999) in H. Murakami, Y. Kuritsubo and T. Tsuge (eds) *Murakami Haruki sutadizu,* Vol. 5, Tokyo: Wakakusa Shobo, pp. 38-60.

—— (2000) 'Suputoniku no koibitu- (kikan) to (senrei) monogatari janku-ka ni koushite', *Yuriika,* 32(4): 204-9.

William Skidelsky (review date 24 January 2005)

SOURCE: Skidelsky, William. "Teenage Kicks." *New Statesman* 134, no. 4723 (24 January 2005): 52-3.

[*In the review below, Skidelsky dismisses* Kafka on the Shore *as childish.*]

Haruki Murakami is one of the world's most successful authors. Few other serious writers enjoy such commercial success: ***Norwegian Wood,*** the novel that made him famous, has sold more than a million copies. Only those who have never read his work are likely to be surprised by this. Murakami's writing, though often strange and complex, has an easygoing accessibility that makes his books hard to put down. The trademark elements of his fiction—a frank approach to sex, a preoccupation with alienation and loss, an effortless-seeming ability to straddle high and popular culture, a strain of overt surrealism—account for his popularity (especially, you suspect, among teenagers) both in Japan and in the west. In addition, Murakami himself is an attractive figure—vaguely mysterious and cultish, but also friendly-looking and cute. To any bookish 17-year-old, he must seem like the epitome of cool.

Is it possible, however, that Murakami is a bit too likeable? The flipside of such hipness is a suspicion that his novels are not terribly profound. It is true that they make frequent and extravagant gestures towards profundity—but that is not the same as actually being so. This suspicion is reinforced by a common misapprehension about his work. Because so much about Murakami's fiction appears reassuringly recognisable, it is tempting to assume that he is an author whose primary concern is real life. We feel the urge to identify with his protagonists, to see their concerns as mirroring our own. In fact, there is nothing remotely lifelike about his fiction: his imagination takes off from the point at which reality stops. For all their cleverness and surface complexity, his novels are essentially works of escapism.

The narrator of Murakami's latest novel [*Kafka on the Shore*] is a characteristically precocious 15-year-old named Kafka Tamura. He is not really called Kafka: that is the name he adopts when, at the beginning of the story, he runs away from home. Kafka has lived alone in Tokyo with his father, a celebrated sculptor, ever since his mother left home (taking his older sister with her) when he was four. We never learn Kafka's real name, nor anything else about his home life, other than the terrible, Sophoclean prophecy his father has made—that after sleeping with both his mother and sister, he will commit patricide. Thus Murakami introduces one of his favourite themes—the conflict between destiny and individual volition. In absconding from home, is Kafka running away from or is he embracing his fate?

Kafka travels to the faraway town of Takamatsu, where he hopes he can disappear completely. As is invariably the case in Murakami, however, a series of strange coincidences occurs. On the coach, Kafka meets a girl who is the same age as his sister. Can she really be her? You would think not, but this being Murakami, nothing is ruled out. It is not long before she gives Kafka a hand job, thus taking care of the first part of his father's prophecy (sort of). In Takamatsu, Kafka visits a library and is befriended by the head librarian, an exquisitely cultivated transvestite called Oshima, but of greater interest is the library's mysterious and beautiful owner, Mrs Saeki. Besides being the right age to be Kafka's mother, Mrs Saeki is unable to account for a large part of her past. Kafka feels irresistibly drawn to her, particularly when he starts receiving nightly visits from her 15-year-old ghost. After losing his virginity to this accommodating apparition, Kafka embarks on an affair with the flesh-and-blood Mrs Saeki.

As if all that weren't strange enough, Murakami throws in a separate plot strand involving an old man called Nakata. As a child during the war, Nakata was involved in an incident of collective hypnosis in the woods. (Murakami documents this in the form of an X-file.) The episode left him mentally subnormal but with the ability to converse with cats. In Tokyo, Nakata runs into Kafka's father who, posing in the guise of Johnnie Walker (yes, I really do mean the man on the whisky bottle), is going about slaughtering the city's feline population. Outraged by this, Nakata kills Johnnie Walker and himself sets off for Takamatsu. Committing the murder causes Nakata to lose the ability to communicate with cats; he is, however, able to make fish fall from the sky. As becomes clear, his

experiences are in some way bound up with Kafka's destiny—although, as this connection can be explained only by reference to an object called the "entrance stone", its nature remains tantalisingly hazy.

It would be conventional at this point to say that none of this is as silly as it sounds. Unfortunately, however, it is. *Kafka on the Shore* is an extraordinarily silly novel—and not just because of its specious metaphysical musings. No less ridiculous is Kafka's obsession with his genitalia. He is a boy who cannot take his clothes off without gazing lovingly at his "fresh-out-of-its-foreskin cock", or remarking on his "porcelain-hard erection". Not surprisingly, this habit only grows more pronounced when he begins his affair with Mrs Saeki. While there is nothing implausible about a 15-year-old being obsessed with sex, the way Murakami has Kafka talk about his penis makes it clear that what is really being expressed here is a middle-aged man's fixation with the idea of nascent sexuality.

Add to this the slow pace at which the story unfolds, and it is impossible to avoid concluding that *Kafka on the Shore* is a serious let-down. No doubt thousands will read it and believe they have discovered fundamental truths about life. One must hope that most of them will have the excuse of being teenagers.

Haruki Murakami and Sean Wilsey (interview date 2005)

SOURCE: Murakami, Haruki, and Sean Wilsey. "Sean Wilsey Talks with Haruki Murakami." In *The Believer Book of Writers Talking to Writers*, edited by Vendela Vida, pp. 241-50. San Francisco, Calif.: Believer Books, 2005.

[*In the following interview, Wilsey and Murakami discuss the author's writing schedule, his literary influences, and the role of motifs such as music and money in his work.*]

Haruki Murakami has published thirteen books in English, of which the majority are great, and two are better—that is, deeper, funnier, lonelier, more life-affirming and breath-taking and sleep-depriving—than anything I've ever read.

A rough sketch of Murakami's pre-writing years goes like this: born in 1949, in Kyoto, his self-described uneventful suburban childhood was enlivened by voracious reading of Dostoevsky and Raymond Chandler (the latter in paperbacks left behind by American sailors). A few years as a middling university student in Tokyo introduced him to the two loves of his life, jazz music and his wife, Yōko; he married and opened a jazz club, called Peter Cat (cats being a third love), which was such a success that Murakami's life seemed set on its course—comfortable, bohemian—until, as he told an audience in 1992, "Suddenly one day in April 1978, I felt like writing a novel . . . I was at a baseball game . . . in the outfield stands, drinking beer . . . My favorite team was the Yakult Swallows. They were playing the Hiroshima Carps. The Swallows' first batter in the bottom of the first inning was an American, Dave Hilton. You've probably never heard of him. He never made a name for himself in the States, so he came to play ball in Japan. I'm pretty sure he was the leading hitter that year. Anyhow, he sent the first ball pitched to him that day into left field for a double. And that's when the idea struck me: I could write a novel."

So he wrote a novel. Every night after closing Peter Cat Murakami sat at his kitchen table, drank beer, and in six months produced the short, Vonnegut-like *Hear the Wind Sing* (1979). He submitted the novel for a literary award, and when it won Murakami went to get Dave Hilton's autograph—"I feel he was a lucky charm for me"—then went back to the kitchen table and wrote another novel, *Pinball, 1973* (1980). This book (coupled with a movie deal on the first) was successful enough to allow him to sell the jazz club and become a full-time writer at age thirty-two.

Established, Murakami moved back to the suburbs and began work on *A Wild Sheep Chase* (1982), technically the final book in a trilogy that began with the first two—the trilogy of the rat—though he considers it his first novel, because it's where he found his voice. (An unfortunate footnote to his success story is that neither *Hear the Wind Sing* or *Pinball, 1973* will ever be available in the United States because, as Murakami bluntly told *Publishers Weekly* in 1991, they are "weak.")

Style found, weakness behind him, lifestyle then changed. Murakami began exercising religiously, running marathons, eating meticulously, drinking moderately—living with a Shinto purity in order to maintain the rigorous work habits that have permitted him to be so consistently productive. He also began translating, mostly American writers, dividing his days between his own writing and the rendering into Japanese of Americans'. With his regime in place Murakami produced some astounding books, beginning with the hyper-experimental *Hard-Boiled Wonderland and the End of the World* (1985, and still his personal favorite), and then, in pursuit of a wider audience, changing course to write what he described to *Publishers Weekly* as a "totally realistic, very straight" story, its title aimed directly at the mainstream: *Norwegian Wood* (1987). The novel was so huge that he fled Japan to escape the unprecedented, pop-star scale of his success. On the lam he wrote *Dance Dance Dance* (1988), a rollicking sequel to *A Wild Sheep Chase* (making a two-thirds-suppressed trilogy into a half-suppressed quadrilogy) and *South of the Border, West of the Sun* (1992), an elegiac version of *Norwegian Wood*—quieter and more mature.

Then, working as a professor in the United States, he began his masterpiece, *The Wind-up Bird Chronicle* (1994-1995), in which he took the best of his experimental and realistic voices, plus a new sense of history and morality, and closed in on what makes a writer immortal. *The Wind-up Bird Chronicle* was published in Japan in three volumes in 1994-1995, and in the U.S. in 1997, in a single abridged edition. Since then Murakami has returned to Japan. Short stories have always come naturally, and he has written some of his best in the past few years, collecting them in the 200-page tour de force *After the Quake* (2002). He's also written a nonfiction book, *Underground* (2000), about the poison gas attacks on the Tokyo subway, and two more novels, *Sputnik Sweetheart* (1999) and *Kafka on the Shore* (2005).

For this interview we communicated by email; I wrote questions in English, and he responded in Japanese. Jay Rubin, translator of *The Wind-up Bird Chronicle* and author of the indispensable biography *Haruki Murakami and the Music of Words* (2002), translated the answers into English.

As an interviewee Murakami does not open up the deepest recess of his heart and soul. As a writer he opens up yours.

[*Wilsey*]: *It occurs to me that the most malevolent figure in your work is a sort of professional interviewee (Noboru Wataya in* **The Wind-Up Bird Chronicle***); and you equate his facility with the media (and the slipperiness of his opinions) with his evil and soullessness. You seem to be saying if a person is too good at opening his mouth in public he's empty inside. Then again, one of the most illuminating interviews I've ever read with anyone on any subject was the* New York Times's *interview with you on the subject of 9/11, and its similarities to the Tokyo subway gas attacks. There you said, speaking of cult leaders, and their relationship with their followers, "If you have questions, there is always someone to provide the answers. In a way, things are very easy and clear, and you are happy as long as you believe." How does one speak publicly without becoming a professional/Noboru Wataya, or stopping people from thinking for themselves?*

[Murakami]: often get calls from newspapers asking my opinion on some news event or other—for example, "What do you think about Japan's decision to dispatch Self-Defense Force troops to Iraq?" or "What's your view of the twelve-year-old girl who cut her classmate's throat?" and such.

I do of course have my own reasonably clear personal opinions about such events. But there is a definite difference between my having an opinion as an individual and "novelist Haruki Murakami"'s having an opinion. Still, it goes without saying that any personal opinion of mine appearing in the newspaper will be read by the public as the opinion of novelist Haruki Murakami. And so I make it a rule never to respond to questions from the media.

I am not, of course, saying that novelists must not express their personal opinions. It is my belief, however, that, rather than expressing his views on a number of diverse matters, the role of the novelist would seem most properly to lie in his depicting as precisely as possible (as Kafka described his execution machine in chillingly minute detail) the personal bases and environmental forces that give rise to those views. To put it in a more extreme manner, what the novelist needs is not diverse opinions but a personal system of storytelling upon which his opinions can take a firm stand.

In that sense, Noboru Wataya's stance is, as you suggest, shallow and superficial. Precisely because his opinions are shallow and superficial, they communicate with great speed, and they have great practical impact. What I wanted to convey to the reader through my portrait of Noboru Wataya was the dangerous influence that contemporary media gladiators, who use such rhetoric as a weapon, exert on our society and our minds: the special cruelty they deploy below the surface. We are practically surrounded by such people in our daily lives. Often, the opinions we assume to be our own turn out on closer inspection to be nothing but the parroting of theirs. It is chilling to think that in many instances we view the world through the media and speak to each other in the words of the media.

The only thing we can do sometimes to avoid straying into such a sealed labyrinth, is to go down alone into a deep well the way the protagonist Watanabe does: to recover one's own point of view, one's own language. This is not an easy thing to do, of course, and sometimes it involves danger. The job of the novelist, perhaps, is to act as a seasoned guide to such dangerous journeys. And, in some cases, in the story we can simulate for the reader the experience of undertaking such a task of self-exploration. For me, the story is a powerful vehicle that performs many such functions.

What Shoko Asahara, the founder of the Aum Shinrikyo [the cult that released poison gas on the Tokyo subway], did was to undertake the deliberate abuse—

and misuse—of such functions of the story. The circuit of the story he offered was oppressive and firmly closed off from external input. By contrast, the circuit of a genuine story must be fundamentally spontaneous and always open to the outside. We must reject all things Wataya-like and Asahara-like. This may well be the marrow of the story I am trying to write.

I responded to the *New York Times*'s request for an interview because I wanted to speak about my general view of the world and of the novel, not to give my personal opinions or to play rhetorical games. There is a major difference here. Wouldn't you say that Noboru Wataya is less an interviewee than a commentator?

Let me ask novelist Haruki Murakami about writing. You've talked about loving and being influenced by Carver, Chandler, Dostoevsky, and Kafka. I love Dostoevsky (The Possessed *is one of my favorite novels), and I have always found him very funny; do these writers also make you laugh?*

I agree that *The Possessed* is one of Dostoevsky's funniest novels. Carver and Chandler, too, have wonderful senses of humor. Kafka's novels and stories are weirdly comical in their very structure. Humor plays a big role in my fiction, too. I suspect that you can't have genuine seriousness without an element of humor.

What do you think about cuteness? Modern Japan, or at least the Japan we see over here, at its most extreme, seems like a nation swinging between its obsessions with either the extremely cute, or the extremely efficient (Hello Kitty; Honda Civic).

You've said that violence is the key to Japan. **The Wind-Up Bird Chronicle** *is the book in which you wrestle most directly and harrowingly with Japan's history of violence, and the character you use to wrestle with it is called Cinnamon—a very cute name. What are you saying about cuteness? Is Japan's obsession with cuteness a means of wrestling with the violence of its recent history?*

I myself am not much interested in the cute and the efficient, so I can't really answer your questions. The commodification of the cute and the efficient is not something unique to Japan. Mickey Mouse is cute, after all, and the Swiss Army Knife is efficient. And nations are violent systems by definition. I feel it can be dangerous to explain whole cultures with buzzwords.

The Japanese artist I most closely identify you with is Hayao Miyazaki, whose (sometimes cute) characters have to struggle with tragedy or loneliness or loss. As artists you both seem to know loss and deal with it in somewhat similar ways. Do you like or identify with Miyazaki?

I have never seen any of Miyazaki's films. I don't know why, but I have never been much interested in *anime*. I like to keep a sharp division between things that interest me and things that don't in order to use the limited time allotted to me in life most economically, and anime just happens to belong to the category of things that don't interest me.

I've noticed that female musicians in your work tend to be classically trained, and somewhat cursed (Reiko from **Norwegian Wood***; Miu from* **Sputnik Sweetheart***), while the men are happy cads who play jazz, like Tony Takitani's dad [from the short story* "Tony Takitani"*]. Reiko and Miu possess great skill and dedication, but insufficient emotion, and, ultimately, following deeply scarring emotional incidents, which they are each incapable of translating into art, they give up on music. As someone who used to run a jazz club, and who has said in numerous interviews that* "concentration" *is the most important tool a writer can possess (rather than emotion), what are you saying about the creative process? Is music really that different from writing? (There's a great deal of music in your sentences.) Why do your female musicians always have such a hard time?*

Women often act as mediums in my novels. They guide the protagonist to "places out of the ordinary," and they make the story move. As you know, music (along with dance) is the art most deeply imbued with ritualism. In that sense, a woman with musical ambitions may be an important presence in my work. Both Reiko and Miu might be said to be "mediums who have been abandoned by the gods." For them, their having given music up (their having been forced to give music up) is equivalent to their having severed a special tie with the world. (Now, don't forget this is entirely my personal opinion, not the opinion of novelist Haruki Murakami.)

I believe that concentration plays an equally central role in both music and the creation of a novel. Only the outward appearance of that "concentration" is different. The performance itself is usually the final expressive form in the case of music, and so the appearance of that concentration inevitably turns out to be more short-term, more expressive, more tangible. In the case of the creation of a novel, the concentration has to be more long-term, more introspective, more enduring. The way I see it, emotion is more an ordinary part of everyday life. It exists in everyone. Human beings devoid of emotion simply don't exist (do they?). In order to get a firm grasp on an emotion and express it with precision in an objective medium, however, what is required is strong enough powers of concentration to bring time to a temporary standstill. And for that what you need is the physical strength and stamina to maintain that concentration as long as possible. This is not something available to just anyone.

At the same time, I think that having made my living through most of my twenties as the owner of a jazz club taught me a lot about music and played an important role in my writing of novels. It might be true to say that I imported my methodology as-is into my novels—the importance of rhythm, for example, the joy of improvisation, the importance of establishing empathy with an audience. This is not a metaphor. For me, writing and the performance of music (though I don't actually perform music) have a direct and literal link in the air.

Your male narrators are often unemployed, or unconventionally employed, but they always make it clear that money is a non-issue. There are some meditations on money in your early books, but the subject dropped out of your fiction quite quickly. Why doesn't money interest you?

For no special reason. I suppose I'm just more interested in other things. I grew up in a family that was neither over-supplied with money nor troubled by a shortage of money, so, for better or worse, I probably never had to think seriously about it. As an adult, of course, I had to start dealing with money problems as a practical matter, but I suspect that one's childhood experience plays a big role in these things.

You get up early in the morning and write on a set schedule every day. How much note-taking do you do outside of this schedule? Does the writing part of your brain turn off when you finish writing, or are you always writing?

As a rule, I don't think too much about my fiction when I'm not sitting at my desk. If anything, I try hard to think about something else (or about nothing at all)—to switch gears in my head by doing sports or listening to music or reading or cooking. Maybe, in some remote corner of my mind, I'm thinking about my novel. Not even I know how my brain works.

Do you ever just decide to take a break and not write?

For me, writing is like breathing. I'm always writing something. When it's not fiction, I'm translating or writing essays and stuff like that. Writing is like training for an athlete or practice for a musician. If you stop entirely, it takes a long time to get your pace back.

But in your periods of less intensely sustained labor, how do you fill your time?

I'm happiest when I'm making the rounds of the used record stores.

You wrote your first novel at a table drinking beer, and there's a lot of beer in it. (In fact, by my informal count, there are an average of three beers consumed on each page of your first two books.) Do you still drink beer? Do you have a favorite beer?

I still like beer and often have a drink. I like Bass Ale and Samuel Adams. I'm not a big drinker, though. I like a bottle or two in the evening, maybe with a little whiskey or wine afterwards.

In addition to your medium-like women, your books often contain a cursed place or thing—in **Dance Dance Dance** *it's the Dolphin Hotel and the Maserati ("The curse of the Maserati"). In* **The Wind-Up Bird Chronicle** *it's the abandoned house. Where do these things come from?*

I don't know, maybe those places (or places like them) exist inside me. I really can't say much more than that writing about such places is entirely natural for me. Unnatural things occur quite naturally there.

Can you talk a bit about where you might be going next? I've noticed that you seem to be writing in new ways, about both younger and older characters.

What I want to do is write about lots of different characters in lots of different situations, and that way to create stories with greater breadth. New character types are beginning to appear in my books because I know now how to write them.

Ila Goody (essay date 2005)

SOURCE: Goody, Ila. "'Fin de Siècle, Fin du Globe'; Intercultural Choronotopes of Memory and Apocalypse in the Fictions of Murakami Haruki and Kazuo Ishiguro." In *Intercultural Explorations*, pp. 95-103. Amsterdam: Rodopi, 2005.

[*In the following essay, Goody examines the relation between borders and the end of the world in* Hard-Boiled Wonderland and the End of the World *and works by other contemporary Japanese writers.*]

> "Fin de siècle," murmured Lord Henry.
> "Fin du globe," answered his hostess.
>
> —Oscar Wilde

> ". . . I had an intense sensation of the presence of a border, invisible but uncrossable. . . . To see the border, however, one does not need sight."
>
> Karatani Kojin

The border which Karatani Kojin at the close of the third Anyone conference in Barcelona, found untraversable in spite of its invisibility is literally that of Port-Bou, a Franco-Spanish town on the coast of the Mediterranean where Walter Benjamin took his life in 1940 and where he is buried. It stands, however, for the diverse intercultural borders which still persist in the waning years of this century. And it stands as well for the border into a new century and a new millennium, which, moreover, must be crossed despite the terrible tensions and anxieties which surround it. At the same time, the very notion of an intercultural border is being redefined and redesignated in literary and artistic production. *Fin du globe* this time round marks not only the fascination with decay exemplified by Wilde's *Dorian Gray,* but even more the recognition of the end of the old totalizing concepts of this globe, the end of the old geography and the literature predicated upon it. The notion of the stable frontier is now vanishing, just as the ideas of the ego and the *cogito* disappeared in early modernist literature to be replaced by shifting, fragmentary, flickering territories, one layered transparently upon another. Increasingly, narratives interrogating the borders of culture (along with similar artistic and architectural texts) appear, in novels as diverse as Janet Turner Hospital's *Borderline* (1985), Cees Nooteboom's *In the Dutch Mountains* (1984), and Carlos Fuentes' *The Old Gringo.* Nooteboom's story is set in a vast Netherlands extending southward "several days' drive from Amsterdam or The Hague" to the highest peaks of Europe and on towards the end of the world. According to Fuentes, the Mexican border in fact begins at the Mason-Dixon line, and the dust of the one-time frontier sweeps back from Mexico "over the shrub and the wheat fields, the plains and the smoky mountains, the long deep green rivers", right up to "the shore, of the Potomac, the Atlantic, the centre of the world". For Fuentes, the shifting, repositioned border is the subject of the new narrative, "a perpetual rebeginning of stories perpetually unfinished", whether linking Aztec Mexico and imperial Seville in "The Two Shores" (1992) or the heartland of hegemonic America and its southernmost frontiers in *The Old Gringo.* And it is in this way, by renewing and reconstituting old narratives in an intercultural *topos* that Fuentes, along with so many other contemporary/postmodern writers, resolves the disillusionment and sense of exhaustion that had characterized *fin-de-siècle* and late imperial fiction until very recently.

A similar narrative phenomenon that of what might be termed "fiction of the place between" or fiction of the frontier, marks contemporary/postmodern Japanese narrative and narratives of Japanese literature and cultures particularly those by Murakami Haruki, Ka-zuo Ishiguro, and Cees Nooteboom. In these instances, however, the chronotope of the border only occasion-ally offers an escape from or a positive alternative to the end of the world and the shattering of culture. It would appear that a vision of culture in fragments and a correlatively disjunctive narrative mode, is the predominant characteristic of these texts. Murakami's ***Hard-Boiled Wonderland and the End of the World*** (1991), the ur-novel of the group, alternates between two narrative frames one set in near-contemporary Tokyo office buildings amid a war between rival data-processing "gangs", the other located in a timeless realm of the unconscious called "the end of the world". The borders of the narrator's identity shift, in the course of Murakami's story back and forth across this destabilizing chasm, until the two realms converge in the obliteration of his conscious experience, and thus in the logical end of the story. Several boundaries are tiers suggested between the narrator's right and left brain, between the conscious and unconscious minds between Japanese and Western culture. For a very brief time/space—the chronotope of the novel—the narrator has the ability to travel freely between these diverse territories. Muraka invokes the contrasting metaphors of the elevator and the well-bucket in presenting access to these territories, using the latter image in particular—with all its resonances in such Noh plays as *Izutsu* ("the well-curb")—as the mode by which the atavistic state of Japanese identity can be attained. As a reader of ancient dreams embedded in the skulls of unicorns, the traditional Chinese mythical creature, Murakami's narrator mediates between the roots of his culture in Asia, and its contemporary manifestations amid the glittering shards of Western cultural artifacts and commodities. The narrator of ***Hard-Boiled Wonderland*** [***The Hard-Boiled Wonder-land and the End of the World***] is thus a bricoleur of cultural memory and experience travelling both verti-cally into Eastern and Western historical tradition, and horizontally into a borderless kaleidoscope of intercul-tural elements. Murakami's presentation of "the end of the world" is a chronotope that straddles both Eastern and Western models of historical belief, invoking both the European sense of apocalyptic space/time and the Buddhist sense of *mappo,* the degenerate last days of the law. The descent of the novel's protagonist, moreover, into a dark underworld to confront the IN-Klings (a.k.a. Infra-Nocturnal Kappa) threatening the upper region is an obvious expression of the basic Western topos in which the hero descends under-ground, fights monsters and reascends to the ordinary world. (And, as I have pointed out elsewhere, the litmus have other manifest affinities with European culture: not only do they resemble the Morlocks in H.

G. Wells's *The Time Machine,* but the Inklings was also the name of the select Oxford circle revolving around C. S. Lewis, to whom J. R. R. Tolkien read chapters of *The Lord of the Rings*—his saga of spiritual quest through Middle Earth—as it was being com-posed. At the same time, it also invokes memories of the traditional mythic descent in the *Kojiki* (Record of Ancient Matters) of the god Izanagi into the under-world to find his deceased sister-wife Izanami "living" in a body disfigured by the putrefaction of death. The giant fish, moreover worshipped by the monstrous and filthy INKlings in their subterranean lair recalls the huge catfish (*namazu*) said to coil around the island at the bottom of the lake in the mediaeval text *Chiku-bushima engi* (History of Chikubushima). At the core of ***Hard-Boiled Wonderland,*** then, are repeated, embedded invocations of native Japanese as well as Chinese tradition from the folkloric Kappa, to the figuration of P'eng-lai or Horai, the mountain of the immortals. However, this virtual well of memory can be visited only briefly and inconclusively, before the protagonist is sent back up literally to the surface of his cultural awareness. As in the Noh play *Izutsu* ("the well-curb"), retrieval of the memory of the past is evanescent and merely situational: the waters of the well provide images from the past, but, like the wife of Narihira, Murakami's narrator—and Murakami himself in this text—can never permanently possess them and remains fixed on the border, haunting the edges and gazing elegiacally into the depths.

Still another set of images of an apocalyptic world in fragments appears in Murakami's short stories, published in English as the collection *The Elephant Vanishes* (1993). Several of these stories may be considered the literary manifestation of what one contemporary anthropologist of Japanese culture has termed "discourses of the vanishing", writerly displace-ments of national-cultural losses in the modern/post-modern period. In the title story an elephant vanishes from the town zoo by shrinking through its chains and absconding along with its complicitous keeper, in another a little green monster shrivels up, dissolves and disappears when the housewife to whom it has preferred its love expels it from her house, and in still another a set of television people, who are like a trompe l'œil painting of reduced perspective appear 20 or 30% smaller than ordinary people and accurately forecast the dematerialization and disappearance of the narrator's wife. The vanishings in these stories are, moreover, not merely personal, at the conclusion of "A Slow Boat to China" the narrator envisages the apocalyptic disintegration of Tokyo and the entire civilization it represents: "In a flash, the buildings will crumble . . . Slowly, gradually, until nothing remains."

More than merely a comment on tectonic instability, this is a proposition that contemporary Tokyo is not as one of the main characters suggests any longer a place for human occupation or significant social interaction.

Recently Murakami seems to have moved away from this somewhat negative view of the end of the world we know into a more positive millennial stance. In an interview with Kawai Hayao, Murakami comments that he has now shifted his focus away from detachment and pithiness, as well as from the hero's search for an elusive "kind of Holy Grail". These modes of fragmentation have now been replaced in *The Wind-Up Bird Chronicle* with a more decided figuration of connectedness, which Murakami expresses in terms of "the vertical thread of history" and the renewed digging of a well that reaches very deep and is also connected to Nomonhan: "if you dig a well, and dig and dig and dig, eventually you can cross the wall that seemed to make any connection impossible, and be joined."

Such a resumption of connectedness, through the writing of historical fictions of cultural memory, is entirely missing in the most recent narratives of Kazuo Ishigurog which seem only to intensify the split and fractured memorial structures of his earlier novel. It is possible that Ishiguro's intense sensitivity to cultural fragmentation arises from his specific situation as a Japanese raised in Britain, that his acute awareness of destabilized borders is a unique case of the intercultural writer as an elegiac mourner for a coherently demarcated imperium. It is, however, more likely that this phenomenon—while intensified in a postmodern world—is itself part of the mode of modernist Japanese narrative stretching from Soseki through Kawabata and Kaiko Ken, as well as through architects, designers and filmmakers such as Isozaki Arata and Teshigahara Hiroshi. In that textual mode, cultural experience is fractured and shattered, the present is often conceived as discontinuous, transitional, and ultimately degenerative, and the world of moral absolutes has vanished irretrievably. The narrator of Kaiko Ken's *Darkness in Summer* briefly recovers a sense of wholeness by going fishing in a lake somewhere outside a divided Berlin, where he encounters an enormous, magical pike with mysterious life-giving powers. The experience, however, is insufficiently powerful to prevent him from returning as a journalist, not to Japan, but to Viet Nam to report on the Asian-American conflict. In *Kokoro*, Soseki's character *sensei,* as the representative mentor within the story, embodies a feeling of absolute loneliness, dislocation, and disenchantment that casts its pall not only over the student-narrator, but as Dennis Washburn points out, over much subsequent twentieth-century Japanese

fiction. Thus, for example, Washburn proposes that in his masterpiece, *Yama no oto* (The Sound of the Mountain), Kawabata portrays Japan as a country that has lost its cultural memory just as the protagonist Shingo has lost his personal one. Shingo attempts to replace lost memories by creating new narratives but he realizes that in so doing he may be putting things together incorrectly as indeed he does near the end of the narrative when he mistakenly assumes that a middle-aged man and a young woman sitting together on a train are father and daughter. Whereas Kawabata presents this fracturing of the generations from perspective of the fathers who Iona., for the re-establishment of harmonious social integration however, Ishiguro flips the point of view over to that of his own younger cohort, many of whom are determined to reject old cultural allegiances. This problematic of the decline and shattering of traditional cultural hegemonies has been Ishiguro's major concern throughout his early career, whether the focus has been on Japan (*A Painter of Our Time*), England (*The Remains of the Day*) or the first novel that initiated this series, the text-in-between the two cultural frontiers, *A Pale View of Hills*. From one perspective, it might be proposed that all these texts deal, as do so many of Kawabata's, with "the remains of the days that they are souvenirs of belatedness, of the sense of an ending, of the cultural *Nachlass.* But, at least in *A Pale View of Hills,* Ishiguro's point of view is more overtly balanced between those generational characters whose allegiances are to the realms of the fathers and those who, significantly passing over the sons, perceive and acknowledge the rising dominion of the daughters In evoking such a recognition, Ishiguro draws on the thread of increasingly dominant female characters in modern Japanese narrative, from Sachiko as the *locus* of greatest stability and moral authority in *Sasameyuki* (The Makioka Sisters) to Shingo's daughter-in-law Kikuko in *Yama no oto.* The Sachiko figure in *A Pale View of Hills,* far from being the embodiment of stability, wavers continuously between emigrating to America with a new, though unreliable, male protector, and returning to her uncle's house near Nagasaki, a house which is unusually large and spacious, with plenty of room for herself and her daughter. That house, however, she sees as unduly empty and silent; and Sachiko, like her own daughter who flirts precariously near the edges of mountains and wastelands, prefers to explore the frontiers of new cultural experiences however risky they may be. This Sachiko, unlike Tanizaki's, remains on the dangerous edge of the border into a new history, unbound by the forms of discipline and loyalty that once constituted social coherence. She is a kind of stranded object, without appropriate placement in either culture.

Although Ishiguro's stranded cultural figures (Sachiko, Stevens, the painter Ono Masuji) partially mourn their losses, however, they also manifest an eerily cool pragmatism towards the possibilities of cultural adaptation. In contrast the elegiac demeanour of Kawabata's transitional novels, of which these are the intertextual completions, Ishiguro's narratives do not really lament that man is in love and loves what vanishes (Yeats). Ishiguro's "discourses of the vanishing" point instead to the strategies not only for what he will make "of a diminished thing", but even more to how lie will incorporate into his texts the aesthetic of MA, of Isozaki Arata's disjunctive architectonics of the fragmentary "space-between". The "void centre" of MA, as Isozaki conceives it, possesses strong affinities with the void of Lao Tzu, a void not of thorough hollowness but, as Nakaniehi Susumu suggests, "an empty space for free movement or transfiguration". And just as Isozaki's Tsukuba Science City, which he says possesses the "complex structure of a long novel", aims at a shifting, revolving, flickering style" between historical periods and national cultures, an architecture of suggestive ruins, so Ishiguro's most recent long narrative, *The Unconsoled,* constitutes the disintegration of traditional novelistic architecture into an almost total breakdown of narrative coherence. Plot, chronotope, dialogue, point of view, are all stretched and fragmented, as well as distorted anamorphically, so that the dominant mode of reading the text becomes the one of carefully negotiating its hermeneutic gaps. The greatest of all Ishiguro's cultural adaptors across fissures and schisms is the narrator of *The Unconsoled,* Ryder, who quite literally seems to ride the waves between its disjunctive narrative elements. Waking up in a strange, anonymous, presumably European town, Ryder is aware that he has promised to give a concert, for which, is true dreamscape fashion, he is insufficiently prepared, and he is aware as well that he has forgotten most of his past, "a cloud of uncertain memory, punctuated by black holes of sheer oblivion". The notional town in which Ryder finds himself—which resembles the town in which Murakami's dreamer also finds *himself*—is clearly, from the chronotope of its buildings and location, as well as the diverse names of its denizens (Christoff, Boris, Sophie, Gustav, Henze) centrally European; and, even more than Stevens the butler, Ryder has to decide how he will deal with the raging voices of anguished cultural belatedness, for whom he must arrange new auditions, performances, and justifications. The moral voice of Ishiguro would seem to be suggesting here that the social obligations of memory exist even for those, like Ryder, who themselves have no clear recollection of either responsibility or involvement. He is surrounded by the clamorous demands of the "unconsoled", those poignant, legitimate claimants for reclamation, justice,

attention who, like the hungry ghosts of Buddhist scrolls beleaguering the priests, assert their grotesquely pitifully hungry hopes that, at last, old wrongs will be redressed. Like Kafka, Beckett, and Dostoevski, whom Ishiguro has cited among his favourite authors and possible influences, Ishiguro knows that virtually nothing is to be done and searching for who is to blame is futile. In the end there can only be a dance-like segue between the fragmentary segments of discourse, along the ever-shifting, newly-repositioned borders of stories perpetually unfinished and reborn.

The rebirth of stories from the hoard of cultural memory occurs nowhere with more elegance than in Cees Nooteboom's recasting of Kawabata's *Thousand Cranes* in his novel *Rituals.* For Kawabata, the narrative of *Thousand Cranes* (Sembazuru) was not so much are-invocation of the social and aesthetic harmonies of the art of tea (chanoyu) as of its breakdown, representing the decadence of Japanese social space from the pleasant meeting-ground of friends to the poisonous locus of defiled antagonists. In *Sembazuru* the anti-heroine, Kurimoto increasingly expands her territory, rather like an expert player of *go,* until she has either moved into or destroyed all the homes of her fellow-players, so that the "green oasis" of the tea hut now becomes a wasteland. For Nooteboom the tearoom also becomes the location of death, this time of a puristic connoisseur of ceramics who envisages himself as the re-incarnation of Sea no Rikyu and the aesthetics of his circle and tradition. Here, as at the conclusion of *Sembazuru,* the teabowl is shattered, a sign of the end of an age. Whereas, however, Rikyu's suicide was demanded by Hideyoshi as a socio-political act, that of Nooteboom's hero is more, like the compromises of Soseki's *sensei* and the defeat of Kawabata's Kikuji, the expression of an individual's disenchantment with his own isolation.

At the third Anyone conference Arata Akira spoke, along with Isozaki Aratal, of another *fin de siècle,* that of the 18th century, closer in spirit to our own than the 19th, and, in particular to its play of significant styles. His *locus classicus* here is Sir John Soane's own house in London, now a museum, a postmodernist text even wore resonant than Las Meninas. In Soane's house we find suspended ceilings, skylights, crypts, and convex mirrors that create a site of multiple layers of labyrinthine meaning—a true *locus* of the *unheimlich,* as wall as of the archaeology of knowledge. In 1872 Nietzsche wrote a fragment entitled "The Last Man", in which the last man develops a schizophrenic dialogue with his own voice. The voices of Murakami, Ishiguro, Nooteboom are in diverse ways ricocheting signifiers within the crypts of postmodernist, intercultural discourses, in which cultural memory establishes boundaries-of infinite reverberation . . . The palimpsest of cultural memory may begin with the end—with the ruins of discourse, whether Hiroshima, Berlin, or other figurations of the apocalypse—but it will begin again with the retelling of old stories within newly expanded borders, among the re-constructions of those ruins. Out of the crypts of intercultural memory and the fictions of the frontier will arise repositioned passages to the *emplacement* of future texts, which, like Isozaki's MA, offer a new literary architecture and an inviting "space-between" in which to accommodate the border that once existed between East and West.

Chloë Schama (essay date 23 October 2006)

SOURCE: Schama, Chloë. "The Escape Artist." *New Republic* 235, no. 17 (23 October 2006): 34-7.

[*In this essay, Schama explains that although Murakami seems to reject Japan by focusing extensively on the West in his fiction, his writing actually tackles subjects that relate directly to Japanese culture.*]

Plenty of successful writers have infelicitous beginnings. The writer who is condemned at the same time that he is commended is rarer. When, in Japan in 1979, the Gunzo Award for New Writers was given to Haruki Murakami for his first novel, *Hear the Wind Sing,* the award committee found itself unable to explain its decision. One member ranked the book "somewhere between sixty and eighty-five" out of a hundred, only later conceding that it was "a good work." Another member of the committee chose the book because it was the least bad of the choices. The strongest defense offered was that the novel demonstrated a thorough understanding of American popular literature—faint praise for what was meant to be the best debut novel of the year in Japan.

But this tepid endorsement understood something that was critical to Murakami's writing at this early stage: his indifference toward Japanese tradition or even Japanese society. The narrator of *Hear the Wind Sing,* which Murakami began writing in English, is concerned with decidedly non-Japanese matters: President Kennedy's assassination and the life lessons from an invented American writer. This was a conscious decision on Murakami's part: "All I could think about when I began writing fiction in my youth was how to run as far as I could from the 'Japanese Condition,'" he would say later. "I wanted to distance myself as much as possible from the curse of the Japanese."

Murakami did not start writing until he was twenty-nine, but the great escape began early. He claims (to the likely chagrin of his parents, who were both teachers of Japanese literature) that he stopped reading

Japanese writers in his teens, turning instead to nineteenth-century Europeans (Chekhov, Dostoyevsky, Flaubert, Dickens) and then to Americans (Vonnegut, Brautigan, Capote). He has called Raymond Carver—whose work he has translated into Japanese—"the greatest teacher I have ever had."

Taking all this into account, the insubstantial praise of the Gunzo committee was more precise than it seemed. Murakami is probably the most famous contemporary Japanese writer, yet his fiction often appears as though it could be set in almost any industrialized society. On the surface, the stories in *Blind Willow, Sleeping Woman* follow this pattern, taking place in hotels, restaurants, apartment buildings, and hospitals. Not one is set in a temple or a tea room. But the matter is not quite so simple. It is not easy to make a perfect escape. These stories have the rootless feel that characterizes much of Murakami's fiction, but they also reveal that Murakami might be more engaged with the culture he inherited than most would guess.

Murakami is a literary phenomenon. *Norwegian Wood* (1987), the book that catapulted him to an international reputation, has sold more than four million copies in Japan alone. According to Jay Rubin's biography of Murakami, the writer's publisher, Kodansha, draped red and green banners across its Tokyo offices after *Norwegian Wood*'s extraordinary success so that the building resembled the cover of the novel. One newspaper coined a term—"The Norway Tribe"—for devotees who traipsed to the various places where scenes from the novel take place. A Japanese critic wrote in a review of Murakami's most recent novel, *Kafka on the Shore,* that "in any heavy storm there are always writers who hoist a torchlight in front of people. . . . Whatever happens in the world, I will watch his light."

And the enthusiasm of his fans goes beyond Japan: "Devotees . . . not only remember the books, but we remember where we were when we first read them," claims the British writer David Mitchell. In my own experience, Mitchell's theory holds. When a colleague spotted *South of the Border, West of the Sun* (1992) on my desk a dreamy look stole across his face. He told me that he first read the book on a bus traveling from Narita to Tokyo. He was dead tired after a long flight but he could not stop reading. I could see from his face that he had been entranced.

But stunning statistics and a cult-like following do not prove literary merit. Descriptions of Murakami's writing rarely help to elucidate the evidence for or against his talent—too often they are either mired in admiration for his mysticism or frustrated by that same attribute. "Read it to your cat," wrote one critic in a glowing review of *Kafka on the Shore* in *The*

Washington Post. "You can sense his peculiar grasp of the fathomless," gushed another. Of course the fathomless may also be formless. The novel has a "willful disregard for any kind of coherence," complained a less enthusiastic reviewer.

Fans and critics should not be chastised too severely for their inability to pinpoint Murakami's skill (or lack of it). His writing consistently relies on the idea that indefinite forces are the most affecting. In Murakami's work, the portentous and unsatisfying word "something" is never far away when a story or a novel reaches a critical point. Consider a few examples from the latest collection: "There was something special about the sixties"; "Something had happened, he thought, and the world had changed"; "His heart felt enclosed by something formless"; "At first it seemed like I could forget, but something remained inside me"; "Something had been lost." It's no wonder that his fans have a hard time explaining what they like. They like something.

The reason for Murakami's sensational impact may be more concrete: he writes protest literature, an irresistible form that is re-invented with every generation, and which no generation wants to be without. Murakami's protest speaks not only to his own generation, but to generations younger and older; and not only to the Japanese, but to people scattered across the globe. His protagonists are teenaged (Kafka from ***Kafka on the Shore***), college-aged (Toru from ***Norwegian Wood***), middle-aged (Hajime from ***South of the Border, West of the Sun***), and elderly (Nakata from ***Kafka on the Shore***). The rebel figure, set against conformity and commodity, appears throughout Murakami's work, and his presence graces much of ***Blind Willow, Sleeping Woman***.

Murakami has been criticized for the very universality that seems so fundamental to his appeal. Kenzaburō Ōe characterized Murakami's writing as failing to "appeal to intellectuals in the broad sense with models for Japan's present and future." This is a typical view among critics who dislike Murakami for his apparent reluctance to engage with Japanese problems. But for all his attention to global consumerism, there has always been more to Murakami than lifestyle studies. Whether the protests in which he has engaged amount to more than a raised fist against a vague (non-Japanese) entity, or whether they constitute a thoughtful model for Japan—well, that is the great Murakami question; and his coyness about it may be his finest trick.

The stories in ***Blind Willow, Sleeping Woman,*** which were written throughout the course of Murakami's career, can be regarded as an inventory of his evolving discontents, demonstrating both his universal appeal as a writer of protest lit and his specific dissatisfactions with the Japanese literary establishment, with the failure of the student movements of the 1960s, and with what he sees as a dangerous historical forgetfulness. He shows evidence of a social consciousness, but these stories also demonstrate the nature of that social consciousness—veiled and metaphorical; obscure, and often willfully so. Whatever his vision of the world in which he lives, however engaged or disengaged with Japan, Murakami's power is mainly as a stylist. This is often the case with protest literature (even if it prides itself on its high substance), and it is what makes Murakami's writing seem universal.

"The Rise and Fall of Sharpie Cakes" is the most explicit example of Murakami's protest against authority. Murakami writes in the preface that the story "reveals my impressions of the literary world at the time of my debut." He is referring to the remnants of the *bundan* guild, an elite group of writers and critics who set the standards (didactic, moral, and uplifting) for "pure" literature in Japan for much of the twentieth century. This group conceived of itself as the defender of quality in the face of pulp, porn, and pop—particularly important after World War II, when the literary strictures of the pre-war era were loosened. The influence of the *bundan* guild was waning when Murakami began writing, but it still had its defenders, Ōe among them.

In **"Sharpie Cakes,"** [**"The Rise and Fall of Sharpie Cakes"**] Murakami attacks them head-on. The narrator enters a contest to invent a new recipe for a popular snack food, the sharpie cake. Realizing that the prevailing recipe is hopelessly outdated, he creates something more palatable to younger consumers. He almost wins, but the "Sharpie Crows," unappealing creatures with "globs of white fat" for eyes and bodies "swollen to the point of bursting," who are the ultimate authority within the company, cannot handle the narrator's innovation. When offered the cakes, the crows create a frenzied "free-for-all, blood calling forth more blood, rage leading to rage." The narrator then scolds the managing director of the company: "Now look what you've done! . . . You just threw the cakes in front of them like that all of a sudden. The stimulus was too strong." The lack of subtlety here is actually a strength; the bizarre and repulsive image of crows gone wild would hardly be effective in a less Boschian incarnation. The very specific object of Murakami's disgruntlement (an object that no longer seems relevant) becomes a larger emblem of authority, made grotesque and bloodthirsty to augment its absurdity.

"A Folklore for My Generation: A Pre-History of Late-Stage Capitalism" shows the hippie-era side of Murakami's protest writing. But this story is compelling not because of the narrator's counterculture attitude, but because of the way Murakami expresses it. The story is narrated by a disappointed middle-aged man reminiscing on the failings of the 1960s. "I was born in 1949," it begins, "entered junior high in 1961, and college in 1967. And reached my long-awaited twentieth birthday . . . during the height of the boisterous slapstick that was the student movement." The relevance of these temporal markers quickly dissipates in a wave of timelessly clichéd language; this was a time of "momentum and energy . . . tremendous spark of promise. . . . Heroism and villainy, ecstasy and disillusionment, martyrdom and betrayal." Violence and rock-and-roll, additional markers of ageless discontent, are invoked: "there were doors we had to kick in, right in front of us, and you better believe we kicked them in!"; "Jim Morrison, the Beatles, and Dylan blast[ed] out the sound track to our lives." It is a nice irony, the narrator relying on trite language to emphasize his generation's uniqueness. In interviews Murakami has repeatedly spoken of the frustrations that his generation went through. In this story, those frustrations are less interesting than the narrator's convincingly self-deluded voice.

More and more, Murakami has used Japan's modern history—and the whitewashing of that history—as the locus of his discontent. This protest, of course, demands a certain amount of cultural specificity. It is here that Murakami uses the Japanese experience to the greatest extent; it is here that substance almost dominates over style. In **"Tony Takitani,"** Tony's father, a jazz musician, escapes from Japan during World War II to live a life of decadence in China while the bombs fall elsewhere. He is a man who "possessed not the slightest hint of will or introspection . . . [who] wanted nothing more than to be able to play his trombone, eat three meals a day, and have a few women nearby." Murakami's rebuke is indirect; it is the son, not the father, who suffers most in the course of the story. (Like his father, Tony is generally apathetic about ethical contemplation and demanding emotional matters. When he is finally forced to face these things, the experience brings him more pain than joy.) But the moral is acute: responsibility does not die with each passing generation.

This type of didacticism is very evident in ***The Wind-Up Bird Chronicle*** (1997), a novel that juxtaposes the Japanese invasion of Manchuria with the daily activities of an unemployed paralegal (making spaghetti, looking for a lost cat, picking up clothes at the cleaners). The invasion scenes are painfully graphic. Mongolian soldiers kill a man by removing his skin "slowly, carefully, almost lovingly" so that "the entire skin of Yamamoto's right arm [comes] off in a single thin sheet. . . . After that he skinned both legs, cut off the penis and testicles, and removed the

ears." This goes on for many pornographically sickening pages. And violent action is not confined to the Mongolians. In a similarly lengthy scene, Japanese soldiers execute Chinese prisoners with bayonets: "they twisted the blades so as to rip the men's internal organs, and thrust the tips upward. . . . Their sliced-up bodies poured prodigious amounts of blood on the ground, but even with their organs shredded they went on twitching slightly for some time."

The point is to show the convergence between this world of savagery and the seemingly tranquil world of modern-day Japan. "I bet it's a lot easier to kill somebody than people think," muses a bored teenager, echoing the Mongolian soldiers' mantra while she tans. When Murakami was asked why his "generation should take responsibility for a war that ended before it was born," he answered, "Because we're Japanese." And when Ian Buruma profiled Murakami for *The New Yorker,* he reported that Murakami felt that violence was "the key to Japan." It is an old idea, though some of Murakami's readers may find it to their punk and grunge tastes, an Irvine Welsh from Japan.

Perhaps Murakami is responding to Ōe's criticism, accepting a *sensei* role by forcing the Japanese to confront the past. A few months ago Murakami publicly condemned Shintaro Ishihara, the right-wing governor of Tokyo, as "a very dangerous man." Ishihara has been criticized for visiting the Yasukuni shrine that commemorates Japanese citizens who died in World War II, including convicted war criminals. Murakami told a reporter for the *South China Morning Post* that Japan's rightward political trajectory concerned him: "I feel I have a responsibility as a novelist to do something." The novel that he is currently writing is said to include a critique of Japanese nationalism.

Murakami's real strength is not as a moral guide, as an indefatigable protestor. Whatever the sources of their inspiration, the stories in ***Blind Willow, Sleeping Woman*** are nothing like a serious critical evaluation of a national identity. These stories are a succession of disparate and abstracted discontents that do not add up to a political position. A protest against the universe is a pre-political protest, crippled by its own generality, best carried out by teenagers and lunatics. What redeems Murakami's writing from its puerility is its aestheticism: its haunting imagery, its credible voices, its allegorical play, its skill for surprise.

The stories are full of sly and unexpected combinations: the blending of a real world with a surreal world, the mixing of formulaic fictional structures with literary and linguistic experiment. **"The Year of Spaghetti,"** for example, transforms a habit into a manifestation of contemporary anomie. The narrator's obsession with spaghetti, not an otherworldly call from "a girl so indistinct that, by four thirty, she might very well disappear altogether," becomes the truly odd element of the story. Peculiar details punctuate his ordinary actions: he cooks in a pot "big enough to hold a German shepherd." By the end of the story, his routine has morphed from banal to bizarre to an illustration of modern isolation: "Can you imagine how astonished the Italians would be if they knew that what they were exporting in 1971 was *loneliness*?"

"Where I'm Likely to Find It," which begins like a hard-boiled detective story, illustrates Murakami's adept manipulation of clichéd literary forms. A woman (with great legs, of course) asks a private investigator to locate her missing husband. The woman remains in the narrator's consciousness, clicking about in her high heels, but what really captivates him is her apartment building—more specifically, the landings of the staircase. He becomes fixated, visiting the staircase every day. He gathers no clues, but this stasis doesn't bother him. Nor does it seem important; whodunit expectations deflate with the expansion of his strange fascination. The search for the missing husband turns into a search for "something that could very well be shaped like a door. Or . . . an umbrella, or a doughnut. Or an elephant." Perhaps there is symbolism behind these objects, perhaps not. It seems more likely that their randomness is meant to suggest that pat answers to mysteries, especially when you expect them, are most unlikely.

If Murakami is going to provide his country with any type of "torchlight"—and it is emphatically not the responsibility of the novelist to do so—it will come in the illumination of psychic implications where you least expect to find them: in a culinary routine, in the lonely landing of a staircase, in a refrigerator. "If it's art or literature you're looking for, you'd do well to read the Greeks," he wrote in *Hear the Wind Sing.* "Mere humans who root through their refrigerators at three o'clock in the morning can only produce writing that matches what they do." Even if the refrigerator is much less than the world, Murakami's remarkable talent is for showing us how much of the world may be found in the refrigerator.

Reiko Abe Auestad (essay date 2006)

SOURCE: Auestad, Reiko Abe. "Implications of Globalization for the Reception of Modern Japanese Literature."[1] In *Global Literary Field,* pp. 22-40. Newcastle, UK: Cambridge Scholars Press, 2006.

[*In the essay below, Auestad studies Murakami's role in the globalization of literature, commenting on the author's Western influences and his translating of English-language texts.*]

. . . few have tackled the Oedipal tale with as much wit, verve and retail success as Japan's Haruki Murakami has in *Kafka on the Shore.* The book sold 550,000 copies in its first month on his home soil in 2002. . . . *Kafka* [*Kafka on the Shore.*] has become a best seller in Germany, South Korea and China, and now the English-language version has become a U.K. best seller.[2]

Murakami Haruki's works have now been translated into at least fifteen languages in eighteen countries.[3] He has become a very popular writer indeed, not only in Japan but also in the U.S.A., Europe and other parts of the world—Taiwan, China, Russia, Korea and even Siberia. Gary Fiskertjon, Murakami's editor at Knopf, refers to him as "the breakthrough Japanese writer in the West."[4] Murakami's success has no doubt made it easier for other Japanese writers to appear on the international scene. A few special anthologies of Japanese contemporary authors have come out, and many other popular writers have followed his lead in recent years.[5]

Besides his obvious success on the international book market, there are two factors that make Murakami interesting as an object of study in thinking about the implications of globalization for literature. First of all, he is not only a writer but also a translator. He was under considerable influence of Raymond Carver, Kurt Vonnegut and other American writers when he began his writing career. His narrators' distanced, casual pop-style with a subdued sense of humour definitely owes a lot to his reading/translating of these authors. His "magic realism" with fantastic and surrealistic elements and a detective novel style plot full of suspense would not have been the same without his familiarity with postmodern American writers.[6] Even after his success as a writer Murakami continued to translate.[7] In many of his translation projects, he has closely collaborated with an American literature expert, Shibata Motoyuki, who is known for his translation of Paul Auster in Japan, and their mutual influence is well documented. Murakami's writing is an excellent example of "phantasmagoric" text, concealing "the influences of distant social forces and processes," which is an inevitable corollary of globalization.[8]

Another interesting twist to his career is his age. Murakami (b. 1949) has now turned fifty-seven. At this writing, twenty-seven years have passed since his debut novel appeared in Japan; twenty-five years since his first translation of an American author in Japanese came out; seventeen years since his first translated novel in English had a breakthrough outside Japan.[9] This means we now have a young generation of not only Japanese but also American and foreign readers who "grew up" with Murakami and have been influenced by his literary corpus (his own literature and translation).[10] In talking about "influence" in relation to Murakami's work one must consider the ever more multidimensional implications of cultural globalization. According to Miura Masashi, a whole new generation of young Japanese authors cite Murakami Haruki and translated American contemporary authors (rather than Kawabata or Ôe) as their mentors.[11] Murakami is also presumably exerting back some influence on young American readers/authors. The questions are: in the context of such a global literary field, does it make sense to talk about "Japaneseness", or "Americanization" for that matter? Are these characteristics so context-bound that it makes less sense to talk about them in the increasingly globalized world? Or would "hybridity" be a new buzz term that would explain away all the differences?

Second, there has been a critical debate over whether or not Murakami's 2002 *Kafka on the Shore* should be read in the "Japanese" historical context. This relates back to the issues I just raised above. Even if our everyday experience is penetrated by distant events and relations and even if it might make less sense to talk about "Japaneseness," the fact remains that we all "continue to lead local lives—in the sense that 'the constraints of the body ensure that all individuals, at every moment, are contextually situated in time and space.'" "In this fundamental sense the ties of culture to location can never be completely severed."[12] The question here is how we can meet the challenge of "deterritorialization" inherent in globalization and preserve "the ties of culture to location" in the way that literature's "mission" as the source of social critique/the avant-garde remains effective (if one agrees that literature still has such a mission).

THE RECEPTION OF MURAKAMI'S LITERATURE IN JAPAN

AMERICANIZED STYLE AND COMMERCIAL SUCCESS

Despite (or rather, because of) his popularity, the recognition by the literary establishment in Japan was slow to come by. His 1979 debut book, *Hear the Wind Sing,* brought him a literary prize but he never won the prestigious Akutagawa prize, an award given to young, promising authors. Even though his 1982 *Wild Sheep Chase* and 1985 *Hard-Boiled Wonderland* [*Hard-Boiled Wonderland and the End of the World*] won him some critical recognition, it is his 1987 *Norwegian Wood,* a runaway best-seller, that brought him a real national breakthrough. *Norwegian Wood* is a nostalgic story of loss and love in realistic style, quite a-typical of Murakami. The novel nevertheless struck the right chord among Japanese youth. Released just before Christmas, the book was enticingly pack-

aged in two red and green volumes. The sales-record reached 3,500,000 volumes by the end of 1988, giving Murakami a superstar status. The industries were quick to take advantage of the fever. Green "Norwegian" forests showed up everywhere in advertising. A new CD featuring an orchestrated version of "Norwegian Wood" was launched (as is described in the first chapter of the novel), and the original Beatles song went up in sales as well.[13]

Paradoxically, however, Murakami became so famous that he felt as if "everyone hated him," he recalls in his recent interview, adding that it was surprisingly "the most unhappy time of [his] life."[14] The frenzied media attention drove him to prolong his sojourn abroad and he ended up spending the next eight years in Europe and the U.S. in virtual "exile." Professionally, too, it is not unproblematic for an author to be so commercially successful. In Jay Rubin's words, "many commentators, most of them far senior to Murakami's main readership, take his popularity as a sign that there is something wrong, not only with Murakami's writing but with all of contemporary Japanese literature."[15] The literary establishment considered his novels entertaining page-turners and his elevation to pop-star status only increased his distance from the literary establishment.

Outside Japan, Masao Miyoshi, a Japanese expatriate critic resident in California, who is also a friend and admirer of Ôe Kenzaburô (the 1994 Nobel Laureate), is known to be a harsh critic of Murakami. In his 1991 *Off Center,* Miyoshi deplored the absence of a critical stance in modern Japanese literature, a trend most prominently displayed by commercially successful writers such as Murakami Haruki. In contrast to Murakami's literature which is "all sophisticated stylizations of trivia, flying over the boredom and irritation of everyday life," Miyoshi refers to Ôe Kenzaburô as "the only serious writer with a sizeable readership in Japan" who has undeservedly received little attention abroad. Miyoshi also seemed to suggest that Murakami's commercial success outside Japan was largely due to his cleverness to "custom-tailor [his] goods to [his] clients abroad" by "exhibiting an exotic Japan" in its most internationalized version.[16]

Ôe Kenzaburô himself did not have much better to say about Murakami's literature which was all about "how a person who lacks an active posture can live a pleasant and fashionable life in today's affluent, urban, consumer society." For someone like Ôe with a classical modernist view of literature, the lack of an "active posture" is a fatal flaw because, in his opinion, a willingness "to create around him an integrated world encompassing social and political situations" is what makes a work "novel."[17]

Tatsumi Takayuki, Professor in American literature, on the other hand, was quick to compliment Murakami's sensitivity in catching on to the hip currents in post-modern "global" literature.[18] In his *Nihon Henryû bun-gaku* (Japanese Slipstream literature; 1998) he elaborates on the development of the wall as a metaphor in Murakami's works. One thinks of the "wall" as in the walled city in **Hard-Boiled Wonder-land and the End of the World** first as a "border" one crosses to escape into another world. The protagonist eventually realizes, however, that there is no "other world," because the walled city itself is a product of his own mind, and it is impossible to escape from "himself." The wall which used to divide the world neatly into two in the cold-war era, now collapses the distinction between "right"/"left," and "dream"/ "reality," "subject/object," deconstructing reality itself—generating an acute sense of lost reality typical of hypermedia society in advanced capitalism. Citing similar examples of surrealistic images of a wall in American slipstream literature and English TV series, Tatsumi argues Murakami's strength lies in his ability to "capture and allegorize moments in which reality turns into such alternative, virtual realities riddled with mysteries that are never solved."[19]

BECOMING "JAPANESE" ENOUGH?

As far as the *bundan* (the literary establishment) is concerned, things seemed to change for the better for Murakami with his 1994 **The Wind-Up Bird Chronicle.** As Rubin puts it, this novel "did much to change the attitude of the Japanese literary establishment towards Murakami."[20] The novel not only won the hearts of his readers, but of senior critics and authors in the literary establishment, bringing him the prestigious Forty-Seventh Yomiuri (Newspaper) Liter-ary Prize for 1995. Most noteworthy was that one of his harshest critics, Ôe Kenzaburô, was on the prize committee and gave him compliments at the ceremony, referring to the book as "beautiful" and "important." He even read aloud the passage in Book Two, Chapter 4, "Divine Grace Lost," portraying Lieutenant Mamiya's "failure to experience a revelation in the light that floods down into the Mongolian well in which he has been left to die."[21]

As is clear from Ôe's reference to Lt. Mamiya, one of the things in the novel that impressed senior critics was what they saw as Murakami's new willingness to engage with "Japan" in the way he never did earlier. By looking into some of the lesser known aspects of the Japanese warfare on the Asian continent, the novel tried to grapple with the meaning of being "Japanese" in the post-war era without the first hand experience of the war. The novel has engrossing accounts of the Kwantung Army's secret cross-border espionage into

Mongolia—an expedition that later developed into the so-called Nomonhan Incident. Lt. Mamiya is one of the two survivors of this failed expedition and the nar-rator of these meta-stories.

Another war-related story is told by a female character who goes by the nickname Nutmeg. Over a dinner table she tells the protagonist about his father's tragicomic experience as the vet of a local zoo in Hsin-ching, the "Special New Capital City" of Manchukuo, which the modern Japanese state has constructed in the wilderness. In August 1945, just a few days before the Soviet Far East Command was expected to arrive in the city, the director and his soldiers are ordered to "liquidate" the fierce animals in the zoo without using gunpowder, which was becoming too precious. Equipped with no poison to execute the order, the director makes enquiries to the Kwantung Army Headquarters. Most of the high-ranking officers, however, have already disappeared. The Chinese soldiers in the Manchuko Army assigned to defend the city have also deserted. Knowing that the animals are going to starve anyway, the director instructs his soldiers to shoot them after all.

> They killed the leopards. They killed the wolves. They killed the bears. Shooting the bears took the most time. Even after the two gigantic animals had taken dozens of rifle slugs, they continued to crash against the bars of their cage, roaring at the men and slobbering, fangs bared. . . . When the soldiers at last succeeded in extinguishing all signs of life in the bears, they were so exhausted they were ready to collapse on the spot. . . . The young soldier who would be beaten to death by a Soviet soldier seventeen months later in a coal mine near Irkutsk took several deep breaths in succession, averting his gaze from the bears' corpses. He was engaged in a fierce struggle to force back the nausea that had worked its way up to his throat.[22]

The protagonist, Okada Tôru, who is too young to have had the first-hand experience of the war, listens attentively. The powerful and moving accounts of the absurdities of violence and killing in these incidents certainly create one of the climaxes in the novel, albeit only marginally tied to the main story line.[23]

The year after the publication of **The Wind-Up Bird Chronicle,** Japan was struck by two catastrophes; In January more then 5,000 people died in an earthquake in Kobe; in March twelve people died and more than 5,000 were injured in the subway in Tokyo as a result of the sarin gas attack by the Aum Shinri Kyo cult. Murakami followed up on his social engagement by producing three works related to these events; **Under-ground, The Place that was Promised: Underground 2,** both non-fictional accounts of his interviews with the members of the cult and the victims, and **After the Quake,** six short stories related to the earthquake. By questioning how and why this could happen and what the appeal of the Aum was, in a thoughtful afterword titled "Blind Nightmare: Where are we Japanese Going?" in *Underground,* Murakami lived up to the critics' expectations to take up specifically Japanese issues.[24]

THE RECEPTION OF MURAKAMI'S LITERATURE
OUTSIDE JAPAN AND ISSUES RELATED TO
TRANSLATION

READER-FRIENDLINESS ON THE INTERNATIONAL MARKET

Jay Rubin has the following to say about the translation of Murakami's *A Wild Sheep Chase,* his international breakthrough novel that "caught the attention of the English-speaking readers."

> If Alfred Birnbaum can be credited with having discovered Murakami for an English-speaking readership, Elmer Luke can be credited with having saved his discovery. He began working with Birnbaum to improve the appeal of *A Wild Sheep Chase* to an international readership. They removed dates and other signs linking the action to the 1970s, giving it a more contemporary feel—even going so far as to include a Reagan-era chapter title, "One for the Kipper", that chimed with the translation's hip new style, if not to the book's chronology. (Set in 1978, the novel should not have contained—and does not in the original—this allusion to the famous movie line "Make it one for the Gipper," which flourished during the Reagan years after 1980.)[25]

Rubin goes on to inform us that Elmer Luke and other foreign editors managed to persuade a somewhat sceptical Murakami and Kôdansha to support this translation project with a 50,000 US dollar advertising budget. The year was 1989, two years after the phenomenal success of *Norwegian Wood* in Japan. Alfred Birnbaum's translation of *Norwegian Wood* came out the same year, so time was ripe to launch Murakami on the global literary market with a fanfare. As Rubin says "there is no doubt that Alfred's jazzy translation of *A Wild Sheep Chase* is what caught the attention of English-speaking readers," so one must say that Elmer Luke and Kôdansha's strategy worked.[26] With the help from Birnbaum and Luke, Murakami made a successful entry into the "international" book market in the U.S. *The New Yorker* published two short stories by Murakami in 1990, **"TV People"** and **"The Wind-up Bird and Tuesday's Women."** Supported by editors favourable to Murakami, he has become one of the most published writers in the magazine of any nationality.

I must point out, however, that removing "dates and other signs linking the action to the 1970s" in *A Wild Sheep Chase* is a drastic measure that raises a question that goes far beyond style. Although the novel

came out in 1982, the main story is set in 1978, as Rubin points out. The first chapter is symbolically titled "1970/11/25," the date of Mishima Yukio's spectacular death, and gives in a flashback the protagonist's recollection of that "strange afternoon" spent with his girlfriend who later committed suicide. A sense of loss and disarray that permeates the whole novel is closely connected with the collapse of the student movement that started in 1970. As Matthew Strecher points out, "few [Japanese] readers" at the time "needed reminding" that "Japan's greatest political struggle in the post-war era—Zenkyôtô, the popular student uprising against the U.S-Japan Security Treaty ("Ampo")—collapsed in utter defeat." He continues:

> Indeed, from the time AMPO was automatically renewed in 1970, the unifying causes of the Zenkyôtô movement were eliminated one by one. R. Nixon's peace initiative with China in 1971 began to thaw the dangerously confrontational situation on both sides . . .; Okinawa was returned to Japanese sovereignty in 1972. U.S. troop withdrawal from Vietnam began [ending the war in 1975]. At home, the Japanese economy was about to embark on its now-famous "bubble" growth period, ushering in a level of affluence unseen even in the era of "rapid" growth.[27]

Thrown into sharp relief is a poignant sense of disillusionment for Japanese youth in 1978 standing at the threshold of a new affluent era. The importance of "dates and other signs linking the action to the 1970s" can hardly be exaggerated. By changing the setting to the Reagan era to give a "contemporary feel" in 1989 when the translation was scheduled to come out, they turned *A Wild Sheep Chase* into a very different novel, to which I will come back later.[28]

This manipulation with the original text was carried over into other languages because the English version served as the "standard" text in many countries that published Murakami's books by retranslating from English. The Norwegian edition that came out in 1993 is no exception. It has dropped the American "One for the Kipper" as the title of a chapter, opting for just "Kipper," but, all the references to the 1970s in the chapter titles remained unmentioned. Preserving the original context in translation is no longer taken for granted on the increasingly global literary market.

On a related note, we might consider another episode concerning the translation of Murakami. In an essay from 2000, Irmela Hijiya-Kirschnereit, a German Japanologist, expresses her outrage over the fact that DuMont, a German publisher, retranslated Murakami's **Wind-Up Bird Chronicle** into German from Jay Rubin's English translation. At the request of Murakami's American publisher, Knopf, Jay Rubin had to make considerable cuts in translating **Wind-Up Bird Chronicle** and the same cuts were, therefore, transferred to the German edition. The whole thing developed into a public debate in Germany involving a few other professors and critics. DuMont and Murakami issued a "joint declaration" on the website recognizing the merit of a direct translation but at the same time admitting that "in the interest of speed Murakami was willing to accept translation into other languages from the English."[29] Hijiya-Kirschnereit criticizes Murakami for endorsing the "English-language-centred cultural imperialism" by taking such a compromising attitude, an argument that would probably win sympathy among scholars and critics who are less concerned about saleability of books and timing of publications.[30] Jay Rubin, on the other hand, emphasizes that he collaborated closely with Murakami in the process of translation and making cuts, and shows a more understanding attitude toward commercial/pragmatic interests, such as reader-friendliness and speed.

SPEED OF TRANSLATION

It took eight years before his first novel, **Hear the Wind Sing,** was available in English. **Norwegian Wood** was his first work that was translated so quickly, two years after the original publication. After **The Wind-Up Bird Chronicle,** whose English edition came out after three years (the translation work started even before the book was finished in Japanese), it has taken only two to three years before the English translations came out. Both **Underground,** and **After the Quake** were promptly translated (even though they were by no means the most commercially successful books by Murakami). There was a dramatic increase in the number of reviews in international magazines and journals after the publication of **The Wind-up Bird Chronicle.**

It is pointless to deny the crucial roles played by the publishers and editors in deciding whose works, which texts, how and when to translate in promoting foreign literature. These decisions must take saleability of the products and the market reaction into consideration—decisions which, in turn, influence the future possibilities of that particular author on the international market. Rubin goes as far as to argue that "without an editor who believes in a writer, there is no way for a publisher to promote that writer's career."[31] Reader-friendliness and speed are apparently some of the more important factors to which editors must give thought. In response to criticism about the cuts made in **The Wind-up Bird Chronicle,** Murakami's US editor, Gary Fisketjon, writes on Knopf's website: "My reaction was that it couldn't be published successfully at such length, which indeed would do harm to Haruki's cause

in this country."[32] As he seems to be suggesting, failing to give a good impression in one translation may have a serious consequence for the author's career in that country. Once an author gets noticed by a sizeable native readership as being worthwhile, however, it takes perhaps less remarkable works to sell his products.

TRANSLATIONS AS INDEPENDENT PRODUCTS: RETERRITORIALIZATION

Discussing Alfred Birnbaum's translation of **A Wild Sheep Chase** published in 1989, Aoyama Minami notes that the book was received positively in the U.S. as something which criticized "Japan Inc." that Americans felt increasingly antagonistic about in the late 1980s.[33] As already noted, the novel was originally published in 1982 and set in 1978, but the translation took pains to place its setting in the Reagan era by erasing traces from the 1970s. The novel was consequently read in the light of the strained U.S.-Japan relationship over the trade imbalance which had been gaining momentum for some time. "Japan bashing" had already been full-blown with Theodore White's article "The Danger from Japan" in 1985. White compares the German trade surplus with the Japanese, and concludes that "the Germans, somehow, evoke little American bitterness because we understand their culture," whereas "the Japanese provoke American wrath because they are a locked and closed civilization that reciprocates our hushed fear with veiled contempt."[34]

Sony's purchase of Columbia Pictures in 1989 only exacerbated the anti-Japanese feelings among Americans. In the pervasive mood of such Japanese-culture bashing, the "jazzy" tone in **A Wild Sheep Chase** perhaps provided a relieving respite from the fear of the impenetrable "Japanese" which, for many, was represented by "the insular nature" of their fiction. A reviewer from *Chicago Tribune* writes:

> We've been going through a long period of explaining to ourselves why the Japanese have been taking all of our business away from us. A lot of the reasons we come up with have to do with the differences between Japanese culture and our own. Ah, the strangeness of it all, we sometimes croon to ourselves, as we watch their profits-and our debts-mount. And readers who from time to time expand their borders to include some of the best Japanese novelists in translation-Kawabata, Abe, Endo and others-have recognized the insular nature of the fiction. . . .

> Now, however, readers will have to take into account the fiction of Haruki Murakami, whose **A Wild Sheep Chase** is the first of his best-selling novels to appear in English. The 40-year-old Murakami appears to turn the notion of Japanese insularity on its head; his novel, in a lively translation by Alfred Birnbaum, is a greatly entertaining piece of fiction that will remind U.S. readers of the first time they read Tom Robbins or how much they miss Thomas Pynchon.

A Wild Sheep Chase is a buoyant critique of everything in Japanese culture that we believe confounds us. . . .[35]

It is difficult to tell whether or not Elmer Luke and Birnbaum had such reactions in mind when they removed the dates linking the novel to 1970s Japan. But, their recontextualization of the setting resonated well with the American readers' needs in 1989 and it was most likely what made it a success on the American market.

As Aoyama points out, it is interesting to note that the reception of *A Wild Sheep Chase* was far less favourable in England where Birnbaum's translation appeared half a year later. Without the American context of Japan bashing in the 1980s, and without the original Japanese context of the collapse of the student uprising in the 1970s, *A Wild Sheep Chase* may have appeared like a big enigma to many British readers. Devoid of any specific contexts, the novel seems to have been read as a mysterious allegory, which was more mysterious than interesting.[36] It was received in the similar vein in Norway, too, when it first appeared in 1993. I wrote a book review myself for a Norwegian newspaper, *Morgenbladet,* after reading the Norwegian translation (which was retranslated from Birnbaum's English translation), and remember feeling that the whole novel was a confounding riddle with little relevance to historical reality of any kind.[37]

Gary Fisketjon, editor at Knopf, put together Murakami's short stories into one volume, and titled it *The Elephant Vanishes* in 1993, the first Murakami anthology in English. Five of them were taken from the Japanese anthology titled *The Second Bakery Attack* (1986), but the rest was taken from other sources, and the combination was entirely new.[38]

British publisher Harvill Press brought out an anthology of short stories, *Birthday Stories; Selected and Introduced by Haruki Murakami,* to commemorate Murakami's 55th birthday in January 2004. The anthology contained eleven stories by American, British, and Irish authors, and one by Murakami himself. Even though it is an English version of the original Japanese edition, being a part of the English anthology in translation gives Murakami's story a special "para-text," which, in turn, makes this product an independent global (British?) product severed from the local Japanese context.[39] The British editor was primarily interested in having "something of Murakami's to publish in Britain while waiting for the translation of *Kafka on the Shore* to be completed."[40] These projects illustrate not only how important editors can be in promoting foreign literature, but also how they can play a role in assimilating foreign literature into their native framework, making it, as it were, their own.

KAFKA ON THE SHORE (2002) IN THE POST-9/11 WORLD

"Listening to a lot of other people's stories is very healing for me," Murakami told the psychologist Hayao Kawai. "Yes, yes," Kawai replied, "that's what we do, we heal and are ourselves healed."[41]

Murakami's 2002 novel, *Kafka on the Shore,* was released in English in January 2005, and has been making headlines in newspapers and magazines. The book was actually making headlines before the publication as a way of advertisement. Even though some reviewers express their frustrations over too many "loose ends" hanging in the air, their overall impressions seem positive.[42]

The critics' reception of *Kafka on the Shore* in Japan, however, is more mixed. Particularly noteworthy is the divided opinion among the so called serious critics over the book's impact, which makes an interesting contrast to the reception of *The Wind-Up Bird Chronicle.* While the established fans of Murakami such as Katô Norihiro and Kawai Hayao have received the book with enthusiasm, some left-wing literary critics have expressed concern over what they consider to be a Jungian, psychological turn in the novel.[43] *Kafka* [*Kafka on the Shore*] displays a disturbing tendency to approach problems of "Japanese" identity in increasingly psychological terms. In order to fully understand their criticism, one must consider the historical context in which *Kafka* came out. *Kafka* was published in the autumn of 2002, a year after the September 11 attacks in New York and Washington, when there was a heated public debate over Japan's role in international politics in the post-9/11 world.

THE WORLDLY CONTEXT: READING AGAINST THE NATIVE GRAIN?

The point is that texts have ways of existing that even in their most rarefied form are always enmeshed in circumstance, time, place, and society—in short, they are in the world, and hence worldly[44]

After the economic "bubble" burst in the early 1990s, Japanese search for national identity seems to have entered a new phase. Unemployment rates went up and the life-time employment system was collapsing. Heinous crimes by juvenile delinquents were drawing attention in the media. For many, the saringas attack by the Aum-cult confirmed their suspicion that something was going terribly wrong. The educational system (with its notorious examination hell) came under severe criticism, and the Ministry of Education launched a reform program, aiming at liberalization and deregulation. The negative aspects of too much homogeneity, and "me-too" thinking was pointed out.

"Individuality" was a new key-word, which was to solve the problems of standardization and supposed lack of creativity in the educational system.

Their emphasis on individuality was, however, carefully orchestrated with the idea of social responsibility, which was to distinguish individuality from mere "selfishness." The implication was that the idea of social responsibility was to be extended to national and eventually to international responsibility. The point of departure for a proper sense of self should be anchored in national identity, which the Japanese of the post-war era had had too little of, owing to the unfortunate historical circumstances. In order to imbue the right sense of social, national, and international responsibility into the young Japanese mind, the flag and national anthem came suddenly into focus. In 1999 a law was passed to make the salute to these national symbols obligatory at school ceremonies. A committee was appointed to re-examine the relevance of the Fundamental Law of Education implemented under the American Occupation which does not mention such "core" values as "community, home, and nation." Some of the exponents of the education reform even supported the project to revise what was seen as an overtly "masochistic" view of modern Japanese history. To strengthen the moral profile in education, the Ministry of Education in 2000 distributed free of charge "moral" handbooks, titled "Kokoro no nôto" (Your mind notes), to all children in primary and junior-high school.[45]

The handbook's pedagogical intention is fairly obvious. The handbook at each level is organized according to the same principle; it is supposed to function as a kind of sounding board for the pupil's mind. He/she is encouraged to make notes on his/her feelings and thoughts in the book as he/she encounters everyday problems. "What do you like about yourself? Were you able to perform all the 'good' things today as you are supposed to? It feels terrible to tell a lie, doesn't it? Do you have a secret? Do you like having one? What can you do to make your class better? And your town? And your country?"[46]

What is noteworthy is that these notes are kept at school, and are subject to teacher's supervision. Many of the questions clearly anticipate "correct" answers, toward which children will be guided. Critics of "Kokoro no nôto" have pointed out that it is a cleverly devised form of mind control, making it easier for the teacher to monitor what the children are thinking. The notes close with a personal message to *you* from Kawai Hayao, a leading psychologist in Japan, who was responsible for planning the notes; "These notes are full of your feelings and thoughts. I hope they will give you strength whenever you remember to open

them in the future." Hayao Kawai is a great fan of Murakami, an admirer of *Kafka,* and their friendship is well-known. So what, you may ask. What does this have to do with a reading of Murakami's *Kafka on the Shore*? Some might say "nothing," while others might say "a lot."

NAKATA AND MISS SAEKI IN KAFKA ON THE SHORE

Since the scope of this paper does not allow a full discussion of the novel, I will comment on a few aspects pertaining to two of the side characters, Nakata and Miss Saeki, which I believe are relevant to a reading of *Kafka* in the context of its time and place. The novel is presented in alternating chapters with plot-lines that converge and cross. The odd-numbered chapters are narrated by Kafka Tamura, a 15 year old boy who, cursed by his father's prophesy that he would kill his father and sleep with his mother, decides to run away from home. The other story-line in the even-numbered chapters follows the fate of an old, half-witted man named Nakata. Miss Saeki is a fifty year old female proprietor of the library where Kafka seeks refuge, and is a mother-like figure with whom Kafka falls in love.

Both Nakata and Miss Saeki are victims of meaningless violence, for which they have suffered most of their life. Nakata is one of the school children who briefly fell into a coma under mysterious circumstances at the end of the WWII. Most likely as a result of their young female teacher's violent "fit" that only Nakata experienced, he never fully recovered from the trauma of the incidence and lost his memory. The night before going on an excursion with the children, the teacher dreamed about having sex with her fiancé, who had been sent to war. Experiencing an unexpected menstruation which she believed was related to the dream knocked her completely off balance. When she discovered a young Nakata bringing her a handkerchief soiled with her own blood, she started hitting him in spite of herself, a move which she regretted later, but gave a fatal blow to the young Nakata's sensitive mind.

Miss Saeki had a childhood lover to whom she was totally dedicated. He died, however, a completely meaningless death in the midst of student demonstrations in the 1960s. While he was delivering some food to his friends participating in the student uprising, he was mistaken for being a spy from the enemy faction and was beaten to death. Miss Saeki never recovered from this loss and has lived a life like a zombie.

The novel ends with the death of Nakata and Miss Saeki. Both of them willingly depart this world after finishing their "errands," although Miss Saeki's errand is never made entirely clear. Miss Saeki asks Nakata to burn her memoirs about her lover and their past and close a shrine gate in the local forest that Miss Saeki has mistakenly opened earlier. Nakata faithfully executes Miss Saeki's requests with the help of his good friend, Hoshino, and thereby closes the gateway into the "past" where surviving deserters from World War II are still wandering. And all this seems to coincide with Kafka's recovery from his nightmare and his coming of age. Kafka has learned a lesson and can start his life afresh by going back to his home town in Tokyo.

A strong sense of fate and passivity permeates the novel. Violence and killing simply occur in the meaningless ensemble of cruel coincidences. No one is to blame for the wounds that were inflicted on Nakata and Miss Saeki; no one can take responsibility for their suffering. In a similar vein, the question of agency is blurred in the psychological drama in which wanting to have someone killed, or dreaming about it, is enough to induce the act of killing itself. Who is to blame for murdering Johnny Walker/Kafka's father? Nakata or Kafka himself?

Suffering is a necessary part of "growing up" and the healing process which all must go through. As Kawai Hayao suggests, by telling stories, "we heal and are ourselves healed" as we channel destructive energies into positive ones, making our life more bearable. The solution to suffering is ultimately psychological and never political. A parallel in post-war Japanese history can be easily made. Is it not about time that "Japan" as a nation liberates itself from the haunting memory of the painful past? By taking a psychoanalytic journey into "Japan's" own collective subconscious, "Japan" can cure itself from its self-inflicted paranoia. Is it not about time, indeed, that "Japan," by leaving behind the legacy of the war, starts playing a more active role in the post 9/11 world order? If the message is not that direct and obvious, some critics would still argue that *Kafka* did play a considerable role in influencing the "world" opinion in Japan at the time its future role in the post 9/11-order was fiercely debated.[47]

Conclusion

THE WORLDLY CONTEXT: READING AGAINST WHICH NATIVE GRAIN?

Edward Said famously emphasized the importance of reading a text in its "worldly context." In an increasingly globalized society, however, one inevitably faces a problem of deciding which worldly context one should be discussing, as the case of reading *Kafka on the Shore* illustrates. What should we expect from the British readers of *Kafka on the Shore,* who have been

"warming up" for this translation by reading Murakami's birthday anthology? Should they have been reading Japanese history instead? How about Chinese and Korean readers, who, while having much more at stake in remembering the "Japanese" context, are more prone to be fascinated by the magical power of Murakami's "hip" storytelling techniques ? The popularity of *Kafka* in China, for example, seems to demonstrate that it is being read in its own "historical" context—in which the lure of the "exotic" in its most internationalized version (as in Miyoshi's words) is more powerful than "politics."

As Tomlinson points out, we should remember that "where there is deterritorialization there is also reterritorialization."[48] It is "important to avoid overstating the cultural flux of globalization and losing sight of the tendency of cultural mixtures to re-embed themselves, however briefly, into 'stable' identity positions." Murakami's literature, which is already a "cultural mixture," is not only constantly reinterpreted, translated, and re-contextualized in new environments, but is also being "re-embedded" into "stable" identity positions, claiming a new authority, a new cultural "home," so to speak. Just as J. D. Salinger and Paul Auster can lay claim to having created a cultural "home" for many young Japanese readers through their popular Japanese translators (Shibata Motoyuki and Murakami Haruki), Murakami's literature in China and Korea or in the U.S. might be gaining ground as a new cultural home/homes, creating their own "paratexts" and interpretative parameters.

Many critics have attempted to describe this process of "deterritorialization" and "reterritorialization" in terms of the "global-local" nexus, and insert the notion of "hybridization" to give justice to the intricate process of "the local negotiation with globalizing forces" in which both differences and similarities are relativized.[49] We should bear in mind, however, that "hybridization" here does not mean a single-handed celebration of cultural mixing in which the foreign is always assimilated into the familiar by reterritorialization. In order for a concept like "hybridity" to be critically viable, it has to be defined as something that can intervene in this stabilizing process by inserting "otherness" that resists complete assimilation. We need "hybridity" that does not coagulate into a fixed subject-position, allowing us the conceptual space to think beyond the binary-opposition that always divides our world into "we" against "others."

In this connection, Iwabuchi makes a valuable distinction between "hybridity" and "hybridism" which is often thought of as a "key feature of Japanese national identity." "Japan is said to be a vociferously assimilating cultural entity: The Japanese modern experience is described in terms of appropriation, domestication, and indigenization of the foreign (predominantly associated with the West) in a way that reinforces an exclusivist notion of Japanese national/cultural identity."[50] Iwabuchi criticizes hybridism for strategically "essential[izing] hybridity and hybridization as an organic and ahistorical aspect of Japanese national/cultural identity." He continues:

> Hybridism is based upon the concentric assimilation of culture, while hybridity emphasizes the incommensurability of cultural difference. Hybridism assumes that anything foreign can be domesticated into the familiar, whereas hybridity assumes an "awareness of the untranslatable bit that lingers on in translation" (Papastergiadis 1995, 18). Hybridity thus destabilizes the very notion of identity, whereas hybridism does not create such a liminal space in which fixed and exclusive national/cultural boundaries can be blurred. Rather, it reinforces the rigidity of these boundaries. Hybridism might be called a fluid essentialism.[51]

Since there is no space for a close textual analysis in this essay to examine "hybridity" in relation to Murakami's literature, I hope that Iwabuchi's warning about the need for this distinction can give us a hint about the possible critical directions to be explored further.

With its mixing of global and local cultural products, such as Johnny Walker, Colonel Sanders, Murasaki Shikibu, Franz Kafka, and Natsume Sôseki, is **Kafka on the Shore** emblematic of the Japanese "strategic hybridism" that exploits the power of "hybridization" just to catch the reader's attention? Can Kafka represent a true hybrid identity "in-between," and become a spokesman for the very difficulty of, and the ambivalence of, being a fifteen year old "Japanese" in the post-9/11-world? Is there any "untranslatable bit that lingers on" in Kafka's identity after every secret corner of his "heart" (*kokoro*) has been elaborated on to the reader? Can Murakami's literature represent "hybridity" and not "hybridism"? I believe some of his novels can, while I have some serious doubts about **Kafka.** Hoping to find another opportunity to pursue this theme in the future, I would like to end this essay by saying that it is up to us, the reader, to judge whether or not his literature manages to establish such a hybrid identity that resists being just another "new product" for the international market, and to maintain some of its critical edge as the source of social critique.

Notes

1. I would like to thank my students Magne Toerring and Morten J. Vatn for having inspired me to write about Murakami Haruki. Thanks are also due to Irena Hayter for her thoughtful comments. Japanese names are written with the last name first except when they appear in the opposite order in English-language sources.

2. Donald Morrison, "It's raining sardines," *Time Europe Magazine,* February 14, 2005, 58.

3. Jay Rubin, *Haruki Murakami and the Music of Words* (London: Vintage, 2003), 5.

4. Ibid., 320.

5. Alfred Birnbaum, ed. *Monkey Brain Sushi: New Tastes in Japanese Fiction* (Tokyo: Kôdansha, 1993) and Helen Mitsios, ed., *New Japanese Voices: The Best Contemporary Fiction from Japan* (New York: The Atlantic Monthly Press, 1991). Many writers are selling well in English, among whom are Murakami Ryû and mystery writers such as Kirino Natsuo and Miyabe Miyuki.

6. Here I use "magic realism" simply to mean a literature in which the real is formally infused with the magic. See Lois Parkinson Zamora, "Introduction: Daiquiri Birds and Flaubertian Parrot(ie)s," in *Magic Realism: Theory, History, Community,* ed. Lois Parkinson *Zamora* and Wendy B. Faris (Durham: Duke University Press, 1995), 1-11.

7. The list of American authors he has translated includes F. Scott Fitzgerald, Raymond Carver, John Irving, Paul Theroux, Truman Capote, Tim O'Brien and J. D. Salinger.

8. John Tomlinson, *Globalization and Culture* (Cambridge: Polity, 1999), 52.

9. *Hear the Wing Song* (1979); F. Scott Fitzgerald's "My Lost City" and other stories (1981); *A Wild Sheep Chase* in Alfred Birnbaum's translation (1989). The Korean translation of *Norwegian Wood* was also published in 1989.

10. I have had a young Norwegian Murakami fan in my class who says he read Dostoevsky because he saw his name pop up in a book by Murakami.

11. See Miura Masashi, *Murakami Haruki to Shibata Motoyuki no môhitotsu no amerika* (Another America: Murakami Haruki and Shibata Motoyuki) (Tokyo: Shinshokan, 2003), 6-7, 19.

12. Tomlinson, 149.

13. Rubin, 160-61.

14. Stephen Phelan, "Found in Translation," *Sunday Herald,* January 2, 2005, 3.

15. Rubin, 6.

16. Masao Miyoshi, *Off Center* (Cambridge, Mass.: Harvard University Press, 1991), 235.

17. Kenzaburô Ôe, *Japan, the Ambiguous and Myself: the Nobel Prize Speech and Other Lectures* (Tokyo: Kôdansha International, 1995).

18. He credits Shiga Takao and Numano Mitsuyoshi for being among the first to have appreciated the same tendency in Murakami's literature. See Tatsumi Takayuki, *Nihon henryû bungaku* (Tokyo: Shinchôsha. 1998), 112.

19. Tatsumi, 99 (My translation).

20. Rubin, 234.

21. Ibid., 235.

22. Haruki Murakami, *The Wind-up Bird Chronicle* (London: Vintage, 2003), 407.

23. Another powerful storyline is the portrayal of Wataya Noboru, the main character's "enemy." The protagonist suspects that Wataya, despite his appearance as a successful politician and a stylish man of the media, has inherited the murky legacy of Japan's expansionist ambitions and is hatching secret plans to manipulate the future of Japan.

24. Alfred Birnbaum and Philip Gabriel, trans., *Underground: The Tokyo Gas Attack and the Japanese Psyche* (London: Harvill Press, 2000), which includes *Yakusoku sareta basho de: andaaguraundo 2* (*The Place That Was Promised: Underground 2*); Jay Rubin, trans., *After the Quake: Stories* (New York: Alfred A. Knopf, 2002).

25. Rubin, 189.

26. Ibid., 320.

27. Matthew Strecher, "Magic Realism and the Search for Identity in the Fiction of Murakami Haruki," *Journal of Japanese Studies* 25, no. 2 (1999): 264.

28. However, it should be pointed out that an attentive reader would have guessed that the setting must be the 1970s since Mishima Yukio's (1925-1970) appearance on the TV is mentioned in the first chapter.

29. Rubin, 307-8.

30. Ibid., 208-9. Consider also the following quote: "A delightful story, *The Wind-Up Bird Chronicle* demonstrates the enormity of Murakami's literary imagination and his thoughtful insight into the meaning of postmodern reality. The translation, capturing the style and aura of the original, is equally enjoyable. It is regrettable, however, that the English version has been subjected to extensive cutting, undoubtedly under pressure from the publisher." (Yoshiko Yokochi Samuel, *World Literature Today,* Spring 1999, in "Murakami Haruki," *The Complete Review: A Literary Saloon and Site of Review,* 2001-2005, http://www.complete-review.com/authors/ murkamh.htm). A reviewer in *The Complete Review* concludes: "If it bothers you—and it should—contact the publishers and tell them that you don't want them making stupid editorial decisions like this on your behalf: translations (already a crime against literature) should be as true to the original as possible—and that certainly means NO cuts under ANY circumstances."

31. Rubin, 315.

32. Ibid., 306.

33. Aoyama Minami, *Eigo ni natta Nippon shôsetsu* (Japanese Novels That Have Become English) (Tokyo: Shûeisha, 1996), 94.

34. Miyoshi, 63.

35. Alan Cheuse, "Of Japan's Insular Values and a Quest for a Mythical Sheep," *Chicago Tribune,* November 19, 1989, 6.

36. Aoyama cites a review in *Guardian,* July 6, 1990 (Aoyama, 95).

37. "Murakami Harukis Sauejakten" (Murakami Haruki's Wild Sheep Chase) *Morgenbladet,* 1993.

38. Rubin, 315.

39. Gerard Genette, *Paratexts: Thresholds of Interpretation* (Cambridge: Cambridge University Press, 1997).

40. Rubin, 300.

41. Ibid., 5.

42. Haruki Murakami, *Kafka on the Shore* (London: Harvill Press, 2005). See John Updike, "Subconscious Tunnels: Haruki Murakami's Dreamlike New Novel," *The New Yorker,* January 24 and 31, 2005; "*Kafka on the Shore* by Murakami Haruki," *The Complete Review,* 2004-2005; http://www.complete-review.com/ reviews/murakamih/kafkaots.htm (accessed June 25, 2005) and Knut Ebeltoft, "Noen virkeligheter flyter mer enn andre" (Some Realities Are More Floating Than Others), *Bokkilden.no,* http:// www.bokkilden.no/Article.aspx?ArticleID=7674 (accessed June 25, 2005).

43. Personal correspondence with Shimamura Teru, April 26, 2005.

44. Edward Said, *The World, the Text, and the Critic* (Cambridge, Mass.: Harvard University Press, 1983), 35.

45. See Masayoshi Kakinuma and Tsuneo Nagano, eds., *Kokoro no nôto kenkyû* (Study of Your Mind Notes) (Tokyo: Hihyôsha, 2003) and *Aikokushin no kenkyû* (Study of Patriotism) (Tokyo: Hihyôsha, 2004).

46. *Kokoro no nôto: shôgakkô ichi 'ninen* (Your Mind Notes for Sixth and Seventh Graders) (Tokyo: Bunkeidô, 2003) compiled by Ministry of Education, Culture, Sports, Science and Technology.

47. Komori Yôichi has written a book on this theme (personal correspondence, March, 2005). See his *Murakami Harukiron: Umibe no kafuka o seidoku suru* (On Murakami Haruki: A close reading of *Kafka on the Shore*) (Tokyo: Heibon sha, 2006).

48. Tomlinson, 148.

49. As Iwabuchi summarizes, "in the study of transnational cultural flows, the concepts of hybridity and hybridization, together with others such as creoliza-

tion (Hannerz 1991) and indigenization (Appadurai 1996), also articulate the dynamic, ongoing, uneven but creative process of cultural interconnection, transgression, appropriation, reworking and crossfertilization." See Kôichi Iwabuchi, *Recentering globalization: Popular culture and Japanese transnationalism* (Durham and London: Duke University Press, 2002), 51.

50. Iwabuchi, 53.

51. Ibid., 54.

Amy Ty Lai (essay date March 2007)

SOURCE: Lai, Amy Ty. "Memory, Hybridity, and Creative Alliance in Haruki Murakami's Fiction." *Mosaic* 40, no. 1 (March 2007): 163-79.

[*In this essay, Lai surveys the role of animal imagery in Murakami's fiction.*]

> The couple . . . were able to open a cosy little establishment in a western suburb of Tokyo in 1974. They called it "Peter Cat" after an old pet of Haruki's.
>
> —Jay Rubin *Haruki Murakami and the Music of Words*

This essay attempts to fill the gap in the criticism on Haruki Murakami by exploring the use of animals in his major fiction. While it will critique and expand the critical works on the author, especially those by Matthew Strecher and Jay Rubin, it will also expose insufficiencies in the established concepts regarding animals in the postmodern arts, specifically those of Steve Baker. As such, the essay aims to enrich the already abundant criticism on the author, and open new directions in conceptualizing animal imagery in contemporary literature.

Haruki Murakami's fiction first appeared in the 1970s. Yoshio Iwamoto notes that Murakami's characters are often haunted by "a sense of loss," the content of which "is never spelled out" ("Voice" 297); while they avoid confronting other people, whom they view as functional objects, they pay "fetishistic attention" to consumer goods and trivial things, which furnish them with "a grip on a recalcitrant reality" (297-98). As Celeste Loughman argues, Murakami believes that neither materialism itself, nor the preference for Western popular culture, is the root of current problems, but "that's all there is." The confused or lost identity, caused by an absence of "idealism" or any source of self-fulfilment, is further severed by a loss of connection with the past, including the nation's cultural past ("No" 90).[1] Such is true not only of Murakami's many nameless protagonists, but of the named ones in his

most conventional novel, *Norwegian Wood* (*Noruwei no mori*): the protagonists aim at being different from other people, yet are not "truly unique and individualistic" (Okada 65-66). Eager to do away with social obligations, they are nonetheless very much conditioned by Japanese group-oriented mentality (72-73).

Steve Baker, in *The Postmodern Animal,* quotes Nina Lykke's "Between Monsters, Goddesses and Cyborgs: Feminist Confrontations with Science," claiming that modernity was a "repressive process of purification" that worked to ensure that any monster or hybrid that threatened to transgress the border between human and non-human was reclassified to either the human or the non-human sphere. In the cyborg world of post-industrial and postmodern society, however, such creatures or creations are becoming increasingly common, and their repression, less and less successful ("Leopards" 99). Citing Margrit Shildrick's "Posthumanism and the Monstrous Body," he argues that the proliferation of animals and the embrace of impurity, hybridity, even monstrosity in the postmodern arts could be a positive and creative trend, and that the "humanist politics of norms and identity" might give way to "a politics of hybrids" (100). In the vein of Deleuze and Guattari, Baker stresses that "becoming-animal," which provides a creative escape from a repressive society and other conservative forces, is not equivalent to "resembling, imitating or identifying with" an animal, nor does it happen in the imagination, dreams or fantasies, or necessarily entail a bodily metamorphosis (120-21). While Deleuze and Guattari claim in *A Thousand Plateaus,* "becoming-animal produces nothing other than itself. What is real is the becoming itself" (Baker 121), Baker defines "becoming-animal" as "human being's creative opportunity to think themselves other-than-in-identity," hence the precise relationship between the human and the animal as one of "alliance" (125-26). Therefore, in contrast to recent theoretical works on cyborgs, hybrids, and monsters, there is no dissolution of bodily identity: "separate bodies enter into alliances in order to do things," but neither is "undone" by the process (132-33).

Baker's conceptualization naturally brings up the other extreme, envisioned by science fiction writers from H. G. Wells to Octavia Butler and David Icke, who dramatize dystopic threats represented by alien figures of human-animal hybrids and use their works as allegories for political concerns such as the explosion of biotechnology. We are also reminded of the hybrid characters in the works of many contemporary artists, and the rock paintings and carvings from the dawn of time that have been discovered and widely reported all over the world. Interestingly, "Becoming animal" is the title of a recent exhibition at Mass MoCa, a museum of contemporary art in Western Massachusetts, showing works by twelve internationally-renowned artists to demonstrate the boundaries and interactions, hostilities and resonances between humans and animals. Indeed, "becoming-animal" and human-animal hybrids constitute a key feature and recurrent theme both in primitive and in postmodern art; as such, to see it as wholly creative or destructive would not be a very productive approach in literary enquiry.

It is close to impossible not to read Murakami's animals in a meaningful way. **"The Kangaroo Communiqué"** (**"Kangarū Tsūshin"**), for instance, turns the life of the kangaroo into an analogy for the protagonist's stranded and monotonous existence. Nonetheless, Baker's conceptualization has more value in those cases where animals are more subtle and find a more intertextualized existence in Murakami's works. A good example is the elephant, which is briefly mentioned in *Hear the Wind Sing* (*Kaze no uta o kike*) (6). It evolves into the "elephants' graveyard" in *Pinball, 1973* (*1973-nen no pinbōru*), a parallel for the timeless warehouse of pinball machines and a label for the depths of the unconscious (155). The "elephant factory" in *The Dancing Dwarf* (*Odoru kobito*) describes the manufacture of genuine elephants (245-46), associating the elephant with "a creative process, the power of the imagination" (Rubin, *Haruki* 107). These are followed by the Professor's remark in *Hard-boiled Wonderland and the End of the World* (*Sekai no owari to hādoboirudo wandārando*), which compares the inner mind, or core consciousness, with the "great unexplored 'elephant graveyard,'" which he quickly corrects to the "elephant factory," stating that it is not only a burial ground for collected dead memories, but a place where "you sort through countless memories and bits of knowledge, [. . .] and finally make up a cognitive system" (256).

The association between the elephant and the core consciousness, memories, and imagination is not as arbitrary as it might seem, as the animal conjures such positive qualities as strength, stability, and gracefulness. It would sound reductionist to put too much emphasis on the elephant's association with Buddhism and Shintoism, yet the author, by using an animal that has strong religious meaning to symbolize the human mind, does seem to suggests that the belief in one's selfhood is as important as traditional religion in the contemporary world, if not taking its place altogether.

Compared with the elephant, the unicorn plays an even more pivotal role in *Hard-boiled Wonderland and the End of the World,* which is made up of dual, interlocking narratives. In **"Hard-boiled Wonderland,"** the unnamed male inhabitant is enmeshed in a deadly information war between the "System," a government-business hybrid, and the "Factory," a shadowy organization seeking to undermine the System's power, in a slightly futuristic but recognizable Tokyo. In **"The End of the World,"** the protagonist, who has lost his own "Shadow," struggles to remember how he came to live in the "Town," surrounded by an impenetrable wall and homing herds of sad-looking unicorns. Whereas the former's job is to "launder" and "shuffle" information, with the mechanism built in his mind by the "Professor," the latter engages in "dreamreading," assigned to him by the "Gatekeeper," by placing his fingertips on the temples of unicorns' skulls so as to draw out their warmth and images.

Indeed, **"The End of the World"** is not the first time that unicorns have appeared in Murakami's fiction. The protagonist in **"A Poor-Aunt Story"** (**"Binbō na obsan no hanashi"**) looks across the water at a pair of bronze unicorns outside the Meiji Memorial Picture Gallery, the front hooves of which "thrust out in angry protest against the flow of time for abandoning them in its wake." Rubin labels the unicorns "representations of the timeless core of the unconscious mind" ("Murakami" 186). The unicorns in *Hard-boiled Wonderland and the End of the World* evoke "primordial memories" (13), and, as they hear the horn that summons them, there seems to be "an indelible intimacy of memories long departed from their eyes" (14). Later, the protagonist in **"Hard-boiled Wonderland"** learns that the unicorn is "a product of fantasy" (95) and "an imaginary animal" (97) in Western and Eastern imaginations, and despite obscure records of their existence, their single-horned nature makes them something of an "evolutionary anomaly" (98), which could only have managed to survive in "a lost world" (103). Such rarity, even mythological in origin, turns the animal into an apt symbol for precious memories that form part of the self or mind, even if such memories do not really exist and have to be invented. It is not a surprise when the "Librarian" informs the protagonist that the minds of the Town's inhabitants are in fact absorbed by the unicorns, which ferry them across the wall to the outside world; their skulls are scraped and buried for a full year to leech away the minds' energies, taken to the library stacks, and kept there until the dreamreader's hands "release the last glimmers of mind into the air" (335-36).

Strecher reads the "System" as a metaphor for the late-capitalist consumerist state ("Beyond" 362). As the plot unfolds, the two narratives gradually merge: the protagonist in **"Hard-boiled Wonderland,"** through an error on the part of the Professor, is destined to carry on his life in a state of complete oblivion until the End of the World, signifying that he is completely overtaken by the state. Memory is the weapon for resistance. While Murakami acknowledges the destructive aspect of memory, in particular the fixation on one's past, Stephen Snyder contends that the obscure mention of Marcel Proust at the beginning of *Hard-boiled Wonderland and the End of the World* invites the reader to treat the text as "a meditation on memory or the possibility of the reinvention of memory" (70-71). Susan Napier, nonetheless, sees the novel's ending as highly uncertain, and the overall picture of Tokyo that of "a bleak and alienating city, a world based on mindless consumption of products that range from Italian food to data information" (211-12). It is true that the protagonist refuses to leave the Town, for which he believes he is fully responsible as its true creator, yet, as Strecher argues, much of the landscape is in fact not the protagonist's own perception, but a fabrication by the Professor who draws on his experience as a film editor ("Beyond" 363-65).

As the protagonist can do nothing but dreamread the unicorns' skulls, instead of forming any kind of alliance with the unicorns, he is complicit with the System. How, then, is Baker's "becoming-animal" useful to the understanding of the novel? Jay Rubin notices the birds flitting back and forth over the wall surrounding the Town, which "separates the inner core of self from the part of the mind that is most in touch with the world of reality" ("Other" 497). Indeed, the protagonist's Shadow claims repeatedly to have been inspired by them (Murakami, *Hard-boiled* [*Hard-boiled Wonderland and the End of the World*] 247, 249). When it is time for Shadow to escape the Town, he once again makes an allusion to the birds: "Nothing can keep us in this Town any longer. We are free as the birds" (399). Whether Shadow can truly escape from the Town after plunging into the Pool is not clear, but the novel ends with a scene of complete desolation, where the protagonist contrasts himself with the birds, indicating that he is likely to remain trapped in a state of mindlessness: "Through the driving snow, I see a single white bird take flight. The bird wings over the Wall and into the flurried clouds of the southern sky. All that is left to me is the sound of the snow underfoot" (400).

The creative alliances with animals do not always end in obscurity and failure, and **"The Elephant Vanishes"** (**"Zō no shōmetsu"**) illustrates the success of such an endeavour by describing the mysterious disappearance of an old and feeble elephant from a Tokyo suburb with his human zookeeper. The alliance between them is first suggested by the striking similarities in their physical appearances, and later through the protagonist's eyes, in which the animal seems to undergo some kind of metamorphosis not long before the two of them disappear: it is uncertain whether the animal is becoming-man, or the man is becoming-animal, or

both—though by getting smaller and smaller the animal could indeed have freed itself much more easily: "It was a mysterious sight. Looking through the vent, I had the feeling that a different, chilling kind of time was flowing through the elephant house—but nowhere else. And it seemed to me, too, that the elephant and the keeper were gladly giving themselves over to this new order that was trying to envelop them—or that had already partially succeeded in enveloping them" (326). The harmonious human-animal relationship in "this new order" would indeed be possible in the religious worldview of Shintoism that, as the Japanese state religion, dominated the thinking of its people until the end of the World War II. In Shintoism, all human and non-human objects participate in what is known as "kami"[2] (Kitagawa 12; cited in Loughman, "Japan" 434). The magic in the story would only be credible with a reversion of time, which, quite ironically, also indicates that humans and animals cannot find their peace in the here and now. Given the metaphorical meaning of the elephant in Murakami's fiction, the animal's disappearance also indicates the obliteration of memory and core consciousness in the protagonist in **"The Elephant Vanishes."** Accordingly, he enjoys even greater success in his advertising career in a fast-paced society that has little regard for the animal—and, hence what it represents—and is soon oblivious to the whole incident.

Rat, a close friend of the protagonist, has been left out in my brief mention of *Hear the Wind Sing* and *Pinball, 1973,* and in such subsequent works as *A Wild Sheep Chase* (*Hitsuji o meguru bōken*) and *Dance Dance Dance* (*Dansu dansu dansu*). In *A Wild Sheep Chase,* the protagonist, having used a landscape photograph from Rat in the bulletin of a life insurance company, is approached by the secretary of the "Boss," head of a mysterious powerful syndicate, who forces him to reveal the origin of the photograph. Unwilling to betray his friend, he is coerced into hunting for the sheep with the brownish star on his back pictured in the photograph in Hokkaido, with the help of his unnamed girlfriend. He meets up with strange people, including the "Sheep Professor" and the "Sheep Man," before seeing Rat again, who has by then committed suicide. The Sheep Professor says that the sheep initially entered his body while he was sleeping at the Mongolia-Siberia border, and used him as its first host to make its way into Japan, before entering the Boss to build up a huge, obscure company. Strecher contends that this company, which is neither government, business, industry, nor media, but holds all of these powers at its disposal, is a metaphor for the postmodern state, "hidden, elusive, and unaccountable" all at once (*Dances* 35). Accordingly, the sheep becomes an image of "dominant social ideology of control, of materialism, of desire and easy gratification" in the postmodern, affluent societies of "easy, yet meaningless pleasures, operated by obscure organs of state power" (61). Rather than providing escape for humans, it tempts them to succumb to a dominant power and become more enslaved than they ever have been.

Rat reveals that he was one of the sheep's victims, and he has long recognized the danger of losing himself to the state: "Give your body over to it and everything goes. Consciousness, values, emotions, pain, everything. Gone" (283). As an individual who refuses to lose his selfhood, Rat hangs himself when the sheep inside him is asleep, indicating his preference for death to a life of mindless and painless consumerism. Although the novel was published in the 1980s and is set against the Japan of the 1970s, Rat is regarded as a nostalgic figure belonging to the 1960s, before the end of Zenkyōtō, which led to the downfall of selfhood in post-1970s (*Dances* 154, 169-174).[3] Rubin suggests that the nickname "Rat" identifies him with "a dark, unnerving creature that burrows into shadowy hidden spaces," and his appearance in Murakami's first piece of work implies that the author was already "rooting around in his psychic past among half-forgotten memories and half-understood images that would surface unpredictably from the 'other world'" in his later works (*Haruki* 33). *A Wild Sheep Chase* nonetheless suggests more meaning to the animal than Rubin suggests. Rats are treated as household pests, not unlike the true individual who is out of place among Generation X in a post-industrialized society. Ironically, while the household pest might still manage to carry out its marginal existence in the household. Rat apparently cannot defend himself against the rapidly-expanding capitalist society.

Though Rat commits suicide, he was nonetheless invaded by the sheep, which had already eliminated part of his mind in order to replace it with itself, and this explains the strange, broken language uttered by Sheep Man. Sheep Man is also found in *Dance, Dance, Dance,* which begins with the protagonist's quest for his ex-girlfriend in Hokkaido. On this quest, he encounters a number of characters: Gotanda, a famous film star and classmate from his junior high school days; Yuki the teenager, who leads him to her father Kiraku Makimura, a famous media personality; prostitutes, not only Kiki (the ex-girlfriend), but other members of an international call girl club; and Yumiyoshi, a simple-minded hotelier. Critics believe that Sheep Man, who stays in a dark, abandoned room that sometimes appears on the sixteenth floor of the hotel, may be whatever the author allows the reader to think

he is: "phantom, conscience, elder wise man, sci-fi figment, symbol of goodness in a rotten world, maybe all of these" (Mitgang). Strecher believes that "from his grotesque appearance to his confused and diffuse personality," the character illustrates the "peculiar reality of combining mainstream and counterculture in a single body" (*Dances* 146). Owing to its darkness, one can read the abandoned room on the sixteenth floor as the realm of the unconscious, where the ultimate source of the self is rooted and which still lays hidden in the new Dolphin hotel. Sheep Man's advice to the protagonist suggests that as long as he keeps dancing to the music, to exercise his mind and willpower, he will not be swallowed by the system, words that strongly echo Shadow's advice in *Hardboiled Wonderland and the End of the World.* Indeed, while many characters die in *Dance, Dance, Dance*—including Gotanda, who is closer to a commercial product than a person, as well as the prostitutes who are traded as mere sex machines—indicating that they are engulfed by the state, Yuki and Yumiyoshi not only stay alive, but are aware of the existence of Sheep Man, meaning they still retain their selfhood. Yumiyoshi, in particular, manages to restore an atmosphere of pastoral simplicity in the rapidly urbanizing Hokkaido—that the protagonist finally makes his way back to Yumiyoshi indicates that he can now "initiate an authentic relationship in the 'real' world" (Iwamoto, "Japan" 889).

The use of human-animal hybrids as metaphor for the postmodern self continues in *The Wind-up Bird Chronicle* (*Nejimakidori kuronikuru*), which is made up of three major narratives interconnected by the mysterious "wind-up bird." The main narrative, set in 1984-85, describes Toru Okada's quest for his cat, and later, his wife Kumiko, both having disappeared from his house, his conflict with Kumiko's brother Noboru Wataya, and his encounters with the Kano sisters. A minor narrative depicts the Nomonhan battle back in 1939 and the friendship between Honda, who later became a fortune-teller and Toru's friend, and Mamiya, who describes their story to Toru. These two narratives roughly make up Book One and Book Two; in Book Three, Toru encounters Nutmeg Akasaka and her son Cinnamon, who help him to become a "healer" of women suffering from unconscious imbalances and, later, to solve the mystery of Kumiko's disappearance.

The Wind-up Bird Chronicle exposes underlying violent events in Japan's recent history, indicating that despite the end of imperialism, there could be a return of barbarism (Fisher 166). As in his analyses of *A Wild Sheep Chase, Dance, Dance, Dance,* and in *Hard-boiled Wonderland and the End of the World,* Strecher treats Noboru, an academic who later turns into the leading politician of Japan, as an symbol of the state, both imperial and postmodern, and Toru's struggle with him, a tension between the individual's will and state power (*Dances* 36, 41). The strongest support for Strecher's thesis is how Noboru strips Creto Kano and Kimiko of their core identities, leaving their conscious and unconscious selves divided and lost (46). Strecher even suggests that Noboru is actually Toru's "other" self, or the dark aspects in his unconscious, which he explores after his descent into the well (50-51). As Toru later becomes a healer, his own equilibrium is restored by the flow of sexual and psychic energies among he and his patients when they rub against and penetrate each other during the therapies, and symbolized by the water that fills and rejuvenates the dry well (53-60).

The slaughter of the zoo animals in the Hsin-Ching Zoo in Manchukuo (Book 3, Ch. 9), one of the most graphically violent scenes in the author's works, as has been noted by several critics. Through Nutmeg's father, the veterinarian in charge of the zoo, we see how Japanese soldiers execute, or "liquidate," the animals that could not be fed during the coming battle. The animals become "sacrificial victims," "emblematic of the uncountable, unnamed human casualties of the war" (Fisher 164). More subtle, however, is this scene's association with Toru's early reference to how horses' behaviour is affected by the phases of the moon, which he compares to Kumiko's pre-menstrual syndrome (29-30). The first slaughter is soon followed by the second one (Book 3, Ch. 26), in which a Chinese prisoner-of-war is executed with a baseball bat, another graphically violent scene that strengthens the parallel between animals and humans.

In *Hard-boiled Wonderland and the End of the World,* the Librarian sadly informs the protagonist that their minds—or the postmodern self—"are not taken in whole," but are "scattered, in different pieces among different beasts, all mixed with pieces from others" (351). In *The Wind-up Bird Chronicle,* after Miyami witnesses how an intelligence officer is skinned alive by the Soviet intelligence officer, "Boris the Manskinner," he feels "like an empty shell" (171), and after the vet witnesses how the zoo animals and the Chinese soldier were executed, he suffers similar feelings. Parallels of how the state violates individuals are found in the stories of the 1980s: Neither Kumiko nor Creta Kano, after being "defiled" by Noboru, ever feel the same again, despite the fact that Creta Kato manages to become a better person with Malta's support. Such irrevocable mutilations done to the self are not merely hinted at by graphic violence, but vividly manifested in the form of the mutilations of animals and human-animal hybrids. Toru's pet cat is a good example. Being a beloved, intimate member of the childless couple, it is symbolically appropriate that he disappears at a

time when the lives of the young couple start to fall apart; he returns when Toru becomes a psychic healer and feels that things are going better in his life. Nonetheless, in his dream, Toru admits to Malta that the cat's tail does not seem to have that big of a bend after his return (536), which means that Malta's earlier prediction, that the cat would not return without some major change, has been right ("Barring some major change, the cat will never come back" [178]). Most surprising, however, is that the tail is all of a sudden found on Malta's body (536), which turns her into a cat-human hybrid.

Such a metamorphosis is not too far-fetched, considering Malta's role as a clairvoyant, whose supernatural power resembles those of a witch, and given the affinity between witches and cats. However, an even more striking and gruesome metamorphosis in the dream is Noboru's fawning secretary, Ushikawa, who appears with a dog's body, reminding us that he is not a full human, but, as a servant of Noboru, his self is split and dehumanized (534-35). In this way, animals not only serve as metaphors for human qualities, but by turning into human-animal hybrids, in a manner that is both dreamy and haunting, they capture the essence of the postmodern identity. Yet the cat's significance can only be appreciated in relation to the wind-up bird. The bird is clearly symbolic of the State, under which people are no more than "dolls set on tabletops, the springs in their backs wound up tight" (526). As such, it resembles the stone statue of a bird that looks as if it is trying to escape from the vacant house in the neighborhood (14), and serves as a stark contrast to the birds flying freely across the wall in *Hard-boiled Wonderland and the End of the World.* Strecher prefers to read it as "a metaphor for time and history," its task being "to keep time flowing forward, creating temporal distance between past and present." Toru gives himself the nickname "Mr. Wind-up Bird," because he ultimately restores the equilibrium in others and himself (Haruki 61-62). This interpretation, nonetheless, is somehow discredited by the way Toru brings a stop to his fantasy of being a wind-up bird after he has got down to the well, thinking he "couldn't go on having fun forever" (256-57).

Why is such a fantasy no good to him? The answer points to one of the riddles left unsolved in the novel: why would the couple name their beloved cat after the much-hated Noboru Wataya? Because their so-called resemblance is unconvincing. The naming, I argue, implies that Toru, who contains a destructive "other" inside him, sometimes exerts his power upon a less powerful animal through the act of naming. If this is the case, the cat's disappearance takes on a more ironic significance, as it dramatizes its resistance to such power. That Toru renames him "Mackerel" is ambiguous (378). It indicates that Toru tries to respect the new self acquired by the cat, yet that he names his cat after a fish, instead of giving him a more "proper" name, might indicate that the cat's resistance to his power has not been all that successful.

Cats continue to be described anthropomorphically in one of Murakami's latest novels, *Kafka on the Shore* (*Umibe no Kafuka*). Following the "spirit" of *Hard-boiled Wonderland and the End of the World* (Rubin, *Haruki* 270), the novel is made up of two interlocking narratives: one describes fifteen-year-old Kafka Tamura's attempted escape from his father's prophecy, his journey to Shikoku, and his finding a place in a small corner of its library; the other recounts the story of old Nakata, who has lost all his memories after a bizarre childhood affliction, and who works as a tracker of lost cats, owing to his strange ability to converse with the animals. Later, Kafka acts out what his father has prophesized—that he will murder his father and have sex with the mother and sister who mysteriously left the family when he was only four, particularly as Nakata's murder of the cat-killer in his attempt to save the cats occurs at exactly the same time as the murder of Kafka's father is reported to have taken place.

As its English translation only came out in 2005, the novel and its multilayered symbols have yet to be explored by critics working in English. Rubin prefers to read it as a story of initiation as much as a positive version of *Hard-boiled Wonderland and the End of the World,* in which Kafka's maturation depends on his decision not to remain in the library, "the other world's suspended state," but to go back to Tokyo and take his place as a responsible member of society (*Haruki* 274). Following the vein of Strecher's analyses, one can easily detect the presence of the state in Kafka's father, who never appears directly in the novel, but re-invents himself as the cat-killer. The cat-killer, by calling himself "Johnnie Walker," the name one of the world's most famous brand names of Scottish whiskey, also transforms himself into a commercial icon, a symbol of globalization and its sweeping power. While his mass killing of cats and his murder by Nakata indicate the cruelty of war and the danger of countering violence with violence, the senseless slaughtering of cats might well be read as a metaphor of how humans, appearing as anthropomorphized cats, are mutilated by the state, be it imperial or post-capitalist. This is not the end of the symbolism in this incident: Nakata's salvation of the cats (hence humans) is soon followed by the tumbling of fish from the sky. As fish are a symbol of Jesus Christ, Nakata's prophecy about the fish, which has come from nowhere, interestingly likens him to the Christian Saviour.

In his post-1995 works, Murakami does not merely use animals as symbols of the fragmented self, he dramatizes how they inspire his characters, rendering Baker's conceptualization much more relevant. At the end of *Hard-boiled Wonderland and the End of the World,* Toru meets up with his young teenage friend May Kasahara, who regrets not being able to show him the "Duck People":

> The duck people have these flat orange feet that are really cute, like they're wearing little kids' rain boots, but they're not made for walking on ice, I guess, because I see them slipping and sliding all over the place, and some even fall on their bottoms. They must not have non-slip treads. So winter is not really a fun season for the duck people. I wonder what they think, deep down inside, about ice and stuff. I bet they don't hate it all that much. It just seems that way to me from watching them. They look like they're living happily enough, even if it's winter, probably just grumbling to themselves, "Ice again? Oh, well. . . ."
>
> (592)

May's affection for the ducks, which, in her eyes have become half-duck, half-human, suggests that she has formed some sort of alliance with them. Like humans, they are subject to more ominous forces (in her description, the cold weather), but unlike most humans, they do not seem much disturbed and manage to retain their autonomy. Having quit school to work anonymously at a wig factory, May manages to find contentment and to think seriously as an individual; by comparison, the protagonist, who seldom thought "seriously" even when he was an adolescent, and only starts to do so as an adult, obviously pales by comparison.

Kafka on the Shore emphasizes the creative value of "becoming-animal." Nataka, always addressing himself in the third person, gives us the feeling that he is coming out of his human self and becoming even closer to the cats with which he converses. The black cat comments that despite Nakata's childhood affliction and its damaging effects, his simple life is "a pretty good life" after all (50). The cat has probably felt that Nakata's life is very similar to his own. Despite leading a simple life, the black cat is portrayed as possessing a strong individuality. Upon noticing that Nakata's shadow is very faint (which associates him with the protagonist in the Town of *Hard-boiled Wonderland and the End of the World*), he urges him to reclaim the other half of his shadow (53-54), meaning to make his selfhood become whole again.

The creative alliance between human and animal is nonetheless best exemplified in "the boy named Crow" who, as the plot unfolds, reveals himself to be Kafka's alter-ego, spurring him on his journey, and conversing with him at some critical points of his life. In the un-numbered chapter entitled "The Boy Named Crow," found between Chapter 46 and Chapter 47, the crow attacks the cat-killer, who seems to have been resurrected from his death after his murder by Nakata in Chapter 16 and is once again describing how he uses the souls of the cats to make up a huge flute for no particular reason. While the episode makes us skeptical of whether the cat-killer and what he symbolizes can ever be eradicated (as there is no evidence that he is killed, even in this chapter), it also strengthens the link between Nakata and Kafka, who never cross paths in the novel, and makes the boy named Crow's message to Kafka, that he must get his "self" back (417), much more urgent.[4] Kafka, unlike the protagonist in *Hard-boiled Wonderland and the End of the World,* indeed comes out of his journey as "the world's toughest 15-year-old" and returns to his society (4,505). As Nataka in the novel is not only an old man, but serves as the "other" of Kafka, his death should not be read tragically or as a sign that he has failed to reclaim his shadow and his selfhood.

That these creative alliances are found in works after 1995, the year when the Kobe earthquake and the sarin gas attack took place, is not coincidental, and my discussion will move onto **"Honey Pie" ("Hachimitsu pai"),** the last story in *After the Quake* (*Kami no kodomotachi wa mina odoru*), before fleshing out further the significance of such a creative turn. **"Honey Pie"** tells of Junpei, who has secretly loved Sayoko throughout the years despite her marriage to, and subsequent divorce from, his best friend, Takatsuki. Takatsuki urges Junpei to marry Sayoko, even revealing to him that she is also in love with him, but Junpei thinks that this violates his standard of "decency." It is only after the earthquake has struck Japan that he is plagued by a feeling of rootlessness, suddenly feeling that he is not "connected" to anyone or anything at all, that he considers a life with Sayoko (124).

After the earthquake, Sayoko's daughter Sala has nightmares in which she finds a scary "Earthquake Man" threatening to stuff all the people into a small box, and so Junpei comes to the house to make up bedtime stories for her. He invents Masakichi, a bear who collects honey to sell to the humans in town, which he has modelled after his own personality; he also invents Tonkichi, a bear who catches salmon and trades it for Masakichi's honey, modelled after Takatsuki. When all the fish flee from the river, Tonkichi refuses the free honey from Masakichi. Masakichi and Tonkichi finally come up with a solution: Tonkichi will make honey pies out of Masakichi's honey, and Masakichi will sell them to the town. As he finishes his fable, Junpei decides to follow his desire to form a happy family with Sayoko and Sala.

While the story of the bears can be taken as a simple allegory of Junpei's own life, there is more to the character of Masakichi, who speaks human language. As Junpei describes him: "Meanwhile, Masakichi looked just like a bear, and so the people would say, 'OK, he knows how to count, and he can talk and all, but when you get right down to it he's still a bear.' So Masakichi didn't really belong to either world—the bear world or the people world" (**"Honey Pie"** 105).

That the "bear" falls in between the bear world and the human world, belonging to neither, means that in the process of its creation it has turned into a "hybrid." Junpei learns from his own creation, which enables him to think much more creatively than he normally could. Having claimed his selfhood, he feels that no one can ever threaten to put him and others in the small box of Sala's dream, so reminiscent of the state so prominent in Murakami's other fiction.

It should be noted that Murakami does not glorify the power of "becoming-animal." **"Super-Frog Saves Tokyo" ("Kaeru-kun, Tôkyô o sukuu"),** also in *After the Quake,* offers a dystopian version of "becoming-animal," in the form of "becoming-monster." Katagiri finds a giant frog in his apartment one day, who urges him to help save Tokyo from a second earthquake caused by Worm, a monster residing underground who has been aroused from his slumber. He will not have to do any real fighting, only stand behind Frog and offer him verbal and spiritual support during the fight. Before the battle takes place, Katagiri gets shot by a man, but when he wakes up in the hospital, the nurse tells him that no earthquake has struck Tokyo, and he was found passed out on the ground unharmed. After the nurse leaves, Frog appears to Katagiri again, reassuring him that Worm has been defeated, and the "whole fight occurred in the area of imagination," which is the "precise location of the battlefield" (98-99).

We are inclined to interpret Frog as an imagined character existing in Katagiri's mind, borne out of his desire for recognition. Frog, though realistically portrayed as an animal, appears well-educated and well-read, and claims to have "the profoundest respect" for Katagiri (89), who has an unglamorous job at the bank and who has sacrificed his life to care single-handedly for his ungrateful younger brothers and sisters. By agreeing to support Frog, Katagiri attempts to form a creative alliance with this superior animal, which he hopes will enable him to escape from a society that labels him a "loser." The animal is nonetheless insufficient by human standards: he possesses no "balls," and when he laughs, he shows that he has no teeth either (95). After he has fallen asleep, worms and other insects crawl out of his body and devour him; they then swarm the room and invade Katagiri's body, and only disappear as the nurse enters and turns on the light.

Frog's predicament is reminiscent of Kafka's protagonist in *Metamorphoses,* who turns into an insect and finally dies, making the story a statement of life's absurdity and despair. Roland Kelts contends that the meditative power of the stories in *After the Quake* derive from "the characters' discovery of their hollowness" and their "often uncertain attempts to fill it." While Junpei in **"Honey Pie"** is optimistic that his future will be rid of uncertainty, Katagiri remains unsure about this. Murakami, while discussing **"Super-Frog,"** [**"Super-Frog Saves Tokyo"**] vaguely mentions that the "evil" comes from "within" (Kelts 2002), a remark that echoes Frog's "The enemy is.. . . . inside me" (100). "Becoming-animal" therefore offers only a possibility of freedom, but the animal is obviously no more reliable than the human; Frog's fatigue and exhaustion, which lead him to be devoured by worms, indicate the importance of faith and perseverance in humans.

In *Underground: The Tokyo Gas Attack and the Japanese Psyche* (*Andaguraundo*), made up of interviews of the sarin gas attack victims and the Aum cult members, Murakami describes the danger of losing one's ego and "self" (201) and of offering some part of it to "greater System or Order" (203). The animals in his fiction confirm the importance that he accords to the self, as well as necessitating a reconceptualization of the postmodern animal. While Baker focuses on how "becoming-animal" offers a creative way of escaping from state repression, Murakami uses animals as an emblem of selfhood, human-animal hybrids as manifestations of the fragmented self, and "becoming-animal" as an inspiring and creative process in which humans can fare better in a late-capitalist society that is never entirely free from the imperial shadow. This, perhaps, explains why the elephants are spared in the zoo massacre in *The Wind-up Bird Chronicle,* after all other animals have been killed: because they are "too large" to be done away with, their survival suggests that even though human lives are readily wiped out, their consciousness is not, and should not readily be obliterated.

"Becoming-animal," with its tinge of optimism, has become more prominent in his post-1995 works. **"Honey Pie,"** the story of a writer, even looks like Murakami's own signature of such creativity, imagination, and optimism. All these signs of optimism might indicate his concern for his fellow Japanese, for and about whom he has always been writing (Gregory, Miyawaki, and McCaffery). His message is that they should live their lives creatively and imaginatively,

adding that such creativity and imagination should be sustained by faith and perseverance. Katagiri, a middle-aged man, seems to lack these attributes, but children and teenage characters in *The Wind-up Bird Chronicle, Kafka on the Shore* and others tend to inspire adults or are simply superior to them. The favourable portraits of the younger generations in Murakami's work is not surprising: he describes what he calls a "generational sense of responsibility," namely that he feels the need to pass something onto his young readers (Rubin, *Haruki* 291-92). It is not too much to suggest that with no children of his own, he enjoys an intimacy with his young characters, who are like his young readers: both are dear to him, like his own children.

Notes

1. Loughman uses *A Slow Boat to China* (*Chūgokuyuki no surō bōto,* 1980) to suggest Japanese loss of connection with their cultural past, of which China and Chinese culture form a significant part.

2. Kami is translated as "gods, deities, or spirits," but also means "above," "superior," or the "numinous or sacred nature" (Kitagawa 12).

3. Rat wishes that he had been born in nineteenth century Russia, gotten involved in the "something-or-other Rebellion" and finally been exiled to Siberia (76); in reality, he has gone to the wilderness of Hokkaido, a place which had yet to be urbanized at that time, in order to detach himself from the city.

4. Kafka in fact means "crow" in Czech; the crow also reminds the reader of the cult movie, *The Crow* (1994), where the bird, as the carrier of dead souls, helps the dead protagonist to seek revenge on his enemies.

Works Cited

Baker, Steve. "Leopards in the Temple." *The Postmodern Animal.* London: Reaktion Books, 2000. 99-134.

Fisher, Susan. "An Allegory of Return: Murakami Haruki's *The Wind-Up Bird Chronicle.*" *Comparative Literature Studies* 37.2 (Summer 2000): 155-70.

Gregory, Sinda, Toshifumi Miyawaki, and Larry McCaffery. "It Don't Mean a Thing, If It Ain't Got That Swing: An Interview with Haruki Murakami." *The Review of Contemporary Fiction* 22.2 (June 2002): 111-27.

Iwamoto, Yoshio. "Japan—*Dance Dance Dance*" (book review). *World Literature Today* 68.4 (Autumn 1994): 889.

———. "A Voice from Postmodern Japan: Haruki Murakami." *World Literature Today* 27.2 (Spring 1993): 295-300.

Kelts, Roland. "Quake II: Haruki Murakami vs The End of the World." *Village Voice* 25 September-1 October 2002 <http://www.villagevoice.com/news/0239,kelts,38605,1.html (21 February 2006).

Kitagawa, Joseph M. *Religion in Japanese History.* New York: Columbia UP, 1966.

Loughman, Celeste. "Japan—*The Elephant Vanishes.*" (book review). *World Literature Today* 68.2 (Spring 1994): 434.

———. "No Place I Was Meant to Be: Contemporary Japan in the Short Fiction of Haruki Murakami." *World Literature Today* 71.1 (Winter 1997): 87-94.

Mitgang, Herbert. "Looking for America, or Is It Japan?" *New York Times* 3 January 1994 <www.murakami.ch/about_hm/bookreviews/bookreview_the_elephant_vanishes.html (12 Febraury 2006).

Murakami, Haruki. *Dance Dance Dance.* 1988. Trans. Alfred Birnbaum. London: Vintage, 2003.

———. "The Dancing Dwarf." 1984. *The Elephant Vanishes.* Trans. Alfred Birnbaum. London: Vintage, 2003. 241-65.

———. "The Elephant Vanishes." 1986. *The Elephant Vanishes.* Trans. Alfred Birnbaum. London: Vintage, 2003. 307-27.

———. *Hard-boiled Wonderland and the End of the World.* 1985. Trans. Alfred Birnbaum. London: Vintage, 1993.

———. *Hear the Wind Sing.* 1979. Trans. Alfred Birnbaum. Tokyo: Kodansha International, 1987.

———. "Honey Pie." 2000. *after the quake.* Trans. Alfred Birnbaum. London: Vintage, 2003. 103-32.

———. *Kafka on the Shore.* 2002. Trans. Phillip Gabriel. London: Harvill, 2005.

———. "The Kangaroo Communique." 1983. *The Elephant Vanishes.* Trans. Alfred Birnbaum. London: Vintage, 2003. 51-65.

———. *Pinball, 1973.* 1980. Trans. Alfred Birnbaum. Tokyo: Kodansha International, 1985.

———. "A Poor-Aunt Story." 1980. *New Yorker* 77.38 (3 Dec 2001): 8.

———. "Super-Frog Saves Tokyo." 2000. *after the quake.* Trans. Alfred Birnbaum. London: Vintage, 2003. 82-102.

———. *Underground: The Tokyo Gas Attack and the Japanese Psyche.* Trans. Alfred Birnbaum. London: Vintage, 2001.

———. *A Wild Sheep Chase.* 1982. Trans. Alfred Birnbaum. London: Vintage, 2003.

———. *The Wind-up Bird Chronicle.* 1994-95. Trans. Alfred Birnbaum. London: Vintage, 2003.

Napier, Susan. "The Dystopian Imagination: From the Asylum through the Labyrinth to the End of the World." *The Fantastic in Modern Japanese Literature: The Subversion of Modernity.* London: Routledge, 1996. 181-223.

Okada, Sumie. "Traces of a Different Sort of 'Groupism' in *Norwegian Wood* by Haruki Murakami." *Japanese Writers and the West.* Basingstoke: Palgrave Macmillan, 2003. 61-73.

Rubin, Jay. *Haruki Murakami and the Music of Words.* 2003. London: Vintage, 2005.

———. "Murakami Haruki's Two Poor Aunts Tell Everything They Know About Sheep, Wells, Unicorns, Proust, Elephants, and Magpies." *Ōe and Beyond: Fiction in Contemporary Japan.* Eds. Stephen Snyder and Philip Gabriel. Honolulu: U of Hawaii P, 1999. 177-98.

———. "The Other World of Murakami Haruki." *Japan Quarterly* 39.4 (1992): 490-500.

Strecher, Matthew. "Beyond 'Pure' Literature: Mimesis, Formula, and the Postmodern in the Fiction of Murakami Haruki." *The Journal of Asian Studies* 57.2 (May 1998): 354-78.

———. *Dances with Sheep: The Quest for Identity in the Fiction of Murakami Haruki.* Ann Arbor, MI: Center for Japanese Studies, University of Michigan, 2002.

———. *Haruki Murakami's The Wind-up Bird Chronicle: A Reader's Guide.* London: The Continuum International Publishing Group Inc., 2002.

———. "Magical Realism and the Search for Identity in the Fiction of Murakami Haruki." *The Journal of Japanese Studies* 25.2 (Summer 1999): 263-98.

Snyder, Stephen. "Two Murakamis and Marcel Proust: Memory as Form in Contemporary Japanese Fiction." *In Pursuit of Contemporary East Asian Culture.* Eds. Xiaobing Tang and Stephen Snyder. Boulder: Westview Press, 1996. 69-83.

Daniel Trilling (review date 4 June 2007)

SOURCE: Trilling, Daniel. "Culture Industry." *New Statesman* 136, no. 4847 (4 June 2007): 58.

[*In the following review, Trilling remarks that* After Dark *focuses on portraying modern city life rather than connecting the reader to the characters or the plot.*]

"People's memories are the fuel they burn to stay alive," says a character in Haruki Murakami's **After Dark.** "Advertising fillers in the newspaper, philosophy books, dirty pictures in a magazine, a bundle of ten-thousand-yen bills: when you feed 'em to the fire, they're all just paper."

Murakami's internationally popular novels use elements such as these as their building blocks. His characters inhabit worlds crammed full with the detritus of consumer capitalism: a starting point for novels characterised by the barroom philosophising of his characters and a beguiling narrative style that skips between realism and the supernatural. For readers, it is a kind of comfort food; an easy way into the work.

In *After Dark,* a short novel that takes place over the course of a single night, we are shown a world made almost entirely from clichés: somewhere at the heart of a neon-lit city a girl in an all-night diner (Mari) is approached by a young man (Takahashi). The city is Japanese, but from all we know it could just as easily be London or Beijing or New York. Mari is reluctant to talk at first, but Takahashi perseveres. He is a musician on his way to band practice; she is running away from something, but won't say what. The action moves from the diner to a seedy hotel where we encounter a beaten-up prostitute and her Chinese gangster pimps. Naturally, the gangsters are out for revenge.

It is almost as if Murakami doesn't want the physical details of plot, character and location to trouble the reader's attention too much. They appear almost incidental to the novel's aim of evoking the sense of altered perception that comes to us during the hours when we should be sleeping. From the book's opening passage, where we swoop down on the city through the eyes of a bird, Murakami seeks to detach us from the action.

The effect is otherworldly, but it's also creepy. Mari has a sister, the stunningly beautiful Eri, who went to sleep one day a few months ago and hasn't woken up since. In chapters interspersed with the main narrative, Murakami takes us into her bedroom, where a dream-like sequence involving a flickering TV screen unfolds. A third-person narrator conspires with us as we spy on the sleeping woman: "The room is dark, but our eyes gradually adjust to the darkness," he tells us. Most of the women in this novel are there to be used or abused—be it Mari as she is pursued by Takahashi, or the hotel worker who has fled a violent past, or indeed the Chinese prostitute—and in the character of Eri, Murakami has placed a good-looking woman in suspended animation, seemingly for our viewing pleasure. It's a device more normally associated with cinema, and there is a knowing nod to Jean-Luc Godard in the name of the hotel: Alphaville.

This is a strange approach to fiction. While films necessarily alienate us to some extent from the people on screen, novels are often seen as a way of exploring the inner worlds of their characters. In previous novels, Murakami has done just that. But here, the psychology has been stripped away so that the endlessly repeated banalities of modern city life can float freely.

In the novel's opening and its conclusion, cities are described as machine-like, where every inhabitant is forced to live both as an individual and as "a nameless part of the collective entity". But even here, the author doesn't appear to be making an explicit point.

The narrator of Murakami's 1994 novel *Dance Dance Dance,* a journalist who makes a living writing PR puff-pieces and fillers for glossy magazines, likens his vocation to shovelling "cultural snow". Throughout his career, Murakami has been engaged in a similar pursuit, only he doesn't shovel; he sculpts. *After Dark,* in its brevity, is less a sculpture than an intricately formed snowflake. It's pretty, for sure, but look at it for too long and it's liable to melt into nothingness.

Rio Otomo (essay date June 2007)

SOURCE: Otomo, Rio. "Narratives, the Body and the 1964 Tokyo Olympics." *Asian Studies Review* 31, no. 2 (June 2007): 117-32.

[*In the following essay, Otomo comments on* A Wild Sheep Chase *and* Sydney! *to demonstrate how texts written about the Olympic Games reveal the social and political climate at the time.*]

INTRODUCTION

In this paper I investigate media representations of the 1964 Tokyo Olympic Games by tracing the stories of three Olympic athletes that were prominent in the mass media at the time. In revisiting them, my aim is to explore the relationship between the spectacles of sporting performances and the narratives that are generated around them. I focus in particular on the ways in which these narratives interact with the production of broader social discourses.

The body in action generally evokes story-telling in viewers. The initial story, the body-text authored by the actor, is a private and unique inscription on his or her body. This body-text is, however, often overlayed by other narratives to generate different meanings. The relationships between such narratives are unsettling, giving evidence to each other while approaching different ends. The spectacles of the performing body exhibited at sporting events always spawn various narratives, through which we can observe aspects of the social and cultural norms of the time. A single performance can be brought to viewers as multiple stories that disseminate fast and far through the electronic media, and some of which have a disempowering effect on the performer. Three stories from the 1964 Tokyo Olympic Games that I introduce in this essay exemplify such instances. All three exhibit traces of the modern discourse of the body—the human body to be disciplined and managed and to be "clean-and-proper", as part of Japan's on-going modernisation project since the Meiji period (1868-1912)—which was revitalised by the mass media during the Tokyo Olympic Games.[1] By re-telling these stories, I wish to critique the ways in which this particular discourse undermined the agency of the performer and assisted the dominant paradigm of postwar Japan—namely, the ethics of hard work (the body as a means) and the belief in moving forward. This essay, therefore, does not have an ambition to present alternative accounts of history, but wishes to further enrich the growing body of critiques of sports, media and 1960s Japan.

The decade after 1960 occupies a special place in my memory, which has, in hindsight, been driven by and to a certain degree shaped my research in literary studies to date. In the lead up to 10 October 1964, primary-school children, myself included, were told to learn from Baron de Coubertin, the father of the modern Olympic Games, that the most important thing in life was not to come first, but to take part; and not to have conquered, but to have fought well. Once the Games started, however, the mood of the classroom quickly shifted, and talk was all about medals, heroes and our national strength. In the preceding years preparations for the *Tōkyō orinpikku* had already set in motion rapid changes in the social landscape not only in the metropolitan areas but throughout Japan: the disappearance of rice paddies, the appearance of new roads, new buildings, and in our homes new electronic appliances one after another. It was felt by many that our lives were improving and that achieving a better life was within our reach. The spectacles of the performing body seen during the Games manifested and paraded the ethics of hard work that matched the emotions of the viewers, who felt ready to work harder to rise higher.

The date, 10 October 1964, was thus marked in the minds of many ordinary Japanese as the beginning of Japan's "rise". And this "rise" was imagined communally through the images of athletic bodies, which we watched through the mediation of TV cameras, and through the stories that were brought to us by the media en masse. The narratives of individual athletes were told in such a way that they would draw forth in the viewers a sense of national unity and pride in an autonomous nation. These narratives that accompanied spectacles of athletes' bodies emphasised that they

were the embodiment of will-power, self-discipline and self-control. In short these (model) individuals were highlighted as *self*-motivated and *auto*-powered. What is behind the story-telling as such is the inadvertent approval of the systemic operation of power on the private body. By encouraging citizens' self-governance of their own bodies, state power can operate more efficiently and thoroughly without manifesting itself as an oppressive authority.[2] One could say that those who led the government after the war without a fundamental shift in their thinking were thus able to realise their nationalist goals without evoking the word "Emperor". Indeed, as state power went underground or became inconspicuous in the postwar period, it became harder to imagine sources of oppression. Yet, as I attempt to argue in this paper, the private body was not altogether less subjugated than it had been under the militarist regime, and its passivity was intensified as people internalised the project of modernity as their own.

Being fascinated by their newly acquired TV screens, the people tasted the pleasure of being *spectators* whose own bodies were rendered inert and passive. The early 1960s saw the beginning of Japan's consumer society, in which people believed what they saw on the screen to reflect their reality or achievable utopian dreams. Hosting the Olympic Games was the culmination of Japan's postwar economic recovery and at the same time symbolised the recovery of a once-dispersed spirituality, national unity and pride.[3] By watching the smaller figures of Japanese athletes competing well against the much larger physiques of Europeans, Americans and Russians, Japanese audiences could re-imagine Japan as a unified nation-state.[4] The momentum of this, which was imagined as the birth of a renewed nation, was produced through a particular discourse of the body which, as I mentioned, harks back to Japan's modernisation project from the Meiji period.[5] Japan in the 1960s entertained the same ideals that it had before the war, and the effect of the war on the discourse of the body was interruption rather than a shift of paradigm, which I underscore through my stories below.[6]

The electronic board in the main stadium displayed three words in Latin—*"faster, higher and stronger"*—through which one could trace a belief in European Enlightenment Humanism, representing the limitless potential of mankind. In the Japanese context these words are the very motto for economic recovery, signifying the dominant mode of production for factory workers—"produce *faster, more and better.*" As a late-developing capitalist state Japan prioritised the interests of large corporations, and as a result, corporations provided citizens with the time and facilities needed for sporting activities. The benefit for corporations was three-fold: the sense of unity among employees; character-building to become company warriors; and advertising. It was also considered to be effective in keeping at bay the union movement and strikes.[7] The Tokyo Olympic Games took place in this climate and produced much needed folk heroes, and through the images of their bodies the discourse of winning was disseminated to all walks of life, continuing a discourse from 1930s' prewar Japan rather than merely reacting to defeat in the war.

For the purpose of this paper—to revisit 1960s Japan and analyse the dominant discourse of the body—I propose a device through which a critical standpoint should emerge. It is to draw on the articles written by Mishima Yukio (1925-70),[8] who is more pertinent to this topic than most other writers from that era. Mishima was more prolific as a novelist in the 1950s, but it was in the 1960s that he became exceptionally versatile in his work and came to perform the role of cultural guru. His ubiquitous presence in the mass media was such that whenever one turns a stone to research any aspect of that era, one is likely to come across Mishima's name. Although he later gained notoriety for his suicide and came to be regarded as an eccentric, he wrote conservatively, always attuned to the needs of the general public, which earned him a large readership. He frequently published essays for women's magazines and newspapers in addition to his regular contributions to literary magazines; Mishima Yukio was "media-savvy" even by today's standards.[9]

During the Tokyo Olympic Games Mishima took on the role of sports reporter, gaining an official pass to access the various sporting venues. On the one hand, he shared the heightened emotions of the spectators and the TV viewers, and hence his writing reflected the general atmosphere of the time, which serves this discussion effectively. On the other hand, the issue of the human body was his personal and literary interest, which he tackled throughout his life. This places him in a unique and privileged position in this discussion. In 1955, at the age of 30, Mishima began bodybuilding, and by the time of the Tokyo Olympics he had accomplished a masculinist makeover of his body and started to pursue martial arts. The discourse of the body in question which highlights one's willpower to manage and train one's body is known to be immanent in all kinds of martial arts. Mishima internalised this discourse and put it into practice, which became evident in his essays and dialogues published between 1965 and 1969 in *Eirei no koe* [*Voice of the spirits*], *Taiwa: Nihonjin ron* [*A dialogue: On Japanese*], *Hagakure nyūmon* [*Hagakure for beginners*], *Taiyō to tetsu* [*Sun and steel*] and *Bunka bōei ron* [*On the defence of our culture*]. It should be noted that the full list of his writings exhibits a shift after his involvement in the Olympic Games, and that these books

were written in the subsequent years. The ways in which the discourse of the body that Mishima embodied may have precipitated the writer towards his death, however, are beyond the scope of this paper.[10]

The three stories that I tell below arethose of: the women's volleyball team, which won the gold medal; the leader of the male gymnastics team, who performed in spite of injury; and the marathon bronze medallist, who later killed himself, leaving letters of apology behind. I call these stories: 'Managing the woman's body', 'Overcoming pain' and 'Resistance of the body'. As a coda to these three stories, I consider contemporary writer Murakami Haruki (b. 1949) in the final section 'Notes on the discourse of *konjō* [willpower]'. Murakami's report on the Sydney Olympic Games (2000) reveals a stark contrast to Mishima's Tokyo Olympics reports, which offers us a small opening to contemplate a possible shift between 1960s and present-day Japan.

MANAGING THE WOMAN'S BODY

Mishima Yukio, not yet viewed as an ultranationalist in 1964, wrote enthusiastic newspaper articles as a sports reporter, putting into words the shared emotions of the people at large. One of the highlights Mishima featured was the final match of the women's volleyball competition—the USSR vs Japan—which resulted in a gold medal to Japan. The whole nation was glued to the TV screen and together shed tears of joy at the end of the game. The title of Mishima's article reads *'Kanojo mo naita, watashi mo naita: joshi barē'* [Her tears, and my tears, too: the women's volleyball][11]:

> The volleyball court is like a shiny man-made lawn, spread on the shiny surface of the floor. It shows clearly the reflections of white shoes, red shorts and judges' yellow flags. That is why the members of the Japanese team often take a little towel out of their green shorts and wipe their sweat off the floor in a womanly manner, looking as if they were polishing the floor . . . Kasai [the team leader and the setter] is a wonderful party host who can tell at a glance which of her guests are finishing their dish and directs her waiters to serve the table immaculately. The Soviet Union team utterly exhausted themselves by receiving such an elaborate banquet.

The Japanese athletes performed their signature innovation, a roiling receive, which often made the floor wet with their sweat. Wiping the floor straight away to avoid slipping on it was the quick solution to the problem in a game in which time mattered. These athletes had been named the "Witches from the East" in Europe two years earlier for their superlative skills in the sport. Volleyball is not about femininity; it is about skill. In Japanese media reports, however, their womanliness—that is, their "Japanese" womanliness—

came to the fore, as in Mishima's article above. In other words, the narratives of their sports performances were predetermined to be narratives of virtuous women's self-sacrificial deeds for the nation.[12] Here is my attempt to tell a different story about these athletes.

One of the growing industries in postwar Japan was textile production. In the novel *Kinu to meisatsu* (1964) (*Silk and Insight*) published in the same month as the Olympics, Mishima had written about the conditions of textile workers.[13] This novel depicts the nascent stage of Japanese-style corporate management, in which the capitalist plays the role of a father and manages his workers and production through the use of the family metaphor. The novel anticipates the proliferation of the style of management that later acquired universal renown as the (alleged) key to Japan's so-called "economic miracle". As a part of Japan's modernisation project, which began in the Meiji period, corporations were keen to develop a personnel management system that emphasised harmony by re-imagining the factory as a family-like moral community consisting of a caring employer (as the father) and faithful employees (as his children). This style of management tapped into the minds of ordinary Japanese who were already accustomed to a private life under social constraints; that is, constrained for the greater cause of achieving the unity of the whole. As early as 1913, an American model of modern management was adopted by textile companies such as Kanebō and Nichibō, along with Mitsubishi Electric and Nihon Electric.[14] In the postwar years the same management system, one that was supported by the story of a corporation as a big family, was reintroduced, in order to improve production levels and quality control.

By 1954 large textile and electronics companies in the Tokyo, Osaka and Nagoya districts were systematically recruiting their factory workers from regional Japan, where family farming was not profitable enough to cope with inflation. Rural agricultural communities, recently decimated by the war, were now made increasingly unsustainable by the open market economy, the introduction of machinery, and the frenzy of land development led by the government. Although this trend started as soon as industrialisation began in Japan, its extent in the 1950s and 1960s far surpassed previous eras. The twenty years of running the *shūdan shūshoku* [the mass recruitment transport scheme] trains involved more than 550,000 young people aged either fifteen or eighteen, reaching its peak in 1964. In this year alone 100,000 of them boarded these trains.[15] The *shūdan shūshoku* was organised by a collaboration between local governments, industries, schools and the National Rail, which offered discount group tickets and additional train services. From 1965 onwards more students proceeded to complete their high-school education and consequently became harder to recruit. The scheme eventually ended, with the last train arriving at Tokyo's Ueno Station in 1975. During this period the junior high-school graduate recruits were dubbed the "Golden Eggs", a name that reflects the role that these young people, who were actually 15 year-old child workers, played in the rapid economic growth of postwar Japan.

In March every year a large number of these young girls, freshly graduated from both junior high and high school, were sent in groups to textile firm dormitories where they could choose to continue their education through evening school along with their full-time work.[16] They could also pursue their interest in various sports by joining company teams. Japanese textile companies were always keen to promote their company names through sporting events, which is still the case today. They could recruit young female athletes from their own pool of workers living in the dormitories and give them training over a period of years to make successful athletes. These women were separated from their families, going home only once or twice a year, for the New Year celebration in winter and the *Bon* festival in summer. They were often financially contributing to their family at home. The 1964 women's volleyball gold medal team consisted of such women.[17] Behind the team's success, there were hundreds of similar women who shared the same dream but did not make it to the national team.

The official documentary film of the Tokyo Olympics was directed by Ichikawa Kon.[18] After briefly showing the girls' emotionally charged faces at the winning moment, the camera's gaze comes to rest on the man on the bench, their coach Daimatsu Hirofumi, whose name later circulated throughout Japan as the real hero behind this success. Four years later Daimatsu became a parliamentarian, with the support of the conservative Liberal Democratic Party. A popular narrative that repeatedly appeared in the media was that Coach Daimatsu would never allow the girls to take a day off from their training, even when they were experiencing period pain. He himself writes:

> I can tell when the players have their periods. Their sweat during practice is different from the others': they sweat greasy sweat. Yet, as they keep practising a year or two even with their periods, they will have bodies that can endure the same practice even with cramps. They cease to have downtime. In short, whenever they face games, their period no longer hampers their performance.[19]

Daimatsu emphasised his knowledge of the female body and the importance of overcoming it, statements that the popular media faithfully replicated in print.[20]

This Spartan coach, whom these girls adored, was narrativised in the media as a trustworthy and insightful man. He was, in a sense, the ideal father that, as a nation, Japan needed, particularly after the head of state lost his political power and spiritual charisma. The famous words of *"oni no Daimatsu"* [Daimatsu, the Demon] as he was affectionately called, are *"damatte, ore ni tsuitekoi"* [Just trust and follow me without question] and *"naseba naru"* [Where there is a will, there is a way], phrases that one can easily relate to the words of the emperor—as in the wartime propaganda—and hence the dominant discourses of the 1930s that effectively mobilised the nation for military expansion. The spectacle of the performance of the women's volleyball team that captured the nation's heart was thus quickly replaced by the words of the Father who managed and controlled the women's bodies. This reveals that the male-dominated sports journalism of the time was sensitive to the clash between an imagined femininity and the masculine properties of sporting performance. It was more appropriate to present these physically and mentally strong women as enduring and dutiful daughters than as heroes, despite their heroic achievement. The women themselves did not articulate their cause at the time (and perhaps do not even now), choosing to speak the same language as their coach.[21]

Following the Olympics, there was a period of volleyball frenzy among schoolgirls throughout Japan. In 1966, I found myself one of just over 100 girls putting their names down for the volleyball club at my junior high school; more than half of the 13 year-old girls were willing to go through mock-Daimatsu training every day after school.[22] In following years came series of *manga*, TV dramas and animations that are called *"supokon-kei"* [or *supōtsu-konjō-kei*] which can be translated as the "willpower-in-sports-genre". Among these, some popular titles shown as TV series are *Sain wa V* (*The sign is V,* 1968), *Atakku nanbā wan* (*Attack no. 1,* 1969), *Kyojin no hoshi* (*Star of the Giants,* 1968), *Ashita no Jō* (*Tomorrow's Jo,* 1970) and *Ēsu o nerae* (*Aim at the ace,* 1973).[23] These stories, which featured attractive young athletes, continued to send young viewers monological messages about the importance of endurance, patience, self-sacrifice, faithfulness and teamwork. The essence of the sentiments narrated in such stories, I would add, was not a far cry from that of the prewar militarist discourse.

OVERCOMING PAIN

Ono Takashi, the highly accomplished gymnast and team leader of the entire Japanese Olympic team, had already won gold medals for the horizontal bar at both the Melbourne Olympics (1956) and the Rome Olympics (1960), along with other medals over three

Olympics, by the time he was asked to lead the Tokyo Olympic team at the age of 32. There was a phrase that caught on in the media: *"oni ni kanabō, ono ni tetsubō"* which rhymed as "the iron bar for *Oni* [the ogre],[24] and the horizontal bar for Ono". The Japanese Men's Gymnastic Team was aiming at the team gold medal, and Ono's performance on the bar was a crucial element in achieving this. Trying to overcome he handicap anticipated his relatively advanced age would be, Ono overtrained and damaged his right shoulder in the lead up to his horizontal bar performance. The team doctor injected anaesthetic into his shoulder to reduce the pain, which inadvertently made him lose sensation in his whole arm. Ono then exercised vigorously to regain the sensation but with limited success, which resulted in further excruciating pain. He resorted to electric acupuncture and performed his horizontal bar routine despite the pain. While the nation watched Ono's performance, eagerly awaiting news of the team gold medal, reporters and commentators repeatedly reminded the audience of the fact that Ono was performing *despite the pain* for the sake of the team, and the nation. The spectacle of the beautiful performance of Ono's body was overtaken by a narrative about his pain and his willpower. Mishima, viewing this performance from the close distance of the journalists' seating area, wrote:

> The horizontal bar had been cruelly attacking his shoulder for some time. His shoulder then became the enemy of the perfection that he [Ono] was aiming to achieve. It was assaulting him from within, as if it had been a spy who sold his soul to the enemy camp.[25]

Mishima uses military metaphors such as "spy" and "enemy", while he also defines gymnastics as a meeting point of beauty and power, and the kind of sport that is closest to art.

> Of all sports gymnastics approaches art; the more it emphasises the value of the form, the closer it gets to art . . . If our body is a door with rusty hinges . . . the body of gymnasts is like a revolving door. It endlessly vacillates from extreme flexibility to extreme tension and from emptiness to sudden fullness, transporting its power at will. And the performance which requires the highest levels of balance and strength is presented quietly in the most graceful form. At that very moment we are seeing not the human body, but the unworldly form created by human spirits.[26]

Mishima thus saw gymnastics as the site at which man's will-power overcame the body, and in his imagination this was done for the sake of art. But there is another story that contrasts with Mishima's storytelling.

The team leader for the women's gymnastic team was Ono Kiyoko, the wife of Ono Takashi. When given the chance, she could not turn down the opportunity to lead the Olympic team, even though she had given birth to their second child just one year before the Olympics.[27] As her husband approached the horizontal bar to perform with his partially numbed arm, she whispered into his ear, "Please do not die; we have children".[28] If his shoulder should give way, he could have had a fatal fall during his performance. What she meant to tell him was, "Please do not die for the country, but live for me and our children. Be father and husband before being a national hero", words that immediately resonate with *"Kimi shinitamou koto na-kare"*, Yosano Akiko's widely-loved early poem (1904) in which she tells her brother not to die in the war, and because of which she was accused of disloyalty to the Emperor and the country.[29] Even in the 1960s Ono Kiyoko did not wish to risk any criticism of this kind, and she did not tell her story until much later, in the year 2000. In the same interview she recalled a time when she was asked by her home prefecture to represent the district in *kokutai* [the National Sports Festival] just three months after her first baby was born. She says, "The men who make decisions do not know a woman's body".[30] Ono Kiyoko later had a successful political career with the right-wing faction of the Liberal Democratic Party, and her role included the area of women's health. Incidentally, Ono Kiyoko was one of the female TV demonstrators on *rajio taisō* [radio exercises], the formalised body movements that were practised in unison by schools and communities as the standard exercise regime. This was more than the pursuit of good health; it was also a symbolic act of good citizenship. This was at the time when every TV program was broadcast live; Ono had to get up before 5 am to make the 6 o'clock shows on the NHK, the national broadcaster. The TV viewers did not know while watching her mechanical movements and her impassive face that she was juggling motherhood, university teaching and competitive gymnastics. She was expected to move as precisely as a machine, and the narration that overlayed her performance was an equally mechanical man's voice that gave instructions, "one, two, three and four, now swing your arms widely . . . ."

RESISTANCE OF THE BODY

Tsuburaya Kōkichi, bronze medallist in the marathon at the Tokyo Olympics, was found dead in his room in the barracks of the Self-Defence Forces on 9 January 1968. Tsuburaya had slashed his wrists to end his life, leaving behind two letters: a will addressed to his family, and an apology to the Forces. The first was an unusual suicide note that echoed an incantation-like rhythm—a sound reminiscent of pre-modern Japan—and therefore attracted the attention of the writers of modern literature. After giving thanks for each individual dish that he had been served at his parents'

home during the New Year holiday, Tsuburaya briefly stated that he could not run any more and wished he were with his parents:

> Dear Father, dear Mother, the *mikka-tororo* soup was so delicious, as were the dried persimmons and *mochi* rice cakes,
>
> Dear Brother Toshio, dear sister,[31] the *sushi* was so delicious,
>
> Dear Brother Katsumi, dear sister, the wine and the apples were so delicious,
>
> Dear Brother Iwao, dear sister, the *shiso* herb rice and the *nanban zuke* pickles were so delicious,
>
> Dear Brother Kikuzō, dear sister, the grape juice and the Yōmeishu wine were so delicious, and thank you for always helping me with my washing,
>
> Dear Brother Kōzō, dear sister, thank you for giving me a lift home and back, the *mongō* cuttlefish was so delicious,
>
> Dear Brother Masao, dear sister, I am so sorry for making you worried,
>
> Dear Sachio, Hideo, Mikio, Toshiko, Hideko, Ryōsuke, Takahisa, Miyoko, Yukie, Mitsue, Akira, Yoshiyuki, Keiko, Kōei, Yō, Kī, and Masatsugu,[32] please grow up to be good people.
>
> Father, Mother, your Kōkichi is exhausted and cannot run any more.
>
> Please forgive him.
>
> He is sorry for always making you worried, causing you trouble and disturbing your restful minds.
>
> Your Kōkichi wanted to live at your side.[33]

In "Chōkyori rannā no isho" (1979) (The Will of a Long-Distance Runner), Sawaki Kōtaro describes this text as being written "as if to reawaken native souls which had been sleeping in the villages deep in mountainous areas" unaffected by the modernisation of the land.[34] Kawabata Yasunari, the Nobel Prize laureate, quoted this text in full in his essay soon after Tsuburaya's death, finding its style of writing both beautiful and humbling for a professional writer (Kawabata, 1978, pp. 292-95). Kara Jūrō, the dramatist of the 1960s alternative theatre movement, wrote the play *Koshimaki Osen: Furisode Kaji no maki* (1969) (*Osen in her Undergarments: A chapter on the 1657 Edo fire*), in which he used this text to wrap around the body to ward off evil.

The second letter was much shorter than Tsuburaya letter to his family; in it, he apologises to his superiors at the Forces' Sports School and wishes Japan success in the Mexico Olympics, which were to take place later in the same year. Kimihara Kenji, his Olympic co-runner, sent a telegraph to his funeral: "May your soul rest in heaven. I swear to raise the red Sun in

Mexico to carry out your wishes" (Sawaki, 1979, p. 137), which he later achieved, winning a silver medal. Tsuburaya had joined the Forces after high school and found they suited his personality and upbringing.[35] The Self-Defence Forces were formally established in 1954 and took their original form in 1950, soon after the outbreak of the Korean War, when the United States anticipated a strategic use for Japanese armed forces in the near future. Owing to domestic controversy over their legal status, their ideological ambiguity, and the social antipathy towards their war-provoking image, the survival of the Forces largely depended on how well they performed in recruitment campaigns and overall public relations.[36] The slogan that they used in 1957 was *"ai sareru jieitai"* (The Well-liked Forces), and their primary imperative was to win public approval (Uchiumi, 1993). In that climate, good performance in sporting events was regarded as an immediate duty, or an achievement akin to winning a battle. On 1 April 1964, six months before the Olympics, the principal of the Forces' sports school made a welcoming speech to its new members that included the following:

> In the final battlefield of the Tokyo Olympics you must keep your faith in winning the war as a member of the forces and fight until the last moment, becoming finalists, raising the flag of the rising sun and living up to the expectations of the citizens and the entire membership of the forces . . .[37]

Of the 22 members who participated in the Tokyo Olympics, bronze medallist Tsuburaya and weightlifting gold medallist Miyake Yoshinobu received the Forces' highest award. But unlike Miyake, whose sporting achievements at his university had earned him an invitation to join the Forces, Tsuburaya was a soldier before he was an athlete. Thereafter, he gave frequent public talks and appearances, often at the expense of his training schedule.[38]

Mishima Yukio gives his own version of a voiceover of Tsuburaya's suicide, narrativising it as an ideal warrior's death and a highly respectable action. He concedes that even though the Olympic Games are the only opportunity for the army to represent the country and demonstrate national strength, ordinary people cannot regard the Olympic Games as an eternal "justice" to die for (Mishima 1989, vol. 3, p. 452). But Tsuburaya's illusion, Mishima claims, comes from the glory that he once experienced at the Olympic Games, and his death should be justified for it:

> It was a suicide brought about by his sensitive, masculine and beautiful pride. . . . He could have lived for many years to come, filling a new role as an instructor for the next generation of athletes or such . . . But, even if he successfully killed his pride and

lived on, that would be just his body which survived . . . It is in fact simple; there is only one solution to this. To let one's pride live on, one has to kill the body which is breaking down. . . . And in wrenching the body off his pride, it was necessary for him to give another reason—the responsibilities and the honour of an army officer's pride.[39]

In reading Tsuburaya's will, Mishima, who was also a discerning literary critic, did not hear what many other writers did—the powerful sound of the text that was devoid of the central "I."[40] He instead focused on the justification for the suicide act.

In 1964, contrary to the expectation that a medal would go to Kimihara, it was Tsuburaya who came into the stadium on the last day of the Olympic Games in second place, following a charismatic runner, the Ethiopian Imperial Guard Abebe Bikila. On finishing, Bikila conducted a light cooling down exercise, leaving the spectators in awe that he had any energy left in his thin body. Bikila had had his appendix removed only six weeks before the Games. He mentioned later that any of his colleagues in the Imperial Guard could win the marathon; this audacious comment was given credence when one of his colleagues did win a gold medal in Mexico in 1968. Tsuburaya, on the other hand, was overtaken by another runner during his last lap and received the bronze medal. The expectation for him to run for another Olympics and receive a higher medal was internalised from then on by both Tsuburaya and his supporters, especially those in the Forces. Three years later, after celebrating the New Year at his parents' home, he was as usual running back to his army base along the national route, with his brother driving alongside. To his brother's surprise, Tsuburaya stopped and got into the car after only ten minutes or so, saying he could not run any more. During the holiday, he had been hit with the news that his long-term girlfriend had married another man. Tsuburaya had made the decision to follow the Forces' order—not to get married until winning a medal at the Mexico Olympics—and yet, he had been hampered by a series of injuries that made even competing a diminishing prospect. He was 28 years of age. He had lived, as all athletes do, the conflict of his own body: the body that thrived in performing to its limit, and the body that resisted the will to achieve.

Mishima's article romanticising Tsuburaya's final action as the way of the *samurai* demonstrates the writer's own ideals—the twisted image of masculinity that is closely connected to a will to die. Successfully going through his own physical makeover, Mishima by then held a strong belief in Man's willpower; he was determined not to belong to what Nietzsche called "the priestly class"—men who are introverted, self-reflective and inactive by nature. Instead, he wished to embody the class of the "knightly" which was in his own historical context the *samurai* warrior class.[41] Mishima upheld the way of the samurai, drawing his own warrior codes from *The book of hagakure*.[42] He saw the body as the blank canvas that a man could paint in different colours freely and at will. Tsuburaya's action in terminating his body's functions was thus painted by Mishima as the story of a man who possessed the ultimate masculinity of the *samurai,* which was demonstrated by his will to die. Mishima's response to this incident did not represent the general public's view, but indicated a direction, which the pursuit of the ultimate management of the body that appeared in both Western modernity and the *samurai* codes could lead us to. Within three years from Tsuburaya's death Mishima rushed to his own, performing an antiquated *samurai* death.[43] Despite Mishima's voiceover, it appears that Tsuburaya's "body" in the end resisted his "will to achieve" and payed the price for it.

Notes on the Discourse of *Konjo*/Willpower

Murakami Haruki is one of the most well-read contemporary Japanese novelists outside Japan. He started his writing career when Mishima's ended. One of Murakami's earlier novels, **Hitsuji o meguru bōken** (1982) (*A Wild Sheep Chase,* 1989) begins with a university campus scene in which the young protagonist and his girlfriend are munching hotdogs and talking about having sex. In the background the muted TV screen is showing Mishima giving a final propaganda speech in his theatrical uniform and with a kamikaze-style headband around his head. Murakami thus gives his own version of a voiceover to Mishima's performance, which highlights the fact that Mishima's ultranationalism fell on deaf ears. Karatani Kōjin makes the observation that the target of Murakami's "chase" in this novel is Mishima, and the novel is an attempt to overcome Mishima and what he represents (Karatani, 1995, p. 122)—namely, a masculinity tightly connected to nationalism, or vice versa.

During the 2000 Sydney Olympic Games Murakami went to Sydney as an Olympics reporter. His reports were published as two volumes entitled **Sydney!** in 2001. An avid long-distance runner himself, Murakami focuses on the marathon. He demonstrates his knowledge of the sport and offers an insider's view of the technicalities of the race. The book begins with a novelistic piece featuring Arimori Yūko and a psychological transcript of her race at the 1996 Atlanta Olympics.

> —The idea of quitting never occurred to her. To complete whatever she started was her way of life. "*Konjō?* No, it is not the matter of *konjō*. I run for my own self worth. I run, swallowing my own blood.—If I went home without a medal, no one would listen to me. People are only going to listen to those who come home with the goods. And I have a lot to say. For that alone I must get a medal, because people only understand when they are shown something tangible". But at the same time, she really could not care less about medals. "I have twice been thrown into this cruel giant mincing machine called the Olympics, and each time I completed the race, staking my own dignity. Each time was a valuable achievement of my own. I'd never let it be judged by whether or not I got a medal, never by that single flag of the Sun—". Emotions akin to anger were always there deep down in her mind.[44]

Murakami's novelistic treatment of this gold medallist, who did not even participate in the Sydney Games, demonstrates his critical stance on the Olympics, the supposed theme of his book. Through the Arimori story above, he is from the start setting a tone that is antinationalist and anti-glorification, pre-empting any expectation of that sort from his readers. Murakami spends time in describing the taste of his breakfast, a meat pie in the stadium, and just like in his novels, he drinks beer after beer. His detailed descriptions of food, transport and other mundane affairs have the effect of diffusing, dispersing and dislocating the "extraordinary" space of the Olympic Games. Murakami's reports are devoid of nationalistic sentiment, and he describes female marathon runners without a hint of gender specificity. The contrast Murakami provides with Mishima is intentionally stark. Mishima attempted to capture the extraordinariness of the occasion, peppering his writing with words of grandiosity, celebration and excitement. On the one hand, Mishima's articles conveyed the very emotions that the whole nation was immersed in at the time of the Olympics, and their focus was on the spiritual values such as perseverance and endurance—*konjō*—that the athletes supposedly demonstrated through their performances. Murakami, on the other hand, denounces this term through his description of the internal landscape of a marathon woman. Arimori's monologue represents today's Japan, which does not value self-sacrificial modes of performance in the same way it did in the 1960s. It nevertheless still talks about a pain that cannot be relieved in producing a bodily performance, and about the media who would not give her a chance to express herself without being decorated with a medal. She denounces the concept of *konjō,* but she has one internally. On this point the discourse of the body remains in the same orbit of the narrative of overcoming the resisting body.

Yōko Zetterlund, a professional volleyball player who grew up in Japan and made it to the US national team for the Atlanta Olympics, has a Japanese website for her fans, on which she writes comments on various issues surrounding sports. In one article she wonders why Japan has not performed as well in sporting events in recent years despite the richer environment available for athletes. Admitting that the term *konjō* is outdated, she implies that this is what is missing in the sporting culture of contemporary Japan. The Daimatsu-*esque* spiritual emphasis—a return of *konjō*—is projected onto her catch phrase: "Make Everything Possible: there is no mission that is impossible", the coach's motto of *"naseba naru"* in translation.[45] While sporting events are positive social and cultural practices from the perspectives of the participating individuals and local communities,[46] the discourse of *konjō* as such can mislead those who prefer stories with simple structures. Monological stories are easy to take in as one's own story, since they obviate the complex negotiations one otherwise has to tackle in life. The discourse of *konjō* was one of the grand narratives of postwar Japan that urged people to give up their own story-making and follow the simple and linear story of success. What it suppressed most in the process was the human body as a private locale that harbours happiness and pleasure.

Forty years after the Tokyo Olympics, we keep watching athletes run faster, jump higher and perform more intricate movements than their predecessors ever did. The spectacle of the Japanese athletes' bodies no longer engenders national unity to the same degree as it did in 1964. If what we read in the monologue written by Murakami reflects the reality of an elite woman athlete, she seems in control without being coerced by her male coach, or her country. It tells us that the discourse surrounding the body has shifted to one that is more individualistic. It also seems that the systemic intervention in the woman's body no longer operates in the same manner as it did before. Nevertheless, coercion can occur through the complex workings of an enlarged and empowered mass media that creates voiceover of various narratives, producing discourses that are in favour of certain interest groups. The spectacle of the body attracts viewers, and therefore the human body is still easy prey for media punters. Every four years, Olympic Games continue to remind us of national boundaries and our sense of belonging, which is often more divisive than inclusive. On 31 August 2006 the Governor of Tokyo, Ishihara Shin-tarō, announced his city's victory over Fukuoka to become Japan's candidate to host 2016 Olympic Games. Ishihara's ultranationalist and racist stance has not been critically discussed and condemned by the media to date.[47] His performance as the public face of the Olympic Games is likely to create a further divide between nations and may revive the sense of sporting games being wars by other means. The narratives accompanying the spectacles of the body will still require our constant attention.

Notes

1. The body is marginalised in the modernist concept of the subject, in which the self is imagined to be a clean-and-proper unified entity. Julia Kristeva first used these terms to critique the oppression of the symbolic realm in Lacanian psychoanalysis in *Powers of Horror* (1982). Michel Foucault's critique of the modern nation-state demonstrates the same concept in *The Birth of the Clinic* (1994) and *Discipline and Punish* (1995). This approach to the body was consistent with the pre-existing *samurai* code of ethics that was popularised in support of the militarist cause in the mid-Meiji period. See Yoshikuni Igarashi, *Bodies of Memory: Narratives of war in postwar Japanese culture, 1945-70* (2000), which effectively demonstrates a Foucauldian reading of the body in postwar Japan. Japanese names are given surname first throughout this essay, unless they are authors of English publications such as Igarashi.

2. The state-citizens equation that I use here can be replaced by the corporation-workers relationship in the context of postwar Japan. The difficulty in locating power in this period is compounded by the tight collaboration between the state and large corporations.

3. The modern Olympic Games were initially held as the opening performance of the World Exposition, which functioned as a vehicle for imperialist projects (Yoshimi, 1992; 1999; 2002; and Tomotsune, 1995).

4. Prior to the Tokyo Olympics, television had already created a national hero—a professional wrestler called Rikidōzan (1924-63)—who, using the "native" technique of *karate-choppu,* always defeated American wrestlers at the end of the match. He was of Korean descent, and started his sporting career as a *sumō* wrestler in Japan.

5. For historical accounts of the ways in which sports were incorporated into rising militarism in prewar Japan, see Kimura (1978, pp. 117-78).

6. This view is underscored by recent research, such as work by Yoshimi Shun'ya (1992; 1999; 2002).

7. It has been pointed out that the development of sporting activities went in parallel with the country's industrialisation process; hence the absence of club-based civil sports was notable until recently (Todoroki, 1993, pp. 13-32)

8. Among the novels written by Mishima Yukio are *Kamen no kokuhaku* (1949) (Confessions of a mask), *Kinkakuji* (1956) (The temple of the golden pavilion) and the four volumes of *Hōjō no umi* (1965-71) (The sea of fertility).

9. Mishima appeared in six films as an actor. Twenty-one of his novels have been made into films, and *Shiosai* (1954) (The sound of waves) was remade five times over twenty years. His playfully written

articles such as *Fudōtoku kyōlku kōza* (1958-59) (Unethical educational lectures, Mishima 1989, vol. 3, pp. 15-222) and *Han teijo daigaku* (1966) (Lessons not to become a faithful wife) were originally serialised in popular magazines.

10. See Otomo. "'The way of the samurai": *Ghost Dog*, Mishima, and modernity's *Other*' (2000) for further discussion on this point.

11. Mishima (1989, vol. 4, pp. 347-48). The original article was published in *Hōchi shinbun,* 24 October 1964. English translation of Japanese quotations is mine throughout.

12. Igarashi describes the ways in which the nation-wide expectation for the team to compete in the Tokyo Olympic Games altered their plan to retire after winning the world championship in 1962. See 'Nostalgia for Bodies in Pain' (Igarashi, 2000, pp. 155-63).

13. There are well-publicised non-fiction works such as Hosoi Wakizō's *Jokō aishi* (1925) and Yamamoto Shigemi's *Aa Nomugitōge* (1968) which documented the hard conditions of young textile workers in the Meiji-Taisho periods. Mishima's fiction focused more on the family rhetoric used by the company owner and the innocent youths involved in the early Shows period.

14. Frederick W. Taylor's *The Principles of Scientific Management* (1911) was translated into Japanese as early as 1912, and its methodology was modified and promoted through a governmental institution. The Industrial Efficiency Research Institute was set up in 1921 to promote the concept. See William Tsutsui's *Manufacturing Ideology* (1998).

15. I owe this information to 'Nunmin no sengoshi: shūdan shūshoku, dekasegi and rettō no fuchi' (Sunouchi, 2001, pp. 195-218).

16. Although there were also a large number of boys who were recruited in this way, they were considered to be lifetime employees, while girls were there for a limited period and regularly replaced by a fresh intake.

17. The Olympic team was based on Nichibō Kaizuka (Nihon Bōseki Kōgyō, later called Yunichika), which is now owned by Tōre (Tōkyō Reiyon). The members were Kasai Masae, Miyamoto Emiko, Yada Kinuko, Handa Yuriko, Matsumura Yoshiko, Isobe Sada, Matsumura Masami, Shinozaki Yōko, Sasaki Setsuko, Fujimoto Yūko, Kondō Masako and Shibuki Ayano.

18. *Tōkyo orinpikku,* 1965, Tōkyo orinpikku eiga kyōkai.

19. The extract from Daimatsu's *Nasebanaru* (1964) (When there is a will, there is a way) is translated and cited by Igarashi in *Bodies of Memory,* 2000, p. 157.

20. Igarashi makes a fascinating connection between Daimatsu's wartime experience as a POW and his philosophy of winning and managing women's bodies (2000, pp. 155-63).

21. Looking back, team leader Kasai recently mentioned that girls owed everything to Coach Daimatsu, who loved them and taught them so much through the hardest training. (http://www.joc.or.jp/stories/tokyo/20041021_tokyo.html)

22. Extra-curricular sporting activity is called *bukatsudō* in Japanese. Peter Cave points out the changing culture of school sports in '*Bukatsudō*: The educational role of Japanese school clubs' (2004).

23. Saitō Tamaki (2003, pp. 153-59 and appendix). Saitō points out that the *supokon* genre survives through the 1980s but as a parody of the earlier works, found for example in *Toppu o nerae* (1988) which is an obvious parody of *Ēsu o nerae.*

24. The *oni,* a powerful creature of Japanese folk mythology, is always represented bearing an iron bar.

25. Mishima (1989, vol. 4, p. 346), originally published in *Mainichi shinbun,* 21 October 1964.

26. Ibid (pp. 345-346).

27. The couple convey in an interview just before the Games that they are longing to have a normal family life with their children. (See 'Chanoma no kin medaru' in *Bungei shunjū ni miru supōtsu showa shi* vol. 2, pp. 330-35).

28. 'Ase to namida to egao no yonjū-ni nen' (Forty-two years of sweat, tears and smiles), *Shūkan Asahi,* 7 July 2000.

29. The poem was written as a letter to her younger brother, who was a conscript in the Russo-Japanese War (1904-05) in which 60,000 young soldiers died in less than two years.

30. Op. cit., 'Ase to namida to egao no yonjū-ni nen'.

31. All nameless "sisters" are his sisters-in-law.

32. These are the names of his nephews and nieces.

33. The original Japanese text can be found on the web, or in print (Kawabata, 1978. pp. 292-93; Sawaki, 1979, p. 100). My translation fails to convey the starkly detached tone which runs through this poem (as I would prefer to call it); even in the last sentence the poet refers to himself in the third person.

34. Sawaki (1979, p. 101). For the biography of Tsuburaya, see also Hashimato Katsuhiko (1999).

35. Ibid. Sawaki describes Tsuburaya's good relationship with his father, who was a man of principles and a patriarch who both loved his children and raised them in a highly disciplined manner.

36. Their public relations strategies must have been effective, since my childhood memory of the Self Defence Forces in my hometown is a warm and happy one: the big fair of their camp Open Day; my excitement at climbing on top of a tank; the reassuring presence of strong but friendly men in uniform.

37. Uchiumi (1993, p. 272), the extract from *Taiiku gakkō shi* (Jieitai taiiku gakkō, 1964, p. 93).

38. The media in general talked of public expectations as the cause of Tsuburaya's suicide. Uchiumi and others, however, emphasise that the nature of the Self-Defence Forces was the key factor (Uchiumi, 1993; Nagaoka, 1977; Aoyama, 1980; Kawamoto, 1979).

39. Mishima (1989, vol. 3, p. 452).

40. Modern Japanese literature strove to construct the solid presence of the speaking "I", a project that Mishima was part of. At the time of Tsuburaya's suicide, however, Mishima was departing from that project, as demonstrated in *Hōjō no umi* (The sea of fertility).

41. The quoted terms are Nietzschean terms. See *On the Genealogy of Morals* (Nietzsche, 1989, First essay, sections 6 and 7). For Mishima's understanding of Nietzsche see Seikai Ken (1992) and Roy Starrs (1994).

42. Mishima (1989, vol. 1, pp. 688-734). The English translation is found in *The samurai ethic and modern Japan: Yukio Mishima and Hagakure* (1992). *The book of hagakure* was written in the eighteenth century by Yamamoto Tsunetomo and read only by his associates in a region away from the central Edo government. It was revived and taken seriously during Japan's modernisation in the Meiji period as representing a value system peculiar to Japan.

43. Henry Scott-Stokes (1975) gives a detailed description of Mishima's suicide. For a more literary interpretation of Mishima, see John Nathan (1974), and the film by Paul Schrader (1985). It goes without saying that in Japanese there books are constantly being written on Mishima and his works, one of the most recent being Dōmoto Masaki's memoir (2005), which openly discusses Mishima's sexuality and its relevance to his final action.

44. Murakami (2004, pp. 24-25).

45. The original article on *konjō* that included her criticism of Japanese athletes has been removed from the current website http://www.yoko2.com, which may also reveal the view of the general public. There are, however, various articles found on this website that convey similar sentiments, and her motto remains the same. Incidentally, Zetterlund was coached by her mother, who was herself once trained by Coach Daimatsu, over seven years.

46. There are numerous positive stories of communal involvement in sports in contemporary Japan. See for example, Light and Yasaki's account of how the J. League has constructed local identity (2000).

47. One example of Ishihara's racially derogatory remarks is cited by John Brinsley and Keiichi Yamamura (9 February 2007):

[Roppongi] is now virtually a foreign neighborhood. Africans—I don't mean African-Americans—who don't speak English are there doing who knows what—This is leading to new forms of crime such as car theft," he [Ishihara] said. "We should be letting in people who are intelligent". (http://www.bloomberg.com/apps/news?pid = newsarchive&sid = avIXVIIvqIKo)

See also the controversial article written by Ishihara (*Sankel shinbun*, 8 May 2001). Morisu Hiroshi and Kan. Sanjun point out the Japanese media's apparent inability to critique Ishihara's racism in *Nasionarizumu no kokufuku* (2002, pp. 22-23).

References

Aoyama, Ichirō (1977) *Eikō to kodoku no kanata e: Tsuburaya Kōkichi monogatari* (Bēsubōru magajinsha).

Brinsley, John and Yamamura Keiichi (2007) Japan threatened by China, its own timidity: Ishihara (update 1). 9 February 2007. (http://www.bloomberg.com/apps/news?pid=newsarchive&sid=avIXVIIvqIKo, last accessed 3 March 2007)

Cave, Peter (2004) Bukatsudō: The educational role of Japanese school clubs, *The Journal of Japanese Studies* 30(2), pp. 383-415.

Dōmoto, Masaki (2005) *Kaisō: kaiten tobira no Mishima Yukio* (Bungei shunjū).

Foucault, Michel (1994) *The birth of the clinic: An archaeology of medical perception,* trans. A. M. Sheridan Smith (New York: Vintage Books).

———. (1995) *Discipline and punish: The birth of the prison,* trans. Alan Sheridan (Harmondsworth: Penguin).

Hashimoto, Katsuhiko (1999) *Orinpikku ni ubawareta inochi* (Shōgakukan).

Hosoi, Wakizō (1925) *Jokō aishi* (Kaizōsha).

Ichikawa, Kon (director) (1965) *Tokyo orinpikku,* (a film) distributed by Tokyo orinpikku eiga kyōkai.

Igarashi, Yoshikuni (2000) *Bodies of memory: Narratives of war in postwar Japanese culture, 1945-1970* (Princeton, NJ: Princeton University Press).

Karatani, Kōjin (1995) Murakami Haruki no fūkei: 1973 nen no pinbōru, in *Shūen o megutte,* pp. 89-137 (Kōdansha).

Kawabata, Yasunari (1973) *Issō Jkka* (Mainichi shinbunsha).

Kawamoto, Nobumasa (1976) *Supōtsu no gendaishi* (Taishūkan shoten).

Kimura, Kichiji (1978) Nihon ni okeru supōtsu to nashonarizumu, in Nakamura Toshio et al. (eds) *Supōtsu nashonarizumu,* pp. 117-78 (Taishūkan shoten).

Kristeva, Julia (1982) *Powers of horror: An essay on abjection,* trans. Leon S. Roudiez (New York: Columbia University Press).

Light, Richard and Yasaki Wataru (2002) J league soccer and the rethinking of regional identity in Japan, *Sporting Traditions* 18(2), pp. 31-46.

Mishima, Yukio (1949) *Kamen no kokuhaku* (Kawade shobō) [1993. *Confessions of a mask,* trans. Meredith Weatherby. London: Flamingo].

―――. (1954) *Shiosai* (Shinchōsha) [c1956. *The sound of waves,* trans. Meredith Weatherby, Tokyo: C. E. Tuttle].

―――. (1956) *Kinkakuji* (Shinchōsha) [1987. *The temple of the golden pavilion,* trans. Ivan Morris, Penguin Books].

―――. (1962) *Yūkoku* (Chūō kōronsha) [1995. *Patriotism,* trans. Geoffrey W. Sargent. New York: New Directions Books].

―――. (1964) *Kinu to meisatsu* (Kōdansha) [1998, *Silk and insight,* trans. Hiroaki Sato. New York: M. E. Sharpe].

―――. (1968) *Taiyō to tetsu* (Kōdansha) [1971, *Sun and steel,* trans. John Bester. London, Secker and Warburg].

―――. (1966) *Han teijo daigaku* (Shinchōsha).

―――. (1971) *Hōjō no umi* (Shinchōsha) [1985. *The sea of fertility,* trans. Michael Gallagher, et. al. Penguin Books].

―――. (1989) *Mishima Yukio hyōron zenshū,* 4 vols (Shinchōsha).

―――. (1992) *The samurai ethic and modern Japan: Yukio Mishima and Hagakure,* trans. Kathryn Sparling (Tokyo: CE Tuttle).

Morisu, Hiroshi and Kan Sanjun (2002) *Nashonarizumu no kokufuku* (Shūeisha).

Murakami, Haruki (1982) *Hitsuji o meguru bōken* (Kōdansha) [1989, *A wild sheep chase,* trans. Alfred Birnbaum. Tokyo and New York: Kodansha International].

―――. (2004) *Shidonii! koara junjōhen* (Bungei shunjū).

Nagaoka, Tamio (1977) *Mō, hashiremasen: Tsuburaya Kokichi no eikō to shi* (Kodansha).

Nathan, John (1974) *Mishima, a biography* (London: Hamilton).

Nietzsche, Friedrich (1989) *On the genealogy of morals,* trans. and ed. Walter Kaufmann (New York: Vintage Books).

Ono, Kiyoko (2000) Ase to mamida to egao no yonjū-ni nen, *Shūkan Asahi,* 7 July 2000.

Ono, Takashi and Ono Kiyoko (1988) Chanoma no kin medaru, n *Bungei shunjū ni miru supōtsu shōwa shi,* vol. 2, pp. 330-35 (Bungei shunjū).

Otomo, Rio (2000) "The way of the samurai": *Ghost Dog,* Mishima, and modernity's *Other, Japanese* Studies 21(1), pp. 31-43.

Saitō, Tamaki (2003) *Sentō bishōjo no seishin bunseki* (ōta shuppan).

Sawaki, Kōtaro (1979) Chōkyori rannā no isho, in *Yaburezaru monotachi,* pp. 97-142 (Bunshun Bunko).

Scott-Stokes, Henry (1975) *The life and death of Yukio Mishima* (London: Peter Owen).

Schrader, Paul (director and co-scripted) (1985) *A Mishima: Life in four chapters* (a film) distributed by Warner Bros.

Seikai, Ken (1992) *Mishima Yukio to Nīche* (Seikyūsha).

Starrs, Roy (1994) *Deadly dialectics: Sex, violence and nihilism in the world of Yukio Mishima* (Kent: Japan Library).

Sunouchi, Keiji (2001) Nanmin no sengoshi: shūdan shūshoku, dekasegi to rettō no fuchi, in Uemura Tadao, et al. (eds) *Rekishi ga kakikaerareru toki,* pp. 195-218 (Iwanami shoten).

Taylor, Frederick W. (1911) *The priniciples of scientific management* (New York: Harper Bros.).

Todoroki, Kenji (1993) *Kigyō, supōtsu, shizen: kabushiki gaisha Nippon no supōtsu* (Taishūkan).

Tomotsune, Tsutomu (1995) *1940 nen Tōkyō bankokuhaku, orinpikku to hisabetsu buraku e no manazashi.* (http://www.asahi-net.or.jp/~1s9r-situ/tomoar1.html last accessed 27 January 2007)

Tsutsui, William W. (1993) *Manufacturing ideology: Scientific management in twentieth-century Japan* (Princeton, NJ: Princeton University Press).

Uchiumi, Kazuo (1993) Jieitai to supōtsu: jieitai ni totte no Tōkyō Orinpikku, in *Sengo supōtsu taisei no kakuritsu,* pp. 256-85 (Fumaidō).

Yamamoto, Shigemi (1968) *Aa nomugitoge* (Asahi shinbunsha).

Yosano, Akiko. ??

Yoshimi, Shun'ya, ed. (1992) *Hakurankai no seijigaku: manazashi no kindai* (Chūō kōron shinsha).

―――. (1999) *Undōkai to nihon kindai* (Seikyūsha).

―――. (2002) *1930 nendai no media to shintai* (Seikyūsha).

Zetterlund, Yoko. No mission is impossible, the official home page. (http://www.yoko2.com, last accessed 27 January 2007).

Steffen Hantke (essay date fall 2007)

SOURCE: Hantke, Steffen. "Postmodernism and Genre Fiction as Deferred Action: Haruki Murakami and the Noir Tradition." *Critique: Studies in Contemporary Fiction* 49, no. 1 (fall 2007): 3-23.

[*In the following essay, Hantke investigates the character of the hard-boiled detective in Murakami's fiction, arguing that the author uses this figure to critique and deconstruct literary theories and genres.*]

In recent years, Haruki Murakami's reputation has not only started to spread outside of his native Japan—the man has arrived. I discovered him in 1993 when my science fiction reading group selected the Vintage paperback of **Hard-boiled Wonderland and the End of the World** as its book of the month. Published in 1993, only two years after its original Japanese release, the English translation of the novel coincided with Knopf's publication of the short-story collection **The Elephant Vanishes,** both following the 1990 Penguin edition of **A Wild Sheep Chase.** His career began in his native Japan around 1980, and he began to reach an English-speaking audience during the early 1990s with this wave of translations. At roughly the same time, his work was also being translated into a number of languages other than English, a clear sign that he had attained the status as a writer of international acclaim. His novels are now released simultaneously in a number of languages, and the release of **Kafka on the Shore,** one of his more recent novels, was staged by publishers around the world as a major event. In fact, the *New York Times* listed **Kafka on the Shore** as one of "The Ten Best Books of 2005." Praised by an anonymous reviewer as "the work of a powerfully confident writer," it was the only novel out of the five works of fiction on the list that was a translation.

As I cannot read Murakami in his original Japanese—a considerable handicap—I will refer to critical sources better equipped to deal with the finer points of style and diction in Japanese. However, because the point of this essay will be to argue Murakami's cosmopolitanism and situate his writing in a context of textual production and reception across cultural boundaries, this handicap strikes me as oddly appropriate. True, it does impose limits on interpretation but also implicates me as a reader in the same global contexts in which Murakami operates. As much as any proliferation of contextual awareness carries the risk of producing misreadings, it also opens up new interpretive options that remain unavailable to those operating within a single cultural framework.

Murakami's international success is even more of an accomplishment given that Japanese writers with more sterling credentials, such as Nobel Prize winner Kenzaburō Ōe, have not yet secured a readership outside of their native country as large as Murakami's. Western readers may find aspects of Murakami's work that are grounded in Japanese culture and tradition as baffling or impenetrable as those in Ōe's or other idiosyncratically "Japanese" writers. But what reconciles those readers with Murakami is, I believe, his ability to integrate elements into his work that are utterly familiar to Western readers.[1] Many have noted the "copious pop references" cropping up in his writing (Rubin 17). Among these references, the creative variations he teases out of the American hard-boiled mystery are the most conspicuous and significant. In tone and theme, Murakami's novels are about as noir as contemporary fiction in a slipstream mode gets, which raises the question: What is the appeal of the hard-boiled detective to the Japanese writer?[2]

The Japanese Writer as Hard-boiled Detective

In an essay on Raymond Chandler, Pico Iyer credits Murakami with "quietly revolution[zing] Japanese literature with his everyday mysteries of identity and disappearance (who am I, and what happened to that memory—that girl—that was here a moment ago?)" (87). Iyer's tongue-in-cheek summary is dead on: Murakami manages to take the formula of hard-boiled detective fiction and, with its help, raise questions of cognition and identity with respect to the personal lives of his characters, questions that were background material for the likes of Hammett or Chandler. Murakami's "mysteries of identity and disappearance" have steered the hard-boiled detective story away from the exploration of milieu and toward encounters with the unknowable. His heroes, if they arrive at a solution to the mystery at all, do so by means other than rational analysis; their modus operandi, as well as their mode of existence, is existential, ironically playful, and largely textual.

Murakami has been experimenting with the hardboiled variant of noir since **A Wild Sheep Chase,** published early in his career in 1982. In the novel, the detective is in pursuit of an elusive, mysterious sheep, a MacGuffin reminiscent of Dashiell Hammett's Maltese Falcon or "the big whatsit" in Robert Aldrich's production of Mickey Spillane's *Kiss Me, Deadly* (1955). In a lecture in Berkeley, Murakami talks about "one West Coast reader [who] saw the connection.

Referring to Chandler's *The Big Sleep,* he called my novel *The Big Sheep.* I felt honored by this" (qtd. in Rubin 81). Murakami's exploration of the genre continued with **Dance Dance Dance** (1988), the sequel to **A Wild Sheep Chase,** and elements of noir still figure prominently in more recent novels such as **The Sputnik Sweetheart** (1999).

On the most basic level, Chandler and the hard-boiled detective tradition have provided Murakami with a blueprint for protagonist and plot. A detective figure, not always a professional investigator, is called on to solve a case that reveals itself as more complex than is apparent at first glance. The investigation begins inconspicuously, revolves around an act of violence or a disappearance, and features a female character whose allure overcomes the protagonist's initial reluctance to involve himself in something that spells trouble. Ultimately, no clear moral lesson emerges. Although the truth, fully or partially, emerges, people are killed, justice proves elusive, and the world remains a dangerous and godforsaken place.

More important than this sequence of events and crucial to the tone of the novels is the detective himself. It is this figure for which Murakami is particularly indebted to Chandler and his frequently quoted dictum that the hero in hard-boiled fiction "is everything" ("Simple" 18). Although plot and setting have their attractions, it is for the sake of this character, for the sake of his voice and world-weary cynicism, that readers return to hard-boiled fiction. Critics have noted the consistency with which Murakami employs this protagonist throughout his work, often leaving him nameless to allow for the reader's projection of continuity from one novel to the next.[3] The figure appears even in stories and novels that are not overtly modeled on the hard-boiled formula, suggesting that Murakami has succeeded in deriving the character from the formula, but then making him so uniquely his own that he can function independent of his indigenous fictional environment.

Murakami's professional background explains, to some extent, his working with formulaic elements of noir isolated from the totality of the genre. Not only did Murakami begin "his career by translating Chandler, among others, into kanji and katakana script" (Iyer 87) but also served as the Japanese translator of Raymond Carver, a writer who manages to sustain a laconic hard-boiled voice in the absence of the typical genre trappings of noir. Murakami's intense study of Carver may have taught him that certain noir elements are sustainable apart from their generic origins, and that recontextualizing these elements can serve his own idiosyncratic voice and vision.

The typical Murakami protagonist, the result of this generic eclecticism, never refers to himself by using the formal *watashi* or *watakashi,* the conventional first-person pronoun favored in Japanese literature that serves as an unambiguous marker of "literariness." Instead, he calls himself *boku,* "another pronoun-like word for 'I', but an unpretentious one used primarily by young men in informal circumstances" (Rubin 37). Endowed with "a generous fund of curiosity and a cool, detached, bemused acceptance of the inherent strangeness of life" (37), this narrator is a unique yet readily recognizable variation on Chandler's detective. Even when un- or underemployed, Murakami's Japanese middle-class Everyman remains strangely unconcerned with money, career, or social prestige. That peculiar lethargy latent in Hammett's Sam Spade or Chandler's Philip Marlowe is brought into the foreground with Murakami's protagonists. They derive pleasure from the minutiae of small household chores, like ironing a shirt or cooking pasta—activities that are explicitly coded as domestic or feminine. Sometimes they are deserted by wives or girlfriends, divorced, abandoned without explanation, or demoted to the status of househusbands after leaving their jobs or being fired. They are slow to get involved in the mysteries life deposits at their doorsteps and often seem incapable of explaining why they persist on the course that has taken them out of their comfortable, aimless daily routines. They are tempted by the women around them, but, on the whole, they respond according to Chandler's demand that they should be neither eunuchs nor satyrs ("Simple" 18). When they resist temptation, it is less because they adhere to Chandler's code of chivalric honor and more because of a lack of energy, initiative, or sexual appetite.

Discussing this unique recurring narrator and unpacking his significance has become a staple of Murakami criticism.[4] But while many critics identify the character as a hallmark of Murakami's style and philosophical outlook, few elaborate on the connection between Murakami's *boku* and the hard-boiled detective. Perhaps they underestimate or even overlook the link because few of Murakami's protagonists actually are detectives. Most of them end up in this role by accident, because they are energized by some small mystery that enters their field of vision, or they drift aimlessly into the gravitational field of an enigmatic event. This deprofessionalization of the detective figure sets Murakami's *boku* apart from the Spades and Marlowes. At Chandler's own strong insistence, these figures are in it for the money, as professionals making a living, although they already "mark a transitional stage between detecting as a fine art and as a large-scale organized profession" (Mandel 36).

Murakami makes no secret of his penchant for hard-boiled pastiche. Despite his admission that hard-boiled detective fiction is not the only "pop structure" he is interested in ("I've been using [. . .] science fiction structures, for example. I'm also using love story or romance structures" [qtd. in Gregory, Miyawaki, and McCaffery 114]), he gives a reason why the figure of the hard-boiled detective is of such crucial importance to his work that cuts more to the quick of his serious intentions as a writer. As far as "my thinking about the hard-boiled style" is concerned, Murakami explains, "I'm interested in the fact that [hard-boiled detectives] are very individualist in orientation. The figure of the loner. I'm interested in that because it isn't easy to live in Japan as an individualist or a loner. I'm always thinking about this I'm a novelist and I'm a loner, an individualist" (114).[5] Although the loner may be a figure of normative individualism in American culture, its significance changes within Japanese culture. Especially "the lack of a 'subsystem'—a means of defining oneself outside the parameters of ordinary life as a *sarariiman* (white-collar worker), factory worker, or other predefined role"—leaves little room for highly idiosyncratic and individualistic activities, like those of a fiction writer (Strecher 281). By adopting the central character, the structures, and the tone of the hard-boiled detective novel, Murakami finds an instrument that invests his profession with a modicum of glamour and adventure, which are conspicuously absent from a profession coded as domestic and thus deficient in masculinity, or just plain antisocial. But noir is not just a tool of vicarious self-aggrandizement; to the degree that the hard-boiled detective is an anachronism in a postmodern world—and perhaps an exotic, maladapted figure in Japanese society—it also helps Murakami reflect critically on his own activity as a writer, or, more specifically, as a contemporary Japanese writer.

A psychological reading of Murakami's central character suggests that hard-boiled weariness functions as a defense mechanism against the trauma of modernity. Murakami's protagonists "embody the intuition, ubiquitous in late modernity, that the inexplicable has become commonplace: it is normal that abnormal things occur" (Cassegard 82). Because they have traded in vulnerability for "a masochistically tinged resignation which borders on indifference," their "instinctual needs and fundamental impulses become channeled in such a way that their gratification is made less dependent on relations to other people" (85, 86). The *boku*'s self-sufficiency becomes a hallmark of the postmodernity of Murakami's writing; it aligns itself with the texts' frequent forays into a fantastic mode that transgresses the rules of verisimilitude, with the pastiche of the hard-boiled detective novel and the

powerlessness writers experience in a culture in which literature functions primarily as cultural commodity without its traditional role of social arbiter. A "masochistically tinged resignation" strikes me as a valid response to this situation.[6]

Given the ubiquity of Murakami's *boku* and the self-reflexive quality in his use of the hard-boiled detective genre, it is necessary to revise the earlier critical discussion of Murakami in one respect. The hard-boiled tradition is not one of the key elements of Murakami's literary cosmopolitanism; it is the key element. It is a means for Murakami of mapping out a narrative position from which writing fiction becomes possible. It allows him to reflect on himself as a cosmopolitan writer working in a tradition extraneous to traditional Japanese culture and thus as a spokesperson for Japan in its contemporary role within the global economy and emerging global culture. It also allows him to reflect on himself as a man in a profession coded as feminine, someone whose activity is not on a par with the *sarariiman*'s productivity but more along the lines of ironing shirts or cooking pasta. It is the association with the hard-boiled detective that transforms the novelist's deprofessionalization from social stigma into a prerequisite of heroic independence. In other words, it invites reflection on writing fiction as a socially responsible activity, both inside the mechanisms of a capitalist market and yet oddly undisciplined; a shadowy profession, socially coded as a nonprofession, and thus in need of validation through either commercial success or the trappings of academic respectability.

This is a particularly urgent issue for Murakami because, on the one hand, his popularity nudges him toward the role of the public intellectual while, on the other hand, his investment in an ostensibly lowbrow and, more important, explicitly non-Japanese cultural tradition seems to bar him from just this role. Writers of serious standing have not had to legitimize themselves professionally in the way Murakami has; in fact, their cultural marginality, when framed by a high modernist ideology, appears as a privileged position. A writer such as Ōe, "whose traditional business [it] is to define what is popular and what is legitimate" (Ross 5), is not so much part of popular culture as he is occupying a position outside or above it. An emphasis on "being Japanese" would then, as in the case of Ōe, tie the writer back into the community as a public intellectual. A popular Japanese writer like Murakami, however, "hopelessly in love with the cultural classlessness in whose republicanist name [American pop culture] conquers internal and external resistance the world over" (Ross 7), might be perceived to be a participant in popular culture rather than a critical commentator.[7] His status as a public intellectual would be compromised not only by his association with popular culture but also more specifically by the non-Japanese aspect of contemporary Japanese culture. By introducing a figure that epitomizes, glorifies, and mythologizes American individualism into the Japanese cultural context, Murakami's work opens a line of inquiry into the flexibility of Japanese society, or the lack thereof. By taking on additional significance as a means of generic self-reflexivity, the *boku* serves as a stand-in for the postmodern author and his options of how to participate in, and respond to, the culture that has created him.

THE PANOPTIC VIEW OF GENRE: NOIR AS DEFERRED ACTION

Given this complex meshing of biographical and cultural forces in Murakami's background, it is hardly surprising that his use of hard-boiled or noir tropes shows all the self-consciousness of an author who has come to noir as an outsider and with a degree of belatedness. Take, for example, the scene in ***Hard-boiled Wonderland*** [***Hard-boiled Wonderland and the End of the World***] in which two toughs barge into the apartment of the nameless private eye "like a wrecking ball" (131). Undaunted by the physical threat, the narrator dubs one "the hulk" or "Big Boy" and the other "Junior." While they intimidate and interrogate him, he has time for a few wisecracks: "Junior didn't say a word, choosing instead to contemplate the lit end of his cigarette [. . .] This was where the Jean-Luc Godard scene would have been titled *Il regardait le feu de son tabac.* My luck that Godard films were no longer fashionable" (132; emphasis in original).

No one is surprised, least of all the *boku* himself, that in the scene that follows, the two thugs politely yet systematically trash his apartment. After all, they are in character, and this is what "muscle" in the noir universe usually does. The narrator's calmly self-reflective response to the physical danger and his reframing of the scene as a piece of movie trivia place Big Boy and Junior in a line of noir thugs reminiscent, for example, of Moose Malloy in Chandler's *Farewell, My Lovely,* or the men sent to kill Jean-Pierre Melville's protagonist in *Le Samouraï* (1967). But the fact that Murakami has his narrator reveal his textual savvy by an intertextual reference that is poignantly not to a classic film places the text self-consciously in a position of extreme ironic distance from the noir tradition. Godard's ambivalence toward American pop culture and its global influence would make genuine nostalgia for the hard-boiled detective or film noir difficult, if not impossible. Godard is relevant here, but only as a marker of historical obsolescence; after all, his "films were no longer fashionable." Despite the insistence on ironic distancing, there is an obvious af-

fection for the noir style that shines through every line of ***Hard-boiled Wonderland.*** It originates from a position even further removed from the genre's fashionable critical distance. We have traveled through a critical assessment of the hard-boiled style into a phase in which nostalgia, albeit a self-conscious nostalgia, becomes possible again—from modern parody to postmodern pastiche.

Film noir historians have identified this position Murakami occupies as one of cultural belatedness, or "deferred action—*Nachtraeglichkeit,*" as Thomas Elsaesser calls it (423).[8] Elsaesser's terminology reflects a critical consensus in cinema studies that has begun to coalesce around the idea that, in a sense, there never was such a thing as film noir. Elsaesser himself comes to this conclusion after examining what might be called a foundational myth of film noir, the "connection between German Expressionist cinema and American film noir" (420).[9] Ever since this story about noir's origins has solidified into one of the "commonplaces of film history," Elsaesser argues, it has become difficult to see film noir for what it really is, "an imaginary entity whose meaning resides in a set of shifting signifiers" (420).[10] He concludes:

> film noir has no essence, [. . .] its most stable characteristic is its "absent-centredness", its displacements, its over-determinedness, whose ghostly existence as too many discourses, instead of canceling each other out, merely seems to amplify the term's resonance and suggestiveness. Most noticeable is the term's historical imaginary as deferred action (*Nachtraeglichkeit*).
>
> (423)

James Naremore follows Elsaesser's lead in pursuing this constructionist approach. Film noir, he writes, "belongs to the history of ideas as much as to the history of cinema; in other words, it has less to do with a group of artifacts than with a discourse" (11). To the degree that it is "a loose, evolving system of arguments and readings that helps to shape commercial strategies and aesthetic ideologies" (11), it has not only "become useful to the movie industry" (38) but also to academics, film historians, and, by proxy, writers like Murakami who are influenced by these traditions. Naremore points out that, because noir is "a concept that was generated ex post facto," it can easily be transformed into "a dream image of bygone glamour" (39). This transfer of an ideological construct from critical discourse into "a worldwide mass memory" entails a process of fetishization, which, in turn, "represses as much history as it recalls, usually in the service of cinephilia and commodification" (39). From Elsaesser's and Naremore's comments, film noir emerges as a commodity that is simultaneously material and immaterial, an object of exchange as much as an object of desire. In both of these capacities, noir is produced by the studios, with their directors and producers, and by critics and reviewers, who are invested in the term as the coinage of professional and cultural capital.

This fetishizing of noir seems most starkly visible to critics approaching U.S. culture from the outside. For Marc Vernet, for example, noir is deeply implicated in the ways American culture circulates through global markets in the years after World War II. His reading of noir's precarious ontology, aside from echoing Elsaesser's and Naremore's essential tenet, eloquently elaborates on this dimension of the outside of noir—geographically and culturally—as an essential prerequisite for the genre's critical understanding:

> As an object or corpus of films, *film noir* does not belong to the history of cinema; it belongs as a notion to the history of film criticism, or, if one prefers, to the history of those who wanted to love the American cinema even in its middling production and to form an image of it. *Film noir* is a collector's idea that, for the moment, can only be found in books.
>
> (26; emphasis in original)

All three critics operate from a perspective of doubly deferred action, or, to use Elsaesser's term, *Nachtraeglichkeit,* which allows for a panoptic view of the genre's historical development. Their vantage point, in the second half of the 1990s, is also that of Murakami. It encompasses first the cycle of classic noir films themselves, as well as their subsequent critical assessment by French and American critics from the 1950s to the 1970s, from Borde and Chaumeton to Schrader's "Notes on Film Noir" (1972). Historically speaking, the panoptic width of their perspective is that of contemporary directors and writers who are also invested in film noir, yet treat it not so much as a preexisting phenomenon, an accomplished cultural fact, but as a construct to be dismantled and reassembled at will.

Murakami's biographical background fits in with this historical model of doubly deferred action. He belongs to a generation that came of age "in the late 1960s and early 1970s, after their country had been assiduously importing American culture for more than two decades" (Walley 41), the first generation "to be born in the postwar period, without memories of hardship in the Second World War or participation in the reconstruction of Japan following it" (Strecher 264-65). Toshifumi Miyawaki describes this generation as the "emerging shinjinrui (literally 'New Human Race') generation of Japanese youth" (Gregory, Miyawaki, and McCaffery 112), while Rubin calls Murakami "the first genuinely 'post-post-war writer', the first to cast

off the 'dank, heavy atmosphere' of the post-war period and to capture in literature the new Americanized mood of lightness" (17). Postwar Japanese culture as Murakami has experienced it and as he describes it in his fiction has embraced American cultural imports for so long that they are virtually taken for granted.[11] The historical phase in which postwar Japan experienced the intrusion of American culture as a cause for alarm and trigger of cultural crisis has passed. What used to raise problems of national identity is now accomplished fact. By the late 1960s, which Murakami himself pinpoints as the beginning of his political and cultural awareness, Japan was as culturally colonized by the United States as most European countries, having reached a degree of saturation at which the boundaries between indigenous and imported culture were beginning to blur.[12] Noir would still carry the mark of cultural otherness, but the rough edges of the exotic, of genuine cultural otherness, would have eroded over time. By the time Murakami's generation encounters noir, it already exists as something established and fully formed. As Murakami himself approaches noir both as someone removed from the genre's geographical and historical origins, his use of the genre fits in with the accounts of noir that recent film scholarship has provided in refutation of the idea that there is such a thing as "noir" predating the critical discourse about it.

THE NOIR CITY AND ITS OTHER: ESCAPING TO THE RESIDUAL ZONE

An essential means by which noir discourse in literature and film has always reflected on its own status as a cultural construct, from the classic cycle on, is the motif of the spatial other. It postulates the existence of a space outside the noir universe, a universe that traditionally appears claustrophobic and deterministic, vast, unknowable, and of uncertain dimensions.[13] The idea of a refuge from this nightmare serves as an object of utopian desire or postlapsarian nostalgia for characters weighed down by existential pressures, chafing against urban grittiness, and suffering from isolation and alienation. It is a place of vague memories or unfulfilled promises. In the attempt to escape, characters must cross the boundaries that encircle the noir universe, or at least bump up against them when the attempted escape fails, which is almost always the case. Through the attempted transgression, the boundaries are made visible. Once reified, they become available as a self-reflexive metaphor through which noir discourse examines its own origins and effects.

Examples of this trope in classic noir and hard-boiled discourse abound, from the brief rural idyll at the end of David Goodis's *Down There* (1956, filmed as *Shoot the Piano Player,* 1960) and the desperate dash across the border in Chandler's *The Long Goodbye* (1953), to Joe Gillis's aborted attempt to return to his native Ohio in Billy Wilder's *Sunset Boulevard* (1950) and Dix Handley's failed return to the Kentucky farm of his youth in John Huston's production of W. R. Burnett's *The Asphalt Jungle* (1950). Neo-noir is equally enamored of the trope. The final sequence of David Fincher's *Se7en* (1995) takes us out of the city with the promise of narrative and dramatic resolution. *Dark City,* written and directed by Alex Proyas (1998), features a place called Shell Beach, vaguely remembered by John Murdoch, the film's protagonist, as a childhood sanctuary to which he tries to return. Other noir hybrids, such as Josef Rusniak's *The Thirteenth Floor* (1999) and Andy and Larry Wachowski's *The Matrix* (1999), feature key scenes that stage the literal breaking through of the boundaries around the noir space. In keeping with noir's cynicism and determinism, most of these attempted escapes fail: Handley collapses at the moment of arrival, Gillis ends up floating in Norma Desmond's pool, and Fincher's two detectives are reeled back into the iron maw of the city. But even these spectacular failures shed light on the existence of boundaries and paradoxically confirm rather than cast doubts on the existence of an outside, a spatial other.[14]

Murakami's two novels published, respectively, before and after *Hard-boiled Wonderland* handle this trope largely in accordance with classic American noir in film and fiction. *A Wild Sheep Chase* begins in Tokyo, presented as a space of postindustrial urban alienation worthy of Chandler's Los Angeles or Wilder's Hollywood. From there, the novel's protagonist is sent on a mission that takes him to Sapporo on the northern island of Hokkaido. The shift in location is accompanied by a shift in climate. Murakami draws attention to the cold, snow, and wind, all elements of a natural world that has been completely obliterated from the urban space in which the novel starts. But despite its remoteness, Hokkaido does not offer an escape from the corruption and political machinations in Tokyo. As in most noir discourse, the island merely promises an escape that it ultimately fails to deliver. It is merely an extension of the urban noir space, its periphery, not its outside.

The sequel to *A Wild Sheep Chase,* in which Murakami explores the spatial logic of noir further, begins with the protagonist revisiting the locations of the earlier novel. But then *Dance Dance Dance* reverses the topographic sequence, as the more substantial part of the novel takes place not on Hokkaido but in Tokyo. This move from the periphery to the center suggests that there is no escape from the noir space. To the same degree that this is a sign of resignation in the

face of an inescapable spatial and ideological totality, it also signals Murakami's willingness to conform to the rules of the genre. The forces of postindustrial capitalism associated with the urban environment have extended their reach far enough that no uncolonized spaces are left; their control of the narrative universe is total.

Or so it seems, because embedded in this totality are small niches or lacunae exempt from the forces that dominate the noir city. These spaces, it turns out, do not follow the logic of center versus periphery, but presuppose instead a spatial model closer to that of the field. This field is humming with informational density and postmodern paranoia. It is organized through an infinite connectedness that signals vitality, agency, and emplotment (at least to the degree that noir cynicism permits). Any space exempt, consequently, is coded as dead, inert, static, and void.

A Wild Sheep Chase and *Dance Dance Dance* feature a building—the Dolphin Hotel in Sapporo—that functions as the novels' primary metaphor of such exemption or spatial otherness.[15] "Its undistinguishedness was metaphysical," the protagonist tells us when he first sets foot inside the Dolphin Hotel in *A Wild Sheep Chase* (163). He calls it "incomprehensible" (166), uneasily noticing the grasp of entropic forces: "It wasn't particularly old; still it was strikingly run-down." When he revisits this postmodern haunted mansion in *Dance Dance Dance,* he is stunned to find that the old building has been "transformed into a gleaming twenty-six story Bauhaus Modern-Art Deco symphony of glass and steel, with flags of various nations waving along the driveway," grandly renamed "l' Hotel Dauphin" (21). Although, at first glance, the pressure-cooker of modernization seems to have eliminated the dead space that used to be the old Dolphin Hotel, the protagonist discovers that its essence has merely been condensed into a spatial ghost contained within the building. This ghost now lurks behind the gleaming façade that so stridently denies the existence of an unresolved past or of history altogether. The elevator stops on the wrong floor, the doors open, and a darkness that is "deathly absolute" will "entrap the unsuspecting guest" (74). Time, which had already slowed down in the Dolphin Hotel to an endless undifferentiated series of days and nights, now comes to a complete standstill.

The urban landscape in Murakami's novels is riddled with such holes, neglected or unexplored pockets and enclosures, which function in radical opposition to the social and economic bustle around them. In *The Wind-up Bird Chronicle,* a dry well in a neighbor's back yard, abandoned and half-forgotten, becomes both a trap and a sanctuary to the protagonist. A dead alley behind his house has the same connotations. "It was not an alley in the proper sense of the word," Murakami's narrator tells us, but "then there was probably no word for what it was. It wasn't a 'road' or a 'path' or even a 'way'. Properly speaking, a 'way' should be a pathway or channel with an entrance and an exit, which takes you somewhere if you follow it. But our 'alley' had neither entrance nor exit [. . .]. The alley had not one dead end but two" (12). The circumstances under which this dead space within the busy metropolis of Tokyo came to be are similarly charged with allegorical overtones:

> [. . .] the story was [. . .] that it used to have both an entrance and an exit [. . .]. But with the rapid economic growth of the mid-fifties, rows of new houses came to fill the empty lots on either side of the road [. . .]. People didn't like strangers passing so close to their houses and yards, so before long, one end of the path was blocked off [. . .]. Then one local citizen decided to enlarge his yard and completely sealed off his end of the alley.
>
> (12)

Rubin, in his study of Murakami, has two interpretations to offer for these dead spaces. "Underground" is associated with "lack of rational understanding, forgetting, free association, [which] open the deep wells and dark passageways to the timeless other world that exists in parallel with this one" (33-34).[16] As Murakami's characters enter these spaces, they begin to explore their own inner space, recover what has been lost, and, in the process, address their sense of displacement and isolation. But in the process of recentering the self through voluntary sequestration at the bottom of the well, the protagonist of *The Wind-up Bird Chronicle* also discovers that his own narrative is bound up with suppressed memories of the Japanese atrocities in Manchuria. The psychological amnesia, which begins to dissolve as a result of the protagonist's self-imposed sequestration, remains a collective cultural blind spot. Because the protagonist's self-recognition remains an atypical event in the larger Japanese culture, Rubin concludes that the space functions as an allegory of the 1980s, "a vacant, stagnant, dissatisfying decade, just beneath the surface of which lurks a violent history" (213).

The collective aspect of Rubin's reading strikes me as particularly relevant for the dead back alley that features so prominently in *The Wind-up Bird Chronicle.* Postwar economic growth on one side and xenophobia on the other side are "squeezing down" this space. This condensation is not a process that ends in a moment of explosion. Instead, it squeezes, figuratively speaking, the air out of the space. It is a dead space, hostile and uninhabitable. It is ejected from the Lacanian symbolic order and placed in the

realm of abjection, Julia Kristeva's term for the prelinguistic space of the mother that must be rejected before the adult self can come into being. As a postmodern author, Murakami sees abjection less in Kristeva's terms of psychological individuation, and more as a technologically mediated process that creates the self, from the outside in, as an extension of industrial capitalism.[17] To be outside the economic order, cut off from the formative powers of circulation, constitutes abjection. Following this logic, the origins of the mysterious back alley are relegated to the realm of conjecture and myth. To the extent that the space does not altogether fall into the realm of the unspeakable, it appears as a piece of urban legend, passed on in an informal noncommodified oral tradition. Except for this form of transmission, which is either pre-industrial or functions largely outside the commercial mechanisms of industrial culture, the space has no existence at all. Its peculiar nature cannot be captured in language because it is nothing "in the proper sense of the word."

Rubin's psychological and historical reading of the topography is convincing, especially in its account of the opposition between the ordinary and extraordinary nature of both spaces. But by the same token, Rubin is unconcerned with the fact that Murakami borrows strongly from the generic conventions of noir film and fiction. These conventions, Murakami himself admits somewhat paradoxically, appeal to him because of their "authenticity" (Gregory, Miyawaki, and McCaffery 114). To associate them, of all things, with "authenticity" requires a frame of mind that completely ignores Elsaesser's and Naremore's account of noir—an inventory of prefabricated elements, self-consciously reconfigured in plain view. Murakami's neo-noir narrators, hence, are hardly authentic; rather, they are masks the author wears to reflect back on his own social role and the limited range of his influence ("it isn't easy to live in Japan as an individualist or a loner. I'm always thinking about this. I'm a novelist and I'm a loner, an individualist" [Gregory, Miyawaki, and McCaffery 114]).

In the context of Murakami's noir pastiche, social allegory takes its place next to individual psychology. The "dead spaces" in his fiction are reminiscent of Fredric Jameson's description of postmodernism as the historical stage at which modernism's project has finally been completed. "In modernism," Jameson argues:

> [S]ome residual zones of "nature" or "being," of the old, the older, the archaic, still subsist; culture can still do something to that nature and work at transforming that "referent." Postmodernism is what you have when the modernization process is complete and nature is

gone for good. It is a more fully human world than the older one, but one in which "culture" has become a veritable "second nature."

(ix)

Jameson's categorization places Murakami's writing at the modern end of the spectrum of contemporary culture, which is surprising given Murakami's reputation as a quintessential postmodern author. The double *Nachtraeglichkeit* in regard to noir I have discussed earlier raises the question of whether Murakami intends these "residual zones" to stand for "'nature' or 'being,' [. . .] the old, the older, the archaic," as Jameson puts it. In Murakami, these zones still require the kind of cultural labor Jameson regards as a prerequisite for their completed colonization by modernism. But it is doubtful whether this labor is progressive, pushing the entire field toward a state of completed modernization, or whether this labor is already part of a postmodern nostalgia that recuperates these spaces in the same manner in which Murakami "constructs" noir discourse. True, Murakami's "residual zones" are associated with nature—the snowy countryside of Hokkaido, for example, to which the protagonist of *A Wild Sheep Chase* and *Dance Dance Dance* travels. Tokyo, by comparison, has "weather" or "climate" only in the figurative sense of the word, while Sapporo and the mountainous countryside of Hokkaido are under the sway of nature—exposed to snow, wind, and rain. But the transformation of the Dolphin Hotel into "I' Hotel Dauphin" transfers the scene of postmodern transformation from nature to culture. The "residual zone" survives behind the seamless postmodern façade of the hotel, cut off from the image-obsessed frenzy of what is already a postindustrial economy. Jameson suggests that these residual zones have been overlooked or temporarily neglected by the forces of social and economic development, or have successfully resisted invasion. But Murakami explains their existence by seeing them created by the pressures of "progress" itself, a kind of inadvertent secondary product of the process of postmodernization at the moment when it starts writing its own history as a struggle toward completion.

INSIDE ON THE OUTSIDE: NOIR DYSTOPIA AND PREINDUSTRIAL NOSTALGIA

The ways in which these pressures are written into the generic codes by which we imagine the postmodern, Murakami explores in his most accomplished "everyday myster[y] of identity and disappearance" to date, *Hard-boiled Wonderland and the End of the World.* Critical consensus has singled the book out as Murakami's most mature, most consistently developed work from this phase of his career. Although it did not sell as well as Murakami's later novel *Norwegian Wood* (1987), which made Murakami a household name in Japan, it constitutes a breakthrough for Murakami because in it, he perfects the pastiche of American hard-boiled detective fiction that underlies his entire work.[18]

Hard-boiled Wonderland and the End of the World deploys the self-reflexive spatial tropes of noir I have pointed out in Murakami's other fiction. In a discussion of Kim Newman's novel *The Night Mayor,* Rob Latham coins the term "VR noir." By this he means "an offshoot of SF noir [mostly associated with cyberpunk authors like William Gibson, Bruce Sterling, and Pat Cadigan] that deploys computer-based technologies of simulation, such as virtual reality, as interfaces between a realm of private consciousness and a larger public system of images and collective fantasy" (96). Latham's descriptions of "VR noir" is highly reminiscent of Murakami's postmodern sensibility: a heady amalgamation of "the stylish pell-mell action" harking back to Alfred Bester's 1950s science fiction, a "pop sophistication combined with an undercurrent of camp" borrowed from such TV shows as *The Avengers,* and Chandler's "tone of simmering world-weariness that conveys both alienation from, and anger at, a system of corrupt, irresponsible power" (95).

Continuing the line of nameless first-person narrators from his earlier novels, Murakami's private eye in *Hard-boiled Wonderland* is a Chandleresque figure "just doing his job" yet trying to extricate himself from a complicated cabal that revolves around the content of his brain. The cognitive breakthrough his investigation is headed for will reveal that reality is not what it seems and that the fate of the universe depends on him, as the novel mixes noir's anxieties with science fiction's technophilic exaltation. One part of the novel's setting is a neo-noir Tokyo in which two technology giants, ominously and vaguely referred to as "the System" and "the Factory," battle for economic domination in "a classic cops-and-robbers routine" (33). Fitting the postindustrial nature of the economy, the object of their competition is information, that multipurpose MacGuffin of the postindustrial economic imagination. While the Factory traffics "in illegally obtained data and other information on the black market, making megaprofits," the System, operating in a "quasi-governmental status," tries to safeguard the data (33). The protagonist works as an agent who rents out his brain as storage space for sensitive or valuable data, which are encoded by a process called "shuffling" as they are moved from one half of his brain to the other and rendered illegible even to himself. The competition is fierce, both sides play dirty, and the differences between the two factions are negligible. In short, it is noir's dog-eat-dog nightmare of capitalism run amok.

Alternating with the chapters that are set in this "VR noir" Tokyo are chapters that take place in a preindustrial or postapocalyptic village in an unspecified location and moment in history. This is the "End of the World," as opposed to the noir chapters of the "Hard-boiled Wonderland" in the novel's title. Chapters in **Hard-boiled Wonderland** are told in the past tense, while chapters in the End of the World are told in the present tense, suggesting a perpetual narrative "now" outside of the flow of history.[19] Surrounded by a high wall, the village is as much a shelter as it is a prison. Time is regulated by the cyclical patterns of nature, by the seasons of the year and the labors and rituals heralded by their recurrence. In the opening of the first chapter that takes place in the village, Murakami either uses primary colors, associated with the world of myth and fairy tale, or earth tones, associated with natural materials and substances. Unicorns graze on summer meadows. Their fur is "golden" at the "approach of autumn"; it is "black and sandy gray, white and ruddy brown" in the spring (12). Similar colors are also used in descriptions of the raw materials used in the making of buildings and objects. The narrative contemplation of the change of seasons echoes the nostalgia for a preindustrial Japan enshrined in novels such as Kawabata Yasunari's *Snow Country*: "Spring passed, summer ended, and just now as the light takes on a diaphanous glow and the first gusts of autumn ripple the waters of the streams, change becomes visible in the beasts" (Murakami, **Hard-boiled** [**Hard-boiled Wonderland and the End of the World**] 12-13). This elegiac style, "almost meditative in [its] stillness" (12), marks a dramatic departure from the hard-boiled narration in the alternate chapters. It is in keeping with the town as a metaphor for "a timeless 'original place' inside the deep wells of the mind" or "a repository of legend and dream [. . .] inaccessible to conscious thought" (Rubin 116).

At first glance, the interplay of the two separate locations recapitulates the motif of the escape from the noir space to its spatial other. Aligning itself with this motif, Hard-boiled Wonderland becomes the dystopian present or future, named with the typical sarcasm of the genre, whereas the End of the World is the refuge from it—the re-creation of one's personal or cultural past or of a topographically removed safe haven, uncontaminated by the corrupting forces of industrial capitalism. In noir film, place in the corrupt world can be represented by Huston's Asphalt Jungle or Proyas's Dark City, while the haven is represented by the Kentucky boyhood farm of *Asphalt Jungle* protagonist Handley or Murdoch's Shell Beach in *Dark City*.

But this is where the similarities end. Murakami's protagonist succeeds in making it to the village at the beginning of the novel. Contrary to the genre conven-

tions of noir, by which the escape must end in failure, his escape from Hard-boiled Wonderland appears to have been successful. More significantly, Murakami keeps the alternating chapters in balance until the end, withholding the explanation as to the exact relationship between the two locations. As the two protagonists are revealed to be one and the same person, the book ends with this person trying to escape from the village at the end of the world.

Before this happens, however, Murakami keeps the two halves of the book separate, inviting the reader to fill the ellipses within the novel's paratactic blueprint. When the story lines in both locations and alternating chapters finally dovetail, the End of the World is revealed as literally a place "inside the deep wells of the mind," to use Rubin's words. It is a mental construct inside the protagonist's brain, its constituent elements self-reflexively referred to in the novel as "the stuff writers make into novels" (262). The explanation of this central idea of the novel is so convoluted that it requires roughly twenty pages (254-74) and features a drawing of a circuit as a visual aid (271). Its metaphoric conceit is that the End of the World is the protagonist's "core consciousness," the "world in [his] mind" (270). This world is ticking down to a countdown that ends with the protagonist's consciousness entrapped in a permanent state of solipsism.

Within the larger structure of the novel, the End of the World is embedded inside the ontologically more authentic Hard-boiled Wonderland. This would follow the logic of noir inherent in the motif of the spatial other, albeit with inverted connotations, as the utopian haven is revealed as a dystopian prison. But the use of the word *and* between the two halves of the novel's title marks a departure from the noir formula. The classic noir motif would demand an *or*. Literally speaking, a person can only be in one place at a time; figuratively speaking, a person can be in two places at once, but only if the relationship between the two places corresponds to the ontological difference between the tenor and the vehicle of a metaphor.

But Murakami casts significant doubts on the superior degree of authenticity of Hard-boiled Wonderland. Just as noir's spatial other falls conspicuously short of its utopian promises, the noir universe itself is revealed to be lacking in authenticity as well. In it, there are, for example, creatures called INKlings that haunt the subterranean caverns underneath the city. Whereas the mechanisms of "shuffling" or data storage inside the human brain are naturalized through cybertechnological rhetoric, the INKlings are nightmare creatures out of horror or fantasy fiction, explicable only in reference to the supernatural. Their presence alone precludes any reading of Hard-boiled Wonderland as a place of social realism set up in conscious opposition to the mythic End of the World.

Murakami also undermines the relative proximity of Hard-boiled Wonderland to the reader's own reality by subtly undercutting the cyberpunk discourse that is supposed to anchor neo-noir Tokyo in the discursive space of extrapolative science fiction. Although "Murakami denies that [William] Gibson's work was a source for the novel," the similarities between Gibson's style of cyberpunk, which includes Rob Latham's "VR noir" as a sub-subgenre, and Murakami's novel—or at least half of it—are striking (Rubin 121). And yet the differences are far more crucial. Gibson's style is so densely allusive in its derivations from the rhetoric of science that it tends to obscure its own metaphorical significance, while Murakami draws attention to just that representational dimension. Side by side with a pastiche of Gibson's high-tech jargon (for example, "I input the data-as-given into my right brain then after converting it via a totally unrelated sign-pattern, I transfer it to my left brain, which I then output as completely recoded numbers [. . .]" 32), Murakami has his protagonist supply a crude hand-drawn sketch of the human brain split in two. The drawing depicts the brain with deadpan childish simplicity as a cracked egg.[20] With tongue-in-cheek humor, the left side is marked "LEFT BRAIN" and the right side "RIGHT BRAIN." The placement of this drawing amidst chunks of Gibsonian technobabble demystifies the rhetorical device, pointing to the conceptual simplicity underneath the complex language. Readers are reminded that the rhetoric carries, or perhaps conceals, a metaphoric level of communication identical to that of a world in which shadows are severed with the thrust of a knife from their owners, and dreams are embedded in the skulls of unicorns.

It is no coincidence that the first chapter of the novel begins with an interminably long and slow ride in an elevator, down into Tokyo's underworld. The elevator is another "dead space," a residual zone typical of Murakami. The scene recalls *Gravity's Rainbow* by Thomas Pynchon, which, unbeknownst to the reader, begins inside a nightmare about the horrors of a night-time evacuation of London during the Blitz. The scene in *Gravity's Rainbow* also functions as an elevator ride down into the world of the novel, inviting us to "wake up" to a reality that is waiting for us somewhere outside of the dream. However, when the novel begins "for real" many pages later, it is set in an unreal London that is so removed from empirical and historical reality that it is just as much a nightmare as the one from which we just woke up. This repeated deferral of the moment of truth always arrives. Like *Gravity's Rainbow*, **Hard-boiled Wonderland** never really

reaches safe ontological ground. What promised to be a safe haven turns out to be a prison inside one's own mind, embedded inside—not located outside—the world from which one had tried to escape.

It is important to keep in mind that the noir sections of **Hard-boiled Wonderland** have no claim on a higher degree of verisimilitude. Critics in pursuit of the novel's allegorical significance rely on the assumption that the End of the World is a projection, a compensatory construct that originates in Hard-boiled Wonderland. Consequently, they see "the walled, amnesia-stricken community [as] a metaphor for a Japan that hesitates to come to terms with its past or actively define a global role for its future" (Snyder 75). Murakami does indeed show us a projection of Japan, cast in terms of a popular nostalgia for preindustrial times. In Japan, this nostalgia might be based on either a conservative or even reactionary politics, while, in the West, it might be linked to an exotic image of Japan popularized in Orientalist discourse. My point of departure from other critics, however, starts with the assumption that this nostalgia is motivated by a historical reality in which contemporary Japan does indeed look like the Japan in Gibson's cyberpunk rhapsodizing—"the global imagination's default setting for the future"; "a mirror world, an alien planet we can actually do business with, a future." Murakami puts a stop to such conceptualizing of Japan. The two halves of the novel, of the narrator's consciousness, and thus of the sociohistorical allegory, are balanced in the sense that they are equally inauthentic. If the End of the World is supposed to be a projection emanating from an authentic historical Japan, then the Hard-boiled Wonderland of the novel cannot be this place. It is a noir fabrication, self-consciously assembled, baring its artificiality at every turn.

Why, then, does Murakami go to such lengths, in his self-conscious deployment of noir tropes, to distance both halves of the novel from contemporary Japan? Why does he present both visions of Japan as projections—projections from where, and by whom? What we can say with certainty is that, although his text is still recognizably noir, albeit in a contemporary slipstream format, Murakami has dismantled that favorite noir trope—the attempted escape to a spatial other. His unique accomplishment lies in the fact that this rewriting of the trope does not fall back on noir cynicism. That is, the denial of an escape from the noir space does not confirm genre as an inescapable totality. **Hard-boiled Wonderland** does not compel the reader's claustrophobic resignation or masochist submission. Instead, Murakami calls our attention to the fact that both sides of the boundary—what we perceive as inside and outside—are, in fact, projections. The only firm ground to stand on is the one that emerges from the process of negotiation between these multiple spaces, a position reminiscent of Bakhtinian heteroglossia. We arrive at the collectively assembled consensus about empirical reality, which is another way of saying "the world of the reader," through a perpetual process of dialogue between imaginary spaces. Japan is neither the nostalgic village at the End of the World, nor is it the "future we can do business with." It does, however, participate in both images, depending on whoever does the speaking. Murakami's use of noir shows his awareness that "noir in its heyday was already a symptomatic form, marking a crisis in classical narrative's capacity for depicting our world, for telling its story" (Telotte 188). One step removed even from neo-noir, which "seems intent on extending its skepticism to include the raw materials from which we fashion those narratives," **Hard-boiled Wonderland** marks the inclusion of noir itself into the inventory of "raw materials." It indicts popular genres, just as it indicts the nostalgic and potentially reactionary myths of an idyllic, preindustrial past, because they arrest the processes by which we conceptualize the world and transfer their constituent concepts into a static vocabulary of images. It is the world outside the text, Murakami insists, that other space shared by reader and author, that is constantly in flux, and thus always open to renegotiation and transformation.

Notes

1. This may have antagonized critics engaged in "the quasi-religious rhapsodizing about the spiritual superiority or unique magic of Japanese that has passed for serious intellectual commentary in Japan" (Rubin 233).

2. Critics have called Murakami's novels "cautionary parables about the dangers of life under late capitalism—dangers which included information overload, the irrelevance of human values and spirituality in a world dominated by the inhuman logic of postindustrial capitalism, and the loss of contact with other human beings" (Gregory, Miyawaki, and McCaffery 112).

3. Exceptions are *A Wild Sheep Chase* and *Dance Dance Dance,* in which the protagonist is explicitly identified as the same person.

4. Jay Rubin devotes a lengthy discussion to the figure of the *boku* in his book *Haruki Murakami and the Music of Words* (36-41).

5. Murakami also expresses a fondness for the taciturnity of the hard-boiled detectives in regard to past trauma and present misfortune. Apart from their independence, Murakami praises the fact that they "never [complain] about their misfortune" (Gregory, Miyawaki, and McCaffery 114). These comments show that he has discovered an affinity between this most American of cultural icons on the one hand

and, on the other hand, a Japanese culture that, in the eyes of outsiders, places tight strictures and rigid limitations on the expression of emotion.

6. Rubin points out that some of Murakami's more outspoken critics consider this pose a form of commercial compromise, which must be understood not from the author's point of view but with an eye on the audience he is courting. "One especially outspoken critic of Murakami is the ever-argumentative Masao Miyoshi [. . .] Like Yukio Mishima, says Miyoshi, Murakami custom-tailors his goods to his readers abroad." Whereas "Mishima displayed an exotic Japan, its nationalist side," Murakami exhibits "an exotic Japan, its international version"; he is "preoccupied with Japan, or, to put it more precisely, with what [he] imagine[s] the foreign buyers like to see in it" (Rubin 6-7).

7. It is important to note that there is, of course, an oversimplification implied in this binary model—a writer may not be "either" this "or" that. Within the binary model, however, the political flip side of Murakami's position has certain advantages, too. His association with American popular culture can be seen as a conscious move against the politics of the serious Japanese intellectual, a conservative agenda that, at its extreme right-wing end, might be associated with the heritage of Japanese militarism and imperialism.

8. Elsaesser borrows the concept of *Nachtraeglichkeit* from Freud's description of "the child [receiving] an impression to which he is unable to react adequately; he is only able to understand it and be moved by it when the impression is revived in him" at later stages in his development. Only much later "is he able to grasp with his conscious mental processes what was then going on in him" (Elsaesser 415n).

9. Quotations from Elsaesser are from his book *Weimar Cinema and After* (2000), although this specific argument was published originally in "A German Ancestry to Film Noir? Film History and its Imaginary," *iris* 21 (Spring 1996): 129-44.

10. Following a critical rather than a cinematic tradition, he traces the consolidation of the genre's identity back to the interventions of German exiles like Siegfried Kracauer and Lotte Eisner, and then on to Nino Frank and Raymond Borde and Etienne Chaumeton, wondering what role they played not in the discovery or classification of film noir, but in its invention or construction (422).

11. The import of Western culture did not begin during the years after World War II, but it had been a feature of Japanese culture since the late 1850s and especially during the Meiji restoration. This would include prewar adoption of early American film and hard-boiled detective fiction, which, as a result of rising nationalism in the prewar years, was either curtailed or culturally reframed.

12. "It is important to note here that Japan in the 1960s is Japan before its period of 'rapid growth' (kodo seicho). American influence was in many spheres immense, but once the difficult period of the 1960 *Ampo* (US-Japan Security Treaty) riots had passed, that influence turned almost entirely cultural. In a sense Murakami's protagonist is symbolic of the freedom—or perhaps aimlessness—of jazz, perhaps of American culture in general" (Tamotsu 268).

13. In its visual style, film noir accounts for this mood and for the somewhat paradoxical meshing of the claustrophobic and the agoraphobic in its use of deep-focus shots and, especially in the work of directors like Orson Welles, in its use of wide-angle lenses. Both devices open the frame up so that more visual information can be included and thus suggest a larger, less easily controllable field of vision. Simultaneously, however, both devices also crowd the frame, and especially the wide-angle lens brings objects so close that they are enlarged to the point of visual intimidation.

14. For a discussion of claustrophobia in noir and its origins, see Porfirio.

15. A closer look reveals that there are spaces that function, so to speak, as secondary enclosures of this type. In *A Wild Sheep Chase,* for example, a limo picks up the protagonist, enveloping him "in near total silence"; being inside is "as quiet as sitting at the bottom of a lake wearing earplugs" (65, 66). *Hard-boiled Wonderland* opens with a lengthy scene in which the protagonist is trapped in an elevator's "impossibly slow ascent" so unnerving in its smoothness that there "was no telling for sure" whether it is ascending or descending—"all sense of direction simply vanished" (1). Clearly, these are transitory spaces—an automobile, an elevator—serving as a foreshadowing of the place to which they are transporting the protagonist.

16. It is fitting that Murakami has called his series of investigative interviews with survivors of the AUM gas attack on the Tokyo subway *Underground* (2000).

17. For further information on the terminology used here, see Creed, and for a discussion of individuation within the sociohistorical and cultural contexts of late capitalism, see Seltzer.

18. Miyawaki calls the novel "perhaps his masterpiece to date" (Gregory, Miyawaki, and McCaffery 112), and Rubin declares that he has "been able to enjoy almost everything of Murakami's knowing that he was the creator of that incredible mind trip *Hard-boiled Wonderland and the End of the World.*" He places the novel at the center of Murakami's oeuvre, reading it as a key to the entire work; "echoes of [it] are to be found in everything he has written since" (285). Critics in Japan agreed with these assessments when they awarded the novel the prestigious Tanizaki Literary Prize in 1985.

19. This is, however, a reading of the English translation rather than Murakami's original Japanese. In the original, Murakami splits "his narrator-hero into Boku and Watashi, assigning the formal Watashi-T to the more realistic world of a vaguely futuristic Tokyo, and the informal Boku-T to the inner, fantastic world of 'The Town and Its Uncertain Walls'" (Rubin 117). The title in the quotation refers to an earlier short story by Murakami that provides the thematic basis for the novel.

20. It also alludes to the map of the village at the End of the World that can be found in the opening of the novel (placed before the beginning of pagination). The village is split down the middle into two cerebral hemispheres by a river, much like a brain. The association with the child's drawing of the cracked egg demystifies the map, in its generic function as part of high fantasy.

Works Cited

The Asphalt Jungle. Dir. John Huston. Perf. Sterling Hayden, Louis Calhern, and Jean Hagen. MGM, 1950.

Burnett, W. R. *The Asphalt Jungle.* New York: Knopf, 1949.

Cassegard, Carl. "Haruki Murakami and the Naturalization of Modernity." *International Journal of Japanese Sociology* 10 (2001): 80-92.

Chandler, Raymond. *Farewell, My Lovely.* New York: Knopf, 1940.

———. *The Long Goodbye.* 1953. New York: Vintage, 1992.

———. "The Simple Art of Murder: An Essay." 1944. *The Simple Art of Murder.* New York: Vintage, 1988. 1-19.

Creed, Barbara. "Kristeva, Femininity, Abjection." Gelder 64-71.

Dark City. Dir. Alex Proyas. Perf. Rufus Sewell and William Hurt. New Line Cinema, 1998.

Elsaesser, Thomas. *Weimar Cinema and After: Germany's Historical Imaginary.* New York: Routledge, 2000.

Freud, Sigmund. "From the History of an Infantile Neurosis ('Wolf Man')." *The Freud Reader.* Ed. Peter Gay. New York: Norton, 1989. 400-29.

Gelder, Ken, ed. *The Horror Reader.* New York: Routledge, 2000.

Gibson, William. "Modern Boys and Mobile Girls." *Guardian Unlimited* 1 Apr. 2001 <http://observer.guardian.co.uk/life/story/0,6903,466391,00.html>.

Goodis, David. *Down There.* Greenwich: Fawcett, 1956.

Gregory, Sinda, Toshifumi Miyawaki, and Larry Mc-Caffery. "It Don't Mean a Thing, If It Ain't Got That Swing: An Interview with Haruki Murakami." *Review of Contemporary Fiction* 22.2 (Summer 2002): 111-19.

Hammett, Dashiell. *The Maltese Falcon.* New York: Knopf, 1930.

Iyer, Pico. "The Mystery of Influence: Why Raymond Chandler Persists While So Many More Respected Writers Are Forgotten." *Harper's Magazine* Oct. 2002: 85-91.

Jameson, Fredric. *Postmodernism, or, the Cultural Logic of Late Capitalism.* Durham: Duke UP. 1991.

Kiss Me Deadly. Dir. Robert Aldrich. Perf. Ralph Meeker. United Artists, 1955.

Latham, Rob. "VR Noir: Kim Newman's *The Night Mayor.*" *Paradoxa: Studies in World Literary Genres* 16 (2001): 95-109.

Mandel, Ernest. *Delightful Murder: A Social History of the Crime Story.* Minneapolis: U of Minnesota P, 1984.

The Matrix. Dir. Andy Wachowski and Larry Wachowski. Perf. Keanu Reeves and Laurence Fishburne. Warner Bros., 1999.

Murakami, Haruki. *Dance Dance Dance.* New York: Vintage, 1994.

———. *The Elephant Vanishes.* New York: Knopf, 1993.

———. *Hard-boiled Wonderland and the End of the World.* New York: Vintage, 1993.

———. *Kafka on the Shore.* New York: Knopf, 2005.

———. *Norwegian Wood.* 1987. New York: Vintage, 2000.

———. *The Sputnik Sweetheart.* 1999. New York: Knopf, 2001.

———. *Underground: The Tokyo Gas Attack and the Japanese Psyche.* London: Harvill, 2000.

———. *A Wild Sheep Chase.* New York: Penguin, 1990.

———. *The Wind-up Bird Chronicle.* 1997. London: Vintage, 2003.

Naremore, James. *More than Night: Film Noir in Its Contexts.* Berkeley: U of California P, 1998.

Porfirio, Robert. "No Way Out: Existential Motifs in the *Film Noir.*" Silver and Ursini 77-95.

Pynchon, Thomas. *Gravity's Rainbow.* New York: Viking, 1972.

Ross, Andrew. *No Respect: Intellectuals and Popular Culture.* London: Routledge, 1989.

Rubin, Jay. *Haruki Murakami and the Music of Words.* London: Harvill, 2002.

Le Samouraï [U.S. title: *The Godson*]. 1967. Dir. Jean-Pierre Melville. Perf. Alain Delon. 1967. Artists Intl., 1972.

Schrader, Paul. "Notes on Film Noir." Silver and Ursini 53-65.

Seltzer, Mark, "The Serial Killer as a Type of Person." Gelder 97-111.

Se7en [Seven]. Dir. David Fincher. Perf. Brad Pitt, Morgan Freeman, and Gwyneth Paltrow. New Line Cinema, 1995.

Shoot the Piano Player [Tirez sur le pianiste], 1960. Dir. François Truffaut. Perf. Charles Aznavour and Marie Dubois. Astor Pictures, 1962.

Silver, Alain, and James Ursini, eds. *Film Noir Reader.* New York: Limelight, 1996.

Snyder, Stephen. "Two Murakamis and Marcel Proust: Memory as Form in Japanese Fiction." *In Pursuit of Contemporary East Asian Culture,* Ed. Xiaobing Tang and Stephen Snyder. Boulder: Westview, 1996. 69-83.

Spillane, Mickey. *Kiss Me, Deadly.* New York: Dutton, 1952.

Strecher, Matthew. "Magical Realism and the Search for Identity in the Fiction of Murakami Haruki." *Journal of Japanese Studies* 25.2 (Summer 1999): 269-98.

Sunset Boulevard. Dir. Billy Wilder. Perf. William Holden, Gloria Swanson, and Erich von Stroheim. Paramount, 1950.

Tamotsu, Aoki. "Murakami Haruki and Contemporary Japan." Trans. Matthew Strecher. Ed. John Whittier Treat. *Contemporary Japan and Popular Culture.* Honolulu: U of Hawaii P, 1996. 265-75.

Telotte, J. P. "Lost Memory and New Noir." *Paradoxa: Studies in World Literary Genres* 16 (2001): 177-89.

"The Ten Best Books of 2005." *New York Times* 11 Dec. 2005 <www.nytimes.com/2005/12/11/books/review/tenbest.html.

The Thirteenth Floor. Dir. Josef Rusnak. Perf. Craig Bierko and Armin Mueller-Stahl. Columbia Pictures, 1999.

Vernet, Marc. "Film Noir on the Edge of Doom." *Shades of Noir: A Reader.* Ed. Joan Copjec. New York: Verso, 1993, 1-33.

Walley, Glynne. "Two Murakamis and Their American Influence." *Japan Quarterly* 44.1 (Jan.-Mar. 1997): 41-50.

Keya Mitra (review date May-June 2008)

SOURCE: Mitra, Keya. "Enigmatic Magic." *American Book Review* 29, no. 4 (May-June 2008): 18-19.

[*In the following review, Mitra praises* After Dark *for its mysterious tone and for the uncertainty in the story's plot.*]

In Haruki Murakami's *After Dark,* "we," the reader and the unknown narrator, witness intimate moments of these characters' lives—the supernatural experience of a Sleeping Beauty sucked into a television screen and the transient but poignant encounters Mari Asai, the protagonist, shares with a musician, an ex-professional wrestler and owner of a twenty-four-hour love hotel, and a battered Chinese prostitute. As readers, we are in a position of constant unease as we are sucked into the movement of a city that at night resembles "a single gigantic creature—or more like a single collective entity created by many intertwining organisms." Murakami writes: "The district plays by its own rules at a time like this." In this suspenseful but subtle novel set in Japan, we witness a series of surrealistic and miraculous events transpire after dark, when characters are at the mercy of the wiles of the city.

In Murakami's novel, a shift occurs at night—the city's inhabitants relinquish their autonomy and get sucked into the inexorable movement of street life. Characters try to control time: from her table by a window at Denny's, Mari, a college freshman reading alone, glances down at the street below, which is flooded with people "trying to hold time back and people trying to urge it forward." Mari tries to "buy herself more time" at this twenty- four-hour diner by ordering a sandwich. However, Mari has no control over time, just as she has virtually no control over her independence. She has come to a diner to escape from family and to read alone, but at night it seems that even those seeking isolation are drawn into the lives of strangers in the city. After dark, lives intersect, and strangers acquire dimension and humanity.

Within the first two paragraphs of the novel, Murakami establishes an ominous tone. Though the "peak of activity has passed," the "basal metabolism that maintains life continues undiminished, producing the basso continuo of the city's moan, a monotonous sound that neither rises nor falls but is pregnant with foreboding." The city's moan signals a pervasive desperation that we sense in the novel's characters as well. In this vast city, the camera hones in on Mari sitting in the diner. Mari isn't instantly likeable by any means; when approached at the Denny's by a young man, an acquaintance from the past, with a smile

"meant to show he means no harm," she "looks at him with eyes that could be looking at an overgrown bush in the corner of a garden." She responds tersely to his conversation and seems constantly on guard. Unlike many novels, in which the reader is allowed access to the thoughts and emotions of the characters, we are never allowed to enter Mari's mind or inspect her thoughts. We never feel entirely comfortable because we are voyeurs embarking on a sinister journey with strangers whose thoughts are off-limits to us. Murakami takes on the daunting task of creating character without interiority, and he rises to the challenge admirably, developing enigmatic but complex and compelling characters.

Murakami tests our patience when it comes to the minutiae of his characters lives—even the most minor of details are sometimes withheld. For example, when Mari asks the young man conversing with her his name, he manages to dodge the question: "'I don't mind if you forget my name. It's about as ordinary as a name can be. Even I feel like forgetting it sometimes.'" In fact, it isn't until thirty-two pages into the novel that Kaoru, another stranger Mari encounters who owns a love hotel named Alphaville, reveals the man's name, Murakami's characters demand our faith and endurance. However, if we exercise patience, *After Dark* can be an immensely satisfying read.

Initially, Mari is an impenetrable character. However, once Kaoru exposes Mari to a situation outside her comfort zone—one in which a young Chinese prostitute at a "love hotel" has been physically beaten by a Japanese businessman (her customer), and Mari must translate her account of what happened—Mari's vulnerabilities begin to emerge. She forms a strange connection with Kaoru, a "'big hunk of a woman,'" and the battered Chinese girl whose story she translates. We soon discover during Mari's conversation with the young man that her sister, Eri, has been in a deep sleep for a long time, and the details of Mari's family life are gradually revealed. Though we cannot travel inside the minds of these characters, we come to embrace the strangeness of their circumstances. Even Eri, Mari's beautiful sister (also referred to as "Sleeping Beauty" or "Snow White") who we mostly see in slumber, comes alive as a character as she emerges, through conversation, as a complicated, haunted woman.

Though the novel is slow in revealing the essence of its characters, Murakami maintains in his narrative a continual tension and suspense. At times, we are confronted with magical and unexplainable circumstances: a television flickers on in Eri's room though it is not plugged in, and on the screen we see a masked man sitting in a chair in the same room in which Eri is sleeping. The narrator confirms our suspicion that "something is about to happen in this room. Something of great significance." Initially, it seems we are watching a scene straight out of a horror movie like *The Ring* (2002); at any moment we expect a creature from the dead to suck Eri into the nightmarish world of the television.

But Murakami is far too skilled a writer to lapse into melodrama or horror. Eri is drawn into the television and transported to a world on "the other side," but we can never pinpoint the sinister forces at work in this world. Although we frequently witness otherworldly occurrences. Murakami does not attempt to answer these mysteries. We do not witness either the downfall or redemption of Mari's gorgeous sleeping sister—unlike Sleeping Beauty or Snow White, she is not conveniently rescued or saved. Magic operates in small ways in Murakami's narrative, and readers anticipating anything more dramatic will inevitably be disappointed. The world of this novel is beautiful and mystical, but it challenges us to absorb the reality before us without seeking resolution. At times, the lack of character interiority can be infuriating; as we watch a Chinese businessman who, hours ago, brutally attacked a young woman, complete sit-ups on his office floor, we crave some insight into his motivations, his emotions. Of course, we never get such answers, for violence, like magic, remains unexplained. As readers, we must accept the uncertainty of the narrative.

After Dark is a wonderfully understated, enigmatic novel in which questions are raised without being answered, relationships are developed without a guarantee of continuation, and supernatural forces are at work that we cannot identify. In the midst of all this uncertainty. Murakami's ending seems somewhat conventional and sentimental. However, perhaps in a novel so steeped in ambiguity and nuance, virtually no conclusion would seem satisfactory. The story ends as abruptly and mysteriously as it begins. Like the characters, we must give in to the powerful forces at work here and revel in the mystical experience of inhabiting Murakami's world while it lasts.

Matthew Richard Chozick (essay date 2008)

SOURCE: Chozick, Matthew Richard. "De-Exoticizing Haruki Murakami's Reception." *Comparative Literature Studies* 45, no. 1 (2008): 62-73.

[*In the following essay, Chozick considers how Japanese and American readers have each interpreted Murakami's writing as exotic, with Japanese critics pointing to Murakami's references to American culture, and*

American reviewers discussing Murakami's fiction in terms of his Japanese background. This essay originally contained ideographic characters, which have been silently removed for this reprinting.]

> "Japan is a pure invention. There is no such country, there are no such people."
>
> —Oscar Wilde

Little scholarship has accounted for the contradictory international reception of Haruki Murakami's corpus of literature. Japanese literati have derided Murakami, who lived outside of Japan for much of two decades, as being Americanized or as pandering his style to an American audience. For instance, scholar Masao Miyoshi argued in *Off Center* that Murakami writes not of Japan, but of "what the foreign [book] buyers like to see in it."[1] Nobel laureate Kenzaburō Ōe has said that "Murakami writes in Japanese, but his writing isn't really Japanese . . . it can be read very naturally in New York."[2] In 1998, the year Murakami's critically acclaimed novel, [*The Wind-Up Bird Chronicle*], went into English print, the author himself professed that Japanese culture had become unfamiliar to him due to a "self-imposed exile [from Japan]."[3]

In contrast to Murakami's Japanese reception, American reviewers often treat the author's fiction as inseparable from his cultural heritage. For instance, A. O. Scott, writing in *Newsday,* said that Murakami's *The Wind-Up Bird Chronicle* embodied "a vision no American novelist could have invented."[4] Elizabeth Ward, a reviewer for *Washington Post Book World,* deemed Murakami's *The Wind-Up Bird Chronicle* an endeavor to "stuff all of modern Japan into a single fictional edifice."[5] Yet curiously enough, the first two volumes of *The Wind-Up Bird Chronicle* were researched and penned in Princeton, New Jersey; the final volume was completed in Cambridge, Massachusetts. Apropos of this, Murakami said in an interview with Jay Rubin—leading scholar and translator of *The Wind-Up Bird Chronicle*—that he "could not have written *The Wind-Up Bird Chronicle* if he had not been living in the United States."[6]

Nevertheless, American brands, song lyrics, and political references were in Haruki Murakami's writings before he ever set foot outside of Japan. Indeed, in *1973* [*Pinball, 1973*]—written three years before the author first traveled internationally—he described these game machines as containing:

> [An awfully large amount of copper, enough to construct statues of all the presidents in American history (though you may not like Richard M. Nixon enough to build a statue of him).][7]

This quip at President Nixon's expense, of course, does not require a footnote for most of Murakami's

American readership. This degree of accessibility for Americans, sometimes at the expense of Japanese, is a tendency throughout Murakami's books.

Murakami's works rarely mention contemporary Japanese culture, corporations, composers, or artists. The protagonists do not cite the lyrics of Japanese pop stars, fit diligent "salaryman" stereotypes, or patron karaoke establishments. In contrast, internationally distinguished American and British companies, films, authors, and bands are frequently referenced. *The Wind-Up Bird Chronicle*'s central character, Toru, discusses jazz, munches cookies, hears of Allen Ginsberg and Keith Richards, drinks coffee, listens to Michael Jackson, writes with a Mont Blanc pen, and meets Japanese with non-Japanese names—such as Cinnamon, Nutmeg, and Malta. With all of these recognizable cultural references, how might *Newsday*'s book review of *The Wind-Up Bird Chronicle* describe the text as "a vision no American novelist could have invented"?

I propose to answer this question by reconciling the seemingly incompatible readings of Murakami's works in Japan and in America with the author's texts as well as cultural-historical concomitants. Such an analysis requires a critical theory of how exoticism has functioned as a commodity in the Japanese and American reception of Murakami's writings. Translator and scholar Philip Gabriel examined Murakami's travel writing from a relevant perspective. Gabriel's journal article, "Back to the Unfamiliar," treated Murakami's works as "a repeated pattern, a path outwards that in the final analysis spirals inwards, an ostensible attempt to confront the exotic and the unfamiliar that ends up obsessed with the familiar."[8] In Gabriel's article, the interchange between exoticism (non-Japaneseness) and familiarity (Japaneseness) was foregrounded, but Gabriel did not analyze how readers from "unfamiliar" or "other" cultures experience Murakami's texts in translation. I will expand this comparatively vis-à-vis Murakami's reception.

In this paper I argue that several different, but complementary mechanisms—in Japan and in America—naturalize Murakami's fiction as almost universally "foreign," while at the same time universally accessible. This paradox is textually contingent on three narratological features. First, Japanese and American readers are generally quite familiar with the allusions, themes, textualized political events, and authorial techniques Murakami selects to write with and about. Second, conscious recognition of this familiarity is then obfuscated by an exotic façade of foreign language loan words, recognizable cultural objects described in unexpected ways, and an array of apposite book covers that conjure the myth of exoti-

cism. Lastly, Murakami's works also remain open to contradictory interpretations as a corollary of unresolved ambiguities in plot, character, setting, diction, and physical descriptions. But before continuing with the present conjecture, let us discuss a concrete example to build upon.

CULTURAL CONFUSION, PLURALITY, AND APPROPRIATION

In 2006, Alan Cheuse reviewed Haruki Murakami's [*Kafka on the Shore*] on America's *National Public Radio* and said this about the title: "*Kafka on the Shore*? I suppose it might seem equally as suggestive and mysterious to Japanese readers if they picked up a novel like 'Lady Murasaki of the Loop' or 'Genji on the Hudson.'"[9]

Cheuse's assessment is terribly problematic. Cheuse claimed that Franz Kafka is as endemically American as Chicago's "Loop" or New York's "Hudson"—and while Americans tend to overuse and maltreat the expression "Kafkaesque," it is absurd to reason that Kafka stands as a monument to the United States. Also, Cheuse alleged that Kafka's name would be unknown or "mysterious," to Japanese. This usage of "mysterious," this linguistic sign, consists of two components: the signifier (mysterious) and the signified concept (Kafka's German-language literature being foreign or unknown to Japanese readers, but not to Americans). Thus, Cheuse represented the Japanese as literarily insular, while paradoxically classifying *Kafka on the Shore* as the product of a Japanese author. No doubt, Japanese literati would lament Cheuse's tenuous statement if it were better publicized. Might Cheuse have more productively considered Murakami's novel as liminal, as existing in a gulf between cultures?

Hayao Kawai, a Japanese psychoanalyst who writes extensively on Murakami, read *Kafka on the Shore* as a novel of utmost liminality. Kawai interpreted the name [Kafuka], as an attempt to combine opposite etymons [ka] (possible, good) and [fuka] (not possible, not good), which are normally separated, but here are merged into one boundary-less sign.[10] "Ka-fuka" superimposes consciousness and unconsciousness, success and failure, the possible and the impossible. In *Murakami Haruki: The Simulacrum in Contemporary Japanese Culture,* scholar Michael Seats agreed with Kawai and added that Murakami's use of liminal symbols is like Jacques Derrida's exegesis of the pharmakon, in which meaning "remains obscure."[11] In Seats's reading of *Kafka on the Shore,* interpretations are open to contradiction; multiple opposing explications may both be correct as "options and possibilities" (338). Is it in this way that Murakami's texts are reversibly interpretable as either American or as Japanese?

Part of the difficulty in understanding and classifying Haruki Murakami is that he may represent a new cultural plurality that cannot be easily fit into common historical conceptions of national identity or literary canons. To this end, in this journal, scholar Naomi Matsuoka advocated for Murakami to be canonically grouped with others of stylistic similarity instead of by Japanese nationality: "we may consider them contemporary fictions rather than classifying them by countries."[12] But whether or not canonization is reformed, the point stands that Murakami has much in common with American writers. Jay Rubin wrote that Murakami was "heavily influenced by the rhythms of his favorite [American] authors. . . . Raymond Chandler, then Truman Capote, F. Scott Fitzgerald, and Kurt Vonnegut."[13] Not only the rhythm, but also the musical cadence of America has been incorporated into many of Murakami's works. For instance, the title [*Dance Dance Dance*] was originally a Dells number and [*South of the Border, West of the Sun*] references a Nat King Cole tune. Clearly these book names resonate with many American and Japanese readers by evoking shared nostalgia. However, the titles are also repositories of foreign culture in Japan, which points towards well-known but exotic references in the English foreign language.

Let us revisit the argument that Haruki Murakami's success has been contingent upon a perceived exoticism. This contains two lines of reasoning: Murakami's novels must be branded as somewhat American in Japan, but more Japanese in America. In either country, the content of Murakami's novels ought to be largely recognizable—despite any exotic façades. English-language versions of Murakami's novels are outwardly exotic, not due to foreign language song names printed on the covers, but through the use of images of Japanese women. Erotic photographs are not on the Japanese editions of Murakami's works. On the front of an English-language edition of [*Sputnik Sweetheart*], a bare Japanese model waits in bed for the reader. The undressed woman does not reveal her culture, yet her culture is explicit with the word "Japanese" printed numerous times on the book. The pictorial representation of Japan is a culturally neutered portrayal, ultimately suited to come across as not too foreign and not too pedestrian. Murakami's cover girls never wear traditional or modern Japanese clothing such as *yukata, kimono*—or conversely—farmer Johns, Levi's jeans, or Gap t-shirts. This is a literary example of Daryl J. Bem's social psychological research, in which marginally exotic encounters,

"exotic—but not too exotic," were shown to heighten arousal.[14] Murakami's book covers have been just that; the photographs are exotic, but do not estrange American readers by either incorporating unrecognizably foreign or overly familiar Western images. Thus, Japan appears as familiar or as mysterious as the non-Japanese reader negotiates it to be. One might envision the eroticized girl on *Sputnik Sweetheart* dressed anachronistically. The nude body is a blank canvas for cultural ascription.

Encountering Murakami's book covers is a starkly different experience for Japanese than for Americans, but of comparable foreignness. Murakami's Japanese book jackets display non-Japanese art in the form of English language maps, Russian spacecrafts, Balinese contemporary painting, Italian sculpture, Czech text, and so forth. In addition, Japanese readers must often use English—Japanese dictionaries to decode the covers; insofar as the "neologic" book titles include English words such as [chronicle], [pinball], [hardboiled], [dance], [dark], [wonderland], [people], and more.

In translation, the covers and titles pose an ironic problem: the nuance of Murakami's English cannot be rendered back into English. The visual exoticism of the *katakana* phonetic script used to type non-Japanese words, the unclear meanings, and the dual language stylization cannot be preserved in English translations. What might the English in Murakami's titles signify to his Japanese readership? Jacques Derrida once wrote that "a name . . . immediately says more than the name."[15] Certainly this is true with English titles appropriated into Japanese that are nuanced as exotic, yet written in the familiar Japanese *katakana* script. The fashionable amalgamation of English nomenclature into the Japanese lexicon has a remarkable history. Japan's unconditional surrender to the United States took place on August 15, 1945, but by September 1945 the *Japanese-American Conversation Booklet* comprised a top-selling position of sales in the country; as a consequence, scholar Shunya Yoshimi has argued, America became "inscribed in the identities of the Japanese people."[16] But how does this remotely inscribed identity differ from the identity of Americans?

MULTIPLE IDENTITIES AND SKIN TONES

As discussed above, Haruki Murakami's characterization is often conveyed by non-Japanese cultural references and affiliations. Some of these references are straightforward such as a woman introduced in [*Hard-Boiled Wonderland and the End of the World*] as a J. D. Salinger and George Harrison fan. But often, foreign references are re-interpreted and function independently of what, for example, American readers may recognize as familiar. For instance, the cast of characters in *Kafka on the Shore* features Kentucky Fried Chicken's Colonel Sanders as well as the Scottish whiskey icon Johnnie Walker. These cultural icons represent a postmodernism that is antonymous with any corporate ties. Murakami does not follow prescribed notion of what these printed names signify, even though he exploits the significations for an effect that is defamiliarizing. For instance, the whiskey magnate Johnnie Walker collects cats from his neighborhood in Tokyo and eats their hearts to make a giant flute to somehow destroy the universe.

Johnnie Walter demonstrates his heart collection process to a mentally handicapped man while singing "Heigh-Ho" from Disney's *Snow White*:

> [Johnnie Walker's eyes narrowed. For a while, he gently pets the cat's head. He then runs the tip of his index finger up and down the cat's soft belly. Without warning, Johnnie Walker, using the scalpel in his right hand, does not hesitate to slice a straight line down the young feline's belly. . . . The abdomen separates, gapes open, and red colored organs spill out. . . . Then while whistling "Heigh-Ho," he sticks his hand inside the cat's body. With a tiny scalpel, Johnnie Walker skillfully slices the heart free from the body and then pulls out the cat's heart. . . . As if it were a totally natural thing to do, he stuck the heart inside of his mouth.][17]

This passage juxtaposes a very immediate sense of reality—activating all five senses—with the absurdity of Johnnie Walker butchering a feline to the Seven Dwarves' harmony. It is noteworthy that preexisting schemata on the whiskey icon cannot be negotiated for comprehension. Readers must eschew reliance on familiarity and accept a system of coding multiple possible identities to Johnnie Walker. In this way, Murakami's characters, familiar to both Japanese and Americans, are defamiliarized.

Achieving the same uncanny effect, Kentucky Fried Chicken's Colonel Sanders plays the role of a pimp in *Kafka on the Shore*. This personality lauds one of his prostitutes:

> [Voluptuous breasts, tender skin, a curvy waist, dripping wet. A hot, sex machine.][18]

Notice that in this quotation, Colonel Sanders's speech does not describe the prostitute's beauty in visual terms—even though pale flesh is widely considered an aesthetic asset in Japan. Murakami's characters are almost never depicted with skin color. Consequently, these imaginary individuals might be visualized as racially Icelandic, Indian, or Japanese; it is of no textual significance.

In *Wind-Up Bird Chronicle,* a Mongolian soldier peels the flesh off a Japanese soldier and improbably, skin

color again is not remarked on, even though other body organs are described fully:

> [Lastly, the bear-like Mongolian officer spread the skin from Yamamoto's torso, which he had stripped skillfully. On it were even Yamamoto's nipples. Someone grabbed the skin and spread it out like a sheet to dry. . . . A lump of red, bloody, skinless meat was on the ground. . . . From amid the mass of blood and flesh were two large white eyeballs peering out. Yamamoto's mouth was stuck wide open as if screaming. His teeth were bared.][19]

In this passage, Murakami's corporeal descriptions are all universally valid in terms of color. Humans share the same appearance of internal organs and "white eyeballs." Consequently, Americans are not pushed to imagine Japanese individuals; once more, the characters are as exotic or as pedestrian as readers negotiate them to be.

Likewise, in a short story published in *The New Yorker* titled, **"Shinagawa Monkey",** Murakami introduced a psychotherapist—an unconventional Japanese occupation—as "a pleasant, heavyset woman in her late forties. Her short hair was dyed a light brown, her broad face wreathed in an amiable smile."[20] This description, like many of Murakami's, might appear straightforward to the magazine's subscribers. However, in a closer reading, it ought to seem peculiar that the therapist's hair color is dyed brown, as opposed to blonde. For American readers, this difference again reinforces the exoticism of Murakami's writing, even though brown hair is ubiquitous in the United States.

MURAKAMI AND AMERICAN BASEBALL

In April 1978, Haruki Murakami attended a Japanese baseball game starring an American hitter named Dave Hilton. Hilton got into position to swing, pulled back his bat, and whacked a ball scoring a double. Murakami saw this—sitting in the outfield with a beer—and suddenly thought for no reason whatsoever, "the idea struck me: I could write a novel . . . I went to a stationery store and bought a fountain pen and paper."[21] This was the serendipitous way in which Murakami became an author at the age of twenty-nine. The metaphor found in baseball—of one man batting alone, but supporting others, pitted against an entire lineup, corporation, supernatural being, or government—has been persistent in virtually every piece Murakami has published. Equally striking is the number of baseball references Murakami has included in his texts.

In *The Wind-Up Bird Chronicle,* the protagonist, Toru, grips a baseball bat to move through space and levels of consciousness. This bat not only assists in transporting Toru, but at the end of the novel, he finds victory in combating the malevolent character Noburu Wataya by employing the baseball bat as a weapon. The narrator describes the scene:

> [I got a hit in with the bat somewhere near my rival's clavicle. . . . Then I landed a compact backswing with the bat on my rival's body. I took another try in the same direction, but changed the angle to be slightly higher. . . . On the third swing, I struck home with a hit in his face.][22]

Notice Murakami's diction is drawn directly from baseball: "compact backswing" is katakana English pronounced as "konpakuto swingu"; "struck home" translates from the Japanese baseball term [meichuu]. Moreover, in terms of narrative structure, this final scene replicates baseball's theatrical three-swing system, which builds towards a climax and resolution by counting off the times at bat.

Like in *The Wind-Up Bird Chronicle*, baseball also facilitates plot development and resolution in *Kafka on the Shore*. Hoshino the truck driver, a character with the same surname as a former player and coach of the Chunichi Dragons, meets Colonel Sanders. Just after making his acquaintance, Colonel Sanders says:

> [I always call Chunichi Dragon fans Hoshino-chan.][23]

In this line of dialogue, Sanders inappropriately refers to Hoshino with the informal "chan." Sanders explains his casual elocution as a kind of baseball camaraderie, which then helps the two speakers bond (right off the bat). Many American readers are, no doubt, familiar with the process of how sports fans bond through team talk, though the nuanced transgression of formality in this scene may be difficult for non-Japanese to understand. Regardless, this social setting, discussing sports to establish rapport, is recognizable to Americans.

Walt Whitman once wrote that baseball "belongs as much to our [American] institutions . . . as our Constitution's laws."[24] Indeed, baseball is known as the "national pastime." But this familiar "all-American sport" has a longstanding history in the "land of the rising sun." Horace Wilson, an American professor at Tokyo University, introduced baseball to Japan in 1872. Since this time, baseball has become Japan's principal spectator sport. Tokyo houses a Baseball Hall of Fame with plaques displaying team names redolent of foreign counterparts such as the Buffaloes, Lions, Bay-stars, Lotte Marines, Softbank Hawks, Yumiuri Giants, and so forth. As a consequence, the baseball references in Murakami's novels are particularly familiar to both Japanese and Americans; but the contexts—for instance, between a pimp from Kentucky and a Japanese truck-driver, or between an astral projecting man and a Diet member—once more defamiliarize and exoticize the texts.

CONCLUSION

Reviews and critics all over the world write of Murakami's fiction as foreign, yet his record-breaking sales—garnered in over twenty languages—demonstrate a universal compatibility. This success depends on both Murakami's ability to make his books accessible internationally and also on how readers perceive Japan. Concerning Americans, many come to expect, appreciate, and inculcate notions of Japanese exoticism. For instance, in *The New Yorker*, November 27, 2006, a two-page comic with the ubiquitous title: "Turning Japanese, I Really Think So" spoofed the process of an American reading manga for the first time. This cartoon inducts a fictional character into a bizarre world of parody. To appreciate this kooky cartoon, the reader must have at least a modicum of prior exposure to manga; spoofing depends on familiarity. Much like in the case of Haruki Murakami, this kind of familiarity with Japan is exoticized.

Haruki Murakami's writings have been widely interpreted as foreign, which I attributed above to cultural concomitants that function in concert with narratological devices in the author's works. A number of mechanisms—such as Murakami's use of loan words, references, and exotic book covers—play more than a mere soupçon role in evoking the author's foreignness. In both Japan and America, Murakami's success has been contingent on his capacity to package narratives as exotic, but filled with recognizable content. This acrobatic feat requires not only adroit writing, but also a global modernity in which the miscegenation of cultures has occurred through technological advancements.

Recall my analysis of Alan Cheuse's National Public Radio review of *Kafka on the Shore*. Cheuse spoke of Franz Kafka as belonging more to America than to Japan. Cheuse's misappropriation of Kafka as his own literature, suggests that foreign culture can be interpreted as ontologically part of new global ethos—an ethos that spreads beyond topography and language, an ethos that unites nations through narrative. However, constituents cannot be equally, simultaneously of numerous lands. And it is through conceptualizing modern culture as inherently fragmented, disjunctive, and like the pop artist and historian Takashi Murakami once argued, a "number of distinct layers [merged] into one," that the incompatible reviews presented by Japanese and Americans, for example, can be understood as not separate but within the same "literary ecosystem."[25]

This essay explored the psychological construction of exoticism as an aesthetic of unperceived familiarity. Forthcoming papers might continue to examine how this understanding could be applied to other circumstances or in additional capacities. In the future, writers of critical theory and cultural studies will no doubt be ever more concerned with how technology and the dissemination of media rapidly alter the face of global communities—and by extension human identity. To suggest that Murakami could even be Japanese or could even be American is to conceptualize identity based on a nationalistic paradigm that may no longer hold much value. After all, in Murakami's world, Colonel Sanders is a pimp and a Chunichi Dragon fan.

Notes

1. Masao Miyoshi, *Off Center* (Cambridge: Harvard UP, 1991), 234.

2. Kenzaburō Ōe and Kazuo Shiguro, "The Novelist in Today's World: A Conversation," *boundary 2* 18.3 (1991): 118.

3. Haruki Murakami, *Underground,* trans. Alfred Birnbaum and Philip Gabriel (New York: Vintage, 2001), 235.

4. A. Scott, "TOKYO NOIR/Haruki Murakami's Paranoid Style," *Newsday,* October 19, 1997, B09.

5. Elizabeth Ward, *"The Wind-Up Bird Chronicle,"* The *Washington Post Book World,* November 9, 1997, X08.

6. Jay Rubin, *Haruki Murakami and the Music of Words* (London: Vintage, 2003), 229-30.

7. Haruki Murakami, *1973-nen no pinboru* (Tokyo: Kodansha, 1980), 29. Unless otherwise noted, translations into English are by the author.

8. Philip Gabriel, "Back to the Unfamiliar: The Travel Writings of Murakami Haruki," *Japanese Language and Literature* 36.2 (2002): 151.

9. Alan Cheuse, "Off the Air: Book Reviews from National Public Radio (*Kafka on the Shore* and *Zorro*)," *World Literature* 80.1 (2006): 27.

10. Hayao Kawai, "Kyokai taiken no monogatari: Murakami Haruki umibe no kafuka," *Shincho* 99.12 (2002): 234.

11. Michael Seats, *Murakami Haruki: The Simulacrum in Contemporary Japanese Culture* (Lanham: Lexington Books, 2006), 337.

12. Naomi Matsuoka, "Murakami Haruki and Raymond Carver: The American Scene," *Comparative Literature Studies* 30.4 (1993): 423-38.

13. Jay Rubin, *Modern Japanese Writers* (New York: Scribner's & Gale, 2001), 229.

14. Daryl Bem, "Exotic Becomes Erotic: A Developmental Theory of Sexual Orientation," *Psychological Review* 103.2 (1996): 325.

15. Jacques Derrida, *Writing and Difference,* trans. Alan Bass (Chicago: U of Chicago P, 1980), 221.

16. Shunya Yoshimi, "'America' as Desire and Violence: Americanization in Postwar Japan and Asia during the Cold War," trans. David Buist, *Inter-Asia Cultural Studies* 4.3 (2003): 444.

17. Haruki Murakami, *Umibe no kafuka* (Tokyo: Shinchosha, 2002), 1:305-6.

18. Ibid., 2:94.

19. Haruki Murakami, *Nejimakidori kuronikuru* (Tokyo: Shinchosha, 1994), 1:290.

20. Haruki Murakami, "A Shinagawa Monkey," trans. Philip Gabriel, *The New Yorker,* February 3, 2006, 152.

21. Rubin, *Modern Japanese Writers,* 227.

22. Haruki Murakami, *Nejimakidori kuronikuru* (Tokyo: Shinchosha, 1995), 3:470.

23. Murakami, *Umibe no kafuka,* 2:67.

24. Walt Whitman, quoted in Edward Folsom, "America's 'Hurrah Game': Baseball and Walt Whitman," *Iowa Review* 68.77 (1980): 11.

25. Takashi Murakami, *Superflat* (Tokyo: Madra, 2000), 4.

FURTHER READING

Criticism

Barnacle, Hugo. "The Master's Sketchbook." *New Statesman* 1345, no. 4799 (3 July 2006): 66.

 Offers a positive assessment of the short story collection *Blind Willow, Sleeping Woman.*

Boulter, Jonathan. "Writing Guilt: Haruki Murakami and the Archives of National Mourning." *English Studies in Canada* 32, no. 1 (March 2006): 125-45.

 Explores themes of trauma, guilt, and memory in *Underground: The Tokyo Gas Attack and the Japanese Psyche* and *After the Quake.*

Evenson, Brian. Review of *Sputnik Sweetheart,* by Haruki Murakami. *Review of Contemporary Fiction* 21, no. 3 (fall 2001): 215.

 Praises *Sputnik Sweetheart* for its combination of the "postmodern and the pastoral."

Flutsch, Maria. "Girls and the Unconscious in Murakami Haruki's *Kafka on the Shore.*" *Japanese Studies* 26, no. 1 (May 2006): 69-79.

Examines female characters in *Kafka on the Shore* from a psychoanalytic perspective.

Holguin, Catalina. "Something for Myself." *Boston Review* 32, no. 6 (November-December 2007): 35-7.

Contrasts Murakami's fiction and non-fictional works, focusing on narrative arcs and characterization.

Miah, Andy. "Inside the Mind of a Marathon Runner." *Nature* 454, no. 7204 (31 July 2008): 583-84.

A review of *What I Talk About When I Talk About Running,* in which Miah asserts that Murakami's discussion about his love of running in this work provides a deeper look at the auhor's personality.

Reynolds, J. Wyatt. "'I'm Just an Ordinary Guy': The Rise and Reclamation of the Anti-Hero in Haruki Murakami's *Dance Dance Dance. The Image of the Hero in Literature, Media, and Society,* edited by Will Wright and Steven Kaplan, pp. 427-31. Pueblo: Colorado State University, 2004.

Considers Murakami's use of protagonists antithetical to traditional themes of heroism.

Seltzer, Mark. "Murder/Media/Modernity." *Canadian Review of American Studies* 38, no. 1 (2008): 11-41.

Explores the true crime genre using *Underground: The Tokyo Gas Attack and the Japanese Psyche,* among others, as examples.

Suter, Rebecca. "Chainizu Bokkusu/Ireko: Modernism and Postmodernism in 'Tairando' and 'Airon No Aru Fūkei' by Murakami Haruki." In *Contact Zones; Rewriting Genre Across the East-West Border,* pp. 107-31. Naples, Italy: Liguori Editore, 2003.

Suter analyzes two short stories—"Airon no aru fūkei" and "Tairando"—to show the relationship between Japan and the West, as well as to examine Murakami's place in both the modernist and postmodernist theories.

Review of *After the Quake: Stories,* by Haruki Murakami. *Virginia Quarterly Review* 79, no. 1 (winter 2003): 22-3.

Applauds Murakami for creating an accessible and nuanced portrait of contemporary Japan.

Welch, Patricia. "Haruki Murakami's Storytelling World." *World Literature Today* 79, no. 1 (January-April 2005): 55-9.

Surveys Murakami's writing career, highlighting the author's narrative choices.

Additional coverage of Murakami's life and career is contained in the following sources published by Gale: *Contemporary Authors,* **Vol. 165;** *Contemporary Authors New Revision Series,* **Vol. 102, 146;** *Contemporary Literary Criticism,* **Vol. 150;** *Literature Resource Center; Modern Japanese Writers; Reference Guide to World Literature,* **Ed. 3;** *Short Stories for Students,* **Vol. 23; and** *St. James Guide to Science Fiction Writers,* **Ed. 4.**

How to Use This Index

The main references

> **Calvino, Italo**
> 1923-1985 .... **CLC 5, 8, 11, 22, 33, 39,**
> **73; SSC 3, 48**

list all author entries in the following Gale Literary Criticism series:

AAL = Asian American Literature
BG = The Beat Generation: A Gale Critical Companion
BLC = Black Literature Criticism
BLCS = Black Literature Criticism Supplement
CLC = Contemporary Literary Criticism
CLR = Children's Literature Review
CMLC = Classical and Medieval Literature Criticism
DC = Drama Criticism
FL = Feminism in Literature: A Gale Critical Companion
GL = Gothic Literature: A Gale Critical Companion
HLC = Hispanic Literature Criticism
HLCS = Hispanic Literature Criticism Supplement
HR = Harlem Renaissance: A Gale Critical Companion
LC = Literature Criticism from 1400 to 1800
NCLC = Nineteenth-Century Literature Criticism
NNAL = Native North American Literature
PC = Poetry Criticism
SSC = Short Story Criticism
TCLC = Twentieth-Century Literary Criticism
WLC = World Literature Criticism, 1500 to the Present
WLCS = World Literature Criticism Supplement

The cross-references

> See also CA 85-88, 116; CANR 23, 61;
> DAM NOV; DLB 196; EW 13; MTCW 1, 2;
> RGSF 2; RGWL 2; SFW 4; SSFS 12

list all author entries in the following Gale biographical and literary sources:

AAYA = Authors & Artists for Young Adults
AFAW = African American Writers
AFW = African Writers
AITN = Authors in the News
AMW = American Writers
AMWR = American Writers Retrospective Supplement
AMWS = American Writers Supplement
ANW = American Nature Writers
AW = Ancient Writers
BEST = Bestsellers
BPFB = Beacham's Encyclopedia of Popular Fiction: Biography and Resources
BRW = British Writers
BRWS = British Writers Supplement
BW = Black Writers
BYA = Beacham's Guide to Literature for Young Adults
CA = Contemporary Authors
CAAS = Contemporary Authors Autobiography Series
CABS = Contemporary Authors Bibliographical Series
CAD = Contemporary American Dramatists
CANR = Contemporary Authors New Revision Series
CAP = Contemporary Authors Permanent Series
CBD = Contemporary British Dramatists
CCA = Contemporary Canadian Authors
CD = Contemporary Dramatists
CDALB = Concise Dictionary of American Literary Biography

CDALBS = *Concise Dictionary of American Literary Biography Supplement*
CDBLB = *Concise Dictionary of British Literary Biography*
CMW = *St. James Guide to Crime & Mystery Writers*
CN = *Contemporary Novelists*
CP = *Contemporary Poets*
CPW = *Contemporary Popular Writers*
CSW = *Contemporary Southern Writers*
CWD = *Contemporary Women Dramatists*
CWP = *Contemporary Women Poets*
CWRI = *St. James Guide to Children's Writers*
CWW = *Contemporary World Writers*
DA = *DISCovering Authors*
DA3 = *DISCovering Authors 3.0*
DAB = *DISCovering Authors: British Edition*
DAC = *DISCovering Authors: Canadian Edition*
DAM = *DISCovering Authors: Modules*
   DRAM: *Dramatists Module;* **MST:** *Most-studied Authors Module;*
   MULT: *Multicultural Authors Module;* **NOV:** *Novelists Module;*
   POET: *Poets Module;* **POP:** *Popular Fiction and Genre Authors Module*
DFS = *Drama for Students*
DLB = *Dictionary of Literary Biography*
DLBD = *Dictionary of Literary Biography Documentary Series*
DLBY = *Dictionary of Literary Biography Yearbook*
DNFS = *Literature of Developing Nations for Students*
EFS = *Epics for Students*
EW = *European Writers*
EWL = *Encyclopedia of World Literature in the 20th Century*
EXPN = *Exploring Novels*
EXPP = *Exploring Poetry*
EXPS = *Exploring Short Stories*
FANT = *St. James Guide to Fantasy Writers*
FW = *Feminist Writers*
GFL = *Guide to French Literature,* Beginnings to 1789, 1798 to the Present
GLL = *Gay and Lesbian Literature*
HGG = *St. James Guide to Horror, Ghost & Gothic Writers*
HW = *Hispanic Writers*
IDFW = *International Dictionary of Films and Filmmakers: Writers and Production Artists*
IDTP = *International Dictionary of Theatre: Playwrights*
LAIT = *Literature and Its Times*
LAW = *Latin American Writers*
JRDA = *Junior DISCovering Authors*
MAICYA = *Major Authors and Illustrators for Children and Young Adults*
MAICYAS = *Major Authors and Illustrators for Children and Young Adults Supplement*
MAWW = *Modern American Women Writers*
MJW = *Modern Japanese Writers*
MTCW = *Major 20th-Century Writers*
NCFS = *Nonfiction Classics for Students*
NFS = *Novels for Students*
PAB = *Poets: American and British*
PFS = *Poetry for Students*
RGAL = *Reference Guide to American Literature*
RGEL = *Reference Guide to English Literature*
RGSF = *Reference Guide to Short Fiction*
RGWL = *Reference Guide to World Literature*
RHW = *Twentieth-Century Romance and Historical Writers*
SAAS = *Something about the Author Autobiography Series*
SATA = *Something about the Author*
SFW = *St. James Guide to Science Fiction Writers*
SSFS = *Short Stories for Students*
TCWW = *Twentieth-Century Western Writers*
WLIT = *World Literature and Its Times*
WP = *World Poets*
YABC = *Yesterday's Authors of Books for Children*
YAW = *St. James Guide to Young Adult Writers*

Literary Criticism Series
Cumulative Author Index

Ammons, A.R. 1926-2001 .. **CLC 2, 3, 5, 8, 9, 25, 57, 108; PC 16**
See also AITN 1; AMWS 7; CA 9-12R; 193; CANR 6, 36, 51, 73, 107, 156; CP 1, 2, 3, 4, 5, 6, 7; CSW; DAM POET; DLB 5, 165, 342; EWL 3; MAL 5; MTCW 1, 2; PFS 19; RGAL 4; TCLE 1:1

Ammons, Archie Randolph
See Ammons, A.R.

Amo, Tauraatua i
See Adams, Henry (Brooks)

Amory, Thomas 1691(?)-1788 .... **LC 48**
See also DLB 39

Anand, Mulk Raj 1905-2004 ..... **CLC 23, 93, 237**
See also CA 65-68; 231; CANR 32, 64; CN 1, 2, 3, 4, 5, 6, 7; DAM NOV; DLB 323; EWL 3; MTCW 1, 2; MTFW 2005; RGSF 2

Anatol
See Schnitzler, Arthur

Anaximander c. 611B.C.-c. 546B.C. .... **CMLC 22**

Anaya, Rudolfo A. 1937- . **CLC 23, 148, 255; HLC 1**
See also AAYA 20; BYA 13; CA 45-48; CAAS 4; CANR 1, 32, 51, 124, 169; CLR 129; CN 4, 5, 6, 7; DAM MULT, NOV; DLB 82, 206, 278; HW 1; LAIT 4; LLW; MAL 5; MTCW 1, 2; MTFW 2005; NFS 12; RGAL 4; RGSF 2; TCWW 2; WLIT 1

Anaya, Rudolpho Alfonso
See Anaya, Rudolfo A.

Andersen, Hans Christian 1805-1875 .... **NCLC 7, 79; SSC 6, 56; WLC 1**
See also AAYA 57; CLR 6, 113; DA; DA3; DAB; DAC; DAM MST, POP; EW 6; MAICYA 1, 2; RGSF 2; RGWL 2, 3; SATA 100; TWA; WCH; YABC 1

Anderson, C. Farley
See Mencken, H(enry) L(ouis); Nathan, George Jean

Anderson, Jessica (Margaret) Queale 1916- .... **CLC 37**
See also CA 9-12R; CANR 4, 62; CN 4, 5, 6, 7; DLB 325

Anderson, Jon (Victor) 1940- .... **CLC 9**
See also CA 25-28R; CANR 20; CP 1, 3, 4, 5; DAM POET

Anderson, Lindsay (Gordon) 1923-1994 .... **CLC 20**
See also CA 125; 128; 146; CANR 77

Anderson, Maxwell 1888-1959 .... **TCLC 2, 144**
See also CA 105; 152; DAM DRAM; DFS 16, 20; DLB 7, 228; MAL 5; MTCW 2; MTFW 2005; RGAL 4

Anderson, Poul 1926-2001 .... **CLC 15**
See also AAYA 5, 34; BPFB 1; BYA 6, 8, 9; CA 1-4R, 181; 199; CAAE 181; CAAS 2; CANR 2, 15, 34, 64, 110; CLR 58; DLB 8; FANT; INT CANR-15; MTCW 1, 2; MTFW 2005; SATA 90; SATA-Brief 39; SATA-Essay 106; SCFW 1, 2; SFW 4; SUFW 1, 2

Anderson, Robert 1917-2009 .... **CLC 23**
See also AITN 1; CA 21-24R; CANR 32; CD 6; DAM DRAM; DLB 7; LAIT 5

Anderson, Robert Woodruff
See Anderson, Robert

Anderson, Roberta Joan
See Mitchell, Joni

Anderson, Sherwood 1876-1941 ... **SSC 1, 46, 91; TCLC 1, 10, 24, 123; WLC 1**
See also AAYA 30; AMW; AMWC 2; BPFB 1; CA 104; 121; CANR 61; CDALB 1917-1929; DA; DA3; DAB; DAC; DAM MST, NOV; DLB 4, 9, 86; DLBD 1; EWL

3; EXPS; GLL 2; MAL 5; MTCW 1, 2; MTFW 2005; NFS 4; RGAL 4; RGSF 2; SSFS 4, 10, 11; TUS

Anderson, Wes 1969- .... **CLC 227**
See also CA 214

Andier, Pierre
See Desnos, Robert

Andouard
See Giraudoux, Jean(-Hippolyte)

Andrade, Carlos Drummond de
See Drummond de Andrade, Carlos

Andrade, Mario de
See de Andrade, Mario

Andreae, Johann V(alentin) 1586-1654 .... **LC 32**
See also DLB 164

Andreas Capellanus fl. c. 1185- .... **CMLC 45**
See also DLB 208

Andreas-Salome, Lou 1861-1937 ... **TCLC 56**
See also CA 178; DLB 66

Andreev, Leonid
See Andreyev, Leonid (Nikolaevich)

Andress, Lesley
See Sanders, Lawrence

Andrew, Joseph Maree
See Occomy, Marita (Odette) Bonner

Andrewes, Lancelot 1555-1626 .... **LC 5**
See also DLB 151, 172

Andrews, Cicily Fairfield
See West, Rebecca

Andrews, Elton V.
See Pohl, Frederik

Andrews, Peter
See Soderbergh, Steven

Andrews, Raymond 1934-1991 .... **BLC 2:1**
See also BW 2; CA 81-84; 136; CANR 15, 42

Andreyev, Leonid (Nikolaevich) 1871-1919 .... **TCLC 3**
See also CA 104; 185; DLB 295; EWL 3

Andrezel, Pierre
See Blixen, Karen (Christentze Dinesen)

Andric, Ivo 1892-1975 .... **CLC 8; SSC 36; TCLC 135**
See also CA 81-84; 57-60; CANR 43, 60; CDWLB 4; DLB 147, 329; EW 11; EWL 3; MTCW 1; RGSF 2; RGWL 2, 3

Androvar
See Prado (Calvo), Pedro

Angela of Foligno 1248(?)-1309 .... **CMLC 76**

Angelique, Pierre
See Bataille, Georges

Angell, Judie
See Angell, Judie

Angell, Judie 1937- .... **CLC 30**
See also AAYA 11, 71; BYA 6; CA 77-80; CANR 49; CLR 33; JRDA; SATA 22, 78; WYA; YAW

Angell, Roger 1920- .... **CLC 26**
See also CA 57-60; CANR 13, 44, 70, 144; DLB 171, 185

Angelou, Maya 1928- ...... **BLC 1:1; CLC 12, 35, 64, 77, 155; PC 32; WLCS**
See also AAYA 7, 20; AMWS 4; BPFB 1; BW 2, 3; BYA 2; CA 65-68; CANR 19, 42, 65, 111, 133; CDALBS; CLR 53; CP 4, 5, 6, 7; CPW; CSW; CWP; DA; DA3; DAB; DAC; DAM MST, MULT, POET, POP; DLB 38; EWL 3; EXPN; EXPP; FL 1:5; LAIT 4; MAICYA 2; MAICYAS 1; MAL 5; MBL; MTCW 1, 2; MTFW 2005; NCFS 2; NFS 2; PFS 2, 3; RGAL 4; SATA 49, 136; TCLE 1:1; WYA; YAW

Angouleme, Marguerite d'
See de Navarre, Marguerite

Anna Comnena 1083-1153 .... **CMLC 25**

Annensky, Innokentii Fedorovich
See Annensky, Innokenty (Fyodorovich)

Annensky, Innokenty (Fyodorovich) 1856-1909 .... **TCLC 14**
See also CA 110; 155; DLB 295; EWL 3

Annunzio, Gabriele d'
See D'Annunzio, Gabriele

Anodos
See Coleridge, Mary E(lizabeth)

Anon, Charles Robert
See Pessoa, Fernando

Anouilh, Jean 1910-1987 ..... **CLC 1, 3, 8, 13, 40, 50; DC 8, 21; TCLC 195**
See also AAYA 67; CA 17-20R; 123; CANR 32; DAM DRAM; DFS 9, 10, 19; DLB 321; EW 13; EWL 3; GFL 1789 to the Present; MTCW 1, 2; MTFW 2005; RGWL 2, 3; TWA

Ansa, Tina McElroy 1949- .... **BLC 2:1**
See also BW 2; CA 142; CANR 143; CSW

Anselm of Canterbury 1033(?)-1109 .... **CMLC 67**
See also DLB 115

Anthony, Florence
See Ai

Anthony, John
See Ciardi, John (Anthony)

Anthony, Peter
See Shaffer, Anthony; Shaffer, Peter

Anthony, Piers 1934- .... **CLC 35**
See also AAYA 11, 48; BYA 7; CA 200; CAAE 200; CANR 28, 56, 73, 102, 133; CLR 118; CPW; DAM POP; DLB 8; FANT; MAICYA 2; MAICYAS 1; MTCW 1, 2; MTFW 2005; SAAS 22; SATA 84, 129; SATA-Essay 129; SFW 4; SUFW 1, 2; YAW

Anthony, Susan B(rownell) 1820-1906 .... **TCLC 84**
See also CA 211; FW

Antiphon c. 480B.C.-c. 411B.C. .... **CMLC 55**

Antoine, Marc
See Proust, (Valentin-Louis-George-Eugene) Marcel

Antoninus, Brother
See Everson, William (Oliver)

Antonioni, Michelangelo 1912-2007 .... **CLC 20, 144, 259**
See also CA 73-76; 262; CANR 45, 77

Antschel, Paul 1920-1970 .... **CLC 10, 19, 53, 82; PC 10**
See also CA 85-88; CANR 33, 61; CDWLB 2; DLB 69; EWL 3; MTCW 1; PFS 21; RGHL; RGWL 2, 3

Anwar, Chairil 1922-1949 .... **TCLC 22**
See also CA 121; 219; EWL 3; RGWL 3

Anyidoho, Kofi 1947- .... **BLC 2:1**
See also BW 3; CA 178; CP 5, 6, 7; DLB 157; EWL 3

Anzaldua, Gloria (Evanjelina) 1942-2004 .... **CLC 200; HLCS 1**
See also CA 175; 227; CSW; CWP; DLB 122; FW; LLW; RGAL 4; SATA-Obit 154

Apess, William 1798-1839(?) .... **NCLC 73; NNAL**
See also DAM MULT; DLB 175, 243

Apollinaire, Guillaume 1880-1918 .... **PC 7; TCLC 3, 8, 51**
See also CA 104; 152; DAM POET; DLB 258, 321; EW 9; EWL 3; GFL 1789 to the Present; MTCW 2; PFS 24; RGWL 2, 3; TWA; WP

Apollonius of Rhodes
See Apollonius Rhodius

Apollonius Rhodius c. 300B.C.-c. 220B.C. .... **CMLC 28**
See also AW 1; DLB 176; RGWL 2, 3

Appelfeld, Aharon 1932- ... **CLC 23, 47; SSC 42**
See also CA 112; 133; CANR 86, 160; CWW 2; DLB 299; EWL 3; RGHL; RGSF 2; WLIT 6

Appelfeld, Aron
See Appelfeld, Aharon

Apple, Max (Isaac) 1941- .... **CLC 9, 33; SSC 50**
See also AMWS 17; CA 81-84; CANR 19, 54; DLB 130

Appleman, Philip (Dean) 1926- .... **CLC 51**
See also CA 13-16R; CAAS 18; CANR 6, 29, 56

Appleton, Lawrence
See Lovecraft, H. P.

Apteryx
See Eliot, T(homas) S(tearns)

Apuleius, (Lucius Madaurensis) c. 125-c. 164 .... **CMLC 1, 84**
See also AW 2; CDWLB 1; DLB 211; RGWL 2, 3; SUFW; WLIT 8

Aquin, Hubert 1929-1977 .... **CLC 15**
See also CA 105; DLB 53; EWL 3

Aquinas, Thomas 1224(?)-1274 ..... **CMLC 33**
See also DLB 115; EW 1; TWA

Aragon, Louis 1897-1982 .... **CLC 3, 22; TCLC 123**
See also CA 69-72; 108; CANR 28, 71; DAM NOV, POET; DLB 72, 258; EW 11; EWL 3; GFL 1789 to the Present; GLL 2; LMFS 2; MTCW 1, 2; RGWL 2, 3

Arany, Janos 1817-1882 .... **NCLC 34**

Aranyos, Kakay 1847-1910
See Mikszath, Kalman

Aratus of Soli c. 315B.C.-c. 240B.C. .... **CMLC 64**
See also DLB 176

Arbuthnot, John 1667-1735 .... **LC 1**
See also DLB 101

Archer, Herbert Winslow
See Mencken, H(enry) L(ouis)

Archer, Jeffrey 1940- .... **CLC 28**
See also AAYA 16; BEST 89:3; BPFB 1; CA 77-80; CANR 22, 52, 95, 136; CPW; DA3; DAM POP; INT CANR-22; MTFW 2005

Archer, Jeffrey Howard
See Archer, Jeffrey

Archer, Jules 1915- .... **CLC 12**
See also CA 9-12R; CANR 6, 69; SAAS 5; SATA 4, 85

Archer, Lee
See Ellison, Harlan

Archilochus c. 7th cent. B.C.- .... **CMLC 44**
See also DLB 176

Ard, William
See Jakes, John

Arden, John 1930- .... **CLC 6, 13, 15**
See also BRWS 2; CA 13-16R; CAAS 4; CANR 31, 65, 67, 124; CBD; CD 5, 6; DAM DRAM; DFS 9; DLB 13, 245; EWL 3; MTCW 1

Arenas, Reinaldo 1943-1990 .. **CLC 41; HLC 1; TCLC 191**
See also CA 124; 128; 133; CANR 73, 106; DAM MULT; DLB 145; EWL 3; GLL 2; HW 1; LAW; LAWS 1; MTCW 2; MTFW 2005; RGSF 2; RGWL 3; WLIT 1

Arendt, Hannah 1906-1975 .... **CLC 66, 98; TCLC 193**
See also CA 17-20R; 61-64; CANR 26, 60, 172; DLB 242; MTCW 1, 2

Aretino, Pietro 1492-1556 .... **LC 12, 165**
See also RGWL 2, 3

Arghezi, Tudor
See Theodorescu, Ion N.

Arguedas, Jose Maria 1911-1969 .... **CLC 10, 18; HLCS 1; TCLC 147**
See also CA 89-92; CANR 73; DLB 113; EWL 3; HW 1; LAW; RGWL 2, 3; WLIT 1

Argueta, Manlio 1936- .... **CLC 31**
See also CA 131; CANR 73; CWW 2; DLB 145; EWL 3; HW 1; RGWL 3

Arias, Ron 1941- .... **HLC 1**
See also CA 131; CANR 81, 136; DAM MULT; DLB 82; HW 1, 2; MTCW 2; MTFW 2005

Ariosto, Lodovico
See Ariosto, Ludovico

Ariosto, Ludovico 1474-1533 ... **LC 6, 87; PC 42**
See also EW 2; RGWL 2, 3; WLIT 7

Aristides
See Epstein, Joseph

Aristophanes 450B.C.-385B.C. .... **CMLC 4, 51; DC 2; WLCS**
See also AW 1; CDWLB 1; DA; DA3; DAB; DAC; DAM DRAM, MST; DFS 10; DLB 176; LMFS 1; RGWL 2, 3; TWA; WLIT 8

Aristotle 384B.C.-322B.C. .... **CMLC 31; WLCS**
See also AW 1; CDWLB 1; DA; DA3; DAB; DAC; DAM MST; DLB 176; RGWL 2, 3; TWA; WLIT 8

Arlt, Roberto (Godofredo Christophersen) 1900-1942 .... **HLC 1; TCLC 29**
See also CA 123; 131; CANR 67; DAM MULT; DLB 305; EWL 3; HW 1, 2; IDTP; LAW

Armah, Ayi Kwei 1939- . **BLC 1:1, 2:1; CLC 5, 33, 136**
See also AFW; BRWS 10; BW 1; CA 61-64; CANR 21, 64; CDWLB 3; CN 1, 2, 3, 4, 5, 6, 7; DAM MULT, POET; DLB 117; EWL 3; MTCW 1; WLIT 2

Armatrading, Joan 1950- .... **CLC 17**
See also CA 114; 186

Armin, Robert 1568(?)-1615(?) .... **LC 120**

Armitage, Frank
See Carpenter, John (Howard)

Armstrong, Jeannette (C.) 1948- .... **NNAL**
See also CA 149; CCA 1; CN 6, 7; DAC; DLB 334; SATA 102

Arnette, Robert
See Silverberg, Robert

Arnim, Achim von (Ludwig Joachim von Arnim) 1781-1831 .. **NCLC 5, 159; SSC 29**
See also DLB 90

Arnim, Bettina von 1785-1859 ...... **NCLC 38, 123**
See also DLB 90; RGWL 2, 3

Arnold, Matthew 1822-1888 ..... **NCLC 6, 29, 89, 126; PC 5, 94; WLC 1**
See also BRW 5; CDBLB 1832-1890; DA; DAB; DAC; DAM MST, POET; DLB 32, 57; EXPP; PAB; PFS 2; TEA; WP

Arnold, Thomas 1795-1842 .... **NCLC 18**
See also DLB 55

Arnow, Harriette (Louisa) Simpson 1908-1986 ...... **CLC 2, 7, 18; TCLC 196**
See also BPFB 1; CA 9-12R; 118; CANR 14; CN 2, 3, 4; DLB 6; FW; MTCW 1, 2; RHW; SATA 42; SATA-Obit 47

Arouet, Francois-Marie
See Voltaire

Arp, Hans
See Arp, Jean

Arp, Jean 1887-1966 .... **CLC 5; TCLC 115**
See also CA 81-84; 25-28R; CANR 42, 77; EW 10

Arrabal
See Arrabal, Fernando

Arrabal (Teran), Fernando
See Arrabal, Fernando

Arrabal, Fernando 1932- ... **CLC 2, 9, 18, 58**
See also CA 9-12R; CANR 15; CWW 2; DLB 321; EWL 3; LMFS 2

Arreola, Juan Jose 1918-2001 .... **CLC 147; HLC 1; SSC 38**
See also CA 113; 131; 200; CANR 81; CWW 2; DAM MULT; DLB 113; DNFS 2; EWL 3; HW 1, 2; LAW; RGSF 2

Arrian c. 89(?)-c. 155(?) .... **CMLC 43**
See also DLB 176

Arrick, Fran
See Angell, Judie

Arrley, Richmond
See Delany, Samuel R., Jr.

Artaud, Antonin (Marie Joseph) 1896-1948 .... **DC 14; TCLC 3, 36**
See also CA 104; 149; DA3; DAM DRAM; DFS 22; DLB 258, 321; EW 11; EWL 3; GFL 1789 to the Present; MTCW 2; MTFW 2005; RGWL 2, 3

Arthur, Ruth M(abel) 1905-1979 ..... **CLC 12**
See also CA 9-12R; 85-88; CANR 4; CWRI 5; SATA 7, 26

Artsybashev, Mikhail (Petrovich) 1878-1927 .... **TCLC 31**
See also CA 170; DLB 295

Arundel, Honor (Morfydd) 1919-1973 .... **CLC 17**
See also CA 21-22; 41-44R; CAP 2; CLR 35; CWRI 5; SATA 4; SATA-Obit 24

Arzner, Dorothy 1900-1979 .... **CLC 98**

Asch, Sholem 1880-1957 .... **TCLC 3**
See also CA 105; DLB 333; EWL 3; GLL 2; RGHL

Ascham, Roger 1516(?)-1568 .... **LC 101**
See also DLB 236

Ash, Shalom
See Asch, Sholem

Ashbery, John 1927- ... **CLC 2, 3, 4, 6, 9, 13, 15, 25, 41, 77, 125, 221; PC 26**
See also AMWS 3; CA 5-8R; CANR 9, 37, 66, 102, 132, 170; CP 1, 2, 3, 4, 5, 6, 7; DA3; DAM POET; DLB 5, 165; DLBY 1981; EWL 3; GLL 1; INT CANR-9; MAL 5; MTCW 1, 2; MTFW 2005; PAB; PFS 11, 28; RGAL 4; TCLE 1:1; WP

Ashbery, John Lawrence
See Ashbery, John

Ashbridge, Elizabeth 1713-1755 .... **LC 147**
See also DLB 200

Ashdown, Clifford
See Freeman, R(ichard) Austin

Ashe, Gordon
See Creasey, John

Ashton-Warner, Sylvia (Constance) 1908-1984 .... **CLC 19**
See also CA 69-72; 112; CANR 29; CN 1, 2, 3; MTCW 1, 2

Asimov, Isaac 1920-1992 ..... **CLC 1, 3, 9, 19, 26, 76, 92**
See also AAYA 13; BEST 90:2; BPFB 1; BYA 4, 6, 7, 9; CA 1-4R; 137; CANR 2, 19, 36, 60, 125; CLR 12, 79; CMW 4; CN 1, 2, 3, 4, 5; CPW; DA3; DAM POP; DLB 8; DLBY 1992; INT CANR-19; JRDA; LAIT 5; LMFS 2; MAICYA 1, 2; MAL 5; MTCW 1, 2; MTFW 2005; NFS 29; RGAL 4; SATA 1, 26, 74; SCFW 1, 2; SFW 4; SSFS 17; TUS; YAW

Askew, Anne 1521(?)-1546 .... **LC 81**
See also DLB 136

Assis, Joaquim Maria Machado de
See Machado de Assis, Joaquim Maria

Astell, Mary 1666-1731 .... **LC 68**
See also DLB 252, 336; FW

Beauchamp, Kathleen Mansfield
1888-1923 . **SSC 9, 23, 38, 81; TCLC 2, 8, 39, 164; WLC 4**
 See also BPFB 2; BRW 7; CA 104; 134; DA; DA3; DAB; DAC; DAM MST; DLB 162; EWL 3; EXPS; FW; GLL 1; MTCW 2; RGEL 2; RGSF 2; SSFS 2, 8, 10, 11; TEA; WWE 1

Beaumarchais, Pierre-Augustin Caron de
1732-1799 .... **DC 4; LC 61**
 See also DAM DRAM; DFS 14, 16; DLB 313; EW 4; GFL Beginnings to 1789; RGWL 2, 3

Beaumont, Francis 1584(?)-1616 .. **DC 6; LC 33**
 See also BRW 2; CDBLB Before 1660; DLB 58; TEA

Beauvoir, Simone de 1908-1986 .... **CLC 1, 2, 4, 8, 14, 31, 44, 50, 71, 124; SSC 35; WLC 1**
 See also BPFB 1; CA 9-12R; 118; CANR 28, 61; DA; DA3; DAB; DAC; DAM MST, NOV; DLB 72; DLBY 1986; EW 12; EWL 3; FL 1:5; FW; GFL 1789 to the Present; LMFS 2; MTCW 1, 2; MTFW 2005; RGSF 2; RGWL 2, 3; TWA

Beauvoir, Simone Lucie Ernestine Marie Bertrand de
 See Beauvoir, Simone de

Becker, Carl (Lotus) 1873-1945 ..... **TCLC 63**
 See also CA 157; DLB 17

Becker, Jurek 1937-1997 .... **CLC 7, 19**
 See also CA 85-88; 157; CANR 60, 117; CWW 2; DLB 75, 299; EWL 3; RGHL

Becker, Walter 1950- .... **CLC 26**

Becket, Thomas a 1118(?)-1170 .... **CMLC 83**

Beckett, Samuel 1906-1989 ... **CLC 1, 2, 3, 4, 6, 9, 10, 11, 14, 18, 29, 57, 59, 83; DC 22; SSC 16, 74; TCLC 145; WLC 1**
 See also BRWC 2; BRWR 1; BRWS 1; CA 5-8R; 130; CANR 33, 61; CBD; CDBLB 1945-1960; CN 1, 2, 3, 4; CP 1, 2, 3, 4; DA; DA3; DAB; DAC; DAM DRAM, MST, NOV; DFS 2, 7, 18; DLB 13, 15, 233, 319, 321, 329; DLBY 1990; EWL 3; GFL 1789 to the Present; LATS 1:2; LMFS 2; MTCW 1, 2; MTFW 2005; RGSF 2; RGWL 2, 3; SSFS 15; TEA; WLIT 4

Beckford, William 1760-1844 .... **NCLC 16**
 See also BRW 3; DLB 39, 213; GL 2; HGG; LMFS 1; SUFW

Beckham, Barry (Earl) 1944- .... **BLC 1:1**
 See also BW 1; CA 29-32R; CANR 26, 62; CN 1, 2, 3, 4, 5, 6; DAM MULT; DLB 33

Beckman, Gunnel 1910- .... **CLC 26**
 See also CA 33-36R; CANR 15, 114; CLR 25; MAICYA 1, 2; SAAS 9; SATA 6

Becque, Henri 1837-1899 .... **DC 21; NCLC 3**
 See also DLB 192; GFL 1789 to the Present

Becquer, Gustavo Adolfo
1836-1870 .... **HLCS 1; NCLC 106**
 See also DAM MULT

Beddoes, Thomas Lovell 1803-1849 .. **DC 15; NCLC 3, 154**
 See also BRWS 11; DLB 96

Bede c. 673-735 .... **CMLC 20**
 See also DLB 146; TEA

Bedford, Denton R. 1907-(?) .... **NNAL**

Bedford, Donald F.
 See Fearing, Kenneth (Flexner)

Beecher, Catharine Esther
1800-1878 .... **NCLC 30**
 See also DLB 1, 243

Beecher, John 1904-1980 .... **CLC 6**
 See also AITN 1; CA 5-8R; 105; CANR 8; CP 1, 2, 3

Beer, Johann 1655-1700 .... **LC 5**
 See also DLB 168

Beer, Patricia 1924- .... **CLC 58**
 See also BRWS 14; CA 61-64; 183; CANR 13, 46; CP 1, 2, 3, 4, 5, 6; CWP; DLB 40; FW

Beerbohm, Max
 See Beerbohm, (Henry) Max(imilian)

Beerbohm, (Henry) Max(imilian)
1872-1956 .... **TCLC 1, 24**
 See also BRWS 2; CA 104; 154; CANR 79; DLB 34, 100; FANT; MTCW 2

Beer-Hofmann, Richard
1866-1945 .... **TCLC 60**
 See also CA 160; DLB 81

Beg, Shemus
 See Stephens, James

Begiebing, Robert J(ohn) 1946- .... **CLC 70**
 See also CA 122; CANR 40, 88

Begley, Louis 1933- .... **CLC 197**
 See also CA 140; CANR 98, 176; DLB 299; RGHL; TCLE 1:1

Behan, Brendan (Francis)
1923-1964 .... **CLC 1, 8, 11, 15, 79**
 See also BRWS 2; CA 73-76; CANR 33, 121; CBD; CDBLB 1945-1960; DAM DRAM; DFS 7; DLB 13, 233; EWL 3; MTCW 1, 2

Behn, Aphra 1640(?)-1689 .. **DC 4; LC 1, 30, 42, 135; PC 13, 88; WLC 1**
 See also BRWS 3; DA; DA3; DAB; DAC; DAM DRAM, MST, NOV, POET; DFS 16, 24; DLB 39, 80, 131; FW; TEA; WLIT 3

Behrman, S(amuel) N(athaniel)
1893-1973 .... **CLC 40**
 See also CA 13-16; 45-48; CAD; CAP 1; DLB 7, 44; IDFW 3; MAL 5; RGAL 4

Bekederemo, J. P. Clark
 See Clark Bekederemo, J.P.

Belasco, David 1853-1931 .... **TCLC 3**
 See also CA 104; 168; DLB 7; MAL 5; RGAL 4

Belcheva, Elisaveta Lyubomirova
1893-1991 .... **CLC 10**
 See also CA 178; CDWLB 4; DLB 147; EWL 3

Beldone, Phil "Cheech"
 See Ellison, Harlan

Beleno
 See Azuela, Mariano

Belinski, Vissarion Grigoryevich
1811-1848 .... **NCLC 5**
 See also DLB 198

Belitt, Ben 1911- .... **CLC 22**
 See also CA 13-16R; CAAS 4; CANR 7, 77; CP 1, 2, 3, 4, 5, 6; DLB 5

Belknap, Jeremy 1744-1798 .... **LC 115**
 See also DLB 30, 37

Bell, Gertrude (Margaret Lowthian)
1868-1926 .... **TCLC 67**
 See also CA 167; CANR 110; DLB 174

Bell, J. Freeman
 See Zangwill, Israel

Bell, James Madison 1826-1902 ..... **BLC 1:1; TCLC 43**
 See also BW 1; CA 122; 124; DAM MULT; DLB 50

Bell, Madison Smartt 1957- ..... **CLC 41, 102, 223**
 See also AMWS 10; BPFB 1; CA 111; 183; CAAE 183; CANR 28, 54, 73, 134, 176; CN 5, 6, 7; CSW; DLB 218, 278; MTCW 2; MTFW 2005

Bell, Marvin (Hartley) 1937- ...... **CLC 8, 31; PC 79**
 See also CA 21-24R; CAAS 14; CANR 59, 102; CP 1, 2, 3, 4, 5, 6, 7; DAM POET; DLB 5; MAL 5; MTCW 1; PFS 25

Bell, W. L. D.
 See Mencken, H(enry) L(ouis)

Bellamy, Atwood C.
 See Mencken, H(enry) L(ouis)

Bellamy, Edward 1850-1898 ..... **NCLC 4, 86, 147**
 See also DLB 12; NFS 15; RGAL 4; SFW 4

Belli, Gioconda 1948- .... **HLCS 1**
 See also CA 152; CANR 143; CWW 2; DLB 290; EWL 3; RGWL 3

Bellin, Edward J.
 See Kuttner, Henry

Bello, Andres 1781-1865 .... **NCLC 131**
 See also LAW

Belloc, (Joseph) Hilaire (Pierre Sebastien Rene Swanton) 1870-1953 .... **PC 24; TCLC 7, 18**
 See also CA 106; 152; CLR 102; CWRI 5; DAM POET; DLB 19, 100, 141, 174; EWL 3; MTCW 2; MTFW 2005; SATA 112; WCH; YABC 1

Belloc, Joseph Peter Rene Hilaire
 See Belloc, (Joseph) Hilaire (Pierre Sebastien Rene Swanton)

Belloc, Joseph Pierre Hilaire
 See Belloc, (Joseph) Hilaire (Pierre Sebastien Rene Swanton)

Belloc, M. A.
 See Lowndes, Marie Adelaide (Belloc)

Belloc-Lowndes, Mrs.
 See Lowndes, Marie Adelaide (Belloc)

Bellow, Saul 1915-2005 ...... **CLC 1, 2, 3, 6, 8, 10, 13, 15, 25, 33, 34, 63, 79, 190, 200; SSC 14, 101; WLC 1**
 See also AITN 2; AMW; AMWC 2; AMWR 2; BEST 89:3; BPFB 1; CA 5-8R; 238; CABS 1; CANR 29, 53, 95, 132; CDALB 1941-1968; CN 1, 2, 3, 4, 5, 6, 7; DA; DA3; DAB; DAC; DAM MST, NOV, POP; DLB 2, 28, 299, 329; DLBD 3; DLBY 1982; EWL 3; MAL 5; MTCW 1, 2; MTFW 2005; NFS 4, 14, 26; RGAL 4; RGHL; RGSF 2; SSFS 12, 22; TUS

Belser, Reimond Karel Maria de
1929- .... **CLC 14**
 See also CA 152

Bely, Andrey
 See Bugayev, Boris Nikolayevich

Belyi, Andrei
 See Bugayev, Boris Nikolayevich

Bembo, Pietro 1470-1547 .... **LC 79**
 See also RGWL 2, 3

Benary, Margot
 See Benary-Isbert, Margot

Benary-Isbert, Margot 1889-1979 .... **CLC 12**
 See also CA 5-8R; 89-92; CANR 4, 72; CLR 12; MAICYA 1, 2; SATA 2; SATA-Obit 21

Benavente (y Martinez), Jacinto
1866-1954 .... **DC 26; HLCS 1; TCLC 3**
 See also CA 106; 131; CANR 81; DAM DRAM, MULT; DLB 329; EWL 3; GLL 2; HW 1, 2; MTCW 1, 2

Benchley, Peter 1940-2006 .... **CLC 4, 8**
 See also AAYA 14; AITN 2; BPFB 1; CA 17-20R; 248; CANR 12, 35, 66, 115; CPW; DAM NOV, POP; HGG; MTCW 1, 2; MTFW 2005; SATA 3, 89, 164

Benchley, Peter Bradford
 See Benchley, Peter

Benchley, Robert (Charles)
1889-1945 .... **TCLC 1, 55**
 See also CA 105; 153; DLB 11; MAL 5; RGAL 4

Benda, Julien 1867-1956 .... **TCLC 60**
 See also CA 120; 154; GFL 1789 to the Present

Benedict, Ruth 1887-1948 .... **TCLC 60**
 See also CA 158; CANR 146; DLB 246

Booth, Wayne C. 1921-2005 .... **CLC 24**
See also CA 1-4R; 244; CAAS 5; CANR 3, 43, 117; DLB 67

Booth, Wayne Clayson
See Booth, Wayne C.

Borchert, Wolfgang 1921-1947 .... **TCLC 5**
See also CA 104; 188; DLB 69, 124; EWL 3

Borel, Petrus 1809-1859 .... **NCLC 41**
See also DLB 119; GFL 1789 to the Present

Borges, Jorge Luis 1899-1986 ... **CLC 1, 2, 3, 4, 6, 8, 9, 10, 13, 19, 44, 48, 83; HLC 1; PC 22, 32; SSC 4, 41, 100; TCLC 109; WLC 1**
See also AAYA 26; BPFB 1; CA 21-24R; CANR 19, 33, 75, 105, 133; CDWLB 3; DA; DA3; DAB; DAC; DAM MST, MULT; DLB 113, 283; DLBY 1986; DNFS 1, 2; EWL 3; HW 1, 2; LAW; LMFS 2; MSW; MTCW 1, 2; MTFW 2005; PFS 27; RGHL; RGSF 2; RGWL 2, 3; SFW 4; SSFS 17; TWA; WLIT 1

Borne, Ludwig 1786-1837 .... **NCLC 193**
See also DLB 90

Borowski, Tadeusz 1922-1951 .... **SSC 48; TCLC 9**
See also CA 106; 154; CDWLB 4; DLB 215; EWL 3; RGHL; RGSF 2; RGWL 3; SSFS 13

Borrow, George (Henry)
1803-1881 .... **NCLC 9**
See also BRWS 12; DLB 21, 55, 166

Bosch (Gavino), Juan 1909-2001 ..... **HLCS 1**
See also CA 151; 204; DAM MST, MULT; DLB 145; HW 1, 2

Bosman, Herman Charles
1905-1951 .... **TCLC 49**
See also CA 160; DLB 225; RGSF 2

Bosschere, Jean de 1878(?)-1953 ... **TCLC 19**
See also CA 115; 186

Boswell, James 1740-1795 ... **LC 4, 50; WLC 1**
See also BRW 3; CDBLB 1660-1789; DA; DAB; DAC; DAM MST; DLB 104, 142; TEA; WLIT 3

Boto, Eza
See Biyidi, Alexandre

Bottomley, Gordon 1874-1948 .... **TCLC 107**
See also CA 120; 192; DLB 10

Bottoms, David 1949- .... **CLC 53**
See also CA 105; CANR 22; CSW; DLB 120; DLBY 1983

Boucicault, Dion 1820-1890 .... **NCLC 41**
See also DLB 344

Boucolon, Maryse
See Conde, Maryse

Bourcicault, Dion
See Boucicault, Dion

Bourdieu, Pierre 1930-2002 .... **CLC 198**
See also CA 130; 204

Bourget, Paul (Charles Joseph)
1852-1935 .... **TCLC 12**
See also CA 107; 196; DLB 123; GFL 1789 to the Present

Bourjaily, Vance (Nye) 1922- .... **CLC 8, 62**
See also CA 1-4R; CAAS 1; CANR 2, 72; CN 1, 2, 3, 4, 5, 6, 7; DLB 2, 143; MAL 5

Bourne, Randolph S(illiman)
1886-1918 .... **TCLC 16**
See also AMW; CA 117; 155; DLB 63; MAL 5

Boursiquot, Dionysius
See Boucicault, Dion

Bova, Ben 1932- .... **CLC 45**
See also AAYA 16; CA 5-8R; CAAS 18; CANR 11, 56, 94, 111, 157; CLR 3, 96; DLBY 1981; INT CANR-11; MAICYA 1, 2; MTCW 1; SATA 6, 68, 133; SFW 4

Bova, Benjamin William
See Bova, Ben

Bowen, Elizabeth (Dorothea Cole)
1899-1973 . **CLC 1, 3, 6, 11, 15, 22, 118; SSC 3, 28, 66; TCLC 148**
See also BRWS 2; CA 17-18; 41-44R; CANR 35, 105; CAP 2; CDBLB 1945-1960; CN 1; DA3; DAM NOV; DLB 15, 162; EWL 3; EXPS; FW; HGG; MTCW 1, 2; MTFW 2005; NFS 13; RGSF 2; SSFS 5, 22; SUFW 1; TEA; WLIT 4

Bowering, George 1935- .... **CLC 15, 47**
See also CA 21-24R; CAAS 16; CANR 10; CN 7; CP 1, 2, 3, 4, 5, 6, 7; DLB 53

Bowering, Marilyn R(uthe) 1949- .... **CLC 32**
See also CA 101; CANR 49; CP 4, 5, 6, 7; CWP; DLB 334

Bowers, Edgar 1924-2000 .... **CLC 9**
See also CA 5-8R; 188; CANR 24; CP 1, 2, 3, 4, 5, 6, 7; CSW; DLB 5

Bowers, Mrs. J. Milton 1842-1914
See Bierce, Ambrose (Gwinett)

Bowie, David
See Jones, David Robert

Bowles, Jane (Sydney) 1917-1973 ..... **CLC 3, 68**
See also CA 19-20; 41-44R; CAP 2; CN 1; EWL 3; MAL 5

Bowles, Jane Auer
See Bowles, Jane (Sydney)

Bowles, Paul 1910-1999 ..... **CLC 1, 2, 19, 53; SSC 3, 98; TCLC 209**
See also AMWS 4; CA 1-4R; 186; CAAS 1; CANR 1, 19, 50, 75; CN 1, 2, 3, 4, 5, 6; DA3; DLB 5, 6, 218; EWL 3; MAL 5; MTCW 1, 2; MTFW 2005; RGAL 4; SSFS 17

Bowles, William Lisle 1762-1850 . **NCLC 103**
See also DLB 93

Box, Edgar
See Vidal, Gore

Boyd, James 1888-1944 .... **TCLC 115**
See also CA 186; DLB 9; DLBD 16; RGAL 4; RHW

Boyd, Nancy
See Millay, Edna St. Vincent

Boyd, Thomas (Alexander)
1898-1935 .... **TCLC 111**
See also CA 111; 183; DLB 9; DLBD 16, 316

Boyd, William 1952- .... **CLC 28, 53, 70**
See also CA 114; 120; CANR 51, 71, 131, 174; CN 4, 5, 6, 7; DLB 231

Boyesen, Hjalmar Hjorth
1848-1895 .... **NCLC 135**
See also DLB 12, 71; DLBD 13; RGAL 4

Boyle, Kay 1902-1992 .... **CLC 1, 5, 19, 58, 121; SSC 5, 102**
See also CA 13-16R; 140; CAAS 1; CANR 29, 61, 110; CN 1, 2, 3, 4, 5; CP 1, 2, 3, 4, 5; DLB 4, 9, 48, 86; DLBY 1993; EWL 3; MAL 5; MTCW 1, 2; MTFW 2005; RGAL 4; RGSF 2; SSFS 10, 13, 14

Boyle, Mark
See Kienzle, William X.

Boyle, Patrick 1905-1982 .... **CLC 19**
See also CA 127

Boyle, T. C.
See Boyle, T. Coraghessan

Boyle, T. Coraghessan 1948- ..... **CLC 36, 55, 90; SSC 16**
See also AAYA 47; AMWS 8; BEST 90:4; BPFB 1; CA 120; CANR 44, 76, 89, 132; CN 6, 7; CPW; DA3; DAM POP; DLB 218, 278; DLBY 1986; EWL 3; MAL 5; MTCW 2; MTFW 2005; SSFS 13, 19

Boz
See Dickens, Charles (John Huffam)

Brackenridge, Hugh Henry
1748-1816 .... **NCLC 7**
See also DLB 11, 37; RGAL 4

Bradbury, Edward P.
See Moorcock, Michael

Bradbury, Malcolm (Stanley)
1932-2000 .... **CLC 32, 61**
See also CA 1-4R; CANR 1, 33, 91, 98, 137; CN 1, 2, 3, 4, 5, 6, 7; CP 1; DA3; DAM NOV; DLB 14, 207; EWL 3; MTCW 1, 2; MTFW 2005

Bradbury, Ray 1920- ... **CLC 1, 3, 10, 15, 42, 98, 235; SSC 29, 53; WLC 1**
See also AAYA 15; AITN 1, 2; AMWS 4; BPFB 1; BYA 4, 5, 11; CA 1-4R; CANR 2, 30, 75, 125, 186; CDALB 1968-1988; CN 1, 2, 3, 4, 5, 6, 7; CPW; DA; DA3; DAB; DAC; DAM MST, NOV, POP; DLB 2, 8; EXPN; EXPS; HGG; LAIT 3, 5; LATS 1:2; LMFS 2; MAL 5; MTCW 1, 2; MTFW 2005; NFS 1, 22, 29; RGAL 4; RGSF 2; SATA 11, 64, 123; SCFW 1, 2; SFW 4; SSFS 1, 20; SUFW 1, 2; TUS; YAW

Bradbury, Ray Douglas
See Bradbury, Ray

Braddon, Mary Elizabeth
1837-1915 .... **TCLC 111**
See also BRWS 8; CA 108; 179; CMW 4; DLB 18, 70, 156; HGG

Bradfield, Scott 1955- .... **SSC 65**
See also CA 147; CANR 90; HGG; SUFW 2

Bradfield, Scott Michael
See Bradfield, Scott

Bradford, Gamaliel 1863-1932 .... **TCLC 36**
See also CA 160; DLB 17

Bradford, William 1590-1657 .... **LC 64**
See also DLB 24, 30; RGAL 4

Bradley, David, Jr. 1950- ...... **BLC 1:1; CLC 23, 118**
See also BW 1, 3; CA 104; CANR 26, 81; CN 4, 5, 6, 7; DAM MULT; DLB 33

Bradley, David Henry, Jr.
See Bradley, David, Jr.

Bradley, John Ed 1958- .... **CLC 55**
See also CA 139; CANR 99; CN 6, 7; CSW

Bradley, John Edmund, Jr.
See Bradley, John Ed

Bradley, Marion Zimmer
1930-1999 .... **CLC 30**
See also AAYA 40; BPFB 1; CA 57-60; 185; CAAS 10; CANR 7, 31, 51, 75, 107; CPW; DA3; DAM POP; DLB 8; FANT; FW; GLL 1; MTCW 1, 2; MTFW 2005; SATA 90, 139; SATA-Obit 116; SFW 4; SUFW 2; YAW

Bradshaw, John 1933- .... **CLC 70**
See also CA 138; CANR 61

Bradstreet, Anne 1612(?)-1672 .... **LC 4, 30, 130; PC 10**
See also AMWS 1; CDALB 1640-1865; DA; DA3; DAC; DAM MST, POET; DLB 24; EXPP; FW; PFS 6; RGAL 4; TUS; WP

Brady, Joan 1939- .... **CLC 86**
See also CA 141

Bragg, Melvyn 1939- .... **CLC 10**
See also BEST 89:3; CA 57-60; CANR 10, 48, 89, 158; CN 1, 2, 3, 4, 5, 6, 7; DLB 14, 271; RHW

Brahe, Tycho 1546-1601 .... **LC 45**
See also DLB 300

Braine, John (Gerard) 1922-1986 . **CLC 1, 3, 41**
See also CA 1-4R; 120; CANR 1, 33; CDBLB 1945-1960; CN 1, 2, 3, 4; DLB 15; DLBY 1986; EWL 3; MTCW 1

Butts, Mary 1890(?)-1937 ... **SSC 124; TCLC 77**
See also CA 148; DLB 240

Buxton, Ralph
See Silverstein, Alvin; Silverstein, Virginia B(arbara Opshelor)

Buzo, Alex
See Buzo, Alexander (John)

Buzo, Alexander (John) 1944- .... **CLC 61**
See also CA 97-100; CANR 17, 39, 69; CD 5, 6; DLB 289

Buzzati, Dino 1906-1972 .... **CLC 36**
See also CA 160; 33-36R; DLB 177; RGWL 2, 3; SFW 4

Byars, Betsy 1928- .... **CLC 35**
See also AAYA 19; BYA 3; CA 33-36R, 183; CAAE 183; CANR 18, 36, 57, 102, 148; CLR 1, 16, 72; DLB 52; INT CANR-18; JRDA; MAICYA 1, 2; MAICYAS 1; MTCW 1; SAAS 1; SATA 4, 46, 80, 163; SATA-Essay 108; WYA; YAW

Byars, Betsy Cromer
See Byars, Betsy

Byatt, Antonia Susan Drabble
See Byatt, A.S.

Byatt, A.S. 1936- .... **CLC 19, 65, 136, 223; SSC 91**
See also BPFB 1; BRWC 2; BRWS 4; CA 13-16R; CANR 13, 33, 50, 75, 96, 133; CN 1, 2, 3, 4, 5, 6; DA3; DAM NOV, POP; DLB 14, 194, 319, 326; EWL 3; MTCW 1, 2; MTFW 2005; RGSF 2; RHW; SSFS 26; TEA

Byrd, William II 1674-1744 .... **LC 112**
See also DLB 24, 140; RGAL 4

Byrne, David 1952- .... **CLC 26**
See also CA 127

Byrne, John Keyes 1926-2009 .... **CLC 19**
See also CA 102; CANR 78, 140; CBD; CD 5, 6; DFS 13, 24; DLB 13; INT CA-102

Byron, George Gordon (Noel) 1788-1824 ..... **DC 24; NCLC 2, 12, 109, 149; PC 16, 95; WLC 1**
See also AAYA 64; BRW 4; BRWC 2; CDBLB 1789-1832; DA; DA3; DAB; DAC; DAM MST, POET; DLB 96, 110; EXPP; LMFS 1; PAB; PFS 1, 14, 29; RGEL 2; TEA; WLIT 3; WP

Byron, Robert 1905-1941 .... **TCLC 67**
See also CA 160; DLB 195

C. 3. 3.
See Wilde, Oscar

Caballero, Fernan 1796-1877 .... **NCLC 10**

Cabell, Branch
See Cabell, James Branch

Cabell, James Branch 1879-1958 .... **TCLC 6**
See also CA 105; 152; DLB 9, 78; FANT; MAL 5; MTCW 2; RGAL 4; SUFW 1

Cabeza de Vaca, Alvar Nunez 1490-1557(?) .... **LC 61**

Cable, George Washington 1844-1925 .... **SSC 4; TCLC 4**
See also CA 104; 155; DLB 12, 74; DLBD 13; RGAL 4; TUS

Cabral de Melo Neto, Joao 1920-1999 .... **CLC 76**
See also CA 151; CWW 2; DAM MULT; DLB 307; EWL 3; LAW; LAWS 1

Cabrera Infante, G. 1929-2005 ... **CLC 5, 25, 45, 120; HLC 1; SSC 39**
See also CA 85-88; 236; CANR 29, 65, 110; CDWLB 3; CWW 2; DA3; DAM MULT; DLB 113; EWL 3; HW 1, 2; LAW; LAWS 1; MTCW 1, 2; MTFW 2005; RGSF 2; WLIT 1

Cabrera Infante, Guillermo
See Cabrera Infante, G.

Cade, Toni
See Bambara, Toni Cade

Cadmus and Harmonia
See Buchan, John

Caedmon fl. 658-680 .... **CMLC 7**
See also DLB 146

Caeiro, Alberto
See Pessoa, Fernando

Caesar, Julius
See Julius Caesar

Cage, John (Milton), (Jr.) 1912-1992 .... **CLC 41; PC 58**
See also CA 13-16R; 169; CANR 9, 78; DLB 193; INT CANR-9; TCLE 1:1

Cahan, Abraham 1860-1951 .... **TCLC 71**
See also CA 108; 154; DLB 9, 25, 28; MAL 5; RGAL 4

Cain, Christopher
See Fleming, Thomas

Cain, G.
See Cabrera Infante, G.

Cain, Guillermo
See Cabrera Infante, G.

Cain, James M(allahan) 1892-1977 .. **CLC 3, 11, 28**
See also AITN 1; BPFB 1; CA 17-20R; 73-76; CANR 8, 34, 61; CMW 4; CN 1, 2; DLB 226; EWL 3; MAL 5; MSW; MTCW 1; RGAL 4

Caine, Hall 1853-1931 .... **TCLC 97**
See also RHW

Caine, Mark
See Raphael, Frederic (Michael)

Calasso, Roberto 1941- .... **CLC 81**
See also CA 143; CANR 89

Calderon de la Barca, Pedro 1600-1681 . **DC 3; HLCS 1; LC 23, 136**
See also DFS 23; EW 2; RGWL 2, 3; TWA

Caldwell, Erskine 1903-1987 ... **CLC 1, 8, 14, 50, 60; SSC 19; TCLC 117**
See also AITN 1; AMW; BPFB 1; CA 1-4R; 121; CAAS 1; CANR 2, 33; CN 1, 2, 3, 4; DA3; DAM NOV; DLB 9, 86; EWL 3; MAL 5; MTCW 1, 2; MTFW 2005; RGAL 4; RGSF 2; TUS

Caldwell, (Janet Miriam) Taylor (Holland) 1900-1985 .... **CLC 2, 28, 39**
See also BPFB 1; CA 5-8R; 116; CANR 5; DA3; DAM NOV, POP; DLBD 17; MTCW 2; RHW

Calhoun, John Caldwell 1782-1850 .... **NCLC 15**
See also DLB 3, 248

Calisher, Hortense 1911-2009 .... **CLC 2, 4, 8, 38, 134; SSC 15**
See also CA 1-4R; CANR 1, 22, 117; CN 1, 2, 3, 4, 5, 6; DA3; DAM NOV; DLB 2, 218; INT CANR-22; MAL 5; MTCW 1, 2; MTFW 2005; RGAL 4; RGSF 2

Callaghan, Morley Edward 1903-1990 ..... **CLC 3, 14, 41, 65; TCLC 145**
See also CA 9-12R; 132; CANR 33, 73; CN 1, 2, 3, 4; DAC; DAM MST; DLB 68; EWL 3; MTCW 1, 2; MTFW 2005; RGEL 2; RGSF 2; SSFS 19

Callimachus c. 305B.C.-c. 240B.C. .... **CMLC 18**
See also AW 1; DLB 176; RGWL 2, 3

Calvin, Jean
See Calvin, John

Calvin, John 1509-1564 .... **LC 37**
See also DLB 327; GFL Beginnings to 1789

Calvino, Italo 1923-1985 .... **CLC 5, 8, 11, 22, 33, 39, 73; SSC 3, 48; TCLC 183**
See also AAYA 58; CA 85-88; 116; CANR 23, 61, 132; DAM NOV; DLB 196; EW

13; EWL 3; MTCW 1, 2; MTFW 2005; RGHL; RGSF 2; RGWL 2, 3; SFW 4; SSFS 12; WLIT 7

Camara Laye
See Laye, Camara

Cambridge, A Gentleman of the University of
See Crowley, Edward Alexander

Camden, William 1551-1623 .... **LC 77**
See also DLB 172

Cameron, Carey 1952- .... **CLC 59**
See also CA 135

Cameron, Peter 1959- .... **CLC 44**
See also AMWS 12; CA 125; CANR 50, 117, 188; DLB 234; GLL 2

Camoens, Luis Vaz de 1524(?)-1580
See Camoes, Luis de

Camoes, Luis de 1524(?)-1580 . **HLCS 1; LC 62; PC 31**
See also DLB 287; EW 2; RGWL 2, 3

Camp, Madeleine L'Engle
See L'Engle, Madeleine

Campana, Dino 1885-1932 .... **TCLC 20**
See also CA 117; 246; DLB 114; EWL 3

Campanella, Tommaso 1568-1639 .... **LC 32**
See also RGWL 2, 3

Campbell, Bebe Moore 1950-2006 . **BLC 2:1; CLC 246**
See also AAYA 26; BW 2, 3; CA 139; 254; CANR 81, 134; DLB 227; MTCW 2; MTFW 2005

Campbell, John Ramsey
See Campbell, Ramsey

Campbell, John W(ood, Jr.) 1910-1971 .... **CLC 32**
See also CA 21-22; 29-32R; CANR 34; CAP 2; DLB 8; MTCW 1; SCFW 1, 2; SFW 4

Campbell, Joseph 1904-1987 .... **CLC 69; TCLC 140**
See also AAYA 3, 66; BEST 89:2; CA 1-4R; 124; CANR 3, 28, 61, 107; DA3; MTCW 1, 2

Campbell, Maria 1940- .... **CLC 85; NNAL**
See also CA 102; CANR 54; CCA 1; DAC

Campbell, Ramsey 1946- ... **CLC 42; SSC 19**
See also AAYA 51; CA 57-60, 228; CAAE 228; CANR 7, 102, 171; DLB 261; HGG; INT CANR-7; SUFW 1, 2

Campbell, (Ignatius) Roy (Dunnachie) 1901-1957 .... **TCLC 5**
See also AFW; CA 104; 155; DLB 20, 225; EWL 3; MTCW 2; RGEL 2

Campbell, Thomas 1777-1844 .... **NCLC 19**
See also DLB 93, 144; RGEL 2

Campbell, Wilfred
See Campbell, William

Campbell, William 1858(?)-1918 ..... **TCLC 9**
See also CA 106; DLB 92

Campbell, William Edward March 1893-1954 .... **TCLC 96**
See also CA 108; 216; DLB 9, 86, 316; MAL 5

Campion, Jane 1954- .... **CLC 95, 229**
See also AAYA 33; CA 138; CANR 87

Campion, Thomas 1567-1620 . **LC 78; PC 87**
See also CDBLB Before 1660; DAM POET; DLB 58, 172; RGEL 2

Camus, Albert 1913-1960 ...... **CLC 1, 2, 4, 9, 11, 14, 32, 63, 69, 124; DC 2; SSC 9, 76; WLC 1**
See also AAYA 36; AFW; BPFB 1; CA 89-92; CANR 131; DA; DA3; DAB; DAC; DAM DRAM, MST, NOV; DLB 72, 321, 329; EW 13; EWL 3; EXPN; EXPS; GFL 1789 to the Present; LATS 1:2; LMFS 2; MTCW 1, 2; MTFW 2005; NFS 6, 16; RGHL; RGSF 2; RGWL 2, 3; SSFS 4; TWA

Casares, Adolfo Bioy
   See Bioy Casares, Adolfo
Casas, Bartolome de las 1474-1566
   See Las Casas, Bartolome de
Case, John
   See Hougan, Carolyn
Casely-Hayford, J(oseph) E(phraim)
   1866-1903 .... **BLC 1:1; TCLC 24**
   See also BW 2; CA 123; 152; DAM MULT
Casey, John (Dudley) 1939- .... **CLC 59**
   See also BEST 90:2; CA 69-72; CANR 23,
   100
Casey, Michael 1947- .... **CLC 2**
   See also CA 65-68; CANR 109; CP 2, 3;
   DLB 5
Casey, Patrick
   See Thurman, Wallace (Henry)
Casey, Warren (Peter) 1935-1988 .... **CLC 12**
   See also CA 101; 127; INT CA-101
Casona, Alejandro
   See Alvarez, Alejandro Rodriguez
Cassavetes, John 1929-1989 .... **CLC 20**
   See also CA 85-88; 127; CANR 82
Cassian, Nina 1924- .... **PC 17**
   See also CWP; CWW 2
Cassill, R(onald) V(erlin)
   1919-2002 .... **CLC 4, 23**
   See also CA 9-12R; 208; CAAS 1; CANR
   7, 45; CN 1, 2, 3, 4, 5, 6, 7; DLB 6, 218;
   DLBY 2002
Cassiodorus, Flavius Magnus c. 490(?)-c.
   583(?) .... **CMLC 43**
Cassirer, Ernst 1874-1945 .... **TCLC 61**
   See also CA 157
Cassity, (Allen) Turner 1929- .... **CLC 6, 42**
   See also CA 17-20R, 223; CAAE 223;
   CAAS 8; CANR 11; CSW; DLB 105
Cassius Dio c. 155-c. 229 .... **CMLC 99**
   See also DLB 176
Castaneda, Carlos (Cesar Aranha)
   1931(?)-1998 .... **CLC 12, 119**
   See also CA 25-28R; CANR 32, 66, 105;
   DNFS 1; HW 1; MTCW 1
Castedo, Elena 1937- .... **CLC 65**
   See also CA 132
Castedo-Ellerman, Elena
   See Castedo, Elena
Castellanos, Rosario 1925-1974 .... **CLC 66;
   HLC 1; SSC 39, 68**
   See also CA 131; 53-56; CANR 58; CD-
   WLB 3; DAM MULT; DLB 113, 290;
   EWL 3; FW; HW 1; LAW; MTCW 2;
   MTFW 2005; RGSF 2; RGWL 2, 3
Castelvetro, Lodovico 1505-1571 .... **LC 12**
Castiglione, Baldassare 1478-1529 ..... **LC 12,
   165**
   See also EW 2; LMFS 1; RGWL 2, 3;
   WLIT 7
Castiglione, Baldesar
   See Castiglione, Baldassare
Castillo, Ana 1953- .... **CLC 151**
   See also AAYA 42; CA 131; CANR 51, 86,
   128, 172; CWP; DLB 122, 227; DNFS 2;
   FW; HW 1; LLW; PFS 21
Castillo, Ana Hernandez Del
   See Castillo, Ana
Castle, Robert
   See Hamilton, Edmond
Castro (Ruz), Fidel 1926(?)- .... **HLC 1**
   See also CA 110; 129; CANR 81; DAM
   MULT; HW 2
Castro, Guillen de 1569-1631 .... **LC 19**
Castro, Rosalia de 1837-1885 ... **NCLC 3, 78;
   PC 41**
   See also DAM MULT
Castro Alves, Antonio de
   1847-1871 .... **NCLC 205**
   See also DLB 307; LAW

Cather, Willa (Sibert) 1873-1947 . **SSC 2, 50,
   114; TCLC 1, 11, 31, 99, 132, 152;
   WLC 1**
   See also AAYA 24; AMW; AMWC 1;
   AMWR 1; BPFB 1; CA 104; 128; CDALB
   1865-1917; CLR 98; DA; DA3; DAB;
   DAC; DAM MST, NOV; DLB 9, 54, 78,
   256; DLBD 1; EWL 3; EXPN; EXPS; FL
   1:5; LAIT 3; LATS 1:1; MAL 5; MBL;
   MTCW 1, 2; MTFW 2005; NFS 2, 19;
   RGAL 4; RGSF 2; RHW; SATA 30; SSFS
   2, 7, 16, 27; TCWW 1, 2; TUS
Catherine II
   See Catherine the Great
Catherine, Saint 1347-1380 .... **CMLC 27**
Catherine the Great 1729-1796 .... **LC 69**
   See also DLB 150
Cato, Marcus Porcius
   234B.C.-149B.C. .... **CMLC 21**
   See also DLB 211
Cato, Marcus Porcius, the Elder
   See Cato, Marcus Porcius
Cato the Elder
   See Cato, Marcus Porcius
Catton, (Charles) Bruce 1899-1978 . **CLC 35**
   See also AITN 1; CA 5-8R; 81-84; CANR
   7, 74; DLB 17; MTCW 2; MTFW 2005;
   SATA 2; SATA-Obit 24
Catullus c. 84B.C.-54B.C. .... **CMLC 18**
   See also AW 2; CDWLB 1; DLB 211;
   RGWL 2, 3; WLIT 8
Cauldwell, Frank
   See King, Francis (Henry)
Caunitz, William J. 1933-1996 .... **CLC 34**
   See also BEST 89:3; CA 125; 130; 152;
   CANR 73; INT CA-130
Causley, Charles (Stanley)
   1917-2003 .... **CLC 7**
   See also CA 9-12R; 223; CANR 5, 35, 94;
   CLR 30; CP 1, 2, 3, 4, 5; CWRI 5; DLB
   27; MTCW 1; SATA 3, 66; SATA-Obit
   149
Caute, (John) David 1936- .... **CLC 29**
   See also CA 1-4R; CAAS 4; CANR 1, 33,
   64, 120; CBD; CD 5, 6; CN 1, 2, 3, 4, 5,
   6, 7; DAM NOV; DLB 14, 231
Cavafy, C. P.
   See Kavafis, Konstantinos Petrou
Cavafy, Constantine Peter
   See Kavafis, Konstantinos Petrou
Cavalcanti, Guido c. 1250-c.
   1300 .... **CMLC 54**
   See also RGWL 2, 3; WLIT 7
Cavallo, Evelyn
   See Spark, Muriel
Cavanna, Betty
   See Harrison, Elizabeth (Allen) Cavanna
Cavanna, Elizabeth
   See Harrison, Elizabeth (Allen) Cavanna
Cavanna, Elizabeth Allen
   See Harrison, Elizabeth (Allen) Cavanna
Cavendish, Margaret Lucas
   1623-1673 .... **LC 30, 132**
   See also DLB 131, 252, 281; RGEL 2
Caxton, William 1421(?)-1491(?) .... **LC 17**
   See also DLB 170
Cayer, D. M.
   See Duffy, Maureen (Patricia)
Cayrol, Jean 1911-2005 .... **CLC 11**
   See also CA 89-92; 236; DLB 83; EWL 3
Cela (y Trulock), Camilo Jose
   See Cela, Camilo Jose
Cela, Camilo Jose 1916-2002 .... **CLC 4, 13,
   59, 122; HLC 1; SSC 71**
   See also BEST 90:2; CA 21-24R; 206;
   CAAS 10; CANR 21, 32, 76, 139; CWW
   2; DAM MULT; DLB 322; DLBY 1989;
   EW 13; EWL 3; HW 1; MTCW 1, 2;
   MTFW 2005; RGSF 2; RGWL 2, 3

Celan, Paul
   See Antschel, Paul
Celine, Louis-Ferdinand
   See Destouches, Louis-Ferdinand
Cellini, Benvenuto 1500-1571 .... **LC 7**
   See also WLIT 7
Cendrars, Blaise
   See Sauser-Hall, Frederic
Centlivre, Susanna 1669(?)-1723 .... **DC 25;
   LC 65**
   See also DLB 84; RGEL 2
Cernuda (y Bidon), Luis
   1902-1963 .... **CLC 54; PC 62**
   See also CA 131; 89-92; DAM POET; DLB
   134; EWL 3; GLL 1; HW 1; RGWL 2, 3
Cervantes, Lorna Dee 1954- ..... **HLCS 1; PC
   35**
   See also CA 131; CANR 80; CP 7; CWP;
   DLB 82; EXPP; HW 1; LLW; PFS 30
Cervantes (Saavedra), Miguel de
   1547-1616 .... **HLCS; LC 6, 23, 93; SSC
   12, 108; WLC 1**
   See also AAYA 56; BYA 1, 14; DA; DAB;
   DAC; DAM MST, NOV; EW 2; LAIT 1;
   LATS 1:1; LMFS 1; NFS 8; RGSF 2;
   RGWL 2, 3; TWA
Cesaire, Aime
   See Cesaire, Aime
Cesaire, Aime 1913-2008 .... **BLC 1:1; CLC
   19, 32, 112; DC 22; PC 25**
   See also BW 2, 3; CA 65-68; 271; CANR
   24, 43, 81; CWW 2; DA3; DAM MULT,
   POET; DLB 321; EWL 3; GFL 1789 to
   the Present; MTCW 1, 2; MTFW 2005;
   WP
Cesaire, Aime Fernand
   See Cesaire, Aime
Chaadaev, Petr Iakovlevich
   1794-1856 .... **NCLC 197**
   See also DLB 198
Chabon, Michael 1963- ... **CLC 55, 149, 265;
   SSC 59**
   See also AAYA 45; AMWS 11; CA 139;
   CANR 57, 96, 127, 138; DLB 278; MAL
   5; MTFW 2005; NFS 25; SATA 145
Chabrol, Claude 1930- .... **CLC 16**
   See also CA 110
Chairil Anwar
   See Anwar, Chairil
Challans, Mary 1905-1983 ...... **CLC 3, 11, 17**
   See also BPFB 3; BYA 2; CA 81-84; 111;
   CANR 74; CN 1, 2, 3; DA3; DLBY 1983;
   EWL 3; GLL 1; LAIT 1; MTCW 2;
   MTFW 2005; RGEL 2; RHW; SATA 23;
   SATA-Obit 36; TEA
Challis, George
   See Faust, Frederick (Schiller)
Chambers, Aidan 1934- .... **CLC 35**
   See also AAYA 27; CA 25-28R; CANR 12,
   31, 58, 116; JRDA; MAICYA 1, 2; SAAS
   12; SATA 1, 69, 108, 171; WYA; YAW
Chambers, James .... **CLC 21**
   See also CA 124; 199
Chambers, Jessie
   See Lawrence, D(avid) H(erbert Richards)
Chambers, Robert W(illiam)
   1865-1933 .... **SSC 92; TCLC 41**
   See also CA 165; DLB 202; HGG; SATA
   107; SUFW 1
Chambers, (David) Whittaker
   1901-1961 .... **TCLC 129**
   See also CA 89-92; DLB 303
Chamisso, Adelbert von
   1781-1838 .... **NCLC 82**
   See also DLB 90; RGWL 2, 3; SUFW 1
Chamoiseau, Patrick 1953- .... **CLC 268**
   See also CA 162; CANR 88; EWL 3;
   RGWL 3

YAS 1; MAL 5; MTCW 1, 2; MTFW
2005; RGAL 4; SATA 7, 48, 81; TUS;
WYA; YAW

Chin, Frank (Chew, Jr.) 1940- .... **AAL; CLC
135; DC 7**
See also CA 33-36R; CAD; CANR 71; CD
5, 6; DAM MULT; DLB 206, 312; LAIT
5; RGAL 4

Chin, Marilyn (Mei Ling) 1955- .... **PC 40**
See also CA 129; CANR 70, 113; CWP;
DLB 312; PFS 28

Chislett, (Margaret) Anne 1943- ...... **CLC 34**
See also CA 151

Chitty, Thomas Willes 1926- .... **CLC 6, 11**
See also CA 5-8R; CN 1, 2, 3, 4, 5, 6; EWL
3

Chivers, Thomas Holley
1809-1858 .... **NCLC 49**
See also DLB 3, 248; RGAL 4

Chlamyda, Jehudil
See Peshkov, Alexei Maximovich

Ch'o, Chou
See Shu-Jen, Chou

Choi, Susan 1969- .... **CLC 119**
See also CA 223; CANR 188

Chomette, Rene Lucien 1898-1981 .. **CLC 20**
See also CA 103

Chomsky, Avram Noam
See Chomsky, Noam

Chomsky, Noam 1928- .... **CLC 132**
See also CA 17-20R; CANR 28, 62, 110,
132, 179; DA3; DLB 246; MTCW 1, 2;
MTFW 2005

Chona, Maria 1845(?)-1936 .... **NNAL**
See also CA 144

Chopin, Kate
See Chopin, Katherine

Chopin, Katherine 1851-1904 .... **SSC 8, 68,
110; TCLC 127; WLCS**
See also AAYA 33; AMWR 2; BYA 11, 15;
CA 104; 122; CDALB 1865-1917; DA3;
DAB; DAC; DAM MST, NOV; DLB 12,
78; EXPN; EXPS; FL 1:3; FW; LAIT 3;
MAL 5; MBL; NFS 3; RGAL 4; RGSF 2;
SSFS 2, 13, 17, 26; TUS

Chretien de Troyes c. 12th cent. - . **CMLC 10**
See also DLB 208; EW 1; RGWL 2, 3;
TWA

Christie
See Ichikawa, Kon

Christie, Agatha (Mary Clarissa)
1890-1976 .. **CLC 1, 6, 8, 12, 39, 48, 110**
See also AAYA 9; AITN 1, 2; BPFB 1;
BRWS 2; CA 17-20R; 61-64; CANR 10,
37, 108; CBD; CDBLB 1914-1945; CMW
4; CN 1, 2; CPW; CWD; DA3; DAB;
DAC; DAM NOV; DFS 2; DLB 13, 77,
245; MSW; MTCW 1, 2; MTFW 2005;
NFS 8; RGEL 2; RHW; SATA 36; TEA;
YAW

Christie, Ann Philippa
See Pearce, Philippa

Christie, Philippa
See Pearce, Philippa

Christine de Pisan
See Christine de Pizan

Christine de Pizan 1365(?)-1431(?) ...... **LC 9,
130; PC 68**
See also DLB 208; FL 1:1; FW; RGWL 2,
3

Chuang-Tzu c. 369B.C.-c.
286B.C. .... **CMLC 57**

Chubb, Elmer
See Masters, Edgar Lee

Chulkov, Mikhail Dmitrievich
1743-1792 .... **LC 2**
See also DLB 150

Churchill, Caryl 1938- .... **CLC 31, 55, 157;
DC 5**
See also BRWS 4; CA 102; CANR 22, 46,
108; CBD; CD 5, 6; CWD; DFS 25; DLB
13, 310; EWL 3; FW; MTCW 1; RGEL 2

Churchill, Charles 1731-1764 .... **LC 3**
See also DLB 109; RGEL 2

Churchill, Chick
See Churchill, Caryl

Churchill, Sir Winston (Leonard Spencer)
1874-1965 .... **TCLC 113**
See also BRW 6; CA 97-100; CDBLB
1890-1914; DA3; DLB 100, 329; DLBD
16; LAIT 4; MTCW 1, 2

Chute, Carolyn 1947- .... **CLC 39**
See also CA 123; CANR 135; CN 7

Ciardi, John (Anthony) 1916-1986 . **CLC 10,
40, 44, 129; PC 69**
See also CA 5-8R; 118; CAAS 2; CANR 5,
33; CLR 19; CP 1, 2, 3, 4; CWRI 5; DAM
POET; DLB 5; DLBY 1986; INT
CANR-5; MAICYA 1, 2; MAL 5; MTCW
1, 2; MTFW 2005; RGAL 4; SAAS 26;
SATA 1, 65; SATA-Obit 46

Cibber, Colley 1671-1757 .... **LC 66**
See also DLB 84; RGEL 2

Cicero, Marcus Tullius
106B.C.-43B.C. .... **CMLC 3, 81**
See also AW 1; CDWLB 1; DLB 211;
RGWL 2, 3; WLIT 8

Cimino, Michael 1943- .... **CLC 16**
See also CA 105

Cioran, E(mil) M. 1911-1995 .... **CLC 64**
See also CA 25-28R; 149; CANR 91; DLB
220; EWL 3

Circus, Anthony
See Hoch, Edward D.

Cisneros, Sandra 1954- .... **CLC 69, 118, 193;
HLC 1; PC 52; SSC 32, 72**
See also AAYA 9, 53; AMWS 7; CA 131;
CANR 64, 118; CLR 123; CN 7; CWP;
DA3; DAM MULT; DLB 122, 152; EWL
3; EXPN; FL 1:5; FW; HW 1, 2; LAIT 5;
LATS 1:2; LLW; MAICYA 2; MAL 5;
MTCW 2; MTFW 2005; NFS 2; PFS 19;
RGAL 4; RGSF 2; SSFS 3, 13, 27; WLIT
1; YAW

Cixous, Helene 1937- .... **CLC 92, 253**
See also CA 126; CANR 55, 123; CWW 2;
DLB 83, 242; EWL 3; FL 1:5; FW; GLL
2; MTCW 1, 2; MTFW 2005; TWA

Clair, Rene
See Chomette, Rene Lucien

Clampitt, Amy 1920-1994 .... **CLC 32; PC 19**
See also AMWS 9; CA 110; 146; CANR
29, 79; CP 4, 5; DLB 105; MAL 5; PFS
27

Clancy, Thomas L., Jr. 1947- ... **CLC 45, 112**
See also AAYA 9, 51; BEST 89:1, 90:1;
BPFB 1; BYA 10, 11; CA 125; 131;
CANR 62, 105, 132; CMW 4; CPW;
DA3; DAM NOV, POP; DLB 227; INT
CA-131; MTCW 1, 2; MTFW 2005

Clancy, Tom
See Clancy, Thomas L., Jr.

Clare, John 1793-1864 .. **NCLC 9, 86; PC 23**
See also BRWS 11; DAB; DAM POET;
DLB 55, 96; RGEL 2

Clarin
See Alas (y Urena), Leopoldo (Enrique
Garcia)

Clark, Al C.
See Goines, Donald

Clark, Brian (Robert)
See Clark, (Robert) Brian

Clark, (Robert) Brian 1932- .... **CLC 29**
See also CA 41-44R; CANR 67; CBD; CD
5, 6

Clark, Curt
See Westlake, Donald E.

Clark, Eleanor 1913-1996 .... **CLC 5, 19**
See also CA 9-12R; 151; CANR 41; CN 1,
2, 3, 4, 5, 6; DLB 6

Clark, J. P.
See Clark Bekederemo, J.P.

Clark, John Pepper
See Clark Bekederemo, J.P.
See also AFW; CD 5; CP 1, 2, 3, 4, 5, 6, 7;
RGEL 2

Clark, Kenneth (Mackenzie)
1903-1983 .... **TCLC 147**
See also CA 93-96; 109; CANR 36; MTCW
1, 2; MTFW 2005

Clark, M. R.
See Clark, Mavis Thorpe

Clark, Mavis Thorpe 1909-1999 ...... **CLC 12**
See also CA 57-60; CANR 8, 37, 107; CLR
30; CWRI 5; MAICYA 1, 2; SAAS 5;
SATA 8, 74

Clark, Walter Van Tilburg
1909-1971 .... **CLC 28**
See also CA 9-12R; 33-36R; CANR 63,
113; CN 1; DLB 9, 206; LAIT 2; MAL 5;
RGAL 4; SATA 8; TCWW 1, 2

Clark Bekederemo, J.P. 1935- .... **BLC 1:1;
CLC 38; DC 5**
See Clark, John Pepper
See also AAYA 79; BW 1; CA 65-68;
CANR 16, 72; CD 6; CDWLB 3; DAM
DRAM, MULT; DFS 13; DLB 117; EWL
3; MTCW 2; MTFW 2005

Clarke, Arthur
See Clarke, Arthur C.

Clarke, Arthur C. 1917-2008 .. **CLC 1, 4, 13,
18, 35, 136; SSC 3**
See also AAYA 4, 33; BPFB 1; BYA 13;
CA 1-4R; 270; CANR 2, 28, 55, 74, 130;
CLR 119; CN 1, 2, 3, 4, 5, 6, 7; CPW;
DA3; DAM POP; DLB 261; JRDA; LAIT
5; MAICYA 1, 2; MTCW 1, 2; MTFW
2005; SATA 13, 70, 115; SATA-Obit 191;
SCFW 1, 2; SFW 4; SSFS 4, 18; TCLE
1:1; YAW

Clarke, Arthur Charles
See Clarke, Arthur C.

Clarke, Austin 1896-1974 .... **CLC 6, 9**
See also CA 29-32; 49-52; CAP 2; CP 1, 2;
DAM POET; DLB 10, 20; EWL 3; RGEL
2

Clarke, Austin C. 1934- .... **BLC 1:1; CLC 8,
53; SSC 45, 116**
See also BW 1; CA 25-28R; CAAS 16;
CANR 14, 32, 68, 140; CN 1, 2, 3, 4, 5,
6, 7; DAC; DAM MULT; DLB 53, 125;
DNFS 2; MTCW 2; MTFW 2005; RGSF
2

Clarke, Gillian 1937- .... **CLC 61**
See also CA 106; CP 3, 4, 5, 6, 7; CWP;
DLB 40

Clarke, Marcus (Andrew Hislop)
1846-1881 .... **NCLC 19; SSC 94**
See also DLB 230; RGEL 2; RGSF 2

Clarke, Shirley 1925-1997 .... **CLC 16**
See also CA 189

Clash, The
See Headon, (Nicky) Topper; Jones, Mick;
Simonon, Paul; Strummer, Joe

Claudel, Paul (Louis Charles Marie)
1868-1955 .... **TCLC 2, 10**
See also CA 104; 165; DLB 192, 258, 321;
EW 8; EWL 3; GFL 1789 to the Present;
RGWL 2, 3; TWA

Claudian 370(?)-404(?) .... **CMLC 46**
See also RGWL 2, 3

Claudius, Matthias 1740-1815 .... **NCLC 75**
See also DLB 97

Comfort, Alex(ander) 1920-2000 .... **CLC 7**
See also CA 1-4R; 190; CANR 1, 45; CN 1, 2, 3, 4; CP 1, 2, 3, 4, 5, 6, 7; DAM POP; MTCW 2

Comfort, Montgomery
See Campbell, Ramsey

Compton-Burnett, I(vy) 1892(?)-1969 .... **CLC 1, 3, 10, 15, 34; TCLC 180**
See also BRW 7; CA 1-4R; 25-28R; CANR 4; DAM NOV; DLB 36; EWL 3; MTCW 1, 2; RGEL 2

Comstock, Anthony 1844-1915 ...... **TCLC 13**
See also CA 110; 169

Comte, Auguste 1798-1857 .... **NCLC 54**

Conan Doyle, Arthur
See Doyle, Sir Arthur Conan

Conde (Abellan), Carmen 1901-1996 .... **HLCS 1**
See also CA 177; CWW 2; DLB 108; EWL 3; HW 2

Conde, Maryse 1937- .... **BLC 2:1; BLCS; CLC 52, 92, 247**
See also BW 2, 3; CA 110, 190; CAAE 190; CANR 30, 53, 76, 171; CWW 2; DAM MULT; EWL 3; MTCW 2; MTFW 2005

Condillac, Etienne Bonnot de 1714-1780 .... **LC 26**
See also DLB 313

Condon, Richard 1915-1996 ...... **CLC 4, 6, 8, 10, 45, 100**
See also BEST 90:3; BPFB 1; CA 1-4R; 151; CAAS 1; CANR 2, 23, 164; CMW 4; CN 1, 2, 3, 4, 5, 6; DAM NOV; INT CANR-23; MAL 5; MTCW 1, 2

Condon, Richard Thomas
See Condon, Richard

Condorcet
See Condorcet, marquis de Marie-Jean-Antoine-Nicolas Caritat

Condorcet, marquis de Marie-Jean-Antoine-Nicolas Caritat 1743-1794 .... **LC 104**
See also DLB 313; GFL Beginnings to 1789

Confucius 551B.C.-479B.C. .... **CMLC 19, 65; WLCS**
See also DA; DA3; DAB; DAC; DAM MST

Congreve, William 1670-1729 ... **DC 2; LC 5, 21; WLC 2**
See also BRW 2; CDBLB 1660-1789; DA; DAB; DAC; DAM DRAM, MST, POET; DFS 15; DLB 39, 84; RGEL 2; WLIT 3

Conley, Robert J. 1940- .... **NNAL**
See also CA 41-44R; CANR 15, 34, 45, 96, 186; DAM MULT; TCWW 2

Connell, Evan S., Jr. 1924- .... **CLC 4, 6, 45**
See also AAYA 7; AMWS 14; CA 1-4R; CAAS 2; CANR 2, 39, 76, 97, 140; CN 1, 2, 3, 4, 5, 6; DAM NOV; DLB 2, 335; DLBY 1981; MAL 5; MTCW 1, 2; MTFW 2005

Connelly, Marc(us Cook) 1890-1980 . **CLC 7**
See also CA 85-88; 102; CAD; CANR 30; DFS 12; DLB 7; DLBY 1980; MAL 5; RGAL 4; SATA-Obit 25

Connolly, Paul
See Wicker, Tom

Connor, Ralph
See Gordon, Charles William

Conrad, Joseph 1857-1924 ..... **SSC 9, 67, 69, 71; TCLC 1, 6, 13, 25, 43, 57; WLC 2**
See also AAYA 26; BPFB 1; BRW 6; BRWC 1; BRWR 2; BYA 2; CA 104; 131; CANR 60; CDBLB 1890-1914; DA; DA3; DAB; DAC; DAM MST, NOV; DLB 10, 34, 98, 156; EWL 3; EXPN; EXPS; LAIT 2; LATS 1:1; LMFS 1; MTCW 1, 2; MTFW 2005; NFS 2, 16; RGEL 2; RGSF 2; SATA 27; SSFS 1, 12; TEA; WLIT 4

Conrad, Robert Arnold
See Hart, Moss

Conroy, Pat 1945- .... **CLC 30, 74**
See also AAYA 8, 52; AITN 1; BPFB 1; CA 85-88; CANR 24, 53, 129; CN 7; CPW; CSW; DA3; DAM NOV, POP; DLB 6; LAIT 5; MAL 5; MTCW 1, 2; MTFW 2005

Constant (de Rebecque), (Henri) Benjamin 1767-1830 .... **NCLC 6, 182**
See also DLB 119; EW 4; GFL 1789 to the Present

Conway, Jill K. 1934- .... **CLC 152**
See also CA 130; CANR 94

Conway, Jill Kathryn Ker
See Conway, Jill K.

Conybeare, Charles Augustus
See Eliot, T(homas) S(tearns)

Cook, Michael 1933-1994 .... **CLC 58**
See also CA 93-96; CANR 68; DLB 53

Cook, Robin 1940- .... **CLC 14**
See also AAYA 32; BEST 90:2; BPFB 1; CA 108; 111; CANR 41, 90, 109, 181; CPW; DA3; DAM POP; HGG; INT CA-111

Cook, Roy
See Silverberg, Robert

Cooke, Elizabeth 1948- .... **CLC 55**
See also CA 129

Cooke, John Esten 1830-1886 .... **NCLC 5**
See also DLB 3, 248; RGAL 4

Cooke, John Estes
See Baum, L(yman) Frank

Cooke, M. E.
See Creasey, John

Cooke, Margaret
See Creasey, John

Cooke, Rose Terry 1827-1892 ...... **NCLC 110**
See also DLB 12, 74

Cook-Lynn, Elizabeth 1930- .... **CLC 93; NNAL**
See also CA 133; DAM MULT; DLB 175

Cooney, Ray .... **CLC 62**
See also CBD

Cooper, Anthony Ashley 1671-1713 .. **LC 107**
See also DLB 101, 336

Cooper, Dennis 1953- .... **CLC 203**
See also CA 133; CANR 72, 86; GLL 1; HGG

Cooper, Douglas 1960- .... **CLC 86**

Cooper, Henry St. John
See Creasey, John

Cooper, J. California (?)- .... **CLC 56**
See also AAYA 12; BW 1; CA 125; CANR 55; DAM MULT; DLB 212

Cooper, James Fenimore 1789-1851 .... **NCLC 1, 27, 54, 203**
See also AAYA 22; AMW; BPFB 1; CDALB 1640-1865; CLR 105; DA3; DLB 3, 183, 250, 254; LAIT 1; NFS 25; RGAL 4; SATA 19; TUS; WCH

Cooper, Susan Fenimore 1813-1894 .... **NCLC 129**
See also ANW; DLB 239, 254

Coover, Robert 1932- .. **CLC 3, 7, 15, 32, 46, 87, 161; SSC 15, 101**
See also AMWS 5; BPFB 1; CA 45-48; CANR 3, 37, 58, 115; CN 1, 2, 3, 4, 5, 6, 7; DAM NOV; DLB 2, 227; DLBY 1981; EWL 3; MAL 5; MTCW 1, 2; MTFW 2005; RGAL 4; RGSF 2

Copeland, Stewart (Armstrong) 1952- .... **CLC 26**

Copernicus, Nicolaus 1473-1543 .... **LC 45**

Coppard, A(lfred) E(dgar) 1878-1957 .... **SSC 21; TCLC 5**
See also BRWS 8; CA 114; 167; DLB 162; EWL 3; HGG; RGEL 2; RGSF 2; SUFW 1; YABC 1

Coppee, Francois 1842-1908 .... **TCLC 25**
See also CA 170; DLB 217

Coppola, Francis Ford 1939- ... **CLC 16, 126**
See also AAYA 39; CA 77-80; CANR 40, 78; DLB 44

Copway, George 1818-1869 .... **NNAL**
See also DAM MULT; DLB 175, 183

Corbiere, Tristan 1845-1875 .... **NCLC 43**
See also DLB 217; GFL 1789 to the Present

Corcoran, Barbara (Asenath) 1911- .... **CLC 17**
See also AAYA 14; CA 21-24R; 191; CAAE 191; CAAS 2; CANR 11, 28, 48; CLR 50; DLB 52; JRDA; MAICYA 2; MAICYAS 1; RHW; SAAS 20; SATA 3, 77; SATA-Essay 125

Cordelier, Maurice
See Giraudoux, Jean(-Hippolyte)

Cordier, Gilbert
See Scherer, Jean-Marie Maurice

Corelli, Marie
See Mackay, Mary

Corinna c. 225B.C.-c. 305B.C. ...... **CMLC 72**

Corman, Cid 1924-2004 .... **CLC 9**
See also CA 85-88; 225; CAAS 2; CANR 44; CP 1, 2, 3, 4, 5, 6, 7; DAM POET; DLB 5, 193

Corman, Sidney
See Corman, Cid

Cormier, Robert 1925-2000 .... **CLC 12, 30**
See also AAYA 3, 19; BYA 1, 2, 6, 8, 9; CA 1-4R; CANR 5, 23, 76, 93; CDALB 1968-1988; CLR 12, 55; DA; DAB; DAC; DAM MST, NOV; DLB 52; EXPN; INT CANR-23; JRDA; LAIT 5; MAICYA 1, 2; MTCW 1, 2; MTFW 2005; NFS 2, 18; SATA 10, 45, 83; SATA-Obit 122; WYA; YAW

Corn, Alfred (DeWitt III) 1943- .... **CLC 33**
See also CA 179; CAAE 179; CAAS 25; CANR 44; CP 3, 4, 5, 6, 7; CSW; DLB 120, 282; DLBY 1980

Corneille, Pierre 1606-1684 .. **DC 21; LC 28, 135**
See also DAB; DAM MST; DFS 21; DLB 268; EW 3; GFL Beginnings to 1789; RGWL 2, 3; TWA

Cornwell, David
See le Carre, John

Cornwell, David John Moore
See le Carre, John

Cornwell, Patricia 1956- .... **CLC 155**
See also AAYA 16, 56; BPFB 1; CA 134; CANR 53, 131; CMW 4; CPW; CSW; DAM POP; DLB 306; MSW; MTCW 2; MTFW 2005

Cornwell, Patricia Daniels
See Cornwell, Patricia

Cornwell, Smith
See Smith, David (Jeddie)

Corso, Gregory 1930-2001 .... **CLC 1, 11; PC 33**
See also AMWS 12; BG 1:2; CA 5-8R; 193; CANR 41, 76, 132; CP 1, 2, 3, 4, 5, 6, 7; DA3; DLB 5, 16, 237; LMFS 2; MAL 5; MTCW 1, 2; MTFW 2005; WP

Cortazar, Julio 1914-1984 ... **CLC 2, 3, 5, 10, 13, 15, 33, 34, 92; HLC 1; SSC 7, 76**
See also BPFB 1; CA 21-24R; CANR 12, 32, 81; CDWLB 3; DA3; DAM MULT, NOV; DLB 113; EWL 3; EXPS; HW 1, 2; LAW; MTCW 1, 2; MTFW 2005; RGSF 2; RGWL 2, 3; SSFS 3, 20; TWA; WLIT 1

Cortes, Hernan 1485-1547 .... **LC 31**

Cortez, Jayne 1936- .... **BLC 2:1**
See also BW 2, 3; CA 73-76; CANR 13, 31, 68, 126; CWP; DLB 41; EWL 3

Crowfield, Christopher
  See Stowe, Harriet (Elizabeth) Beecher
Crowley, Aleister
  See Crowley, Edward Alexander
Crowley, Edward Alexander
  1875-1947 .... **TCLC 7**
  See also CA 104; GLL 1; HGG
Crowley, John 1942- .... **CLC 57**
  See also AAYA 57; BPFB 1; CA 61-64;
  CANR 43, 98, 138, 177; DLBY 1982;
  FANT; MTFW 2005; SATA 65, 140; SFW
  4; SUFW 2
Crowne, John 1641-1712 .... **LC 104**
  See also DLB 80; RGEL 2
Crud
  See Crumb, R.
Crumarums
  See Crumb, R.
Crumb, R. 1943- .... **CLC 17**
  See also CA 106; CANR 107, 150
Crumb, Robert
  See Crumb, R.
Crumbum
  See Crumb, R.
Crumski
  See Crumb, R.
Crum the Bum
  See Crumb, R.
Crunk
  See Crumb, R.
Crustt
  See Crumb, R.
Crutchfield, Les
  See Trumbo, Dalton
Cruz, Victor Hernandez 1949- ... **HLC 1; PC 37**
  See also BW 2; CA 65-68, 271; CAAE 271;
  CAAS 17; CANR 14, 32, 74, 132; CP 1,
  2, 3, 4, 5, 6, 7; DAM MULT, POET; DLB
  41; DNFS 1; EXPP; HW 1, 2; LLW;
  MTCW 2; MTFW 2005; PFS 16; WP
Cryer, Gretchen (Kiger) 1935- .... **CLC 21**
  See also CA 114; 123
Csath, Geza
  See Brenner, Jozef
Cudlip, David R(ockwell) 1933- .... **CLC 34**
  See also CA 177
Cullen, Countee 1903-1946 ..... **BLC 1:1; HR
1:2; PC 20; TCLC 4, 37, 220; WLCS**
  See also AAYA 78; AFAW 2; AMWS 4; BW
  1; CA 108; 124; CDALB 1917-1929; DA;
  DA3; DAC; DAM MST, POET; DLB 4, 48, 51; EWL 3; EXPP; LMFS 2;
  MAL 5; MTCW 1, 2; MTFW 2005; PFS
  3; RGAL 4; SATA 18; WP
Culleton, Beatrice 1949- .... **NNAL**
  See also CA 120; CANR 83; DAC
Culver, Timothy J.
  See Westlake, Donald E.
Culver, Timothy J.
  See Westlake, Donald E.
Cum, R.
  See Crumb, R.
Cumberland, Richard
  1732-1811 .... **NCLC 167**
  See also DLB 89; RGEL 2
Cummings, Bruce F(rederick)
  1889-1919 .... **TCLC 24**
  See also CA 123
Cummings, E(dward) E(stlin)
  1894-1962 .. **CLC 1, 3, 8, 12, 15, 68; PC
5; TCLC 137; WLC 2**
  See also AAYA 41; AMW; CA 73-76;
  CANR 31; CDALB 1929-1941; DA;
  DA3; DAB; DAC; DAM MST, POET;
  DLB 4, 48; EWL 3; EXPP; MAL 5;
  MTCW 1, 2; MTFW 2005; PAB; PFS 1,
  3, 12, 13, 19, 30; RGAL 4; TUS; WP

Cummins, Maria Susanna
  1827-1866 .... **NCLC 139**
  See also DLB 42; YABC 1
Cunha, Euclides (Rodrigues Pimenta) da
  1866-1909 .... **TCLC 24**
  See also CA 123; 219; DLB 307; LAW;
  WLIT 1
Cunningham, E. V.
  See Fast, Howard
Cunningham, J. Morgan
  See Westlake, Donald E.
Cunningham, J(ames) V(incent)
  1911-1985 .... **CLC 3, 31; PC 92**
  See also CA 1-4R; 115; CANR 1, 72; CP 1,
  2, 3, 4; DLB 5
Cunningham, Julia (Woolfolk)
  1916- .... **CLC 12**
  See also CA 9-12R; CANR 4, 19, 36; CWRI
  5; JRDA; MAICYA 1, 2; SAAS 2; SATA
  1, 26, 132
Cunningham, Michael 1952- .... **CLC 34, 243**
  See also AMWS 15; CA 136; CANR 96,
  160; CN 7; DLB 292; GLL 2; MTFW
  2005; NFS 23
Cunninghame Graham, R. B.
  See Cunninghame Graham, Robert
  (Gallnigad) Bontine
**Cunninghame Graham, Robert (Gallnigad)
Bontine** 1852-1936 .... **TCLC 19**
  See also CA 119; 184; DLB 98, 135, 174;
  RGEL 2; RGSF 2
Curnow, (Thomas) Allen (Monro)
  1911-2001 .... **PC 48**
  See also CA 69-72; 202; CANR 48, 99; CP
  1, 2, 3, 4, 5, 6, 7; EWL 3; RGEL 2
Currie, Ellen 19(?)- .... **CLC 44**
Curtin, Philip
  See Lowndes, Marie Adelaide (Belloc)
Curtin, Phillip
  See Lowndes, Marie Adelaide (Belloc)
Curtis, Price
  See Ellison, Harlan
Cusanus, Nicolaus 1401-1464
  See Nicholas of Cusa
Cutrate, Joe
  See Spiegelman, Art
Cynewulf c. 770- .... **CMLC 23**
  See also DLB 146; RGEL 2
Cyrano de Bergerac, Savinien de
  1619-1655 .... **LC 65**
  See also DLB 268; GFL Beginnings to
  1789; RGWL 2, 3
Cyril of Alexandria c. 375-c. 430 . **CMLC 59**
Czaczkes, Shmuel Yosef Halevi
  See Agnon, S.Y.
Dabrowska, Maria (Szumska)
  1889-1965 .... **CLC 15**
  See also CA 106; CDWLB 4; DLB 215;
  EWL 3
Dabydeen, David 1955- .... **CLC 34**
  See also BW 1; CA 125; CANR 56, 92; CN
  6, 7; CP 5, 6, 7; DLB 347
Dacey, Philip 1939- .... **CLC 51**
  See also CA 37-40R, 231; CAAE 231;
  CAAS 17; CANR 14, 32, 64; CP 4, 5, 6,
  7; DLB 105
Dacre, Charlotte c. 1772-1825(?) . **NCLC 151**
Dafydd ap Gwilym c. 1320-c. 1380 ..... **PC 56**
Dagerman, Stig (Halvard)
  1923-1954 .... **TCLC 17**
  See also CA 117; 155; DLB 259; EWL 3
D'Aguiar, Fred 1960- ..... **BLC 2:1; CLC 145**
  See also CA 148; CANR 83, 101; CN 7;
  CP 5, 6, 7; DLB 157; EWL 3
Dahl, Roald 1916-1990 ...... **CLC 1, 6, 18, 79;
TCLC 173**
  See also AAYA 15; BPFB 1; BRWS 4; BYA
  5; CA 1-4R; 133; CANR 6, 32, 37, 62;
  CLR 1, 7, 41, 111; CN 1, 2, 3, 4; CPW;

DA3; DAB; DAC; DAM MST, NOV,
  POP; DLB 139, 255; HGG; JRDA; MAI-
  CYA 1, 2; MTCW 1, 2; MTFW 2005;
  RGSF 2; SATA 1, 26, 73; SATA-Obit 65;
  SSFS 4; TEA; YAW
Dahlberg, Edward 1900-1977 . **CLC 1, 7, 14;
TCLC 208**
  See also CA 9-12R; 69-72; CANR 31, 62;
  CN 1, 2; DLB 48; MAL 5; MTCW 1;
  RGAL 4
Daitch, Susan 1954- .... **CLC 103**
  See also CA 161
Dale, Colin
  See Lawrence, T(homas) E(dward)
Dale, George E.
  See Asimov, Isaac
d'Alembert, Jean Le Rond
  1717-1783 .... **LC 126**
Dalton, Roque 1935-1975(?) ..... **HLCS 1; PC
36**
  See also CA 176; DLB 283; HW 2
Daly, Elizabeth 1878-1967 .... **CLC 52**
  See also CA 23-24; 25-28R; CANR 60;
  CAP 2; CMW 4
Daly, Mary 1928- .... **CLC 173**
  See also CA 25-28R; CANR 30, 62, 166;
  FW; GLL 1; MTCW 1
Daly, Maureen 1921-2006 .... **CLC 17**
  See also AAYA 5, 58; BYA 6; CA 253;
  CANR 37, 83, 108; CLR 96; JRDA; MAI-
  CYA 1, 2; SAAS 1; SATA 2, 129; SATA-
  Obit 176; WYA; YAW
Damas, Leon-Gontran 1912-1978 ... **CLC 84;
TCLC 204**
  See also BW 1; CA 125; 73-76; EWL 3
Dana, Richard Henry Sr.
  1787-1879 .... **NCLC 53**
Dangarembga, Tsitsi 1959- .... **BLC 2:1**
  See also BW 3; CA 163; NFS 28; WLIT 2
Daniel, Samuel 1562(?)-1619 .... **LC 24**
  See also DLB 62; RGEL 2
Daniels, Brett
  See Adler, Renata
Dannay, Frederic 1905-1982 .... **CLC 3, 11**
  See also BPFB 3; CA 1-4R; 107; CANR 1,
  39; CMW 4; DAM POP; DLB 137; MSW;
  MTCW 1; RGAL 4
D'Annunzio, Gabriele 1863-1938 ... **TCLC 6,
40, 215**
  See also CA 104; 155; EW 8; EWL 3;
  RGWL 2, 3; TWA; WLIT 7
Danois, N. le
  See Gourmont, Remy(-Marie-Charles) de
Dante 1265-1321 .... **CMLC 3, 18, 39, 70; PC
21; WLCS**
  See also DA; DA3; DAB; DAC; DAM
  MST, POET; EFS 1; EW 1; LAIT 1;
  RGWL 2, 3; TWA; WLIT 7; WP
d'Antibes, Germain
  See Simenon, Georges (Jacques Christian)
Danticat, Edwidge 1969- . **BLC 2:1; CLC 94,
139, 228; SSC 100**
  See also AAYA 29; CA 152, 192; CAAE
  192; CANR 73, 129, 179; CN 7; DNFS 1;
  EXPS; LATS 1:2; MTCW 2; MTFW
  2005; NFS 28; SSFS 1, 25; YAW
Danvers, Dennis 1947- .... **CLC 70**
Danziger, Paula 1944-2004 .... **CLC 21**
  See also AAYA 4, 36; BYA 6, 7, 14; CA
  112; 115; 229; CANR 37, 132; CLR 20;
  JRDA; MAICYA 1, 2; MTFW 2005;
  SATA 36, 63, 102, 149; SATA-Brief 30;
  SATA-Obit 155; WYA; YAW
Da Ponte, Lorenzo 1749-1838 .... **NCLC 50**
d'Aragona, Tullia 1510(?)-1556 .... **LC 121**
Dario, Ruben 1867-1916 .... **HLC 1; PC 15;
TCLC 4**
  See also CA 131; CANR 81; DAM MULT;
  DLB 290; EWL 3; HW 1, 2; LAW;
  MTCW 1, 2; MTFW 2005; RGWL 2, 3

Donaldson, Stephen R. 1947- ... **CLC 46, 138**
See also AAYA 36; BPFB 1; CA 89-92; CANR 13, 55, 99; CPW; DAM POP; FANT; INT CANR-13; SATA 121; SFW 4; SUFW 1, 2

Donleavy, J(ames) P(atrick) 1926- .... **CLC 1, 4, 6, 10, 45**
See also AITN 2; BPFB 1; CA 9-12R; CANR 24, 49, 62, 80, 124; CBD; CD 5, 6; CN 1, 2, 3, 4, 5, 6, 7; DLB 6, 173; INT CANR-24; MAL 5; MTCW 1, 2; MTFW 2005; RGAL 4

Donnadieu, Marguerite
See Duras, Marguerite

Donne, John 1572-1631 ... **LC 10, 24, 91; PC 1, 43; WLC 2**
See also AAYA 67; BRW 1; BRWC 1; BRWR 2; CDBLB Before 1660; DA; DAB; DAC; DAM MST, POET; DLB 121, 151; EXPP; PAB; PFS 2, 11; RGEL 3; TEA; WLIT 3; WP

Donnell, David 1939(?)- .... **CLC 34**
See also CA 197

Donoghue, Denis 1928- .... **CLC 209**
See also CA 17-20R; CANR 16, 102

Donoghue, Emma 1969- .... **CLC 239**
See also CA 155; CANR 103, 152; DLB 267; GLL 2; SATA 101

Donoghue, P.S.
See Hunt, E. Howard

Donoso (Yanez), Jose 1924-1996 ... **CLC 4, 8, 11, 32, 99; HLC 1; SSC 34; TCLC 133**
See also CA 81-84; 155; CANR 32, 73; CD-WLB 3; CWW 2; DAM MULT; DLB 113; EWL 3; HW 1, 2; LAW; LAWS 1; MTCW 1, 2; MTFW 2005; RGSF 2; WLIT 1

Donovan, John 1928-1992 .... **CLC 35**
See also AAYA 20; CA 97-100; 137; CLR 3; MAICYA 1, 2; SATA 72; SATA-Brief 29; YAW

Don Roberto
See Cunninghame Graham, Robert (Gallnigad) Bontine

Doolittle, Hilda 1886-1961 . **CLC 3, 8, 14, 31, 34, 73; PC 5; WLC 3**
See also AAYA 66; AMWS 1; CA 97-100; CANR 35, 131; DA; DAC; DAM MST, POET; DLB 4, 45; EWL 3; FL 1:5; FW; GLL 1; LMFS 2; MAL 5; MBL; MTCW 1, 2; MTFW 2005; PFS 6, 28; RGAL 4

Doppo
See Kunikida Doppo

Doppo, Kunikida
See Kunikida Doppo

Dorfman, Ariel 1942- .... **CLC 48, 77, 189; HLC 1**
See also CA 124; 130; CANR 67, 70, 135; CWW 2; DAM MULT; DFS 4; EWL 3; HW 1, 2; INT CA-130; WLIT 1

Dorn, Edward (Merton)
1929-1999 .... **CLC 10, 18**
See also CA 93-96; 187; CANR 42, 79; CP 1, 2, 3, 4, 5, 6, 7; DLB 5; INT CA-93-96; WP

Dor-Ner, Zvi .... **CLC 70**

Dorris, Michael 1945-1997 .... **CLC 109; NNAL**
See also AAYA 20; BEST 90:1; BYA 12; CA 102; 157; CANR 19, 46, 75; CLR 58; DA3; DAM MULT, NOV; DLB 175; LAIT 5; MTCW 2; MTFW 2005; NFS 3; RGAL 4; SATA 75; SATA-Obit 94; TCWW 2; YAW

Dorris, Michael A.
See Dorris, Michael

Dorsan, Luc
See Simenon, Georges (Jacques Christian)

Dorsange, Jean
See Simenon, Georges (Jacques Christian)

Dorset
See Sackville, Thomas

Dos Passos, John (Roderigo)
1896-1970 ... **CLC 1, 4, 8, 11, 15, 25, 34, 82; WLC 2**
See also AMW; BPFB 1; CA 1-4R; 29-32R; CANR 3; CDALB 1929-1941; DA; DA3; DAB; DAC; DAM MST, NOV; DLB 4, 9, 274, 316; DLBD 1, 15; DLBY 1996; EWL 3; MAL 5; MTCW 1, 2; MTFW 2005; NFS 14; RGAL 4; TUS

Dossage, Jean
See Simenon, Georges (Jacques Christian)

Dostoevsky, Fedor Mikhailovich
1821-1881 .. **NCLC 2, 7, 21, 33, 43, 119, 167, 202; SSC 2, 33, 44; WLC 2**
See also AAYA 40; DA; DA3; DAB; DAC; DAM MST, NOV; DLB 238; EW 7; EXPN; LATS 1:1; LMFS 1, 2; NFS 28; RGSF 2; RGWL 2, 3; SSFS 8; TWA

Dostoevsky, Fyodor
See Dostoevsky, Fedor Mikhailovich

Doty, Mark 1953(?)- .... **CLC 176; PC 53**
See also AMWS 11; CA 161, 183; CAAE 183; CANR 110, 173; CP 7; PFS 28

Doty, Mark A.
See Doty, Mark

Doty, Mark Alan
See Doty, Mark

Doty, M.R.
See Doty, Mark

Doughty, Charles M(ontagu)
1843-1926 .... **TCLC 27**
See also CA 115; 178; DLB 19, 57, 174

Douglas, Ellen 1921- .... **CLC 73**
See also CA 115; CANR 41, 83; CN 5, 6, 7; CSW; DLB 292

Douglas, Gavin 1475(?)-1522 .... **LC 20**
See also DLB 132; RGEL 2

Douglas, George
See Brown, George Douglas

Douglas, Keith (Castellain)
1920-1944 .... **TCLC 40**
See also BRW 7; CA 160; DLB 27; EWL 3; PAB; RGEL 2

Douglas, Leonard
See Bradbury, Ray

Douglas, Michael
See Crichton, Michael

Douglas, Michael
See Crichton, Michael

Douglas, (George) Norman
1868-1952 .... **TCLC 68**
See also BRW 6; CA 119; 157; DLB 34, 195; RGEL 2

Douglas, William
See Brown, George Douglas

Douglass, Frederick 1817(?)-1895 .. **BLC 1:1; NCLC 7, 55, 141; WLC 2**
See also AAYA 48; AFAW 1, 2; AMWC 1; AMWS 3; CDALB 1640-1865; DA; DA3; DAC; DAM MST, MULT; DLB 1, 43, 50, 79, 243; FW; LAIT 2; NCFS 2; RGAL 4; SATA 29

Dourado, (Waldomiro Freitas) Autran
1926- .... **CLC 23, 60**
See also CA 25-28R; 179; CANR 34, 81; DLB 145, 307; HW 2

Dourado, Waldomiro Freitas Autran
See Dourado, (Waldomiro Freitas) Autran

Dove, Rita 1952- . **BLC 2:1; BLCS; CLC 50, 81; PC 6**
See also AAYA 46; AMWS 4; BW 2; CA 109; CAAS 19; CANR 27, 42, 68, 76, 97, 132; CDALBS; CP 5, 6, 7; CSW; CWP; DA3; DAM MULT, POET; DLB 120; EWL 3; EXPP; MAL 5; MTCW 2; MTFW 2005; PFS 1, 15; RGAL 4

Dove, Rita Frances
See Dove, Rita

Doveglion
See Villa, Jose Garcia

Dowell, Coleman 1925-1985 .... **CLC 60**
See also CA 25-28R; 117; CANR 10; DLB 130; GLL 2

Downing, Major Jack
See Smith, Seba

Dowson, Ernest (Christopher)
1867-1900 .... **TCLC 4**
See also CA 105; 150; DLB 19, 135; RGEL 2

Doyle, A. Conan
See Doyle, Sir Arthur Conan

Doyle, Sir Arthur Conan
1859-1930 ..... **SSC 12, 83, 95; TCLC 7; WLC 2**
See also AAYA 14; BPFB 1; BRWS 2; BYA 4, 5, 11; CA 104; 122; CANR 131; CD-BLB 1890-1914; CLR 106; CMW 4; DA; DA3; DAB; DAC; DAM MST, NOV; DLB 18, 70, 156, 178; EXPS; HGG; LAIT 2; MSW; MTCW 1, 2; MTFW 2005; NFS 28; RGEL 2; RGSF 2; RHW; SATA 24; SCFW 1, 2; SFW 4; SSFS 2; TEA; WCH; WLIT 4; WYA; YAW

Doyle, Conan
See Doyle, Sir Arthur Conan

Doyle, John
See Graves, Robert

Doyle, Roddy 1958- .... **CLC 81, 178**
See also AAYA 14; BRWS 5; CA 143; CANR 73, 128, 168; CN 6, 7; DA3; DLB 194, 326; MTCW 2; MTFW 2005

Doyle, Sir A. Conan
See Doyle, Sir Arthur Conan

Dr. A
See Asimov, Isaac; Silverstein, Alvin; Silverstein, Virginia B(arbara Opshelor)

Drabble, Margaret 1939- ...... **CLC 2, 3, 5, 8, 10, 22, 53, 129**
See also BRWS 4; CA 13-16R; CANR 18, 35, 63, 112, 131, 174; CDBLB 1960 to Present; CN 1, 2, 3, 4, 5, 6, 7; CPW; DA3; DAB; DAC; DAM MST, NOV, POP; DLB 14, 155, 231; EWL 3; FW; MTCW 1, 2; MTFW 2005; RGEL 2; SATA 48; TEA

Drakulic, Slavenka 1949- .... **CLC 173**
See also CA 144; CANR 92

Drakulic-Ilic, Slavenka
See Drakulic, Slavenka

Drapier, M. B.
See Swift, Jonathan

Drayham, James
See Mencken, H(enry) L(ouis)

Drayton, Michael 1563-1631 . **LC 8, 161; PC 98**
See also DAM POET; DLB 121; RGEL 2

Dreadstone, Carl
See Campbell, Ramsey

Dreiser, Theodore 1871-1945 .... **SSC 30, 114; TCLC 10, 18, 35, 83; WLC 2**
See also AMW; AMWC 2; AMWR 2; BYA 15, 16; CA 106; 132; CDALB 1865-1917; DA; DA3; DAC; DAM MST, NOV; DLB 9, 12, 102, 137; DLBD 1; EWL 3; LAIT 2; LMFS 2; MAL 5; MTCW 1, 2; MTFW 2005; NFS 8, 17; RGAL 4; TUS

Dreiser, Theodore Herman Albert
See Dreiser, Theodore

Drexler, Rosalyn 1926- .... **CLC 2, 6**
See also CA 81-84; CAD; CANR 68, 124; CD 5, 6; CWD; MAL 5

Dreyer, Carl Theodor 1889-1968 ...... **CLC 16**
See also CA 116

d'Urfe, Honore
See Urfe, Honore d'

Durfey, Thomas 1653-1723 .... **LC 94**
See also DLB 80; RGEL 2

Durkheim, Emile 1858-1917 .... **TCLC 55**
See also CA 249

Durrell, Lawrence (George)
1912-1990 ..... **CLC 1, 4, 6, 8, 13, 27, 41**
See also BPFB 1; BRWS 1; CA 9-12R; 132;
CANR 40, 77; CDBLB 1945-1960; CN 1,
2, 3, 4; CP 1, 2, 3, 4, 5; DAM NOV; DLB
15, 27, 204; DLBY 1990; EWL 3; MTCW
1, 2; RGEL 2; SFW 4; TEA

Durrenmatt, Friedrich
See Duerrenmatt, Friedrich

Dutt, Michael Madhusudan
1824-1873 .... **NCLC 118**

Dutt, Toru 1856-1877 .... **NCLC 29**
See also DLB 240

Dwight, Timothy 1752-1817 .... **NCLC 13**
See also DLB 37; RGAL 4

Dworkin, Andrea 1946-2005 ..... **CLC 43, 123**
See also CA 77-80; 238; CAAS 21; CANR
16, 39, 76, 96; FL 1:5; FW; GLL 1; INT
CANR-16; MTCW 1, 2; MTFW 2005

Dwyer, Deanna
See Koontz, Dean R.

Dwyer, K.R.
See Koontz, Dean R.

Dybek, Stuart 1942- .... **CLC 114; SSC 55**
See also CA 97-100; CANR 39; DLB 130;
SSFS 23

Dye, Richard
See De Voto, Bernard (Augustine)

Dyer, Geoff 1958- .... **CLC 149**
See also CA 125; CANR 88

Dyer, George 1755-1841 .... **NCLC 129**
See also DLB 93

Dylan, Bob 1941- .... **CLC 3, 4, 6, 12, 77; PC 37**
See also AMWS 18; CA 41-44R; CANR
108; CP 1, 2, 3, 4, 5, 6, 7; DLB 16

Dyson, John 1943- .... **CLC 70**
See also CA 144

Dzyubin, Eduard Georgievich
1895-1934 .... **TCLC 60**
See also CA 170; EWL 3

E. V. L.
See Lucas, E(dward) V(errall)

Eagleton, Terence (Francis) 1943- .. **CLC 63, 132**
See also CA 57-60; CANR 7, 23, 68, 115;
DLB 242; LMFS 2; MTCW 1, 2; MTFW
2005

Eagleton, Terry
See Eagleton, Terence (Francis)

Early, Jack
See Scoppettone, Sandra

East, Michael
See West, Morris L(anglo)

Eastaway, Edward
See Thomas, (Philip) Edward

Eastlake, William (Derry)
1917-1997 .... **CLC 8**
See also CA 5-8R; 158; CAAS 1; CANR 5,
63; CN 1, 2, 3, 4, 5, 6; DLB 6, 206; INT
CANR-5; MAL 5; TCWW 1, 2

Eastman, Charles A(lexander)
1858-1939 .... **NNAL; TCLC 55**
See also CA 179; CANR 91; DAM MULT;
DLB 175; YABC 1

Eaton, Edith Maude 1865-1914 .... **AAL**
See also CA 154; DLB 221, 312; FW

Eaton, (Lillie) Winnifred 1875-1954 .... **AAL**
See also CA 217; DLB 221, 312; RGAL 4

Eberhart, Richard 1904-2005 ...... **CLC 3, 11, 19, 56; PC 76**
See also AMW; CA 1-4R; 240; CANR 2,
125; CDALB 1941-1968; CP 1, 2, 3, 4, 5,
6, 7; DAM POET; DLB 48; MAL 5;
MTCW 1; RGAL 4

Eberhart, Richard Ghormley
See Eberhart, Richard

Eberstadt, Fernanda 1960- .... **CLC 39**
See also CA 136; CANR 69, 128

Ebner, Margaret c. 1291-1351 ...... **CMLC 98**

Echegaray (y Eizaguirre), Jose (Maria Waldo) 1832-1916 .... **HLCS 1; TCLC 4**
See also CA 104; CANR 32; DLB 329;
EWL 3; HW 1; MTCW 1

Echeverria, (Jose) Esteban (Antonino)
1805-1851 .... **NCLC 18**
See also LAW

Echo
See Proust, (Valentin-Louis-George-Eugene)
Marcel

Eckert, Allan W. 1931- .... **CLC 17**
See also AAYA 18; BYA 2; CA 13-16R;
CANR 14, 45; INT CANR-14; MAICYA
2; MAICYAS 1; SAAS 21; SATA 29, 91;
SATA-Brief 27

Eckhart, Meister 1260(?)-1327(?) .. **CMLC 9, 80**
See also DLB 115; LMFS 1

Eckmar, F. R.
See de Hartog, Jan

Eco, Umberto 1932- .... **CLC 28, 60, 142, 248**
See also BEST 90:1; BPFB 1; CA 77-80;
CANR 12, 33, 55, 110, 131; CPW; CWW
2; DA3; DAM NOV, POP; DLB 196, 242;
EWL 3; MSW; MTCW 1, 2; MTFW
2005; NFS 22; RGWL 3; WLIT 7

Eddison, E(ric) R(ucker)
1882-1945 .... **TCLC 15**
See also CA 109; 156; DLB 255; FANT;
SFW 4; SUFW 1

Eddy, Mary (Ann Morse) Baker
1821-1910 .... **TCLC 71**
See also CA 113; 174

Edel, (Joseph) Leon 1907-1997 .. **CLC 29, 34**
See also CA 1-4R; 161; CANR 1, 22, 112;
DLB 103; INT CANR-22

Eden, Emily 1797-1869 .... **NCLC 10**

Edgar, David 1948- .... **CLC 42**
See also CA 57-60; CANR 12, 61, 112;
CBD; CD 5, 6; DAM DRAM; DFS 15;
DLB 13, 233; MTCW 1

Edgerton, Clyde (Carlyle) 1944- ...... **CLC 39**
See also AAYA 17; CA 118; 134; CANR
64, 125; CN 7; CSW; DLB 278; INT CA-
134; TCLE 1:1; YAW

Edgeworth, Maria 1768-1849 ... **NCLC 1, 51, 158; SSC 86**
See also BRWS 3; DLB 116, 159, 163; FL
1:3; FW; RGEL 2; SATA 21; TEA; WLIT
3

Edmonds, Paul
See Kuttner, Henry

Edmonds, Walter D(umaux)
1903-1998 .... **CLC 35**
See also BYA 2; CA 5-8R; CANR 2; CWRI
5; DLB 9; LAIT 1; MAICYA 1, 2; MAL
5; RHW; SAAS 4; SATA 1, 27; SATA-
Obit 99

Edmondson, Wallace
See Ellison, Harlan

Edson, Margaret 1961- ...... **CLC 199; DC 24**
See also AMWS 18; CA 190; DFS 13; DLB
266

Edson, Russell 1935- .... **CLC 13**
See also CA 33-36R; CANR 115; CP 2, 3,
4, 5, 6, 7; DLB 244; WP

Edwards, Bronwen Elizabeth
See Rose, Wendy

Edwards, Eli
See McKay, Festus Claudius

Edwards, G(erald) B(asil)
1899-1976 .... **CLC 25**
See also CA 201; 110

Edwards, Gus 1939- .... **CLC 43**
See also CA 108; INT CA-108

Edwards, Jonathan 1703-1758 .... **LC 7, 54**
See also AMW; DA; DAC; DAM MST;
DLB 24, 270; RGAL 4; TUS

Edwards, Sarah Pierpont 1710-1758 .. **LC 87**
See also DLB 200

Efron, Marina Ivanovna Tsvetaeva
See Tsvetaeva (Efron), Marina (Ivanovna)

Egeria fl. 4th cent. - .... **CMLC 70**

Eggers, Dave 1970- .... **CLC 241**
See also AAYA 56; CA 198; CANR 138;
MTFW 2005

Egoyan, Atom 1960- .... **CLC 151**
See also AAYA 63; CA 157; CANR 151

Ehle, John (Marsden, Jr.) 1925- ...... **CLC 27**
See also CA 9-12R; CSW

Ehrenbourg, Ilya (Grigoryevich)
See Ehrenburg, Ilya (Grigoryevich)

Ehrenburg, Ilya (Grigoryevich)
1891-1967 .... **CLC 18, 34, 62**
See also CA 102; 25-28R; EWL 3

Ehrenburg, Ilyo (Grigoryevich)
See Ehrenburg, Ilya (Grigoryevich)

Ehrenreich, Barbara 1941- .... **CLC 110, 267**
See also BEST 90:4; CA 73-76; CANR 16,
37, 62, 117, 167; DLB 246; FW; MTCW
1, 2; MTFW 2005

Ehrlich, Gretel 1946- .... **CLC 249**
See also ANW; CA 140; CANR 74, 146;
DLB 212, 275; TCWW 2

Eich, Gunter
See Eich, Gunter

Eich, Gunter 1907-1972 .... **CLC 15**
See also CA 111; 93-96; DLB 69, 124;
EWL 3; RGWL 2, 3

Eichendorff, Joseph 1788-1857 .... **NCLC 8**
See also DLB 90; RGWL 2, 3

Eigner, Larry
See Eigner, Laurence (Joel)

Eigner, Laurence (Joel) 1927-1996 ..... **CLC 9**
See also CA 9-12R; 151; CAAS 23; CANR
6, 84; CP 1, 2, 3, 4, 5, 6, 7; DLB 5; WP

Eilhart von Oberge c. 1140-c.
1195 .... **CMLC 67**
See also DLB 148

Einhard c. 770-840 .... **CMLC 50**
See also DLB 148

Einstein, Albert 1879-1955 .... **TCLC 65**
See also CA 121; 133; MTCW 1, 2

Eiseley, Loren
See Eiseley, Loren Corey

Eiseley, Loren Corey 1907-1977 .... **CLC 7**
See also AAYA 5; ANW; CA 1-4R; 73-76;
CANR 6; DLB 275; DLBD 17

Eisenstadt, Jill 1963- .... **CLC 50**
See also CA 140

Eisenstein, Sergei (Mikhailovich)
1898-1948 .... **TCLC 57**
See also CA 114; 149

Eisner, Simon
See Kornbluth, C(yril) M.

Eisner, Will 1917-2005 .... **CLC 237**
See also AAYA 52; CA 108; 235; CANR
114, 140, 179; MTFW 2005; SATA 31,
165

Eisner, William Erwin
See Eisner, Will

Ekeloef, (Bengt) Gunnar
1907-1968 .... **CLC 27; PC 23**
See also CA 123; 25-28R; DAM POET;
DLB 259; EW 12; EWL 3

Epinay, Louise d' 1726-1783 .... **LC 138**
See also DLB 313
Epsilon
See Betjeman, John
Epstein, Daniel Mark 1948- .... **CLC 7**
See also CA 49-52; CANR 2, 53, 90
Epstein, Jacob 1956- .... **CLC 19**
See also CA 114
Epstein, Jean 1897-1953 .... **TCLC 92**
Epstein, Joseph 1937- .... **CLC 39, 204**
See also AMWS 14; CA 112; 119; CANR
50, 65, 117, 164
Epstein, Leslie 1938- .... **CLC 27**
See also AMWS 12; CA 73-76, 215; CAAE
215; CAAS 12; CANR 23, 69, 162; DLB
299; RGHL
Equiano, Olaudah 1745(?)-1797 ..... **BLC 1:2;
LC 16, 143**
See also AFAW 1, 2; CDWLB 3; DAM
MULT; DLB 37, 50; WLIT 2
Erasmus, Desiderius 1469(?)-1536 ..... **LC 16,
93**
See also DLB 136; EW 2; LMFS 1; RGWL
2, 3; TWA
Erdman, Paul E. 1932-2007 .... **CLC 25**
See also AITN 1; CA 61-64; 259; CANR
13, 43, 84
Erdman, Paul Emil
See Erdman, Paul E.
Erdrich, Karen Louise
See Erdrich, Louise
Erdrich, Louise 1954- .... **CLC 39, 54, 120,
176; NNAL; PC 52; SSC 121**
See also AAYA 10, 47; AMWS 4; BEST
89:1; BPFB 1; CA 114; CANR 41, 62,
118, 138; CDALBS; CN 5, 6, 7; CP 6, 7;
CPW; CWP; DA3; DAM MULT, NOV,
POP; DLB 152, 175, 206; EWL 3; EXPP;
FL 1:5; LAIT 5; LATS 1:2; MAL 5;
MTCW 1, 2; MTFW 2005; NFS 5; PFS
14; RGAL 4; SATA 94, 141; SSFS 14,
22; TCWW 2
Erenburg, Ilya (Grigoryevich)
See Ehrenburg, Ilya (Grigoryevich)
See also DLB 272
Erickson, Stephen Michael
See Erickson, Steve
Erickson, Steve 1950- .... **CLC 64**
See also CA 129; CANR 60, 68, 136;
MTFW 2005; SFW 4; SUFW 2
Erickson, Walter
See Fast, Howard
Ericson, Walter
See Fast, Howard
Eriksson, Buntel
See Bergman, Ingmar
Eriugena, John Scottus c.
810-877 .... **CMLC 65**
See also DLB 115
Ernaux, Annie 1940- .... **CLC 88, 184**
See also CA 147; CANR 93; MTFW 2005;
NCFS 3, 5
Erskine, John 1879-1951 .... **TCLC 84**
See also CA 112; 159; DLB 9, 102; FANT
Erwin, Will
See Eisner, Will
Eschenbach, Wolfram von
See von Eschenbach, Wolfram
Eseki, Bruno
See Mphahlele, Es'kia
Esekie, Bruno
See Mphahlele, Es'kia
Esenin, S.A.
See Esenin, Sergei
Esenin, Sergei 1895-1925 .... **TCLC 4**
See also CA 104; EWL 3; RGWL 2, 3
Esenin, Sergei Aleksandrovich
See Esenin, Sergei

Eshleman, Clayton 1935- .... **CLC 7**
See also CA 33-36R, 212; CAAE 212;
CAAS 6; CANR 93; CP 1, 2, 3, 4, 5, 6,
7; DLB 5
Espada, Martin 1957- .... **PC 74**
See also CA 159; CANR 80; CP 7; EXPP;
LLW; MAL 5; PFS 13, 16
Espriella, Don Manuel Alvarez
See Southey, Robert
Espriu, Salvador 1913-1985 .... **CLC 9**
See also CA 154; 115; DLB 134; EWL 3
Espronceda, Jose de 1808-1842 ..... **NCLC 39**
Esquivel, Laura 1950(?)- ... **CLC 141; HLCS
1**
See also AAYA 29; CA 143; CANR 68, 113,
161; DA3; DNFS 2; LAIT 3; LMFS 2;
MTCW 2; MTFW 2005; NFS 5; WLIT 1
Esse, James
See Stephens, James
Esterbrook, Tom
See Hubbard, L. Ron
Esterhazy, Peter 1950- .... **CLC 251**
See also CA 140; CANR 137; CDWLB 4;
CWW 2; DLB 232; EWL 3; RGWL 3
Estleman, Loren D. 1952- .... **CLC 48**
See also AAYA 27; CA 85-88; CANR 27,
74, 139, 177; CMW 4; CPW; DA3; DAM
NOV, POP; DLB 226; INT CANR-27;
MTCW 1, 2; MTFW 2005; TCWW 1, 2
Etherege, Sir George 1636-1692 . **DC 23; LC
78**
See also BRW 2; DAM DRAM; DLB 80;
PAB; RGEL 2
Euclid 306B.C.-283B.C. .... **CMLC 25**
Eugenides, Jeffrey 1960- .... **CLC 81, 212**
See also AAYA 51; CA 144; CANR 120;
MTFW 2005; NFS 24
Euripides c. 484B.C.-406B.C. .... **CMLC 23,
51; DC 4; WLCS**
See also AW 1; CDWLB 1; DA; DA3;
DAB; DAC; DAM DRAM, MST; DFS 1,
4, 6, 25; DLB 176; LAIT 1; LMFS 1;
RGWL 2, 3; WLIT 8
Eusebius c. 263-c. 339 .... **CMLC 103**
Evan, Evin
See Faust, Frederick (Schiller)
Evans, Caradoc 1878-1945 ... **SSC 43; TCLC
85**
See also DLB 162
Evans, Evan
See Faust, Frederick (Schiller)
Evans, Marian
See Eliot, George
Evans, Mary Ann
See Eliot, George
Evarts, Esther
See Benson, Sally
Evelyn, John 1620-1706 .... **LC 144**
See also BRW 2; RGEL 2
Everett, Percival 1956- .... **CLC 57**
See Everett, Percival L.
See also AMWS 18; BW 2; CA 129; CANR
94, 134, 179; CN 7; MTFW 2005
Everett, Percival L.
See Everett, Percival
See also CSW
Everson, R(onald) G(ilmour)
1903-1992 .... **CLC 27**
See also CA 17-20R; CP 1, 2, 3, 4; DLB 88
Everson, William (Oliver)
1912-1994 .... **CLC 1, 5, 14**
See also BG 1:2; CA 9-12R; 145; CANR
20; CP 1; DLB 5, 16, 212; MTCW 1
Evtushenko, Evgenii Aleksandrovich
See Yevtushenko, Yevgeny (Alexandrovich)

Ewart, Gavin (Buchanan)
1916-1995 .... **CLC 13, 46**
See also BRWS 7; CA 89-92; 150; CANR
17, 46; CP 1, 2, 3, 4, 5, 6; DLB 40;
MTCW 1
Ewers, Hanns Heinz 1871-1943 ..... **TCLC 12**
See also CA 109; 149
Ewing, Frederick R.
See Sturgeon, Theodore (Hamilton)
Exley, Frederick (Earl) 1929-1992 .... **CLC 6,
11**
See also AITN 2; BPFB 1; CA 81-84; 138;
CANR 117; DLB 143; DLBY 1981
Eynhardt, Guillermo
See Quiroga, Horacio (Sylvestre)
Ezekiel, Nissim (Moses) 1924-2004 .. **CLC 61**
See also CA 61-64; 223; CP 1, 2, 3, 4, 5, 6,
7; DLB 323; EWL 3
Ezekiel, Tish O'Dowd 1943- .... **CLC 34**
See also CA 129
Fadeev, Aleksandr Aleksandrovich
See Bulgya, Alexander Alexandrovich
Fadeev, Alexandr Alexandrovich
See Bulgya, Alexander Alexandrovich
Fadeyev, A.
See Bulgya, Alexander Alexandrovich
Fadeyev, Alexander
See Bulgya, Alexander Alexandrovich
Fagen, Donald 1948- .... **CLC 26**
Fainzil'berg, Il'ia Arnol'dovich
See Fainzilberg, Ilya Arnoldovich
Fainzilberg, Ilya Arnoldovich
1897-1937 .... **TCLC 21**
See also CA 120; 165; DLB 272; EWL 3
Fair, Ronald L. 1932- .... **CLC 18**
See also BW 1; CA 69-72; CANR 25; DLB
33
Fairbairn, Roger
See Carr, John Dickson
Fairbairns, Zoe (Ann) 1948- .... **CLC 32**
See also CA 103; CANR 21, 85; CN 4, 5,
6, 7
Fairfield, Flora
See Alcott, Louisa May
Falco, Gian
See Papini, Giovanni
Falconer, James
See Kirkup, James
Falconer, Kenneth
See Kornbluth, C(yril) M.
Falkland, Samuel
See Heijermans, Herman
Fallaci, Oriana 1930-2006 .... **CLC 11, 110**
See also CA 77-80; 253; CANR 15, 58, 134;
FW; MTCW 1
Faludi, Susan 1959- .... **CLC 140**
See also CA 138; CANR 126; FW; MTCW
2; MTFW 2005; NCFS 3
Faludy, George 1913- .... **CLC 42**
See also CA 21-24R
Faludy, Gyoergy
See Faludy, George
Fanon, Frantz 1925-1961 ...... **BLC 1:2; CLC
74; TCLC 188**
See also BW 1; CA 116; 89-92; DAM
MULT; DLB 296; LMFS 2; WLIT 2
Fanshawe, Ann 1625-1680 .... **LC 11**
Fante, John (Thomas) 1911-1983 .... **CLC 60;
SSC 65**
See also AMWS 11; CA 69-72; 109; CANR
23, 104; DLB 130; DLBY 1983
Farah, Nuruddin 1945- .. **BLC 1:2, 2:2; CLC
53, 137**
See also AFW; BW 2, 3; CA 106; CANR
81, 148; CDWLB 3; CN 4, 5, 6, 7; DAM
MULT; DLB 125; EWL 3; WLIT 2
Fardusi
See Ferdowsi, Abu'l Qasem

Fiedler, Leslie A(aron) 1917-2003 ..... **CLC 4, 13, 24**
See also AMWS 13; CA 9-12R; 212; CANR 7, 63; CN 1, 2, 3, 4, 5, 6; DLB 28, 67; EWL 3; MAL 5; MTCW 1, 2; RGAL 4; TUS

Field, Andrew 1938- .... **CLC 44**
See also CA 97-100; CANR 25

Field, Eugene 1850-1895 .... **NCLC 3**
See also DLB 23, 42, 140; DLBD 13; MAICYA 1, 2; RGAL 4; SATA 16

Field, Gans T.
See Wellman, Manly Wade

Field, Michael 1915-1971 .... **TCLC 43**
See also CA 29-32R

Fielding, Helen 1958- .... **CLC 146, 217**
See also AAYA 65; CA 172; CANR 127; DLB 231; MTFW 2005

Fielding, Henry 1707-1754 .... **LC 1, 46, 85, 151, 154; WLC 2**
See also BRW 3; BRWR 1; CDBLB 1660-1789; DA; DA3; DAB; DAC; DAM DRAM, MST, NOV; DLB 39, 84, 101; NFS 18; RGEL 2; TEA; WLIT 3

Fielding, Sarah 1710-1768 .... **LC 1, 44**
See also DLB 39; RGEL 2; TEA

Fields, W. C. 1880-1946 .... **TCLC 80**
See also DLB 44

Fierstein, Harvey (Forbes) 1954- ..... **CLC 33**
See also CA 123; 129; CAD; CD 5, 6; CPW; DA3; DAM DRAM, POP; DFS 6; DLB 266; GLL; MAL 5

Figes, Eva 1932- .... **CLC 31**
See also CA 53-56; CANR 4, 44, 83; CN 2, 3, 4, 5, 6, 7; DLB 14, 271; FW; RGHL

Filippo, Eduardo de
See de Filippo, Eduardo

Finch, Anne 1661-1720 ..... **LC 3, 137; PC 21**
See also BRWS 9; DLB 95; PFS 30

Finch, Robert (Duer Claydon)
1900-1995 .... **CLC 18**
See also CA 57-60; CANR 9, 24, 49; CP 1, 2, 3, 4, 5, 6; DLB 88

Findley, Timothy (Irving Frederick)
1930-2002 .... **CLC 27, 102**
See also CA 25-28R; 206; CANR 12, 42, 69, 109; CCA 1; CN 4, 5, 6, 7; DAC; DAM MST; DLB 53; FANT; RHW

Fink, William
See Mencken, H(enry) L(ouis)

Firbank, Louis 1942- .... **CLC 21**
See also CA 117

Firbank, (Arthur Annesley) Ronald
1886-1926 .... **TCLC 1**
See also BRWS 2; CA 104; 177; DLB 36; EWL 3; RGEL 2

Firdaosi
See Ferdowsi, Abu'l Qasem

Firdausi
See Ferdowsi, Abu'l Qasem

Firdavsi, Abulqosimi
See Ferdowsi, Abu'l Qasem

Firdavsii, Abulqosim
See Ferdowsi, Abu'l Qasem

Firdawsi, Abu al-Qasim
See Ferdowsi, Abu'l Qasem

Firdosi
See Ferdowsi, Abu'l Qasem

Firdousi
See Ferdowsi, Abu'l Qasem

Firdousi, Abu'l-Qasim
See Ferdowsi, Abu'l Qasem

Firdovsi, A.
See Ferdowsi, Abu'l Qasem

Firdovsi, Abulgasim
See Ferdowsi, Abu'l Qasem

Firdusi
See Ferdowsi, Abu'l Qasem

Fish, Stanley
See Fish, Stanley Eugene

Fish, Stanley E.
See Fish, Stanley Eugene

Fish, Stanley Eugene 1938- .... **CLC 142**
See also CA 112; 132; CANR 90; DLB 67

Fisher, Dorothy (Frances) Canfield
1879-1958 .... **TCLC 87**
See also CA 114; 136; CANR 80; CLR 71; CWRI 5; DLB 9, 102, 284; MAICYA 1, 2; MAL 5; YABC 1

Fisher, M(ary) F(rances) K(ennedy)
1908-1992 .... **CLC 76, 87**
See also AMWS 17; CA 77-80; 138; CANR 44; MTCW 2

Fisher, Roy 1930- .... **CLC 25**
See also CA 81-84; CAAS 10; CANR 16; CP 1, 2, 3, 4, 5, 6, 7; DLB 40

Fisher, Rudolph 1897-1934 ...... **BLC 1:2; HR 1:2; SSC 25; TCLC 11**
See also BW 1, 3; CA 107; 124; CANR 80; DAM MULT; DLB 51, 102

Fisher, Vardis (Alvero) 1895-1968 .... **CLC 7; TCLC 140**
See also CA 5-8R; 25-28R; CANR 68; DLB 9, 206; MAL 5; RGAL 4; TCWW 1, 2

Fiske, Tarleton
See Bloch, Robert (Albert)

Fitch, Clarke
See Sinclair, Upton

Fitch, John IV
See Cormier, Robert

Fitzgerald, Captain Hugh
See Baum, L(yman) Frank

FitzGerald, Edward 1809-1883 ...... **NCLC 9, 153; PC 79**
See also BRW 4; DLB 32; RGEL 2

Fitzgerald, F(rancis) Scott (Key)
1896-1940 .... **SSC 6, 31, 75; TCLC 1, 6, 14, 28, 55, 157; WLC 2**
See also AAYA 24; AITN 1; AMW; AMWC 2; AMWR 1; BPFB 1; CA 110; 123; CDALB 1917-1929; DA; DA3; DAB; DAC; DAM MST, NOV; DLB 4, 9, 86, 219, 273; DLBD 1, 15, 16; DLBY 1981, 1996; EWL 3; EXPN; EXPS; LAIT 3; MAL 5; MTCW 1, 2; MTFW 2005; NFS 2, 19, 20; RGAL 4; RGSF 2; SSFS 4, 15, 21, 25; TUS

Fitzgerald, Penelope 1916-2000 . **CLC 19, 51, 61, 143**
See also BRWS 5; CA 85-88; 190; CAAS 10; CANR 56, 86, 131; CN 3, 4, 5, 6, 7; DLB 14, 194, 326; EWL 3; MTCW 2; MTFW 2005

Fitzgerald, Robert (Stuart)
1910-1985 .... **CLC 39**
See also CA 1-4R; 114; CANR 1; CP 1, 2, 3, 4; DLBY 1980; MAL 5

FitzGerald, Robert D(avid)
1902-1987 .... **CLC 19**
See also CA 17-20R; CP 1, 2, 3, 4; DLB 260; RGEL 2

Fitzgerald, Zelda (Sayre)
1900-1948 .... **TCLC 52**
See also AMWS 9; CA 117; 126; DLBY 1984

Flanagan, Thomas (James Bonner)
1923-2002 .... **CLC 25, 52**
See also CA 108; 206; CANR 55; CN 3, 4, 5, 6, 7; DLBY 1980; INT CA-108; MTCW 1; RHW; TCLE 1:1

Flaubert, Gustave 1821-1880 .... **NCLC 2, 10, 19, 62, 66, 135, 179, 185; SSC 11, 60; WLC 2**
See also DA; DA3; DAB; DAC; DAM MST, NOV; DLB 119, 301; EW 7; EXPS; GFL 1789 to the Present; LAIT 2; LMFS 1; NFS 14; RGSF 2; RGWL 2, 3; SSFS 6; TWA

Flavius Josephus
See Josephus, Flavius

Flecker, Herman Elroy
See Flecker, (Herman) James Elroy

Flecker, (Herman) James Elroy
1884-1915 .... **TCLC 43**
See also CA 109; 150; DLB 10, 19; RGEL 2

Fleming, Ian 1908-1964 ... **CLC 3, 30; TCLC 193**
See also AAYA 26; BPFB 1; BRWS 14; CA 5-8R; CANR 59; CDBLB 1945-1960; CMW 4; CPW; DA3; DAM POP; DLB 87, 201; MSW; MTCW 1, 2; MTFW 2005; RGEL 2; SATA 9; TEA; YAW

Fleming, Ian Lancaster
See Fleming, Ian

Fleming, Thomas 1927- .... **CLC 37**
See also CA 5-8R; CANR 10, 102, 155; INT CANR-10; SATA 8

Fleming, Thomas James
See Fleming, Thomas

Fletcher, John 1579-1625 . **DC 6; LC 33, 151**
See also BRW 2; CDBLB Before 1660; DLB 58; RGEL 2; TEA

Fletcher, John Gould 1886-1950 .... **TCLC 35**
See also CA 107; 167; DLB 4, 45; LMFS 2; MAL 5; RGAL 4

Fleur, Paul
See Pohl, Frederik

Flieg, Helmut
See Heym, Stefan

Flooglebuckle, Al
See Spiegelman, Art

Flying Officer X
See Bates, H(erbert) E(rnest)

Fo, Dario 1926- .... **CLC 32, 109, 227; DC 10**
See also CA 116; 128; CANR 68, 114, 134, 164; CWW 2; DA3; DAM DRAM; DFS 23; DLB 330; DLBY 1997; EWL 3; MTCW 1, 2; MTFW 2005; WLIT 7

Foden, Giles 1967- .... **CLC 231**
See also CA 240; DLB 267; NFS 15

Fogarty, Jonathan Titulescu Esq.
See Farrell, James T(homas)

Follett, Ken 1949- .... **CLC 18**
See also AAYA 6, 50; BEST 89:4; BPFB 1; CA 81-84; CANR 13, 33, 54, 102, 156; CMW 4; CPW; DA3; DAM NOV, POP; DLB 87; DLBY 1981; INT CANR-33; MTCW 1

Follett, Kenneth Martin
See Follett, Ken

Fondane, Benjamin 1898-1944 ..... **TCLC 159**

Fontane, Theodor 1819-1898 . **NCLC 26, 163**
See also CDWLB 2; DLB 129; EW 6; RGWL 2, 3; TWA

Fonte, Moderata 1555-1592 .... **LC 118**

Fontenelle, Bernard Le Bovier de
1657-1757 .... **LC 140**
See also DLB 268, 313; GFL Beginnings to 1789

Fontenot, Chester .... **CLC 65**

Fonvizin, Denis Ivanovich
1744(?)-1792 .... **LC 81**
See also DLB 150; RGWL 2, 3

Foote, Horton 1916-2009 .... **CLC 51, 91**
See also CA 73-76; CAD; CANR 34, 51, 110; CD 5, 6; CSW; DA3; DAM DRAM; DFS 20; DLB 26, 266; EWL 3; INT CANR-34; MTFW 2005

Foote, Mary Hallock 1847-1938 .. **TCLC 108**
See also DLB 186, 188, 202, 221; TCWW 2

Foote, Samuel 1721-1777 .... **LC 106**
See also DLB 89; RGEL 2

Foote, Shelby 1916-2005 .... **CLC 75, 224**
See also AAYA 40; CA 5-8R; 240; CANR 3, 45, 74, 131; CN 1, 2, 3, 4, 5, 6, 7;

Fraze, Candida (Merrill) 1945- .... **CLC 50**
See also CA 126
Frazer, Andrew
See Marlowe, Stephen
Frazer, J(ames) G(eorge)
1854-1941 .... **TCLC 32**
See also BRWS 3; CA 118; NCFS 5
Frazer, Robert Caine
See Creasey, John
Frazer, Sir James George
See Frazer, J(ames) G(eorge)
Frazier, Charles 1950- .... **CLC 109, 224**
See also AAYA 34; CA 161; CANR 126,
170; CSW; DLB 292; MTFW 2005; NFS
25
Frazier, Charles R.
See Frazier, Charles
Frazier, Charles Robinson
See Frazier, Charles
Frazier, Ian 1951- .... **CLC 46**
See also CA 130; CANR 54, 93
Frederic, Harold 1856-1898 ... **NCLC 10, 175**
See also AMW; DLB 12, 23; DLBD 13;
MAL 5; NFS 22; RGAL 4
Frederick, John
See Faust, Frederick (Schiller)
Frederick the Great 1712-1786 .... **LC 14**
Fredro, Aleksander 1793-1876 .... **NCLC 8**
Freeling, Nicolas 1927-2003 .... **CLC 38**
See also CA 49-52; 218; CAAS 12; CANR
1, 17, 50, 84; CMW 4; CN 1, 2, 3, 4, 5,
6; DLB 87
Freeman, Douglas Southall
1886-1953 .... **TCLC 11**
See also CA 109; 195; DLB 17; DLBD 17
Freeman, Judith 1946- .... **CLC 55**
See also CA 148; CANR 120, 179; DLB
256
Freeman, Mary E(leanor) Wilkins
1852-1930 .... **SSC 1, 47, 113; TCLC 9**
See also CA 106; 177; DLB 12, 78, 221;
EXPS; FW; HGG; MBL; RGAL 4; RGSF
2; SSFS 4, 8, 26; SUFW 1; TUS
Freeman, R(ichard) Austin
1862-1943 .... **TCLC 21**
See also CA 113; CANR 84; CMW 4; DLB
70
French, Albert 1943- .... **CLC 86**
See also BW 3; CA 167
French, Antonia
See Kureishi, Hanif
French, Marilyn 1929- .. **CLC 10, 18, 60, 177**
See also BPFB 1; CA 69-72; CANR 3, 31,
134, 163; CN 5, 6, 7; CPW; DAM DRAM,
NOV, POP; FL 1:5; FW; INT CANR-31;
MTCW 1, 2; MTFW 2005
French, Paul
See Asimov, Isaac
Freneau, Philip Morin 1752-1832 .. **NCLC 1,
111**
See also AMWS 2; DLB 37, 43; RGAL 4
Freud, Sigmund 1856-1939 .... **TCLC 52**
See also CA 115; 133; CANR 69; DLB 296;
EW 8; EWL 3; LATS 1:1; MTCW 1, 2;
MTFW 2005; NCFS 3; TWA
Freytag, Gustav 1816-1895 .... **NCLC 109**
See also DLB 129
Friedan, Betty 1921-2006 .... **CLC 74**
See also CA 65-68; 248; CANR 18, 45, 74;
DLB 246; FW; MTCW 1, 2; MTFW
2005; NCFS 5
Friedan, Betty Naomi
See Friedan, Betty
Friedlander, Saul 1932- .... **CLC 90**
See also CA 117; 130; CANR 72; RGHL
Friedman, B(ernard) H(arper)
1926- .... **CLC 7**
See also CA 1-4R; CANR 3, 48

Friedman, Bruce Jay 1930- ...... **CLC 3, 5, 56**
See also CA 9-12R; CAD; CANR 25, 52,
101; CD 5, 6; CN 1, 2, 3, 4, 5, 6, 7; DLB
2, 28, 244; INT CANR-25; MAL 5; SSFS
18
Friel, Brian 1929- .. **CLC 5, 42, 59, 115, 253;
DC 8; SSC 76**
See also BRWS 5; CA 21-24R; CANR 33,
69, 131; CBD; CD 5, 6; DFS 11; DLB
13, 319; EWL 3; MTCW 1; RGEL 2; TEA
Friis-Baastad, Babbis Ellinor
1921-1970 .... **CLC 12**
See also CA 17-20R; 134; SATA 7
Frisch, Max 1911-1991 ...... **CLC 3, 9, 14, 18,
32, 44; TCLC 121**
See also CA 85-88; 134; CANR 32, 74; CD-
WLB 2; DAM DRAM, NOV; DFS 25;
DLB 69, 124; EW 13; EWL 3; MTCW 1,
2; MTFW 2005; RGHL; RGWL 2, 3
Fromentin, Eugene (Samuel Auguste)
1820-1876 .... **NCLC 10, 125**
See also DLB 123; GFL 1789 to the Present
Frost, Frederick
See Faust, Frederick (Schiller)
Frost, Robert 1874-1963 . **CLC 1, 3, 4, 9, 10,
13, 15, 26, 34, 44; PC 1, 39, 71; WLC 2**
See also AAYA 21; AMW; AMWR 1; CA
89-92; CANR 33; CDALB 1917-1929;
CLR 67; DA; DA3; DAB; DAC; DAM
MST, POET; DLB 54, 284, 342; DLBD
7; EWL 3; EXPP; MAL 5; MTCW 1, 2;
MTFW 2005; PAB; PFS 1, 2, 3, 4, 5, 6,
7, 10, 13; RGAL 4; SATA 14; TUS; WP;
WYA
Frost, Robert Lee
See Frost, Robert
Froude, James Anthony
1818-1894 .... **NCLC 43**
See also DLB 18, 57, 144
Froy, Herald
See Waterhouse, Keith (Spencer)
Fry, Christopher 1907-2005 ... **CLC 2, 10, 14**
See also BRWS 3; CA 17-20R; 240; CAAS
23; CANR 9, 30, 74, 132; CBD; CD 5, 6;
CP 1, 2, 3, 4, 5, 6, 7; DAM DRAM; DLB
13; EWL 3; MTCW 1, 2; MTFW 2005;
RGEL 2; SATA 66; TEA
Frye, (Herman) Northrop
1912-1991 .... **CLC 24, 70; TCLC 165**
See also CA 5-8R; 133; CANR 8, 37; DLB
67, 68, 246; EWL 3; MTCW 1, 2; MTFW
2005; RGAL 4; TWA
Fuchs, Daniel 1909-1993 .... **CLC 8, 22**
See also CA 81-84; 142; CAAS 5; CANR
40; CN 1, 2, 3, 4, 5; DLB 9, 26, 28;
DLBY 1993; MAL 5
Fuchs, Daniel 1934- .... **CLC 34**
See also CA 37-40R; CANR 14, 48
Fuentes, Carlos 1928- .. **CLC 3, 8, 10, 13, 22,
41, 60, 113; HLC 1; SSC 24; WLC 2**
See also AAYA 4, 45; AITN 2; BPFB 1;
CA 69-72; CANR 10, 32, 68, 104, 138;
CDWLB 3; CWW 2; DA; DA3; DAB;
DAC; DAM MST, MULT, NOV; DLB
113; DNFS 2; EWL 3; HW 1, 2; LAIT 3;
LATS 1:2; LAW; LAWS 1; LMFS 2;
MTCW 1, 2; MTFW 2005; NFS 8; RGSF
2; RGWL 2, 3; TWA; WLIT 1
Fuentes, Gregorio Lopez y
See Lopez y Fuentes, Gregorio
Fuertes, Gloria 1918-1998 .... **PC 27**
See also CA 178, 180; DLB 108; HW 2;
SATA 115
Fugard, (Harold) Athol 1932- . **CLC 5, 9, 14,
25, 40, 80, 211; DC 3**
See also AAYA 17; AFW; CA 85-88; CANR
32, 54, 118; CD 5, 6; DAM DRAM; DFS
3, 6, 10, 24; DLB 225; DNFS 1, 2; EWL
3; LATS 1:2; MTCW 1; MTFW 2005;
RGEL 2; WLIT 2

Fugard, Sheila 1932- .... **CLC 48**
See also CA 125
Fujiwara no Teika 1162-1241 .... **CMLC 73**
See also DLB 203
Fukuyama, Francis 1952- .... **CLC 131**
See also CA 140; CANR 72, 125, 170
Fuller, Charles (H.), (Jr.) 1939- ..... **BLC 1:2;
CLC 25; DC 1**
See also BW 2; CA 108; 112; CAD; CANR
87; CD 5, 6; DAM DRAM, MULT; DFS
8; DLB 38, 266; EWL 3; INT CA-112;
MAL 5; MTCW 1
Fuller, Henry Blake 1857-1929 .... **TCLC 103**
See also CA 108; 177; DLB 12; RGAL 4
Fuller, John (Leopold) 1937- .... **CLC 62**
See also CA 21-24R; CANR 9, 44; CP 1, 2,
3, 4, 5, 6, 7; DLB 40
Fuller, Margaret
See Ossoli, Sarah Margaret (Fuller)
Fuller, Roy (Broadbent) 1912-1991 ... **CLC 4,
28**
See also BRWS 7; CA 5-8R; 135; CAAS
10; CANR 53, 83; CN 1, 2, 3, 4, 5; CP 1,
2, 3, 4, 5; CWRI 5; DLB 15, 20; EWL 3;
RGEL 2; SATA 87
Fuller, Sarah Margaret
See Ossoli, Sarah Margaret (Fuller)
Fuller, Thomas 1608-1661 .... **LC 111**
See also DLB 151
Fulton, Alice 1952- .... **CLC 52**
See also CA 116; CANR 57, 88; CP 5, 6, 7;
CWP; DLB 193; PFS 25
Furey, Michael
See Ward, Arthur Henry Sarsfield
Furphy, Joseph 1843-1912 .... **TCLC 25**
See also CA 163; DLB 230; EWL 3; RGEL
2
Furst, Alan 1941- .... **CLC 255**
See also CA 69-72; CANR 12, 34, 59, 102,
159; DLBY 01
Fuson, Robert H(enderson) 1927- .... **CLC 70**
See also CA 89-92; CANR 103
Fussell, Paul 1924- .... **CLC 74**
See also BEST 90:1; CA 17-20R; CANR 8,
21, 35, 69, 135; INT CANR-21; MTCW
1, 2; MTFW 2005
Futabatei, Shimei 1864-1909 .... **TCLC 44**
See also CA 162; DLB 180; EWL 3; MJW
Futabatei Shimei
See Futabatei, Shimei
Futrelle, Jacques 1875-1912 .... **TCLC 19**
See also CA 113; 155; CMW 4
GAB
See Russell, George William
Gaberman, Judie Angell
See Angell, Judie
Gaboriau, Emile 1835-1873 .... **NCLC 14**
See also CMW 4; MSW
Gadda, Carlo Emilio 1893-1973 ...... **CLC 11;
TCLC 144**
See also CA 89-92; DLB 177; EWL 3;
WLIT 7
Gaddis, William 1922-1998 ... **CLC 1, 3, 6, 8,
10, 19, 43, 86**
See also AMWS 4; BPFB 1; CA 17-20R;
172; CANR 21, 48, 148; CN 1, 2, 3, 4, 5,
6; DLB 2, 278; EWL 3; MAL 5; MTCW
1, 2; MTFW 2005; RGAL 4
Gage, Walter
See Inge, William (Motter)
Gaiman, Neil 1960- .... **CLC 195**
See also AAYA 19, 42; CA 133; CANR 81,
129, 188; CLR 109; DLB 261; HGG;
MTFW 2005; SATA 85, 146, 197; SFW
4; SUFW 2
Gaiman, Neil Richard
See Gaiman, Neil

Gass, William H. 1924- . **CLC 1, 2, 8, 11, 15, 39, 132; SSC 12**
See also AMWS 6; CA 17-20R; CANR 30, 71, 100; CN 1, 2, 3, 4, 5, 6, 7; DLB 2, 227; EWL 3; MAL 5; MTCW 1, 2; MTFW 2005; RGAL 4

Gassendi, Pierre 1592-1655 .... **LC 54**
See also GFL Beginnings to 1789

Gasset, Jose Ortega y
See Ortega y Gasset, Jose

Gates, Henry Louis, Jr. 1950- ... **BLCS; CLC 65**
See also BW 2, 3; CA 109; CANR 25, 53, 75, 125; CSW; DA3; DAM MULT; DLB 67; EWL 3; MAL 5; MTCW 2; MTFW 2005; RGAL 4

Gatos, Stephanie
See Katz, Steve

Gautier, Theophile 1811-1872 .. **NCLC 1, 59; PC 18; SSC 20**
See also DAM POET; DLB 119; EW 6; GFL 1789 to the Present; RGWL 2, 3; SUFW; TWA

Gautreaux, Tim 1947- .... **CLC 270**
See also CA 187; CSW; DLB 292

Gay, John 1685-1732 .... **LC 49**
See also BRW 3; DAM DRAM; DLB 84, 95; RGEL 2; WLIT 3

Gay, Oliver
See Gogarty, Oliver St. John

Gay, Peter 1923- .... **CLC 158**
See also CA 13-16R; CANR 18, 41, 77, 147; INT CANR-18; RGHL

Gay, Peter Jack
See Gay, Peter

Gaye, Marvin (Pentz, Jr.)
1939-1984 .... **CLC 26**
See also CA 195; 112

Gebler, Carlo 1954- .... **CLC 39**
See also CA 119; 133; CANR 96, 186; DLB 271

Gebler, Carlo Ernest
See Gebler, Carlo

Gee, Maggie 1948- .... **CLC 57**
See also CA 130; CANR 125; CN 4, 5, 6, 7; DLB 207; MTFW 2005

Gee, Maurice 1931- .... **CLC 29**
See also AAYA 42; CA 97-100; CANR 67, 123; CLR 56; CN 2, 3, 4, 5, 6, 7; CWRI 5; EWL 3; MAICYA 2; RGSF 2; SATA 46, 101

Gee, Maurice Gough
See Gee, Maurice

Geiogamah, Hanay 1945- .... **NNAL**
See also CA 153; DAM MULT; DLB 175

Gelbart, Larry
See Gelbart, Larry (Simon)

Gelbart, Larry (Simon) 1928- ... **CLC 21, 61**
See also CA 73-76; CAD; CANR 45, 94; CD 5, 6

Gelber, Jack 1932-2003 ...... **CLC 1, 6, 14, 79**
See also CA 1-4R; 216; CAD; CANR 2; DLB 7, 228; MAL 5

Gellhorn, Martha (Ellis)
1908-1998 .... **CLC 14, 60**
See also CA 77-80; 164; CANR 44; CN 1, 2, 3, 4, 5, 6 7; DLBY 1982, 1998

Genet, Jean 1910-1986 .. **CLC 1, 2, 5, 10, 14, 44, 46; DC 25; TCLC 128**
See also CA 13-16R; CANR 18; DA3; DAM DRAM; DFS 10; DLB 72, 321; DLBY 1986; EW 13; EWL 3; GFL 1789 to the Present; GLL 1; LMFS 2; MTCW 1, 2; MTFW 2005; RGWL 2, 3; TWA

Genlis, Stephanie-Felicite Ducrest
1746-1830 .... **NCLC 166**
See also DLB 313

Gent, Peter 1942- .... **CLC 29**
See also AITN 1; CA 89-92; DLBY 1982

Gentile, Giovanni 1875-1944 .... **TCLC 96**
See also CA 119

Geoffrey of Monmouth c.
1100-1155 .... **CMLC 44**
See also DLB 146; TEA

George, Jean
See George, Jean Craighead

George, Jean Craighead 1919- .... **CLC 35**
See also AAYA 8, 69; BYA 2, 4; CA 5-8R; CANR 25; CLR 1, 80, 136; DLB 52; JRDA; MAICYA 1, 2; SATA 2, 68, 124, 170; WYA; YAW

George, Stefan (Anton) 1868-1933 . **TCLC 2, 14**
See also CA 104; 193; EW 8; EWL 3

Georges, Georges Martin
See Simenon, Georges (Jacques Christian)

Gerald of Wales c. 1146-c. 1223 ... **CMLC 60**

Gerhardi, William Alexander
See Gerhardie, William Alexander

Gerhardie, William Alexander
1895-1977 .... **CLC 5**
See also CA 25-28R; 73-76; CANR 18; CN 1, 2; DLB 36; RGEL 2

Gerome
See Thibault, Jacques Anatole Francois

Gerson, Jean 1363-1429 .... **LC 77**
See also DLB 208

Gersonides 1288-1344 .... **CMLC 49**
See also DLB 115

Gerstler, Amy 1956- .... **CLC 70**
See also CA 146; CANR 99

Gertler, T. .... **CLC 34**
See also CA 116; 121

Gertrude of Helfta c. 1256-c.
1301 .... **CMLC 105**

Gertsen, Aleksandr Ivanovich
See Herzen, Aleksandr Ivanovich

Ghalib
See Ghalib, Asadullah Khan

Ghalib, Asadullah Khan
1797-1869 .... **NCLC 39, 78**
See also DAM POET; RGWL 2, 3

Ghelderode, Michel de 1898-1962 ..... **CLC 6, 11; DC 15; TCLC 187**
See also CA 85-88; CANR 40, 77; DAM DRAM; DLB 321; EW 11; EWL 3; TWA

Ghiselin, Brewster 1903-2001 .... **CLC 23**
See also CA 13-16R; CAAS 10; CANR 13; CP 1, 2, 3, 4, 5, 6, 7

Ghose, Aurabinda 1872-1950 .... **TCLC 63**
See also CA 163; EWL 3

Ghose, Aurobindo
See Ghose, Aurabinda

Ghose, Zulfikar 1935- .... **CLC 42, 200**
See also CA 65-68; CANR 67; CN 1, 2, 3, 4, 5, 6, 7; CP 1, 2, 3, 4, 5, 6, 7; DLB 323; EWL 3

Ghosh, Amitav 1956- .... **CLC 44, 153**
See also CA 147; CANR 80, 158; CN 6, 7; DLB 323; WWE 1

Giacosa, Giuseppe 1847-1906 .... **TCLC 7**
See also CA 104

Gibb, Lee
See Waterhouse, Keith (Spencer)

Gibbon, Edward 1737-1794 .... **LC 97**
See also BRW 3; DLB 104, 336; RGEL 2

Gibbon, Lewis Grassic
See Mitchell, James Leslie

Gibbons, Kaye 1960- .... **CLC 50, 88, 145**
See also AAYA 34; AMWS 10; CA 151; CANR 75, 127; CN 7; CSW; DA3; DAM POP; DLB 292; MTCW 2; MTFW 2005; NFS 3; RGAL 4; SATA 117

Gibran, Kahlil 1883-1931 ..... **PC 9; TCLC 1, 9, 205**
See also CA 104; 150; DA3; DAM POET, POP; DLB 346; EWL 3; MTCW 2; WLIT 6

Gibran, Khalil
See Gibran, Kahlil

Gibson, Mel 1956- .... **CLC 215**

Gibson, William 1914-2008 .... **CLC 23**
See also CA 9-12R; 279; CAD; CANR 9, 42, 75, 125; CD 5, 6; DA; DAB; DAC; DAM DRAM, MST; DFS 2; DLB 7; LAIT 2; MAL 5; MTCW 2; MTFW 2005; SATA 66; SATA-Obit 199; YAW

Gibson, William 1948- .... **CLC 39, 63, 186, 192; SSC 52**
See also AAYA 12, 59; AMWS 16; BPFB 2; CA 126; 133; CANR 52, 90, 106, 172; CN 6, 7; CPW; DA3; DAM POP; DLB 251; MTCW 2; MTFW 2005; SCFW 2; SFW 4; SSFS 26

Gibson, William Ford
See Gibson, William

Gide, Andre (Paul Guillaume)
1869-1951 .... **SSC 13; TCLC 5, 12, 36, 177; WLC 3**
See also CA 104; 124; DA; DA3; DAB; DAC; DAM MST, NOV; DLB 65, 321, 330; EW 8; EWL 3; GFL 1789 to the Present; MTCW 1, 2; MTFW 2005; NFS 21; RGSF 2; RGWL 2, 3; TWA

Gifford, Barry 1946- .... **CLC 34**
See also CA 65-68; CANR 9, 30, 40, 90, 180

Gifford, Barry Colby
See Gifford, Barry

Gilbert, Frank
See De Voto, Bernard (Augustine)

Gilbert, W(illiam) S(chwenck)
1836-1911 .... **TCLC 3**
See also CA 104; 173; DAM DRAM, POET; DLB 344; RGEL 2; SATA 36

Gilbert of Poitiers c. 1085-1154 .... **CMLC 85**

Gilbreth, Frank B(unker), Jr.
1911-2001 .... **CLC 17**
See also CA 9-12R; SATA 2

Gilchrist, Ellen (Louise) 1935- .. **CLC 34, 48, 143, 264; SSC 14, 63**
See also BPFB 2; CA 113; 116; CANR 41, 61, 104; CN 4, 5, 6, 7; CPW; CSW; DAM POP; DLB 130; EWL 3; EXPS; MTCW 1, 2; MTFW 2005; RGAL 4; RGSF 2; SSFS 9

Gildas fl. 6th cent. - .... **CMLC 99**

Giles, Molly 1942- .... **CLC 39**
See also CA 126; CANR 98

Gill, Eric
See Gill, (Arthur) Eric (Rowton Peter Joseph)

Gill, (Arthur) Eric (Rowton Peter Joseph)
1882-1940 .... **TCLC 85**
See also CA 120; DLB 98

Gill, Patrick
See Creasey, John

Gillette, Douglas .... **CLC 70**

Gilliam, Terry 1940- .... **CLC 21, 141**
See also AAYA 19, 59; CA 108; 113; CANR 35; INT CA-113

Gilliam, Terry Vance
See Gilliam, Terry

Gillian, Jerry
See Gilliam, Terry

Gilliatt, Penelope (Ann Douglass)
1932-1993 .... **CLC 2, 10, 13, 53**
See also AITN 2; CA 13-16R; 141; CANR 49; CN 1, 2, 3, 4, 5; DLB 14

Gilligan, Carol 1936- .... **CLC 208**
See also CA 142; CANR 121, 187; FW

Goldman, William 1931- .... **CLC 1, 48**
See also BPFB 2; CA 9-12R; CANR 29, 69, 106; CN 1, 2, 3, 4, 5, 6, 7; DLB 44; FANT; IDFW 3, 4

Goldman, William W.
See Goldman, William

Goldmann, Lucien 1913-1970 .... **CLC 24**
See also CA 25-28; CAP 2

Goldoni, Carlo 1707-1793 .... **LC 4, 152**
See also DAM DRAM; EW 4; RGWL 2, 3; WLIT 7

Goldsberry, Steven 1949- .... **CLC 34**
See also CA 131

Goldsmith, Oliver 1730(?)-1774 .... **DC 8; LC 2, 48, 122; PC 77; WLC 3**
See also BRW 3; CDBLB 1660-1789; DA; DAB; DAC; DAM DRAM, MST, NOV, POET; DFS 1; DLB 39, 89, 104, 109, 142, 336; IDTP; RGEL 2; SATA 26; TEA; WLIT 3

Goldsmith, Peter
See Priestley, J(ohn) B(oynton)

Goldstein, Rebecca 1950- .... **CLC 239**
See also CA 144; CANR 99, 165; TCLE 1:1

Goldstein, Rebecca Newberger
See Goldstein, Rebecca

Gombrowicz, Witold 1904-1969 .... **CLC 4, 7, 11, 49**
See also CA 19-20; 25-28R; CANR 105; CAP 2; CDWLB 4; DAM DRAM; DLB 215; EW 12; EWL 3; RGWL 2, 3; TWA

Gomez de Avellaneda, Gertrudis
1814-1873 .... **NCLC 111**
See also LAW

Gomez de la Serna, Ramon
1888-1963 .... **CLC 9**
See also CA 153; 116; CANR 79; EWL 3; HW 1, 2

Goncharov, Ivan Alexandrovich
1812-1891 .... **NCLC 1, 63**
See also DLB 238; EW 6; RGWL 2, 3

Goncourt, Edmond (Louis Antoine Huot) de
1822-1896 .... **NCLC 7**
See also DLB 123; EW 7; GFL 1789 to the Present; RGWL 2, 3

Goncourt, Jules (Alfred Huot) de
1830-1870 .... **NCLC 7**
See also DLB 123; EW 7; GFL 1789 to the Present; RGWL 2, 3

Gongora (y Argote), Luis de
1561-1627 .... **LC 72**
See also RGWL 2, 3

Gontier, Fernande 19(?)- .... **CLC 50**

Gonzalez Martinez, Enrique
See Gonzalez Martinez, Enrique

Gonzalez Martinez, Enrique
1871-1952 .... **TCLC 72**
See also CA 166; CANR 81; DLB 290; EWL 3; HW 1, 2

Goodison, Lorna 1947- .... **BLC 2:2; PC 36**
See also CA 142; CANR 88, 189; CP 5, 6, 7; CWP; DLB 157; EWL 3; PFS 25

Goodman, Allegra 1967- .... **CLC 241**
See also CA 204; CANR 162; DLB 244

Goodman, Paul 1911-1972 ..... **CLC 1, 2, 4, 7**
See also CA 19-20; 37-40R; CAD; CANR 34; CAP 2; CN 1; DLB 130, 246; MAL 5; MTCW 1; RGAL 4

Goodweather, Hartley
See King, Thomas

GoodWeather, Hartley
See King, Thomas

Googe, Barnabe 1540-1594 .... **LC 94**
See also DLB 132; RGEL 2

Gordimer, Nadine 1923- ...... **CLC 3, 5, 7, 10, 18, 33, 51, 70, 123, 160, 161, 263; SSC 17, 80; WLCS**
See also AAYA 39; AFW; BRWS 2; CA 5-8R; CANR 3, 28, 56, 88, 131; CN 1, 2, 3, 4, 5, 6, 7; DA; DA3; DAB; DAC; DAM MST, NOV; DLB 225, 326, 330; EWL 3; EXPS; INT CANR-28; LATS 1:2; MTCW 1, 2; MTFW 2005; NFS 4; RGEL 2; RGSF 2; SSFS 2, 14, 19; TWA; WLIT 2; YAW

Gordon, Adam Lindsay
1833-1870 .... **NCLC 21**
See also DLB 230

Gordon, Caroline 1895-1981 . **CLC 6, 13, 29, 83; SSC 15**
See also AMW; CA 11-12; 103; CANR 36; CAP 1; CN 1, 2; DLB 4, 9, 102; DLBD 17; DLBY 1981; EWL 3; MAL 5; MTCW 1, 2; MTFW 2005; RGAL 4; RGSF 2

Gordon, Charles William
1860-1937 .... **TCLC 31**
See also CA 109; DLB 92; TCWW 1, 2

Gordon, Mary 1949- .. **CLC 13, 22, 128, 216; SSC 59**
See also AMWS 4; BPFB 2; CA 102; CANR 44, 92, 154, 179; CN 4, 5, 6, 7; DLB 6; DLBY 1981; FW; INT CA-102; MAL 5; MTCW 1

Gordon, Mary Catherine
See Gordon, Mary

Gordon, N. J.
See Bosman, Herman Charles

Gordon, Sol 1923- .... **CLC 26**
See also CA 53-56; CANR 4; SATA 11

Gordone, Charles 1925-1995 .... **BLC 2:2; CLC 1, 4; DC 8**
See also BW 1, 3; CA 93-96, 180; 150; CAAE 180; CAD; CANR 55; DAM DRAM; DLB 7; INT CA-93-96; MTCW 1

Gore, Catherine 1800-1861 .... **NCLC 65**
See also DLB 116, 344; RGEL 2

Gorenko, Anna Andreevna
See Akhmatova, Anna

Gor'kii, Maksim
See Peshkov, Alexei Maximovich

Gorky, Maxim
See Peshkov, Alexei Maximovich

Goryan, Sirak
See Saroyan, William

Gosse, Edmund (William)
1849-1928 .... **TCLC 28**
See also CA 117; DLB 57, 144, 184; RGEL 2

Gotlieb, Phyllis (Fay Bloom) 1926- .. **CLC 18**
See also CA 13-16R; CANR 7, 135; CN 7; CP 1, 2, 3, 4; DLB 88, 251; SFW 4

Gottesman, S. D.
See Kornbluth, C(yril) M.; Pohl, Frederik

Gottfried von Strassburg fl. c.
1170-1215 .... **CMLC 10, 96**
See also CDWLB 2; DLB 138; EW 1; RGWL 2, 3

Gotthelf, Jeremias 1797-1854 .... **NCLC 117**
See also DLB 133; RGWL 2, 3

Gottschalk, Laura Riding
See Jackson, Laura (Riding)

Gould, Lois 1932(?)-2002 .... **CLC 4, 10**
See also CA 77-80; 208; CANR 29; MTCW 1

Gould, Stephen Jay 1941-2002 .... **CLC 163**
See also AAYA 26; BEST 90:2; CA 77-80; 205; CANR 10, 27, 56, 75, 125; CPW; INT CANR-27; MTCW 1, 2; MTFW 2005

Gourmont, Remy(-Marie-Charles) de
1858-1915 .... **TCLC 17**
See also CA 109; 150; GFL 1789 to the Present; MTCW 2

Gournay, Marie le Jars de
See de Gournay, Marie le Jars

Govier, Katherine 1948- .... **CLC 51**
See also CA 101; CANR 18, 40, 128; CCA 1

Gower, John c. 1330-1408 .... **LC 76; PC 59**
See also BRW 1; DLB 146; RGEL 2

Goyen, (Charles) William
1915-1983 .... **CLC 5, 8, 14, 40**
See also AITN 2; CA 5-8R; 110; CANR 6, 71; CN 1, 2, 3; DLB 2, 218; DLBY 1983; EWL 3; INT CANR-6; MAL 5

Goytisolo, Juan 1931- .... **CLC 5, 10, 23, 133; HLC 1**
See also CA 85-88; CANR 32, 61, 131, 182; CWW 2; DAM MULT; DLB 322; EWL 3; GLL 2; HW 1, 2; MTCW 1, 2; MTFW 2005

Gozzano, Guido 1883-1916 .... **PC 10**
See also CA 154; DLB 114; EWL 3

Gozzi, (Conte) Carlo 1720-1806 .... **NCLC 23**

Grabbe, Christian Dietrich
1801-1836 .... **NCLC 2**
See also DLB 133; RGWL 2, 3

Grace, Patricia Frances 1937- .... **CLC 56**
See also CA 176; CANR 118; CN 4, 5, 6, 7; EWL 3; RGSF 2

Gracian, Baltasar 1601-1658 .... **LC 15, 160**

Gracian y Morales, Baltasar
See Gracian, Baltasar

Gracq, Julien 1910-2007 ..... **CLC 11, 48, 259**
See also CA 122; 126; 267; CANR 141; CWW 2; DLB 83; GFL 1789 to the present

Grade, Chaim 1910-1982 .... **CLC 10**
See also CA 93-96; 107; DLB 333; EWL 3; RGHL

Grade, Khayim
See Grade, Chaim

Graduate of Oxford, A
See Ruskin, John

Grafton, Garth
See Duncan, Sara Jeannette

Grafton, Sue 1940- .... **CLC 163**
See also AAYA 11, 49; BEST 90:3; CA 108; CANR 31, 55, 111, 134; CMW 4; CPW; CSW; DA3; DAM POP; DLB 226; FW; MSW; MTFW 2005

Graham, John
See Phillips, David Graham

Graham, Jorie 1950- .... **CLC 48, 118; PC 59**
See also AAYA 67; CA 111; CANR 63, 118; CP 4, 5, 6, 7; CWP; DLB 120; EWL 3; MTFW 2005; PFS 10, 17; TCLE 1:1

Graham, R(obert) B(ontine) Cunninghame
See Cunninghame Graham, Robert (Gallnigad) Bontine

Graham, Robert
See Haldeman, Joe

Graham, Tom
See Lewis, (Harry) Sinclair

Graham, W(illiam) S(ydney)
1918-1986 .... **CLC 29**
See also BRWS 7; CA 73-76; 118; CP 1, 2, 3, 4; DLB 20; RGEL 2

Graham, Winston (Mawdsley)
1910-2003 .... **CLC 23**
See also CA 49-52; 218; CANR 2, 22, 45, 66; CMW 4; CN 1, 2, 3, 4, 5, 6, 7; DLB 77; RHW

Grahame, Kenneth 1859-1932 ...... **TCLC 64, 136**
See also BYA 5; CA 108; 136; CANR 80; CLR 5, 135; CWRI 5; DA3; DAB; DLB 34, 141, 178; FANT; MAICYA 1, 2; MTCW 2; NFS 20; RGEL 2; SATA 100; TEA; WCH; YABC 1

Granger, Darius John
See Marlowe, Stephen

Grile, Dod
　　See Bierce, Ambrose (Gwinett)
Grillparzer, Franz 1791-1872 .... **DC 14;**
　　NCLC 1, 102; SSC 37
　　　See also CDWLB 2; DLB 133; EW 5;
　　　RGWL 2, 3; TWA
Grimble, Reverend Charles James
　　See Eliot, T(homas) S(tearns)
Grimke, Angelina (Emily) Weld
　　1880-1958 .... **HR 1:2**
　　　See also BW 1; CA 124; DAM POET; DLB
　　　50, 54; FW
Grimke, Charlotte L(ottie) Forten
　　1837(?)-1914 .... **BLC 1:2; TCLC 16**
　　　See also BW 1; CA 117; 124; DAM MULT,
　　　POET; DLB 50, 239
Grimm, Jacob Ludwig Karl
　　1785-1863 .... **NCLC 3, 77; SSC 36, 88**
　　　See also CLR 112; DLB 90; MAICYA 1, 2;
　　　RGSF 2; RGWL 2, 3; SATA 22; WCH
Grimm, Wilhelm Karl 1786-1859 .. **NCLC 3,**
　　77; SSC 36
　　　See also CDWLB 2; CLR 112; DLB 90;
　　　MAICYA 1, 2; RGSF 2; RGWL 2, 3;
　　　SATA 22; WCH
Grimm and Grim
　　See Grimm, Jacob Ludwig Karl; Grimm,
　　Wilhelm Karl
Grimm Brothers
　　See Grimm, Jacob Ludwig Karl; Grimm,
　　Wilhelm Karl
Grimmelshausen, Hans Jakob Christoffel
　　von
　　See Grimmelshausen, Johann Jakob Christ-
　　offel von
Grimmelshausen, Johann Jakob Christoffel
　　von 1621-1676 .... **LC 6**
　　　See also CDWLB 2; DLB 168; RGWL 2, 3
Grindel, Eugene 1895-1952 .... **PC 38; TCLC**
　　7, 41
　　　See also CA 104; 193; EWL 3; GFL 1789
　　　to the Present; LMFS 2; RGWL 2, 3
Grisham, John 1955- .... **CLC 84, 273**
　　　See also AAYA 14, 47; BPFB 2; CA 138;
　　　CANR 47, 69, 114, 133; CMW 4; CN 6,
　　　7; CPW; CSW; DA3; DAM POP; MSW;
　　　MTCW 2; MTFW 2005
Grosseteste, Robert 1175(?)-1253 . **CMLC 62**
　　　See also DLB 115
Grossman, David 1954- .... **CLC 67, 231**
　　　See also CA 138; CANR 114, 175; CWW
　　　2; DLB 299; EWL 3; RGHL; WLIT 6
Grossman, Vasilii Semenovich
　　See Grossman, Vasily (Semenovich)
Grossman, Vasily (Semenovich)
　　1905-1964 .... **CLC 41**
　　　See also CA 124; 130; DLB 272; MTCW 1;
　　　RGHL
Grove, Frederick Philip
　　See Greve, Felix Paul (Berthold Friedrich)
Grubb
　　See Crumb, R.
Grumbach, Doris 1918- .... **CLC 13, 22, 64**
　　　See also CA 5-8R; CAAS 2; CANR 9, 42,
　　　70, 127; CN 6, 7; INT CANR-9; MTCW
　　　2; MTFW 2005
Grundtvig, Nikolai Frederik Severin
　　1783-1872 .... **NCLC 1, 158**
　　　See also DLB 300
Grunge
　　See Crumb, R.
Grunwald, Lisa 1959- .... **CLC 44**
　　　See also CA 120; CANR 148
Gryphius, Andreas 1616-1664 .... **LC 89**
　　　See also CDWLB 2; DLB 164; RGWL 2, 3

Guare, John 1938- .... **CLC 8, 14, 29, 67; DC**
　　20
　　　See also CA 73-76; CAD; CANR 21, 69,
　　　118; CD 5, 6; DAM DRAM; DFS 8, 13;
　　　DLB 7, 249; EWL 3; MAL 5; MTCW 1,
　　　2; RGAL 4
Guarini, Battista 1538-1612 .... **LC 102**
　　　See also DLB 339
Gubar, Susan 1944- .... **CLC 145**
　　　See also CA 108; CANR 45, 70, 139, 179;
　　　FW; MTCW 1; RGAL 4
Gubar, Susan David
　　See Gubar, Susan
Gudjonsson, Halldor Kiljan
　　1902-1998 .... **CLC 25**
　　　See also CA 103; 164; CWW 2; DLB 293,
　　　331; EW 12; EWL 3; RGWL 2, 3
Guedes, Vincente
　　See Pessoa, Fernando
Guenter, Erich
　　See Eich, Gunter
Guest, Barbara 1920-2006 ... **CLC 34; PC 55**
　　　See also BG 1:2; CA 25-28R; 248; CANR
　　　11, 44, 84; CP 1, 2, 3, 4, 5, 6, 7; CWP;
　　　DLB 5, 193
Guest, Edgar A(lbert) 1881-1959 ... **TCLC 95**
　　　See also CA 112; 168
Guest, Judith 1936- .... **CLC 8, 30**
　　　See also AAYA 7, 66; CA 77-80; CANR
　　　15, 75, 138; DA3; DAM NOV, POP;
　　　EXPN; INT CANR-15; LAIT 5; MTCW
　　　1, 2; MTFW 2005; NFS 1
Guevara, Che
　　See Guevara (Serna), Ernesto
Guevara (Serna), Ernesto
　　1928-1967 .... **CLC 87; HLC 1**
　　　See also CA 127; 111; CANR 56; DAM
　　　MULT; HW 1
Guicciardini, Francesco 1483-1540 ..... **LC 49**
Guido delle Colonne c. 1215-c.
　　1290 .... **CMLC 90**
Guild, Nicholas M. 1944- .... **CLC 33**
　　　See also CA 93-96
Guillemin, Jacques
　　See Sartre, Jean-Paul
Guillen, Jorge 1893-1984 . **CLC 11; HLCS 1;**
　　PC 35
　　　See also CA 89-92; 112; DAM MULT,
　　　POET; DLB 108; EWL 3; HW 1; RGWL
　　　2, 3
Guillen, Nicolas (Cristobal)
　　1902-1989 .... **BLC 1:2; CLC 48, 79;**
　　HLC 1; PC 23
　　　See also BW 2; CA 116; 125; 129; CANR
　　　84; DAM MST, MULT, POET; DLB 283;
　　　EWL 3; HW 1; LAW; RGWL 2, 3; WP
Guillen y Alvarez, Jorge
　　See Guillen, Jorge
Guillevic, (Eugene) 1907-1997 .... **CLC 33**
　　　See also CA 93-96; CWW 2
Guillois
　　See Desnos, Robert
Guillois, Valentin
　　See Desnos, Robert
Guimaraes Rosa, Joao 1908-1967 ... **CLC 23;**
　　HLCS 1
　　　See also CA 175; 89-92; DLB 113, 307;
　　　EWL 3; LAW; RGSF 2; RGWL 2, 3;
　　　WLIT 1
Guiney, Louise Imogen
　　1861-1920 .... **TCLC 41**
　　　See also CA 160; DLB 54; RGAL 4
Guinizelli, Guido c. 1230-1276 ...... **CMLC 49**
　　　See also WLIT 7
Guinizzelli, Guido
　　See Guinizelli, Guido

Guiraldes, Ricardo (Guillermo)
　　1886-1927 .... **TCLC 39**
　　　See also CA 131; EWL 3; HW 1; LAW;
　　　MTCW 1
Gumilev, Nikolai (Stepanovich)
　　1886-1921 .... **TCLC 60**
　　　See also CA 165; DLB 295; EWL 3
Gumilyov, Nikolay Stepanovich
　　See Gumilev, Nikolai (Stepanovich)
Gump, P. Q.
　　See Card, Orson Scott
Gump, P.Q.
　　See Card, Orson Scott
Gunesekera, Romesh 1954- .... **CLC 91**
　　　See also BRWS 10; CA 159; CANR 140,
　　　172; CN 6, 7; DLB 267, 323
Gunn, Bill
　　See Gunn, William Harrison
Gunn, Thom(son William)
　　1929-2004 . **CLC 3, 6, 18, 32, 81; PC 26**
　　　See also BRWS 4; CA 17-20R; 227; CANR
　　　9, 33, 116; CDBLB 1960 to Present; CP
　　　1, 2, 3, 4, 5, 6, 7; DAM POET; DLB 27;
　　　INT CANR-33; MTCW 1; PFS 9; RGEL
　　　2
Gunn, William Harrison
　　1934(?)-1989 .... **CLC 5**
　　　See also AITN 1; BW 1, 3; CA 13-16R;
　　　128; CANR 12, 25, 76; DLB 38
Gunn Allen, Paula
　　See Allen, Paula Gunn
Gunnars, Kristjana 1948- .... **CLC 69**
　　　See also CA 113; CCA 1; CP 6, 7; CWP;
　　　DLB 60
Gunter, Erich
　　See Eich, Gunter
Gurdjieff, G(eorgei) I(vanovich)
　　1877(?)-1949 .... **TCLC 71**
　　　See also CA 157
Gurganus, Allan 1947- .... **CLC 70**
　　　See also BEST 90:1; CA 135; CANR 114;
　　　CN 6, 7; CPW; CSW; DAM POP; GLL 1
Gurney, A. R.
　　See Gurney, A(lbert) R(amsdell), Jr.
Gurney, A(lbert) R(amsdell), Jr.
　　1930- .... **CLC 32, 50, 54**
　　　See also AMWS 5; CA 77-80; CAD; CANR
　　　32, 64, 121; CD 5, 6; DAM DRAM; DLB
　　　266; EWL 3
Gurney, Ivor (Bertie) 1890-1937 ... **TCLC 33**
　　　See also BRW 6; CA 167; DLBY 2002;
　　　PAB; RGEL 2
Gurney, Peter
　　See Gurney, A(lbert) R(amsdell), Jr.
Guro, Elena (Genrikhovna)
　　1877-1913 .... **TCLC 56**
　　　See also DLB 295
Gustafson, James M(oody) 1925- ... **CLC 100**
　　　See also CA 25-28R; CANR 37
Gustafson, Ralph (Barker)
　　1909-1995 .... **CLC 36**
　　　See also CA 21-24R; CANR 8, 45, 84; CP
　　　1, 2, 3, 4, 5, 6; DLB 88; RGEL 2
Gut, Gom
　　See Simenon, Georges (Jacques Christian)
Guterson, David 1956- .... **CLC 91**
　　　See also CA 132; CANR 73, 126; CN 7;
　　　DLB 292; MTCW 2; MTFW 2005; NFS
　　　13
Guthrie, A(lfred) B(ertram), Jr.
　　1901-1991 .... **CLC 23**
　　　See also CA 57-60; 134; CANR 24; CN 1,
　　　2, 3; DLB 6, 212; MAL 5; SATA 62;
　　　SATA-Obit 67; TCWW 1, 2
Guthrie, Isobel
　　See Grieve, C(hristopher) M(urray)
Gutierrez Najera, Manuel
　　1859-1895 .... **HLCS 2; NCLC 133**
　　　See also DLB 290; LAW

Hannah, Barry 1942- .. **CLC 23, 38, 90, 270; SSC 94**
See also BPFB 2; CA 108; 110; CANR 43, 68, 113; CN 4, 5, 6, 7; CSW; DLB 6, 234; INT CA-110; MTCW 1; RGSF 2

Hannon, Ezra
See Hunter, Evan

Hanrahan, Barbara 1939-1991 .... **TCLC 219**
See also CA 121; 127; CN 4, 5; DLB 289

Hansberry, Lorraine (Vivian)
1930-1965 ... **BLC 1:2, 2:2; CLC 17, 62; DC 2; TCLC 192**
See also AAYA 25; AFAW 1, 2; AMWS 4; BW 1, 3; CA 109; 25-28R; CABS 3; CAD; CANR 58; CDALB 1941-1968; CWD; DA; DA3; DAB; DAC; DAM DRAM, MST, MULT; DFS 2; DLB 7, 38; EWL 3; FL 1:6; FW; LAIT 4; MAL 5; MTCW 1, 2; MTFW 2005; RGAL 4; TUS

Hansen, Joseph 1923-2004 .... **CLC 38**
See also BPFB 2; CA 29-32R; 233; CAAS 17; CANR 16, 44, 66, 125; CMW 4; DLB 226; GLL 1; INT CANR-16

Hansen, Karen V. 1955- .... **CLC 65**
See also CA 149; CANR 102

Hansen, Martin A(lfred)
1909-1955 .... **TCLC 32**
See also CA 167; DLB 214; EWL 3

Hanson, Kenneth O(stlin) 1922- .... **CLC 13**
See also CA 53-56; CANR 7; CP 1, 2, 3, 4, 5

Hardwick, Elizabeth 1916-2007 .... **CLC 13**
See also AMWS 3; CA 5-8R; 267; CANR 3, 32, 70, 100, 139; CN 4, 5, 6; CSW; DA3; DAM NOV; DLB 6; MBL; MTCW 1, 2; MTFW 2005; TCLE 1:1

Hardwick, Elizabeth Bruce
See Hardwick, Elizabeth

Hardwick, Elizabeth Bruce
See Hardwick, Elizabeth

Hardy, Thomas 1840-1928 . **PC 8, 92; SSC 2, 60, 113; TCLC 4, 10, 18, 32, 48, 53, 72, 143, 153; WLC 3**
See also AAYA 69; BRW 6; BRWC 1, 2; BRWR 1; CA 104; 123; CDBLB 1890-1914; DA; DA3; DAB; DAC; DAM MST, NOV, POET; DLB 18, 19, 135, 284; EWL 3; EXPN; EXPP; LAIT 2; MTCW 1, 2; MTFW 2005; NFS 3, 11, 15, 19; PFS 3, 4, 18; RGEL 2; RGSF 2; TEA; WLIT 4

Hare, David 1947- . **CLC 29, 58, 136; DC 26**
See also BRWS 4; CA 97-100; CANR 39, 91; CBD; CD 5, 6; DFS 4, 7, 16; DLB 13, 310; MTCW 1; TEA

Harewood, John
See Van Druten, John (William)

Harford, Henry
See Hudson, W(illiam) H(enry)

Hargrave, Leonie
See Disch, Thomas M.

Hariri, Al- al-Qasim ibn 'Ali Abu Muhammad al-Basri
See al-Hariri, al-Qasim ibn 'Ali Abu Muhammad al-Basri

Harjo, Joy 1951- ..... **CLC 83; NNAL; PC 27**
See also AMWS 12; CA 114; CANR 35, 67, 91, 129; CP 6, 7; CWP; DAM MULT; DLB 120, 175, 342; EWL 3; MTCW 2; MTFW 2005; PFS 15; RGAL 4

Harlan, Louis R(udolph) 1922- .... **CLC 34**
See also CA 21-24R; CANR 25, 55, 80

Harling, Robert 1951(?)- .... **CLC 53**
See also CA 147

Harmon, William (Ruth) 1938- .... **CLC 38**
See also CA 33-36R; CANR 14, 32, 35; SATA 65

Harper, F. E. W.
See Harper, Frances Ellen Watkins

Harper, Frances E. W.
See Harper, Frances Ellen Watkins

Harper, Frances E. Watkins
See Harper, Frances Ellen Watkins

Harper, Frances Ellen
See Harper, Frances Ellen Watkins

Harper, Frances Ellen Watkins
1825-1911 . **BLC 1:2; PC 21; TCLC 14, 217**
See also AFAW 1, 2; BW 1, 3; CA 111; 125; CANR 79; DAM MULT, POET; DLB 50, 221; MBL; RGAL 4

Harper, Michael S(teven) 1938- ..... **BLC 2:2; CLC 7, 22**
See also AFAW 2; BW 1; CA 33-36R; 224; CAAE 224; CANR 24, 108; CP 2, 3, 4, 5, 6, 7; DLB 41; RGAL 4; TCLE 1:1

Harper, Mrs. F. E. W.
See Harper, Frances Ellen Watkins

Harpur, Charles 1813-1868 .... **NCLC 114**
See also DLB 230; RGEL 2

Harris, Christie
See Harris, Christie (Lucy) Irwin

Harris, Christie (Lucy) Irwin
1907-2002 .... **CLC 12**
See also CA 5-8R; CANR 6, 83; CLR 47; DLB 88; JRDA; MAICYA 1, 2; SAAS 10; SATA 6, 74; SATA-Essay 116

Harris, Frank 1856-1931 .... **TCLC 24**
See also CA 109; 150; CANR 80; DLB 156, 197; RGEL 2

Harris, George Washington
1814-1869 .... **NCLC 23, 165**
See also DLB 3, 11, 248; RGAL 4

Harris, Joel Chandler 1848-1908 ..... **SSC 19, 103; TCLC 2**
See also CA 104; 137; CANR 80; CLR 49, 128; DLB 11, 23, 42, 78, 91; LAIT 2; MAICYA 1, 2; RGSF 2; SATA 100; WCH; YABC 1

Harris, John (Wyndham Parkes Lucas)
Beynon 1903-1969 .... **CLC 19**
See also BRWS 13; CA 102; 89-92; CANR 84; DLB 255; SATA 118; SCFW 1, 2; SFW 4

Harris, MacDonald
See Heiney, Donald (William)

Harris, Mark 1922-2007 .... **CLC 19**
See also CA 5-8R; 260; CAAS 3; CANR 2, 55, 83; CN 1, 2, 3, 4, 5, 6, 7; DLB 2; DLBY 1980

Harris, Norman .... **CLC 65**

Harris, (Theodore) Wilson 1921- ... **BLC 2:2; CLC 25, 159**
See also BRWS 5; BW 2, 3; CA 65-68; CAAS 16; CANR 11, 27, 69, 114; CDWLB 3; CN 1, 2, 3, 4, 5, 6, 7; CP 1, 2, 3, 4, 5, 6, 7; DLB 117; EWL 3; MTCW 1; RGEL 2

Harrison, Barbara Grizzuti
1934-2002 .... **CLC 144**
See also CA 77-80; 205; CANR 15, 48; INT CANR-15

Harrison, Elizabeth (Allen) Cavanna
1909-2001 .... **CLC 12**
See also CA 9-12R; 200; CANR 6, 27, 85, 104, 121; JRDA; MAICYA 1; SAAS 4; SATA 1, 30; YAW

Harrison, Harry 1925- .... **CLC 42**
See also CA 1-4R; CANR 5, 21, 84; DLB 8; SATA 4; SCFW 2; SFW 4

Harrison, Harry Max
See Harrison, Harry

Harrison, James
See Harrison, Jim

Harrison, James Thomas
See Harrison, Jim

Harrison, Jim 1937- .... **CLC 6, 14, 33, 66, 143; SSC 19**
See also AMWS 8; CA 13-16R; CANR 8, 51, 79, 142; CN 5, 6; CP 1, 2, 3, 4, 5, 6; DLBY 1982; INT CANR-8; RGAL 4; TCWW 2; TUS

Harrison, Kathryn 1961- .... **CLC 70, 151**
See also CA 144; CANR 68, 122

Harrison, Tony 1937- .... **CLC 43, 129**
See also BRWS 5; CA 65-68; CANR 44, 98; CBD; CD 5, 6; CP 2, 3, 4, 5, 6, 7; DLB 40, 245; MTCW 1; RGEL 2

Harriss, Will(ard Irvin) 1922- .... **CLC 34**
See also CA 111

Hart, Ellis
See Ellison, Harlan

Hart, Josephine 1942(?)- .... **CLC 70**
See also CA 138; CANR 70, 149; CPW; DAM POP

Hart, Moss 1904-1961 .... **CLC 66**
See also CA 109; 89-92; CANR 84; DAM DRAM; DFS 1; DLB 7, 266; RGAL 4

Harte, (Francis) Bret(t)
1836(?)-1902 ... **SSC 8, 59; TCLC 1, 25; WLC 3**
See also AMWS 2; CA 104; 140; CANR 80; CDALB 1865-1917; DA; DA3; DAC; DAM MST; DLB 12, 64, 74, 79, 186; EXPS; LAIT 2; RGAL 4; RGSF 2; SATA 26; SSFS 3; TUS

Hartley, L(eslie) P(oles) 1895-1972 ... **CLC 2, 22**
See also BRWS 7; CA 45-48; 37-40R; CANR 33; CN 1; DLB 15, 139; EWL 3; HGG; MTCW 1, 2; MTFW 2005; RGEL 2; RGSF 2; SUFW 1

Hartman, Geoffrey H. 1929- .... **CLC 27**
See also CA 117; 125; CANR 79; DLB 67

Hartmann, Sadakichi 1869-1944 ... **TCLC 73**
See also CA 157; DLB 54

Hartmann von Aue c. 1170-c.
1210 .... **CMLC 15**
See also CDWLB 2; DLB 138; RGWL 2, 3

Hartog, Jan de
See de Hartog, Jan

Haruf, Kent 1943- .... **CLC 34**
See also AAYA 44; CA 149; CANR 91, 131

Harvey, Caroline
See Trollope, Joanna

Harvey, Gabriel 1550(?)-1631 .... **LC 88**
See also DLB 167, 213, 281

Harvey, Jack
See Rankin, Ian

Harwood, Ronald 1934- .... **CLC 32**
See also CA 1-4R; CANR 4, 55, 150; CBD; CD 5, 6; DAM DRAM, MST; DLB 13

Hasegawa Tatsunosuke
See Futabatei, Shimei

Hasek, Jaroslav (Matej Frantisek)
1883-1923 .... **SSC 69; TCLC 4**
See also CA 104; 129; CDWLB 4; DLB 215; EW 9; EWL 3; MTCW 1, 2; RGSF 2; RGWL 2, 3

Hass, Robert 1941- ... **CLC 18, 39, 99; PC 16**
See also AMWS 6; CA 111; CANR 30, 50, 71, 187; CP 3, 4, 5, 6, 7; DLB 105, 206; EWL 3; MAL 5; MTFW 2005; RGAL 4; SATA 94; TCLE 1:1

Hassler, Jon 1933-2008 .... **CLC 263**
See also CA 73-76; 270; CANR 21, 80, 161; CN 6, 7; INT CANR-21; SATA 19; SATA-Obit 191

Hassler, Jon Francis
See Hassler, Jon

Hastings, Hudson
See Kuttner, Henry

Hastings, Selina .... **CLC 44**
See also CA 257

POP; DLB 335; DLBY 1985; FANT; MAL 5; MTCW 1, 2; MTFW 2005; SSFS 25; SUFW 2

Helvetius, Claude-Adrien 1715-1771 .. **LC 26**
See also DLB 313

Helyar, Jane Penelope Josephine
1933- .... **CLC 17**
See also CA 21-24R; CANR 10, 26; CWRI 5; SAAS 2; SATA 5; SATA-Essay 138

Hemans, Felicia 1793-1835 ...... **NCLC 29, 71**
See also DLB 96; RGEL 2

Hemingway, Ernest (Miller)
1899-1961 .... **CLC 1, 3, 6, 8, 10, 13, 19, 30, 34, 39, 41, 44, 50, 61, 80; SSC 1, 25, 36, 40, 63, 117; TCLC 115, 203; WLC 3**
See also AAYA 19; AMW; AMWC 1; AMWR 1; BPFB 2; BYA 2, 3, 13, 15; CA 77-80; CANR 34; CDALB 1917-1929; DA; DA3; DAB; DAC; DAM MST, NOV; DLB 4, 9, 102, 210, 308, 316, 330; DLBD 1, 15, 16; DLBY 1981, 1987, 1996, 1998; EWL 3; EXPN; EXPS; LAIT 3, 4; LATS 1:1; MAL 5; MTCW 1, 2; MTFW 2005; NFS 1, 5, 6, 14; RGAL 4; RGSF 2; SSFS 17; TUS; WYA

Hempel, Amy 1951- .... **CLC 39**
See also CA 118; 137; CANR 70, 166; DA3; DLB 218; EXPS; MTCW 2; MTFW 2005; SSFS 2

Henderson, F. C.
See Mencken, H(enry) L(ouis)

Henderson, Mary
See Mavor, Osborne Henry

Henderson, Sylvia
See Ashton-Warner, Sylvia (Constance)

Henderson, Zenna (Chlarson)
1917-1983 .... **SSC 29**
See also CA 1-4R; 133; CANR 1, 84; DLB 8; SATA 5; SFW 4

Henkin, Joshua 1964- .... **CLC 119**
See also CA 161; CANR 186

Henley, Beth .... **CLC 23, 255; DC 6, 14**
See Henley, Elizabeth Becker
See also CABS 3; CAD; CD 5, 6; CSW; CWD; DFS 2, 21, 26; DLBY 1986; FW

Henley, Elizabeth Becker 1952- ...... **CLC 23, 255; DC 6, 14**
See Henley, Beth
See also AAYA 70; CA 107; CABS 3; CAD; CANR 32, 73, 140; CD 5, 6; CSW; DA3; DAM DRAM, MST; DFS 2, 21; DLBY 1986; FW; MTCW 1, 2; MTFW 2005

Henley, William Ernest 1849-1903 .. **TCLC 8**
See also CA 105; 234; DLB 19; RGEL 2

Hennissart, Martha 1929- .... **CLC 2**
See also BPFB 2; CA 85-88; CANR 64; CMW 4; DLB 306

Henry VIII 1491-1547 .... **LC 10**
See also DLB 132

Henry, O. 1862-1910 . **SSC 5, 49, 117; TCLC 1, 19; WLC 3**
See also AAYA 41; AMWS 2; CA 104; 131; CDALB 1865-1917; DA; DA3; DAB; DAC; DAM MST; DLB 12, 78, 79; EXPS; MAL 5; MTCW 1, 2; MTFW 2005; RGAL 4; RGSF 2; SSFS 2, 18, 27; TCWW 1, 2; TUS; YABC 2

Henry, Oliver
See Henry, O.

Henry, Patrick 1736-1799 .... **LC 25**
See also LAIT 1

Henryson, Robert 1430(?)-1506(?) ..... **LC 20, 110; PC 65**
See also BRWS 7; DLB 146; RGEL 2

Henschke, Alfred
See Klabund

Henson, Lance 1944- .... **NNAL**
See also CA 146; DLB 175

Hentoff, Nat(han Irving) 1925- .... **CLC 26**
See also AAYA 4, 42; BYA 6; CA 1-4R; CAAS 6; CANR 5, 25, 77, 114; CLR 1, 52; DLB 345; INT CANR-25; JRDA; MAICYA 1, 2; SATA 42, 69, 133; SATA-Brief 27; WYA; YAW

Heppenstall, (John) Rayner
1911-1981 .... **CLC 10**
See also CA 1-4R; 103; CANR 29; CN 1, 2; CP 1, 2, 3; EWL 3

Heraclitus c. 540B.C.-c. 450B.C. ... **CMLC 22**
See also DLB 176

Herbert, Frank 1920-1986 ... **CLC 12, 23, 35, 44, 85**
See also AAYA 21; BPFB 2; BYA 4, 14; CA 53-56; 118; CANR 5, 43; CDALBS; CPW; DAM POP; DLB 8; INT CANR-5; LAIT 5; MTCW 1, 2; MTFW 2005; NFS 17; SATA 9, 37; SATA-Obit 47; SCFW 1, 2; SFW 4; YAW

Herbert, George 1593-1633 . **LC 24, 121; PC 4**
See also BRW 2; BRWR 2; CDBLB Before 1660; DAB; DAM MST, POET; DLB 126; EXPP; PFS 25; RGEL 2; TEA; WP

Herbert, Zbigniew 1924-1998 ..... **CLC 9, 43; PC 50; TCLC 168**
See also CA 89-92; 169; CANR 36, 74, 177; CDWLB 4; CWW 2; DAM POET; DLB 232; EWL 3; MTCW 1; PFS 22

Herbst, Josephine (Frey)
1897-1969 .... **CLC 34**
See also CA 5-8R; 25-28R; DLB 9

Herder, Johann Gottfried von
1744-1803 .... **NCLC 8, 186**
See also DLB 97; EW 4; TWA

Heredia, Jose Maria 1803-1839 ...... **HLCS 2; NCLC 209**
See also LAW

Hergesheimer, Joseph 1880-1954 ... **TCLC 11**
See also CA 109; 194; DLB 102, 9; RGAL 4

Herlihy, James Leo 1927-1993 .... **CLC 6**
See also CA 1-4R; 143; CAD; CANR 2; CN 1, 2, 3, 4, 5

Herman, William
See Bierce, Ambrose (Gwinett)

Hermogenes fl. c. 175- .... **CMLC 6**

Hernandez, Jose 1834-1886 .... **NCLC 17**
See also LAW; RGWL 2, 3; WLIT 1

Herodotus c. 484B.C.-c. 420B.C. .. **CMLC 17**
See also AW 1; CDWLB 1; DLB 176; RGWL 2, 3; TWA; WLIT 8

Herr, Michael 1940(?)- .... **CLC 231**
See also CA 89-92; CANR 68, 142; DLB 185; MTCW 1

Herrick, Robert 1591-1674 .. **LC 13, 145; PC 9**
See also BRW 2; BRWC 2; DA; DAB; DAC; DAM MST, POP; DLB 126; EXPP; PFS 13, 29; RGAL 4; RGEL 2; TEA; WP

Herring, Guilles
See Somerville, Edith Oenone

Herriot, James 1916-1995
See Wight, James Alfred

Herris, Violet
See Hunt, Violet

Herrmann, Dorothy 1941- .... **CLC 44**
See also CA 107

Herrmann, Taffy
See Herrmann, Dorothy

Hersey, John 1914-1993 .. **CLC 1, 2, 7, 9, 40, 81, 97**
See also AAYA 29; BPFB 2; CA 17-20R; 140; CANR 33; CDALBS; CN 1, 2, 3, 4, 5; CPW; DAM POP; DLB 6, 185, 278, 299; MAL 5; MTCW 1, 2; MTFW 2005; RGHL; SATA 25; SATA-Obit 76; TUS

Hervent, Maurice
See Grindel, Eugene

Herzen, Aleksandr Ivanovich
1812-1870 .... **NCLC 10, 61**
See also DLB 277

Herzen, Alexander
See Herzen, Aleksandr Ivanovich

Herzl, Theodor 1860-1904 .... **TCLC 36**
See also CA 168

Herzog, Werner 1942- .... **CLC 16, 236**
See also CA 89-92

Hesiod fl. 8th cent. B.C.- .... **CMLC 5, 102**
See also AW 1; DLB 176; RGWL 2, 3; WLIT 8

Hesse, Hermann 1877-1962 ... **CLC 1, 2, 3, 6, 11, 17, 25, 69; SSC 9, 49; TCLC 148, 196; WLC 3**
See also AAYA 43; BPFB 2; CA 17-18; CAP 2; CDWLB 2; DA; DA3; DAB; DAC; DAM MST, NOV; DLB 66, 330; EW 9; EWL 3; EXPN; LAIT 1; MTCW 1, 2; MTFW 2005; NFS 6, 15, 24; RGWL 2, 3; SATA 50; TWA

Hewes, Cady
See De Voto, Bernard (Augustine)

Heyen, William 1940- .... **CLC 13, 18**
See also CA 33-36R; 220; CAAE 220; CAAS 9; CANR 98, 188; CP 3, 4, 5, 6, 7; DLB 5; RGHL

Heyerdahl, Thor 1914-2002 .... **CLC 26**
See also CA 5-8R; 207; CANR 5, 22, 66, 73; LAIT 4; MTCW 1, 2; MTFW 2005; SATA 2, 52

Heym, Georg (Theodor Franz Arthur)
1887-1912 .... **TCLC 9**
See also CA 106; 181

Heym, Stefan 1913-2001 .... **CLC 41**
See also CA 9-12R; 203; CANR 4; CWW 2; DLB 69; EWL 3

Heyse, Paul (Johann Ludwig von)
1830-1914 .... **TCLC 8**
See also CA 104; 209; DLB 129, 330

Heyward, (Edwin) DuBose
1885-1940 .... **HR 1:2; TCLC 59**
See also CA 108; 157; DLB 7, 9, 45, 249; MAL 5; SATA 21

Heywood, John 1497(?)-1580(?) .... **LC 65**
See also DLB 136; RGEL 2

Heywood, Thomas 1573(?)-1641 . **DC 29; LC 111**
See also DAM DRAM; DLB 62; LMFS 1; RGEL 2; TEA

Hiaasen, Carl 1953- .... **CLC 238**
See also CA 105; CANR 22, 45, 65, 113, 133, 168; CMW 4; CPW; CSW; DA3; DLB 292; MTCW 2; MTFW 2005

Hibbert, Eleanor Alice Burford
1906-1993 .... **CLC 7**
See also BEST 90:4; BPFB 2; CA 17-20R; 140; CANR 9, 28, 59; CMW 4; CPW; DAM POP; MTCW 2; MTFW 2005; RHW; SATA 2; SATA-Obit 74

Hichens, Robert (Smythe)
1864-1950 .... **TCLC 64**
See also CA 162; DLB 153; HGG; RHW; SUFW

Higgins, Aidan 1927- .... **SSC 68**
See also CA 9-12R; CANR 70, 115, 148; CN 1, 2, 3, 4, 5, 6, 7; DLB 14

Higgins, George V(incent)
1939-1999 .... **CLC 4, 7, 10, 18**
See also BPFB 2; CA 77-80; 186; CAAS 5; CANR 17, 51, 89, 96; CMW 4; CN 2, 3, 4, 5, 6; DLB 2; DLBY 1981, 1998; INT CANR-17; MSW; MTCW 1

Higginson, Thomas Wentworth
1823-1911 .... **TCLC 36**
See also CA 162; DLB 1, 64, 243

Hogg, James 1770-1835 .... **NCLC 4, 109**
See also BRWS 10; DLB 93, 116, 159; GL
2; HGG; RGEL 2; SUFW 1

Holbach, Paul-Henri Thiry
1723-1789 .... **LC 14**
See also DLB 313

Holberg, Ludvig 1684-1754 .... **LC 6**
See also DLB 300; RGWL 2, 3

Holbrook, John
See Vance, Jack

Holcroft, Thomas 1745-1809 .... **NCLC 85**
See also DLB 39, 89, 158; RGEL 2

Holden, Ursula 1921- .... **CLC 18**
See also CA 101; CAAS 8; CANR 22

Holderlin, (Johann Christian) Friedrich
1770-1843 .... **NCLC 16, 187; PC 4**
See also CDWLB 2; DLB 90; EW 5; RGWL
2, 3

Holdstock, Robert 1948- .... **CLC 39**
See also CA 131; CANR 81; DLB 261;
FANT; HGG; SFW 4; SUFW 2

Holdstock, Robert P.
See Holdstock, Robert

Holinshed, Raphael fl. 1580- .... **LC 69**
See also DLB 167; RGEL 2

Holland, Isabelle (Christian)
1920-2002 .... **CLC 21**
See also AAYA 11, 64; CA 21-24R; 205;
CAAE 181; CANR 10, 25, 47; CLR 57;
CWRI 5; JRDA; LAIT 4; MAICYA 1, 2;
SATA 8, 70; SATA-Essay 103; SATA-Obit
132; WYA

Holland, Marcus
See Caldwell, (Janet Miriam) Taylor
(Holland)

Hollander, John 1929- .... **CLC 2, 5, 8, 14**
See also CA 1-4R; CANR 1, 52, 136; CP 1,
2, 3, 4, 5, 6, 7; DLB 5; MAL 5; SATA 13

Hollander, Paul
See Silverberg, Robert

Holleran, Andrew
See Garber, Eric

Holley, Marietta 1836(?)-1926 .... **TCLC 99**
See also CA 118; DLB 11; FL 1:3

Hollinghurst, Alan 1954- .... **CLC 55, 91**
See also BRWS 10; CA 114; CN 5, 6, 7;
DLB 207, 326; GLL 1

Hollis, Jim
See Summers, Hollis (Spurgeon, Jr.)

Holly, Buddy 1936-1959 .... **TCLC 65**
See also CA 213

Holmes, Gordon
See Shiel, M(atthew) P(hipps)

Holmes, John
See Souster, (Holmes) Raymond

Holmes, John Clellon 1926-1988 ...... **CLC 56**
See also BG 1:2; CA 9-12R; 125; CANR 4;
CN 1, 2, 3, 4; DLB 16, 237

Holmes, Oliver Wendell, Jr.
1841-1935 .... **TCLC 77**
See also CA 114; 186

Holmes, Oliver Wendell
1809-1894 .... **NCLC 14, 81; PC 71**
See also AMWS 1; CDALB 1640-1865;
DLB 1, 189, 235; EXPP; PFS 24; RGAL
4; SATA 34

Holmes, Raymond
See Souster, (Holmes) Raymond

Holt, Samuel
See Westlake, Donald E.

Holt, Victoria
See Hibbert, Eleanor Alice Burford

Holub, Miroslav 1923-1998 .... **CLC 4**
See also CA 21-24R; 169; CANR 10; CD-
WLB 4; CWW 2; DLB 232; EWL 3;
RGWL 3

Holz, Detlev
See Benjamin, Walter

Homer c. 8th cent. B.C.- .... **CMLC 1, 16, 61;**
PC 23; WLCS
See also AW 1; CDWLB 1; DA; DA3;
DAB; DAC; DAM MST, POET; DLB
176; EFS 1; LAIT 1; LMFS 1; RGWL 2,
3; TWA; WLIT 8; WP

Hong, Maxine Ting Ting
See Kingston, Maxine Hong

Hongo, Garrett Kaoru 1951- .... **PC 23**
See also CA 133; CAAS 22; CP 5, 6, 7;
DLB 120, 312; EWL 3; EXPP; PFS 25;
RGAL 4

Honig, Edwin 1919- .... **CLC 33**
See also CA 5-8R; CAAS 8; CANR 4, 45,
144; CP 1, 2, 3, 4, 5, 6, 7; DLB 5

Hood, Hugh (John Blagdon) 1928- . **CLC 15,**
28, 273; SSC 42
See also CA 49-52; CAAS 17; CANR 1,
33, 87; CN 1, 2, 3, 4, 5, 6, 7; DLB 53;
RGSF 2

Hood, Thomas 1799-1845 . **NCLC 16; PC 93**
See also BRW 4; DLB 96; RGEL 2

Hooker, (Peter) Jeremy 1941- .... **CLC 43**
See also CA 77-80; CANR 22; CP 2, 3, 4,
5, 6, 7; DLB 40

Hooker, Richard 1554-1600 .... **LC 95**
See also BRW 1; DLB 132; RGEL 2

Hooker, Thomas 1586-1647 .... **LC 137**
See also DLB 24

hooks, bell 1952(?)- .... **BLCS; CLC 94**
See also BW 2; CA 143; CANR 87, 126;
DLB 246; MTCW 2; MTFW 2005; SATA
115, 170

Hooper, Johnson Jones
1815-1862 .... **NCLC 177**
See also DLB 3, 11, 248; RGAL 4

Hope, A(lec) D(erwent) 1907-2000 .... **CLC 3,**
51; PC 56
See also BRWS 7; CA 21-24R; 188; CANR
33, 74; CP 1, 2, 3, 4, 5, 6, 7; DLB 289; EWL
3; MTCW 1, 2; MTFW 2005; PFS 8;
RGEL 2

Hope, Anthony 1863-1933 .... **TCLC 83**
See also CA 157; DLB 153, 156; RGEL 2;
RHW

Hope, Brian
See Creasey, John

Hope, Christopher 1944- .... **CLC 52**
See also AFW; CA 106; CANR 47, 101,
177; CN 4, 5, 6, 7; DLB 225; SATA 62

Hope, Christopher David Tully
See Hope, Christopher

Hopkins, Gerard Manley
1844-1889 .... **NCLC 17, 189; PC 15;**
WLC 3
See also BRW 5; BRWR 2; CDBLB 1890-
1914; DA; DA3; DAB; DAC; DAM MST,
POET; DLB 35, 57; EXPP; PAB; PFS 26;
RGEL 2; TEA; WP

Hopkins, John (Richard) 1931-1998 .. **CLC 4**
See also CA 85-88; 169; CBD; CD 5, 6

Hopkins, Pauline Elizabeth
1859-1930 .... **BLC 1:2; TCLC 28**
See also AFAW 2; BW 2, 3; CA 141; CANR
82; DAM MULT; DLB 50

Hopkinson, Francis 1737-1791 .... **LC 25**
See also DLB 31; RGAL 4

Hopley, George
See Hopley-Woolrich, Cornell George

Hopley-Woolrich, Cornell George
1903-1968 .... **CLC 77**
See also CA 13-14; CANR 58, 156; CAP 1;
CMW 4; DLB 226; MSW; MTCW 2

Horace 65B.C.-8B.C. .... **CMLC 39; PC 46**
See also AW 2; CDWLB 1; DLB 211;
RGWL 2, 3; WLIT 8

Horatio
See Proust, (Valentin-Louis-George-Eugene)
Marcel

Horgan, Paul (George Vincent
O'Shaughnessy) 1903-1995 .. **CLC 9, 53**
See also BPFB 2; CA 13-16R; 147; CANR
9, 35; CN 1, 2, 3, 4, 5; DAM NOV; DLB
102, 212; DLBY 1985; INT CANR-9;
MTCW 1, 2; MTFW 2005; SATA 13;
SATA-Obit 84; TCWW 1, 2

Horkheimer, Max 1895-1973 .... **TCLC 132**
See also CA 216; 41-44R; DLB 296

Horn, Peter
See Kuttner, Henry

Hornby, Nick 1957(?)- .... **CLC 243**
See also AAYA 74; CA 151; CANR 104,
151; CN 7; DLB 207

Horne, Frank (Smith) 1899-1974 ...... **HR 1:2**
See also BW 1; CA 125; 53-56; DLB 51;
WP

Horne, Richard Henry Hengist
1802(?)-1884 .... **NCLC 127**
See also DLB 32; SATA 29

Hornem, Horace Esq.
See Byron, George Gordon (Noel)

Horne Tooke, John 1736-1812 ..... **NCLC 195**

Horney, Karen (Clementine Theodore
Danielsen) 1885-1952 .... **TCLC 71**
See also CA 114; 165; DLB 246; FW

Hornung, E(rnest) W(illiam)
1866-1921 .... **TCLC 59**
See also CA 108; 160; CMW 4; DLB 70

Horovitz, Israel 1939- .... **CLC 56**
See also CA 33-36R; CAD; CANR 46, 59;
CD 5, 6; DAM DRAM; DLB 7, 341;
MAL 5

Horton, George Moses
1797(?)-1883(?) .... **NCLC 87**
See also DLB 50

Horvath, odon von 1901-1938
See von Horvath, Odon
See also EWL 3

Horvath, Oedoen von -1938
See von Horvath, Odon

Horwitz, Julius 1920-1986 .... **CLC 14**
See also CA 9-12R; 119; CANR 12

Horwitz, Ronald
See Harwood, Ronald

Hospital, Janette Turner 1942- .... **CLC 42,**
145
See also CA 108; CANR 48, 166; CN 5, 6,
7; DLB 325; DLBY 2002; RGSF 2

Hosseini, Khaled 1965- .... **CLC 254**
See also CA 225; SATA 156

Hostos, E. M. de
See Hostos (y Bonilla), Eugenio Maria de

Hostos, Eugenio M. de
See Hostos (y Bonilla), Eugenio Maria de

Hostos, Eugenio Maria
See Hostos (y Bonilla), Eugenio Maria de

Hostos (y Bonilla), Eugenio Maria de
1839-1903 .... **TCLC 24**
See also CA 123; 131; HW 1

Houdini
See Lovecraft, H. P.

Houellebecq, Michel 1958- .... **CLC 179**
See also CA 185; CANR 140; MTFW 2005

Hougan, Carolyn 1943-2007 .... **CLC 34**
See also CA 139; 257

Household, Geoffrey (Edward West)
1900-1988 .... **CLC 11**
See also CA 77-80; 126; CANR 58; CMW
4; CN 1, 2, 3, 4; DLB 87; SATA 14;
SATA-Obit 59

Housman, A(lfred) E(dward)
1859-1936 .... **PC 2, 43; TCLC 1, 10;**
WLCS
See also AAYA 66; BRW 6; CA 104; 125;
DA; DA3; DAB; DAC; DAM MST,
POET; DLB 19, 284; EWL 3; EXPP;
MTCW 1, 2; MTFW 2005; PAB; PFS 4,
7; RGEL 2; TEA; WP

Housman, Laurence 1865-1959 .... **TCLC 7**
See also CA 106; 155; DLB 10; FANT;
RGEL 2; SATA 25

Houston, Jeanne Wakatsuki 1934- .... **AAL**
See also AAYA 49; CA 103, 232; CAAE
232; CAAS 16; CANR 29, 123, 167;
LAIT 4; SATA 78, 168; SATA-Essay 168

Hove, Chenjerai 1956- .... **BLC 2:2**
See also CP 7

Howard, Elizabeth Jane 1923- ..... **CLC 7, 29**
See also BRWS 11; CA 5-8R; CANR 8, 62,
146; CN 1, 2, 3, 4, 5, 6, 7

Howard, Maureen 1930- .... **CLC 5, 14, 46,
151**
See also CA 53-56; CANR 31, 75, 140; CN
4, 5, 6, 7; DLBY 1983; INT CANR-31;
MTCW 1, 2; MTFW 2005

Howard, Richard 1929- .... **CLC 7, 10, 47**
See also AITN 1; CA 85-88; CANR 25, 80,
154; CP 1, 2, 3, 4, 5, 6, 7; DLB 5; INT
CANR-25; MAL 5

Howard, Robert E 1906-1936 .... **TCLC 8**
See also BPFB 2; BYA 5; CA 105; 157;
CANR 155; FANT; SUFW 1; TCWW 1,
2

Howard, Robert Ervin
See Howard, Robert E

Howard, Warren F.
See Pohl, Frederik

Howe, Fanny 1940- .... **CLC 47**
See also CA 117, 187; CAAE 187; CAAS
27; CANR 70, 116, 184; CP 6, 7; CWP;
SATA-Brief 52

Howe, Fanny Quincy
See Howe, Fanny

Howe, Irving 1920-1993 .... **CLC 85**
See also AMWS 6; CA 9-12R; 141; CANR
21, 50; DLB 67; EWL 3; MAL 5; MTCW
1, 2; MTFW 2005

Howe, Julia Ward 1819-1910 . **PC 81; TCLC
21**
See also CA 117; 191; DLB 1, 189, 235;
FW

Howe, Susan 1937- .... **CLC 72, 152; PC 54**
See also AMWS 4; CA 160; CP 5, 6, 7;
CWP; DLB 120; FW; RGAL 4

Howe, Tina 1937- .... **CLC 48**
See also CA 109; CAD; CANR 125; CD 5,
6; CWD; DLB 341

Howell, James 1594(?)-1666 .... **LC 13**
See also DLB 151

Howells, W. D.
See Howells, William Dean

Howells, William D.
See Howells, William Dean

Howells, William Dean 1837-1920 ... **SSC 36;
TCLC 7, 17, 41**
See also AMW; CA 104; 134; CDALB
1865-1917; DLB 12, 64, 74, 79, 189;
LMFS 1; MAL 5; MTCW 2; RGAL 4;
TUS

Howes, Barbara 1914-1996 .... **CLC 15**
See also CA 9-12R; 151; CAAS 3; CANR
53; CP 1, 2, 3, 4, 5, 6; SATA 5; TCLE 1:1

Hrabal, Bohumil 1914-1997 ...... **CLC 13, 67;
TCLC 155**
See also CA 106; 156; CAAS 12; CANR
57; CWW 2; DLB 232; EWL 3; RGSF 2

Hrabanus Maurus 776(?)-856 .... **CMLC 78**
See also DLB 148

Hrotsvit of Gandersheim c. 935-c.
1000 .... **CMLC 29**
See also DLB 148

Hsi, Chu 1130-1200 .... **CMLC 42**

Hsun, Lu
See Shu-Jen, Chou

Hubbard, L. Ron 1911-1986 .... **CLC 43**
See also AAYA 64; CA 77-80; 118; CANR
52; CPW; DA3; DAM POP; FANT;
MTCW 2; MTFW 2005; SFW 4

Hubbard, Lafayette Ronald
See Hubbard, L. Ron

Huch, Ricarda (Octavia)
1864-1947 .... **TCLC 13**
See also CA 111; 189; DLB 66; EWL 3

Huddle, David 1942- .... **CLC 49**
See also CA 57-60, 261; CAAS 20; CANR
89; DLB 130

Hudson, Jeffery
See Crichton, Michael

Hudson, Jeffrey
See Crichton, Michael

Hudson, W(illiam) H(enry)
1841-1922 .... **TCLC 29**
See also CA 115; 190; DLB 98, 153, 174;
RGEL 2; SATA 35

Hueffer, Ford Madox
See Ford, Ford Madox

Hughart, Barry 1934- .... **CLC 39**
See also CA 137; FANT; SFW 4; SUFW 2

Hughes, Colin
See Creasey, John

Hughes, David (John) 1930-2005 ..... **CLC 48**
See also CA 116; 129; 238; CN 4, 5, 6, 7;
DLB 14

Hughes, Edward James
See Hughes, Ted

Hughes, (James Mercer) Langston
1902-1967 .. **BLC 1:2; CLC 1, 5, 10, 15,
35, 44, 108; DC 3; HR 1:2; PC 1, 53;
SSC 6, 90; WLC 3**
See also AAYA 12; AFAW 1, 2; AMWR 1;
AMWS 1; BW 1, 3; CA 1-4R; 25-28R;
CANR 1, 34, 82; CDALB 1929-1941;
CLR 17; DA; DA3; DAB; DAC; DAM
DRAM, MST, MULT, POET; DFS 6, 18;
DLB 4, 7, 48, 51, 86, 228, 315; EWL 3;
EXPP; EXPS; JRDA; LAIT 3; LMFS 2;
MAICYA 1, 2; MAL 5; MTCW 1, 2;
MTFW 2005; NFS 21; PAB; PFS 1, 3, 6,
10, 15, 30; RGAL 4; RGSF 2; SATA 4,
33; SSFS 4, 7; TUS; WCH; WP; YAW

Hughes, Richard (Arthur Warren)
1900-1976 .... **CLC 1, 11; TCLC 204**
See also CA 5-8R; 65-68; CANR 4; CN 1,
2; DAM NOV; DLB 15, 161; EWL 3;
MTCW 1; RGEL 2; SATA 8; SATA-Obit
25

Hughes, Ted 1930-1998 . **CLC 2, 4, 9, 14, 37,
119; PC 7, 89**
See also BRWC 2; BRWR 2; BRWS 1; CA
1-4R; 171; CANR 1, 33, 66, 108; CLR 3,
131; CP 1, 2, 3, 4, 5, 6; DA3; DAB; DAC;
DAM MST, POET; DLB 40, 161; EWL
3; EXPP; MAICYA 1, 2; MTCW 1, 2;
MTFW 2005; PAB; PFS 4, 19; RGEL 2;
SATA 49; SATA-Brief 27; SATA-Obit
107; TEA; YAW

Hughes, Thomas 1822-1896 .... **NCLC 207**
See also BYA 3; DLB 18, 163; LAIT 2;
RGEL 2; SATA 31

Hugo, Richard
See Huch, Ricarda (Octavia)

Hugo, Richard F(ranklin)
1923-1982 .... **CLC 6, 18, 32; PC 68**
See also AMWS 6; CA 49-52; 108; CANR
3; CP 1, 2, 3; DAM POET; DLB 5, 206;
EWL 3; MAL 5; PFS 17; RGAL 4

Hugo, Victor (Marie) 1802-1885 .... **NCLC 3,
10, 21, 161, 189; PC 17; WLC 3**
See also AAYA 28; DA; DA3; DAB; DAC;
DAM DRAM, MST, NOV, POET; DLB
119, 192, 217; EFS 2; EW 6; EXPN; GFL
1789 to the Present; LAIT 1, 2; NFS 5,
20; RGWL 2, 3; SATA 47; TWA

Huidobro, Vicente
See Huidobro Fernandez, Vicente Garcia

Huidobro Fernandez, Vicente Garcia
1893-1948 .... **TCLC 31**
See also CA 131; DLB 283; EWL 3; HW 1;
LAW

Hulme, Keri 1947- .... **CLC 39, 130**
See also CA 125; CANR 69; CN 4, 5, 6, 7;
CP 6, 7; CWP; DLB 326; EWL 3; FW;
INT CA-125; NFS 24

Hulme, T(homas) E(rnest)
1883-1917 .... **TCLC 21**
See also BRWS 6; CA 117; 203; DLB 19

Humboldt, Alexander von
1769-1859 .... **NCLC 170**
See also DLB 90

Humboldt, Wilhelm von
1767-1835 .... **NCLC 134**
See also DLB 90

Hume, David 1711-1776 .. **LC 7, 56, 156, 157**
See also BRWS 3; DLB 104, 252, 336;
LMFS 1; TEA

Humphrey, William 1924-1997 .... **CLC 45**
See also AMWS 9; CA 77-80; 160; CANR
68; CN 1, 2, 3, 4, 5, 6; CSW; DLB 6, 212,
234, 278; TCWW 1, 2

Humphreys, Emyr Owen 1919- .... **CLC 47**
See also CA 5-8R; CANR 3, 24; CN 1, 2,
3, 4, 5, 6, 7; DLB 15

Humphreys, Josephine 1945- ..... **CLC 34, 57**
See also CA 121; 127; CANR 97; CSW;
DLB 292; INT CA-127

Huneker, James Gibbons
1860-1921 .... **TCLC 65**
See also CA 193; DLB 71; RGAL 4

Hungerford, Hesba Fay
See Brinsmead, H(esba) F(ay)

Hungerford, Pixie
See Brinsmead, H(esba) F(ay)

Hunt, E. Howard 1918-2007 .... **CLC 3**
See also AITN 1; CA 45-48; 256; CANR 2,
47, 103, 160; CMW 4

Hunt, Everette Howard, Jr.
See Hunt, E. Howard

Hunt, Francesca
See Holland, Isabelle (Christian)

Hunt, Howard
See Hunt, E. Howard

Hunt, Kyle
See Creasey, John

Hunt, (James Henry) Leigh
1784-1859 .... **NCLC 1, 70; PC 73**
See also DAM POET; DLB 96, 110, 144;
RGEL 2; TEA

Hunt, Marsha 1946- .... **CLC 70**
See also BW 2, 3; CA 143; CANR 79

Hunt, Violet 1866(?)-1942 .... **TCLC 53**
See also CA 184; DLB 162, 197

Hunter, E. Waldo
See Sturgeon, Theodore (Hamilton)

Hunter, Evan 1926-2005 .... **CLC 11, 31**
See also AAYA 39; BPFB 2; CA 5-8R; 241;
CANR 5, 38, 62, 97, 149; CMW 4; CN 1,
2, 3, 4, 5, 6, 7; CPW; DAM POP; DLB
306; DLBY 1982; INT CANR-5; MSW;
MTCW 1; SATA 25; SATA-Obit 167;
SFW 4

Hunter, Kristin
See Lattany, Kristin (Elaine Eggleston)
Hunter

Hunter, Mary
See Austin, Mary (Hunter)

Hunter, Mollie 1922- .... **CLC 21**
See also AAYA 13, 71; BYA 6; CANR 37,
78; CLR 25; DLB 161; JRDA; MAICYA
1, 2; SAAS 7; SATA 2, 54, 106, 139;
SATA-Essay 139; WYA; YAW

Hunter, Robert (?)-1734 .... LC 7

Hurston, Zora Neale 1891-1960 ..... BLC 1:2; CLC 7, 30, 61; DC 12; HR 1:2; SSC 4, 80; TCLC 121, 131; WLCS
See also AAYA 15, 71; AFAW 1, 2; AMWS 6; BW 1, 3; BYA 12; CA 85-88; CANR 61; CDALBS; DA; DA3; DAC; DAM MST, MULT, NOV; DFS 6; DLB 51, 86; EWL 3; EXPN; EXPS; FL 1:6; FW; LAIT 3; LATS 1:1; LMFS 2; MAL 5; MBL; MTCW 1, 2; MTFW 2005; NFS 3; RGAL 4; RGSF 2; SSFS 1, 6, 11, 19, 21; TUS; YAW

Husserl, E. G.
See Husserl, Edmund (Gustav Albrecht)

Husserl, Edmund (Gustav Albrecht) 1859-1938 .... TCLC 100
See also CA 116; 133; DLB 296

Huston, John (Marcellus) 1906-1987 .... CLC 20
See also CA 73-76; 123; CANR 34; DLB 26

Hustvedt, Siri 1955- .... CLC 76
See also CA 137; CANR 149

Hutcheson, Francis 1694-1746 .... LC 157
See also DLB 252

Hutchinson, Lucy 1620-1675 .... LC 149

Hutten, Ulrich von 1488-1523 .... LC 16
See also DLB 179

Huxley, Aldous (Leonard) 1894-1963 .... CLC 1, 3, 4, 5, 8, 11, 18, 35, 79; SSC 39; WLC 3
See also AAYA 11; BPFB 2; BRW 7; CA 85-88; CANR 44, 99; CDBLB 1914-1945; DA; DA3; DAB; DAC; DAM MST, NOV; DLB 36, 100, 162, 195, 255; EWL 3; EXPN; LAIT 5; LMFS 2; MTCW 1, 2; MTFW 2005; NFS 6; RGEL 2; SATA 63; SCFW 4; SFW 4; TEA; YAW

Huxley, T(homas) H(enry) 1825-1895 .... NCLC 67
See also DLB 57; TEA

Huygens, Constantijn 1596-1687 .... LC 114
See also RGWL 2, 3

Huysmans, Joris-Karl 1848-1907 ... TCLC 7, 69, 212
See also CA 104; 165; DLB 123; EW 7; GFL 1789 to the Present; LMFS 2; RGWL 2, 3

Hwang, David Henry 1957- .... CLC 55, 196; DC 4, 23
See also CA 127; 132; CAD; CANR 76, 124; CD 5, 6; DA3; DAM DRAM; DFS 11, 18; DLB 212, 228, 312; INT CA-132; MAL 5; MTCW 2; MTFW 2005; RGAL 4

Hyatt, Daniel
See James, Daniel (Lewis)

Hyde, Anthony 1946- .... CLC 42
See also CA 136; CCA 1

Hyde, Margaret O. 1917- .... CLC 21
See also CA 1-4R; CANR 1, 36, 137, 181; CLR 23; JRDA; MAICYA 1, 2; SAAS 8; SATA 1, 42, 76, 139

Hyde, Margaret Oldroyd
See Hyde, Margaret O.

Hynes, James 1956(?)- .... CLC 65
See also CA 164; CANR 105

Hypatia c. 370-415 .... CMLC 35

Ian, Janis 1951- .... CLC 21
See also CA 105; 187

Ibanez, Vicente Blasco
See Blasco Ibanez, Vicente

Ibarbourou, Juana de 1895(?)-1979 .... HLCS 2
See also DLB 290; HW 1; LAW

Ibarguengoitia, Jorge 1928-1983 ..... CLC 37; TCLC 148
See also CA 124; 113; EWL 3; HW 1

Ibn Arabi 1165-1240 .... CMLC 105

Ibn Battuta, Abu Abdalla 1304-1368(?) .... CMLC 57
See also WLIT 2

Ibn Hazm 994-1064 .... CMLC 64

Ibn Zaydun 1003-1070 .... CMLC 89

Ibsen, Henrik (Johan) 1828-1906 .. DC 2, 30; TCLC 2, 8, 16, 37, 52; WLC 3
See also AAYA 46; CA 104; 141; DA; DA3; DAB; DAC; DAM DRAM, MST; DFS 1, 6, 8, 10, 11, 15, 16, 25; EW 7; LAIT 2; LATS 1:1; MTFW 2005; RGWL 2, 3

Ibuse, Masuji 1898-1993 .... CLC 22
See also CA 127; 141; CWW 2; DLB 180; EWL 3; MJW; RGWL 3

Ibuse Masuji
See Ibuse, Masuji

Ichikawa, Kon 1915-2008 .... CLC 20
See also CA 121; 269

Ichiyo, Higuchi 1872-1896 .... NCLC 49
See also MJW

Idle, Eric 1943- .... CLC 21
See also CA 116; CANR 35, 91, 148

Idris, Yusuf 1927-1991 .... SSC 74
See also AFW; DLB 346; EWL 3; RGSF 2, 3; RGWL 3; WLIT 2

Ignatieff, Michael 1947- .... CLC 236
See also CA 144; CANR 88, 156; CN 6, 7; DLB 267

Ignatieff, Michael Grant
See Ignatieff, Michael

Ignatow, David 1914-1997 .... CLC 4, 7, 14, 40; PC 34
See also CA 9-12R; 162; CAAS 3; CANR 31, 57, 96; CP 1, 2, 3, 4, 5, 6; DLB 5; EWL 3; MAL 5

Ignotus
See Strachey, (Giles) Lytton

Ihimaera, Witi (Tame) 1944- .... CLC 46
See also CA 77-80; CANR 130; CN 2, 3, 4, 5, 6, 7; RGSF 2; SATA 148

Il'f, Il'ia
See Fainzilberg, Ilya Arnoldovich

Ilf, Ilya
See Fainzilberg, Ilya Arnoldovich

Illyes, Gyula 1902-1983 .... PC 16
See also CA 114; 109; CDWLB 4; DLB 215; EWL 3; RGWL 2, 3

Imalayen, Fatima-Zohra
See Djebar, Assia

Immermann, Karl (Lebrecht) 1796-1840 .... NCLC 4, 49
See also DLB 133

Ince, Thomas H. 1882-1924 .... TCLC 89
See also IDFW 3, 4

Inchbald, Elizabeth 1753-1821 ...... NCLC 62
See also DLB 39, 89; RGEL 2

Inclan, Ramon (Maria) del Valle
See Valle-Inclan, Ramon (Maria) del

Incogniteau, Jean-Louis
See Kerouac, Jack

Infante, G(uillermo) Cabrera
See Cabrera Infante, G.

Ingalls, Rachel 1940- .... CLC 42
See also CA 123; 127; CANR 154

Ingalls, Rachel Holmes
See Ingalls, Rachel

Ingamells, Reginald Charles
See Ingamells, Rex

Ingamells, Rex 1913-1955 .... TCLC 35
See also CA 167; DLB 260

Inge, William (Motter) 1913-1973 ..... CLC 1, 8, 19
See also CA 9-12R; CAD; CDALB 1941-1968; DA3; DAM DRAM; DFS 1, 3, 5, 8; DLB 7, 249; EWL 3; MAL 5; MTCW 1, 2; MTFW 2005; RGAL 4; TUS

Ingelow, Jean 1820-1897 .... NCLC 39, 107
See also DLB 35, 163; FANT; SATA 33

Ingram, Willis J.
See Harris, Mark

Innaurato, Albert (F.) 1948(?)- ... CLC 21, 60
See also CA 115; 122; CAD; CANR 78; CD 5, 6; INT CA-122

Innes, Michael
See Stewart, J(ohn) I(nnes) M(ackintosh)

Innis, Harold Adams 1894-1952 .... TCLC 77
See also CA 181; DLB 88

Insluis, Alanus de
See Alain de Lille

Iola
See Wells-Barnett, Ida B(ell)

Ionesco, Eugene 1912-1994 ... CLC 1, 4, 6, 9, 11, 15, 41, 86; DC 12; WLC 3
See also CA 9-12R; 144; CANR 55, 132; CWW 2; DA; DA3; DAB; DAC; DAM DRAM, MST; DFS 4, 9, 25; DLB 321; EW 13; EWL 3; GFL 1789 to the Present; LMFS 2; MTCW 1, 2; MTFW 2005; RGWL 2, 3; SATA 7; SATA-Obit 79; TWA

Iqbal, Muhammad 1877-1938 .... TCLC 28
See also CA 215; EWL 3

Ireland, Patrick
See O'Doherty, Brian

Irenaeus St. 130- .... CMLC 42

Irigaray, Luce 1930- .... CLC 164
See also CA 154; CANR 121; FW

Irish, William
See Hopley-Woolrich, Cornell George

Irland, David
See Green, Julien (Hartridge)

Iron, Ralph
See Schreiner, Olive (Emilie Albertina)

Irving, John 1942- . CLC 13, 23, 38, 112, 175
See also AAYA 8, 62; AMWS 6; BEST 89:3; BPFB 2; CA 25-28R; CANR 28, 73, 112, 133; CN 3, 4, 5, 6, 7; CPW; DA3; DAM NOV, POP; DLB 6, 278; DLBY 1982; EWL 3; MAL 5; MTCW 1, 2; MTFW 2005; NFS 12, 14; RGAL 4; TUS

Irving, John Winslow
See Irving, John

Irving, Washington 1783-1859 . NCLC 2, 19, 95; SSC 2, 37, 104; WLC 3
See also AAYA 56; AMW; CDALB 1640-1865; CLR 97; DA; DA3; DAB; DAC; DAM MST; DLB 3, 11, 30, 59, 73, 74, 183, 186, 250, 254; EXPS; GL 2; LAIT 1; RGAL 4; RGSF 2; SSFS 1, 8, 16; SUFW 1; TUS; WCH; YABC 2

Irwin, P. K.
See Page, P(atricia) K(athleen)

Isaacs, Jorge Ricardo 1837-1895 ... NCLC 70
See also LAW

Isaacs, Susan 1943- .... CLC 32
See also BEST 89:1; BPFB 2; CA 89-92; CANR 20, 41, 65, 112, 134, 165; CPW; DA3; DAM POP; INT CANR-20; MTCW 1, 2; MTFW 2005

Isherwood, Christopher 1904-1986 ... CLC 1, 9, 11, 14, 44; SSC 56
See also AMWS 14; BRW 7; CA 13-16R; 117; CANR 35, 97, 133; CN 1, 2, 3; DA3; DAM DRAM, NOV; DLB 15, 195; DLBY 1986; EWL 3; IDTP; MTCW 1, 2; MTFW 2005; RGAL 4; RGEL 2; TUS; WLIT 4

Ishiguro, Kazuo 1954- . CLC 27, 56, 59, 110, 219
See also AAYA 58; BEST 90:2; BPFB 2; BRWS 4; CA 120; CANR 49, 95, 133; CN 5, 6, 7; DA3; DAM NOV; DLB 194, 326; EWL 3; MTCW 1, 2; MTFW 2005; NFS 13; WLIT 4; WWE 1

Ishikawa, Hakuhin
See Ishikawa, Takuboku

Jen, Gish
See Jen, Lillian

Jen, Lillian 1955- .... **AAL; CLC 70, 198, 260**
See also AMWC 2; CA 135; CANR 89, 130; CN 7; DLB 312

Jenkins, (John) Robin 1912- .... **CLC 52**
See also CA 1-4R; CANR 1, 135; CN 1, 2, 3, 4, 5, 6, 7; DLB 14, 271

Jennings, Elizabeth (Joan)
1926-2001 .... **CLC 5, 14, 131**
See also BRWS 5; CA 61-64; 200; CAAS 5; CANR 8, 39, 66, 127; CP 1, 2, 3, 4, 5, 6, 7; CWP; DLB 27; EWL 3; MTCW 1; SATA 66

Jennings, Waylon 1937-2002 .... **CLC 21**

Jensen, Johannes V(ilhelm)
1873-1950 .... **TCLC 41**
See also CA 170; DLB 214, 330; EWL 3; RGWL 3

Jensen, Laura (Linnea) 1948- .... **CLC 37**
See also CA 103

Jerome, Saint 345-420 .... **CMLC 30**
See also RGWL 3

Jerome, Jerome K(lapka)
1859-1927 .... **TCLC 23**
See also CA 119; 177; DLB 10, 34, 135; RGEL 2

Jerrold, Douglas William
1803-1857 .... **NCLC 2**
See also DLB 158, 159, 344; RGEL 2

Jewett, (Theodora) Sarah Orne
1849-1909 . **SSC 6, 44, 110; TCLC 1, 22**
See also AAYA 76; AMW; AMWC 2; AMWR 2; CA 108; 127; CANR 71; DLB 12, 74, 221; EXPS; FL 1:3; FW; MAL 5; MBL; NFS 15; RGAL 4; RGSF 2; SATA 15; SSFS 4

Jewsbury, Geraldine (Endsor)
1812-1880 .... **NCLC 22**
See also DLB 21

Jhabvala, Ruth Prawer 1927- . **CLC 4, 8, 29, 94, 138; SSC 91**
See also BRWS 5; CA 1-4R; CANR 2, 29, 51, 74, 91, 128; CN 1, 2, 3, 4, 5, 6, 7; DAB; DAM NOV; DLB 139, 194, 323, 326; EWL 3; IDFW 3, 4; INT CANR-29; MTCW 1, 2; MTFW 2005; RGSF 2; RGWL 2; RHW; TEA

Jibran, Kahlil
See Gibran, Kahlil

Jibran, Khalil
See Gibran, Kahlil

Jiles, Paulette 1943- .... **CLC 13, 58**
See also CA 101; CANR 70, 124, 170; CP 5; CWP

Jimenez (Mantecon), Juan Ramon
1881-1958 .... **HLC 1; PC 7; TCLC 4, 183**
See also CA 104; 131; CANR 74; DAM MULT, POET; DLB 134, 330; EW 9; EWL 3; HW 1; MTCW 1, 2; MTFW 2005; RGWL 2, 3

Jimenez, Ramon
See Jimenez (Mantecon), Juan Ramon

Jimenez Mantecon, Juan
See Jimenez (Mantecon), Juan Ramon

Jin, Ba 1904-2005 .... **CLC 18**
See also CA 244; CWW 2; DLB 328; EWL 3

Jin, Ha
See Jin, Xuefei

Jin, Xuefei 1956- .... **CLC 109, 262**
See also CA 152; CANR 91, 130, 184; DLB 244, 292; MTFW 2005; NFS 25; SSFS 17

Jodelle, Etienne 1532-1573 .... **LC 119**
See also DLB 327; GFL Beginnings to 1789

Joel, Billy
See Joel, William Martin

Joel, William Martin 1949- .... **CLC 26**
See also CA 108

John, St.
See John of Damascus, St.

John of Damascus, St. c.
675-749 .... **CMLC 27, 95**

John of Salisbury c. 1115-1180 ..... **CMLC 63**

John of the Cross, St. 1542-1591 .... **LC 18, 146**
See also RGWL 2, 3

John Paul II, Pope 1920-2005 .... **CLC 128**
See also CA 106; 133; 238

Johnson, B(ryan) S(tanley William)
1933-1973 .... **CLC 6, 9**
See also CA 9-12R; 53-56; CANR 9; CN 1; CP 1, 2; DLB 14, 40; EWL 3; RGEL 2

Johnson, Benjamin F., of Boone
See Riley, James Whitcomb

Johnson, Charles (Richard) 1948- . **BLC 1:2, 2:2; CLC 7, 51, 65, 163**
See also AFAW 2; AMWS 6; BW 2, 3; CA 116; CAAS 18; CANR 42, 66, 82, 129; CN 5, 6, 7; DAM MULT; DLB 33, 278; MAL 5; MTCW 2; MTFW 2005; RGAL 4; SSFS 16

Johnson, Charles S(purgeon)
1893-1956 .... **HR 1:3**
See also BW 1, 3; CA 125; CANR 82; DLB 51, 91

Johnson, Denis 1949- . **CLC 52, 160; SSC 56**
See also CA 117; 121; CANR 71, 99, 178; CN 4, 5, 6, 7; DLB 120

Johnson, Diane 1934- ...... **CLC 5, 13, 48, 244**
See also BPFB 2; CA 41-44R; CANR 17, 40, 62, 95, 155; CN 4, 5, 6, 7; DLBY 1980; INT CANR-17; MTCW 1

Johnson, E(mily) Pauline 1861-1913 . **NNAL**
See also CA 150; CCA 1; DAC; DAM MULT; DLB 92, 175; TCWW 2

Johnson, Eyvind (Olof Verner)
1900-1976 .... **CLC 14**
See also CA 73-76; 69-72; CANR 34, 101; DLB 259, 330; EW 12; EWL 3

Johnson, Fenton 1888-1958 .... **BLC 1:2**
See also BW 1; CA 118; 124; DAM MULT; DLB 45, 50

Johnson, Georgia Douglas (Camp)
1880-1966 .... **HR 1:3**
See also BW 1; CA 125; DLB 51, 249; WP

Johnson, Helene 1907-1995 .... **HR 1:3**
See also CA 181; DLB 51; WP

Johnson, J. R.
See James, C(yril) L(ionel) R(obert)

Johnson, James Weldon
1871-1938 .... **BLC 1:2; HR 1:3; PC 24; TCLC 3, 19, 175**
See also AAYA 73; AFAW 1, 2; BW 1, 3; CA 104; 125; CANR 82; CDALB 1917-1929; CLR 32; DA3; DAM MULT, POET; DLB 51; EWL 3; EXPP; LMFS 2; MAL 5; MTCW 1, 2; MTFW 2005; NFS 22; PFS 1; RGAL 4; SATA 31; TUS

Johnson, Joyce 1935- .... **CLC 58**
See also BG 1:3; CA 125; 129; CANR 102

Johnson, Judith (Emlyn) 1936- .... **CLC 7, 15**
See also CA 25-28R; 153; CANR 34, 85; CP 2, 3, 4, 5, 6, 7; CWP

Johnson, Lionel (Pigot)
1867-1902 .... **TCLC 19**
See also CA 117; 209; DLB 19; RGEL 2

Johnson, Marguerite Annie
See Angelou, Maya

Johnson, Mel
See Malzberg, Barry N(athaniel)

Johnson, Pamela Hansford
1912-1981 .... **CLC 1, 7, 27**
See also CA 1-4R; 104; CANR 2, 28; CN 1, 2, 3; DLB 15; MTCW 1, 2; MTFW 2005; RGEL 2

Johnson, Paul 1928- .... **CLC 147**
See also BEST 89:4; CA 17-20R; CANR 34, 62, 100, 155

Johnson, Paul Bede
See Johnson, Paul

Johnson, Robert .... **CLC 70**

Johnson, Robert 1911(?)-1938 .... **TCLC 69**
See also BW 3; CA 174

Johnson, Samuel 1709-1784 . **LC 15, 52, 128; PC 81; WLC 3**
See also BRW 3; BRWR 1; CDBLB 1660-1789; DA; DAB; DAC; DAM MST; DLB 39, 95, 104, 142, 213; LMFS 1; RGEL 2; TEA

Johnson, Stacie
See Myers, Walter Dean

Johnson, Uwe 1934-1984 .. **CLC 5, 10, 15, 40**
See also CA 1-4R; 112; CANR 1, 39; CD-WLB 2; DLB 75; EWL 3; MTCW 1; RGWL 2, 3

Johnston, Basil H. 1929- .... **NNAL**
See also CA 69-72; CANR 11, 28, 66; DAC; DAM MULT; DLB 60

Johnston, George (Benson) 1913- .... **CLC 51**
See also CA 1-4R; CANR 5, 20; CP 1, 2, 3, 4, 5, 6, 7; DLB 88

Johnston, Jennifer (Prudence)
1930- .... **CLC 7, 150, 228**
See also CA 85-88; CANR 92; CN 4, 5, 6, 7; DLB 14

Joinville, Jean de 1224(?)-1317 ..... **CMLC 38**

Jolley, Elizabeth 1923-2007 ..... **CLC 46, 256, 260; SSC 19**
See also CA 127; 257; CAAS 13; CANR 59; CN 4, 5, 6, 7; DLB 325; EWL 3; RGSF 2

Jolley, Monica Elizabeth
See Jolley, Elizabeth

Jones, Arthur Llewellyn 1863-1947 . **SSC 20; TCLC 4**
See Machen, Arthur
See also CA 104; 179; DLB 36; HGG; RGEL 2; SUFW 1

Jones, D(ouglas) G(ordon) 1929- ..... **CLC 10**
See also CA 29-32R; CANR 13, 90; CP 1, 2, 3, 4, 5, 6, 7; DLB 53

Jones, David (Michael) 1895-1974 .... **CLC 2, 4, 7, 13, 42**
See also BRW 6; BRWS 7; CA 9-12R; 53-56; CANR 28; CDBLB 1945-1960; CP 1, 2; DLB 20, 100; EWL 3; MTCW 1; PAB; RGEL 2

Jones, David Robert 1947- .... **CLC 17**
See also CA 103; CANR 104

Jones, Diana Wynne 1934- .... **CLC 26**
See also AAYA 12; BYA 6, 7, 9, 11, 13, 16; CA 49-52; CANR 4, 26, 56, 120, 167; CLR 23, 120; DLB 161; FANT; JRDA; MAICYA 1, 2; MTFW 2005; SAAS 7; SATA 9, 70, 108, 160; SFW 4; SUFW 2; YAW

Jones, Edward P. 1950- .. **BLC 2:2; CLC 76, 223**
See also AAYA 71; BW 2, 3; CA 142; CANR 79, 134; CSW; MTFW 2005; NFS 26

Jones, Everett LeRoi
See Baraka, Amiri

Jones, Gayl 1949- .. **BLC 1:2; CLC 6, 9, 131, 270**
See also AFAW 1, 2; BW 2, 3; CA 77-80; CANR 27, 66, 122; CN 4, 5, 6, 7; CSW; DA3; DAM MULT; DLB 33, 278; MAL 5; MTCW 1, 2; MTFW 2005; RGAL 4

Jones, James 1921-1977 ...... **CLC 1, 3, 10, 39**
See also AITN 1, 2; AMWS 11; BPFB 2; CA 1-4R; 69-72; CANR 6; CN 1; DLB 2, 143; DLBD 17; DLBY 1998; EWL 3; MAL 5; MTCW 1; RGAL 4

Jones, John J.
See Lovecraft, H. P.

Jones, LeRoi
See Baraka, Amiri

Jones, Louis B. 1953- .... **CLC 65**
See also CA 141; CANR 73

Jones, Madison 1925- .... **CLC 4**
See also CA 13-16R; CAAS 11; CANR 7,
54, 83, 158; CN 1, 2, 3, 4, 5, 6, 7; CSW;
DLB 152

Jones, Madison Percy, Jr.
See Jones, Madison

Jones, Mervyn 1922- .... **CLC 10, 52**
See also CA 45-48; CAAS 5; CANR 1, 91;
CN 1, 2, 3, 4, 5, 6, 7; MTCW 1

Jones, Mick 1956(?)- .... **CLC 30**

Jones, Nettie (Pearl) 1941- .... **CLC 34**
See also BW 2; CA 137; CAAS 20; CANR
88

Jones, Peter 1802-1856 .... **NNAL**

Jones, Preston 1936-1979 .... **CLC 10**
See also CA 73-76; 89-92; DLB 7

Jones, Robert F(rancis) 1934-2003 .... **CLC 7**
See also CA 49-52; CANR 2, 61, 118

Jones, Rod 1953- .... **CLC 50**
See also CA 128

Jones, Terence Graham Parry
1942- .... **CLC 21**
See also CA 112; 116; CANR 35, 93, 173;
INT CA-116; SATA 67, 127; SATA-Brief
51

Jones, Terry
See Jones, Terence Graham Parry

Jones, Thom (Douglas) 1945(?)- ..... **CLC 81;
SSC 56**
See also CA 157; CANR 88; DLB 244;
SSFS 23

Jong, Erica 1942- .... **CLC 4, 6, 8, 18, 83**
See also AITN 1; AMWS 5; BEST 90:2;
BPFB 2; CA 73-76; CANR 26, 52, 75,
132, 166; CN 3, 4, 5, 6, 7; CP 2, 3, 4, 5,
6, 7; CPW; DA3; DAM NOV, POP; DLB
2, 5, 28, 152; FW; INT CANR-26; MAL
5; MTCW 1, 2; MTFW 2005

Jonson, Ben(jamin) 1572(?)-1637 . **DC 4; LC
6, 33, 110, 158; PC 17; WLC 3**
See also BRW 1; BRWC 1; BRWR 1; CD-
BLB Before 1660; DA; DAB; DAC;
DAM DRAM, MST, POET; DFS 4, 10;
DLB 62, 121; LMFS 1; PFS 23; RGEL 2;
TEA; WLIT 3

Jordan, June 1936-2002 .. **BLCS; CLC 5, 11,
23, 114, 230; PC 38**
See also AAYA 2, 66; AFAW 1, 2; BW 2,
3; CA 33-36R; 206; CANR 25, 70, 114,
154; CLR 10; CP 3, 4, 5, 6, 7; CWP;
DAM MULT, POET; DLB 38; GLL 2;
LAIT 5; MAICYA 1, 2; MTCW 1; SATA
4, 136; YAW

Jordan, June Meyer
See Jordan, June

Jordan, Neil 1950- .... **CLC 110**
See also CA 124; 130; CANR 54, 154; CN
4, 5, 6, 7; GLL 2; INT CA-130

Jordan, Neil Patrick
See Jordan, Neil

Jordan, Pat(rick M.) 1941- .... **CLC 37**
See also CA 33-36R; CANR 121

Jorgensen, Ivar
See Ellison, Harlan

Jorgenson, Ivar
See Silverberg, Robert

Joseph, George Ghevarughese .... **CLC 70**

Josephson, Mary
See O'Doherty, Brian

Josephus, Flavius c. 37-100 ..... **CMLC 13, 93**
See also AW 2; DLB 176; WLIT 8

Josh
See Twain, Mark

Josiah Allen's Wife
See Holley, Marietta

Josipovici, Gabriel 1940- ...... **CLC 6, 43, 153**
See also CA 37-40R; 224; CAAE 224;
CAAS 8; CANR 47, 84; CN 3, 4, 5, 6, 7;
DLB 14, 319

Josipovici, Gabriel David
See Josipovici, Gabriel

Joubert, Joseph 1754-1824 .... **NCLC 9**

Jouve, Pierre Jean 1887-1976 .... **CLC 47**
See also CA 252; 65-68; DLB 258; EWL 3

Jovine, Francesco 1902-1950 .... **TCLC 79**
See also DLB 264; EWL 3

Joyaux, Julia
See Kristeva, Julia

Joyce, James (Augustine Aloysius)
1882-1941 .... **DC 16; PC 22; SSC 3, 26,
44, 64, 118, 122; TCLC 3, 8, 16, 35, 52,
159; WLC 3**
See also AAYA 42; BRW 7; BRWC 1;
BRWR 1; BYA 11, 13; CA 104; 126; CD-
BLB 1914-1945; DA; DA3; DAB; DAC;
DAM MST, NOV, POET; DLB 10, 19,
36, 162, 247; EWL 3; EXPN; EXPS;
LAIT 3; LMFS 1, 2; MTCW 1, 2; MTFW
2005; NFS 7, 26; RGSF 2; SSFS 1, 19;
TEA; WLIT 4

Jozsef, Attila 1905-1937 .... **TCLC 22**
See also CA 116; 230; CDWLB 4; DLB
215; EWL 3

Juana Ines de la Cruz, Sor
1651(?)-1695 ... **HLCS 1; LC 5, 136; PC
24**
See also DLB 305; FW; LAW; RGWL 2, 3;
WLIT 1

Juana Inez de La Cruz, Sor
See Juana Ines de la Cruz, Sor

Juan Manuel, Don 1282-1348 .... **CMLC 88**

Judd, Cyril
See Kornbluth, C(yril) M.; Pohl, Frederik

Juenger, Ernst 1895-1998 .... **CLC 125**
See also CA 101; 167; CANR 21, 47, 106;
CDWLB 2; DLB 56; EWL 3; RGWL 2, 3

Julian of Norwich 1342(?)-1416(?) . **LC 6, 52**
See also BRWS 12; DLB 146; LMFS 1

Julius Caesar 100B.C.-44B.C. .... **CMLC 47**
See also AW 1; CDWLB 1; DLB 211;
RGWL 2, 3; WLIT 8

Jung, Patricia B.
See Hope, Christopher

Junger, Ernst
See Juenger, Ernst

Junger, Sebastian 1962- .... **CLC 109**
See also AAYA 28; CA 165; CANR 130,
171; MTFW 2005

Juniper, Alex
See Hospital, Janette Turner

Junius
See Luxemburg, Rosa

Junzaburo, Nishiwaki
See Nishiwaki, Junzaburo

Just, Ward 1935- .... **CLC 4, 27**
See also CA 25-28R; CANR 32, 87; CN 6,
7; DLB 335; INT CANR-32

Just, Ward Swift
See Just, Ward

Justice, Donald 1925-2004 ... **CLC 6, 19, 102;
PC 64**
See also AMWS 7; CA 5-8R; 230; CANR
26, 54, 74, 121, 122, 169; CP 1, 2, 3, 4,
5, 6, 7; CSW; DAM POET; DLBY 1983;
EWL 3; INT CANR-26; MAL 5; MTCW
2; PFS 14; TCLE 1:1

Justice, Donald Rodney
See Justice, Donald

Juvenal c. 60-c. 130 .... **CMLC 8**
See also AW 2; CDWLB 1; DLB 211;
RGWL 2, 3; WLIT 8

Juvenis
See Bourne, Randolph S(illiman)

K., Alice
See Knapp, Caroline

Kabakov, Sasha .... **CLC 59**

Kabir 1398(?)-1448(?) .... **LC 109; PC 56**
See also RGWL 2, 3

Kacew, Romain 1914-1980 .... **CLC 25**
See also CA 108; 102; DLB 83, 299; RGHL

Kacew, Roman
See Kacew, Romain

Kadare, Ismail 1936- .... **CLC 52, 190**
See also CA 161; CANR 165; EWL 3;
RGWL 3

Kadohata, Cynthia 1956(?)- ..... **CLC 59, 122**
See also AAYA 71; CA 140; CANR 124;
CLR 121; SATA 155, 180

Kafka, Franz 1883-1924 ... **SSC 5, 29, 35, 60;
TCLC 2, 6, 13, 29, 47, 53, 112, 179;
WLC 3**
See also AAYA 31; BPFB 2; CA 105; 126;
CDWLB 2; DA; DA3; DAB; DAC; DAM
MST, NOV; DLB 81; EW 9; EWL 3;
EXPS; LATS 1:1; LMFS 2; MTCW 1, 2;
MTFW 2005; NFS 7; RGSF 2; RGWL 2,
3; SFW 4; SSFS 3, 7, 12; TWA

Kafu
See Nagai, Kafu

Kahanovitch, Pinchas
See Der Nister

Kahanovitsch, Pinkhes
See Der Nister

Kahanovitsh, Pinkhes
See Der Nister

Kahn, Roger 1927- .... **CLC 30**
See also CA 25-28R; CANR 44, 69, 152;
DLB 171; SATA 37

Kain, Saul
See Sassoon, Siegfried (Lorraine)

Kaiser, Georg 1878-1945 .... **TCLC 9, 220**
See also CA 106; 190; CDWLB 2; DLB
124; EWL 3; LMFS 2; RGWL 2, 3

Kaledin, Sergei .... **CLC 59**

Kaletski, Alexander 1946- .... **CLC 39**
See also CA 118; 143

Kalidasa fl. c. 400-455 .... **CMLC 9; PC 22**
See also RGWL 2, 3

Kallman, Chester (Simon)
1921-1975 .... **CLC 2**
See also CA 45-48; 53-56; CANR 3; CP 1,
2

Kaminsky, Melvin .... **CLC 12, 217**
See Brooks, Mel
See also AAYA 13, 48; DLB 26

Kaminsky, Stuart M. 1934- .... **CLC 59**
See also CA 73-76; CANR 29, 53, 89, 161;
CMW 4

Kaminsky, Stuart Melvin
See Kaminsky, Stuart M.

Kamo no Chomei 1153(?)-1216 .... **CMLC 66**
See also DLB 203

Kamo no Nagaakira
See Kamo no Chomei

Kandinsky, Wassily 1866-1944 .... **TCLC 92**
See also AAYA 64; CA 118; 155

Kane, Francis
See Robbins, Harold

Kane, Paul
See Simon, Paul

Kane, Sarah 1971-1999 .... **DC 31**
See also BRWS 8; CA 190; CD 5, 6; DLB
310

Kanin, Garson 1912-1999 .... **CLC 22**
See also AITN 1; CA 5-8R; 177; CAD;
CANR 7, 78; DLB 7; IDFW 3, 4

Kaniuk, Yoram 1930- .... **CLC 19**
See also CA 134; DLB 299; RGHL

Kant, Immanuel 1724-1804 ..... **NCLC 27, 67**
  See also DLB 94

Kantor, MacKinlay 1904-1977 .... **CLC 7**
  See also CA 61-64; 73-76; CANR 60, 63;
  CN 1, 2; DLB 9, 102; MAL 5; MTCW 2;
  RHW; TCWW 1, 2

Kanze Motokiyo
  See Zeami

Kaplan, David Michael 1946- .... **CLC 50**
  See also CA 187

Kaplan, James 1951- .... **CLC 59**
  See also CA 135; CANR 121

Karadzic, Vuk Stefanovic
  1787-1864 .... **NCLC 115**
  See also CDWLB 4; DLB 147

Karageorge, Michael
  See Anderson, Poul

Karamzin, Nikolai Mikhailovich
  1766-1826 .... **NCLC 3, 173**
  See also DLB 150; RGSF 2

Karapanou, Margarita 1946- .... **CLC 13**
  See also CA 101

Karinthy, Frigyes 1887-1938 .... **TCLC 47**
  See also CA 170; DLB 215; EWL 3

Karl, Frederick R(obert)
  1927-2004 .... **CLC 34**
  See also CA 5-8R; 226; CANR 3, 44, 143

Karr, Mary 1955- .... **CLC 188**
  See also AMWS 11; CA 151; CANR 100;
  MTFW 2005; NCFS 5

Kastel, Warren
  See Silverberg, Robert

Kataev, Evgeny Petrovich
  1903-1942 .... **TCLC 21**
  See also CA 120; DLB 272

Kataphusin
  See Ruskin, John

Katz, Steve 1935- .... **CLC 47**
  See also CA 25-28R; CAAS 14, 64; CANR
  12; CN 4, 5, 6, 7; DLBY 1983

Kauffman, Janet 1945- .... **CLC 42**
  See also CA 117; CANR 43, 84; DLB 218;
  DLBY 1986

Kaufman, Bob (Garnell)
  1925-1986 .... **CLC 49; PC 74**
  See also BG 1:3; BW 1; CA 41-44R; 118;
  CANR 22; CP 1; DLB 16, 41

Kaufman, George S. 1889-1961 ...... **CLC 38;**
  DC 17
  See also CA 108; 93-96; DAM DRAM;
  DFS 1, 10; DLB 7; INT CA-108; MTCW
  2; MTFW 2005; RGAL 4; TUS

Kaufman, Moises 1964- .... **DC 26**
  See also CA 211; DFS 22; MTFW 2005

Kaufman, Sue
  See Barondess, Sue K(aufman)

Kavafis, Konstantinos Petrou
  1863-1933 .... **PC 36; TCLC 2, 7**
  See also CA 104; 148; DA3; DAM POET;
  EW 8; EWL 3; MTCW 2; PFS 19; RGWL
  2, 3; WP

Kavan, Anna 1901-1968 .... **CLC 5, 13, 82**
  See also BRWS 7; CA 5-8R; CANR 6, 57;
  DLB 255; MTCW 1; RGEL 2; SFW 4

Kavanagh, Dan
  See Barnes, Julian

Kavanagh, Julie 1952- .... **CLC 119**
  See also CA 163; CANR 186

Kavanagh, Patrick (Joseph)
  1904-1967 .... **CLC 22; PC 33**
  See also BRWS 7; CA 123; 25-28R; DLB
  15, 20; EWL 3; MTCW 1; RGEL 2

Kawabata, Yasunari 1899-1972 ..... **CLC 2, 5,**
  9, 18, 107; SSC 17
  See also CA 93-96; 33-36R; CANR 88;
  DAM MULT; DLB 180, 330; EWL 3;
  MJW; MTCW 2; MTFW 2005; RGSF 2;
  RGWL 2, 3

Kawabata Yasunari
  See Kawabata, Yasunari

Kaye, Mary Margaret
  See Kaye, M.M.

Kaye, M.M. 1908-2004 .... **CLC 28**
  See also CA 89-92; 223; CANR 24, 60, 102,
  142; MTCW 1, 2; MTFW 2005; RHW;
  SATA 62; SATA-Obit 152

Kaye, Mollie
  See Kaye, M.M.

Kaye-Smith, Sheila 1887-1956 .... **TCLC 20**
  See also CA 118; 203; DLB 36

Kaymor, Patrice Maguilene
  See Senghor, Leopold Sedar

Kazakov, Iurii Pavlovich
  See Kazakov, Yuri Pavlovich

Kazakov, Yuri Pavlovich 1927-1982 . **SSC 43**
  See also CA 5-8R; CANR 36; DLB 302;
  EWL 3; MTCW 1; RGSF 2

Kazakov, Yury
  See Kazakov, Yuri Pavlovich

Kazan, Elia 1909-2003 .... **CLC 6, 16, 63**
  See also CA 21-24R; 220; CANR 32, 78

Kazantzakis, Nikos 1883(?)-1957 .... **TCLC 2,**
  5, 33, 181
  See also BPFB 2; CA 105; 132; DA3; EW
  9; EWL 3; MTCW 1, 2; MTFW 2005;
  RGWL 2, 3

Kazin, Alfred 1915-1998 ..... **CLC 34, 38, 119**
  See also AMWS 8; CA 1-4R; CAAS 7;
  CANR 1, 45, 79; DLB 67; EWL 3

Keane, Mary Nesta (Skrine)
  1904-1996 .... **CLC 31**
  See also CA 108; 114; 151; CN 5, 6; INT
  CA-114; RHW; TCLE 1:1

Keane, Molly
  See Keane, Mary Nesta (Skrine)

Keates, Jonathan 1946(?)- .... **CLC 34**
  See also CA 163; CANR 126

Keaton, Buster 1895-1966 .... **CLC 20**
  See also AAYA 79; CA 194

Keats, John 1795-1821 ...... **NCLC 8, 73, 121;**
  PC 1, 96; WLC 3
  See also AAYA 58; BRW 4; BRWR 1; CD-
  BLB 1789-1832; DA; DA3; DAB; DAC;
  DAM MST, POET; DLB 96, 110; EXPP;
  LMFS 1; PAB; PFS 1, 2, 3, 9, 17; RGEL
  2; TEA; WLIT 3; WP

Keble, John 1792-1866 .... **NCLC 87**
  See also DLB 32, 55; RGEL 2

Keene, Donald 1922- .... **CLC 34**
  See also CA 1-4R; CANR 5, 119

Keillor, Garrison 1942- ..... **CLC 40, 115, 222**
  See also AAYA 2, 62; AMWS 16; BEST
  89:3; BPFB 2; CA 111; 117; CANR 36,
  59, 124, 180; CPW; DA3; DAM POP;
  DLBY 1987; EWL 3; MTCW 1, 2; MTFW
  2005; SATA 58; TUS

Keith, Carlos
  See Lewton, Val

Keith, Michael
  See Hubbard, L. Ron

Kell, Joseph
  See Burgess, Anthony

Keller, Gottfried 1819-1890 .... **NCLC 2; SSC**
  26, 107
  See also CDWLB 2; DLB 129; EW; RGSF
  2; RGWL 2, 3

Keller, Nora Okja 1965- .... **CLC 109**
  See also CA 187

Kellerman, Jonathan 1949- .... **CLC 44**
  See also AAYA 35; BEST 90:1; CA 106;
  CANR 29, 51, 150, 183; CMW 4; CPW;
  DA3; DAM POP; INT CANR-29

Kelley, William Melvin 1937- .... **BLC 2:2;**
  CLC 22
  See also BW 1; CA 77-80; CANR 27, 83;
  CN 1, 2, 3, 4, 5, 6, 7; DLB 33; EWL 3

Kellock, Archibald P.
  See Mavor, Osborne Henry

Kellogg, Marjorie 1922-2005 .... **CLC 2**
  See also CA 81-84; 246

Kellow, Kathleen
  See Hibbert, Eleanor Alice Burford

Kelly, Lauren
  See Oates, Joyce Carol

Kelly, M(ilton) T(errence) 1947- ...... **CLC 55**
  See also CA 97-100; CAAS 22; CANR 19,
  43, 84; CN 6

Kelly, Robert 1935- .... **SSC 50**
  See also CA 17-20R; CAAS 19; CANR 47;
  CP 1, 2, 3, 4, 5, 6, 7; DLB 5, 130, 165

Kelman, James 1946- .... **CLC 58, 86**
  See also BRWS 5; CA 148; CANR 85, 130;
  CN 5, 6, 7; DLB 194, 319, 326; RGSF 2;
  WLIT 4

Kemal, Yasar
  See Kemal, Yashar

Kemal, Yashar 1923(?)- .... **CLC 14, 29**
  See also CA 89-92; CANR 44; CWW 2;
  EWL 3; WLIT 6

Kemble, Fanny 1809-1893 .... **NCLC 18**
  See also DLB 32

Kemelman, Harry 1908-1996 .... **CLC 2**
  See also AITN 1; BPFB 2; CA 9-12R; 155;
  CANR 6, 71; CMW 4; DLB 28

Kempe, Margery 1373(?)-1440(?) ... **LC 6, 56**
  See also BRWS 12; DLB 146; FL 1:1;
  RGEL 2

Kempis, Thomas a 1380-1471 .... **LC 11**

Kenan, Randall (G.) 1963- .... **BLC 2:2**
  See also BW 2, 3; CA 142; CANR 86; CN
  7; CSW; DLB 292; GLL 1

Kendall, Henry 1839-1882 .... **NCLC 12**
  See also DLB 230

Keneally, Thomas 1935- .... **CLC 5, 8, 10, 14,**
  19, 27, 43, 117
  See also BRWS 4; CA 85-88; CANR 10,
  50, 74, 130, 165; CN 1, 2, 3, 4, 5, 6, 7;
  CPW; DA3; DAM NOV; DLB 289, 299,
  326; EWL 3; MTCW 1, 2; MTFW 2005;
  NFS 17; RGEL 2; RGHL; RHW

Keneally, Thomas Michael
  See Keneally, Thomas

Kennedy, A. L. 1965- .... **CLC 188**
  See also CA 168, 213; CAAE 213; CANR
  108; CD 5, 6; CN 6, 7; DLB 271; RGSF
  2

Kennedy, Adrienne (Lita) 1931- .... **BLC 1:2;**
  CLC 66; DC 5
  See also AFAW 2; BW 2, 3; CA 103; CAAS
  20; CABS 3; CAD; CANR 26, 53, 82;
  CD 5, 6; DAM MULT; DFS 9; DLB 38,
  341; FW; MAL 5

Kennedy, Alison Louise
  See Kennedy, A. L.

Kennedy, John Pendleton
  1795-1870 .... **NCLC 2**
  See also DLB 3, 248, 254; RGAL 4

Kennedy, Joseph Charles 1929- .. **CLC 8, 42;**
  PC 93
  See Kennedy, X. J.
  See also AMWS 15; CA 1-4R, 201; CAAE
  201; CAAS 9; CANR 4, 30, 40; CLR 27;
  CP 1, 2, 3, 4, 5, 6, 7; CWRI 5; DLB 5;
  MAICYA 2; MAICYAS 1; SAAS 22;
  SATA 14, 86, 130; SATA-Essay 130

Kennedy, William 1928- .. **CLC 6, 28, 34, 53,**
  239
  See also AAYA 1, 73; AMWS 7; BPFB 2;
  CA 85-88; CANR 14, 31, 76, 134; CN 4,
  5, 6, 7; DA3; DAM NOV; DLB 143;
  DLBY 1985; EWL 3; INT CANR-31;
  MAL 5; MTCW 1, 2; MTFW 2005; SATA
  57

Lagerkvist, Paer (Fabian)
1891-1974 .. **CLC 7, 10, 13, 54; SSC 12; TCLC 144**
See also CA 85-88; 49-52; DA3; DAM DRAM, NOV; DLB 259, 331; EW 10; EWL 3; MTCW 1, 2; MTFW 2005; RGSF 2; RGWL 2, 3; TWA

Lagerkvist, Par
See Lagerkvist, Paer (Fabian)

Lagerloef, Selma (Ottiliana Lovisa)
See Lagerlof, Selma (Ottiliana Lovisa)

Lagerlof, Selma (Ottiliana Lovisa)
1858-1940 .... **TCLC 4, 36**
See also CA 108; 188; CLR 7; DLB 259, 331; MTCW 2; RGWL 2, 3; SATA 15; SSFS 18

La Guma, Alex 1925-1985 .. **BLCS; CLC 19; TCLC 140**
See also AFW; BW 1, 3; CA 49-52; 118; CANR 25, 81; CDWLB 3; CN 1, 2, 3; CP 1; DAM NOV; DLB 117, 225; EWL 3; MTCW 1, 2; MTFW 2005; WLIT 2; WWE 1

Lahiri, Jhumpa 1967- .... **SSC 96**
See also AAYA 56; CA 193; CANR 134, 184; DLB 323; MTFW 2005; SSFS 19, 27

Laidlaw, A. K.
See Grieve, C(hristopher) M(urray)

Lainez, Manuel Mujica
See Mujica Lainez, Manuel

Laing, R(onald) D(avid) 1927-1989 . **CLC 95**
See also CA 107; 129; CANR 34; MTCW 1

Laishley, Alex
See Booth, Martin

Lamartine, Alphonse (Marie Louis Prat) de
1790-1869 .... **NCLC 11, 190; PC 16**
See also DAM POET; DLB 217; GFL 1789 to the Present; RGWL 2, 3

Lamb, Charles 1775-1834 ..... **NCLC 10, 113; SSC 112; WLC 3**
See also BRW 4; CDBLB 1789-1832; DA; DAB; DAC; DAM MST; DLB 93, 107, 163; RGEL 2; SATA 17; TEA

Lamb, Lady Caroline 1785-1828 ... **NCLC 38**
See also DLB 116

Lamb, Mary Ann 1764-1847 ...... **NCLC 125; SSC 112**
See also DLB 163; SATA 17

Lame Deer 1903(?)-1976 .... **NNAL**
See also CA 69-72

Lamming, George (William)
1927- . **BLC 1:2, 2:2; CLC 2, 4, 66, 144**
See also BW 2, 3; CA 85-88; CANR 26, 76; CDWLB 3; CN 1, 2, 3, 4, 5, 6, 7; CP 1; DAM MULT; DLB 125; EWL 3; MTCW 1, 2; MTFW 2005; NFS 15; RGEL 2

L'Amour, Louis 1908-1988 .... **CLC 25, 55**
See also AAYA 16; AITN 2; BEST 89:2; BPFB 2; CA 1-4R; 125; CANR 3, 25, 40; CPW; DA3; DAM NOV, POP; DLB 206; DLBY 1980; MTCW 1, 2; MTFW 2005; RGAL 4; TCWW 1, 2

Lampedusa, Giuseppe (Tomasi) di
See Tomasi di Lampedusa, Giuseppe

Lampman, Archibald 1861-1899 .. **NCLC 25, 194**
See also DLB 92; RGEL 2; TWA

Lancaster, Bruce 1896-1963 .... **CLC 36**
See also CA 9-10; CANR 70; CAP 1; SATA 9

Lanchester, John 1962- .... **CLC 99**
See also CA 194; DLB 267

Landau, Mark Alexandrovich
See Aldanov, Mark (Alexandrovich)

Landau-Aldanov, Mark Alexandrovich
See Aldanov, Mark (Alexandrovich)

Landis, Jerry
See Simon, Paul

Landis, John 1950- .... **CLC 26**
See also CA 112; 122; CANR 128

Landolfi, Tommaso 1908-1979 .... **CLC 11, 49**
See also CA 127; 117; DLB 177; EWL 3

Landon, Letitia Elizabeth
1802-1838 .... **NCLC 15**
See also DLB 96

Landor, Walter Savage
1775-1864 .... **NCLC 14**
See also BRW 4; DLB 93, 107; RGEL 2

Landwirth, Heinz
See Lind, Jakov

Lane, Patrick 1939- .... **CLC 25**
See also CA 97-100; CANR 54; CP 3, 4, 5, 6, 7; DAM POET; DLB 53; INT CA-97-100

Lane, Rose Wilder 1887-1968 ...... **TCLC 177**
See also CA 102; CANR 63; SATA 29; SATA-Brief 28; TCWW 2

Lang, Andrew 1844-1912 .... **TCLC 16**
See also CA 114; 137; CANR 85; CLR 101; DLB 98, 141, 184; FANT; MAICYA 1, 2; RGEL 2; SATA 16; WCH

Lang, Fritz 1890-1976 .... **CLC 20, 103**
See also AAYA 65; CA 77-80; 69-72; CANR 30

Lange, John
See Crichton, Michael

Langer, Elinor 1939- .... **CLC 34**
See also CA 121

Langland, William 1332(?)-1400(?) .... **LC 19, 120**
See also BRW 1; DA; DAB; DAC; DAM MST, POET; DLB 146; RGEL 2; TEA; WLIT 3

Langstaff, Launcelot
See Irving, Washington

Lanier, Sidney 1842-1881 . **NCLC 6, 118; PC 50**
See also AMWS 1; DAM POET; DLB 64; DLBD 13; EXPP; MAICYA 1; PFS 14; RGAL 4; SATA 18

Lanyer, Aemilia 1569-1645 .... **LC 10, 30, 83; PC 60**
See also DLB 121

Lao-Tzu
See Lao Tzu

Lao Tzu c. 6th cent. B.C.-3rd cent. B.C. .... **CMLC 7**

Lapine, James (Elliot) 1949- .... **CLC 39**
See also CA 123; 130; CANR 54, 128; DFS 25; DLB 341; INT CA-130

Larbaud, Valery (Nicolas)
1881-1957 .... **TCLC 9**
See also CA 106; 152; EWL 3; GFL 1789 to the Present

Larcom, Lucy 1824-1893 .... **NCLC 179**
See also AMWS 13; DLB 221, 243

Lardner, Ring
See Lardner, Ring(gold) W(ilmer)

Lardner, Ring W., Jr.
See Lardner, Ring(gold) W(ilmer)

Lardner, Ring(gold) W(ilmer)
1885-1933 ..... **SSC 32, 118; TCLC 2, 14**
See also AMW; BPFB 2; CA 104; 131; CDALB 1917-1929; DLB 11, 25, 86, 171; DLBD 16; MAL 5; MTCW 1, 2; MTFW 2005; RGAL 4; RGSF 2; TUS

Laredo, Betty
See Codrescu, Andrei

Larkin, Maia
See Wojciechowska, Maia (Teresa)

Larkin, Philip (Arthur) 1922-1985 ... **CLC 3, 5, 8, 9, 13, 18, 33, 39, 64; PC 21**
See also BRWS 1; CA 5-8R; 117; CANR 24, 62; CDBLB 1960 to Present; CP 1, 2, 3, 4; DA3; DAB; DAM MST, POET;

DLB 27; EWL 3; MTCW 1, 2; MTFW 2005; PFS 3, 4, 12; RGEL 2

La Roche, Sophie von
1730-1807 .... **NCLC 121**
See also DLB 94

La Rochefoucauld, Francois
1613-1680 .... **LC 108**
See also DLB 268; EW 3; GFL Beginnings to 1789; RGWL 2, 3

Larra (y Sanchez de Castro), Mariano Jose de 1809-1837 .... **NCLC 17, 130**

Larsen, Eric 1941- .... **CLC 55**
See also CA 132

Larsen, Nella 1893(?)-1963 ... **BLC 1:2; CLC 37; HR 1:3; TCLC 200**
See also AFAW 1, 2; AMWS 18; BW 1; CA 125; CANR 83; DAM MULT; DLB 51; FW; LATS 1:1; LMFS 2

Larson, Charles R(aymond) 1938- ... **CLC 31**
See also CA 53-56; CANR 4, 121

Larson, Jonathan 1960-1996 .... **CLC 99**
See also AAYA 28; CA 156; DFS 23; MTFW 2005

La Sale, Antoine de c. 1386-1460(?) . **LC 104**
See also DLB 208

Las Casas, Bartolome de
1474-1566 .... **HLCS; LC 31**
See also DLB 318; LAW; WLIT 1

Lasch, Christopher 1932-1994 .... **CLC 102**
See also CA 73-76; 144; CANR 25, 118; DLB 246; MTCW 1, 2; MTFW 2005

Lasker-Schueler, Else 1869-1945 ... **TCLC 57**
See also CA 183; DLB 66, 124; EWL 3

Lasker-Schuler, Else
See Lasker-Schueler, Else

Laski, Harold J(oseph) 1893-1950 . **TCLC 79**
See also CA 188

Latham, Jean Lee 1902-1995 .... **CLC 12**
See also AITN 1; BYA 1; CA 5-8R; CANR 7, 84; CLR 50; MAICYA 1, 2; SATA 2, 68; YAW

Latham, Mavis
See Clark, Mavis Thorpe

Lathen, Emma
See Hennissart, Martha

Lathrop, Francis
See Leiber, Fritz (Reuter, Jr.)

Lattany, Kristin
See Lattany, Kristin (Elaine Eggleston) Hunter

Lattany, Kristin (Elaine Eggleston) Hunter
1931- .... **CLC 35**
See also AITN 1; BW 1; BYA 3; CA 13-16R; CANR 13, 108; CLR 3; CN 1, 2, 3, 4, 5, 6; DLB 33; INT CANR-13; MAICYA 1, 2; SAAS 10; SATA 12, 132; YAW

Lattimore, Richmond (Alexander)
1906-1984 .... **CLC 3**
See also CA 1-4R; 112; CANR 1; CP 1, 2, 3; MAL 5

Laughlin, James 1914-1997 .... **CLC 49**
See also CA 21-24R; 162; CAAS 22; CANR 9, 47; CP 1, 2, 3, 4, 5, 6; DLB 48; DLBY 1996, 1997

Laurence, Jean Margaret Wemyss
See Laurence, Margaret

Laurence, Margaret 1926-1987 ..... **CLC 3, 6, 13, 50, 62; SSC 7**
See also BYA 13; CA 5-8R; 121; CANR 33; CN 1, 2, 3, 4; DAC; DAM MST; DLB 53; EWL 3; FW; MTCW 1, 2; MTFW 2005; NFS 11; RGEL 2; RGSF 2; SATA-Obit 50; TCWW 2

Laurent, Antoine 1952- .... **CLC 50**

Lauscher, Hermann
See Hesse, Hermann

Livesay, Dorothy (Kathleen)
1909-1996 .... CLC **4, 15, 79**
See also AITN 2; CA 25-28R; CAAS 8;
CANR 36, 67; CP 1, 2, 3, 4, 5; DAC;
DAM MST, POET; DLB 68; FW; MTCW
1; RGEL 2; TWA

Livius Andronicus c. 284B.C.-c.
204B.C. .... CMLC **102**

Livy c. 59B.C.-c. 12 .... CMLC **11**
See also AW 2; CDWLB 1; DLB 211;
RGWL 2, 3; WLIT 8

Li Yaotang
See Jin, Ba

Lizardi, Jose Joaquin Fernandez de
1776-1827 .... NCLC **30**
See also LAW

Llewellyn, Richard
See Llewellyn Lloyd, Richard Dafydd Vivian

Llewellyn Lloyd, Richard Dafydd Vivian
1906-1983 .... CLC **7, 80**
See also CA 53-56; 111; CANR 7, 71; DLB
15; SATA 11; SATA-Obit 37

Llosa, Jorge Mario Pedro Vargas
See Vargas Llosa, Mario

Llosa, Mario Vargas
See Vargas Llosa, Mario

Lloyd, Manda
See Mander, (Mary) Jane

Lloyd Webber, Andrew 1948- .... CLC **21**
See also AAYA 1, 38; CA 116; 149; DAM
DRAM; DFS 7; SATA 56

Llull, Ramon c. 1235-c. 1316 .... CMLC **12**

Lobb, Ebenezer
See Upward, Allen

Locke, Alain (Le Roy)
1886-1954 .... BLCS; HR **1:3**; TCLC **43**
See also AMWS 14; BW 1, 3; CA 106; 124;
CANR 79; DLB 51; LMFS 2; MAL 5;
RGAL 4

Locke, John 1632-1704 .... LC **7, 35, 135**
See also DLB 31, 101, 213, 252; RGEL 2;
WLIT 3

Locke-Elliott, Sumner
See Elliott, Sumner Locke

Lockhart, John Gibson 1794-1854 .. NCLC **6**
See also DLB 110, 116, 144

Lockridge, Ross (Franklin), Jr.
1914-1948 .... TCLC **111**
See also CA 108; 145; CANR 79; DLB 143;
DLBY 1980; MAL 5; RGAL 4; RHW

Lockwood, Robert
See Johnson, Robert

Lodge, David 1935- .... CLC **36, 141**
See also BEST 90:1; BRWS 4; CA 17-20R;
CANR 19, 53, 92, 139; CN 1, 2, 3, 4, 5,
6, 7; CPW; DAM POP; DLB 14, 194;
EWL 3; INT CANR-19; MTCW 1, 2;
MTFW 2005

Lodge, Thomas 1558-1625 .... LC **41**
See also DLB 172; RGEL 2

Loewinsohn, Ron(ald William)
1937- .... CLC **52**
See also CA 25-28R; CANR 71; CP 1, 2, 3,
4

Logan, Jake
See Smith, Martin Cruz

Logan, John (Burton) 1923-1987 .... CLC **5**
See also CA 77-80; 124; CANR 45; CP 1,
2, 3, 4; DLB 5

Lo-Johansson, (Karl) Ivar
1901-1990 .... TCLC **216**
See also CA 102; 131; CANR 20, 79, 137;
DLB 259; EWL 3; RGWL 2, 3

Lo Kuan-chung 1330(?)-1400(?) .... LC **12**

Lomax, Pearl
See Cleage, Pearl

Lomax, Pearl Cleage
See Cleage, Pearl

Lombard, Nap
See Johnson, Pamela Hansford

Lombard, Peter 1100(?)-1160(?) ... CMLC **72**

Lombino, Salvatore
See Hunter, Evan

London, Jack 1876-1916
See London, John Griffith

London, John Griffith 1876-1916 .... SSC **4,
49**; TCLC **9, 15, 39**; WLC **4**
See also AAYA 13, 75; AITN 2; AMW;
BPFB 2; BYA 4, 13; CA 110; 119; CANR
73; CDALB 1865-1917; CLR 108; DA;
DA3; DAB; DAC; DAM MST, NOV;
DLB 8, 12, 78, 212; EWL 3; EXPS;
JRDA; LAIT 3; MAICYA 1, 2,; MAL 5;
MTCW 1, 2; MTFW 2005; NFS 8, 19;
RGAL 4; RGSF 2; SATA 18; SFW 4;
SSFS 7; TCWW 1, 2; TUS; WYA; YAW

Long, Emmett
See Leonard, Elmore

Longbaugh, Harry
See Goldman, William

Longfellow, Henry Wadsworth
1807-1882 .... NCLC **2, 45, 101, 103**; PC
30; WLCS
See also AMW; AMWR 2; CDALB 1640-
1865; CLR 99; DA; DA3; DAB; DAC;
DAM MST, POET; DLB 1, 59, 235;
EXPP; PAB; PFS 2, 7, 17; RGAL 4;
SATA 19; TUS; WP

Longinus c. 1st cent. - .... CMLC **27**
See also AW 2; DLB 176

Longley, Michael 1939- .... CLC **29**
See also BRWS 8; CA 102; CP 1, 2, 3, 4, 5,
6, 7; DLB 40

Longstreet, Augustus Baldwin
1790-1870 .... NCLC **159**
See also DLB 3, 11, 74, 248; RGAL 4

Longus fl. c. 2nd cent. - .... CMLC **7**

Longway, A. Hugh
See Lang, Andrew

Lonnbohm, Armas Eino Leopold
See Lonnbohm, Armas Eino Leopold

Lonnbohm, Armas Eino Leopold
1878-1926 .... TCLC **24**
See also CA 123; EWL 3

Lonnrot, Elias 1802-1884 .... NCLC **53**
See also EFS 1

Lonsdale, Roger .... CLC **65**

Lopate, Phillip 1943- .... CLC **29**
See also CA 97-100; CANR 88, 157; DLBY
1980; INT CA-97-100

Lopez, Barry (Holstun) 1945- .... CLC **70**
See also AAYA 9, 63; ANW; CA 65-68;
CANR 7, 23, 47, 68, 92; DLB 256, 275,
335; INT CANR-7, CANR-23; MTCW 1;
RGAL 4; SATA 67

Lopez de Mendoza, Inigo
See Santillana, Inigo Lopez de Mendoza,
Marques de

Lopez Portillo (y Pacheco), Jose
1920-2004 .... CLC **46**
See also CA 129; 224; HW 1

Lopez y Fuentes, Gregorio
1897(?)-1966 .... CLC **32**
See also CA 131; EWL 3; HW 1

Lorca, Federico Garcia
See Garcia Lorca, Federico

Lord, Audre
See Lorde, Audre

Lord, Bette Bao 1938- .... AAL; CLC **23**
See also BEST 90:3; BPFB 2; CA 107;
CANR 41, 79; INT CA-107; SATA 58

Lord Auch
See Bataille, Georges

Lord Brooke
See Greville, Fulke

Lord Byron
See Byron, George Gordon (Noel)

Lord Dunsany
See Dunsany, Edward John Moreton Drax
Plunkett

Lorde, Audre 1934-1992 .... BLC **1:2, 2:2**;
CLC **18, 71**; PC **12**; TCLC **173**
See also AFAW 1, 2; BW 1, 3; CA 25-28R;
142; CANR 16, 26, 46, 82; CP 2, 3, 4, 5;
DA3; DAM MULT, POET; DLB 41; EWL
3; FW; GLL 1; MAL 5; MTCW 1, 2;
MTFW 2005; PFS 16; RGAL 4

Lorde, Audre Geraldine
See Lorde, Audre

Lord Houghton
See Milnes, Richard Monckton

Lord Jeffrey
See Jeffrey, Francis

Loreaux, Nichol .... CLC **65**

Lorenzini, Carlo 1826-1890 .... NCLC **54**
See also CLR 5, 120; MAICYA 1, 2; SATA
29, 100; WCH; WLIT 7

Lorenzo, Heberto Padilla
See Padilla (Lorenzo), Heberto

Loris
See Hofmannsthal, Hugo von

Loti, Pierre
See Viaud, (Louis Marie) Julien

Lottie
See Grimke, Charlotte L(ottie) Forten

Lou, Henri
See Andreas-Salome, Lou

Louie, David Wong 1954- .... CLC **70**
See also CA 139; CANR 120

Louis, Adrian C. .... NNAL
See also CA 223

Louis, Father M.
See Merton, Thomas (James)

Louise, Heidi
See Erdrich, Louise

Lovecraft, H. P. 1890-1937 .... SSC **3, 52**;
TCLC **4, 22**
See also AAYA 14; BPFB 2; CA 104; 133;
CANR 106; DA3; DAM POP; HGG;
MTCW 1, 2; MTFW 2005; RGAL 4;
SCFW 1, 2; SFW 4; SUFW

Lovecraft, Howard Phillips
See Lovecraft, H. P.

Lovelace, Earl 1935- .... CLC **51**
See also BW 2; CA 77-80; CANR 41, 72,
114; CD 5, 6; CDWLB 3; CN 1, 2, 3, 4,
5, 6, 7; DLB 125; EWL 3; MTCW 1

Lovelace, Richard 1618-1658 ..... LC **24, 158**;
PC **69**
See also BRW 2; DLB 131; EXPP; PAB;
RGEL 2

Low, Penelope Margaret
See Lively, Penelope

Lowe, Pardee 1904- .... AAL

Lowell, Amy 1874-1925 ... PC **13**; TCLC **1, 8**
See also AAYA 57; AMW; CA 104; 151;
DAM POET; DLB 54, 140; EWL 3;
EXPP; LMFS 2; MAL 5; MBL; MTCW
2; MTFW 2005; PFS 30; RGAL 4; TUS

Lowell, James Russell 1819-1891 ... NCLC **2,
90**
See also AMWS 1; CDALB 1640-1865;
DLB 1, 11, 64, 79, 189, 235; RGAL 4

Lowell, Robert (Traill Spence, Jr.)
1917-1977 .... CLC **1, 2, 3, 4, 5, 8, 9, 11,
15, 37, 124**; PC **3**; WLC **4**
See also AMW; AMWC 2; AMWR 2; CA
9-12R; 73-76; CABS 2; CAD; CANR 26,
60; CDALBS; CP 1, 2; DA; DA3; DAB;
DAC; DAM MST, NOV; DLB 5, 169;
EWL 3; MAL 5; MTCW 1, 2; MTFW
2005; PAB; PFS 6, 7; RGAL 4; WP

Lowenthal, Michael 1969- .... CLC **119**
See also CA 150; CANR 115, 164

Lowenthal, Michael Francis
See Lowenthal, Michael

MacInnes, Helen (Clark)
1907-1985 .... **CLC 27, 39**
See also BPFB 2; CA 1-4R; 117; CANR 1,
28, 58; CMW 4; CN 1, 2; CPW; DAM
POP; DLB 87; MSW; MTCW 1, 2;
MTFW 2005; SATA 22; SATA-Obit 44

Mackay, Mary 1855-1924 .... **TCLC 51**
See also CA 118; 177; DLB 34, 156; FANT;
RGEL 2; RHW; SUFW 1

Mackay, Shena 1944- .... **CLC 195**
See also CA 104; CANR 88, 139; DLB 231,
319; MTFW 2005

Mackenzie, Compton (Edward Montague)
1883-1972 .... **CLC 18; TCLC 116**
See also CA 21-22; 37-40R; CAP 2; CN 1;
DLB 34, 100; RGEL 2

Mackenzie, Henry 1745-1831 .... **NCLC 41**
See also DLB 39; RGEL 2

Mackey, Nathaniel 1947- .... **BLC 2:3; PC 49**
See also CA 153; CANR 114; CP 6, 7; DLB
169

Mackey, Nathaniel Ernest
See Mackey, Nathaniel

MacKinnon, Catharine A. 1946- .... **CLC 181**
See also CA 128; 132; CANR 73, 140, 189;
FW; MTCW 2; MTFW 2005

Mackintosh, Elizabeth
1896(?)-1952 .... **TCLC 14**
See also CA 110; CMW 4; DLB 10, 77;
MSW

Macklin, Charles 1699-1797 .... **LC 132**
See also DLB 89; RGEL 2

MacLaren, James
See Grieve, C(hristopher) M(urray)

MacLaverty, Bernard 1942- ...... **CLC 31, 243**
See also CA 116; 118; CANR 43, 88, 168;
CN 5, 6, 7; DLB 267; INT CA-118; RGSF
2

MacLean, Alistair (Stuart)
1922(?)-1987 .... **CLC 3, 13, 50, 63**
See also CA 57-60; 121; CANR 28, 61;
CMW 4; CP 2, 3, 4, 5, 6, 7; CPW; DAM
POP; DLB 276; MTCW 1; SATA 23;
SATA-Obit 50; TCWW 2

Maclean, Norman (Fitzroy)
1902-1990 .... **CLC 78; SSC 13**
See also AMWS 14; CA 102; 132; CANR
49; CPW; DAM POP; DLB 206; TCWW
2

MacLeish, Archibald 1892-1982 ... **CLC 3, 8,
14, 68; PC 47**
See also AMW; CA 9-12R; 106; CAD;
CANR 33, 63; CDALBS; CP 1, 2; DAM
POET; DFS 15; DLB 4, 7, 45; DLBY
1982; EWL 3; EXPP; MAL 5; MTCW 1,
2; MTFW 2005; PAB; PFS 5; RGAL 4;
TUS

MacLennan, (John) Hugh
1907-1990 .... **CLC 2, 14, 92**
See also CA 5-8R; 142; CANR 33; CN 1,
2, 3, 4; DAC; DAM MST; DLB 68; EWL
3; MTCW 1, 2; MTFW 2005; RGEL 2;
TWA

MacLeod, Alistair 1936- .. **CLC 56, 165; SSC
90**
See also CA 123; CCA 1; DAC; DAM
MST; DLB 60; MTCW 2; MTFW 2005;
RGSF 2; TCLE 1:2

Macleod, Fiona
See Sharp, William

MacNeice, (Frederick) Louis
1907-1963 .... **CLC 1, 4, 10, 53; PC 61**
See also BRW 7; CA 85-88; CANR 61;
DAB; DAM POET; DLB 10, 20; EWL 3;
MTCW 1, 2; MTFW 2005; RGEL 2

MacNeill, Dand
See Fraser, George MacDonald

Macpherson, James 1736-1796 .... **CMLC 28;
LC 29; PC 97**
See also BRWS 8; DLB 109, 336; RGEL 2

Macpherson, (Jean) Jay 1931- .... **CLC 14**
See also CA 5-8R; CANR 90; CP 1, 2, 3, 4,
6, 7; CWP; DLB 53

Macrobius fl. 430- .... **CMLC 48**

MacShane, Frank 1927-1999 .... **CLC 39**
See also CA 9-12R; 186; CANR 3, 33; DLB
111

Macumber, Mari
See Sandoz, Mari(e Susette)

Madach, Imre 1823-1864 .... **NCLC 19**

Madden, (Jerry) David 1933- .... **CLC 5, 15**
See also CA 1-4R; CAAS 3; CANR 4, 45;
CN 3, 4, 5, 6, 7; CSW; DLB 6; MTCW 1

Maddern, Al(an)
See Ellison, Harlan

Madhubuti, Haki R. 1942- .... **BLC 1:2; CLC
2; PC 5**
See also BW 2, 3; CA 73-76; CANR 24,
51, 73, 139; CP 2, 3, 4, 5, 6, 7; CSW;
DAM MULT, POET; DLB 5, 41; DLBD
8; EWL 3; MAL 5; MTCW 2; MTFW
2005; RGAL 4

Madison, James 1751-1836 .... **NCLC 126**
See also DLB 37

Maepenn, Hugh
See Kuttner, Henry

Maepenn, K. H.
See Kuttner, Henry

Maeterlinck, Maurice 1862-1949 .... **DC 32;
TCLC 3**
See also CA 104; 136; CANR 80; DAM
DRAM; DLB 192, 331; EW 8; EWL 3;
GFL 1789 to the Present; LMFS 2; RGWL
2, 3; SATA 66; TWA

Maginn, William 1794-1842 .... **NCLC 8**
See also DLB 110, 159

Mahapatra, Jayanta 1928- .... **CLC 33**
See also CA 73-76; CAAS 9; CANR 15,
33, 66, 87; CP 4, 5, 6, 7; DAM MULT;
DLB 323

Mahfouz, Nagib
See Mahfouz, Naguib

Mahfouz, Naguib 1911(?)-2006 . **CLC 52, 55,
153; SSC 66**
See also AAYA 49; AFW; BEST 89:2; CA
128; 253; CANR 55, 101; DA3; DAM
NOV; DLB 346; DLBY 1988; MTCW 1,
2; MTFW 2005; RGSF 2; RGWL 2, 3;
SSFS 9; WLIT 2

Mahfouz, Naguib Abdel Aziz Al-Sabilgi
See Mahfouz, Naguib

Mahfouz, Najib
See Mahfouz, Naguib

Mahfuz, Najib
See Mahfouz, Naguib

Mahon, Derek 1941- .... **CLC 27; PC 60**
See also BRWS 6; CA 113; 128; CANR 88;
CP 1, 2, 3, 4, 5, 6, 7; DLB 40; EWL 3

Maiakovskii, Vladimir
See Mayakovski, Vladimir (Vladimirovich)

Mailer, Norman 1923-2007 ... **CLC 1, 2, 3, 4,
5, 8, 11, 14, 28, 39, 74, 111, 234**
See also AAYA 31; AITN 2; AMW; AMWC
2; AMWR 2; BPFB 2; CA 9-12R; 266;
CABS 1; CANR 28, 74, 77, 130; CDALB
1968-1988; CN 1, 2, 3, 4, 5, 6, 7; CPW;
DA; DA3; DAB; DAC; DAM MST, NOV,
POP; DLB 2, 16, 28, 185, 278; DLBD 3;
DLBY 1980, 1983; EWL 3; MAL 5;
MTCW 1, 2; MTFW 2005; NFS 10;
RGAL 4; TUS

Mailer, Norman Kingsley
See Mailer, Norman

Maillet, Antonine 1929- .... **CLC 54, 118**
See also CA 115; 120; CANR 46, 74, 77,
134; CCA 1; CWW 2; DAC; DLB 60;
INT CA-120; MTCW 2; MTFW 2005

Maimonides, Moses 1135-1204 ..... **CMLC 76**
See also DLB 115

Mais, Roger 1905-1955 .... **TCLC 8**
See also BW 1, 3; CA 105; 124; CANR 82;
CDWLB 3; DLB 125; EWL 3; MTCW 1;
RGEL 2

Maistre, Joseph 1753-1821 .... **NCLC 37**
See also GFL 1789 to the Present

Maitland, Frederic William
1850-1906 .... **TCLC 65**

Maitland, Sara (Louise) 1950- .... **CLC 49**
See also BRWS 11; CA 69-72; CANR 13,
59; DLB 271; FW

Major, Clarence 1936- ...... **BLC 1:2; CLC 3,
19, 48**
See also AFAW 2; BW 2, 3; CA 21-24R;
CAAS 6; CANR 13, 25, 53, 82; CN 3, 4,
5, 6, 7; CP 2, 3, 4, 5, 6, 7; CSW; DAM
MULT; DLB 33; EWL 3; MAL 5; MSW

Major, Kevin (Gerald) 1949- .... **CLC 26**
See also AAYA 16; CA 97-100; CANR 21,
38, 112; CLR 11; DAC; DLB 60; INT
CANR-21; JRDA; MAICYA 1, 2; MAIC-
YAS 1; SATA 32, 82, 134; WYA; YAW

Maki, James
See Ozu, Yasujiro

Makin, Bathsua 1600-1675(?) .... **LC 137**

Makine, Andrei 1957-
See Makine, Andrei

Makine, Andrei 1957- .... **CLC 198**
See also CA 176; CANR 103, 162; MTFW
2005

Malabaila, Damiano
See Levi, Primo

Malamud, Bernard 1914-1986 .. **CLC 1, 2, 3,
5, 8, 9, 11, 18, 27, 44, 78, 85; SSC 15;
TCLC 129, 184; WLC 4**
See also AAYA 16; AMWS 1; BPFB 2;
BYA 15; CA 5-8R; 118; CABS 1; CANR
28, 62, 114; CDALB 1941-1968; CN 1, 2,
3, 4; CPW; DA; DA3; DAB; DAC; DAM
MST, NOV, POP; DLB 2, 28, 152; DLBY
1980, 1986; EWL 3; EXPS; LAIT 4;
LATS 1:1; MAL 5; MTCW 1, 2; MTFW
2005; NFS 27; RGAL 4; RGHL; RGSF 2;
SSFS 8, 13, 16; TUS

Malan, Herman
See Bosman, Herman Charles; Bosman,
Herman Charles

Malaparte, Curzio 1898-1957 .... **TCLC 52**
See also DLB 264

Malcolm, Dan
See Silverberg, Robert

Malcolm, Janet 1934- .... **CLC 201**
See also CA 123; CANR 89; NCFS 1

Malcolm X
See Little, Malcolm

Malebranche, Nicolas 1638-1715 .... **LC 133**
See also GFL Beginnings to 1789

Malherbe, Francois de 1555-1628 .... **LC 5**
See also DLB 327; GFL Beginnings to 1789

Mallarme, Stephane 1842-1898 ...... **NCLC 4,
41, 210; PC 4**
See also DAM POET; DLB 217; EW 7;
GFL 1789 to the Present; LMFS 2; RGWL
2, 3; TWA

Mallet-Joris, Francoise 1930- .... **CLC 11**
See also CA 65-68; CANR 17; CWW 2;
DLB 83; EWL 3; GFL 1789 to the Present

Malley, Ern
See McAuley, James Phillip

Mallon, Thomas 1951- .... **CLC 172**
See also CA 110; CANR 29, 57, 92

Mallowan, Agatha Christie
See Christie, Agatha (Mary Clarissa)

Maloff, Saul 1922- .... **CLC 5**
See also CA 33-36R

Malone, Louis
See MacNeice, (Frederick) Louis

Marquis de Sade
See Sade, Donatien Alphonse Francois
Marric, J. J.
See Creasey, John
Marryat, Frederick 1792-1848 .... **NCLC 3**
See also DLB 21, 163; RGEL 2; WCH
Marsden, James
See Creasey, John
Marsh, Edward 1872-1953 .... **TCLC 99**
Marsh, (Edith) Ngaio 1895-1982 .. **CLC 7, 53**
See also CA 9-12R; CANR 6, 58; CMW 4;
CN 1, 2, 3; CPW; DAM POP; DLB 77;
MSW; MTCW 1, 2; RGEL 2; TEA
Marshall, Alan
See Westlake, Donald E.
Marshall, Allen
See Westlake, Donald E.
Marshall, Garry 1934- .... **CLC 17**
See also AAYA 3; CA 111; SATA 60
Marshall, Paule 1929- .... **BLC 1:3, 2:3; CLC
27, 72, 253; SSC 3**
See also AFAW 1, 2; AMWS 11; BPFB 2;
BW 2, 3; CA 77-80; CANR 25, 73, 129;
CN 1, 2, 3, 4, 5, 6, 7; DA3; DAM MULT;
DLB 33, 157, 227; EWL 3; LATS 1:2;
MAL 5; MTCW 1, 2; MTFW 2005;
RGAL 4; SSFS 15
Marshallik
See Zangwill, Israel
Marsilius of Inghen c.
1340-1396 .... **CMLC 106**
Marsten, Richard
See Hunter, Evan
Marston, John 1576-1634 .... **LC 33**
See also BRW 2; DAM DRAM; DLB 58,
172; RGEL 2
Martel, Yann 1963- .... **CLC 192**
See also AAYA 67; CA 146; CANR 114;
DLB 326, 334; MTFW 2005; NFS 27
Martens, Adolphe-Adhemar
See Ghelderode, Michel de
Martha, Henry
See Harris, Mark
Marti, Jose
See Marti (y Perez), Jose (Julian)
Marti (y Perez), Jose (Julian)
1853-1895 ..... **HLC 2; NCLC 63; PC 76**
See also DAM MULT; DLB 290; HW 2;
LAW; RGWL 2, 3; WLIT 1
Martial c. 40-c. 104 .... **CMLC 35; PC 10**
See also AW 2; CDWLB 1; DLB 211;
RGWL 2, 3
Martin, Ken
See Hubbard, L. Ron
Martin, Richard
See Creasey, John
Martin, Steve 1945- .... **CLC 30, 217**
See also AAYA 53; CA 97-100; CANR 30,
100, 140; DFS 19; MTCW 1; MTFW
2005
Martin, Valerie 1948- .... **CLC 89**
See also BEST 90:2; CA 85-88; CANR 49,
89, 165
Martin, Violet Florence 1862-1915 .. **SSC 56;
TCLC 51**
Martin, Webber
See Silverberg, Robert
Martindale, Patrick Victor
See White, Patrick (Victor Martindale)
Martin du Gard, Roger
1881-1958 .... **TCLC 24**
See also CA 118; CANR 94; DLB 65, 331;
EWL 3; GFL 1789 to the Present; RGWL
2, 3
Martineau, Harriet 1802-1876 ...... **NCLC 26,
137**
See also DLB 21, 55, 159, 163, 166, 190;
FW; RGEL 2; YABC 2

Martines, Julia
See O'Faolain, Julia
Martinez, Enrique Gonzalez
See Gonzalez Martinez, Enrique
Martinez, Jacinto Benavente y
See Benavente (y Martinez), Jacinto
Martinez de la Rosa, Francisco de Paula
1787-1862 .... **NCLC 102**
See also TWA
Martinez Ruiz, Jose 1873-1967 .... **CLC 11**
See also CA 93-96; DLB 322; EW 3; EWL
3; HW 1
Martinez Sierra, Gregorio
See Martinez Sierra, Maria
Martinez Sierra, Gregorio
1881-1947 .... **TCLC 6**
See also CA 115; EWL 3
Martinez Sierra, Maria 1874-1974 .. **TCLC 6**
See also CA 250; 115; EWL 3
Martinsen, Martin
See Follett, Ken
Martinson, Harry (Edmund)
1904-1978 .... **CLC 14**
See also CA 77-80; CANR 34, 130; DLB
259, 331; EWL 3
Martyn, Edward 1859-1923 .... **TCLC 131**
See also CA 179; DLB 10; RGEL 2
Marut, Ret
See Traven, B.
Marut, Robert
See Traven, B.
Marvell, Andrew 1621-1678 .... **LC 4, 43; PC
10, 86; WLC 4**
See also BRW 2; BRWR 2; CDBLB 1660-
1789; DA; DAB; DAC; DAM MST,
POET; DLB 131; EXPP; PFS 5; RGEL 2;
TEA; WP
Marx, Karl (Heinrich)
1818-1883 .... **NCLC 17, 114**
See also DLB 129; LATS 1:1; TWA
Masaoka, Shiki -1902
See Masaoka, Tsunenori
Masaoka, Tsunenori 1867-1902 ..... **TCLC 18**
See also CA 117; 191; EWL 3; RGWL 3;
TWA
Masaoka Shiki
See Masaoka, Tsunenori
Masefield, John (Edward)
1878-1967 .... **CLC 11, 47; PC 78**
See also CA 19-20; 25-28R; CANR 33;
CAP 2; CDBLB 1890-1914; DAM POET;
DLB 10, 19, 153, 160; EWL 3; EXPP;
FANT; MTCW 1, 2; PFS 5; RGEL 2;
SATA 19
Maso, Carole 1955(?)- .... **CLC 44**
See also CA 170; CANR 148; CN 7; GLL
2; RGAL 4
Mason, Bobbie Ann 1940- ... **CLC 28, 43, 82,
154; SSC 4, 101**
See also AAYA 5, 42; AMWS 8; BPFB 2;
CA 53-56; CANR 11, 31, 58, 83, 125,
169; CDALBS; CN 5, 6, 7; CSW; DA3;
DLB 173; DLBY 1987; EWL 3; EXPS;
INT CANR-31; MAL 5; MTCW 1, 2;
MTFW 2005; NFS 4; RGAL 4; RGSF 2;
SSFS 3, 8, 20; TCLE 1:2; YAW
Mason, Ernst
See Pohl, Frederik
Mason, Hunni B.
See Sternheim, (William Adolf) Carl
Mason, Lee W.
See Malzberg, Barry N(athaniel)
Mason, Nick 1945- .... **CLC 35**
Mason, Tally
See Derleth, August (William)
Mass, Anna .... **CLC 59**
Mass, William
See Gibson, William

Massinger, Philip 1583-1640 .... **LC 70**
See also BRWS 11; DLB 58; RGEL 2
Master Lao
See Lao Tzu
Masters, Edgar Lee 1868-1950 ...... **PC 1, 36;
TCLC 2, 25; WLCS**
See also AMWS 1; CA 104; 133; CDALB
1865-1917; DA; DAC; DAM MST,
POET; DLB 54; EWL 3; EXPP; MAL 5;
MTCW 1, 2; MTFW 2005; RGAL 4;
TUS; WP
Masters, Hilary 1928- .... **CLC 48**
See also CA 25-28R; 217; CAAE 217;
CANR 13, 47, 97, 171; CN 6, 7; DLB
244
Masters, Hilary Thomas
See Masters, Hilary
Mastrosimone, William 1947- .... **CLC 36**
See also CA 186; CAD; CD 5, 6
Mathe, Albert
See Camus, Albert
Mather, Cotton 1663-1728 .... **LC 38**
See also AMWS 2; CDALB 1640-1865;
DLB 24, 30, 140; RGAL 4; TUS
Mather, Increase 1639-1723 .... **LC 38, 161**
See also DLB 24
Mathers, Marshall
See Eminem
Mathers, Marshall Bruce
See Eminem
Matheson, Richard 1926- .... **CLC 37, 267**
See also AAYA 31; CA 97-100; CANR 88,
99; DLB 8, 44; HGG; INT CA-97-100;
SCFW 1, 2; SFW 4; SUFW 2
Matheson, Richard Burton
See Matheson, Richard
Mathews, Harry 1930- .... **CLC 6, 52**
See also CA 21-24R; CAAS 6; CANR 18,
40, 98, 160; CN 5, 6, 7
Mathews, John Joseph 1894-1979 .. **CLC 84;
NNAL**
See also CA 19-20; 142; CANR 45; CAP 2;
DAM MULT; DLB 175; TCWW 1, 2
Mathias, Roland 1915-2007 .... **CLC 45**
See also CA 97-100; 263; CANR 19, 41;
CP 1, 2, 3, 4, 5, 6, 7; DLB 27
Mathias, Roland Glyn
See Mathias, Roland
Matsuo Basho 1644(?)-1694 ...... **LC 62; PC 3**
See also DAM POET; PFS 2, 7, 18; RGWL
2, 3; WP
Mattheson, Rodney
See Creasey, John
Matthew of Vendome c. 1130-c.
1200 .... **CMLC 99**
See also DLB 208
Matthews, (James) Brander
1852-1929 .... **TCLC 95**
See also CA 181; DLB 71, 78; DLBD 13
Matthews, Greg 1949- .... **CLC 45**
See also CA 135
Matthews, William (Procter III)
1942-1997 .... **CLC 40**
See also AMWS 9; CA 29-32R; 162; CAAS
18; CANR 12, 57; CP 2, 3, 4, 5, 6; DLB
5
Matthias, John (Edward) 1941- .... **CLC 9**
See also CA 33-36R; CANR 56; CP 4, 5, 6,
7
Matthiessen, F(rancis) O(tto)
1902-1950 .... **TCLC 100**
See also CA 185; DLB 63; MAL 5
Matthiessen, Peter 1927- ... **CLC 5, 7, 11, 32,
64, 245**
See also AAYA 6, 40; AMWS 5; ANW;
BEST 90:4; BPFB 2; CA 9-12R; CANR
21, 50, 73, 100, 138; CN 1, 2, 3, 4, 5, 6,

McGinley, Phyllis 1905-1978 .... **CLC 14**
See also CA 9-12R; 77-80; CANR 19; CP
1, 2; CWRI 5; DLB 11, 48; MAL 5; PFS
9, 13; SATA 2, 44; SATA-Obit 24

McGinniss, Joe 1942- .... **CLC 32**
See also AITN 2; BEST 89:2; CA 25-28R;
CANR 26, 70, 152; CPW; DLB 185; INT
CANR-26

McGivern, Maureen Daly
See Daly, Maureen

McGivern, Maureen Patricia Daly
See Daly, Maureen

McGrath, Patrick 1950- .... **CLC 55**
See also CA 136; CANR 65, 148; CN 5, 6,
7; DLB 231; HGG; SUFW 2

McGrath, Thomas (Matthew)
1916-1990 .... **CLC 28, 59**
See also AMWS 10; CA 9-12R; 132; CANR
6, 33, 95; CP 1, 2, 3, 4, 5; DAM POET;
MAL 5; MTCW 1; SATA 41; SATA-Obit
66

McGuane, Thomas 1939- .. **CLC 3, 7, 18, 45, 127**
See also AITN 2; BPFB 2; CA 49-52;
CANR 5, 24, 49, 94, 164; CN 2, 3, 4, 5,
6, 7; DLB 2, 212; DLBY 1980; EWL 3;
INT CANR-24; MAL 5; MTCW 1;
MTFW 2005; TCWW 1, 2

McGuane, Thomas Francis III
See McGuane, Thomas

McGuckian, Medbh 1950- .... **CLC 48, 174; PC 27**
See also BRWS 5; CA 143; CP 4, 5, 6, 7;
CWP; DAM POET; DLB 40

McHale, Tom 1942(?)-1982 .... **CLC 3, 5**
See also AITN 1; CA 77-80; 106; CN 1, 2,
3

McHugh, Heather 1948- .... **PC 61**
See also CA 69-72; CANR 11, 28, 55, 92;
CP 4, 5, 6, 7; CWP; PFS 24

McIlvanney, William 1936- .... **CLC 42**
See also CA 25-28R; CANR 61; CMW 4;
DLB 14, 207

McIlwraith, Maureen Mollie Hunter
See Hunter, Mollie

McInerney, Jay 1955- .... **CLC 34, 112**
See also AAYA 18; BPFB 2; CA 116; 123;
CANR 45, 68, 116, 176; CN 5, 6, 7; CPW;
DA3; DAM POP; DLB 292; INT CA-123;
MAL 5; MTCW 2; MTFW 2005

McIntyre, Vonda N. 1948- .... **CLC 18**
See also CA 81-84; CANR 17, 34, 69;
MTCW 1; SFW 4; YAW

McIntyre, Vonda Neel
See McIntyre, Vonda N.

McKay, Claude
See McKay, Festus Claudius

McKay, Festus Claudius
1889-1948 ...... **BLC 1:3; HR 1:3; PC 2; TCLC 7, 41; WLC 4**
See also AFAW 1, 2; AMWS 10; BW 1, 3;
CA 104; 124; CANR 73; DA; DAB;
DAC; DAM MST, MULT, NOV; DLB
DLB 4, 45, 51, 117; EWL 3; EXPP; GLL
2; LAIT 3; LMFS 2; MAL 5; MTCW 1,
2; MTFW 2005; PAB; PFS 4; RGAL 4;
TUS; WP

McKuen, Rod 1933- .... **CLC 1, 3**
See also AITN 1; CA 41-44R; CANR 40;
CP 1

McLoughlin, R. B.
See Mencken, H(enry) L(ouis)

McLuhan, (Herbert) Marshall
1911-1980 .... **CLC 37, 83**
See also CA 9-12R; 102; CANR 12, 34, 61;
DLB 88; INT CANR-12; MTCW 1, 2;
MTFW 2005

McMahon, Pat
See Hoch, Edward D.

McManus, Declan Patrick Aloysius
See Costello, Elvis

McMillan, Terry 1951- .. **BLCS; CLC 50, 61, 112**
See also AAYA 21; AMWS 13; BPFB 2;
BW 2, 3; CA 140; CANR 60, 104, 131;
CN 7; CPW; DA3; DAM MULT, NOV,
POP; MAL 5; MTCW 2; MTFW 2005;
RGAL 4; YAW

McMurtry, Larry 1936- .... **CLC 2, 3, 7, 11, 27, 44, 127, 250**
See also AAYA 15; AITN 2; AMWS 5;
BEST 89:2; BPFB 2; CA 5-8R; CANR
19, 43, 64, 103, 170; CDALB 1968-1988;
CN 2, 3, 4, 5, 6, 7; CPW; CSW; DA3;
DAM NOV, POP; DLB 2, 143, 256;
DLBY 1980, 1987; EWL 3; MAL 5;
MTCW 1, 2; MTFW 2005; RGAL 4;
TCWW 1, 2

McMurtry, Larry Jeff
See McMurtry, Larry

McNally, Terrence 1939- ... **CLC 4, 7, 41, 91, 252; DC 27**
See also AAYA 62; AMWS 13; CA 45-48;
CAD; CANR 2, 56, 116; CD 5, 6; DA3;
DAM DRAM; DFS 16, 19; DLB 7, 249;
EWL 3; GLL 1; MTCW 2; MTFW 2005

McNally, Thomas Michael
See McNally, T.M.

McNally, T.M. 1961- .... **CLC 82**
See also CA 246

McNamer, Deirdre 1950- .... **CLC 70**
See also CA 188; CANR 163

McNeal, Tom .... **CLC 119**
See also CA 252; CANR 185; SATA 194

McNeile, Herman Cyril
1888-1937 .... **TCLC 44**
See also CA 184; CMW 4; DLB 77

McNickle, (William) D'Arcy
1904-1977 .... **CLC 89; NNAL**
See also CA 9-12R; 85-88; CANR 5, 45;
DAM MULT; DLB 175, 212; RGAL 4;
SATA-Obit 22; TCWW 1, 2

McPhee, John 1931- .... **CLC 36**
See also AAYA 61; AMWS 3; ANW; BEST
90:1; CA 65-68; CANR 20, 46, 64, 69,
121, 165; CPW; DLB 185, 275; MTCW
1, 2; MTFW 2005; TUS

McPhee, John Angus
See McPhee, John

McPherson, James Alan, Jr.
See McPherson, James Alan

McPherson, James Alan 1943- . **BLCS; CLC 19, 77; SSC 95**
See also BW 1, 3; CA 25-28R; 273; CAAE
273; CAAS 17; CANR 24, 74, 140; CN
3, 4, 5, 6; CSW; DLB 38, 244; EWL 3;
MTCW 1; MTFW 2005; RGAL 4;
RGSF 2; SSFS 23

McPherson, William (Alexander)
1933- .... **CLC 34**
See also CA 69-72; CANR 28; INT
CANR-28

McTaggart, J. McT. Ellis
See McTaggart, John McTaggart Ellis

McTaggart, John McTaggart Ellis
1866-1925 .... **TCLC 105**
See also CA 120; DLB 262

Mda, Zakes 1948- .... **BLC 2:3; CLC 262**
See also CA 205; CANR 151, 185; CD 5,
6; DLB 225

Mda, Zanemvula
See Mda, Zakes

Mda, Zanemvula Kizito Gatyeni
See Mda, Zakes

Mead, George Herbert 1863-1931 . **TCLC 89**
See also CA 212; DLB 270

Mead, Margaret 1901-1978 .... **CLC 37**
See also AITN 1; CA 1-4R; 81-84; CANR
4; DA3; FW; MTCW 1, 2; SATA-Obit 20

Meaker, M. J.
See Meaker, Marijane

Meaker, Marijane 1927- .... **CLC 12, 35**
See also AAYA 2, 23; BYA 1, 7, 8; CA 107;
CANR 37, 63, 145, 180; CLR 29; GLL 2;
INT CA-107; JRDA; MAICYA 1, 2; MAI-
CYAS 1; MTCW 1; SAAS 1; SATA 20,
61, 99, 160; SATA-Essay 111; WYA;
YAW

Meaker, Marijane Agnes
See Meaker, Marijane

Mechthild von Magdeburg c. 1207-c.
1282 .... **CMLC 91**
See also DLB 138

Medoff, Mark (Howard) 1940- .... **CLC 6, 23**
See also AITN 1; CA 53-56; CAD; CANR
5; CD 5, 6; DAM DRAM; DFS 4; DLB
7; INT CANR-5

Medvedev, P. N.
See Bakhtin, Mikhail Mikhailovich

Meged, Aharon
See Megged, Aharon

Meged, Aron
See Megged, Aharon

Megged, Aharon 1920- .... **CLC 9**
See also CA 49-52; CAAS 13; CANR 1,
140; EWL 3; RGHL

Mehta, Deepa 1950- .... **CLC 208**

Mehta, Gita 1943- .... **CLC 179**
See also CA 225; CN 7; DNFS 2

Mehta, Ved 1934- .... **CLC 37**
See also CA 1-4R, 212; CAAE 212; CANR
2, 23, 69; DLB 323; MTCW 1; MTFW
2005

Melanchthon, Philipp 1497-1560 .... **LC 90**
See also DLB 179

Melanter
See Blackmore, R(ichard) D(oddridge)

Meleager c. 140B.C.-c. 70B.C. ...... **CMLC 53**

Melies, Georges 1861-1938 .... **TCLC 81**

Melikow, Loris
See Hofmannsthal, Hugo von

Melmoth, Sebastian
See Wilde, Oscar

Melo Neto, Joao Cabral de
See Cabral de Melo Neto, Joao

Meltzer, Milton 1915- .... **CLC 26**
See also AAYA 8, 45; BYA 2, 6; CA 13-
16R; CANR 38, 92, 107; CLR 13; DLB
61; JRDA; MAICYA 1, 2; SAAS 1; SATA
1, 50, 80, 128; SATA-Essay 124; WYA;
YAW

Melville, Herman 1819-1891 ..... **NCLC 3, 12, 29, 45, 49, 91, 93, 123, 157, 181, 193; PC 82; SSC 1, 17, 46, 95; WLC 4**
See also AAYA 25; AMW; AMWR 1;
CDALB 1640-1865; DA; DA3; DAB;
DAC; DAM MST, NOV; DLB 3, 74, 250,
254; EXPN; EXPS; GL 3; LAIT 1, 2; NFS
7, 9; RGAL 4; RGSF 2; SATA 59; SSFS
3; TUS

Members, Mark
See Powell, Anthony

Membreno, Alejandro .... **CLC 59**

Menand, Louis 1952- .... **CLC 208**
See also CA 200

Menander c. 342B.C.-c. 293B.C. .... **CMLC 9, 51, 101; DC 3**
See also AW 1; CDWLB 1; DAM DRAM;
DLB 176; LMFS 1; RGWL 2, 3

Menchu, Rigoberta 1959- .. **CLC 160; HLCS 2**
See also CA 175; CANR 135; DNFS 1;
WLIT 1

Miller, Sue 1943- .... **CLC 44**
    See also AMWS 12; BEST 90:3; CA 139;
    CANR 59, 91, 128; DA3; DAM POP;
    DLB 143
Miller, Walter M(ichael, Jr.)
    1923-1996 .... **CLC 4, 30**
    See also BPFB 2; CA 85-88; CANR 108;
    DLB 8; SCFW 1, 2; SFW 4
Millett, Kate 1934- .... **CLC 67**
    See also AITN 1; CA 73-76; CANR 32, 53,
    76, 110; DA3; DLB 246; FW; GLL 1;
    MTCW 1, 2; MTFW 2005
Millhauser, Steven 1943- ... **CLC 21, 54, 109;**
    SSC 57
    See also AAYA 76; CA 110; 111; CANR
    63, 114, 133, 189; CN 6, 7; DA3; DLB 2;
    FANT; INT CA-111; MAL 5; MTCW 2;
    MTFW 2005
Millhauser, Steven Lewis
    See Millhauser, Steven
Millin, Sarah Gertrude 1889-1968 ... **CLC 49**
    See also CA 102; 93-96; DLB 225; EWL 3
Milne, A. A. 1882-1956 .... **TCLC 6, 88**
    See also BRWS 5; CA 104; 133; CLR 1,
    26, 108; CMW 4; CWRI 5; DA3; DAB;
    DAC; DAM MST; DLB 10, 77, 100, 160;
    FANT; MAICYA 1, 2; MTCW 1, 2;
    MTFW 2005; RGEL 2; SATA 100; WCH;
    YABC 1
Milne, Alan Alexander
    See Milne, A. A.
Milner, Ron(ald) 1938-2004 .. **BLC 1:3; CLC**
    56
    See also AITN 1; BW 1; CA 73-76; 230;
    CAD; CANR 24, 81; CD 5, 6; DAM
    MULT; DLB 38; MAL 5; MTCW 1
Milnes, Richard Monckton
    1809-1885 .... **NCLC 61**
    See also DLB 32, 184
Milosz, Czeslaw 1911-2004 .... **CLC 5, 11, 22,**
    31, 56, 82, 253; PC 8; WLCS
    See also AAYA 62; CA 81-84; 230; CANR
    23, 51, 91, 126; CDWLB 4; CWW 2;
    DA3; DAM MST, POET; DLB 215, 331;
    EW 13; EWL 3; MTCW 1, 2; MTFW
    2005; PFS 16, 29; RGHL; RGWL 2, 3
Milton, John 1608-1674 ..... **LC 9, 43, 92; PC**
    19, 29; WLC 4
    See also AAYA 65; BRW 2; BRWR 2; CD-
    BLB 1660-1789; DA; DA3; DAB; DAC;
    DAM MST, POET; DLB 131, 151, 281;
    EFS 1; EXPP; LAIT 1; PAB; PFS 3, 17;
    RGEL 2; TEA; WLIT 3; WP
Min, Anchee 1957- .... **CLC 86**
    See also CA 146; CANR 94, 137; MTFW
    2005
Minehaha, Cornelius
    See Wedekind, Frank
Miner, Valerie 1947- .... **CLC 40**
    See also CA 97-100; CANR 59, 177; FW;
    GLL 2
Minimo, Duca
    See D'Annunzio, Gabriele
Minot, Susan (Anderson) 1956- ...... **CLC 44,**
    159
    See also AMWS 6; CA 134; CANR 118;
    CN 6, 7
Minus, Ed 1938- .... **CLC 39**
    See also CA 185
Mirabai 1498(?)-1550(?) .... **LC 143; PC 48**
    See also PFS 24
Miranda, Javier
    See Bioy Casares, Adolfo
Mirbeau, Octave 1848-1917 .... **TCLC 55**
    See also CA 216; DLB 123, 192; GFL 1789
    to the Present
Mirikitani, Janice 1942- .... **AAL**
    See also CA 211; DLB 312; RGAL 4

Mirk, John (?)-c. 1414 .... **LC 105**
    See also DLB 146
Miro (Ferrer), Gabriel (Francisco Victor)
    1879-1930 .... **TCLC 5**
    See also CA 104; 185; DLB 322; EWL 3
Misharin, Alexandr .... **CLC 59**
Mishima, Yukio
    See Hiraoka, Kimitake
Mishima Yukio
    See Hiraoka, Kimitake
Miss C. L. F.
    See Grimke, Charlotte L(ottie) Forten
Mister X
    See Hoch, Edward D.
Mistral, Frederic 1830-1914 .... **TCLC 51**
    See also CA 122; 213; DLB 331; GFL 1789
    to the Present
Mistral, Gabriela
    See Godoy Alcayaga, Lucila
Mistry, Rohinton 1952- ... **CLC 71, 196, 274;**
    SSC 73
    See also BRWS 10; CA 141; CANR 86,
    114; CCA 1; CN 6, 7; DAC; DLB 334;
    SSFS 6
Mitchell, Clyde
    See Ellison, Harlan; Silverberg, Robert
Mitchell, Emerson Blackhorse Barney
    1945- .... **NNAL**
    See also CA 45-48
Mitchell, James Leslie 1901-1935 .... **TCLC 4**
    See also BRWS 14; CA 104; 188; DLB 15;
    RGEL 2
Mitchell, Joni 1943- .... **CLC 12**
    See also CA 112; CCA 1
Mitchell, Joseph (Quincy)
    1908-1996 .... **CLC 98**
    See also CA 77-80; 152; CANR 69; CN 1,
    2, 3, 4, 5, 6; CSW; DLB 185; DLBY 1996
Mitchell, Margaret (Munnerlyn)
    1900-1949 .... **TCLC 11, 170**
    See also AAYA 23; BPFB 2; BYA 1; CA
    109; 125; CANR 55, 94; CDALBS; DA3;
    DAM NOV, POP; DLB 9; LAIT 2; MAL
    5; MTCW 1, 2; MTFW 2005; NFS 9;
    RGAL 4; RHW; TUS; WYAS 1; YAW
Mitchell, Peggy
    See Mitchell, Margaret (Munnerlyn)
Mitchell, S(ilas) Weir 1829-1914 .... **TCLC 36**
    See also CA 165; DLB 202; RGAL 4
Mitchell, W(illiam) O(rmond)
    1914-1998 .... **CLC 25**
    See also CA 77-80; 165; CANR 15, 43; CN
    1, 2, 3, 4, 5, 6; DAC; DAM MST; DLB
    88; TCLE 1:2
Mitchell, William (Lendrum)
    1879-1936 .... **TCLC 81**
    See also CA 213
Mitford, Mary Russell 1787-1855 ... **NCLC 4**
    See also DLB 110, 116; RGEL 2
Mitford, Nancy 1904-1973 .... **CLC 44**
    See also BRWS 10; CA 9-12R; CN 1; DLB
    191; RGEL 2
Miyamoto, (Chujo) Yuriko
    1899-1951 .... **TCLC 37**
    See also CA 170, 174; DLB 180
Miyamoto Yuriko
    See Miyamoto, (Chujo) Yuriko
Miyazawa, Kenji 1896-1933 .... **TCLC 76**
    See also CA 157; EWL 3; RGWL 3
Miyazawa Kenji
    See Miyazawa, Kenji
Mizoguchi, Kenji 1898-1956 .... **TCLC 72**
    See also CA 167
Mo, Timothy (Peter) 1950- .... **CLC 46, 134**
    See also CA 117; CANR 128; CN 5, 6, 7;
    DLB 194; MTCW 1; WLIT 4; WWE 1
Modarressi, Taghi (M.) 1931-1997 ... **CLC 44**
    See also CA 121; 134; INT CA-134

Modiano, Patrick (Jean) 1945- .... **CLC 18,**
    218
    See also CA 85-88; CANR 17, 40, 115;
    CWW 2; DLB 83, 299; EWL 3; RGHL
Mofolo, Thomas (Mokopu)
    1875(?)-1948 .... **BLC 1:3; TCLC 22**
    See also AFW; CA 121; 153; CANR 83;
    DAM MULT; DLB 225; EWL 3; MTCW
    2; MTFW 2005; WLIT 2
Mohr, Nicholasa 1938- .... **CLC 12; HLC 2**
    See also AAYA 8, 46; CA 49-52; CANR 1,
    32, 64; CLR 22; DAM MULT; DLB 145;
    HW 1, 2; JRDA; LAIT 5; LLW; MAICYA
    2; MAICYAS 1; RGAL 4; SAAS 8; SATA
    8, 97; SATA-Essay 113; WYA; YAW
Moi, Toril 1953- .... **CLC 172**
    See also CA 154; CANR 102; FW
Mojtabai, A(nn) G(race) 1938- ..... **CLC 5, 9,**
    15, 29
    See also CA 85-88; CANR 88
Moliere 1622-1673 ..... **DC 13; LC 10, 28, 64,**
    125, 127; WLC 4
    See also DA; DA3; DAB; DAC; DAM
    DRAM, MST; DFS 13, 18, 20; DLB 268;
    EW 3; GFL Beginnings to 1789; LATS
    1:1; RGWL 2, 3; TWA
Molin, Charles
    See Mayne, William (James Carter)
Molnar, Ferenc 1878-1952 .... **TCLC 20**
    See also CA 109; 153; CANR 83; CDWLB
    4; DAM DRAM; DLB 215; EWL 3;
    RGWL 2, 3
Momaday, N. Scott 1934- ...... **CLC 2, 19, 85,**
    95, 160; NNAL; PC 25; WLCS
    See also AAYA 11, 64; AMWS 4; ANW;
    BPFB 2; BYA 12; CA 25-28R; CANR 14,
    34, 68, 134; CDALBS; CN 2, 3, 4, 5, 6,
    7; CPW; DA; DA3; DAB; DAC; DAM
    MST, MULT, NOV, POP; DLB 143, 175,
    256; EWL 3; EXPP; INT CANR-14;
    LAIT 4; LATS 1:2; MAL 5; MTCW 1, 2;
    MTFW 2005; NFS 10; PFS 2, 11; RGAL
    4; SATA 48; SATA-Brief 30; TCWW 1,
    2; WP; YAW
Monette, Paul 1945-1995 .... **CLC 82**
    See also AMWS 10; CA 139; 147; CN 6;
    GLL 1
Monroe, Harriet 1860-1936 .... **TCLC 12**
    See also CA 109; 204; DLB 54, 91
Monroe, Lyle
    See Heinlein, Robert A.
Montagu, Elizabeth 1720-1800 .... **NCLC 7,**
    117
    See also FW
Montagu, Mary (Pierrepont) Wortley
    1689-1762 .... **LC 9, 57; PC 16**
    See also DLB 95, 101; FL 1:1; RGEL 2
Montagu, W. H.
    See Coleridge, Samuel Taylor
Montague, John (Patrick) 1929- ..... **CLC 13,**
    46
    See also CA 9-12R; CANR 9, 69, 121; CP
    1, 2, 3, 4, 5, 6, 7; DLB 40; EWL 3;
    MTCW 1; PFS 12; RGEL 2; TCLE 1:2
Montaigne, Michel (Eyquem) de
    1533-1592 .... **LC 8, 105; WLC 4**
    See also DA; DAB; DAC; DAM MST;
    DLB 327; EW 2; GFL Beginnings to
    1789; LMFS 1; RGWL 2, 3; TWA
Montale, Eugenio 1896-1981 ... **CLC 7, 9, 18;**
    PC 13
    See also CA 17-20R; 104; CANR 30; DLB
    114, 331; EW 11; EWL 3; MTCW 1; PFS
    22; RGWL 2, 3; TWA; WLIT 7
Montesquieu, Charles-Louis de Secondat
    1689-1755 .... **LC 7, 69**
    See also DLB 314; EW 3; GFL Beginnings
    to 1789; TWA
Montessori, Maria 1870-1952 ...... **TCLC 103**
    See also CA 115; 147

Montgomery, (Robert) Bruce
1921(?)-1978 .... **CLC 22**
See also CA 179; 104; CMW 4; DLB 87;
MSW

Montgomery, L(ucy) M(aud)
1874-1942 .... **TCLC 51, 140**
See also AAYA 12; BYA 1; CA 108; 137;
CLR 8, 91; DA3; DAC; DAM MST; DLB
92; DLBD 14; JRDA; MAICYA 1, 2;
MTCW 2; MTFW 2005; RGEL 2; SATA
100; TWA; WCH; WYA; YABC 1

Montgomery, Marion, Jr. 1925- .... **CLC 7**
See also AITN 1; CA 1-4R; CANR 3, 48,
162; CSW; DLB 6

Montgomery, Marion H. 1925-
See Montgomery, Marion, Jr.

Montgomery, Max
See Davenport, Guy (Mattison, Jr.)

Montherlant, Henry (Milon) de
1896-1972 .... **CLC 8, 19**
See also CA 85-88; 37-40R; DAM DRAM;
DLB 72, 321; EW 11; EWL 3; GFL 1789
to the Present; MTCW 1

Monty Python
See Chapman, Graham; Cleese, John
(Marwood); Gilliam, Terry; Idle, Eric;
Jones, Terence Graham Parry; Palin,
Michael

Moodie, Susanna (Strickland)
1803-1885 .... **NCLC 14, 113**
See also DLB 99

Moody, Hiram
See Moody, Rick

Moody, Hiram F. III
See Moody, Rick

Moody, Minerva
See Alcott, Louisa May

Moody, Rick 1961- .... **CLC 147**
See also CA 138; CANR 64, 112, 179;
MTFW 2005

Moody, William Vaughan
1869-1910 .... **TCLC 105**
See also CA 110; 178; DLB 7, 54; MAL 5;
RGAL 4

Mooney, Edward 1951- .... **CLC 25**
See also CA 130

Mooney, Ted
See Mooney, Edward

Moorcock, Michael 1939- ...... **CLC 5, 27, 58, 236**
See also AAYA 26; CA 45-48; CAAS 5;
CANR 2, 17, 38, 64, 122; CN 5, 6, 7;
DLB 14, 231, 261, 319; FANT; MTCW 1,
2; MTFW 2005; SATA 93, 166; SCFW 1,
2; SFW 4; SUFW 1, 2

Moorcock, Michael John
See Moorcock, Michael

Moorcock, Michael John
See Moorcock, Michael

Moore, Al
See Moore, Alan

Moore, Alan 1953- .... **CLC 230**
See also AAYA 51; CA 204; CANR 138,
184; DLB 261; MTFW 2005; SFW 4

Moore, Brian 1921-1999 ... **CLC 1, 3, 5, 7, 8, 19, 32, 90**
See also BRWS 9; CA 1-4R; 174; CANR 1,
25, 42, 63; CCA 1; CN 1, 2, 3, 4, 5, 6;
DAB; DAC; DAM MST; DLB 251; EWL
3; FANT; MTCW 1; MTFW 2005;
RGEL 2

Moore, Edward
See Muir, Edwin

Moore, G. E. 1873-1958 .... **TCLC 89**
See also DLB 262

Moore, George Augustus
1852-1933 .... **SSC 19; TCLC 7**
See also BRW 6; CA 104; 177; DLB 10,
18, 57, 135; EWL 3; RGEL 2; RGSF 2

Moore, Lorrie
See Moore, Marie Lorena

Moore, Marianne (Craig)
1887-1972 .... **CLC 1, 2, 4, 8, 10, 13, 19, 47; PC 4, 49; WLCS**
See also AMW; CA 1-4R; 33-36R; CANR
3, 61; CDALB 1929-1941; CP 1; DA;
DA3; DAB; DAC; DAM MST, POET;
DLB 45; DLBD 7; EWL 3; EXPP; FL 1:6;
MAL 5; MBL; MTCW 1, 2; MTFW 2005;
PAB; PFS 14, 17; RGAL 4; SATA 20;
TUS; WP

Moore, Marie Lorena 1957- ...... **CLC 39, 45, 68, 165**
See also AMWS 10; CA 116; CANR 39,
83, 139; CN 5, 6, 7; DLB 234; MTFW
2005; SSFS 19

Moore, Michael 1954- .... **CLC 218**
See also AAYA 53; CA 166; CANR 150

Moore, Thomas 1779-1852 .... **NCLC 6, 110**
See also DLB 96, 144; RGEL 2

Moorhouse, Frank 1938- .... **SSC 40**
See also CA 118; CANR 92; CN 3, 4, 5, 6,
7; DLB 289; RGSF 2

Mora, Pat 1942- .... **HLC 2**
See also AMWS 13; CA 129; CANR 57,
81, 112, 171; CLR 58; DAM MULT; DLB
209; HW 1, 2; LLW; MAICYA 2; MTFW
2005; SATA 92, 134, 186

Moraga, Cherrie 1952- ... **CLC 126, 250; DC 22**
See also CA 131; CANR 66, 154; DAM
MULT; DLB 82, 249; FW; GLL 1; HW 1,
2; LLW

Moran, J.L.
See Whitaker, Rod

Morand, Paul 1888-1976 .... **CLC 41; SSC 22**
See also CA 184; 69-72; DLB 65; EWL 3

Morante, Elsa 1918-1985 .... **CLC 8, 47**
See also CA 85-88; 117; CANR 35; DLB
177; EWL 3; MTCW 1, 2; MTFW 2005;
RGHL; RGWL 2, 3; WLIT 7

Moravia, Alberto
See Pincherle, Alberto

Morck, Paul
See Rolvaag, O.E.

More, Hannah 1745-1833 ...... **NCLC 27, 141**
See also DLB 107, 109, 116, 158; RGEL 2

More, Henry 1614-1687 .... **LC 9**
See also DLB 126, 252

More, Sir Thomas 1478(?)-1535 ... **LC 10, 32, 140**
See also BRWC 1; BRWS 7; DLB 136, 281;
LMFS 1; NFS 29; RGEL 2; TEA

Moreas, Jean
See Papadiamantopoulos, Johannes

Moreton, Andrew Esq.
See Defoe, Daniel

Moreton, Lee
See Boucicault, Dion

Morgan, Berry 1919-2002 .... **CLC 6**
See also CA 49-52; 208; DLB 6

Morgan, Claire
See Highsmith, Patricia

Morgan, Edwin 1920- .... **CLC 31**
See also BRWS 9; CA 5-8R; CANR 3, 43,
90; CP 1, 2, 3, 4, 5, 6, 7; DLB 27

Morgan, Edwin George
See Morgan, Edwin

Morgan, (George) Frederick
1922-2004 .... **CLC 23**
See also CA 17-20R; 224; CANR 21, 144;
CP 2, 3, 4, 5, 6, 7

Morgan, Harriet
See Mencken, H(enry) L(ouis)

Morgan, Jane
See Cooper, James Fenimore

Morgan, Janet 1945- .... **CLC 39**
See also CA 65-68

Morgan, Lady 1776(?)-1859 .... **NCLC 29**
See also DLB 116, 158; RGEL 2

Morgan, Robin (Evonne) 1941- .... **CLC 2**
See also CA 69-72; CANR 29, 68; FW;
GLL 2; MTCW 1; SATA 80

Morgan, Scott
See Kuttner, Henry

Morgan, Seth 1949(?)-1990 .... **CLC 65**
See also CA 185; 132

**Morgenstern, Christian (Otto Josef
Wolfgang)** 1871-1914 .... **TCLC 8**
See also CA 105; 191; EWL 3

Morgenstern, S.
See Goldman, William

Mori, Rintaro
See Mori Ogai

Mori, Toshio 1910-1980 ... **AAL; SSC 83, 123**
See also CA 116; 244; DLB 312; RGSF 2

Moricz, Zsigmond 1879-1942 .... **TCLC 33**
See also CA 165; DLB 215; EWL 3

Morike, Eduard (Friedrich)
1804-1875 .... **NCLC 10, 201**
See also DLB 133; RGWL 2, 3

Morin, Jean-Paul
See Whitaker, Rod

Mori Ogai 1862-1922 .... **TCLC 14**
See also CA 110; 164; DLB 180; EWL 3;
MJW; RGWL 3; TWA

Moritz, Karl Philipp 1756-1793 .... **LC 2, 162**
See also DLB 94

Morland, Peter Henry
See Faust, Frederick (Schiller)

Morley, Christopher (Darlington)
1890-1957 .... **TCLC 87**
See also CA 112; 213; DLB 9; MAL 5;
RGAL 4

Morren, Theophil
See Hofmannsthal, Hugo von

Morris, Bill 1952- .... **CLC 76**
See also CA 225

Morris, Julian
See West, Morris L(anglo)

Morris, Steveland Judkins (?)-
See Wonder, Stevie

Morris, William 1834-1896 . **NCLC 4; PC 55**
See also BRW 5; CDBLB 1832-1890; DLB
18, 35, 57, 156, 178, 184; FANT; RGEL
2; SFW 4; SUFW

Morris, Wright (Marion) 1910-1998 . **CLC 1, 3, 7, 18, 37; TCLC 107**
See also AMW; CA 9-12R; 167; CANR 21,
81; CN 1, 2, 3, 4, 5, 6; DLB 2, 206, 218;
DLBY 1981; EWL 3; MAL 5; MTCW 1,
2; MTFW 2005; RGAL 4; TCWW 1, 2

Morrison, Arthur 1863-1945 .... **SSC 40; TCLC 72**
See also CA 120; 157; CMW 4; DLB 70,
135, 197; RGEL 2

Morrison, Chloe Anthony Wofford
See Morrison, Toni

Morrison, James Douglas
1943-1971 .... **CLC 17**
See also CA 73-76; CANR 40

Morrison, Jim
See Morrison, James Douglas

Morrison, John Gordon 1904-1998 ... **SSC 93**
See also CA 103; CANR 92; DLB 260

Morrison, Toni 1931- . **BLC 1:3, 2:3; CLC 4, 10, 22, 55, 81, 87, 173, 194; WLC 4**
See also AAYA 1, 22, 61; AFAW 1, 2;
AMWC 1; AMWS 3; BPFB 2; BW 2, 3;
CA 29-32R; CANR 27, 42, 67, 113, 124;
CDALB 1968-1988; CLR 99; CN 3, 4, 5,
6, 7; CPW; DA; DA3; DAB; DAC; DAM
MST, MULT, NOV, POP; DLB 6, 33, 143,
331; DLBY 1981; EWL 3; EXPN; FL 1:6;
FW; GL 3; LAIT 2, 4; LATS 1:2; LMFS
2; MAL 5; MBL; MTCW 1, 2; MTFW

2005; NFS 1, 6, 8, 14; RGAL 4; RHW; SATA 57, 144; SSFS 5; TCLE 1:2; TUS; YAW

Morrison, Van 1945- .... **CLC 21**
See also CA 116; 168

Morrissy, Mary 1957- .... **CLC 99**
See also CA 205; DLB 267

Mortimer, John 1923-2009 .... **CLC 28, 43**
See also CA 13-16R; CANR 21, 69, 109, 172; CBD; CD 5, 6; CDBLB 1960 to Present; CMW 4; CN 5, 6, 7; CPW; DA3; DAM DRAM, POP; DLB 13, 245, 271; INT CANR-21; MSW; MTCW 1, 2; MTFW 2005; RGEL 2

Mortimer, John Clifford
See Mortimer, John

Mortimer, Penelope (Ruth)
1918-1999 .... **CLC 5**
See also CA 57-60; 187; CANR 45, 88; CN 1, 2, 3, 4, 5, 6

Mortimer, Sir John
See Mortimer, John

Morton, Anthony
See Creasey, John

Morton, Thomas 1579(?)-1647(?) .... **LC 72**
See also DLB 24; RGEL 2

Mosca, Gaetano 1858-1941 .... **TCLC 75**

Moses, Daniel David 1952- .... **NNAL**
See also CA 186; CANR 160; DLB 334

Mosher, Howard Frank 1943- .... **CLC 62**
See also CA 139; CANR 65, 115, 181

Mosley, Nicholas 1923- .... **CLC 43, 70**
See also CA 69-72; CANR 41, 60, 108, 158; CN 1, 2, 3, 4, 5, 6, 7; DLB 14, 207

Mosley, Walter 1952- .... **BLCS; CLC 97, 184**
See also AAYA 57; AMWS 13; BPFB 2; BW 2; CA 142; CANR 57, 92, 136, 172; CMW 4; CN 7; CPW; DA3; DAM MULT, POP; DLB 306; MSW; MTCW 2; MTFW 2005

Moss, Howard 1922-1987 . **CLC 7, 14, 45, 50**
See also CA 1-4R; 123; CANR 1, 44; CP 1, 2, 3, 4; DAM POET; DLB 5

Mossgiel, Rab
See Burns, Robert

Motion, Andrew 1952- .... **CLC 47**
See also BRWS 7; CA 146; CANR 90, 142; CP 4, 5, 6, 7; DLB 40; MTFW 2005

Motion, Andrew Peter
See Motion, Andrew

Motley, Willard (Francis)
1909-1965 .... **CLC 18**
See also AMWS 17; BW 1; CA 117; 106; CANR 88; DLB 76, 143

Motoori, Norinaga 1730-1801 .... **NCLC 45**

Mott, Michael (Charles Alston)
1930- .... **CLC 15, 34**
See also CA 5-8R; CAAS 7; CANR 7, 29

Mountain Wolf Woman 1884-1960 . **CLC 92; NNAL**
See also CA 144; CANR 90

Moure, Erin 1955- .... **CLC 88**
See also CA 113; CP 5, 6, 7; CWP; DLB 60

Mourning Dove 1885(?)-1936 .... **NNAL**
See also CA 144; CANR 90; DAM MULT; DLB 175, 221

Mowat, Farley 1921- .... **CLC 26**
See also AAYA 1, 50; BYA 2; CA 1-4R; CANR 4, 24, 42, 68, 108; CLR 20; CPW; DAC; DAM MST; DLB 68; INT CANR-24; JRDA; MAICYA 1, 2; MTCW 1, 2; MTFW 2005; SATA 3, 55; YAW

Mowat, Farley McGill
See Mowat, Farley

Mowatt, Anna Cora 1819-1870 ..... **NCLC 74**
See also RGAL 4

Mo Yan
See Moye, Guan

Moye, Guan 1956(?)- .... **CLC 257**
See also CA 201; EWL 3; RGWL 3

Mo Yen
See Moye, Guan

Moyers, Bill 1934- .... **CLC 74**
See also AITN 2; CA 61-64; CANR 31, 52, 148

Mphahlele, Es'kia 1919-2008 .... **BLC 1:3; CLC 25, 133**
See also AFW; BW 2, 3; CA 81-84; 278; CANR 26, 76; CDWLB 3; CN 4, 5, 6; DA3; DAM MULT; DLB 125, 225; EWL 3; MTCW 2; MTFW 2005; RGSF 2; SATA 119; SATA-Obit 198; SSFS 11

Mphahlele, Ezekiel
See Mphahlele, Es'kia

Mphahlele, Zeke
See Mphahlele, Es'kia

Mqhayi, S(amuel) E(dward) K(rune Loliwe)
1875-1945 .... **BLC 1:3; TCLC 25**
See also CA 153; CANR 87; DAM MULT

Mrozek, Slawomir 1930- .... **CLC 3, 13**
See also CA 13-16R; CAAS 10; CANR 29; CDWLB 4; CWW 2; DLB 232; EWL 3; MTCW 1

Mrs. Belloc-Lowndes
See Lowndes, Marie Adelaide (Belloc)

Mrs. Fairstar
See Horne, Richard Henry Hengist

M'Taggart, John M'Taggart Ellis
See McTaggart, John McTaggart Ellis

Mtwa, Percy (?)- .... **CLC 47**
See also CD 6

Mueller, Lisel 1924- .... **CLC 13, 51; PC 33**
See also CA 93-96; CP 6, 7; DLB 105; PFS 9, 13

Muggeridge, Malcolm (Thomas)
1903-1990 .... **TCLC 120**
See also AITN 1; CA 101; CANR 33, 63; MTCW 1, 2

Muhammad 570-632 .... **WLCS**
See also DA; DAB; DAC; DAM MST; DLB 311

Muir, Edwin 1887-1959 . **PC 49; TCLC 2, 87**
See also BRWS 6; CA 104; 193; DLB 20, 100, 191; EWL 3; RGEL 2

Muir, John 1838-1914 .... **TCLC 28**
See also AMWS 9; ANW; CA 165; DLB 186, 275

Mujica Lainez, Manuel 1910-1984 ... **CLC 31**
See also CA 81-84; 112; CANR 32; EWL 3; HW 1

Mukherjee, Bharati 1940- ..... **AAL; CLC 53, 115, 235; SSC 38**
See also AAYA 46; BEST 89:2; CA 107, 232; CAAE 232; CANR 45, 72, 128; CN 5, 6, 7; DAM NOV; DLB 60, 218, 323; DNFS 1, 2; EWL 3; FW; MAL 5; MTCW 1, 2; MTFW 2005; RGAL 4; RGSF 2; SSFS 7, 24; TUS; WWE 1

Muldoon, Paul 1951- .... **CLC 32, 72, 166**
See also BRWS 4; CA 113; 129; CANR 52, 91, 176; CP 2, 3, 4, 5, 6, 7; DAM POET; DLB 40; INT CA-129; PFS 7, 22; TCLE 1:2

Mulisch, Harry (Kurt Victor)
1927- .... **CLC 42, 270**
See also CA 9-12R; CANR 6, 26, 56, 110; CWW 2; DLB 299; EWL 3

Mull, Martin 1943- .... **CLC 17**
See also CA 105

Muller, Wilhelm .... **NCLC 73**

Mulock, Dinah Maria
See Craik, Dinah Maria (Mulock)

Multatuli 1820-1881 .... **NCLC 165**
See also RGWL 2, 3

Munday, Anthony 1560-1633 .... **LC 87**
See also DLB 62, 172; RGEL 2

Munford, Robert 1737(?)-1783 .... **LC 5**
See also DLB 31

Mungo, Raymond 1946- .... **CLC 72**
See also CA 49-52; CANR 2

Munro, Alice 1931- .... **CLC 6, 10, 19, 50, 95, 222; SSC 3, 95; WLCS**
See also AITN 2; BPFB 2; CA 33-36R; CANR 33, 53, 75, 114, 177; CCA 1; CN 1, 2, 3, 4, 5, 6, 7; DA3; DAC; DAM MST, NOV; DLB 53; EWL 3; MTCW 1, 2; MTFW 2005; NFS 27; RGEL 2; RGSF 2; SATA 29; SSFS 5, 13, 19; TCLE 1:2; WWE 1

Munro, H(ector) H(ugh) 1870-1916 . **SSC 12, 115; TCLC 3; WLC 5**
See also AAYA 56; BRWS 6; BYA 11; CA 104; 130; CANR 104; CDBLB 1890-1914; DA; DA3; DAB; DAC; DAM MST, NOV; DLB 34, 162; EXPS; LAIT 2; MTCW 1, 2; MTFW 2005; RGEL 2; SSFS 1, 15; SUFW

Munro, Hector H.
See Munro, H(ector) H(ugh)

Murakami, Haruki 1949- .... **CLC 150, 274**
See also CA 165; CANR 102, 146; CWW 2; DLB 182; EWL 3; MJW; RGWL 3; SFW 4; SSFS 23

Murakami Haruki
See Murakami, Haruki

Murasaki, Lady
See Murasaki Shikibu

Murasaki Shikibu 978(?)-1026(?) .. **CMLC 1, 79**
See also EFS 2; LATS 1:1; RGWL 2, 3

Murdoch, Iris 1919-1999 .. **CLC 1, 2, 3, 4, 6, 8, 11, 15, 22, 31, 51; TCLC 171**
See also BRWS 1; CA 13-16R; 179; CANR 8, 43, 68, 103, 142; CBD; CDBLB 1960 to Present; CN 1, 2, 3, 4, 5, 6; CWD; DA3; DAB; DAC; DAM MST, NOV; DLB 14, 194, 233, 326; EWL 3; INT CANR-8; MTCW 1, 2; MTFW 2005; NFS 18; RGEL 2; TCLE 1:2; TEA; WLIT 4

Murfree, Mary Noailles 1850-1922 .. **SSC 22; TCLC 135**
See also CA 122; 176; DLB 12, 74; RGAL 4

Murglie
See Murnau, F.W.

Murnau, Friedrich Wilhelm
See Murnau, F.W.

Murnau, F.W. 1888-1931 .... **TCLC 53**
See also CA 112

Murphy, Richard 1927- .... **CLC 41**
See also BRWS 5; CA 29-32R; CP 1, 2, 3, 4, 5, 6, 7; DLB 40; EWL 3

Murphy, Sylvia 1937- .... **CLC 34**
See also CA 121

Murphy, Thomas (Bernard) 1935- ... **CLC 51**
See also CA 101; DLB 310

Murphy, Tom
See Murphy, Thomas (Bernard)

Murray, Albert 1916- .... **BLC 2:3; CLC 73**
See also BW 2; CA 49-52; CANR 26, 52, 78, 160; CN 7; CSW; DLB 38; MTFW 2005

Murray, Albert L.
See Murray, Albert

Murray, James Augustus Henry
1837-1915 .... **TCLC 117**

Murray, Judith Sargent
1751-1820 .... **NCLC 63**
See also DLB 37, 200

Murray, Les(lie Allan) 1938- .... **CLC 40**
See also BRWS 7; CA 21-24R; CANR 11, 27, 56, 103; CP 1, 2, 3, 4, 5, 6, 7; DAM POET; DLB 289; DLBY 2001; EWL 3; RGEL 2

Murry, J. Middleton
See Murry, John Middleton
Murry, John Middleton
1889-1957 .... **TCLC 16**
See also CA 118; 217; DLB 149
Musgrave, Susan 1951- .... **CLC 13, 54**
See also CA 69-72; CANR 45, 84, 181;
CCA 1; CP 2, 3, 4, 5, 6, 7; CWP
Musil, Robert (Edler von)
1880-1942 ... **SSC 18; TCLC 12, 68, 213**
See also CA 109; CANR 55, 84; CDWLB
2; DLB 81, 124; EW 9; EWL 3; MTCW
2; RGSF 2; RGWL 2, 3
Muske, Carol
See Muske-Dukes, Carol
Muske, Carol Anne
See Muske-Dukes, Carol
Muske-Dukes, Carol 1945- .... **CLC 90**
See also CA 65-68, 203; CAAE 203; CANR
32, 70, 181; CWP; PFS 24
Muske-Dukes, Carol Ann
See Muske-Dukes, Carol
Muske-Dukes, Carol Anne
See Muske-Dukes, Carol
Musset, Alfred de 1810-1857 . **DC 27; NCLC 7, 150**
See also DLB 192, 217; EW 6; GFL 1789
to the Present; RGWL 2, 3; TWA
Musset, Louis Charles Alfred de
See Musset, Alfred de
Mussolini, Benito (Amilcare Andrea)
1883-1945 .... **TCLC 96**
See also CA 116
Mutanabbi, Al-
See al-Mutanabbi, Ahmad ibn al-Husayn
Abu al-Tayyib al-Jufi al-Kindi
My Brother's Brother
See Chekhov, Anton (Pavlovich)
Myers, L(eopold) H(amilton)
1881-1944 .... **TCLC 59**
See also CA 157; DLB 15; EWL 3; RGEL
2
Myers, Walter Dean 1937- ...... **BLC 1:3; 2:3; CLC 35**
See also AAYA 4, 23; BW 2; BYA 6, 8, 11;
CA 33-36R; CANR 20, 42, 67, 108, 184;
CLR 4, 16, 35, 110; DAM MULT, NOV;
DLB 33; INT CANR-20; JRDA; LAIT 5;
MAICYA 1, 2; MAICYAS 1; MTCW 2;
MTFW 2005; SAAS 2; SATA 41, 71, 109,
157, 193; SATA-Brief 27; WYA; YAW
Myers, Walter M.
See Myers, Walter Dean
Myles, Symon
See Follett, Ken
Nabokov, Vladimir (Vladimirovich)
1899-1977 .... **CLC 1, 2, 3, 6, 8, 11, 15, 23, 44, 46, 64; SSC 11, 86; TCLC 108, 189; WLC 4**
See also AAYA 45; AMW; AMWC 1;
AMWR 1; BPFB 2; CA 5-8R; 69-72;
CANR 20, 102; CDALB 1941-1968; CN
1, 2; CP 2; DA; DA3; DAB; DAC; DAM
MST, NOV; DLB 2, 244, 278, 317; DLBD
3; DLBY 1980, 1991; EWL 3; EXPS;
LATS 1:2; MAL 5; MTCW 1, 2; MTFW
2005; NCFS 4; NFS 9; RGAL 4; RGSF
2; SSFS 6, 15; TUS
Naevius c. 265B.C.-201B.C. .... **CMLC 37**
See also DLB 211
Nagai, Kafu 1879-1959 .... **TCLC 51**
See also CA 117; 276; DLB 180; EWL 3;
MJW
Nagai, Sokichi
See Nagai, Kafu
Nagai Kafu
See Nagai, Kafu
na gCopaleen, Myles
See O Nuallain, Brian

na Gopaleen, Myles
See O Nuallain, Brian
Nagy, Laszlo 1925-1978 .... **CLC 7**
See also CA 129; 112
Naidu, Sarojini 1879-1949 .... **TCLC 80**
See also EWL 3; RGEL 2
Naipaul, Shiva 1945-1985 .... **CLC 32, 39; TCLC 153**
See also CA 110; 112; 116; CANR 33; CN
2, 3; DA3; DAM NOV; DLB 157; DLBY
1985; EWL 3; MTCW 1, 2; MTFW 2005
Naipaul, Shivadhar Srinivasa
See Naipaul, Shiva
Naipaul, V.S. 1932- .. **CLC 4, 7, 9, 13, 18, 37, 105, 199; SSC 38, 121**
See also BPFB 2; BRWS 1; CA 1-4R;
CANR 1, 33, 51, 91, 126; CDBLB 1960
to Present; CDWLB 3; CN 1, 2, 3, 4, 5,
6, 7; DA3; DAB; DAC; DAM MST,
NOV; DLB 125, 204, 207, 326, 331;
DLBY 1985, 2001; EWL 3; LATS 1:2;
MTCW 1, 2; MTFW 2005; RGEL 2;
RGSF 2; TWA; WLIT 4; WWE 1
Nakos, Lilika 1903(?)-1989 .... **CLC 29**
Napoleon
See Yamamoto, Hisaye
Narayan, R.K. 1906-2001 ...... **CLC 7, 28, 47, 121, 211; SSC 25**
See also BPFB 2; CA 81-84; 196; CANR
33, 61, 112; CN 1, 2, 3, 4, 5, 6, 7; DA3;
DAM NOV; DLB 323; DNFS 1; EWL 3;
MTCW 1, 2; MTFW 2005; RGEL 2;
RGSF 2; SATA 62; SSFS 5; WWE 1
Nash, Frediric Ogden
See Nash, Ogden
Nash, Ogden 1902-1971 ...... **CLC 23; PC 21; TCLC 109**
See also CA 13-14; 29-32R; CANR 34, 61,
185; CAP 1; CP 1; DAM POET; DLB 11;
MAICYA 1, 2; MAL 5; MTCW 1, 2;
RGAL 4; SATA 2, 46; WP
Nashe, Thomas 1567-1601(?) . **LC 41, 89; PC 82**
See also DLB 167; RGEL 2
Nathan, Daniel
See Dannay, Frederic
Nathan, George Jean 1882-1958 .... **TCLC 18**
See also CA 114; 169; DLB 137; MAL 5
Natsume, Kinnosuke
See Natsume, Soseki
Natsume, Soseki 1867-1916 .... **TCLC 2, 10**
See also CA 104; 195; DLB 180; EWL 3;
MJW; RGWL 2, 3; TWA
Natsume Soseki
See Natsume, Soseki
Natti, (Mary) Lee 1919- .... **CLC 17**
See also CA 5-8R; CANR 2; CWRI 5;
SAAS 3; SATA 1, 67
Navarre, Marguerite de
See de Navarre, Marguerite
Naylor, Gloria 1950- . **BLC 1:3; CLC 28, 52, 156, 261; WLCS**
See also AAYA 6, 39; AFAW 1, 2; AMWS
8; BW 2, 3; CA 107; CANR 27, 51, 74,
130; CN 4, 5, 6, 7; CPW; DA; DA3;
DAC; DAM MST, MULT, NOV, POP;
DLB 173; EWL 3; FW; MAL 5; MTCW
1, 2; MTFW 2005; NFS 4, 7; RGAL 4;
TCLE 1:2; TUS
Neal, John 1793-1876 .... **NCLC 161**
See also DLB 1, 59, 243; FW; RGAL 4
Neff, Debra .... **CLC 59**
Neihardt, John Gneisenau
1881-1973 .... **CLC 32**
See also CA 13-14; CANR 65; CAP 1; DLB
9, 54, 256; LAIT 2; TCWW 1, 2
Nekrasov, Nikolai Alekseevich
1821-1878 .... **NCLC 11**
See also DLB 277

Nelligan, Emile 1879-1941 .... **TCLC 14**
See also CA 114; 204; DLB 92; EWL 3
Nelson, Alice Ruth Moore Dunbar
1875-1935 .... **HR 1:2**
See also BW 1, 3; CA 122; 124; CANR 82;
DLB 50; FW; MTCW 1
Nelson, Willie 1933- .... **CLC 17**
See also CA 107; CANR 114, 178
Nemerov, Howard 1920-1991 .... **CLC 2, 6, 9, 36; PC 24; TCLC 124**
See also AMW; CA 1-4R; 134; CABS 2;
CANR 1, 27, 53; CN 1, 2, 3; CP 1, 2, 3,
4, 5; DAM POET; DLB 5, 6; DLBY 1983;
EWL 3; INT CANR-27; MAL 5; MTCW
1, 2; MTFW 2005; PFS 10, 14; RGAL 4
Nepos, Cornelius c. 99B.C.-c.
24B.C. .... **CMLC 89**
See also DLB 211
Neruda, Pablo 1904-1973 .. **CLC 1, 2, 5, 7, 9, 28, 62; HLC 2; PC 4, 64; WLC 4**
See also CA 19-20; 45-48; CANR 131; CAP
2; DA; DA3; DAB; DAC; DAM MST,
MULT, POET; DLB 283, 331; DNFS 2;
EWL 3; HW 1; LAW; MTCW 1, 2;
MTFW 2005; PFS 11, 28; RGWL 2, 3;
TWA; WLIT 1; WP
Nerval, Gerard de 1808-1855 ... **NCLC 1, 67; PC 13; SSC 18**
See also DLB 217; EW 6; GFL 1789 to the
Present; RGSF 2; RGWL 2, 3
Nervo, (Jose) Amado (Ruiz de)
1870-1919 .... **HLCS 2; TCLC 11**
See also CA 109; 131; DLB 290; EWL 3;
HW 1; LAW
Nesbit, Malcolm
See Chester, Alfred
Nessi, Pio Baroja y
See Baroja, Pio
Nestroy, Johann 1801-1862 .... **NCLC 42**
See also DLB 133; RGWL 2, 3
Netterville, Luke
See O'Grady, Standish (James)
Neufeld, John (Arthur) 1938- .... **CLC 17**
See also AAYA 11; CA 25-28R; CANR 11,
37, 56; CLR 52; MAICYA 1, 2; SAAS 3;
SATA 6, 81, 131; SATA-Essay 131; YAW
Neumann, Alfred 1895-1952 .... **TCLC 100**
See also CA 183; DLB 56
Neumann, Ferenc
See Molnar, Ferenc
Neville, Emily Cheney 1919- .... **CLC 12**
See also BYA 2; CA 5-8R; CANR 3, 37,
85; JRDA; MAICYA 1, 2; SAAS 2; SATA
1; YAW
Newbound, Bernard Slade 1930- .... **CLC 11, 46**
See also CA 81-84; CAAS 9; CANR 49;
CCA 1; CD 5, 6; DAM DRAM; DLB 53
Newby, P(ercy) H(oward)
1918-1997 .... **CLC 2, 13**
See also CA 5-8R; 161; CANR 32, 67; CN
1, 2, 3, 4, 5, 6; DAM NOV; DLB 15, 326;
MTCW 1; RGEL 2
Newcastle
See Cavendish, Margaret Lucas
Newlove, Donald 1928- .... **CLC 6**
See also CA 29-32R; CANR 25
Newlove, John (Herbert) 1938- .... **CLC 14**
See also CA 21-24R; CANR 9, 25; CP 1, 2,
3, 4, 5, 6, 7
Newman, Charles 1938-2006 .... **CLC 2, 8**
See also CA 21-24R; 249; CANR 84; CN
3, 4, 5, 6
Newman, Charles Hamilton
See Newman, Charles
Newman, Edwin (Harold) 1919- ...... **CLC 14**
See also AITN 1; CA 69-72; CANR 5

Newman, John Henry 1801-1890 . **NCLC 38, 99**
See also BRWS 7; DLB 18, 32, 55; RGEL 2

Newton, (Sir) Isaac 1642-1727 ...... **LC 35, 53**
See also DLB 252

Newton, Suzanne 1936- .... **CLC 35**
See also BYA 7; CA 41-44R; CANR 14; JRDA; SATA 5, 77

New York Dept. of Ed. .... **CLC 70**

Nexo, Martin Andersen
1869-1954 .... **TCLC 43**
See also CA 202; DLB 214; EWL 3

Nezval, Vitezslav 1900-1958 .... **TCLC 44**
See also CA 123; CDWLB 4; DLB 215; EWL 3

Ng, Fae Myenne 1956- .... **CLC 81**
See also BYA 11; CA 146

Ngcobo, Lauretta 1931- .... **BLC 2:3**
See also CA 165

Ngema, Mbongeni 1955- .... **CLC 57**
See also BW 2; CA 143; CANR 84; CD 5, 6

Ngugi, James T.
See Ngugi wa Thiong'o

Ngugi, James Thiong'o
See Ngugi wa Thiong'o

Ngugi wa Thiong'o 1938- .... **BLC 1:3, 2:3; CLC 3, 7, 13, 36, 182**
See also AFW; BRWS 8; BW 2; CA 81-84; CANR 27, 58, 164; CD 3, 4, 5, 6, 7; CD-WLB 3; CN 1, 2; DAM MULT, NOV; DLB 125; DNFS 2; EWL 3; MTCW 1, 2; MTFW 2005; RGEL 2; WWE 1

Niatum, Duane 1938- .... **NNAL**
See also CA 41-44R; CANR 21, 45, 83; DLB 175

Nichol, B(arrie) P(hillip) 1944-1988 . **CLC 18**
See also CA 53-56; CP 1, 2, 3, 4; DLB 53; SATA 66

Nicholas of Autrecourt c.
1298-1369 .... **CMLC 108**

Nicholas of Cusa 1401-1464 .... **LC 80**
See also DLB 115

Nichols, John 1940- .... **CLC 38**
See also AMWS 13; CA 9-12R, 190; CAAE 190; CAAS 2; CANR 6, 70, 121, 185; DLBY 1982; LATS 1:2; MTFW 2005; TCWW 1, 2

Nichols, Leigh
See Koontz, Dean R.

Nichols, Peter (Richard) 1927- .... **CLC 5, 36, 65**
See also CA 104; CANR 33, 86; CBD; CD 5, 6; DLB 13, 245; MTCW 1

Nicholson, Linda .... **CLC 65**

Ni Chuilleanain, Eilean 1942- .... **PC 34**
See also CA 126; CANR 53, 83; CP 5, 6, 7; CWP; DLB 40

Nicolas, F. R. E.
See Freeling, Nicolas

Niedecker, Lorine 1903-1970 ..... **CLC 10, 42; PC 42**
See also CA 25-28; CAP 2; DAM POET; DLB 48

Nietzsche, Friedrich (Wilhelm)
1844-1900 .... **TCLC 10, 18, 55**
See also CA 107; 121; CDWLB 2; DLB 129; EW 7; RGWL 2, 3; TWA

Nievo, Ippolito 1831-1861 .... **NCLC 22**

Nightingale, Anne Redmon 1943- .... **CLC 22**
See also CA 103; DLBY 1986

Nightingale, Florence 1820-1910 ... **TCLC 85**
See also CA 188; DLB 166

Nijo Yoshimoto 1320-1388 .... **CMLC 49**
See also DLB 203

Nik. T. O.
See Annensky, Innokenty (Fyodorovich)

Nin, Anais 1903-1977 ..... **CLC 1, 4, 8, 11, 14, 60, 127; SSC 10**
See also AITN 2; AMWS 10; BPFB 2; CA 13-16R; 69-72; CANR 22, 53; CN 1, 2; DAM NOV, POP; DLB 2, 4, 152; EWL 3; GLL 2; MAL 5; MBL; MTCW 1, 2; MTFW 2005; RGAL 4; RGSF 2

Nisbet, Robert A(lexander)
1913-1996 .... **TCLC 117**
See also CA 25-28R; 153; CANR 17; INT CANR-17

Nishida, Kitaro 1870-1945 .... **TCLC 83**

Nishiwaki, Junzaburo 1894-1982 .... **PC 15**
See also CA 194; 107; EWL 3; MJW; RGWL 3

Nissenson, Hugh 1933- .... **CLC 4, 9**
See also CA 17-20R; CANR 27, 108, 151; CN 5, 6; DLB 28, 335

Nister, Der
See Der Nister

Niven, Larry 1938- .... **CLC 8**
See also AAYA 27; BPFB 2; BYA 10; CA 21-24R, 207; CAAE 207; CAAS 12; CANR 14, 44, 66, 113, 155; CPW; DAM POP; DLB 8; MTCW 1, 2; SATA 95, 171; SCFW 1, 2; SFW 4

Niven, Laurence VanCott
See Niven, Larry

Nixon, Agnes Eckhardt 1927- .... **CLC 21**
See also CA 110

Nizan, Paul 1905-1940 .... **TCLC 40**
See also CA 161; DLB 72; EWL 3; GFL 1789 to the Present

Nkosi, Lewis 1936- .... **BLC 1:3; CLC 45**
See also BW 1, 3; CA 65-68; CANR 27, 81; CBD; CD 5, 6; DAM MULT; DLB 157, 225; WWE 1

Nodier, (Jean) Charles (Emmanuel)
1780-1844 .... **NCLC 19**
See also DLB 119; GFL 1789 to the Present

Noguchi, Yone 1875-1947 .... **TCLC 80**

Nolan, Brian
See O Nuallain, Brian

Nolan, Christopher 1965-2009 .... **CLC 58**
See also CA 111; CANR 88

Noon, Jeff 1957- .... **CLC 91**
See also CA 148; CANR 83; DLB 267; SFW 4

Norden, Charles
See Durrell, Lawrence (George)

Nordhoff, Charles Bernard
1887-1947 .... **TCLC 23**
See also CA 108; 211; DLB 9; LAIT 1; RHW 1; SATA 23

Norfolk, Lawrence 1963- .... **CLC 76**
See also CA 144; CANR 85; CN 6, 7; DLB 267

Norman, Marsha (Williams) 1947- . **CLC 28, 186; DC 8**
See also CA 105; CABS 3; CAD; CANR 41, 131; CD 5, 6; CSW; CWD; DAM DRAM; DFS 2; DLB 266; DLBY 1984; FW; MAL 5

Normyx
See Douglas, (George) Norman

Norris, (Benjamin) Frank(lin, Jr.)
1870-1902 . **SSC 28; TCLC 24, 155, 211**
See also AAYA 57; AMW; AMWC 2; BPFB 2; CA 110; 160; CDALB 1865-1917; DLB 12, 71, 186; LMFS 2; MAL 5; NFS 12; RGAL 4; TCWW 1, 2; TUS

Norris, Kathleen 1947- .... **CLC 248**
See also CA 160; CANR 113

Norris, Leslie 1921-2006 .... **CLC 14**
See also CA 11-12; 251; CANR 14, 117; CAP 1; CP 1, 2, 3, 4, 5, 6, 7; DLB 27, 256

North, Andrew
See Norton, Andre

North, Anthony
See Koontz, Dean R.

North, Captain George
See Stevenson, Robert Louis (Balfour)

North, Captain George
See Stevenson, Robert Louis (Balfour)

North, Milou
See Erdrich, Louise

Northrup, B. A.
See Hubbard, L. Ron

North Staffs
See Hulme, T(homas) E(rnest)

Northup, Solomon 1808-1863 ...... **NCLC 105**

Norton, Alice Mary
See Norton, Andre

Norton, Andre 1912-2005 .... **CLC 12**
See also AAYA 14; BPFB 2; BYA 4, 10, 12; CA 1-4R; 237; CANR 2, 31, 68, 108, 149; CLR 50; DLB 8, 52; JRDA; MAI-CYA 1, 2; MTCW 1; SATA 1, 43, 91; SUFW 1, 2; YAW

Norton, Caroline 1808-1877 .. **NCLC 47, 205**
See also DLB 21, 159, 199

Norway, Nevil Shute 1899-1960 .... **CLC 30**
See also BPFB 3; CA 102; 93-96; CANR 85; DLB 255; MTCW 2; NFS 9; RHW 4; SFW 4

Norwid, Cyprian Kamil
1821-1883 .... **NCLC 17**
See also RGWL 3

Nosille, Nabrah
See Ellison, Harlan

Nossack, Hans Erich 1901-1977 .... **CLC 6**
See also CA 93-96; 85-88; CANR 156; DLB 69; EWL 3

Nostradamus 1503-1566 .... **LC 27**

Nosu, Chuji
See Ozu, Yasujiro

Notenburg, Eleanora (Genrikhovna) von
See Guro, Elena (Genrikhovna)

Nova, Craig 1945- .... **CLC 7, 31**
See also CA 45-48; CANR 2, 53, 127

Novak, Joseph
See Kosinski, Jerzy

Novalis 1772-1801 .... **NCLC 13, 178**
See also CDWLB 2; DLB 90; EW 5; RGWL 2, 3

Novick, Peter 1934- .... **CLC 164**
See also CA 188

Novis, Emile
See Weil, Simone (Adolphine)

Nowlan, Alden (Albert) 1933-1983 ... **CLC 15**
See also CA 9-12R; CANR 5; CP 1, 2, 3; DAC; DAM MST; DLB 53; PFS 12

Noyes, Alfred 1880-1958 ...... **PC 27; TCLC 7**
See also CA 104; 188; DLB 20; EXPP; FANT; PFS 4; RGEL 2

Nugent, Richard Bruce
1906(?)-1987 .... **HR 1:3**
See also BW 1; CA 125; DLB 51; GLL 2

Nunez, Elizabeth 1944- .... **BLC 2:3**
See also CA 223

Nunn, Kem .... **CLC 34**
See also CA 159

Nussbaum, Martha Craven 1947- .. **CLC 203**
See also CA 134; CANR 102, 176

Nwapa, Flora (Nwanzuruaha)
1931-1993 .... **BLCS; CLC 133**
See also BW 2; CA 143; CANR 83; CD-WLB 3; CWRI 5; DLB 125; EWL 3; WLIT 2

Nye, Robert 1939- .... **CLC 13, 42**
See also BRWS 10; CA 33-36R; CANR 29, 67, 107; CN 1, 2, 3, 4, 5, 6, 7; CP 1, 2, 3, 4, 5, 6, 7; CWRI 5; DAM NOV; DLB 14, 271; FANT; HGG; MTCW 1; RHW; SATA 6

MAICYA 1, 2; MAICYAS 1; MTCW 1;
SATA 13, 53, 92, 133; WYA; YAW

Paterson, Katherine Womeldorf
See Paterson, Katherine

Patmore, Coventry Kersey Dighton
1823-1896 .... **NCLC 9; PC 59**
See also DLB 35, 98; RGEL 2; TEA

Paton, Alan 1903-1988 ..... **CLC 4, 10, 25, 55,
106; TCLC 165; WLC 4**
See also AAYA 26; AFW; BPFB 3; BRWS
2; BYA 1; CA 13-16; 125; CANR 22;
CAP 1; CN 1, 2, 3, 4; DA; DA3; DAB;
DAC; DAM MST, NOV; DLB 225;
DLBD 17; EWL 3; EXPN; LAIT 4;
MTCW 1, 2; MTFW 2005; NFS 3, 12;
RGEL 2; SATA 11; SATA-Obit 56; TWA;
WLIT 2; WWE 1

Paton Walsh, Gillian
See Paton Walsh, Jill

Paton Walsh, Jill 1937- .... **CLC 35**
See also AAYA 11, 47; BYA 1, 8; CA 262;
CAAE 262; CANR 38, 83, 158; CLR 2,
6, 128; DLB 161; JRDA; MAICYA 1, 2;
SAAS 3; SATA 4, 72, 109, 190; SATA-
Essay 190; WYA; YAW

Patsauq, Markoosie 1942- .... **NNAL**
See also CA 101; CLR 23; CWRI 5; DAM
MULT

Patterson, (Horace) Orlando (Lloyd)
1940- .... **BLCS**
See also BW 1; CA 65-68; CANR 27, 84;
CN 1, 2, 3, 4, 5, 6

Patton, George S(mith), Jr.
1885-1945 .... **TCLC 79**
See also CA 189

Paulding, James Kirke 1778-1860 ... **NCLC 2**
See also DLB 3, 59, 74, 250; RGAL 4

Paulin, Thomas Neilson
See Paulin, Tom

Paulin, Tom 1949- .... **CLC 37, 177**
See also CA 123; 128; CANR 98; CP 3, 4,
5, 6, 7; DLB 40

Pausanias c. 1st cent. - .... **CMLC 36**

Paustovsky, Konstantin (Georgievich)
1892-1968 .... **CLC 40**
See also CA 93-96; 25-28R; DLB 272;
EWL 3

Pavese, Cesare 1908-1950 .... **PC 13; SSC 19;
TCLC 3**
See also CA 104; 169; DLB 128, 177; EW
12; EWL 3; PFS 20; RGSF 2; RGWL 2,
3; TWA; WLIT 7

Pavic, Milorad 1929- .... **CLC 60**
See also CA 136; CDWLB 4; CWW 2; DLB
181; EWL 3; RGWL 3

Pavlov, Ivan Petrovich 1849-1936 . **TCLC 91**
See also CA 118; 180

Pavlova, Karolina Karlovna
1807-1893 .... **NCLC 138**
See also DLB 205

Payne, Alan
See Jakes, John

Payne, Rachel Ann
See Jakes, John

Paz, Gil
See Lugones, Leopoldo

Paz, Octavio 1914-1998 . **CLC 3, 4, 6, 10, 19,
51, 65, 119; HLC 2; PC 1, 48; TCLC
211; WLC 4**
See also AAYA 50; CA 73-76; 165; CANR
32, 65, 104; CWW 2; DA; DA3; DAB;
DAC; DAM MST, MULT, POET; DLB
290, 331; DLBY 1990, 1998; DNFS 1;
EWL 3; HW 1, 2; LAW; LAWS 1; MTCW
1, 2; MTFW 2005; PFS 18, 30; RGWL 2,
3; SSFS 13; TWA; WLIT 1

p'Bitek, Okot 1931-1982 . **BLC 1:3; CLC 96;
TCLC 149**
See also AFW; BW 2, 3; CA 124; 107;
CANR 82; CP 1, 2, 3; DAM MULT; DLB
125; EWL 3; MTCW 1, 2; MTFW 2005;
RGEL 2; WLIT 2

Peabody, Elizabeth Palmer
1804-1894 .... **NCLC 169**
See also DLB 1, 223

Peacham, Henry 1578-1644(?) .... **LC 119**
See also DLB 151

Peacock, Molly 1947- .... **CLC 60**
See also CA 103, 262; CAAE 262; CAAS
21; CANR 52, 84; CP 5, 6, 7; CWP; DLB
120, 282

Peacock, Thomas Love
1785-1866 .... **NCLC 22; PC 87**
See also BRW 4; DLB 96, 116; RGEL 2;
RGSF 2

Peake, Mervyn 1911-1968 .... **CLC 7, 54**
See also CA 5-8R; 25-28R; CANR 3; DLB
15, 160, 255; FANT; MTCW 1; RGEL 2;
SATA 23; SFW 4

Pearce, Ann Philippa
See Pearce, Philippa

Pearce, Philippa 1920-2006 .... **CLC 21**
See also BYA 5; CA 5-8R; 255; CANR 4,
109; CLR 9; CWRI 5; DLB 161; FANT;
MAICYA 1; SATA 1, 67, 129; SATA-Obit
179

Pearl, Eric
See Elman, Richard (Martin)

Pearson, Jean Mary
See Gardam, Jane

Pearson, Thomas Reid
See Pearson, T.R.

Pearson, T.R. 1956- .... **CLC 39**
See also CA 120; 130; CANR 97, 147, 185;
CSW; INT CA-130

Peck, Dale 1967- .... **CLC 81**
See also CA 146; CANR 72, 127, 180; GLL
2

Peck, John (Frederick) 1941- .... **CLC 3**
See also CA 49-52; CANR 3, 100; CP 4, 5,
6, 7

Peck, Richard 1934- .... **CLC 21**
See also AAYA 1, 24; BYA 1, 6, 8, 11; CA
85-88; CANR 19, 38, 129, 178; CLR 15,
142; INT CANR-19; JRDA; MAICYA 1,
2; SAAS 2; SATA 18, 55, 97, 110, 158,
190; SATA-Essay 110; WYA; YAW

Peck, Richard Wayne
See Peck, Richard

Peck, Robert Newton 1928- .... **CLC 17**
See also AAYA 3, 43; BYA 1, 6; CA 81-84,
182; CAAE 182; CANR 31, 63, 127; CLR
45; DA; DAC; DAM MST; JRDA; LAIT
3; MAICYA 1, 2; NFS 29; SAAS 1; SATA
21, 62, 111, 156; SATA-Essay 108; WYA;
YAW

Peckinpah, David Samuel
See Peckinpah, Sam

Peckinpah, Sam 1925-1984 .... **CLC 20**
See also CA 109; 114; CANR 82

Pedersen, Knut 1859-1952 .. **TCLC 2, 14, 49,
151, 203**
See also AAYA 79; CA 104; 119; CANR
63; DLB 297, 330; EW 8; EWL 8; MTCW
1, 2; RGWL 2, 3

Peele, George 1556-1596 .... **DC 27; LC 115**
See also BRW 1; DLB 62, 167; RGEL 2

Peeslake, Gaffer
See Durrell, Lawrence (George)

Peguy, Charles (Pierre)
1873-1914 .... **TCLC 10**
See also CA 107; 193; DLB 258; EWL 3;
GFL 1789 to the Present

Peirce, Charles Sanders
1839-1914 .... **TCLC 81**
See also CA 194; DLB 270

Pelagius c. 350-c. 418 .... **CMLC 112**

Pelecanos, George P. 1957- .... **CLC 236**
See also CA 138; CANR 122, 165; DLB
306

Pelevin, Victor 1962- .... **CLC 238**
See also CA 154; CANR 88, 159; DLB 285

Pelevin, Viktor Olegovich
See Pelevin, Victor

Pellicer, Carlos 1897(?)-1977 .... **HLCS 2**
See also CA 153; 69-72; DLB 290; EWL 3;
HW 1

Pena, Ramon del Valle y
See Valle-Inclan, Ramon (Maria) del

Pendennis, Arthur Esquir
See Thackeray, William Makepeace

Penn, Arthur
See Matthews, (James) Brander

Penn, William 1644-1718 .... **LC 25**
See also DLB 24

PEPECE
See Prado (Calvo), Pedro

Pepys, Samuel 1633-1703 ... **LC 11, 58; WLC
4**
See also BRW 2; CDBLB 1660-1789; DA;
DA3; DAB; DAC; DAM MST; DLB 101,
213; NCFS 4; RGEL 2; TEA; WLIT 3

Percy, Thomas 1729-1811 .... **NCLC 95**
See also DLB 104

Percy, Walker 1916-1990 .... **CLC 2, 3, 6, 8,
14, 18, 47, 65**
See also AMWS 3; BPFB 3; CA 1-4R; 131;
CANR 1, 23, 64; CN 1, 2, 3, 4; CPW;
CSW; DA3; DAM NOV, POP; DLB 2;
DLBY 1980, 1990; EWL 3; MAL 5;
MTCW 1, 2; MTFW 2005; RGAL 4; TUS

Percy, William Alexander
1885-1942 .... **TCLC 84**
See also CA 163; MTCW 2

Perdurabo, Frater
See Crowley, Edward Alexander

Perec, Georges 1936-1982 .... **CLC 56, 116**
See also CA 141; DLB 83, 299; EWL 3;
GFL 1789 to the Present; RGHL; RGWL
3

**Pereda (y Sanchez de Porrua), Jose Maria
de** 1833-1906 .... **TCLC 16**
See also CA 117

Pereda y Porrua, Jose Maria de
See Pereda (y Sanchez de Porrua), Jose
Maria de

Peregoy, George Weems
See Mencken, H(enry) L(ouis)

Perelman, S(idney) J(oseph)
1904-1979 .. **CLC 3, 5, 9, 15, 23, 44, 49;
SSC 32**
See also AAYA 79; AITN 1, 2; BPFB 3;
CA 73-76; 89-92; CANR 18; DAM
DRAM; DLB 11, 44; MTCW 1, 2; MTFW
2005; RGAL 4

Peret, Benjamin 1899-1959 .... **PC 33; TCLC
20**
See also CA 117; 186; GFL 1789 to the
Present

Peretz, Isaac Leib
See Peretz, Isaac Loeb

Peretz, Isaac Loeb 1851(?)-1915 ...... **SSC 26;
TCLC 16**
See also CA 109; 201; DLB 333

Peretz, Yitzkhok Leibush
See Peretz, Isaac Loeb

Perez Galdos, Benito 1843-1920 ..... **HLCS 2;
TCLC 27**
See also CA 125; 153; EW 7; EWL 3; HW
1; RGWL 2, 3

Prus, Boleslaw 1845-1912 .... **TCLC 48**
See also RGWL 2, 3

Prynne, William 1600-1669 .... **LC 148**

Prynne, Xavier
See Hardwick, Elizabeth

Pryor, Aaron Richard
See Pryor, Richard

Pryor, Richard 1940-2005 .... **CLC 26**
See also CA 122; 152; 246

Pryor, Richard Franklin Lenox Thomas
See Pryor, Richard

Przybyszewski, Stanislaw
1868-1927 .... **TCLC 36**
See also CA 160; DLB 66; EWL 3

Pseudo-Dionysius the Areopagite fl. c. 5th
cent. - .... **CMLC 89**
See also DLB 115

Pteleon
See Grieve, C(hristopher) M(urray)

Puckett, Lute
See Masters, Edgar Lee

Puig, Manuel 1932-1990 .... **CLC 3, 5, 10, 28,
65, 133; HLC 2**
See also BPFB 3; CA 45-48; CANR 2, 32,
63; CDWLB 3; DA3; DAM MULT; DLB
113; DNFS 1; EWL 3; GLL 1; HW 1, 2;
LAW; MTCW 1, 2; MTFW 2005; RGWL
2, 3; TWA; WLIT 1

Pulitzer, Joseph 1847-1911 .... **TCLC 76**
See also CA 114; DLB 23

Pullman, Philip 1946- .... **CLC 245**
See also AAYA 15, 41; BRWS 8; BYA 8,
13; CA 127; CANR 50, 77, 105, 134;
CLR 20, 62, 84; JRDA; MAICYA 1, 2;
MAICYAS 1; MTFW 2005; SAAS 17;
SATA 65, 103, 150, 198; SUFW 2; WYAS
1; YAW

Purchas, Samuel 1577(?)-1626 .... **LC 70**
See also DLB 151

Purdy, A(lfred) W(ellington)
1918-2000 .... **CLC 3, 6, 14, 50**
See also CA 81-84; 189; CAAS 17; CANR
42, 66; CP 1, 2, 3, 4, 5, 6, 7; DAC; DAM
MST, POET; DLB 88; PFS 5; RGEL 2

Purdy, James 1923-2009 .... **CLC 2, 4, 10, 28,
52**
See also AMWS 7; CA 33-36R; CAAS 1;
CANR 19, 51, 132; CN 1, 2, 3, 4, 5, 6, 7;
DLB 2, 218; EWL 3; INT CANR-19;
MAL 5; MTCW 1; RGAL 4

Purdy, James Amos
See Purdy, James

Pure, Simon
See Swinnerton, Frank Arthur

Pushkin, Aleksandr Sergeevich
See Pushkin, Alexander (Sergeyevich)

Pushkin, Alexander (Sergeyevich)
1799-1837 .... **NCLC 3, 27, 83; PC 10;
SSC 27, 55, 99; WLC 5**
See also DA; DA3; DAB; DAC; DAM
DRAM, MST, POET; DLB 205; EW 5;
EXPS; PFS 28; RGSF 2; RGWL 2, 3;
SATA 61; SSFS 9; TWA

P'u Sung-ling 1640-1715 .... **LC 49; SSC 31**

Putnam, Arthur Lee
See Alger, Horatio, Jr.

Puttenham, George 1529(?)-1590 ...... **LC 116**
See also DLB 281

Puzo, Mario 1920-1999 .... **CLC 1, 2, 6, 36,
107**
See also BPFB 3; CA 65-68; 185; CANR 4,
42, 65, 99, 131; CN 1, 2, 3, 4, 5, 6; CPW;
DA3; DAM NOV, POP; DLB 6; MTCW
1, 2; MTFW 2005; NFS 16; RGAL 4

Pygge, Edward
See Barnes, Julian

Pyle, Ernest Taylor 1900-1945 .... **TCLC 75**
See also CA 115; 160; DLB 29; MTCW 2

Pyle, Ernie
See Pyle, Ernest Taylor

Pyle, Howard 1853-1911 .... **TCLC 81**
See also AAYA 57; BYA 2, 4; CA 109; 137;
CLR 22, 117; DLB 42, 188; DLBD 13;
LAIT 1; MAICYA 1, 2; SATA 16, 100;
WCH; YAW

Pym, Barbara (Mary Crampton)
1913-1980 .... **CLC 13, 19, 37, 111**
See also BPFB 3; BRWS 2; CA 13-14; 97-
100; CANR 13, 34; CAP 1; DLB 14, 207;
DLBY 1987; EWL 3; MTCW 1, 2; MTFW
2005; RGEL 2; TEA

Pynchon, Thomas 1937- .. **CLC 2, 3, 6, 9, 11,
18, 33, 62, 72, 123, 192, 213; SSC 14,
84; WLC 5**
See also AMWS 2; BEST 90:2; BPFB 3;
CA 17-20R; CANR 22, 46, 73, 142; CN
1, 2, 3, 4, 5, 6, 7; CPW 1; DA; DA3;
DAB; DAC; DAM MST, NOV, POP;
DLB 2, 173; EWL 3; MAL 5; MTCW 1,
2; MTFW 2005; NFS 23; RGAL 4; SFW
4; TCLE 1:2; TUS

Pythagoras c. 582B.C.-c. 507B.C. . **CMLC 22**
See also DLB 176

Q
See Quiller-Couch, Sir Arthur (Thomas)

Qian, Chongzhu
See Ch'ien, Chung-shu

Qian, Sima 145B.C.-c. 89B.C. .... **CMLC 72**

Qian Zhongshu
See Ch'ien, Chung-shu

Qroll
See Dagerman, Stig (Halvard)

Quarles, Francis 1592-1644 .... **LC 117**
See also DLB 126; RGEL 2

Quarrington, Paul 1953- .... **CLC 65**
See also CA 129; CANR 62, 95

Quarrington, Paul Lewis
See Quarrington, Paul

Quasimodo, Salvatore 1901-1968 .... **CLC 10;
PC 47**
See also CA 13-16; 25-28R; CAP 1; DLB
114, 332; EW 12; EWL 3; MTCW 1;
RGWL 2, 3

Quatermass, Martin
See Carpenter, John (Howard)

Quay, Stephen 1947- .... **CLC 95**
See also CA 189

Quay, Timothy 1947- .... **CLC 95**
See also CA 189

Queen, Ellery
See Dannay, Frederic; Hoch, Edward D.;
Lee, Manfred B.; Marlowe, Stephen;
Sturgeon, Theodore (Hamilton); Vance,
Jack

Queneau, Raymond 1903-1976 ..... **CLC 2, 5,
10, 42**
See also CA 77-80; 69-72; CANR 32; DLB
72, 258; EW 12; EWL 3; GFL 1789 to
the Present; MTCW 1, 2; RGWL 2, 3

Quevedo, Francisco de 1580-1645 ...... **LC 23,
160**

Quiller-Couch, Sir Arthur (Thomas)
1863-1944 .... **TCLC 53**
See also CA 118; 166; DLB 135, 153, 190;
HGG; RGEL 2; SUFW 1

Quin, Ann 1936-1973 .... **CLC 6**
See also CA 9-12R; 45-48; CANR 148; CN
1; DLB 14, 231

Quin, Ann Marie
See Quin, Ann

Quincey, Thomas de
See De Quincey, Thomas

Quindlen, Anna 1953- .... **CLC 191**
See also AAYA 35; AMWS 17; CA 138;
CANR 73, 126; DA3; DLB 292; MTCW
2; MTFW 2005

Quinn, Martin
See Smith, Martin Cruz

Quinn, Peter 1947- .... **CLC 91**
See also CA 197; CANR 147

Quinn, Peter A.
See Quinn, Peter

Quinn, Simon
See Smith, Martin Cruz

Quintana, Leroy V. 1944- ...... **HLC 2; PC 36**
See also CA 131; CANR 65, 139; DAM
MULT; DLB 82; HW 1, 2

Quintilian c. 40-c. 100 .... **CMLC 77**
See also AW 2; DLB 211; RGWL 2, 3

Quiroga, Horacio (Sylvestre)
1878-1937 ... **HLC 2; SSC 89; TCLC 20**
See also CA 117; 131; DAM MULT; EWL
3; HW 1; LAW; MTCW 1; RGSF 2;
WLIT 1

Quoirez, Francoise 1935-2004 ... **CLC 3, 6, 9,
17, 36**
See also CA 49-52; 231; CANR 6, 39, 73;
CWW 2; DLB 83; EWL 3; GFL 1789 to
the Present; MTCW 1, 2; MTFW 2005;
TWA

Raabe, Wilhelm (Karl) 1831-1910 . **TCLC 45**
See also CA 167; DLB 129

Rabe, David (William) 1940- .. **CLC 4, 8, 33,
200; DC 16**
See also CA 85-88; CABS 3; CAD; CANR
59, 129; CD 5, 6; DAM DRAM; DFS 3,
8, 13; DLB 7, 228; EWL 3; MAL 5

Rabelais, Francois 1494-1553 .... **LC 5, 60;
WLC 5**
See also DA; DAB; DAC; DAM MST;
DLB 327; EW 2; GFL Beginnings to
1789; LMFS 1; RGWL 2, 3; TWA

Rabi'a al-'Adawiyya c. 717-c.
801 .... **CMLC 83**
See also DLB 311

Rabinovitch, Sholem 1859-1916 .... **SSC 33;
TCLC 1, 35**
See also CA 104; DLB 333; TWA

Rabinovitsh, Sholem Yankev
See Rabinovitch, Sholem

Rabinowitz, Sholem Yakov
See Rabinovitch, Sholem

Rabinowitz, Solomon
See Rabinovitch, Sholem

Rabinyan, Dorit 1972- .... **CLC 119**
See also CA 170; CANR 147

Rachilde
See Vallette, Marguerite Eymery; Vallette,
Marguerite Eymery

Racine, Jean 1639-1699 .. **DC 32; LC 28, 113**
See also DA3; DAB; DAM MST; DLB 268;
EW 3; GFL Beginnings to 1789; LMFS
1; RGWL 2, 3; TWA

Radcliffe, Ann (Ward) 1764-1823 ... **NCLC 6,
55, 106**
See also DLB 39, 178; GL 3; HGG; LMFS
1; RGEL 2; SUFW; WLIT 3

Radclyffe-Hall, Marguerite
See Hall, Radclyffe

Radiguet, Raymond 1903-1923 ...... **TCLC 29**
See also CA 162; DLB 65; EWL 3; GFL
1789 to the Present; RGWL 2, 3

Radishchev, Aleksandr Nikolaevich
1749-1802 .... **NCLC 190**
See also DLB 150

Radishchev, Alexander
See Radishchev, Aleksandr Nikolaevich

Radnoti, Miklos 1909-1944 .... **TCLC 16**
See also CA 118; 212; CDWLB 4; DLB
215; EWL 3; RGHL; RGWL 2, 3

Rado, James 1939- .... **CLC 17**
See also CA 105

Radvanyi, Netty 1900-1983 .... **CLC 7**
See also CA 85-88; 110; CANR 82; CD-
WLB 2; DLB 69; EWL 3

Renan, Joseph Ernest 1823-1892 . **NCLC 26, 145**
See also GFL 1789 to the Present

Renard, Jules(-Pierre) 1864-1910 .. **TCLC 17**
See also CA 117; 202; GFL 1789 to the Present

Renart, Jean fl. 13th cent. - .... **CMLC 83**

Renault, Mary
See Challans, Mary

Rendell, Ruth 1930- .... **CLC 28, 48, 50**
See also BEST 90:4; BPFB 3; BRWS 9; CA 109; CANR 32, 52, 74, 127, 162; CN 5, 6, 7; CPW; DAM POP; DLB 87, 276; INT CANR-32; MSW; MTCW 1, 2; MTFW 2005

Rendell, Ruth Barbara
See Rendell, Ruth

Renoir, Jean 1894-1979 .... **CLC 20**
See also CA 129; 85-88

Rensie, Willis
See Eisner, Will

Resnais, Alain 1922- .... **CLC 16**

Revard, Carter 1931- .... **NNAL**
See also CA 144; CANR 81, 153; PFS 5

Reverdy, Pierre 1889-1960 .... **CLC 53**
See also CA 97-100; 89-92; DLB 258; EWL 3; GFL 1789 to the Present

Reverend Mandju
See Su, Chien

Rexroth, Kenneth 1905-1982 .... **CLC 1, 2, 6, 11, 22, 49, 112; PC 20, 95**
See also BG 1:3; CA 5-8R; 107; CANR 14, 34, 63; CDALB 1941-1968; CP 1, 2, 3; DAM POET; DLB 16, 48, 165, 212; DLBY 1982; EWL 3; INT CANR-14; MAL 5; MTCW 1, 2; MTFW 2005; RGAL 4

Reyes, Alfonso 1889-1959 .... **HLCS 2; TCLC 33**
See also CA 131; EWL 3; HW 1; LAW

Reyes y Basoalto, Ricardo Eliecer Neftali
See Neruda, Pablo

Reymont, Wladyslaw (Stanislaw) 1868(?)-1925 .... **TCLC 5**
See also CA 104; DLB 332; EWL 3

Reynolds, John Hamilton 1794-1852 .... **NCLC 146**
See also DLB 96

Reynolds, Jonathan 1942- .... **CLC 6, 38**
See also CA 65-68; CANR 28, 176

Reynolds, Joshua 1723-1792 .... **LC 15**
See also DLB 104

Reynolds, Michael S(hane) 1937-2000 .... **CLC 44**
See also CA 65-68; 189; CANR 9, 89, 97

Reza, Yasmina 1959- .... **DC 34**
See also AAYA 69; CA 171; CANR 145; DFS 19; DLB 321

Reznikoff, Charles 1894-1976 .... **CLC 9**
See also AMWS 14; CA 33-36; 61-64; CAP 2; CP 1, 2; DLB 28, 45; RGHL; WP

Rezzori, Gregor von
See Rezzori d'Arezzo, Gregor von

Rezzori d'Arezzo, Gregor von 1914-1998 .... **CLC 25**
See also CA 122; 136; 167

Rhine, Richard
See Silverstein, Alvin; Silverstein, Virginia B(arbara Opshelor)

Rhodes, Eugene Manlove 1869-1934 .... **TCLC 53**
See also CA 198; DLB 256; TCWW 1, 2

R'hoone, Lord
See Balzac, Honore de

Rhys, Jean 1890-1979 .... **CLC 2, 4, 6, 14, 19, 51, 124; SSC 21, 76**
See also BRWS 2; CA 25-28R; 85-88; CANR 35, 62; CDBLB 1945-1960; CD-WLB 3; CN 1, 2; DA3; DAM NOV; DLB 36, 117, 162; DNFS 2; EWL 3; LATS 1:1; MTCW 1, 2; MTFW 2005; NFS 19; RGEL 2; RGSF 2; RHW; TEA; WWE 1

Ribeiro, Darcy 1922-1997 .... **CLC 34**
See also CA 33-36R; 156; EWL 3

Ribeiro, Joao Ubaldo (Osorio Pimentel) 1941- .... **CLC 10, 67**
See also CA 81-84; CWW 2; EWL 3

Ribman, Ronald (Burt) 1932- .... **CLC 7**
See also CA 21-24R; CAD; CANR 46, 80; CD 5, 6

Ricci, Nino 1959- .... **CLC 70**
See also CA 137; CANR 130; CCA 1

Ricci, Nino Pio
See Ricci, Nino

Rice, Anne 1941- .... **CLC 41, 128**
See also AAYA 9, 53; AMWS 7; BEST 89:2; BPFB 3; CA 65-68; CANR 12, 36, 53, 74, 100, 133; CN 6, 7; CPW; CSW; DA3; DAM POP; DLB 292; GL 3; GLL 2; HGG; MTCW 2; MTFW 2005; SUFW 2; YAW

Rice, Elmer (Leopold) 1892-1967 ...... **CLC 7, 49**
See also CA 21-22; 25-28R; CAP 2; DAM DRAM; DFS 12; DLB 4, 7; EWL 3; IDTP; MAL 5; MTCW 1, 2; RGAL 4

Rice, Tim(othy Miles Bindon) 1944- .... **CLC 21**
See also CA 103; CANR 46; DFS 7

Rich, Adrienne 1929- ..... **CLC 3, 6, 7, 11, 18, 36, 73, 76, 125; PC 5**
See also AAYA 69; AMWR 2; AMWS 1; CA 9-12R; CANR 20, 53, 74, 128; CDALBS; CP 1, 2, 3, 4, 5, 6, 7; CSW; CWP; DA3; DAM POET; DLB 5, 67; EWL 3; EXPP; FL 1:6; FW; MAL 5; MBL; MTCW 1, 2; MTFW 2005; PAB; PFS 15, 29; RGAL 4; RGHL; WP

Rich, Barbara
See Graves, Robert

Rich, Robert
See Trumbo, Dalton

Richard, Keith
See Richards, Keith

Richards, David Adams 1950- .... **CLC 59**
See also CA 93-96; CANR 60, 110, 156; CN 7; DAC; DLB 53; TCLE 1:2

Richards, I(vor) A(rmstrong) 1893-1979 .... **CLC 14, 24**
See also BRWS 2; CA 41-44R; 89-92; CANR 34, 74; CP 1, 2; DLB 27; EWL 3; MTCW 2; RGEL 2

Richards, Keith 1943- .... **CLC 17**
See also CA 107; CANR 77

Richardson, Anne
See Roiphe, Anne

Richardson, Dorothy Miller 1873-1957 .... **TCLC 3, 203**
See also BRWS 13; CA 104; 192; DLB 36; EWL 3; FW; RGEL 2

Richardson (Robertson), Ethel Florence Lindesay 1870-1946 .... **TCLC 4**
See also CA 105; 190; DLB 197, 230; EWL 3; RGEL 2; RGSF 2; RHW

Richardson, Henrietta
See Richardson (Robertson), Ethel Florence Lindesay

Richardson, Henry Handel
See Richardson (Robertson), Ethel Florence Lindesay

Richardson, John 1796-1852 .... **NCLC 55**
See also CCA 1; DAC; DLB 99

Richardson, Samuel 1689-1761 ...... **LC 1, 44, 138; WLC 5**
See also BRW 3; CDBLB 1660-1789; DA; DAB; DAC; DAM MST, NOV; DLB 39; RGEL 2; TEA; WLIT 3

Richardson, Willis 1889-1977 .... **HR 1:3**
See also BW 1; CA 124; DLB 51; SATA 60

Richler, Mordecai 1931-2001 .... **CLC 3, 5, 9, 13, 18, 46, 70, 185, 271**
See also AITN 1; CA 65-68; 201; CANR 31, 62, 111; CCA 1; CLR 17; CN 1, 2, 3, 4, 5, 7; CWRI 5; DAC; DAM MST, NOV; DLB 53; EWL 3; MAICYA 1, 2; MTCW 1, 2; MTFW 2005; RGEL 2; RGHL; SATA 44, 98; SATA-Brief 27; TWA

Richter, Conrad (Michael) 1890-1968 .... **CLC 30**
See also AAYA 21; AMWS 18; BYA 2; CA 5-8R; 25-28R; CANR 23; DLB 9, 212; LAIT 1; MAL 5; MTCW 1, 2; MTFW 2005; RGAL 4; SATA 3; TCWW 1, 2; TUS; YAW

Ricostranza, Tom
See Ellis, Trey

Riddell, Charlotte 1832-1906 .... **TCLC 40**
See also CA 165; DLB 156; HGG; SUFW

Riddell, Mrs. J. H.
See Riddell, Charlotte

Ridge, John Rollin 1827-1867 ...... **NCLC 82; NNAL**
See also CA 144; DAM MULT; DLB 175

Ridgeway, Jason
See Marlowe, Stephen

Ridgway, Keith 1965- .... **CLC 119**
See also CA 172; CANR 144

Riding, Laura
See Jackson, Laura (Riding)

Riefenstahl, Berta Helene Amalia 1902-2003 .... **CLC 16, 190**
See also CA 108; 220

Riefenstahl, Leni
See Riefenstahl, Berta Helene Amalia

Riffe, Ernest
See Bergman, Ingmar

Riffe, Ernest Ingmar
See Bergman, Ingmar

Riggs, (Rolla) Lynn 1899-1954 .... **NNAL; TCLC 56**
See also CA 144; DAM MULT; DLB 175

Riis, Jacob A(ugust) 1849-1914 ..... **TCLC 80**
See also CA 113; 168; DLB 23

Rikki
See Ducornet, Erica

Riley, James Whitcomb 1849-1916 .... **PC 48; TCLC 51**
See also CA 118; 137; DAM POET; MAICYA 1, 2; RGAL 4; SATA 17

Riley, Tex
See Creasey, John

Rilke, Rainer Maria 1875-1926 .... **PC 2; TCLC 1, 6, 19, 195**
See also CA 104; 132; CANR 62, 99; CD-WLB 2; DA3; DAM POET; DLB 81; EW 9; EWL 3; MTCW 1, 2; MTFW 2005; PFS 19, 27; RGWL 2, 3; TWA; WP

Rimbaud, (Jean Nicolas) Arthur 1854-1891 ... **NCLC 4, 35, 82; PC 3, 57; WLC 5**
See also DA; DA3; DAB; DAC; DAM MST, POET; DLB 217; EW 7; GFL 1789 to the Present; LMFS 2; PFS 28; RGWL 2, 3; TWA; WP

Rinehart, Mary Roberts 1876-1958 .... **TCLC 52**
See also BPFB 3; CA 108; 166; RGAL 4; RHW

Ringmaster, The
See Mencken, H(enry) L(ouis)

Ringwood, Gwen(dolyn Margaret) Pharis 1910-1984 .... **CLC 48**
See also CA 148; 112; DLB 88

Rio, Michel 1945(?)- .... **CLC 43**
See also CA 201

Rooke, Leon 1934- .... **CLC 25, 34**
See also CA 25-28R; CANR 23, 53; CCA 1; CPW; DAM POP

Roosevelt, Franklin Delano
1882-1945 .... **TCLC 93**
See also CA 116; 173; LAIT 3

Roosevelt, Theodore 1858-1919 ..... **TCLC 69**
See also CA 115; 170; DLB 47, 186, 275

Roper, Margaret c. 1505-1544 .... **LC 147**

Roper, William 1498-1578 .... **LC 10**

Roquelaure, A. N.
See Rice, Anne

Rosa, Joao Guimaraes 1908-1967
See Guimaraes Rosa, Joao

Rose, Wendy 1948- . **CLC 85; NNAL; PC 13**
See also CA 53-56; CANR 5, 51; CWP; DAM MULT; DLB 175; PFS 13; RGAL 4; SATA 12

Rosen, R.D. 1949- .... **CLC 39**
See also CA 77-80; CANR 62, 120, 175; CMW 4; INT CANR-30

Rosen, Richard
See Rosen, R.D.

Rosen, Richard Dean
See Rosen, R.D.

Rosenberg, Isaac 1890-1918 .... **TCLC 12**
See also BRW 6; CA 107; 188; DLB 20, 216; EWL 3; PAB; RGEL 2

Rosenblatt, Joe
See Rosenblatt, Joseph

Rosenblatt, Joseph 1933- .... **CLC 15**
See also CA 89-92; CP 3, 4, 5, 6, 7; INT CA-89-92

Rosenfeld, Samuel
See Tzara, Tristan

Rosenstock, Sami
See Tzara, Tristan

Rosenstock, Samuel
See Tzara, Tristan

Rosenthal, M(acha) L(ouis)
1917-1996 .... **CLC 28**
See also CA 1-4R; 152; CAAS 6; CANR 4, 51; CP 1, 2, 3, 4, 5, 6; DLB 5; SATA 59

Ross, Barnaby
See Dannay, Frederic; Lee, Manfred B.

Ross, Bernard L.
See Follett, Ken

Ross, J. H.
See Lawrence, T(homas) E(dward)

Ross, John Hume
See Lawrence, T(homas) E(dward)

Ross, Martin 1862-1915
See Martin, Violet Florence
See also DLB 135; GLL 2; RGEL 2; RGSF 2

Ross, (James) Sinclair 1908-1996 ... **CLC 13; SSC 24**
See also CA 73-76; CANR 81; CN 1, 2, 3, 4, 5, 6; DAC; DAM MST; DLB 88; RGEL 2; RGSF 2; TCWW 1, 2

Rossetti, Christina 1830-1894 ... **NCLC 2, 50, 66, 186; PC 7; WLC 5**
See also AAYA 51; BRW 5; BYA 4; CLR 115; DA; DA3; DAB; DAC; DAM MST, POET; DLB 35, 163, 240; EXPP; FL 1:3; LATS 1:1; MAICYA 1, 2; PFS 10, 14, 27; RGEL 2; SATA 20; TEA; WCH

Rossetti, Christina Georgina
See Rossetti, Christina

Rossetti, Dante Gabriel 1828-1882 . **NCLC 4, 77; PC 44; WLC 5**
See also AAYA 51; BRW 5; CDBLB 1832-1890; DA; DAB; DAC; DAM MST, POET; DLB 35; EXPP; RGEL 2; TEA

Rossi, Cristina Peri
See Peri Rossi, Cristina

Rossi, Jean-Baptiste 1931-2003 .... **CLC 90**
See also CA 201; 215; CMW 4; NFS 18

Rossner, Judith 1935-2005 .... **CLC 6, 9, 29**
See also AITN 2; BEST 90:3; BPFB 3; CA 17-20R; 242; CANR 18, 51, 73; CN 4, 5, 6, 7; DLB 6; INT CANR-18; MAL 5; MTCW 1, 2; MTFW 2005

Rossner, Judith Perelman
See Rossner, Judith

Rostand, Edmond (Eugene Alexis)
1868-1918 .... **DC 10; TCLC 6, 37**
See also CA 104; 126; DA; DA3; DAB; DAC; DAM DRAM, MST; DFS 1; DLB 192; LAIT 1; MTCW 1; RGWL 2, 3; TWA

Roth, Henry 1906-1995 ..... **CLC 2, 6, 11, 104**
See also AMWS 9; CA 11-12; 149; CANR 38, 63; CAP 1; CN 1, 2, 3, 4, 5, 6; DA3; DLB 28; EWL 3; MAL 5; MTCW 1, 2; MTFW 2005; RGAL 4

Roth, (Moses) Joseph 1894-1939 ... **TCLC 33**
See also CA 160; DLB 85; EWL 3; RGWL 2, 3

Roth, Philip 1933- ... **CLC 1, 2, 3, 4, 6, 9, 15, 22, 31, 47, 66, 86, 119, 201; SSC 26, 102; WLC 5**
See also AAYA 67; AMWR 2; AMWS 3; BEST 90:3; BPFB 3; CA 1-4R; CANR 1, 22, 36, 55, 89, 132, 170; CDALB 1968-1988; CN 3, 4, 5, 6, 7; CPW 1; DA; DA3; DAB; DAC; DAM MST, NOV, POP; DLB 2, 28, 173; DLBY 1982; EWL 3; MAL 5; MTCW 1, 2; MTFW 2005; NFS 25; RGAL 4; RGHL; RGSF 2; SSFS 12, 18; TUS

Roth, Philip Milton
See Roth, Philip

Rothenberg, Jerome 1931- .... **CLC 6, 57**
See also CA 45-48; CANR 1, 106; CP 1, 2, 3, 4, 5, 6, 7; DLB 5, 193

Rotter, Pat .... **CLC 65**

Roumain, Jacques (Jean Baptiste)
1907-1944 .... **BLC 1:3; TCLC 19**
See also BW 1; CA 117; 125; DAM MULT; EWL 3

Rourke, Constance Mayfield
1885-1941 .... **TCLC 12**
See also CA 107; 200; MAL 5; YABC 1

Rousseau, Jean-Baptiste 1671-1741 ...... **LC 9**

Rousseau, Jean-Jacques 1712-1778 .... **LC 14, 36, 122; WLC 5**
See also DA; DA3; DAB; DAC; DAM MST; DLB 314; EW 4; GFL Beginnings to 1789; LMFS 1; RGWL 2, 3; TWA

Roussel, Raymond 1877-1933 .... **TCLC 20**
See also CA 117; 201; EWL 3; GFL 1789 to the Present

Rovit, Earl (Herbert) 1927- .... **CLC 7**
See also CA 5-8R; CANR 12

Rowe, Elizabeth Singer 1674-1737 ..... **LC 44**
See also DLB 39, 95

Rowe, Nicholas 1674-1718 .... **LC 8**
See also DLB 84; RGEL 2

Rowlandson, Mary 1637(?)-1678 .... **LC 66**
See also DLB 24, 200; RGAL 4

Rowley, Ames Dorrance
See Lovecraft, H. P.

Rowley, William 1585(?)-1626 ... **LC 100, 123**
See also DFS 22; DLB 58; RGEL 2

Rowling, J.K. 1965- .... **CLC 137, 217**
See also AAYA 34; BYA 11, 13, 14; CA 173; CANR 128, 157; CLR 66, 80, 112; MAICYA 2; MTFW 2005; SATA 109, 174; SUFW 2

Rowling, Joanne Kathleen
See Rowling, J.K.

Rowson, Susanna Haswell
1762(?)-1824 .... **NCLC 5, 69, 182**
See also AMWS 15; DLB 37, 200; RGAL 4

Roy, Arundhati 1960(?)- .... **CLC 109, 210**
See also CA 163; CANR 90, 126; CN 7; DLB 323, 326; DLBY 1997; EWL 3; LATS 1:2; MTFW 2005; NFS 22; WWE 1

Roy, Gabrielle 1909-1983 .... **CLC 10, 14**
See also CA 53-56; 110; CANR 5, 61; CCA 1; DAB; DAC; DAM MST; DLB 68; EWL 3; MTCW 1; RGWL 2, 3; SATA 104; TCLE 1:2

Royko, Mike 1932-1997 .... **CLC 109**
See also CA 89-92; 157; CANR 26, 111; CPW

Rozanov, Vasilii Vasil'evich
See Rozanov, Vassili

Rozanov, Vasily Vasilyevich
See Rozanov, Vassili

Rozanov, Vassili 1856-1919 .... **TCLC 104**
See also DLB 295; EWL 3

Rozewicz, Tadeusz 1921- ...... **CLC 9, 23, 139**
See also CA 108; CANR 36, 66; CWW 2; DA3; DAM POET; DLB 232; EWL 3; MTCW 1, 2; MTFW 2005; RGHL; RGWL 3

Ruark, Gibbons 1941- .... **CLC 3**
See also CA 33-36R; CAAS 23; CANR 14, 31, 57; DLB 120

Rubens, Bernice (Ruth) 1923-2004 . **CLC 19, 31**
See also CA 25-28R; 232; CANR 33, 65, 128; CN 1, 2, 3, 4, 5, 6, 7; DLB 14, 207, 326; MTCW 1

Rubin, Harold
See Robbins, Harold

Rudkin, (James) David 1936- .... **CLC 14**
See also CA 89-92; CBD; CD 5, 6; DLB 13

Rudnik, Raphael 1933- .... **CLC 7**
See also CA 29-32R

Ruffian, M.
See Hasek, Jaroslav (Matej Frantisek)

Rufinus c. 345-410 .... **CMLC 111**

Ruiz, Jose Martinez
See Martinez Ruiz, Jose

Ruiz, Juan c. 1283-c. 1350 .... **CMLC 66**

Rukeyser, Muriel 1913-1980 . **CLC 6, 10, 15, 27; PC 12**
See also AMWS 6; CA 5-8R; 93-96; CANR 26, 60; CP 1, 2, 3; DA3; DAM POET; DLB 48; EWL 3; FW; GLL 2; MAL 5; MTCW 1, 2; PFS 10, 29; RGAL 4; SATA-Obit 22

Rule, Jane 1931-2007 .... **CLC 27, 265**
See also CA 25-28R; 266; CAAS 18; CANR 12, 87; CN 4, 5, 6, 7; DLB 60; FW

Rule, Jane Vance
See Rule, Jane

Rulfo, Juan 1918-1986 .. **CLC 8, 80; HLC 2; SSC 25**
See also CA 85-88; 118; CANR 26; CD-WLB 3; DAM MULT; DLB 113; EWL 3; HW 1, 2; LAW; MTCW 1, 2; RGSF 2; RGWL 2, 3; WLIT 1

Rumi, Jalal al-Din 1207-1273 ...... **CMLC 20; PC 45**
See also AAYA 64; RGWL 2, 3; WLIT 6; WP

Runeberg, Johan 1804-1877 .... **NCLC 41**

Runyon, (Alfred) Damon
1884(?)-1946 .... **TCLC 10**
See also CA 107; 165; DLB 11, 86, 171; MAL 5; MTCW 2; RGAL 4

Rush, Norman 1933- .... **CLC 44**
See also CA 121; 126; CANR 130; INT CA-126

Rushdie, Salman 1947- .... **CLC 23, 31, 55, 100, 191, 272; SSC 83; WLCS**
See also AAYA 65; BEST 89:3; BPFB 3; BRWS 4; CA 108; 111; CANR 33, 56, 108, 133; CLR 125; CN 4, 5, 6, 7; CPW

Saltykov, Mikhail Evgrafovich
1826-1889 .... **NCLC 16**
See also DLB 238:

Saltykov-Shchedrin, N.
See Saltykov, Mikhail Evgrafovich

Samarakis, Andonis
See Samarakis, Antonis

Samarakis, Antonis 1919-2003 .... **CLC 5**
See also CA 25-28R; 224; CAAS 16; CANR
36; EWL 3

Samigli, E.
See Schmitz, Aron Hector

Sanchez, Florencio 1875-1910 .... **TCLC 37**
See also CA 153; DLB 305; EWL 3; HW 1;
LAW

Sanchez, Luis Rafael 1936- .... **CLC 23**
See also CA 128; DLB 305; EWL 3; HW 1;
WLIT 1

Sanchez, Sonia 1934- . **BLC 1:3, 2:3; CLC 5,
116, 215; PC 9**
See also BW 2, 3; CA 33-36R; CANR 24,
49, 74, 115; CLR 18; CP 2, 3, 4, 5, 6, 7;
CSW; CWP; DA3; DAM MULT; DLB 41;
DLBD 8; EWL 3; MAICYA 1, 2; MAL 5;
MTCW 1, 2; MTFW 2005; PFS 26; SATA
22, 136; WP

Sancho, Ignatius 1729-1780 .... **LC 84**

Sand, George 1804-1876 .... **DC 29; NCLC 2,
42, 57, 174; WLC 5**
See also DA; DA3; DAB; DAC; DAM
MST, NOV; DLB 119, 192; EW 6; FL 1:3;
FW; GFL 1789 to the Present; RGWL 2,
3; TWA

Sandburg, Carl (August) 1878-1967 . **CLC 1,
4, 10, 15, 35; PC 2, 41; WLC 5**
See also AAYA 24; AMW; BYA 1, 3; CA
5-8R; 25-28R; CANR 35; CDALB 1865-
1917; CLR 67; DA; DA3; DAB; DAC;
DAM MST, POET; DLB 17, 54, 284;
EWL 3; EXPP; LAIT 2; MAICYA 1, 2;
MAL 5; MTCW 1, 2; MTFW 2005; PAB;
PFS 3, 6, 12; RGAL 4; SATA 8; TUS;
WCH; WP; WYA

Sandburg, Charles
See Sandburg, Carl (August)

Sandburg, Charles A.
See Sandburg, Carl (August)

Sanders, (James) Ed(ward) 1939- .... **CLC 53**
See also BG 1:3; CA 13-16R; CAAS 21;
CANR 13, 44, 78; CP 1, 2, 3, 4, 5, 6, 7;
DAM POET; DLB 16, 244

Sanders, Edward
See Sanders, (James) Ed(ward)

Sanders, Lawrence 1920-1998 .... **CLC 41**
See also BEST 89:4; BPFB 3; CA 81-84;
165; CANR 33, 62; CMW 4; CPW; DA3;
DAM POP; MTCW 1

Sanders, Noah
See Blount, Roy, Jr.

Sanders, Winston P.
See Anderson, Poul

Sandoz, Mari(e Susette) 1900-1966 .. **CLC 28**
See also CA 1-4R; 25-28R; CANR 17, 64;
DLB 9, 212; LAIT 2; MTCW 1, 2; SATA
5; TCWW 1, 2

Sandys, George 1578-1644 .... **LC 80**
See also DLB 24, 121

Saner, Reg(inald Anthony) 1931- .... **CLC 9**
See also CA 65-68; CP 3, 4, 5, 6, 7

Sankara 788-820 .... **CMLC 32**

Sannazaro, Jacopo 1456(?)-1530 .... **LC 8**
See also RGWL 2, 3; WLIT 7

Sansom, William 1912-1976 . **CLC 2, 6; SSC
21**
See also CA 5-8R; 65-68; CANR 42; CN 1,
2; DAM NOV; DLB 139; EWL 3; MTCW
1; RGEL 2; RGSF 2

Santayana, George 1863-1952 .... **TCLC 40**
See also AMW; CA 115; 194; DLB 54, 71,
246, 270; DLBD 13; EWL 3; MAL 5;
RGAL 4; TUS

Santiago, Danny
See James, Daniel (Lewis)

**Santillana, Inigo Lopez de Mendoza,
Marques de** 1398-1458 .... **LC 111**
See also DLB 286

Santmyer, Helen Hooven
1895-1986 .... **CLC 33; TCLC 133**
See also CA 1-4R; 118; CANR 15, 33;
DLBY 1984; MTCW 1; RHW

Santoka, Taneda 1882-1940 .... **TCLC 72**

Santos, Bienvenido N(uqui)
1911-1996 ... **AAL; CLC 22; TCLC 156**
See also CA 101; 151; CANR 19, 46; CP 1;
DAM MULT; DLB 312, 348; EWL;
RGAL 4; SSFS 19

Santos, Miguel
See Mihura, Miguel

Sapir, Edward 1884-1939 .... **TCLC 108**
See also CA 211; DLB 92

Sapper
See McNeile, Herman Cyril

Sapphire 1950- .... **CLC 99**
See also CA 262

Sapphire, Brenda
See Sapphire

Sappho fl. 6th cent. B.C.- ... **CMLC 3, 67; PC
5**
See also CDWLB 1; DA3; DAM POET;
DLB 176; FL 1:1; PFS 20; RGWL 2, 3;
WLIT 8; WP

Saramago, Jose 1922- ..... **CLC 119; HLCS 1**
See also CA 153; CANR 96, 164; CWW 2;
DLB 287, 332; EWL 3; LATS 1:2; NFS
27; SSFS 23

Sarduy, Severo 1937-1993 .... **CLC 6, 97;
HLCS 2; TCLC 167**
See also CA 89-92; 142; CANR 58, 81;
CWW 2; DLB 113; EWL 3; HW 1, 2;
LAW

Sargeson, Frank 1903-1982 ..... **CLC 31; SSC
99**
See also CA 25-28R; 106; CANR 38, 79;
CN 1, 2, 3; EWL 3; GLL 2; RGEL 2;
RGSF 2; SSFS 20

Sarmiento, Domingo Faustino
1811-1888 .... **HLCS 2; NCLC 123**
See also LAW; WLIT 1

Sarmiento, Felix Ruben Garcia
See Dario, Ruben

Saro-Wiwa, Ken(ule Beeson)
1941-1995 .... **CLC 114; TCLC 200**
See also BW 2; CA 142; 150; CANR 60;
DLB 157

Saroyan, William 1908-1981 ... **CLC 1, 8, 10,
29, 34, 56; DC 28; SSC 21; TCLC 137;
WLC 5**
See also AAYA 66; CA 5-8R; 103; CAD;
CANR 30; CDALBS; CN 1, 2; DA; DA3;
DAB; DAC; DAM DRAM, MST, NOV;
DFS 17; DLB 7, 9, 86; DLBY 1981; EWL
3; LAIT 4; MAL 5; MTCW 1, 2; MTFW
2005; RGAL 4; RGSF 2; SATA 23; SATA-
Obit 24; SSFS 14; TUS

Sarraute, Nathalie 1900-1999 .... **CLC 1, 2, 4,
8, 10, 31, 80; TCLC 145**
See also BPFB 3; CA 9-12R; 187; CANR
23, 66, 134; CWW 2; DLB 83, 321; EW
12; EWL 3; GFL 1789 to the Present;
MTCW 1, 2; MTFW 2005; RGWL 2, 3

Sarton, May 1912-1995 ... **CLC 4, 14, 49, 91;
PC 39; TCLC 120**
See also AMWS 8; CA 1-4R; 149; CANR
1, 34, 55, 116; CN 1, 2, 3, 4, 5, 6; CP 1,
2, 3, 4, 5, 6; DAM POET; DLB 48; DLBY
1981; EWL 3; FW; INT CANR-34; MAL

5; MTCW 1, 2; MTFW 2005; RGAL 4;
SATA 36; SATA-Obit 86; TUS

Sartre, Jean-Paul 1905-1980 . **CLC 1, 4, 7, 9,
13, 18, 24, 44, 50, 52; DC 3; SSC 32;
WLC 5**
See also AAYA 62; CA 9-12R; 97-100;
CANR 21; DA; DA3; DAB; DAC; DAM
DRAM, MST, NOV; DFS 5, 26; DLB 72,
296, 321, 332; EW 12; EWL 3; GFL 1789
to the Present; LMFS 2; MTCW 1, 2;
MTFW 2005; NFS 21; RGHL; RGSF 2;
RGWL 2, 3; SSFS 9; TWA

Sassoon, Siegfried (Lorraine)
1886-1967 .... **CLC 36, 130; PC 12**
See also BRW 6; CA 104; 25-28R; CANR
36; DAB; DAM MST, NOV, POET; DLB
20, 191; DLBD 18; EWL 3; MTCW 1, 2;
MTFW 2005; PAB; PFS 28; RGEL 2;
TEA

Satterfield, Charles
See Pohl, Frederik

Satyremont
See Peret, Benjamin

Saul, John III
See Saul, John

Saul, John 1942- .... **CLC 46**
See also AAYA 10, 62; BEST 90:4; CA 81-
84; CANR 16, 40, 81, 176; CPW; DAM
NOV, POP; HGG; SATA 98

Saul, John W.
See Saul, John

Saul, John W. III
See Saul, John

Saul, John Woodruff III
See Saul, John

Saunders, Caleb
See Heinlein, Robert A.

Saura (Atares), Carlos 1932-1998 .... **CLC 20**
See also CA 114; 131; CANR 79; HW 1

Sauser, Frederic Louis
See Sauser-Hall, Frederic

Sauser-Hall, Frederic 1887-1961 ..... **CLC 18,
106**
See also CA 102; 93-96; CANR 36, 62;
DLB 258; EWL 3; GFL 1789 to the
Present; MTCW 1; WP

Saussure, Ferdinand de
1857-1913 .... **TCLC 49**
See also DLB 242

Savage, Catharine
See Brosman, Catharine Savage

Savage, Richard 1697(?)-1743 .... **LC 96**
See also DLB 95; RGEL 2

Savage, Thomas 1915-2003 .... **CLC 40**
See also CA 126; 132; 218; CAAS 15; CN
6, 7; INT CA-132; SATA-Obit 147;
TCWW 2

Savan, Glenn 1953-2003 .... **CLC 50**
See also CA 225

Savonarola, Girolamo 1452-1498 ...... **LC 152**
See also LMFS 1

Sax, Robert
See Johnson, Robert

Saxo Grammaticus c. 1150-c.
1222 .... **CMLC 58**

Saxton, Robert
See Johnson, Robert

Sayers, Dorothy L(eigh) 1893-1957 . **SSC 71;
TCLC 2, 15**
See also BPFB 3; BRWS 3; CA 104; 119;
CANR 60; CDBLB 1914-1945; CMW 4;
DAM POP; DLB 10, 36, 77, 100; MSW;
MTCW 1, 2; MTFW 2005; RGEL 2;
SSFS 12; TEA

Sayers, Valerie 1952- .... **CLC 50, 122**
See also CA 134; CANR 61; CSW

Sayles, John (Thomas) 1950- .... **CLC 7, 10,
14, 198**
See also CA 57-60; CANR 41, 84; DLB 44

Scamander, Newt
See Rowling, J.K.
Scammell, Michael 1935- .... **CLC 34**
See also CA 156
Scannel, John Vernon
See Scannell, Vernon
Scannell, Vernon 1922-2007 .... **CLC 49**
See also CA 5-8R; 266; CANR 8, 24, 57,
143; CN 1, 2; CP 1, 2, 3, 4, 5, 6, 7; CWRI
5; DLB 27; SATA 59; SATA-Obit 188
Scarlett, Susan
See Streatfeild, Noel
Scarron 1847-1910
See Mikszath, Kalman
Scarron, Paul 1610-1660 .... **LC 116**
See also GFL Beginnings to 1789; RGWL
2, 3
Schaeffer, Susan Fromberg 1941- ..... **CLC 6,
11, 22**
See also CA 49-52; CANR 18, 65, 160; CN
4, 5, 6, 7; DLB 28, 299; MTCW 1, 2;
MTFW 2005; SATA 22
Schama, Simon 1945- .... **CLC 150**
See also BEST 89:4; CA 105; CANR 39,
91, 168
Schama, Simon Michael
See Schama, Simon
Schary, Jill
See Robinson, Jill
Schell, Jonathan 1943- .... **CLC 35**
See also CA 73-76; CANR 12, 117, 187
Schelling, Friedrich Wilhelm Joseph von
1775-1854 .... **NCLC 30**
See also DLB 90
Scherer, Jean-Marie Maurice
1920- .... **CLC 16**
See also CA 110
Schevill, James (Erwin) 1920- .... **CLC 7**
See also CA 5-8R; CAAS 12; CAD; CD 5,
6; CP 1, 2, 3, 4, 5
Schiller, Friedrich von 1759-1805 ...... **DC 12;
NCLC 39, 69, 166**
See also CDWLB 2; DAM DRAM; DLB
94; EW 5; RGWL 2, 3; TWA
Schisgal, Murray (Joseph) 1926- .... **CLC 6**
See also CA 21-24R; CAD; CANR 48, 86;
CD 5, 6; MAL 5
Schlee, Ann 1934- .... **CLC 35**
See also CA 101; CANR 29, 88; SATA 44;
SATA-Brief 36
Schlegel, August Wilhelm von
1767-1845 .... **NCLC 15, 142**
See also DLB 94; RGWL 2, 3
Schlegel, Friedrich 1772-1829 .... **NCLC 45**
See also DLB 90; EW 5; RGWL 2, 3; TWA
Schlegel, Johann Elias (von)
1719(?)-1749 .... **LC 5**
Schleiermacher, Friedrich
1768-1834 .... **NCLC 107**
See also DLB 90
Schlesinger, Arthur M., Jr.
1917-2007 .... **CLC 84**
See Schlesinger, Arthur Meier
See also AITN 1; CA 1-4R; 257; CANR 1,
28, 58, 105, 187; DLB 17; INT CANR-
28; MTCW 1, 2; SATA 61; SATA-Obit
181
Schlink, Bernhard 1944- .... **CLC 174**
See also CA 163; CANR 116, 175; RGHL
Schmidt, Arno (Otto) 1914-1979 ...... **CLC 56**
See also CA 128; 109; DLB 69; EWL 3
Schmitz, Aron Hector 1861-1928 ..... **SSC 25;
TCLC 2, 35**
See also CA 104; 122; DLB 264; EW 8;
EWL 3; MTCW 1; RGWL 2, 3; WLIT 7

Schnackenberg, Gjertrud 1953- ...... **CLC 40;
PC 45**
See also AMWS 15; CA 116; CANR 100;
CP 5, 6, 7; CWP; DLB 120, 282; PFS 13,
25
Schnackenberg, Gjertrud Cecelia
See Schnackenberg, Gjertrud
Schneider, Leonard Alfred
1925-1966 .... **CLC 21**
See also CA 89-92
Schnitzler, Arthur 1862-1931 ..... **DC 17; SSC
15, 61; TCLC 4**
See also CA 104; CDWLB 2; DLB 81, 118;
EW 8; EWL 3; RGSF 2; RGWL 2, 3
Schoenberg, Arnold Franz Walter
1874-1951 .... **TCLC 75**
See also CA 109; 188
Schonberg, Arnold
See Schoenberg, Arnold Franz Walter
Schopenhauer, Arthur 1788-1860 . **NCLC 51,
157**
See also DLB 90; EW 5
Schor, Sandra (M.) 1932(?)-1990 ..... **CLC 65**
See also CA 132
Schorer, Mark 1908-1977 .... **CLC 9**
See also CA 5-8R; 73-76; CANR 7; CN 1,
2; DLB 103
Schrader, Paul (Joseph) 1946- . **CLC 26, 212**
See also CA 37-40R; CANR 41; DLB 44
Schreber, Daniel 1842-1911 .... **TCLC 123**
Schreiner, Olive (Emilie Albertina)
1855-1920 .... **TCLC 9**
See also AFW; BRWS 2; CA 105; 154;
DLB 18, 156, 190, 225; EWL 3; FW;
RGEL 2; TWA; WLIT 2; WWE 1
Schulberg, Budd 1914- .... **CLC 7, 48**
See also AMWS 18; BPFB 3; CA 25-28R;
CANR 19, 87, 178; CN 1, 2, 3, 4, 5, 6, 7;
DLB 6, 26, 28; DLBY 1981, 2001; MAL
5
Schulberg, Budd Wilson
See Schulberg, Budd
Schulman, Arnold
See Trumbo, Dalton
Schulz, Bruno 1892-1942 .. **SSC 13; TCLC 5,
51**
See also CA 115; 123; CANR 86; CDWLB
4; DLB 215; EWL 3; MTCW 2; MTFW
2005; RGSF 2; RGWL 2, 3
Schulz, Charles M. 1922-2000 .... **CLC 12**
See also AAYA 39; CA 9-12R; 187; CANR
6, 132; INT CANR-6; MTFW 2005;
SATA 10; SATA-Obit 118
Schulz, Charles Monroe
See Schulz, Charles M.
Schumacher, E(rnst) F(riedrich)
1911-1977 .... **CLC 80**
See also CA 81-84; 73-76; CANR 34, 85
Schumann, Robert 1810-1856 ...... **NCLC 143**
Schuyler, George Samuel 1895-1977 . **HR 1:3**
See also BW 2; CA 81-84; 73-76; CANR
42; DLB 29, 51
Schuyler, James Marcus 1923-1991 .. **CLC 5,
23; PC 88**
See also CA 101; 134; CP 1, 2, 3, 4, 5;
DAM POET; DLB 5, 169; EWL 3; INT
CA-101; MAL 5; WP
Schwartz, Delmore (David)
1913-1966 . **CLC 2, 4, 10, 45, 87; PC 8;
SSC 105**
See also AMWS 2; CA 17-18; 25-28R;
CANR 35; CAP 2; DLB 28, 48; EWL 3;
MAL 5; MTCW 1, 2; MTFW 2005; PAB;
RGAL 4; TUS
Schwartz, Ernst
See Ozu, Yasujiro
Schwartz, John Burnham 1965- .... **CLC 59**
See also CA 132; CANR 116, 188

Schwartz, Lynne Sharon 1939- .... **CLC 31**
See also CA 103; CANR 44, 89, 160; DLB
218; MTCW 2; MTFW 2005
Schwartz, Muriel A.
See Eliot, T(homas) S(tearns)
Schwarz-Bart, Andre 1928-2006 .... **CLC 2, 4**
See also CA 89-92; 253; CANR 109; DLB
299; RGHL
Schwarz-Bart, Simone 1938- . **BLCS; CLC 7**
See also BW 2; CA 97-100; CANR 117;
EWL 3
Schwerner, Armand 1927-1999 .... **PC 42**
See also CA 9-12R; 179; CANR 50, 85; CP
2, 3, 4, 5, 6; DLB 165
**Schwitters, Kurt (Hermann Edward Karl
Julius)** 1887-1948 .... **TCLC 95**
See also CA 158
Schwob, Marcel (Mayer Andre)
1867-1905 .... **TCLC 20**
See also CA 117; 168; DLB 123; GFL 1789
to the Present
Sciascia, Leonardo 1921-1989 .. **CLC 8, 9, 41**
See also CA 85-88; 130; CANR 35; DLB
177; EWL 3; MTCW 1; RGWL 2, 3
Scoppettone, Sandra 1936- .... **CLC 26**
See also AAYA 11, 65; BYA 8; CA 5-8R;
CANR 41, 73, 157; GLL 1; MAICYA 2;
MAICYAS 1; SATA 9, 92; WYA; YAW
Scorsese, Martin 1942- .... **CLC 20, 89, 207**
See also AAYA 38; CA 110; 114; CANR
46, 85
Scotland, Jay
See Jakes, John
Scott, Duncan Campbell
1862-1947 .... **TCLC 6**
See also CA 104; 153; DAC; DLB 92;
RGEL 2
Scott, Evelyn 1893-1963 .... **CLC 43**
See also CA 104; 112; CANR 64; DLB 9,
48; RHW
Scott, F(rancis) R(eginald)
1899-1985 .... **CLC 22**
See also CA 101; 114; CANR 87; CP 1, 2,
3, 4; DLB 88; INT CA-101; RGEL 2
Scott, Frank
See Scott, F(rancis) R(eginald)
Scott, Joan .... **CLC 65**
Scott, Joanna 1960- .... **CLC 50**
See also AMWS 17; CA 126; CANR 53,
92, 168
Scott, Joanna Jeanne
See Scott, Joanna
Scott, Paul (Mark) 1920-1978 ...... **CLC 9, 60**
See also BRWS 1; CA 81-84; 77-80; CANR
33; CN 1, 2; DLB 14, 207, 326; EWL 3;
MTCW 1; RGEL 2; RHW; WWE 1
Scott, Ridley 1937- .... **CLC 183**
See also AAYA 13, 43
Scott, Sarah 1723-1795 .... **LC 44**
See also DLB 39
Scott, Sir Walter 1771-1832 .... **NCLC 15, 69,
110, 209; PC 13; SSC 32; WLC 5**
See also AAYA 22; BRW 4; BYA 2; CD-
BLB 1789-1832; DA; DAB; DAC; DAM
MST, NOV, POET; DLB 93, 107, 116,
144, 159; GL 3; HGG; LAIT 1; RGEL 2;
RGSF 2; SSFS 10; SUFW 1; TEA; WLIT
3; YABC 2
Scribe, (Augustin) Eugene 1791-1861 . **DC 5;
NCLC 16**
See also DAM DRAM; DLB 192; GFL
1789 to the Present; RGWL 2, 3
Scrum, R.
See Crumb, R.
Scudery, Georges de 1601-1667 .... **LC 75**
See also GFL Beginnings to 1789
Scudery, Madeleine de 1607-1701 .. **LC 2, 58**
See also DLB 268; GFL Beginnings to 1789

Soderbergh, Steven 1963- .... **CLC 154**
    See also AAYA 43; CA 243
Soderbergh, Steven Andrew
    See Soderbergh, Steven
Sodergran, Edith (Irene) 1892-1923
    See Soedergran, Edith (Irene)
Soedergran, Edith (Irene)
    1892-1923 .... **TCLC 31**
    See also CA 202; DLB 259; EW 11; EWL
    3; RGWL 2, 3
Softly, Edgar
    See Lovecraft, H. P.
Softly, Edward
    See Lovecraft, H. P.
Sokolov, Alexander V(sevolodovich)
    1943- .... **CLC 59**
    See also CA 73-76; CWW 2; DLB 285;
    EWL 3; RGWL 2, 3
Sokolov, Raymond 1941- .... **CLC 7**
    See also CA 85-88
Sokolov, Sasha
    See Sokolov, Alexander V(sevolodovich)
Solo, Jay
    See Ellison, Harlan
Sologub, Fedor
    See Teternikov, Fyodor Kuzmich
Sologub, Feodor
    See Teternikov, Fyodor Kuzmich
Sologub, Fyodor
    See Teternikov, Fyodor Kuzmich
Solomons, Ikey Esquir
    See Thackeray, William Makepeace
Solomos, Dionysios 1798-1857 .... **NCLC 15**
Solwoska, Mara
    See French, Marilyn
Solzhenitsyn, Aleksandr 1918-2008 ... **CLC 1,**
    2, 4, 7, 9, 10, 18, 26, 34, 78, 134, 235;
    SSC 32, 105; WLC 5
    See also AAYA 49; AITN 1; BPFB 3; CA
    69-72; CANR 40, 65, 116; CWW 2; DA;
    DA3; DAB; DAC; DAM MST, NOV;
    DLB 302, 332; EW 13; EWL 3; EXPS;
    LAIT 4; MTCW 1, 2; MTFW 2005; NFS
    6; RGSF 2; RGWL 2, 3; SSFS 9; TWA
Solzhenitsyn, Aleksandr I.
    See Solzhenitsyn, Aleksandr
Solzhenitsyn, Aleksandr Isayevich
    See Solzhenitsyn, Aleksandr
Somers, Jane
    See Lessing, Doris
Somerville, Edith Oenone
    1858-1949 .... **SSC 56; TCLC 51**
    See also CA 196; DLB 135; RGEL 2; RGSF
    2
Somerville & Ross
    See Martin, Violet Florence; Somerville,
    Edith Oenone
Sommer, Scott 1951- .... **CLC 25**
    See also CA 106
Sommers, Christina Hoff 1950- ...... **CLC 197**
    See also CA 153; CANR 95
Sondheim, Stephen 1930- .. **CLC 30, 39, 147;**
    DC 22
    See also AAYA 11, 66; CA 103; CANR 47,
    67, 125; DAM DRAM; DFS 25; LAIT 4
Sondheim, Stephen Joshua
    See Sondheim, Stephen
Sone, Monica 1919- .... **AAL**
    See also DLB 312
Song, Cathy 1955- .... **AAL; PC 21**
    See also CA 154; CANR 118; CWP; DLB
    169, 312; EXPP; FW; PFS 5
Sontag, Susan 1933-2004 ... **CLC 1, 2, 10, 13,**
    31, 105, 195
    See also AMWS 3; CA 17-20R; 234; CANR
    25, 51, 74, 97, 184; CN 1, 2, 3, 4, 5, 6, 7;
    CPW; DA3; DAM POP; DLB 2, 67; EWL
    3; MAL 5; MBL; MTCW 1, 2; MTFW
    2005; RGAL 4; RHW; SSFS 10

Sophocles 496(?)B.C.-406(?)B.C. .... **CMLC 2,**
    47, 51, 86; DC 1; WLCS
    See also AW 1; CDWLB 1; DA; DA3;
    DAB; DAC; DAM DRAM, MST; DFS 1,
    4, 8, 24; DLB 176; LAIT 1; LATS 1:1;
    LMFS 1; RGWL 2, 3; TWA; WLIT 8
Sordello 1189-1269 .... **CMLC 15**
Sorel, Georges 1847-1922 .... **TCLC 91**
    See also CA 118; 188
Sorel, Julia
    See Drexler, Rosalyn
Sorokin, Vladimir .... **CLC 59**
    See also CA 258; DLB 285
Sorokin, Vladimir Georgievich
    See Sorokin, Vladimir
Sorrentino, Gilbert 1929-2006 .... **CLC 3, 7,**
    14, 22, 40, 247
    See also CA 77-80; 250; CANR 14, 33, 115,
    157; CN 3, 4, 5, 6, 7; CP 1, 2, 3, 4, 5, 6,
    7; DLB 5, 173; DLBY 1980; INT
    CANR-14
Soseki
    See Natsume, Soseki
Soto, Gary 1952- ... **CLC 32, 80; HLC 2; PC**
    28
    See also AAYA 10, 37; BYA 11; CA 119;
    125; CANR 50, 74, 107, 157; CLR 38;
    CP 4, 5, 6, 7; DAM MULT; DFS 26; DLB
    82; EWL 3; EXPP; HW 1, 2; INT CA-
    125; JRDA; LLW; MAICYA 2; MAIC-
    YAS 1; MAL 5; MTCW 2; MTFW 2005;
    PFS 7, 30; RGAL 4; SATA 80, 120, 174;
    WYA; YAW
Soupault, Philippe 1897-1990 .... **CLC 68**
    See also CA 116; 147; 131; EWL 3; GFL
    1789 to the Present; LMFS 2
Souster, (Holmes) Raymond 1921- .... **CLC 5,**
    14
    See also CA 13-16R; CAAS 14; CANR 13,
    29, 53; CP 1, 2, 3, 4, 5, 6, 7; DA3; DAC;
    DAM POET; DLB 88; RGEL 2; SATA 63
Southern, Terry 1924(?)-1995 .... **CLC 7**
    See also AMWS 11; BPFB 3; CA 1-4R;
    150; CANR 1, 55, 107; CN 1, 2, 3, 4, 5,
    6; DLB 2; IDFW 3, 4
Southerne, Thomas 1660-1746 .... **LC 99**
    See also DLB 80; RGEL 2
Southey, Robert 1774-1843 .... **NCLC 8, 97**
    See also BRW 4; DLB 93, 107, 142; RGEL
    2; SATA 54
Southwell, Robert 1561(?)-1595 .... **LC 108**
    See also DLB 167; RGEL 2; TEA
Southworth, Emma Dorothy Eliza Nevitte
    1819-1899 .... **NCLC 26**
    See also DLB 239
Souza, Ernest
    See Scott, Evelyn
Soyinka, Wole 1934- .. **BLC 1:3, 2:3; CLC 3,**
    5, 14, 36, 44, 179; DC 2; WLC 5
    See also AFW; BW 2, 3; CA 13-16R;
    CANR 27, 39, 82, 136; CD 5, 6; CDWLB
    3; CN 6, 7; CP 1, 2, 3, 4, 5, 6 ,7; DA;
    DA3; DAB; DAC; DAM DRAM, MST,
    MULT; DFS 10, 26; DLB 125, 332; EWL
    3; MTCW 1, 2; MTFW 2005; PFS 27;
    RGEL 2; TWA; WLIT 2; WWE 1
Spackman, W(illiam) M(ode)
    1905-1990 .... **CLC 46**
    See also CA 81-84; 132
Spacks, Barry (Bernard) 1931- .... **CLC 14**
    See also CA 154; CANR 33, 109; CP 3, 4,
    5, 6, 7; DLB 105
Spanidou, Irini 1946- .... **CLC 44**
    See also CA 185; CANR 179
Spark, Muriel 1918-2006 .... **CLC 2, 3, 5, 8,**
    13, 18, 40, 94, 242; PC 72; SSC 10, 115
    See also BRWS 1; CA 5-8R; 251; CANR
    12, 36, 76, 89, 131; CDBLB 1945-1960;
    CN 1, 2, 3, 4, 5, 6, 7; CP 1, 2, 3, 4, 5, 6,

7; DA3; DAB; DAC; DAM MST, NOV;
    DLB 15, 139; EWL 3; FW; INT CANR-
    12; LAIT 4; MTCW 1, 2; MTFW 2005;
    NFS 22; RGEL 2; TEA; WLIT 4; YAW
Spark, Muriel Sarah
    See Spark, Muriel
Spaulding, Douglas
    See Bradbury, Ray
Spaulding, Leonard
    See Bradbury, Ray
Speght, Rachel 1597-c. 1630 .... **LC 97**
    See also DLB 126
Spence, J. A. D.
    See Eliot, T(homas) S(tearns)
Spencer, Anne 1882-1975 ...... **HR 1:3; PC 77**
    See also BW 2; CA 161; DLB 51, 54
Spencer, Elizabeth 1921- .... **CLC 22; SSC 57**
    See also CA 13-16R; CANR 32, 65, 87; CN
    1, 2, 3, 4, 5, 6, 7; CSW; DLB 6, 218;
    EWL 3; MTCW 1; RGAL 4; SATA 14
Spencer, Leonard G.
    See Silverberg, Robert
Spencer, Scott 1945- .... **CLC 30**
    See also CA 113; CANR 51, 148; DLBY
    1986
Spender, Stephen 1909-1995 ..... **CLC 1, 2, 5,**
    10, 41, 91; PC 71
    See also BRWS 2; CA 9-12R; 149; CANR
    31, 54; CDBLB 1945-1960; CP 1, 2, 3, 4,
    5, 6; DA3; DAM POET; DLB 20; EWL
    3; MTCW 1, 2; MTFW 2005; PAB; PFS
    23; RGEL 2; TEA
Spengler, Oswald (Arnold Gottfried)
    1880-1936 .... **TCLC 25**
    See also CA 118; 189
Spenser, Edmund 1552(?)-1599 ...... **LC 5, 39,**
    117; PC 8, 42; WLC 5
    See also AAYA 60; BRW 1; CDBLB Before
    1660; DA; DA3; DAB; DAC; DAM MST,
    POET; DLB 167; EFS 2; EXPP; PAB;
    RGEL 2; TEA; WLIT 3; WP
Spicer, Jack 1925-1965 .... **CLC 8, 18, 72**
    See also BG 1:3; CA 85-88; DAM POET;
    DLB 5, 16, 193; GLL 1; WP
Spiegelman, Art 1948- .... **CLC 76, 178**
    See also AAYA 10, 46; CA 125; CANR 41,
    55, 74, 124; DLB 299; MTCW 2; MTFW
    2005; RGHL; SATA 109, 158; YAW
Spielberg, Peter 1929- .... **CLC 6**
    See also CA 5-8R; CANR 4, 48; DLBY
    1981
Spielberg, Steven 1947- .... **CLC 20, 188**
    See also AAYA 8, 24; CA 77-80; CANR
    32; SATA 32
Spillane, Frank Morrison
    See Spillane, Mickey
Spillane, Mickey 1918-2006 .. **CLC 3, 13, 241**
    See also BPFB 3; CA 25-28R; 252; CANR
    28, 63, 125; CMW 4; DA3; DLB 226;
    MSW; MTCW 1, 2; MTFW 2005; SATA
    66; SATA-Obit 176
Spinoza, Benedictus de 1632-1677 .. **LC 9, 58**
Spinrad, Norman (Richard) 1940- ... **CLC 46**
    See also BPFB 3; CA 37-40R, 233; CAAE
    233; CAAS 19; CANR 20, 91; DLB 8;
    INT CANR-20; SFW 4
Spitteler, Carl 1845-1924 .... **TCLC 12**
    See also CA 109; DLB 129, 332; EWL 3
Spitteler, Karl Friedrich Georg
    See Spitteler, Carl
Spivack, Kathleen (Romola Drucker)
    1938- .... **CLC 6**
    See also CA 49-52
Spivak, Gayatri Chakravorty
    1942- .... **CLC 233**
    See also CA 110; 154; CANR 91; FW;
    LMFS 2

DA3; DAB; DAC; DAM MST, POET; DLB 54, 342; EWL 3; EXPP; MAL 5; MTCW 1, 2; PAB; PFS 13, 16; RGAL 4; TUS; WP

Stevenson, Anne (Katharine) 1933- .. **CLC 7, 33**
See also BRWS 6; CA 17-20R; CAAS 9; CANR 9, 33, 123; CP 3, 4, 5, 6, 7; CWP; DLB 40; MTCW 1; RHW

Stevenson, Robert Louis (Balfour)
1850-1894 ...... **NCLC 5, 14, 63, 193; PC 84; SSC 11, 51; WLC 5**
See also AAYA 24; BPFB 3; BRW 5; BRWC 1; BRWR 1; BYA 1, 2, 4, 13; CD-BLB 1890-1914; CLR 10, 11, 107; DA; DA3; DAB; DAC; DAM MST, NOV; DLB 18, 57, 141, 156, 174; DLBD 13; GL 3; HGG; JRDA; LAIT 1, 3; MAICYA 1, 2; NFS 11, 20; RGEL 2; RGSF 2; SATA 100; SUFW; TEA; WCH; WLIT 4; WYA; YABC 2; YAW

Stewart, J(ohn) I(nnes) M(ackintosh)
1906-1994 .... **CLC 7, 14, 32**
See also CA 85-88; 147; CAAS 3; CANR 47; CMW 4; CN 1, 2, 3, 4, 5; DLB 276; MSW; MTCW 1, 2

Stewart, Mary (Florence Elinor)
1916- .... **CLC 7, 35, 117**
See also AAYA 29, 73; BPFB 3; CA 1-4R; CANR 1, 59, 130; CMW 4; CPW; DAB; FANT; RHW; SATA 12; YAW

Stewart, Mary Rainbow
See Stewart, Mary (Florence Elinor)

Stewart, Will
See Williamson, John Stewart

Stifle, June
See Campbell, Maria

Stifter, Adalbert 1805-1868 ... **NCLC 41, 198; SSC 28**
See also CDWLB 2; DLB 133; RGSF 2; RGWL 2, 3

Still, James 1906-2001 .... **CLC 49**
See also CA 65-68; 195; CAAS 17; CANR 10, 26; CSW; DLB 9; DLBY 01; SATA 29; SATA-Obit 127

Sting 1951- .... **CLC 26**
See also CA 167

Stirling, Arthur
See Sinclair, Upton

Stitt, Milan 1941-2009 .... **CLC 29**
See also CA 69-72

Stockton, Francis Richard
1834-1902 .... **TCLC 47**
See also AAYA 68; BYA 4, 13; CA 108; 137; DLB 42, 74; DLBD 13; EXPS; MAI-CYA 1, 2; SATA 44; SATA-Brief 32; SFW 4; SSFS 3; SUFW; WCH

Stockton, Frank R.
See Stockton, Francis Richard

Stoddard, Charles
See Kuttner, Henry

Stoker, Abraham 1847-1912 . **SSC 62; TCLC 8, 144; WLC 6**
See also AAYA 23; BPFB 3; BRWS 3; BYA 5; CA 105; 150; CDBLB 1890-1914; DA; DA3; DAB; DAC; DAM MST, NOV; DLB 304; GL 3; HGG; LATS 1:1; MTFW 2005; NFS 18; RGEL 2; SATA 29; SUFW; TEA; WLIT 4

Stoker, Bram
See Stoker, Abraham

Stolz, Mary 1920-2006 .... **CLC 12**
See also AAYA 8, 73; AITN 1; CA 5-8R; 255; CANR 13, 41, 112; JRDA; MAICYA 1, 2; SAAS 3; SATA 10, 71, 133; SATA-Obit 180; YAW

Stolz, Mary Slattery
See Stolz, Mary

Stone, Irving 1903-1989 .... **CLC 7**
See also AITN 1; BPFB 3; CA 1-4R; 129; CAAS 3; CANR 1, 23; CN 1, 2, 3, 4; CPW; DA3; DAM POP; INT CANR-23; MTCW 1, 2; MTFW 2005; RHW; SATA 3; SATA-Obit 64

Stone, Oliver 1946- .... **CLC 73**
See also AAYA 15, 64; CA 110; CANR 55, 125

Stone, Oliver William
See Stone, Oliver

Stone, Robert 1937- .... **CLC 5, 23, 42, 175**
See also AMWS 5; BPFB 3; CA 85-88; CANR 23, 66, 95, 173; CN 4, 5, 6, 7; DLB 152; EWL 3; INT CANR-23; MAL 5; MTCW 1; MTFW 2005

Stone, Robert Anthony
See Stone, Robert

Stone, Ruth 1915- .... **PC 53**
See also CA 45-48; CANR 2, 91; CP 5, 6, 7; CSW; DLB 105; PFS 19

Stone, Zachary
See Follett, Ken

Stoppard, Tom 1937- ... **CLC 1, 3, 4, 5, 8, 15, 29, 34, 63, 91; DC 6, 30; WLC 6**
See also AAYA 63; BRWC 1; BRWR 2; BRWS 1; CA 81-84; CANR 39, 67, 125; CBD; CD 5, 6; CDBLB 1960 to Present; DA; DA3; DAB; DAC; DAM DRAM, MST; DFS 2, 5, 8, 11, 13, 16; DLB 13, 233; DLBY 1985; EWL 3; LATS 1:2; MTCW 1, 2; MTFW 2005; RGEL 2; TEA; WLIT 4

Storey, David (Malcolm) 1933- . **CLC 2, 4, 5, 8**
See also BRWS 1; CA 81-84; CANR 36; CBD; CD 5, 6; CN 1, 2, 3, 4, 5, 6; DAM DRAM; DLB 13, 14, 207, 245, 326; EWL 3; MTCW 1; RGEL 2

Storm, Hyemeyohsts 1935- ... **CLC 3; NNAL**
See also CA 81-84; CANR 45; DAM MULT

Storm, (Hans) Theodor (Woldsen)
1817-1888 ... **NCLC 1, 195; SSC 27, 106**
See also CDWLB 2; DLB 129; EW; RGSF 2; RGWL 2, 3

Storni, Alfonsina 1892-1938 . **HLC 2; PC 33; TCLC 5**
See also CA 104; 131; DAM MULT; DLB 283; HW 1; LAW

Stoughton, William 1631-1701 .... **LC 38**
See also DLB 24

Stout, Rex (Todhunter) 1886-1975 ..... **CLC 3**
See also AAYA 79; AITN 2; BPFB 3; CA 61-64; CANR 71; CMW 4; CN 2; DLB 306; MSW; RGAL 4

Stow, (Julian) Randolph 1935- ... **CLC 23, 48**
See also CA 13-16R; CANR 33; CN 1, 2, 3, 4, 5, 6, 7; CP 1, 2, 3, 4; DLB 260; MTCW 1; RGEL 2

Stowe, Harriet (Elizabeth) Beecher
1811-1896 .... **NCLC 3, 50, 133, 195; WLC 6**
See also AAYA 53; AMWS 1; CDALB 1865-1917; CLR 131; DA; DA3; DAB; DAC; DAM MST, NOV; DLB 1, 12, 42, 74, 189, 239, 243; EXPN; FL 1:3; JRDA; LAIT 2; MAICYA 1, 2; NFS 6; RGAL 4; TUS; YABC 1

Strabo c. 64B.C.-c. 25 .... **CMLC 37**
See also DLB 176

Strachey, (Giles) Lytton
1880-1932 .... **TCLC 12**
See also BRWS 2; CA 110; 178; DLB 149; DLBD 10; EWL 3; MTCW 2; NCFS 4

Stramm, August 1874-1915 .... **PC 50**
See also CA 195; EWL 3

Strand, Mark 1934- .. **CLC 6, 18, 41, 71; PC 63**
See also AMWS 4; CA 21-24R; CANR 40, 65, 100; CP 1, 2, 3, 4, 5, 6, 7; DAM

POET; DLB 5; EWL 3; MAL 5; PAB; PFS 9, 18; RGAL 4; SATA 41; TCLE 1:2

Stratton-Porter, Gene(va Grace)
1863-1924 .... **TCLC 21**
See also ANW; BPFB 3; CA 112; 137; CLR 87; CWRI 5; DLB 221; DLBD 14; MAI-CYA 1, 2; RHW; SATA 15

Straub, Peter 1943- .... **CLC 28, 107**
See also BEST 89:1; BPFB 3; CA 85-88; CANR 28, 65, 109; CPW; DAM POP; DLBY 1984; HGG; MTCW 1, 2; MTFW 2005; SUFW 2

Straub, Peter Francis
See Straub, Peter

Strauss, Botho 1944- .... **CLC 22**
See also CA 157; CWW 2; DLB 124

Strauss, Leo 1899-1973 .... **TCLC 141**
See also CA 101; 45-48; CANR 122

Streatfeild, Mary Noel
See Streatfeild, Noel

Streatfeild, Noel 1897(?)-1986 .... **CLC 21**
See also CA 81-84; 120; CANR 31; CLR 17, 83; CWRI 5; DLB 160; MAICYA 1, 2; SATA 20; SATA-Obit 48

Stribling, T(homas) S(igismund)
1881-1965 .... **CLC 23**
See also CA 189; 107; CMW 4; DLB 9; RGAL 4

Strindberg, (Johan) August
1849-1912 ... **DC 18; TCLC 1, 8, 21, 47; WLC 6**
See also CA 104; 135; DA; DA3; DAB; DAC; DAM DRAM, MST; DFS 4, 9; DLB 259; EW 7; EWL 3; IDTP; LMFS 2; MTCW 2; MTFW 2005; RGWL 2, 3; TWA

Stringer, Arthur 1874-1950 .... **TCLC 37**
See also CA 161; DLB 92

Stringer, David
See Roberts, Keith (John Kingston)

Stroheim, Erich von 1885-1957 ..... **TCLC 71**

Strugatskii, Arkadii (Natanovich)
1925-1991 .... **CLC 27**
See also CA 106; 135; DLB 302; SFW 4

Strugatskii, Boris (Natanovich)
1933- .... **CLC 27**
See also CA 106; DLB 302; SFW 4

Strugatsky, Arkadii Natanovich
See Strugatskii, Arkadii (Natanovich)

Strugatsky, Boris (Natanovich)
See Strugatskii, Boris (Natanovich)

Strummer, Joe 1952-2002 .... **CLC 30**

Strunk, William, Jr. 1869-1946 ...... **TCLC 92**
See also CA 118; 164; NCFS 5

Stryk, Lucien 1924- .... **PC 27**
See also CA 13-16R; CANR 10, 28, 55, 110; CP 1, 2, 3, 4, 5, 6, 7

Stuart, Don A.
See Campbell, John W(ood, Jr.)

Stuart, Ian
See MacLean, Alistair (Stuart)

Stuart, Jesse (Hilton) 1906-1984 ... **CLC 1, 8, 11, 14, 34; SSC 31**
See also CA 5-8R; 112; CANR 31; CN 1, 2, 3; DLB 9, 48, 102; DLBY 1984; SATA 2; SATA-Obit 36

Stubblefield, Sally
See Trumbo, Dalton

Sturgeon, Theodore (Hamilton)
1918-1985 .... **CLC 22, 39**
See also AAYA 51; BPFB 3; BYA 9, 10; CA 81-84; 116; CANR 32, 103; DLB 8; DLBY 1985; HGG; MTCW 1, 2; MTFW 2005; SCFW; SFW 4; SUFW

Sturges, Preston 1898-1959 .... **TCLC 48**
See also CA 114; 149; DLB 26

Styron, William 1925-2006 .. **CLC 1, 3, 5, 11, 15, 60, 232, 244; SSC 25**
See also AMW; AMWC 2; BEST 90:4; BPFB 3; CA 5-8R; 255; CANR 6, 33, 74, 126; CDALB 1968-1988; CN 1, 2, 3, 4, 5, 6, 7; CPW; CSW; DA3; DAM NOV, POP; DLB 2, 143, 299; DLBY 1980; EWL 3; INT CANR-6; LAIT 2; MAL 5; MTCW 1, 2; MTFW 2005; NCFS 1; NFS 22; RGAL 4; RGHL; RHW; TUS

Styron, William Clark
See Styron, William

Su, Chien 1884-1918 .... **TCLC 24**
See also CA 123; EWL 3

Suarez Lynch, B.
See Bioy Casares, Adolfo; Borges, Jorge Luis

Suassuna, Ariano Vilar 1927- .... **HLCS 1**
See also CA 178; DLB 307; HW 2; LAW

Suckert, Kurt Erich
See Malaparte, Curzio

Suckling, Sir John 1609-1642 . **LC 75; PC 30**
See also BRW 2; DAM POET; DLB 58, 126; EXPP; PAB; RGEL 2

Suckow, Ruth 1892-1960 .... **SSC 18**
See also CA 193; 113; DLB 9, 102; RGAL 4; TCWW 2

Sudermann, Hermann 1857-1928 .. **TCLC 15**
See also CA 107; 201; DLB 118

Sue, Eugene 1804-1857 .... **NCLC 1**
See also DLB 119

Sueskind, Patrick 1949- .... **CLC 182**
See Suskind, Patrick
See also BPFB 3; CA 145; CWW 2

Suetonius c. 70-c. 130 .... **CMLC 60**
See also AW 2; DLB 211; RGWL 2, 3; WLIT 8

Su Hsuan-ying
See Su, Chien

Su Hsuean-ying
See Su, Chien

Sukenick, Ronald 1932-2004 ..... **CLC 3, 4, 6, 48**
See also CA 25-28R, 209; 229; CAAE 209; CAAS 8; CANR 32, 89; CN 3, 4, 5, 6, 7; DLB 173; DLBY 1981

Suknaski, Andrew 1942- .... **CLC 19**
See also CA 101; CP 3, 4, 5, 6, 7; DLB 53

Sullivan, Vernon
See Vian, Boris

Sully Prudhomme, Rene-Francois-Armand
1839-1907 .... **TCLC 31**
See also CA 170; DLB 332; GFL 1789 to the Present

Su Man-shu
See Su, Chien

Sumarokov, Aleksandr Petrovich
1717-1777 .... **LC 104**
See also DLB 150

Summerforest, Ivy B.
See Kirkup, James

Summers, Andrew James
See Summers, Andy

Summers, Andy 1942- .... **CLC 26**
See also CA 255

Summers, Hollis (Spurgeon, Jr.)
1916- .... **CLC 10**
See also CA 5-8R; CANR 3; CN 1, 2, 3; CP 1, 2, 3, 4; DLB 6; TCLE 1:2

Summers, (Alphonsus Joseph-Mary Augustus) Montague
1880-1948 .... **TCLC 16**
See also CA 118; 163

Sumner, Gordon Matthew
See Sting

Sun Tzu c. 400B.C.-c. 320B.C. ...... **CMLC 56**

Surdas c. 1478-c. 1583 .... **LC 163**
See also RGWL 2, 3

Surrey, Henry Howard 1517-1574 ... **LC 121; PC 59**
See also BRW 1; RGEL 2

Surtees, Robert Smith 1805-1864 .. **NCLC 14**
See also DLB 21; RGEL 2

Susann, Jacqueline 1921-1974 .... **CLC 3**
See also AITN 1; BPFB 3; CA 65-68; 53-56; MTCW 1, 2

Su Shi
See Su Shih

Su Shih 1036-1101 .... **CMLC 15**
See also RGWL 2, 3

Suskind, Patrick .... **CLC 182**
See Sueskind, Patrick
See also BPFB 3; CA 145; CWW 2

Suso, Heinrich c. 1295-1366 .... **CMLC 87**

Sutcliff, Rosemary 1920-1992 .... **CLC 26**
See also AAYA 10; BYA 1, 4; CA 5-8R; 139; CANR 37; CLR 1, 37, 138; CPW; DAB; DAC; DAM MST, POP; JRDA; LATS 1:1; MAICYA 1, 2; MAICYAS 1; RHW; SATA 6, 44, 78; SATA-Obit 73; WYA; YAW

Sutherland, Efua (Theodora Morgue)
1924-1996 .... **BLC 2:3**
See also AFW; BW 1; CA 105; CWD; DLB 117; EWL 3; IDTP; SATA 25

Sutro, Alfred 1863-1933 .... **TCLC 6**
See also CA 105; 185; DLB 10; RGEL 2

Sutton, Henry
See Slavitt, David R.

Su Yuan-ying
See Su, Chien

Su Yuean-ying
See Su, Chien

Suzuki, D. T.
See Suzuki, Daisetz Teitaro

Suzuki, Daisetz T.
See Suzuki, Daisetz Teitaro

Suzuki, Daisetz Teitaro
1870-1966 .... **TCLC 109**
See also CA 121; 111; MTCW 1, 2; MTFW 2005

Suzuki, Teitaro
See Suzuki, Daisetz Teitaro

Svareff, Count Vladimir
See Crowley, Edward Alexander

Svevo, Italo
See Schmitz, Aron Hector

Swados, Elizabeth 1951- .... **CLC 12**
See also CA 97-100; CANR 49, 163; INT CA-97-100

Swados, Elizabeth A.
See Swados, Elizabeth

Swados, Harvey 1920-1972 .... **CLC 5**
See also CA 5-8R; 37-40R; CANR 6; CN 1; DLB 2, 335; MAL 5

Swados, Liz
See Swados, Elizabeth

Swan, Gladys 1934- .... **CLC 69**
See also CA 101; CANR 17, 39; TCLE 1:2

Swanson, Logan
See Matheson, Richard

Swarthout, Glendon (Fred)
1918-1992 .... **CLC 35**
See also AAYA 55; CA 1-4R; 139; CANR 1, 47; CN 1, 2, 3, 4, 5; LAIT 5; NFS 29; SATA 26; TCWW 1, 2; YAW

Swedenborg, Emanuel 1688-1772 ..... **LC 105**

Sweet, Sarah C.
See Jewett, (Theodora) Sarah Orne

Swenson, May 1919-1989 ...... **CLC 4, 14, 61, 106; PC 14**
See also AMWS 4; CA 5-8R; 130; CANR 36, 61, 131; CP 1, 2, 3, 4; DA; DAB; DAC; DAM MST, POET; DLB 5; EXPP; GLL 2; MAL 5; MTCW 1, 2; MTFW 2005; PFS 16, 30; SATA 15; WP

Swift, Augustus
See Lovecraft, H. P.

Swift, Graham 1949- .... **CLC 41, 88, 233**
See also BRWC 2; BRWS 5; CA 117; 122; CANR 46, 71, 128, 181; CN 4, 5, 6, 7; DLB 194, 326; MTCW 2; MTFW 2005; NFS 18; RGSF 2

Swift, Jonathan 1667-1745 ..... **LC 1, 42, 101; PC 9; WLC 6**
See also AAYA 41; BRW 3; BRWC 1; BRWR 1; BYA 5, 14; CDBLB 1660-1789; CLR 53; DA; DA3; DAB; DAC; DAM MST, NOV, POET; DLB 39, 95, 101; EXPN; LAIT 1; NFS 6; PFS 27; RGEL 2; SATA 19; TEA; WCH; WLIT 3

Swinburne, Algernon Charles
1837-1909 ... **PC 24; TCLC 8, 36; WLC 6**
See also BRW 5; CA 105; 140; CDBLB 1832-1890; DA; DA3; DAB; DAC; DAM MST, POET; DLB 35, 57; PAB; RGEL 2; TEA

Swinfen, Ann .... **CLC 34**
See also CA 202

Swinnerton, Frank (Arthur)
1884-1982 .... **CLC 31**
See also CA 202; 108; CN 1, 2, 3; DLB 34

Swinnerton, Frank Arthur
1884-1982 .... **CLC 31**
See also CA 108; DLB 34

Swithen, John
See King, Stephen

Sylvia
See Ashton-Warner, Sylvia (Constance)

Symmes, Robert Edward
See Duncan, Robert

Symonds, John Addington
1840-1893 .... **NCLC 34**
See also BRWS 14; DLB 57, 144

Symons, Arthur 1865-1945 .... **TCLC 11**
See also BRWS 14; CA 107; 189; DLB 19, 57, 149; RGEL 2

Symons, Julian (Gustave)
1912-1994 .... **CLC 2, 14, 32**
See also CA 49-52; 147; CAAS 3; CANR 3, 33, 59; CMW 4; CN 1, 2, 3, 4, 5; CP 1, 3, 4; DLB 87, 155; DLBY 1992; MSW; MTCW 1

Synge, (Edmund) J(ohn) M(illington)
1871-1909 .... **DC 2; TCLC 6, 37**
See also BRW 6; BRWR 1; CA 104; 141; CDBLB 1890-1914; DAM DRAM; DFS 18; DLB 10, 19; EWL 3; RGEL 2; TEA; WLIT 4

Syruc, J.
See Milosz, Czeslaw

Szirtes, George 1948- .... **CLC 46; PC 51**
See also CA 109; CANR 27, 61, 117; CP 4, 5, 6, 7

Szymborska, Wislawa 1923- ... **CLC 99, 190; PC 44**
See also AAYA 76; CA 154; CANR 91, 133, 181; CDWLB 4; CWP; CWW; DA3; DLB 232, 332; DLBY 1996; EWL 3; MTCW 2; MTFW 2005; PFS 15, 27; RGHL; RGWL 3

T. O., Nik
See Annensky, Innokenty (Fyodorovich)

Tabori, George 1914-2007 .... **CLC 19**
See also CA 49-52; 262; CANR 4, 69; CBD; CD 5, 6; DLB 245; RGHL

Tacitus c. 55-c. 117 .... **CMLC 56**
See also AW 2; CDWLB 1; DLB 211; RGWL 2, 3; WLIT 8

Tadjo, Veronique 1955- .... **BLC 2:3**
See also EWL 3

Tagore, Rabindranath 1861-1941 .... **PC 8; SSC 48; TCLC 3, 53**
See also CA 104; 120; DA3; DAM DRAM, POET; DFS 26; DLB 323, 332; EWL 3; MTCW 1, 2; MTFW 2005; PFS 18; RGEL 2; RGSF 2; RGWL 2, 3; TWA

Taine, Hippolyte Adolphe
1828-1893 .... **NCLC 15**
See also EW 7; GFL 1789 to the Present

Talayesva, Don C. 1890-(?) .... **NNAL**

Talese, Gay 1932- .... **CLC 37, 232**
See also AITN 1; AMWS 17; CA 1-4R; CANR 9, 58, 137, 177; DLB 185; INT CANR-9; MTCW 1, 2; MTFW 2005

Tallent, Elizabeth 1954- .... **CLC 45**
See also CA 117; CANR 72; DLB 130

Tallmountain, Mary 1918-1997 .... **NNAL**
See also CA 146; 161; DLB 193

Tally, Ted 1952- .... **CLC 42**
See also CA 120; 124; CAD; CANR 125; CD 5, 6; INT CA-124

Talvik, Heiti 1904-1947 .... **TCLC 87**
See also EWL 3

Tamayo y Baus, Manuel
1829-1898 .... **NCLC 1**

Tammsaare, A(nton) H(ansen)
1878-1940 .... **TCLC 27**
See also CA 164; CDWLB 4; DLB 220; EWL 3

Tam'si, Tchicaya U
See Tchicaya, Gerald Felix

Tan, Amy 1952- ..... **AAL; CLC 59, 120, 151, 257**
See also AAYA 9, 48; AMWS 10; BEST 89:3; BPFB 3; CA 136; CANR 54, 105, 132; CDALBS; CN 6, 7; CPW 1; DA3; DAM MULT, NOV, POP; DLB 173, 312; EXPN; FL 1:6; FW; LAIT 3, 5; MAL 5; MTCW 2; MTFW 2005; NFS 1, 13, 16; RGAL 4; SATA 75; SSFS 9; YAW

Tandem, Carl Felix
See Spitteler, Carl

Tandem, Felix
See Spitteler, Carl

Tania B.
See Blixen, Karen (Christentze Dinesen)

Tanizaki, Jun'ichiro 1886-1965 ... **CLC 8, 14, 28; SSC 21**
See also CA 93-96; 25-28R; DLB 180; EWL 3; MJW; MTCW 2; MTFW 2005; RGSF 2; RGWL 2

Tanizaki Jun'ichiro
See Tanizaki, Jun'ichiro

Tannen, Deborah 1945- .... **CLC 206**
See also CA 118; CANR 95

Tannen, Deborah Frances
See Tannen, Deborah

Tanner, William
See Amis, Kingsley

Tante, Dilly
See Kunitz, Stanley

Tao Lao
See Storni, Alfonsina

Tapahonso, Luci 1953- .... **NNAL; PC 65**
See also CA 145; CANR 72, 127; DLB 175

Tarantino, Quentin (Jerome)
1963- .... **CLC 125, 230**
See also AAYA 58; CA 171; CANR 125

Tarassoff, Lev
See Troyat, Henri

Tarbell, Ida M(inerva) 1857-1944 . **TCLC 40**
See also CA 122; 181; DLB 47

Tarchetti, Ugo 1839(?)-1869 .... **SSC 119**

Tardieu d'Esclavelles,
    Louise-Florence-Petronille
See Epinay, Louise d'

Tarkington, (Newton) Booth
1869-1946 .... **TCLC 9**
See also BPFB 3; BYA 3; CA 110; 143; CWRI 5; DLB 9, 102; MAL 5; MTCW 2; RGAL 4; SATA 17

Tarkovskii, Andrei Arsen'evich
See Tarkovsky, Andrei (Arsenyevich)

Tarkovsky, Andrei (Arsenyevich)
1932-1986 .... **CLC 75**
See also CA 127

Tartt, Donna 1964(?)- .... **CLC 76**
See also AAYA 56; CA 142; CANR 135; MTFW 2005

Tasso, Torquato 1544-1595 .... **LC 5, 94**
See also EFS 2; EW 2; RGWL 2, 3; WLIT 7

Tate, (John Orley) Allen 1899-1979 .. **CLC 2, 4, 6, 9, 11, 14, 24; PC 50**
See also AMW; CA 5-8R; 85-88; CANR 32, 108; CN 1, 2; CP 1, 2; DLB 4, 45, 63; DLBD 17; EWL 3; MAL 5; MTCW 1, 2; MTFW 2005; RGAL 4; RHW

Tate, Ellalice
See Hibbert, Eleanor Alice Burford

Tate, James (Vincent) 1943- ..... **CLC 2, 6, 25**
See also CA 21-24R; CANR 29, 57, 114; CP 1, 2, 3, 4, 5, 6, 7; DLB 5, 169; EWL 3; PFS 10, 15; RGAL 4; WP

Tate, Nahum 1652(?)-1715 .... **LC 109**
See also DLB 80; RGEL 2

Tauler, Johannes c. 1300-1361 ...... **CMLC 37**
See also DLB 179; LMFS 1

Tavel, Ronald 1936-2009 .... **CLC 6**
See also CA 21-24R; CAD; CANR 33; CD 5, 6

Taviani, Paolo 1931- .... **CLC 70**
See also CA 153

Taylor, Bayard 1825-1878 .... **NCLC 89**
See also DLB 3, 189, 250, 254; RGAL 4

Taylor, C(ecil) P(hilip) 1929-1981 .... **CLC 27**
See also CA 25-28R; 105; CANR 47; CBD

Taylor, Edward 1642(?)-1729 ..... **LC 11, 163; PC 63**
See also AMW; DA; DAB; DAC; DAM MST, POET; DLB 24; EXPP; RGAL 4; TUS

Taylor, Eleanor Ross 1920- .... **CLC 5**
See also CA 81-84; CANR 70

Taylor, Elizabeth 1912-1975 .... **CLC 2, 4, 29; SSC 100**
See also CA 13-16R; CANR 9, 70; CN 1, 2; DLB 139; MTCW 1; RGEL 2; SATA 13

Taylor, Frederick Winslow
1856-1915 .... **TCLC 76**
See also CA 188

Taylor, Henry 1942- .... **CLC 44**
See also CA 33-36R; CAAS 7; CANR 31, 178; CP 6, 7; DLB 5; PFS 10

Taylor, Henry Splawn
See Taylor, Henry

Taylor, Kamala 1924-2004 .... **CLC 8, 38**
See also BYA 13; CA 77-80; 227; CN 1, 2, 3, 4, 5, 6, 7; DLB 323; EWL 3; MTFW 2005; NFS 13

Taylor, Mildred D. 1943- .... **CLC 21**
See also AAYA 10, 47; BW 1; BYA 3, 8; CA 85-88; CANR 25, 115, 136; CLR 9, 59, 90; CSW; DLB 52; JRDA; LAIT 3; MAICYA 1, 2; MTFW 2005; SAAS 5; SATA 135; WYA; YAW

Taylor, Peter (Hillsman) 1917-1994 .. **CLC 1, 4, 18, 37, 44, 50, 71; SSC 10, 84**
See also AMWS 5; BPFB 3; CA 13-16R; 147; CANR 9, 50; CN 1, 2, 3, 4, 5; CSW; DLB 218, 278; DLBY 1981, 1994; EWL 3; EXPS; INT CANR-9; MAL 5; MTCW 1, 2; MTFW 2005; RGSF 2; SSFS 9; TUS

Taylor, Robert Lewis 1912-1998 .... **CLC 14**
See also CA 1-4R; 170; CANR 3, 64; CN 1, 2; SATA 10; TCWW 1, 2

Tchekhov, Anton
See Chekhov, Anton (Pavlovich)

Tchicaya, Gerald Felix 1931-1988 .. **CLC 101**
See also CA 129; 125; CANR 81; EWL 3

Tchicaya U Tam'si
See Tchicaya, Gerald Felix

Teasdale, Sara 1884-1933 .... **PC 31; TCLC 4**
See also CA 104; 163; DLB 45; GLL 1; PFS 14; RGAL 4; SATA 32; TUS

Tecumseh 1768-1813 .... **NNAL**
See also DAM MULT

Tegner, Esaias 1782-1846 .... **NCLC 2**

Teilhard de Chardin, (Marie Joseph) Pierre
1881-1955 .... **TCLC 9**
See also CA 105; 210; GFL 1789 to the Present

Temple, Ann
See Mortimer, Penelope (Ruth)

Tennant, Emma 1937- .... **CLC 13, 52**
See also BRWS 9; CA 65-68; CAAS 9; CANR 10, 38, 59, 88, 177; CN 3, 4, 5, 6, 7; DLB 14; EWL 3; SFW 4

Tenneshaw, S.M.
See Silverberg, Robert

Tenney, Tabitha Gilman
1762-1837 .... **NCLC 122**
See also DLB 37, 200

Tennyson, Alfred 1809-1892 ... **NCLC 30, 65, 115, 202; PC 6; WLC 6**
See also AAYA 50; BRW 4; CDBLB 1832-1890; DA; DA3; DAB; DAC; DAM MST, POET; DLB 32; EXPP; PAB; PFS 1, 2, 4, 11, 15, 19; RGEL 2; TEA; WLIT 4; WP

Teran, Lisa St. Aubin de
See St. Aubin de Teran, Lisa

Terence c. 184B.C.-c. 159B.C. ...... **CMLC 14; DC 7**
See also AW 1; CDWLB 1; DLB 211; RGWL 2, 3; TWA; WLIT 8

Teresa de Jesus, St. 1515-1582 .... **LC 18, 149**

Teresa of Avila, St.
See Teresa de Jesus, St.

Terkel, Louis
See Terkel, Studs

Terkel, Studs 1912-2008 .... **CLC 38**
See also AAYA 32; AITN 1; CA 57-60; 278; CANR 18, 45, 67, 132; DA3; MTCW 1, 2; MTFW 2005; TUS

Terkel, Studs Louis
See Terkel, Studs

Terry, C. V.
See Slaughter, Frank G(ill)

Terry, Megan 1932- .... **CLC 19; DC 13**
See also CA 77-80; CABS 3; CAD; CANR 43; CD 5, 6; CWD; DFS 18; DLB 7, 249; GLL 2

Tertullian c. 155-c. 245 .... **CMLC 29**

Tertz, Abram
See Sinyavsky, Andrei (Donatevich)

Tesich, Steve 1943(?)-1996 .... **CLC 40, 69**
See also CA 105; 152; CAD; DLBY 1983

Tesla, Nikola 1856-1943 .... **TCLC 88**

Teternikov, Fyodor Kuzmich
1863-1927 .... **TCLC 9**
See also CA 104; DLB 295; EWL 3

Tevis, Walter 1928-1984 .... **CLC 42**
See also CA 113; SFW 4

Tey, Josephine
See Mackintosh, Elizabeth

Thackeray, William Makepeace
1811-1863 ...... **NCLC 5, 14, 22, 43, 169; WLC 6**
See also BRW 5; BRWC 2; CDBLB 1832-1890; DA; DA3; DAB; DAC; DAM MST,

NOV; DLB 21, 55, 159, 163; NFS 13; RGEL 2; SATA 23; TEA; WLIT 3

Thakura, Ravindranatha
See Tagore, Rabindranath

Thames, C. H.
See Marlowe, Stephen

Tharoor, Shashi 1956- .... **CLC 70**
See also CA 141; CANR 91; CN 6, 7

Thelwall, John 1764-1834 .... **NCLC 162**
See also DLB 93, 158

Thelwell, Michael Miles 1939- .... **CLC 22**
See also BW 2; CA 101

Theo, Ion
See Theodorescu, Ion N.

Theobald, Lewis, Jr.
See Lovecraft, H. P.

Theocritus c. 310B.C.- .... **CMLC 45**
See also AW 1; DLB 176; RGWL 2, 3

Theodorescu, Ion N. 1880-1967 .... **CLC 80**
See also CA 167; 116; CDWLB 4; DLB 220; EWL 3

Theriault, Yves 1915-1983 .... **CLC 79**
See also CA 102; CANR 150; CCA 1; DAC; DAM MST; DLB 88; EWL 3

Therion, Master
See Crowley, Edward Alexander

Theroux, Alexander 1939- .... **CLC 2, 25**
See also CA 85-88; CANR 20, 63; CN 4, 5, 6, 7

Theroux, Alexander Louis
See Theroux, Alexander

Theroux, Paul 1941- .... **CLC 5, 8, 11, 15, 28, 46, 159**
See also AAYA 28; AMWS 8; BEST 89:4; BPFB 3; CA 33-36R; CANR 20, 45, 74, 133, 179; CDALBS; CN 1, 2, 3, 4, 5, 6, 7; CP 1; CPW 1; DA3; DAM POP; DLB 2, 218; EWL 3; HGG; MAL 5; MTCW 1, 2; MTFW 2005; RGAL 4; SATA 44, 109; TUS

Theroux, Paul Edward
See Theroux, Paul

Thesen, Sharon 1946- .... **CLC 56**
See also CA 163; CANR 125; CP 5, 6, 7; CWP

Thespis fl. 6th cent. B.C.- .... **CMLC 51**
See also LMFS 1

Thevenin, Denis
See Duhamel, Georges

Thibault, Jacques Anatole Francois
1844-1924 .... **TCLC 9**
See also CA 106; 127; DA3; DAM NOV; DLB 123, 330; EWL 3; GFL 1789 to the Present; MTCW 1, 2; RGWL 2, 3; SUFW 1; TWA

Thiele, Colin 1920-2006 .... **CLC 17**
See also CA 29-32R; CANR 12, 28, 53, 105; CLR 27; CP 1, 2; DLB 289; MAICYA 1, 2; SAAS 2; SATA 14, 72, 125; YAW

Thiong'o, Ngugi Wa
See Ngugi wa Thiong'o

Thistlethwaite, Bel
See Wetherald, Agnes Ethelwyn

Thomas, Audrey (Callahan) 1935- .... **CLC 7, 13, 37, 107; SSC 20**
See also AITN 2; CA 21-24R, 237; CAAE 237; CAAS 19; CANR 36, 58; CN 2, 3, 4, 5, 6, 7; DLB 60; MTCW 1; RGSF 2

Thomas, Augustus 1857-1934 .... **TCLC 97**
See also MAL 5

Thomas, D.M. 1935- ..... **CLC 13, 22, 31, 132**
See also BPFB 3; BRWS 4; CA 61-64; CAAS 11; CANR 17, 45, 75; CDBLB 1960 to Present; CN 4, 5, 6, 7; CP 1, 2, 3, 4, 5, 6, 7; DA3; DLB 40, 207, 299; HGG; INT CANR-17; MTCW 1, 2; MTFW 2005; RGHL; SFW 4

Thomas, Dylan (Marlais) 1914-1953 .... **PC 2, 52; SSC 3, 44; TCLC 1, 8, 45, 105; WLC 6**
See also AAYA 45; BRWS 1; CA 104; 120; CANR 65; CDBLB 1945-1960; DA; DA3; DAB; DAC; DAM DRAM, MST, POET; DLB 13, 20, 139; EWL 3; EXPP; LAIT 3; MTCW 1, 2; MTFW 2005; PAB; PFS 1, 3, 8; RGEL 2; RGSF 2; SATA 60; TEA; WLIT 4; WP

Thomas, (Philip) Edward 1878-1917 . **PC 53; TCLC 10**
See also BRW 6; BRWS 3; CA 106; 153; DAM POET; DLB 19, 98, 156, 216; EWL 3; PAB; RGEL 2

Thomas, J.F.
See Fleming, Thomas

Thomas, Joyce Carol 1938- .... **CLC 35**
See also AAYA 12, 54; BW 2, 3; CA 113; 116; CANR 48, 114, 135; CLR 19; DLB 33; INT CA-116; JRDA; MAICYA 1, 2; MTCW 1, 2; MTFW 2005; SAAS 7; SATA 40, 78, 123, 137; SATA-Essay 137; WYA; YAW

Thomas, Lewis 1913-1993 .... **CLC 35**
See also ANW; CA 85-88; 143; CANR 38, 60; DLB 275; MTCW 1, 2

Thomas, M. Carey 1857-1935 .... **TCLC 89**
See also FW

Thomas, Paul
See Mann, (Paul) Thomas

Thomas, Piri 1928- .... **CLC 17; HLCS 2**
See also CA 73-76; HW 1; LLW

Thomas, R(onald) S(tuart)
1913-2000 .... **CLC 6, 13, 48**
See also BRWS 12; CA 89-92; 189; CAAS 4; CANR 30; CDBLB 1960 to Present; CP 1, 2, 3, 4, 5, 6, 7; DAB; DAM POET; DLB 27; EWL 3; MTCW 1; RGEL 2

Thomas, Ross (Elmore) 1926-1995 .. **CLC 39**
See also CA 33-36R; 150; CANR 22, 63; CMW 4

Thompson, Francis (Joseph)
1859-1907 .... **TCLC 4**
See also BRW 5; CA 104; 189; CDBLB 1890-1914; DLB 19; RGEL 2; TEA

Thompson, Francis Clegg
See Mencken, H(enry) L(ouis)

Thompson, Hunter S. 1937(?)-2005 .. **CLC 9, 17, 40, 104, 229**
See also AAYA 45; BEST 89:1; BPFB 3; CA 17-20R; 236; CANR 23, 46, 74, 77, 111, 133; CPW; CSW; DA3; DAM POP; DLB 185; MTCW 1, 2; MTFW 2005; TUS

Thompson, James Myers
See Thompson, Jim

Thompson, Jim 1906-1977 .... **CLC 69**
See also BPFB 3; CA 140; CMW 4; CPW; DLB 226; MSW

Thompson, Judith (Clare Francesca)
1954- .... **CLC 39**
See also CA 143; CD 5, 6; CWD; DFS 22; DLB 334

Thomson, James 1700-1748 .... **LC 16, 29, 40**
See also BRWS 3; DAM POET; DLB 95; RGEL 2

Thomson, James 1834-1882 .... **NCLC 18**
See also DAM POET; DLB 35; RGEL 2

Thoreau, Henry David 1817-1862 .. **NCLC 7, 21, 61, 138, 207; PC 30; WLC 6**
See also AAYA 42; AMW; ANW; BYA 3; CDALB 1640-1865; DA; DA3; DAB; DAC; DAM MST; DLB 1, 183, 223, 270, 298; LAIT 2; LMFS 1; NCFS 3; RGAL 4; TUS

Thorndike, E. L.
See Thorndike, Edward L(ee)

Thorndike, Edward L(ee)
1874-1949 .... **TCLC 107**
See also CA 121

Thornton, Hall
See Silverberg, Robert

Thorpe, Adam 1956- .... **CLC 176**
See also CA 129; CANR 92, 160; DLB 231

Thorpe, Thomas Bangs
1815-1878 .... **NCLC 183**
See also DLB 3, 11, 248; RGAL 4

Thubron, Colin 1939- .... **CLC 163**
See also CA 25-28R; CANR 12, 29, 59, 95, 171; CN 5, 6, 7; DLB 204, 231

Thubron, Colin Gerald Dryden
See Thubron, Colin

Thucydides c. 455B.C.-c. 395B.C. . **CMLC 17**
See also AW 1; DLB 176; RGWL 2, 3; WLIT 8

Thumboo, Edwin Nadason 1933- .... **PC 30**
See also CA 194; CP 1

Thurber, James (Grover)
1894-1961 .. **CLC 5, 11, 25, 125; SSC 1, 47**
See also AAYA 56; AMWS 1; BPFB 3; BYA 5; CA 73-76; CANR 17, 39; CDALB 1929-1941; CWRI 5; DA; DA3; DAB; DAC; DAM DRAM, MST, NOV; DLB 4, 11, 22, 102; EWL 3; EXPS; FANT; LAIT 3; MAICYA 1, 2; MAL 5; MTCW 1, 2; MTFW 2005; RGAL 4; RGSF 2; SATA 13; SSFS 1, 10, 19; SUFW; TUS

Thurman, Wallace (Henry)
1902-1934 .. **BLC 1:3; HR 1:3; TCLC 6**
See also BW 1, 3; CA 104; 124; CANR 81; DAM MULT; DLB 51

Tibullus c. 54B.C.-c. 18B.C. .... **CMLC 36**
See also AW 2; DLB 211; RGWL 2, 3; WLIT 8

Ticheburn, Cheviot
See Ainsworth, William Harrison

Tieck, (Johann) Ludwig
1773-1853 ..... **NCLC 5, 46; SSC 31, 100**
See also CDWLB 2; DLB 90; EW 5; IDTP; RGSF 2; RGWL 2, 3; SUFW

Tiger, Derry
See Ellison, Harlan

Tilghman, Christopher 1946- .... **CLC 65**
See also CA 159; CANR 135, 151; CSW; DLB 244

Tillich, Paul (Johannes)
1886-1965 .... **CLC 131**
See also CA 5-8R; 25-28R; CANR 33; MTCW 1, 2

Tillinghast, Richard (Williford)
1940- .... **CLC 29**
See also CA 29-32R; CAAS 23; CANR 26, 51, 96; CP 2, 3, 4, 5, 6, 7; CSW

Tillman, Lynne (?)- .... **CLC 231**
See also CA 173; CANR 144, 172

Timrod, Henry 1828-1867 .... **NCLC 25**
See also DLB 3, 248; RGAL 4

Tindall, Gillian (Elizabeth) 1938- ...... **CLC 7**
See also CA 21-24R; CANR 11, 65, 107; CN 1, 2, 3, 4, 5, 6, 7

Ting Ling
See Chiang, Pin-chin

Tiptree, James, Jr.
See Sheldon, Alice Hastings Bradley

Tirone Smith, Mary-Ann 1944- .... **CLC 39**
See also CA 118; 136; CANR 113; SATA 143

Tirso de Molina 1580(?)-1648 .... **DC 13; HLCS 2; LC 73**
See also RGWL 2, 3

Titmarsh, Michael Angelo
See Thackeray, William Makepeace

Tocqueville, Alexis (Charles Henri Maurice Clerel Comte) de 1805-1859 .. **NCLC 7, 63**
See also EW 6; GFL 1789 to the Present; TWA

Toe, Tucker
See Westlake, Donald E.

Toer, Pramoedya Ananta
1925-2006 .... **CLC 186**
See also CA 197; 251; CANR 170; DLB 348; RGWL 3

Toffler, Alvin 1928- .... **CLC 168**
See also CA 13-16R; CANR 15, 46, 67, 183; CPW; DAM POP; MTCW 1, 2

Toibin, Colm 1955- .... **CLC 162**
See also CA 142; CANR 81, 149; CN 7; DLB 271

Tolkien, John Ronald Reuel
See Tolkien, J.R.R

Tolkien, J.R.R 1892-1973 ...... **CLC 1, 2, 3, 8, 12, 38; TCLC 137; WLC 6**
See also AAYA 10; AITN 1; BPFB 3; BRWC 2; BRWS 2; CA 17-18; 45-48; CANR 36, 134; CAP 2; CDBLB 1914-1945; CLR 56; CN 1; CPW 1; CWRI 5; DA; DA3; DAB; DAC; DAM MST, NOV, POP; DLB 15, 160, 255; EFS 2; EWL 3; FANT; JRDA; LAIT 1; LATS 1:2; LMFS 2; MAICYA 1, 2; MTCW 1, 2; MTFW 2005; NFS 8, 26; RGEL 2; SATA 2, 32, 100; SATA-Obit 24; SFW 4; SUFW; TEA; WCH; WYA; YAW

Toller, Ernst 1893-1939 .... **TCLC 10**
See also CA 107; 186; DLB 124; EWL 3; RGWL 2, 3

Tolson, M. B.
See Tolson, Melvin B(eaunorus)

Tolson, Melvin B(eaunorus)
1898(?)-1966 .... **BLC 1:3; CLC 36, 105; PC 88**
See also AFAW 1, 2; BW 1, 3; CA 124; 89-92; CANR 80; DAM MULT, POET; DLB 48, 76; MAL 5; RGAL 4

Tolstoi, Aleksei Nikolaevich
See Tolstoy, Alexey Nikolaevich

Tolstoi, Lev
See Tolstoy, Leo (Nikolaevich)

Tolstoy, Aleksei Nikolaevich
See Tolstoy, Alexey Nikolaevich

Tolstoy, Alexey Nikolaevich
1882-1945 .... **TCLC 18**
See also CA 107; 158; DLB 272; EWL 3; SFW 4

Tolstoy, Leo (Nikolaevich)
1828-1910 . **SSC 9, 30, 45, 54; TCLC 4, 11, 17, 28, 44, 79, 173; WLC 6**
See also AAYA 56; CA 104; 123; DA; DA3; DAB; DAC; DAM MST, NOV; DLB 238; EFS 2; EW 7; EXPS; IDTP; LAIT 2; LATS 1:1; LMFS 1; NFS 10, 28; RGSF 2; RGWL 2, 3; SATA 26; SSFS 5; TWA

Tolstoy, Count Leo
See Tolstoy, Leo (Nikolaevich)

Tomalin, Claire 1933- .... **CLC 166**
See also CA 89-92; CANR 52, 88, 165; DLB 155

Tomasi di Lampedusa, Giuseppe
1896-1957 .... **TCLC 13**
See also CA 111; 164; DLB 177; EW 11; EWL 3; MTCW 2; MTFW 2005; RGWL 2, 3; WLIT 7

Tomlin, Lily 1939(?)- .... **CLC 17**
See also CA 117

Tomlin, Mary Jane
See Tomlin, Lily

Tomlin, Mary Jean
See Tomlin, Lily

Tomline, F. Latour
See Gilbert, W(illiam) S(chwenck)

Tomlinson, (Alfred) Charles 1927- .... **CLC 2, 4, 6, 13, 45; PC 17**
See also CA 5-8R; CANR 33; CP 1, 2, 3, 4, 5, 6, 7; DAM POET; DLB 40; TCLE 1:2

Tomlinson, H(enry) M(ajor)
1873-1958 .... **TCLC 71**
See also CA 118; 161; DLB 36, 100, 195

Tomlinson, Mary Jane
See Tomlin, Lily

Tonna, Charlotte Elizabeth
1790-1846 .... **NCLC 135**
See also DLB 163

Tonson, Jacob fl. 1655(?)-1736 .... **LC 86**
See also DLB 170

Toole, John Kennedy 1937-1969 ..... **CLC 19, 64**
See also BPFB 3; CA 104; DLBY 1981; MTCW 2; MTFW 2005

Toomer, Eugene
See Toomer, Jean

Toomer, Eugene Pinchback
See Toomer, Jean

Toomer, Jean 1894-1967 ... **BLC 1:3; CLC 1, 4, 13, 22; HR 1:3; PC 7; SSC 1, 45; TCLC 172; WLCS**
See also AFAW 1, 2; AMWS 3, 9; BW 1; CA 85-88; CDALB 1917-1929; DA3; DAM MULT; DLB 45, 51; EWL 3; EXPP; EXPS; LMFS 2; MAL 5; MTCW 1, 2; MTFW 2005; NFS 11; RGAL 4; RGSF 2; SSFS 5

Toomer, Nathan Jean
See Toomer, Jean

Toomer, Nathan Pinchback
See Toomer, Jean

Torley, Luke
See Blish, James (Benjamin)

Tornimparte, Alessandra
See Ginzburg, Natalia

Torre, Raoul della
See Mencken, H(enry) L(ouis)

Torrence, Ridgely 1874-1950 .... **TCLC 97**
See also DLB 54, 249; MAL 5

Torrey, E. Fuller 1937- .... **CLC 34**
See also CA 119; CANR 71, 158

Torrey, Edwin Fuller
See Torrey, E. Fuller

Torsvan, Ben Traven
See Traven, B.

Torsvan, Benno Traven
See Traven, B.

Torsvan, Berick Traven
See Traven, B.

Torsvan, Berwick Traven
See Traven, B.

Torsvan, Bruno Traven
See Traven, B.

Torsvan, Traven
See Traven, B.

Toson
See Shimazaki, Haruki

Tourneur, Cyril 1575(?)-1626 .... **LC 66**
See also BRW 2; DAM DRAM; DLB 58; RGEL 2

Tournier, Michel 1924- .... **CLC 6, 23, 36, 95, 249; SSC 88**
See also CA 49-52; CANR 3, 36, 74, 149; CWW 2; DLB 83; EWL 3; GFL 1789 to the Present; MTCW 1, 2; SATA 23

Tournier, Michel Edouard
See Tournier, Michel

Tournimparte, Alessandra
See Ginzburg, Natalia

Towers, Ivar
See Kornbluth, C(yril) M.

Towne, Robert (Burton) 1936(?)- ..... **CLC 87**
See also CA 108; DLB 44; IDFW 3, 4

Townsend, Sue
See Townsend, Susan Lilian

Townsend, Susan Lilian 1946- .... **CLC 61**
See also AAYA 28; CA 119; 127; CANR 65, 107; CBD; CD 5, 6; CPW; CWD; DAB; DAC; DAM MST; DLB 271; INT CA-127; SATA 55, 93; SATA-Brief 48; YAW

Townshend, Pete
See Townshend, Peter

Townshend, Peter 1945- .... **CLC 17, 42**
See also CA 107

Townshend, Peter Dennis Blandford
See Townshend, Peter

Tozzi, Federigo 1883-1920 .... **TCLC 31**
See also CA 160; CANR 110; DLB 264; EWL 3; WLIT 7

Trafford, F. G.
See Riddell, Charlotte

Traherne, Thomas 1637(?)-1674 .. **LC 99; PC 70**
See also BRW 2; BRWS 11; DLB 131; PAB; RGEL 2

Traill, Catharine Parr 1802-1899 .. **NCLC 31**
See also DLB 99

Trakl, Georg 1887-1914 .... **PC 20; TCLC 5**
See also CA 104; 165; EW 10; EWL 3; LMFS 2; MTCW 2; RGWL 2, 3

Trambley, Estela Portillo
See Portillo Trambley, Estela

Tranquilli, Secondino
See Silone, Ignazio

Transtroemer, Tomas Gosta
See Transtromer, Tomas

Transtromer, Tomas (Gosta)
See Transtromer, Tomas

Transtromer, Tomas 1931- .... **CLC 52, 65**
See also CA 117; 129; CAAS 17; CANR 115, 172; CWW 2; DAM POET; DLB 257; EWL 3; PFS 21

Transtromer, Tomas Goesta
See Transtromer, Tomas

Transtromer, Tomas Gosta
See Transtromer, Tomas

Transtromer, Tomas Gosta
See Transtromer, Tomas

Traven, B. 1882(?)-1969 .... **CLC 8, 11**
See also CA 19-20; 25-28R; CAP 2; DLB 9, 56; EWL 3; MTCW 1; RGAL 4

Trediakovsky, Vasilii Kirillovich
1703-1769 .... **LC 68**
See also DLB 150

Treitel, Jonathan 1959- .... **CLC 70**
See also CA 210; DLB 267

Trelawny, Edward John
1792-1881 .... **NCLC 85**
See also DLB 110, 116, 144

Tremain, Rose 1943- .... **CLC 42**
See also CA 97-100; CANR 44, 95, 186; CN 4, 5, 6, 7; DLB 14, 271; RGSF 2; RHW

Tremblay, Michel 1942- .... **CLC 29, 102, 225**
See also CA 116; 128; CCA 1; CWW 2; DAC; DAM MST; DLB 60; EWL 3; GLL 1; MTCW 1, 2; MTFW 2005

Trevanian
See Whitaker, Rod

Trevisa, John c. 1342-c. 1402 .... **LC 139**
See also BRWS 9; DLB 146

Trevor, Glen
See Hilton, James

Trevor, William 1928- ... **CLC 1, 2, 3, 4, 5, 6, 7; SSC 21, 58**
See also BRWS 4; CA 9-12R; CANR 4, 37, 55, 76, 102, 139; CBD; CD 5, 6; DAM NOV; DLB 14, 139; EWL 3; INT CANR-37; LATS 1:2; MTCW 1, 2; MTFW 2005; RGEL 2; RGSF 2; SSFS 10; TCLE 1:2; TEA

Unsworth, Barry 1930- .... **CLC 76, 127**
See also BRWS 7; CA 25-28R; CANR 30, 54, 125, 171; CN 6, 7; DLB 194, 326

Unsworth, Barry Forster
See Unsworth, Barry

Updike, John 1932-2009 .... **CLC 1, 2, 3, 5, 7, 9, 13, 15, 23, 34, 43, 70, 139, 214; PC 90; SSC 13, 27, 103; WLC 6**
See also AAYA 36; AMW; AMWC 1; AMWR 1; BPFB 3; BYA 12; CA 1-4R; CABS 1; CANR 4, 33, 51, 94, 133; CDALB 1968-1988; CN 1, 2, 3, 4, 5, 6, 7; CP 1, 2, 3, 4, 5, 6, 7; CPW 1; DA; DA3; DAB; DAC; DAM MST, NOV, POET, POP; DLB 2, 5, 143, 218, 227; DLBD 3; DLBY 1980, 1982, 1997; EWL 3; EXPP; HGG; MAL 5; MTCW 1, 2; MTFW 2005; NFS 12, 24; RGAL 4; RGSF 2; SSFS 3, 19; TUS

Updike, John Hoyer
See Updike, John

Upshaw, Margaret Mitchell
See Mitchell, Margaret (Munnerlyn)

Upton, Mark
See Sanders, Lawrence

Upward, Allen 1863-1926 .... **TCLC 85**
See also CA 117; 187; DLB 36

Urdang, Constance (Henriette)
1922-1996 .... **CLC 47**
See also CA 21-24R; CANR 9, 24; CP 1, 2, 3, 4, 5, 6; CWP

Urfe, Honore d' 1567(?)-1625 .... **LC 132**
See also DLB 268; GFL Beginnings to 1789; RGWL 2, 3

Uriel, Henry
See Faust, Frederick (Schiller)

Uris, Leon 1924-2003 .... **CLC 7, 32**
See also AITN 1, 2; BEST 89:2; BPFB 3; CA 1-4R; 217; CANR 1, 40, 65, 123; CN 1, 2, 3, 4, 5, 6; CPW 1; DA3; DAM NOV, POP; MTCW 1, 2; MTFW 2005; RGHL; SATA 49; SATA-Obit 146

Urista (Heredia), Alberto (Baltazar)
1947- .... **HLCS 1; PC 34**
See also CA 45-48R; CANR 2, 32; DLB 82; HW 1; LLW

Urmuz
See Codrescu, Andrei

Urquhart, Guy
See McAlmon, Robert (Menzies)

Urquhart, Jane 1949- .... **CLC 90, 242**
See also CA 113; CANR 32, 68, 116, 157; CCA 1; DAC; DLB 334

Usigli, Rodolfo 1905-1979 .... **HLCS 1**
See also CA 131; DLB 305; EWL 3; HW 1; LAW

Usk, Thomas (?)-1388 .... **CMLC 76**
See also DLB 146

Ustinov, Peter (Alexander)
1921-2004 .... **CLC 1**
See also AITN 1; CA 13-16R; 225; CANR 25, 51; CBD; CD 5, 6; DLB 13; MTCW 2

U Tam'si, Gerald Felix Tchicaya
See Tchicaya, Gerald Felix

U Tam'si, Tchicaya
See Tchicaya, Gerald Felix

Vachss, Andrew 1942- .... **CLC 106**
See also CA 118, 214; CAAE 214; CANR 44, 95, 153; CMW 4

Vachss, Andrew H.
See Vachss, Andrew

Vachss, Andrew Henry
See Vachss, Andrew

Vaculik, Ludvik 1926- .... **CLC 7**
See also CA 53-56; CANR 72; CWW 2; DLB 232; EWL 3

Vaihinger, Hans 1852-1933 .... **TCLC 71**
See also CA 116; 166

Valdez, Luis (Miguel) 1940- ..... **CLC 84; DC 10; HLC 2**
See also CA 101; CAD; CANR 32, 81; CD 5, 6; DAM MULT; DFS 5; DLB 122; EWL 3; HW 1; LAIT 4; LLW

Valenzuela, Luisa 1938- .... **CLC 31, 104; HLCS 2; SSC 14, 82**
See also CA 101; CANR 32, 65, 123; CD-WLB 3; CWW 2; DAM MULT; DLB 113; EWL 3; FW; HW 1, 2; LAW; RGSF 2; RGWL 3

Valera y Alcala-Galiano, Juan
1824-1905 .... **TCLC 10**
See also CA 106

Valerius Maximus .... **CMLC 64**
See also DLB 211

Valery, (Ambroise) Paul (Toussaint Jules)
1871-1945 .... **PC 9; TCLC 4, 15**
See also CA 104; 122; DA3; DAM POET; DLB 258; EW 8; EWL 3; GFL 1789 to the Present; MTCW 1, 2; MTFW 2005; RGWL 2, 3; TWA

Valle-Inclan, Ramon (Maria) del
1866-1936 .... **HLC 2; TCLC 5**
See also CA 106; 153; CANR 80; DAM MULT; DLB 134, 322; EW 8; EWL 3; HW 2; RGSF 2; RGWL 2, 3

Vallejo, Antonio Buero
See Buero Vallejo, Antonio

Vallejo, Cesar (Abraham)
1892-1938 .... **HLC 2; TCLC 3, 56**
See also CA 105; 153; DAM MULT; DLB 290; EWL 3; HW 1; LAW; PFS 26; RGWL 2, 3

Valles, Jules 1832-1885 .... **NCLC 71**
See also DLB 123; GFL 1789 to the Present

Vallette, Marguerite Eymery
1860-1953 .... **TCLC 67**
See also CA 182; DLB 123, 192; EWL 3

Valle Y Pena, Ramon del
See Valle-Inclan, Ramon (Maria) del

Van Ash, Cay 1918-1994 .... **CLC 34**
See also CA 220

Vanbrugh, Sir John 1664-1726 .... **LC 21**
See also BRW 2; DAM DRAM; DLB 80; IDTP; RGEL 2

Van Campen, Karl
See Campbell, John W(ood, Jr.)

Vance, Gerald
See Silverberg, Robert

Vance, Jack 1916- .... **CLC 35**
See also CA 29-32R; CANR 17, 65, 154; CMW 4; DLB 8; FANT; MTCW 1; SCFW 1, 2; SFW 4; SUFW 1, 2

Vance, John Holbrook
See Vance, Jack

Van Den Bogarde, Derek Jules Gaspard Ulric Niven 1921-1999 .... **CLC 14**
See also CA 77-80; 179; DLB 14

Vandenburgh, Jane .... **CLC 59**
See also CA 168

Vanderhaeghe, Guy 1951- .... **CLC 41**
See also BPFB 3; CA 113; CANR 72, 145; CN 7; DLB 334

van der Post, Laurens (Jan)
1906-1996 .... **CLC 5**
See also AFW; CA 5-8R; 155; CANR 35; CN 1, 2, 3, 4, 5, 6; DLB 204; RGEL 2

van de Wetering, Janwillem
1931-2008 .... **CLC 47**
See also CA 49-52; 274; CANR 4, 62, 90; CMW 4

Van Dine, S. S.
See Wright, Willard Huntington

Van Doren, Carl (Clinton)
1885-1950 .... **TCLC 18**
See also CA 111; 168

Van Doren, Mark 1894-1972 .... **CLC 6, 10**
See also CA 1-4R; 37-40R; CANR 3; CN 1; CP 1; DLB 45, 284, 335; MAL 5; MTCW 1, 2; RGAL 4

Van Druten, John (William)
1901-1957 .... **TCLC 2**
See also CA 104; 161; DLB 10; MAL 5; RGAL 4

Van Duyn, Mona 1921-2004 .... **CLC 3, 7, 63, 116**
See also CA 9-12R; 234; CANR 7, 38, 60, 116; CP 1, 2, 3, 4, 5, 6, 7; CWP; DAM POET; DLB 5; MAL 5; MTFW 2005; PFS 20

Van Dyne, Edith
See Baum, L(yman) Frank

van Herk, Aritha 1954- .... **CLC 249**
See also CA 101; CANR 94; DLB 334

van Itallie, Jean-Claude 1936- .... **CLC 3**
See also CA 45-48; CAAS 2; CAD; CANR 1, 48; CD 5, 6; DLB 7

Van Loot, Cornelius Obenchain
See Roberts, Kenneth (Lewis)

van Ostaijen, Paul 1896-1928 .... **TCLC 33**
See also CA 163

Van Peebles, Melvin 1932- .... **CLC 2, 20**
See also BW 2, 3; CA 85-88; CANR 27, 67, 82; DAM MULT

van Schendel, Arthur(-Francois-Emile)
1874-1946 .... **TCLC 56**
See also EWL 3

Van See, John
See Vance, Jack

Vansittart, Peter 1920-2008 .... **CLC 42**
See also CA 1-4R; 278; CANR 3, 49, 90; CN 4, 5, 6, 7; RHW

Van Vechten, Carl 1880-1964 ... **CLC 33; HR 1:3**
See also AMWS 2; CA 183; 89-92; DLB 4, 9, 51; RGAL 4

van Vogt, A(lfred) E(lton) 1912-2000 . **CLC 1**
See also BPFB 3; BYA 13, 14; CA 21-24R; 190; CANR 28; DLB 8, 251; SATA 14; SATA-Obit 124; SCFW 1, 2; SFW 4

Vara, Madeleine
See Jackson, Laura (Riding)

Varda, Agnes 1928- .... **CLC 16**
See also CA 116; 122

Vargas Llosa, Jorge Mario Pedro
See Vargas Llosa, Mario

Vargas Llosa, Mario 1936- .. **CLC 3, 6, 9, 10, 15, 31, 42, 85, 181; HLC 2**
See also BPFB 3; CA 73-76; CANR 18, 32, 42, 67, 116, 140, 173; CDWLB 3; CWW 2; DA; DA3; DAB; DAC; DAM MST, MULT, NOV; DLB 145; DNFS 2; EWL 3; HW 1, 2; LAIT 5; LATS 1:2; LAW; LAWS 1; MTCW 1, 2; MTFW 2005; RGWL 2, 3; SSFS 14; TWA; WLIT 1

Varnhagen von Ense, Rahel
1771-1833 .... **NCLC 130**
See also DLB 90

Vasari, Giorgio 1511-1574 .... **LC 114**

Vasilikos, Vasiles
See Vassilikos, Vassilis

Vasiliu, George
See Bacovia, George

Vasiliu, Gheorghe
See Bacovia, George

Vassa, Gustavus
See Equiano, Olaudah

Vassilikos, Vassilis 1933- .... **CLC 4, 8**
See also CA 81-84; CANR 75, 149; EWL 3

Vaughan, Henry 1621-1695 .... **LC 27; PC 81**
See also BRW 2; DLB 131; PAB; RGEL 2

Vaughn, Stephanie .... **CLC 62**

Vazov, Ivan (Minchov) 1850-1921 . **TCLC 25**
See also CA 121; 167; CDWLB 4; DLB 147

Wellman, Mac
See Wellman, John McDowell; Wellman, John McDowell

Wellman, Manly Wade 1903-1986 ... **CLC 49**
See also CA 1-4R; 118; CANR 6, 16, 44; FANT; SATA 6; SATA-Obit 47; SFW 4; SUFW

Wells, Carolyn 1869(?)-1942 .... **TCLC 35**
See also CA 113; 185; CMW 4; DLB 11

Wells, H(erbert) G(eorge) 1866-1946 . **SSC 6, 70; TCLC 6, 12, 19, 133; WLC 6**
See also AAYA 18; BPFB 3; BRW 6; CA 110; 121; CDBLB 1914-1945; CLR 64, 133; DA; DA3; DAB; DAC; DAM MST, NOV; DLB 34, 70, 156, 178; EWL 3; EXPS; HGG; LAIT 3; LMFS 2; MTCW 1, 2; MTFW 2005; NFS 17, 20; RGEL 2; RGSF 2; SATA 20; SCFW 1, 2; SFW 4; SSFS 3; SUFW; TEA; WCH; WLIT 4; YAW

Wells, Rosemary 1943- .... **CLC 12**
See also AAYA 13; BYA 7, 8; CA 85-88; CANR 48, 120, 179; CLR 16, 69; CWRI 5; MAICYA 1, 2; SAAS 1; SATA 18, 69, 114, 156; YAW

Wells-Barnett, Ida B(ell)
1862-1931 .... **TCLC 125**
See also CA 182; DLB 23, 221

Welsh, Irvine 1958- .... **CLC 144**
See also CA 173; CANR 146; CN 7; DLB 271

Welty, Eudora 1909-2001 .... **CLC 1, 2, 5, 14, 22, 33, 105, 220; SSC 1, 27, 51, 111; WLC 6**
See also AAYA 48; AMW; AMWR 1; BPFB 3; CA 9-12R; 199; CABS 1; CANR 32, 65, 128; CDALB 1941-1968; CN 1, 2, 3, 4, 5, 6, 7; CSW; DA; DA3; DAB; DAC; DAM MST, NOV; DFS 26; DLB 2, 102, 143; DLBD 12; DLBY 1987, 2001; EWL 3; EXPS; HGG; LAIT 3; MAL 5; MBL; MTCW 1, 2; MTFW 2005; NFS 13, 15; RGAL 4; RGSF 2; RHW; SSFS 2, 10, 26; TUS

Welty, Eudora Alice
See Welty, Eudora

Wen I-to 1899-1946 .... **TCLC 28**
See also EWL 3

Wentworth, Robert
See Hamilton, Edmond

Werewere Liking 1950- .... **BLC 2:2**
See also EWL 3

Werfel, Franz (Viktor) 1890-1945 ... **TCLC 8**
See also CA 104; 161; DLB 81, 124; EWL 3; RGWL 2, 3

Wergeland, Henrik Arnold
1808-1845 .... **NCLC 5**

Werner, Friedrich Ludwig Zacharias
1768-1823 .... **NCLC 189**
See also DLB 94

Werner, Zacharias
See Werner, Friedrich Ludwig Zacharias

Wersba, Barbara 1932- .... **CLC 30**
See also AAYA 2, 30; BYA 6, 12, 13; CA 29-32R, 182; CAAE 182; CANR 16, 38; CLR 3, 78; DLB 52; JRDA; MAICYA 1, 2; SAAS 2; SATA 1, 58; SATA-Essay 103; WYA; YAW

Wertmueller, Lina 1928- .... **CLC 16**
See also CA 97-100; CANR 39, 78

Wescott, Glenway 1901-1987 .. **CLC 13; SSC 35**
See also CA 13-16R; 121; CANR 23, 70; CN 1, 2, 3, 4; DLB 4, 9, 102; MAL 5; RGAL 4

Wesker, Arnold 1932- .... **CLC 3, 5, 42**
See also CA 1-4R; CAAS 7; CANR 1, 33; CBD; CD 5, 6; CDBLB 1960 to Present; DAB; DAM DRAM; DLB 13, 310, 319; EWL 3; MTCW 1; RGEL 2; TEA

Wesley, Charles 1707-1788 .... **LC 128**
See also DLB 95; RGEL 2

Wesley, John 1703-1791 .... **LC 88**
See also DLB 104

Wesley, Richard (Errol) 1945- .... **CLC 7**
See also BW 1; CA 57-60; CAD; CANR 27; CD 5, 6; DLB 38

Wessel, Johan Herman 1742-1785 .... **LC 7**
See also DLB 300

West, Anthony (Panther)
1914-1987 .... **CLC 50**
See also CA 45-48; 124; CANR 3, 19; CN 1, 2, 3, 4; DLB 15

West, C. P.
See Wodehouse, P(elham) G(renville)

West, Cornel 1953- .... **BLCS; CLC 134**
See also CA 144; CANR 91, 159; DLB 246

West, Cornel Ronald
See West, Cornel

West, Delno C(loyde), Jr. 1936- .... **CLC 70**
See also CA 57-60

West, Dorothy 1907-1998 ...... **HR 1:3; TCLC 108**
See also AMWS 18; BW 2; CA 143; 169; DLB 76

West, Edwin
See Westlake, Donald E.

West, (Mary) Jessamyn 1902-1984 ... **CLC 7, 17**
See also CA 9-12R; 112; CANR 27; CN 1, 2, 3; DLB 6; DLBY 1984; MTCW 1, 2; RGAL 4; RHW; SATA-Obit 37; TCWW 2; TUS; YAW

West, Morris L(anglo) 1916-1999 ..... **CLC 6, 33**
See also BPFB 3; CA 5-8R; 187; CANR 24, 49, 64; CN 1, 2, 3, 4, 5, 6; CPW; DLB 289; MTCW 1, 2; MTFW 2005

West, Nathanael 1903-1940 ...... **SSC 16, 116; TCLC 1, 14, 44**
See also AAYA 77; AMW; AMWR 2; BPFB 3; CA 104; 125; CDALB 1929-1941; DA3; DLB 4, 9, 28; EWL 3; MAL 5; MTCW 1, 2; MTFW 2005; NFS 16; RGAL 4; TUS

West, Owen
See Koontz, Dean R.

West, Paul 1930- .... **CLC 7, 14, 96, 226**
See also CA 13-16R; CAAS 7; CANR 22, 53, 76, 89, 136; CN 1, 2, 3, 4, 5, 6, 7; DLB 14; INT CANR-22; MTCW 2; MTFW 2005

West, Rebecca 1892-1983 ... **CLC 7, 9, 31, 50**
See also BPFB 3; BRWS 3; CA 5-8R; 109; CANR 19; CN 1, 2, 3; DLB 36; DLBY 1983; EWL 3; FW; MTCW 1, 2; MTFW 2005; NCFS 4; RGEL 2; TEA

Westall, Robert (Atkinson)
1929-1993 .... **CLC 17**
See also AAYA 12; BYA 2, 6, 7, 8, 9, 15; CA 69-72; 141; CANR 18, 68; CLR 13; FANT; JRDA; MAICYA 1, 2; MAICYAS 1; SAAS 2; SATA 23, 69; SATA-Obit 75; WYA; YAW

Westermarck, Edward 1862-1939 . **TCLC 87**

Westlake, Donald E. 1933-2008 ... **CLC 7, 33**
See also BPFB 3; CA 17-20R; 280; CAAS 13; CANR 16, 44, 65, 94, 137; CMW 4; CPW; DAM POP; INT CANR-16; MSW; MTCW 2; MTFW 2005

Westlake, Donald E. Edmund
See Westlake, Donald E.

Westlake, Donald Edwin
See Westlake, Donald E.

Westlake, Donald Edwin Edmund
See Westlake, Donald E.

Westmacott, Mary
See Christie, Agatha (Mary Clarissa)

Weston, Allen
See Norton, Andre

Wetcheek, J. L.
See Feuchtwanger, Lion

Wetering, Janwillem van de
See van de Wetering, Janwillem

Wetherald, Agnes Ethelwyn
1857-1940 .... **TCLC 81**
See also CA 202; DLB 99

Wetherell, Elizabeth
See Warner, Susan (Bogert)

Whale, James 1889-1957 .... **TCLC 63**
See also AAYA 75

Whalen, Philip (Glenn) 1923-2002 .... **CLC 6, 29**
See also BG 1:3; CA 9-12R; 209; CANR 5, 39; CP 1, 2, 3, 4, 5, 6, 7; DLB 16; WP

Wharton, Edith (Newbold Jones)
1862-1937 . **SSC 6, 84, 120; TCLC 3, 9, 27, 53, 129, 149; WLC 6**
See also AAYA 25; AMW; AMWC 2; AMWR 1; BPFB 3; CA 104; 132; CDALB 1865-1917; CLR 136; DA; DA3; DAB; DAC; DAM MST, NOV; DLB 4, 9, 12, 78, 189; DLBD 13; EWL 3; EXPS; FL 1:6; GL 3; HGG; LAIT 2, 3; LATS 1:1; MAL 5; MBL; MTCW 1, 2; MTFW 2005; NFS 5, 11, 15, 20; RGAL 4; RGSF 2; RHW; SSFS 6, 7; SUFW; TUS

Wharton, James
See Mencken, H(enry) L(ouis)

Wharton, William 1925-2008 ..... **CLC 18, 37**
See also CA 93-96; 278; CN 4, 5, 6, 7; DLBY 1980; INT CA-93-96

Wheatley (Peters), Phillis
1753(?)-1784 .... **BLC 1:3; LC 3, 50; PC 3; WLC 6**
See also AFAW 1, 2; CDALB 1640-1865; DA; DA3; DAC; DAM MST, MULT, POET; DLB 31, 50; EXPP; FL 1:1; PFS 13, 29; RGAL 4

Wheelock, John Hall 1886-1978 .... **CLC 14**
See also CA 13-16R; 77-80; CANR 14; CP 1, 2; DLB 45; MAL 5

Whim-Wham
See Curnow, (Thomas) Allen (Monro)

Whisp, Kennilworthy
See Rowling, J.K.

Whitaker, Rod 1931-2005 .... **CLC 29**
See also CA 29-32R; 246; CANR 45, 153; CMW 4

Whitaker, Rodney
See Whitaker, Rod

Whitaker, Rodney William
See Whitaker, Rod

White, Babington
See Braddon, Mary Elizabeth

White, E. B. 1899-1985 .... **CLC 10, 34, 39**
See also AAYA 62; AITN 2; AMWS 1; CA 13-16R; 116; CANR 16, 37; CDALBS; CLR 1, 21, 107; CPW; DA3; DAM POP; DLB 11, 22; EWL 3; FANT; MAICYA 1, 2; MAL 5; MTCW 1, 2; MTFW 2005; NCFS 5; RGAL 4; SATA 2, 29, 100; SATA-Obit 44; TUS

White, Edmund 1940- .... **CLC 27, 110**
See also AAYA 7; CA 45-48; CANR 3, 19, 36, 62, 107, 133, 172; CN 5, 6, 7; DA3; DAM POP; DLB 227; MTCW 1, 2; MTFW 2005

White, Edmund Valentine III
See White, Edmund

White, Elwyn Brooks
See White, E. B.

White, Hayden V. 1928- .... **CLC 148**
See also CA 128; CANR 135; DLB 246

Woiwode, Larry (Alfred) 1941- ... **CLC 6, 10**
See also CA 73-76; CANR 16, 94; CN 3, 4, 5, 6, 7; DLB 6; INT CANR-16
Wojciechowska, Maia (Teresa)
1927-2002 .... **CLC 26**
See also AAYA 8, 46; BYA 3; CA 9-12R, 183; 209; CAAE 183; CANR 4, 41; CLR 1; JRDA; MAICYA 1, 2; SAAS 1; SATA 1, 28, 83; SATA-Essay 104; SATA-Obit 134; YAW
Wojtyla, Karol (Jozef)
See John Paul II, Pope
Wojtyla, Karol (Josef)
See John Paul II, Pope
Wolf, Christa 1929- ...... **CLC 14, 29, 58, 150, 261**
See also CA 85-88; CANR 45, 123; CD-WLB 2; CWW 2; DLB 75; EWL 3; FW; MTCW 1; RGWL 2, 3; SSFS 14
Wolf, Naomi 1962- .... **CLC 157**
See also CA 141; CANR 110; FW; MTFW 2005
Wolfe, Gene 1931- .... **CLC 25**
See also AAYA 35; CA 57-60; CAAS 9; CANR 6, 32, 60, 152; CPW; DAM POP; DLB 8; FANT; MTCW 2; MTFW 2005; SATA 118, 165; SCFW 2; SFW 4; SUFW 2
Wolfe, Gene Rodman
See Wolfe, Gene
Wolfe, George C. 1954- .... **BLCS; CLC 49**
See also CA 149; CAD; CD 5, 6
Wolfe, Thomas (Clayton)
1900-1938 .... **SSC 33, 113; TCLC 4, 13, 29, 61; WLC 6**
See also AMW; BPFB 3; CA 104; 132; CANR 102; CDALB 1929-1941; DA; DA3; DAB; DAC; DAM MST, NOV; DLB 9, 102, 229; DLBD 2, 16; DLBY 1985, 1997; EWL 3; MAL 5; MTCW 1, 2; NFS 18; RGAL 4; SSFS 18; TUS
Wolfe, Thomas Kennerly, Jr. 1931- .. **CLC 1, 2, 9, 15, 35, 51, 147**
See also AAYA 8, 67; AITN 2; AMWS 3; BEST 89:1; BPFB 3; CA 13-16R; CANR 9, 33, 70, 104; CN 5, 6, 7; CPW; CSW; DA3; DAM POP; DLB 152, 185 185; EWL 3; INT CANR-9; LAIT 5; MTCW 1, 2; MTFW 2005; RGAL 4; TUS
Wolfe, Tom
See Wolfe, Thomas Kennerly, Jr.
Wolff, Geoffrey 1937- .... **CLC 41**
See also CA 29-32R; CANR 29, 43, 78, 154
Wolff, Geoffrey Ansell
See Wolff, Geoffrey
Wolff, Sonia
See Levitin, Sonia
Wolff, Tobias 1945- .... **CLC 39, 64, 172; SSC 63**
See also AAYA 16; AMWS 7; BEST 90:2; BYA 12; CA 114; 117; CAAS 22; CANR 54, 76, 96; CN 5, 6, 7; CSW; DA3; DLB 130; EWL 3; INT CA-117; MTCW 2; MTFW 2005; RGAL 4; RGSF 2; SSFS 4, 11
Wolitzer, Hilma 1930- .... **CLC 17**
See also CA 65-68; CANR 18, 40, 172; INT CANR-18; SATA 31; YAW
Wollstonecraft, Mary 1759-1797 .... **LC 5, 50, 90, 147**
See also BRWS 3; CDBLB 1789-1832; DLB 39, 104, 158, 252; FL 1:1; FW; LAIT 1; RGEL 2; TEA; WLIT 3
Wonder, Stevie 1950- .... **CLC 12**
See also CA 111
Wong, Jade Snow 1922-2006 .... **CLC 17**
See also CA 109; 249; CANR 91; SATA 112; SATA-Obit 175
Wood, Ellen Price
See Wood, Mrs. Henry

Wood, Mrs. Henry 1814-1887 ...... **NCLC 178**
See also CMW 4; DLB 18; SUFW
Wood, James 1965- .... **CLC 238**
See also CA 235
Woodberry, George Edward
1855-1930 .... **TCLC 73**
See also CA 165; DLB 71, 103
Woodcott, Keith
See Brunner, John (Kilian Houston)
Woodruff, Robert W.
See Mencken, H(enry) L(ouis)
Woodward, Bob 1943- .... **CLC 240**
See also CA 69-72; CANR 31, 67, 107, 176; MTCW 1
Woodward, Robert Upshur
See Woodward, Bob
Woolf, (Adeline) Virginia 1882-1941 .. **SSC 7, 79; TCLC 1, 5, 20, 43, 56, 101, 123, 128; WLC 6**
See also AAYA 44; BPFB 3; BRW 7; BRWC 2; BRWR 1; CA 104; 130; CANR 64, 132; CDBLB 1914-1945; DA; DA3; DAB; DAC; DAM MST, NOV; DLB 36, 100, 162; DLBD 10; EWL 3; EXPS; FL 1:6; FW; LAIT 3; LATS 1:1; LMFS 2; MTCW 1, 2; MTFW 2005; NCFS 2; NFS 8, 12, 28; RGEL 2; RGSF 2; SSFS 4, 12; TEA; WLIT 4
Woollcott, Alexander (Humphreys)
1887-1943 .... **TCLC 5**
See also CA 105; 161; DLB 29
Woolman, John 1720-1772 .... **LC 155**
See also DLB 31
Woolrich, Cornell
See Hopley-Woolrich, Cornell George
Woolson, Constance Fenimore
1840-1894 .... **NCLC 82; SSC 90**
See also DLB 12, 74, 189, 221; RGAL 4
Wordsworth, Dorothy 1771-1855 . **NCLC 25, 138**
See also DLB 107
Wordsworth, William 1770-1850 .. **NCLC 12, 38, 111, 166, 206; PC 4, 67; WLC 6**
See also AAYA 70; BRW 4; BRWC 1; CD-BLB 1789-1832; DA; DA3; DAB; DAC; DAM POET; DLB 93, 107; EXPP; LATS 1:1; LMFS 1; PAB; PFS 2; RGEL 2; TEA; WLIT 3; WP
Wotton, Sir Henry 1568-1639 .... **LC 68**
See also DLB 121; RGEL 2
Wouk, Herman 1915- .... **CLC 1, 9, 38**
See also BPFB 2, 3; CA 5-8R; CANR 6, 33, 67, 146; CDALBS; CN 1, 2, 3, 4, 5, 6; CPW; DA3; DAM NOV, POP; DLBY 1982; INT CANR-6; LAIT 4; MAL 5; MTCW 1, 2; MTFW 2005; NFS 7; TUS
Wright, Charles 1932-2008 ... **BLC 1:3; CLC 49**
See also BW 1; CA 9-12R; 278; CANR 26; CN 1, 2, 3, 4, 5, 6, 7; DAM MULT, POET; DLB 33
Wright, Charles 1935- ... **CLC 6, 13, 28, 119, 146**
See also AMWS 5; CA 29-32R; CAAS 7; CANR 23, 36, 62, 88, 135, 180; CP 3, 4, 5, 6, 7; DLB 165; DLBY 1982; EWL 3; MTCW 1, 2; MTFW 2005; PFS 10
Wright, Charles Penzel, Jr.
See Wright, Charles
Wright, Charles Stevenson
See Wright, Charles
Wright, Frances 1795-1852 .... **NCLC 74**
See also DLB 73
Wright, Frank Lloyd 1867-1959 .... **TCLC 95**
See also AAYA 33; CA 174
Wright, Harold Bell 1872-1944 .... **TCLC 183**
See also BPFB 3; CA 110; DLB 9; TCWW 2

Wright, Jack R.
See Harris, Mark
Wright, James (Arlington)
1927-1980 .... **CLC 3, 5, 10, 28; PC 36**
See also AITN 2; AMWS 3; CA 49-52; 97-100; CANR 4, 34, 64; CDALBS; CP 1, 2; DAM POET; DLB 5, 169, 342; EWL 3; EXPP; MAL 5; MTCW 1, 2; MTFW 2005; PFS 7, 8; RGAL 4; TUS; WP
Wright, Judith 1915-2000 ... **CLC 11, 53; PC 14**
See also CA 13-16R; 188; CANR 31, 76, 93; CP 1, 2, 3, 4, 5, 6, 7; CWP; DLB 260; EWL 3; MTCW 1, 2; MTFW 2005; PFS 8; RGEL 2; SATA 14; SATA-Obit 121
Wright, L(aurali) R. 1939- .... **CLC 44**
See also CA 138; CMW 4
Wright, Richard 1908-1960 .. **BLC 1:3; CLC 1, 3, 4, 9, 14, 21, 48, 74; SSC 2, 109; TCLC 136, 180; WLC 6**
See also AAYA 5, 42; AFAW 1, 2; AMW; BPFB 3; BW 1; BYA 2; CA 108; CANR 64; CDALB 1929-1941; DA; DA3; DAB; DAC; DAM MST, MULT, NOV; DLB 76, 102; DLBD 2; EWL 3; EXPN; LAIT 3, 4; MAL 5; MTCW 1, 2; MTFW 2005; NCFS 1; NFS 1, 7; RGAL 4; RGSF 2; SSFS 3, 9, 15, 20; TUS; YAW
Wright, Richard B. 1937- .... **CLC 6**
See also CA 85-88; CANR 120; DLB 53
Wright, Richard Bruce
See Wright, Richard B.
Wright, Richard Nathaniel
See Wright, Richard
Wright, Rick 1945- .... **CLC 35**
Wright, Rowland
See Wells, Carolyn
Wright, Stephen 1946- .... **CLC 33**
See also CA 237
Wright, Willard Huntington
1888-1939 .... **TCLC 23**
See also CA 115; 189; CMW 4; DLB 306; DLBD 16; MSW
Wright, William 1930- .... **CLC 44**
See also CA 53-56; CANR 7, 23, 154
Wroth, Lady Mary 1587-1653(?) .... **LC 30, 139; PC 38**
See also DLB 121
Wu Ch'eng-en 1500(?)-1582(?) .... **LC 7**
Wu Ching-tzu 1701-1754 .... **LC 2**
Wulfstan c. 10th cent. -1023 .... **CMLC 59**
Wurlitzer, Rudolph 1938(?)- .... **CLC 2, 4, 15**
See also CA 85-88; CN 4, 5, 6, 7; DLB 173
Wyatt, Sir Thomas c. 1503-1542 . **LC 70; PC 27**
See also BRW 1; DLB 132; EXPP; PFS 25; RGEL 2; TEA
Wycherley, William 1640-1716 .... **LC 8, 21, 102, 136**
See also BRW 2; CDBLB 1660-1789; DAM DRAM; DLB 80; RGEL 2
Wyclif, John c. 1330-1384 .... **CMLC 70**
See also DLB 146
Wylie, Elinor (Morton Hoyt)
1885-1928 .... **PC 23; TCLC 8**
See also AMWS 1; CA 105; 162; DLB 9, 45; EXPP; MAL 5; RGAL 4
Wylie, Philip (Gordon) 1902-1971 ... **CLC 43**
See also CA 21-22; 33-36R; CAP 2; CN 1; DLB 9; SFW 4
Wyndham, John
See Harris, John (Wyndham Parkes Lucas) Beynon
Wyss, Johann David Von
1743-1818 .... **NCLC 10**
See also CLR 92; JRDA; MAICYA 1, 2; SATA 29; SATA-Brief 27

Xenophon c. 430B.C.-c. 354B.C. ... **CMLC 17**
See also AW 1; DLB 176; RGWL 2, 3;
WLIT 8

Xingjian, Gao 1940- .... **CLC 167**
See also CA 193; DFS 21; DLB 330;
MTFW 2005; RGWL 3

Yakamochi 718-785 .... **CMLC 45; PC 48**

Yakumo Koizumi
See Hearn, (Patricio) Lafcadio (Tessima
Carlos)

Yamada, Mitsuye (May) 1923- .... **PC 44**
See also CA 77-80

Yamamoto, Hisaye 1921- .... **AAL; SSC 34**
See also CA 214; DAM MULT; DLB 312;
LAIT 4; SSFS 14

Yamauchi, Wakako 1924- .... **AAL**
See also CA 214; DLB 312

Yan, Mo
See Moye, Guan

Yanez, Jose Donoso
See Donoso (Yanez), Jose

Yanovsky, Basile S.
See Yanovsky, V(assily) S(emenovich)

Yanovsky, V(assily) S(emenovich)
1906-1989 .... **CLC 2, 18**
See also CA 97-100; 129

Yates, Richard 1926-1992 .... **CLC 7, 8, 23**
See also AMWS 11; CA 5-8R; 139; CANR
10, 43; CN 1, 2, 3, 4, 5; DLB 2, 234;
DLBY 1981, 1992; INT CANR-10; SSFS
24

Yau, John 1950- .... **PC 61**
See also CA 154; CANR 89; CP 4, 5, 6, 7;
DLB 234, 312; PFS 26

Yearsley, Ann 1753-1806 .... **NCLC 174**
See also DLB 109

Yeats, W. B.
See Yeats, William Butler

Yeats, William Butler 1865-1939 . **DC 33; PC
20, 51; TCLC 1, 11, 18, 31, 93, 116;
WLC 6**
See also AAYA 48; BRW 6; BRWR 1; CA
104; 127; CANR 45; CDBLB 1890-1914;
DA; DA3; DAB; DAC; DAM DRAM,
MST, POET; DLB 10, 19, 98, 156, 332;
EWL 3; EXPP; MTCW 1, 2; MTFW
2005; NCFS 3; PAB; PFS 1, 2, 5, 7, 13,
15; RGEL 2; TEA; WLIT 4; WP

Yehoshua, A.B. 1936- .... **CLC 13, 31, 243**
See also CA 33-36R; CANR 43, 90, 145;
CWW 2; EWL 3; RGHL; RGSF 2; RGWL
3; WLIT 6

Yehoshua, Abraham B.
See Yehoshua, A.B.

Yellow Bird
See Ridge, John Rollin

Yep, Laurence 1948- .... **CLC 35**
See also AAYA 5, 31; BYA 7; CA 49-52;
CANR 1, 46, 92, 161; CLR 3, 17, 54, 132;
DLB 52, 312; FANT; JRDA; MAICYA 1,
2; MAICYAS 1; SATA 7, 69, 123, 176;
WYA; YAW

Yep, Laurence Michael
See Yep, Laurence

Yerby, Frank G(arvin) 1916-1991 . **BLC 1:3;
CLC 1, 7, 22**
See also BPFB 3; BW 1, 3; CA 9-12R; 136;
CANR 16, 52; CN 1, 2, 3, 4, 5; DAM
MULT; DLB 76; INT CANR-16; MTCW
1; RGAL 4; RHW

Yesenin, Sergei Aleksandrovich
See Esenin, Sergei

Yevtushenko, Yevgeny (Alexandrovich)
1933- ...... **CLC 1, 3, 13, 26, 51, 126; PC
40**
See also CA 81-84; CANR 33, 54; CWW
2; DAM POET; EWL 3; MTCW 1; PFS
29; RGHL; RGWL 2, 3

Yezierska, Anzia 1885(?)-1970 .... **CLC 46;
TCLC 205**
See also CA 126; 89-92; DLB 28, 221; FW;
MTCW 1; NFS 29; RGAL 4; SSFS 15

Yglesias, Helen 1915-2008 .... **CLC 7, 22**
See also CA 37-40R; 272; CAAS 20; CANR
15, 65, 95; CN 4, 5, 6, 7; INT CANR-15;
MTCW 1

Y.O.
See Russell, George William

Yokomitsu, Riichi 1898-1947 .... **TCLC 47**
See also CA 170; EWL 3

Yolen, Jane 1939- .... **CLC 256**
See also AAYA 4, 22; BPFB 3; BYA 9, 10,
11, 14, 16; CA 13-16R; CANR 11, 29, 56,
91, 126, 185; CLR 4, 44; CWRI 5; DLB
52; FANT; INT CANR-29; JRDA; MAI-
CYA 1, 2; MTFW 2005; SAAS 1; SATA
4, 40, 75, 112, 158, 194; SATA-Essay 111;
SFW 4; SUFW 2; WYA; YAW

Yonge, Charlotte (Mary)
1823-1901 .... **TCLC 48**
See also CA 109; 163; DLB 18, 163; RGEL
2; SATA 17; WCH

York, Jeremy
See Creasey, John

York, Simon
See Heinlein, Robert A.

Yorke, Henry Vincent 1905-1974 ...... **CLC 2,
13, 97**
See also BRWS 2; CA 85-88; 175; 49-52;
DLB 15; EWL 3; RGEL 2

Yosano, Akiko 1878-1942 ... **PC 11; TCLC 59**
See also CA 161; EWL 3; RGWL 3

Yoshimoto, Banana
See Yoshimoto, Mahoko

Yoshimoto, Mahoko 1964- .... **CLC 84**
See also AAYA 50; CA 144; CANR 98, 160;
NFS 7; SSFS 16

Young, Al(bert James) 1939- .... **BLC 1:3;
CLC 19**
See also BW 2, 3; CA 29-32R; CANR 26,
65, 109; CN 2, 3, 4, 5, 6, 7; CP 1, 2, 3, 4,
5, 6, 7; DAM MULT; DLB 33

Young, Andrew (John) 1885-1971 ...... **CLC 5**
See also CA 5-8R; CANR 7, 29; CP 1;
RGEL 2

Young, Collier
See Bloch, Robert (Albert)

Young, Edward 1683-1765 .... **LC 3, 40**
See also DLB 95; RGEL 2

Young, Marguerite (Vivian)
1909-1995 .... **CLC 82**
See also CA 13-16; 150; CAP 1; CN 1, 2,
3, 4, 5, 6

Young, Neil 1945- .... **CLC 17**
See also CA 110; CCA 1

Young Bear, Ray A. 1950- ... **CLC 94; NNAL**
See also CA 146; DAM MULT; DLB 175;
MAL 5

Yourcenar, Marguerite 1903-1987 ... **CLC 19,
38, 50, 87; TCLC 193**
See also BPFB 3; CA 69-72; CANR 23, 60,
93; DAM NOV; DLB 72; DLBY 1988;
EW 12; EWL 3; GFL 1789 to the Present;
GLL 1; MTCW 1, 2; MTFW 2005;
RGWL 2, 3

Yuan, Chu 340(?)B.C.-278(?)B.C. . **CMLC 36**

Yu Dafu 1896-1945 .... **SSC 122**
See also DLB 328; RGSF 2

Yurick, Sol 1925- .... **CLC 6**
See also CA 13-16R; CANR 25; CN 1, 2,
3, 4, 5, 6, 7; MAL 5

Zabolotsky, Nikolai Alekseevich
1903-1958 .... **TCLC 52**
See also CA 116; 164; EWL 3

Zabolotsky, Nikolay Alekseevich
See Zabolotsky, Nikolai Alekseevich

Zagajewski, Adam 1945- .... **PC 27**
See also CA 186; DLB 232; EWL 3; PFS
25

Zakaria, Fareed 1964- .... **CLC 269**
See also CA 171; CANR 151, 188

Zalygin, Sergei -2000 .... **CLC 59**

Zalygin, Sergei (Pavlovich)
1913-2000 .... **CLC 59**
See also DLB 302

Zamiatin, Evgenii
See Zamyatin, Evgeny Ivanovich

Zamiatin, Evgenii Ivanovich
See Zamyatin, Evgeny Ivanovich

Zamiatin, Yevgenii
See Zamyatin, Evgeny Ivanovich

Zamora, Bernice (B. Ortiz) 1938- .. **CLC 89;
HLC 2**
See also CA 151; CANR 80; DAM MULT;
DLB 82; HW 1, 2

Zamyatin, Evgeny Ivanovich
1884-1937 .... **SSC 89; TCLC 8, 37**
See also CA 105; 166; DLB 272; EW 10;
EWL 3; RGSF 2; RGWL 2, 3; SFW 4

Zamyatin, Yevgeny Ivanovich
See Zamyatin, Evgeny Ivanovich

Zangwill, Israel 1864-1926 ... **SSC 44; TCLC
16**
See also CA 109; 167; CMW 4; DLB 10,
135, 197; RGEL 2

Zanzotto, Andrea 1921- .... **PC 65**
See also CA 208; CWW 2; DLB 128; EWL
3

Zappa, Francis Vincent, Jr. 1940-1993
See Zappa, Frank
See also CA 108; 143; CANR 57

Zappa, Frank .... **CLC 17**
See Zappa, Francis Vincent, Jr.

Zaturenska, Marya 1902-1982 ..... **CLC 6, 11**
See also CA 13-16R; 105; CANR 22; CP 1,
2, 3

Zayas y Sotomayor, Maria de 1590-c.
1661 .... **LC 102; SSC 94**
See also RGSF 2

Zeami 1363-1443 .... **DC 7; LC 86**
See also DLB 203; RGWL 2, 3

Zelazny, Roger 1937-1995 .... **CLC 21**
See also AAYA 7, 68; BPFB 3; CA 21-24R;
148; CANR 26, 60; CN 6; DLB 8; FANT;
MTCW 1, 2; MTFW 2005; SATA 57;
SATA-Brief 39; SCFW 1, 2; SFW 4;
SUFW 1, 2

Zephaniah, Benjamin 1958- .... **BLC 2:3**
See also CA 147; CANR 103, 156, 177; CP
5, 6, 7; DLB 347; SATA 86, 140, 189

Zhang Ailing
See Chang, Eileen

Zhdanov, Andrei Alexandrovich
1896-1948 .... **TCLC 18**
See also CA 117; 167

Zhukovsky, Vasilii Andreevich
See Zhukovsky, Vasily (Andreevich)

Zhukovsky, Vasily (Andreevich)
1783-1852 .... **NCLC 35**
See also DLB 205

Ziegenhagen, Eric .... **CLC 55**

Zimmer, Jill Schary
See Robinson, Jill

Zimmerman, Robert
See Dylan, Bob

Zindel, Paul 1936-2003 ...... **CLC 6, 26; DC 5**
See also AAYA 2, 37; BYA 2, 3, 8, 11, 14;
CA 73-76; 213; CAD; CANR 31, 65, 108;
CD 5, 6; CDALBS; CLR 3, 45, 85; DA;
DA3; DAB; DAC; DAM DRAM, MST,
NOV; DFS 12; DLB 7, 52; JRDA; LAIT
5; MAICYA 1, 2; MTCW 1, 2; MTFW
2005; NFS 14; SATA 16, 58, 102; SATA-
Obit 142; WYA; YAW

Literary Criticism Series
Cumulative Topic Index

This index lists all topic entries in Gale's *Children's Literature Review* (CLR), *Classical and Medieval Literature Criticism* (CMLC), *Contemporary Literary Criticism* (CLC), *Drama Criticism* (DC), *Literature Criticism from 1400 to 1800* (LC), *Nineteenth-Century Literature Criticism* (NCLC), *Short Story Criticism* (SSC), and *Twentieth-Century Literary Criticism* (TCLC). The index also lists topic entries in the Gale Critical Companion Collection, which includes the following publications: *The Beat Generation* (BG), *Feminism in Literature* (FL), *Gothic Literature* (GL), and *Harlem Renaissance* (HR).

461

Topic Index

Topic Index

CLC Cumulative Nationality Index

Nationality Index

CLC-274 Title Index

ISBN-13: 978-1-4144-3447-6
ISBN-10: 1-4144-3447-2

90000

9 781414 434476